**FOR REFERENCE**

**Date Due**

|  |  |  |  |
|---|---|---|---|
|  |  |  |  |
|  |  |  |  |
|  |  |  |  |
|  |  |  |  |
|  |  |  |  |
|  |  |  |  |
|  |  |  |  |
|  |  |  |  |
|  |  |  |  |
|  |  |  |  |
|  |  |  |  |
|  |  |  |  |
|  |  |  |  |
|  |  |  |  |
|  |  |  |  |

BRODART, CO.     Cat. No. 23-233     Printed in U.S.A.

# HANDBOOK OF RESEARCH ON EDUCATIONAL COMMUNICATIONS AND TECHNOLOGY

## THIRD EDITION

# HANDBOOK OF RESEARCH ON EDUCATIONAL COMMUNICATIONS AND TECHNOLOGY

## THIRD EDITION

EDITED BY

J. MICHAEL SPECTOR
M. DAVID MERRILL
JEROEN VAN MERRIËNBOER
MARCY P. DRISCOLL

Routledge
Taylor & Francis Group

NEW YORK AND LONDON

Routledge
Taylor & Francis Group
270 Madison Avenue
New York, NY 10016

Routledge
Taylor & Francis Group
2 Park Square
Milton Park, Abingdon
Oxon OX14 4RN

© 2008 by Taylor & Francis Group, LLC
Routledge is an imprint of Taylor & Francis Group, an Informa business

Transferred to Digital Printing 2009

International Standard Book Number-13: 978-0-8058-5849-5 (Hardcover)

**Visit the Taylor & Francis Web site at**
**http://www.taylorandfrancis.com**

**and Routledge Web site at**
**http://www.routledge.com**

# Dedication

We dedicate this volume to David H. Jonassen, who edited the first two editions of the *Handbook of Research on Educational Communications and Technology*. His contributions have been many and substantial over the years, including the advice given on this edition and coauthoring a chapter on problem-based learning.

*Mike Spector, Dave Merrill, Jeroen van Merriënboer, and Marcy Driscoll*

# Contents

**Part IV. Models**

**Part VI. Methodological Issues**

# Foreword

## TECHNOLOGY AND EDUCATION

Karl Benz's invention of an automobile with a built-in internal combustion engine in 1885 caused a worldwide revolution, not only in the technological field but also in all segments of human life, such as economics, culture, family structure, urbanization, women and youth emancipation, and climate change. A car, however, seems more suited to solve mobility problems than to serve educational goals. The rise of personal computers and network facilities in the second half of the 20th century eventually converged in a digital World Wide Web (WWW) that revolutionized information development and exchange. Increasing miniaturization, integrated functionalities, and wireless use now comprise a communication hyperspace in a global world. In contrast to the gas-fueled engine, information and communication technologies suggest sensitivity toward lifelong human learning issues. This is what the *Handbook of Research on Educational Communications and Technology* is all about.

Because education is a critical topic in all societies and cultures, it is a common social impulse to (try to) use available technology for schooling purposes. Though linking technology and education seems at first glance to be a rather natural endeavor, it is by no means a smooth and progressive enterprise. Indeed, the history of educational technology documents a long and often difficult process of mutual adaptation, hesitation, and integration. Closer scrutiny of this history reveals some cracks or fissures in a less than smooth process of progressive development; these breaks are successively stimulated by promises of producers of new media and technologies. From their backgrounds in business or technology, these self-proclaimed educational reformers make a linear forecast of efficient and effective output for learning and instruction but neglect the complexity of multidimensional and multilevel educational settings. Moreover, these overly optimistic promises are formulated before any valid empirical evidence for success has been found. Entire lists of sayings about that promised *techno-land* are abundantly available on the Internet. Teachers, parents, and school directors, either genuine innovators themselves or pressed by policymakers, hold strong beliefs about the positive impact of new devices. They are sensible to the societal need for implementing technology in modern schools and using new technologies as external means for serving an internal need for innovation (the Trojan horse phenomenon). In most cases, however, experience with technologies brings more difficulties and less productivity than expected at the beginning, an observation that often causes frustration even in the research community. One waits, then, until the next, more powerful tool is available. This resembles the myth of Sisyphus, a king of Corinth who was condemned forever to roll a boulder up a hill in Hades only to have it roll down again as he neared the top.

Indeed, media and technologies were invented and developed for out-of-school purposes, which means that they are initially not natural but foreign organs in the education organism; therefore, we are in dire need of transplantation knowledge to cope with the school's immune system. Building this transplantation knowledge—to stick with our metaphor—is not a mere technological issue; it also has to receive an empirical grounding in a multidisciplinary, broad-spectrum, and multi-vocal research approach. In this way, research on learning and instruction, philosophy, curriculum, methods, school organization, technology, and user characteristics could converge in educational innovation strategies that take into account increasing complexity.

## EVOLUTION IN MEDIA AND TECHNOLOGY

Depending on the attributes of the different media or technologies and the educational contexts in which they are embedded, different answers are given or need to be given to build up a fruitful interaction between technology and education. Some speak in this context of a marriage. A quick scan of evolutions in media and technology reveals various stages of development; however, rather than suggesting a definite break between each developmental step, which leads inevitably to isolation or compartmentalization, it seems more apt to use the concept of a wave. Educational technology is a cumulative endeavor in which knowledge from earlier phases can be absorbed smoothly in more recent waves. To mention only a few examples, former research on the effects of media attributes or symbol systems can easily be integrated into a complementary view on different symbol systems in multimedia systems; early investigations on hypercard and hypertext continue to yield insight into the characteristics of hypermedia; research on mental effort can be integrated into the so-called cognitive load theory; and research on peer learning with personal computers can shed light on key aspects of learning communities in an Internet environment.

Evolutions in technology can be summarized in three successive developments. After World War II, information representation media were expected to support traditional teaching and learning, mostly in classrooms. Such media were supposed to bring the real world into the stuffy classroom with the use of radio, television, slideshows, film, and video. This kind of technology was conceived of as an extension of verbal and textual symbol systems contained in teacher lectures and books; however, the traditional school format hindered the flexible adaptation of these new media due to locked time slots, predefined curricula, teachers' resistance toward change, and limited organizational flexibility, infrastructure, and finances. If used, media were a mere add-on that brought about no fundamental change in teaching and learning approaches.

From 1970 on, the increasing use of computers in society created a dual argument for integrating computers into educational settings. On the one hand, society claimed that youths had to be prepared to live in an information society, equipped with the computer skills necessary for driving on the information highway (though nowadays youths seem to outperform their teachers and parents in their use of digital technology). On the other hand, the attributes of computers allowed for interactive data processing, symbol transformation, and information storage, which seemed compatible with human information processing and knowledge construction. The personal computer was loaded with software, ranging from drill-and-practice programs to simulations and open tools. In terms of innovation strategy, most governments assumed that filling schools with computers would automatically enhance learning processes and higher-order skill acquisition. Research has shown, however, that computers only create learning output if sufficient support is available and computer use is an integral part of the curriculum or learning environment.

Since the last decade of the 20th century, the closed position of personal computers has been opened by the communication facilities of networked computers. Computers are no longer personal or even computing machines that manipulate digits. They are tools that activate human communication. On the one hand, these tools complement, correct, or fine-tune information embedded in educational software or available on the Internet; on the other hand, they can be used to develop new information and shared knowledge through computer interaction. This human shield allows for many interactions among experts, coaches, teachers, peers, parents, and learners. Computers are communication tools in an information-rich environment and are used by myriad technology-enhanced communities of learners and communities of practice.

## INNOVATIVE RESEARCH ON EDUCATIONAL TECHNOLOGY

The shared feeling that recent communication and information technologies are much closer to education than their nondigital predecessors could lead to a smoother educational use. This opinion can be sustained, at least from a logical perspective; however, innovations in instruction and learning are dependent not only on logical perspectives but also on *psychological* motives. Surveys on computer use indicate that only a fraction of the time spent with computers is used for educational or learning purposes. Contrary to the simple procedure of finding useful information on the Internet, learning and knowledge building are developmental processes that integrate new knowledge into already existing prior knowledge and lead to increasing abstraction, comprehension, and conceptual change. Learning is cumulative and an object of mental effort, motivation, and cognitive skilfulness. Learning is not so much defined by the quantity of information available but by the gradual transformation of relevant information into knowledge. This is not a matter of mere information delivery in an information society. It is essentially the way novices are supported in building their own knowledge out of available information in a long-lasting effort and a long-term perspective, as well. Learning is essentially a developmental activity.

Although research on educational technology is often tuned toward evolution in the field, it started with many studies at a microlevel of complexity: assessment of the effectiveness and efficiency of computer software, detection of minimal conditions for implementation of technology in schools, insight into the main characteristics of learners confronted with technology, and so on. Later on, when not only technological tools but also human interactions with tools and peers became dominant, research was more complex and situated at the mesolevel of complexity. Integral school innovation, integration of computers in curricula, and interaction between offline and online learning or between face-to-face and distant learning are topics that require intensive research. The rise of both the complexity and the range of technology use in education calls for adapted research approaches. If the entire educational system is to become the object of research, the only answer is a systemic approach. *Systemic* means that both the conceptual coherence and the empirical method contribute to a better understanding of the complexity, leading toward better designs. Instead of a proliferation of terminology, approaches, methods, and variables, research should aim at accumulation. The centrifugal trend needs to be transformed into a centripetal one: bringing researchers together through strong research programs.

Complexity cannot be solved by simple or monodisciplinary approaches. Because the system consists of many subcomponents that refer to different backgrounds and interpretation frameworks, the solution lies in an interdisciplinary research endeavor. Indeed, technology, curriculum development, courseware development, distance teaching, innovation strategies, philosophy, social psychology, anthropology, learning paradigms, organizational issues, and ethics all define the value of modern technology use. This is simply due to the fact that at the macrolevel of complexity highly organized blended learning includes and integrates technology and human interactions among the individual, group, and community levels of organization.

The research question is no longer how individual studies contribute to evidence-based uses of technology but how these studies can be brought together in multidisciplinary and multilevel research programs. This includes an emphasis on interactions between variables and levels rather than on individual, flat studies; for example, because open technological environments call for learner control, self-regulation, and group learning, the nature of technology support has to be defined in the complex relationship between learner control and environmental (technological) support. In this way, research programs can take into account long-term goals and flexible adaptation toward changes in the environment.

Most technology research is focused on a limited sample (mostly college students) with a restricted set of one-shot research questions. We know little about evolutions in technology use or about developmental characteristics in the transition from novice to expert. There is a need for more longitudinal studies that can shed light on this evolutionary perspective.

Since the early times of design and development of learning software, emphasis has been placed on the designer and on his or her expertise. If, however, learners are to codesign their learning environment as partners in a learning community, it will be necessary to conduct research on the users: the complex mindset of policymakers, school directors, coaches, teachers, and students, as well as their competencies in cobuilding environments. This includes the required instructional knowledge for contributing to optimal learning environments.

The information made available in this *Handbook* by acknowledged scholars depicts many contributions to the foundation, strategies, technologies, models, design and development, and methodology of educational communications and technology. One of the expected outcomes of this immense knowledge base is the creation of a new generation of research and development, in which conceptual alignment, empirical richness, and synergy are spearheads of educational innovation.

*Joost Lowyck*
Professor Emeritus, Leuven University, Belgium

# Preface

## HISTORY

Early in 2005, Phil Harris, Executive Director of the Association of Educational Communications and Technology, approached Mike Spector and asked if he would like to lead the development of the third edition of the *Handbook of Research on Educational Communications and Technology*. Spector consulted with Dave Jonassen, editor of the previous two editions, and with Lane Akers, Senior Education Editor at Routledge Publishers. A strategy was then developed to make the third edition more international in terms of scope and contributions and to have an editorial team rather than an individual editor lead the effort. Spector, Harris, Akers, and Jonassen then discussed who might comprise that editorial team. By May 2005, the editorial team of Mike Spector, Dave Merrill, Jeroen van Merriënboer, and Marcy Driscoll was formed.

The strategy developed to determine the contents had four major steps: (1) extended conversations with Jonassen to take lessons learned from the first two editions into this edition; (2) a survey of AECT members to get their reactions to the second edition and recommendations for the third edition; (3) presentations at the annual meetings of AECT in 2005 and again in 2006 to get direct feedback from AECT members about plans for the third edition; and (4) ongoing discussions among the editors via teleconference, videoconference, and occasional face-to-face meetings about the *Handbook*.

Nearly 200 persons responded to the *Handbook* survey, which asked about general use, individual chapters in the second edition, and their desires for the third edition. Responses indicated that the *Handbook* is used primarily by doctoral students initiating a research review for their dissertation studies, by faculty as an additional resource for teaching courses on related topics, and by researchers seeking a quick review on a specific topic. Recommendations for the third edition included addressing more topics and having shorter chapters with more references to recent research. We followed these recommendations to the best of our ability.

At the 2005 AECT meeting, the editorial team developed the basic organization of the *Handbook* around four parts: (1) Strategies, (2) Technologies, (3) Models, and (4) Design and Development. These parts reflect major aspects involved in deploying informa-tion and communications technologies (ICT) for educational purposes; they are preceded by a Foundations part and followed by a Research Methodologies part. Each part was led by one of the coeditors with assistance from a second coeditor and several external reviewers.

Also at that meeting, the editorial team with significant input from Jonassen developed an initial list of desired contributors. The agreement with our publisher, Lawrence Erlbaum Associates, was that the second edition would remain available online through the AECT website to AECT members, so some excellent chapters in that edition were not included in this third edition. Author guidelines were developed that reflected the outcomes of the survey and the organizational framework developed by the editorial team. Specifically, we asked for shorter chapters with longer bibliographies, and we also requested keywords with definitions to be included in a glossary and an indication (via asterisks in the reference section) of core references.

A general call for contributions was issued to the AECT membership. The lead editor for each part of the *Handbook* was responsible for determining the contributing authors to that part and for coordinating drafts and reviews of that part of the *Handbook*. In short, the editorial team functioned as a team, with coeditors having and taking responsibility for the various parts of this *Handbook*.

We made a conscious effort from the very beginning to include many more non-American contributors. Rather than simply ask those who had contributed to the first two editions to again make a contribution, we determined that we ought to think ahead to the fourth edition. We also knew that the second edition would remain available for the indefinite future. As a consequence, when we eventually approached authors, we expressed a preference for pairing a highly experienced author with a promising young scholar who conceivably could lead a contribution in the next edition. The intent in selecting authors was to ensure that chapters would be broadly representative of the relevant research in a particular area rather than reflecting only one view or approach.

The *Handbook* took shape in late 2005. At that time, we had as many as 100 chapters targeted for development. The editorial team narrowed that list to about 65 in early 2006 when development of individual chapters took place. Along the way, a few contributors decided they could not make the contributions they had wanted to make and withdrew from the process. One of the most distinguished contributors who had also made valuable contributions to the first two editions, Bill Winn, passed away unexpectedly. Bill cannot be replaced; however, his chapter on computer-mediated technologies was a critical one. Art Graesser agreed to take on the formidable task of leading the development of that chapter in a short period of only six months. In the end, the third edition of this *Handbook* consists of 56 chapters divided into six parts.

## CONTENTS

As already noted, the third edition is divided into six parts. Part I, Foundations, led by Marcy Driscoll, is expected to remain fairly stable over the years and require only minor updating every five years or so. The Foundations part includes historical, theoretical, and methodological foundations and perspectives. This initial part of the *Handbook* is aimed at the various sets of assumptions that underlie research in educational communications and technology. Some of these assumptions are based on what has gone before. Others are based on developments in other disciplines. The goal in this part of the *Handbook* is to make these assumptions explicit, summarize key developments, and provide pointers to exemplary work that has implications for research in educational communications and technology.

Part II, led by Dave Merrill, is focused on strategies. The various chapters in the Strategies part cover both instructional and learning strategies, although the emphasis is on implications for design and development. These various strategies can be linked with subsequent chapters in Parts III, IV, and V of the *Handbook*, in accordance with our organizational framework.

Part III, led by Mike Spector, is focused on technologies. The editorial team collectively decided that the distinction between hard and soft technologies was too facile and not especially meaningful, and it was dropped in this edition. The Technologies part of the *Handbook* consists of 17 chapters on both digital and non-electronic technologies, intelligent and non-intelligent technologies, and planning and evaluation technologies, as well as technologies for implementation.

Part IV, led by Jeroen van Merriënboer, focuses on models. Issues concerned with various types of and approaches to learning are discussed. These models clearly inform design and development and can be linked to various instructional strategies covered in Part II. The Models part includes general models directed toward learning in schools as well as outside schools and models that focus on learning in specific domains such as medicine, science, and reading.

Part V, led by Dave Merrill, focuses on design and development. This part of the *Handbook* discusses research that pertains directly to professional practice. Readers will find chapters on familiar topics such as competency development, task analysis, change agency, and performance assessment. The Design and Development part also covers innovative treatments of design languages, design and development teams, and user-centered design and development.

Part VI, led by Jeroen van Merriënboer, focuses on methodological issues. This part follows the empirical cycle through theory development, experimental design, and data collection and analysis. Design sections adhere to the main parts of the *Handbook* and treat, in order, research on strategies, technologies, models, and design and development. For data collection, special requirements for (virtual) laboratories are discussed. Analysis methods include the analysis of learning processes, interactions, and complex performances. The Methodological Issues part ends with a discussion by the editorial team of a research agenda that should help our field to build a strong scientific foundation for the future.

## USE

The division into four core parts that represent key aspects of using information and communications technologies to support learning and instruction, preceded by a Foundations section and followed by a Methodological Issues section, is intended to facilitate use of this research handbook. We have intentionally kept titles brief and descriptive to help facilitate those who wish to follow a thread through the four core parts of the *Handbook*.

An example of a thread concerned with research on instructional modeling and representation might involve the chapters on representation strategies, modeling technologies, model-facilitated learning, and design languages. Many such threads are possible. Individual chapters were primarily developed to represent stand-alone treatments of specific topics within the framework and guidelines provided. All chapters have extensive lists of references that should prove useful to researchers new to a particular area of research and to doctoral students conducting their background research.

It is our belief that professional practitioners and educational researchers will benefit from the chapters in Parts I and VI. These chapters, as well as many others in the *Handbook*, are likely to be useful for those responsible for leading graduate seminars in the areas of educational technology, instructional systems, or learning environment design and development. It is our hope that this edition of the *Handbook* will be as useful as the previous two editions. Time will tell. In any case, we invite you to give us your feedback, which we will pass along to whoever is selected to lead the development of the fourth edition.

Learn, educate and persevere.

*Mike Spector, Dave Merrill,*
*Jeroen van Merriënboer, and Marcy Driscoll*

# Acknowledgments

We have many people to thank for bringing this volume to fruition. David Jonassen provided valuable advice and insight with regard to the framework for and potential contributors to this third edition of the *Handbook*. Lane Akers, Senior Education Editor at Routledge Publishers, provided assistance throughout the process, beginning in the preplanning phases through to the final production phase. Phil Harris, Executive Director of the Association for Educational Communications and Technology, supported the effort throughout as well. AECT hosted an online survey to which nearly 200 persons provided feedback on the second edition and what they would like to see in the third edition. Thanks to Rick Xavier for supporting the development and deployment of that online survey. A number of external reviewers provided valuable feedback on various drafts. Two graduate assistants helped us keep track of manuscripts and manage the review process: ChanMin Kim and JungMi Lee, both at Florida State University. Several universities contributed resources, including Florida State University, the Open University of the Netherlands, and Syracuse University. Finally, we thank the contributors—this research handbook would not exist without their substantial efforts.

# Contributors

## THE EDITORS

**J. Michael Spector**
Professor and Associate Director
Learning Systems Institute
Florida State University
Tallahassee, Florida

**M. David Merrill**
Professor Emeritus
Utah State University
Logan, Utah
and
Visiting Research Professor
Florida State University
Tallahassee, Florida

**Jeroen J. G. van Merriënboer**
Professor and Research Program Director
Educational Technology Expertise Center
Open University of the Netherlands
Heerlen, the Netherlands

**Marcy P. Driscoll**
Dean, College of Education
Florida State University
Tallahassee, Florida


## CONTRIBUTING AUTHORS

**Robert Atkinson**
College of Education
Arizona State University
Tempe, Arizona

**Paul Ayres**
School of Education
University of New South Wales
Sydney, Australia

**Eun-Ok Baek**
College of Education
California State University
San Bernardino, California

**Eva L. Baker**
National Center for Research on Evaluation,
    Standards, and Student Testing (CRESST)
Graduate School of Education and Information Studies
University of California, Los Angeles
Los Angeles, California

**Sasha A. Barab**
School of Education
Indiana University
Bloomington, Indiana

**Matthew Barclay**
College of Education and Human Services
Utah State University
Logan, Utah

**Brian Beabout**
College of Education
Pennsylvania State University
University Park, Pennsylvania

**Laura Blasi**
College of Education
University of Central Florida
Orlando, Florida

**Elizabeth Boling**
School of Education
Indiana University
Bloomington, Indiana

**Eddy Boot**
Department of Training and Instruction
TNO Human Factors
Soesterberg, the Netherlands

**Henny P. A. Boshuizen**
Educational Technology Expertise Centre
Open University of the Netherlands
Heerlen, the Netherlands

**Luca Botturi**
NewMinE Lab
University of Lugano
Lugano, Switzerland

**Clint A. Bowers**
College of Arts and Sciences
University of Central Florida
Orlando, Florida

**Robert Maribe Branch**
College of Education
University of Georgia
Athens, Georgia

**Kerry J. Burner**
College of Education
Florida State University
Tallahassee, Florida

**John K. Burton**
School of Education
Virginia Polytechnic Institute and State University
Blacksburg, Virginia

**Kursat Cagiltay**
Computer Education and Instructional Technology
Middle East Technical University
Ankara, Turkey

**Janis A. Cannon-Bowers**
Institute for Simulation and Training
University of Central Florida
Orlando, Florida

**Alison A. Carr-Chellman**
College of Education
Pennsylvania State University
University Park, Pennsylvania

**Bryan L. Chapman**
Brandon Hall Research/Chapman Alliance
Sunnyvale, California

**Patrick Chipman**
Institute for Intelligent Systems
University of Memphis
Memphis, Tennessee

**Gregory K. W. K. Chung**
National Center for Research on Evaluation,
  Standards, and Student Testing (CRESST)
Graduate School of Education and Information Studies
University of California, Los Angeles
Los Angeles, California

**Geraldine Clarebout**
Centre for Instructional Psychology and Technology
Katholike Universiteit Leuven
Leuven, Belgium

**Roy B. Clariana**
College of Education
Pennsylvania State University
Malvern, Pennsylvania

**Richard E. Clark**
Center for Cognitive Technology
Rossier School of Education
University of Southern California
Los Angeles, California

**Ruth Colvin Clark**
Clark Training and Consulting
Cortez, Colorado

**L. K. Curda**
College of Education
University of West Florida
Pensacola, Florida

**Ton de Jong**
Department of Instructional Technology
Faculty of Behavioral Sciences
University of Twente
Enschede, the Netherlands

**Girlie C. Delacruz**
National Center for Research on Evaluation,
  Standards, and Student Testing (CRESST)
Graduate School of Education and Information Studies
University of California, Los Angeles
Los Angeles, California

**Vanessa P. Dennen**
College of Education
Florida State University
Tallahassee, Florida

**Tyler Dodge**
School of Education
Indiana University
Bloomington, Indiana

**Tim Dornan**
Manchester Medical School
University of Manchester
Manchester, England

**Ian Douglas**
Learning Systems Institute
Florida State University
Tallahassee, Florida

**Aaron R. Duley**
Ames Research Center
National Aeronautics and Space Administration
Moffett Field, California

**Charles Dziuban**
Research Initiative for Teaching Effectiveness
University of Central Florida
Orlando, Florida

**Sean Early**
Center for Cognitive Technology
Rossier School of Education
University of Southern California
Los Angeles, California.

**Jan Elen**
Faculty of Psychology and Educational Sciences
Katholike Universiteit Leuven
Leuven, Belgium

**David F. Feldon**
College of Education
University of South Carolina
Columbia, South Carolina

**Stephen M. Fiore**
Cognitive Sciences Program
Department of Philosophy and Institute for Simulation
  and Training
University of Central Florida
Orlando, Florida

**Eric J. Fox**
College of Arts and Sciences
Western Michigan University
Kalamazoo, Michigan

**Theodore Frick**
School of Education
Indiana University
Bloomington, Indiana

**James E. Gall**
College of Education and Behavioral Sciences
University of Northern Colorado
Greeley, Colorado

**Andrew S. Gibbons**
Instructional Psychology and Technology
McKay School of Education
Brigham Young University
Provo, Utah

**Peter Goodyear**
CoCo Research Centre
University of Sydney
Sydney, Australia

**Barbara L. Grabowski**
Instructional Systems Program
Pennsylvania State University
University Park, Pennsylvania

**Arthur C. Graesser**
Institute for Intelligent Systems
University of Memphis
Memphis, Tennessee

**Sabine Graf**
Women's Postgraduate College for Internet
  Technologies
Vienna University of Technology
Vienna, Austria

**Charles R. Graham**
Instructional Psychology and Technology
McKay School of Education
Brigham Young University
Provo, Utah

**Koeno Gravemeijer**
Freudenthal Institute for Science and Mathematics
  Education and Langeveld Institute
Utrecht University
Utrecht, the Netherlands

**Peter A. Hancock**
College of Science
University of Central Florida
Orlando, Florida

**Michael J. Hannafin**
Learning and Performance Support Laboratory
University of Georgia
Athens, Georgia

**Robert D. Hannafin**
Neag School of Education
University of Connecticut
Storrs, Connecticut

**John Hedberg**
School of Education
Macquarie University
North Ryde, New South Wales, Australia

**Janette R. Hill**
College of Education
University of Georgia
Athens, Georgia

**Woei Hung**
Educational Technology
University of Arizona South
Sierra Vista, Arizona

**David W. Johnson**
College of Education and Human Development
University of Minnesota
Minneapolis, Minnesota

**Roger T. Johnson**
College of Education and Human Development
University of Minnesota
Minneapolis, Minnesota

**Tristan E. Johnson**
Learning Systems Institute
Florida State University
Tallahassee, Florida

**David H. Jonassen**
School of Information Science and
  Learning Technologies
University of Missouri
Columbia, Missouri

**Yael Kali**
Technion-Israel Institute of Technology
Technion City
Haifa, Israel

**Liesbeth Kester**
Educational Technology Expertise Center
Open University of the Netherlands
Heerlen, the Netherlands

**ChanMin Kim**
College of Education
Florida State University
Tallahassee, Florida

**Brandon G. King**
Institute for Intelligent Systems
University of Memphis
Memphis, Tennessee

**Kinshuk**
School of Computing and Information Systems
Athabasca University
Athabasca, Alberta, Canada

**James D. Klein**
College of Education
Arizona State University
Tempe, Arizona

**Rob Koper**
Educational Technology Expertise Centre
Open University of the Netherlands
Heerlen, the Netherlands

**Tiffany A. Koszalka**
Instructional Design, Development, and Evaluation
Syracuse University
Syracuse, New York

**Wilmad Kuiper**
University of Twente
Faculty of Behavioral Sciences
Enschede, the Netherlands

**Miriam B. Larson**
Educational Research and Outreach
Virginia Polytechnic Institute and State University
Blacksburg, Virginia

**Hyeon Woo Lee**
College of Education
Pennsylvania State University
University Park, Pennsylvania

**Jung Lee**
The Richard Stockton College of New Jersey
Pomona, New Jersey

**JungMi Lee**
College of Education
Florida State University
Tallahassee, Florida

**Kyu Yon Lim**
College of Education
Pennsylvania State University
University Park, Pennsylvania

**Marcia C. Linn**
Graduate School of Education
University of California at Berkeley
Berkeley, California

**Rude Liu**
Educational Psychology
Beijing Normal University
Beijing, China

**Barbara B. Lockee**
School of Education
Virginia Polytechnic Institute and State University
Blacksburg, Virginia

**Linda L. Lohr**
College of Education and Behavioral Sciences
University of Northern Colorado
Greeley, Colorado

**Joost Lowyck**
Center for Instructional Psychology and Technology
Leuven University
Leuven, Belgium

**M. David Merrill**
College of Education and Human Services
Utah State University
Logan, Utah
and
Learning Systems Institute
Florida State University
Tallahassee, Florida

**Michael Molenda**
School of Education
Indiana University
Bloomington, Indiana

**D. Michael Moore**
Educational Research and Outreach
Virginia Polytechnic Institute and State University
Blacksburg, Virginia

**Konrad Morgan**
School of Applied Media and Information Technology
Northern Alberta Institute of Technology
Edmonton, Alberta, Canada

**Gary R. Morrison**
College of Education
Old Dominion University
Norfolk, Virginia

**Som Naidu**
Educational Technology
University of Melbourne
Victoria, Australia

**Susanne Narciss**
Learning and Instruction
Technische Universitaet Dresden
Dresden, Germany

**Jon Nelson**
Department of Instructional Technology
Utah State University
Logan, Utah

**Delia Neuman**
College of Information Studies
University of Maryland
College Park, Maryland

**Frank Nguyen**
San Diego State University
San Diego, California

**Xiaopeng Ni**
College of Education
University of Georgia
Athens, Georgia

**Dale S. Niederhauser**
College of Human Sciences
Iowa State University
Ames, Iowa

**Mary Niemczyk**
College of Technology and Applied Sciences
Arizona State University–Polytechnic
Mesa, Arizona

**Fleurie Nievelstein**
Educational Technology Expertise Center
Open University of the Netherlands
Heerlen, the Netherlands

**Debra L. O'Connor**
Intelligent Decision Systems, Inc.
Williamsburg, Virginia

**Eunjung Oh**
College of Education
University of Georgia
Athens, Georgia

**Ron Owston**
Institute for Research on Learning Technologies
York University
Toronto, Ontario, Canada

**Fred Paas**
Educational Technology Expertise Center
Open University of the Netherlands
Heerlen, the Netherlands

**Ok-Choon Park**
Institute of Education Sciences
Washington, D.C.

**Jay Pfaffman**
College of Education, Health, and Human Sciences
University of Tennessee
Knoxville, Tennessee

**Caroline Phythian-Sence**
College of Arts and Sciences
Florida State University
Tallahassee, Florida

**Frans J. Prins**
Educational Technology Expertise Center
Open University of the Netherlands
Heerlen, the Netherlands

**Tillman J. Ragan**
Instructional Psychology and Technology Program
University of Oklahoma
Norman, Oklahoma

**Thomas C. Reeves**
College of Education
University of Georgia
Athens, Georgia

**Charles M. Reigeluth**
School of Education
Indiana University
Bloomington, Indiana

**Rita C. Richey**
College of Education
Wayne State University
Detroit, Michigan

**Remy M. J. P. Rikers**
Psychology Department
Erasmus University
Rotterdam, Zuid-Holland, the Netherlands

**Rhonda Robinson**
Department of Educational Technology,
  Research, and Assessment
Northern Illinois University
DeKalb, Illinois

**Steven M. Ross**
Center for Research in Educational Policy
University of Memphis
Memphis, Tennessee

**Thomas Satwicz**
College of Education
University of Georgia
Athens, Georgia

**Wilhelmina Savenye**
College of Education
Arizona State University
Tempe, Arizona

**Albert Scherpbier**
Medical Informatics
Maastricht University
Maastricht, the Netherlands

**Richard F. Schmid**
Centre for the Study of Learning and Performance
Concordia University
Montreal, Quebec, Canada

**Kathy L. Schuh**
College of Education
University of Iowa
Iowa City, Iowa

**Norbert M. Seel**
College of Education
Florida State University
Tallahassee, Florida
and
University of Freiburg
Freiburg, Germany

**Valerie J. Shute**
College of Education
Florida State University
Tallahassee, Florida

**Roderick C. Sims**
School of Education
Capella University
Woodburn, New South Wales, Australia

**Kennon M. Smith**
School of Education
Indiana University
Bloomington, Indiana

**Patricia L. Smith**
Instructional Psychology and Technology Program
University of Oklahoma
Norman, Oklahoma

**J. Michael Spector**
Learning Systems Institute
Florida State University
Tallahassee, Florida

**John Spencer**
School of Medical Education Development
University of Newcastle
Newcastle, England

**Reed Stevens**
Cognitive Studies in Education
University of Washington
Seattle, Washington

**Johannes Strobel**
Educational Technology and Centre for the
  Study of Learning and Performance
Concordia University
Montreal, Quebec, Canada

**John Sweller**
School of Education
University of New South Wales
Sydney, New South Wales, Australia

**Jan van den Akker**
Faculty of Behavioral Sciences
University of Twente
Enschede, the Netherlands

**Geerdina Maria van der Aalsvoort**
Pedagogische Wetenschappen
Leiden University
Leiden, the Netherlands

**Tamara van Gog**
Educational Technology Expertise Center
Open University of the Netherlands
Heerlen, the Netherlands

**Wouter R. van Joolingen**
Department of Instructional Technology
Faculty of Behavioral Sciences
University of Twente
Enschede, the Netherlands

**Jeroen J. G. van Merriënboer**
Educational Technology Expertise Center
Open University of the Netherlands
Heerlen, the Netherlands

**Andrew van Schaak**
Vanderbilt University
Nashville, Tennessee

**Richard K. Wagner**
Florida Center for Reading Research
Florida State University
Tallahassee, Florida

**Paul Ward**
Department of Psychology and Learning
  Systems Institute
Florida State University
Tallahassee, Florida

**Sunnie Lee Watson**
School of Education
Indiana University
Bloomington, Indiana

**William R. Watson**
School of Engineering and Technology
Indiana University–Purdue University Indianapolis
Indianapolis, Indiana

**David A. Wiley**
Center for Open and Sustainable Learning
College of Education and Human Services
Utah State University
Logan, Utah

**Kenneth A. Yates**
Rossier School of Education
University of Southern California
Los Angeles, California

**Michael Young**
School of Education
University of Connecticut
Storrs, Connecticut

**Diego Zapata-Rivera**
Research and Development
Educational Testing Service
Princeton, New Jersey

# REVIEWERS

**Sharon Ainsworth**
Learning Sciences Research Institute
University of Nottingham
Nottingham, England

**Bonnie H. Armstrong**
College of Education
Florida State University
Tallahassee, Florida

**Theo J. Bastiaens**
Institut für Bildungswissenschaft und
 Medienforschung
Fern Universität Hagen
Hagen, Germany

**Saskia Brand-Gruwel**
Educational Technology Expertise Center
Open University of the Netherlands
Heerlen, the Netherlands

**L. K. Curda**
College of Professional Studies
University of West Florida
Pensacola, Florida

**Sanne Dijkstra**
Behavioral Sciences
University of Twente
Enschede, the Netherlands

**Tyler Dodge**
School of Education
Indiana University
Bloomington, Indiana

**Philip L. Doughty**
School of Education
Syracuse University
Syracuse, New York

**Gijsbert Erkens**
College of Liberal Arts and Sciences
Universiteit Utrecht
Utrecht, the Netherlands

**Begoña Gros-Salvat**
Department of Education
University of Barcelona
Barcelona, Spain

**Dirk Ifenthaler**
Department of Education
Albert-Ludwigs-Universität
Freiburg, Germany

**Tristan E. Johnson**
Learning Systems Institute
Florida State University
Tallahassee, Florida

**Paul A. Kirschner**
Educational Psychology and ICT and
 Research Centre Learning in Interaction
Utrecht University
Utrecht, the Netherlands

**Ard W. Lazonder**
Behavioral Sciences
University of Twente
Enschede, the Netherlands

**Detlev Leutner**
School of Education
Duisburg-Essen University
Essen, Germany

**M. David Merrill**
College of Education and Human Services
Utah State University
Logan, Utah
and
Learning Systems Institute
Florida State University
Tallahassee, Florida

**Konrad Morgan**
Human Computer Interaction and InterMedia
 Research Centre
University of Bergen
Bergen, Norway

**Richard A. Schwier**
College of Education
University of Saskatchewan
Saskatoon, Saskatchewan, Canada

**H. Barbara Sorensen**
United States Air Force Research Laboratory
Mesa, Arizona

**J. Michael Spector**
Learning Systems Institute
Florida State University
Tallahassee, Florida

**Jan-Willem Strijbos**
Department of Educational Sciences
Leiden University
Leiden, the Netherlands

**Carla van Boxtel**
Graduate School of Teaching and Learning
University of Amsterdam
Amsterdam, the Netherlands

**Marcel van der Klink**
Educational Technology Expertise Center
Open University of the Netherlands
Heerlen, the Netherlands

**Hans van der Meij**
Behavioral Sciences
University of Twente
Enschede, the Netherlands

**Jeroen J. G. van Merriënboer**
Professor and Research Program Director
Educational Technology Expertise Center
Open University of the Netherlands
Heerlen, the Netherlands

**Andrew van Schaack**
College of Education and Human Development
Vanderbilt University
Nashville, Tennessee

**Monique Volman**
Centre for Educational Training, Assessment,
 and Research (CETAR)
Vrije Universiteit Amsterdam
Amsterdam, the Netherlands

**Hui-Ling Wu**
College of Education and Human Development
Texas A&M University
College Station, Texas

# Part I
## Foundations

This Foundations part of the *Handbook* was led by Marcy P. Driscoll with assistance from J. Michael Spector. The Foundations are expected to remain fairly stable over the years. The relevant Foundations include historical, theoretical, and methodological developments, theories, and perspectives. This initial part of the *Handbook* is aimed at the various sets of assumptions that underlie research in educational communications and technology. Some of these assumptions are based on what has gone before. Others are based on developments in other disciplines. The goal in this part of the *Handbook* is to make these assumptions explicit, summarize key developments, and provide pointers to exemplary work that has implications for research in educational communications and technology. This part of the *Handbook* consists of seven chapters covering: (1) historical foundations, (2) theoretical foundations, (3) complexity theory, (4) experiential perspectives, (5) empirical perspectives, (6) contextualistic perspectives, and (7) philosophical perspectives.

# 1

# Historical Foundations

*Michael Molenda*
Indiana University, Bloomington, Indiana

## CONTENTS

## ABSTRACT

Research and practice in educational technology are rooted in a primordial human drive to find ways of teaching in ways that are more efficient. Every civilization has developed formal methods of education more efficacious than the trial-and-error of everyday living. In the first decades of the 20th century, individuals and, later, groups of affiliated professionals made that quest a central focus, thus establishing educational technology as a field. Their first activities aimed at enriching the learning experience with visual and later audio-visual resources. As radio broadcasting grew in the 1930s and then television in the 1950s, these mass media were accepted as ways to reach even larger audiences, in and out of school, with educative audio-visual programs. In the 1960s, the wave of interest in teaching machines incorporating programmed instruction based on behaviorist psychology engulfed the field, engendering a shift in identity. The proper study of the field expanded from audio-visual technologies to all technologies, including psychological ones. By the 1980s, the center of gravity had shifted to the design of instructional systems, especially the adroit application of instructional methods, enlivened by fresh insights from cognitive and constructivist perspectives. As computers became ubiquitous in the 1990s, they became the delivery system of choice due to their interactive capabilities. With the rapid global spread of the World Wide Web after 1995, networked computers took on communication functions as well as storage and processing functions. The 21st century began with educational technology increasingly focused on distance education, the latest paradigmatic framework for its ageless mission to help more people learn faster, better, and more affordably.

## KEYWORDS

*Constructivism:* In learning theory, a set of assumptions about human learning emphasizing the central role of the mind's active construction of new knowledge.

*Distance education:* An educational program characterized by the separation, in time or place, between instructor and student and in which communications media are used to allow interchange.

*Technology:* The application of scientific or other organized knowledge to practical tasks.

## INTRODUCTION

The area of research surveyed in this handbook—educational communications and technology—is broad and complex. The constructs on which the individual chapters focus sometimes have vague boundaries and often overlap with other constructs. The research surveyed is rooted in many different disciplines, each with its own history and subculture. Any attempt to impose a coherent story line on such a variegated drama must necessarily be a bit complicated, with plot lines that crisscross frequently. This brief history makes no claim to originality or heterodoxy. It strives for the opposite effect: to tell the story of the evolution of educational communications and technology as it is understood by mainstream observers. It draws heavily on well-known sources, such as Saettler's (1990) comprehensive history and the most recent overview of the main constructs of the field (Januszewski and Molenda, 2008). It is animated by the editors' goal of beginning this handbook by making explicit the assumptions on which research has been based. It takes the vantage point of the membership and readership of the Association for Educational Communications and Technology (AECT) and its predecessors over the past century. For simplicity's sake, the term *educational technology* will be used as the name of the field whose story is being told.

## HISTORICAL FOUNDATIONS OF WHAT?

### The Very Beginning

Humans have succeeded as a species largely due to their ability to learn from their experiences and to pass along their wisdom to succeeding generations. Much learning and acculturation happens spontaneously, without planning or structure. Through the ages, as human society has become increasingly complex and organized, communities have consciously set up particular arrangements, such as apprenticeships, schools, and other educational institutions, to help their members develop the cognitive and functional skills needed to survive and flourish.

The history of organized education and training can be viewed as a long struggle to extend opportunities to more people and to devise means of helping those people learn better than through the events of everyday life. Institutions established for education and training revolve around activities intended to help people learn productively, individually or in groups, in classrooms or at a distance. Schools, colleges, corporate training centers, and other educational institutions provide many sorts of facilities to facilitate learning.

Learning goals in educational settings are often complex, difficult, and protracted. Throughout history, educators have devised means to help people learn that are easier, faster, surer, or less expensive than previous means. Some of these means could be classified as technological, by which we mean applying scientific or other organized knowledge to the attainment of practical ends, a definition proposed by John Kenneth Galbraith (1967). These developments may take the form of hard technologies, including materials and physical inventions, or soft technologies, including special work processes or carefully designed instructional templates that are applicable beyond a single case. This chapter aims to recount some of the milestones in the history of these developments.

### Precursors of the Modern Era

The ideas that have propelled educational technology during its modern history have their roots in philosophical, pedagogical, and psychological theories stretching back to the 5th century B.C., when Athenian culture was at its zenith in the West and when Confucius was establishing his philosophy, which came to dominate East Asian thinking. (Confucian thought, however, was not known in the Western world until the translations of Italian Jesuit missionary Matteo Ricci around 1600.)

In classical Athens, the Sophists taught provocative, often relativistic, notions of epistemology. The works of Socrates, Plato, and Aristotle in organizing philosophical thought can be seen as a reaction against the Sophists' position that a good argument is one that prevails, if only through rhetorical manipulation, regardless of truth value. Their frameworks for discussion of cognition and knowledge were largely lost during the Dark Ages in Europe but were gradually rediscovered and reexamined as medieval scholars gained access to texts saved in Arabic. During the 15th century, Yi T'oegye in Korea was developing a neo-Confucian philosophy that focused on moral principles but also treated epistemology. His Steps of Practical Self-Cultivation, procedures for thinking through problems, are comparable to the maieutic method of Socrates. (Socrates considered his educational practice to be similar to midwifery in that he helped individuals deliver ideas; see Kim, 2003.)

By the Renaissance era, European philosophers of education such as Comenius were elaborating pedagogical principles and practices that are recognizable to the modern educator—for example, arranging the classroom for efficient management, systematically incorporating visuals into text presentations, organizing the curriculum according to the developmental stages of learners, and engaging children in playful activities instead of punishing drills.

Advances in communications media came to education slowly in the 18th and 19th centuries. Maps, globes, and scientific apparatus were standard equipment in the better schools and colleges in the 18th century, but it was not until early in the 19th century that a new general-purpose media format—the blackboard—came into widespread use. The Scots claim that the blackboard was invented by James Pillans, headmaster of the Old High School in Edinburgh in the early 1800s, who used a blackboard and colored chalks to teach geography (Scots Community, 2007). By 1830, the blackboard, usually locally made by painting planks with black paint, had become an essential part of classroom furnishings. Its ability to make teacher or student writing or drawings visible to a large group expanded the teacher's capabilities exponentially. Bumstead (1841, p. viii) proclaimed that the "inventor or introducer of the blackboard system deserves to be ranked among the best contributors to learning and science, if not among the greatest benefactors of mankind."

The hand-held stereoscope became popular in education in the mid-1850s, promoted by Sir David Brewster in England, who carried out basic research in stereoscopy and became a firm advocate of its value in visualizing the curriculum (Anderson, 1962).

# EARLY VISUAL MEDIA

## Slide Projection

The origins of the modern field of educational technology can be traced to the efforts of practitioners in the late 19th and early 20th century to use projected visual images to supplement lectures. Slide projection evolved from 17th-century handpainted slides illuminated by oil lamps. The so-called magic lantern provided entertainment for paying audiences throughout the 19th century (Petroski, 2006). The use of slide projection in education was restricted by the high cost of purchasing and operating these early devices. They ran on gas, oil, or hydrogen combined with lime (so-called limelight, first used in the Covent Garden Theatre in London in 1837), all of which had a high cost per hour of use. Edison's invention in the 1890s of incandescent lighting powered by electricity made slide projection affordable, and by the end of the 19th century lantern slides were in common use in education.

## Silent Films in Education

The direct ancestors of educational films were the non-theatrical short films that began to emerge around 1910. British and French cinematographers exhibited films showing amazing sights such as microscopic creatures, insects in flight, and underwater seascapes. Films of news events and travel adventures played to rapt audiences. Silent films began to be used in schools as early as 1910 (Saettler, 1990). In 1912, the Lycée Hoche de Versailles in France had gained international notice for its exemplary incorporation of films into science teaching. By the 1920s, many different individuals, companies, nonprofit organizations, and government agencies attempted to supplement the existing supply of theatrical films and newsreels. Educators could find many types of films to use: theatrical films edited for special purposes, industrial films, government films, and a smaller number of films produced specifically for the classroom. Schools that wanted to be viewed as progressive rushed to build collections of films. Despite the marginal value of many of the available films, interest and usage continued to grow, and by the end of the 1920s many education agencies had units devoted to film or visual education, and thick catalogs documented the thousands of films available to educators.

# VISUAL INSTRUCTION MOVEMENT

Enthusiasm for the use of still pictures and motion pictures as educational resources grew to become the Visual Instruction movement, an increasingly organized effort by enthusiasts to promote wider use of these new technologies. This movement is regarded as the first paradigm in which the field found its identity. Under this paradigm, advocates sought to make visual materials widely available throughout school districts, postsecondary institutions, and adult education institutions. At first these resources were included in the collections of educational museums; the first in the United

States was established in St. Louis, Missouri, in 1905, based on exhibits saved from the World's Fair held in that city in 1904 (Saettler, 1990). Later, collections of visual media were gathered into visual resources centers of their own, and the leaders of the emerging field of visual instruction were the directors of these centers.

The earliest formal research on educational applications of media was Lashley and Watson's program of studies on the use of World War I military training films on the prevention of venereal disease with civilian audiences (Lashley and Watson, 1921). An early large-scale effort to design and produce a set of films specifically for schools was the *Chronicles of America Photoplays*, produced by Yale University in the late 1920s. Knowlton and Tilton (1929) studied the use of these history films in seventh-grade classrooms. One of their major conclusions was that the educational value of such films lay not only in the quality of the materials but also in how well teachers used them. This finding, that the instructional value of any media product is determined largely by how it is used, would be rediscovered by each succeeding generation with its new media: radio, then television, then programmed instruction, then computer-based instruction, and now Internet-based learning environments.

The making of films for educational use in the early years was not explicitly guided by pedagogical theories. Producers generally chose subjects that were visual in nature then applied the methodology of one of the existing film genres: drama, travelogue, documentary, ethnography, historical reenactment, nature study, scientific experiment or demonstration, lecture, procedural guide, and the like.

During the 1920s, visual instruction enthusiasts formed a number of organizations. In 1923, one of them, the National Education Association's Department of Visual Instruction (DVI), emerged to become the preeminent organization of professionals concerned with the use of visual media to improve instruction. The name changed to Department of Audio-Visual Instruction (DAVI) in 1947 as its boundaries expanded to include auditory media: sound films and various forms of recorded sound, beginning with phonographs and later including radio broadcasting, sound filmstrips, and audiocassettes.

## AUDIO-VISUAL INSTRUCTION

The phonograph record, introduced in 1910, was the first widely available format for recorded sound and was used almost exclusively for music. Although magnetic tape displaced the phonograph for recording purposes in the 1950s, vinyl records remain in use into the 21st century. As soon as the phonograph was invented, film producers tried various methods of using this new technology to add sound to motion pictures, but in the late 1920s the technique of adding an optical sound track to the film itself became the preferred format for sound films. Interestingly, there was considerable resistance to sound films in the education community. Some methodologists felt that the practice of having the classroom teacher add narration to silent films added a level of customization and personalization to film showings. Administrators worried about their installed base, the large investment they had made in silent film projectors. As late as 1936, a survey showed that schools owned ten times more silent film projectors than sound film projectors (Saettler, 1990). The slide format had become standardized at the $2 \times 2$-inch frame size, using 35-mm film, which was also used for the filmstrip, which later became the most popular format for commercially produced audio-visual materials. Audio resources were added to the growing base of visual resources. By the 1930s, schools maintained equipment pools that contained (in order of frequency): lantern slide projectors, radio receivers, 16-mm silent film projectors, 35-mm silent film projectors, filmstrip projectors, opaque projectors, micro-slide projectors, 16-mm sound film projectors, and 35-mm sound film projectors (Saettler, 1990).

## EDUCATIONAL RADIO

### Initiation of Radio Services

In the 1920s and 1930s, broadcast radio became the prime mass communication medium around the world. In most countries, broadcasting facilities were directly managed by the government, although after the founding of the British Broadcasting Corporation (BBC) in 1927, many countries (such as Japan's NHK and Canada's CBC) followed its model of a quasi-autonomous public corporation. Providing cultural and educational programming was assumed to be a primary responsibility of these organizations; such programs were often among the first to be broadcast. The first school programs in Canada began in 1925, in England in 1926. By the mid-1930s, there were school broadcasting services in virtually every European country as well as in Australia, Japan, South Africa, and India.

### Educational Radio in Japan

Japan's NHK initiated nationwide school broadcasts in 1935 and soon developed a policy of programs to complement the school curriculum, "to fill in areas unreached by the conventional teaching" (De Vera, 1967, p. 23). Following reorganization after World War II, NHK went on to become an international exemplar for its ambitious and high-quality programming in radio and later (beginning in 1953) in television.

## Educational Radio in North America

In Canada, the first large-scale school broadcasts were actually offered by the Canadian National Railways (CNR) system. This radio service was established to entertain rail travelers, but it also reached the towns and cities along its route, and the CNR broadcasters were quick to provide programming that would appeal to school audiences. The CNR school service built a loyal audience by deliberately building participative activities into the programs. The service was subsumed into the CBC in 1933. In the early 1920s, many American universities obtained licenses to operate radio stations, often as technical experiments in electrical engineering. A large proportion of these died out in competition with commercial stations, but some put down roots. The operations that prospered were the ones in which radio played an integral part in the university's mission—bringing educational opportunities to audiences beyond the campus (Wood and Wylie, 1977).

## Educational Radio Programming

By the mid-1930s, many Ameican school districts operated radio stations, which developed sophisticated educational programming, often incorporating innovative pedagogical techniques. At the Cleveland, Ohio, Board of Education's radio station, WBOE, in the 1930s they pretested programs by creating rough drafts and trying them out with student audiences. This practice foreshadowed the later notion of improving lessons and validating their worth through formative and summative evaluation (Cambre, 1978). Educational broadcasters offered programs in every conceivable subject, including foreign languages, health, social studies, home economics, science, music, art, and many other subjects. BBC programmers worked closely with advisory boards of teachers in every subject area to find niches into which audio material might add value (Bailey, 1957). They reached thousands of schools in each country; for example, in 1936 in England and Wales some 4600 schools were registered users (Parker, 1939). However, in the Americas and many European countries, programming tended to be what Levenson and Stasheff (1952) referred to as "informally educative" rather than directly instructional. Radio services had difficulty playing core instructional roles. For one thing, the advantage of broadcasting is its coverage of a broad area, but that meant crossing school district and even state and provincial boundaries. It was difficult to create any lesson that would meet the content, scope, sequence, and timing demands of multiple schools across multiple jurisdictions. For another thing, teachers, the gatekeepers of the classroom, were reluctant to turn over responsibility for core subject matter, sensing that it would threaten their authority. This pattern of consigning technology-based programming to a supplementary role was to be repeated with television, programmed instruction, and computer-assisted instruction.

## EDUCATIONAL MEDIA IN WORLD WAR II

During World War II both the Allies and Axis powers used motion pictures extensively for home-front propaganda purposes, with the German director Leni Riefenstahl setting new aesthetic standards with psychologically powerful documentaries, such as *Triumph of the Will*. Such films provided rich material for a generation of researchers in psychology and media studies in the United States and Europe. The need for rapid mass training of literally millions of combatants and industrial workers brought films to the forefront of military training. The British and American armed forces made extensive use of 16-mm films for training and motivational purposes, but the U.S. effort was the most pervasive of any of the combatant nations. Between 1941 and 1945, the Division of Visual Aids for Military Training—with major participation by Hollywood directors and actors—produced over 400 sound films and over 400 silent filmstrips, enabling a military mobilization far broader and faster than the Axis strategists had expected (Saettler, 1990).

During the war, as films were being produced and used in training, the U.S. Army commissioned a series of psychological studies, later published as *Experiments on Mass Communication* (Hovland et al., 1949), which tested hypotheses about various filmic techniques and their instructional effectiveness. Because of the concentration of time, money, effort, and research expended on these productions, a genre of instructional film came into its own. New filmic conventions were established, for example, showing procedural tasks from the performer's viewpoint rather than the viewer's and using a first-person stream of consciousness narration to model the thought process of the performer.

# EDUCATIONAL MEDIA IN THE POST-WAR PERIOD

## Research on Media

After the war, instructional film research continued under U.S. Navy sponsorship at Pennsylvania State University, a research program that yielded over a hundred publications (Hoban and Van Ormer, 1970). Some of the experiments dealt with utilization techniques, but most explored presentation variables, such as camera angles, pacing, narration, music, and color (Saettler, 1990). The U.S. Air Force also commissioned a series of studies in the early 1950s that explored the possible interactions between film and programmed instruction techniques and broadly examined the value of learner response during film or video viewing. Research within the field received a major stimulus with the founding in 1953 of the journal *Audio-Visual Communication Review* by DAVI, the predecessor of AECT. The National Defense Education Act passed in 1958 provided a flood of funding in the United States for audio-visual research under Title VII.

## Basic Research

Most of the basic research on visual and auditory perception has been done outside the field of educational technology. The most relevant strand of visual learning research began in Germany with Gestalt psychology in the first half of the 20th century, pioneered by Max Wertheimer (1944) and elaborated by Kurt Koffka and Wolfgang Köhler. They were attempting to describe how humans and other primates perceived stimuli and used cognitive processes to understand and solve problems. Another strand, focusing on the formation of mental models, was begun by Kenneth Craik (1943) in England and elaborated by Johnson-Laird (1983). Generalizations gathered from these sorts of basic research were compiled by Fleming and Levie (1978) in the form of message design principles.

## Audio-Visual Instruction in Practice

The period between World War II and the advent of personal computers in 1982 could be viewed as the audio-visual instruction period. Immediately after World War II, educational technology practice revolved around the media formats that had become widely available to teachers by 1946: 16-mm films, 35-mm slide/filmstrip projectors, opaque projectors, radio receivers, and record players. These formats were owned by schools at the rate of at least 1 per 100 teachers. Television receivers reached this status in 1958 and overhead projectors in 1960 (Finn et al., 1962). Magnetic tape recording was invented in Germany in 1935 and was introduced to the United States by servicemen who brought back recorders after the war. By 1956, reel-to-reel tape recorders had joined the ranks of media devices found in mass use in schools (Finn et al., 1962). Cassette audio recorders were introduced by Philips in the Netherlands in 1962 and became the standard audio format in schools around the world by the early 1970s.

Meanwhile, the actual rate of use of audio-visual media by K–12 teachers during this era would have to be characterized as moderate. Utilization rates were strongly affected by accessibility. Teachers were likely to use materials that were stored in their own classrooms, somewhat less likely to use those housed in a center in their building, and even less likely to use items, such as 16-mm films, that had to be delivered from outside the building on a scheduled basis. Surveys in the 1940s and 1950s in the United States indicated that about 40% of elementary teachers and 20% of secondary teachers used films frequently. Evidence from various sources indicates that the average teacher used about one film per month (Cuban, 1986, pp. 14–18). The reasons given by teachers for the low rate of use of film and similar media, in addition to accessibility, included lack of training in the technology, unreliability of projection equipment, limited school budgets (for rental of films and purchase of projectors), and difficulty integrating the material into the curriculum. Surveys in the 1990s identified the identical barriers to teachers' use of computers.

The animating vision of the audio-visual paradigm, represented by Hoban et al. (1937), was to replace empty verbalism or rote memorization with meaningful learning. Dale (1946), an early advocate of rich learning environments, expanded the notion of visual instruction by proposing in his Cone of Experience that learning experiences—including direct personal experiences, field trips, and dramatizations as well as audio and visual media—could be arrayed in a spectrum from concrete to abstract, each with its proper place in the tool kit.

# EDUCATIONAL TELEVISION (ETV)

The BBC began regular television broadcasts in 1936, and regular programs were being offered in the United States, Germany, France, and the Soviet Union before World War II, which brought developments to a standstill. After the war, television grew rapidly; for example, the NBC commercial network was broadcasting by 1947, and NHK began regular television service in

1953. In most European countries, the radio formula was carried over to television, with the state broadcasting agencies expanding into this new medium, funded by license fees, and continuing their tradition of bringing cultural and educational programming to the populace.

## ETV in Europe

The BBC began school broadcasts in 1957; by 1974, over 80% of all schools were making regular use of BBC programs (British Information Services, 1974), a pattern that carried on into the 21st century. Guided since the early days of radio by a School Broadcasting Council that includes strong representation of teachers, programs are carefully designed to be integrated into the national curriculum. In other European countries, the general pattern is for the state television corporation to devote a small percentage of its broadcast hours to programming aimed at in-school audiences and adult education.

## ETV in North America

Like the United Kingdom, Canada also operates a national television network, the CBC, which is supported in part by commercial advertising. The CBC began to provide school broadcasts when television operations commenced in 1952. They continued to offer a limited schedule of in-school programs throughout the 1960s and 1970s as the various provinces gradually undertook their own program production. Just as in the United States, Canada's K–12 education system is controlled by provincial authorities rather than the national government, and by the mid-1960s most of the provinces were producing in-school programs tailored to their specific needs. Beginning in 1970, TVOntario, a public noncommercial network serving Ontario, offered school-oriented programs, some of which attained international recognition and distribution; thus, both national and provincial programs are available for school use.

During the 1950s, dozens of noncommercial television licenses were granted to universities and community groups in the United States, and educational television programs began to be beamed to school and college audiences (the first being KUHT at the University of Houston in 1953) and adults and children at home. Many of the same parties that had experimented with radio also did so with television, essentially replaying the radio scenario. Because this was a period of rapid school population growth there was a general shortage of qualified teachers. Television was seen by some as a way to reduce the need for additional teachers by replacing the presentation function with broadcast lessons.

In the late 1950s and through the 1960s in the United States, programs were distributed on a regional basis, such as by the Eastern Educational Network and the Midwest Program of Airborne Television Instruction (MPATI, a precursor of satellite broadcasting), and a few on a national basis, such as Continental Classroom. During this period, the Ford Foundation and the federal government were subsidizing the expansion of television in higher education through grants for closed-circuit TV construction and program production. By the end of the decade of the 1960s, tens of millions of school and college students were receiving televised instruction on a daily basis. After the popularization of videotape recording (later, videocassette recording), ETV programming was increasingly created and used as off-the-shelf packaged units rather than being received through broadcasting.

## ETV Programming

As with educational films, ETV programs tended to emulate the familiar genres: lecture, demonstration, voice-over visualization, interview, panel discussion, dramatization, field trip, or documentary (Wood and Wylie, 1977). The production processes were comparable to those used in commercial radio and television: "We borrowed from commercial television certain ideas about what constitutes a program, and we have not shaken free from these concepts" (Suchman, 1966, p. 30). American ETV presentations, particularly those beamed to college audiences, tended to be more verbal (featuring the so-called talking heads) than European productions (Tanner and Woerdehoff, 1964). European programs, particularly those of the BBC, were notable for their emphasis on visualization. The BBC collection became a major international archive of exemplary programming that was drawn upon by producers from around the globe.

A break from this expository pattern began in the 1960s under the influence of the so-called Cognitive Revolution, which suggested that television should be participative rather than passive. It should ask questions, pose challenging problems, and spark discussion and search for answers. In short, it should trigger inquiry (McBride, 1966). The discovery learning movement eventually led to the production of a number of educational television series, especially in science and social studies, that portrayed problematic situations and invited learners to discuss them. The *Jasper Woodbury Problem Solving Series* in the 1990s represented the culmination of this movement.

## ETV in Developing Countries

As television was later in coming to the less industrialized countries, so were educational applications. In many countries educational television came with the financial and technical support of industrialized countries, intending to help expand educational opportunities as part of nation building; for example, in 1961 UNESCO and the Ford Foundation established a pilot project in Delhi, India, to offer televised physics, chemistry, and English lessons to secondary students in that city (Mohanty, 1984). In 1966, a project was initiated for communicating agricultural information to farmers in some 80 villages outside of Delhi; the programs were viewed communally and were followed by group discussion.

This pattern of urban in-school programs and rural agricultural development support was followed in many other developing countries. During the 1960s and 1970s, educational television projects were undertaken in more than a dozen countries in Latin America (e.g., El Salvador and Colombia) and like numbers in Africa (e.g., Ivory Coast and Niger) and Asia (e.g., South Korea and India). In Oceania, the entire educational system of American Samoa was restructured around television in the 1960s.

In many cases, these projects were not intended to be permanent; in any event, most were not sustained. Tiffin's (1978) system analysis of ETV projects in Latin America indicated that although the lessons themselves were educationally effective the overall projects suffered from systemic problems. Clayton's (1979) analysis echoed these findings, noting that systems in which major components are absent or dysfunctional tended to perish.

In the post-colonial era, ETV was viewed as a means of expanding the reach of disadvantaged education systems while improving the quality of the education that was offered. The evidence indicated that from a strictly economic standpoint these early projects were difficult to justify. Reform based on television may be a faster means of changing the curriculum and improving teaching methods but it is also more expensive in these settings and often not locally sustainable (Carnoy, 1975).

# THE COMMUNICATION PARADIGM

## Information Theory

During the later days of educational radio and the earlier days of educational television, communication theory became a dominant paradigm both in the physical and social sciences. Flowing from Shannon and Weaver's (Shannon, 1949) information theory, through Wiener's (1950) cybernetics and Berlo's (1960) Process of Communication model, thinkers in educational technology were viewing teaching/learning problems as communication problems. Improvement of communication depended on detecting where the weak points in the process were and ameliorating them: choosing a more visual medium, building more redundancy into the message, matching the receiver's language capability better, providing the sender with better feedback about the receiver's response, and the like.

## Semantics

During the 1940s and 1950s, theories of communication not only sparked the emergence of information science but also attracted attention in the social sciences. General Semantics, conceived by Korzybski (1933) and interpreted and popularized by Hayakawa (1941), offered a new way of studying the meanings evoked when humans communicated through various media. It added the human dimension to the technical process of communication addressed in other communication theories.

## A New Paradigm for Audio-Visual Education

The communication perspective became a new paradigm for defining the audio-visual instruction field. It was embraced wholeheartedly by a segment of the field; for example, the name of the academic program at Syracuse University changed from Audio-Visual Education to Educational Media to Instructional Communications in the mid-1960s. The first formal definition of the field in 1963 used the term *audiovisual communications* as the central concept. When the time came to change the name of DAVI in 1971, there was nearly equal support for *communications* and *technology* as the key terms, so both were incorporated into the new name: Association for Educational Communications and Technology (AECT).

# RADICAL BEHAVIORISM

## Application to Instruction

The term *behaviorism* refers collectively to several related but different theories in psychology. One of them, radical behaviorism, has had the greatest practical impact on educational technology due to the application of its primary technique, operant conditioning, to teaching-learning problems (Burton et al., 2004). As discussed in the chapter by Lockee and colleagues in the Technologies part of this handbook, B.F. Skinner's analysis of the problems of group-based traditional instruction led him to the invention of a mechanical device for applying operant conditioning to academic instruction (Skinner, 1954). Referred to as a *teaching machine*, the device gained national attention. The arrangement of stimuli, responses, and reinforcers in teaching machines became known as *programmed instruction*, and programmed instruction lessons in book format were published in great profusion in the 1960s.

## Impact of Teaching Machines

The Department of Audiovisual Instruction (the hyphen between audio and visual was dropped in 1960) joined the new programmed instruction movement by publishing *Teaching Machines and Programmed Learning: A Source Book* (Lumsdaine and Glaser, 1960). The 1959 DAVI convention program had a single paper devoted to programmed instruction, but there was a major session in 1960 entitled "Programmed Instructional Materials for Use in Teaching Machines." This title gives a clue to the link between audio-visual administrators and programmed instruction: the machines that were initially used to deliver the programmed lessons. When schools and colleges acquired teaching machines someone had to take care of them: the audio-visual coordinator! The primacy of the machine was indicated by the name that marked this special-interest group at the next several DAVI conventions: the Teaching Machine Group.

## Emergence of Educational Technology Paradigm

Gradually the emphasis shifted to the process of designing self-instructional systems. This design process dovetailed with the notion promoted earlier by James D. Finn that instructional technology could be viewed as a way of thinking about instruction, not just a conglomeration of devices. Thereafter, technology began to take on the dual meanings of application of scientific thinking and the various communications media and devices (parallel to the distinction between hard and soft technologies found in the second edition of this handbook). Further, by the mid-1960s, Skinner also came to view programmed instruction as a practical application of scientific knowledge to education, and he referred to his instructional strategies as a *technology of teaching* (Skinner, 1965, 1968). Other authors converted this term to *educational technology*;

an early example is *Educational Technology: Readings in Programmed Instruction* (DeCecco, 1964).

Between 1960 and 1970, the research focus of what had been the audio-visual education field shifted sharply toward work on teaching machines and programmed instruction, prompting the change of the name of the field from audio-visual education to educational technology. Torkelson (1977) examined the contents of articles published in *AV Communication Review* between 1953 and 1977 and found that the topics of teaching machines and programmed instruction dominated the journal in the 1960s. In fact, between 1963 and 1967, these topics represented a plurality of all articles published in that journal.

This reorientation of the field can be seen as a major paradigm shift, from the creation and use of audio-visual media or the communication of messages to the design of learning environments according a specific set of psychological specifications. The dominant psychological theories would change over time, but the role of applied psychologist would remain at the core.

## Behavioral Technologies

Research and development in behaviorism led to other innovations such as programmed tutoring, Direct Instruction, and Personalized System of Instruction, which are discussed at greater length in the chapter by Lockee and colleagues in Part III. These technologies established an enviable record when compared with so-called conventional instruction in experiments in which paper-and-pencil tests were used as the measure of learner achievement (Lockee et al., 2004). As communication technology advanced, these frameworks were incorporated in mechanical, electromechanical, and ultimately digital formats, such as computer-assisted instruction and online distance education.

# SYSTEMS APPROACH TO INSTRUCTIONAL DESIGN

## Evolution of Systems Approach

The essence of the systems approach is to subdivide the instructional planning process into steps, to arrange those steps in logical order, then to use the output of each step as the input of the next. The systems approach traces its origins to concepts that emerged from military research during World War II. An analytical technique that grew out of submarine hunting was called *operations research*, in which computers were used to make the calculations required. After the war, this approach to analyzing, creating, and managing man/machine operations, now referred to as the *systems approach*, was applied to the development of training materials and programs.

During the post-war period, each of the U.S. military services developed its own model for training development, and all of them were based on the systems approach, a soft science version of systems analysis, itself an offshoot of operations research. The systems approach was viewed in the military as a paradigm for combining the human element with the machine elements in man–machine systems, an antidote to purely mechanistic thinking. From the entry of the systems approach into the field of educational technology, it was recognized by its advocates as a loose set of guidelines that were applicable to the complex problems of human learning only by analogy and not the sort of completely deterministic and tightly controlled methodology described by some of its detractors.

The concept of systems approach probably was introduced to educational technology leaders in the United States by Charles F. Hoban in his keynote address, "A Systems Approach to Audio-Visual Communication," presented at the second Lake Okoboji leadership conference in 1956 (Noel and Noel, 1965). The conference spotlight coincided with a series of articles by James D. Finn published around the same time. Together, they helped create momentum behind the idea of the systems approach, which eventually became a hallmark of the field.

## Instructional Systems Development Models

During the 1960s, the systems approach began to appear in procedural models of Instructional Systems Development (ISD) in American higher education. Barson's (1967) Instructional Systems Development project, conducted at Michigan State University and three other universities between 1961 and 1965, produced an influential model and a set of heuristic guidelines for developers. During this same period, Leonard Silvern at the University of Southern California began offering the first course in applying the systems approach to instruction (Designing Instructional Systems), which was based on his military and aerospace experience. He also produced a detailed procedural model that influenced later model builders (Silvern, 1965).

### A Model for Schools

These early activities in the consortium that included Syracuse, Michigan State, U.S. International University, and the University of Southern California (later joined by Indiana University) culminated in a joint project, known as the Instructional Development Institute (IDI). The IDI was a packaged training program on instructional development for teachers, and between 1971 and 1977 it was offered to hundreds of groups of educators. Because it was usually conducted by faculty and graduate students from nearby universities, the IDI became an extremely influential vehicle for disseminating ideas about the ISD process among educational technology faculty and students across the United States.

### A Model for the Military Services

The Center for Performance Technology at Florida State University was selected in 1973 by the U.S. Department of Defense to develop procedures to substantially improve Army training. As recounted by Branson (1978), the ISD procedures developed for the Army evolved into a model, the Interservice Procedures for Instructional Systems Development (IPISD), that was adopted by the Army, Navy, Air Force, and Marines. The detailed procedures clustered around five major functions: analyze, design, develop, implement, and control. The IPISD model eventually had enormous influence in military and industrial training because its use was mandated not only in all of the U.S. armed services but also among all defense contractors.

### A Generic ISD Model

The 1980s brought a proliferation of ISD models for education and training. They differed in details but typically adhered to the common conceptual framework of analyze, design, develop, implement, and evaluate. This conceptual framework came to be called by its acronym, ADDIE. During the 1970s and 1980s, advocates for the systems approach attempted to promote its use in K–12 and higher education. These efforts were largely unsuccessful, possibly for reasons related to the social and economic dynamics of these institutions; however, ISD was welcomed in corporate and military training, where it became the reigning paradigm for the next 20 years as a way to standardize design practices and make training more efficient and effective.

## ISD as a Paradigm Shift

The ISD movement can be viewed as another paradigm shift in the history of educational technology. By the end of the 1980s, skill in instructional design was viewed as the core competency of the educational technology professional. By contrast, the development and production of audio-visual materials became a niche specialization, one that was often outsourced.

## Critical Questioning of ISD

By the late 1990s, however, an accumulation of pressures—new digital capabilities, intense cost competition and the need to reduce human resources costs, and the increasing pace of change—led to increasingly critical questioning of the ISD orthodoxy (discussed from an international perspective in Tennyson et al., 1997). In particular, the design of more complex computer-based learning environments in which learners are expected to take the initiative in pursuing knowledge and to collaborate with others in doing so challenges conventional ISD procedures (Häkkinen, 2002). Lowyck and Pöysä (2001), among others, have called for new models that emphasize co-construction of knowledge and indeed co-design of the learning environment.

## ADVENT OF COMPUTERS IN EDUCATION

### Mainframe Era

The first attempts to use computers to present and control instruction began in the early 1960s before the microprocessor, when mainframe computers used punched cards for input. The early experiments in computer-assisted instruction (CAI) began just at the time that programmed instruction was at its peak, so many of the early CAI programs followed a drill-and-practice or tutorial format. A correct response was confirmed, while an incorrect response might branch the learner to a remedial sequence or an easier question. Beginning in the mid-1960s, the CAI research and development program at Stanford University, later the Computer Curriculum Corporation, created successful drill-and-practice materials in mathematics and reading, later adding foreign languages (Saettler, 1990).

### Minicomputer Era

More innovative and more learner-centered programs were developed in the TICCIT project at Brigham Young University in the 1970s after the introduction of the microprocessor and the proliferation of minicomputers. These sophisticated programs yielded successful programs in mathematics and English composition; however, both the Stanford and TICCIT programs failed to gain major adoption in their intended sectors: K–12 and community college education (Saettler, 1990).

The PLATO project at the University of Illinois began in 1961 and was aimed at producing cost-efficient instruction using networked inexpensive terminals and a simplified programming language for instruction, TUTOR (Saettler, 1990). Most of the early programs were basically drill-and-practice with some degree of branching, but a wide variety of subject matter was developed at the college level. Over time, terminals at outlying universities were connected to the central mainframe in a timesharing system, growing to hundreds of sites and thousands of hours of material available across the college curriculum. As software development continued, many innovative display systems evolved, including a graphical Web browser. With experience and with more capable hardware, more varied sorts of instructional strategies became possible, including laboratory and discovery oriented methods.

The PLATO system pioneered online forums and message boards, e-mail, chat rooms, instant messaging, remote screen sharing, and multiplayer games, leading to the emergence of what was perhaps the world's first online community (Woolley, 1994). It continued to grow and evolve right through the early 2000s, sparking the expansion of local CAI development and finding a niche in military and vocational education.

## COGNITIVIST AND CONSTRUCTIVIST THEORIES

### Cognitivism

Like behaviorism, *cognitivism* is a label for a variety of diverse theories in psychology that endeavor to explain internal mental functions through scientific methods. From this perspective, learners use their memory and thought processes to generate strategies as well as store and manipulate mental representations and ideas. The Scottish psychologist Kenneth Craik (1943) theorized that thinking and reasoning take place through the internal manipulation of mental models. A generation later, Johnson-Laird (1983) built on Craik's foundation, elaborating a theory that when people participate in discourse they construct a mental model of the situation being discussed. Other theories that would later become very influential were being developed in the 1920s and 1930s by Jean Piaget in Switzerland and Lev Vygotsky in Russia, but these did not have significant impact on American educational psychology until translations were widely circulated in the 1960s. Cognitive theories gained momentum in the United States with the publication of Jerome

Bruner's *The Process of Education* in 1960, the dissemination of Piaget's and Vygotsky's works, and the emergence of information-processing theory (leading to cognitive load theory) in the 1960s. By 1970, when the journal *Cognitive Psychology* was born, the cognitive perspective had gained not only legitimacy but also dominance.

## Constructivism

A perspective on learning and instruction known as *constructivism* entered the vocabulary of the educational technology field in North America by means of a provocative presentation by David Jonassen at the 1990 meeting of Professors of Instructional Design and Technology (PIDT), a presentation later recorded and amplified in Jonassen's column (1990) in *Educational Technology* and in a lead article in *Educational Technology Research and Development* (1991). He challenged instructional design and technology people to question the "objectivist epistemology" underlying practice in the field. He attributed the field's failure to change in a revolutionary way to its acceptance of this epistemology, which he claimed undergirded both behaviorist learning theories and cognitivist learning theories.

Early advocates of constructivism used the term as an umbrella term for a wide range of innovative instructional methods drawn primarily from recent developments in cognitive psychology (see Bednar et al., 1991; Duffy and Cunningham, 1996; Duffy and Jonassen, 1992). Piaget and Vygotsky were frequently cited as foundational influences on the development of this perspective. Because of the importance of social and cultural influences in Vygotsky's theory, it is termed a sociocultural approach to learning and the branch that follows this theory is often termed *social constructivism*.

The difficulty of defining a canonical version of constructivism is discussed in Robinson et al. (2008). In view of these many differing streams of thought, Driscoll (2005) concludes "there is no single constructivist theory of instruction" (p. 386), and she cites as constructivism's common denominator the assumption "that knowledge is constructed by learners as they attempt to make sense of their experiences" (p. 387). This assumption actually overlaps with those of earlier cognitivist theories of learning. Where constructivists (some of them) seem to differ from cognitivists, according to Driscoll, is that they argue that "knowledge constructions do not necessarily bear any correspondence to external reality" (Driscoll, 2005, p. 388). This subjectivism aligns with the epistemology of von Glasersfeld (1984, 1992), the founder of radical constructivism.

### Constructivist Movement

Irrespective of ambiguity about its theoretical basis, the constructivist message struck a chord among many academics in educational technology. For those attracted to postmodernism, constructivism shared a foundation in a subjectivist epistemology. For those leery of behaviorism's reductionist tendencies, constructivism projected a vision of holism. It hearkened back to the era in which Bruner called for a learner-centered approach to meaningful learning. Perhaps most importantly for those in educational technology, it coincided with the new capabilities of digital media.

Constructivism recommended instructional strategies that followed several broad principles, according to Driscoll (2005, pp. 394–395):

1. Embed learning in complex, realistic, and relevant environments.
2. Provide for social negotiation as an integral part of learning.
3. Support multiple perspectives and the use of multiple modes of representation.
4. Encourage ownership in learning.
5. Nurture self-awareness of the knowledge construction process.

At least the first three of these principles lend themselves better to technology-based delivery than face-to-face conventional instruction. First, complex, realistic environments (or microworlds) can be created using simulation software. Second, e-mail, chat rooms, and threaded discussions can facilitate social negotiation. Third, the World Wide Web platform enables designers to link pictures and moving animation clips to verbal presentations, all of which can be navigated according to individual needs and interests.

Many of the instructional strategies promoted by constructivists were mentioned in the early article by Bednar et al. (1991): situated cognition (associated with cognitive apprenticeship), anchored instruction, problem-based learning, and collaborative learning. These strategies were subsequently supported by the American Psychological Association's *Learner-Centered Psychological Principles* (APA, 1995), an authoritative position paper on approaches to teaching and learning.

### Constructivism as a New Paradigm

Advocates on the American side, such as Thomas Duffy and David Jonassen, and on the European side, such as Joost Lowyck, converged on several joint projects (see Duffy et al., 1993), contributing to a growing wave of interest on both sides of the Atlantic. Having gained momentum by the mid-1990s as the constructivist movement, this could be viewed as another paradigm shift in the identity of the field. From that time to the present, the conversation has centered on using the tools of educational technology to create learning environments suited to experiential learning: WebQuests, problem-based learning, microworlds, simulations and games, blogs, and wikis.

### Emerging Syntheses

In recent years, theorists have been seeking a resolution to the paradigm wars among the competing learning theories. A synthesis offered by M. David Merrill (2002) suggests a lesson design framework incorporating behaviorist, cognitivist, and constructivist conceptions. Merrill's (2002) framework, which he refers to as *first principles of instruction*, proposes four phases to the instructional process: (1) activation of prior experience, (2) demonstration of skills, (3) application of skills, and (4) integration of these skills into real-world activities, with all four phases revolving around a problem or realistic task. Diana Laurillard (2002) of the British Open University characterizes academic instruction as essentially a conversation, an iterative dialog between a teacher and a student that is focused on a particular topic or goal. She proposes that media may play four roles in the instructional dialog: discursive, adaptive, interactive, or reflective. These roles reflect the emphasis of the different psychological perspectives; hence, Laurillard's model also may be viewed as an attempt at a theoretical synthesis.

# THE DIGITAL AGE

## Microcomputers and Personal Computers

The role of computers in education began to change dramatically with the development of microcomputers in France and in the United States in the 1960s and 1970s. Microcomputers became increasingly commercially successful after the introduction of new models in 1977 by Apple and RadioShack and in 1981 by IBM. By the end of 1982, the rapid proliferation of the personal computer was acknowledged by *Time* magazine by being named Machine of the Year, a break from the magazine's tradition of Man of the Year. Apple's Macintosh model in 1984 enticed even more novices to venture into the computer world. Previously, students encountered mainframe or minicomputers in labs, where they served as tutors that typically controlled drill-and-practice exercises. Now, both students and teachers could have access to user-friendly desktop computers in the classroom and at home as well as productivity tools such as word-processing programs for writing, spreadsheets for organizing quantitative data, and presentation software to create graphs and slide shows.

## School Adoption of Computers

An international survey in 1989 revealed that in most industrialized countries widespread school adoption of computers began around 1983 and increased at a steady rate each year thereafter. By 1989, several countries (Luxembourg, Switzerland, the Netherlands, France, United States, and British Columbia in Canada) had reached the plateau of having approximately one computer per classroom; however, as had been discovered earlier in the audio-visual era, access to the hardware does not equate to use. This survey as well as later surveys indicated that only a small percentage of teachers who had access to computers actually integrated their use significantly into their teaching (Pelgrum and Plomp, 1991; Plomp and Pelgrum, 1993). In these early years, student usage was primarily to learn about computers rather than to learn with computers.

As access to computers grew, eventually reaching recommended levels by about 2005, student usage continued to lag behind availability. In the mid-1990s, student use was still rather mundane, often limited to a few hours per week of drill programs or routine word-processing applications (Anderson and Ronnkvist, 1999). By the mid-2000 decade, it appeared that more students were using computers for many more hours (U.S. Department of Education, 2005) and possibly for uses more central to the curriculum, although this is debatable.

From the 1980s through the 1990s, the pendulum was swinging from analog media to digital media as the primary source of instructional materials in schools, colleges, and corporate training centers; however, traditional media formats such as textbooks, the overhead projector, and videocassettes have continued to be used heavily by teachers at all levels right up to the present. As an example, three fourths of all corporate trainers reported that they use manuals and textbooks and over one half use videocassettes (Dolezalek, 2004, p. 34).

## Internet and World Wide Web

As profoundly as personal computers changed the information environment in the 1980s, the advent of the Internet in the 1990s changed it even more. The rapid increase in connections to the Internet in the early 1990s vastly expanded the potential for sharing information at a distance. The invention of graphical user interfaces allowed the World Wide Web to become the most popular Internet protocol around 1993. Because of its ubiquity it became the *de facto* standard platform for sharing resources. Being structured according to hypermedia principles (links and nodes) it largely displaced the earlier concept of hypermedia programs residing in a local computer system. With programs residing on the Web, they could be tapped from any place in the world that could access the Internet.

## Distance Education

What is now known as distance education can be traced back at least to 1840 in England, when Isaac Pitman began offering shorthand lessons through the medium of mail. Correspondence study was well established in Germany, as well, before the first American correspondence study program (Society to Encourage Studies at Home) began in 1873 in Boston. Correspondence study attained respectability in the United States when major programs were offered at the University of Chicago and Columbia University early in the 20th century. In 1956, Chicago City Junior College launched TV College, using broadcast television to offer post-secondary education degrees to viewers in the Chicago area. It was immensely popular and it also happened to be on the itinerary of a visiting group of professors from the United Kingdom in 1964, a group known as the Brynmor Jones Committee. The 1965 report of this committee (*Audio-Visual Aids in Higher Scientific Education*) was a watershed in the evolution of educational technology in the United Kingdom (MacKenzie, 2005), and it inspired the vision of an "open university," which became part of the Labour Party's platform in 1963.

### The British Open University

The establishment in 1969 of the British Open University became a landmark in distance education in several regards. First, it was designed as an open-access, degree-granting institution. Second, it was expected to scale up to serve tens of thousands of students at a time. Third, although broadcast television in partnership with the BBC provided the most visible part of its instruction, it was designed to integrate television, other audio-visual media, print, telephone help systems, and face-to-face tuition in a seamless whole. The British Open University eventually became the model for most of the distance universities that came later. In particular, the broadcasting partnership has been emulated by the Open University of Hong Kong, the Bangladesh Open University, and the Korean National Open University (Bates, 2005).

### Mega-Universities

The subsequent years have seen the flowering of a series of large-scale distance universities, referred to as *mega-universities* by Daniel (1996), such as the China TV University System, the French Centre National d'Enseignement à Distance, Indira Gandhi National Open University, and Indonesia's Universitas Terbuka, among others. Perhaps the largest is Anadolu University, based in Turkey, which serves over 500,000 students from Germany to Cyprus.

### Web-Based Courses

The impact of the computer on distance education was first manifested through courses based on computer conferencing. Boise State University was offering a master's degree program in educational technology via computer conferencing in the 1990s. More recently, however, it is the mushrooming of the World Wide Web that has fueled growth in distance education. The Web makes it feasible for higher education institutions and corporate training operations to offer their courses at a distance economically. Instead of requiring video studios and expensive transmission systems, Web-based courses use existing computer infrastructure at no extra cost to deliver their courses to users. Web-based courses began to appear around 1995. The University of British Columbia offered its first entirely Web-based credit courses in 1996 (Bates, 2005).

These demonstrated successes created a brief land-rush mentality among American universities in the late 1990s to try to capture a commanding share of the market for online distance education. By the end of the 1990s, courses delivered via Internet were offered at 60% of all colleges, compared with 22% only 5 years earlier (U.S. Department of Education, 1999). Within a few years, the investment fever had waned and the field was left to the slow-but-steady providers of reliable, good-quality courses. Over 30 states formed distance learning consortia to pool their resources and give students a wider menu of choices. Consortia such as UMassOnline and Illinois Virtual Campus experienced double-digit growth in enrollments between 2000 and 2006 (Bichelmeyer and Molenda, 2006). In Europe, the Open University of Catalonia, which opened in 1996 as a public, fully online university, was serving 25,000 students by 2004 (Bates, 2005).

### Virtual Schools

During the past decade distance education also became a major phenomenon at the K–12 level in the United States. Many school districts, especially those in urban centers facing competition from home schooling, charter schools, and private alternatives, started virtual schools to try to retain students who were drifting outside the public school system. A major national survey in 2003 found that students in more than one third of public school districts enrolled in distance education courses: 76% at the high-school level and another 15% in combined or ungraded schools (Setzer and Lewis, 2005).

### Computer-Based Residential Courses

The use of the Web grew not only for off-campus distance courses but also for on-campus residential courses. By 2004, most American universities had adopted a standard course management system (CMS), a suite of applications, tying together Web presentations, e-mail, discussion forums, and other applications. Blackboard.com, introduced its first CMS, CourseInfo, in 1999. By 2006, Blackboard had merged with its largest rival, WebCT, and dominated the field of college and university CMSs, although rival open-source software CMSs were also being developed, such as Moodle and Sakai. The widespread adoption of CMSs blurred the line between distance and residential courses, as it allowed residential students to carry out more of their course activities on a computer, making distance a matter of degree rather than of kind.

Growth in distance education created a demand for distance course designers and developers, making this one of the key growth areas for educational technologists. By 2006, the work of educational technology had shifted heavily into the digital domain, moving the field closer to the field of informatics; however, the identity forged in the pre-computer era—the designer of learning environments—remains central, supplemented by the even earlier identity as promoter of sensorially rich learning experiences.

## CONCLUSION

Since its inception, the field of educational communications and technology has been characterized by changes in technology and radical shifts in its underlying paradigms. Beginning as visual instruction, then audio-visual instruction, adherents were attracted by the prospect of enriching the learning experience through involvement of the senses. Advances in broadcasting technology encouraged another vision: to bring educational opportunities to audiences hitherto beyond the reach of schooling. New psychological theories came along, holding out the promise of devising frameworks for lessons that would facilitate learning in dramatically improved ways. Then digital technol-

ogies captured the field, enabling designers to create learning environments in which verbal and visual media could be combined under the inspiration of various pedagogical theories into expository lessons, problem-solving laboratories, collaborative work spaces, or hybrids thereof—all made available to almost anyone, anywhere.

The field has also been and continues to be thoroughly interdisciplinary. Certain individuals and institutions have provided a measure of continuity over the years, but discontinuity has been a recurrent problem. Each media revolution and each paradigm change bring new people with different backgrounds into the field. From visual instruction to radio, from audio-visual media to programmed instruction, from instructional design to distance education—each transition has tended to mean reinventing the wheel in terms of the questions asked in research and in terms of grand dreams about revolutionizing education.

Likewise, the field has been and continues to be international in scope. Although the geographically diffuse components of the field are only loosely articulated, ideas have been able to flow sufficiently to allow rich cross-fertilization of both theories and practices. As the Internet has made communication and collaboration an order of magnitude easier, it appears that the coming years will knit participants even more tightly together.

## References

Anderson, C. (1962). *Technology in American Education 1650–1900*. Washington, D.C.: U.S. Department of Health, Education, and Welfare.

Anderson, R. E. and Ronnkvist, A. (1999). *The Presence of Computers in American Schools*. Irvine, CA: Center for Research on Information Technology and Organizations, University of California.

APA. (1995). *Learner-Centered Psychological Principles: A Framework for School Reform and Redesign*. Washington, D.C.: Board of Educational Affairs, American Psychological Association (http://www.apa.org/ed/lcpnewtext.html).

Bailey, K. V. (1957). *The Listening Schools: Educational Broadcasting by Sound and Television*. London: British Broadcasting Corporation.

Barson, J. (1967). *Instructional Systems Development: A Demonstration and Evaluation Project*, U.S. Office of Education Title II-B Project OE-16-025. East Lansing, MI: Michigan State University.

Bates, A. W. (2005). *Technology, e-Learning and Distance Education*, 2nd ed. New York: Routledge.

Bednar, A. K., Cunningham, D., Duffy, T. M., and Perry, J. D. (1991). Theory into practice: how do we link? In *Instructional Technology: Past, Present and Future*, edited by G. Anglin, pp. 17–34. Denver, CO: Libraries Unlimited.

Berlo, D. K. (1960). *The Process of Communication: An Introduction to Theory and Practice*. New York: Holt, Rinehart and Winston.

Bichelmeyer, B. and Molenda, M. (2006). Issues and trends in instructional technology: gradual growth atop tectonic shifts. In *Educational Media and Technology Yearbook*, Vol. 31, edited by M. Orey, V. J. McClendon, and R. M. Branch, pp. 3–32. Englewood, CO: Libraries Unlimited.

Branson, R. K. (1978). The interservice procedures for instructional systems development. *Educ. Technol.*, 18(3), 11–14.

British Information Services. (1974). *Educational Television and Radio in Britain*. London: British Information Services.

Bruner, J. (1960). *The Process of Education*. Cambridge, MA: Harvard University Press.

Brynmor–Jones Committee. (1965). *Audio-Visual Aids in Higher Scientific Education*. London: HMSO.

Bumstead, J. F. (1841). *The Blackboard in the Primary Schools*. Boston: Perkins & Marvin.

Burton, J. K., Moore, D. M., and Magliaro, S. G. (2004). Behaviorism and instructional technology. In *Handbook of Research on Educational Communications and Technology*, 2nd ed., edited by D. H. Jonassen, pp. 3–36. Mahwah, NJ: Lawrence Erlbaum.

Cambre, M. A. (1978). The Development of Formative Evaluation Procedures for Instructional Film and Television: The First Fifty Years, unpublished Ph.D. dissertation. Bloomington, IN: Indiana University.

Carnoy, M. (1975). The economic costs and returns to educational television. *Econ. Devel. Cult. Change*, 23(2), 207–248.

Clayton, J. S. (1979). Inhibitors to the application of technology [comment]. *Educ. Commun. Technol. J.*, 27, 157–163.

Craik, K. (1943). *The Nature of Explanation*. Cambridge, U.K.: Cambridge University Press.

Cuban, L. (1986). *Teachers and Machines: The Classroom Use of Technology Since 1920*. New York: Teachers College Press.*

Dale, E. (1946). *Audio-Visual Methods in Teaching*. New York: The Dryden Press.

Daniel, J. S. (1996). *Mega-Universities and Knowledge Media*. London: Kogan Page.

DeCecco, J. P. (1964). *Educational Technology: Readings in Programmed Instruction*. New York: Holt, Rinehart and Winston.

De Vera, J. M. (1967). *Educational Television in Japan*. Tokyo: Sophia University and Charles E. Tuttle.

Dolezalek, H. (2004). Industry report 2004. *Training*, 41(10), 20–36.

Driscoll, M. P. (2005). *Psychology of Learning for Instruction*, 3rd ed. Boston: Allyn & Bacon.

Duffy, T. M. and Cunningham, D. J. (1996). Constructivism: implications for the design and delivery of instruction. In *Handbook of Research for Educational Communications and Technology*, edited by D. H. Jonassen, pp. 170–198. New York: Macmillan Library Reference USA.

Duffy, T. M. and Jonassen, D. H., Eds. (1992). *Constructivism and the Technology of Instruction: A Conversation*. Hillsdale, NJ: Lawrence Erlbaum Associates.

Duffy, T. M., Lowyck, J., and Jonassen, D. H., Eds. (1993). *Designing Environments for Constructive Learning*. New York: Springer-Verlag.

Finn, J. D., Perrin, D. G., and Campion, L. E. (1962). *Studies in the Growth of Instructional Technology. I. Audio-Visual Instrumentation for Instruction in the Public Schools, 1930–1960: A Basis for Take-Off*. Washington, D.C.: National Education Association.

Fleming, M. and Levie, W. H. (1978). *Instructional Message Design: Principles from the Behavioral Sciences*. Englewood Cliffs, NJ: Educational Technology Publications.

Galbraith, J. K. (1967). *The New Industrial State*. Boston: Houghton Mifflin.

Häkkinen, P. (2002). Challenges for design of computer-based learning environments. *Br. J. Educ. Technol.*, 33(4), 461–469.

Hayakawa, S. I. (1941). *Language in Action: A Guide to Accurate Thinking, Reading and Writing*. New York: Harcourt, Brace.

Hoban, C. F., Hoban, Jr., C .F., and Zisman, S. B. (1937). *Visualizing the Curriculum*. New York: The Cordon Company.

Hoban, C. F. and Van Ormer, E. B. (1970). *Instructional Film Research 1918–1950*. New York: Arno Press.

Hovland, C. I., Lumsdaine, A. A., and Sheffield, F. D. (1949). *Studies in Social Psychology in World War II*. Vol. 3. *Experiments on Mass Communication*. Princeton, NJ: Princeton University Press.

Januszewski, A. and Molenda, M. (2008). *Educational Technology: A Definition with Commentary*. New York: Lawrence Erlbaum Associates.*

Johnson-Laird, P. N. (1983). *Mental Models: Towards a Cognitive Science of Language, Inference, and Consciousness*. Cambridge, U.K.: Cambridge University Press.

Jonassen, D. H. (1990). Thinking technology: toward a constructivist view of instructional design. *Educ. Technol.*, 30(9), 32–34.

Jonassen, D. H. (1991). Objectivism versus constructivism: do we need a new philosophical paradigm? *Educ. Technol. Res. Devel.*, 39(3), 5–14.

Kim, Y. (2003). An information literacy initiative adopting a moral philosophy for cyberspace: based on Yi Toegye's neo-Confucian pedagogy for self cultivation of one's mind and heart. *Media Educ.*, 10, 1–11.

Knowlton, D. C. and Tilton, J. W. (1929). *Motion Pictures in History Teaching*. New Haven, CT: Yale University Press.

Korzybski, A. (1933). *Science and Sanity: An Introduction to Non-Aristotelian Systems and General Semantics*. Lancaster, PA: International Non-Aristotelian Library Publishing.

Lashley, K. S. and Watson, J. B. (1922). *A Psychological Study of Motion Pictures in Relation to Venereal Disease Campaigns*. Washington, D.C.: U.S. Interdepartmental Social Hygiene Board.

Laurillard, D. (2002). *Rethinking University Teaching*, 2nd ed. New York: RoutledgeFalmer.

Levenson, W. B. and Stasheff, E. (1952). *Teaching Through Radio and Television*, rev. ed. New York: Rinehart & Co.

Lockee, B., Moore, D. M., and Burton, J. (2004). Foundations of programmed instruction. In *Handbook of Research on Educational Communications and Technology*, 2nd ed., edited by D. H. Jonassen, pp. 545–569. Mahwah, NJ: Lawrence Erlbaum Associates.

Lowyck, J. and Pöysä, J. (2001). Design of collaborative learning environments. *Comput. Hum. Behav.*, 17(6), 507–516.

Lumsdaine, A. A. and Glaser, R., Eds. (1960). *Teaching Machines and Programmed Learning: A Source Book*. Washington, D.C.: Department of Audiovisual Instruction, National Education Association.

MacKenzie, N. (2005). Genesis: the Brynmor Jones report. *Br. J. Educ. Technol.*, 36(5), 711–723.

McBride, W., Ed. (1966). *Inquiry: Implications for Televised Instruction*. Washington, D.C.: National Education Association.

Merrill, M. D. (2002). First principles of instruction. *Educ. Technol. Res. Devel.*, 50(3), 43–59.

Mohanty, J. (1984). *Educational Broadcasting: Radio and Television in Education*. New Delhi, India: Sterling Publishers.

Noel, F. W. and Noel, E. S. (1965). *Audio-Visual Leadership*, a summary of the Lake Okoboji Audio-Visual Leadership Conferences held at the Iowa Lakeside Laboratory, Milford, Iowa, during the years 1955–1959. Iowa City, IA: State University of Iowa Extension Division.

Parker, L. W. (1939). British school broadcasting. *English J.*, 28(4), 296–302.

Pelgrum, W. J. and Plomp, T. (1993). The worldwide use of computers: a description of main trends. *Comput. Educ.*, 20(4), 323–332.

Petroski, H. (2006). *Success Through Failure: The Paradox of Design*. Princeton, NJ: Princeton University Press.

Plomp, T. and Pelgrum, W. J. (1991). Introduction of computers in education: state of the art in eight countries. *Comput. Educ.*, 17(3), 249–258.

Robinson, R., Molenda, M., and Rezabek, L. (2008). Facilitating learning. In *Educational Technology: A Definition with Commentary*, edited by A. Januszewski and M. Molenda. New York: Lawrence Erlbaum Associates.

Saettler, P. (1990). *The Evolution of American Educational Technology*. Englewood, CO: Libraries Unlimited.*

Scots Community. (2007). Inventing Scots, http://www.scotscommunity.com/HISTORY/Famous%20Scots/Inventions.htm.

Setzer, J. and Lewis, L. (2005). *Distance Education Courses for Public Elementary and Secondary School Students: 2002–2003*, NCES 2005-101. Washington, D.C.: U.S. Department of Education, National Center for Education Statistics.

Shannon, C. E. (1949). *The Mathematical Theory of Communication*. Urbana, IL: University of Illinois Press.

Silvern, L. C. (1965). *Basic Analysis*. Los Angeles, CA: Education and Training Consultants.

Skinner, B. F. (1954). The science of learning and the art of teaching. *Harvard Educ. Rev.*, 24, 86–97.

Skinner, B. F. (1965). The technology of teaching. *Proc. R. Soc. Lond. B*, 162, 427–443.

Skinner, B. F. (1968). *The Technology of Teaching*. New York: Appleton-Century-Crofts.

Suchman, J. R. (1966). The pattern of inquiry. In *Inquiry: Implications for Televised Instruction*, edited by W. McBride, pp. 23–30. Washington, D.C.: National Education Association.

Tanner, D. and Woerdehoff, F. J. (1964). Profiles of instructional methodology for selected television courses. *School Rev.*, 72(2), 201–208.

Tennyson, R. D., Schott, F., Seel, N. M., and Dijkstra, S. (1997). *Instructional Design: International Perspectives*, Vols. 1 and 2. Mahwah, NJ: Lawrence Erlbaum Associates.

Tiffin, J. W. (1978). Problems in instructional television in Latin America. *Revista de Tecnologia Educativa*, 4(2), 163–235.

Torkelson, G. M. (1977). AVCR—one quarter century: evolution of theory and research. *AV Commun. Rev.*, 25(4), 317–358.

U.S. Department of Education. (1999). *Distance Education at Postsecondary Education Institutions: 1997–98*, NCES 2000-013. Washington, D.C.: National Center for Education Statistics.

U.S. Department of Education. (2005). *Rates of Computer and Internet Use by Children in Nursery School and Students in Kindergarten through Twelfth Grade: 2003*, Issue Brief 2005-111. Washington, D.C.: Institute of Education Sciences, National Center for Education Statistics.

von Glasersfeld, E. (1984). An introduction to radical constructivism. In *The Invented Reality*, edited by P. Watzlawick, pp. 17–40. New York: W.W. Norton.

von Glasersfeld, E. (1992). *Aspects of Radical Constructivism and Its Educational Recommendations*, presented at the Seventh International Congress on Mathematical Education (ICMe-7), Working Group 4, Quebec, Canada.

Wertheimer, M. (1944). Gestalt theory [English translation of *Über Gestalttheorie*, 1924/1925]. *Social Res.*, 11, 78–99.

Wiener, N. (1950). *The Human Use of Human Beings: Cybernetics and Society*. Boston: Houghton Mifflin.

Wood, D. N. and Wylie, D. G. (1977). *Educational Telecommunications*. Belmont, CA: Wadsworth.*

Woolley, D. R. (1994). *PLATO: The Emergence of Online Community*, http://www.thinkofit.com/plato/dwplato.htm.

---

\* Indicates a core reference.

# 2

# Theoretical Foundations

*J. Michael Spector*
Florida State University, Tallahassee, Florida

## CONTENTS

## ABSTRACT

This chapter addresses the theoretical foundations for research in educational communications and technology. Four relevant areas are explored: (1) the psychology of learning, (2) communications theory, (3) human–computer interaction, and (4) instructional design and development. Past work in these four areas can be viewed as providing a theoretical foundation for further research and development in educational communications and technology.

## KEYWORDS

*Educational communications:* Forms, means, and methods of expressing and sharing ideas, information, and knowledge to support learning and instruction.

*Educational technology:* The disciplined application of scientific principles and theoretical knowledge to support and enhance human learning and performance.

*Theoretical foundation:* A related set of rules and principles that can be brought to bear as a basis for making predictions and providing explanations for a variety of phenomena.

## INTRODUCTION

"May you have a strong foundation when the winds of changes shift." (from Bob Dylan's "Forever Young")

A fundamental aspect of educational communications and technology is change. Television was a new communications technology that influenced (for better or worse) learning and instruction 50 years ago. Since then, there have been many other new technologies and innovations in educational communications; however, the general problems for educational researchers have remained relatively constant—for example, how to make effective use of a specific technology in a particular educational context. In conducting research for such a purpose, one can proceed on the basis of prior work. What, then, is the nature of theoretical foundations in educational communications and technology?

## The Approach

The quick answer is that theoretical foundations are the basis for conducting research in an area. In this chapter, rather than review specific research foundations and cite appropriate sources along the way, I describe the general features of the educational communications and technology research landscape, citing only a very few sources in the main body of this chapter. I have included an extended bibliography at the end of the chapter to help readers extend their investigations in directions that seem useful and appropriate to them (an asterisk in the extended bibliography indicates a critical reference).

There are two reasons for selecting this approach: (1) *the lay of the land*—the general things relevant to most educational technology research are worth discussing as part of our intellectual heritage and identity, and (2) *my lack of expertise*—I do not regard myself as an expert in most of the areas to be mentioned, so the best I can do is to point to things that I believe are relevant. I certainly do not mean to imply that the framework presented here or the items listed in the bibliography are exhaustive or even the most salient aspects of educational technology research. They are simply the things I have stumbled across in my wandering around this intriguing landscape in the last 20 years.

## Nature of Research and Theory

The basic question that research aims to answer is why things happen the way they do. Developing an answer to such a question often involves a general rule or principle that has explanatory power or that will be predictive, as we often ask about future events—what will happen if we manipulate or change one or more things in the situation? A related set of rules and principles that has been shown to be reliable in many situations might be regarded as a theory.

Of course, there are different kinds of research questions and a variety of research objects. Appropri- ate methods depend on the nature of the questions and the objects investigated. Example question types for educational technology researchers include: (1) What will help these students learn this material? (2) Why do those students have difficulty in learning that material? (3) When will this technology and that form of communication be effective with those learners? (4) How can we explain the effects of that change in the instruction? Other types of questions can be framed, as well.

When specific questions are put forth in concrete contexts, one can identify appropriate methods of investigation. Oftentimes in exploratory research involving a new form of communications or a new technology, qualitative methods (e.g., action research, case studies, ethnographic research) are useful in gaining an understanding of and interpreting relevant aspects and factors that seem to influence learning and performance. On the other hand, when developing a general explanation for which factors systematically result in particular outcomes, one might use quantitative methods (e.g., controlled studies with randomized samples, quasi-experimental studies). In some cases, a study might involve both qualitative and quantitative methods depending on the questions being investigated and the research objects involved.

What confounds this already complex area of research and theory is that educational technologists are generally trying to find means to improve learning and performance. When a general instructional approach is devised, initial evidence of its efficacy must be developed. This may involve a formative evaluation that is aimed at making subsequent modifications to improve outcomes. Moreover, in the area of learning and instruction, there are many differences that make it difficult to develop general explanations and predictive theories. What works with one kind of learning task and a particular group of learners may not work with others. The circumstances in which learning occurs may also affect outcomes.

It is a wonder that instructional science has made such progress in the last 50 years given the nature of these obstacles. Some researchers are inclined to abandon the traditional scientific approach altogether, but doing so might be a hasty and unwarranted decision. A more modest approach is to use traditional research methods and make adaptations and modifications as they seem appropriate for particular research circumstances. The starting point of a research inquiry, as suggested earlier, is the admission that one lacks a good explanation for why things happen the way they do. This point of departure across the research landscape involves both *humility* (one begins an inquiry not knowing the outcome) and *openness* (one journeys

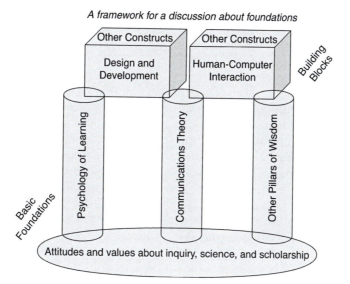

*A framework for a discussion about foundations*

**Figure 2.1** A framework for discussing theoretical foundations.

forth open to a variety of outcomes). These two aspects of traditional research and theory—humility and openness—ought to be retained as the core of our theoretical foundations.

## Four Foundation Areas

The notion of foundations in a discipline is not new. Having foundations implies having a history. Moreover, foundations imply that there is a solid basis for further work—research and development, in this case. In other words, foundations look both to the past and to the future. In looking to the past, it seems to me that psychology is obviously a critical foundation area—especially the psychology of learning. Human behavior and the development of knowledge and skills are perhaps the bedrock on which educational communications and technology rest. This idea is confirmed by the many graduate curricula in educational technology and instructional systems that include a core course requirement in the psychology of learning (or closely related subject such as the principles of learning). One section of this chapter briefly introduces this foundation area.

The nature of communications and its many forms and variations also seems critical to educational technology. Relevant theories exist to guide both the representation of information and the transmission of information from one place, person, or system to another place, person, or system.

Thus far, I have identified what I regard as two basic foundation areas: what people do (psychology) and what people say (communications). The other two foundation areas to be discussed below are more spe-cific and applied in that they address the ways and means of facilitating what people do and say, especially with regard to their interactions with others (e.g., teachers and students) and with learning materials and instructional systems. One can easily imagine basic values and scientific attitudes in addition to the two cited here—humility and openness (see Figure 2.1). One can also identify other basic foundations and building blocks to support and motivate research in educational communications and technology. The framework presented here (see Figure 2.1) is intended only for purposes of discussion and as an arbitrary point of departure.

In each of these four areas, I identify relevant past research and developments and suggest how these might influence future research and development in educational communications and technology.

## PSYCHOLOGY OF LEARNING

In *How We Think*, Dewey (1910) argued that we need to understand the nature of thought to be able to devise appropriate means and methods to train thought. Along the way, Dewey distinguished abstract from concrete thinking and indicated that many training regimens proceeded from the concrete to the abstract. Piaget (1929) identified a parallel progress in the development of reasoning in children. Dewey cited implications for his theory of thought for instructional planning—namely, he argued that effective training involves a balance of many things, including especially information, observation, imagination, reflection, playfulness, and seriousness.

Bruner (1966) made explicit the close relationship between intellectual development as investigated by Piaget (1929) and the practical task of devising support for learning of the kind suggested by Dewey (1910). Since that time, other researchers have devised instructional design frameworks based on new psychological research (see, for example, Merrill and Twitchell, 1993; Reigeluth, 1983, 1999; van Merriënboer, 1997). Meanwhile, the psychology of learning has undergone basic changes, evolving from behaviorism (see, for example, Skinner, 1938) to cognitivism (e.g., Anderson, 1983) to constructivism (e.g., Ford, 1987). Associated with these changes have been changes in how researchers and developers think about instruction (e.g., Driscoll, 2000; Lesgold et al., 1978; Reigeluth, 1983, 1999; Spector and Anderson, 2000).

What seems clear is that there is much more to understand about human psychology and learning. As a consequence, models of instruction are likely to continue to evolve based on our understanding of human behavior, cognition, and emotion. New areas of exploration in psychology that are likely to impact instructional design research include the linkages between neural mechanisms and problem solving as well as the structure of memory and its role in both learning and unlearning.

## COMMUNICATIONS THEORY

The second basic foundation to be discussed here is communications theory. The reason for this is that nearly all learning involves language (Vygotsky, 1962, 1978). The relationship of language, thinking, and learning appears in many philosophical analyses; see, for example, Dewey's (1910) *How We Think* and Wittgenstein's (1953) *Philosophical Investigations*. The notion of the central role of language games in thinking and problem solving was elaborated by Wittgenstein (1953). A language game is a rule-governed means of communication adopted by an identifiable community. In the case of learning and instruction, one might regard the professional communities of practice and the language games they have adopted as fundamental units of analysis.

One can find connections between language and learning elaborated in the ancient works of Plato as well as in modern philosophy (Klein et al., 2004; Spector, 1994). In short, language is fundamental to thinking and learning. The many techniques and tools for the expression and sharing of language—communications—are then fundamental aspects of thinking and learning. Moreover, methods of communications are likely to influence learning outcomes and impact the design, deployment, and evaluation of instructional systems and performance environments.

The notion of language games associated with Wittgenstein (1953) places particular emphasis on the use of language. The underlying notion is that it is use and context that give meaning to words and statements, which, without a context and accepted or expected use, are basically lifeless. Although use and context are certainly fundamental to meaning, communications theorists have examined much more with regard to the fundamental aspects of language. For example, Charles Sanders Peirce, Ferdinand de Saussure, Claude Shannon, and others developed and elaborated theories of signs and the rules that govern their use in various contexts (Hardwick, 1977; Saussure, 1959; Shannon, 1948). Saussure (1959) made a clear distinction between the sign and that which is signified. Peirce added a third category—the notion of an icon—and argued that the sign by itself was devoid of meaning. This argument was based on a pragmatic view of language and introduced the notion of language in use that permeates Wittgenstein's *Investigations*. Shannon extended these concepts to include the computer as a user of signs; he created a mathematical treatment of symbol systems that has been widely influential in the computer and information science communities.

As with the other pillars of educational communications and technology mentioned in this chapter, many more things could be cited as fundamental to inquiry and scholarship. Before turning to two applied foundation areas, it is worth mentioning one additional aspect of communications theory that is particularly pertinent to the world of digital media—namely, the notion of visualization as a form of communicating. Tufte (1977) argues that graphics are a form of expression—a language—that can be used more or less effectively in accordance with how well certain rules and guidelines governing their use are followed. Those who are interested in designing effective graphics are well advised to look at Tufte's (1977) writings, which might be considered one of many bridges between the basic foundation area of communications theory and the more applied foundation area of human–computer interaction.

## HUMAN–COMPUTER INTERACTION

How one person represents something to another person and the particular form of expression used to convey that representation influence what is likely to be understood. That is why communications theory is a fundamental consideration in learning and why so much emphasis is placed on the design of instructional messages. Given the widespread use of computers to support learning and the growing use of handheld devices, it seems quite natural to treat the exchange of information between humans and the computers with which they interact as a distinct area. There are certainly psychological aspects to human–computer interaction, as well as communications issues. As a consequence, in this simple framework, human–computer interaction is considered an applied foundation area of educational communications and technology research.

Many aspects of human–computer interaction have been investigated. They include basic human factor issues such as the colors and fonts that are easily discernible on a computer monitor and the various types of control devices and how they can be designed to facilitate human use. Other human use issues include when and how systems might support multiple learners who might be working or learning in different places and at different times. The types of computer-generated messages that are likely to be supportive of learning and performance have been studied in many different contexts and comprise an important area of human–computer interaction research.

Just as different disciplines have specific research methods that are considered appropriate for particular problems, these foundation areas have preferred or commonly used research methods. One of the widely used methods in human–computer interaction studies involves activity theory (Leont'ev, 1975; Nardi, 1996). Activity theory is a framework for studying humans and their use of artifacts. Emphasis is placed on an object's purpose and how it is used by an individual often working with others to achieve a particular goal. Activity theory emphasizes purposeful social interactions and might well be considered a research extension of the notion of a language game.

Perhaps the most well known instructional theory that involves human–computer interaction is Merrill's (1980) component display theory (CDT). An interesting aspect of CDT is that it introduced the issue of learner control and provided guidelines for when control should pass from the instructional computing system to the learner and what should be included in that control. CDT also provided an early version of what was reasonable to display on the computer screen given the current state of a learner's progress through a set of learning materials. These concepts would of course evolve and have given rise to many subsequent studies and instructional design frameworks, which are discussed next.

## INSTRUCTIONAL DESIGN AND DEVELOPMENT

The final foundation area to be briefly discussed involves what might be regarded as the core area of professional practice in educational communications and technology—namely, instructional design and development. This is a rich area of empirical research. Given the dynamic nature of learning and instruction and the introduction of new technologies and forms of communications, it is unlikely that this research area will ever be exhausted. In closing out this discussion of theoretical foundations, a model to guide investigations of instructional design and development issues is presented.

Instructional design and development are human activities. The general purpose of these activities is to facilitate and support human learning and performance. To achieve desired outcomes, instructional designers have developed instructional design models and principles, based in large part on the psychology of learning and what is known about effective communications (Gustafson and Branch, 2002). These models suggest that different instructional methods and strategies are likely to be effective in different circumstances (Gagné, 1985; Merrill and Twitchell, 1993). Instructional design principles have been developed that link back specifically to the psychology of learning and human perception (Gagné et al., 1992). Specific instructional design models have been developed to fit particular types of learning outcomes.

One of the more robust and well elaborated of these models in the four-component instructional design (4C/ID) model developed by van Merriënboer (1997). In 4C/ID there is a fundamental distinction between recurrent and nonrecurrent tasks—that is to say, those tasks whose performance remains relatively constant in spite of variations or changes in the surrounding conditions (recurrent tasks) and those requiring significant changes in performance due to changes in the surrounding conditions (nonrecurrent tasks). Instructional support for the former might include part-task training aiming for automaticity of task performance; instructional support for the latter might include whole-task demonstrations and practice in a variety of circumstances guided by heuristics and a mentor or coach.

A theoretical framework that accommodates all of these different models and associated research can be found in Reigeluth (1983). Reigeluth argues that a basic difference between psychological research on learning and instructional design research is that the former is primarily descriptive (these learners under those conditions achieved particular outcomes), whereas the latter is primarily prescriptive (to achieve a desired outcome given certain conditions, one ought to use that instructional strategy). This instructional design research framework can be applied at the lesson level or for an entire course or program.

Some researchers have challenged the descriptive–prescriptive distinction as being a naïvely objectivist view that overlooks the fact that values are involved in descriptive research just as they are obviously involved in prescriptive research. While I happen to acknowledge the fundamental nature of attitudes and values for all human activity (recall Figure 2.1), I believe that Reigeluth's framework remains a valid guide for ongoing research in our discipline. Indeed, I believe instructional design research and theory would become a marginalized craft without much influence or impact on education without such a sound theoretical foundation.

## CONCLUSION

It is my hope that a basis for ongoing dialog about theoretical foundations has been established in this chapter. I realize that I have traversed much landscape but not provided very much detail. I acknowledge having ignored much that is relevant. These errors of commission and omission could form the basis for discussion and leave the author of the Theoretical Foundations chapter in the next edition of this *Handbook* much more about which to write.

In closing I would like to return briefly to the two basic values that provided a point of departure: humility and openness. It is clear to me that a great many have contributed to our knowledge about educational communications and technology. I have chosen to include an extended bibliography rather than a simple list of references so as to emphasize that fact. Indeed, we stand on the shoulders of giants. The problem is deciding whose shoulders to use for a meaningful boost up and look over the landscape. Part of developing a sense of humility is realizing the significance of what so many who have preceded us have accomplished.

A second pathway to humility is realizing how limited our own understanding is on any particular issue of any complexity at all. I have adopted the following mantra for this purpose—surely it would be a remarkable coincidence if the limits of my imagination happened to coincide with the limits of reality. Openness follows naturally from a sense of humility and the realization that others often have excellent ideas.

As educational researchers, we might wonder what will come from what we have done, are now doing, and are likely to do in the future. We conduct studies, we write articles and books, we pile up accomplishments, and yet there is always more to be done, new territory to be explored, alternative explanations to investigate, new methods to try, and so on. I am reminded of a sonnet written by Percy Bysshe Shelly (1818) with which I close:

*Ozymandias*

> I met a traveler from an antique land
> Who said: Two vast and trunkless legs of stone
> Stand in the desert ... Near them, on the sand,
> Half sunk, a shattered visage lies, whose frown,
> And wrinkled lip, and sneer of cold command,
> Tell that its sculptor well those passions read
> Which yet survive, stamped on these lifeless things,
> The hand that mocked them, and the heart that fed;
> And on the pedestal these words appear:
> "My name is Ozymandias, king of kings:
> Look on my works, ye Mighty, and despair!"
> Nothing beside remains. Round the decay
> Of that colossal wreck, boundless and bare
> The lone and level sands stretch far away.

## Extended Bibliography*

Alessi, S. M. and Trollip, S. R. (1991). *Computer-Based Instruction: Methods and Development*. Englewood Cliffs, NJ: Prentice-Hall.

Anderson, J. R. (1983). *The Architecture of Cognition*. Cambridge, MA: Harvard University Press.

Anglin, G. J., Ed. (1995). *Instructional Technology: Past, Present, and Future*, 2nd ed. Englewood, CO: Libraries Unlimited.

Ausubel, D. P. (1960). The use of advance organizers in the learning and retention of meaningful verbal material. *J. Educ. Psychol.*, 51, 267–272.

Banathy, B. (1973). *Developing a Systems View of Education*. Belmont, CA: Lear Siegler, Inc./Fearon Publishers.

Banathy, B. (1991). *Systems Design of Education: A Journey to Create the Future*. Englewood Cliffs, NJ: Educational Technology Publications.

Banathy, B. (2000). *Guided Societal Evolution: A Systems View*. New York: Plenum Press.

Bloom, B. S., Engelhart, M. D., Furst, E. J., Hill, W. H., and Krathwohl, D. R. (1956). *Taxonomy of Educational Objectives, Handbook I: Cognitive Domain*. New York: McKay.

Bransford, J. D., Brown, A. L., and Cocking, R. R. (1999). *How People Learn: Brain, Mind, Experience, and School*. Washington, D.C.: National Academy Press.*

Brethower, D. M., Markle, D. G., Rummler, G. A., Schrader, A. W., and Smith, D. E. P. (1965). *Programmed Learning: A Practicum*. Ann Arbor, MI: Ann Arbor Publishers.

---

* Rather than list only those sources cited, this extended reference list includes other sources relevant to the theoretical foundations of educational communications and technology.

Bruner, J. S. (1966). *Toward a Theory of Instruction*. Cambridge, MA: Harvard University Press.*

Collins, A. (1991). Cognitive apprenticeship and instructional technology. In *Educational Values and Cognitive Instruction: Implications for Reform*, edited by L. Idol and B. F. Jones, pp. 121–138. Hillsdale, NJ: Lawrence Erlbaum Associates.

Cunningham, D. J. (1987). Outline of an education semiotic. *Am. J. Semiotics*, 5, 201–216.

Davydov, V. V. (1988). Learning activity: the main problems needing further research. *Activity Theory*, 1(1–2), 29–36.

Dean, P. J. and Ripley, D. E., Eds. (1997). *Performance Improvement Pathfinders: Models for Organizational Learning Systems*. Washington, D.C.: International Society for Performance Improvement.

Dewey, J. (1910). *How We Think*. Boston: Heath.*

Dewey, J. (1938). *Experience and Education*. New York: Kappa Delta Pi.

Dills, C. R. and Romiszowski, A. J., Eds. (1997). *Instructional Development Paradigms*. Englewood Cliffs, NJ: Educational Technology Publications.

Dörner, D. (1996). *The Logic of Failure: Why Things Go Wrong and What We Can Do to Make Them Right*, translated by Rita and Robert Kimber. New York: Holt, Rinehart and Winston.*

Dreyfus, H. L. and Dreyfus, S. E. (1986). *Mind over Machine: The Power of Human Intuition and Expertise in the Era of the Computer*. New York: Macmillan.

Driscoll, M. P. (2000). *Psychology of Learning for Instruction*, 2nd ed. Boston: Allyn & Bacon.*

Duffy, T. M. and Jonassen, D. H. (1991). Constructivism: new implications for instructional design? *Educ. Technol.*, 31, 7–12.

Eco, U. (1976). *A Theory of Semiotics*. Bloomington, IN: Indiana University Press.

Ertmer, P. A. and Quinn, J., Eds. (1999). *The ID Casebook: Case Studies in Instructional Design*. Upper Saddle River, NJ: Merrill.

Ford, D. H. (1987). *Humans As Self-Constructing Living Systems: A Developmental Perspective on Behavior and Personality*. Hillsdale, NJ: Lawrence Erlbaum Associates.

Friedman, S. L., Klivington, K. A., and Peterson, R. W., Eds. (1986). *The Brain, Cognition and Education*. Orlando, FL: Academic Press.

Gagné, R. M. (1985). *The Conditions of Learning and Theory of Instruction*, 4th ed. New York: Holt, Rinehart and Winston.*

Gagné, R. M. (1989). *Studies of Learning: 50 Years of Research*. Tallahassee, FL: Learning Systems Institute.

Gagné, R. M., Briggs, L., and Wager, W. (1992). *Principles of Instructional Design*, 4th ed. Englewood Cliffs, NJ: Prentice-Hall.

Gentner, D. and Stevens, A. L., Eds. (1983). *Mental Models*. Hillsdale, NJ: Lawrence Erlbaum Associates.

Gilbert, T. F. (1978). *Human Competence: Engineering Worthy Performance*. New York: McGraw-Hill.

Gustafson, K. and Branch, R. (2002). *Survey of Instructional Development Models*, 4th ed. Syracuse, NY: ERIC Clearinghouse on Information and Technology.

Hardwick, C. S., Ed. (1977). *Semiotics and Significs: The Correspondence between Charles S. Peirce and Lady Victoria Welby*. Bloomington, IN: Indiana University Press.

Havelock, R. G. with Zlotolow, S. (1995). *The Change Agent's Guide*, 2nd ed. Englewood Cliffs, NJ: Educational Technology Publications.

Hlynka, D. and Belland, J. C., Eds. (1991). *Paradigms Regained: The Uses of Illuminative, Semiotic and Post-Modern Criticism As Modes of Inquiry in Educational Technology*. Englewood Cliffs, NJ: Educational Technology Publications.

Jonassen, D. H. and Land, S., Eds. (2000). *Theoretical Foundations of Learning Environments*. Mahwah, NJ: Lawrence Erlbaum Associates.

Jonassen, D. H., Tessmer, M., and Hannum, W. H. (1999). *Task Analysis Methods for Instructional Design*. Mahwah, NJ: Lawrence Erlbaum Associates.

Kaufman, R. (1998). *Strategic Thinking: A Guide to Identifying and Solving Problems*, rev. ed. Washington, D.C.: International Society for Performance Improvement.

Kaufman, R. (2000). *Mega Planning: Practical Tools for Organizational Success*. Thousand Oaks, CA. Sage Publications.

Khan, B. H., Ed. (1997). *Web-Based Instruction*. Englewood Cliffs, NJ: Educational Technology Publications.

Kintsch, W. (1974). *The Representation of Meaning in Memory*. Hillsdale, NJ: Lawrence Erlbaum Associates.

Klein, J. D., Spector, J. M., Grabowski, B., and de la Teja, I. (2004). *Instructor Competencies: Standards for Face-to-Face, Online and Blended Settings*. Greenwich, CT: Information Age Publishing.

Koschmann, T. (1996). Paradigm shifts and instructional technology: an introduction. In *CSCL: Theory and Practice of an Emerging Paradigm*, edited by T. Koschmann, pp. 1–23. Mahwah, NJ: Lawrence Erlbaum Associates.

Kozma, R. B. (1994). Will media influence learning? Reframing the debate. *Educ. Technol. Res. Devel.*, 42(2), 11–14.

Lajoie, S. P. (1993). Computer environments as cognitive tools for enhancing learning. In *Computers as Cognitive Tools*, edited by S. P. Lajoie and S. J. Derry, pp. 261–288. Hillsdale, NJ: Lawrence Erlbaum Associates.

Langdon, D. (2000). *Aligning Performance: Improving People, Systems, and Organizations*. San Francisco, CA: Jossey-Bass/Pfeiffer.

Lave, J. (1988). *Cognition in Practice: Mind, Mathematics and Culture in Everyday Life*. New York: Cambridge University Press.

Leont'ev, A. N. (1975). *Activity, Consciousness, and Personality*. New York: Prentice Hall.

Lesgold, A. M., Pellegrino, J. W., Fokkema, S. D., and Glaser, R. D., Eds. (1978). *Cognitive Psychology and Instruction*. New York: Plenum Press.

Mager, R. F. (1997). *Preparing Instructional Objectives: A Critical Tool in the Development of Effective Instruction*, 3rd ed. Atlanta, GA: Center for Effective Performance.

McGilly, K., Ed. (1994). *Classroom Lessons: Integrating Cognitive Theory and Classroom Practice*. Cambridge MA: Bradford/MIT.

Merrill, M. D. (1980). Learner control in computer based learning. *Comput. Educ.*, 4, 77–95.

Merrill, M. D. and Twitchell, D. G., Eds. (1993). *Instructional Design Theory*. Englewood Cliffs, NJ: Educational Technology Publications.*

Merrill, M. D., Tennyson, R. D., and Possey, L. O. (1992). *Teaching Concepts: An Instructional Design Guide*, 2nd ed. Englewood Cliffs, NJ: Educational Technology Publications.

Nardi, B. A., Ed. (1996). *Context and Consciousness: Activity Theory and Human–Computer Interaction*. Cambridge, MA: MIT Press.

Norman, D. A. (1990). *The Design of Everyday Things*. Hillsdale, NJ: Lawrence Erlbaum Associates.

Palmer, P. J. (1998). *The Courage to Teach: Exploring the Inner Landscape of a Teacher's Life*. San Francisco, CA: Jossey-Bass.

Papert, S. (1999). *Mindstorms: Children, Computers, and Powerful Ideas*. New York: Basic Books.

Piaget, J. (1929). *The Child's Conception of the World*. New York: Harcourt Brace Jovanovich.

Plomp, T. and Ely, D. (1996). *International Encyclopedia of Educational Technology*, 2nd ed. Tarrytown, NY: Elsevier.

Polanyi, M. (1967). *The Tacit Dimension*. New York: Doubleday Anchor.

Posavec, E. and Carey, R. (1997). *Program Evaluation: Methods and Case Studies*, 5th ed. Upper Saddle River, NJ: Prentice-Hall.

Reigeluth, C. M. (1983). *Instructional Design Theories and Models: An Overview of Their Current Status*. Hillsdale, NJ: Lawrence Erlbaum Associates.*

Reigeluth, C. M., Ed. (1999). *Instructional Design Theories and Models: A New Paradigm of Instructional Theory*, Vol. 2. Hillsdale, NJ: Lawrence Erlbaum Associates.*

Resnick, L. B., Ed. (1989). *Knowing, Learning, and Instruction: Essays in Honor of Robert Glaser*. Hillsdale, NJ: Lawrence Erlbaum Associates.

Resnick, L., Levine, J. M., and Teasley, S., Eds. (1991), *Perspectives on Socially Shared Cognition*. Washington, D.C.: APA Press.

Richey, R. C., Fields, D. C., and Foxon, M., with Roberts, R. C., Spannaus, T., and Spector, J. M. (2001). *Instructional Design Competencies: The Standards*, 3rd ed. Syracuse, NY: ERIC Clearinghouse on Information and Technology.

Rossett, A. (1999). *First Things Fast: A Handbook for Performance Analysis*. San Diego, CA: Pfeiffer.

Rummler, G. A. and Brache, A. P. (1990). *Improving Performance: How to Manage the White Space on the Organization Chart*. San Francisco, CA: Jossey-Bass.

Sales, G. and Dempsey, J., Eds. (1993). *Interactive Instruction and Feedback*. Englewood Cliffs, NJ: Educational Technology.

Salomon, G., Ed. (1993). *Distributed Cognitions: Psychological and Educational Considerations*. New York: Cambridge University Press.

Saussure, F. (1959). The object of linguistics—nature of the linguistic sign, a course in general linguistics. In *Semiotics: An Introductory Anthology*, edited by R. E. Innis, pp. 28–40. London: Hutchinson.

Scardamalia, M. (2004). Instruction, learning, and knowledge building: harnessing theory, design, and innovation dynamics. *Educ. Technol.*, 44(3), 30–33.

Schank, R. C. and Abelson, R. P. (1977). *Scripts, Plans, Goals and Understanding: An Inquiry into Human Knowledge*. Hillsdale, NJ: Lawrence Erlbaum Associates.

Shannon, C. E. (1948). A mathematical theory of communication. *Bell System Tech. J.*, 27, 379–423; 623–656.

Shelly, P. B. (1818). Ozymandias. *The Examiner*, February 1, p. 13.

Shrock, S. A. and Coscarelli, W. C. C. (1989). *Criterion-Referenced Test Development: Technical and Legal Guidelines for Corporate Training*. Reading, MA: Addison-Wesley.

Simon, H. A. (1981). *The Sciences of the Artificial*, 2nd ed. Cambridge, MA: Harvard University Press.

Skinner, B. F. (1938). *The Behavior of Organisms: An Experimental Analysis*. Englewood Cliffs, NJ: Prentice-Hall.*

Skinner, B. F. (1969). *Contingencies of Reinforcement: A Theoretical Analysis*. New York: Appleton-Century-Crofts.

Smith, P. L. and Ragan, T. J. (1999). *Instructional Design*, 2nd ed. Upper Saddle River, NJ: Merrill.

Spector, J. M. (1994). Integrating instructional science, learning theory, and technology. In *Automating Instructional Design, Development, and Delivery*, edited by R. D. Tennyson, pp. 243–260. Brussels, Belgium: Springer-Verlag.

Spector, J. M. (1998a). The role of epistemology in instructional design. *Instruct. Sci.*, 26, 193–203.

Spector, J. M. (1998b). The future of instructional theory: a synthesis of European and American perspectives. *J. Structural Learning Intelligent Syst.*, 13(2), 115–128.

Spector, J. M. (2000). Towards a philosophy of instruction. *Educ. Technol. Soc.*, 3(3), 522–525.

Spector, J. M. (2001). A philosophy of instructional design for the 21st century? *J. Structural Learning Intelligent Syst.*, 14(4), 307–318.

Spector, J. M. and Anderson, T. M., Eds. (2000). *Integrated and Holistic Perspectives on Learning, Instruction and Technology: Understanding Complexity*. Dordrecht: Kluwer Academic Press.

Spector, J. M., Polson, M. C., and Muraida, D. J., Eds. (1993). *Automating Instructional Design: Concepts and Issues*. Englewood Cliffs, NJ: Educational Technology.

Spector, J. M., Ohrazda, C., Van Schaack, A., and Wiley, D. A., Eds. (2005). *Innovations in Instructional Technology: Essays in Honor of M. David Merrill*. Mahwah, NJ: Lawrence Erlbaum Associates.

Sterman, J. D. (1994). Learning in and about complex systems. *Syst. Dynam. Rev.*, 10(2/3), 291–300.

Stolovitch, H. D. and Keeps, E. J., Eds. (1999). *Handbook of Human Performance Technology: Improving Individual and Organizational Performance Worldwide*, 2nd ed. San Francisco, CA: Jossey-Bass/Pfeiffer.

Sweller, J. (1999). *Instructional Design in Technical Areas*. Australia: Stylus Publications.

Tennyson, R. D., Schott, F., Seel, N. M., and Dijkstra, S. (1997). *Instructional Design International Perspectives: Theory, Research, and Models*. Mahwah, NJ: Lawrence Erlbaum Associates.

Tufte, E. R. (1997). *Visual Explanations: Images and Quantities, Evidence and Narrative*. Cheshire, CN: Graphics Press.

van Merriënboer, J. J. G. (1997). *Training Complex Cognitive Skills: A Four Component Instructional Design Model*. Englewood Cliffs, NJ: Educational Technology Publications.*

Vygotsky, L. S. (1962). *Thought and Language*. Cambridge, MA: MIT Press.

Vygotsky, L. S. (1978). *Mind in Society: The Development of Higher Psychological Processes*. Cambridge, MA: Harvard University Press.

Wenger, E. (1987). *Artificial Intelligence and Tutoring Systems: Computational and Cognitive Approaches to the Communication of Knowledge*. Los Altos, CA: Morgan Kaufmann.

Wilson, B. G. (1996). *Constructivist Learning Environments: Case Studies in Instructional Design*. Englewood Cliffs, NJ: Educational Technology Publications.

Winograd, T. and Flores, F. (1986). *Understanding Computers and Cognition: A New Foundation for Design*. Norwood, NJ: Ablex.

Wittgenstein, L. (1953). *Philosophical Investigations*, translated by G. E. M. Anscombe. New York: Macmillan.

---

* Indicates a core reference.

# 3

# Complexity Theory

*Xiaopeng Ni and Robert Maribe Branch*
University of Georgia, Athens, Georgia

## CONTENTS

Introduction ............................................................................................................................30
    The Concept of Complexity ...........................................................................................30
    Complexity Theory .........................................................................................................30
    Complexity in Practice ...................................................................................................31
Conclusion ..............................................................................................................................32
References ...............................................................................................................................32

## ABSTRACT

Complexity is a common phenomenon existing in biological organisms, geological formations, and social constructions. Educational researchers and educational practitioners routinely encounter complex situations as a function of study and practice. Managing complex situations has become a common necessity for educational technology researchers to make sense of complicated situations; however, complexity as a factor in educational technology research tends to be maligned, oversimplified, or otherwise insufficiently addressed, thereby rendering the results of many research studies about educational technology lacking in generalizability. A conceptual, theoretical, and practical understanding of complexity offers a framework for research on educational technology that addresses the issues associated with nonlinear and complicated relationships. Complexity theory is predicated on a phenomenon possessing five attributes: (1) it contains independent complicated entities, (2) multiple entities are contained within, (3) the entities within the phenomenon perform interrelated functions, (4) the phenomenon seeks a common goal, and (5) uncertainty is generated because of unpredictable interactions within itself and between itself and the environment. A summary of the main conceptual, theoretical, and practical aspects of complexity is presented as it relates to educational communications and technology.

## KEYWORDS

*Complex:* Pertains to a group of multiple independent entities with interrelated functions seeking a common goal through adaptive processes.
*Complicated:* Consisting of many interconnecting parts or elements; intricate; involving many different and confusing aspects.
*System:* An interdependent entity that is responsive, systematic, and bound by the open or closed nature of the context in which it is located.
*Uncertainty:* Nonlinear patterns that are usually the result of unpredictable interactions.

# INTRODUCTION

Research designs in the field of educational communications and technology feature strategies intended to reduce or control the number of naturally occurring relationships during an intervention to isolate a subset of relations for further scrutiny. Isolating certain variables and controlling selected relationships is common practice for social and behavioral scientists. Managing the number of variables is a reasonable practice for educational technology researchers seeking to make sense of complicated situations. Educational technology research often involves the study of complex entities interacting within complicated environments. A complex phenomenon is a group of multiple independent entities with interrelated functions seeking a common goal through adaptive processes.

Complexity is a common phenomenon existing in biological organisms, geological formations, and social constructions. Although a complex entity is a unique phenomenon, it is important to understand the relationships that exist within it and the relationships between itself and the environment to abstract information common to multiple phenomena, to gain meaning, and to make generalizations: "Somewhere between the specific that has no meaning and the general that has no content there must be, for each purpose and at each level of abstraction, an optimum degree of generality" (Banathy and Jenlink, 2003, p. 38). Complexity as a factor in educational technology research tends to be malaligned, oversimplified, or otherwise insufficiently addressed, thereby rendering the results of many research studies about educational technology lacking in generalizability or application. A conceptual, theoretical, and practical understanding of complexity can offer a guiding framework for research on educational technology that addresses the issues associated with nonlinear and complicated relationships.

## The Concept of Complexity

Complexity, as an independent research concept, emerged from the fields of mathematics and physics. Levy (1992) defined a complex system as one whose components interact with sufficient intricacy such that they cannot be predicted by standard linear equations. Levy added that multiple variables interact nonlinearly such that the overall behavior of a complex entity can only be understood as an emergent consequence of the holistic sum of all the myriad behaviors embedded within. Levy's definition focused on dynamic relationships and unpredictable patterns in nonlinear systems. Law and Mol (2001) claimed there is complexity: (1)

if things relate to each other but do not add up, (2) if events occur but not within the processes of linear time, and (3) if phenomena share a space but cannot be mapped in terms of a single set of three-dimensional coordinates. What has come to be called complexity science first arose in the confluence of several fields—including cybernetics, systems theory, artificial intelligence, and nonlinear dynamics—many of which had begun to appear in the physical sciences in the mid-20th century. Complexity is the concept used to describe phenomena that produce increasing amount of information, energy, hierarchy, variability, relationship, and components, which in turn increase the possible outcomes and reduce certainty and predictability. The concept of complexity applies here because outcomes associated with educational communications and technology are commonly characterized by increasing amounts of information and an increased number of outcomes.

## Complexity Theory

Complexity implies that natural and social systems are nonlinear and dynamic. Education certainly classifies as a nonlinear, dynamic, natural, and social system: "Complexity theories have come to be taken up in the social sciences in many and various ways ranging from the highly technical, philosophical, narrative and more recently the applied" (Davis et al., 2004, p. 2). Educational technologists can arrange classrooms in various configurations, schedule mutually agreeable meeting times, and prepare and sequence instructional materials to satisfy a linear order of events, but even educational technologists cannot guarantee the same linear order of a student's learning experience nor interaction patterns among peers, teachers, media, and context. Complexity theory is predicated on a phenomenon possessing five attributes: (1) it contains independent complicated entities, (2) multiple entities are contained within, (3) the entities within the phenomenon perform interrelated functions, (4) the phenomenon seeks a common goal through a process of adaptation, and (5) uncertainty is generated because of unpredictable interactions within itself and between itself and the environment. Complex phenomena are individual entities that can be divided into smaller entities. Each entity has its own characteristic and function and can be divided into subentities. The human body is a perfect example of a phenomenon that possesses all five attributes and is divided into smaller independent complicated entities such as the head, trunk, and limbs. Each of the human body's entities is made of subentities, such as bone, tissue, and blood. Likewise, each subentity of the human body can be further divided into all kinds of cells, and so forth. An entity can be deconstructed into many parts (sometimes beyond our comprehension), and each part can still be a complex entity but at a micro level. A drop of water can be as complex as the universe; therefore, theoretically, everything is complex relative to the space in which it exists. A single entity may be able to fulfill one task independently in a relatively simple context. A group of entities may be required to fulfill multiple tasks interdependently within a complex context.

Complexity also means that a phenomenon possesses multiple configurations and multiple functions, which is consistent with systems theory. Each part of a system relies on other parts for information and production and therefore interacts with each other. The human system relies on entities such as muscle, bone, nerve, and blood, collaborating with each other to perform bodily functions. A system is synergistic, where the whole is greater than the sum of its parts. Uncertainty is generated because of unpredictable interactions. Many natural and social systems are complicated, and complexity theory can be used as a framework for understanding these systems. Complexity theory also provides a way to examine complicated systems such as educational communications and technology.

## Complexity in Practice

Educational technology is complex because it is formed by multiple interactions within itself and between itself and the environment. Educational technology is the study and ethical practice of facilitating learning and improving performance by creating, using, and managing appropriate technological processes and resources (Association for Educational Communications and Technology, 2007). Practice, within a research context, refers to "interventions that are designed solely to enhance the well-being of an individual patient or client and that have a reasonable expectation of success" (DHEW, 1979, p. 3). Educational technologists develop and implement products, processes, and programs designed to promote the well being of students with expectations of success. Gagné et al. (2005) summarized nine instructional events to describe optimum instructional arrangements based on a cognitive processing model. An instructional event is a relatively small unit that provides the external conditions that complement a learner's internal condition. Branch (1999) defined a set of instructional events that form a discrete teaching–learning session as an instructional episode. An instructional episode is

an entity that guides a learner toward defined knowledge and skill. A complex process is required to accommodate the myriad of complicated variables and relationships associated with educational technology.

Learning refers to the process of acquiring knowledge and skill. Intentional learning refers to learning that happens through purposefully arranged information, human resources, and environments to achieve a certain purpose. Intentional learning is complex because of the nature of knowledge and nonlinear interactions among multiple entities. According to You (1993), learning is complex because knowledge is a dynamic system and an active construction of dynamic reality comprised of an interconnected Web of patterns. Branch (1999) called such a dynamic system as referred to by You an intentional learning space. Branch identified eight entities that are always present within intentional learning space: student, content, media, teacher, peers, time, goal, and context. Branch purported that each of these eight entities is inherently complex. The student is complex because of the physical, emotional, social, and mental development of human beings, as well as the effect of intelligence, cognitive styles, motivation, cultural norms, creativity, and socioeconomic status on behavior patterns. Content is complex because it is a collection of concepts, rules, propositions, procedures, and socially constructed information. Moreover, the information types may be attribute, categorical, classification, component parts, dimension, elaboration, goal, hierarchical, kinds, matrix, prerequisite, procedural, rule, skills, and type. A peer is a complex entity because of all the social negotiations that occur among persons of the same age, status, or ability. Media are channels of communication that come in a multitude of forms. The teacher or teacher function assumes the executive decision-making role, such as identifying appropriate goals and expectations, analyzing learning needs, arranging content information, choosing media, selecting instructional methods, and conducting assessments on instruction and students. Time is a complex entity because it is omnipresent and can be measured by assigning discrete increments and intervals but not controlled. Context is the complex entity that refers to those conditions that directly and indirectly influence situations, environments, and communities. Contextual conditions are formed by physical, political, economical, and cultural settings—in other words, human ecology. Intentional learning space is the place where educational entities and nonlinear behavior coexist. Educational technologists study, experiment, and practice within intentional learning spaces; thus, the practice of intentional learning is complex.

## CONCLUSION

Complexity is a basic characteristic of educational technology; however, the aspects of complexity in educational technology research tend to be insufficiently addressed. Although existing perspectives regarding complexity provide foundational information for instructional designers and educational technologists, more study is needed about nonlinear patterns to understand education as a complex phenomenon.

## REFERENCES

Association for Educational Communications and Technology. (2007). Definition and Terminology Committee, http://www.aect.org/about/div_.asp?DivisionID=18.

Banathy, B. H. and Jenlink, P. M. (2003). Systems inquiry and its application in education. In *Handbook of Research on Educational Communications and Technology*, edited by D. H. Jonassen, pp. 37–57. New York: Macmillan.*

Branch, R. (1999). Instructional design: a parallel processor for navigating learning space. In *Design Approaches and Tools in Education and Training*, edited by J. van den Akker, R. Branch, K. L. Gustafson, N. Nieveen, and T. Plomp, pp. 145–154. Dordrecht: Kluwer.

Davis, B., Phelps, R., and Wells, K. (2004). Complexity: an introduction and a welcome. *Complicity Int. J. Complexity Educ.*, 1(1), 1–8.

DHEW. (1979). *The Belmont Report: Ethical Principles and Guidelines for the Protection of Human Subjects of Research*. Washington, D.C.: The National Commission for the Protection of Human Subjects of Biomedical and Behavioral Research, Department of Health, Education, and Welfare.

Gagné, R. M., Wager, W. W., Golas, K. C., and Keller, J. M. (2005). *Principles of Instructional Design*, 5th ed., Belmont, CA: Wadsworth/Thomson Learning.

Law, J. and Mol, A. (2002). *Complexities: Social Studies of Knowledge Practices*. Durham, NC: Duke University Press.

Levy, S. (1992). *Artificial Life*. New York: Random House.*

You, Y. (1993). What we can learn from chaos theory? An alternative approach to instructional systems design. *Educ. Technol. Res. Devel.*, 41(3), 17–32.*

---

* Indicates a core reference.

# 4

# Experiential Perspectives

*Konrad Morgan*
Northern Alberta Institute of Technology, Edmonton, Alberta, Canada

## CONTENTS

## ABSTRACT

A review of modern perspectives on learning would not be complete without some mention of the increasing awareness that we now have of the importance of experiential learning and its relationship in developing not only domain skills within the learner but also an understanding of new applications for such domain skills. Although experiential learning was first proposed by David Kolb in his 1984 paper titled *Experiential Learning: Experience as the Source of Learning and Development*, the principles outlined in this work can be traced back to the concept of the craft apprenticeships in the Middle Ages. Kolb also referred to an old aphorism accredited to Confucius around 450 B.C.: "Tell me, and I will forget. Show me, and I may remember. Involve me, and I will understand." This chapter discusses experiential learning in a modern perspective and provides the reader with a deeper understanding of the concepts associated with these ideas and the likely future directions for applying experiential leaning within the context of technology-enhanced lifetime learning.

## KEYWORDS

*Active learning:* Proponents of experiential learning often refer to active learning, and by this phrase they refer to the participatory nature of experiential learning. Learners take an active role in their own learning, and this often also implies that learners have to take some responsibility for their own learning and advancement of understanding.

*Apprenticeship:* An apprenticeship is a traditional learning paradigm in which a student learns by working with a master; this method of education was practiced widely in the Middle Ages. Many crafts and skills involved a 7-year period where a student was regarded as an apprentice; only after some formal test, which often involved the unsupervised creation of an object or completion of a task, was the student graduated. A longer process was required before graduates could attain the additional practical experience required for recognition as a master of their crafts or trades. The concept of a lengthy apprenticeship fell from favor with the establishment of mass education in the 20th century.

*Learning style:* A learning style involves a theoretical model that proposes that individuals have preferred ways in which they learn. These learning styles typically involve visual representation, vocal explanations, and practical examples. Experiential learning proposes several ways in which an educator can accommodate these learning styles, although all such styles have a bias toward practical expression and less emphasis on theoretical expressions of learning.

*Reflection:* Reflection is proposed to be a key element in the model of experiential learning where the learner has some inner mental consideration of the consequences of the actions they have taken in practical learning. Some mental models are implied that are necessary for reflection to be an effective element within learning in the experiential approach.

## INTRODUCTION

For the sake of the discussion in this chapter on experiential learning, the following terms are being used as indicated in the keyword definitions and below:

- *Active learning*—Proponents of experiential learning often refer to active learning, and by this phrase they refer to the participatory nature of experiential learning. Learners take an active role in their own learning, and this often also implies that learners have to take some responsibility for their own learning and advancement of understanding.
- *Apprenticeship*—An apprenticeship is a traditional learning paradigm in which a student learns by working with a master. This method of education was practiced widely in the Middle Ages. Many crafts and skills involved a 7-year period where a student was regarded as an apprentice. Only after some formal test, which often involved the unsupervised creation of an object or completion of a task, was the student graduated. A longer process was required before graduates could attain

the additional practical experience required for recognition as a master of their crafts or trades. The concept of a lengthy apprenticeship fell from favor with the establishment of mass education in the 20th century.

- *Learning style*—A learning style involves a theoretical model that proposes that individuals have preferred ways in which they learn. These learning styles typically involve visual representation, vocal explanations, and practical examples. Experiential learning proposes several ways in which an educator can accommodate these learning styles, although all such styles have a bias toward practical expression and less emphasis on theoretical expressions of learning.
- *Reflection*—Reflection is proposed to be a key element in the model of experiential learning where the learner has some inner mental consideration of the consequences of the actions they have taken in practical learning. Some mental models are implied that are necessary for reflection to be an effective element within learning in the experiential approach.

The concept of practice-based education had a long history before the inspirational paper by Kolb and Fry (1975). In fact, before the 20th century when education had a less mass market approach, one-to-one apprenticeship training was the main method of learning in the arts or sciences.

The major change that started in the late nineteenth century was that mass education had become the major method of education with a focus on the theoretical and rote learning of set items of information that were presented as facts (Dewey, 1933). Lessons and assessment then focused on the student learning one single set of view or facts, and the student was expected to extrapolate these facts into a systematic approach to a topic. This learning of the theoretical aspects of a domain made great economic sense but tended to produce students who had less practical experience and who often could not extrapolate the set knowledge they had been taught into the working world after they had graduated.

This type of theoretical and rote learning of the factual elements of a topic was especially prevalent in the early educational technology systems. Even the early models of simulation-based learning environments had weaknesses in that they did not permit students to learn by practical experimentation. In the best students this was not a problem because such gifted individuals were able to learn a topic in spite of the way in which the material was presented; however, for the majority of students it is more effective for them to be able to experience the practical effects of different behaviors and strategies in a learning situation than to passively observe them. This was why the ideas presented in David Kolb's papers (1976, 1981, 1984) and by his associate Roger Fry (Kolb and Fry, 1975) were a revolution in educational theory and practice.

The 1975 paper by Kolb and Fry stated a central hypothesis that learning was made more effective by allowing the learner to experience the real-world situation involved in the target discipline (Smith, 2001). Kolb and Fry (1975) and later Kolb together with other colleagues (Kolb, 1976, 1981, 1984; Kolb et al., 1995; Osland et al., 2007) argued that experiential learning allowed the learner to make sense of concrete experience and that this concrete experience made enormous differences to the effectiveness and application of teaching.

Kolb and Fry (1975) made many references to various sources for their ideas. One of the most convincing arguments in support of experiential learning appears in Kolb's influential paper *Experiential Learning: Experience as the Source of Learning and Development* (1984), which made reference to a quote attributed to the Chinese philosopher Confucius (450 B.C.):

> "Tell me, and I will forget. Show me, and I may remember. Involve me, and I will understand."

This attribution, however, may be apocryphal as there was already a well-established history of praxis-based learning in most traditional arts, and in many disciplines (such as medicine and law) the concept of a lengthy apprenticeship has remained an established part of their profession.

## Concepts of Experiential Learning

Having examined the basis and historical perspective for the idea, we can now discuss the elements of experiential learning (Borzak, 1981; Brookfield, 1983; Houle, 1980). Kolb's model has four key elements in any effective experiential learning situation: (1) concrete experience, (2) observation and reflection, (3) formation of abstract concepts, and (4) testing in new situations (Kolb, 1984). Kolb's work has referred to the elements of this learning cycle as activists, reflectors, theorists, and pragmatists, respectively.

There is some discussion within the literature as to whether there is an optimum starting point in the proposed cycle of these stages of learning (see Figure 4.1); however, it is likely that many of these stages are not discrete; given the nature of neural parallelism in the human brain, these stages probably occur

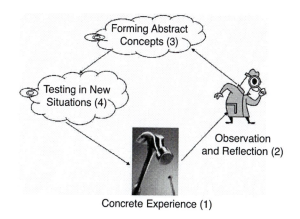

**Figure 4.1** Phases of experiential learning.

simultaneously while a student is involved in experiential learning.

It is interesting that this model involves several stages that are purely internal and conceptual. A lot of the focus in experiential learning has been based on the objective physical stages of enabling practical active experience with less emphasis on the internal mental manipulations that Kolb's model proposes.

It is also appropriate to mention that, however appealing this model appears, in fact very little empirical evidence supports or contests that these phases of learning are involved in any actual learning situations. The reader must therefore realize when dealing with the topic of experiential learning that it is more akin to a teaching philosophy than a science of education.

One of the key claims for experiential learning is how it effectively allows the student to learn the key aspects of a subject and then extrapolate those key concepts to different situations and act independently (Mezirow, 1997; Tennant, 1997). Again the reader should recognize that experiential learning theories do not provide detailed advice about how an educator should organize experiential-based educational activities to anticipate the best way or approach to teach any specific type of topic or subject.

Because experiential learning is more of a teaching philosophy than a scientific theory, it is important for the reader to recognize that there is very little evidence from cognitive science that provides theoretical or objective confirmation or denial of the key tenets of experiential learning. It is clear, however, that the actual experience of participation has a very strong role within experiential learning. Although the tenets of experiential learning are not necessarily supported within any cognitive or neural science explanations of learning, this may be a fertile area of further investigation for researchers interested in exploring links between neuroscience and learning.

**TABLE 4.1**
**Experiential Learner Types**

| Converger | Diverger | Assimulator | Accommodator |
|---|---|---|---|
| Abstract conceptualization and active experimentation | Concrete experience and active experimentation | Abstract concepts and reflective observation | Concrete experience and active experimentation |
| Strong in practical application of ideas; deductive reasoning; unemotional; high levels of concentration | Strong imaginative ability; good at new ideas and different perspectives; social and group orientation | Theoretical models; inductive reasoning; abstract concepts; not thought to be a social person | Doing; risk taking; immediate response; intuitive problem solving |

*Source:* Tennant, M., *Psychology and Adult Learning*, 2nd ed., Routledge, London, 1997. With permission.

## LEARNING STYLES AND EXPERIENTIAL LEARNING

The original papers that form the basis for experiential learning make clear the importance the influence of Piaget (Jean Piaget Archives Foundation, 1989). It should not be surprising to find that a major aspect of experiential learning is the idea of learning styles: converger, diverger, assimilator, and accommodator (Table 4.1) (Kolb, 1984). These styles provide some practical guidance for how to structure learning activities so as to match the preferred learning style of the students. Unfortunately, no definitive guide exists for how to determine the learning style for a student, and again it must be recognized that relatively little empirical evidence exists to support these proposed learning styles, nor is it recognized that educators themselves will have preferred teaching styles, which must also be taken into account for truly effective learning to take place. On the positive side, however, the concept of these learning styles does remove a single dimension of learning such as social skills or intelligence and also shows the strengths and weaknesses of any single learning style. Tennant (1997) elaborated basic learning styles within experiential learning as shown in Table 4.1.

## DIFFERENT USES OF EXPERIENTIAL LEARNING

The researcher will often find that there are two ways in which the term *experiential learning* may be encountered in the literature related to technology-enhanced learning (TEL). The first is as a way of learning that is a direct experience of real life (Borzak, 1981; Brookfield, 1983). This would be in contrast to the second and more common use of the term within TEL as the chance to experience a simulation of the various tasks, communications, and activities that are associated with a particular topic of learning (Houle, 1980). Both of these uses of the term are different from the study of the theoretical aspects of a topic or its history or a highly formalized and abstract series of steps as the more traditional ways in which a topic is taught.

### Further Developments in Experiential Learning

Weil and McGill (1989) proposed four interpretations or *villages* associated with experiential learning within the literature:

- *Village One* assesses and accredits learning from life and work experience.
- *Village Two* focuses on experiential learning as the basis for bringing change into the structures of post school education.
- *Village Three* emphasizes experiential learning as a basis for group consciousness raising.
- *Village Four* is concerned about personal growth and self awareness.

Although these definitions are useful it is important to realize that the major use of experiential learning within TEL will be for practical work-related simulations that are closely linked to real-world practice.

These uses of the term do not make problematic the notion of experience itself. Jarvis (1994, 1995) makes a case for how experiential learning theories can cope with learning through secondary or indirect experience, such as through communication. For example, it is obvious that learners can develop considerable knowledge and expertise simply by reading, and little mention is made of this within the experiential learning literature.

# CRITICISMS

As already mentioned, one of the more major criticisms of experiential learning is the lack of empirical validity for the theory or the learning styles that have been proposed. Further, strong evidence from neuroscience suggests that any stages of learning would be largely simultaneous, so the ideas of fixed stages must be regarded as being for the ease of designing learning situations or for explaining the central concepts behind the theory. There has also been some criticism that the experiential learning literature pays insufficient attention to the process of reflection (Boud and Miller, 1983; Schön, 1983). In addition, little consideration is given to how social or cultural issues can be included within the experiential learning model (Anderson, 1988; Brookfield, 1983; Fraser, 1995; Johnson and Johnson, 2002). These critiques of experiential learning may serve as the basis for further research in this area.

# CONCLUDING REMARKS

In spite of the criticisms, based on this review of the literature it is clear that the central concepts within experiential learning contain some extremely valuable principles for simulation-based learning in TEL. Further research should take the concepts and begin to address how the various ideas within experiential learning could be empirically tested to allow deeper insights into how the findings from neuroscience could be applied to technology-enhanced learning so as to maximize effective learning in digital environments.

# REFERENCES

Anderson, J. A. (1988). Cognitive styles and multicultural populations, *J. Teacher Educ.*, 39(1), 2–9.

Borzak, L., Ed. (1981). *Field Study: A Source Book for Experiential Learning*. Beverley Hills, CA: Sage Publications.*

Boud. D. and Miller, N., Eds. (1983). *Working with Experience: Animating Learning*, London: Routledge.*

Brookfield, S. D. (1983). *Adult Learning, Adult Education and the Community.* Milton Keynes, U.K.: Open University Press.*

Dewey, J. (1933). *How We Think.* New York: Heath.

Fraser, W. (1995). *Learning from Experience: Empowerment or Incorporation.* Leicester, U.K.: National Institute of Adult Continuing Education.

Houle, C. (1980). *Continuing Learning in the Professions.* San Francisco, CA: Jossey-Bass.*

Jarvis, P. (1994). *Learning: ICE301 Lifelong Learning, Unit 1(1).* London: YMCA George Williams College.

Jarvis, P. (1995). *Adult and Continuing Education: Theory and Practice*, 2nd ed. London: Routledge.*

Jean Piaget Archives Foundation. (1989). *The Jean Piaget Bibliography.* Geneva: Jean Piaget Archives Foundation.

Johnson, D. W. and Johnson, F. P. (2002). *Joining Together: Group Theory and Group Skills*, 8th ed. Boston, MA: Allyn & Bacon.

Kolb, A. and Kolb, D. A. (2001). *Experiential Learning Theory Bibliography 1971–2001.* Boston, MA: McBer.

Kolb, D. A. (1976). *The Learning Style Inventory: Technical Manual.* Boston, MA: McBer.*

Kolb, D. A. (1981). Learning styles and disciplinary differences. In *The Modern American College*, edited by A. W. Chickering, pp. 232–255. San Francisco, CA: Jossey-Bass.

Kolb, D. A. (1984). *Experiential Learning: Experience as the Source of Learning and Development.* Englewood Cliffs, NJ: Prentice-Hall.*

Kolb, D. A. and Fry, R. (1975). Toward an applied theory of experiential learning, In *Theories of Group Process*, edited by C. Cooper, pp. 33–57. London: John Wiley & Sons.

Kolb, D. A., Osland, J., and Rubin, I. (1995). *Organizational Behavior: An Experiential Approach to Human Behavior in Organizations*, 6th ed. Englewood Cliffs, NJ: Prentice Hall.

Mezirow, J. (1997). *Transformative Dimensions of Adult Learning.* San Francisco, CA: Jossey-Bass.*

Osland, J., Turner, M. E., and Kolb, D. A. (2007). *The Organizational Behavior Reader*, 8th ed. Englewood Cliffs, NJ: Prentice Hall.

Schön, D. A. (1983). *The Reflective Practitioner.* New York: Basic Books.

Smith, M. K. (2001). *The Encyclopedia of Informal Education: David A. Kolb on Experiential Learning*, http://www.infed.org/b-explrn.htm.

Tennant, M. (1997). *Psychology and Adult Learning*, 2nd ed. London: Routledge.*

Weil, S. W. and McGill, I., Eds. (1989). *Making Sense of Experiential Learning: Diversity in Theory and Practice.* Milton Keynes, U.K.: Open University Press.

Witkin, H. and Goodenough, D. (1981). *Cognitive Styles, Essences and Origins: Field Dependence and Field Independence.* New York: International Universities Press.

* Indicates a core reference.

# 5

# Empirical Perspectives on Memory and Motivation

*Norbert M. Seel*

Florida State University, Tallahassee, Florida; University of Freiburg, Freiburg, Germany

## CONTENTS

## ABSTRACT

This chapter is concerned with empirical research on memory and motivation within the realm of educational communication and technology. A variety of research methods and methodologies are described, with emphasis on the accessibility of theoretical constructs such as memory and motivation and the validity and reliability of assessments. The abundance of issues surrounding the topics of memory and motivation is narrowed to a few which appear repeatedly in the literature and are dominant in the domains under discussion in current instructional psychology. Several theoretical approaches to the architecture of cognition and models of human memory are described and discussed with regard to the question of how experiences with media and human memory interact. Accordingly, cognitive load theory and dual-code processing, as well as the theories of schemata and mental models, are reviewed critically and evaluated with regard to their advantages and drawbacks for learning with media. This chapter furthermore introduces relevant motivational research issues concerning technology-enhanced learning. After a description of several theoretical approaches concerning relevant motivational factors (such as flow and self-efficacy), the empirical research dealing with the question of how media and motivation interact are critically reviewed and evaluated.

## KEYWORDS

*Information processing:* The modeling of sensory input and cognitive transformations as a series of processing stages.

*Memory:* The mental faculty of retaining and recalling past experiences.

*Mental model:* A mental representation that people use to organize their experience about themselves, others, the environment, and the things with which they interact; its functional role is to provide predictive and explanatory power for understanding these phenomena.

*Schemata:* Data structures for representing both generic and specific knowledge.

## INTRODUCTION

We do not learn only through experience; rather, media and technological artifacts also play a central role in the formation of our knowledge of the world. Accordingly, *learning with media* has been at the core of instructional research for more than six decades, and there is not any medium or feature of a medium that has not been investigated with regard to its effectiveness on learning. The use of media may change the characteristic features of learning environments, bringing about effects on cognitive operations, representational formats, interactivity, visualization of semantic structures, and feedback. More specifically, the perceptual organization of messages affects how learners encode information because it is responsible for the nature of the mental representations that learners construct as a result of interaction with media of communication (Seel and Winn, 1997).

Media that combines visual and auditory presentation modes is called *multimedia*, and much research has been done on how people process audio-visual information. This research on *audio-video redundancy* has led to the development of several theoretical approaches over the past decades. Although Severin's

(1967) cue-summation theory was a promising approach in the 1960s, Paivio's (1971) dual-code theory emerged in the 1970s and was then combined with Sweller's (1988) cognitive load theory (CLT) in the 1980s. Both dual-code theory and CLT operate with the stage model of memory, which presupposes sequential information processing. In contrast, cognitive psychologists emphasize parallel information processing and functional capabilities that a memory system requires to support performance in a broad range of cognitive tasks. Important movements are the *levels of processing* approach (Craik and Lockhart, 1972), *parallel distributed processing* (PDP) *models*, as well as *connectionist models* of information processing (McClelland et al., 1986). Finally, *dual-process memory models* have influenced the understanding of recognition memory over the past 30 years. Dual-process memory models distinguish between a *recall-like process* in which episodic information is retrieved at the time of recognition and a *fluency-based process* in which general *familiarity* is used as a basis for recognition (Kelley and Jacoby, 2000). Dual-process models focus on the relationships between semantic and episodic memory, for which research shows the importance of *subjectivity* in remembering. Indeed, memories are constructions made in accordance with present needs and desires, and they are often accompanied by feelings and emotions (Schacter, 1996). This corresponds with studies that show that multimedia learning can enhance the *motivation* of students (Cheung et al., 2003). Consequently, more researchers are proposing connecting motivational and cognitive features of interaction with multimedia (Hede, 2002).

This chapter describes the major lines of research on *memory and motivation* within the realm of multimedia learning. It follows the current discussion about the need for sound models of multimedia learning in which cognitive and motivational factors of information processing are integrated to achieve a better and instructionally relevant understanding of the effectiveness of learning.

## METHODOLOGICAL ISSUES

Theoretical constructs such as memory, learning, and motivation are scientific inventions that serve to describe phenomena that cannot be observed and therefore must be inferred from observable data. Cognitive psychology has at its disposal a great variety of methods for assessing cognition, ranging from naturalistic observation to computer simulation, from experimental methods to verbal protocols, from recording electrical impulses of the brain to collecting reaction times (Simon and Kaplan, 1989). Correspondingly, we can find two major methodologies of memory research based on these methods. The first methodology corresponds to a *physical* approach and applies psychophysical methods (such as EEG or PET) to assess mental states. The other methodology corresponds with *functional* aspects of cognition and infers mental operations from observable behavior. The functional methodology is at the core of experimental methods. It contains traditional tests, questionnaires, the time needed for learning, the frequency and type of errors in performing tasks, drawings, eye fixations during task accomplishment, and so on. In natural settings, *verbal communication* is convenient for mediating ideas, thoughts, and feelings. Taking into account the prime importance of *language* for communication, it is evident that different methods of verbalization play a central role in the diagnosis of cognition. Psychologists often consider think-aloud protocols as an adequate method for verbalizing thoughts, explanations, inferences, speculations, and justifications. From a methodological perspective, an important effect of the infusion of information technologies into education consists in the potential of the computer to assess knowledge and cognitive skills. Computer-based approaches to *cognitive modeling* are considered effective methods for assessing concepts, ideas, and thoughts concerning a particular subject matter domain; however, these methods presuppose special tools (e.g., concept maps) for the assessment of knowledge.

## LEARNING AND MEMORY

### Theories of Human Memory

Theories are constructed to explain complex concepts and ideas. They are often difficult to talk about because they are not clear cut or concrete. Memory, for instance, is a fairly abstract concept, and a number of theories have been developed to explain how people store information in such a way that it can be retrieved when needed. Although all of these theories describe the basic function of memory as enabling the retention of information and personal experiences and the recall of that information and those experiences, there is no universally accepted model of human memory. Often, models of human memory are based on common-sense assumptions about how information is processed and stored.

A popular model of memory is the *stage model* of information processing (Atkinson and Shiffrin, 1968). This model proposes three stages of information pro-cessing: sensory memory, short-term memory, and long-term memory. Information is thought to be processed in a serial, discontinuous manner as it moves from one stage to the next. A central component of a modified version of the stage model is *working memory* with a limited processing capacity (Baddeley and Hitch, 1974). This idea goes back to Ebbinghaus (1885) and Miller (1956), who argued that humans can deal with about $7 \pm 2$ elements of information at a time without overloading working memory.

Several alternative theories of information processing, however, do not correspond with the stage model; for example, the Soar architecture is a theory of cognition that also presupposes the notion of a working memory but in a different sense than the stage model (Newell, 1990). In Soar, the working memory is a more elaborate temporary memory structure that holds information pertaining to the state of the current problem-solving context. The functions of working memory are distributed across multiple components of the architecture, including long-term production memory, which enables the cognitive system to handle complex tasks that require large quantities of information by relying on recognition-based long-term working memory.

The levels-of-processing (LOP) approach, dual-process memory models, and connectionist models do not include the conception of working memory; rather, the LOP approach argues that all stimuli that activate a receptor cell are permanently stored in memory but different levels of processing contribute to the ability to access or retrieve information from memory. Connectionist models, which are currently at the core of cognitive psychology (McLeod et al., 1998), and PDP models suggest that information is stored in multiple locations throughout the brain in the form of networks of connections. At a molar level, however, PDP models operate with the theoretical constructs of *schemata* and *mental models* to explain human information processing (Rumelhart et al., 1986).

The fact that memory is studied in a range of disciplines often leads to academic suspicion. Educational psychologists focus on the stage model of memory, whereas cognitive psychologists focus on parallel associative memory. The question comes up as to whether educational psychologists and cognitive scientists are really addressing the same phenomena when they focus on human memory.

### Cognitive Multimedia Learning and Memory

An analysis of the literature on multimedia learning shows that mainstream educational psychology agrees on a cognitive architecture that corresponds to

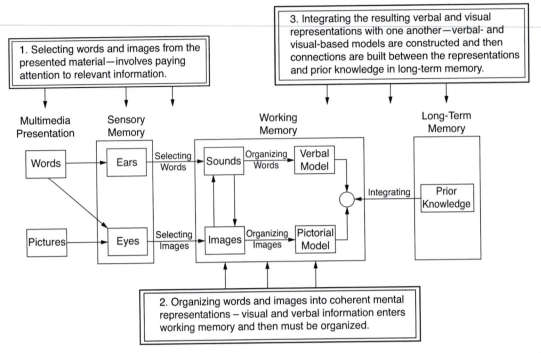

**Figure 5.1** The cognitive theory of multimedia learning. (From Mayer, R.E., *Multimedia Learning*, Cambridge University Press, Cambridge, U.K., 2002. With permission.)

the stage model of information processing (Reed, 2006). In this model, restrictions in the processing of information occur at specific points, especially within the working memory with its limited capacity. In accordance with this assumption, Mayer (2002) has presented a cognitive theory of multimedia learning in which he also refers to Paivio's (1971) dual-code theory of information processing. Paivio suggests that there are two cognitive channels, one specialized in processing nonverbal objects by means of imagery and the other specialized in dealing with language. Learning is better when information is processed through both channels instead of only one, but the working memory limits the amount of information that can be processed in each channel at one time. The capacity may be increased through the simultaneous use of both channels when the corresponding visual and verbal representations are contiguously present in working memory. In addition, by creating connections between corresponding verbal and visual information along with relevant prior knowledge, the learner organizes this information into a coherent representation both verbally and visually. The complete model is described in Figure 5.1.

Because working memory can only process limited amounts of new information, an overload can result if the learning task is too complex. This is the central assumption of the *cognitive load* approach

(Sweller, 1988). Cognitive load may be affected by the mental effort necessary to process new information (*intrinsic cognitive load*), the manner in which the material is presented (*extraneous cognitive load*), or the effort required for activating schemata (*germane cognitive load*). Earlier, Berlyne (1971) had already introduced the simple idea of information overload and suggested that the more elements a pattern contained, the more complex that pattern would be. The cognitive load approach deals with complexity using a single construct: *element interactivity*. If many elements interact, element interactivity is high; if few interact, element interactivity is low. To bypass the limitations of working memory, cognitive load theory stresses the activation of *schemata* that may encapsulate numerous elements of information in a single chunk. The activation of schemata allows automatic processing and thus minimizes the load of working memory. Skilled performance develops through the construction of an increasing number of ever more complex and abstract schemata (Sweller, 1994).

Cognitive load theory is an instructional design theory that aims to reduce the cognitive load caused by poorly designed learning tasks (Sweller et al., 1998), whereas Mayer's cognitive theory of multimedia learning can be easily integrated into the field of research on audio-video redundancy.

## Results of Research on Audio-Video Redundancy

Many attempts employing the concept of *audio-video redundancy* have been made to understand how people integrate and learn information presented verbally and visually—for example, through a text enriched with static pictures or through dynamic pictures (animation or video) accompanied by narration. This research on how people process audiovisual information has highlighted many complexities and inconsistencies (Lang, 1995); for example, people have better short-term recall of auditory than of visual information (Penney, 1989), and they need narration to receive effective instruction from animation (Mayer and Anderson, 1991). Furthermore, Nugent (1992) found increased achievement for combinations of audio and images but not for audio and text, whereas other studies (Mayer and Gallini, 1990) revealed that visual cues amplify and explain text and facilitate the recall of new knowledge because visual cues create imagery during learning that is critical to memory processes. Obviously, information across two channels can serve as reciprocal reinforcement and enhance both recall and comprehension (Levie and Lentz, 1982).

These observations correspond with the *cue-summation theory*, which states that learning is increased as the number of available stimuli are increased (Severin, 1967). Multiple-channel communications are superior to single-channel communications when relevant cues are summated across channels, are neither superior nor inferior when the cues provided on the two channels are redundant, and are inferior when irrelevant cues are combined, presumably because irrelevant cues cause interference between the two channels. If the stimuli provided on different channels are not reciprocally relevant, the distraction causes a decrease rather than an increase in learning and retention (Brashears et al., 2005).

Another issue is the perception of complex visualizations, which can be difficult to perceive and interpret. Several studies (Lowe, 2003; Tversky et al., 2002) have shown that perceptual features of visualizations can interfere with successful comprehension. Although Lowe found an advantage for predictions drawn from animation, this advantage was limited to perceptually *salient* features. However, novice learners often were distracted by perceptually salient features of an animation at the expense of more important content information. Thus, the interpretation and use of visualizations may be affected greatly by perceptual qualities of the visualization. In a comprehensive study on the effects of static and dynamic complexity on children's attention to and recall of televised instruction, Watt and Welch

(1983) showed that increasing static detail on the screen by using complex sets, elaborate graphics, and long shots *decreases recall* while leaving recognition unaffected, whereas increases in visual dynamic complexity produce decreases in recall coupled with increases in recognition. An analysis of the entire viewing process revealed that visual attention was only of minor importance in the learning process, whereas static and dynamic complexities were found to have different effects on learning involving a verbal recall process than learning requiring only visual recognition. Although the visual attention was not significant in this study on television viewing, Mayer and Moreno (1998) found that presenting instruction in both auditory and visual modes can cause a split-attention effect in which students have to divide their attention across multiple inputs, resulting in reduced processing of information. These findings were explained from the perspective of cognitive load theory (CLT), which is at the core of current educational psychology (Paas and van Gog, 2006). Although the results of CLT research are important for instructional design, there are some limitations from both a methodological and a theoretical perspective. Advocates of the cognitive load approach, such as Mayer and Moreno (1998), have pointed out that the limitations of CLT studies include the fact that the participants were usually college students; however, numerous studies indicate that the capacity of memory and the application of memory search strategies increase with development (Harris, 1978). Evidently, adults can refer to more perceptual experiences and can use more effective strategies for the retrieval of knowledge representations than children (Lindberg, 1980; Seel, 1984). Another limitation of CLT studies is that the instructional episodes have been short and only how-it-works material has been used (Mayer and Moreno, 1998).

### Alternative Theories and Predictions

Cognitive load theory and the dual-code theory presuppose a working memory with a limited capacity. The notion of a working memory refers to computational mechanisms that maintain and provide access to information to be retrieved during the performance of a task. Any computational system must support such functionality because computation is inherently a process that requires the temporary storage of information; however, in cognitive science reaction times longer than 6500 msec are treated as outliers of the working memory (e.g., Reijnen et al., 2005).

The question comes up whether theoretical approaches of educational psychology, such as CLT or dual-code theory, are compatible with theories on information processing within the realm of cognitive science.

Actually, Young and Lewis (1999) argue that complex cognitive tasks simply *cannot* be performed with a storage capacity of $7 \pm 2$ items. A problem-solving task involving inner speech, for example, may occur over tens of seconds or even minutes according to thought-monitoring studies (Franklin et al., 2005). To capture the involvement of memory in dealing with complexity, Ericsson and Kintsch (1995) introduced the notion of a *long-term working memory*, and Logie (1995) identified several conceptions of working memory, including the idea of working memory as *controlled attention*. This corresponds with the argumentation of Shiffrin and Schneider (1977) that individual differences on measures of cognitive limitations primarily reflect differences in the ability of controlled processing. It seems that memory theories of cognitive science are, to a large extent, incompatible with the stage model and related theories; however, if alternative theories exist and make differing predictions, we can test a prediction of the theory and a prediction of a competing theory at the same time. When the two predictions are incompatible, a *strong inference* (Platt, 1964) results. In contrast to CLT, dual-process models, for example, argue that *conscious* recollection and familiarity contribute to memory performance. Memory judgments are made by setting some level of familiarity as a response criterion and accepting items that exceed this criterion. A comparison of each information unit to long-term memory produces a continuous familiarity value that is used to make recognition judgments. This process can be appropriately explained by signal-detection theory.

Another example is schema construction, which plays an important role in CLT. Bransford (1984) has pointed out that schema activation and schema construction are two different problems. Although it is possible to activate existing schemata with a given topic, it does not necessarily follow that a learner can use this activated knowledge to develop new knowledge and skills. Furthermore, a major criticism of schema theories is that they are basically *assimilation* models that fail to answer questions on how existing conceptions are modified in the face of inconsistent input and how such theories deal with novelty (Brown, 1979).

## Learning and Remembering in Cognitive Psychology

Whereas educational psychologists (Clark, 2006) emphasize the importance of automated knowledge for learning and memory, cognitive psychologists focus on the role of *consciousness* in information processing because much of human cognition functions by means of continuous interactions between contents of information and various memory systems. Franklin and colleagues (2005) call these interactions *cognitive cycles*. Human computational ability has been estimated at 10 cognitive cycles per second, where each cycle is able to recognize or select information. Although these cycles can overlap, producing parallel actions, they must preserve consciousness. This corresponds with the basic assumption of cognitive psychology that humans store information in memory by relating new information to what is already known. This process is *semantic* in nature because information is stored in terms of its meaning, as defined by its associations to other information in the memory. The capacity for such storage is essentially unlimited, and the cognitive system can handle complex tasks that require large quantities of information by relying on a *recognition-based long-term memory*, which works in concert with the external environment.

Humans have some basic abilities that are essential for processing information and acting successfully in different environments. According to Rumelhart and colleagues (1986), one of these abilities is that humans are very good at *pattern matching* to quickly settle on an interpretation of any input pattern. Times for object recognition, counting, and selection tasks vary from 25 to 170 msec (with 70 msec as the average). Potter and Levy (1969) cited ranges from 50 msec to 300 msec for the processing of single pictures with low to high levels of visual noise, and their studies demonstrate that the accuracy of visual recognition improves as display times increase from 125 msec (16% accuracy) to 1000 msec (80% accuracy). A second basic ability of humans is that they are very good at *modeling* their worlds; that is, they can anticipate the new state of affairs resulting from actions or from an event they observe. This ability is based on building up expectations and assumptions and is crucial for inferential learning (Seel, 1991). Third, humans are good at *manipulating* their environments. This can be considered as a version of "man the tool user" and is perhaps the crucial skill in forming a culture. Especially important here is the ability to manipulate the environment so it comes to represent something. Rumelhart and colleagues (1986) argue that these three basic cognitive abilities involve the interplay between two units of memory: an *interpretation network*, which corresponds to the activation of *schemata*, and the construction of a *model of the world*.

### *Parallel Distributed Processing, Schemata, and Mental Models*

In cognitive psychology, schemata are defined as large-scale slot-filler structures that play critical roles in the interpretation of input data, the guiding of action, and the storage of knowledge in memory (Anderson,

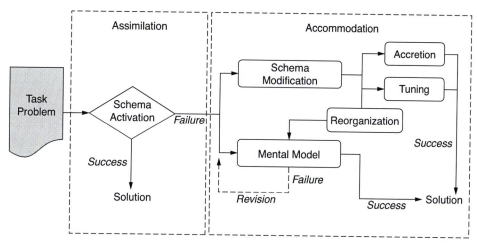

**Figure 5.2** Schemata and mental models as means of assimilation and accommodation. (From Seel, N.M. et al., *Technol. Instruct. Cognit. Learn.*, 4(4), 273–299, 2006. With permission.)

1984). PDP models, however, do not work with concepts such as schemata but rather conceptualize, consistent with recent brain research, memory by means of *constraint networks* resulting from the sum of excitatory and inhibitory influences on a unit. Input comes into the cognitive system and activates a set of units that tend to act together as response to certain patterns of the input. These tightly interconnected units correspond to what has been called a *schema* in cognitive psychology. A schema is the state that maximizes the particular set of constraints acting at a given moment. This conception, of course, contradicts the conventional story that schemata are stored in memory. In PDP models, they are the major content of memory, but *nothing stored corresponds to a schema*. What is stored is a set of connection strengths which, when activated, contains the ability to generate mental states that correspond to an instantiated schemata.

Similarly, mental models consist of *relaxation networks*, which take as input some specification of the actions we intend to carry out and produce an interpretation of what would happen if we did that. It is not necessary for world events to have really happened. In the case that they have not, the cognitive system replaces the inputs from the world with inputs from a model of the world. In PDP models, schemata and mental models are defined at a molar level of cognition, at which individuals organize symbols of experience or thought in such a way that they form a systematic representation of this experience or thought as a means of understanding.

Mental models and schemata are basic formats of *mental representation* that fulfill, in terms of Piaget's epistemology, the functions of assimilation and accommodation. Schemata regulate the assimilation of new information into cognitive structures. If a schema does not fit with a new task it can be adjusted to meet the task requirements by means of accretion, tuning, or reorganization. If this is not successful, accommodation must take place for the individual to reorganize the available knowledge to construct a mental model (Seel, 1991). This can be illustrated as in Figure 5.2.

Mental models are dynamic representations constructed to serve several functions, such as (1) the simplification of an investigation to particular and relevant phenomena in a domain, (2) the envisioning of complex structures (to make visible the invisible), (3) analogical reasoning, and (4) mental simulation in the sense of thought experiments (Seel, 1991). There are two procedures for coming to a mental model: either by means of constructing an analogy with the known or, if this is not possible, by integrating relevant bits of generic knowledge into a coherent structure to meet the requirements of a phenomenon to be explained. Both procedures require quite a lot of time and mental effort. A central component of modeling consists in the process of *fleshing out* (Johnson-Laird, 1983), which can be understood as the step-by-step completion of an initial model to a more complete model. While a schema is a slot-filler structure, a mental model contains assumptions that must be justified by observations. The justification of the assumptions is connected with a *reduction to absurdity* (Seel, 1991). This is a process of testing continuously whether a model can be replaced with a better model. As long as this is not possible, the model is considered as suitable.

### Research on Schemata and Mental Models

The schema concept has been an influential construct of cognitive psychology since the early 1970s and has inspired an abundance of studies in the field of text and picture processing as well as television viewing. In many studies, the role of human memory has been ignored, but some researchers (e.g., Watt and Welch, 1983) have referred explicitly to the interplay among perception, attention, and memory. In these studies, it became evident that both the context and complexity of, for example, pictorial information can play an important role for learning and remembering. Friedman (1979) found that unexpected (i.e., schema-dissonant) objects embedded in a complex scenario can be recalled better than expected objects because dissonant information evokes a focus of attention that is not necessary in the case of schema-congruent information.

The research on memory for schema-relevant information has produced contradictory results. Some studies demonstrate memory selectivity for schema-consistent information, whereas others demonstrate memory selectivity for schema-inconsistent information. A meta-analysis by Rojahn and Pettigrew (1992) on a sample of 60 independent studies with 165 comparative tests suggested a slight overall memory advantage for schema-inconsistent information. In addition, a study by Seel (1984) demonstrated that learners' attention to local information within a complex scenario as well as the processing of this information and its retrieval from memory are dependent on age-related development. First-graders could encode the global and local information of complex scenarios by referring to scene schemata, but they could not recall the pictorial details with a quantity and quality comparable to older children and adults. Visual attention runs from a small area with high resolution to a broad area with a loss of details, and focusing attention on a specific object can lead to a neglect of other objects (Shaw, 1982). Obviously, the *salience* of specific local information plays a central role for comprehension and remembering. Finally, the study by Seel (1984) demonstrated that the content of complex scenarios can evoke emotional reactions with a resulting focal attention on salient features of the scenarios due to a novelty effect.

Text and picture processing has also been a central issue of mental model research since its beginning in the 1980s. The effects of graphical diagrams or even helpful video on the construction of mental models have been investigated (Hegarty and Just, 1993; Sharp et al., 1995). Evidently, diagrams of complex technical systems, for example, proved to be effective not only for the representation of the complex real scenarios but also for the simulation of their processes; however, the success of such media presupposes that the learner is semantically sensitive to their model-relevant characteristics. The concept of semantic sensitivity was introduced by Anzai and Yokoyama (1984), who argued that individuals spontaneously respond to the information from the environment to generate a basic

understanding of it. Numerous studies demonstrate the semantic sensitivity of learners acting in learning environments that demand the construction of a mental model (Anzai and Yokoyama, 1984; Seel, 1995).

Despite these promising results, several authors (Snow, 1990) have criticized the early research on mental models because it was regularly done piecemeal in small-scale, specialized contexts. In many of these early studies (Kieras and Bovair, 1984), the following method was applied. After an initial training in which the subjects had to generate an initial mental model and again after an experimentally varied learning phase, the subjects performed specific tasks considered indicative of successful model construction. Since the 1990s, however, alternative approaches have emerged that focus on instructional research on constructing and revising mental models. These approaches of model-oriented learning and instruction follow an understanding of learning as an active, constructive, and cumulative process, which has been described by Norman (1981, p. 284) as follows:

> I have estimated that experts at a task may spend 5000 hours acquiring their skills: that is not such a long time; it is 2-1/2 years of full-time study, 40 hours a week, 50 weeks a year. Not much time to become a professional tennis player, or computer programmer, or linguist. What goes on during that time? Whatever it is, it is slow, continuous. No magic dose of knowledge in form of pill or lecture. Just a lot of slow, continual exposure to the topic, probably accompanied by several bouts of restructuring of the underlying mental representations, reconceptualizations of the concepts, plus many hours of accumulation of large quantities of facts.

Accordingly, approaches to model-oriented learning and teaching emphasize long-time learning and the accumulation of knowledge. Model-oriented teaching focuses on the patterns of participation and discourse in the classroom, where learners construct their understanding of some phenomenon (Buckley and Boulter, 1999). This is accomplished mainly with the help of *external representations*, provided and guided by the teacher or a multimedia program. Model-based learning, on the other hand, focuses on the construction of mental models of the phenomena under study. When the model is used successfully, it is reinforced and may eventually become a precompiled, stable model or even, after many repetitions, a schema. If the model is not satisfactory, it may be revised or rejected in a progression of mental models.

At the moment, several research groups are concerned with model-oriented learning and teaching (Lesh and Doerr, 2003; Penner, 2001). This line of research is characterized by references to the traditional use of models in math and science instruction, but it does not refer to theories and research on human memory.

Alternatively, my own studies (Seel et al., 2000) correspond with PDP models of information processing and are concerned with complex problem solving and the learning-dependent progression of mental models. The main results of different replication studies (in total with more than 600 students of various ages and backgrounds) can be summarized as follows:

- Mental models are not fixed structures that can be retrieved from memory but are constructed when needed to master the specific demands of a new learning situation.
- Students dynamically modify and restructure their initial mental models when they evaluate externally provided information as being more plausible and convincing than their prior knowledge. This can be interpreted as an indicator of the learners' semantic sensitivity with regard to relevant information from the environment. The learning environment serves as an information resource from which the learners extract the information they need to construct an explanatory model.
- With regard to the stability and change of mental models, the various studies agreed on the observation that mental models are highly situation dependent. Although they were not constructed independently from each other at various points of measurement, their structures were obviously different. Naturally, it was cognitively less demanding for the students to construct new models at each point of measurement than to remember previously constructed models.
- Mental models proved to be effective for mentally simulating the relevant properties of complex systems to be cognitively mastered (Seel et al., 2006).

The results of these studies indicate that the time needed for successful model-based learning was not sufficient with regard to the emergence of a schema, defined here as an automated routine that can be used to access and apply stored knowledge structures without mental effort.

The instructional research on mental models has highlighted several complexities and consistencies. One consistency is concerned with the development of a new methodology for assessing the learning-dependent progression of mental models. The principles of this methodology include embedding the diagnosis of mental models in a complex problem situation, collecting data in a longitudinal design, providing valid and reliable quantitative data, and enabling a methodologically straightforward analysis and interpretation of the data collected (Seel et al., 2007). At the core of this methodology are the SMD (Surface, Matching, Deep Structure) Technology and MIToCaR (Model Inspection Trace of Concepts and Relations). These can be combined with alternative methods for assessing mental models, such as think-aloud protocols, structure-formation techniques, concept-mapping tools, and causal diagrams, all of which have been applied successfully in mental model research (Seel, 1999). Another consistency of mental model research consists in new instructional approaches for improving the construction and refinement of effective mental models (Seel, 2003).

*Summary and Criticism*

Modern psychology regards the human being as playing an active and selective role in approaching each new environment. Cognitive theorists place much greater emphasis on the fact that individuals bring to each environment preestablished schemata based on previous experiences. These schemata have been built up in the course of many previous interactions with the environment as well as further reflections upon these experiences during mental rehearsal. Some of these schemata are more complex, integrated, organized, or differentiated than others; however, although the activation of schemata plays a central role in different psychological approaches, such as the cognitive load theory, we still do not know enough about the construction of schemata. For example, it is not clear under which conditions mental models merge to schemata. Recent research (Seel et al., 2006) has demonstrated that it takes a lot of time and repetitions of successful construction of mental models within a domain until they become precompiled and stable and merge to a schema.

All of the theoretical conceptions and related research that have been considered in the foregoing sections are concerned with structures and functions of the semantic memory; however, in cognitive psychology a distinction has been made between semantic and episodic memory as specializations of the declarative memory.

### Episodic Memory

A simple definition of *episodic memory* is that it encompasses everything we remember as opposed to everything we know. The latter is usually called *semantic memory*, upon which episodic memory is believed to be built. A memory of the last family vacation is an episodic memory; however, if someone asks what color a ripe banana is, semantic memory is used to answer. The notion of episodic memory was first proposed some 30 years ago by Tulving and Thomson (1973). At that time episodic memory was defined in terms of materials and tasks. Today, episodic memory is understood as a neurocognitive system, uniquely different from other memory systems that enable human beings to remember past experiences (Tulving, 2002). It includes time, place, and associated *emotions* that affect the quality of the memorization. Interestingly, an *autobiographical memory* has been introduced as a specialization of the episodic memory. It is related with the investigation everyday memory, which refers to memory operations that routinely occur in one's daily environment, and eyewitness testimony, which has inspired a lot of research into its accuracy (Loftus, 1975). Evidently, human memory for events is fragile and susceptible to distortion.

Although the notion of episodic memory plays a central role in research on human memory, it does not play this role in the cognitive architectures for multimedia learning. Indeed, in the most recent overview by Reed (2006), neither episodic memory nor autobiographical memory is mentioned. Nevertheless, we can learn from the theoretical conceptions and research on this topic that memories are constructions made in accordance with present needs, desires, social influences, etc. Accordingly, memories are often accompanied by strong feelings and emotions that increase the recall of the stored events from episodic memory. Finally, memory usually involves awareness of the memory (Schacter, 1996).

Memory is the retention of, and ability to recall, information, personal experiences, and procedures. A memory system is fairly universally agreed to have three high-level activities: encoding, storage, and retrieval. Most lost memories are lost because they were never elaborately encoded. Perception is mostly a filtering and fragmenting process. Our interests and needs affect perception, but most of what is available to us as potential sense data will never be processed, and most of what is processed will be forgotten. We do not forget simply to avoid being reminded of unpleasant things. We forget because we either did not perceive closely in the first place or did not encode the experience (Schacter, 1996); thus, a central feature of human memory is the subjectivity of remembering. This leads to the next section of this chapter, where motivational aspects of multimedia learning are emphasized.

## LEARNING WITH MEDIA AND MOTIVATION

Motivation is a fairly difficult area, and a number of theories have been developed to try to explain why people behave in the ways that they do and predict or guess what people actually will do on the basis of these theories. Although motivation is generally considered a key variable in learning, it is surprising that so little attention is apparently paid to studies on motivation in multimedia learning as well as, *vice versa*, to learning and cognition in the motivation literature. Indeed, an analysis by Elliott and Dweck (2005) shows that, among more than 5000 citations, no reference is made to cognitive load theory and the stage model of information processing. On the other side, Lowe (2003), for instance, divorced the motivational aspects of animation from its instructive power. It seems apparent that there are two large groups of researchers who are not making much use of each other's insights.

As a consequence, we can find only a few theoretical approaches that aim at integrating motivation into comprehensive models of multimedia learning (Astleitner and Wiesner, 2004; Samaras et al., 2006); however, these models lack substantial empirical evidence, and future research is necessary to analyze the interrelations of the motivational and cognitive variables. The infusion of motivation in multimedia learning is a complex challenge. Motivation might be intrinsic, extrinsic, mixed, or absent altogether. There is some evidence that intrinsic motivation encourages the learner to become cognitively engaged with the multimedia material and improves learning.

Nevertheless, extrinsic motivational factors such as the design features of a multimedia package are thought to provide some initial incentive for learners to access the material, but sustained effort occurs only when they encounter intrinsic motivational factors provided by interesting and challenging content (Najjar, 1998). This may lead to *cognitive engagement*, which is the process whereby learners become motivated to take full control of their own learning. Generally, it has been argued that multimedia and computers have the capacity to allow for external regulation and autonomy support (Stefanou et al., 2004). Technology may also provide for context and variety in learning tasks that theoretically could be exploited to situate motivation. Hede (2002) sees the various motivational factors as impacting learner control or, more specifically, the time and effort learners devote to engaging with multimedia. Beyond Hede's model, there are three approaches to integrating motivation into multimedia learning: (1) schema-based approaches, (2) flow-based approaches, and (3) the uses-and-gratifications approach.

## Schema-Based Approaches to Motivation in Multimedia Learning

In correspondence with Piaget's (1952) theory of *disequilibrium*, a class of theoretical models postulates strong relationships between cognition and emotions. Eckblad (1981), for example, argued that each resistance for assimilating new information into existing schemata evokes affects and emotions of a specific nature. Similarly, Stein and Levine (1991) argued that attempts to assimilate new information into schemata are associated with emotional experiences. When the incoming information is novel, it causes a mismatch with existing schemata and results in arousal of the autonomic nervous system. When this arousal occurs in conjunction with a cognitive appraisal of the situation, a more or less specific emotional reaction occurs. Plans or anticipatory schemata are not only specific to situations; they also involve search and selection strategies related to the kind of information to be processed. When the strategies for processing new materials and specific anticipations match well with the information we actually confront in a new setting, we generally experience positive affects, joy, or a general sense of well-being. If, however, our anticipatory schemata or plans for processing information are inadequate, we may experience negative emotions (Singer and Singer, 1983).

The basic assumption of schema-based research on motivation is that deep comprehension occurs when learners confront contradictions, anomalous events, obstacles to goals, salient contrasts, perturbations, surprises, equivalent alternatives, and other stimuli or experiences that fail to match schema-based expectations (Mandler, 1999). Cognitive disequilibrium has a high likelihood of activating conscious and effortful cognitive deliberation, questions, and inquiry that aim to restore cognitive equilibrium. The affective states of confusion and perhaps frustration are likely to occur during cognitive disequilibrium. Recent research (Rozin and Cohen, 2003) has indeed pointed to confusion as an important affective state for learning. Confusion indicates an uncertainty about what to do next or how to act; thus, confusion often accompanies cognitive disequilibrium. Similarly, states of perturbation and hesitation often indicate the need for clarification or more information.

In four experiments, Schutzwohl (1998) investigated the effects of stimuli discrepant with schemata of varying strength on three components of surprise: (1) the interruption of ongoing activities (indexed by response time increase), (2) the focusing of attention on the schema-discrepant event (indexed by memory performance), and (3) the feeling of surprise (indexed by self-reports). Response times were consistently found to increase with schema strength. This effect was attributed to the increasing difficulty of schema revision. In contrast, memory for the schema-discrepant event was not affected by schema strength, supporting the hypothesis that schema-discrepant stimuli are stored in memory with a distinct tag. Finally, self-reports of surprise intensity varied with schema strength only if they were made immediately after the surprising event without any intervening questions, suggesting that self-reports of surprise are highly susceptible to memory distortions.

Emotional and motivational aspects of learning and remembering are also discussed in connection with cognitive load theory; for example, Early (2006) argued that it may be useful to separate factors that affect learner motivation into distinct groups: the variables or values of variables that increase learner motivation and the variables or values that decrease or fail to influence learner motivation. Custers and Aarts (2005) have identified positive affect as an example of a variable value that increases future goal pursuit via choice. The memory of the pleasurable sensation associated with prior goal pursuit may, over time, become automated and lead to an active choice of novel goals; however, excess burden on working memory may serve as an example of a variable value that decreases goal pursuit by decreasing effort or persistence.

This corresponds with Berlyne's (1971) precept that another process at the other extreme of information overload is boredom. Overly simple visual fields, for example, may lead to the uncomfortable feeling of boredom. One response to boredom with the external environment is to switch to internal information processing (for example, to daydream). Another interesting experiment is that of Ashcraft and Kirk (2001), who investigated the impact of anxiety on working memory. Individuals with high math anxiety demonstrated a reduced working memory capacity, which led to a pronounced increase in reaction time and errors when mental addition was performed concurrently with a memory load task. The effects of the reduction also generalized to a working-memory-intensive transformation task. Overall, the results demonstrated that anxiety affects performance in tasks and that this effect can be interpreted as a transitory disruption of working memory.

## Flow, Engagement, and Self-Efficacy

According to the constructivist theoretical frameworks, a person's affective states are expected to systematically influence how they process new material. The intrinsic motivation literature has identified affective states such as *curiosity* as indicators of motivation level and learning. Learners with more intrinsic motivation and interest display greater levels of pleasure, more active involvement in tasks (Tobias, 1994), more task persistence and lower levels of boredom (Miserandino, 1996), and less anxiety and anger (Patrick et al., 1993). Furthermore, because a person's affective state is linked to their motivation level, intrinsically motivated learners who are engaged should demonstrate more engagement and persistence in performing tasks. A deeper understanding of the materials should be one important consequence.

In an exploratory study, Craig and colleagues (2004) investigated the role of several affective states (frustration, boredom, flow, confusion, eureka, and neutral) that potentially occur during learning with an intelligent tutoring system for dialogs in natural language. Observational analyses revealed significant relationships between learning and the affective states of boredom, flow, and confusion. Other research suggests that interest increases as anxiety decreases and attitude improves and that such motivation assists the achievement of self-efficacy in virtual learning environments (Dyck and Smither, 1994).

These findings indicating that learning correlates negatively with boredom and positively with engagement are consistent with predictions from Csikszentmihalyi's (1975) anaysis of flow experiences. *Flow* describes a state of complete absorption or engagement in an activity and refers to the optimal experience. During optimal experiences, individuals are in a psychological state where they are so involved with the goal-driven activity that nothing else seems to matter. Past research has shown that the flow state has a positive impact on learning (Salanova et al., 2006; Webster et al., 1993) and should be taken into account when designing learning materials. The flow theory is used by Kiili (2005) as a framework for facilitating positive user experience and engagement to maximize the impact of digital learning environments. The purpose of the study was to support an active learning process, creative participation, and learner engagement in learning with a multimedia environment. In addition, Kiili integrated assumptions of cognitive load theory into a participatory multimedia learning model in which learners had to produce learning materials by themselves. The proposed model was studied through an educational game with university-level students. Questionnaires and interviews revealed that content creation was reported as being the main activity causing flow. Additionally, a positive connection between flow and learning was found.

Another promising field of research that is related to flow and engagement includes such topics as emotions and *self-efficacy*. There is considerable evidence regarding the positive effects of self-efficacy on performance and well-being in different domains, such as the workplace, school, and sports (Bandura, 1997). Self-efficacy has shown its power as a buffer in stress processes, and it has also been associated with better health, better self-development, and greater social integration. In addition, there is also evidence regarding the effects of self-efficacy on multimedia learning; for example, Reid (2006) developed an integrated model of playfulness and flow in a virtual reality. Key elements in the model include self-efficacy and volition, which the author sees as necessary characteristics for influencing flow and playfulness for activity in a virtual reality. More specifically, Reid studied how flow is related to playfulness. The findings supported previous research on self-efficacy and volition as children and adults reported that being in control was important and stressed the value of being able to do new things. Playfulness was expressed as the ability to feel presence with the activity.

More generally, it is evident that self-efficacy can be enhanced through experiences with technology. Cheung and colleagues (2003), for example, examined the effects of a multimedia learning system on the self-efficacy of learners and found that software usefulness and software ease of use affected the self-efficacy of students. Furthermore, longer usage of the multimedia learning system led to improvements in self-efficacy in learning but did not make the improvement faster. Self-efficacy also depends on several personal factors, such as anxiety and attitudes. Especially for mature students, the links between these personal factors can increase the burden on the student (negative past experiences with technology). Cavanaugh et al. (2000) hypothesized that technology self-efficacy will affect participants' attitudes toward technology and their perceptions of the effectiveness of training. The results indicate that attitudes toward technology mediate the relationships among technology, self-efficacy, and different measures of effectiveness. Meyer and Sternberger (2005) examined self-efficacy, self-reliance, and motivation in a quasi-experimental study with university students. Post-tests and course grades demonstrated no significance, whereas results of an item-to-item analysis of a questionnaire showed overall satisfaction with the teaching methodology and varied results for self-efficacy, self-reliance, and motivation.

## The Uses-and-Gratifications Approach

This approach has an influential tradition in media research and focuses on *why* people use particular media rather than on their content. The uses-and-gratification approach goes back to Blumler and Katz (1974), who suggested that media users play an active role in choosing and using the media that best fulfills the needs of the user. From the perspective of motivation psychology, the uses-and-gratifications approach can be considered a specific variant of expectation-value models of motivation. These models traditionally assume that both expectancy and value are required for goal commitment.

For a long time, the focus of the uses-and-gratifications approach was clearly on mass media, such as television. Sufficient evidence suggests that television viewing use is often habitual, ritualistic, and unselective (Barwise and Ehrenberg, 1988) but television viewing can sometimes also be an *aesthetic* experience involving *intrinsic motivation*. Furthermore, Zillmann (cited by McQuail, 1987, p. 236) has shown the influence of *mood* on media choice: Boredom encourages the choice of exciting content, whereas stress encourages a choice of relaxing content.

Due to the fact that the World Wide Web has become a major contemporary mass medium, the uses-and-gratifications approach has been applied for studying the Web as a whole and for examining specific types of sites on the Web. Kaye (2002), for example, examined the uses and gratifications of accessing online sources for political information. A factor analysis revealed four primary motivations for connecting to online political information, among which the need for entertainment is of motivational concern. Interestingly, Grace-Farfaglia and colleagues (2005) investigated the issue of gender and Internet uses and gratifications with a representative sample recruited from Internet users in different countries. In general, men still maintain higher Internet skills and self-efficacy in computer applications, but the gender gap is narrowing in each country. Indeed, a regression analysis of Internet gratification factors found gender differences in Internet motivations and online community participation. The data suggest that real-world social motivations impact participation in the virtual space.

An analysis of the recent literature shows that motivations relating to the use of the Internet have been well researched (Parker and Plank, 2000; Song et al., 2006); however, these studies remain to a great extent within the realm of the traditional uses-and-gratifications approach, providing a typology of use motivations, and fail to develop new Internet-specific gratifications (Stafford et al., 2004).

## SUMMARY

When we take the major fields of research on memory and motivation into consideration with regard to their implications for the design of instruction, we find a tension between strong (those that lead to very precise conclusions) and weak (those that lead to less precise conclusions) assumptions. Strong assumptions are helpful when the assumptions apply, but they often do not apply, which then invalidates the conclusions prescribed by the model. Weak assumptions are less helpful in creating specific instructional systems and learning activities, but they are more generally applicable and less likely to be invalidated. Finding the right balance is the challenge for professional practitioners. Extending the research so weak models become stronger and more useful is the challenge for instructional design research.

## REFERENCES

Anderson, R. C. (1984). Some reflections on the acquisition of knowledge. *Educ. Res.*, 13(9), 5–10.

Anzai, Y. and Yokoyama, T. (1984). Internal models in physics problem solving. *Cognit. Instruct.*, 1, 397–450.

Ashcraft, M. H. and Kirk, E. P. (2001). The relationships among working memory, math anxiety, and performance. *J. Exp. Psychol. Gen.*, 130(2), 224–237.

Astleitner, H. and Wiesner, C. (2004). An integrated model of multimedia learning and motivation. *J. Educ. Multimedia Hypermedia*, 13 (1), 3–21.

Atkinson, R. C. and Shiffrin, R. M. (1968). Human memory: a proposed system and its control processes. In *The Psychology of Learning and Motivation: Advances in Research and Theory*, Vol. 2, edited by K. W. Spence and J. T. Spence, pp. 89–195. New York: Academic Press.*

Baddeley, A. D. and Hitch, G. J. (1974). Working memory. In *The Psychology of Learning and Motivation*, Vol. 8, edited by G. H. Bower, pp. 47–90. New York: Academic Press.

Bandura, A. (1997). *Self-Efficacy: The Exercise of Control*. New York: Freeman.

Barwise, D. and Ehrenberg, A. (1988): *Television and Its Audience*. London: Sage.

Berlyne, D. E. (1971). *Aesthetics and Psychobiology*. New York: Appleton-Century-Crofts.

Blumler J. G. and Katz, E. (1974). *The Uses of Mass Communications: Current Perspectives on Gratifications Research*. Beverly Hills, CA: Sage.

Bransford, J. D. (1984). Schema activation versus schema acquisition. In *Learning to Read in American Schools: Basal Readers and Content Texts*, edited by R. C. Anderson, J. Osborn, and R. Tierney, pp. 259–272. Hillsdale, NJ: Lawrence Erlbaum Associates.

Brashears, T., Akers, C., and Smith, J. (2005). The effects of multimedia cues on student cognition in an electronically delivered high school unit of instruction. *J. South. Agric. Educ. Res.*, 55(1), 5–18.

Brown, A. L. (1979). Theories of memory and the problems of development: activity, growth, and knowledge. In *Levels of Processing in Human Memory*, edited by L. S. Cermak and F. I. M. Craik, pp. 225–258. Hillsdale, NJ: Lawrence Erlbaum Associates.

Buckley, B. C. and Boulter, C. J. (1999). Analysis of representation in model-based teaching and learning in science. In *Visual Representations and Interpretations*, edited by R. Paton and I. Neilsen, pp. 289–294. London: Springer.

Cavanaugh, M. A., Milkovich, J. G., and Tang, J. (2000). *The Effective Use of Multimedia Distance Learning Technology: The Role of Technology, Self-Efficacy, Attitudes, Reliability, Use, and Distance in a Global Multimedia Distance Learning Classroom*, CAHRS Working Paper Series, 00-01. Ithaca, NY: Cornell University.

Cheung, W., Li, E. Y., and Yee, L. W. (2003). Multimedia learning system and its effect on self-efficacy in database modeling and design: an exploratory study. *Comput. Educ.*, 41(3), 249–270.

Clark, R. E. (2006). Not knowing what we don't know: reframing the importance of automated knowledge for educational research. In *Avoiding Simplicity, Confronting Complexity: Advances in Studying and Designing (Computer-Based) Powerful Learning Environments*, edited by G. Clarebout and J. Elen, pp. 3–14. Rotterdam, the Netherlands: Sense Publishers.

Craig, S. D., Driscoll, D., and Gholson, B. (2004). Constructing knowledge from dialog in an intelligent tutoring system: interactive learning, vicarious learning, and pedagogical agents. *J. Educ. Multimedia Hypermedia*, 13, 163–183.

Craik, F. I. M. and Lockhart, R. S. (1972). Levels of processing: a framework for memory research. *J. Verbal Learn. Verbal Behav.*, 11, 671–684.

Csikszentmihalyi, M. (1975). *Beyond Boredom and Anxiety*. San Francisco, CA: Jossey-Bass.

Custers, R. and Aarts, H. (2005). Positive affect as implicit motivator: on the nonconscious operation of behavioral goals. *J. Person. Soc. Psychol.*, 89(2), 129–142.

Dyck, J. L. and Smither, J. A. (1994). Age differences in computer anxiety: the role of computer experience, gender and education. *J. Educ. Comput. Res.*, 10(3), 239–248.

Early, S. (2006). Motivational load in instructional design. In *Avoiding Simplicity, Confronting Complexity: Advances in Studying and Designing (Computer-Based) Powerful Learning Environments*, edited by G. Clarebout and J. Elen, pp. 97–108. Rotterdam, the Netherlands: Sense Publishers.

Ebbinghaus, H. (1885). *Über das Gedächtnis: Untersuchungen zur experimentellen Psychologie* (Neuaufl. 1985) [*About Memory: Studies of Experimental Psychology*]. Darmstadt: Wissenschaftliche Buchgesellschaft.

Eckblad, G. (1981). *Scheme Theory. A Conceptual Framework for Cognitive-Motivational Processes*. London: Academic Press.

Elliott, A. J. and Dweck, C. S., Eds. (2005). *Handbook of Competence and Motivation*. New York: Guilford Press.

Ericsson, K. A. and Kintsch, W. (1995). Long-term working memory. *Psychol. Rev.*, 102, 211–245.*

Franklin, S., Baars, B. J., Ramamurthy, U., and Ventura, M. (2005). *The Role of Consciousness in Memory*, Digital Peer Publishing, http://www.dipp.nrw.de/lizenzen/dppl/dppl/DPPL_v2_en_06-2004.html.

Friedman, A. (1979). Framing pictures: the role of knowledge in automatized encoding and memory for gist. *J. Exp. Psychol. Gen.*, 108, 316–355.

Grace-Farfaglia, P., Peters. L., Dekkers, A. C., and Park, S. H. (2005). Gender Differences in the Uses and Gratifications of Internet Use for the United States, the Netherlands, and South Korea. Paper presented at ASSA/AEA Annual Meeting, January 7–9, 2005, Philadelphia, PA.

Harris, P. L. (1978). Developmental aspects of memory: a review. In *Practical Aspects of Memory*, edited by M. M. Gruneberg, P. E. Morris, and R. N. Sykes, pp. 369–377. London: Academic Press.

Hede, A. (2002). An integrated model of multimedia effects on learning. *J. Educ. Multimedia Hypermedia*, 11(2), 177–191.

Hegarty, M. and Just, M. A. (1993). Constructing mental models of machines from text and diagrams. *J. Mem. Language*, 32, 717–742.

Johnson-Laird, P. N. (1983). *Mental Models: Towards a Cognitive Science of Language, Inference, and Consciousness*. Cambridge, U.K.: Cambridge University Press.*

Kaye, B. K. (2002). Online and in the know: uses and gratifications of the Web for political information. *J. Broadcasting Electron. Media*, 46(1), 54–71.

Kelley, C. M. and Jacoby, L. L. (2000). Recollection and familiarity: process-dissociation. In *The Oxford Handbook of Memory*, edited by E. Tulving, F. Craik, and I. M. Fergus, pp. 215–228. London: Oxford University Press.

Kieras, D. E. and Bovair, S. (1984). The role of a mental model in learning to operate a device. *Cognit. Sci.*, 8, 255–273.

Kiili, K. (2005). Participatory multimedia learning: engaging learners. *Australasian J. Educ. Technol.*, 21(3), 303–322.

Lang, A. (1995). Defining audio/video redundancy from a limited-capacity information processing perspective. *Commun. Res.*, 22(1), 86–115.

Lesh, R. and Doerr, H. M., Eds. (2003). *Beyond Constructivism. Models and Modelling Perspectives on Mathematics Problem Solving, Learning, and Teaching*. Mahwah, NJ: Lawrence Erlbaum Associates.*

Levie, W. and Lentz, R. (1982). Effects of text illustrations: a review of research. *Educ. Commun. Technol. J.*, 30, 195–232.

Lindberg, M. A. (1980). Is knowledge base development a necessary and sufficient condition for memory development? *J. Exp. Child Psychol.*, 30, 401–410.

Logie, R. H. (1995). *Visuo-Spatial Working Memory*. Hove, U.K.: Lawrence Erlbaum Associates.

Loftus, E. F. (1975). Leading questions and the eyewitness report. *Cognit. Psychol.*, 7, 560–572.

Lowe, R. K. (2003). Animation and learning: selective processing of information in dynamic graphics. *Learn. Instruct.*, 13, 156–176.

Mandler, G. (1999). Emotion. In *Cognitive Science: Handbook of Perception and Cognition*, 2nd ed., edited by B. M. Bly and D. E. Rumelhart, pp. 367–384. San Diego, CA: Academic Press.

Mayer, R. E. (2002). *Multimedia Learning*. Cambridge, UK: Cambridge University Press.

Mayer, R. E. and Anderson, R. B. (1991). Animations need narrations: an experimental test of a dual-coding hypothesis. *J. Educ. Psychol.*, 83(4), 484–490.

Mayer, R. E. and Gallini, J. K. (1990). When is an illustration worth ten thousand words? *J. Educ. Psychol.*, 82(6), 715–726.

Mayer, R. E. and Moreno, R. (1998). A split-attention effect in multimedia learning: evidence for dual processing systems in working memory. *J. Educ. Psychol.*, 90(2), 312–320.

McClelland, J. L., Rumelhart, D. E., and The PDP Research Group. (1986). *Parallel Distributed Processing: Explorations in the Microstructure of Cognition*. Vol. 2. *Psychological and Biological Models*. Cambridge, MA: The MIT Press.

McLeod, P., Plunkett, K., and Rolls, E. T. (1998). *Introduction to Connectionist Modelling of Cognitive Processes*. Oxford: Oxford University Press.

McQuail, D. (1987). *Mass Communication Theory: An Introduction*, 2nd ed. London: Sage.

Meyer, L. H. and Sternberger, C. S. (2005). Self-efficacy, self-reliance, and motivation in an asynchronous learning environment. *Trans. Eng. Comput. Technol.*, 8, 225–229.

Miller, G. A. (1956). The magical number seven, plus or minus two: some limits on our capacity for processing information. *Psychol. Rev.*, 63, 81–97.

Miserandino, M. (1996). Children who do well in school: individual differences in perceived competence and autonomy in above-average children. *J. Educ. Psychol.*, 88, 203–214.

Najjar, L. J. (1998). Principles of educational multimedia interface design. *Hum. Factors*, 40(2), 311–323.

Newell, A. (1990). *Unified Theories of Cognition.* Cambridge, MA: Harvard University Press.

Norman, D. A. (1981). Twelve issues for cognitive science. In *Perspectives on Cognitive Science*, edited by D. A. Norman, pp. 265–295. Norwood, NJ: Ablex.

Nugent, G. G. (1992). Pictures, audio, and print: symbolic representation and effect on learning. *Educ. Commun. Technol. J.*, 30 (3), 163–174.

Paas, F. and van Gog, T., Eds. (2006). Recent worked examples research: managing cognitive load to foster learning and transfer. *Learn. Instruct.*, 16(2), special issue.

Paivio, A. (1971). *Imagery and Verbal Processes.* New York: Holt, Rinehart and Winston.*

Parker, B. J. and Plank, R. E. (2000). A uses and gratifications perspective on the Internet as a new information source. *Am. Bus. Rev.*, 18 (2), 43–49.

Patrick, B., Skinner, E., and Connell, J. (1993). What motivates children's behavior and emotion? Joint effects of perceived control and autonomy in the academic domain. *J. Person. Soc. Psychol.*, 65, 781–791.

Penner, D. E. (2001). Cognition, computers, and synthetic science: building knowledge and meaning through modeling. *Rev. Res. Educ.*, 25, 1–35.

Penney, C. G. (1989). Modality effects and the structure of short-term memory. *Mem. Cognit.*, 17(4), 398–422.

Piaget, J. (1952). *The Origins of Intelligence in Children.* New York: International Universities Press.

Platt, J. R. (1964). Strong inference. *Science*, 146, 347–353.

Potter, M. C. and Levy, E. I. (1969). Recognition memory for a rapid sequence of pictures. *J. Exp. Psychol.*, 81 (1), 10–15.

Reed, S. K. (2006). Cognitive architectures for multimedia learning. *Educ. Psychol.*, 41(2), 87–98.

Reijnen, W., Walder, F., Stöcklin, M., Wallach, D., and Opwis, K. (2005). Measuring the components of attention in a single task: an exploratory study. In *Proceedings of KogWis05: The German Cognitive Science Conference 2005*, edited by K. Opwis and I.K. Penner, pp. 155–160. Basel: Schwabe.

Reid, D. (2006). A model of playfulness and flow in virtual reality interactions. *Presence*, 13(4), 451–462.

Rojahn, K. and Pettigrew, T. F. (1992). Memory for schema-relevant information: a meta-analytic resolution. *Br. J. Soc. Psychol.*, 31(2), 81–109.

Rozin, P. and Cohen, A. B. (2003). Confusion infusions, suggestives, correctives, and other medicines. *Emotion*, 3, 92–96.

Rumelhart, D. E., Smolensky, P., McClelland, J. L., and Hinton, G. E. (1986). Schemata and sequential thought processes in PDP models. In *Parallel Distributed Processing: Explorations in the Microstructure of Cognition.* Vol. 2. *Psychological and Biological Models*, edited by J. L. McClelland, D. E. Rumelhart, and The PDP Research Group, pp. 7–57. Cambridge, MA: MIT Press.*

Salanova, M., Bakker, A. B., and Llorens, S. (2006). Flow at work: evidence for an upward spiral of personal and organizational resources. *J. Happiness Studies*, 7, 1–22.

Samaras, H., Giouvanakis, T., Bousiou, D., and Tarabanis, K. (2006). Towards a new generation of multimedia learning research. *Assoc. Adv. Comput. Educ. J.*, 14(1), 3–30.

Schacter, D. L. (1996). *Searching for Memory: The Brain, the Mind, and the Past.* New York: Basic Books.

Schutzwohl, A. (1998). Surprise and schema strength. *J. Exp. Psychol. Learn. Mem. Cognit.*, 24(5), 1182–1199.

Seel, N. M. (1984). Entwicklungsverläufe der Verarbeitung von Bildinformationen [Developmental trends of the processing of pictorial information]. *Unterrichtswissenschaft*, 12(1), 18–31.

Seel, N. M. (1991). *Weltwissen und mentale Modelle* [World knowledge and mental models]. Göttingen: Hogrefe.

Seel, N. M. (1995). Mental models, knowledge transfer, and teaching strategies. *J. Struct. Learn. Intell. Syst.*, 12(3), 197–213.

Seel, N. M. (1999). Education diagnosis of mental models: assessment problems and technology-based solutions. *J. Struct. Learn. Intell. Syst.*, 14(2), 153–185.

Seel, N. M. (2003). Model-centered learning and instruction. *Techn. Instruct. Cognit. Learn.*, 1(1), 59–85.*

Seel, N. M. (2006). Mental models and complex problem solving: instructional effects. In *Handling Complexity in Learning Environments: Theory and Research*, edited by J. Elen and R. E. Clark, pp. 43–66. Amsterdam: Kluwer.

Seel, N. M. and Winn, W. D. (1997). Research on media and learning: distributed cognition and semiotics. In *Instructional Design: International Perspectives.* Vol. I. *Theories and Models of Instructional Design*, edited by R. D. Tennyson, F. Schott, N. M. Seel, and S. Dijkstra, pp. 293–326. Mahwah, NJ: Lawrence Erlbaum Associates.*

Seel, N. M., Al-Diban, S., and Blumschein, P. (2000). Mental models and instructional planning. In *Integrated and Holistic Perspectives on Learning, Instruction and Technology: Understanding Complexity*, edited by J. M. Spector and T. M. Anderson, pp. 129–158. Dordrecht: Kluwer.

Seel, N. M., Darabi, A. A., and Nelson, D. W. (2006). A dynamic mental model approach to examine schema development in performing a complex troubleshooting task: retention of mental models. *Technol. Instruct. Cognit. Learn.*, 4(4), 273–299.

Seel, N. M., Ifenthaler, D., and Pirnay-Dummer, P. N. (2007). Mental models and problem solving: technological solutions for measurement and assessment of the development of expertise. In *Learning by Modeling*, edited by P. Blumschein, J. Strobel, D. Jonassen, and W. Hung. Rotterdam: Sense Publishers.

Severin, W. J. (1967). Another look at cue summation. *Audio Visual Commun. Rev.*, 15, 233–245.

Sharp, D. L. M., Bransford, J. D., Goldman, S. R., Risko, V. J., Kinzer, C. K., and Vye, N. J. (1995). Dynamic visual support for story comprehension and mental model building by young, at-risk children. *Educ. Technol. Res. Devel.*, 43(4), 25–42.

Shaw, M. L. (1982). Attending to multiple sources of information. I. The integration of information in decision making. *Cognit. Psychol.*, 14, 353–409.

Shiffrin, R. M. and Schneider, W. (1977). Controlled and automatic human information processing. II. Perceptual learning, automatic attention, and a general theory. *Psychol. Rev.*, 84, 127–190.

Simon, H. A. and Kaplan, C. A. (1989). Foundations of cognitive science. In *Foundations of Cognitive Science*, edited by M. I. Posner, pp. 1–47. Cambridge, MA: The MIT Press.

Singer, J. L. and Singer, D. G. (1983). Implications of childhood television viewing for cognition, imagination, and emotion. In *Children's Understanding of Television: Research on Attention and Comprehension*, edited by J. Bryant and D. R. Anderson, pp. 265–295. New York: Academic Press.

Song, I., Larose, R., Eastin, M. S., and Lin, C. A. (2006). Internet gratifications and internet addiction: on the uses and abuses of new media. *CyberPsychol. Behav.*, 7(4), 384–394.

Snow, R. E. (1990). New approaches to cognitive and conative assessment in education. *Int. J. Educ. Res.*, 14(5), 455–473.

Stafford, T. F., Stafford, M. R., and Schkade, L. L. (2004). Determining uses and gratifications for the Internet. *Decision Sci.*, 35(2), 259–288.

Stefanou, C. R., Perencevich, K. C., DiCintio, M., and Turner, J. C. (2004). Supporting autonomy in the classroom: ways of teachers encourage student decision making and ownership. *Educ. Psychol.*, 39(2), 97–110.

Stein, N. and Levine, L. J. (1991). Making sense out of emotion In *Memories, Thoughts, and Emotions: Essays in Honour of George Mandler*, edited by W. Kessen, A. Ortony, and F. Craik, pp. 295–322. Hillsdale, NJ: Lawrence Erlbaum Associates.

Sweller, J. (1988). Cognitive load during problem solving: effects on learning. *Cognit. Sci.*, 12, 257–285.*

Sweller, J. (1994). Cognitive load theory, learning difficulty, and instructional design. *Learn. Instruct.*, 4, 295–312.

Sweller, J., van Merrienboër, J. J. G., and Paas, F. (1998). Cognitive architecture and instructional design. *Educ. Psychol. Rev.*, 10, 251–296.

Tobias, S. (1994). Interest, prior knowledge, and learning. *Rev. Educ. Res.*, 64, 37–54.

Tulving, E. (2002). Episodic memory: from mind to brain. *Annu. Rev. Psychol.*, 53, 1–25.

Tulving, E. and Thomson, D. M. (1973). Encoding specificity and retrieval processes in episodic memory. *Psychol. Rev.*, 80, 352–373.

Tversky, B., Morrison, J. B., and Betrancourt, M. (2002). Animation: can it facilitate? *Int. J. Hum.–Comput. Studies*, 57, 247–262.

Watt, Jr., J. H. and Welch, A. J. (1983). Effects of static and dynamic complexity on children's attention and recall of televised instruction. In *Children's Understanding of Television: Research on Attention and Comprehension*, edited by J. Bryant and D. R. Anderson, pp. 69–102. New York: Academic Press.

Webster, J., Trevino, L., and Ryan, L. (1993). The dimensionality and correlates of flow in human–computer interaction. *Comput. Hum. Behav.*, 9, 411–426.

Young, R. M. and Lewis, R. L. (1999). The Soar cognitive architecture and human working memory. In *Models of Working Memory: Mechanisms of Active Maintenance and Executive Control*, edited by A. Miyake and P. Shah, pp. 224–256. New York: Cambridge University Press.

---

* Indicates a core reference.

# 6

# Contextualistic Perspectives

*Eric J. Fox*
Western Michigan University, Kalamazoo, Michigan

## CONTENTS

## ABSTRACT

This chapter provides an overview of Stephen Pepper's philosophical worldviews (1942) as a way of clarifying the philosophical assumptions of different perspectives. A detailed analysis of contextualism is provided, and the manner in which this worldview relates to both constructivist and behavioral theories in instructional design is explicated.

## KEYWORDS

*Contextualism:* A philosophical worldview in which any event is interpreted as an ongoing act inseparable from its current and historical context and in which a radically functional approach to truth and meaning is adopted. The root metaphor of contextualism is the *act-in-context*, and the truth criterion of contextualism is *successful working* or *effective action*.

*Descriptive contextualism:* A variant of contextualism that has as its primary goal an understanding of the complexity and richness of a whole event through an appreciation of its participants and features. It seeks the construction of knowledge that is specific, personal, ephemeral, and spatiotemporally restricted, like a historical narrative.

*Functional contextualism:* A philosophy of science and variant of contextualism that has as its primary goal the prediction and influence of events with precision, scope, and depth using empirically based concepts and rules. It seeks the construction of knowledge that is general, abstract, and spatiotemporally unrestricted, like a scientific principle.

## INTRODUCTION

It can be difficult to fully appreciate the role philosophical assumptions play in the development of theory, science, and technology. This is particularly true in applied disciplines such as instructional design, where scholars and practitioners often leave core assumptions unstated, cobble together patchwork theories or techniques in the hope of embracing diverse perspectives, or trust that brute-force empiricism will reveal all of the relevant facts. Unfortunately, such practices make it difficult to clearly discern philosophical differences and are unlikely to contribute to the development of a coherent and progressive discipline. Those who do not specify their core assumptions or claim that they have none are typically just adopting those of the mainstream culture; those who carelessly integrate diverse theories run the risk of trying to combine mutually exclusive tenets and producing little more than incoherence; and those who trust in merely amassing raw empirical data are advocating a strategy that can be grossly inefficient, uncharacteristic of scientific research, and ill suited to the development of true technological innovation. Theories, and the philosophical assumptions that guide their construction and evaluation, are the foundation of scientific and technological progress.

"Theory" has a wide variety of meanings in intellectual discourse, but we will restrict our discussion to a relatively simple interpretation: statements that are relatively precise and have relatively broad scope. *Precision* refers to the number of ways a particular phenomenon can be explained with a given set of analytic concepts (the fewer, the better), and *scope* refers to the range of phenomena that can be explained with those concepts (the wider, the better). Theories are valuable because they allow for conceptual economy and parsimony, provide guidance for confronting new problems or situations, and prevent a discipline from becoming increasingly disorganized and incoherent (Hayes et al., 1999).

There are many different theories or statements we can generate to describe, interpret, and understand the events of our world. What determines the types of theories we construct and value? Philosophy. Whereas many theories are obviously tied to empirical data, philosophical assumptions nonetheless guide the creation, assessment, and evaluation of knowledge claims and theories. Regardless of the empirical support a particular theory might enjoy, for example, it is typically not difficult to find scholars or practitioners who eschew it. Sometimes this is because the critics have different criteria (or respect) for empirical support, sometimes it is because they do not view the theory as compatible with their belief system, and sometimes it is because they have a competing theory that can account for the same data. In all of these cases, philosophical assumptions are impacting their evaluation of the theory. As suggested earlier, however, individuals often do not clearly reveal or explicate these assumptions when engaging in theoretical debates. It seems that clarity about such issues might allow more productive discussions and comparisons.

One approach to illuminating underlying philosophical assumptions is the root metaphor or worldview approach offered by Stephen Pepper in his book *World Hypotheses: A Study in Evidence* (1942). Pepper was what some would call a meta-philosopher: he philosophized about philosophy. In particular, Pepper was interested in identifying key similarities and differences among the many different schools of philosophy that have emerged over the centuries. As Morris (1997, p. 531) notes, Pepper was "simply trying to make sense of the welter of philosophical and scientific ideas and concepts found in his day."

Pepper claimed that any philosophy can be categorized by the overarching metaphorical language it uses (its root metaphor) and the rules of evidence it embraces (its truth criterion). A *world hypothesis* or *worldview* consists of a distinctive root metaphor and truth criterion, and Pepper observed that well-developed philosophies tend to cluster around one of several such worldviews. The categories and concepts derived from a worldview's root metaphor serve as the basis for constructing theories or statements about the world, and its truth criterion provides the rules used to evaluate theories and knowledge claims. Pepper's framework can prove very useful for revealing the essential components, assumptions, and concerns of different discourse communities, and for this reason his work has recently received renewed attention in many areas (Ambrose, 1998; Berry, 1984; Berzins, 1979; Biglan,

1995; Bredo, 1994; Fox, 2006; Hayes et al., 1988; Lyddon, 1989; Minton, 1992; Morris, 1988; Overton, 1984; Prawat and Floden, 1994; Quina, 1982; Reese, 1991; Seifert, 2000).

This chapter briefly reviews Pepper's primary worldviews and then focuses on one that seems to inform a great variety of instructional design theory: contextualism. Varieties of contextualism are described and related to the field of instructional design, and the role that contextualism could play in developing a more coherent, pragmatic, and progressive science of learning and instruction is outlined.

# PHILOSOPHICAL WORLDVIEWS

Pepper (1942) wrote that a philosophical worldview is characterized by a root metaphor and truth criterion. A root metaphor is a well-known, familiar object or idea that serves as the basic analogy by which an analyst attempts to understand the complexities of the world. Those who adhere to the worldview of mechanism, for example, use the root metaphor of a machine to interpret events: the entire universe is considered to be like a machine, and the mechanist seeks to discover the discrete parts of this machine and understand how they relate to one another. A worldview's truth criterion, inextricably linked to its root metaphor, provides the basis for evaluating the validity of analyses.

Root metaphors roughly correspond to ontological assumptions, or views about the nature of being or existence (e.g., whether or not the universe is deterministic). Truth criteria roughly correspond to epistemological assumptions or views about the nature of knowledge and truth (e.g., whether it is discovered or constructed). Morris (1997) noted that a worldview (e.g., mechanism) is a broad category that consists of an informally organized epistemology and ontology, whereas a specific philosophy (e.g., logical positivism) represents a more formally systemized version of its worldview's epistemology and ontology. As will be revealed later, particular philosophies operating under the same worldview can appear rather dissimilar due to differences in how they formalize their ontological and epistemological assumptions.

Like theories, worldviews can be evaluated by their degree of precision and scope. Pepper, in fact, uses these criteria to identify "relatively adequate" worldviews: those that strive for complete scope with absolute precision. Although theories typically have good scope with regard to events in a particular domain, worldviews strive for unlimited scope with regard to *all* events. There are many different worldviews, and none has perfect scope and precision, but Pepper

claims that these come closest while maintaining good internal consistency: *formism*, *mechanism*, *contextualism*, and *organicism*.

Before examining the worldviews in more detail, it is worth considering some of the cautions Pepper (1942) offered with regard to evaluating. One is that the adequacy of one worldview cannot legitimately be determined by another worldview, nor do the shortcomings of one worldview necessarily strengthen the position of another. If one considers the assumptions of a worldview to be analogous to the rules for playing a game (they are, in a sense, rules for playing the game of philosophy), it is easy to see why this would be inappropriate. It would be similar to a baseball player criticizing tennis for its lack of home runs—the criticism is illegitimate, obviously, because tennis is played under an entirely different set of rules. Likewise, it is illegitimate to criticize one worldview's analysis using a different worldview's rules for conducting analyses. A degree of philosophical humility is prudent for everyone, as no degree of empirical evidence will ever "prove" that one worldview is superior to another. Philosophical assumptions *enable* analysis, they are not the *result* of analysis (Hayes, 1993).

A second noteworthy caution is that eclecticism, at the level of philosophical assumptions, is confusing and unproductive. This is because the root metaphors of the worldviews are autonomous and mutually exclusive. Keeping with our games analogy, this would be similar to trying to play a game that combines all of the rules of both baseball and tennis. Most of the rules of these two sports could not be implemented simultaneously. When "game eclecticism" is pursued, it becomes virtually impossible to determine scoring, fouls, and winners (the game of Calvinball from the comic strip *Calvin and Hobbes* by Bill Watterson illustrates this point beautifully). When philosophical eclecticism is pursued, it likewise becomes virtually impossible to evaluate theories or knowledge claims in any kind of clear, coherent, or systematic way. Both forms of eclecticism can be highly amusing, but neither is likely to produce very meaningful results.

## Formism

*Similarity* is the root metaphor of formism, and *correspondence* is its truth criterion. The two major variants of formism are termed *immanent* and *transcendent*. In immanent formism, the root metaphor is based on the perception that two or more objects are similar or alike (e.g., "these two apples are similar"). In transcendent formism, the root metaphor is based on the perception that objects conform to a preconceived form or pattern (e.g., "these apples are examples of the transcendent *apple* form"). A key process of formist analysis is either describing the similarities and differences between two objects, or naming and/or describing the forms of which the objects are examples. The measure of truth inherent in this root metaphor is "the degree of similarity which a description has to its object or reference" (Pepper, 1942, p. 181), or the *correspondence* between a description and its referent. Formism is said to be dispersive, with facts assumed to be unrelated unless proven otherwise. It is perhaps the oldest relatively adequate world hypothesis, and students of philosophy will recognize it as the worldview of Plato (and possibly Aristotle).

## Mechanism

In mechanism, the events, objects, and laws of nature are not assumed to be instances of separate and unconnected forms as in formism, but integrated parts of a single system. That system is characterized by mechanism's root metaphor of the *machine*. This worldview assumes the universe to be organized *a priori* into a vast structure of interrelated parts—a machine—with truth determined by "the way ever more ambitious verbal formulae reveal the assumed organization of the world" (Hayes, 1993, p. 12). Constructivists may recognize mechanism as what they call objectivism or positivism, and it is the worldview underlying most of cognitive psychology. The mechanistic truth criterion is a more elaborate version of the *correspondence* truth criterion of formism but might be better termed "predictive verification," as truth statements about the assumed organization of the world (i.e., predictions) are generally tested on new phenomena (Hayes, 1993). This form of analysis dominates much of the research in psychology and education, where there is a "long-standing tradition of developing and validating models of hypothetical constructs that predict behavior" (Biglan and Hayes, 1996, p. 50).

## Organicism

The root metaphor of organicism can be described as *organic development*, and its truth criterion is that of *coherence*. Organicists view events as integrated organic systems that are living, growing, and changing, and truth is realized when "systems of belief ... become more encompassing and integrative, leading towards an absolute, complete understanding" (Prawat and Floden, 1994, p. 42). Like mechanists, organicists consider all events and facts of the world to be interrelated. Unlike mechanists, however, organicists do not consider the whole (i.e., the organic system) to be merely a compilation of its parts; rather, the whole is

primary, and the parts are meaningful only as they relate to the overall system. Flux is an inherent characteristics of an organic system, and organicists thus accept change and novelty as a given, whereas stability and constancy are events to be explained. This quality is seen in developmental theories of learning and psychology that rely on stage models, such as the work of Piaget (Hayes et al., 1988).

## CONTEXTUALISM

Contextualism is a worldview based on philosophical pragmatism, a tradition heavily influenced by the work of figures such as Charles Sanders Pierce, William James, Oliver Wendell Holmes, Jr., George Herbert Mead, and John Dewey. As Menand (2001, p. xi) noted in the preface to his historical treatment of the emergence of pragmatism in America:

> If we strain out the differences, personal and philosophical, they had with one another, we can say that what these ... thinkers had in common was not a group of ideas, but a single idea—an idea about ideas. They all believed that ideas are not "out there" waiting to be discovered, but are tools—like forks and knives and microchips—that people devise to cope with the world in which they find themselves.

In pragmatism and contextualism, the truth and meaning of words lie in their function or utility, not in how well they are said to mirror reality. The truth criterion of contextualism is thus dubbed *successful working*, in which an analysis is said to be true or valid insofar as it leads to effective action, or achievement of some goal. This notion of truth does not require—and is not concerned with—the existence of absolute, foundational truths or assumptions about the universe. As James (1907/1948, p. 161) wrote, "The truth of an idea is not a stagnant property inherent in it. Truth *happens* to an idea. It *becomes* true, is *made* true by events."

For the contextualist, an idea's meaning is defined by its practical consequences and its truth by the degree to which those consequences reflect successful action. This extremely functional approach to meaning reflects Charles Darwin's influence on pragmatism, as his views on natural selection were just gaining widespread appeal among scholar's during the era in which pragmatism appeared (Menand, 2001). Pragmatism can be viewed as an application of Darwin's selectionism to epistemology: "In pragmatism, ideas are 'selected' (to be retained as true or valid) if they lead to successful action, just as in natural selection traits are selected (to be retained by the species) if they lead to reproductive success" (Fox, 2006, p. 10).

The root metaphor for contextualism is the commonsense notion of the ongoing *act in context*, such as reading a book, eating a sandwich, or teaching a class. Such events are practical, concrete actions that are "being performed by someone for some purpose in some context" (Reese, 1993, p. 72). In contextualism, context refers to both the current *and* historical context of an act; in fact, it is more context as history than context as place (Morris, 1997). Although the current context of an act is important, to understand the meaning, function, and purpose of the act one must also have an appreciation of the historical context. It seems Pepper was basing his use of the term "context" on Dewey's notion of context as "the historical situatedness of the meaning and function of behavior" (Morris, 1997, p. 533). For these reasons, Pepper also referred to contextualism's root metaphor as "the historic event" (1942, p. 232).

Contextualists analyze all phenomena as acts in context. Events and their contexts are considered integrated wholes and are separated into distinct parts only to achieve some practical purpose, *not* to reveal the true structure or organization of the world (as a mechanist might claim to be doing). In contextualism, such divisions are utilitarian, not foundational. Further, the entire universe and all of time are considered part of the full context of any event. How, then, does a contextualist know how much and which features of the potentially infinite context must be included to adequately characterize an act? The answer to this question is ultimately a pragmatic one (of course): It depends on one's purpose for attempting to characterize the act in the first place. Essentially, whichever features of the context aid in achieving the goal of the analysis may be included. This answer highlights the important role analytic goals play in the contextualism.

## Analytic Goals

Pepper (1942, pp. 250–251) noted that, in contextualism, "serious analysis … is always either directly or indirectly practical … there is no importance in analysis just for analysis." Analysis without some ultimate purpose is problematic in contextualism because neither the root metaphor nor the truth criterion makes much sense without a clear analytic goal. The *successful working* truth criterion is rendered meaningless in an analysis without an explicit goal because success can only be measured in relation to the achievement of some objective (Dewey, 1916/1953). Similarly, the root metaphor of the *act in context* is difficult to mount without an explicit goal because there would be no basis on which to restrict the analysis to a subset of the infinite expanse of the act's historical and environ-mental context (Gifford and Hayes, 1999). It is very difficult for a contextualist without an explicit goal to construct or share knowledge (Hayes, 1993).

## Varieties of Contextualism

As noted earlier, worldviews are broad categories that can contain many specific philosophies. Analytic goals play such an important role in contextualism that the specific instances of this worldview can be distinguished by them (Hayes, 1993). The types of analyses conducted by contextualists and the kinds of knowledge they value are greatly impacted by their analytic goals. Even within the same domain (e.g., human learning), their goals and approaches can be quite different. Some may be interested in establishing a natural science, for example, while others may be interested in establishing a natural history (Morris, 1993). Such differences in purpose can result in systems of inquiry that, despite being based on the same worldview, appear quite dissimilar. Contextualistic theories can be divided into two general categories, based on their overarching analytic goals: *descriptive contextualism* and *functional contextualism* (Hayes, 1993).

Descriptive contextualists seek to understand the complexity and richness of a whole event through a personal and aesthetic appreciation of its participants and features (see Rosnow and Georgoudi, 1986). This approach reveals a strong adherence to the root metaphor of contextualism and can be likened to the enterprise of history, in which stories of the past are constructed in an attempt to understand whole events. There is no one complete or true account of any event, however; each account is localized to an individual with personal and aesthetic meaning and value, rather than global and final (Gifford and Hayes, 1999). Thus, knowledge constructed by the descriptive contextualist is like a historical narrative—personal, ephemeral, specific, and spatiotemporally restricted (Morris, 1993). Social constructivism (Gergen, 1985; Rosnow and Georgoudi, 1986), dramaturgy (Scheibe, 1993), hermeneutics (Dougher, 1993), and narrative approaches (Sarbin, 1986) are all instances of descriptive contextualism.

Functional contextualists, on the other hand, seek to predict and influence events using empirically based concepts and rules (Biglan and Hayes, 1996; Fox, 2006; Gifford and Hayes, 1999; Hayes, 1993). This approach reveals a strong adherence to contextualism's extremely practical truth criterion and can be likened to the enterprise of science or engineering, in which general rules and principles are used to predict and influence events. Rules or theories that cannot potentially contribute to the prediction and influence of the events of interest are rejected or considered incomplete. Knowledge constructed by the functional contextualist is general, abstract, and spatiotemporally unrestricted (Morris, 1993). Like a scientific principle, it is knowledge that is likely to be applicable to all (or many) similar such events, regardless of time or place. The distinction between descriptive contextualism and functional contextualism is analogous to the distinction between natural history and natural science (Morris, 1993).

## DESCRIPTIVE CONTEXTUALISM AND INSTRUCTIONAL DESIGN

Descriptive contextualism has had a significant impact on the field of instructional design in recent years, primarily in the form of approaches commonly grouped under the label of *constructivism*. Constructivists view knowledge not as "something we *acquire* but something that we *produce*" (Mautner, 1996, p. 83) and have challenged many of the traditional practices of the field on epistemological grounds. They consider both behavioral and cognitive psychology, which have informed many instructional design principles, to be representative of objectivism. Objectivist epistemology holds that the real world exists externally to the knower and that it has a complete and correct structure—or meaning—determined by its entities, properties, and relations (Lakoff, 1987). Because objectivism is antithetical to their view of knowledge, constructivists have been critical of many of the instructional practices informed by behavioral and cognitive psychology, such as the emphasis on instructional objectives, the use of task and content analyses, and the reliance on criterion-referenced assessment techniques (Jonassen, 1991). Instead, they recommend a range of different techniques for enhancing instruction, such as providing complex, realistic learning environments; using cooperative learning, problem-based learning, and discovery learning strategies; employing advance organizers and concept maps; and nurturing self-awareness of the knowledge construction process (Driscoll, 2000; Morrison et al., 2007).

### Clarifying Constructivism

Constructivists in education rarely identify themselves as pragmatists or contextualists, but it is clear that most forms of constructivism are based on the contextualistic worldview. Constructivism's defining premise—that knowledge is constructed rather than discovered—is merely a restatement of the pragmatic/contextualistic view on truth and meaning. The functional

truth criterion of contextualism is also evident when constructivists reject the absolute truths and structuralism of objectivism, and the root metaphor of contextualism is apparent when constructivists emphasize the cultural and historical context in which education occurs or champion the design of authentic learning environments. Further, many prominent constructivist figures, including Dewey, Gergen, Bruner, and Vygotsky, are typically considered contextualists (Capaldi and Proctor, 1999; Reese, 1993). The relation between constructivism and contextualism is so apparent that Mancuso (1993, p. 120) claimed that "the basic tenets of constructivism as an epistemology demand an acceptance of a contextualist worldview."

Constructivism is difficult to adequately characterize, however, because the term "refers to many ideas, joined by the merest thread of family resemblance and often expressing quite contradictory views" (Burbules, 2000, p. 308). There are perhaps dozens of different strains of constructivism, and Matthews (2000) suggested that there are more than 20 variants of educational constructivism alone. Recent books on constructivism in education (see, for example, Larochelle et al., 1998; Phillips, 2000) reveal the vastness and complexity of the constructivist landscape and provide a sense of the great theoretical variation that exists within the different constructivist systems.

The many variants of constructivism can be distinguished by a careful analysis of what they mean by "knowledge" and how they are claiming it is "constructed." The primary dimension on which the forms can be differentiated is whether they focus on the ways an individual constructs knowledge and meaning or on the ways communities or social groups negotiate knowledge or truth (Phillips, 2000). Constructivist perspectives that emphasize individual knowledge construction are often identified as forms of *radical constructivism* (or sometimes *psychological constructivism*) (Phillips, 2000), whereas those that emphasize the construction of public domains of knowledge are generally considered forms of *social constructivism*. Theorists can vary considerably with regard to how much they gravitate toward either of these two poles and often disagree on the process by which knowledge is constructed or negotiated (Phillips, 1995; Prawat and Floden, 1994). Such differences can lead to surprisingly different suggestions on how best to improve educational practices and make it easy to understand the proliferation of constructivisms in the educational literature.

In instructional design, authors rarely specify the type of constructivism to which they subscribe and frequently seem unable to maintain philosophical fidelity to a single strain. Jonassen (1994), for example, operating under the general banner of constructivism, initially took a radical constructivist position that "learners construct their own reality or at least interpret it based upon their perceptions of experiences" (p. 34), yet in the very next paragraph adopted a social constructivist stance that "much of reality is shared through a process of social negotiation" (p. 35). Although these two statements are not necessarily logically incompatible, they do represent the thinking of quite different perspectives—perspectives that definitely have different goals and may even be based on entirely different worldviews. It has been argued that radical constructivism is based on organicism (Hayes et al., 1988; Prawat and Floden, 1994), whereas social constructivism is clearly contextualistic.

This lack of clarity in constructivist writing has no doubt contributed to the many questions and debates the movement has inspired: Does an extreme constructivist position make the practice of designing instruction pointless or impossible (Winn, 1993)? Why do some constructivists seem to embrace information-processing theory, but others reject it (Prawat and Floden, 1994)? Can constructivism serve as a prescriptive theory of instruction at all (Jonassen, 1994)? Why is it that, when constructivist models are proceduralized, they seem so similar to traditional instructional design models (Dick, 1996)? Can constructivism be both an educational philosophy and a method (Lebow, 1993)? And, perhaps most importantly, "is constructivism destined to join discovery learning in the long list of educational enthusiasms that come and go, never articulated clearly enough to be tested, or in vogue long enough to prove their theoretical interest or practical worth?" (Cobb, 1999, p. 16).

Recognizing the contextualistic worldview underlying most constructivist theories may help resolve some of the confusion surrounding constructivism. By taking different approaches to defining "knowledge" and "construction," constructivists are actually adopting different analytic goals and content areas. Because the purpose of analysis in contextualism guides how the root metaphor is used and how truth is determined, the different constructivist theories are evolving (or have evolved) into contextualistic systems that value and develop different types of knowledge and analyses. This makes it difficult for different types of constructivists to engage in meaningful or useful discourse and makes it particularly unwise to treat the variety of constructivist perspectives as though they represent a singular theoretical perspective.

Although there are important differences among the constructivist theories in education, most can be accurately characterized as forms of descriptive contextualism. The clearest evidence of this is in their strong preference for qualitative research methodologies. Savenye and Robinson (2004, p. 1046) noted that qualitative research is based on the notion that "humans construct their own reality" and typically involves "highly detailed rich descriptions of human behaviors and opinions." Such research typically includes ethnographies, case studies, surveys, interviews, and historical and document analyses (Denzin and Lincoln, 1998). All of these methods closely resemble historical narrative, which exemplifies the type of knowledge pursued and constructed by descriptive contextualists.

## Limitations

As forms of descriptive contextualism, constructivist theories get their strength from their close adherence to contextualism's root metaphor of the act in context. Descriptive contextualism's goal of achieving a personal understanding and description of the whole event aligns perfectly with the root metaphor, and for this reason the position is remarkably consistent (Gifford and Hayes, 1999).

Such theories, however, also share the inherent weaknesses of descriptive contextualism (Gifford and Hayes, 1999; Hayes, 1993). The first is that it is difficult to determine when the somewhat ill-defined goal of descriptive contextualism has been accomplished (Hayes, 1993). When is the narrative complete, or when has the story been told well enough? This problem is clearly recognized by many descriptive contextualists: "Qualitative narratives all have as their objective an authentic and holistic portrayal of an intact social or cultural scene ... [but] the issue of what constitutes an authentic and holistic portrayal has become hotly contested territory" (LeCompte et al., 1992, p. xv). Debates over the accuracy and completeness of different historical accounts of events also reflect these difficulties.

Another problem faced by descriptive contextualists is that the accomplishment of their goal does not necessarily result in any practical knowledge or benefits. A personal, holistic appreciation of a specific event may or may not yield information that is helpful for achieving any other goals held by the analyst or anyone else (Hayes, 1993). This is probably the most vexing problem facing constructivists in education, as they struggle to develop empirically verified practical applications of their theory (Cobb, 1999; Driscoll, 2000). By virtue of its own overarching purpose, constructivism is a *descriptive* theory of learning or knowledge, not a *prescriptive* theory of instruction (Jonassen, 1994). Descriptive contextualists and constructivists are typically not concerned about this lack of practical knowledge (it is not their purpose, after all). In advocating activity theory, for example, Jonassen (2006, p. 44) noted that it "is not a theory of learning from which instructional prescriptions can be reasonably drawn." Some constructivists even criticize functional contextualism for its explicit focus on being "pragmatic" and "useful" (Hannafin, 2006, p. 40).

Though strong in its adherence to contextualism's root metaphor, descriptive contextualism is not well suited to the development of practical knowledge. This view certainly has advantages and has made important contributions to the field, but it is difficult to use as a philosophy of science or as the foundation for an applied academic discipline like instructional design (Fox, 2006).

## FUNCTIONAL CONTEXTUALISM AND INSTRUCTIONAL DESIGN

Functional contextualism has been offered as a philosophy of science that underlies modern behavioral psychology and that could also serve as a strong foundation for instructional design (Biglan, 1995; Fox, 2006; Gifford and Hayes, 1999; Hayes, 1993). As a philosophy that embraces the scientific principles of learning and conditioning developed in the field of behavior analysis, functional contextualism supports many of the guidelines for instructional development behavioral psychologists have developed over the years (see Chapter 15 in this volume; see also Burton et al., 2004; Fredrick and Hummel, 2004; West and Hamerlynck, 1992). In addition, recent functional-contextual research on language and cognition (Hayes et al., 2001) promises to provide a more pragmatically useful way of speaking about complex human behavior that could have a significant impact on instructional practices. It has been argued that functional contextualism, although sharing the same worldview as most constructivist approaches, may offer a more cohesive view for conducting a science of learning and instruction "with increased clarity, precision, and concern for the construction of practical knowledge" (Fox, 2006, p. 21).

Behavioral psychology has traditionally been characterized as mechanistic, objectivistic, realistic, positivistic, and reductionistic. Whereas this is accurate for some versions of behaviorism (and there are more than a dozen varieties; see O'Donohue and Kitchener, 1999), it is not entirely true for the system developed by Skinner. Behavior analysis has contained elements of both mechanism and contextualism (Hayes et al., 1988), primarily due to philosophical inconsistencies in Skinner's writings and the gradual evolution of his ideas (Gifford and Hayes, 1999; Hayes et al., 1988;

Moxley, 1999, 2001). Skinner's early work was decidedly more mechanistic and positivistic, but by 1945 his work reflected a much closer connection to pragmatism, selectionism, and contextualism (Moxley, 1999, 2001). When Skinner described scientific knowledge as "a corpus of rules for effective action, and these is a special sense in which it could be 'true' if it yields the most effective action possible" (1974, p. 235), he was clearly embracing the pragmatic truth criterion and rejecting the objectivist and realist view of knowledge. In fact, many behavioral psychologists now explicitly embrace contextualism as the philosophy underlying their work (e.g., Barnes-Holmes, 2000; Biglan, 1995; Gifford and Hayes, 1999; Hayes et al., 1993; Lee, 1988; Morris, 1988; Odom and Haring, 1994; Roche, 1999). Functional contextualism can be seen as a clarification and refinement of the pragmatic philosophy underlying Skinner's later work and modern behavioral psychology.

### Implications of the Analytic Goal

Due to differences in analytic goals, work based on functional contextualism (e.g., behavior analysis) appears quite dissimilar to work based on descriptive contextualism (e.g., social constructivism). Whereas descriptive contextualism is focused on creating a descriptive natural history of events, functional contextualism is focused on creating a pragmatic natural science that seeks "the development of an organized system of empirically based verbal concepts and rules that allow behavioral phenomena to be predicted and influenced with precision, scope, and depth" (Biglan and Hayes, 1996, pp. 50–51). Functional contextualists study the current and historical context in which behavior evolves in an effort to construct general laws, principles, and rules that are useful for predicting and changing psychological events in a variety of settings.

Adopting the analytic goal of the prediction *and* influence of psychological events has important ramifications for a science of behavior (Biglan and Hayes, 1996; Fox, 2006). First, analyses focus on functional relations between psychological events and manipulable (at least in principle) events in the environment. Much of educational and psychological theorizing focuses on relations between one type of psychological event (e.g., cognitive schema) and another (e.g., overt performance on a task). This is not productive for the functional contextualist, because we can only directly manipulate events in a person's environment (or the context of their behavior) (Hayes and Brownstein, 1986). By emphasizing relations between two types of psychological events, cognitive theories provide little guidance on how to influence either event; it is like focusing on a correlation between two dependent variables rather than a functional relation between an independent variable and a dependent variable.

Although functional contextualists agree with constructivists that "the learner is an active, changing entity" (Hannafin and Hill, 2002, p. 77), they do not downplay the vital roles the environment and experience play in how the learner acts or changes. The learner does not act or change in a vacuum, after all. Thus, behavior analysts attempt to identify aspects of the manipulable environment that influence the occurrence, incidence, prevalence, or probability of both private and overt psychological events. Cognition and other internal mental events are interpreted by appealing to a person's learning history, rather than assuming they are underlying processes causing and controlling other psychological events or behavior.

In addition, the ultimate purpose of prediction and influence demands an emphasis on experimental research. To examine the impact a particular contextual variable has on an event, it is necessary to systematically vary that variable and measure the resulting impact on the event of interest; in other words, it is necessary to conduct an experiment (Biglan, 1995; Hayes, 1993). Purely descriptive or correlational research does not isolate which features of the context are influencing changes in the psychological event. Functional contextualists favor experimental techniques but value any methodology that may contribute to their pragmatic goals (Biglan and Hayes, 1996). Both traditional group designs and time-series analyses of individual behavior can be employed effectively for the purposes of functional contextualism, and even correlational or predictive research can be useful for suggesting which contextual variables might be relevant to the event of interest. Qualitative methodologies also have their uses in functional contextualism but are not as effective as experimental procedures for testing the influence of environmental variables on behavior or for verifying the general utility of principles.

## Behavioral Principles and Applications

The most well-established principles for predicting and influencing psychological events are those related to classical and operant conditioning. This relatively small set of principles and concepts provides a precise way of speaking about learning that also has remarkable scope. For several decades, the concepts and principles constructed by behavior analysts have proven remarkably effective in allowing teachers, parents, therapists, managers, administrators, trainers, and many others to change and improve the behavior of both humans and animals in many different contexts

(Austin and Carr, 2000; Biglan, 1995; Dougher, 1999; Martin and Pear, 2003; Mattaini and Thyer, 1996).

Procedures derived from behavior analysis are typically considered best practice in the treatment and education of individuals with developmental disabilities; for example, Scotti et al. (1996) and Matson et al. (1996) reported on over 550 studies showing the efficacy of such methods with persons with autism. In clinical psychology, a 1995 report by the American Psychological Association's theoretically diverse Task Force on Promotion and Dissemination of Psychological Procedures indicated that over 20 of the 27 clinical interventions listed as empirically validated are behavior therapy techniques (as cited in O'Donohue and Kitchener, 1999).

In instructional design, most are familiar with the considerable influence Skinner's programmed instruction movement (1954, 1968) has had on both instructional systems design and human performance technology (HPT) (Binder, 1995; Reiser, 2001) but may be unaware of other behavioral contributions to education. Instructional methods, such as the Personalized System of Instruction (PSI) (Fox, 2004; Keller, 1968), Direct Instruction (Becker and Carnine, 1980; Engelmann and Carnine, 1991; Kinder and Carnine, 1991), Precision Teaching (Merbitz et al., 2004a,b), Headsprout Reading Basics (Layng et al., 2004), the Comprehensive Application of Behavior Analysis to Schooling (CABAS) (Greer, 2002), and the Morningside Model of Generative Instruction (Johnson and Layng, 1992; Johnson and Street, 2004), are all explicitly based on behavioral principles and enjoy an extensive amount of empirical support (see Moran and Malott, 2004, for a review of many of these methods). Because most constructivists mistakenly consider behavioral psychology to be objectivistic or mechanistic, they often reject these empirically supported methods simply because they are "inconsistent with those espoused by constructivists" (Hannafin, 2006, p. 39). When the pragmatic core of modern behavioral psychology is elucidated, as it is with functional contextualism, it is difficult to understand what quarrel constructivists could have with these methods.

Functional contextualists do not reject instructional methods simply because they originate from a different worldview or perspective. If a technique has been demonstrated to reliably enhance learning and performance, functional contextualists will embrace it (although they may speak of the learning process in a manner more consistent with their perspective). Contextualism as a worldview is particularly well suited to technological eclecticism because of its pragmatic truth criterion—contextualists can readily adopt techniques and methods of other worldviews if it helps them achieve their analytic goal (Hayes et al., 1988).

Recent advances in behavioral research on language and cognition also hold great promise for education. In particular, Relational Frame Theory (RFT) (Hayes et al., 2001) is an approach to understanding complex human behavior that is based on functional contextualism and basic behavioral principles. RFT also introduces a new behavioral principle that explains how basic stimulus functions—such as reinforcing, punishing, motivational, and discriminative functions—can be altered by verbal processes and relations. This new principle, while entirely consistent with operant theory, has important implications for how complex learning can be influenced (via instructional means or otherwise) and provides a functional account of the structure of verbal knowledge and cognition. A full account of RFT, its empirical support, and its implications is not possible here, but interested readers are referred to a comprehensive text on the theory (Hayes et al., 2001), an online tutorial introducing its basic concepts (Fox, 2005), a text on some of its applied extensions (Hayes et al., 1999), a special issue of the *Journal of Organizational Behavior Management* (Austin, 2006), and the RFT section of the website for the Association for Contextual Behavioral Science (ACBS, 2005).

# CONCLUSION

Pepper's worldview analysis (1942) can be useful for clarifying underlying philosophical assumptions. By highlighting the contextualistic worldview shared by both constructivist and behavioral theories, shared assumptions and key differences are illuminated. Both constructivism and behaviorism have contributed significantly to instructional design and educational technology but often reach contrary conclusions regarding instructional practices. A better understanding of their common philosophical heritage may lead to improved communication and collaboration, with the understanding that the relative value of each perspective will depend upon purpose and context (Morris, 1993).

# REFERENCES

ACBS. (2005). *Relational Frame Theory*, Association for Contextual Behavioral Science, http://www.contextualpsychology.org/rft.

Ambrose, D. (1998). Comprehensiveness of conceptual foundations for gifted education: a world-view analysis. *J. Educ. Gifted*, 21(4), 452–470.

Austin, J., Ed. (2006). Acceptance and mindfulness at work: applying acceptance and commitment therapy and relational frame theory to organizational behavior management. *J. Org. Behav. Manage.*, 26(1/2), special issue.

Austin, J., and Carr, J. E., Eds. (2000). *Handbook of Applied Behavior Analysis*. Reno, NV: Context Press.

Barnes-Holmes, D. (2000). Behavioral pragmatism: no place for reality and truth. *Behav. Anal.*, 23, 191–202.

Becker, W. C. and Carnine, D. W. (1980). Direct instruction: an effective approach to educational intervention with disadvantaged and low performers. In *Advances in Clinical Child Psychology*, Vol. 3, edited by B. B. Lahey and A. E. Kazdin, pp. 429–473. New York: Plenum Press.

Berry, F. M. (1984). An introduction to Stephen C. Pepper's philosophical system via *World Hypotheses: A Study in Evidence*. *Bull. Psychonom. Soc.*, 22(5), 446–448.

Berzins, J. I. (1979). Discussion: androgyny, personality theory, and psychotherapy. *Psychol. Women Q.*, 3(3), 248–254.

Biglan, A. (1995). *Changing Culture Practices: A Contextualistic Framework for Intervention Research*. Reno, NV: Context Press.

Biglan, A. and Hayes, S. C. (1996). Should the behavioral sciences become more pragmatic? The case for functional contextualism in research on human behavior. *Appl. Prev. Psychol. Curr. Sci. Perspect.*, 5, 47–57.*

Binder, C. (1995). Promoting HPT innovation: a return to our natural science roots. *Perform. Improv. Q.*, 8(2), 95–113.

Bredo, E. (1994). Reconstructing educational psychology: situated cognition and Deweyian pragmatism. *Educ. Psychol.*, 29(1), 23–35.

Burbules, N. C. (2000). Moving beyond the impasse. In *Constructivism in Education: Opinions and Second Opinions on Controversial Issues*, edited by D. C. Phillips, pp. 308–330. Chicago: National Society for the Study of Education.

Burton, J. K., Moore, D. M., and Magliaro, S. G. (2004). Behaviorism and instructional technology. In *Handbook of Research on Educational Communications and Technology*, 2nd ed., edited by D. H. Jonassen, pp. 3–36. Mahwah, NJ: Lawrence Erlbaum Associates.

Capaldi, E. J. and Proctor, R. W. (1999). *Contextualism in Psychological Research? A Critical Review*. Thousand Oaks, CA: SAGE.

Cobb, T. (1999). Applying constructivism: a test for the learner as scientist. *Educ. Technol. Res. Dev.*, 47(3), 15–31.

Denzin, N. K. and Lincoln. Y. S., Eds. (1998). *Strategies of Qualitative Inquiry*. Thousand Oaks, CA: SAGE.

Dewey, J. (1916/1953). *Essays in Experimental Logic*. New York: Dover.

Dick, W. (1996). The Dick and Carey model: will it survive the decade? *Educ. Technol. Res. Dev.*, 44(3), 55–63.

Dougher, M. J. (1993). Interpretive and hermeneutic research methods in the contextualistic analysis of verbal behavior. In *Varieties of Scientific Contextualism*, edited by S. C. Hayes, L. J. Hayes, H. W. Reese, and T. R. Sarbin, pp. 211–221. Reno, NV: Context Press.

Dougher, M. J., Ed. (1999). *Clinical Behavior Analysis*. Reno, NV: Context Press.

Driscoll, M. P. (2000). *Psychology of Learning for Instruction*, 2nd ed. Needham Heights, MA: Allyn & Bacon.

Engelmann, S. and Carnine, D. (1991). *Theory of Instruction: Principles and Applications*, rev. ed. Eugene, OR: ADI Press.

Fox, E. J. (2004). The personalized system of instruction: a flexible and effective approach to mastery learning. In *Evidence-Based Educational Methods*, edited by D. J. Moran and R. W. Malott, pp. 201–221. San Diego, CA: Academic Press.

Fox, E. J. (2005). *An Introduction to Relational Frame Theory*, http://www.contextualpsychology.org/rft_tutorial.

Fox, E. J. (2006). Constructing a pragmatic science of learning and instruction with functional contextualism. *Educ. Technol. Res. Dev.*, 54, 5–36.*

Fredrick, L. D. and Hummel, J. H. (2004). Reviewing the outcomes and principles of effective instruction. In *Evidence-Based Educational Methods*, edited by D. J. Moran and R. W. Malott, pp. 9–22. San Diego, CA: Academic Press.

Gergen, K. J. (1985). The social constructionist movement in modern psychology. *Am. Psychol.*, 40, 266–275.

Gifford, E. V. and Hayes, S. C. (1999). Functional contextualism: a pragmatic philosophy for behavioral science. In *Handbook of Behaviorism*, edited by W. O'Donohue and R. Kitchener, pp. 285–327. San Diego, CA: Academic Press.*

Greer, R. D. (2002). *Designing Teaching Strategies: An Applied Behavior Analysis Systems Approach.* San Diego, CA: Academic Press.

Hannafin, M. J. (2006). Functional contextualism in learning and instruction: pragmatic science or objectivism revisited? *Educ. Technol. Res. Dev.*, 54(1), 37–41.

Hannafin, M. J. and Hill, J. R. (2002). Epistemology and the design of learning environments. In *Trends and Issues in Instructional Design and Technology*, edited by R. A. Reiser and J. V. Dempsey, pp. 70–82. Upper Saddle River, NJ: Prentice Hall.

Hayes, S. C. (1993). Analytic goals and the varieties of scientific contextualism. In *Varieties of Scientific Contextualism*, edited by S. C. Hayes, L. J. Hayes, H. W. Reese, and T. R. Sarbin, pp. 11–27. Reno, NV: Context Press.*

Hayes, S. C. and Brownstein, A. J. (1986). Mentalism, behavior–behavior relations, and a behavior-analytic view of the purposes of science. *Behav. Anal.*, 9 (2), 175–190.

Hayes, S. C., Hayes, L. J., and Reese, H. W. (1988). Finding the philosophical core: a review of Stephen C. Pepper's *World Hypotheses*. *J. Exp. Anal. Behav.*, 50, 97–111.*

Hayes, S. C., Hayes, L. J., Reese, H. W., and Sarbin. T. R., Eds. (1993). *Varieties of Scientific Contextualism.* Reno, NV: Context Press.*

Hayes, S. C., Strosahl, K. D., and Wilson, K. G. (1999). *Acceptance and Commitment Therapy: An Experiential Approach to Behavior Change.* New York: The Guilford Press.

Hayes, S. C., Barnes-Holmes, D., and Roche, B., Eds. (2001). *Relational Frame Theory: A Post-Skinnerian Account of Human Language and Cognition.* New York: Kluwer/Plenum.

James, W. (1907/1948). *Essays in Pragmatism.* New York: Hafner.

Johnson, K. R. and Layng. T. V. (1992). Breaking the structuralist barrier: literacy and numeracy with fluency. *Am. Psychol.*, 47(11), 1475–1490 (special issue on reflections on B. F. Skinner and psychology).

Johnson, K. R. and Street, E. M. (2004). *The Morningside Model of Generative Instruction: What It Means to Leave No Child Behind.* Concord, MA: Cambridge Center for Behavioral Studies.

Jonassen, D. H. (1991). Objectivism versus constructivism: do we need a new philosophical paradigm? *Educ. Technol. Res. Dev.*, 39(3), 5–14.*

Jonassen, D. H. (1994). Thinking technology: toward a constructivist design model. *Educ. Technol.*, 34(4), 34–37.*

Jonassen, D. H. (2006). A constructivist's perspective on functional contextualism. *Educ. Technol. Res. Dev.*, 54(1), 43–47.

Keller, F. S. (1968). "Goodbye teacher... ." *J. Appl. Behav. Anal.*, 1, 79–89.

Kinder, D. and Carnine, D. (1991). Direct instruction: what it is and what it is becoming. *J. Behav. Educ.*, 1(2), 193–213.

Lakoff, G. (1987). *Women, Fire, and Dangerous Things: What Categories Reveal About the Mind.* Chicago: University of Chicago Press.

Larochelle, M., Bednarz, N., and Garrison, J., Eds. (1998). *Constructivism and Education.* Cambridge, U.K.: Cambridge Press.*

Layng, T. V. J., Twyman, J. S., and Stikeleather, G. (2004). Selected for success: how Headsprout Reading Basics™ teaches beginning reading. In *Evidence-Based Educational Methods*, edited by D. J. Moran and R. W. Malott, pp. 171–197. San Diego, CA: Academic Press.

Lebow, D. (1993). Constructivist values for instructional systems design: five principles toward a new mindset. *Educ. Technol. Res. Dev.*, 41(3), 4–16.

LeCompte, M. D., Millroy, W. L., and Preissle, J., Eds. (1992). *The Handbook of Qualitative Research in Education.* San Diego, CA: Academic Press.

Lee, V. L. (1988). *Beyond Behaviorism.* Hillsdale, NJ: Lawrence Erlbaum Associates.

Lyddon, W. J. (1989). Root metaphor theory: a philosophical framework for counseling and psychotherapy. *J. Counsel. Dev.*, 67(8), 442–448.

Mancuso, J. C. (1993). Personal construct systems in the context of action. In *Varieties of Scientific Contextualism*, edited by S. C. Hayes, L. J. Hayes, H. W. Reese, and T. R. Sarbin, pp. 111–133. Reno, NV: Context Press.

Martin, G. L. and Pear, J. J. (2003). *Behavior Modification: What It Is and How to Do It*, 7th ed. Englewood Cliffs, NJ: Prentice Hall.

Matson, J. L., Benavidez, D. A., Compton, L. S., Paclwaskyj, T., and Baglio, C. (1996). Behavioral treatment of autistic persons: a review of research from 1980 to the present. *Res. Dev. Disabilities*, 7, 388–451.

Mattaini, M. A. and Thyer, B. A., Eds. (1996). *Finding Solutions to Social Problems: Behavioral Strategies for Change.* Washington, D.C.: American Psychological Association.

Matthews, M. R. (2000). Appraising constructivism in science and mathematics education. In *Constructivism in Education: Opinions and Second Opinions on Controversial Issues*, edited by D. C. Phillips, pp. 161–192. Chicago: National Society for the Study of Education.

Mautner, T. (1996). *The Penguin Dictionary of Philosophy.* London: Penguin Books.

Menand, L. (2001). *The Metaphysical Club: A Story of Ideas in America.* New York: Farrar, Straus, and Giroux.

Merbitz, C., Vieitez, D., Merbitz, N. H., and Binder, C. (2004a). Precision teaching: applications in education and beyond. In *Evidence-Based Educational Methods*, edited by D. J. Moran and R. W. Malott, pp. 63–80. San Diego, CA: Academic Press.

Merbitz, C., Vieitez, D., Merbitz, N. H., and Pennypacker, H. S. (2004b). Precision teaching: foundations and classroom applications. In *Evidence-Based Educational Methods*, edited by D. J. Moran and R. W. Malott, pp. 47–62. San Diego, CA: Academic Press.

Minton, H. L. (1992). Root metaphors and the evolution of American social psychology. *Canad. J. Psychol.*, 33(3), 547–553.

Moran, D. J. and Malott, R. W., Eds. (2004). *Evidence-Based Educational Methods.* San Diego, CA: Academic Press.*

Morris, E. K. (1988). Contextualism: the world view of behavior analysis. *J. Exp. Child Psychol.*, 46, 289–323.

Morris, E. K. (1993). Contextualism, historiography, and the history of behavior analysis. In *Varieties of Scientific Contextualism*, edited by S. C. Hayes, L. J. Hayes, H. W. Reese, and T. R. Sarbin, pp. 137–165. Reno, NV: Context Press.*

Morris, E. K. (1997). Some reflections on contextualism, mechanism, and behavior analysis. *Psychol. Rec.*, 47, 529–542.

Morrison, G. R., Ross, S. M., and Kemp, J. E. (2007). *Designing Effective Instruction*, 5th ed. Hoboken, NJ: Wiley.

Moxley, R. A. (1999). The two Skinners: modern and postmodern. *Behav. Philos.*, 27, 97–125.

Moxley, R. A. (2001). The modern/postmodern context of Skinner's selectionist turn in 1945. *Behav. Philos.*, 29, 121–153.

Odom, S. L. and Haring, T. G. (1994). Contextualism and applied behavior analysis: implications for early childhood education for children with disabilities. In *Behavior Analysis in Education: Focus on Measurably Superior Instruction*, edited by R. Gardner III, D. M. Sainato, J. O. Cooper, T. E. Heron, W. L. Heward, J. Eshleman, and T. A. Grossi, pp. 87–100. Pacific Grove, CA: Brooks/Cole.

O'Donohue, W. and Kitchener, R., Eds. (1999). *Handbook of Behaviorism*. San Diego, CA: Academic Press.

Overton, W. F. (1984). World views and their influence on psychological theory and research: Kuhn–Lakatos–Laudan. In *Advances in Child Development and Behavior*, Vol. 18, edited by H. W. Reese, pp. 191–226. New York: Academic Press.

Pepper, S. C. (1942). *World Hypotheses: A Study in Evidence*. Berkeley, CA: University of California Press.*

Phillips, D. C. (1995). The good, the bad, and the ugly: the many faces of constructivism. *Educ. Res.*, 24 (7), 5–12.

Phillips, D. C., Ed. (2000). *Constructivism in Education: Opinions and Second Opinions on Controversial Issues*. Chicago: The National Society for the Study of Education.*

Prawat, R. S. and Floden, R. E. (1994). Philosophical perspectives on constructivist views of learning. *Educ. Psychol.*, 29(1), 37–48.

Quina, J. (1982). Root metaphor and interdisciplinary curriculum: designs for teaching literature in secondary schools. *J. Mind Behav.*, 3, 345–356.

Reiser, R. A. (2001). A history of instructional design and technology. In *Trends and Issues in Instructional Design and Technology*, edited by R. A. Reiser and J. V. Dempsey, pp. 26–53. Upper Saddle River, NJ: Prentice Hall.

Reese, H. W. (1991). Contextualism and developmental psychology. In *Advances in Child Development and Behavior*, edited by H. W. Reese, pp. 187–230. New York: Academic Press.

Reese, H. W. (1993). Contextualism and dialectical materialism. In *Varieties of Scientific Contextualism*, edited by S. C. Hayes, L. J. Hayes, H. W. Reese, and T. R. Sarbin, pp. 71–110. Reno, NV: Context Press.

Roche, B. (1999). "New wave" analysis. *Psychologist*, 12(10), 498–499.

Rosnow, R. L. and Georgoudi, M., Eds. (1986). *Contextualism and Understanding in Behavioral Science: Implications for Research and Theory*. New York: Praeger.

Sarbin, T. R. (1986). The narrative as a root metaphor for psychology. In *Narrative Psychology: The Storied Nature of Human Conduct*, edited by T. R. Sarbin, pp. 3–22. New York: Praeger.

Savenye, W. C. and Robinson, R. S. (2004). Qualitative research issues and methods: an introduction for educational technologists. In *Handbook of Research on Educational Communications and Technology*, 2nd ed., edited by D. H. Jonassen, pp. 1045–1071. Mahwah, NJ: Lawrence Erlbaum Associates.

Scheibe, K. E. (1993). Dramapsych: getting serious about context. In *Varieties of Scientific Contextualism*, edited by S. C. Hayes, L. J. Hayes, H. W. Reese, and T. R. Sarbin, pp. 191–205. Reno, NV: Context Press.

Scotti, J. R., Ujcich, K. J., Weigle, K. L., and Holland, C. M. (1996). Interventions with challenging behavior of persons with developmental disabilities: a review of current research practices. *J. Assoc. Persons Severe Handicaps*, 21(3), 123–134.

Seifert, K. L. (2000). Uniformity and diversity in everyday views of the child. In *Variability in the Social Construction of the Child: New Directions for Child and Adolescent Development #87*, edited by S. Harkness, C. Raeff, and C. Super, pp. 75–92. San Francisco, CA: Jossey-Bass.

Skinner, B. F. (1954). The science of learning and the art of teaching. *Harvard Educ. Rev.*, 24, 86–97.

Skinner, B. F. (1968). *The Technology of Teaching*. New York: Appleton-Century-Crofts.

Skinner, B. F. (1974). *About Behaviorism*. New York: Knopf.

West, R. P. and Hamerlynck, L. A., Eds. (1992). *Designs for Excellence in Education: The Legacy of B. F. Skinner*. Longmont, CO: Sopris West.

Winn, W. D. (1993). A constructivist critique of the assumptions of instructional design. In *Designing Environments for Constructive Learning*, edited by T. Duffy, J. Lowyck, and D. Jonassen, pp. 189–212. New York: Springer.

---

* Indicates a core reference.

# 7

# Philosophical Perspectives

*Kathy L. Schuh*
University of Iowa, Iowa City, Iowa

*Sasha A. Barab*
Indiana University, Bloomington, Indiana

## CONTENTS

## ABSTRACT

Philosophical perspectives are worldviews that define the nature of the world, the individual's place in it, and the possible relationships to that world and its parts. Learning and instructional theories are developed with respect to a particular set of assumptions regarding what it means to know and learn. It is our contention that when situational variables require some decision on the part of the educator (and we believe this is always the case), an underlying set of assumptions (whether they be tacit or explicit) will, and should, drive the decision. In this chapter we provide overview descriptions of five psychological perspectives, contrasted in terms of epistemology, ontology, unit of analysis, and whether they suggest dualist relationships. These theories (behaviorism, cognitivism, cognitive constructivism, sociocultural/historicism, and situativity theory) provide frameworks for describing learning and designing instruction. It is the goal of this chapter to clarify these distinctions and the underlying assumptions so instructional designers, teachers, and researchers may make pedagogical decisions more explicitly.

## KEYWORDS

*Behaviorism:* An objectivist and monist perspective with regard to individual actions and decisions.

*Cognitive constructivism:* A form of realism that stresses the reorganization of mental structures of an individual making sense of the world.

*Cognitivism:* An objectivist and rationalist perspective with regard to individual cognitive structures.

*Dualism:* When two apparently related items are treated as separate and distinct (e.g., mind/body or individual/environment).

*Empiricism:* An epistemology that states that knowledge comes from experience and through the senses.

*Epistemology:* How we come to know about what exists.

*Idealism:* A view of reality as mental, implying that the world is not separate from the mind.

*Objectivism:* An ontological and epistemological view that contends that reality exists outside of the individual and consists of specific entities.

*Ontology:* What exists in the world.

*Pragmatism:* The view that knowledge is derived from interaction among groups of individuals and the artifacts in their environment, which together create a reality.

*Rationalism:* An epistemological view where reason is the principle source of knowledge.

*Realism:* A form of objectivism that assumes that there is some sort of reality that is separate from the mind and that knowing involves a correspondence between the world and the mind.

*Relativism:* A general principle that places the meaning of experiential and physical events in the relationships that exist among them.

*Situativity theory:* A form of realism that stresses an individual's direct perception of events and phenomena.

*Sociocultural/historicism:* A relativist perspective that emphasizes relations and processes between the individual and society.

*Unit of analysis:* Boundaries of the phenomena of interest.

# INTRODUCTION

Theoretical perspectives such as behaviorism, cognitivism, cognitive constructivism, sociocultural/historicism, and situativity theory provide frameworks for describing learning and designing instruction. Finding roots in philosophy, these perspectives differ with respect to their ontological and epistemological assumptions. Learning theories and instructional theories are developed and linked to a particular set of assumptions, supposedly consistent with one of the theoretical perspectives. Duffy and Jonassen (1992) argued that instructional strategies and methods are clearly influenced by the philosophical assumptions and that theories of knowing and learning are implicit in the instructional design. If not implemented entirely by a cookbook approach, then when situational variables require some decision on the part of the educator an underlying set of assumptions (whether they be tacit or explicit) will drive the decision (Barab and Duffy, 2000). It is inconceivable that a teacher or instructional designer would advocate a particular lesson or activity without at least a tacit theory of how students think and learn.

In the literature, we see various classifications for these different perspectives; for example, Greeno et al. (1996) described behaviorist/empiricist, cognitivist/rationalist, and situative/pragmatist-sociohistorical perspectives. Prawat and Floden (1994) used worldviews to define their classifications: mechanistic (including information processing approaches), organismic (including radical constructivism), and contextualist (including social constructivism). Wood (1995) grounded his categories in the application of learning theory to technology: Skinner and neo-behaviorism, Piaget and constructivist theory, Vygotsky and social constructivism and situated cognition.

Unfortunately, when considering theoretical perspectives and the learning theories that have developed within them, it is not always clear what the underlying philosophical roots are. In fact, it becomes confusing when considering the descriptions from authors distinguishing differently among theoretical perspectives. Driscoll (1994), for example, stated that Piaget's developmental theory and constructivism were interpretivist based. Cobb (1994), when distinguishing among the cognitive and socioconstructivists, aligned the cognitive constructivist with the views of von Glasersfeld (1989), who used Piaget as his example; yet, von Glasersfeld described the basis as pragmatist. Greeno and colleagues (1996), Cobb (1994), and Driscoll (1994) placed the socioconstructivist or sociohistorical perspective under the roots of pragmatism as well, calling on the views of Vygotsky. Phillips (1995) distin-

guished among the various sects of constructivism, placing the perspectives by Piaget and Vygotsky together based on the unit of analysis. Greeno and colleagues (1996) classified constructivism along with cognitivism, finding roots in rationalism. Ertmer and Newby (1993) located cognitivism and behaviorism within the objectivist perspective, with cognitivism as well as constructivism being rationalism.

To further confound things, Garrison (1995) equated contemporary social constructivism with what he defined as pragmatic social behaviorism based on the work of Dewey, indicating a relationship between constructivism and adaptations of behaviorism. Garrison also stated that situated cognition (classified within the situative/pragmatist-sociohistoric category by Greeno et al., 1996) has made an important contribution to social constructivism. Greeno (1998) stated that the situative perspective could subsume both the behaviorist and the cognitivist perspectives. Whereas Prawat and Floden (1994) combined social constructivism and situativity perspectives, Derry (1992) distinguished between constructivist and culturally situated learning views. Among situated perspectives, Lave (1997) further divided what she termed cognition plus, interpretivist views, and her situated social practice view.

What factors are being used to distinguish the above theoretical perspectives? Epistemological or ontological assumptions? For seasoned theorists in the field, these distinctions may be trivial to sort out, or maybe some believe that these distinctions have little practical significance. For those beginning their scholarship in the field, confusion seems to reign. Further, for those interested in designing practical applications of instruction and seeking the grounding that a theoretical foundation can provide, it may be difficult to understand the foundation on which they are building.

It is in response to these questions, and with the goal of providing sharper boundaries among these categories to inform learning architects, that we have written this chapter. We describe theoretical perspectives as subsumed under five categories and clarify these categories by defining the mind/body relations, epistemology, ontology, and the unit of analysis. Then, we turn to the instructional implications of these five categories. It is important to recognize that these distinctions are situated within the context of providing sharper boundaries and stimulating discussion. As such, we have drawn lines among perspectives that may seem overly defined and may not even exist within other contexts and for other purposes; for example, some theorists would not separate situativity and constructivist perspectives or would not build connections between objectivism and cognitivism. In writing this paper, therefore, we have made epistemological and ontological commitments—a process that we suggest is useful for instructional designers and educational psychologists to undertake.

This is not to imply that we have simply constructed these distinctions based on our fancy; in fact, we have aligned each conjecture with citations from colleagues in the field, stacking our allies if you will (Latour, 1987). Our hesitancy in forwarding these categories is that readers will take these brief and overly simplified categories as fixed and rigid rules or, even worse, as substitutes for involved study of the particular philosophical works discussed. It is our intention that these categories should not be used for compartmentalizing but should serve as a backdrop for continued discussion and for broader discourse among our colleagues.

# BACKGROUND

## Epistemology

Epistemology and ontology are within the foundational realm of philosophy and mutually support one another (Lombardo, 1987; Reber, 1995). Epistemology addresses the "origins, nature, methods, and limits of human knowledge" (Reber, 1995, p. 256), focusing on questions about knowledge and the nature of knowledge (Everitt and Fisher, 1995). Those interested in learning and instruction thus have an epistemological purpose (i.e., supporting learners in coming to know) regardless of the perspective with which they choose to be aligned. Understanding how a learner comes to know and how that process can be facilitated forms a basis for research in learning and instruction.

## Ontology

Ontology is a branch of philosophy (within metaphysics) that addresses the nature of being and reality (Lombardo, 1987; Reber, 1995); in other words, an ontology defines what is real in the world, whether physical or abstract structures. Those interested in learning and instruction indicate their ontological preference by specifying what are considered truths about knowledge, information, and the world. To be redundant, yet succinct, ontology refers to "what exists" while epistemology is concerned with "how we come to know about" what exists (Barab et al., 1999; Jonassen, 1991).

## Unit of Analysis

The unit of analysis, from an assessment perspective, refers to the phenomenon of interest or, more specifically, the boundaries of the phenomenon that one is attempting to measure (Young et al., 1997). Salomon (1991), for example, distinguished between the analytic approach, in which units are studied in isolation because they are considered to be discrete, and the systemic approach, in which the units are considered to be interdependent and inseparable. Units of analysis are not objective features that are selected independently of a theoretical perspective; rather, the boundaries of the phenomenon that one is attempting to measure are influenced by a theoretical perspective (Barab and Duffy, 2000). If one views knowledge as structures existing in the brain, then a viable unit of analysis would be to examine the individual (or the cognitive structures of that individual) in isolation, whereas one who views knowledge as situationally constructed would pay more homage and would necessarily expand the unit of analysis to include the surrounding context in which thinking is occurring. This is not to imply there is a one-to-one correspondence between unit of analysis and philosophical assumptions; instead, the unit of analysis is influenced and constrained by underlying ontological and epistemological assumptions. In this chapter, we describe what is an appropriate (viable) unit of analysis given a particular set of assumptions.

## Dualisms

The Cartesian dualism, in which the mind is considered distinct from the body, has been talked about in philosophy and psychology since the inception of these two disciplines. Turvey and Shaw (1995) identified four dualisms that have been central to psychology: mind–body, symbol–matter, subjective–objective, and perception–action. They claim that the organism–environment dualism subsumes these other four. In this dualism, the organism or knower is considered to be independent of the environment or what is known. Nowhere have these dualisms been more apparent than in theories regarding perception (Barab et al., 1999; Reed, 1996). Various theories have been forwarded in an attempt to explain how the mind perceives objects based on the meaningless points of light reaching the eye; for example, in addition to the dualist theory of the structuralists and the monist theory of the materialists, functionalism has been forwarded in which it is postulated that mental states exist as a function of a system. In other words, the way the system is put together is what is critical, rather than the material that the system is made of, thus allowing that a system, and not necessarily the human brain, can give rise to mental states (Fodor, 1994). From a functionalist lens, the mind and brain are viewed as one, with "the mind being viewed as

---

**TABLE 7.1**

**Characteristics for Differentiating among Philosophical Perspectives**

| Factors | Definition |
|---|---|
| Ontology | What exists in the world |
| Epistemology | How we come to know about what exists |
| Unit of analysis | Boundaries of the phenomenon of interest |
| Dualisms | When two items are treated as separate (e.g., mind/body or individual/environment) |

---

'the brain looked at from the inside' and the brain as 'the mind looked at from the outside'" (Turvey and Shaw, 1995, p. 146).

## Categories Summarized

It is these categories that will provide a basis for distinguishing among philosophical perspectives. Table 7.1 provides a summary of these categories.

## PHILOSOPHICAL PERSPECTIVES

Philosophical perspectives reflect certain assumptions with respect to the nature of the world and how we come to know about it; however, these are sets of beliefs and are not open to proof in the positivist sense of the word: "There is no way to elevate one over another on the basis of ultimate, foundational criteria" (Guba and Lincoln, 1983, p. 108). This does not mean that we submit to a radical relativist posture (Bereiter, 1994a; Guba, 1992). These perspectives represent certain sets of assumptions and commitments with respect to worldviews, and advocates of a particular perspective must rely on persuasiveness, assemblage of allies (other colleagues) (Latour, 1987), and utility rather than proof in arguing their position (Bereiter, 1994b). In this section, we present our interpretations (again, citing our colleagues to ground and add credibility to our conjectures) on the defining characteristics of these categories.

## Objectivism

Objectivism is described as both an ontology and epistemology (Lakoff, 1987). Ontologically, "all reality consists of entities, which have fixed properties and relations holding among them at any instant" (Lakoff, 1987, p. 160). The world consists of these entities, their properties, and the relations that exist among them. Reality exists through the structures of these entities and is independent of any human understanding (Lakoff, 1987); thus, the world is real and exists

outside of the individual (Bednar et al., 1995; Driscoll, 1994; Jonassen, 1991; Jonassen et al., 1993). Epistemologically, the mind functions as a mirror of nature, creating representations of the real world that require a correspondence to the external world. To know is to have these correct representations (Lakoff, 1987).

## Realism

Realism is an ontological view of which objectivism is one form (Lakoff, 1987). Both realism and objectivism support the existence of a real, physical world that is external to individuals and includes human experience. Although objectivism provides a specific description of what the real world must be, in terms of entities and properties, realism "merely assumes that there is a reality of some sort" (Lombardo, 1987, p. 159). From this point of view, the physical world is a separate reality from perception and the mind (Mackay, 1997; Reber, 1995) and truth or knowledge is ascertained as having a correspondence between the structures of the mind and what is present in the world (Prawat, 1995).

## Empiricism

As "typified by Locke and Thorndike, [empiricism] emphasizes consistency of knowledge with experience" (Greeno et al., 1996, p. 16). It is an epistemological perspective that holds that knowledge builds from experience, more specifically, from the senses (Driscoll, 1994; Ertmer and Newby, 1993; Gardner, 1985; Lombardo, 1987; Reber, 1995; Traiger, 1994). Empiricism rejects the notion that the human mind enters the world with *a priori* ideas and concepts that exist independently of personal experience (Reber, 1995); thus, what is learned comes from interactions with the environment (Ertmer and Newby, 1993). An empiricist would choose actual data over theoretical conjectures and would formulate an argument based on the evidence of experience.

## Rationalism and Idealism

Rationalism is generally discussed from an epistemological view. From a rationalist perspective, reason is the principle source of knowledge (Lombardo, 1987; Reber, 1995; Traiger, 1994). This reasoning power imposes upon the sensory experience that arises in the world, thus creating the world itself (Gardner, 1985). Early versions of rationalism posited that everything existed in one's mind *a priori*, and a learner's task was to discover what was already there, as in Plato's *Meno* (Plato, 1977). The ontological base of idealism, more pronounced than what might be implied by rationalism, holds that reality is psychological and all knowledge and experience are formed by these mental representations (Reber, 1995); thus, a separate world of physical entities or matter is not supported (Lombardo, 1987).

## Relativism

Relativism, a general principle rather than specifically a philosophical perspective, puts the meaning of experiential and physical events in the relationships that exist among them. In this, there is no intrinsic meaning that is independent of other events (Reber, 1995). Reality from this perspective is socially and experientially based, being local and specific to observer and context (Guba and Lincoln, 1983). There is no absolute truth to the world; instead, there are individual constructions that are highly dependent on the individual building the constructions.

## Pragmatism

Based on an Aristotelian heritage, a line of thought emerged that challenged the analytic, static, and segmented thought of absolute dualism. This was particularly evident in the natural sciences, where "the structures and capacities of animals were described relative to their ways of life within an environment; in turn, the environment was described relative to the ways of life of animals" (Lombardo, 1987, p. 5). In psychology, the pragmatists (also called functionalists) were less concerned with the inherent structure of the mind than with what the mind could do. The central focus of pragmatists (C.S. Peirce, William James, and John Dewey) was on what adaptive purposes justify the existence of mind (Turvey and Shaw, 1996). Rorty (1991) stated that pragmatism requires neither "a metaphysics [ontology] or an epistemology. They [pragmatists] view truth as, in William James' phrase, what is good for *us* to believe" (p. 22, emphasis in original). The truth, or knowledge, is equivalent to the consequences that derive from these interactions (Reber, 1995). What makes a particular stance count as a truth is not some correspondence with the real world but its appropriateness in terms of whether it is progressive (functional) (Barab and Squire, 2004; Bereiter, 1994b).

## Philosophical Views: Summarized

The above by no means accounts for all philosophical perspectives. We have chosen to define those that will be most salient to our discussion of psychological perspectives as they relate to learning and instruction. Table 7.2 contains a summary of these philosophical perspectives.

**TABLE 7.2**
**Philosophical Perspectives Summarized**

| Philosophical Perspective | Definition |
| --- | --- |
| Objectivism | Ontological and epistemological view that contends that reality (the world) exists outside of the individual and consists of specific entities; to know is to have a mirroring of this world |
| Realism | Form of objectivism that assumes that some sort of reality is separate from the mind (ontology); to know is to have a correspondence between the word and the mind (epistemology) |
| Empiricism | Epistemology that states that knowledge comes from experience and through the senses |
| Rationalism | Essentially an epistemological view where reason is the principle source of knowledge |
| Idealism | Defines reality as mental, meaning that the world is not separate from the mind (ontology) |
| Relativism | A general principle that places the meaning of experiential and physical events in the relationships that exist among them |
| Pragmatism | Neither an epistemology or an ontology; knowledge is derived from interaction among groups of individuals and the artifacts in their environment, both of which create a reality |

## PSYCHOLOGICAL PERSPECTIVES DISTINGUISHED

Considering ontological and epistemological assumptions, units of analysis, and the mind–body relation, we propose a classification model that includes five main categories of current psychological perspectives which have provided a foundation for learning and instructional theories. It is not our intent to add to the myriad of terms used to describe theoretical categories; consider, for example, the many names of various types of constructivism: information-processing constructivism (Prawat and Floden, 1994), cognitive information processing, (Derry, 1992), radical constructivism or cognitive constructivism (Cobb, 1994; Derry, 1992; Duffy and Cunningham, 1996; Prawat and Floden, 1994; von Glasersfeld, 1995), and sociocultural constructivism (sociohistorical) (Cobb, 1994; Duffy and Cunningham, 1996; Prawat and Floden, 1994).

With that in mind, we have chosen the following categories: behaviorism, cognitivism, cognitive constructivism (to keep in the forefront the focus on individual mind), sociocultural/historicism (to keep in the forefront the focus on interactions among individuals and among individuals and society), and situativity theory (to keep in the forefront the focus on interactions among individuals and the situations in which they are acting). As Greeno and colleagues (1996) stated about the boundaries for the three perspectives they outlined, boundaries are, of course, relatively arbitrary. The categories we discuss are not intended to define single boundaries among perspectives but rather to illuminate distinctions that become clear only by looking at the jigsaw that emerges as one variable (ontology, epistemology, unit of analysis, dualism) provides a distinction among two perspectives while another variable suggests their similarity.

## Behaviorism

Behaviorism was the predominant psychological school of thought during the first half the 20th century. Proponents of the field were Pavlov, Thorndike, Watson, Tolman, Hull, and Skinner.

### Ontology/Epistemology

There seems to be much agreement that behaviorism's ontological roots are objectivist (Driscoll, 1994; Duffy and Jonassen, 1992; Ertmer and Newby, 1993; Greeno et al., 1996; Jonassen, 1991). The world is real and exists outside of the individual. To come to know something within a behaviorist framework is to come to engage in specific behaviors in the context of particular stimuli. Burton et al. (1996) summarize three types of learning through which this can occur: respondent learning (e.g., use of classical conditioning where involuntary actions are elicited), operant conditioning (development of a relationship between a stimulus and response), and observational learning (change of behavior brought about by experience of observing others, of which Bandura's work is an example). Thus, the epistemological framework for behaviorism also finds roots in empiricism (Ertmer and Newby, 1993; Greeno et al., 1996).

### Unit of Analysis

To illuminate the focal point of knowledge, from a behaviorist perspective the unit of analysis is the behavior of an individual and the stimuli that elicit it. The mind is considered beyond inspection and not relevant to explaining behavior—no need to open up the black box (Gardner, 1985).

### Dualism Perspective

Because of its objectivist ontological roots, behaviorism supports a type of dualism that distinguishes between knower and world; however, behaviorism is considered an anti-Cartesian school of psychology, as "all mentalist terms can be redefined in terms of observable, physically describable behavior" (Garfield, 1995, p. 336), thus nothing can have a mental property without a physical property. Rather than dualism, behaviorism is a form of monism.

## Cognitivism

Cognitivism, as we describe it here, is that which initially emerged with the cognitive revolution during the 1950s, stressing a renewed focus on mind. As described by Bruner (1990, p. 1), the "revolution was intended to bring the 'mind' back into the human sciences after a long cold winter of objectivism." They "were not out to 'reform' behaviorism, but to replace it" (1990, p. 3). Cognitivism grew from structuralism, where mental states are viewed as the computational states of a Turing machine or as the time-evolving states of a connectionist (neural network) machine" (Turvey and Shaw, 1995, pp. 146–147). This focus on mind, in which the mind was viewed as an information-processing system as exemplified by the mind-as-computer metaphor that emerged, sought an understanding of the organization, encoding, and retrieval of knowledge. We consider symbolic information processing as described by Greeno et al. (1996) and cognitive symbolic processing (Derry, 1992) to be synonymous and exemplify this view.

### Ontology/Epistemology

Although, as Bruner (1990) stated, the cognitive revolution was a reaction to the cold winter of objectivism, cognitivism still finds roots in objectivism as an ontological base. As stated by Ertmer and Newby (1993), behaviorism and cognitivism are both primarily objective, and the world is real and external to the learner. Duffy and Jonassen (1992, p. 3) stated that much of the information-processing view in cognitive psychology is based on an objectivist epistemology, supporting this statement by citing the "independent existence of information and the acquisition of that information." A direct mapping of the world, a knowledge base of expert information, can be accomplished through learning. Although this acquisition of a knowledge structure does underlie the cognitive perspective, we feel that a rationalist epistemological base provides the distinction required to define a meaningful boundary between behaviorism and cognitivism (Ertmer and Newby, 1993). Greeno and colleagues' (1996) theoretical conceptualization is based on issues about the nature of knowing, essentially epistemology, as well as learning, transfer, motivation, and engagement, and describes behaviorism as objectivism and cognitivism as rationalism as well.

### Unit of Analysis

Like the behaviorists, the unit of analysis remains with the individual; however, rather than behavior, it is an analysis of an individual's mind structure and the representations developed.

### Dualism Perspective

With cognitivism's roots in rationalism, mind and environment would not be separated, the world existing only through mind; however, this is an extreme interpretation of rationalism as applied to cognitivism. Bredo (1994) itemized a number of dualisms that arise within this view: language and reality, mind and body, and individual and group. For our discussion, we align more with Turvey and Shaw (1995), who described cognitivism as growing out of 19th-century structuralism, where the mind and body are seen as separate and interactive.

## Cognitive Constructivism

Cognitive constructivism is generally aligned with the work of Piaget. This link to Piaget synthesized the various names that had been applied to this perspective: radical constructivism (Derry, 1996; von Glasersfeld, 1995), cognitive constructivism (Cobb, 1994; Duffy and Cunningham, 1996), psychological constructivism (Prawat, 1995), and constructivism (Bednar et al., 1995). This view, we believe, has emerged as an entity separate from cognitivism and social constructivism based on ontological differences on the one hand and the unit of analysis on the other.

### Ontology/Epistemology

From the cognitive constructivist perspective, there is a real world that we experience (Duffy and Jonassen, 1992), thus appearing to find an ontological base in objectivism; however, this world cannot be directly known (Derry, 1992; von Glaserfeld, 1995), which broadens the nature of the ontology to realism. That reality exists is not denied; however, what we know of the world is only an interpretation based on our experiences (von Glasersfeld, 1995). As such, cognitive constructivism is subjective and relativist, providing for no absolute in what is right or wrong and also has a base in empiricism (Bednar et al., 1995). Cognitive constructivism also finds its epis-

temological basis largely in rationalism (Greeno et al. 1996). The emphasis in knowing is in the cognitive activity of an individual as they make sense of the world (Cobb, 1994).

### Unit of Analysis

The unit of analysis within the cognitive constructivist perspective remains with the individual as in cognitivism but focuses on the conceptual reorganization of one's knowledge rather than on the extant structure of an individual's knowledge. Looking at the cognitive self-organization of the individual, Cobb (1994, p. 15) stated that "constructivists are typically concerned with the quality of individual interpretive activity."

### Dualism Perspective

As described by Cobb (1994), the cognitive constructivist perspective places the mind in the head of the individual. Culture and context play a role in the meaning making of each individual. The individual mind, although influenced by social context, is not one with the social context (Bereiter, 1994b); thus, mind is separate from environment (Prawat and Floden, 1994).

## Sociocultural/Historicism

Socioculturalism is often distinguished from cognitive constructivism (Cobb, 1994; Duffy and Cunningham, 1996; Phillips, 1995; Wood, 1995). Generally, this distinction is noted either through the name of constructivism as socioconstructivism, sociocultural constructivism (Cobb, 1994), social constructivism, or sociohistoricism (Strauss, 1993) or by distinguishing among the proponents of the perspective. Socioconstructivism, as we will identify it, has traditionally been aligned with the views of Vygotsky.

### Ontology/Epistemology

Distinguishing among the forms of constructivism is largely an epistemological distinction (Cobb, 1994; Phillips, 1995). In this perspective, knowing is distributed in the world, among objects and individuals. Knowledge creation is a shared rather than an individual experience (Prawat and Floden, 1994) and evolves through social negotiation (Savery and Duffy, 1995). Phillips (1995) described this emphasis on sociopolitical processes or consensus as a tendency toward relativism, where meaning was only incurred with respect to relationships, thus providing an epistemological distinction among constructivist theoretical perspectives. Prawat and Floden (1994) discussed socioconstructivism from a contextualist worldview, supporting the notion that from this perspective knowledge by verification is linked to actions and events that occur. Thus, ontologically, as with the cognitive constructivists, reality exists through interpretations; however, from the sociocultural perspective, society and an individual's relationship to society have a primary role in the shaping of that reality (Prawat and Floden, 1994).

## Unit of Analysis

Socioculturalists are distinctive in their insistence that knowledge creation is a shared rather than an individual experience (Prawat and Floden, 1994). It is this process, rather than the mental structures of the individual or the environment, that is the unit of analysis (Strauss, 1993); thus, the mind is placed in society, and the individual's cognitive structure as a unit of analysis is essentially meaningless.

## Dualism Perspective

To understand the view on dualism from this perspective, we find Bakhurst's description on the nature of thought as cited in Cobb (1994, p. 14) to be helpful:

> [T]hought should be viewed as something essentially "on the surface," as something located ... on the borderline between the organism and the outside world. For thought ... has a life only in an environment of socially constituted meanings.

Thus, a type of dualism is supported between individual and environment. Although a thought may only exist in the socially constructed world, the individual and environment are not one and the same.

## Situativity Theory

Young (1993) and Greeno (1998) have discussed the ecological tenets of situativity theory—that is, the notion of direct perception without the need for mediating variables that exist in one's head. Other roots to situativity theory can be found in the work of various anthropologists such as Lave and Wenger (1991), describing learning and cognition in the everyday world (Kirshner and Whitson, 1997). For our discussion, we will not distinguish among these perspectives of theory, choosing features of each which, to us, clarify the essence of situativity theory and distinguish it from the other psychological perspectives discussed above.

## Ontology/Epistemology

Lombardo (1987) described the ontological roots of ecological psychology as ecological reciprocity, the dynamical relationships that occur among aspects of the environment. The environment, in this perspective, is not distinct from the individual; the individual is merely a part of a highly interconnected system of relationships (Barab and Roth, 2006). Within this environment, we perceive and act based upon the affordances and constraints of the environment and the situations that arise within it. The epistemological basis of situativity, although seemingly not distinguishable from its ontology, was described by Lombardo (1996) as direct realism, which was foundational to the work of Gibson. Rather than viewing experiences as constituting the mind, the issue becomes what adaptive purposes exist to justify the existence of the mind (Turvey and Shaw, 1995).

A fundamental notion for the situativity theorist from the anthropological view is that "cognition must be viewed as an integral part of the physical, social, and cultural contexts to which it belongs" (Barab and Plucker, 2002; Derry, 1996, p. 416). Learning, or coming to know, has a defining characteristic of an individual involved in legitimate peripheral participation within the practices of a community (Lave and Wenger, 1991). From this perspective, knowing, identity, and context stand in dialectic, not dualistic, relations and are all constituted in the learning process (Barab and Duffy, 2000; Lave, 1997). Not only does this learning take place within the practices of the community, but also the social practices of the world are developed through this process. Thus, a reciprocity emerges as also defined from the ecological view.

## Unit of Analysis

The unit of analysis in this perspective is the "sociocultural setting in which the activities are embedded" (Kirshner and Whitson, 1997, p. 5). More so, it is the ecosystem that exists of which the learner is one part, and it is the individual–ecosystem interactions that must be captured from this perspective (Barab and Kirshner, 2001)

## Dualism Perspective

The situative perspective requires unification of cognition and nature (Turvey and Shaw, 1995). In this, there is not a dualism of mind and environment; instead, there exists, as described by Turvey and Shaw, organism– environment mutuality and reciprocity. Thus, we find a distinction between the situative perspective and

**TABLE 7.3**

**Psychological Perspectives: Epistemology, Ontology, Unit of Analysis, and Dualism Perspective**

| | Epistemology/ Ontology | Unit of Analysis | Dualism Perspective |
|---|---|---|---|
| Behaviorism | Objectivism | Behavior of the individual | Monism |
| Cognitivism | Objectivism Rationalism | Cognitive structures of the individual | Mind/environment |
| Cognitive constructivism | Rationalism Realism | Reorganization of mental structures of an individual making sense of the world | Mind/environment |
| Sociocultural/historicism | Relativism | Relation (and processes) between the individual and society | Individual/environment |
| Situativity theory | Ecological realism | Ecosystem of which the individual is a part | Mutualism |

the social constructivist perspective. Situativity theory defines no borderline between an organism and the environment as did Bakhurst; instead, from a situativity perspective they are one.

## Psychological Views: Summarized

We have outlined five categories of psychological perspectives that provide a basis in describing learning and instruction. Epistemology, ontology, unit of analysis, and the position on mind–environment relationships define these categories as we see them. Table 7.3 provides a summary.

## IMPLICATIONS FOR LEARNING THEORY AND INSTRUCTIONAL METHODS

Theoretical perspectives have been used as a foundation for learning theories and, in turn, instructional theories and their associated methods. Learning theories are descriptive (Prawat, 1992; Reigeluth, 1999b), describing how learning occurs within a particular instance. An example of a learning theory within the cognitive perspective is schema theory, which describes how learning occurs through accretion, tuning, and restructuring (Rumelhart, 1981). In contrast, instructional theories are prescriptive and provide guidance about how to design instruction to facilitate learning. An instructional theory identifies methods to be used and, more importantly, identifies situations in which these methods should or should not be used.

The *elaboration theory* (Reigeluth, 1999a) is an example of an instructional theory identifying how instruction should be sequenced so the learning process can be meaningful and motivational for learning, allowing for simplification of content without deconstructing the learning task into meaningless, decontextualized pieces. An *instructional theory* is probabilis-

tic, rather than deterministic, increasing the chances of achieving learning goals rather than guaranteeing them. The methods identified within an instructional theory provide specific ways in which to support and facilitate learning. The *simplifying conditions method* provides a means to analyze, select, and sequence the content of what is to be learned for an instructional designer who is subscribing to the elaboration theory in designing a learning activity (Reigeluth, 1999a).

Instructional theories and their associated methods are based on learning theories, providing an important linkage between how learning occurs and how to facilitate that process. Learning theories reflect the theoretical perspective, defining learning in terms of the nature of knowledge of the world and how one comes to know about these; however, the linkages among psychological perspective, learning theory, and instructional theory and associated methods are not necessarily simple and direct. Historically, learning theories may have been confined to a single psychological perspective (C. M. Reigeluth, pers. comm., August 24, 1998); for example, there is little question that operant conditioning is aligned with behaviorism. Yet, this clear distinction may not be the norm as psychological perspectives are further delineated and new and existing theories are considered in light of those perspectives; for example, Reigeluth (pers. comm., August 24, 1998) stated the following about his theories:

> While the cognitive perspective provides rationale for many of the prescriptions in the elaboration theory, constructivism provides rationale for others, and behaviorism could even provide rationale for some. Also, the elaboration theory can be used in different ways depending on the philosophical orientation of the user. For example, it could be a central part of self-directed, problem-based learning, or it could be used to sequence behaviorist instruction. I think we often do a disservice by trying to pigeon-hole particular methods into different philosophical and descriptive-theoretical orientation. I find that the real world is a bit more complex than such simplistic categorizations.

We agree with Reigeluth's concern about categorizing particular theories and methods with particular philosophical perspectives; however, we also believe that those who are designing instruction (instructional designers as well as classroom instructors) will benefit from a discussion of the differences in learning theories and instructional theories. What these theories imply about the nature of the world, knowledge, and the learning unit that is of interest provides a theoretical basis for designing instruction.

In the following paragraphs, we discuss the learning and instructional implications of each of the five identified theoretical perspectives. For each theoretical perspective, we identify a learning theory and instructional theory or method that we feel is an exemplar given our description of the psychological perspective. The description provided of each exemplar is brief, allowing the reader to rely on his or her own resources for a more involved description of the theories. It is important, again, to keep in mind the fragileness and contextual nature of the boundaries we have defined.

## Behaviorism

Because of its objectivist roots, those basing instruction on the behaviorist theoretical perspective find it appropriate to define the learning that will occur, describing specific observable outcomes that are indicative of the learning. Because of the role of knowledge as a mirror of the world, instructional content can be preplanned, organized, and programmed with specific outcomes defined. An exemplar learning theory that aligns with this perspective as we have described it is Skinner's operant conditioning. In this theory, learning is viewed as conditioning where behavior that is followed by a reinforcer will increase in frequency or probability. Ways of arranging the contingencies between the desired behavior and the reinforcer as well as schedules for determining the effects of reinforcers are specified (Barker, 1994; Goetz et al., 1992).

From this learning theory, programmed instruction provides an example of an instructional method that facilitates learning by utilizing reinforcement and feedback. The content is analyzed and preplanned based on an objective ontology, providing the learner with a direct map of what specifically is to be learned. Teaching machines and computer-aided instruction, descendants of programmed instruction, provide technological vehicles to facilitate this reinforcement process. Although technology has facilitated the process of this instructional method, the important aspect of these methods is the "arrangements of the materials so that the student could make correct responses and receive reinforcement when the correct responses were

made" (Saettler, 1995, p. 294). Given the focus of mapping correct responses to the learner, this theory and method align well with behaviorism's objective tradition. The behavior of the learner, that of providing correct responses, provides the unit of analysis we have identified.

## Cognitivism

Cognitivism retains the objectivist ontological look at the world, thus having some of the same design goals as behaviorism. Material is analyzed and sequenced, again often in a simple to complex or hierarchical type of organization (Gagné et al., 1992). The rationalist epistemology guides the focus on the study of learners' knowledge structures, thus providing for their cognitive structures as a meaningful unit of analysis. With this focus on rationalist knowledge building, it is possible to detach the learner from the environment, thus supporting a dualist view.

Learning theories within this perspective focus on the organization of the information to facilitate its acquisition by the learner. In his discussion of *meaningful reception learning*, Ausubel (1977) described a cognitive structure in learners where ideas were organized hierarchically and which contained inclusive concepts under which were subsumed subconcepts and other information. The cognitive structures were existing, were organized for stability and clarity, and influenced learning and retention (Ausubel, 1963), and learning was the process of subsuming new meaningful material into this structure. Instructionally, content was presented in its final form (Ausubel, 1961), and "the learner [was] required to internalize the information in a form that will be available for later use" (Driscoll, 1994, p. 115), thus aligning with the objectivist ontology while at the same time acknowledging the role of cognitive structure as needed for the rationalist epistemology.

Gagné's (1985) theory of instruction provides an exemplar within the cognitive perspective. In his *Conditions of Learning*, he described five types of learning capabilities: intellectual skills, verbal information, cognitive strategies, motor skills, and attitudes. Within these comprehensive categories he defines the conditions by which learning can be facilitated; for example, within cognitive strategies, internal conditions for the learner require an encoding strategy. As with the behaviorists, the resulting learning objective or outcome can be made explicit and objective. The instructional process is designed to align with the components and stages central to an information-processing type of learning theory, an early learning theory in the cognitive perspective.

Within this theoretical perspective encoding and retrieval strategies align with the rationalist epistemology, the objective ontological view found in the explicitly defined skills and knowledge that the learner will produce. Although the learning outcome may be a behavior, the unit of analysis is the learner's knowledge structure formed through a mapping of well-structured information to the learner.

## Cognitive Constructivism

With its realist roots, cognitive constructivism supports that the world exists, with learning proceeding from an individual's uniquely and individually constructed interpretation of that world. As with the cognitivist, the rationalist epistemology provides for the importance of the development of cognitive structures; however, in contrast to the cognitive view, information is not prestructured and presumed to be mapped into an individual's mind.

Von Glasersfeld (1995) identified Piaget's work as providing a learning theory that is consistent with the cognitive constructivist perspective as we have described it. Von Glasersfeld (1989, p. 125), describing Piaget as the "most prolific constructivist in our century," stated that Piaget's schemes were adaptable conceptual structures and could never be representations of the real world, always being based on the individual's experiential world. Piaget's scheme provided a means for individuals to construct their world using assimilation, a process by which an individual fits an experience into an existing conceptual structure. Should the experience and scheme not fit together well, perturbation develops, and the new experience will not be assimilated into the existing structure. Accommodation then occurs, and a new scheme is developed. In Piaget's scheme, both assimilation and accommodation are based on subjective experiences where the individual is constructing a personal interpretation of the world (von Glasersfeld, 1995).

Instructionally, sense-making opportunities are provided for learners to experience and thus construct new understandings. Teachers take a more interactive, less directive role in the instructional process of learners (Greeno, 1998). Discovery methods of instruction provide for this type of learning. Ausubel (1961) described the difference between reception learning and discovery learning; in the former, all the content is given to the learner, whereas in the latter the learner is to rearrange the information to integrate it into his or her own existing cognitive structure (i.e., discover it). Bruner (1961) described discovery learning in his early work. He included in discovery not just "finding

out something that was unknown to mankind, but ... [to] include all forms of obtaining knowledge for oneself by the use of one's own mind" (Bruner, 1961, p. 22). His view of learning was that it was an "active process of imposing organization or order on experience" (Goetz et al., 1992, p. 313). From this, discovery learning was intended to support the experience that allowed learners to explore new concepts and develop new skills. The realist ontology provided that what was discovered or made sense of did exist, and a correspondence was developed between the world and the mind. Of interest was the development of the structures of the learner, the order that a learner imposed upon the experience, thus supporting the restructuring of cognitive structures of the learner as a unit of analysis.

## Sociocultural/Historicism

The unit of analysis provides the most informative distinction between cognitive constructivism and socioculturalism. Seeking to understand learning from this perspective required a look at the process by which it occurred among individuals. Although other perspectives also support interaction and peer collaboration as ways of constructing or acquiring knowledge, socioculturalism requires that this process occur; thus, the knowledge developed is not with the individual but in the interactions among individuals.

For a learning theory within this perspective we draw on the work of Vygotsky. According to Vygotsky (1978), learning, in particular good learning, takes place in advance of development in what he termed the *zone of proximal development*. The zone of proximal development is the distance between the actual developmental level of the learner and what he or she is capable of performing with the assistance of an adult or more capable peer. Learning was also not an individual endeavor, relying on the interactions in which the child participates (Vygotsky, 1978, p. 90):

> [L]earning awakens a variety of internal developmental processes that are able to operate only when the child is interacting with people in his environment and in cooperation with his peers. These processes are internalized, they become part of the child's independent developmental achievement.

Knowledge exists in the interactions between the learner and adult, although the interaction is internalized by the learner, becoming a new function for the learner. This internalization of knowledge from interaction is termed *appropriation* (Wertsch, 1998).

An instructional strategy within this perspective that focused on the zone of proximal development is

**TABLE 7.4**

**Psychological Perspectives: Exemplars of Associated Learning Theories and Instructional Theories or Methods**

| Psychological Perspective | Learning Theory | Instruction Theory or Method |
|---|---|---|
| Behaviorism | Skinner's operant conditioning | Programmed instruction and computer-aided instruction |
| Cognitivism | Ausubel's meaningful reception learning | Gagné's conditions of learning |
| Cognitive constructivism | Piaget's scheme theory | Discovery learning |
| Sociocultural/historicism | Vygotsky's zone of proximal development | Reciprocal teaching or scaffolding |
| Situativity theory | Lave and Wenger's legitimate peripheral participant | Anchored instruction |

the use of instructional scaffolding as described by Collins et al. (1989). The idea is that instructional supports are provided that allow the learner to develop increasing competence, at which time the extra supports can be removed. It is in this way that the learner can engage in activities at the upper limit of his or her zone of proximal development. This support allows the tasks to remain complex and motivating yet still within the learner's level of functioning.

## Situativity Theory

The learning theory that we identify for the situativity perspective draws on the work of Lave and Wenger (1991). In contrast to the internalization process, which was evident in the other perspectives, learning, from this perspective, involves the whole person and the role of that person as he or she becomes a fully participating participant of a community (Barab et al., 1999). Based on a theory of social practice, the emphasis is on "the relational interdependencies of agent and world, activity, meaning, cognition, learning, and knowing" (Barab and Duffy, 2000, p. 50). Learning as a legitimate peripheral participant is an evolving form of membership where the learner also reproduces and transforms the community of practice of which they seek membership. The unit of analysis is thus the entire system of which the learner is a part, with knowledge residing in the dynamic relationship of the system. Becoming knowledgeably skillful involves appropriating the practices of the community, emphasizing community-defined practices that wed individuals to a community, instead of cognitive processing.

Instructionally, the situated perspective is often grouped with the sociocultural view. In fact, Garrison (1995) described situated cognition as making an important contribution to social constructivism. For our purposes, we draw on the work of the Cognition and Technology Group at Vanderbilt (1993) to provide an instructional theory (method) for this perspective,

focusing on characteristics that distinguish it from socioculturalism. Anchored instruction situates learning activities in information-rich video environments. Within the environment, learners are presented complex, realistic problems that they solve using information that is embedded within the anchoring story presented. To solve the problem, learners will engage in a number of problem-solving activities such as mathematical problem solving as presented in the *Jasper Woodbury Problem Solving Series*.

As an example of ecological realism, the anchor on which the instruction is built is viewed in terms of affordances as described by Gibson; the anchors are designed to support certain types of teaching and learning activities. That is, the learning opportunities emerge as a result of the learner's problem-solving role within the instruction; the anchor is designed to set up a rich macrocontext in which conceptual tools can be used to address the anchor problem (CTGV, 1993). Although the *Jasper* series lacks the authenticity of a problem-solving encounter that exists in the real world, it provides the opportunity for the learner to participate in a simulated type of world. Thus, even in this technology-based world, the unit of analysis rests not with the learner but with the learner as a part of the system in which the problem solving takes place.

## Implications for Learning Theory and Instructional Methods: Summary

We have identified an exemplar learning theory and instructional theory or method that captures the characteristics of each of the five theoretical perspectives outlined above. Within each perspective there is ample room for debate and discussion about the merits of including these theories within a perspective as well as what other theories and methods might better exemplify the characteristics. Table 7.4 provides a summary of the learning theories and instructional theories or methods used in our discussion.

## CONCLUDING REMARKS

Philosophical perspectives are worldviews that define the nature of the world, the individual's place in it, and the possible relationships to that world and its parts. These perspectives form the foundation for any line of inquiry, including those associated with a particular discipline. As such, it is essential before beginning a line of inquiry or the profession of teaching that individuals examine their ontological and epistemological commitments. In this article, we presented five main categories of psychological perspectives and contrasted them in terms of epistemology, ontology, unit of analysis, and whether they suggested dualist relationships.

In terms of the domain of psychology, we have seen the emergence of psychological perspectives arising from varying philosophical commitments. It is important to acknowledge that philosophies with respect to epistemological and ontological assumptions are not instructional methods and that methods are not philosophies. It has been argued, however, that instructional strategies and methods are clearly influenced by the philosophical assumptions and that theories of knowing and learning are implicit to the instructional design (Barab and Duffy, 2000; Duffy and Jonassen, 1991; Reigeluth, 1999b). We find it inconceivable that a teacher or instructional designer would advocate a particular lesson or activity without at least a tacit theory of how students think and learn. In this article, we have differentiated among philosophical perspectives and suggested alignments between assumptions associated with various perspectives and learning and instructional theories. Obviously, these alignments only scratch the surface and may not be consistent with those advanced by others; however, we have found these alignments useful in that they begin to capture some of the relationships and serve as beginnings for discussion.

We hope this chapter pushes educators to examine and question their ontological and epistemological assumptions and whether or not their instructional practices are consistent with those assumptions. If there is incongruency between philosophical assumptions and instructional practices, then, we argue, it is important to ask oneself "Why the inconsistency?" and "How do I best resolve it?" We have found this reflective practice to be most useful in terms of our own teaching and research. At times, this has meant changing teaching practices and at other times challenging philosophical assumptions (see Glaser and Strauss, 1967, for a discussion of grounded theory development). Some educators have advocated for eclecticism in which one draws from various philosophies and

learning and instructional theories depending on the task at hand (Ertmer and Newby, 1993; Reigeluth, 1999b; Sfard, 1998). In spite of the merit of not getting trapped and closed-minded, we have found it useful in moving forward with a research and teaching program to make ontological and epistemological commitments. From here, we as researchers and reflective practitioners can then empirically examine the merits of such a commitment; that is, we can consider how our theoretical assumptions align with empirical observation and adjust accordingly.

We have noted that the categories and descriptions forwarded in this article are not hard and fast rules or socially negotiated truths agreed upon by the community; rather, they are based on our understandings and on a review and interpretation of the literature and were written in the context of this paper. There is no way to prove, in the conventional positivistic sense, that one theory is better than another. This is partly because the methods one would use to make such arguments are based on a set of ontological and epistemological commitments as well (Greeno, 1997). As such, we expect theoretical debates to remain an important practice in the field. We have aligned our categories with colleagues in the field and, at the very least, argue that much of our conjectures are consistent with some of the socially negotiated meanings and inconsistent with others. But, again, our goal is for this chapter to provide a springboard for discussion and to prompt educators to question the relationships among philosophical assumptions, psychological perspectives, learning and instructional theories, and instructional practice, not to suggest indisputable facts.

## References

Ausubel, D. P. (1961). In defense of verbal learning. *Educ. Theory*, 11(1), 15–25.*

Ausubel, D. P. (1963). Cognitive structure and the facilitation of meaning verbal learning. *J. Teacher Educ.*, 14(2), 217–222.

Ausubel, D. P. (1977). The use of advance organizers in the learning and retention of meaningful verbal material. In *Learning and Instruction*, edited by M. C. Wittrock, pp. 148–155. Berkeley, CA: McCutchan Publishing.

Barab, S. A. and Duffy, T. (2000). From practice fields to communities of practice. In *Theoretical Foundations of Learning Environments*, edited by D. Jonassen and S. M. Land, pp. 25–56. Mahwah, NJ: Lawrence Erlbaum Associates.*

Barab, S. A. and Kirshner, D. (2001). Methodologies for capturing learner practices occurring as part of dynamic learning environments. *J. Learn. Sci.*, 10(1/2), 5–15.

Barab, S. A. and Plucker, J. A. (2002). Smart people or smart contexts? Cognition, ability, and talent development in an age of situated approaches to knowing and learning. *Educ. Psychol.*, 37(3), 165–182.

Barab, S. A. and Roth, W.-M. (2006). Intentionally-bound systems and curricular-based ecosystems: an ecological perspective on knowing. *Educ. Res.*, 35(5), 3–1

Barab, S. A. and Squire, K. D. (2004). Design-based research: putting our stake in the ground. *J. Learn. Sci.*, 13(1), 1–14.

Barab, S. A., Cherkes-Julkowski, M., Swenson, R., Garrett. S., Shaw, R. E., and Young, M. F. (1999). Principles of self-organization: ecologizing the learner-facilitator system. *J. Learn. Sci.*, 8(3/4), 349–390.

Barker, L. M. (1994). *Learning and Behavior: A Psychobiological Perspective*. New York: Macmillan.

Bednar, A. K., Cunningham, D. J., Duffy, T. M., and Perry, J. D. (1995). Theory into practice: how do we link? In *Instructional Technology: Past, Present, and Future*, edited by G. J. Anglin, pp. 100–112. Englewood, CO: Libraries Unlimited, Inc.

Bereiter, C. (1994a). Constructivism, socioculturalism, and Popper's world, 3. *Educ. Res.*, 23(7), 21–23.*

Bereiter, C. (1994b). Implications of postmodernism for science, or, science as progressive discourse. *Educ. Psychol.*, 29, 3–12.

Bredo, E. (1994). Reconstructing educational psychology: situated cognition and Deweyian pragmatism. *Educ. Psychologist*, 29(1), 23–35.

Bruner, J. S. (1961). The act of discovery. *Harvard Educ. Rev.*, 31(1), 21–32.*

Bruner, J. S. (1990). *Acts of Meaning*. Cambridge, MA: Harvard University Press.*

Burton, J. K., Moore, D. M., and Magliaro, S. G. (1996). Behaviorism and instructional technology. In *Handbook of Research for Educational Communications and Technology*, edited by Jonassen, D. H., pp. 46–73. New York: Macmillan.

Cobb, P. (1994). Where is the mind? Constructivist and sociocultural perspectives on mathematical development. *Educ. Res.*, 23, 13–20.*

Cognition and Technology Group at Vanderbilt (CTGV). (1993). Anchored instruction and situated cognition revisited. *Educ. Technol.*, 33, 52–70.

Collins, A., Brown, J. S., and Newman, S. E. (1989). Cognitive apprenticeship: teaching the crafts of reading, writing, and mathematics. In *Knowing, Learning, and Instruction: Essays in Honor of Robert Glaser*, edited by L. B. Resnick, pp. 453–494. Hillsdale, NJ: Lawrence Erlbaum Associates.

Derry, S. J. (1992). Beyond symbolic processing: expanding horizons for educational psychology. *J. Educ. Psychol.*, 84, 413–418.

Derry, S. J. (1996). Cognitive schema theory in the constructivist debate. *Educ. Psychol.*, 31(3/4), 163–174.

Dewey, J. (1963). *Experience and Education*. New York: Collier Macmillan.

Driscoll, M. P. (2005). *Psychology of Learning for Instruction,* 3rd ed. Boston, MA: Allyn & Bacon.

Duffy, T. M. and Cunningham, D. J. (1996). Constructivism: implications for the design and delivery of instruction. In *Handbook of Research for Educational Communications and Technology*, edited by D. H. Jonassen, pp. 170–198. New York: Macmillan.*

Duffy, T. M. and Jonassen, D. H. (1992). Constructivism: new implications for instructional technology. In *Constructivism and the Technology of Instruction*, edited by T. Duffy and D. Jonassen, pp. 1–16. Hillsdale, NJ: Lawrence Erlbaum Associates.

Ertmer, P. A. and Newby, T. J. (1993). Behaviorism, cognitivism, constructivism: comparing critical features from an instructional design perspective. *Perform. Improve. Q.*, 6(4), 50–72.

Everitt, N. and Fisher, A. (1995). *Modern Epistemology: A New Introduction*. New York: McGraw-Hill.*

Fodor, J. (1994). The mind–body problems. *Sci. Am.*, 244(1), 114–123. (Reprinted in Klemke, E. D. et al., Eds., *Philosophy: Contemporary Perspectives on Perennial Issues*, 4th ed., pp. 197–214. New York: St. Martin Press.)*

Gagné, R. M. (1985). *The Conditions of Learning*, 4th ed. New York: Holt, Rinehart and Winston.

Gagné, R. M., Briggs, L. J., and Wager, W. W. (1992). *Principles of Instructional Design*, 4th ed. Fort Worth, TX: Harcourt Brace Jovanovich College Publishers.

Gardner, H. (1985). *The Mind's New Science: A History of the Cognitive Revolution*. New York: HarperCollins.

Garfield, J. (1995). Philosophy: foundations of cognitive science. In *Cognitive Science: An Introduction*, 2nd ed., edited by N. A. Stilling, S. E. Weisler, C. H. Chase, M. H. Feinstein, J. L. Garfield, and E. L. Rissland, pp. 331–377. Cambridge, MA: MIT Press.

Garrison, J. (1995). Deweyan pragmatism and the epistemology of contemporary social constructivism. *Am. Educ. Res. J.*, 32(4), 716–740.

Gibson, J. J. (1996). *The Sense Considered as Perceptual Systems*. Boston, MA: Houghton Mifflin.*

Glaser, B. G. and Strauss, A. L. (1967). *The Discovery of Grounded Theory: Strategies for Qualitative Research*. Chicago, IL: Aldine.

Goetz, E. T., Alexander, P. A., and Ash, M. J. (1992). *Education Psychology: A Classroom Perspective*. New York: Macmillan.

Greeno, J. G. (1997). On claims and answering the wrong questions. *Educ. Res.*, 26(1), 5–17.

Greeno, J. G., Collins, A. M., and Resnick, L. B. (1996). Cognition and learning. In *Handbook of Educational Psychology*, edited by D. C. Berliner and R. C. Calfee, pp. 15–46. New York: Macmillan.*

Greeno, J. G. and the Middle School Mathematics Through Applications Project Group. (1998). The situativity of knowing, learning, and research. *Am. Psychol.*, 53(1), 5–26

Guba, E. G. (1992). Relativism. *Curric. Inquiry*, 22, 17–24.

Guba, E. G. and Lincoln, Y. S. (1983). Epistemological and methodological bases of naturalistic inquiry. In *Evaluation Models: Viewpoints on Educational and Human Services Evaluation*, edited by G. F. Madaus, M. S. Scriven, and D. L. Stufflebeam, pp. 311–334. Boston, MA: Kluwer-Nijhoff.

Jonassen, D. H. (1991). Objectivism versus constructivism: do we need a new philosophical paradigm? *Educ. Technol. Res. Dev.*, 3(93), 5–14.

Jonassen, D. H., Wilson, B. G., Wang, S., and Grabinger, R. S. (1993). Constructivist uses of expert systems to support learning. *J. Comput. Based Instruct.*, 20(3), 86–94.

Kirshner, D. and Whitson, J. A. (1997). Editors' introduction to situated cognition: social, semiotic, and psychological perspectives. In *Situated Cognition: Social, Semiotic, and Psychological Perspectives*, edited by D. Kirshner and J. A. Whitson, pp. 1–16. Mahwah, NJ: Lawrence Erlbaum Associates.

Lakoff, G. (1987). *Women, Fire, and Dangerous Things: What Categories Reveal About the Mind*. Chicago, IL: The University of Chicago Press.*

Latour, B. (1987). *Science in Action: How to Follow Scientists and Engineers Through Society*. Cambridge, MA: Harvard University Press.

Lave, J. (1997). The culture of acquisition and the practice of understanding. In *Situated Cognition: Social, Semiotic, and Psychological Perspectives*, edited by D. Kirshner and J. A. Whitson, pp. 63–82. Mahwah, NJ: Lawrence Erlbaum Associates.

Lave, J., and Wenger, E. (1991). *Situated Learning: Legitimate Peripheral Participation*. New York: Cambridge University Press.*

Lombardo, T. J. (1987). *The Reciprocity of Perceive and Environment: The Evolution of James J. Gibson's Ecological Psychology*. Hillsdale, NJ: Lawrence Erlbaum Associates.

Mackay, N. (1997). Constructivism and the logic of explanation. *J. Construct. Psychol.*, 10, 339–361.

Phillips, D. C. (1995). The good, the bad, and the ugly: the many faces of constructivism. *Educ. Res.*, 24(7), 5–12.

Plato. (1977). Meno. In *Learning and Instruction*, edited by M. C. Wittrock, pp. 14–21. Berkeley, CA: McCutchan.

Prawat, R. S. (1992). Teachers' beliefs about teaching and learning: a constructivist perspective. *Am. J. Educ.*, 100, 354–395.

Prawat, R. S. (1995). Misreading Dewey: reform projects and the language game. *Educ. Res.*, 24(7), 13–22.

Prawat, R. S. and Floden, R. E. (1994). Philosophical perspectives on constructivist views of learning. *Educ. Psychol.*, 29(1), 37–48.

Reber, A. S. (1995). *The Penguin Dictionary of Psychology*. New York: Penguin Books.

Reed, R. S. (1996). *Encountering the World: Toward an Ecological Psychology*. New York: Oxford University Press.

Reigeluth, C. M. (1999a). The elaboration theory: guidance for scope and sequence decisions. In *Instructional-Design Theories and Models: A New Paradigm of Instructional Theory*, Vol. 2, edited by C. M. Reigeluth, pp. 425–453. Hillsdale, NJ: Lawrence Erlbaum Associates.

Reigeluth, C. M. (1999b). What is instructional design theory and how is it changing? In *Instructional-Design Theories and Models: A New Paradigm of Instructional Theory*, Vol. 2, edited by C. M. Reigeluth, pp. 5–29. Hillsdale, NJ: Lawrence Erlbaum Associates.

Rorty, R. (1991). *Objectivity, Relativism, and Truth: Philosophical Papers*, Vol. 1. Cambridge, U.K.: Cambridge University Press.*

Rumelhart, D. E. (1981). Schemata: the building blocks of cognition. In *Cognitive Skills and Their Acquisition*, edited by J. R. Anderson, pp. 33–58. Hillsdale, NJ: Lawrence Erlbaum Associates.

Saettler, P. J. (1990). *The Evolution of American Educational Technology*. Englewood, CO: Libraries Unlimited.

Salomon, G. (1991). Transcending the qualitative-quantitative debate: the analytic and systematic approaches to educational research. *Educ. Res.*, 20(6), 10–18.

Savery, J. R. and Duffy, T. M. (1995). Problem based learning: an instructional model and its constructivist framework. In *Constructivist Learning Environments*, edited by B. G. Wilson, pp. 135–148. Englewood Cliffs, NJ: Educational Technology Publications.

Sfard, A. (1998). On two metaphors for learning and the dangers of choosing just one. *Educ. Res.*, 27(2), 4–13.*

Strauss, A. L. (1993). Theories of learning and development of academics and educators. *Educ. Psychol.*, 28(3), 191–203.

Traiger, S. (1994). The secret operations of the mind. *Minds Machines*, 4, 303–315.

Turvey, M. T. and Shaw, R. E. (1995). Toward an ecological physics and a physical psychology. In *The Science of the Mind: 2001 and Beyond*, edited by R. L. Solso and D. W. Massaro, pp. 144–169. New York: Oxford.

von Glasersfeld, E. (1989). Cognition, construction of knowledge, and teaching. *Synthese*, 80, 121–140.

von Glasersfeld, E. (1995). *Radical Constructivism: A Way of Knowing and Learning*. London: The Falmer Press.*

Vygotsky, L. S. (1978). *Mind in Society: The Development of Higher Psychological Processes*. Cambridge, MA: Harvard University Press.*

Wertsch, J. V. (1998). *Mind as Action*. New York: Oxford University Press.

Wood, D. (1995). Theory, training, and technology, part 1. *Educ. Train.*, 37(1), 12–16.

Young, M. F. (1993). Instructional design for situated learning. *Educ. Technol. Res. Dev.*, 41, 43–58.

Young, M. F., Kulikowich, J. M., and Barab, S. A. (1997). The unit of analysis for situated assessment. *Instruct. Sci.*, 25, 133–150.

* Indicates a core reference.

# Part II
## Strategies

This Strategies part of the *Handbook* was led by M. David Merrill. The various chapters in Strategies cover both instructional and learning strategies, although the emphasis is on implications for design and development. These various strategies can be linked with subsequent chapters in Parts III, IV, and V of the *Handbook*, in accordance with our organizational framework. This part of the *Handbook* consists of seven chapters covering: (1) representation strategies, (2) experiential strategies, (3) generative strategies, (4) practice and feedback strategies, (5) support strategies, (6) collaboration strategies, and (7) strategies for different outcomes. This part of the *Handbook* provides readers with a comprehensive review of recent research pertaining to a variety of instructional strategies that can be linked with Technologies in Part III, with Models in Part IV, and with Design and Development in Part V.

# 8

# Representation Strategies

*Linda L. Lohr and James E. Gall*
University of Northern Colorado, Greeley, Colorado

## CONTENTS

## ABSTRACT

Throughout the history of education as a social science, empirical research has been conducted on various representation modes of knowledge and their impact on learners. Although a number of nonobjectivist philosophies have been put forth in education, research in knowledge representations continues to be dominated by a paradigm of knowledge transfer. This chapter uses a three-tier toolbox metaphor for media-based instructional design. The top tier addresses learning theories, the middle tier addresses multimedia models, and the bottom tier addresses specific text, visuals, audio, and animation/video design guidelines.

## KEYWORDS

*Baddeley's memory model:* An information-processing model that emphasizes the different short-term memory stores for visual (the sketchpad) and auditory (the phonological loop) information.

*Cognitive load theory:* Cognitive model of information processing that emphasizes a conceptual mental workload in understanding human thought.

*Cognitive models:* Descriptions of human thought processes via metaphorical constructs. These constructs may or may not represent actual biological structures. The value of any model is judged by its utility in representing or predicting actual thought, not by the degree of accuracy in depicting brain structure.

*Construction–integration model:* Cognitive model for understanding the processing of text; this model suggests a continual multi-leveled process of building and confirming a cohesive mental model from a text document and a reader's prior knowledge.

*Dual-coding theory:* Cognitive model of information processing that emphasizes the unique contributions of verbal and visual subsystems in understanding human cognition.

*Extraneous load:* In cognitive load theory, the workload component associated with information that is not directly relevant to a particular content area.

*Germane load:* In cognitive load theory, the workload component associated with strategies that require processing but in doing so make the relevant content more accessible.

*Interactive multimedia:* The use of more than one form of media (such as text, visuals, video, animation, and audio) in a way in which a user has a great deal of control over the choice or progress of the program.

*Intrinsic load:* In cognitive load theory, the workload component associated with a particular content area and its level of complexity.

*Long-term memory:* Component of the information-processing model of cognition that represents information stored, presumably for the life of an individual.

*Phonological loop:* In Baddeley's memory model a short-term memory component devoted to retaining auditory information.

*Redundancy:* The presentation of information multiple times either in the same or in different forms; the value of redundancy in communication is context dependent and debated.

*Sensory memory:* Component of the information-processing model of cognition that describes the initial input of information (such as vision or hearing).

*Short-term memory:* Component of the information-processing model of cognition that describes a person's attention.

*Visual sketchpad:* In Baddeley's memory model a short-term memory component devoted to visual and spatial information.

*Visuals:* A form of media in which information is presented visually; text may or may not be considered a visual form.

*Zone of learnability:* In the construction-integration model of text processing, a hypothesized optimal overlap between a text document and a reader's prior knowledge.

## INTRODUCTION

This chapter presents a number of research-based guidelines for using media to support learning. Advances in technology and easy access to images, sound, video, and animation, make the development of information-rich learning environments within the reach of most instructional designers today. Although these media are increasingly sophisticated and varied, access does not necessarily turn the average designer into an expert one. Efforts to enhance instruction are equally capable of the opposite effect when media are poorly implemented.

Increasingly experimental, modality-specific, and cognitively focused research provides new ways to measure and map brain activity in the context of media-facilitated instruction. Today's instructional designer is equipped with a growing body of skills and knowledge, a metaphorical toolbox overflowing with information. Knowing how to use this information is increasingly challenging. For one, the toolbox is messy, as is the process of design (Meikle, 2005) and models used by instructional designers (Bichelmeyer, 2005). Unclear guidelines and the nature of academic rhetoric contribute to the confusion.

The purpose of this chapter is to break from convention to untangle some of the confusion. Recent developments in cognitive load theory (Merriënboer and Sweller, 2005) restate the importance of decreasing content complexity to increase meaningful learning. In keeping with this goal, we share here a simplified view of media research, returning to a number of selected theories and guidelines considered worthy of attention. Given their observed application in a number of settings they possess an arguable degree of merit.

## AN ORGANIZATION SCHEME FOR DESIGN PRINCIPLES

Figure 8.1 uses a toolbox analogy to illustrate a suggested framework for organizing media-based design principles. A three-tier approach consists of general

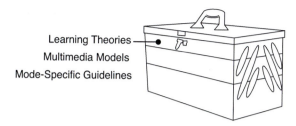

Figure 8.1 Instructional design toolbox.

learning theories at the top tier, multimedia-learning theories at the middle tier, and specific mode-based guidelines for text, visuals, audio, and animations/ video at the lowest and most easily accessed tier.

## Four Related Learning Theories

Theories of learning contribute to our understanding of how media might be presented for effective learning and performance, particularly those theories that are based in the cognitive sciences, the study of how knowledge is acquired. Four related learning theories important to designers and researcher are summarized: (1) information-processing theory, (2) dual-coding theory, (3) cognitive load theory, and (4) Baddeley's model of memory (see Figure 8.2). Information-processing theory provides an overview and perspective of memory structure important to the understanding the significance of dual-coding theory, cognitive load theory, and Baddeley's model of memory.

### Information-Processing Theory

A number of theories describe the transfer of information through memory (Atkinson and Shiffrin, 1968; Broadbent, 1984; Lockhart and Craik, 1994; Norman and Bobrow, 1975; Waugh and Norman, 1965). Atkinson and Shiffrin (1968) proposed a model based on two types of memory: short-term memory (including sensory and working memory) and long-term memory. This dual-store model of memory is commonly referred to as information-processing theory. In this model, short-term memory is very limited in duration (only seconds) and capacity. A component of short-term memory is working memory, a system that performs an executive capacity by managing and manipulating information that constitutes a learner's current attention. Long-term memory has a seemingly infinite duration and capacity.

The interaction of short-term and long-term components is the focus of learning. Although virtually anyone can attend to a particular stimulus, learning is dependant on the transfer of relevant information to long-term memory and its retrieval when performance is required. Instructional designers are fundamentally concerned with the function of working memory. Regardless of the medium, relevant information must gain the attention of the learner, be held in working memory, and ideally be in a form that is readily incorporated into long-term memory.

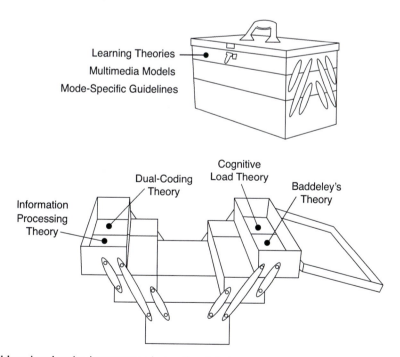

Figure 8.2 Four related learning theories important to instructional design.

### Dual-Coding Theory

Pavio's research (1971, 1986) extended the general information-processing theory by suggesting separate verbal and visual subsystems of memory. Information presented in either form, verbal or visual, is coded in either a visual memory store or a verbal memory store. These separate memory systems are each capable of activating the other, as well as converting information from one form to another. Words can be coded in a verbal format but are also capable of being converted to an image format, if prior knowledge allows. The same can be said for images whose form can be converted to a verbal description. From Paivio's point of view, the connection between the visual and verbal codes strengthens memory. To information designers, presenting the combination of visual and verbal information is likely to increase the chances of recognition and recall, due to the strengthened associations afforded by dual coding.

### Cognitive Load Theory

Cognitive load theory (CLT) relies on the core components of the information-processing model (short-term, working, and long-term memory) but focuses particularly on the limitations of working memory. From the perspective of cognitive load theory, instructional materials should be created for a theoretical optimal cognitive load. In other words, cognitive overload impairs learning; cognitive underload does not generate interest. Cognitive load theory is particularly applicable to instructional designers, and this chapter. According to Sweller et al. (1998, p. 262), "Limited working memory is one of the defining aspects of human cognitive architecture and, accordingly, all instructional designs should be analyzed from a cognitive load perspective."

Cognitive load refers to the amount of information presented and how well that amount compares with the size of working memory. Optimal load varies, based on the level of learner expertise. Novice learners with limited prior knowledge are more likely to process simple, sequential structures with limited threats to overloading memory. Expert learners, on the other hand, are able to accommodate richer, more complex information loads due to their developed schemas or knowledge representations that make integration of new information possible. Optimally, the designer's task is to structure information that fits within existing schema (i.e., prior knowledge). Individual differences in both prior knowledge and effective working memory size are particularly troublesome when designing materials to be used by wide ranges of learners.

The research on cognitive load describes three categories of load: intrinsic load, extraneous load, and germane load (Paas et al., 2003). *Intrinsic load* refers to the nature of the content and its level of complexity. Complexity can be defined in terms of element interactivity, or the extent to which a learner must understand instructional content that overlaps and interacts with other instructional content. High content interactivity describes complex relationships in which the various components can only be understood as part of a larger system. Low content interactivity describes information that is more easily understood in isolation, because it requires an understanding of fewer elements. Learning concepts, for example, would be more likely to involve high element interactivity than learning facts, which would involve low element interactivity. An instructional designer cannot modify intrinsic load because it refers to the complexity of the information itself.

*Extraneous load* can be thought of as the noise, or superfluous elements of communication, that act as barriers to learning due to the increased load they place on memory. For example, using a large number of fonts in a section of text does not add to the content but rather adds to the extraneous load as the reader attempts to assign meaning to the various changes.

*Germane load* can be thought of as those things that a designer can do to facilitate optimal load, such as chunking content, sequencing it, and providing analogies that can help people understand new information more quickly. A designer can work to reduce a high intrinsic load by both reducing extraneous and increasing germane load.

Although cognitive load theory is particularly well suited for the discussion of issues regarding the creation of instructional materials, it is not the sole model for understanding mental workload. Terms such as *exerted mental effort* are often used in research studies, but other than a gross comparison of higher and lower load or difficulty, the concept is not well defined. A mental workload example from human factors describes a model in which a limited amount of attention resources must be shared by perception, working memory functions, metacognitive oversight, and execution of a response (Wickens, 1984).

### Baddeley's Model of Memory

Baddeley's research (2000) attempted to further clarify the capacities of working memory. Working memory is composed of a central executive function. This central executive function is involved in focusing attention, switching attention, and dividing attention. In Baddeley's model, the executive function monitors a

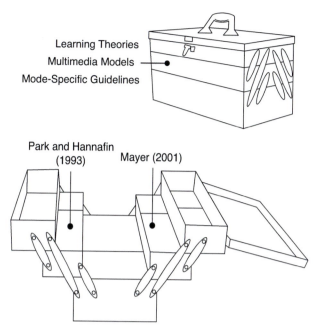

Learning Theories
Multimedia Models
Mode-Specific Guidelines

Park and Hannafin
(1993)          Mayer (2001)

**Figure 8.3** Multimedia guidelines.

visual sketchpad (visual and spatial memory), a pho-nological loop (auditory memory), and an episodic buffer. This episodic buffer is the area that interfaces with the visual sketchpad and the phonological loop and binds or integrates this information. In a sense, Baddeley's model attempts to reconcile the under-standing of short- and long-term memory from infor-mation processing with the channels of different infor-mation streams from dual coding.

Of interest to instructional designers is the idea that the episodic buffer is not considered part of long-term memory. It may be possible to design and organize information for optimal use of this buffer. If the learner does not need to perform low-level integration and organization, more mental effort would be freed to per-form other functions conducive to long-term storage and recall. Working memory can retrieve information from the episodic buffer, creating relatively new repre-sentations while at the same time also retrieving infor-mation from long-term memory. The unique juxtapo-sition of information in the episodic buffer may explain some aspects of problem solving and creativity.

## MULTIMEDIA GUIDELINES

Two prominent theories of multimedia (see Figure 8.3) (Mayer, 2001, Park and Hannafin, 1993) suggest a number of guidelines, which are summarized in Table 8.1. Park and Hannafin (1993) based their work on an extensive review of the research and proposed an over-

arching framework for interactive multimedia design using 20 design principles. Recently, Mayer's (2001) multimedia theory suggested seven design principles that focus specifically on the interaction of audio, text, and visuals in a number of controlled experiments. Table 8.1 provides the authors' classification of com-bined multimedia design principles in the context of cognitive load theory. Principles are placed in cell loca-tions most directly related to their connotation with the purpose of showing potential connections between theories.

## Presentation Guidelines for Text, Visuals, Audio, and Animation/Video

Guidelines for text, visuals, audio, and animation/video are reviewed in this section (see Figure 8.4).

### Text Guidelines

Textual information has long been the backbone of formal education. Although the use visual and spoken language information predates the development of written text in human history, the use of text as an augment to human memory provided a great leap for-ward in educational settings. The guidelines in this section of the chapter focus on the work of Walther Kintsch (1998). Whereas many forms of mediated instruction have been used only over the last 100 years, written text has been used and developed for thousands of years. During the 1970s, in part as an attempt to

**TABLE 8.1**
**Cognitive Framework for Multimedia**

| CLT Theory Components | Park and Hannafin (1993) | Mayer (2001) |
|---|---|---|
| | *Principles that address the importance of:* | *Principles that address the importance of:* |
| Increasing germane load | Prior knowledge and learner familiarity (principles 1, 2, 4, 6) Authentic contexts (principle 10) Adaptive, individual attention and feedback (principles 17, 18, 19) | Visuals for low knowledge and high-spatial learners (principle 7) |
| Reducing intrinsic load | Organization to complement cognitive processes/internal organization (principles 3, 7, 9) Multiple perspectives and cross-referencing (principle 11) Organizing activities (invested mental effort, elaboration, articulation, knowledge differentiation (principles 5, 8, 12, 14) | Using words and pictures rather than words alone (principle 1) Placing words and visuals close together (principle 2) Simultaneously presenting words and pictures (principle 3) |
| Reducing extraneous load | Clear system features, procedures, access, and visual representations (principles 15, 16, 20) Structure and feedback relevancy (principle 13) | Excluding extraneous words, pictures and sounds (principle 4) Using animation and narration rather than animation and on-screen text or animation, on-screen text, and narration (principles 5, 6) |

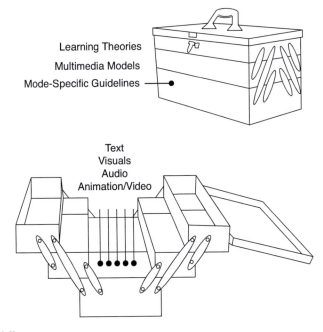

Learning Theories
Multimedia Models
Mode-Specific Guidelines

Text
Visuals
Audio
Animation/Video

**Figure 8.4** Mode-specific guidelines.

represent knowledge with computers, two key ideas for further understanding of text processing were explored: proposition representation and schema theory.

From the perspective of text processing, a proposition is a predicate and a number of arguments that together form an idea or unit of information. For those doing research with text, it was important to distinguish between an idea and the multiple ways of expressing that idea into English or any other language. Decoding natural language into propositions, or a propositional network (complex ideas required

that propositions could refer to other propositions in a tree-like structure of meaning), provided a standardized way of referring to meaning that attempted to minimize variations in language, word choice, or other subtleties of expression.

Whereas propositions focused on lower-level understanding that would be built up, schema theory provided a top-down view of understanding. Although propositions could explain understanding in terms of basic units of understanding, it did very little to explain the advantages of prior knowledge. Rarely are we forced to interpret new information or situations that are so foreign that previous knowledge does not play a large role. Proponents of schema theory have pointed out that a very large proportion of situations we encounter are actually routine in nature. These routines can be expressed as schemas, which are scripts or templates for understanding. Although the details and exceptions can be numerous, the concept of schema provided an essential top-down unifying structure and reflected the pattern-seeking behavior of individuals. When presented with novel situations, it is not uncommon for learners to attempt to make the information fit a preexisting schema.

Propositional representation and schema theory have provoked numerous studies and research in the areas of linguistics, computer science, and cognitive psychology. Over a period of years, Kintsch developed a model of text comprehension that built on this pioneering work. In 1998, he summarized his construction–integration model in a text appropriately called *Comprehension: A Paradigm for Cognition* (Kintsch, 1988).

The construction–integration model proposes two phases to understanding text. First, during the construction phase, readers create an approximate, but incoherent, mental model from textual input and their own goals and prior knowledge. The second (integration) phase involves consolidating local constructions into a cohesive meaning and discarding those local constructions that do not fit. These phases occur at the word level, at the sentence level, and with larger portions of text. They are performed automatically with familiar material and under learner control by active readers. The construction–integration model takes into account both bottom-up and top-down processing. It also provides a way to understand very different types of textual comprehension (e.g., metaphors, humor, abstractions) with simple, robust processes. Kintsch made an important distinction between the textbase, which is a representation of the information contained in the text, and the situational model, which is the information the reader takes from the text, including elaborations and connections based on prior knowledge.

Although Kintsch's construction–integration model has many implications for both researchers and instructional designers, those that are particularly relevant to this chapter are provided in Table 8.2. These are consistent with generally accepted guidelines for writing texts simply because the model was constructed to subsume findings from previous research, and the model suggests that empirical data provide the foundation for creating good instructional texts for readers.

One aspect of the model that is particularly important to point out is Kintsch's *zone of learnability*. This is an intentional analog to Vygotsky's zone of proximal development (1978). Kintsch described a good text as one that provides an appropriate amount of overlap between the new information in the text and the learner's situational model (i.e., relevant prior knowledge). An obvious implication is that if there is too much overlap the reader can gain no new information from the text. The less obvious implication is that the presence of familiar information in terms or words, structure, and other content is a necessary scaffold to promote deeper understanding. A minimal text, in which information is broken down and context is removed, may be as ineffective as an overly complex text. Additional and redundant text may be necessary to support the construction of deeper meaning.

As with earlier theoretical work with text, the construction–integration model has spawned further research that may extend the model or suggest alternatives. It has also led to a particular method of study—latent semantic analysis—which provides additional computational techniques for understanding text.

### Visual/Graphic Guidelines

The instructional benefit of visuals has a long history in the research (Tversky et al., 2002) and perhaps is best summarized in Mayer's (2001, p. 184) multimedia principle: "Students learn better from words and pictures than from words alone." The terms *visual*, *graphic*, and *image* are used interchangeably in the literature. A visual is typically thought of as a form of communication that is not verbal. Braden (1996) identified five categories of visuals that have been studied by educational researchers:

- Semiotics and film/video conventions
- Signs, symbols, and icons
- Images and illustrations
- Multi-images
- Graphic representation, including text as visuals

Saunders (1994) defined graphics as a prepared form of visual communication. Graphics can be:

- Symbols (pictographic or abstract)
- Maps
- Graphs
- Diagrams
- Illustrations or rendered pictures (realistic to abstract)
- Models
- Composite graphics (multi-images)
- Photographs (still or moving)

**TABLE 8.2**
**Cognitive Framework for Text**

| | Characteristics | Recommendation |
|---|---|---|
| Good readers | Good readers are good word decoders. | The use of familiar words frees more processing for higher level functioning. |
| | | Good decoding leads to increased vocabulary, so new vocabulary should be systematically added in familiar contexts. |
| | | Poor decoders can take more time or use higher order processing to compensate. |
| | Good readers have language skills (specifically, the ability to derive meaning from lexical structures). | Use of familiar text structures aids in the understanding of text material. |
| | | Good language skills allow readers to make inferences and construct greater meaning from the text. |
| | | A deficit in language skills can be overcome by making inferences explicit or prompting readers to make them. |
| | Good readers have domain knowledge (i.e., reading is more easily peformed in familiar domains). | Creating texts around familiar domains reduces the limitations of poor decoding and language skills. |
| | | Unfamiliar domains require a greater emphasis on decoding and language skills. |
| | | Because of their extensive domain knowledge, experts are able to derive meaning from even poorly written texts and therefore may be poor judges of the value of those texts to nonexperts. |
| Good texts | Good texts use words consistently with little ambiguity. | Explicitly define words with special connotations within the text. |
| | | When choosing words, select those that are most familiar and less ambiguous. |
| | | Use the appropriate domain when selecting words. |
| | Good texts use explicit structures that support meaning. | Structural cues should be explicit. |
| | | The organization of the text is as important to the meaning as the words themselves. |
| | | Redundancy of content provides an important function of reducing ambiguity, particularly for longer texts. |
| | The explicitness of the text is appropriate for the intended audience. | When a complete, explicit text is used, less prior knowledge is required by the reader. |
| | | When readers have extensive prior knowledge, prompting higher level processing, less explicit texts can be used. |
| Matching readers to texts | The text and the situational model of the reader must overlap, but not too much (zone of learnability). | When there is no overlap between the text and the prior knowledge of the reader, the text will be too difficult to comprehend (all processing will be at the lowest literal level). |
| | | When there is too much overlap between the text and the prior knowledge of the reader, the text has no educational value for that reader. |
| | | To determine the appropriateness of texts for groups of like readers, empirical data provide the most effective method. |

*Source:* Adapted from Kintsch, W., *Comprehension: A Paradigm for Cognition*, Cambridge University Press, Cambridge, U.K., 1998.

Guidelines for the design of visuals based on cognitive theory are presented in Table 8.3 (Lohr, 2007). These guidelines are based on Mayer's learning principles of (1) selection, (2) organization, and (3) integration and are directly related to the three parts of learner memory: short-term memory, working memory, and long-term memory.

*Auditory Guidelines*

Educationally, auditory information is generally thought of in the form of spoken language. Although semantically similar, the information found in spoken vs. written language is processed differently. Auditory information also describes nonsemantic information,

**TABLE 8.3**

**Guidelines for the Design of Instructional Visuals**

| Learning Principle | Description | Guidelines for Text, Images, and Data Displays |
|---|---|---|
| Selection | The selection process addresses the mind's tendency to organize information into figure and ground categories. | Make figure and ground distinctions as clear as possible to reduce the amount of information that memory needs to process. |
| | | Contrast type, shape, color, and size in graphic and data displays to separate important from less important information. |
| | | (Principle is related to Park and Hannafin's principles 3, 7, and 9 to structure information in ways that complement the cognitive process and internal representations. |
| Organization | Organization is based on the mind's tendency to process and remember chunks of information that in turn are arranged hierarchically. | Shape information structures to show subordinate, superordinate, and coordinate relationships, including those related to time and direction. Outlines, arrows, and lists are commonly used to establish hierarchy in a visual. |
| | | Align type and shapes to indicate relationships. Vertical and horizontal alignment establishes relationships based on cultural interpretation and reading order. Western cultures assign more importance to items on the top and left because reading takes place in a top-down, left-right sequence. |
| | | Repeat color, size, and type for elements with equal status. |
| | | Place similar items in closer proximity than dissimilar items. |
| Integration | The integration principle is based on the Gestalt theory that that the whole is greater than the sum of its parts. A person's prior experience allows him or her to see that whole, even when presented with only a part. | Use grid structures to organize and integrate information. |
| | | Group items into meaningful units. Greater understanding is achieved when parts, or elements of a message, are attended to as a whole, not selectively. |
| | | Mayer's principle 7 focuses on the importance of presenting information in ways that require less cognitive effort from the learner—in other words, reduce the cognitive load yet maintain a focus on the parts-to-whole relationships. |
| | | Repeat and align text, shape, color, and size to connect items. |
| | | Place similar items in closer proximity than dissimilar items. |

such as alarms and sound effects, and highly specialized information in the form of music. In the case of music, some skills such as recognizing relative pitch may be taught; however, others, such as the recognition of absolute pitch (requiring a stable long-term memory of a reference pitch), may involve specialized brain mechanisms and require acquisition relatively early in life (Levitin and Rogers, 2005).

Bishop and Cates (2001) provided a framework for thinking of instructional sound from a cognitive perspective (see Table 8.4). Although their primary goal was investigating the potential of sound in support of instructional software, the framework also is useful for considering the medium of sound in isolation. The three types of noise come from the work of Shannon and Weaver, which has been interpreted by Bishop and

**TABLE 8.4**

**Cognitive Framework for Instructional Sound**

| To overcome: | *Acquisition noise*<br>Level A: Technical problems. Competing internal and external stimuli cause message-transmission problems. | *Processing noise*<br>Level B: Semantic problems. Missing interpretive frameworks cause message-interpretation problems. | *Retrieval noise*<br>Level C: Effectiveness problems. Prompt/schema mismatches cause message-understanding problems. |
|---|---|---|---|
| The message should contain: | *Content redundancy* to amplify the content for message transmission (encourages noise-defeating learner acquisition states) | Context redundancy to supply the context for message interpretation (encourages noise-defeating learning processing strategies) | Construct redundancy to cue appropriate constructs for message understanding (encourages noise-defeating learner retrieval schemes) |
| Selection | 1. Use sound to help learners direct attention. | 2. Use sound to help learners isolate information. | 3. Use sound to help learners tie into previous knowledge. |
| Analysis | 4. Use sound to help learners focus attention. | 5. Use sound to help learners organize information. | 6. Use sound to help learners build on existing knowledge. |
| Synthesis | 7. Use sound to help learners hold attention. | 8. Use sound to help learners elaborate on information. | 9. Use sound to help learners prepare knowledge for later use. |

*Source:* Adapted from Bishop, M. J. and Cates, W.M., *Educ. Technol. Res. Dev.*, 49(3), 5–22, 2001.

Cates (2001) from a cognitive instructional viewpoint. Acquisition noise interferes with the reception of an instructional message. Processing noise refers to problems with understanding the message that has been received. Retrieval noise is a mismatch between an understood message and prior knowledge, experience, or attitudes.

Redundancy in auditory information is important to understand in the context of the temporally based nature of the medium. Baddeley's phonological loop (2001) is the short-term memory related to auditory information. Although his focus was on the processing of spoken language, one can consider the short-term memory of other forms of sound (such as music or sound effects) as being under the same limitations. Neisser (1967) referred to this as *echoic memory*. Upon hearing a sound, a person is able to replay a brief portion of it in this short-term memory for further processing. This partially explains the "cocktail party effect," in which a person is engaged in a conversation to the exclusion of numerous others talking in the same room. Short-term audio memory allows that person, in a limited sense, to monitor and switch attention to a different conversation upon hearing his or her name or some other attention-grabbing piece of information.

Bishop and Cates (2001) (see Table 8.4) suggested the use of redundancy to overcome the temporal nature of audio communication. Content redundancy refers to the retransmission or amplification of the audio information. Context redundancy involves presenting semantic information in multiple ways to ensure that it is perceived correctly. Finally, construct redundancy attempts to emphasize the link between the information and prior knowledge.

### Animation/Video Guidelines

Animation and video are described together because they share similar characteristics (e.g., a time component, presentation of motion or change). In addition, the advent of digital technologies for both animation and video production has blurred the distinction between artificial and real representations. Researchers who examine the impact of animation in education must consider the critiques leveled at any media comparison study. As is often the case, animation provides a simplified visual view of a process or behavior that otherwise might be presented in a classroom with models or via video footage; however, animation may be able to uniquely portray an educational concept that might otherwise be difficult to visualize. It may also be used for financial or logistical reasons in lieu of another approach; for example, Adamo-Villani and Beni (2004) described a system that uses realistic three-dimensional animation for the purpose of teaching finger spelling via sign language. Research focused on the use of animation most often describes its use with other forms of presentation. In general, guidelines for its effectiveness can be categorized using a cognitive framework similar to the one used for multimedia. Table 8.5 categorizes findings from a number of studies within the context of the components of cognitive load theory.

## THE NEED FOR CONTINUED RESEARCH

Although no single cognitive theory of learning or multimedia model can explain in sufficient detail all the functions of memory, the theories and models presented in this chapter have much to offer to an understanding of instructional media design. Perhaps a more complex theory and model will be eventually proposed that subsumes a majority of research in cognitive psychology and instructional multimedia; however, it is likely that such a complicated theory and model would be more difficult to translate into prescriptions for practice.

Although most of the guidelines in this chapter represent the work of many experimental studies, their selection and categorization are dependent on the authors' interpretation of the research and are therefore subject to the biases of their perspectives. A comprehensive review of new research will be necessary on a periodic basis to ensure that the most worthy design guidelines are shared. Some might consider a more rigorous approach to the assignment of guideline classifications needed.

Perhaps most needed is a more integrative set of guidelines within the various presentation modes. Whereas visual and animation/video media share an organizational theme similar to the multimedia framework, the text and audio guidelines have unique organization schemes, which makes the relationships between the different models more difficult to understand.

Other topics of future research include the comparison of research-based guidelines to the guidelines used in settings that are more applied and less research oriented. The restrictions encountered by the realities of production are worthy of investigation. Although design focuses on optimal presentation, dynamics within the workplace often curtail the effectiveness of a product. As a case in point, the first author's graphic design textbook promoted guidelines for the effective display of graphics that were clearly violated by the book itself due to the overriding importance of reducing publication costs. Knowing ahead of time what these realities are would be beneficial to the designer.

**TABLE 8.5**
**Cognitive Framework for Animation/Video**

| Theory Components | Description | Guideline |
|---|---|---|
| Increasing germane load | Hays (1996) demonstrated that low-spatial-ability participants made greater gains when animations were used as opposed to static graphics or no graphics. Schnotz and Rasch (2005) described the value of animations for learners with low learning prerequisites. Learners with high learning prerequisites received more value from manipulating pictures themselves. Bishop and Cates (2001) described the technique of visual description that provides access to television, movies, etc., for individuals with visual impairments. They suggested that the technique might also be useful for promoting comprehension for those with average vision. | Design effects are stronger for low-knowledge learners than for high-knowledge learners and for high spatial learners rather than low spatial learners (Mayer's principle 7). |
| Reducing intrinsic load | Reiber (1996) found that animated graphic feedback could produce gains in tacit knowledge when compared with text-only feedback. Garcia (1998) described the benefit of students creating animations in their understanding of science content. Catrambone and Seay (2002) found that animations aided in students' understanding of algorithms when compared to the same text followed by still frames. It was particularly helpful for students in a weak-text vs. an improved-text condition. Bodemer et al. (2005) demonstrated how exposure to static sources of information prior to work with dynamic, interactive visualizations can support learning. Koroghlanian and Klein (2004) found that participants exposed to animations will spend more time in the instruction than those given only static images. Hegarty et al. (2003) found no difference between static and dynamic diagrams in the understanding of dynamic processes; however, they suggested that participants' ability to create animated mental models from static diagrams might be the reason for the lack of difference. | Employ organizing activities (invested mental effort, elaboration, articulation, knowledge differentiation) (Park and Hannafin's principles 5, 8, 12, and 14). Present corresponding words and pictures simultaneously rather than successively (Mayer's principle 3). |
| Reducing extraneous load | Linebarger (2001) found that the use of captions with video programs resulted in greater word recognition for young children and related positive effects. The researcher also reported that captions lessened attention to visual and audio distractions in the video presentation. Caspi et al. (2005) found that video recordings of lectures did influence the message being delivered to students and that mismatches of the medium and the message may have a negative result on cognitive and affective outcomes. | Finding conflicts with Mayer's principle to use animation and narration rather than animation, narration, and text (Mayer's principle 5). Exclude rather than include extraneous words, pictures, or sounds (Mayer's principle 4). |

## SUMMARY

This chapter presents a three-tier toolbox metaphor for guiding the design of a number of presentation media. The designer typically reaches for the elements on the third tier, the most concrete and accessible elements of design: text, visuals, audio, and animation/video. Understanding first-tier elements that include cognitively based theories of learning (information-processing theory, dual-coding theory, cognitive load theory, and Baddeley's memory theory) in turn helps the designer more clearly understand second-tier multimedia models (Mayer, 2001; Park and Hannafin, 1993) and their relationship to mode-based guidelines. The relationship between the three tiers is appealing, but more research is needed to articulate a more fully integrative design toolbox.

## REFERENCES

Adamo-Villani, N. and Beni, G. (2004). Automated finger spelling by highly realistic 3D animation. *Br. J. Educ. Technol.*, 35(3), 345–362.

Alessi, S. M. and Trollip, S. R. (2001). *Multimedia for Learning: Methods and Development*, 3rd ed. Boston: Allyn & Bacon.

Anderson, J. R. (1985). *Cognitive Psychology and Its Implications*, 2nd ed. New York: W.H. Freeman.

Atkinson, R. L. and Shiffrin, R. M. (1968). Human memory: a proposed system and its control processes. In *The Psychology of Learning and Motivation: Advances in Research and Theory*, Vol. 2, edited by K. W. Spence and J. T. Spence. New York: Academic Press.

Baddeley, A. D. (2000). The episodic buffer: a new component in working memory? *Trends Cogn. Sci.*, 4(1), 417–423.

Bauer, J. and Gall, J. (2006). Digital video production and editing for preservice teachers. In *Proceedings of Society for Information Technology and Teacher Education International Conference 2006*, edited by C. Crawford et al., pp. 3147–3149. Chesapeake, VA: AACE.

Bichelmeyer, B. (2005). *The ADDIE Model: A Metaphor for the Lack of Clarity in the Field of IDT*, http://www.indiana.edu/~idt/shortpapers/documents/IDTf_Bic.pdf.

Bishop, M. J. and Cates, W. M. (2001). Theoretical foundations for sound's use in multimedia instruction to enhance learning. *Educ. Technol. Res. Dev.*, 49(3), 5–22.

Bodemer, D. R., Ploetzner, R., Bruchmuller, K., and Hucker, S. (2005). Supporting learning with interactive multimedia through active integration of representations. *Instruct. Sci.*, 33(1), 73–95.

Braden, R. A. (1996). Visual literacy. In *Handbook of Research for Educational Communications and Technology*, edited by D. H. Jonassen, pp. 491–520. New York: Simon & Schuster.

Broadbent, D. E. (1984). The Maltese cross: a new simplistic model for memory. *Behav. Brain Sci.*, 7, 55–94.

Caspi, A., Gorsky, P., and Privman, M. (2005). Viewing comprehension: students' learning preferences and strategies when studying from video. *Instruct. Sci.*, 33(1), 31–47.

Catrambone, R. and Seay, A. F. (2002). Using animation to help students learn computer algorithms. *Hum. Factors*, 44(3), 495–511.

Chi, M. T. H., Glaser, R., and Farr, M., Eds. (1988). *The Nature of Expertise*. Hillsdale, NJ: Lawrence Erlbaum Associates.

Davenport, T. (1999). From data to knowledge. *CIO Mag.*, April 12 (http://www.cio.com/archive/040199/think.html).

Gagné, R. M. (1965). *The Conditions of Learning*, 1st ed. New York: Holt, Rinehart and Winston.

Gagné, R. M. (1985). *The Conditions of Learning*, 4th ed. New York: Holt, Rinehart and Winston.

Garcia, C. E. (1998). Exploring the use of animation software with young bilingual students learning science. *J. Educ. Comput. Res.*, 19, 247–267.

Gardner, H. E. (1987). *The Mind's New Science: A History of the Cognitive Revolution*. New York: Basic.

Goetz, E. T. and Sadoski, M. (1995). The perils of seduction: distracting details or incomprehensible abstractions? [commentary]. *Reading Res. Q.*, 30(3), 500–511.

Guthrie, J. T. and Mosenthal, P. (1987). Literacy as multidimensional: locating information and reading comprehension. *Educ. Psychol.*, 22(4), 279–297.

Harp, S. F. and Mayer, R. E. (1998). How seductive details do their damage: a theory of cognitive interest in science learning. *J. Educ. Psychol.*, 90(3), 414–434.

Hays, T.A. (1996). Spatial abilities and the effects of computer animation on short-term and long-term comprehension. *J. Educ. Comput. Res.*, 14(2), 139–155.

Hegarty, M., Kriz, S., and Cate, C. (2003). The roles of mental animations and external animations in understanding mechanical systems. *Cogn. Instruct.*, 21(4), 325–360.

Jacobson, R. (2000). Introduction: why information design matters. In *Information Design*, edited by R. Jacobson. Cambridge, MA: MIT Press.

Kintsch, W. (1998). *Comprehension: A Paradigm for Cognition*. Cambridge, U.K.: Cambridge University Press.*

Koroghlanian, C. and Klein, J. D. (2004). The effect of audio and animation in multimedia instruction. *J. Educ. Multimedia Hypermedia*, 13(1), 23–46.

Landauer, T. K., Foltz, P. W., and Laham, D. (1998). Introduction to latent semantic analysis. *Discourse Processes*, 25, 259–284.

Levitin, D. J. and Rogers, S. E. (2005). Absolute pitch: perception, coding, and controversies. *Trends Cogn. Sci.*, 9(1), 26–33.

Linebarger, D. L. (2001). Learning to read from television: the effects of using captions and narration. *J. Educ. Psychol.*, 93(2), 288–298.

Lockhart, R. S. and Craik, F. I. M. (1990). Levels of processing: a retrospective commentary on a framework for memory research. *Can. J. Psychol.*, 44, 87–112.

Lohr, L. L. (2007). *Creating Graphics for Learning and Performance: Lessons in Visual Literacy*. Upper Saddle River, NJ: Prentice Hall.

Mathewson, J. H. (1999). Visual-spatial thinking: an aspect of science overlooked by educators. *Sci. Educ.*, 83(1), 33–54.

Mayer, R. E. (1984). Aids to text comprehension. *Educ. Psychol.*, 19, 30–42.

Mayer, R. E. (1989). Models for understanding. *Rev. Educ. Res.*, 59, 43–64.

Mayer, R. E. (2001). *Multimedia Learning*. New York: Cambridge University Press.*

Meeter, M. and Murre, J. M. J. (2004). Consolidation of long-term memory: evidence and alternatives. *Psychol. Bull.*, 130(6), 843–857.

Meikle, J. L. (2005). Ghosts in the machine: why it's hard to write about design. *Technol. Cult.*, 46(2), 385–392.

Merrienboer, J. G. and Sweller, J. (2005). Cognitive load theory and complex learning: recent developments and future directions. *Educ. Psychol. Rev.*, 17(2), 147–177.*

Neisser U. (1967). *Cognitive Psychology*. New York: Appleton-Century-Crofts.

Norman, D. A. (1980). Twelve issues for cognitive science. *Cogn. Sci. Multidiscip. J.*, 4(1), 1–32.

Norman, D. A. and Bobrow, D. G. (1975). On data limited and resource limited processes. *Cogn. Psychol.*, 7, 44–64.

Paas, F., Renkl, A., and Sweller, J. (2003). Cognitive load theory and instructional design: recent developments. *Educ. Psychol.*, 38(1), 1–4.

Park, I. and Hannafin, J. (1993). Empirically based guidelines for the design of interactive media. *Educ. Technol. Res. Dev.*, 41(3), 63–85.

Pavio, A. (1965). Abstractness, imagery, and meaningfulness in paired–associate learning. *J. Verbal Learn. Verbal Behav.*, 4, 32–38.

Pavio, A. (1990). *Mental Representations: A Dual Coding Approach*, 2nd ed. New York: Oxford University Press.

Reiber, L. P. (1996). Seriously considering play: designing interactive learning environments based on the blending of microworlds, simulations, and games. *Educ. Technol. Res. Dev.*, 44(2), 43-58.

Schnotz, W. and Rasch, T. (2005). Enabling, facilitating, and inhibiting effects of animations in multimedia learning: why reduction of cognitive load can have negative results on learning. *Educ. Technol. Res. Dev.*, 53(3), 47–58.

Tversky, B., Morrison, J. B., and Betrancourt, M. (2002). Animation: can it facilitate? *Int. J. Hum.–Comput. Stud.*, 57, 247–262.

Vidal-Abarca, E., Martinez, G., and Gilabert, R. (2000). Two procedures to improve instructional text: effects on memory and learning. *J. Educ. Psychol.*, 92(1), 107–116.

Vygotsky, L. S. (1978). *Mind and Society: The Development of Higher Mental Processes*. Cambridge, MA: Harvard University Press.

Waugh, N. C. and Norman, D. A. (1965). Primary memory. *Psychol. Rev.*, 72, 89–104.

Wertheimer, M. (1987). *A Brief History of Psychology*, 3rd ed. New York: Harcourt Brace Jovanovich.

Wickens, C. D. (1984). *Engineering Psychology and Human Performance*. Columbus, OH: Merrill.

* Indicates a core reference.

# 9

# Strategies for Designing Embodied Curriculum

*Sasha A. Barab and Tyler Dodge*
Indiana University, Bloomington, Indiana

## CONTENTS

## ABSTRACT

This chapter provides a conceptual framework related to designing for situational embodiment; discusses three types of curricular designs, ranging from designed and emergent simulation models to participation models; and overviews various strategies for achieving each design, including examples from the literature. Specifically, we discuss designed simulation models (e.g., anchored instruction, problem-based learning, and cognitive apprenticeship); emergent simulation models (e.g., case-based reasoning, project-based learning, and classroom learning communities); and participation models (e.g., participatory simulations, academic play spaces, and communities of practice). Looking across the different examples, we also discern tensions that emerge in working toward curricular embodiment—namely, tensions concerning the quality of the context (noisy vs. tailored) and the quality of the formalisms (explicit vs. implicit).

## KEYWORDS

*Authenticity:* Learner-perceived relations between the associated practices and one's projected or envisioned use value of those practices.

*Formalism:* The formal structure and abstract principles that underlie the conceptual framework of the content area; for example, the concept of erosion is a formalism in science, division is a formalism in mathematics, and metaphor is a type of formalism in language arts

*Participation models of authenticity:* Models that establish a sense of authenticity by engaging learners in the authentic practices as they work on real-world tasks as part of authentic communities and in contexts that value the outcomes of those tasks.

*Simulation models of authenticity:* Models that build upon the assumption that classroom activity should be made to resemble as much as possible the activities in which real-world practitioners engage.

*Situational embodiment:* When to-be-learned content is experienced in relation to a particular context of use that provides legitimacy to the content and student actions and a meaningful goal and set of actions for the learner and on which learner actions have some consequence.

## INTRODUCTION

A number of theorists have argued that the cognitive revolution has consisted of two phases. In the first phase, it was individual thinkers and their isolated minds that were the emphasis (Gardner, 1985). Clearly, during this period theorists attempted to de emphasize context (partly in an attempt to remove the behaviorist shackles fastened by Skinner and others) and focus on the individual mind as disembodied from the environmental particulars in which it is situated (Fodor, 1975; Shannon, 1988). The second phase relocated cognitive functioning within its social, cultural, and historical framework (Barron et al., 1995) and is central to many so-called situative perspectives (Brown et al., 1989; Cobb and Yackel, 1995; Greeno, 1989; Kirshner and Whitson, 1998; Suchman, 1987; Young, 1993).

Consistent with ecological notions advanced by Gibson and others (Gibson, 1966, 1979/1986; Reed, 1991; Reed and Jones, 1982; Shaw and Bransford,

1977; Young, 1993), learners were no longer conceived of as isolated from the environment in which learning occurs; rather, both individuals and environments were considered functionally coupled, with intention-contingent practices serving as the bond that weds the two (Reed, 1991). These ecological descriptions challenge the belief that knowledge is a thing to be acquired and that knowing is simply a cognitive act that occurs in the confines of isolated minds. Instead, from an ecological perspective, knowledge refers to an activity (not a thing), is always contextualized (not abstract), is reciprocally constructed as part of the individual–environment interaction (not objectively defined or subjectively created), and involves whole persons (not disembodied minds) (Barab and Duffy, 2000). Cognitions are not acts of the mind or decontextualized bits of knowledge to be transmitted, but contextually embedded practices that engage individuals who are vitally situated within and across rich and meaningful environments.

At its core, this theorizing suggests an emphasis of supporting meaningful participation within experientially rich contexts. Sfard (1998) characterized the shift as a move away from the *acquisition* metaphor, which has guided much of the practice in K–12 schools, toward a *participation* metaphor in which knowledge is considered fundamentally situated in practice. In a very real way, what is being argued for is the primacy of experience, but the arrangement of schools and the focus on supporting abstracted understandings make the adoption of a situated or experiential curriculum difficult. Schools are designed to structure not simply experience in a general sense but also pedagogically useful experiences intended to support the learning of particular content. In this chapter, we first present a brief overview of an embodied curriculum along with a framework for conceptualizing the challenge of truly embodying curricular understandings. This is then followed by an overview of nine instructional approaches that work to situate understandings.

## AN EMBODIED CURRICULUM

Many educators have argued that the didactic format of teaching that concentrates on memorization of factual information promotes the development of superficial conceptual understanding (Lave and Wenger, 1991; Roth, 1996; Ruopp et al., 1993; Wandersee et al., 1994). In response to the limitations of these teacher-centered or lecture-based environments, an increasing number of educators are abandoning such predominantly didactic modes of instruction and moving toward more experiential or situated models of instruction (Barab and Hay, 2001; Barab and Plucker, 2002; Brown, 1992; Brown et al., 1994; Collins et al., 1989; Cognition and Technology Group at Vanderbilt [CTGV], 1991, 1993; Duffy and Jonassen, 1992; Roth, 1996). These participatory learning environments support the natural complexity of content, avoid oversimplification, engage students in the construction of products requiring practices that embody complex contexts, encourage collaboration, and present instruction within both simulated and real-world contexts (Barab and Duffy, 2000).

Central to the various efforts is a common belief that, when the underlying content to be taught becomes situated in terms of authentic use, it changes the essential meanings of that content for the learner. At its core, what is being argued is the need for a *situationally embodied curriculum*, one that is owned by the learner and that evidences the functional value of, and need for, the target formalisms. Building on Nathan's (2005) description of formalisms, this refers to the "formal structure and abstract principles that underlie the conceptual framework of the content area" (p. 5). Each discipline entails core concepts, methodologies, frameworks, tasks, and principles that provide a central organizing role in the discipline (e.g., symbolic equations, graphs and diagrams, scientific laws, rules of grammar, historic patterns, music notations, artistic movements). Formalisms are assumed to bear some generalizable power or utility for illuminating the deep structure of otherwise unrelated contexts; yet, though we agree that formalisms may be powerful for knowledgeable experts, they do not bear the same utility for those only beginning to know a domain. In the latter case, an explicit focus on formalisms abstracted from their functional contexts is not the most productive pedagogical move.

Still, building an embodied curriculum in the context of schools represents a formidable challenge, and at its core is selecting an appropriate context and determining the amount of *noise* required for an underlying formalism to become *embodied*. When a learning environment is overly tailored, it begins to feel more like school work and becomes less experiential (Dewey, 1938/1997); the potential for enmeshment becomes unlikely, and the knowledge is more likely to remain inert (Whitehead, 1929). As one adds more situational aspects, the potential for mystery, reality, and discovery increases, but one sacrifices guidance, efficiency, and clarity. In fact, life itself presents the ultimate noisy context, with schools being developed in part to present formalisms removed from this noise—a place where pure reason can prevail, where explicit focus on formalisms can occur.

As long as educators continue to assign pure thought and disembodied formalisms a reverent quality in terms of the goals of education, we will continue to undermine the meanings and understandings that we wish to support. The goal of a *situationally embodied design* is to evolve the learning trajectory in relation to the curricular narrative framework, thereby grounding content with respect to those situations in which it has value. What makes the curriculum situationally embodied is that the to-be-learned content is experienced in relation to a particular narrative context. For us, a narrative context is not simply any surround, but a storyline that provides legitimacy to the content and student actions and a meaningful goal and set of actions for the learner, and on which learner actions have some consequence. To the extent that a particular formalism is not connected to a related context of use, it runs the risk of becoming a disembodied fact to be memorized, with no contextual anchor by which a student can see its authentic application. It is the learner intentions and use affordances emerging from the context of use that transform a formalism from a disembodied fact to an embedded or even embodied one (Barab et al., 1999). In building a particular context of use, educators must examine the intentions likely to emerge from the core context and understand how satisfying these emergent intentions both requires and validates a particular formalism as a useful tool. Below, we overview nine instructional approaches that work to embody or situate the content, the learner, and the experience.

## DESIGNING EMBODIED CURRICULA

Thus far, we have argued that the meaning of a set of formalisms changes when they are situated within a context of use. A critical challenge, therefore, for those interested in designing embodied curricula is establishing the context for embodiment, and this requires establishing a curricular narrative with an element of authenticity; however, *authenticity* as a term is widely used but poorly defined. In designing an environment for learning, one must determine what is meant by authentic—and to whom (Barab et al., 2000). For example, what is authentic to the designer may not be to the learner, what is authentic to the learner may not be to the designer, and both or neither may be considered authentic by real-world practitioners (Brown et al., 1989).

Authenticity lies in the learner-perceived relations between the associated practices and one's projected or envisioned use value of those practices. With that said, a number of educators have worked to develop both theories and learning environments that help to establish embodiment. Below we review a number of these, first describing those that borrow from a simulation model of authenticity, distinguishing those that are primarily under the direction of the designer vs. those in which the to-be-learned content is more emergent though still not situated within a real-world context. Then, we overview designed spaces that leverage a participatory model, prioritizing the importance of the real-world context in the service of real-world issues (Petraglia, 1998; Radinsky et al., 1998).

## Designed Simulation Models for Establishing Embodiment

Simulation models build upon the assumption that classroom activity should be made to resemble as much as possible the activities in which real-world practitioners engage. This includes featuring elements of *factual* authenticity, wherein the environmental details of the task are designed to be similar to those of the real world; *procedural* or *process* authenticity, in which learner practices are similar to those that would be engaged outside of schools; and *task* authenticity, in which the tasks are similar to those being undertaken by real-world practitioners (Petraglia, 1998). Barab and Duffy (2000), borrowing from Senge (1994), referred to these contexts as *practice fields* because they do not take place in the real fields but, rather, allow learners to practice the sorts of activities that they will later encounter outside of schools. In our thinking, it is more than entailing *authentic* practice that makes these contexts valuable; they also legitimize the worth and meaning of the content being practiced. Although no single set of strategies can capture all of the theories and designs representing simulation models, we overview a number of theories and designs that illuminate what we mean by practice fields.

### Anchored Instruction

Anchored instruction refers to instruction in which the material to be learned is presented in the context of a specific topic or anchor that serves to legitimize the material and, further, allows it to be examined from multiple perspectives. The work of the Cognition and Technology Group at Vanderbilt (1990, 1991, 1993) has primarily focused on video-based *macrocontexts*, intended to overcome inert knowledge (Whitehead, 1929) by anchoring learning—thereby embodying the to-be-learned content—within the context of meaningful problem-solving activities. In contrast to the disconnected *application problems* found at the end of textbook chapters, macrocontexts refer to stories set in

semantically rich, open-ended environments (CTGV, 1993). In these anchoring macrocontexts, students begin with a complex narrative introducing a problem and then use top-down strategies to generate the subgoals necessary to reach the solution. This top-down processing helps students learn the lower-level skills (e.g., mathematical algorithms and facts) in a manner that also gives them insights into the relationships between the skills being learned and the reciprocal opportunities for using them.

One illuminative set of curricula is the *Jasper Woodbury Problem Solving Series*, designed for students in grades 5 and up. Each videodisc contains a short (approximately 17-minute) video adventure that ends with a complex challenge. Like good detective novels, the adventures embed all of the essential data (along with additional, irrelevant data) within the story. In one such story, students must discover and satisfy 17 mathematical subproblems necessary for determining if the main character, Jasper, can reach home (CTGV, 1990). Much of the challenge in these episodes involves distinguishing the noise in the context from those aspects relevant to the problem at hand. The *Jasper* adventures also present embedded didactic scenes that model particular approaches to solving problems and that can be revisited on a just-in-time basis as students need them to solve the challenges. When students use these curricula, they learn mathematics as they work to solve the challenge: they develop concepts and skills through just-in-time instruction.

Significantly, these lessons do not separate the content (e.g., the distance–rate–time formula) from the medium (e.g., the videodisc story in which Jasper's problem is introduced); rather, they simply present a context (i.e., determining whether or not Jasper can reach home). Although anchored instruction may also resemble problem-based learning (PBL; described below), it tends to be less open ended than the latter. Most anchored modules are designed for young learners and so embed all of the data necessary to solve the problem within the modules themselves through an embedded-data design. Also, in contrast to PBL, substantial independent research and data collection are not usually required in anchored modules. As with PBL, the goal is to capture a real problem along with its real-world context, but in anchored instruction there is no pretense that this problem actually exists for the students; instead, learners are invited to engage in a fictitious problem. It is also important to note that, although the first set of anchored episodes designed by the CTGV focused on relatively constrained designed simulation problems, over time they have developed community-linking scaffolds (Barron et al., 1995) and flexibly adaptive designs, the outcomes of which are increasingly determined by the students and teachers (Schwartz et al., 1999).

## Problem-Based Learning

According to Finkle and Torp (1995, p. 1), problem-based learning (PBL) simultaneously develops both problem-solving strategies and disciplinary knowledge bases and skills by placing students in the active role of problem solvers confronted with an ill-structured problem that mirrors real-world problems. Although originally associated specifically with medical curricula and stipulating a sequence of rules to be followed in addressing the ill-structured problems of that field (Barrows and Tamblyn, 1980), problem-based learning has been adopted in a range of other domains, not strictly as a methodology but more broadly, suggesting an approach to instruction. Although not situated in the real world *per se* (participatory authenticity), learners nonetheless experience simulatory authenticity, which affords both meaning and focus. Central to this instructional strategy is the problematic context (Dewey, 1938/1997) or cognitive puzzlement (Savery and Duffy, 1995) that fosters learning through engagement in meaningful domain-related tasks.

In discussing PBL, Savery and Duffy (1995) articulated a series of instructional principles that can be applied to a PBL environment, synthesized as follows. First, the learner must perceive the learning activities as related to a broader task or problem and must accept ownership of the instructional goals and the problem-solving process. In addition, though embedded in a tailored or sheltered context, the learning activities must nonetheless support and challenge the learner and must demand authentic discourse to prepare the learner to function in the complexity of the real-world domain. Finally, the learner must test emergent understandings against alternative views and contexts and must reflect on both what is learned and the process by which learning occurs. This approach differs from such related strategies as case-based reasoning (Kolodner, 2006) in that the students bear responsibility for developing an original solution to the problem rather than studying someone else's solution.

As a workplace simulation situating grade-school children in different positions at a fictitious monetary institution, the Chelsea Bank program is an example of PBL that consists of over a dozen computer-based episodes and engages middle-school students in a variety of finance-related problems through the use of a range of problem-solving strategies, including, for example, making predictions, modifying solutions, and seeking help (Duffy et al., 1996). Indeed, although situated within the domain of finance, the project does not serve as mere vocational training but instead aims to develop skills in basic literacy and problem solving. For example, in assisting a Chelsea customer, students make use of bank manuals, account information, and other resources to decide, from multiple-choice options, what action to take; they must select from the options and justify their answers. A key challenge in the successful implementation of the Chelsea Bank program and other PBL simulations is helping teachers to act as a guide that supports successful inquiry (Duffy et al., 1996).

## Cognitive Apprenticeship

Cognitive apprenticeship is an approach to learning developed by Collins et al. (1989) to take advantage of the rich contexts through which learning in traditional apprenticeships occurred. They developed an instructional model derived from the metaphor of the apprentice working under the master craftsperson in traditional societies, as well as from research related to how people learn and participate in everyday, informal environments (Rogoff and Lave, 1984). Traditional apprenticeships, however, entailed hands-on learning trajectories, evidenced by the product of the craft. In contrast, cognitive apprenticeship emphasizes cognitive learning trajectories through making conceptual processes visible. In this approach, the teacher or more knowledgeable other serves to explicate the thinking underlying the teacher's actions, thereby modeling for students through a form of *cognitive apprenticeship*. The teacher then *coaches* and *scaffolds*, with the goal being to gradually *fade* teacher intervention such that the student can engage in the behavior without the support of the teacher.

Additional instructional strategies include *articulation* as learners are encouraged to verbalize their knowledge and thinking, *reflection* on the learning experience, and *exploration* as they begin to pose problems of their own creation. Central to cognitive apprenticeship is that, rather than simply learning a particular fact or concept, students engage in a rich and meaningful task. Collins et al. (1989, p. 487) suggested that "a critical element in fostering learning is to have students carry out tasks and solve problems in an environment that reflects the multiple uses to which their knowledge will be put in the future." Indeed, Palincsar and Brown's (1984) *reciprocal teaching* of reading involves many of the features of cognitive apprenticeship in that the basic method centers on modeling and coaching students in four strategic skills: formulating questions based on the text, summarizing the text, making predictions about what will ensue, and clarifying difficulties with the text.

The method has been used with small and large groups as well as with individual students. The term *reciprocal teaching* denotes that the teacher and students take turns playing the role of teacher as they come to understand a text. In describing its effectiveness, Palincsar and Brown (1984) argued that working with a text in a discussion format differs greatly from teaching isolated comprehension skills such as identifying the main idea. When students engage in reciprocal teaching, they learn strategies that serve a larger goal, namely both to understand what they are reading and to develop the critical ability to *read and learn*. Another example lies in the domain of mathematics (Schoenfeld, 1996). In this work, the expert thinks aloud as she works through a novel problem and then reflects with other learners on the strategies used and the paths followed. Describing the embodiment of one class, Schoenfeld (1996, p. 213) reported:

> Mathematics was the medium of exchange. We talked about mathematics, explained it to each other, shared the false starts, enjoyed the interaction of personalities. In short, we became mathematical people. It was fun, but it was also natural and felt right. It wasn't a separate "school experience" for a few hours a week. By virtue of this cultural immersion, the students experienced mathematics in a way that made sense.

Schoenfeld (1987) emphasized the importance of creating a microcosm of a mathematician's culture to help students think like mathematicians.

## Emergent Simulation Models for Establishing Embodiment

The designs discussed above involve developing much of the learning context before the learners have even begun. The constraints are primarily built into the resources, and the acceptable outcomes are fairly well defined; the designer, for the most part, knows what a correct solution is, even as the design is being created. In contrast, an emergent simulation model situates much of the interaction within the tasks but leaves the participants to socially negotiate much of the structure of the activities and determine what counts as reasonable evidence for success. In these cases, an important contribution to their authenticity derives from convincing others of the meaning and credibility of one's interpretations. Further, such an approach usually occurs over extended durations and involves both less knowledgeable and more knowledgeable others with whom one collaborates; however, in contrast to participation models, these remain simulations and typically present a task designed for the learning situation as

opposed to a real-world problem that the work may impact. Again, although no single set of strategies can capture all of the theories and designs consistent with this perspective, we overview several theories and designs that illuminate the category of emergent simulation models.

### Case-Based Reasoning

Case-based reasoning (CBR) originated in the pursuit of artificial intelligence within the field of computer science (Schank, 1982), but, influenced by constructivist conceptualizations of learning, the approach now guides a range of educational endeavors. Indeed, as an instructional strategy, a case-based approach affords a rich learning context without necessitating undue design effort. Like PBL, CBR relies on prior knowledge and experience to provide a rich context for problem solving, and, significantly, this foundation extends beyond the compass of the individual learner to allow the knowledge and experience of others in the field to constitute the case (Kolodner, 1993, 2006). As Jonassen (1999, p. 219) wrote:

> Students acquire knowledge and requisite thinking skills by studying cases ... and preparing case summaries or diagnoses. Case learning is anchored in authentic contexts; learners must manage complexity and think like practitioners.

The ill-structured quality of the cases, then, affords a perceived authenticity on the part of the learners (Jonassen and Hernandez-Serrano, 2002). New understandings naturally ensue from the interpretation, consideration, and application of the understandings embedded in the cases, whether experienced personally or vicariously, provided that the learner's experience is informed by "concrete, authentic, and timely feedback" (Kolodner and Guzdial, 2000, p. 220) so as to facilitate an iterative refinement of and fluency with the competencies germane to both the present case and others that complement or contrast with it.

Case libraries bring together cases reflecting a domain of interest, such as legal, scientific, or social work. These cases may be culled not only from the literature of the domain but also from the encounters of other students who have engaged with a domain-related concept or skill (Kolodner, 2006); that is, the experience of one student can be presented to others as a case through which they can vicariously undergo the experience, thus developing individual understandings that emerge from the encounter. In this way, not only case libraries but also class discussions represent tools or structures that can be designed to facilitate learner embodiment. Still, even though cases advance student understanding of domain formalisms, they nonetheless do so by embedding these formalisms in a rich context; while scaffolding how students conceive of the formalisms, the cases achieve this through narrative rather than expository discourse, thus affording an authenticity despite the designed nature of the experience.

Again, although case libraries demonstrate the potential for instructors to design effective learning experiences, engagement with the cases themselves remains grounded in their rich contexts, and learning emerges in a manner emphasizing student ownership of the experience and ensuing understandings. This emergent quality is exemplified by the Balloon Car Challenge discussed by Kolodner (2002). One in a series of activities in a middle-school physical science class, the Balloon Car Challenge employs a number of learning theories including CBR to engage students in science applications that, consistent with the precepts discussed above, embody the development of scientific practices within the iterative testing and refinement of possible solutions. This unit on propulsion requires students to test different numbers of balloons as well as different lengths and diameters of straws connecting the balloons to the vehicles. Ultimately, based on their tests, conjectures, and findings, students combine the various propulsion systems to enable their vehicles to traverse a demanding course. Through these experiences, students develop skills in scientific hypothesis, experimentation, and explanation as well as evidence-based decision making. Moreover, they gain experience and fluency with scientific discourse—that is, "talking and doing science." Through their experiences, they engage themselves in authentic practices of the domain of science.

### Project-Based Learning

Project-based learning involves posing nontrivial problems, in response to which students formulate questions, predictions, experiments, analyses, conclusions, and artifacts (Blumenfeld et al., 1991). Typically of extended duration and collaborative in nature (Bransford and Stein, 1993), these investigations or projects display an authenticity that, for the students, facilitates an embodied curricular experience. In contrast to PBL, which entails designed or structured problems guiding student discovery of "correct" solutions, the outcomes of project-based learning are uncertain, emerging from the practices of the students themselves as they create links between the classroom and the real world and across diverse academic disciplines. In short, although the teacher may establish the learning environment, it

is the student motivation, direction, and achievement that characterize the learning process. Still, though, the teacher must also support this process due to its protracted and often ambiguous nature (Blumenfeld et al., 2006). Two essential aspects of project-based learning deserve reiteration: First, because student-formulated questions drive the inquiry projects, the students construct their own understandings of domain formalisms, and, second, because the projects culminate in concrete, explicit artifacts, the students can reflect on these understandings and revise them based on feedback from others.

In the early 1990s, researchers found middle-school and high-school science education to be problematic: superficial in addressing a broad range of topics at only shallow levels of complexity and artificial in structuring student experience in generic and predictable ways. Further, not only textbooks but also teacher practices failed to recognize the need for students to bring their prior knowledge to bear upon their personal construction of scientific understandings. In response, building on the precepts of project-based learning, several domain-specific projects emerged that together characterized project-based science (Krajcik and Blumenfeld, 2006), including the Center for Learning Technologies in Urban Schools (LeTUS) and the Investigating and Questioning our World through Science and Technology (IQWST) project, both of which developed out of school–university collaborations. Central to the current discussion, these efforts embodied the learning of science practices and concepts within the context of a larger project.

As Krajcik and Blumenfeld (2006) explained, these projects were driven by authentic questions—meaningful and contextualized questions that structured student activity and aligned that activity with academic standards. Second, student activity bore authenticity in that it was situated in the practices and formalisms of the scientific domain; again, students engaged in sustained inquiry resulting in scientific explanations. Third, student work was dependent upon collaboration—not only with other students, who corroborated and critiqued emergent understandings, and not only with the teacher, who helped to structure and support the inquiry process, but also with members of the community beyond the classroom, who helped the students become more fluent with the discourse and practices of the domain. Fourth, these projects leveraged technology tools to not only align student activity with authentic scientific practices but also facilitate student-constructed understandings and artifacts. Indeed, this relates closely to the fifth feature of the project-based science projects discussed by Krajcik and Blumenfeld, namely that the instantiation of student understanding in the creation of artifacts served to advance not only the understandings of other students but also, through feedback and iterative revision, the students' own emergent understandings.

### Classroom Learning Communities

As argued above with respect to cognitive apprenticeship, when one employs a situative perspective to inform classroom practice, the culture of the classroom will—indeed, must—be transformed (Brown, 1992; Schoenfeld, 1988). As Driscoll (2000, p. 175) explained, "The traditional social structure of schools is one in which teachers dispense knowledge to students through classroom activities, textbooks, and possibly other media." Such an arrangement privileges the teacher as controlling student learning and portrays the teacher and the textbook alone as bearing legitimate knowledge. "When a classroom becomes a learning community, however, the social structure transforms into one in which teacher and learners work collaboratively to achieve important goals, goals that may well have been established jointly" (Driscoll, 2000, p. 175). In this way, learning communities instantiate distributed expertise, collaboration, and emergent ownership.

For over a decade, Brown and Campione (Brown, 1992; Brown and Campione, 1990; Brown et al., 1994) have engineered and researched *communities of learners*. In Brown's (1992) seminal work on design experiments, she discussed the process of building a learning community among fifth graders. Their classrooms showed an atmosphere of respect where students' statements were regarded earnestly and their questions were considered seriously; moreover, students developed a community of discourse in which "meaning is negotiated and renegotiated as members of the community develop and share expertise" (Brown et al., 1994, p. 200). Central to these efforts was the use of reciprocal teaching and jigsaw methods to engage students in collaboration. Because reciprocal teaching has been discussed above, the following focuses on the jigsaw method.

This instructional strategy involves students working collaboratively to develop expertise with one component of a larger task; once they have mastered the components for which they are responsible, students engage in reciprocal teaching to share what they have learned with other members of the group. Through these techniques, educators can develop repetitive structures, called *cycles*, to help students gain facility with the various components and recognize their developing mastery over time. Lasting approximately 10 weeks, these cycles begin with a teacher or visiting expert introducing a unit and benchmark lesson and emphasizing a holistic view of the task as well as an analytic perspective of how the various topics interrelate. Students then concentrate on researching their *pieces of the puzzle* and teaching them to others in their groups, with the distributed expertise emerging as students develop competence in the various aspects of their tasks. The teacher models the jigsaw practice throughout the research cycle, and at its completion the groups engage in full reciprocal teaching, with each student participating as an expert of his or her own facet of the topic material.

Significantly, with technology-mediated communication being employed increasingly in educational settings, such structures as e-mail and teleconferencing allow students to collaborate not only face to face but also distributed across space and time and to communicate with not only each other but the wider community as well. Indeed, Scardamalia and Bereiter (Bereiter and Scardamalia, 1996; Scardamalia and Bereiter, 1994, 1996) presented another interesting example that leverages technological resources for supporting collaboration. One exciting aspect of their work is that the community builds a communal database that each new class engages, embodying the learning not only in the immediate classroom rituals but also as part of an extended community evolving over time.

## Participation Models for Establishing Embodiment

Participation models establish a sense of authenticity by engaging learners in the authentic practices as they work on real tasks, frequently as a member of a community including *newcomers* and more established *old timers* (Lave and Wenger, 1991). As with both designed and emergent simulations, participation models entail factual, process, and task authenticity but additionally introduce *ecological* authenticity in that the learner engages real-world tasks within the ecological niche where the tasks bear value. In addition to real-world immersion, these designs also integrate considerable pedagogical scaffolding, including practice scenarios occurring in the classroom as well as simple just-in-time lectures tailored to help learners understand the necessary content and participate more meaningfully in related tasks. In fact, for these types of spaces, an important contingency of their success as contexts for learning is that even such real-world participation is structured so non-experts can succeed, in contrast to contexts that simply immerse learners in a sink-or-swim scenario. Still, all pedagogically structured activities, whether classroom based or not, are embodied in the participatory context of a real-world task with real-world implications.

## Participatory Simulations

The participation model of authenticity is founded on the assumption that the authenticity of a learning activity derives from learners participating in a real-world problem in an authentic context. Participation models designed for school contexts pose challenges because they require that students leave the classroom environment and participate directly with real-world practitioners as members of their communities. One means of establishing participatory authenticity entails fostering student-expert partnerships (SEPs) as part of the educational experience. Central to the SEP model is adopting—that is, learning and doing—the particular content through hands-on, minds-on activities that afford students an opportunity to participate in a project with real-world impact and with significance to both the students and real-world practitioners. Examples of such partnerships include the Global Learning and Observations to Benefit the Environment (GLOBE) project (Finarelli, 1998; Rock and Lawless, 1997), the Global Rivers Environmental Education Network (GREEN) project (Donahue et al., 1998), and Forest Watch (Rock and Lauten, 1996). Central to all these projects is that the practices and outcomes are deemed authentic and owned by the learner as well as the community of practice and that they respond to real-world issues.

Another example, the National Geographic Society's Kids Network curriculum (Bradsher and Hogan, 1995; Karlan et al., 1997), has engaged over 1.5 million children from 50 countries in collaborative investigations of real-world issues. The curriculum consists of 8-week curricular units targeted toward fourth through sixth graders. During implementation, five to ten geographically dispersed classrooms connect through the Kids Network personnel to form a *research team*. The students begin by studying the curriculum area (e.g., global warming, stream erosion) and discussing the general issue in relation to their specific community; the distributed classes work as a team, negotiating how to approach the issues to reflect the local interests of each group. This process of collaboratively determining the particular research issues balances different groups' interests, allows for ownership and legitimacy, and makes possible the global comparisons. Once the research issues have been determined, the groups develop data collection tools and gather samples from their communities, with Kids Network experts helping to discuss issues and offer guidance.

The Kids Network staff receives and integrates data from the different locations. Data summaries are then prepared and sent to participating classrooms; in addition, a practicing scientist sends initial interpretations of the data to model scientific thinking for the students (Bradsher and Hogan, 1995). The students complete the lesson by forming original interpretations of the data, drawing conclusions relevant to their communities, and preparing presentations of the findings for a community audience. These findings and presentations also become incorporated within the network such that subsequent groups can learn from previous efforts. Bradsher and Hogan (1995, p. 39), two National Geographic Society project personnel, characterized the Kids Network curriculum:

> Students pose and research questions about their local community, form hypotheses, collect data through experiments, and analyze results. The answers are largely unknown in advance, and the findings are of interest beyond the classroom.

Although the curriculum is considerably more structured than described here and the findings more prescriptive (Hunter, 1990; Karlan et al., 1997), the approach bears potential for engaging students in authentic scientific problems and discourse alongside other students and scientists. Central to the embodiment is that, through their work, students make significant contributions to their real world communities.

## Academic Play Spaces

Academic play spaces are educational, entertaining, and personally transformative curricular contexts designed according to contemporary theories of learning (Bransford et al., 2000), narrative (Bruner, 2002; Rosenblatt, 1938/1995), interactive narrative (Murray, 1997), and game design (Gee, 2003; Salen and Zimmerman, 2004). Significantly, the structure and content of these spaces align with not only academic standards and domain formalisms but also real-world issues and authentic practices. Certainly, games can establish immersive "worlds" affording a sense of agency and consequentiality, but academic play spaces additionally involve curricular tasks and pedagogical elements to provide for academic learning. These environments support complex forms of participation within interactive narrative frames, wherein learners have agency in determining how these narratives unfold. Central challenges in developing such narrative-based curricula include not only meaningfully situating academic content but also situating the learner in such a way that knowing becomes a process of embodiment and participation. Further, the design should position the disciplinary content so it both yields outcomes in the immediate context and transfers to—that is, relates and applies to—other, future narrative experiences (Bereiter, 1997). In this way, academic play spaces necessarily blur the lines of the *magic circle*, the imaginary boundary between the game world and other non-game worlds (Murray, 1997; Salen and Zimmerman, 2004).

The process of designing academic play spaces to support embodied experiences may be illustrated by the case of Quest Atlantis, a learning and teaching project employing a virtual multi-user environment to immerse children ages 9 to 12 in educational challenges (Barab et al., 2005b). Leveraging strategies from commercial games as well as research on learning and motivation, Quest Atlantis allows children to travel through virtual spaces to perform entertaining, academic activities; they can also text chat with other children and mentors and, through customizing their avatars and project homepages, develop their virtual personae. Additionally, the program advocates a series of pro-social life *commitments* (e.g., environmental awareness, creative expression, diversity affirmation) to foster student awareness and empowerment (Gardner et al., 2001). Children engage with these commitments throughout their participation in the project as well as through the fictional meta-narrative featuring seven teenage Council members on the planet Atlantis. To blur the magic circle of the game, children's in-game identities depend on their successful completion of tasks with their local community, as part of their out-of-school life worlds (Barab and Roth, 2006).

Each Council member champions one of the commitments so children develop rich understandings and ecological perspectives regarding the commitments. Significantly, the curricular tasks often involve engaging in not simply the virtual but the real world as well, such as collecting data about the water quality of nearby rivers to inform others about the process. In this project, children are not simply *audience* to the underlying narrative as it is advanced through novels, comic books, and other regalia, although they find these play structures to be immersive and compelling (Barab et al., 2005a). Rather, they are *participants* in the narrative as they engage in activities, acquiring new potentialities and even contributing to the evolution of the narrative itself through, for example, interacting with the Council members and voting on pertinent issues. Indeed, children's transactions with the narrative, the virtual space, and their out-of-game communities collectively come to afford an embodied experience that is simultaneously virtual and real.

### Communities of Practice

Communities of practice demonstrate many of the aspects of learning communities discussed above but also involve more extended time frames and evolve in authentic contexts. Lave and Wenger (1991) advanced the term *community of practice* to capture the importance of activity in fusing individuals to communities and of communities in legitimizing individual practices. Within this context, learning is regarded as a trajectory along which learners move from being legitimate peripheral participants to core participants in the community of practice. Building on prior conceptualizations (Barab and Duffy, 2000), Barab et al. (2004, p. 55) defined a community of practice as "a persistent, sustained social network of individuals" that demonstrates the following characteristics: (1) shared knowledge, values, and beliefs; (2) overlapping histories among members; (3) mutual interdependence; (4) mechanisms for reproduction; (5) a common practice and/or mutual enterprise; (6) opportunities for interactions and participation; (7) meaningful relationships; and (8) respect for diverse perspectives and minority views. Significantly, communities of practice are nested in, and overlap with, other communities, and they can exist solely in the real world or be supported in part or whole by online sociotechnical structures.

One example of an educational community of practice is the Community of Teachers, a university-based professional development program for pre-service teachers (Barab et al., 2002). The program emphasized fieldwork, with each participant committing to a particular school. They were not assigned to a specific teacher; instead, an apprenticeship relation would develop with a teacher based on social negotiation and mutual recognition of the benefit of a relationship. In this way, students became paired with "old timers" during their first year working toward certification, and they continued to work with these teachers for their duration in the program. Further, each student negotiated membership in a community of students studying to be teachers and, again, remained a part of that community for the duration of their study, sharing their developing understandings and skills and continually negotiating the goals and meanings of both the community and the profession (Barab et al., 2002). As with any community, the Community of Teachers included wizened old timers (students with teaching experience), newcomers (sophomore students), and the levels between, all engaged in a common enterprise.

Further, the program codified a list of 23 Program Expectations that each student satisfied through the apprenticeship (Gregory, 1993), and, indeed, these expectations were realized through embodied practices rather than through lectures or textbooks. Students amassed evidence of their teaching in personal portfolios that demonstrated how, through their experiences, they satisfied the expectations. Because it was

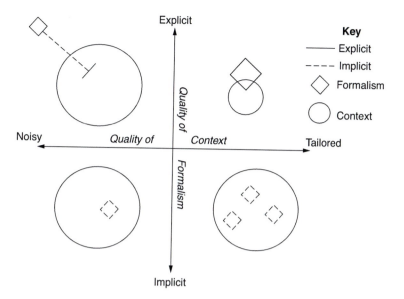

**Figure 9.1** Core tensions in designing for embodiment.

the portfolio that supported the case that a student was ready to enter the profession, over time there grew a collection of personal narratives that came to embody the canonical practices of the community, helping the students to develop a shared language to describe particular group practices. The community fostered a tradition and heritage that was continually inherited and revised by members as they became a part of the program. Moreover, the community trajectory extended across different classrooms and occasions in such a way that individuals came to regard themselves as becoming increasingly central within the nested communities of preservice, practicing, and seasoned teachers. An important component of this program and, more broadly, the community of practice model for establishing embodiment is that the work or practice of the members is situated in both real-world and reflective contexts and that becoming a member of the community and becoming knowledgeably skillful go hand in hand (Wenger, 1998).

## CONCLUDING REMARKS

If situativity theorists are correct and the context in which one learns influences one's coming to know the content to be learned, then understanding strategies for situating content becomes critical. In this chapter, we have provided a conceptual framework and examples from the literature related to designing for situational embodiment. This was not meant to represent an exhaustive list of examples but, rather, an illuminative one. Additionally, we have discussed three types of

curricular designs for embodiment, ranging from *designed* and *emergent simulation models* to *participation models*. It is our conviction that each of these bears advantages and disadvantages. The control and ease of implementation for designed simulations makes them more likely to be adopted in the classroom. Because of the rich dialog and potential agency they afford learners, emergent simulations entail an additional level of authenticity and ownership, but this also complicates their use within K–12 classrooms. Finally, participation models do not require speculation regarding real-world scenarios but actually take place within authentic contexts; yet, this type of embodiment proves to be time consuming, difficult to support, and, indeed, although rich in experience, potentially pedagogically impoverished.

Looking across the different examples, we also discern tensions that emerge in working toward curricular embodiment—namely, tensions concerning the quality of the context (noisy vs. tailored) and the quality of the formalisms (explicit vs. implicit). Indeed, balancing the curricular experience across the four quadrants illustrated in Figure 9.1 poses a key challenge for instructional design and represents an important matter to examine in future research. Specifically, curricula emphasizing explicit formalism risks occasioning an overly school-like experience, while excessive focus on context may be inefficient—especially given the contemporary preoccupation with facilitating students in accumulating standards. Further, prior experience and knowledge likely affect the extent to which narrative is necessary to establish embodiment. For students who already have a rich appreciation of contexts of use, establishing an elaborate narrative context for learning might be ineffectual and potentially counterproductive; instead, attending to explicitly tailored instruction through a lecture format might be optimal.

In general, we posit that a situationally embodied curriculum is not simply a sophisticated word problem such as may be found in a conventional textbook; instead, the design theories described above target a qualitatively different type of curriculum. It is our core argument that, when domain formalisms are situated within a context of use, their meanings and the learner relations with these meanings are usefully transformed, and it is establishing such meaningful relation—not inert content acquisition—that education should support (Dewey, 1938/1997). To situate this argument, we have presented a number of design theories that, in different ways, all embody content within a rich context. Further, they exist not simply as design theories but have been put into practice to produce actual designs, enlist empirical research into their effectiveness, and advance theoretical approaches to instructional design. Within the allotted space, we have not been able to provide enough detail to *embody* the learner within any of these approaches. Instead, our goals were more modest: to provide sketches of and connections among them so the interested reader may pursue them further. Our main goal, however, was to highlight a theory of embodiment and provide an overview of approaches for conceptualizing and possibly even designing embodied curriculum.

## REFERENCES

Barab, S. A. and Duffy, T. (2000). From practice fields to communities of practice. In *Theoretical Foundations of Learning Environments*, edited by D. Jonassen, and S. M. Land, pp. 25–56. Mahwah, NJ: Lawrence Erlbaum Associates.*

Barab, S. A. and Hay, K. (2001). Doing science at the elbows of scientists: issues related to the Scientist Apprentice Camp. *J. Res. Sci. Teach.*, 38(1), 70–102.

Barab, S. A. and Plucker, J. A. (2002). Smart people or smart contexts? Cognition, ability, and talent development in an age of situated approaches to knowing and learning. *Educ. Psychol.*, 37(3), 165–182.

Barab, S. A. and Roth, W.-M. (2006). Curriculum-based ecosystems: supporting knowing from an ecological perspective. *Educ. Res.*, 35(5), pp. 3–13.*

Barab, S. A., Cherkes-Julkowski, M., Swenson, R., Garrett. S., Shaw, R. E., and Young, M. F. (1999). Learning as participation in autocatakinetic systems. *J. Learn. Sci.*, 8(3/4), 349–390.*

Barab, S. A., Squire, K. D., and Dueber, W. (2000). A co-evolutionary model for supporting the emergence of authenticity. *Educ. Technol. Res. Dev.*, 48(2), pp. 37–62.

Barab, S. A., Barnett, M. G., and Squire, K. (2002). Building a community of teachers: navigating the essential tensions in practice. *J. Learn. Sci.*, 11(4), 489–542.*

Barab, S. A., MaKinster, J. G., and Scheckler, R. (2004). Designing system dualities: characterizing an online professional development community. In *Designing for Virtual Communities in the Service of Learning*, edited by S. A. Barab, R. Kling, and J. H. Gray, pp. 53–90. New York: Cambridge University Press.

Barab, S. A., Arici, A., and Jackson, C. (2005a). Eat your vegetables and do your homework: a design-based investigation of enjoyment and meaning in learning. *Educ. Technol.*, 65(1), 15–21.

Barab, S. A., Thomas, M., Dodge, T., Carteaux, B., and Tuzun, H. (2005b). Making learning fun: Quest Atlantis, a game without guns. *Educ. Technol. Res. Dev.*, 53(1), 86–107.

Barron, B., Vye, N. J., Zech, L., Schwartz, D. L., Bransford, J. D., Goldman, S. R., Pellegrino, J., Morris, J., Garrison, S., and Kantor, R. (1995). Creating contexts for community-based problem solving: the *Jasper* challenge series. In *Thinking and Literacy: The Mind at Work*, edited by C. Hedley, P. Antonacci, and M. Rabinowitz, pp. 47–72. Hillsdale, NJ: Lawrence Erlbaum Associates.

Barrows, H. S. and Tamblyn, R. M. (1980). *Problem-Based Learning: An Approach to Medical Education*. New York: Springer.

Bereiter, C. (1997). Situated cognition and how to overcome it. In *Situated Cognition: Social, Semiotic and Psychological Perspectives*, edited by D. Kirshner and J. A. Whitson, pp. 281–300. Mahwah, NJ: Lawrence Erlbaum Associates.

Bereiter, C. and Scardamalia, M. (1996). Rethinking learning. In *Handbook of Education and Human Development: New Models of Learning, Teaching, and Schooling*, edited by D. R. Olson and N. Torrance, pp. 485–513. Cambridge, MA: Basil Blackwell.

Blumenfeld, P., Soloway, E., Marx, R., Krajcik, J., Guzdial, M., and Palincsar, A. (1991). Motivating project-based learning: sustaining the doing, supporting the learning. *Educ. Psychol.*, 26(3&4), 369–398.

Blumenfeld, P. C., Kempler, T. M., and Krajcik, J. S. (2006). Motivation and cognitive engagement in learning environments. In *Cambridge Handbook of the Learning Sciences*, edited by R. K. Sawyer, pp. 475–488. New York: Cambridge University Press.*

Bradsher, M. and Hogan, L. (1995). The Kids Network: student-scientists pool resources. *Educ. Leadership*, 53(2), 38–43.

Bransford, J. D. and Stein, B. S. (1993). *The IDEAL Problem Solver*, 2nd ed. New York: Freeman.

Bransford, T. D., Brown, A. L., and Cocking, R. R., Eds. (2000). *How People Learn: Brain, Mind, Experience, and School*, expanded ed. Washington, D.C.: National Academy Press.*

Brown, A. L. (1992). Design experiments: theoretical and methodological challenges in creating complex interventions in classroom settings. *J. Learn. Sci.*, 2(2), 141–178.*

Brown, A. L. and Campione, J. C. (1990). Communities of learning and thinking, or a context by any other name. In *Contributions to Human Development*. Vol. 21. *Developmental Perspectives on Teaching and Learning Thinking Skills*, edited by D. Kuhn, pp. 108–126. London: Karger.

Brown, A. L., Ash, D., Rutherford, M., Nakagawa, K., Gordon, A., and Campione, J. C. (1994). Distributed expertise in the classroom. In *Organizational Learning*, edited by M. D. Cohen and L. S. Sproull, pp. 188–228. London: SAGE.

Brown, J. S., Collins, A., and Duguid, P. (1989). Situated cognition and the culture of learning. *Educ. Res.*, 18(1), 32–42.*

Bruner, J. (2002). *Making Stories: Law, Literature, Life*. New York: Farrar, Straus and Giroux.

Cobb, P. and Yackel, E. (1995). Constructivist, emergent, and sociocultural perspectives in the context of developmental research. In *Proceedings of the 17th Annual Meeting of the North American Chapter of the International Group for the Psychology of Mathematics Education*, Vol. 1, edited by D. T. Owens, M. K. Reed, and G. M. Millsaps, pp. 3–29. Columbus, OH: ERIC Clearinghouse for Science, Mathematics, and Environmental Education.

Cognition and Technology Group at Vanderbilt (CTGV). (1990). Anchored instruction and its relationship to situated cognition. *Educ. Res.*, 19(6), 2–10.*

Cognition and Technology Group at Vanderbilt (CTGV). (1991). Some thoughts about constructivism and instructional design. *Educ. Technol.*, 31(9), 16–18.

Cognition and Technology Group at Vanderbilt. (1993). Anchored instruction and situated cognition revisited. *Educ. Technol.*, 33(3), 52–70.*

Collins, A., Brown, J. S., and Newman, S. E. (1989). Cognitive apprenticeship: teaching the crafts of reading, writing, and mathematics. In *Knowing, Learning, and Instruction: Essays in Honor of Robert Glaser*, edited by L. B. Resnick, pp. 453–494. Hillsdale, NJ: Lawrence Erlbaum Associates.*

Dewey, J. (1938/1997). *Experience and Education*. New York: Macmillan.*

Donahue, M., Voit, G. M., Gioia, I., Luppino, G., Hughes, J. P., and Stocke, J. T. (1998). A very hot high redshift cluster of galaxies: more trouble for $\Omega_0 = 1$. *Astrophys. J.*, 502(Pt. 1), 550–557.

Driscoll, M. P. (2000). *Psychology of Learning for Instruction*, 2nd ed. Boston: Allyn & Bacon.

Duffy, T. M. and Jonassen, D. H. (1992). Constructivism: new implications for instructional technology. In *Constructivism and the Technology of Instruction: A Conversation*, edited by T. M. Duffy and D. H. Jonassen, pp. 1–16. Hillsdale, NJ: Lawrence Erlbaum Associates.*

Duffy, T. M., Greene, B., Farr, R., and Mikulecky, L. (1996). *Cognitive, Social, and Literacy Competencies: The Chelsea Bank Simulation Project*, year one final report submitted to the Andrew W. Mellon and Russell Sage Foundations. Bloomington, IN: Indiana University.

Finarelli, M. G. (1998). GLOBE: a worldwide environmental science and education partnership. *J. Sci. Educ. Technol.*, 7(1), 77–84.

Finkle, S. and Torp, L. (1995). *Introductory Documents*. Available from the Center for Problem-Based Learning, Illinois Mathematics and Science Academy, 1500 West Sullivan Road, Aurora, IL 60506.

Fodor, J. (1975). *Language of Thought*. Cambridge, MA: Harvard University Press.

Gardner, H. (1985). *Frames of Mind: The Theory of Multiple Intelligences*. New York: Basic Books.

Gardner, H., Csikszentmihalyi, M., and Damon, W. (2001). *Good Work: When Excellence and Ethics Meet*. New York: Basic Books.

Gee, J. P. (2003). *What Videogames Have to Teach Us About Learning and Literacy*. New York: Palgrave Macmillan.*

Gibson, J. J. (1966). *The Senses Considered as Perceptual Systems*. Boston: Houghton Mifflin.

Gibson, J. J. (1979/1986). *The Ecological Approach to Visual Perception*. Hillsdale, NJ: Lawrence Erlbaum Associates.*

Greeno, J. G. (1989). A perspective on thinking. *Am. Psychol.*, 44(2), 134–141.*

Gregory, T. (1993). *Community of Teachers*, unpublished manuscript. Bloomington, IN: Indiana University.

Hunter, B. (1990). Computer-mediated communications support for teacher collaborations: researching new contexts for both teaching and learning. *Educ. Technol.*, 30(10), 46–49.

Jonassen, D. H. (1999). Designing constructivist learning environments. In *Instructional Design Theories and Models: A New Paradigm of Instructional Theory*, Vol. II, edited by C. M. Reigeluth, pp. 215–239. Mahwah, NJ: Lawrence Erlbaum Associates.*

Jonassen, D. H. and Hernandez-Serrano, J. (2002). Case-based reasoning and instructional design: using stories to support problem solving. *Educ. Technol. Res. Dev.*, 50(2), 65–77.

Karlan, J. W., Huberman, M., and Middlebrooks, S. H. (1997). The challenges of bringing the Kids Network to the classroom. In *Bold Ventures*. Vol. 2. *Case Studies of U.S. Innovations in Science Education*, edited by S. A. Raizen and E. D. Britton, pp. 247–394. Boston: Kluwer.

Kirshner, D. and Whitson, J. A. (1998). Obstacles to understanding cognition as situated. *Educ. Res.*, 27(8), 22–28.

Kolodner, J. L. (1993). *Case-Based Reasoning*. San Mateo, CA: Morgan Kaufman Publishers.

Kolodner, J. L. (2002). Facilitating the learning of design practices: lessons learned from an inquiry into science education. *J. Indust. Teacher Educ.*, 39(3), 9–40.

Kolodner, J. L. (2006). Case-based reasoning. In *Cambridge Handbook of the Learning Sciences*, edited by R. K. Sawyer, pp. 225–242. New York: Cambridge University Press.*

Kolodner, J. L. and Guzdial, M. (2000). Theory and practice of case-based learning aids. In *Theoretical Foundations of Learning Environments*, edited by D. H. Jonassen and S. M. Land, pp. 215–242. Mahwah, NJ: Lawrence Erlbaum Associates.

Krajcik, J. S. and Blumenfeld, P. C. (2006). Project-based learning. In *Cambridge Handbook of the Learning Sciences*, edited by R. K. Sawyer, pp. 317–333. New York: Cambridge University Press.*

Lave, J. and Wenger, E. (1991). *Situated Learning: Legitimate Peripheral Participation*. New York: Cambridge University Press.*

Murray, J. (1997). *Hamlet on the Holodeck: The Future of Narrative in Cyberspace*. New York: The Free Press.

Nathan, M. J. (2005). *Rethinking Formalisms in Formal Education*, WCER Working Paper Series No. 2005-11. Madison, WI: Wisconsin Center for Educational Research.

Palincsar, A. S. and Brown, A. L. (1984). Reciprocal teaching of comprehension-fostering and comprehension-monitoring activities. *Cognit. Instruct.*, 1(2), 117–175.*

Petraglia, J. (1998). *Reality by Design: The Rhetoric and Technology of Authenticity in Education*. Mahwah, NJ: Lawrence Erlbaum Associates.*

Radinsky, J., Bouillion, L., Hanson, K., Gomez, L., Vemeer, D., and Fishman, B. (1998). A Framework for Authenticity: Mutual Benefits Partnerships. Paper presented at the annual meeting of the American Educational Research Association, April 13–17, San Diego, CA.

Reed, E. S. (1991). Cognition as the cooperative appropriation of affordances. *Ecol. Psychol.*, 3(2), 135–158.

Reed, E. S. and Jones, R., Eds. (1982). *Reasons for Realism: Selected Essays of James J. Gibson*. Hillsdale, NJ: Lawrence Erlbaum Associates.

Rock, B. N. and Lauten, G. N. (1996). K–12 grade students as active contributors to research investigations. *J. Sci. Technol.*, 5(4), 255–266.

Rock, B. N. and Lawless, J. G. (1997). The GLOBE program: a source of datasets for use in global change studies. *IGBP Newslett.*, 29, 15–17.

Rogoff, B. and Lave, J., Eds. (1984). *Everyday Cognition: Its Development in Social Context*. Cambridge, MA: Harvard University Press.*

Rosenblatt, L. M. (1938/1995). *Literature as Exploration*, 5th ed. New York: Modern Language Association.

Roth, W.-M. (1996). Knowledge diffusion in a grade 4–5 classroom during a unit of civil engineering: an analysis of a classroom community in terms of its changing resources and practices. *Cognit. Instruct.*, 14(2), 170–220.

Roth, W.-M. (1998). *Designing Communities*. Dordrecht: Kluwer.

Ruopp, R., Gal, S., Drayton, B., and Pfister, M., Eds. (1993). *LabNet: Toward a Community of Practice*. Hillsdale, NJ: Lawrence Erlbaum Associates.

Salen, K. and Zimmerman, E. (2004). *Rules of Play: Game Design Fundamentals*. Cambridge, MA: MIT Press.*

Savery, J. R. and Duffy, T. M. (1995). Problem-based learning: an instructional model and its constructivist framework. *Educ. Technol.*, 35(5), 31–38.*

Scardamalia, M. and Bereiter, C. (1994). Computer support for knowledge-building communities. *J. Learn. Sci.*, 3(3), 265–283.*

Scardamalia, M. and Bereiter, C. (1996). Computer support for knowledge building communities. In *CSCL: Theory and Practice of an Emerging Paradigm*, edited by T. Koschmann, pp. 249–268. Mahwah, NJ: Lawrence Erlbaum Associates.

Schank, R. C. (1982). *Dynamic Memory: A Theory of Reminding and Learning in Computers and People*. New York: Cambridge University Press.

Schoenfeld, A. H. (1987). What's all the fuss about metacognition? In *Cognitive Science and Mathematics Education*, edited by A. H. Schoenfeld, pp. 189–215. Hillsdale, NJ: Lawrence Erlbaum Associates.

Schoenfeld, A. H. (1988). When good teaching leads to bad results: the disasters of 'well-taught' mathematics courses. *Educ. Psychol.*, 23(2), 145–166.

Schoenfeld, A. H. (1996). In fostering communities of inquiry, must it matter that the teacher knows the 'answer'? *For Learn. Math.*, 16(3), 11–16.

Schwartz, D. L., Lin, X., Brophy, S., and Bransford, J. D. (1999). Toward the development of flexibly adaptive instructional design. In *Instructional-Design Theories and Models: A New Paradigm of Instructional Theory*, Vol II, edited by C. Reigeluth, pp. 183–213. Mahwah, NJ: Lawrence Erlbaum Associates.*

Senge, P. M. (1994). *The Fifth Discipline: The Art and Practice of the Learning Organization*. New York: Doubleday.

Sfard, A. (1998). On two metaphors for learning and the dangers of choosing just one. *Educ. Res.*, 27(2), 4–13.*

Shannon, B. (1988). Semantic representation of meaning: a critique. *Psychol. Bull.*, 104(1), 70–83.

Shaw, R. E. and Bransford, J. (1977). Introduction: psychological approaches to the problem of knowledge. In *Perceiving, Acting and Knowing*, edited by R. E. Shaw and J. Bransford, pp. 1–39. Hillsdale, NJ: Lawrence Erlbaum Associates.

Suchman, L. (1987). *Plans and Situated Actions: The Problem of Human–Machine Communication*. New York: Cambridge University Press.

Wandersee, J. H., Mintzes, J. J., and Novak, J. D. (1994). Research on alternative conceptions in science. In *Handbook on Science Teaching and Learning*, edited by D. L. Gabel, pp. 177–210. New York: Macmillan.

Wenger, E. (1998). *Communities of Practice: Learning, Meaning, and Identity*. New York: Cambridge University Press.*

Whitehead, A. N. (1929). *The Aims of Education and Other Essays*. New York: Macmillan.*

Young, M. F. (1993). Instructional design for situated learning. *Educ. Technol. Res. Dev.*, 41(1), 43–58.

* Indicates a core reference.

# 10

# Generative Learning: Principles and Implications for Making Meaning

*Hyeon Woo Lee, Kyu Yon Lim, and Barbara L. Grabowski*
Pennsylvania State University, University Park, Pennsylvania

## CONTENTS

## ABSTRACT

The first and second edition of this chapter defined generative learning and its foundations and presented relevant research that tested the theory. The primary goal of this edition is to reconceptualize the processes for making meaning by synthesizing theoretical foundations of generative learning and exploring generative learning effects by different types of learning outcomes. The essence of this model of generative learning is knowledge generation. Only through learners' generation of relationships and meaning themselves can knowledge be generated that is sustainable—this is the essential process of meaning making by the learner. Likewise, only those activities that involve the actual creation of relationships and meaning would be classified as examples of generative learning strategies. A variety of studies reporting on results of generative strategies have shown that, in most cases, active learner involvement produced increased gains in recall, comprehension, and higher order thinking or improvement in self-regulated learning skill. Misconception, providing feedback, and developmental appropriateness are issues that have emerged as unresolved. As such, there is much research left to do to establish specific guidelines that help the designer create a learning environment that stimulates attention and intention, promotes active mental processing at all stages and levels of learning, and provides the learner with appropriate help in the generation process.

## KEYWORDS

*Attention:* Arousal and intention in the brain that influence an individual's learning processes. Without active, dynamic, and selective attending of environmental stimuli, it follows that meaning generation cannot occur.

*Knowledge generation:* Generation of understanding through developing relationships between and among ideas.

*Meaning making:* The process of connecting new information with prior knowledge, affected by one's intention, motivation, and strategies employed.

*Motivation processes:* Wittrock (1991) specified interest and attribution as being the two essential and linked components of motivation processes activated by arousal and intention through the descending reticular activation system.

*Self-regulation:* Active participation in terms of behavior, motivation, and metacognition in one's own learning process (Zimmerman, 1986).

## INTRODUCTION

The internal processes of learning and how they are stimulated are of prime importance to instructional designers. These processes are understood through extensive theoretical conceptions and predictions and empirical evidence about cognitive functioning, processes, and the structure of memory. Using theoretical foundations about learning, designers develop a conception of the thinking that occurs within the learner, and they use this conception to guide the design of learning environments. One important concept explaining these processes is generative learning theory. Generative learning theory, with its companion model, generative teaching, has a foundation in neural research as

well as research regarding the structure of knowledge and cognitive development. Generative learning theory focuses on selecting appropriate, learner-centric instructional activities for the learner. This theory is one that combines the importance of learner and instructional intentionality. Because of this blending, Bonn and Grabowski (2001) call generative learning theory a practical cousin of constructivism. Perhaps it also provides a more complete perspective about learning, making it a second cousin to behaviorism. The theory brings together our understanding of learning processes and the design of external stimuli or instruction. Describing how meaning is made for different types of learning outcomes is the challenge of this chapter.

## MAKING MEANING IN GENERATIVE LEARNING

### Generative Learning Foundations

Wittrock (1974a,b) was the founder of generative learning theory. His beliefs about learning were influenced by research in several areas of cognitive psychology, including cognitive development, human learning, human abilities, information processing, and aptitude treatment interactions. His work explains and prescribes teaching strategies to maximize reading comprehension. In his theory, Wittrock emphasized one very significant and basic assumption: The learner is not a passive recipient of information; rather, he or she is an active participant in the learning process, working to construct meaningful understanding of information found in the environment. Wittrock (1974a, p. 182) stated that, "although a student may not understand sentences spoken to him by his teacher, it is highly likely that a student understands sentences that he generates himself." It is, as Harlen and Osborne (1985, p. 137) call it, "learning through the person."

Designing instruction based on this basic assumption, however, is not as simple or straightforward as it may first appear. Wittrock built his model around four parts based on a neural model of brain functioning (Luria, 1973) and cognitive research on the process of knowing (Wittrock, 1992). As is evident from the empirical results that are reported later in this chapter, those studies that apply a simplistic rather than a holistic perspective result in mixed or unpredicted findings. It is important, therefore, to elaborate on the interrelationship of the four parts to Wittrock's model: generation, motivation, learning, and knowledge creation. Metacognitive processes also play a key role in this model, although in most cases Wittrock folds metacognition into the knowledge creation process.

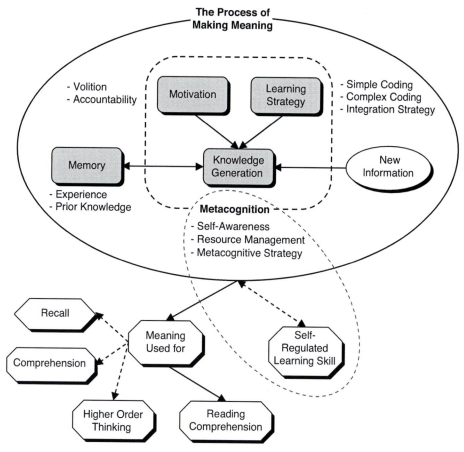

**Figure 10.1** Conceptual understanding of generative learning.

## Interrelationship of the Components of Generative Learning

The concept map in Figure 10.1 is illustrative of our conceptualization of the ideas presented in Wittrock's writings (1974a,b, 1985, 1990, 1991, 1992) and in Grabowski's (2004) concept map regarding the progression of generative learning. As shown inside the dotted rectangle in Figure 10.1, the essence of generative learning is knowledge generation. Only through the *learner's self-generation* of relationships and understanding can knowledge be generated meaningfully. Only those activities that involve the actual creation of relationships and meaning would be classified as examples of generative learning strategies. Restructuring of environmental information by definition requires the learner to generate either organizational or integrated relationships and construct personal meaning. One part of meaning making results from the processes of generating relations between memory including preconceptions, abstract knowledge, everyday experience, domain-specific knowledge, and new

information (Wittrock, 1974b). This connection is shown by the connecting arrows. Generation can result in schema fitting (Rummelhart, 1981; Rummelhart and Ortony, 1977).

Basically, data points or schemata form the knowledge units that are manipulated in generative learning theory. Because of the way knowledge is stored, instructional and learning activities must connect new to existing knowledge so it is easily retrievable. This connection is made by adding information to schema, restructuring, or tuning it. Although connections are made by links, those linkages are not defined or labeled, as in creating a pattern note without labeling the lines. Generative learning theory, on the other hand, is similar in concept to creating a pattern note with all the links labeled. Activities designed by schema theorists would include those that remind learners of prior knowledge and relate the information to what the learners already know. It is less relevant who selects those connection points compared to the fact that they are made.

By definition, learners should become accountable and responsible in learning and mentally active in constructing relations between what they know and what they are learning (Wittrock, 1990). Motivation, the second of Wittrock's components shown inside the dotted rectangle, promotes the impulse or intention to learn or carry out a task (Corno, 2001). Persistence and sustained interest in knowledge generation process is one essential component of the motivation process of this model. Interest can be enhanced only when the learners attribute successful comprehension to their own effort at knowledge generation (Wittrock, 1991).

Learners who are motivated to generate meaning between their memory and new information need to use various learning strategies from simple coding to integration strategies. Depending on their motivation level or memory, such as prior learning on domain or learning strategy, or learners' preference, learners employ different learning strategies in knowledge generation. This process can be explained by information-processing theory: the process of thinking and memory storage—in other words, the stages and levels of processing. What we take from information-processing theory is an emphasis on how we think, rather than on what we think or that we think. Its focus is on that process of transforming external stimuli into some recallable form to be stored in memory. The emphasis of generative learning theory is on the generation of new conceptual understandings, not just on transferring information.

Finally, Wittrock (1991) emphasized that learners should control their own generative processes. Metacognition regulates one's cognitive activities in learning processes and therefore surrounds the three generative learning processes shown in Figure 10.1 (Brown, 1978; Flavell, 1979). Self-monitoring is a vital process here because it informs learners about their progress (Zimmerman, 1998). Based on self-monitoring, learners manage their effort and available resources and change their learning strategies to generate meaning.

In summary, to make meaning, learners actually create relationships among or between their memory and new information. Learners are mentally active and use various learning strategies in this knowledge generation process. Also, learners metacognitively self-regulate this process. The outcome of this knowledge generation was originally investigated in reading comprehension, and many researchers extended this model to investigate a variety of generative learning strategies that were expected to promote different levels of learning in a variety of domains. Recently, researchers have explored higher order thinking and self-regulated learning skills as outcomes of generative learning.

## APPLIED RESEARCH

### Synthesis from the Learning Process Perspective

Learning strategies, as illustrated in Figure 10.1, that are employed to generate knowledge and meaning during the learning process are the most frequently studied component of generative learning theory. For example, many research studies have tested the effects of simple coding strategies such as underlining, note taking, and adjunct or inserted questions; more complex coding organizational strategies, such as the creation of hierarchies, headings, summaries, and concept maps or manipulation of objects; and, finally, elaborative integration strategies such as imaging and creation of examples, interpretations, or analogies (Table 10.1).

An analysis was conducted from this strategy perspective in the first two editions of this chapter. From this perspective, three conclusions could be drawn. First, when comparing generative strategies treatment and control groups, researchers often found no significant differences, indicating that mental activity cannot be strictly controlled by instruction, and this finding raised the issue that requiring an overt response may be more effective in encouraging the desired result (Anderson and Kulhavey, 1972; Peper and Mayer, 1986; Shrager and Mayer, 1989).

Second, investigation of the subject-generated vs. experimenter-provided activity is a relatively common theme in generative learning studies (see, for example, Barnett et al., 1981; Bull and Wittrock, 1973; Doctorow et al., 1978; Rickards and August, 1975; Smith and Dwyer, 1995; Stein and Bransford, 1979). These research results are mixed with learning gains not consistently predicted by this factor.

Third, comparing the various types of generative strategies is another major research theme (Hooper et al., 1994; McKeague and DiVesta, 1996; Wittrock and Alesandrini, 1990). Again, looking at generative learning from this perspective did not result in consistent or definitive guidelines for its use. Although some of the research has found some generative learning strategies to be effective, the results are mixed when examining them by learning strategy type, and they warrant a different type of analysis.

### Synthesis from a Learning Outcomes Perspective

Four categories of criterion measures emerged when examining research on generative learning strategies from a learning outcomes perspective: recall, comprehension, higher order thinking, and self-regulation skill.

## Recall

According to the research summarized in Table 10.1, recall is the most frequently studied criterion measure. Wittrock and Carter (1975) conducted a study examining free recall in generative vs. reproductive treatments. The generative group was directed to organize the hierarchies, whereas the reproductive group was directed to simply copy them. The results showed better performance for the generative treatment groups than for the reproductive groups for the disorganized and randomly organized hierarchies; however, the organized reproductive group performed better on free recall than the unrelated generative group. Burton et al. (1986) investigated the effect of superordinate and subordinate questions by using a secondary task probe technique and a passage about a mythical country. The overall results indicated that more main ideas were recalled than details.

Davis and Hult (1997) studied immediate and delayed free recall in note taking and writing summaries in introductory psychology classes. Their results support the findings of Barnett et al. (1981) that writing summaries during pauses in the lecture note-taking activity significantly improved free recall and delayed retention. King (1992) examined the effect of self-questioning, summarizing, and note taking on immediate and delayed recall of under-prepared college students. On immediate recall, summarizers performed better than self-questioners, who were better than note takers, indicating a progressive generative effect. Self-questioners performed best on the delayed tests, indicating that deeper processing may occur in more generative tasks such as self-questioning. Woods and Bernard (1987) also found effects of adjunct conceptual post-questions on encouraging a greater depth of processing of verbal information among adults 60 years of age and older. From results on intentional and incidental free-recall tests, they found that adjunct questions helped older learners process only intentional text at a greater depth. Shrager and Mayer (1989) reported interesting results regarding aptitude–treatment interaction research. Note takers recalled more than non-note takers for students with low levels of prior knowledge but not for those with high levels of prior knowledge.

To summarize these findings, recall has been often used as dependent variable in the studies for simple coding strategies. In addition, some researchers reported that the higher the level of generativity, the higher the score on delayed recall. Research findings, however, are mixed with regard to the type of strategies, measurement instrument, and the interaction with individual differences.

## Comprehension

In two experiments with elementary-school children, Doctorow et al. (1978) studied the effect of learner-generated vs. experimenter-provided paragraph headings and sentence meanings on comprehension. The combination of text organized through the use of headings plus learner-generated sentences about the paragraphs produced dramatic gains in reading comprehension. This strategy also increased comprehension more for high-ability students than for low-ability students, perhaps because high-ability students have better organizational cognitive abilities to make sense out of disorganized information. Two studies tested the effect of a combination of generative strategies on comprehension. The treatments of Carnine and Kinder (1985) study were images, corrective feedback, and summary to study reading comprehension. They found significant gains from pre- to post-tests for both narrative and expository text. Linden and Wittrock (1981) also tested the effect of images, summary sentences, and analogies, all of which increased and correlated with comprehension.

Several studies have tested the effect of concept mapping on comprehension. Smith and Dwyer (1995) found a significant difference only on lower level terminology tasks, not on a comprehension task, in favor of instructor-provided maps. Similarly, two other studies (Kenny, 1995; Taricani, 2002) found no effects of learner-generated graphic organizers or concept maps on comprehension. In the Taricani (2002) study, feedback was also tested against generativity to evaluate the notion that learner generation can create misconceptions that are corrected before testing; however, the blending of concept mapping and feedback did not assist in overall learning of terminology and comprehension. Wang (2003) also tested the effect of different types of concept mapping strategies on terminology and comprehension. Students who were given partially predeveloped concept maps performed better on all levels of learning outcome, but students who created their own concept map groups performed better only on terminology.

In summary, the effect of complex coding strategies on comprehension is still mixed, but simple coding strategies are consistently reported to be effective for aiding comprehension. Higher levels of generativity when using complex coding strategies (e.g., learner-generated concept map) did not seem to be effective for improving comprehension.

## Higher Order Thinking

Research has also investigated problem solving, reasoning, inference, and application. Among the research, problem solving has been tested by a few

**TABLE 10.1**
**Summary of Selected Applied Generative Research Studies**

| Learning Outcome | Generative Activity | Author/Year | Content | Age Level | Results |
|---|---|---|---|---|---|
| Recall | *Note taking*<br>Note taking, elaborated and simple review; instructor-provided and learner-generated notes | Barnett et al. (1981) | History | Undergraduates | Note taking produced better results than no note taking, but there was no significant difference between elaborated review and simple review of notes.<br>Review of instructor-prepared notes resulted in greater learning than review of learner-generated notes.<br>Delayed retention scores were higher for questions from learner notes. |
| | Writing summaries during note taking | Davis and Hult (1997) | Introductory psychology | Undergraduates | Summary group scored significantly higher on free recall and delayed retention test. |
| | *Adjunct questions*<br>Adjunct questions: super-subordinate post-questions | Burton et al. (1986) | Description of a mythical country | Undergraduates | More main ideas were recalled, and general questions were more engaging than detailed ones. |
| | Adjunct post-questions | Woods and Bernard (1987) | Weather forecasting | Adults ages 60 years or older | Adjunct questions aided recall of intentional ideas only. |
| | *Organizational strategies*<br>Organization hierarchies | Wittrock and Carter (1975) | Mineral tables | Undergraduates | Learner-generated hierarchies for disorganized lists were significantly better than simply reproducing them.<br>Reproducing organized hierarchies was significantly better than learner-generated ones. |
| | *Manipulation of objects*<br>Individual and group concept mapping and object manipulation; sequence of activities | Ritchie and Volkl (2000) | Science | Sixth-grade children | No difference was found between concept mapping and manipulatives on immediate recall and those who worked in teams vs. those who worked individually.<br>Performance was significantly better for those who created concept maps first and then used the manipulatives on the delayed posttest.<br>Interaction was found between strategy and individual/team on immediate and delayed recall; those who created concept maps in teams performed significantly better than those who used the manipulatives in teams. The opposite effect was found for intermediate recall. |
| | *Imaging*<br>Imaging: experimenter provided and learner generated | Bull and Wittrock (1973) | Definitions of nouns | Elementary-school students | Recall was significantly higher for imaging than the verbal/copying strategy. |

116

| | Strategy | Citation | Subject area | Population | Results |
|---|---|---|---|---|---|
| | *Elaborations* | | | | |
| | Elaboration interpretation | Johnsey et al. (1992) | Professional development | Adults | Results favored the use of embedded *vs.* detached elaboration strategies. Elaborations were better than no elaborations. No difference was found between learner-generated and experimenter-provided. |
| | *Combination of coding and integration* | | | | |
| | Self-questioning, summarizing, and note taking | King (1992) | Generic lecture | Underprepared undergraduates | Immediate: Summarizers performed better than self-questioners, who performed better than note takers. Delayed: Self-questioners performed better than summarizers, who performed better than note takers. |
| Comprehension | *Underlining* | | | | |
| | Underlining | Richards and August (1975) | Educational psychology | Undergraduates | Achievement increased on post-test when learner underlined most relevant information. |
| | *Note taking* | | | | |
| | Précising *vs.* rereading, underlining, or signaling | McGuire (1999) | Reading | ESL learners | Précising resulted in higher comprehension over rereading, underlining, or signaling |
| | *Adjunct questions* | | | | |
| | Adjunct pictures | Brody and Legenza (1980) | History | Undergraduates | Post-pictures were more beneficial than pre-pictures |
| | *Organizational strategies* | | | | |
| | Organization headings, sentence meaning | Doctorow et al. (1978) | SRA literature | Elementary-school students | Learner-generated sentences combined with experimenter-provided headings produced increased comprehension, followed by generative only. |
| | Physical manipulation of objects | Sayeki et al. (1991) | Math | Elementary-school students | Post-test showed physical manipulation facilitated graphics increased problem solving over static or computer-manipulated graphics. |
| | Graphic organizers | Kenny (1995) | Nursing elderly patients | University nursing students and faculty | Significantly poorer performance on the immediate learning and retention tests for those given generative graphic organizers than those given a graphic organizer. |
| | *Imaging* | | | | |
| | Verbal and image elaborations: sequence | Kourilsky and Wittrock (1987) | Economics | High-school students | Verbal-to-image elaborations were significantly better than image to verbal or either used singularly. |
| | *Elaborations* | | | | |
| | Elaborations elaborated sentences | Stein and Bransford (1979) | Language arts | Undergraduates | Performance was facilitated only when elaborations clarified precise objectives; prompting encouraged subjects to ask more relevant questions. |
| | Elaboration examples | DiVesta and Peverley (1984) | Fictitious concept | Undergraduates | Students who generated their own examples did significantly better on far-transfer tasks than those given instructor-provided examples. |

117

**TABLE 10.1 (cont.)**
**Summary of Selected Applied Generative Research Studies**

| Learning Outcome | Generative Activity | Author/Year | Content | Age Level | Results |
|---|---|---|---|---|---|
| | *Combination of coding and integration* | | | | |
| | Images, verbalization of the image and summaries, structural adjunct questions | Carnine and Kinder (1985) | Social studies and science | Low-performing elementary-school children | Comprehension increased significantly but not more than when inserted questions on passage structure were used. |
| | Summaries, analogies and question answering in different sequences | BouJaoude and Tamin (1998) | Science | Seventh-grade students | No differences were found for strategy or sequence. Students preferred summaries the most; questions, because they were easy; analogies, for fun; and summaries, for their helpfulness. |
| | *Metacognitive strategy* | | | | |
| | Generative learning processes training | Kourilsky and Wittrock (1992) | Economics | High-school seniors | Generative learning procedures significantly increased confidence and decreased level of misunderstanding. |
| | Generative learning training | Kourilsky (1993) | Economics | Professional teachers | Pre- to post-test gains on both exams were significant when misconceptions were clarified and learning was covered again. |
| Recall and comprehension | *Note taking* | | | | |
| | Note taking | Peper and Mayer (1986) | Auto engines | High-school and college students | Note taking increased achievement for far-transfer problem solving but not near-transfer fact retention. |
| | Note taking | Shrager and Mayer (1989) | How to use a camera | Undergraduates | Confirmed above findings; also, significant differences were found for students with low prior knowledge. |
| | *Organizational strategies* | | | | |
| | Concept maps | Smith and Dwyer (1995) | Human heart | Undergraduates | Learners using instructor-provided concept maps performed better on identification tests only; no other differences were found. |
| | Concept maps: partial and total learner generated by feedback | Taricani (2002) | Human heart | Undergraduates | Providing feedback resulted in higher terminology scores on partially generated map |
| | Concept maps: concept matching mapping, proposition identifying mapping, and student-generated concept mapping | Wang (2003) | Heart content | Undergraduates | Concept matching mapping strategy was the most effective among the three strategies. |
| | *Imaging* | | | | |
| | Imaging | Anderson and Kulhavey (1972) | Fictitious description of a tribe of people | High-school seniors | Significant differences were found in favor of those who actually used an imaging strategy. |

118

| | | Study | Content area | Participants | Findings |
|---|---|---|---|---|---|
| | *Combination of coding and integration* | | | | |
| | Summaries, and analogies | Wittrock and Alesandrini (1990) | Marine life | Undergraduates | Those who generated summaries performed better than those who generated analogies. Students working alone did better than those working in pairs. |
| | Combination of generative strategies, images summary sentences, and analogies/metaphors | Linden and Wittrock (1981) | Reading | Elementary-school students | All generations were increased and correlated with comprehension. More generations were produced when images were produced before verbal elaborations. No difference was found for generation sequence. |
| | Strategy orientation (underlining, headings, and analogies) by guided vs. active activity | McKeague and DiVesta (1996) | Radar | Undergraduates | Results were mixed for factual recall. No effect by strategy was found. Students performed better in the guided activities than the active learner groups. |
| Higher order thinking skill | *Adjunct questions* | | | | |
| | Adjunct questions: frequency, nature of, need for feedback, overt/covert response | Anderson and Biddle (1975) | Across content areas | Across age levels | Learning was better with more frequent questions. No difference was found when feedback was given. Overt response was needed depending on if questions were embedded. |
| | Adjunct postquestions with no overt responses | Sutliff (1986) | Electrical engineering | Low-and upper-ability college students | No significant differences were found between groups |
| | *Organizational strategies* | | | | |
| | Linear, navigational, and generative computer text | Barab et al. (1999) | Social studies | Undergraduates | Navigational and generative group performed better in problem solving. Linear group performed better in reading comprehension. |
| | Generated map vs. completed map | Lee and Nelson (2005) | Designing instruction | Undergraduates | Generative map outperformed completed map in well-structured problem solving. |
| | *Imaging* | | | | |
| | Verbal only, image only, and combined elaborations | Laney (1990) | Economics | Third-grade children | Verbal-only and verbal-to-image integrated strategies facilitated reasoning better than imagery only. |
| | *Metacognitive strategy* | | | | |
| | Instruction on summary writing versus reflection training | Friend (2001) | Reading comprehension | Unskilled undergraduate writers | Instruction on how to write effective summaries was more effective. |
| Comprehension and higher-order thinking skill | *Organizational strategies* | | | | |
| | Concept vs. semantic maps | Beissner et al. (1993) | Human heart | Undergraduates | Learner-generated concept maps were the better strategy for holists. Learner-generated semantic maps were better for serialists for problem-solving learning only. |

119

**TABLE 10.1 (cont.)**
**Summary of Selected Applied Generative Research Studies**

| Learning Outcome | Generative Activity | Author/Year | Content | Age Level | Results |
|---|---|---|---|---|---|
| Recall, comprehension, and higher order thinking skills | *Manipulation of objects*<br>Mouse-manipulated graphics | Haag and Grabowski (1994) | Human heart | Undergraduate | Learner-manipulated graphics increased problem solving over static or computer-manipulated graphics. |
| Higher-order thinking skill and SRL | Organizational strategies<br>Concept mapping | Chularut and DeBacker (2004) | ESL | College students | Concept mapping group scored higher in achievement and self-monitoring.<br>High proficiency group scored higher in achievement, self-monitoring, and self-efficacy.<br>The difference in gains over time in achievement, self-monitoring, and self-efficacy between the concept mapping group and control group were greater for the higher English proficiency group. |

studies. In research comparing note takers and non-note takers who were learning how to use a camera, Shrager and Mayer (1989) concluded that note takers with low prior knowledge solved transfer problems better than non-note takers with low prior knowledge. Barab et al. (1999) also reported that students in the generative activity group performed better in problem solving in a computer-based learning environment. Regarding organizational strategy, Beissner et al. (1993) compared the effects of learner-generated concept maps and serial maps with learner differences at four levels of learning. Their findings showed an interaction between concept vs. semantic maps and serialist or holist learners on the problem-solving questions only, with serialists performing better with semantic maps and holists performing better with concept maps. In a more recent study, Lee and Nelson (2005) compared the effect of learner-generated concept maps and instructor-generated concept maps on problem solving. Research results showed that the learner-generated concept map group outperformed the instructor-generated map group in well-structured problem solving. They also reported an interaction effect with learners' prior knowledge: The high prior knowledge group benefited more from the activity of concept map generation than the low prior knowledge group.

On the other hand, Laney (1990) and Sutliff (1986) examined the effect of generative strategies on reasoning and inference respectively. In Laney's study, the verbal-only strategy and the integration of verbal and imaging strategy were more effective than the imaging-only strategy on the economic reasoning of third-graders. He felt that his results were consistent with Wittrock's notion that the effective use of imaging is developmental. Laney's third-grade subjects had not yet developed this ability and were more familiar with verbal instruction. Sutliff investigated the effect of inserted questions on reducing passivity in a self-instructional slide–tape presentation as evidenced by increased learning of facts and inference. He reported that there were no significant differences between groups, which is in contrast to prior research reporting significantly different effects of questions.

In sum, most of the studies investigating higher order thinking skills dealt with complex coding strategies such as organization. Because it has been only a decade since we have begun investigating this topic with regard to generative learning, the research findings have not collectively supported each other; however, relatively more effort has been directed toward aptitude–treatment interaction research by considering learners' prior knowledge level or learning style.

### Self-Regulation Skill

In recent years, there has been a resurgence of interest in self-regulated learning (SRL). This phenomenon can be explained from two perspectives. First, recent research findings support a positive relationship between students' self-regulating skill and their academic achievement (Azevedo and Cromley, 2004; Kramarski and Gutman, 2006; Pintrich and De Groot, 1990; Zimmerman, 1998; Zimmerman and Schunk, 2001). Second, a major goal of education is to train students to be skillful self-regulators to enable them to be life-long learners (Boekaerts, 1997; Boekaerts and Corno, 2005). "Self-regulated learners are behaviorally, motivationally, and metacognitively active participants in their own learning process" (Zimmerman, 1986). This interpretation is in line with Wittrock's emphasis on learners' motivation, cognitive learning strategy, and metacognitive process in the knowledge generation processes. In other words, self-regulation skills may play a vital role in generative learning, but learners can also develop their self-regulation skills through generative learning activities. Chularut and DeBacker (2004) investigated the effect of a generative learning strategy—concept mapping—on students' achievement and self-regulation and self-efficacy in learning English as a second language. They found that students who were using concept mapping had significantly greater achievement gains at post-test compared to pre-test. In addition to the benefit of achievement, their results showed that a positive effect of engaging in concept mapping increased students' self-regulation and self-efficacy relative to the control group.

### Summary

A variety of studies reporting on results of generative strategies have been summarized here. This section is not intended to be exhaustive; rather, the studies have been selected as representative of the kind of research that has been conducted across content areas, learning types, and age levels; however, all articles that could be found that specify generative learning as the theory being tested are included. In general, results have shown some increased gains in recall, comprehension, and higher order thinking skill as well as improvement in self-regulated learning skill when the learner is an active partner vs. a passive participant in the learning process and when instruction includes activities that relate new information together and new information to prior knowledge. These studies on generative learning have shown that, in many cases, active learner involvement produced increased learning; that is, learner-generated activities have resulted in significant gains in learning, although misconceptions, feedback, and developmental appropriateness require further investigation, and there remain some mixed findings based on generative learning strategies.

## IMPLICATIONS FOR FURTHER RESEARCH

Past research verifies Wittrock's basic premise of active learner engagement; however, further research should explore the interrelationship of the four components as shown in Figure 10.1 (motivation, learning strategy, knowledge generation, metacognition) in making and applying meaning to predict higher recall, greater comprehension, better higher order thinking, and more controlled self-regulation. What appear to be weak or inconsistent results in previous research may be strengthened if all components are taken into account. Two such areas of research are proposed.

### Motivation, Learner, and Knowledge Creation Processes

Identifying strategies that will enhance the perception of learner responsibility is one example of studying the interrelationships of the components. This indicates a need to merge the learner control research with that of generative learning to address such questions as:

- What are the best methods for providing advisory feedback on learner-generated conceptions of the instruction content, and what are their effects?
- What is the effect on learning of directive, embedded, or inductive control when motivation level varies?

### Instructor-Provided or Learner-Generated and Self-Regulation?

In addition, a question remains as to the relationship between generative learning and learners' self-regulation. From Wittrock's definition, learners need to use their self-regulation skill during the knowledge generation process, and consequently the learners may increase not only their comprehension but also their self-regulation skill. Self-regulation seems to be of critical importance when learners are faced with generating their own understanding rather than having the instructor providing understanding, especially where misconceptions are possible. These relationships should be empirically tested by addressing such questions as:

- Is there any interaction between a learner's level of self-regulation skill and generative activities?
- What is the effect of generative learning strategies on a learner's self-regulated learning skill?

## FINAL THOUGHTS

The principles behind generative learning offer the instructional designer much guidance for developing environments that engage the learner in active processing of the information in face-to-face, e-learning, or even informal learning environments. Following Wittrock's principles, one should put the control of learning in the hands of the learner by creating an advisory environment in which learners manipulate information by moving text, graphics, and media around mentally or physically, testing their own understanding of the relationships they are building. This means putting learners in an environment in which success can be guided, rewarded, and reinforced. Generative learning theory is not discovery learning but student-centric learning with specified activities for actively constructing meaning. Generative learning activities require internal processing of external stimuli. A generative learning environment is not limited to open-ended resources, although it could engender those, and it includes carefully crafted external stimuli that are ready for individual processing. Generative activities are what exist between the external stimuli and the learner. Generative learning theory does not assume dominance of the role of the learner or instructor or instruction but rather a partnership in the process.

As a practical cousin to constructivism and a more complete second cousin to behaviorism, generative learning theory is easily applied to any learning or instructional setting. The subtle differences between this theory and other theories account for differences in instructor roles (the role of the sage). For behaviorism, the sage is on the stage. For constructivism, the sage is viewed as a guide. For generative learning theory, the *sage, guide*, and *learner* are in the center. Content, instructional expertise, and instructional intention are expected of the sage and guide. Active engagement, attention, and learning intention are also expected of the learner. Much research must yet be done to support this position, and there is much research left to do to establish specific guidelines that help the designer create a learning environment that stimulates attention and intention, promotes active mental processing at all stages and levels of learning, and provides appropriate support in the generation process. The evidence indicates that generative learning theory is very applicable to instructional design and that research defining types of processing should continue.

# REFERENCES

Anderson, R. C. and Biddle, W. B. (1975). On asking people questions about what they are reading. In *Psychology of Learning and Motivation*, Vol. 9, edited by G. Bower. New York: Academic Press.

Anderson, R. C. and Kulhavey, R. W. (1972). Imagery and prose learning. *J. Educ. Psychol.*, 63(3), 242–243.

Azevedo, R. and Cromley, J. G. (2004). Does training of self-regulated learning facilitate students' learning with hypermedia? *J. Educ. Psychol.*, 96, 523–535.

Barab, S. A., Young, M. F., and Wang, J. (1999). The effects of navigational and generative activities in hypertext learning on problem solving and comprehension. *Int. J. Instruct. Media*, 26(3), 283–309.

Barnett, J. E., DiVesta, F. J., and Rogonzenski, L. T. (1981). What is learned in notetaking? *J. Educ. Psychol.*, 73(2), 181–192.

Beissner, K., Jonassen, D., and Grabowski, B. L. (1993). Using and selecting graphic techniques to convey structural knowledge. In *Proceedings of Selected Research Paper Presentations*, edited by M. R. Simonson, pp. 79–114. Ames: Iowa State University.

Boekaerts, M. (1997). Self-regulated learning: a new concept embraced by researchers, policy makers, educators, teachers, and students. *Learn. Instruct.*, 7(2), 161–186.

Boekaerts, M. and Corno, L. (2005). Self-regulation in the classroom: a perspective on assessment and intervention. *Appl. Psychol. Int. Rev.*, 54(2), 199–231.

Bonn, K. and Grabowski, B. L. (2001). Generative Learning Theory: A Practical Cousin to Constructivism. Paper presented at the Joint Meeting of Mathematics, January 9–14, New Orleans, LA.

BouJaoude, S. and Tamin, R. (1998). Analogies, Summaries, and Question Answering in Middle School Life Science: Effect on Achievement and Perceptions of Instructional Value. Paper presented at the annual meeting of the National Association for Research in Science Teaching, April 19–22, San Diego, CA (ERIC Document ED 420 503).

Brody, P. and Legenza, A. (1980). Can pictorial attributes serve mathemagenic functions? *Educ. Commun. Technol. J.*, 28(1), 25–29

Brown, A. L. (1978). Knowing when, where, and how to remember: a problem of metacognition. In *Advances in Instructional Psychology*, Vol. 1, edited by R. Glaser, pp. 77–165. Hillsdale, NJ: Lawrence Erlbaum Associates.

Bull, B. L. and Wittrock, M. C. (1973). Imagery in the learning of verbal definitions. *Br. J. Educ. Psychol.*, 43(3), 289–293.

Burton, J. K., Niles, J. A., Lalik, R. M., and Reed, M. W. (1986). Cognitive capacity engagement during and following interspersed mathernagenic questions. *J. Educ. Psychol.*, 78(2), 147–152.

Carnine, D. and Kinder, C. (1985). Teaching low-performing students to apply generative and schema strategies to narrative and expository materials. *Remed. Spec. Educ.*, 6(1), 20–30.

Chularut, P. and DeBacker, T. K. (2004). The influence of concept mapping on achievement, self-regulation, and self-efficacy in students of English as a second language. *Contemp. Educ. Psychol.*, 29, 248–263.

Corno, L. (2001). Volitional aspects of self-regulated learning. In *Self-Regulated Learning and Academic Achievement: Theoretical Perspectives*, 2nd ed., edited by B. J. Zimmerman and D. H. Schunk, pp. 191–225. Mahwah, NJ: Lawrence Erlbaum Associates.

Davis, M. and Hult, R. E. (1997). Effects of writing summaries as a generative learning activity during note taking. *Teaching Psychol.*, 24(1), 47–49.

DiVesta, F. T. and Peverley, S. (1984). The effects of encoding variability, processing activity, and rule-examples sequence on the transfer of conceptual rules. *J. Educ. Psychol.*, 76(1), 108–119.

Doctorow, M., Wittrock, M. C., and Marks, C. B. (1978). Generative processes in reading comprehension. *J. Educ. Psychol.*, 70(2), 109–118.

Flavell, J. H. (1979). Metacognition and cognitive monitoring. *Am. Psychol.*, 34, 906–911.

Friend, R. (2001). Effects of strategy instruction on summary writing of college students. *Contemp. Educ. Psychol.*, 26, 3–24.

Grabowski, B. L. (2004). Generative learning contributions to the design of instruction and learning. In *Handbook of Research on Educational Communications and Technology*, 2nd ed., edited by D. H. Jonassen and Association for Educational Communications and Technology, pp. 719–743. Mahwah, NJ: Lawrence Erlbaum Associates.*

Haag, B. B. and Grabowski, B. L. (1994). The effects of varied visual organizational strategies within computer-based instruction on factual, conceptual and problem solving learning. In *16th Annual Proceedings of Selected Research and Development Presentations*, edited by M. R. Simonson, N. Maushak, and K. Abu-Omar, pp. 235–246B. Ames: Iowa State University.

Harlen, W. and Osborne, R. (1985). A model for learning and teaching applied to primary science. *J. Curric. Stud.*, 17(2), 133–146.

Hooper, S., Sales, G., and Rysavy, S. (1994). Generating summaries and analogies alone and in pairs. *Contemp. Educ. Psychol.*, 19, 53–62.

Johnsey, A., Morrison, G. R., and Ross, S. M. (1992). Using elaboration strategies training in computer-based instruction to promote generative learning. *Contemp. Educ. Psychol.*, 17, 125–135.

Kenny, R. (1995). The generative effects of instructional organizers with computer-based interactive video. *J. Educ. Comput. Res.*, 12(3), 275–296.

King, A. (1992). Comparison of self-questioning, summarizing, and note taking review as strategies for learning from lectures. *Am. Educ. Res. J.*, 29, 303–323.

Kourilsky, M. (1993). Economic education and a generative model misleaming and recovery. *J. Econ. Educ.*, 25(Winter), 23–33.

Kourilsky, M. and Wittrock, M. C. (1987). Verbal and graphical strategies in teaching economics. *Teaching Teacher Educ.*, 3(1), 1–12.

Kourilsky, M. and Wittrock, M. C. (1992). Generative teaching: an enhancement strategy for the learning of economics in cooperative groups. *Am. Educ. Res. J.*, 29(4), 861–876.

Kramarski, B. and Gutman, M. (2006). How can self-regulated learning be supported in mathematical e-learning environments? *J. Comput. Assist. Learn.*, 22, 24–33.

Laney, J. D. (1990). Generative teaching and learning of cost benefit analysis: an empirical investigation. *J. Res. Dev. Educ.*, 23(3), 136–144.

Lee, Y. and Nelson, D. W. (2005). Viewing or visualizing: which concept map strategy works best on problem-solving performance? *Br. J. Educ. Technol.*, 36(2), 193–203.

Linden, M. and Wittrock, M. C. (1981). The teaching of reading comprehension according to the model of generative learning. *Reading Res. Q.*, 17(1), 44–57.

Luria, A. (1973). *The Working Brain: An Introduction to Neuropsychology.* New York: Basic Books.

McKeague, C. A. and DiVesta, F. J. (1996). Strategy outcomes, learner activity, and learning outcomes: implications for instructional support of learning. *Educ. Technol. Res. Dev.*, 44(2), 29–42.

Peper, R. J. and Mayer, R. E. (1986). Generative effects of note taking during science lectures. *J. Educ. Psychol.*, 78(1), 34–38.

Pintrich, P. R. and De Groot, E. V. (1990). Motivational and self-regulated learning components of classroom academic performance. *J. Educ. Psychol.*, 82, 33–40.

Rickards, J. P. and August, G. J. (1975). Generative underlining strategies in prose recall. *J. Educ. Psychol.*, 67(6), 860–865.

Ritchie, D. and Volkl, C. (2000). Effectiveness of two generative learning strategies in the science classroom. *School Sci. Math.*, 100(2), 83–90.

Rummelhart, D. E. (1981). *Understanding Understanding* [technical report], ERIC Document 198-497. Washington, D.C.: National Science Foundation.

Rummelhart, D. E. and Ortony, A. (1977). The representation of knowledge in memory. In *Schooling and the Acquisition of Knowledge*, edited by R. C. Anderson, R. J. Spiro, and W. E. Montague, pp. 37–53. Mahwah, NJ: Lawrence Erlbaum Associates.

Sayeki, Y., Ueno, N., and Nagasaka, T. (1991). Mediation as a generative model for obtaining an area. *Learn. Instruct.*, 1, 229–242.

Shrager, L. and Mayer, R. E. (1989). Note-taking fosters generative learning strategies in novices. *J. Educ. Psychol.*, 81(2), 263–264.

Smith, K. and Dwyer, F. M. (1995). The effect of concept mapping strategies in facilitating student achievement. *Int. J. Instruct. Media*, 22(1), 25–31.

Stein, B. S. and Bransford, J. P. (1979). Constraints on effective elaboration: effects of precision and subject generation. *J. Verbal Learn. Verbal Behav.*, 18(6), 769–777.

Sutliff, R. (1986). Effect of adjunct postquestions on achievement. *J. Indust. Teacher Educ.*, 23(3), 45–54.

Taricani, E. (2002). Effect of the Level of Generativity in Concept Mapping with Knowledge of Correct Response Feedback on Learning, unpublished dissertation. University Park, PA: Pennsylvania State University.

Wang, C. X. (2003). The Instructional Effects of Prior Knowledge and Three Concept Mapping Strategies in Facilitation Achievement of Different Educational Objectives, unpublished dissertation. University Park, PA: Pennsylvania State University.

Wittrock, M. C. (1974a). A generative model of mathematics education. *J. Res. Math. Educ.*, 5(4), 181–196.*

Wittrock, M. C. (1974b). Learning as a generative process. *Educ. Psychol.*, 19(2), 87–95.*

Wittrock, M. C. (1985). Teaching learners generative strategies for enhancing reading comprehension. *Theory Pract.*, 24(2), 123–126.*

Wittrock, M. C. (1990). Generative processes of comprehension. *Educ. Psychol.*, 24, 345–376.*

Wittrock, M. C. (1991). Generative teaching of comprehension. *Elem. School J.*, 92, 167–182.*

Wittrock, M. C. (1992). Generative learning processes of the brain. *Educ. Psychol.*, 27(4), 531–541.*

Wittrock, M. C. and Alesandrini, K. (1990). Generation of summaries and analogies and analytic and holistic abilities. *Am. Educ. Res. J.*, 27, 489–502.

Wittrock, M. C. and Carter, J. (1975). Generative processing of hierarchically organized words. *Am. J. Psychol.*, 88(3), 489–501.

Woods, J. H. and Bernard, R. M. (1987). Improving older adults retention of text: a test of an instructional activity. *Educ. Gerontol.*, 13(2), 107–112.

Zimmerman, B. J. (1986). Development of self-regulated academic learning: which are the key subprocesses? *Contemp. Educ. Psychol.*, 16, 307–313.

Zimmerman, B. J. (1998). Developing self-fulfilling cycles of academic regulation: an analysis of exemplary instructional models. In *Self-Regulated Learning: From Teaching to Self-Reflective Practice*, edited by D. H. Schunk and B. J. Zimmerman, pp. 1–19. New York: Guilford Press.*

Zimmerman, B. J. and Schunk, D. H. (2001). *Self-Regulated Learning and Academic Achievement: Theoretical Perspectives*, 2nd ed. Mahwah, NJ: Lawrence Erlbaum Associates.

---

* Indicates a core reference.

# 11

# Feedback Strategies for Interactive Learning Tasks

*Susanne Narciss*
Learning and Instruction, Technische Universitaet Dresden, Germany

## CONTENTS

Susanne Narciss

## ABSTRACT

Modern information technologies increase the range of feedback strategies that can be implemented in computer-based learning environments; however, the design and implementation of feedback strategies are very complex tasks that are often based more on intuition than on psychologically sound design principles. The purpose of this chapter is to present theoretically and empirically based guidelines for the design and evaluation of feedback strategies. To this end, this chapter describes an interactive, two-feedback-loop model that explains core factors and effects of feedback in interactive instruction (Narciss, 2006). Based on these theoretical considerations, a multidimensional view of designing and evaluating multiples feedback strategies under multiple individual and situational conditions is presented. This multidimensional view integrates recommendations of prior research on elaborated feedback (Schimmel, 1988; Smith and Ragan, 1993), task analyses (Jonassen et al., 1999), error analyses (VanLehn, 1990), and tutoring techniques (McKendree, 1990; Merrill et al., 1992).

## KEYWORDS

*Cybernetics:* System theory concerned with the issues of regulation, order, and stability confronting us in the treatment of complex systems and processes.

*Feedback:* Output of a system that is fed back to the controller of the system as an input signal to regulate the system with regard to a reference value (cybernetic definition); post-response information that is provided to learners to inform them of their actual state of learning or performance (instructional context).

*Informative tutoring feedback:* Multiple-try feedback strategies providing elaborated feedback components that guide the learner toward successful task completion without offering immediately the correct response.

*Interactive learning task:* Tasks providing multiple response steps or tries and instructional components such as feedback, guiding questions, prompts, simulation facilities, and so on.

## INTRODUCTION

For almost a century researchers have investigated the factors and effects of feedback involved in instructional contexts; consequently, the body of feedback research is very large. This large body of feedback research has been examined and revisited extensively by Edna Mory in previous editions of this *Handbook* (Mory, 1996, 2004). As space is restricted, the body of feedback research that was included in these previous reviews will be not revisited in detail here, but the insights of this research will be organized and outlined on the basis of a conceptual framework for designing and evaluating feedback for interactive learning tasks. To introduce this conceptual framework, definitions of the term *feedback* will be discussed first.

## FEEDBACK IN INSTRUCTIONAL CONTEXTS: DEFINITION

The term *feedback* is a widely used concept in many technical and scientific domains (e.g., economics, electronics, biology, medicine, psychology). The concept of feedback is derived from cybernetics (Wiener, 1954), which is concerned with the control of systems—that is, with issues of regulation, order, and stability that arise in the context of complex systems and processes. In cybernetics, feedback refers to the output of a system that is fed back to the controller of the system as an input signal. This input/feedback signal closes the feedback loop and, in combination with an externally defined reference value, controls the system. In addition to the reference value and the feedback signal, the controller and the variable to be controlled are key elements. The controller stores the reference value, compares it with the current actual value, and, on the basis of this comparison, assesses what correction is required; hence, the effects of a feedback signal depend not only on this feedback signal but also all the other functional elements of the causal loop.

Since the development of Thorndike's (1913) law of effect, it has become well established in psychology that the consequences of a behavior may influence the rate and intensity of that behavior in future situations. In the domain of learning and instruction, feedback has been considered to be either a fundamental principle for efficient learning (Andre, 1997; Bilodeau, 1969; Bloom, 1976; Fitts, 1962; Taylor, 1987) or at least as an important element of instruction (Collies et al., 2001; Dick et al., 2001).

Some instructional researchers consider feedback in instructional contexts to be any type of information that is provided to learners after they have responded to a learning task (Wager and Wager, 1985). This notion of feedback is far too large because of the large variety of post-response information, and it does not include the idea that the information is presented with the purpose of allowing the learner to compare his or her actual outcome with a desired outcome to regulate or control the next attempt with this learning task. Experimental researchers thus use a more limited notion of feedback. They use the term *informative feedback* to refer to all post-response stimuli that are provided to a learner by an external source of information, according to experimentally defined rules and conditions, to inform the learner on his or her actual state of learning or performance (Annett, 1969; Bilodeau, 1969; Holding, 1965).

According to the cybernetic and experimental definitions, a general definition for feedback in instructional contexts might be as follows: *Feedback is all post-response information that is provided to a learner to inform the learner on his or her actual state of learning or performance.* In instructional contexts, this definition of feedback requires the differentiation among feedback presented by an external source of information and feedback provided by internal sources of information (i.e., information directly perceivable by the learner while task processing, such as proprioceptive information when performing a pointing task). This differentiation is particularly important from a methodological point of view; consequently, in early experimental feedback studies researchers tried to eliminate or control internal sources of feedback to investigate the effects of external feedback on learning and performance (for a review, see Bilodeau, 1969). The differentiation among external and internal feedback is also crucial if one investigates the effects of feedback on the basis of recent instructional models viewing the process of knowledge acquisition as a process of active knowledge construction and communication (Jonassen, 1999) or as a self-regulated learning process (Butler and Winne, 1995). This differentiation should be kept in mind when revisiting feedback research and considering feedback strategies.

External feedback may confirm or complement the internal feedback, or it may contradict the internal feedback. The latter case raises at least three questions:

- How do learners treat or cope with the discrepancy between internal and external feedback?
- What individual and situational factors contribute to a discrepancy between external and internal feedback?
- How can we design and evaluate feedback strategies that support learners regulating their learning process successfully if there is a discrepancy between internal and external feedback?

The first question has been addressed implicitly by the response certitude model of Kulhavy and his collaborators (Kulhavy and Stock, 1989; Kulhavy et al.,

1990a,b; Stock et al., 1992) and by the five-stage model of mindful feedback processing (Bangert-Drowns et al., 1991). Furthermore, it was explicitly the focus of Butler and Winne's theoretical synthesis regarding feedback and self-regulated learning (Butler and Winne, 1995). These models have been described and discussed in detail in Mory's prior reviews (Mory, 1996, 2004).

The second question has been answered indirectly as a result of meta-analyses that showed that external feedback effects are not always positive and thus tried to identify possible moderators for the efficiency of external feedback (Bangert-Drowns et al., 1991; Kluger and DeNisi, 1996). The insights of these meta-analyses are integrated in the conceptual framework elaborated below.

The third question, one of the most crucial questions for instructional design and practice, has been in part addressed by researchers developing and evaluating intelligent tutoring systems (ITSs). Detailed reviews of the insights of ITS research are provided by Anderson et al. (1995) and VanLehn et al. (2005); see also Chapters 24 and 27 in this *Handbook*. Core issues and insights from prior research with regard to this question are discussed below.

# A CONCEPTUAL FRAMEWORK FOR FEEDBACK IN INTERACTIVE INSTRUCTION

This section focuses on feedback for interactive (computer-based) learning tasks that is provided by an external source of information (e.g., an instructional program, a teacher) to contribute to the regulation of the learning process in such a way that learners acquire the knowledge and skills required to master these tasks. As elaborated in the next sections, internal feedback is considered an important factor for treating the information provided by the external feedback. Conceptualizing feedback as an instructional activity that aims at contributing to the regulation of a learning process makes it possible to use the core insights provided by models of instruction and self-regulated learning (Bloom, 1976; Boekaerts, 1996; Carroll, 1963) to analyze possible factors and effects of informative feedback. Instructional models are based on the assumption that the effects an instructional activity can have are determined by the quality of the instructional activity (e.g., scope, nature, and structure of the information provided and form of presentation), individual learning prerequisites (e.g., previous knowledge, metacognitive strategies, motivational dispositions, and strategies), and situational factors in the instructional setting

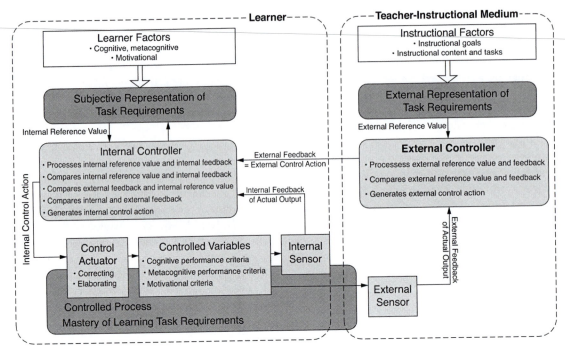

**Figure 11.1** Overview of the components of the ITFL model. (From Narciss, S., *Informatives tutorielles Feedback. Entwicklungs- und Evaluationsprinzipien auf der Basis instruktionspsychologischer Erkenntnisse (Informative Tutoring Feedback)*, Waxmann, Münster, 2006. With permission.)

(instructional goals, learning content, and tasks). The current conceptual framework links these issues with systems theory and attempts to integrate findings from systems theory with recommendations from prior research on elaborated feedback (Schimmel, 1988; Smith and Ragan, 1993), on task analysis (Jonassen et al., 1999), on error analysis (VanLehn, 1990), and on tutoring techniques (Anderson et al., 1995; McKendree, 1990; Merrill et al., 1992; VanLehn et al., 2005).

## Basic Assumptions

The basic components of a generic feedback loop serve as the starting point for formulating a feedback model with two interacting feedback loops: the interactive, two-feedback-loop (ITFL) model:

- Identification or definition of the variables that should be controlled
- Continuous measurement of these controlled variables by a sensor
- Feedback of the actual values of the controlled variables to a controller
- Reference value for each controlled variable that is predefined and stored in the controller
- Comparison of the actual values of the controlled variables with (predefined) reference values by the controller

*Note:* If there is a discrepancy between the actual and the reference value, the controller must transform this discrepancy into a control action.

- Transmission of this control action to a control element (control actuator)
- Execution of the control action by a control actuator

According to systems theory, the control actuator that carries out the control actions, the controlled variables, and a sensor that measures the controlled variable are key elements of the controlled process. To regulate the controlled process, the controller requires the reference value, the actual value provided by feedback, and comparison and transformation procedures for generating the control actions.

In the ITFL model, the controlled process is defined as the carrying out of learning tasks or the mastering of the demands associated with these tasks. Building on models of self-regulated learning (Boekaerts, 1996) as well as the approach of Butler and Winne (1995), this model distinguishes among cognitive, motivational, and metacognitive demands (see Figure 11.1). Quantifiable controlled variables for these criteria could include carefully defined and operationalized cognitive, metacognitive, or motivational indicators of mastery of particular task requirements.

When regulatory paradigms from systems theory are applied to an instructional context containing external feedback, two interacting feedback loops must be considered: (1) an internal feedback loop that processes internal feedback, or the actual values to which the learner has direct access (e.g., confidence in answers, perceived effort); and (2) an external feedback loop that processes the actual values determined by the learning medium (e.g., the instructor, learning program, experimenter).

A distinction between external and internal feedback loops means that it is also necessary to differentiate between the following elements:

- *Sensors*—Internal and external feedback loops require a diagnostic component that registers the actual values of the controlled variables.
- *Reference values*—Control of internal and external feedback loops can only be carried out on the basis of relevant reference values. In the ITFL model, it is assumed that internal reference values are generated on the basis of a subjective representation of the demands of learning tasks, whereas external reference values are based on an external representation of these demands. Subjective task representations are mainly governed by individual prerequisites such as existing knowledge, metacognitive and motivational strategies, and individual learning goals. External representations of task demands are closely related to the features of an instructional context, particularly to the specific instructional goals.
- *Controller*—For the actual values registered by the internal and external sensors to be processed, each requires a component in which reference and actual values can be compared; thus, both external and internal controllers in which this process can be carried out are needed.

In an instructional context that provides external informative feedback, the differentiations made in the ITFL model lead to the following assumptions regarding the interaction between internal and external feedback loops:

- The starting points for internal and external regulatory processes are the relevant controlled variables for the particular controlled process (i.e., mastery of learning task requirements).

- The actual value of the controlled variable or variables is registered by both the learner and by an external actor such as an instructor or a computer-based instructional system.
- External actual values are initially processed externally in the external controller of the teaching medium. The external reference value, the comparison between the reference value and the actual value, and the externally specified rules for calculating the correction value determine the initial value of the external controller. This initial value, which in systems theory would be referred to as an *external correction variable*, is fed to the internal controller as external feedback.
- This external feedback is processed in the internal controller along with the internal actual value (i.e., internal feedback). This means that several comparisons must be carried out by the internal controller. These include comparisons between:
  - Internally measured actual value (internal feedback) and internal reference value
  - External feedback and internal feedback
  - External feedback and internal reference value
- From these comparison processes a correction variable (i.e., an internal correction variable) must be generated. The learner's main task in this case is to locate the source of any discrepancies that are detected between these various values. Such discrepancies can occur when, for example, internal or external sensors register feedback values inaccurately, the quality of internal or external feedback is poor, or the subjective task representation is incorrect or imprecise and thus leads to incorrect reference values. The results of this causal analysis are important for calculating the internal correction variable. This means that the internal correction variable is the result of a number of internal processing procedures.
- The internal correction variable is channeled to the first stage of the controlled process— the control element—where it serves as the basis for selection and activation of corrective measures. These corrective measures can in turn have an impact on the controlled variables.

Susanne Narciss

## Factors Affecting the Efficiency of External Feedback

The assumptions of the ITFL model lead to the conclusion that the efficient regulation of task processing with external feedback may be affected by factors of both the internal and the external feedback loops. Both feedback loops contribute to the regulation of the same controlled process, which is characterized by the requirements of the learning tasks.

### Requirements of Learning Tasks and Instructional Objectives

As mentioned earlier, the starting point for both feedback loops is the controlled process, which can be more or less complex depending on the requirements of the learning tasks and the instructional objectives. For a system to be regulated successfully, it is crucial that its controlled process be described carefully and precisely. At the same time, it is necessary to define which variables will serve as controlled variables that will be measured and regulated, how these are to be measured, and the procedures through which corrections are to be carried out. In instructional contexts, this involves initially analyzing exactly what requirements are associated with the instructional content, goals, and tasks. Moreover, to select corrective measures for the regulation of controlled variables, the errors and difficulties that could arise in connection with mastering task requirements must also be identified, as well as the information and strategies that are necessary to eliminate these errors or difficulties.

Instructional content, goals, and tasks may be more or less complex concerning their requirements. Bloom's revised version of the taxonomy of learning objectives may serve as a basis for categorizing task requirements (Anderson et al., 2001). Analyzing learning task requirements on the basis of this taxonomy makes it clear that it is more difficult to identify precisely the content-related, cognitive, metacognitive, and motivational requirements for complex tasks (i.e., those that require higher order, content-related knowledge or operations) than for simple tasks. As a consequence, one may assume that the internal and external feedback loops might function less efficiently for complex learning tasks. The notion that task complexity affects the internal feedback loop was, for example, identified in Mory's studies, which aimed at generalizing Kulhavy and Stock's model of response certitude (Mory, 1994, 1996, 2004). Mory found that for higher order learning tasks, students' response certitude could not be used as a reliable measure for adapting feedback, because students were not able to assess their answers to these tasks correctly (in terms of the ITFL model, they were not able to generate a reliable internal feedback).

This assumption is also reflected in many studies on elaborated feedback that were conducted to investigate the hypothesis that elaborated feedback is more effective with more complex tasks; however, results of these studies are rather mixed (see reviews by Azevedo and Bernard, 1995; Bangert-Drowns et al., 1991; Mory, 1996, 2004). Yet, feedback studies that developed elaborated feedback on the basis of thorough analyses of task requirements generally found the developed elaborated feedback types to be superior to simple outcome feedback (Birenbaum and Tatsuoka, 1987; Nagata, 1993, 1997; Nagata and Swisher, 1995; Narciss, 2004, 2006; Narciss and Huth, 2004, 2006). In some studies, however, with very complex and difficult tasks or with serious errors, elaborated feedback was not efficient even if it was developed on the basis of task analyses (Birenbaum and Tatsuoka, 1987; Clariana and Lee, 2001; Nagata, 1997).

### Internal Loop Factors: Prior Knowledge, Cognitive, Metacognitive, and Motivational Skills

According to the ITFL model, the learner's representation of task requirements, the learner's ability to assess his or her responses (quality of the internal sensor), the learner's abilities and strategies with regard to analyzing and comparing internal and external information and identifying corrective actions (quality of the internal controller), and, finally, the learner's abilities and motivation in applying these corrective actions (quality of the control actuator) are core factors contributing to the efficiency of the internal feedback loop. All internal factors influence the external feedback loop because the two loops interact.

#### Subjective Task Representation: Prior Knowledge

The starting point for processes in the internal controller is a precise definition of reference values of controlled variables. These reference values are generated on the basis of how learners understand and represent the requirements of the learning tasks. Meaningful reference values can only be generated if the subjective representation of task requirements is adequate. Whether learners are able to represent task requirements adequately and precisely depends on the complexity of these requirements but also on individual factors such as prior knowledge, metacognitive knowledge, and strategies and motivation. How much individual difference in subjective task representations affects the impact of feedback on learning is an interesting question for future research.

## Learners' Self-Assessment Skills

Comparing the reference values with the actual values of controlled variables yields meaningful information only if the actual values of the controlled variables are determined accurately. In the internal loop, this depends a great deal on learners' abilities or skills in assessing their responses and performance (Mory, 1996, 2004). Learners must identify indicators for each task requirement that can help them evaluate the extent to which the task requirements are fulfilled. How external feedback may support the acquisition of self-assessment skills is another interesting issue for future research.

## Learners' Skills and Strategies in Information Processing

To generate an appropriate control action, learners must compare the internal and external feedback, the internal feedback and reference values, and the external feedback and the internal reference values. As discussed in the five-stage model of mindful feedback processing (Bangert-Drowns et al., 1991) and in Butler and Winne's (1995) synthesis on feedback and self-regulated learning, many individual factors may affect how learners process these informational components, particularly when discrepancies exist between the different components.

## Learners' Will and Skills in Overcoming Errors and Obstacles

As shown in studies on feedback seeking, even the most sophisticated feedback is useless if learners do not attend to it (Aleven et al., 2003; Narciss et al., 2004) or are not willing to invest time and effort in error correction. In addition to having the will, students also need the skills necessary to fulfill the requirements related to error correction. Butler and Winne (1995) derived six maladaptive ways of feedback seeking and processing from Chinn and Brewer's (1993) work on how misconceptions may hinder conceptual change: Students may (1) ignore the external feedback, (2) reject the external feedback, (3) judge the external feedback irrelevant, (4) consider external and internal feedback to be unrelated, (5) reinterpret external feedback to make it conform to the internal feedback, or (6) make superficial rather than fundamental changes to their knowledge or beliefs. In all these cases, the effect of the external feedback will be small.

## External Loop Factors: Instructional Goals, Diagnostic Procedures, Feedback Quality

In addition to these internal loop factors, the ITFL model attracts attention to external loop factors that might affect the efficiency of both feedback loops.

These include the external representation of task requirements related to the instructional goals; the accuracy of the diagnostic procedures assessing learners' responses (equal to the quality of the external sensor); the teaching medium abilities and strategies with regard to analyzing learners' responses—namely, errors—and identifying corrective actions with regard to these errors (quality of the external controller); and, finally, the teaching medium's ability in communicating these corrective actions (equal to the quality of the external feedback).

## External Representation of Task Requirements and Instructional Goals

The starting point for processes in the external controller is a precise definition of reference values of controlled variables. In the external loop, these reference values are generated on the basis of how the instructional medium (e.g., teacher, computer-based learning environment) represents the requirements of the learning tasks. As in the internal loop, meaningful reference values can only be generated if the representation of task requirements is adequate. This means that learning goals must be operationalized in such a way that valid and reliably verifiable learning outcomes can be defined in the form of reference values. As mentioned above, this might be more difficult for more complex task requirements.

## Accuracy of Diagnostic Procedures

In the external loop, the controlled variables must also be diagnosed accurately to make the comparison between the reference values with the actual values of controlled variables meaningful. This, in turn, means that the indicators appropriate for measuring different levels of mastery in a valid and reliable way must be determined. How challenging an accurate diagnosis might be was elicited in a recent study of Chi et al. (2004) on the accuracy of human tutors. Chi and her colleagues found that tutors were only able to assess students' understanding from their own perspective, and they were not able to diagnose students' alternative understanding from the perspective of the students' knowledge.

## Quality of External Data Processing and Feedback Design

If a discrepancy between the actual and reference values of controlled variables is detected, a correction variable must be defined. A key issue here is how well the external controller (i.e., the learning medium) is able to transform this discrepancy value into a correction variable that has a high level of information relevant to mastering the task requirements. Especially with difficult and complex learning tasks, a series of transformations may be necessary so learners can obtain information about the external correction variable (external feedback) that they can use to correct errors or overcome obstacles. The starting point for the necessary transformational steps is precise knowledge of the controlled process. It is necessary to know which factors, in the sense of controlled variables, are responsible for the system's performance and thus must be addressed by the correction variable—that is, the external feedback.

## DESIGNING AND EVALUATING (TUTORING) FEEDBACK

Researchers used a large variety of feedback types. Widely used feedback types include:

- *Knowledge of performance* (KP) provides learners with a summative feedback after they have responded to a set of tasks. This feedback contains information on the achieved performance level for this set of tasks (e.g., percentage of correctly solved tasks).
- *Knowledge of result/response* (KR) provides learners with information on the correctness of their actual response (e.g., correct/incorrect).
- *Knowledge of the correct response* (KCR) provides the correct answer to the given task.
- *Answer-until-correct* (AUC) *feedback* provides KR and offers the opportunity of further tries with the same task until the task is answered correctly.
- *Multiple-try feedback* (MTF) provides KR and offers the opportunity of a limited number of further tries with the same task.
- *Elaborated feedback* (EF) provides additional information besides KR or KCR.

Complex elaborated feedback exists in multiple forms and is thus related to a large if not fuzzy set of meanings. Several authors have attempted to classify the numerous feedback types (Dempsey et al., 1993; Kulhavy and Stock, 1989; Mason and Bruning, 2001; Schimmel, 1988). There is some congruency with regard to classifying simple feedback types such as KR or KCR, even though these feedback types are sometimes denoted by different terms (e.g., knowledge of result, confirmation feedback, simple verification feedback, knowledge of the correct answer/response).

The various classifications differ, however, in how they organize the different types of elaborated feedback: Kulhavy and Stock (1989) differentiate among *task-specific* elaborated information, which in cases of multiple-choice tasks is considered to be knowledge of the correct response; *instruction-based* elaborated information (e.g., hints to the section of the instructional text that is relevant for answering the task); and *extra-instructional* elaborated information, which goes beyond the instructional text and might, for example, address metacognitive strategies. Mason and Bruning (2001) differentiate among the following elaborated feedback components: *topic-contingent* (provides item verification and general information concerning the topic), *response-contingent* (provides KR, KCR, and explanations as to why answers are correct or incorrect), *bug-related* (provides KR and error-specific information) (Schimmel, 1988), and *attribute isolation* (provides KR and highlights the relevant attributes of the concept) (Merrill, 1987).

Comparing these classifications reveals that feedback types can vary in functional, content-related, and formal characteristics. One may conclude that the nature and quality of an external feedback message is determined by at least three facets of feedback: (1) functional aspects related to instructional objectives (e.g., cognitive functions such as promoting information processing, motivational functions such as reinforcing correct responses or sustaining effort and persistence); (2) semantic aspects related to the content of the feedback message; and (3) formal and technical aspects related to the presentation of the feedback message (e.g., frequency, timing, mode, amount, form) (Narciss, 2006; Narciss and Huth, 2004).

The purposes of the following sections are (1) to present principles for selecting and specifying the functional, content-related, and formal dimensions of elaborated feedback components that can be implemented in a tutoring feedback algorithm, and (2) to outline implications for future feedback research.

### Selecting and Specifying the Functions of External Feedback

Different theoretical frameworks use different types of feedback and attribute different functions to feedback in learning situations. From a behavioral viewpoint, feedback is considered to reinforce correct responses. In behavioral learning contexts, the focus of interest is therefore more on formal and technical feedback characteristics such as frequency and delay than on the complexity of the feedback contents; hence, behavioral studies use outcome-related feedback types such as knowledge of result or knowledge of the correct

**TABLE 11.1**
**Feedback Functions in Four Sources**

| Cusella (1987) | Sales (1993) | Wager and Mory (1993) | Butler and Winne (1995) |
|---|---|---|---|
| Reinforcing | Stimulating | Confirming | Confirming |
| Informing | Informing | Informing | Informing |
| Indicating | Guiding | Indicating | Indicating |
| Motivating | Motivating | Motivating | Correcting |
| Regulating | Regulating | Correcting | Making suggestions |
| Instructing | Instructing | Instructing | Completing knowledge |
| | Assessing | Assessing | Differentiating |
| | Advising | | Restructuring |

response (for a review, see Kulik and Kulik, 1988). From a cognitive viewpoint, feedback is considered a source of information necessary for the correction of incorrect responses (Anderson et al., 1971; Kulhavy and Stock, 1989). The question of which type of elaborated feedback information is most efficient is of major interest in cognitive feedback studies; however, in most of these studies even elaborated informative feedback has only been conceptualized as seeking to confirm or change a learner's domain knowledge. Feedback models that view feedback in the context of self-regulated learning theorize that the most important function of feedback is tutoring or guiding the learner to regulate the learning process successfully (Butler and Winne, 1995).

This brief summary of prior research reveals that feedback can affect the learning process at various levels and can therefore have numerous different functions. For this reason, a number of authors have made more subtle distinctions (Butler and Winne, 1995; Cusella, 1987; Sales, 1993; Wager and Mory, 1993) (see Table 11.1). A comparison of these differentiated treatments of feedback functions reveals that all of these authors advocate feedback as an acknowledging or reinforcing function, an informing function, and some form of guiding or steering function. Moreover, all of them have postulated a regulatory or correcting function for feedback. In addition, Cusella (1987), Sales (1993), and Wager and Mory (1993) drew attention to the motivational and instructional function of feedback. Butler and Winne (1995) described at least three subfunctions of the instructing function (tuning or completing, differentiating, and restructuring). In addition, these authors have pointed out that feedback can activate metacognitive processes such as monitoring or information seeking.

If external informative feedback is viewed from the standpoint of the current ITFL model, it becomes clear that as a general rule multiple feedback functions

come into play simultaneously, according to how the controlled and command variables are defined. On the basis of the models of good information processors (Pressley, 1986), intelligent novices (Mathan and Koedinger, 2005), and self-directed learning (Boekaerts, 1996), possible feedback functions can be defined from the cognitive, metacognitive, and motivational standpoints. Because finer differentiations of feedback functions make it possible to work out which information will be useful in which settings, careful selection and specification of the intended feedback functions provide the basis for designing tutorial feedback.

*Cognitive Functions*

In the case of complex tasks, incorrect answers and solutions can occur for widely varying reasons (Van-Lehn, 1990). The content-related, procedural, or strategic knowledge elements that a learner needs to arrive at a correct solution may be lacking, erroneous, or imprecise. The necessary knowledge elements may also be incorrectly linked or the conditions for their use incorrect or ill-defined. Feedback can offer information on all of these aspects. A distinction can be made between the following cognitive feedback functions in connection with incorrect responses:

- An informative function in cases where the number, location, and type of error or reason for the error are unknown
- A completion function in cases where the error is attributable to lack of content-related, procedural, or strategic knowledge and the feedback provides information on the missing knowledge
- A corrective function in cases where the error is attributable to erroneous content or erroneous procedural or strategic elements and the feedback provides information that can be used to correct the erroneous elements
- A differentiation function in cases where the error is attributable to imprecise content-related, procedural, or strategic knowledge elements and the feedback provides information that allows for clarification of the imprecise elements
- A restructuring function in cases where the error is attributable to erroneous connections between content, procedural, or strategic elements and the feedback provides information that can be used to restructure these incorrectly connected elements

## *Metacognitive Functions*

According to Butler and Winne (1995), external feedback can have numerous metacognitive functions apart from those listed in Table 11.1; for example, external feedback can address metacognitive strategies and their deployment options, provide criteria for monitoring and evaluating goals, or motivate learners to generate their own monitoring related information. In addition, it can serve as a basis for assessing the suitability of solution strategies employed or of error search and correction strategies; hence, at least the following feedback functions can be differentiated from each other with regard to mastery of metacognitive requirements:

- An informative function in cases where metacognitive strategies or the conditions for their use are unknown and feedback provides information about metacognitive strategies
- A specification function in cases where feedback provides criteria for monitoring goals or where conditions for the use of specific solution strategies or metacognitive strategies are specified
- A corrective function in cases where errors have arisen in the use of metacognitive strategies and the feedback provides information that can be used to correct erroneous strategies
- A guiding function in cases where learners are encouraged (e.g., through leading questions) to generate their own criteria for monitoring or evaluation or to assess the suitability of their own solution strategies or other actions

Recent studies on the effects of feedback addressing metacognitive processes and strategies have provided mixed results (Roll et al., 2006; van den Boom et al., 2004).

## *Motivational Functions*

Even though feedback has been assigned an important role for both achievement and motivation (Hoska, 1993; Kluger and DeNisi, 1996; Mory, 1996), most studies on external informative feedback have focused on learner achievement and neglected the impact of feedback on motivation. At the motivational level, however, it is crucial, despite errors and the resulting negative effect, to maintain the level of effort, persistence, and intensity of task processing. Many theories of motivation suggest that perceived values of task processing and self-perceptions of competence are crucial factors in learners' motivation (Pintrich, 2003).

Generally, all types of feedback contain an evaluative feedback component (i.e., information regarding the correctness or quality of the solution) that reveals success or failure in task processing. Feedback thus has an impact on the attainment value of the task that might result in more effort or strategy investment and might affect performance. Symonds and Chase (1929) and Brown (1932) reported supportive results for this motivational effect of feedback. Recently, a study of Vollmeyer and Rheinberg (2005) revealed that this impact of feedback is present even if feedback is merely announced. Moreover, Ulicsak (2004) found that students spent more time reflecting group activities if they believed that the instructional system was observing them and would provide feedback.

If feedback provides additional elaborated components that guide learners to successful task completion without immediately providing knowledge of the correct response, it offers mastery experiences that can be linked to personal causation. As such, mastery experiences are considered the most important source for developing a positive self-efficacy—in other words, positive perceptions of competence (Bandura, 1997; Usher and Pajares, 2006). Feedback may also affect how the difficulty of such tasks, the prospects of success, and the attributions of success or failure are assessed in future situations; hence, at least the following basic motivational functions should be considered when evaluating informative elaborated feedback:

- An incentive function, in that feedback renders the results of task processing visible
- A task facilitation function to contribute information for overcoming task difficulties
- A self-efficacy enhancing function, if it provides information that makes it possible to master tasks successfully, even if errors are committed or difficulties arise
- A reattribution function, if it provides information that contributes to mastery experiences that can be linked to personal causation

In addition to informative elaborated feedback types, a variety of motivational elaborated feedback types has been investigated by motivational researchers. Such motivational feedback types include reattribution feedback (Dresel and Ziegler, 2006; Schunk, 1983); mastery-oriented feedback, which makes learner's progress visible (Schunk and Rice, 1993); and task vs. competence feedback (Sansone, 1986,

**TABLE 11.2**
**Content-Related Classification of Feedback Components**

| Category | Examples |
|---|---|
| Knowledge of performance (KP) | 15 of 20 correct; 85% correct |
| Knowledge of result/response (KR) | Correct/incorrect |
| Knowledge of the correct results (KCR) | Description/indication of the correct response |
| *Elaborated concepts* | |
| Knowledge about task constraints (KTC) | Hints/explanations on type of task |
| | Hints/explanations on task-processing rules |
| | Hints/explanations on subtasks |
| | Hints/explanations on task requirements |
| Knowledge about concepts (KC) | Hints/explanations on technical terms |
| | Examples illustrating the concept |
| | Hints/explanations on the conceptual context |
| | Hints/explanations on concept attributes |
| | Attribute-isolation examples |
| Knowledge about mistakes (KM) | Number of mistakes |
| | Location of mistakes |
| | Hints/explanations on type of errors |
| | Hints/explanations on sources of errors |
| Knowledge about how to proceed (KH) | Bug-related hints for error correction |
| | Hints/explanations on task-specific strategies |
| | Hints/explanations on task-processing steps |
| | Guiding questions |
| | Worked-out examples |
| Knowledge about metacognition (KMC) | Hints/explanations on metacognitive strategies |
| | Metacognitive guiding questions |

*Source:* Narciss, S., *Informatives tutorielles Feedback. Entwicklungs- und Evaluationsprinzipien auf der Basis instruktionspsychologischer Erkenntnisse (Informative Tutoring Feedback)*, Waxmann, Münster, 2006. With permission.

1989; Senko and Harackiewicz, 2005). In summary, elaborated motivational feedback components that had a positive impact on learners' motivation (namely, on perceptions of competence): (1) stressed the relation between effort, ability, and success; (2) made progress visible; (3) provided task information rather than performance information; or (4) elicited goal discrepancy.

## Selecting and Specifying the Content of Feedback Elements

In general, the content of a feedback message may consist of two components (Kulhavy and Stock, 1989). The first component, the *evaluative* or, in Kulhavy's terms, the *verification* component, relates to the learning outcome and indicates the performance level achieved (e.g., correct/incorrect response, percentage of correct answers, and distance to the learning criterion). This component is attributed a controlling function (Keller, 1983). The second component, the *informational* component, consists of additional information relating to the topic, the task, errors, or solutions. Com-

bining the evaluation and information component of feedback might result in a large variety of feedback contents.

### *Overview on Elaborated Feedback Components*

Table 11.2 presents a content-related classification of feedback components that provides a structured overview of simple and elaborated feedback components by organizing the components with regard to which aspect of the instructional context is addressed. This content-related classification assumes that elaborated information might address: (1) task rules, task constraints, and task requirements; (2) conceptual knowledge; (3) errors or mistakes; (4) procedural knowledge; and (5) metacognitive knowledge. Five categories of elaborated feedback components can thus be defined:

- Elaborated components that provide information on task rules, task constraints, and task requirements are linked by the category of *knowledge on task constraints* (KTC).

- Elaborated components that provide information on conceptual knowledge relevant for task processing are linked by the category of *knowledge about concepts* (KC).
- Elaborated components that provide information on errors or mistakes are linked with the category of *knowledge about mistakes* (KM).
- Elaborated components that provide information on procedural knowledge relevant for task processing are linked by the category *knowledge on how to proceed* or, briefly, *know-how* (KH).
- Elaborated components that provide information on metacognitive knowledge are linked by the category *knowledge on metacognition* (KMC).

To design feedback algorithms with elaborated components, several simple and elaborated feedback components can be combined. In most of the feedback studies, elaborated feedback was designed by combining knowledge of the correct result or knowledge of the result with elaborated components such as explanations of errors or to correct responses.

### Cognitive Task and Error Analyses

Narciss and Huth (2004) derived the steps necessary to select and specify the feedback content from knowledge about cognitive task analysis and error analysis (for a detailed description, see Jonassen et al., 1999; VanLehn, 1990). Similar steps were proposed by VanLehn and his collaborators (2005) and by Rittle-Johnson and Koedinger (2005) based on insights and experiences in developing intelligent tutoring systems.

The first step consists of the selection and specification of instructional objectives (e.g., acquisition of a knowledge domain, mastery of learning tasks, literacy in the given context). The starting point of this step is the curriculum and its objectives, which in general have to be specified to obtain explicit, concrete, and measurable learning outcomes. The revised version of Bloom's taxonomy of educational objectives offers a well-founded framework for this specification of learning objectives (Anderson et al., 2001). The specified concrete learning outcomes provide the basis for the selection of the feedback functions, content, and forms.

Feedback is presented after the accomplishment of learning tasks; consequently, learning tasks are especially relevant to the design of feedback. The second step is, therefore, to select typical learning tasks and match them to the required learning outcomes.

The third step consists of analyzing the requirements for each type of task. The aim of these task analyses is to identify: (1) domain-specific knowledge items (e.g., facts, concepts, events, rules, models, theories); (2) cognitive operations related to these items (e.g., remember, transform, classify, argue, infer); and (3) cognitive and metacognitive skills involved in the mastery of the selected learning tasks. The informative components of a feedback message can refer to each of these aspects of a learning task; hence, the results of these task analyses provide an overview of both task requirements and possible informative components that can be implemented in a feedback message.

As mentioned above, from a cognitive and from a self-regulated learning viewpoint, elaborated or informative feedback is considered a necessary source of information, especially if the learner encounters obstacles or proceeds incorrectly. A next important step for the design of informative feedback is therefore to describe typical errors and typical incorrect steps. Furthermore, it is necessary to identify misconceptions and incorrect or inefficient strategies that can be attributed to the described errors (Crippen and Brooks, 2005; Narciss and Huth, 2004, 2006; Van-Lehn, 1990).

The steps described above are essential prerequisites for the selection and specification of helpful information. The results of the task and error analyses provide information that is necessary to select those informative components that match the task requirements. If the major function of the feedback message is tutoring learners to master the given learning tasks and the related requirements, then feedback should not immediately provide the correct response or explain the correct strategy. This information should only be offered if the learners do not succeed otherwise; hence, offering adequate tutoring when learners encounter obstacles requires providing information that gives knowledge on how to proceed without presenting knowledge of the correct response. Table 11.2 presents examples of such informative tutoring feedback components.

Smith and Ragan (1993) recommended that the content should be tailored to the type of learning tasks; however, it should be kept in mind that studies comparing the efficiency of different types of information with regard to various learning tasks reported rather mixed results (for a detailed review, see Mory, 1996, 2004). Furthermore, with the development of new paradigms for learning and instruction, the question of which knowledge should be addressed by the feedback content is getting more and more complex.

## Selecting and Specifying the Form and Mode of Feedback Presentation

Feedback types vary not only in their content-related aspects but also in formal and technical aspects relevant for feedback presentation. Using formal criteria (e.g., timing, frequency), Holding (1965) differentiated, for example, 32 different types of feedback. The interactive capabilities of modern information technology increase the range of feedback strategies that can be implemented efficiently in computer-based instruction (Hannafin et al., 1993). Using the interactive capabilities of modern information technology, it is, for example, possible to combine elaborated feedback, tutoring, and mastery learning strategies to design *informative tutoring feedback*. The term *informative tutoring feedback* (ITF) refers to feedback strategies that provide elaborated feedback components to guide the learner toward successful task completion. The focus of this elaborated information is on tutoring students to detect errors, overcome obstacles, and apply more efficient strategies for solving the learning tasks. In contrast to elaborated feedback types, which provide learners with immediate knowledge of the correct response and additional information, ITF components are presented without immediate knowledge of the correct response. Additionally, ITF strategies offer the opportunity to apply the feedback information on another try (Narciss, 2006). These ITF strategies are rooted in studies on tutoring activities (McKendree, 1990; Merrill et al., 1992, 1995). The following sections present an overview on important aspects of feedback that must be taken into consideration when choosing the form and mode of feedback presentation.

### *Immediate vs. Delayed Feedback Timing*

An aspect of feedback that received much attention in feedback research is the *timing* of the feedback (Dempsey and Wager, 1988; for a review, see Kulik and Kulik, 1988). From Skinner's operant learning theory, one might assume that the feedback should be provided soon after the response; however, experimental studies that used paradigms similar to those of studies testing the effects of blocked or massed vs. distributed practice found that delaying feedback can be beneficial, especially for retention in a delayed post-test. This effect is referred to as the *delay retention effect* (Brackbill et al., 1963). Kulhavy and Anderson (1972) explained the delay retention effect by an interference perseveration hypothesis, which suggests that immediate feedback might proactively interfere with the incorrect response, and this interference might hinder the acquisition of the correct response. Delayed feedback is not related to proactive interference, because the incorrect response is not present and probably forgotten. Research based on the interference perseveration hypothesis provided mixed results (Kulhavy and Anderson, 1972; Kulhavy and Stock, 1989; Markowotz and Renner, 1966; Peek and Tillema, 1978; Rankin and Trepper, 1978; Schroth and Lund, 1993; Sturges, 1969, 1972, 1978; Surber and Anderson, 1975). Kulik and Kulik (1988) proposed a dual-trace information-processing explanation for the delay retention effect. They pointed out that, with immediate feedback, learners only have one trial, whereas with delayed feedback they have two separate trials with an item. In the case of memorization, two separate trials are better than one, and delayed feedback might be superior to immediate feedback.

Clariana has developed a connectionist description of feedback timing to better explain the existing results and to provide a basis for new insights on immediate and delayed feedback (Clariana, 1999; Clariana et al., 2000). With regard to the potential effects of immediate vs. delayed feedback, Clariana's model proposes a strengthening effect for incorrect responses with delayed feedback, whereas immediate feedback weakens the association between incorrect responses and items. These hypotheses were confirmed by a study of Clariana and Koul (2005); yet, the superiority of delayed feedback (i.e., the delay retention effect) was only found in experimental situations with test items, and it was not found in applied studies (Kulik and Kulik, 1988). Because researchers used a variety of immediate and delayed feedback types—item per item vs. end of session; directly after the session vs. hours or days after session (Dempsey and Wager, 1988)—Mory (2004, p. 256) stated that the field of research on feedback timing is "muddied."

Recently, Mathan and Koedinger (2005) reconsidered the debate on feedback timing from a metacognitive perspective. They suggested that the question of when to provide feedback following an error has to be answered on the basis of a model of desired performance. If this model includes metacognitive skills for error detection and correction, then feedback providing knowledge of the correct response should not be offered immediately, because it does not foster the acquisition of these skills. In contrast, feedback offering knowledge of the result together with knowledge about mistakes implemented in a multiple-try algorithm that requires students to analyze their erroneous responses and to identify error correction steps can be provided immediately (see, for example, Mathan and Koedinger, 2005; Moreno and Valdez, 2005; Narciss and Huth, 2006).

## Single-Try vs. Multiple-Try: Simultaneous vs. Sequential Presentation of Elaborated Feedback

A second formal aspect is related to the question of how many tries are offered to learners after they have received feedback. Many studies offer only a single try per item; that is, learners respond to an item, are provided with feedback, and do not have the opportunity to respond again to this item. Some studies, however, have offered multiple tries after providing feedback. Most of these studies use answer-until-correct (AUC) feedback (for a review, see Clariana, 1993). Clariana's review of 30 studies that compared single-try feedback types (immediate knowledge of result, immediate knowledge of the correct response, delayed feedback, no feedback) to multiple-try feedback/AUC found a superiority of all feedback types over no feedback but no differences between single-try and multiple-try feedback. In a more recent review, Clariana and Koul (2004) contrasted multiple-try feedback effects (AUC) for verbatim outcomes with higher order "more than verbatim" outcomes (i.e., drawing and labeling biological diagrams). This review revealed that AUC is less effective for verbatim outcomes but more effective for higher order outcomes (Clariana and Koul, 2005).

Multiple-try feedback types other than AUC can be developed if one considers a third formal aspect of feedback presentation: Complex elaborated feedback can be presented simultaneously (i.e., all information in one step) or sequentially (cumulatively or step by step). Most studies on complex elaborated feedback provide the elaborated information simultaneously with knowledge of the result or knowledge of the correct response (Kulhavy et al., 1985; Phye, 1979; Phye and Bender, 1989). However, only half of the studies utilizing this simultaneous presentation of elaborated feedback produced significant positive effects (Kulhavy and Stock, 1989; Mory, 1996, 2004).

In addition to these empirical findings on presenting complex elaborated feedback simultaneously, research on cognitive load in instructional contexts would suggest that a sequential presentation of complex elaborated feedback should be superior to a simultaneous presentation (Chandler and Sweller, 1992). Indeed, the few controlled experimental studies that have investigated the tutorial feedback types that present elaborated feedback components sequentially have reported positive effects (Albacete and VanLehn, 2000; Heift, 2004; Nagata, 1993; Nagata and Swisher, 1995; Narciss and Huth, 2006; VanLehn et al., 2005).

Because a sequential presentation of feedback components requires offering multiple tries with the same item, a direct comparison of the effects of simultaneous vs. sequential feedback presentations is very difficult if not impossible. An important issue for future research, however, would be addressing the question of how many feedback steps or cycles are effective under which individual and situational conditions.

## Adaptive vs. Nonadaptive Feedback Presentation

A fourth formal aspect of feedback presentation is whether the feedback is presented in an adaptive or a nonadaptive way. The adaptation issue is related at such questions as these:

- *Which learner characteristics are critical for adaptation?* Crucial characteristics that have been extensively addressed by feedback research and by most research on tutoring systems include the learner's prior knowledge or knowledge state (Albert and Lukas, 1999; Hancock et al., 1995a) and the learner's metacognitive state in general measured by the learner's response certitude (Hancock et al., 1992, 1995b; Mory, 1991, 1994). Other important characteristics that have received attention only in recent studies include the learner's motivation (e.g., self-efficacy) (Narciss, 2004), goal orientation (Senko and Harackiewicz, 2005), and metacognitive skills other than response certitude (Aleven et al., 2006).
- *Which task characteristics are critical for adaptation?* According to Sanz (2004), this question is sometimes neglected by instructional designers; however, adaptation may be more or less necessary for different tasks, and there might be critical task characteristics (i.e., specific task requirements) that can be used as indicators for deciding when and how much adaptation would be reasonable. In the algebra tutoring system Ms. Lindquist, the three feedback strategies are, for example, determined by the exercise and its structure (Heffernan, 2001).
- *How do we diagnose the individual characteristics in a reliable and valid way?* Several approaches to diagnosing learner characteristics have been investigated by researchers who are developing intelligent tutoring systems: manually authored finite-state machines (Koedinger et al., 2004); generative approaches, such as model tracing

(Anderson et al., 1995); evaluative approaches (Mitrovich et al., 2002); and decision theoretic approaches (Murray et al., 2004). Recently, several authors have suggested using observable data on students' activities to infer nonobservable learner characteristics (Kutay and Ho, 2005; Melis and Anders, 2005; Romero et al., 2005).

- *How do we adapt feedback to the critical situational and individual factors?* Adaptive feedback can be implemented in several ways. An approach used frequently in intelligent tutoring systems involves controlling the sequence, content, and instructional activities (program-controlled adaptation). A second type of adaptation is based on the idea that the learner has to take an active part in instruction and thus is presented with a choice of instructional activities (learner-controlled adaptation). Unfortunately, learners sometimes lack the metacognitive skills and motivation required to decide which instructional activities would be best for them (for reviews on the effects of learner- vs. program-controlled instruction, see Steinberg, 1977, 1989; see also Corbett and Anderson, 1990; Narciss et al., 2004). Recent studies and frameworks on adaptive feedback include metacognitive feedback components that should foster the acquisition of metacognitive skills (Aleven et al., 2006; Gouli et al., 2005). A third type of adaptation consists of combining program and learner control, which offers a variety of other possibilities for adapting feedback and raises new issues for future research (e.g., when and how to shift from program to learner control and *vice versa*).

## *Unimodal vs. Multimodal Feedback Presentation*

The capabilities of modern information technologies allow the presentation of feedback not only as written text but also as narrated text (Narciss and Huth, 2004, 2006) or as a static or dynamic graphic. Furthermore, feedback can be provided by animated agents (Moreno, 2004). When and how to apply the principles of multimedia learning derived from Mayer's theory of multimedia learning (Mayer, 2001) for the multimodal presentation of feedback have yet to be investigated.

## Implications for Evaluating (Tutoring) Feedback

The design principles outlined above show that external feedback, particularly informative tutorial feedback, is a multidimensional instructional measure. Moreover, the interactive, two-feedback-loop model described earlier suggests that the effects of external feedback occur through an interaction with the learner (i.e., with a complex information processing system). This in turn means that the effects of external feedback are not general but only emerge in specific situational and individual settings; for example, the amount of time it takes for errors to be eliminated with the help of external feedback depends on: (1) the individual characteristics of the learner; (2) the quality of the external feedback components; (3) the type, complexity, and difficulty of the tasks; and (4) the type of error. In highly skilled learners or for easy tasks or simple slips, for example, knowledge-of-result feedback alone is sufficient to yield a correct response the next time. In learners with a low level of skill, for very complex and difficult tasks, or in the case of serious errors, it is possible that even informative tutorial feedback may not be sufficient for mastering the high demands.

The effects of various feedback strategies also largely depend on how learners process and interpret the information provided. In addition to cognitive requirements (e.g., prior knowledge, strategic knowledge), individual motivational factors, such as self-efficacy and perceived task values, and individual metacognitive factors, such as monitoring competencies and strategies, play a role. To draw differentiated conclusions about the effects of various types of feedback, not only cognitive but also individual motivational and metacognitive factors and the nature of how individuals process the feedback should be controlled.

External feedback can contribute to changes that occur (1) during the treatment, (2) shortly after the treatment, or (3) long after the treatment; thus, evaluating the effects of various feedback strategies requires collecting data both during and after the treatment (Phye, 1991, 2001; Phye and Sanders, 1994). When investigating the effects of various types or strategies of external feedback, it should no longer be a question of which feedback type is the best but rather one of the following questions:

- Under which individual and situational conditions do which feedback components or strategies have high information value for learners?

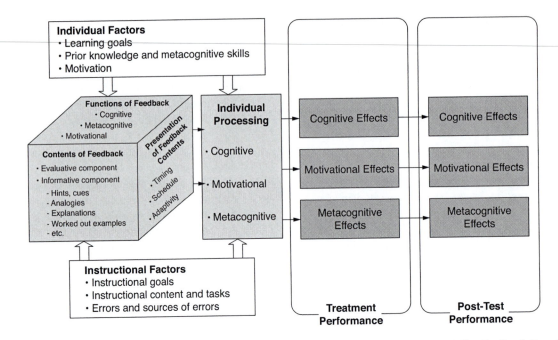

**Figure 11.2** Summary of factors and effects of external feedback. (From Narciss, S., *Informatives tutorielles Feedback. Entwicklungs- und Evaluationsprinzipien auf der Basis instruktionspsychologischer Erkenntnisse (Informative Tutoring Feedback)*, Waxmann, Münster, 2006. With permission.)

- Under these individual and situational conditions, what cognitive, metacognitive, and motivational effects do the various feedback components or strategies have?
- When are these effects expected to occur, and what is their expected duration?

Figure 11.2 summarizes these considerations regarding requirements for and the effects of various kinds of external feedback.

## REFERENCES

Albacete, P. and VanLehn, K. (2000). Evaluating the effectiveness of a cognitive tutor for fundamental physics concepts. In *Proc. of the 22nd Annual Meeting of the Cognitive Science Society*, August 13–15, Philadelphia, PA.

Albert, D. and Lukas, J. (1999). *Knowledge Spaces: Theories, Empirical Research, and Applications*. Mahwah, NJ: Lawrence Erlbaum Associates.

Aleven, V., Stahl, E., Schworm, S., Fischer, F., and Wallace, R. (2003). Help seeking and help design in interactive learning environments. *Rev. Educ. Psychol.*, 62, 148–156.*

Aleven, V., McLaren, B. M., Roll, I., and Koedinger, K. R. (2006). Toward computer-based tutoring: a model of help-seeking with a cognitive tutor. *Int. J. Artif. Intell. Educ.*, 16, 101–130.

Anderson, J. R., Corbett, A. T., Koedinger, K. R., and Pelletier, R. (1995). Cognitive tutors: lessons learned. *J. Learn. Sci.*, 4, 167–207.*

Anderson, L. W., Krathwohl, D. R., Airasian, P. W., Cruikshank, K. A., Mayer, R. E., Pintrich, P. R., Raths, J., and Wittrock, M. C. (2001). *A Taxonomy for Learning, Teaching, and Assessing: A Revision of Bloom's Taxonomy of Educational Objectives*. New York: Longman.

Anderson, R. C., Kulhavy, R. W., and Andre, T. (1971). Feedback procedures in programmed instruction. *J. Educ. Psychol.*, 62, 148–156.*

Andre, T. (1997). Selected microinstructional methods to facilitate knowledge construction: implications for instructional design. In *Instructional Design: International Perspectives*. Vol. 1. *Theory, Research, and Models*, edited by R. D. Tennyson and F. Schott, pp. 243–267. Mahwah, NJ: Lawrence Erlbaum Associates.

Annett, J. (1969). *Feedback and Human Behavior*. Oxford: Penguin Books.*

Azevedo, R. and Bernard, R. M. (1995). A meta-analysis of the effects of feedback in computer-based instruction. *J. Educ. Comput. Res.*, 13, 111–127.

Bandura, A. (1997). *Self-Efficacy: The Exercise of Control*. New York: Holt.

Bangert-Drowns, R. L., Kulik, C. C., Kulik, J. A., and Morgan, M. T. (1991). The instructional effect of feedback in test-like events. *Rev. Educ. Res.*, 61, 213–238.*

Bilodeau, E. A. (1969). *Principles of Skill Acquisition*. New York: Academic Press.*

Birenbaum, M. and Tatsuoka, K. (1987). Effects of 'on-line' test feedback on the seriousness of subsequent errors. *J. Educ. Meas.*, 24, 145–155.

Bloom, B. (1976). *Human Characteristics and School Learning*. New York: McGraw–Hill.

Boekaerts, M. (1996). Self-regulated learning at the junction of cognition and motivation. *Eur. Psychol.*, 1, 100–112.

Brackbill, Y., Blobitt, W. E., Davlin, D., and Wagner, J. E. (1963). Amplitude of response and the delay–retention effect. *J. Exp. Psychol.*, 66, 57–64.

Brown, F. J. (1932). Knowledge of results as an incentive in school room practice. *J. Educ. Psychol.*, 23, 532–552.

Butler, D. L. and Winne, P. H. (1995). Feedback and self–regulated learning: a theoretical synthesis. *Rev. Educ. Res.*, 65, 245–281.*

Carroll, J. B. (1963). A model of school learning. *Teachers College Record*, 64, 723–733.

Chandler, P. and Sweller, J. (1992). The split-attention effect as a factor in the design of instruction. *Br. J. Educ. Psychol.*, 62, 233–246.

Chi, M., Siler, S. A., and Joeng, H. (2004). Can tutors monitor students' understanding accurately? *Cognition and Instruction*, 22, 363–387.

Chinn, C. A. and Brewer, W. F. (1993). The role of anomalous data in knowledge acquisition: a theoretical framework and implications for science instruction. *Rev. Educ. Res.*, 63, 1–49.

Clariana, R. B. (1993). A review multiple-try feedback in traditional and computer-based instruction. *J. Comput. Based Instruct.*, 20, 67–74.

Clariana, R. B. (1999). CBT design: a feedback achievement treatment interaction. *21st Annu. Proc. Assoc. Educ. Commun. Technol.*, 22, 87–92.

Clariana, R. B. and Koul, R. (2004). Multiple-try feedback and higher–order learning outcomes. *Int. J. Instruct. Media*, 32, 239–245.

Clariana, R. B. and Koul, R. (2005). The effects of different forms of feedback on fuzzy and verbatim memory of science principles. *Br. J. Educ. Psychol.*, 75, 1–13.

Clariana, R. B. and Lee, D. (2001). The effects of recognition and recall study tasks with feedback in a computer-based vocabulary lesson. *Educ. Technol. Res. Dev.*, 49, 23–36.

Clariana, R. B., Wagner, D., and Rohrer-Murphy, L. C. (2000). A connectionist description of feedback timing. *Educ. Technol. Res. Dev.*, 48, 5–21.

Collies, B., DeBoer, W., and Slotman, K. (2001). Feedback for Web-based assignments. *J. Comput. Assist. Learn.*, 17, 306–313.

Corbett, A. T. and Anderson, J. R. (1990). The effect of feedback control on learning to program with the Lisp Tutor. In *Proceedings of the Twelfth Annual Conference of the Cognitive Science Society*, July 25–28, Cambridge, MA (http://act–r.psy.cmu.edu/papers/165/FeedbackControl_CorJRA.pdf).

Crippen, K. J. and Brooks, D. W. (2005). The AP descriptive chemistry question: student errors. *J. Comput. Math. Sci. Teach.*, 24, 357–366.

Cusella, L. P. (1987). Feedback, motivation and performance. In *Handbook of Organizational Communication: An Interdisciplinary Perspective*, edited by F. M. Jablin, L. L. Putnam, K. H. Roberts, and L. W. Pooter, pp. 624–678. Newsbury Park, CA: SAGE.

Dempsey, J. V. and Sales, G. C., Eds. (1993). *Interactive Instruction and Feedback*. Englewood Cliffs, NJ: Educational Technology Publications.

Dempsey, J. V., Driscoll, M. P., and Swindell, L. K. (1993). Text-based feedback. In *Interactive Instruction and Feedback*, edited by J. V. Dempsey and G. C. Sales, pp. 21–54. Englewood Cliffs, NJ: Educational Technology Publications.

Dempsey, J. V. and Wager, S. U. (1988). A taxonomy for the timing of feedback in computer-based instruction. *Educ. Psychol.*, 28(10), 20–25.

Dick, W., Carey, L., and Carey, J. O. (2001). *The Systematic Design of Instruction*. New York: Addison, Wesley, Longman.

Dresel, M. and Ziegler, A. (2006). Langfristige Förderung von Fähigkeitsselbstkonzept und impliziter Fähigkeitstheorie durch computerbasiertes attributionales Feedback (Long-term enhancement of academic self-concept and implicit ability theory through computer-based attributional feedback). *Zeitschrift für Pädagogische Psychologie*, 20, 49–64.

Fitts, P. M. (1962). Factors in complex skill training. In *Training Research and Education*, edited by R. Glaser, pp. 177–197. Oxford, England: University of Pittsburgh Press.

Gouli, E., Gogoulou, A., Papanikolaou, K., and Grigoriadou, M. (2005). An adaptive feedback framework to support reflection, tutoring and guiding in assessment. In *Advances in Web-Based Education: Personalized Learning Environments*, edited by G. Magoulas and S. Chen, pp. 178–202. New York: Idea Group Publishing.

Hancock, T. E., Stock, W. A., and Kulhavy, R. W. (1992). Predicting feedback effects from response-certitude estimates. *Bull. Psychonom. Soc.*, 30, 173–176.

Hancock, T. E., Thurman, R. A., and Hubbard, D. C. (1995a). An expanded control model for the use of instructional feedback. *Contemp. Educ. Psychol.*, 20, 410–425.

Hancock, T. E., Thurman, R. A., and Hubbard, D. C. (1995b). Using multiple indicators of cognitive state in logistic models that predict individual performance in machine-mediated learning environments. *Machine-Mediated Learn.*, 5(3), 237–253.

Hannafin, M. J., Hannafin, K. D., and Dalton, D. W. (1993). Feedback and emerging instructional technologies. In *Interactive Instruction and Feedback*, edited by J. V. Dempsey and G. C. Sales, pp. 263–286. Englewood Cliffs, NJ: Educational Technology Publications.

Heffernan, N. T. (2001). Intelligent Tutoring Systems Have Forgotten the Tutor: Adding a Cognitive Model of Human Tutors, Ph.D. dissertation, School of Computer Science, Carnegie Mellon University (http://www.algebratutor.org).

Heift, T. (2004). Corrective feedback and learner uptake in CALL. *ReCall: J. Eurocall*, 16, 416–431.

Holding, D. H. (1965). *Principles of Training*. Oxford, U.K.: Pergamon Press.

Hoska, D. M. (1993). Motivating learners trough CBI feedback: developing a positive learner perspective. In *Interactive Instruction and Feedback*, edited by J. V. Dempsey and G. C. Sales, pp. 105–131. Englewood Cliffs, NJ: Educational Technology.*

Jonassen, D. H. (1999). Designing constructivist learning environments. In *Instructional-Design Theories and Models: A New Paradigm of Instructional Theory*, Vol. II, edited by C. M. Reigeluth, pp. 215–239. Mahwah, NJ: Lawrence Erlbaum Associates.

Jonassen, D. H., Tessmer, M., and Hannum, W. H. (1999). Classifying knowledge and skills from task analysis. In *Task Analysis Methods for Instructional Design*, edited by D. H. Jonassen, M. Tessmer, and W. H. Hannum, pp. 25–32. Mahwah, NJ: Lawrence Erlbaum Associates.

Keller, J. M. (1983). Motivational design of instruction. In *Instructional Design Theories and Models: An Overview of Their Current Status*, edited by C. M. Reigeluth, pp. 386–434. Mahwah, NJ: Lawrence Erlbaum Associates.

Koedinger, K. R., Aleven, V., Heffernan, N., McLaren, B., and Hockenberry, M. (2004). Opening the door to non-programmers: authoring intelligent tutor behavior by demonstration. In *Proceedings of the Seventh International Conference on Intelligent Tutoring System (ITS 2004)*, pp. 162–174. Berlin: Springer Verlag.

Kluger, A. N. and DeNisi, A. (1996). Effects of feedback interventions on performance: a historical review, a meta-analysis, and a preliminary feedback intervention theory. *Psychol. Bull.*, 119, 254–284.*

Kulhavy, R. W. and Anderson, R. C. (1972). Learning-criterion error perseveration in text material. *J. Educ. Psychol.*, 63(5), 505–512.

Kulhavy, R. W. and Stock, W. A. (1989). Feedback in written instruction: the place of response certitude. *Educ. Psychol. Rev.*, 1, 279–308.*

Kulhavy, R. W., White, M. T., Topp, B. W., Chan, A. L., and Adams, J. (1985). Feedback complexity and corrective efficiency. *Contemp. Educ. Psychol.*, 10, 285–291.

Kulhavy, R. W., Stock, W. A., Hancock, T. E., Swindell, L. K., and Hammrich, P. L. (1990a). Written feedback: response certitude and durability. *Contemp. Educ. Psychol.*, 15, 319–332.

Kulhavy, R. W., Stock, W. A., Thornton, N. E., Winston, K. S., and Behrens, J. T. (1990b). Response feedback, certitude and learning from text. *Br. J. Educ. Psychol.*, 60, 161–170.

Kulik, J. A. and Kulik, C. C. (1988). Timing of feedback and verbal learning. *Rev. Educ. Res.*, 58, 79–97.*

Kutay, C. and Ho, P. (2005). Designing agents for feedback using the documents produced in learning. *Int. J. E-Learning*, http://goliath.ecnext.com/coms2/gi_0199-4307620/Designing-agents-for-feedback-using.html.

Markowotz, N. and Renner, K. E. (1966). Feedback and the delay-retention effect. *J. Exp. Psychol.*, 72(3), 452–455.

Mason, J. B. and Bruning, R. (2001). *Providing Feedback in Computer-Based Instruction: What the Research Tells Us*, http://dwb4.unl.edu/dwb/Research/MB/MasonBruning.html.

Mathan, S. A. and Koedinger, K. R. (2005). Fostering the intelligent novice: learning from errors with meta-cognitive tutoring. *Educ. Psychol.*, 40, 257–265.

Mayer, R. E. (2001). *Multimedia Learning*. New York: Cambridge University Press.

McKendree, J. (1990). Effective feedback content for tutoring complex skills. *Hum.–Comput. Interact.*, 5, 381–413.*

Melis, E. and Anders, E. (2005). Global feedback in Activmath. *J. Comput. Math. Sci. Teach.*, 24, 197–220.

Merrill, D. C., Reiser, B. J., Ranney, M., and Trafton, J. G. (1992). Effective tutoring techniques: a comparison of human tutors and intelligent tutoring systems. *J. Learn. Sci.*, 2, 277–305.*

Merrill, D. C., Reiser, B. J., Merrill, S. K., and Landes, S. (1995). Tutoring: guided learning by doing. *Cognit. Instruct.*, 13, 315–372.

Merrill, J. (1987). Levels of questioning and forms of feedback: instructional factors in courseware design. *J. Comput.-Based Instruct.*, 14(1), 18–22.

Mitrovic, A., Martin, B., and Mayo, M. (2002). Using evaluation to shape ITS design: results and experience with SQL-Tutor, *User Model. User-Adapt. Interact.*, 12(2/3), 243–279.

Moreno, R. (2004). Decreasing cognitive load for novice students: effects of explanatory versus corrective feedback in discovery-based multimedia. *Instruct. Sci.*, 32, 99–113.

Moreno, R. and Valdez, A. (2005). Cognitive load and learning effects of having students organize pictures and words in multimedia environments: the role of student interactivity and feedback. *Educ. Technol. Res. Dev.*, 53, 35–45.

Mory, E. H. (1994). Adaptive feedback in computer-based instruction: effects of response certitude on performance, feedback-study time and efficiency. *J. Educ. Comput. Res.*, 11, 263–290.

Mory, E. H. (1996). Feedback research. In *Handbook of Research for Educational Communications and Technology*, edited by D. H. Jonassen, pp. 919–956. New York: Simon & Schuster.*

Mory, E. H. (2004). Feedback research revisited. In *Handbook of Research on Educational Communications and Technology*, 2nd ed., edited by D. H. Jonassen, pp. 745–783. Mahwah, NJ: Lawrence Erlbaum Associates.*

Murray, R. C., VanLehn, K., and Mostow, J. (2004). Looking ahead to select tutorial actions: a decision-theoretic approach. *Int. J. Artif. Intell. Educ.*, 14, 235–278.

Nagata, N. (1993). Intelligent computer feedback for second language instruction. *Modern Lang. J.*, 77, 330–339.

Nagata, N. (1997). An experimental comparison of deductive and inductive feedback generated by a simple parser. *System*, 25, 515–534.

Nagata, N. and Swisher, M. V. (1995). A study of consciousness-raising by computer: the effect of metalinguistic feedback on second language learning. *Foreign Lang. Ann.*, 28, 337–347.

Narciss, S. (2004). The impact of informative tutoring feedback and self–efficacy on motivation and achievement in concept learning. *Experimental Psychology*, 51(3), 214–228.

Narciss, S. (2006). *Informatives tutorielles Feedback. Entwicklungs- und Evaluationsprinzipien auf der Basis instruktionspsychologischer Erkenntnisse (Informative Tutoring Feedback)*. Münster: Waxmann.

Narciss, S. and Huth, K. (2004). How to design informative tutoring feedback for multi–media learning. In *Instructional Design for Multimedia Learning*, edited by H. M. Niegemann, D. Leutner, and R. Brünken, pp. 181–195. Münster: Waxmann.*

Narciss, S. and Huth, K. (2006). Fostering achievement and motivation with bug-related tutoring feedback in a computer-based training for written subtraction. *Learn. Instruct.* 16, 310–322.

Narciss, S., Körndle, H., Reimann, G., and Müller, C. (2004). Feedback-seeking and feedback efficiency in Web-based learning: how do they relate to task and learner characteristics? In *Instructional Design for Effective and Enjoyable Computer–Supported Learning: Proceedings of the First Joint Meeting of the EARLI SIGs Instructional Design and Learning and Instruction with Computers* [CD-ROM], edited by P. Gerjets, P. A. Kirschner, J. Elen, and R. Joiner, pp. 377–388. Tübingen: Knowledge Media Research Center.

Peek, J. and Tillema, H. H. (1978). Delay of feedback and retention of correct and incorrect responses. *J. Exp. Educ.*, 38, 171–178.

Phye, G. D. (1979). The processing of informative feedback about multiple-choice test performance. *Contemp. Educ. Psychol.*, 4, 381–394.

Phye, G. D. (1991). Advice and feedback during cognitive training: effects at acquisition and delayed transfer. *Contemp. Educ. Psychol.*, 16, 87–94.

Phye, G. D. (2001). Problem-solving instruction and problem-solving transfer: the correspondence issue. *J. Exp. Psychol.*, 93, 571–578.

Phye, G. D. and Bender, T. (1989). Feedback complexity and practice: response pattern analysis in retention and transfer. *Contemp. Educ. Psychol.*, 14, 97–110.

Phye, G. D. and Sanders, C. E. (1994). Advice and feedback: elements of practice for problem solving. *Contemp. Educ. Psychol.*, 19, 286–301.

Pintrich, P. R. (2003). Motivation and classroom learning. In *Handbook of Psychology*. Vol. 7. *Educational Psychology*, edited by W. M. Reynolds and G. E. Miller, pp. 103–122. Hoboken, NJ: John Wiley & Sons.

Pressley, M. (1986). The relevance of the good strategy user model to the teaching of mathematics. *Educ. Psychol.*, 21, 139–161.

Rankin, R. J. and Trepper, T. (1978). Retention and delay of feedback in a computer-assisted task. *J. Exp. Educ.*, 64, 67–70.

Rittle-Johnson, B. and Koedinger, K. R. (2005). Designing knowledge scaffolds to support mathematical problem solving. *Cognit. Instruct.*, 23, 313–349.*

Roll, I., Aleven, V., McLaren, B. M., Ryu, E., Baker, R., and Koedinger, K. R. (2006). The help-tutor: does metacognitive feedback improve students' help-seeking actions, skills and learning? In *ITS 2006*, LNCS 4053, edited by M. Ikeda, K. Ashley, and T.-W. Chan, pp. 360–369. Berlin: Springer.

Romero, C., Ventura, S., and DeBra, P. (2005). Knowledge discovery with genetic programming for providing feedback to courseware authors. *User Model. User-Adapt. Interact.*, 14, 425–464.

Sales, G. C. (1993). Adapted and adaptive feedback in technology-based instruction. In *Interactive Instruction and Feedback*, J. V. Dempsey and G. C. Sales, pp. 159–175. Englewood Cliffs, NJ: Educational Technology Publications.

Sansone, C. (1986). A question of competence: the effects of competence and task feedback on intrinsic interest. *J. Person. Soc. Psychol.*, 51, 918–931.

Sansone, C. (1989). Competence feedback, task feedback, and intrinsic interest: an examination of process and context. *J. Exp. Soc. Psychol.*, 25, 343–361.

Sanz, C. (2004). Computer delivered implicit versus explicit feedback in processing instruction. In *Processing Instruction: Theory, Research and Commentary*, edited by B. Van-Patten, pp. 241–255. Mahwah, NJ: Lawrence Erlbaum Associates.

Schimmel, B. J. (1988). Providing meaningful feedback in courseware. In *Instructional Designs for Microcomputer Courseware*, edited by D. H. Jonassen, pp. 183–195. Hillsdale, NJ: Lawrence Erlbaum Associates.

Schroth, M. L. and Lund, E. (1993). Role of delay of feedback on subsequent pattern recognition transfer tasks. *Contemp. Educ. Psychol.*, 18, 15–22.

Schunk, D. H. (1983). Ability versus effort attributional feedback: differential effects on self-efficacy and achievement. *J. Educ. Psychol.*, 75, 848–856.

Schunk, D. H. and Rice, J. M. (1993). Strategy fading and progress feedback: effects on self-efficacy and comprehension among students receiving remedial reading services. *J. Spec. Educ.*, 27, 257–276.

Senko, C. and Harackiewicz, J. M. (2005). Regulation of achievement goals: the role of competence feedback. *J. Educ. Psychol.*, 97, 320–336.

Smith, P. L. and Ragan, T. J. (1993). Designing instructional feedback for different learning outcomes. In *Interactive Instruction and Feedback*, edited by J. V. Dempsey and G. C. Sales, pp. 75–103. Englewood Cliffs, NJ: Educational Technology.*

Steinberg, E. R. (1977). Review of student control in computer-assisted instruction. *J. Comput.-Based Instruct.*, 3, 84–90.

Steinberg, E. R. (1989). Cognition and learner control: a literature review, 1977–1988. *J. Comput.-Based Instruct.*, 16, 117–121.

Stock, W. A., Kulhavy, R. W., Pridemore, D. R., and Krug, D. (1992). Responding to feedback after multiple-choice answers: the influence of response confidence. *Q. J. Exp. Psychol.*, 45A, 649–667.

Sturges, P. T. (1969). Verbal retention as a function of the informativeness and delay of information feedback. *J. Educ. Psychol.*, 60, 11–14.

Sturges; P. T. (1972). Information delay and retention: effect of information in feedback and tests. *J. Educ. Psychol.*, 63, 32–43.

Sturges, P. T. (1978). Delay of informative feedback in computer-assisted testing. *J. Educ. Psychol.*, 70(3), 357–358.

Surber, J. R. and Anderson, R. C. (1975). Delay-retention effect in natural classroom settings. *J. Educ. Psychol.*, 67(2), 170–173.

Swindell, L. K. and Walls, W. F. (1993). Response confidence and the delay retention effect. *Contemp. Educ. Psychol.*, 18, 363–375.

Symonds, P. M. and Chase, D. H. (1929). Practice vs. motivation. *J. Educ. Psychol.*, 20, 19–35.

Taylor, R. (1987). Selecting effective courseware: three fundamental instructional factors. *Contemp. Educ. Psychol.*, 12, 231–243.

Thorndike, E. L. (1913). *Educational Psychology: The Psychology of Learning*. New York: Teachers College Press.

Ulicsak, M. H. (2004) 'How did it know we weren't talking?': an investigation into the impact of self-assessments and feedback in a group activity. *J. Comput. Assist. Learn.*, 20, 205–211.

Usher, E. L. and Pajares, F. (2006). Sources of academic and self-regulatory efficacy beliefs of entering middle school students. *Contemp. Educ. Psychol.*, 31, 125–141.

van den Boom, G., Paas, F., van Mërrienboer, J. J. G., and van Gog, T. (2004). Reflection prompts and tutor feedback in a Web-based learning environment: effects on students' self-regulated learning competence. *Comput. Hum. Behav.*, 20, 551–567.

VanLehn, K. (1990). *Mind Bugs: The Origins of Procedural Misconceptions*. Cambridge, MA: The MIT Press.

VanLehn, K., Lynch, C., Schulze, K., Shapiro, J. A., Shelby, R., Taylor, L., Treacy, D., Weinstein, A., and Wintersgill, M. (2005). The Andes physics tutoring system: lessons learned. *Int. J. Artif. Intell. Educ.*, 15 147–204.*

Vollmeyer, R. and Rheinberg, F. (2005). A surprising effect of feedback on learning. *Learn. Instruct.*, 15, 589–602.

Wager, W. and Mory, E. H. (1993). The role of questions in learning. In *Interactive Instruction and Feedback*, edited by J. V. Dempsey and G. C. Sales, pp. 55–73. Englewood Cliffs, NJ: Educational Technology Publications.

Wager, W. and Wager, S. U. (1985). Presenting questions, processing responses, and providing feedback in CAI. *J. Instruct. Dev.*, 8(4), 2–8.

Wiener, N. (1954). *The Human Use of Human Beings: Cybernetics and Society*. Oxford, England: Houghton Mifflin.

---

* Indicates a core reference.

# 12

# Technology-Enhanced Support Strategies for Inquiry Learning

*Yael Kali*
Technion–Israel Institute of Technology, Haifa, Israel

*Marcia C. Linn*
University of California, Berkeley, California

## CONTENTS

## ABSTRACT

Design studies provide evidence for the effectiveness of specific supports for learning in technology-enhanced environments and suggest guidelines for the design and use of such features. The Design Principles Database is a public collaborative knowledge-building tool that helps capture and synthesize this knowledge using "design principles" as a basic construct. In this chapter, we highlight eight pragmatic design principles from the Design Principles Database that are most likely to support learning, and we provide evidence that shows how learning is supported by features in technologies that apply these principles. We discuss the advantages and limitations of design principles to guide a design process and suggest that, for design principles to be more effective for guiding new innovations, they should be complemented with a design patterns approach.

## KEYWORDS

*Design principles:* Research-based guidelines for instructional design; design principles can be articulated at different grain-sizes: specific principles characterize rationales for designing specific features in a learning environment, pragmatic principles connect rationales behind several features, and meta-principles synthesize a cluster of pragmatic principles.

*Knowledge integration:* The process of adding, distinguishing, organizing, and evaluating accounts of phenomena, situations, and abstractions.

*Learning environment:* A system that incorporates a set of features including a navigation system; learning environments can deliver curricula in any topic area.

*Software features:* Specific applications of technology intended to advance learning; features include designed artifacts such as modeling tools, simulations, micro-worlds, visualizations, collaboration tools, reflection prompts, games, and embedded assessments.

## INTRODUCTION

This chapter synthesizes the benefits of technology-enhanced supports for inquiry learning and is intended to help designers build on past work and help researchers report new findings in the context of current work. To achieve these goals, we take advantage of efforts to collate design principles, such as those devised by Brown (1992), Kali (2006), Kali (in press), Merrill (2002), Quintana et al. (2004), Reigeluth (1999), and van den Akker (1999). We draw on current views of the learner informed by research in cognition and instruction (Bransford et al., 1999; Linn et al., 2004b).

Designers have created and refined numerous supports for inquiry learning. We define support strategies as features of technology-enhanced instruction that the designers report contribute to learning such as guidance, prompts for reflection, and varied representations

of content. We define *inquiry* broadly to refer to any activity that engages the learner in exploring a scientific phenomenon. These supports are embedded in many technology-enhanced inquiry programs that have been tested in classrooms (Barab et al., 2000; Bruer, 1993; diSessa, 2000; Edelson et al., 1999; Krajcik et al., 1998; Linn et al., 2003; Means, 1994; Reiser et al., 2001; Roschelle et al., 2000; Scardamalia and Bereiter, 1996; Schwartz et al., 1999; Songer et al., 2003; Tinker, 2005; White and Frederiksen, 1998).

Studies of inquiry learning show that learners grapple with multiple, conflicting, and often confusing ideas about scientific phenomena. Successful supports for inquiry help learners identify their repertoire of ideas by engaging them in multiple, often authentic problem situations. Successful technology-enhanced instruction often takes advantage of models, simulations, or visualizations to introduce new ideas. Effective instruction does not stop with eliciting and adding ideas, however. To gain durable, generative understanding, students need to devise criteria for sorting out these ideas in varied contexts and at multiple levels of analysis. They need supports that allow them to formulate, often in collaboration with others, more and more nuanced criteria for evaluating ideas. They need time to sort out their ideas and develop an increasingly linked set of views about any phenomenon. In this chapter, we synthesize recent research using technology-enhanced curriculum materials to support inquiry. We identify promising supports for inquiry that emphasize all four processes: eliciting ideas, adding ideas, developing criteria, and sorting out ideas. These processes are the main elements of the knowledge integration framework (Linn, 1995; Linn and Hsi, 2000; Linn et al., 2004b).

Designers often find building on past successes challenging because studies do not tease apart the consequential elements of the innovation (Cognition and Technology Group at Vanderbilt, 1997). We seek ways to facilitate effective use of technology in science learning. In spite of extensive research on supports for inquiry learning, most uses of technology for precollege instruction use drill and practice, word processing, and Web surfing (Fishman et al., 2004). University instruction primarily relies on Web delivery of information (Herrington et al., 2005). Mioduser and colleagues (1999, p. 757) summarized the current uses of technology in education as: "One step ahead for the technology, two steps back for the pedagogy."

To identify promising elements of supports for inquiry, we synthesize findings from design research. Design researchers conduct iterative refinements to develop successful innovations (Bell et al., 2004; Design-Based Research Collective, 2003; Simon,

1969). Studies comparing alternative designs or sequences of refinements provide evidence for the effectiveness of specific supports, shed light on the mechanism behind supports, and suggest guidelines for implementation. These studies often summarize findings in design principles, learning principles, patterns, and related synthesis methods to capture both the innovations and the mechanisms that govern their success. Brown (1992) offered learning principles to synthesize her research findings. Collins (1992) called for guidelines to capture research-based practical design knowledge. These efforts echo practices in other design-based fields that have found principles helpful, including architecture (Alexander et al., 1977), graphical communication (Tufte, 1983), and computer science (Gamma et al., 1995).

The current synthesis starts with features of inquiry innovations captured by Kali (2006) and Kali (in press) in the Design Principles Database (http://www.design-principles.org). The current entries in the Design Principles Database represent the contributions of over 50 individual researchers. The database includes about 100 features (mainly from physical, life, and earth sciences). The database connects: (1) descriptions of promising features, (2) the rationale for the feature, and (3) evidence for the impact of the feature to pragmatic design principles. Pragmatic principles are abstracted guidelines that connect similar rationales behind features in different learning environments. Although features are entered in the database as independent entities, they are often parts of sequences of features that comprise a learning environment.

The database is organized around meta-principles. Meta-principles are overarching ideas that synthesize a cluster of pragmatic principles. The meta-principles in the database include make thinking visible, make science accessible, help learners learn from each other, and promote autonomous lifelong learning.

The structure of the Design Principles Database emerged from longitudinal research on technology-enhanced science learning (Linn and Hsi, 2000; Linn et al., 2004b). The Computer as Learning Partner research program identified the 4 meta-principles and the first 14 pragmatic principles in their 20-year-long effort to iteratively refine effective interactive science experiences (Linn and Hsi, 2000). The Design Principles Database has grown with contributions from participants in workshops, from course activities, and from the public (Kali et al., 2002). It serves as a collaborative knowledge-building tool for communities who design and explore educational technologies (Kali, 2006). The Design Principles Database enables designers to explain the pedagogical rationales behind each feature in a learning environment and for com-

munity members to respond and add their experiences. It is based on the idea that explaining the rationale of a feature can be useful for other designers. Researchers have added additional principles (Linn et al., 2004b) and applied the ideas to design of assessments (Clark and Linn, 2003), professional development (Williams and Linn, 2003), and learning environments (Linn et al., 2003). Researchers can explore the application of principles in new contexts and add their findings back to the Design Principles Database. The design knowledge grows as principles are debated, refined, or warranted with additional field-based evidence.

# SUPPORTS FOR INQUIRY LEARNING

To synthesize supports for inquiry learning, we start with the four meta-principles in the Design Principles Database and select pragmatic principles that connect with the largest number of software features. We have highlighted two promising features for each pragmatic principle. The features vary in their grain size; some represent whole learning environments (such as Model-It), some represent tools in a learning environment (such as the inquiry map in WISE), and others represent elements in software (such as the manipulative animated three-dimensional illustrations in Geo3D). Table 12.1 shows the features and their connections with pragmatic and meta-principles. We describe the meta-principles, associated pragmatic principles, and illustrative features to characterize supports for inquiry learning.

## Meta-Principle: Make Science Accessible

Designers seek to make science accessible for learners to elicit the full repertoire of ideas. They create supports that increase the relevance of science for all learners—those aspiring to careers in science and those taking their last science course. These supports respond to the common complaint that science is not relevant or useful. They also remedy the often inadequate images of science held by students (Hofer and Pintrich, 2002). Two pragmatic principles that follow this meta-principle call for communicating the diversity of science inquiry and for connecting to personally relevant examples.

### Pragmatic Principle: Communicate the Diversity of Science Inquiry

This principle calls on designers to expose learners to the rich diversity of the inquiry process. Far too often students leave science class with an image of inquiry

**TABLE 12.1**
**Features Described in This Chapter and Their Connections to Pragmatic and Meta-Principles**

| Pragmatic Principles | Features |
|---|---|
| *Meta-Principle: Make Science Accessible* | |
| Communicate the diversity of science inquiry | Inquiry map in WISE |
| | SenseMaker in WISE |
| Connect to personally relevant examples | Authentic contexts in the *Jasper* project |
| | Contextualized definition in TELS |
| *Meta-Principle: Make Thinking Visible* | |
| Provide students with templates to organize ideas | Principle Maker in WISE |
| | Design rule-of-thumb template in SMILE |
| Provide knowledge representation tools | Model-It |
| | Causal Mapper |
| Enable three-dimensional manipulation | Three-dimensional illustrations in Geo3D |
| | Scaffolds to support student use of molecular modeling software |
| *Meta-Principle: Help Learners Learn from Each Other* | |
| Encourage learners to learn from others | Automated gathering of peer-evaluation outcomes in CeLS |
| | Supports for collaboration in eStep |
| *Meta-Principle: Promote Autonomous Lifelong Learning* | |
| Enable manipulation of factors in models and simulation | Manipulable models of molecules in Molecular Workbench |
| | Modeling derivatives in Visual Mathematics |
| Encourage reflection | Prompts for reflection on action in CASES |
| | Note taking in WISE |

as dogmatic and inflexible or abstract and incomprehensible (Linn et al., 2004a). Technology-enhanced learning environments can help students become aware of the diversity of science inquiry by engaging students in a variety of inquiry processes. We exemplify how this principle is applied in two different features that are part of the Web-Based Inquiry Science Environment (WISE) (Slotta, 2004).

## Inquiry Map in WISE

To help students explore inquiry processes, WISE uses an inquiry map, which is a dynamic-graphic guide shown in each of the WISE projects (Figure 12.1). It graphically represents the steps of the inquiry in the project. This enables students to get an overview of the project and the inquiry strategies it includes. The inquiry map also expands and collapses each project into its

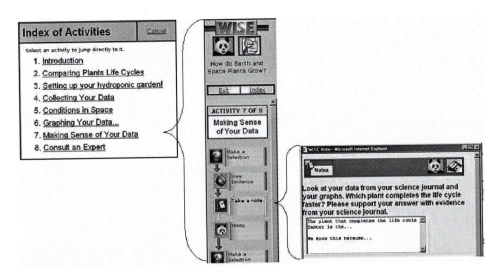

**Figure 12.1** WISE inquiry map (in middle) with index of activities (left) and reelection note (right).

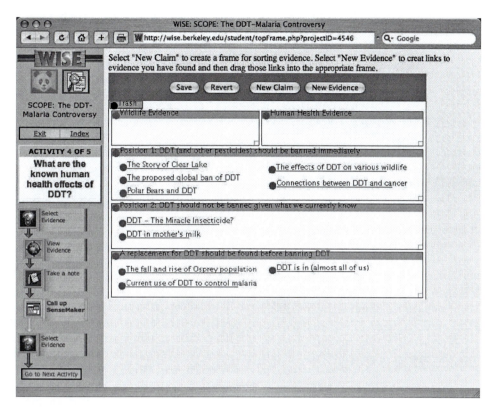

**Figure 12.2** Sorting of evidence Web pages in SenseMaker.

main inquiry components. Teachers using WISE indicate that the map makes students more independent in their inquiry activities, thus strengthening their understanding of the diversity of inquiry processes. In many cases, the inquiry map provides answers to "What do I do now?" questions, making the inquiry process more self-directed. The map also helps students get a better understanding of how each step in the project relates to the whole inquiry process (Linn and Hsi, 2000).

*SenseMaker in WISE*

Another feature that communicates the idea of diversity in science inquiry engages students in controversial scientific debates (Bell, 2004). The WISE Sense-Maker tool (Figure 12.2) helps students figure out the relationships that exist between different Web resources. As they investigate pieces of Web-based evidence, students organize the items into categories in SenseMaker. This sorting of pieces of evidence helps students consolidate their own stance about the controversy and prepare for a class debate. During the debate, the graphical representations of student arguments are displayed. Students can see the diversity of inquiry strategies by comparing their arguments to those of other students and of experts (Bell, 2004). SenseMaker can support debates about such issues as the threat of malaria. Students explore the ethical

trade-offs between protecting human life (by spraying DDT) and protecting wildlife and the environment (by banning the use of DDT) (Seethaler and Linn, 2004). Research shows that engaging students in such debates and supporting their inquiry process with SenseMaker can help students develop a more integrated understanding of complex science topics (Bell, 2004).

***Pragmatic Principle: Connect to Personally Relevant Examples***

Personally relevant problems, such as determining how to keep a drink cold, make science accessible because they elicit intuitive ideas to fuel inquiry (Linn and Hsi, 2000; Songer and Linn, 1991). Linn et al. (2004b) showed that eliciting the broad range of student ideas about science and engaging these ideas enables students to build more coherent, durable scientific views. This principle advocates using personally relevant examples as contexts for scientific inquiry. The examples below show how this principle was applied by two research groups.

*Authentic Contexts in the Jasper Project*

The *Jasper* project, using the anchored instruction approach (Cognition and Technology Group at Vanderbilt, 1990, 1997), was one of the earliest large endeavors

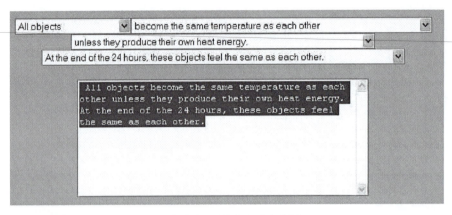

**Figure 12.3** Scaffolding students in the creation of principles with Principle Maker.

to use technology to anchor instruction in authentic contexts. *Jasper* includes a set of 12 video-based adventures that focus on mathematical problem solving. Each video ends in a complex challenge. The adventures are designed like good detective novels, and all the data necessary to solve the adventure are embedded in the story. The *Jasper* adventures present a believable story that has interesting characters, a complex and important challenge, and extensions to a variety of curricular areas. To solve the challenge, the students combine problem-solving skills, mathematics concepts, and the information in the video. The adventures were designed to bridge the gap between everyday and school problems. They provide a common context for instruction, an authentic task, and a chance to see that school knowledge can be used to solve real problems.

### Contextualized Definitions in TELS Modules

The Technology Enhanced Learning in Science (TELS) *Hanging with Friends, Velocity Style!* module (Tate, 2005) embeds scientific terms in the context of an interview with a teenager. The purpose of the interview is to find the teenager's velocity, but the context of the interview is her trip from Lake Park to the movie theater to meet her friends. The interviewee speaks in everyday language while communicating the information needed to determine her velocity, saying, for example, "I was running a bit late and almost didn't get a seat. I arrived at the movie theatre at 5:05 p.m. This is referred to as my final time." The discourse blends everyday language and events (being late to a movie) with information needed to determine velocity. By bringing everyday events (a conversation or interview) into play, the feature draws students into the activity and helps them place it in a familiar context. They compute the velocity of each friend to see if all will arrive in time. The feature motivates students to understand the specific terms and data needed to compute velocity for an everyday event.

## Meta-Principle: Make Thinking Visible

To promote inquiry, designers often encourage students and teachers to make their thinking visible. When students make thinking visible, they can inspect their own knowledge integration processes and deliberately guide their learning (Bransford et al., 1999; Collins et al., 1991; Linn, 1995). To support these processes, designers create tools that students use to map their ideas and externalize their thoughts at different stages of the learning process. Designers also use models or visualizations embedded in inquiry projects to make complex concepts and scientific phenomena visible. We highlight three pragmatic principles that follow this meta-principle. The first two are intended to help students make their own thinking visible, and the third is intended to make complex scientific phenomena visible. We exemplify each pragmatic principle with two features from different contexts.

### Pragmatic Principle: Provide Students with Templates to Organize Ideas

To support students in articulating complex scientific ideas, designers have created what might be called *templates*. Templates scaffold students in representing their ideas and revising them as they complete complex activities (Kolodner et al., 2004). Below are two examples that show software features from two contexts that apply this principle.

### Principle Maker in WISE

One feature that exemplifies how templates can help organize ideas, is the Principle Maker (Clark and Sampson, 2007). The Principle Maker (Figure 12.3) is a tool in the WISE environment that helps students synthesize data that they have collected or experienced into a principle. By providing building-block phrases,

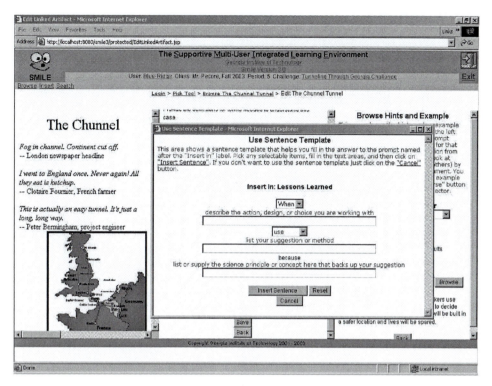

**Figure 12.4** Design rule-of-thumb template in SMILE.

the tool scaffolds the task and gives students clear alternatives without dictating ideas. The Principle Maker is part of a TELS project called *Thermodynamics: Probing Your Surroundings*. Research conducted by Clark and Sampson (2007) suggests that scaffolding students in the creation of principles helps make student ideas explicit. Clark and Sampson take advantage of the principles students build to set up discussions that include groups with opposing ideas. They argue that this process promotes dialogical argumentation. By making thinking visible, the Principle Maker enables a more sophisticated form of argumentation than is found in typical science classrooms. As a result, students have a good sense of the views of their peers and can spend their time supporting, evaluating, and critiquing ideas.

*Design Rule of Thumb Template in SMILE*

Another feature designed according to this principle is part of the Learning by Design classrooms, and the Supporting Multiuser Interactive Learning Environment (SMILE) (Kolodner et al., 2004). This feature assists students in generating and revising design rules of thumb throughout a project experience. Design rules of thumb are lessons that are learned from experience. The template includes constructs that help students construct a design rule of thumb in

the following format: When/If (describe the action, design, or choice you are working within) use/connect/build/employ/measure (list your suggestion or method) because (list or supply the evidence or science principle or concept that backs up your suggestion) (Figure 12.4). Students initially attempt to generate these rules of thumb in small groups based on their experimental results or on cases they are reading. They discuss the rules of thumb as a class and revise them. Ideally, students notice ideas they cannot explain and identify the science they need to learn. Research shows that, before use of the template, students were often unable to make the appropriate connections to science. When templates were used in the context of a class, teachers were better able to introduce the appropriate scientific concepts. When the teacher helped students create rules of thumb as a class before using the software, students using the software created better rules of thumb (with a richer situation description and justification) than students who did not have the template available in the software (Kolodner et al., 2004). This principle calls for providing learners with tools with which they can visually represent, at different learning stages, their understanding of scientific ideas. Linn et al. (2004b) claim that knowledge representation tools can promote interpretation and theorizing about evidence.

151

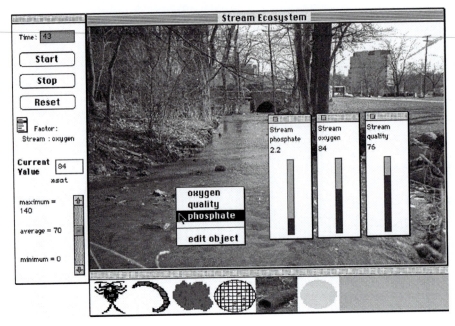

**Figure 12.5** Running a simulation built by students in Model-It.

### Pragmatic Principle: Provide Knowledge Representation Tools

#### Model-It

An example of a tool that enables students to represent and test their knowledge is Model-It, developed at the University of Michigan. Model-It is a learner-centered tool for building dynamic, qualitative-based models. Model-It was designed to support students, even those with only very basic mathematical skills, in building dynamic models of scientific phenomena and running simulations with their models to verify and analyze the results (Jackson et al., 2000). For example, students can build models of water quality and then test how various pollutants would affect water quality. Model-It provides an easy-to-use visual structure with which students can plan, build, and test their models (Figure 12.5). Model-It has been used with thousands of students and their teachers in both urban and suburban areas. Research shows that when properly integrated into the curriculum, Model-It allows students to take part in a variety of scientific practices such as testing, debugging, building relationships, specifying variables, and synthesis (Jackson et al., 2000).

#### Causal Mapper

Another example of a feature that enables students to represent their understanding is Causal Mapper. This feature, developed by Baumgartner (2004), is a stand-alone application that allows learners to make sense of a set of causal relationships. Causal mapping refers to the use of directed node and link graphs—similar to concept maps, in some ways—to represent a set of causal relationships within a system. The causal map shown in Figure 12.6, for example, reflects the representation by two sixth-grade girls of the factors that contribute to the health of a stream. Causal mapping is more structured than concept mapping, in that links capture causal relations. Students can develop a shared representation for causality, and groups can quickly examine and critique each other's causal maps and discuss complex causal chains. Baumgartner (2004) showed that, when students map their own data using Causal Mapper, they develop their ability to interpret their data and use it as evidence for their investigations.

### Pragmatic Principle: Enable Three-Dimensional Manipulation

In the earlier description of the "make thinking visible" meta-principle, we mentioned that one aspect is animating complex scientific phenomena. "Enable three-dimensional manipulation" is a pragmatic principle that emphasizes making scientific phenomena visible. Many students have difficulty perceiving three-dimensional (3D) structures, that are presented in textbooks as two-dimensional (2D) representations. Technology can provide tools that enable students to manipulate representations of these structures. Visualizations can enable students to rotate objects being studied and thus view them from various directions (Dori et al., 2003; Hsi et al., 1997; Kali et al., 1997). Other types of 3D visualizations can also improve understanding, as described in the following two features:

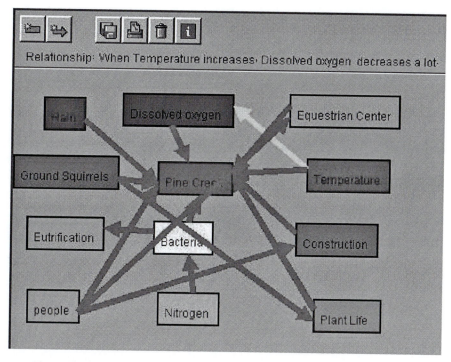

**Figure 12.6** Map created by students with Causal Mapper to represent water-quality factors.

### Three-Dimensional Illustrations in Geo3D

Geo3D was designed to respond to the spatial abilities required in structural geology and the difficulties that high-school students have in the perception of geological structures (Kali and Orion, 1996). In Geo3D, students can visually bisect illustrations of geological structures (see Figure 12.7). They explore relationships between observable and unseen properties of the geological structures. These relationships strengthen the perceptions of geological structures created by folding, uplifting, and erosion (Kali et al., 1997). Even short interactions with these animations (1 to 2 hours) improves students' skills in the visualization of geological structures.

### Scaffolds to Support Student Use of Molecular Modeling Software

Many students have difficulties relating symbolic representation of molecules to 2D and 3D models, especially when organic compounds are involved. Dori et al. (2003) and Barak and Dori (2005) designed a suite of activities that takes advantage of molecular modeling software originally designed for experts, such as WebLab Viewer and ISIS/Draw. To use software designed for experts, learning materials must highlight the salient information for students (Edelson et al., 1999). Guided by this suit of activities, students construct 2D representations of chemical substances using ISIS/Draw and then use WebLab to transform the 2D

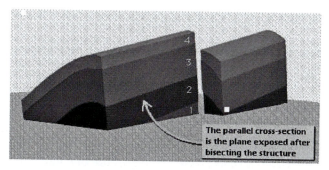

**Figure 12.7** Animation showing bisection of a geological structure in Geo3D.

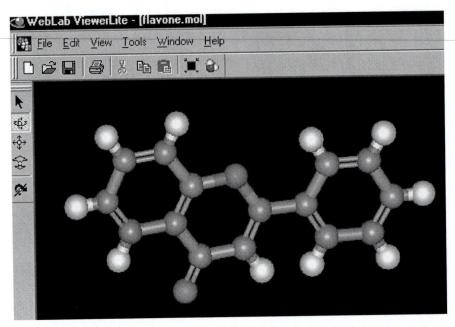

**Figure 12.8** Ball-and-stick model created by a student using the scaffolding activities for the WebLab tool.

representations into a 3D image (framework, ball-and-stick, or space-filling) (Figure 12.8). Students compare their representations to those of their peers. Dori et al. (2006) showed that these activities increase students' understanding of the physical and chemical properties of simple and complex compounds.

## Meta-Principle: Help Learners Learn from Each Other

To help students develop criteria and distinguish among ideas, designers embed social supports in inquiry activities. These opportunities encourage students to listen and learn from others and take advantage of the collective knowledge in the classroom community. Encouraging students to analyze and build on ideas from peers can introduce new perspectives and motivate students to form criteria (Scradamalia and Bereiter, 1994). Additionally, when students interact, they bring to light the alternative views held by learners and the criteria used to interpret ideas (Bransford et al., 1999). We highlight one pragmatic principle that follows this meta-principle and describe two features that show its use in different contexts.

### Pragmatic Principle: Encourage Learners to Learn from Others

This principle emphasizes helping learners to listen and learn from others. When students explain their thoughts to other students, they sort out their own ideas

and learn new ideas from others. Students can help their peers understand an idea by articulating concepts using familiar vocabulary and relevant examples.

### Automated Gathering of Peer-Evaluation Outcomes in CeLS

One example of this principle involves automating peer evaluation. CeLS (Collaborative e-Learning Structures; http://www.mycels.net) allows instructors to construct online structured collaborative activities, including peer evaluation. CeLS automatically gathers and analyzes information submitted by students and shows it in various customizable forms. Figure 12.9 shows an example of the type of information that can be presented in a peer evaluation activity designed in CeLS, including statistical analysis, a histogram, and a collection of student justifications for their grading (presented anonymously). Kali and Ronen (2005) used a peer-evaluation activity designed with CeLS in a philosophy of education course. Undergraduate students constructed a conceptual model of their "ideal school" and developed more sophisticated epistemologies as a result of peer evaluation.

### Supports for Collaboration in eStep

Another example of technology supports that encourage learners to learn from others is the eStep system (Derry et al., 2005; Hmelo-Silver et al., 2005). In eStep, learners read and view a case study that presents a classroom dilemma. They individually reflect on the dilemma and propose an initial solution, then they

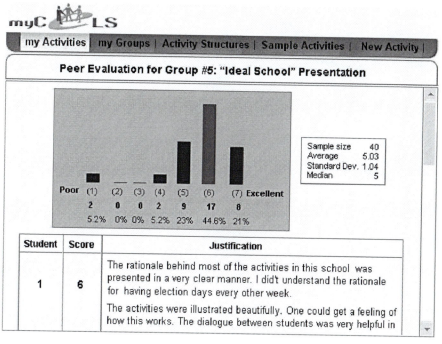

**Figure 12.9** Peer evaluation activity designed with CeLS.

collaborate with other learners to collectively arrive at a revised solution. The lesson ends with individual critiques of the group solution and reflection on the learning, collaboration, lesson design, and usefulness of the solution to their own professional practice. Derry et al. (2005) reported that eStep produced significant increases in teacher and learner abilities to think deeply about student understanding and that the course was more effective at producing transfer than a traditional lecture-based approach covering the same material.

## Meta-Principle: Promote Autonomous Lifelong Learning

To become lifelong learners, students need supports that help them guide their own learning, recognize new ideas, and develop a view of effective inquiry. They need to engage in sustained project work so they can connect personally relevant problems to class topics and reflect on experience using a robust inquiry process in diverse contexts (Linn et al., 2004b). Students benefit from learning to monitor their progress. To encourage autonomy, designers scaffold comprehensive inquiry processes that students can apply to varied problems, both in class and throughout their lives, to explore ways to ensure that these practices are internalized. We present two pragmatic principles from the Design Principles Database that apply this meta-principle and exemplify each, with two features.

### Pragmatic Principle: Enable Manipulation of Factors in Models and Simulations

Interactive models, simulations, and visualizations support autonomy but often frustrate learners because they are too complex or too sophisticated (Hegarty et al., 1999). To enable students to benefit from models, simulations, and visualizations, designers guide interactions and seek ways to promote autonomy. Models, simulations, and visualizations enable learners to connect everyday, microscopic, and symbolic representations of phenomena. They can be used in virtual labs when it is impossible, dangerous, difficult, expensive, or unethical (in the case of animal studies) to conduct a hands-on experiment. They can illustrate many fields, such as finance, mathematics, physics, meteorology, biology, or social sciences. Shternberg and Yerushalmy (2003) distinguished between models that illustrate concepts (such as the relationship between a function and its derivative) and models of physical phenomena such as chemical reactions. In both types, students need strategies for exploring how the model behaves under varied conditions. Many computer-based models allow learners to explore the effect of each variable in a system by holding others constant. Oftentimes, instructional materials help learners internalize the strategies appropriate for exploring complex models and simulations. For example, students need skill in identifying extreme situations and exploring limitations of models.

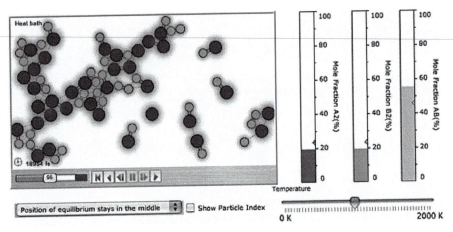

**Figure 12.10** Model for exploring reversible chemical reaction designed with Molecular Workbench.

Students also need to connect computer simulations to hands-on experiments. Ways to guide students to explore inquiry strategies for models and simulations are exemplified in the following features.

### Models of Molecules in Molecular Workbench

The Molecular Workbench software allows designers to create dynamic visualizations to illustrate scientific ideas (Pallant and Tinker, 2004). Students can manipulate visualizations that link atomic-level models with observable phenomena to conceptualize events such as the production of greenhouse gases. An understanding of atomic-level interactions is essential to most of modern science. The idea that many macroscopic phenomena emerge from large numbers of simple interactions is both simple and profound. For example, the example model shown in Figure 12.10 enables students to view how their manipulation of the temperature and the mole fraction of various substances changes the speed of movement of the particles and the reactions between them. To promote autonomy, Molecular Workbench visualizations have an intuitive interface. Typical students using Molecular Workbench demonstrate large gains in understanding of atomic- and molecular-level interactions, reasoning about atoms and molecules, and transfer to understanding of new problems (http://www.concord.org).

### Modeling Derivatives

To help students develop a qualitative understanding of the relationship between a function and its derivative, even before they are taught the formality of mathematics, Shternberg and Yerushalmy (2002) developed the function and derivative model (Figure 12.11) as part of the Visual Math project (http://www.cet.ac.il/math/function/english/). The model allows comparison of two views: a function view at the top and a derivative view at the bottom. Using a set of seven graphical icons, learners can build their own function. As they build and manipulate the function, they view how the derivative changes. This model can be used for student-initiated problems or as part of the activities in the Visual Math curriculum.

### Pragmatic Principle: Encourage Reflection

A well-established method for promoting lifelong learning is to encourage learners to reflect on their own learning and generate explanations. Linn and Hsi (2000) found that, when learners reflect, they monitor their progress and reach new insights. The pattern of conducting an exploration and then reflecting improves understanding (Davis, 2006). Combining an experiment, investigation, or research endeavor with reflection can improve both activities. In contrast to text materials, technology-enhanced materials can prompt students to reflect and capture student ideas while they are learning. Finding the appropriate amount and type of reflection requires iterative design and depends heavily on the context. Designing prompts that elicit reflection is challenging. Some prompts just lead students to conclude that they were successful (Davis and Linn, 2000). The examples below show how this principle helps teachers and learners.

### Prompts for Reflection on Action in CASES

Prompts for reflection are a part of a teachers' online journal tool in CASES (Davis, 2006). They appear as sentence starters or questions listed on the left side of the journal. Two to six prompts are listed under each of three different categories: thinking about today, planning ahead, and general thoughts. A teacher selects a prompt from the left column and the prompts appear in the journal. The prompts are designed to elicit information

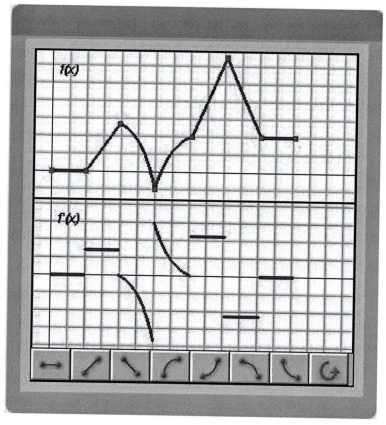

**Figure 12.11** Function and derivative model in Visual Math.

that may otherwise remain tacit, such as justifications for curricular decisions. This reflection on action influences student learning outcomes by helping teachers to think critically about their lessons and teaching methods and to make more effective decisions in real time in the classroom (Davis and Krajcik, 2005).

*Note Taking in WISE*

The WISE environment allows designers to embed notes and students to view them at any time. Prompts direct students to explain their ideas, make connections, or make predictions (see Figure 12.1). Slotta (2004) showed that reflection notes can help students monitor their own learning.

## DISCUSSION AND CONCLUSIONS

In summary, to identify promising supports for inquiry learning we took advantage of a community resource—the Design Principles Database. We organized the discussion around the meta-principles to capture essential elements of effective instruction. To illustrate the meta-principles, we selected the pragmatic principles that connected to the largest number

of features. We provided evidence for the pragmatic principles by describing research on illustrative features. These features communicate the complexity of inquiry instruction as well as the insights emerging in recent research programs.

These results, other findings in the Design Principles Database, and related research all provide strong support for the four meta-principles. First, effective supports for inquiry make science accessible by connecting to the interests or ideas held by the learner (Krajcik et al., 1998; Linn and Hsi, 2000). When students grapple with everyday examples, they can evaluate their intuitive ideas and distinguish them from normative views. Second, effective supports make thinking about scientific phenomena visible to teachers and learners by animating, visualizing, articulating, or representing complex phenomena in multiple ways (Linn et al., 2006). Modern technologies offer a window on unseen scientific phenomena, combined with supports that enable interpretation of these events. Third, effective supports help students learn from each other by asking students to explain their ideas and to critique the ideas of others (Davis, 2006). When students discuss their ideas, they can develop criteria to distinguish them. Fourth, effective supports promote autonomy by stimulating learners to monitor their progress and reflect on their learning (White and Frederiksen, 1998). When students evaluate their own ideas, they can learn to think critically about their progress.

As these examples reveal, designers of inquiry environments have created powerful features that can give new designers a head start on building effective inquiry instruction. The value of the full set of metaprinciples is also reflected in the connections among the features in the Design Principles Database and in the characteristics of learning environments that include multiple features. Features are linked to the pragmatic principle that they illustrate, but some features also have elements that connect to other pragmatic principles. For example, the features that enable three-dimensional manipulation of scientific phenomena also have elements that promote autonomy by asking students to reflect on their observations. Learning environments such as WISE and Model-It typically include features that connect to all four meta-principles; for example, WISE includes SenseMaker, Principle Maker, online discussions, and reflection notes. Evidence in the Design Principles Database suggests that it is reasonable to conclude that effective supports for inquiry should take advantage of all four metaprinciples.

Another way to evaluate the features is to examine how they support the process of knowledge integration described in the introduction. The features in the Design Principles Database support one or more of the four processes of knowledge integration: eliciting ideas, adding ideas, developing criteria, and sorting out ideas. Features such as collaborative brainstorming or reflections on everyday phenomena elicit student ideas. Features such as representations or animations of scientific phenomena add new ideas to those held by the learner. Features such as peer evaluation or SenseMaker encourage students to develop criteria for distinguishing among ideas. Features such as Causal Mapper or prompts for reflection encourage learners to sort out their ideas. These connections between features and the processes of knowledge integration prompted the development of design patterns that describe promising combinations of features (Linn, 2006; Linn and Eylon, 2006).

A design pattern is a sequence of activities followed by teachers and students in a classroom. Linn and Eylon (2006) synthesized a broad range of research on inquiry science to identify patterns that employ the four knowledge integration processes in productive ways. These four processes play out in ten design patterns that research has shown to promote knowledge integration; for example, the pattern using modeling or simulation to enable knowledge integration starts by eliciting predictions about an observable phenomenon such as heating water. The pattern then adds ideas using a feature such as Molecular Workbench. Next, the pattern might guide learners to form conjectures and compare them using a feature such as Principle Maker. Finally, the pattern might help learners consolidate ideas with a feature such as note taking. We are currently linking design principles and design patterns.

The Design Principles Database is effective when it is built into a structured design process and used in a social context, such as a graduate course or a workshop (Kali et al., 2007). Participants in such courses found that the design principles approach assisted them in brainstorming ideas for activities, in generating alternatives, and in designing specific activities; however, they found that the Design Principles Database did not provide sufficient guidance for putting these activities together to create learning environments.

Design patterns can help with this dilemma by suggesting sequences of activities. The Design Principles Database helps when designers seek ways to implement the activities in the sequence. By testing and refining these resources for designers and by adding additional resources that capture the experiences of designers, the field can become more cumulative.

The Design Principles Database is a work in progress. As more designers add their features, new pragmatic principles may emerge, and existing principles may need revisions. The Design Principles Database can help the field become more cumulative by capturing the interplay between the learning context and the design guidelines. Many instructional designers use the analyze, design, develop, implement, and evaluate (ADDIE) framework to create and test innovations (Dick et al., 2001). Those committed to design research acknowledge the importance of the iterative refinement process, in which designs are tested multiple times (Barab and Squire, 2004; Bell et al., 2004; Collins et al., 2004; Design-Based Research Collective, 2003). Both approaches yield results that can be added to the database. In addition, we continue to sponsor opportunities to add and refine features and principles. These activities will elaborate and improve our understanding of supports for inquiry learning.

## ACKNOWLEDGMENTS

This material is based on work supported by the National Science Foundation under grants Nos. 9873180, 9805420, 0087832, 9720384, and 0334199. Any opinions, findings, and conclusions or recommendations expressed in this material are those of the authors and do not necessarily reflect the views of the National Science Foundation. The authors gratefully acknowledge helpful discussions of these ideas with members of the Web-based Inquiry Science Environment group and the Technology Enhanced Learning in Science center. We would like to thank all the people who helped shape the framework and contributed features and principles to the Design Principles Database. Special thanks go to Tamar Ronen-Fuhrmann and Yaakov Snyder for eliciting designers' features and principles as part of the Design Principles Database editorial board effort. The authors appreciate the help in production of this manuscript from David Crowell and Jonathan Breitbart.

## REFERENCES

Alexander, C., Ishikawa, S., and Silverstein, M. (1977). *A Pattern Language: Towns, Buildings, and Construction*. New York: Oxford University Press.

Barab, S. A. and Squire, K. D. (2004). Design-based research: putting our stake in the ground. *J. Learn. Sci.*, 13(1), 1–14.

Barab, S. A., Hay, K. E., Barnett, M. G., and Keating, T. (2000). Virtual solar system project: building understanding through model building. *J. Res. Sci. Teach.*, 37(7), 719–756.

Barak, M. and Dori, Y. J. (2005). Enhancing undergraduate students' chemistry understanding through project-based learning in an IT environment. *Sci. Educ.*, 89(1), 117–139.

Baumgartner, E. (2004). Synergy research and knowledge integration: customizing activities around stream ecology. In *Internet Environments for Science Education*, edited by M. C. Linn, E. A. Davis, and P. Bell, pp. 73–85. Mahwah, NJ: Lawrence Erlbaum Associates.

Bell, P. (2004). The educational opportunities of contemporary controversies in science. In *Internet Environments for Science Education*, edited by M. C. Linn, E. A. Davis, and P. Bell, pp. 115–144. Mahwah, NJ: Lawrence Erlbaum Associates.

Bell, P., Hoadley, C. M., and Linn, M. C. (2004). Design-based research in education. In *Internet Environments for Science Education*, edited by M. C. Linn, E. A. Davis, and P. Bell, pp. 73–85. Mahwah, NJ: Lawrence Erlbaum Associates.*

Bransford, J. D., Brown, A. L., and Cocking, R. R., Eds. (1999). *How People Learn: Brain, Mind, Experience, and School*. Washington, D.C.: National Research Council.*

Brown, A. L. (1992). Design experiments: theoretical and methodological challenges in creating complex interventions in classroom settings. *J. Learn. Sci.*, 2(2), 141–178.

Bruer, J. T. (1993). *Schools for Thought: A Science of Learning in the Classroom*. Cambridge, MA: MIT Press.

Clark, D. B. and Linn, M. C. (2003). Designing for knowledge integration: the impact of instructional time. *J. Learn. Sci.*, 12(4), 451–494.*

Clark, D. B. and Sampson, V. (2007). Personally seeded discussions to scaffold online argumentation. *Int. J. Sci. Educ.*, 29(3), 253–277.

Cognition and Technology Group at Vanderbilt. (1990). Anchored instruction and its relationship to situated cognition. *Educ. Res.*, 19(6), 2–10.*

Cognition and Technology Group at Vanderbilt. (1997). *The Jasper Project: Lessons in Curriculum, Instruction, Assessment, and Professional Development*. Mahwah, NJ: Lawrence Erlbaum Associates.

Collins, A. (1992). Toward a design science of education. In *New Directions in Educational Technology*, edited by E. Scanlon and T. O'Shea, pp. 15–22. Berlin: Springer-Verlag.*

Collins, A., Brown, J. S., and Holum, A. (1991). Cognitive apprenticeship: making thinking visible. *Am. Educ.*, 15(3), 6–11, 38–39.

Collins, A., Joseph, D., and Bielaczyc, K. (2004). Design research: theoretical and methodological issues. *J. Learn. Sci.*, 13(1), 15–42.

Davis, E. A. (2006). Characterizing productive reflection among preservice elementary teachers: seeing what matters. *Teach. Teacher Educ.*, 22(3), 281–301.

Davis, E. A. and Krajcik, J. S. (2005). Designing educative curriculum materials to promote teacher learning. *Educ. Res.*, 34(3), pp. 3–14.

Davis, E. A. and Linn, M. C. (2000). Scaffolding students' knowledge integration: prompts for reflection in KIE. *Int. J. Sci. Educ.*, 22, 819–837.

Derry, S. J., Hmelo-Silver, C. E., and Feltovich, J. (2005). Making a mesh of it: a STELLAR approach to teacher professional development. In *Proc. of the 2005 Computer Supported Collaborative Learning (CSCL): Learning 2005—The Next 10 Years!*, May 30–June 4, Taipei.

Design-Based Research Collective. (2003). Design-based research: an emerging paradigm for educational inquiry. *Educ. Res.*, 32(1), 5–8.

Dick, W., Carey, L., and Carey, J. O. (2001). *The Systematic Design of Instruction*, 5th ed. New York: Longman.

diSessa, A. A. (2000). *Changing Minds: Computers, Learning and Literacy*. Cambridge, MA: MIT Press.*

Dori, Y. J., Barak, M., and Adir, N. (2003). A Web-based chemistry course as a means to foster freshmen learning. *J. Chem. Educ.*, 80(9), 1084–1092.

Dori, Y. J., Barak, M., Herscovitz, O., and Carmi, M. (2006). Preparing pre- and in-service teachers to teach high school science with technology. In *Preparing Teachers to Teach with Technology*, edited by C. Vrasidas and G. V. Glass. Greenwich, CT: Information Age.

Edelson, D. C. (1999). Addressing the challenges of inquiry-based learning through technology and curriculum design. *J. Learn. Sci.*, 8(3/4), 391–450.

Edelson, D. C., Gordin, D., and Pea, R. D. (1999). Addressing the challenges of inquiry-based learning through technology and curriculum design. *J. Learn. Sci.*, 8(3/4), 391–450.

Fishman, B., Marx, R., Blumenfeld, P., Krajcik, J. S., and Soloway, E. (2004). Creating a framework for research on systemic technology innovations. *J. Learn. Sci.*, 13(1), 43–76.

Gamma, E., Helm, R., Johnson, R., and Vlissides, J. (1995). *Design Patterns: Elements of Reusable Object-Oriented Software*. Reading, MA: Addison-Wesley.

Hegarty, M., Quilici, J., Narayan, N. H., Homquist, S., and Moreno, R. (1999). Multimedia instruction: lessons from evaluation of a theory-based design. *J. Educ. Multimedia Hypermedia*, 8(2), 1119–1150.

Herrington, J., Reeves, T. C., and Oliver, R. (2005). Online learning as information delivery: digital myopia. *J. Interact. Learn. Res.*, 16(4), p. 353–367.

Hmelo-Silver, C., Derry, S., Woods, D., DelMarcelle M., and Chernobilsky, E. (2005). From parallel play to meshed interaction: the evolution of the eSTEP system. In *Proc. of the 2005 Computer Supported Collaborative Learning (CSCL): Learning 2005—The Next 10 Years!*, May 30–June 4, Taipei.

Hofer, B. K. and Pintrich, P. R., Eds. (2002). *Personal Epistemology: The Psychology of Beliefs About Knowledge and Knowing*. Mahwah, NJ: Lawrence Erlbaum Associates.

Hsi, S., Linn, M. C., and Bell, J. (1997). The role of spatial reasoning in engineering and the design of spatial instruction. *J. Eng. Educ.*, 86(2), 151–158.

Jackson, S., Krajcik, J., and Soloway, E. (2000). Model-It: a design retrospective. In *Advanced Designs for the Technologies of Learning: Innovations in Science and Mathematics Education*, edited by M. Jacobson and R. Kozma, pp. 77–116. Hillsdale, NJ: Lawrence Erlbaum Associates.

Kali, Y. (2006). Collaborative knowledge building using the Design Principles Database. *Int. J. Comput. Support Collab. Learn.*, 1(2), 187–201.

Kali, Y. (in press). The Design Principles Database as means for promoting design-based research. In *Handbook of Design Research Methods in Education*, edited by A. E. Kelly and R. Lesh. Mahwah, NJ: Lawrence Erlbaum Associates.

Kali, Y. and Orion, N. (1996). Spatial abilities of high-school students in the perception of geologic structures. *J. Res. Sci. Teach.*, 33, 369–391.

Kali, Y. and Ronen, M. (2005). Design principles for online peer-evaluation: fostering objectivity. In *Proc. of the 2005 Computer Supported Collaborative Learning (CSCL): Learning 2005—The Next 10 Years!*, May 30–June 4, Taipei.

Kali, Y., Orion, N., and Mazor, E. (1997). Software for assisting high school students in the spatial perception of geological structures. *J. Geosci. Educ.*, 45, 10–21.

Kali, Y., Bos, N., Linn, M., Underwood, J., and Hewitt, J. (2002). Design principles for educational software. In *Proc. of the 2002 Computer Supported Collaborative Learning (CSCL)*, January 7–11, Boulder, CO.

Kali, Y. and Ronen-Fuhrmann, T. (2007). How can the design of educational technologies affect graduate students' epistemologies about learning? In *Computer Supported Collaborative Learning 2007: Mice, Minds and Society*, edited by C. Hmelo-Silver and A. O'Donnell. Mahwah, NJ: Lawrence Erlbaum Associates.

Kolodner, J. L., Owensby, J. N., and Guzdial, M. (2004). Case-based learning aids. In *Handbook of Research for Education Communications and Technology*, 2nd ed., edited by D. H. Jonassen, pp. 829–861. Mahwah, NJ: Lawrence Erlbaum Associates.*

Krajcik, J. S., Blumenfeld, P. C., Marx, R. W., Bass, K. M., Fredricks, J., and Soloway, E. (1998). Inquiry in project-based science classrooms: initial attempts by middle school students. *J. Learn. Sci.*, 7(3/4), 313–350.

Linn, M. C. (1995). Designing computer learning environments for engineering and computer science: the scaffolded knowledge integration framework. *J. Sci. Educ. Technol.*, 4(2), 103–126.

Linn, M. C. and Eylon, B.-S. (2006). Science education: integrating views of learning and instruction. In *Handbook of Educational Psychology*, 2nd ed., edited by A. Alexander and P. H. Winne, pp. 511–544. Mahwah, NJ: Lawrence Erlbaum Associates.*

Linn, M. C. and Hsi, S. (2000). *Computers, Teachers, Peers: Science Learning Partners*. Mahwah, NJ: Lawrence Erlbaum Associates.

Linn, M. C., Clark, D. B., and Slotta, J. D. (2003). WISE design for knowledge integration. *Sci. Educ.*, 87(4), 517–538.

Linn, M. C., Bell, P., and Davis, E. A. (2004a). Specific design principles: elaborating the scaffolded knowledge integration framework. In *Internet Environments for Science Education*, edited by M. C. Linn, E. A. Davis, and P. Bell, pp. 315–340. Mahwah, NJ: Lawrence Erlbaum Associates.

Linn, M. C., Davis, E. A., and Bell, P., Eds. (2004b). *Internet Environments for Science Education*. Mahwah, NJ: Lawrence Erlbaum Associates.

Linn, M. C., Lee, H.-S., Tinker, R., Husic, F., and Chiu, J. L. (2006). Teaching and assessing knowledge integration. *Science*, 313, 1049–1050.

Means, B. (1994). *Technology and Education Reform: The Reality Behind the Promise*. San Francisco, CA: Jossey-Bass.

Merrill, M. D. (2002). First principles of instruction. *Educ. Technol. Res. Dev.*, 50(3), 43–59.*

Mioduser, D., Nachmias, R., Oren, A., and Lahav, O. (1999). Web-based learning environments (WBLES): current implementation and evolving trends. *J. Netw. Comput. Appl.*, 22, 233–247.

Pallant, A. and Tinker, R. (2004). Reasoning with atomic-scale molecular dynamic models. *J. Sci. Educ. Technol.*, 13(1), 51–66.

Quintana, C., Reiser, B. J., Davis, E. A., Krajcik, J., Fretz, E., Golan-Duncan R. et al. (2004). A scaffolding design framework for software to support science inquiry, *J. Learn. Sci.*, 13(3), 337–386.

Reigeluth, C. M. (1999). *Instructional Design Theories and Models: A New Paradigm of Instructional Theory*, Vol. II. Mahwah, NJ: Lawrence Erlbaum Associates.*

Reiser, B. J., Tabak, I., Sandoval, W. A., Smith, B. K., Steinmuller, F., and Leone, A. J. (2001). BGuILE: strategic and conceptual scaffolds for scientific inquiry in biology classrooms. In *Cognition and Instruction: Twenty-Five Years of Progress*, edited by S. M. Carver and D. Klahr, pp. 263–305. Mahwah, NJ: Lawrence Erlbaum Associates.

Roschelle, J., Pea, P., Hoadley, C., Gordin, D., and Means, B. (2000). Changing how and what children learn in school with computer-based technologies. *The Future of Children and Computer Technology*, 10(2), 76–101.

Schwartz, D. L., Lin, X., Brophy, S., and Bransford, J. D. (1999). Toward the development of flexibly adaptive instructional designs. In *Instructional Design Theories and Models*, Vol. II, edited by C. M. Reigeluth, pp. 183–213. Mahwah, NJ: Lawrence Erlbaum Associates.

Scradamalia, M. and Bereiter, C. (1994). Computer support for knowledge-building communities. *J. Learn. Sci.*, 3(3), 265–283.

Scardamalia, M. and Bereiter, C. (1996). Computer support for knowledge-building communities. In *CSCL: Theory and Practice of an Emerging Paradigm*, edited by T. Koschmann, pp. 249–268. Mahwah, NJ: Lawrence Erlbaum Associates.*

Seethaler, S. and Linn, M. C. (2004). Genetically modified food in perspective: an inquiry-based curriculum to help middle school students make sense of tradeoffs. *Int. J. Sci. Educ.*, 26(14), 1765–1785.

Shternberg, B. and Yerushalmy, M. (2003). Models of functions and models of situations: on design of a modeling based learning environment In *Beyond Constructivism: A Model and Modeling Perspective on Teaching, Learning, and Problem Solving in Mathematics Education*, edited by H. M. Doerr and R. Lesh, pp. 479–500. Mahwah, NJ: Lawrence Erlbaum Associates.

Simon, H. A. (1969). *The Sciences of the Artificial*. Cambridge, MA: MIT Press.

Slotta, J. D. (2004). The Web-based Inquiry Science Environment (WISE): scaffolding teachers to adopt inquiry and technology. In *Internet Environments for Science Education*, edited by M. C. Linn, P. Bell, and E. A. Davis, pp. 203–232. Mahwah, NJ: Lawrence Erlbaum Associates.

Songer, N. B. and Linn, M. C. (1991). How do students' views of science influence knowledge integration? *J. Res. Sci. Teach.*, 28(9), 761–784.

Songer, N. B., Lee, H.-S., and McDonald, S. (2002). Research towards an expanded understanding of inquiry science beyond one idealized standard. *Sci. Educ.*, 87(4), 454–467.

Tate, E. (2005). Hanging with Friends, Velocity Style! A Preliminary Investigation of How Technology-Enhanced Instruction Impacts Students' Understanding of Multiple Representations of Velocity. Poster presented at the annual meeting of the American Educational Research Association, April 11–15, Montreal, Canada.

Tinker, R. (2005). Five lessons: a taste of the future, today. *The Concord Consortium Newsletter: Realizing the Promise of Educational Technology*, Fall (http://www.concord.org/publications/newsletter/2005-fall/five.html).

Tufte, E. R. (1983). *The Visual Display of Quantitative Information*. Cheshire, CT: Graphics Press.

White, B. Y. and Frederiksen, J. R. (1998). Inquiry, modeling, and metacognition: making science accessible to all students. *Cognit. Instruct.*, 16(1), 3–118.

Williams, M. and Linn, M. C. (2003). Collaborating with WISE scientists. *Sci. Child.*, 41(1), 31–35.

van den Akker, J. (1999). Principles and methods of development research. In *Design Methodology and Developmental Research in Education and Training*, edited by J. van den Akker, N. Nieveen, R. M. Branch, K. L. Gustafson, and T. Plomp, pp. 1–14. Dordrecht: Kluwer.

* Indicates a core reference.

# 13

# A Distributed Perspective on Collaborative Activity

*Thomas Satwicz*
University of Georgia, Athens, Georgia

*Reed Stevens*
University of Washington, Seattle, Washington

## CONTENTS

## ABSTRACT

Collaborative learning is often cited as a means to a productive educational experience for students. With this in mind, designers and researchers have taken to building technologies that support various forms of collaborative activity in schools and other learning environments. In this chapter, we take a look at how studies of collaborative learning have developed over time in relation to a shift away from exclusively individualistic conceptions of human activity in educational research and design. We use *prescriptions* for and *descriptions* of collaborative learning as two general categories for understanding research and design. By prescriptions, we mean ideas, principles, and representations of designs for collaboration. By descriptions, we mean empirical accounts of collaboration. In our view, a broad survey of writing on collaborative activity displays an imbalance; we are light on descriptions and heavy on prescriptions. Toward tipping this imbalance back, we argue that a productive perspective for casting descriptions of collaborative learning is a *distributed* one. A distributed perspective is one that considers human activity in relation to both other people and things. We use some of our own work to illustrate this perspective. We conclude by using the distributed perspective to challenge researchers to consider technological artifacts as inherently collaborative and to move their work forward under this assumption.

## KEYWORDS

*Collaboration:* Activity involving multiple people developing shared meaning while working together on a common problem; often involves harmonious cooperation but is not contingent upon it.

*Descriptive accounts:* Analysis of naturally occurring instances of human activity.

*Distributed perspective:* An analytic approach to understanding human activity that distributes agency across people *and* material artifacts.

*Prescriptive accounts:* Designed tools, strategies, and interventions.

## INTRODUCTION

Over the last 15 to 20 years, educational researchers have taken a special interest in sustaining and understanding collaborative learning. In our chapter, we offer a necessarily incomplete survey of the concepts, methods, and technologies used in research on collaboration. We use two general categories to characterize work on collaborative learning. The first category, *prescriptions* for collaboration, includes designed tools, strategies, and interventions to support collaborative learning. The purpose of this research is to develop new technologies and methods based on theories of learning to support collaboration in classrooms and other settings. The second category, which represents much less research literature, we call *descriptions* of collaboration. Descriptive work focuses analysis on examples of collaboration that naturally occur in social situations or have been designed but are studied as naturally occurring events.

The purpose of descriptive accounts is to understand collaboration on multiple levels, at the moment-to-moment unfolding of collaborative activity and at a larger social organizational level (Becker, 1996; Hall

and Stevens, 1995). Our view is that descriptions beget prescriptions and prescriptions need description, but the field is too light on careful descriptions (Stevens, 2001). Our goal in this chapter, beyond highlighting this imbalance, is to show how basic ethnographic descriptions of collaboration are helpful to understanding and designing for collaboration and for working with the essential tension of the individual and the group in learning situations. From there, we suggest that a distributed perspective on human activity is generally useful for research on collaboration, and we sketch some of the core concepts and studies that take this perspective. The distributed perspective reconsiders how we account for collaboration through an analysis of interactions between humans and nonhumans, to use terms from Bruno Latour (1987, 1996).

In this chapter, we use Hutchins' definition of learning as "adaptive reorganization in a complex system" (Hutchins, 1995a, p. 289) to guide our look at examples of collaboration and their impact on learning. While using this notion of learning we keep in mind that the "relevant complex system includes a Web of *coordination* [italics added] among media and processes inside and outside the individual task performers" (Hutchins, 1995a, p. 289). We take collaboration to be activity that involves multiple people developing *shared meaning* while working together on a common problem (Stahl et al., 2006); this often involves harmonious cooperation but is not contingent upon it (Pea, 1994; Stevens, 2000). Our take is that a key aspect of working together involves coordinating people and representational devices, including computers and other forms of media (Hutchins, 1995a). We see the study of collaborative learning as being about the emergent coordination of people and representational devices to accomplish a set of tasks (Stevens, 2000; Stevens and Hall, 1998). Coordination is a part of what sets adaptive reorganization apart from just any reorganization. In our view, adaptive reorganization implies a reaction to a new task or chronic snag (de la Rocha, 1986); to successfully resolve the snag or accomplish the task coordination of people and objects is necessary. As a concept, then, the complex system is useful for considering how interactions between people and the objects they use change during collaborative activity.

We consider, in light of Hutchins' definition, individual change to be an important aspect of the learning process, but we want to highlight that our view of learning extends beyond individuals. Much of the work we draw on in this chapter comes from perspectives that consider learning primarily as an individual process and measures the results of collaboration based on individual notions of learning. We use this work in an attempt to build a bridge between the two perspectives so individualist terms are not the only way to conceive of learning. Along these lines, we do not have any easy solutions for measuring individual change with the distributed perspective; however, in particular domains (e.g., video gaming, math, science, cooking) we suggest that accessing one's ability to develop a distributed system where people and tools are effectively coordinated is a potential starting point.

By casting learning as a process that extends beyond individual change we are attempting to confront a mismatch present in much of the research on collaboration. As Barron (2003, p. 352) pointed out, "much of the empirical research on collaboration has utilized individually defined traits and outcomes." In other words, collaboration as a process with multiple actors—both human and nonhuman—is often held up to measures that only account for abilities in individuals (Stevens, 2000). With Hutchins' definition as a starting point, we are attempting to move beyond this mismatch.

# CONCEPTS, METHODOLOGIES, AND TECHNOLOGIES

The relatively recent focus on collaboration occurred as research on learning and cognition expanded its perspective to include socially situated human activity. For most of the 20th century, educational research on learning was closely tied to mainstream psychology. Before the 1970s, mainstream psychology and a great deal of educational research took the form of behaviorism, which concerned itself with focusing individuals on narrowly defined tasks. Eventually, the paradigm of behaviorism gave way to the so-called "cognitive revolution" (Bruner, 1997), which offered a more complex view of human learning but one that still focused on individuals. It is beyond the scope of this chapter to dwell on the details of how research on learning is shifting with more global paradigm shifts from behaviorism to cognitivism and beyond (Stevens et al., 2005); however, we would like to point out that, for much of the history of learning research, the concern has been with individuals and what goes on inside their heads (Bransford et al., 2000). Our look at collaborative learning begins at a time when sociocultural and situated perspectives on learning compete with mainstream psychology's mentalistic approach. The shift was based in part on a move from mentalist conceptions of human learning to a perspective that treats concepts such as *practice* and *activity* as primary (Cole, 1996; Lave, 1988; Vygotsky, 1962; Wertsch, 1998).

# Sociocultural Research on Learning and Situated Action

The expanded influence of interests beyond mainstream psychology on educational research is due, in part, to sociocultural perspectives on learning having taken hold among designers and researchers. The sociocultural view of human activity is based in part on Vygotskian notions of human action which stresses the role that culture, tools, and artifacts play in human thinking (Cole, 1996; Wertsch, 1998). The expansion beyond mainstream psychology to include a situated action perspective that focuses less on the properties of the human mind and more on social and material aspects of a learning context has not been without controversy (Anderson et al., 1996; Greeno, 1997). A strong element of the situated action movement has been to understand collaboration as an important element of learning.

One of the more common ways in which the sociocultural perspective has found its way into designed technologies for learning is through scaffolded learning environments that attempt to engage students in collaborative scientific inquiry. These prescriptions are based on the idea that students are able to achieve more with guided support from a knowledgeable helper than they would on their own (Wood et al., 1976). Scaffolding technologies are designed to aid students in collaborative activities such as scientific inquiry (Kolodner et al., 2003) and argumentation (Bell, 2001). Scaffolded environments build off the idea that learners are able to achieve more in a context where external supports, either social or material, provide for more complex and difficult thinking. It is postulated that over time the students will no longer need the technological or social supports due to conceptual change and the development of new inquiry practices. In other words, learners internalize relevant aspects of the scaffold. Research on scaffolded learning environments often takes a prescriptive form, arguing for new ways to engage students in collaborative scientific inquiry (Kolodner et al., 2003). The primary focus of this work is to better understand how to engage students in scientific inquiry to promote conceptual change.

Roschelle (1992) attempted the integration of two theoretical ideas—conceptual change and a collaborative-interactional perspective—to understand how two or more people develop shared meanings. His work is one example of how descriptions have been used to identify aspects of student interactions with technology that are relevant to collaboration. He analyzed the interactions of two young girls using software that simulated velocity and acceleration from the perspective of Newtonian physics. Over several iterations of displaying, confirming, and repairing actions, the two girls developed a set of shared meanings for the concepts at hand. Roschelle showed *how* their interactions led to new ideas about the way the physical world works. His analysis, which focused on their conceptual change, revealed that "conversational interaction can enable students to construct relational meanings incrementally" (Roschelle, 1992, p. 237). The importance of this work was to integrate collaboration and conceptual change through careful description of moment-to-moment action. Its contribution was in identifying conceptual change as a process that involves social and material aspects of an environment and the development of shared meaning across students.

Stevens and Hall's (1998) descriptive comparison of a tutor assisting a student through mathematical problem solving and two civil engineers working collaboratively provides a nice complement to the study by Roschelle. They, too, found that over time a convergence of shared meaning occurred incrementally, resulting in the emergent coordination of people and objects; however, rather than cast two people in the roles of learners as Roschelle did, Stevens and Hall looked at naturally occurring asymmetrical pairs who were working together. They showed how a student's and a junior engineer's perception of mathematical representations, what they characterized as *disciplined perception*, changed through interactions with a more knowledgeable collaborator.

Brigid Barron (2003) expanded Roschelle's (1992) study of collaboration and conceptual change to better understand how problem-solving space is used in successful collaborative groups. Barron's (2003) work, another descriptive account, compared successful collaborative groups with unsuccessful groups. As a condition, she found that successful groups have a *relational space* and a *content space*. The relational space exists for interactional challenges and opportunities, while the content space is for the problem to be solved. The existence of these different spaces meant successful groups had fewer challenges achieving joint attention and were able to better capitalize on their members' insights. Her work reinforced the idea that cognitive limitations are not sufficient in explaining why groups fail.

## Computer-Supported Collaborative Learning

The expansion beyond individualist notions of human activity also led to the development of a field known as *computer-supported collaborative learning* (CSCL) (Koschmann, 1994). CSCL work involves designing, developing, and describing technologies to support collaboration in learning environments. In CSCL, the "focus [is] no longer on what might be taking place in the heads of individual learners, but what [is] taking place between them in their interactions" (Stahl et al., 2006, p. 415). Two of the earliest and most established CSCL environments, the Computer-Supported Intentional Learning Environment (CSILE) and the Fifth Dimension, are representative of the difference between a focus on changes in social interactions and mental states as outcomes of collaboration.

### The Computer-Supported Intentional Learning Environment (CSILE)

The Computer-Supported Intentional Learning Environment (now referred to as Knowledge Forum) was one of the earliest examples of a technological prescription for enabling collaborative learning (Scardamalia and Bereiter, 1994). The environment was designed to promote learning by encouraging the development of collaborative knowledge-building communities rather than focusing students on specific tasks. A collaborative knowledge-building community acts somewhat like a small version of a scientific community where big ideas are collectively constructed over time by a group of people (Latour, 1987). With CSILE and Knowledge Forum, students post graphical or text-based notes to relay questions, research plans, and newly found information. These notes can then be linked to form a kind of collaborative inquiry over a local networked environment.

Almost two decades of work on CSILE and Knowledge Forum have demonstrated how networked environments can be used to promote collaborative knowledge building. In a knowledge-building community in school, "learning is not asymptotic because what one person does in adapting changes the environment so that others must readapt" (Scardamalia and Bereiter, 1994, p. 267). In other words, individual contributions raise the standard that others must work for and the nature of learning changes when compared with a traditional classroom. This notion, where learning involves adapting to changes in the context created through social interactions, echoes the sentiments of Hutchins' definition of learning as "adaptive reorganization in a complex system" (Hutchins, 1995a, p. 289) and may be an example of how the coordination of people and objects can impact an individual's thinking. Gilbert and Driscoll (2002) built off the work on CSILE in an attempt to better understand what conditions are necessary for knowledge-building communities. They employed four learning principles to support collaborative knowledge building in a graduate level course. Their principles involve setting a collective goal, using cooperative groups, allowing for selection of materials to support ownership, and using technological tools to archive work and facilitate communication.

### The Fifth Dimension

Another early CSCL environment was the Fifth Dimension (5th D) project initiated by Mike Cole and others at the Laboratory for Comparative Human Cognition (LCHC). The primary focus here was to develop an activity system in after-school clubs that provided "optimal conditions for children's learning and development" (Kaptelinin and Cole, 2001, p. 307). The design of this social system to support collaborative computer game playing is also based on a sociocultural perspective of human activity (Cole, 1996). The primary contribution of this work has been a sustainable model of social interaction that minimizes the power differential between children and adults through a variety of artifacts in the environment. Ito has provided important descriptive accounts of 5th D and shown, in part, that children appropriate the technologies in the environment to accomplish their own goals, which are often at odds with those of the adults (Ito, 1997, 2002, 2005, 2006). The work surrounding the 5th D is a good example of how a descriptive analysis can be applied to the design of a collaborative system.

### CSCL: A Field for Prescription and Description

Supporting collaborative learning with technological tools is an important element of CSCL projects along with a host of other design efforts. A challenge for CSCL, then, is to attend to both the technical and the social aspects of collaboration (Kirschner et al., 2004). Our perspective is that rich descriptions of collaboration that analyze interactions between people and technologies will be productive in achieving that challenge. Along these lines, Stahl et al. (2006) view the field of CSCL as having both descriptive and prescriptive elements that play off each other (Stevens, 2001).

## Distance Education

The Internet has opened many opportunities for collaborative learning, particularly in distance education (Reeves et al., 2004). This prescription often has an explicit focus on fostering online collaborative learning. Additionally, researchers have taken care to craft descriptions for a better understanding of how to get the most out of collaboration in online environments. For example, O'Neill (2001) described how collaborations with professional scientists over networked environments influenced activity in science class-

rooms. He found that students were better able to work within scientific genres when they discussed and shared ideas with professionals. Others looked at how activities in online courses support collaborative learning and confirmed that good pedagogy is as important if not more important than the technology in use (Moallem, 2003). Kato and colleagues (2001) investigated uses of video for distance learning, based on findings from observational studies of how people interact in real settings. Their approach was to design features into a system to allow students and instructors the ability to use gestures, an important aspect of naturally occurring human activity. In another example, Fischer and Mandl (2005) looked at how different representational tools and conditions influenced collaboration during video conferencing and found that in all of their prescribed conditions groups often did not share knowledge. Many of the recommendations from studies of distance learning involve distributing properties of a system across people and artifacts by creating shared objects and assigning individual tasks. As Moallem (2003) contends, successful online collaborative learning is about more than engaging students in the same project, but also about developing shared meaning and knowledge socially.

### Design-Based Research

The shift in our understanding of learning from an individual mental process to socially situated activity has created a methodological challenge for developing collaborative learning environments. If aspects of a context such as materials and relationships are important to supporting learning, then environments for collaboration can be quite complex. Much of the work on scaffolding scientific inquiry, convergent conceptual change, CSCL, and distance education was developed using design-based research (Baumgartner et al., 2003; Brown, 1992; Collins, 1992; Reeves, 2006) to meet the methodological challenges. Design-based research uses iterative cycles of design and observation to build prescriptions for new learning techniques. The implementation of observational methods in the design process helps researchers identify new means for supporting collaboration.

## A DISTRIBUTED PERSPECTIVE

From our position, descriptive accounts influenced by a distributed perspective can be used to better understand the relationship between material objects and the social world in collaborative learning; for example, consider the CSILE environment described above. Where students engage in a knowledge-building community, a distributed look will take the coordinated reorganization of the notes and messages as a learning outcome. The distributed perspective we use here is principally informed by four related approaches to understanding culture, society, and human activity (Bateson, 1972; Becker, 1982; Hutchins, 1995a,b; Latour, 1996). Taken together these approaches emphasize looking beyond individual action to understand human behavior as much of the work on collaborative learning described above already does. What a distributed perspective adds is an increased focus on the material environment as an important aspect of collaboration. In other words, extending the boundary of analysis beyond an individual is applied to nonhuman artifacts as well, a point that lends itself well to a community concerned with the design of learning technologies.

The anthropologist Gregory Bateson (1972) influenced the distributed perspective by expanding conceptualizations of the mind beyond the skin as a means to better explain human behavior. "The mental world—the mind—the world of information processing is not limited by the skin" (Bateson, 1972, p. 454). Bateson explained this expansion of the mind by asking where the mental system of a blind person, using a white cane, begins: Does it begin at the handle, at the end of the stick, or at the sidewalk? He settled the dilemma by including all parts of the system and suggested that the approach was applicable to other behaviors: "If what you are trying to explain is a given piece of behavior, such as the locomotion of the blind man, then, for this purpose, you will need the street, the stick, the man; the street, the stick, and so on, round and round" (Bateson, 1972, p. 459).

The sociologist Howard Becker studied social worlds—a concept similar to communities of practice (Lave and Wenger, 1991; Wenger, 1999)—in art, education, and medicine. In his study of art worlds (Becker, 1982), he analyzed how sets of conventions from art worlds guide the production of new work. Conventions are built into a range of artifacts, from the tools that artists use to the funding mechanisms that support their craft, and make the production of new work possible. "Members of art worlds coordinate the activities by which work is produced by referring to a body of conventional understandings embodied in common practice and in frequently used artifacts" (Becker, 1982, p. 34). His point was that each work of art represents more than the efforts of an individual artist and is a kind of collaboration made possible because of conventions distributed across the objects artists use and the practices they engage in.

Similarly, Latour (1996) has argued that much of what humans can do is built into the material world. In reference to common interactions in a post office, he asked: "How could you compute the daily balance of an office without formulae, receipts, accounts, ledgers—and how can one miss the solidity of the paper, the durability of the ink, the etching of the chips, the shrewdness of the staples and the shock of a rubber stamp?" (Latour, 1996, p. 235). Latour was trying to highlight that much of what humans can do goes beyond the abilities built into the people and is built into the properties of the nonhuman objects themselves. It is the physical nature that gives objects durability in time and space and forms a frame for society. In other words, human behavior is to be best understood as a distribution across people and artifacts.

Finally, Hutchins (1995a,b) took the expansion of the mind and the agency of artifacts and applied it to his ethnographic observations. The result is a human less dependant on complex mental processes and a view of successful activity in the world that is distributed across people *and* artifacts: "This system-level cognitive view directs our attention beyond the cognitive properties of individuals to the properties of external representations and to the interactions between internal and external representations" (Hutchins, 1995b, p. 287).

## PRESCRIPTIONS AND DESCRIPTIONS

Common approaches to promoting collaboration in educational settings could be recast using the distributed perspective. By recasting them we can see relevant aspects of particular systems and how people and objects come into coordination in successful collaborations. Prescriptive research includes work on collaborative problem solving where students are organized into groups and given a variety of tools to scaffold scientific inquiry (Kolodner et al., 2003). Research has also been done to test the effectiveness of conditions for collaboration (Fischer and Mandl, 2005) such as setting collective goals, providing opportunities for ownership, and developing appropriate representational tools. The distributed perspective would consider the emergent coordination of tools and people while students accomplish particular tasks as an important element of learning; therefore, in recasting with this perspective the embodied practices that develop with the use of these tools is foregrounded, and internationalization of the properties of a tool or scaffold is less of a concern. The distributed perspective can be extended to a range of prescriptions, including online environments (Reeves et al., 2004), efforts for teaching collaboration skills (Nath and Ross, 2001), and teacher development programs where collaboration is a means to improving instructional practices. We contend that this is an analytic approach that lends itself well to pushing new designs forward and advancing reiteration in old designs, because understanding the emergent coordination of people, objects, and practices cannot be taken lightly when learning is of concern.

We note that there are many important descriptive accounts of collaboration out there that benefit from a distributed perspective. This work highlights the importance of ensuring that there are spaces where ideas can be heard from all group members (Barron, 2003). It also taught us that collaborative technologies are often not the latest innovation (Stevens, 2000). Additionally descriptive accounts remind us that learners come with their own agendas, which play a role in how the technology gets used (Ito, 2006).

A notable description outside the field of education, but relevant to technology use, took place at the Xerox Palo Alto Research Center (Xerox PARC), where Lucy Suchman (1987) carefully described the interactions between users and copy machine help guides. What is important to take from this work and is relevant to the distributed perspective on collaboration is that Suchman showed that users of intelligent help systems employed the artificial intelligence as a resource rather than a scripted plan. The help systems, from a prescription perspective, are not intended to be a collaborative technology but ended up serving as a resource for collaboration when they came into coordination with the users' activity.

Our ethnographic work on young people's video gaming practices is an example of how we are attempting to roll findings from descriptive research into designed artifacts using a distributed perspective (Satwicz, 2006; Stevens et al., 2007). We began this work, in part, to empirically investigate many of the claims that have been made regarding learning and video games (Gee, 2003; Johnson, 2005). Additionally, because game systems are often designed for use by multiple people and are commonly used in social situations, we saw game play as a place likely for naturally occurring instances of collaboration. Currently, we are beginning to use our descriptions as a means to think about prescriptions for collaborative learning.

In our observations, we have seen kids come up with a host of collaborative learning arrangements. In some situations, more experienced players apprenticed younger players by creating spaces for observation and easy enrollment into the game (Lave and Wenger, 1991). At other times, our participants traded off roles of expert and novice as the tasks they were working on changed. Additionally, we have seen the same game played in quite different ways by different players, suggesting that learning was not programmed into the media but coordinated by the players themselves. We have also seen players use some surprising tools in their collaborations, such as characters and actions in the game. On the whole, we find these instances productive for understanding the many ways in which collaborative learning can happen.

One lesson we are beginning to learn is that the conventions embodied in gaming materials and practices make it easy for kids to organize their own collaborative learning arrangements; for example, we have had our participants describe to us how the consistency of button combinations across games and the design of the controllers make it easy for new games to be taken up and learned. Additionally, because video games are frequently played in family living rooms using television screens viewable by many people at one time, it is easy for players to communicate and share ideas. One design we are in the process of developing is a piece of software that utilizes the conventions built into gaming materials but provides a resource for families to discuss the complexities of institutionalized education and how to be a successful student. The artifact, at this point, is immature, so the ongoing design process is one that will require further descriptive work for a successful, well-grounded prescription.

Video Traces is a medium, designed by the second author, that we describe here as a concrete example of how descriptions of collaborative learning situations can lead to prescriptions in the form of designed artifacts. Across a range of settings, Stevens observed a common pattern of interaction; when working together, people made joint progress through the coordinated use of talk, gesture, and drawing over the surface of drawings or objects that all participants in an interaction could see (Hall and Stevens, 1995; Stevens, 2000, 2007; Stevens and Hall, 1997, 1998). As an example, architects often shared ideas by using their hands or pencils in coordination with their speech to point at and envision possible designs over the surface of drawings. These moments were completely ordinary—they happened all the time—but Stevens found this coordinated use of these ordinary resources to be essential to how people learned and taught together.

Video Traces capitalizes on this coordinated suite of resources by allowing users to record annotations over still or moving images through watching, talking, and pointing (or drawing). This allows people to communicate and share their ideas around a common object in ways that resemble face-to-face collaborative learning situations but without having to be face to face; in essence, Video Traces borrows the technical form of interactional turns in face-to-face interaction and records them. Video Traces has proved useful in a wide range of learning and teaching contexts, including teacher education, museums, dance education, conducting, architecture, and collegiate sports (Stevens, 2007). The important point from the perspective of this chapter is that research involving close description of a range of collaborative settings led to a generalization about collaborative learning that in turn led to a prescription that was embodied in the design digital medium that supports collaboration in a new way.

# DISCUSSION

Our purpose here has been to show some of the conceptual, methodological, and technological milestones in research on collaborative learning. We have indicated that the increase in attention to supporting collaborative learning over the last decade and a half mirrors an expansion of the influences on educational research to include sociocultural and situated perspectives on human activity. Our suggestion is that the next direction in this work should continue this expansion to include a distributed perspective. We pointed to descriptive accounts of collaboration that show how activity is distributed across people and artifacts.

We want to keep pushing for good descriptive accounts that challenge the notion that learning is a process of change *inside* a person (Stevens, 2001); by doing this, we begin to see emergent and unanticipated uses of technology not as a sign of a failed design but as constitutive features of a learning experience. We also remind the reader that when learners do something unexpected, as descriptions show, we have an important foundation to work from. If collaborative learning happens with things that are not designed to be collaborative learning technologies (e.g., paper, single-player video games), then as designers we should take note if we are going to move the field forward.

These ideas echo those of Howard Becker, who has pointed out that the purpose of descriptive work is to find elements of a context that can help us answer our questions: "The object of any description is not to reproduce the object completely—why bother when we have the object already?—but rather to pick out its relevant aspects, details which can be abstracted from the totality of details that make it up so that we can answer some questions we have" (Becker, 1996, p. 64).

Our questions about how collaborative learning is distributed across people and artifacts are well suited for good descriptive accounts. We will end with a final caution on the distributed perspective we advocate for here. Following Suchman (2001), we do not intend to attribute full human agency to machines; however, we do want to push the line. Using Latour's terms, we want to put humans and designed things on the same level. Unlike Latour, however, we do not want to give objects the same kind of agency that we give to people in our analyses. Humans have unique qualities that our descriptive accounts should recognize. The differences, however, are an open question and for us a reason to continue this line of work.

# REFERENCES

Anderson, J. R., Reder, L. M., and Simon, H. A. (1996). Situated learning and education. *Educ. Res.*, 25(4), 5–11.

Barron, B. (2003). When smart groups fail. *J. Learn. Sci.*, 12(3), 307–359.

Bateson, G. (1972). Form, substance, and difference. In *Steps to An Ecology of Mind*, edited by G. Bateson, pp. 448–466. New York: Ballantine Books.*

Baumgartner, E., Bell, P., Brophy, S., Hoadley, C., Hsi, S., Joseph, D. et al. (2003). Design-based research: an emerging paradigm for educational inquiry. *Educ. Res.*, 32(1), 5–8.

Becker, H. S. (1982). *Art Worlds*. Berkeley, CA: University of California Press.

Becker, H. S. (1996). The epistemology of qualitative research. In *Essays on Ethnography and Human Development*, edited by R. Jessor, A. Colby, and R. Schweder, pp. 53–71. Chicago, IL: University of Chicago Press.*

Bell, P. (2001). Using argument map representations to make thinking visible for individuals and groups. In *CSCL 2: Carrying Forward the Conversation*, edited by T. Koschmann, R. Hall, and N. Miyake, pp. 449–485. Mahway, NJ: Lawrence Erlbaum Associates.

Bransford, J. D., Brown, A. L., and Cocking, R. R., Eds. (2000). *How People Learn: Brain, Mind, Experience, and School*. Washington, D.C.: National Academy Press.

Brown, A. L. (1992). Design experiments: theoretical and methodological challenges in creating complex interventions in classroom settings. *J. Learn. Sci.*, 2(2), 141–178.

Bruner, J. (1997). Will cognitive revolutions ever stop? In *The Future of the Cognitive Revolution*, edited by D. M. Johnson and C. E. Erneling, pp. 279–292. New York: Oxford.

Cole, M. (1996). *Cultural Psychology: A Once and Future Discipline*. Cambridge, MA: Harvard University Press.

Collins, A. (1992). Toward a design science of education. In *New Directions in Educational Technology*, edited by E. Scanlon and T. O'Shea, pp. 15–22. New York: Springer-Verlag.

de la Rocha, O. L. (1986). Problems of Sense and Problems of Scale: An Ethnographic Study of Arithmetic in Everyday Life. Ph.D. dissertation. Irvine, CA: University of California.

Fischer, F. and Mandl, H. (2005). Knowledge convergence in computer-supported collaborative learning: the role of external representation tools. *J. Learn. Sci.*, 4(3), 405–441.

Gee, J. P. (2003). *What Video Games Have to Teach Us About Learning and Literacy*. New York: Palgrave.

Gilbert, N. J. and Driscoll, M. P. (2002). Collaborative knowledge building: a case study. *Educ. Technol. Res. Dev.*, 50(1), 59–79.

Greeno, J. G. (1997). On claims that answer the wrong questions. *Educ. Res.*, 26(1), 5–17.

Hall, R. and Stevens, R. (1995). Making space: a comparison of mathematical work in school and professional design practices. In *The Cultures of Computing*, edited by S. L. Star, pp. 118–145. Oxford: Blackwell Publishers.

Hutchins, E. (1995a). *Cognition in the Wild*. Cambridge, MA: MIT Press.*

Hutchins, E. (1995b). How a cockpit remembers its speeds. *Cognit. Sci.*, 19, 265–188.

Ito, M. (1997). Kids and Simulation Games: Subject Formation Through Human–Machine Interaction. Paper presented at the Annual Meeting of the Society for the Social Studies of Science (4S), October 23–26, Tucson, AZ.

Ito, M. (2002). Engineering Play: Children's Software and the Productions of Everyday Life. Ph.D. dissertation. Palo Alto, CA: Stanford University.

Ito, M. (2005). Mobilizing fun in the production and consumption of children's software. *Ann. Am. Acad. Polit. Soc. Sci.*, 597(1), 82–102.

Ito, M. (2006). Engineering play: children's software and the cultural politics of edutainment. *Discourse: Stud. Cult. Polit. Educ.*, 27(2), 139–160.

Johnson, S. (2005). *Everything Bad Is Good for You: How Today's Popular Culture Is Actually Making Us Smarter*. New York: Riverhead Books.

Kaptelinin, V. and Cole, M. (2001). Individual and collective activities in educational computer game playing. In *CSCL 2: Carrying Forward the Conversation*, edited by T. Koschmann, R. Hall, and N. Miyake, pp. 303–316. Mahwah, NJ: Lawrence Erlbaum Associates.

Kato, H., Yamazaki, K., Suzuki, H., Kuzuoka, H., Hiroyuki, M., and Yamazaki, A. (2001). Designing a video-mediated collaboration system based on a body metaphor. In *CSCL 2: Carrying Forward the Conversation*, edited by T. Koschmann, R. Hall, and N. Miyake, pp. 409–423. Mahwah, NJ: Lawrence Erlbaum Associates.

Kirschner, P., Strijbos, J.-W., Kreijns, K., and Beers, P. J. (2004). Designing electronic collaborative learning environments. *Educ. Technol. Res. Dev.*, 52(3), 47–66.

Kolodner, J. L., Camp, P. J., Crismond, D., Fasse, B., Gray, J., Holbrook, J., Puntambekar, S., and Ryan, M. (2003). Problem-based learning meets case-based reasoning in the middle-school science classroom: putting Learning by Design™ into practice. *J. Learn. Sci.*, 12(4), 495–547.

Koschmann, T. (1994). Toward a theory of computer support for collaborative learning. *J. Learn. Sci.*, 3(3), 219–225.*

Latour, B. (1987). *Science in Action*. Milton Keynes, U.K.: Open University.*

Latour, B. (1996). On interobjectivity. *Mind Cult. Activ.*, 3(4), 228–245.*

Lave, J. (1988). *Cognition in Practice: Mind, Mathematics and Culture in Everday Life*. Cambridge, U.K.: Cambridge University Press.*

Lave, J. and Wenger, E. (1991). *Situated Learning: Legitimate Peripheral Participation*. Cambridge, U.K.: Cambridge University Press.

Moallem, M. (2003). An interactive online course: a collaborative design model. *Educ. Technol. Res. Dev.*, 51(4), 85–103.

Nath, L. R. and Ross, S. M. (2001). The influence of a peer-tutoring training model for implementing cooperative groupings with elementary students. *Educ. Technol. Res. Dev.*, 49(2), 41–56.

O'Neill, D. K. (2001). Knowing when you've brought them in: scientific genre knowledge and communities of practice. *J. Learn. Sci.*, 10(3), 223–264.

Pea, R. D. (1994). Seeing what we build together: distributed multimedia learning environments for transformative communications. *J. Learn. Sci.*, 3(3), 285–299.

Reeves, T. C. (2006). Design research from the technology perspective. In *Educational Design Research*, edited by J. V. Akker, K. Gravemeijer, S. McKenney, and N. Nieveen, pp. 86–109. London: Routledge.

Reeves, T. C., Herrington, J., and Oliver, R. (2004). A development research agenda for online collaborative learning. *Educ. Technol. Res. Dev.*, 52(4), 53–65.

Roschelle, J. (1992). Learning by collaborating: convergent conceptual change. *J. Learn. Sci.*, 2(3), 235–276.*

Satwicz, T. (2006). Technology at Play: An Ethnographic Study of Young People's Video Gaming Practices. Ph.D. dissertation. Seattle, WA: University of Washington.

Scardamalia, M. and Bereiter, C. (1994). Computer support for knowledge-building communities. *J. Learn. Sci.*, 3(3), 265–283.

Stahl, G., Koschmann, T., and Suthers, D. D. (2006). Computer-supported collaborative learning. In *The Cambridge Handbook of the Learning Sciences*, edited by R. K. Sawyer, pp. 409–425. New York: Cambridge University Press.

Stevens, R. (2000). Divisions of labor in school and in the workplace: comparing computer and paper-supported activities across settings. *J. Learn. Sci.*, 9(4), 373–401.

Stevens, R. (2001). Keeping it complex in an era of big education. In *CSCL 2: Carrying Forward the Conversation*, edited by T. Koschmann, R. Hall, and N. Miyake, pp. 269–273. Mahwah, NJ: Lawrence Erlbaum Associates.

Stevens, R. (2007). Capturing ideas in digital things: a new twist on the old problem of inert knowledge. In *Video Research in the Learning Sciences*, edited by R. Goldman, S. Derry, R. Pea, and B. Barron. Mahwah, NJ: Lawrence Erlbaum Associates.

Stevens, R. and Hall, R. (1997). Seeing tornado: how Video Traces mediate visitor understandings of (natural?) spectacles in a science museum. *Sci. Educ.*, 18(6), 735–748.

Stevens, R. and Hall, R. (1998). Disciplined perception: learning to see in technoscience. In *Talking Mathematics in School: Studies of Teaching and Learning*, edited by M. Lampert and M. L. Blunk, pp. 107–149. Cambridge, U.K.: Cambridge University Press.

Stevens, R., Satwicz, T., and McCarthy, L. (2007). In game, in room, in world: reconnecting video game play to the rest of kids' lives. In *Ecology of Games*, edited by K. Salen. Chicago, IL: MacArthur Foundation.

Stevens, R., Wineburg, S., Herrenkohl, L., and Bell, P. (2005). The comparative understanding of school subjects: past, present and future. *Rev. Educ. Res.*, 75(2), 125–157.

Suchman, L. (1987). *Plans and Situated Action: The Problem of Human–Machine Communication*. Cambridge, U.K.: Cambridge University Press.*

Suchman, L. (2001). *Human/Machine Reconsidered*, http://www.comp.lancs.ac.uk/sociology/soc040ls.html.

Vygotsky, L. S. (1962). *Thought and Language*. Cambridge, MA: MIT Press.

Wenger, E. (1999). *Communities of Practice: Learning, Meaning, and Identity*. Cambridge, U.K.: Cambridge University Press.

Wertsch, J. V. (1998). *Mind as Action*. New York: Oxford University Press.*

Wood, D., Bruner, J., and Ross, G. (1976). The role of tutoring in problem solving. *J. Child Psychol. Psychiatry*, 17, 89–100.

---

* Indicates a core reference.

# 14

# Prescriptive Principles for Instructional Design

*M. David Merrill*
Florida State University, Tallahassee, Florida

*Matthew Barclay*
Utah State University, Logan, Utah

*Andrew van Schaak*
Vanderbilt University, Nashville, Tennessee

## CONTENTS

## ABSTRACT

This chapter reviews some of the prescriptive principles that, based on research or experience, have been identified for facilitating effective, efficient, and engaging instruction. For the purposes of this chapter, *instruction* is defined as a deliberate attempt to design a product or environment that facilitates the acquisition of specified learning goals. This chapter first reviews the *first principles of instruction* identified by Merrill (2002a). In the second section, recent specifications of instructional design principles are compared to these first principles. The final section reviews approaches for designing instruction centered in whole tasks.

## KEYWORDS

*4C/ID:* Four-component instructional design model (van Merriënboer, 1997).

*Activation principle:* Learning is promoted when learners activate relevant cognitive structures.

*Application principle:* Learning is promoted when learners engage in application of their newly acquired knowledge or skill.

*Cognitive training model:* A five-task instructional design model (Foshay et al., 2003).

*Cycle of instruction:* The activation–demonstration–application–integration cycle of the first principles.

*Demonstration principle:* Learning is promoted when learners observe a demonstration of the skills to be learned.

*e-Learning principles:* Prescriptive principles for designing e-learning; see multimedia learning principles.

*First principles of instruction:* Five principles fundamental to effective, efficient, and engaging learning.

*Instructional design:* Creating blueprints for effective, efficient, and engaging instruction.

*Integration principle:* Learning is promoted when learners integrate their new knowledge into their everyday life.

*Minimalist principles:* Instructional design principles for sparse instruction.

*Multimedia learning principles:* Likely effects of text, animation, audio, and graphics on learning.

*Pebble-in-the-Pond instructional design:* A content-first approach to designing instruction.

*Problem-centered instruction:* See task-centered instruction principle and strategy.

*Scaled instructional strategies:* Hypothesis that application of the first principles has an accumulating performance effect for complex skills.

*Structure–guidance–coaching–reflection cycle:* Instructional assistance within the activation–demonstration–application–reflection cycle of instruction.

*Task-centered instruction principle:* The central principle that learning is promoted when learners are engaged in a task-centered approach.

*Task-centered instructional strategy:* Teaching component skills in the context of a progression of real-world whole tasks.

*Topic-centered instructional strategy:* Teaching component skills in sequence prior to their application to a whole task.

## FIRST PRINCIPLES OF INSTRUCTION

Merrill reviewed a number of instructional design theories and models (Dijkstra et al., 1997; Gagné, 1985; Glaser, 1992; Marzano et al., 2001; McCarthy, 1996; Reigeluth, 1983, 1987, 1999; Reigeluth and Carr-Chellman, in press; Tennyson et al., 1997; van Merriënboer, 1997) in an attempt to identify underlying prescriptive principles common to all or most of these approaches. He concluded that they do share common principles and that they do not incorporate fundamentally different principles Merrill (2002a,b; 2006a,b; 2007; in press a,b). These *first principles* are:

- *Task-centered approach*—Learning is promoted when learners are engaged in a task-centered approach, which includes demonstration and application of component skills. A task-centered approach is enhanced when learners undertake a progression of whole tasks.

- *Activation principle*—Learning is promoted when learners activate relevant cognitive structures by being directed to recall, describe, or demonstrate relevant prior knowledge or experience. Activation is enhanced when learners recall or acquire a structure for organizing the new knowledge.

- *Demonstration principle*—Learning is promoted when learners observe a demonstration of the skills to be learned that is consistent with the type of content being taught. Demonstrations are enhanced when learners receive guidance that relates instances to generalities. Demonstrations are enhanced when learners observe media relevant to the content.

- *Application principle*—Learning is promoted when learners engage in the application of their newly acquired knowledge or skill that is consistent with the type of content being taught. Application is effective only when learners receive intrinsic or corrective feedback. Application is enhanced when learners are coached and when this coaching is gradually withdrawn for each subsequent task.

- *Integration principle*—Learning is promoted when learners integrate their new knowledge into their everyday life by being directed to reflect on, discuss, or defend their new knowledge or skill. Integration is enhanced when learners create, invent, or extrapolate personal ways to use their new knowledge or skill to situations in their world. Integration is enhanced when learners publicly demonstrate their new knowledge or skill.

In this chapter, we summarize some recent presentations of prescriptive principles and compare them to the first principles identified by Merrill. Here, a *prescriptive principle* is a relationship that is always true under appropriate conditions regardless of program or practice. A *practice* is a specific instructional activity. A *program* is a set of prescribed practices. The principles identified in this chapter are underlying relationships rather than alternative instructional models. A given practice, program, or model always implements or fails to implement underlying principles, whether or not these principles are specified. These same principles can be implemented by a wide variety of programs and practices. The principles identified in this chapter share the following properties: First, learning from a given program will be facilitated in direct proportion to its implementation of these principles. Second, these principles of instruction can be implemented in any delivery system or using any instructional architecture (Clark, 2003). Third, these principles of instruction are design oriented rather than learning oriented. They relate to creating learning environments and products rather than describing how learners acquire knowledge and skill from these environments or products.

Our premise is that these design principles apply regardless of the instructional program or practices prescribed by a given theory or model. If this premise is true, research will demonstrate that, when a given instructional program or practice violates or fails to implement one or more of these underlying principles, there will be a decrement in learning and performance.

## Elaboration of First Principles

These principles are familiar to many instructional designers and educators. They have been stated in one form or another for at least the past 200 years. Clark (1999) indicated that J. F. Herbart's (1776–1841) followers designed a five-step teaching method that is remarkably similar to the first principles described earlier:

- Prepare the pupils to be ready for the new lesson (activation).
- Present the new lesson (presentation).
- Associate the new lesson with ideas studied earlier (activation, guidance, and coaching).
- Use examples to illustrate the lesson's major points (demonstration).
- Test pupils to ensure they have learned the new lesson (application).

Even though these principles seem to have been available for some time, they are not often used in instructional materials. An extensive survey of 1400 online courses in marriage relationships from five countries demonstrated that most of the instructional programs reviewed failed to implement even one of these principles (Barclay et al., 2004).

### Four-Phase Cycle of Instruction

The identification of the first principles does more than merely collect a set of prescriptive principles that might be used to select or design effective instruction. These principles are interrelated to one another. The four-phase cycle of instruction consists of activation, demonstration, application, and integration. Effective instruction involves all four of these activities repeated as required for different problems or whole tasks. A similar four-phase cycle (4-MAT) of instruction consisting of meaning (activation), conceptualizing (demonstration), operationalizing (application), and renewing (integration) was described by McCarthy (1996). The Vanderbilt group described a learning cycle consisting of a set of challenges (task or problem), the generation of ideas (activation), multiple perspectives (demonstration), research and revision (demonstration/application), testing your mettle (application), going public (integration), and looking ahead and reflecting back (integration) (Schwartz et al., 1999).

### Problem-Centered Instruction

Perhaps the most important notion of the first principles is that engaging instruction is problem centered; that is, individual instructional components are most effectively taught in the context of a progression of real-world problems where the student is shown a problem, then taught the components, and then shown how the components are used to solve the problem or do the whole task. Van Merriënboer's 4C/ID model for training complex learning tasks makes a very strong research-based argument for centering instruction in whole real-world tasks and then teaching component knowledge and skill in the context of these tasks (van Merriënboer, 1997; van Merriënboer and Kirschner, 2007).

The first principles and 4C/ID identify a task-centered approach that combines the solving of problems with more direct instruction of problem components as contrasted with problem-based approaches in which students are placed in collaborative groups, given resources and a problem, and left to construct their own solution for the problem. Research supports this guided instruction approach over more pure learner-centered approaches with less guidance. Klahr and Nigam (2004) compared guided direct instruction with a discovery learning approach for children learning about confounding variables in scientific experiments. The children were actively involved in performing experiments. The direct instruction group observed demonstration experiments (demonstration–guidance), whereas the discovery group did their own experiments. Klahr and Nigam (2004, p. 661) demonstrated that "many more children learned from direct instruction than from discovery learning" and that children in the direct instruction group made broader and richer scientific judgments about science-fair posters than those in the discovery group. Two important research reviews have argued that instruction involving minimal guidance including problem-based teaching does not work, whereas task-centered approaches involving guidance and coaching are more effective (Kirschner et al., 2006; Mayer, 2004).

### Levels of Instructional Strategies

Previous papers (Merrill, 2006a,b) emphasized that the first principles promote enhanced performance on complex tasks. To assess the affects of the first principles it is necessary to assess learners' scaled performance on these complex tasks. Some methods for determining level of performance include: (1) the number of tasks completed in a progression of subsequently more difficult tasks, (2) the amount of coaching required for satisfactory performance on difficult tasks, and (3) the number of stages performed satisfactorily in a nested complex task.

Merrill (2006a) further suggests scaled instructional strategies based on the first principles. He labeled information-only as a level 0 instructional

strategy and suggested a series of yet-to-be-tested hypotheses for scaled strategies: (1) A level 1 instructional strategy that adds consistent demonstration to a level 0 information-only strategy promotes a higher performance level on scaled complex tasks. (2) A level 2 instructional strategy that adds consistent application with corrective feedback to a level 1 instructional strategy consisting of information plus demonstration promotes an additional level of performance on complex real-world tasks. (3) A level 3 instructional strategy that consists of a task-centered instructional strategy that includes consistent demonstration and consistent application with corrective feedback promotes an additional increment in the level of performance on complex tasks. (4) Providing or recalling relevant experience promotes an additional increment in learning efficiency, effectiveness, and engagement when added to a level 1, level 2, or level 3 instructional strategies. (5) Providing activation–structure promotes an additional increment in learning efficiency, effectiveness, and engagement when added to level 1, level 2, or level 3 instructional strategies. (6) Adding reflection–integration to any of the above instructional strategies promotes an additional increment in learning efficiency, effectiveness, and engagement. (7) Adding create–integrate to any of the above instructional strategies promotes transfer of the newly acquired knowledge and skill to performance on similar tasks in the real world beyond the instructional situation.

### Structure–Guidance–Coaching–Reflection Cycle

Based on a meta-analysis of research on instruction, Marzano and colleagues (2001, p. 32) stated that: "In general, research has demonstrated that making students aware of specific structures in information helps them summarize that information [and subsequently be able to use this information more effectively]" (see also Marzano, 1998). Rosenshine (1997) indicated that when students organize information, summarize information, and compare old material to new material these activities require processing that strengthens cognitive structures and helps students develop more appropriate mental models. These findings suggest that during activation students should be provided or helped to develop a structure for organizing the to-be-learned information. During the demonstration phase, guidance should help the students relate the new information to this structure. During the application phase coaching should help students use this structure to complete the task. During the integration phase, reflection helps students to incorporate this structure into their mental model for subsequent application.

## Applications of the First Principles

The authors are aware of several attempts to use versions of this approach for the development of instructional materials. In consultation with M.D. Merrill, Thompson/NETg applied a version of this approach to the revision of their course for Excel (Thomson, 2002). The resulting scenario-based course taught Excel commands in the context of five spreadsheet problems. The test was to prepare three additional spreadsheet tasks without using the help system in Excel. Thompson/NETg undertook a study to validate the first principles of instruction and the Pebble-in-the-Pond model for instructional development. Their development group, with consultation from Merrill, developed scenarios for a course in Excel. They then developed a strategy of problem–progression–component–instruction with guidance for teaching this course as prescribed by the first principles and Pebble-in-the-Pond. The investigators selected study participants from among NETg customers who volunteered to participate in the study.

The customers were divided into three groups: Group 1, the scenario group ($n = 49$), received instruction as prescribed by the first principles. Group 2, the straight e-learning group ($n = 49$), received the existing commercial version of the NETg Excel course. This commercial version of the course systematically teaches all of the commands and operations of Excel using a guided demonstration that instructs learners to execute a command or series of commands and then to observe the consequence of their action on the screen. This same instruction was used for the component instruction in the scenario group. Both groups had access to the same guided demonstration instruction of individual Excel commands. Group 3, a control group ($n = 30$), received the final three authentic scenarios without any prior instruction in Excel. The instruction was delivered online from a company website that also provided frequently asked questions and access to an online mentor for both experimental groups.

On the three authentic tasks, the scenario group scored an average of 89%, the guided demonstration group scored 68%, and the control group scored 34%. All differences are statistically significant beyond the .001 level. Further, the mean times required to complete the three authentic tasks were 29 minutes for the scenario group and 49 minutes for the guided demonstration group. Most of the control group failed to finish the tasks so no time data were recorded. These differences are also statistically significant beyond the .001 level. Finally, on a qualitative questionnaire, the scenario group expressed considerably more satisfaction with the course than did the guided demonstration group.

The first principles formed the basis of a tool used by Shell EP to evaluate and redesign their courses (Collis and Margaryan, 2005, 2007; Margaryan, 2006). Their instrument was applied to over 65 courses that were redesigned to be in greater compliance with the first principles. Twelve courses were studied in detail. The course-scan values (score on the first principles plus) were compared with participant evaluation data and instructors' reflections. The findings indicate that both the students and the instructors felt that the work-based model increased the business relevance of the courses, led to deeper learning processes and more effective performance, and enabled more immediate application of the content to their jobs (Margaryan, 2006).

An entrepreneur course for distance delivery to students in developing countries was developed at Brigham Young University–Hawaii using the first principles and Pebble-in-the-Pond (Mendenhall et al., 2006a,b). Six principles for starting a business were taught in the context of five small businesses. A final exam required evaluating a business plan for a sixth small business. A pilot study compared performance on this exam by 8 business majors who had completed several previous business courses to 12 non-business majors who had completed only this one new course. Of the 12 non-business majors, 7 scored as well as the business majors. At this writing, further development and evaluation of the course are in progress.

Frick et al. (2007) administered an instructor evaluation form that included items that allowed students to report the extent to which the first principles were implemented in numerous courses at multiple institutions. These items were then correlated with student self-report of academic learning time, learning achievement, and learner satisfaction. Preliminary results showed that the use of the first principles in a course is highly correlated with academic learning time (Spearman's $\rho = 0.682, p < .0005, n = 111$), self-reported student learning achievement ($\rho = 0.823, p < .0005, n = 110$), and student satisfaction ($\rho = 0.830, p < .0005, n = 112$). The internal consistency reliability of the first principles scale was 0.941 (Cronbach's alpha). Frick suggests that the inclusion of the first principles in instructor evaluations would increase the ability of such instruments to assess instructional quality.

## OTHER INSTRUCTIONAL DESIGN PRINCIPLES

Some recent prescriptive books on designing effective instruction have stated prescriptive principles for instructional design. Merrill (2007) presented a

**TABLE 14.1**
**Clark and Mayer's Principles for e-Learning Aligned with Merrill's First Principles**

| E-Learning Principles (Clark and Mayer, 2003) | First Principles (Merrill, 2002) |
| --- | --- |
| Interactions should mirror the job (p. 153). | Task-centered |
| Critical tasks require more [distributed] practice (p. 159). | Task-centered–progression |
| Use job contexts to teach problem-solving processes (p. 251). | Task-centered |
| Incorporate job-specific problem-solving processes (p. 264). | Task-centered |
| Use job-realistic or varied worked examples (p. 186). | Task-centered |
| | Demonstration |
| Replace some practice problems with worked examples (p. 177). | Demonstration–guidance |
| Apply the media elements principles to examples (p. 179). | Demonstration–media |
| Apply the media elements principles to practice exercises (p. 164). | Application |
| Train learners to self-question during receptive e-lessons (p. 166). | Integration–reflect |
| Teach learners to self-explain examples (p. 190). | Integration–reflect |
| Make learners aware of their problem-solving processes (p. 260). | Integration–reflect |
| Focus training on thinking processes vs. job knowledge (p. 256). | Integration–extrapolate |

synthesis of some of these sources as they relate to the first principles of instruction. The following summarizes some of the principles identified by other authors and attempts to relate them to the first principles of instructional design.

## Principles for Multimedia Learning

Based on extensive research, Clark and Mayer (Clark and Mayer, 2003; Mayer, 2001) have identified principles for multimedia learning. These principles elaborate the demonstration principle for relevant media (Mayer, 2001):

- Students learn better from words and pictures than from words alone (p. 63).
- Students learn better when corresponding words and pictures are presented near rather than far from each other on the page or screen (p. 81).
- Students learn better when corresponding words and pictures are presented simultaneously rather than successively (p. 96).
- Students learn better when extraneous material is excluded rather than included (p. 113).
- Students learn better from animation and narration than from animation and on-screen text (p. 134).
- Students learn better from animation and narration than from animation and narration and text (p. 147).
- Design effects are stronger for low-knowledge learners than for high-knowledge learners and for high-spatial learners rather than low-spatial learners (p. 161).

## Principles for e-Learning

In addition to the multimedia principles Clark and Mayer (2003) recommend additional instructional principles (Table 14.1). Correspondence to the first principles is indicated in the right column for each of these principles. It should be evident to the reader that some of these principles have a close correspondence, some of these principles provide more elaboration than the first principles, and some are not included in the first principles. They include personalization, collaboration, and learner-control principles; the first principles do not include principles related to implementation of instruction, such as personalization, collaboration, learner control, and navigation. Perhaps they should. Allen (2003) identified some effective principles for e-learning in three major categories: learner motivation, navigation, and instructional interactivity. Table 14.2 summarizes his keys for motivating e-learning and his checklist for good instructional interactions.

## Minimalist Principles

Van der Meij (1998) identified heuristics for designing minimalist instruction (Table 14.3). The task-centered orientation of these heuristics is apparent. Some of these demonstration, application, guidance, and coaching heuristics provide more specific prescriptions than the first principles.

## Cognitive Training Model

Foshay et al. (2003) presented a cognitive training model that identifies five tasks learners have to complete when learning: (1) select the information to attend to,

**TABLE 14.2**

**Allen's e-Learning Principles Aligned with Merrill's First Principles**

| e-Learning Principles (Allen, 2003) | First Principles (Merrill, 2002) |
|---|---|
| Have the learner perform multistep tasks; having people attempt real (or "authentic") tasks is much more interesting than having them repeat or mimic one step at a time (p. 209). | Task-centered |
| The learner must apply genuine, authentic skills and knowledge; activities should be as similar to the necessary on-the-job performance as possible (p. 276). | Task-centered |
| Good interactions are purposeful in the mind of the learner; learners understand what they can accomplish through participation in the interaction (p. 276). | Task-centered Activation |
| Build on anticipated outcomes; help learners see how their involvement in the e-learning will produce outcomes they care about (p. 158). | Activation (show the whole problem) |
| Select the right content for each learner; if it is meaningless or learners already know it, it is not going to be an enjoyable learning experience (p. 179). | Activation–prior knowledge |
| Use an appealing context; novelty, suspense, fascinating graphics, humor, sound, music, and animation all draw learners in when done well (p. 193).[a] | Demonstration–media |
| Provide intrinsic feedback: Seeing the positive consequences of good performance is better feedback than being told, "Yes, that was good" (p. 214); the feedback demonstrates to learners the ineffectiveness (even risks) of poor responses and the value of good responses (p. 276). | Application–intrinsic feedback |
| Delay judgment; if learners have to wait for confirmation, they will typically reevaluate for themselves while the tension mounts—essentially reviewing and rehearsing (p. 220). | Application–feedback |
| Put learners at risk; if learners have something to lose they pay attention (p. 169). | Integration–publicly demonstrate |

[a] When implementing this guideline one would do well to remember Mayer's (2001) multimedia principles.

**TABLE 14.3**

**Minimalist Instruction and Merrill's First Principles**

| Minimalist Principles (van Meij, 1998) | First Principles (Merrill, 2002) |
|---|---|
| Provide an immediate opportunity to act (p. 22). | Task-centered |
| Select or design instructional activities that are real tasks (p. 29). | Task-centered |
| Be sure the components of the task reflect the task structure (p. 31). | Task-centered–components |
| Prevent mistakes whenever possible (p. 35). | Demonstration–guidance |
| Provide error information that supports detection, diagnosis, and recovery (p. 38). | Demonstration–guidance |
| Be brief; do not spell out everything (p. 43). | Demonstration |
| Provide closure for chapters (p. 44). | Guidance and coaching |
| Respect the integrity of the user's activity (p. 25). | Application |
| Provide on-the-spot error information (p. 41). | Application–coaching |
| Provide error information when actions are error prone or when correction is difficult (p. 37). | Application–coaching |
| Encourage and support exploration and innovation (p. 23). | Integration–reflect, extrapolate |

(2) link the new information with existing knowledge, (3) organize the information, (4) assimilate the new knowledge into existing knowledge, and (5) strengthen the new knowledge in memory. In association with these tasks, they identify 17 elements (prescriptive principles for design) of a training lesson (Table 14.4).

## Instructional Principles Based on Learning Principles

Seidel et al. (2004) identified factors influencing the acquisition and transfer of learning as empirically established in the learning literature. From these learn-ing principles they derived guidelines for more effective instructional design. They organized their principles around four domains: the cognitive domain, the affective domain, the psychomotor domain, and the interpersonal domain. Table 14.5 summarizes their design guidelines for the cognitive domain.

## 4C/ID Instructional Design

Perhaps the most complete recent presentation of instructional strategies is the work of van Merriënboer (1997; van Merriënboer and Kirschner, 2007). The model presents an analysis and design approach that

**TABLE 14.4**
**The Cognitive Training Model and Merrill's First Principles**

| Cognitive Training Model Principles (Foshay et al., 2003, p. 29) | First Principles (Merrill, 2002) |
|---|---|
| Answer the question "What's in it for me?" for the learners. | Task-centered (show the task to be completed) |
| Specify both the desired behavior and the knowledge to be learned. | Task-centered (they are more accepting of traditional objectives) |
| Gain and focus learners' attention on the new knowledge. | Activation |
| Bring to the forefront the prerequisite existing (old) knowledge that forms the base on which the new knowledge is built. | Activation–prior knowledge |
| Organize text presentation to help learners organize new knowledge. | Activation–structure |
| Tell the learners "You can do it!" regarding learning new knowledge. | Activation (not included in first principles) |
| Demonstrate real-life examples of how the new knowledge works when it is applied. | Task-centered |
| Organize and limit the amount of new knowledge presented to match human information processing capacity. | Demonstration |
| | Demonstration |
| Use well-designed illustrations to assist learners' organization and assimilation of new knowledge. | Demonstration |
| Using a different approach for each type of knowledge, present the new knowledge in a way that makes it easiest to understand. | Demonstration–consistency (see Gagné, 1985; Merrill, 1994) |
| Involve learners by having them do something with the new knowledge. | Application |
| Let learners know how well they have done in using the new knowledge, what problems they're having, and why. | Application–feedback (could be both intrinsic and extrinsic) |
| Present the structure of the content again, including the entire structure of knowledge. | Activation–structure with demonstration guidance |
| Have the learners use the new knowledge again, this time to prove to themselves, you, and their employer that they have met the objectives of the training. | Application |
| Have learners use new knowledge in a structured way on the job to ensure they "use it, not lose it." | Integration–extrapolate |

**TABLE 14.5**
**Instructional Principles for the Cognitive Domain and Merrill's First Principles**

| Instructional Principles (Seidel et al., 2004, p. 24) | First Principles (Merrill, 2002) |
|---|---|
| Provide multiple context environments to facilitate positive transfer within and across domains. | Task-centered–progression of tasks |
| Use advanced organizers to facilitate integrative skill acquisition and capitalize on prior knowledge. | Activation–structure (coupled with the structure–guidance–coaching–reflection cycle) |
| Apply the operant principles of minimizing errors, using small steps, and providing immediate reinforcement for acquisition of initial elements of domain knowledge. | Demonstration–consistency (especially for acquiring information) |
| Use part-task training to break up complex tasks into manageable chunks. | Task-centered |
| | Demonstration–component skills |

encompass all of the first principles of instruction.* 4C/ID identifies four layers of activity in the instructional development process: (1) principled skill decomposition, (2) analysis of constituent skills and related knowledge, (3) selection of instructional methods, and (4) development of a learning strategy. The

first principles have little to say about decomposing a complex skill into a hierarchy of constituent skills; however, the analysis of these constituent skills in 4C/ID is similar to the analysis of a problem to identify the component knowledge and skill for a given task (see Figure 14.1). "At the heart of this training method is whole-task practice, in which more and more complex versions of the whole complex cognitive skill are practiced" (progression of whole tasks) (van Merriënboer, 1997, p. 8). The constituent skills required for

---

* 4C/ID is an integrated approach for which individual prescriptive statements are difficult to isolate. We have tried to summarize key aspects of this model and relate them to the first principles.

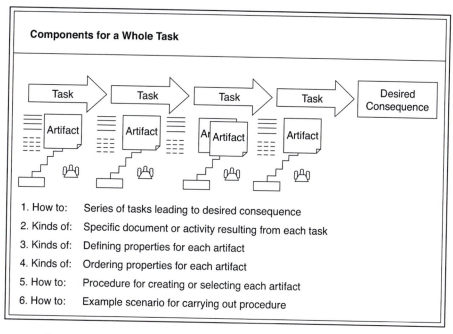

**Figure 14.1** Components for a whole task. (From Merrill, M.D., *Learning Objects for Task-Centered Instruction*, 2006, http://cito.byuh.edu/merrill/Merrill_1/Merrill-1.html.)

performance of the whole task are presented as they are required by the task (task-centered approach). Key aspects of the just-in-time information presentation include partitioning, demonstration (consistent demonstration and guidance), and fading (coaching). The model stresses the identification of cognitive schemata that underlie the performance of nonrecurrent aspects of complex tasks. To promote schema induction, in addition to teaching the recurrent constituent skills presented just in time, the model also includes presentation of heuristic information to help with unfamiliar aspects of problems (structure–activation). The "basic claim of the 4C/ID-model is that its application leads to reflective expertise and, consequently, to increased transfer performance" (integration) (van Merriënboer, 1997, p. 73).

## DESIGNING TASK-CENTERED INSTRUCTION

Figure 14.2 illustrates a Pebble-in-the-Pond approach to instructional development that assists designers to systematically incorporate the first principles into their instructional design (Merrill, 2002b). The steps in this approach are to: (1) specify a whole task, (2) specify a progression of whole tasks, (3) specify the component knowledge and skills required for each task, (4) specify an instructional strategy, (5) specify the user interface, and (6) produce the course.

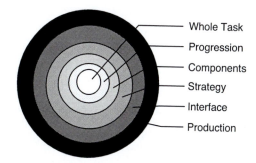

Pebble-in-the-Pond Instructional Design

**Figure 14.2** The Pebble-in-the-Pond approach to instruction. (From Merrill, M.D., *Perform. Improve.*, 41(7), 39–44, 2002. With permission.)

Merrill (2006c) elaborated the analysis required to specify the component knowledge and skill for each task in terms of portrayals of specific artifacts and information for component concepts (kinds of) and component procedures (how to) (Merrill, 1997). This component analysis (Figure 14.1) consists of the following steps: (1) find a portrayal of the artifact that is a consequence of completing the whole task (kind of); (2) identify a series of subtasks (information) leading to the desired consequence (how to); (3) for each subtask, find a portrayal of the artifact that is a consequence of completing this subtask (kind of); (4) identify the defining properties of each artifact (kind of); (5) identify the ordering properties of each artifact

181

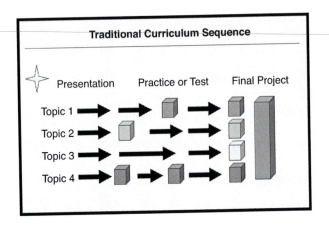

**Figure 14.3** Topic-centered instructional sequencing. (From Mendenhall, A. et al., *Introduction to Entrepreneurship: How to Start Your Own Business*, 2006, http://cito.byuh.edu/entrepreneur/ main.swf.)

(kind of); (6) identify the procedure for creating or selecting the artifact (how to); and (7) identify a portrayal of a scenario illustrating this procedure (Merrill, 2006c).

Figure 14.3 illustrates a typical topic-centered instructional strategy. In this strategy, each topic is taken in turn. Information is presented and demonstrated. Periodic evaluation is administered to assess the information that is presented. Figure 14.4 illustrates a task-centered instructional strategy consistent with the first principles of instruction and the Pebble-in-the-Pond approach to instructional design. In this strategy, a whole task is demonstrated; some level of each of the relevant topics is presented and then demonstrated in the first task. A second whole task is then presented. The learner is asked to apply those topics that were presented to the new task. An expanded version of the topics relevant to the second task is presented and demonstrated for the second task. This strategy is repeated for several more tasks until all the topics have been expanded as much as required by the final tasks and the student is able to apply the topics to a new task unaided.

A new book designed to help designers use the 4C/ID model adapts the Pebble-in-the-Pond model of content-first instructional development as a recommended application of the ten steps to designing instruction for complex skills (van Merriënboer and Kirschner, 2007). Table 14.6 compares the ten development steps of van Merriënboer and Kirschner to the ripples in the Pebble-in-the-Pond model for instructional design.

## CONCLUSION

Considerable agreement exists with regard to the prescriptive instructional design principles that are fundamental to effective, efficient, and engaging instruction, and the first principles of instructional design appear

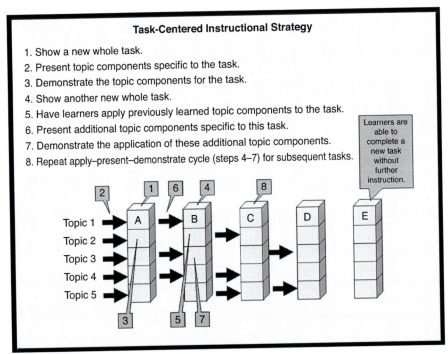

**Figure 14.4** Task-centered instructional sequencing. (Adapted from Mendenhall, A. et al., *Introduction to Entrepreneurship: How to Start Your Own Business*, 2006, http://cito.byuh.edu/entrepreneur/main.swf; Merrill, M.D., *J. Res. Technol. Educ.*, in press.)

**TABLE 14.6**
**Pebble-in-the-Pond and Ten Steps to Complex Learning**

| Pebble-in-the-Pond | Ten Steps to Complex Learning |
|---|---|
| Identify a whole task or problem. | Design learning tasks. |
| Specify a progression of whole tasks. | Sequence task classes. |
| Analyze the component skills for each task. | Set performance objectives.[c] |
| Specify an instructional strategy.[a] | Design supportive information. |
| Determine user interface.[b] | Analyze cognitive strategies. |
| Produce the course. | Analyze mental models. |
| | Design procedural information. |
| | Analyze cognitive rules. |
| | Analyze prerequisite information. |
| | Design part-task practice. |

[a] van Merriënboer and Kirschner (2007) combine analysis and strategy as they discuss component skills; Pebble-in-the-Pond separates these two design functions.
[b] Ten Steps has only a minimal discussion on interface, delivery, and production; their emphasis is on the design aspects of instructional development.
[c] Pebble-in-the-Pond does not specify assessment criteria for the tasks. This is an area where the model should be improved.

*Source:* van Merriënboer, J.J.G. and Kirschner, P.A., *Ten Steps to Complex Learning*, Lawrence Erlbaum Associates, Mahwah, NJ, 2007. With permission.

to have a fair amount of agreement. The limited data available indicate that, when these principles are implemented in instructional products and environments, the instructional quality increases; however, far too much instruction seems to ignore these fundamental principles. It is hoped that this chapter has provided a starting point for more rigorous research to assess the validity of these principles in more situations, for more students, and for a greater variety of subject matters. In the meantime, a greater effort should be made to implement these principles in our instructional products.

# REFERENCES

Allen, M. W. (2003). *Michael Allen's Guide to e-Learning*. New York: John Wiley & Sons.

Barclay, M. W., Gur, B., and Wu, C. (2004). The Impact of Media on the Family: Assessing the Availability and Quality of Instruction on the World Wide Web for Enhancing Marriage Relationship. Paper presented at the UN International Year of the Family Conference, Asia Pacific Dialogue, October 11–13, Kuala Lumpur, Malaysia.

Clark, D. (1999). *A Time Capsule of Training and Learning*, http://www.nwlink.com/~donclark/hrd/history/history.html.

Clark, R. C. (2003). *Building Expertise: Cognitive Methods for Training and Performance Improvement*, 2nd ed. Washington D.C.: International Society for Performance Improvement.*

Clark, R. C. and Mayer, R. E. (2003). *e-Learning and the Science of Instruction*. San Francisco, CA: Pfeiffer.*

Collis, B. and Margaryan, A. (2005). Merrill plus: blending corporate strategy with instructional design. *Educ. Technol.*, 45(3), 54–59.

Collis, B. and Margaryan, A. (in press). Evaluating flexible learning in terms of course quality. In *Flexible Learning in an Information Society*, edited by B. Kahn. Hershey, PA: Idea Group.

Dijkstra, S., Seel, N. M., Schott, F., and Tennyson, R. D., Eds. (1997). *Instructional Design International Perspective: Solving Instructional Design Problems*, Vol. 2. Mahwah, NJ: Lawrence Erlbaum Associates.

Foshay, W. R. R., Silber, K. H., and Stelnicki, M. B. (2003). *Writing Training Materials That Work: How to Train Anyone to Do Anything*. San Francisco, CA: Pfeiffer.*

Frick, T., Chadha, R., Wang, Y., Watson, C., and Green, P. (2007). *Course Evaluations: How Valid Are They?* Unpublished manuscript, Bloomington, IN.

Gagné, R. M. (1985). *The Conditions of Learning and Theory of Instruction*, 4th ed. New York: Holt, Rinehart and Winston.*

Glaser, R. (1992). *Advances in Instructional Psychology*. Hillsdale, NJ: Lawrence Erlbaum Associates.*

Kirschner, P. A., Sweller, J., and Clark, R. E. (2006). Why minimal guidance during instruction does not work: an analysis of the failure of constructivist, discovery, problem-based, experiential, and inquiry-based teaching. *Educ. Psychol.*, 41(2), 75–86.

Klahr, D. and Nigam, M. (2004). The equivalence of learning paths in early science instruction. *Psychol. Sci.*, 15(10), 661–667.

Margaryan, A. (2006). Work-Based Learning: A Blend of Pedagogy and Technology. Ph.D. dissertation. Enschede, the Netherlands: University of Twente.

Marzano, R. J. (1998). *A Theory-Based Meta-Analysis of Research on Instruction*. Aurora, CO: Midcontinent Research Laboratory for Education and Learning.

Marzano, R. J., Pickering, D. J., and Pollock, J. E. (2001). *Classroom Instruction That Works: Research-Based Strategies for Increasing Student Achievement*. Alexandria, VA: Association for Supervision and Curriculum Development.

Mayer, R. E. (2001). *Multimedia Learning*. Cambridge, U.K.: Cambridge University Press.*

Mayer, R. E. (2004). Should there be a three-strikes rule against pure discovery learning? *Am. Psychol.*, 59(1), 14–19.

McCarthy, B. (1996). *About Learning*. Barrington, IL: Excel.

Mendenhall, A., Buhanan, C. W., Suhaka, M., Mills, G., Gibson, G. V., and Merrill, M. D. (2006a). *Introduction to Entrepreneurship: How to Start Your Own Business*, http://cito.byuh.edu/entrepreneur/main.swf.

Mendenhall, A., Buhanan, C. W., Suhaka, M., Mills, G., Gibson, G. V., and Merrill, M. D. (2006b). A task-centered approach to entrepreneurship. *TechTrends*, 50(4), 84–89.

Merrill, M. D. (1994). *Instructional Design Theory*. Englewood Cliffs, NJ: Educational Technology Publications.*

Merrill, M. D. (1997). Instructional strategies that teach. *CBT Solutions*, (Nov./Dec.), 1–11.

Merrill, M. D. (2002a). First principles of instruction. *Educ. Technol. Res. Dev.*, 50(3), 43–59.*

Merrill, M. D. (2002b). A pebble-in-the-pond model for instructional design. *Perform. Improve.*, 41(7), 39–44.*

Merrill, M. D. (2006a). Hypothesized performance on complex tasks as a function of scaled instructional strategies. In *Handling Complexity in Learning Environments: Theory and Research*, edited by J. Elen and R. E. Clark, pp. 265–281. Amsterdam: Elsevier.

Merrill, M. D. (2006b). Levels of instructional strategy. *Educ. Technol.*, 46(4), 5–10.

Merrill, M. D. (2006c). *Learning Objects for Task-Centered Instruction*, http://cito.byuh.edu/merrill/Merrill_1/Merrill-1.html (see also http://cito.byuh.edu/merrill/Merrill_2/Merrill-2.html, http://cito.byuh.edu/merrill/Merrill_3/Merrill-3.html).

Merrill, M. D. (2007). First principles of instruction: a synthesis. In *Trends and Issues in Instructional Design and Technology*, 2nd ed., edited by R. A. Reiser and J. V. Dempsey, pp. 62–71. Upper Saddle River, NJ: Prentice Hall.

Merrill, M. D. (in press a). Converting e sub3 learning to e 3rd power learning: an alternative instructional design method for e-learning. In *E-Learning: Lessons Learned, Challenges Ahead (Voices from Academe and Industry)*, edited by S. Carliner and P. Shank. San Francisco, CA: Pfeiffer.

Merrill, M. D. (in press b). First principles of instruction. In *Instructional-Design Theories and Models*, Vol. III, edited by C. M. Reigeluth and A. Carr-Chellman. Mahwah, NJ: Lawrence Erlbaum Associates.

Merrill, M. D. (in press c). A task-centered instructional strategy. *J. Res. Technol. Educ.*

Reigeluth, C. M., Ed. (1983). *Instructional-Design Theories and Models: An Overview of Their Current Status*. Hillsdale, NJ: Lawrence Erlbaum Associates.*

Reigeluth, C. M., Ed. (1987). *Instructional Theories in Action: Lessons Illustrating Selected Theories and Models*. Hillsdale, NJ: Lawrence Erlbaum Associates.

Reigeluth, C. M., Ed. (1999). *Instructional-Design Theories and Models: A New Paradigm of Instructional Theory*, Vol. II. Mahwah, NJ: Lawrence Erlbaum Associates Publishers.*

Reigeluth, C. M. and Carr-Chellman, A. (in press). *Instructional Design Theories and Models*, Vol. III. Mahwah, NJ: Lawrence Erlbaum Associates.

Rosenshine, B. (1997). Advances in research on instruction. In *Issues in Educating Students with Disabilities*, edited by E. J. Lloyd, E. J. Kameanui, and D. Chard, pp. 197–221. Mahwah, NJ: Lawrence Erlbaum.

Schwartz, D. L., Lin, X., Brophy, S., and Bransford, J. D. (1999). Toward the development of flexibly adaptive instructional designs. In *Instructional-Design Theories and Models: A New Paradigm of Instructional Theory*, Vol. II, edited by C. M. Reigeluth, pp. 183–213. Mahwah, NJ: Lawrence Erlbaum Associates.

Seidel, R. J., Perencevich, K. C., and Kett, A. L. (2004). *From Principles of Learning to Strategies for Instruction: Empirically Based Ingredients to Guide Instructional Development*. New York: Springer.*

Tennyson, R. D., Schott, F., Seel, N. M., and Dijkstra, S., Eds. (1997). *Instructional Design International Perspective: Theory, Research, and Models*, Vol. 1. Mahwah, NJ: Lawrence Erlbaum Associates.

Thomson. (2002). *Thomson Job Impact Study: The Next Generation of Learning*. Naperville, IL: NETg (www.netg.com).

van der Meij, H. (1998). Principles and heuristics for designing minimalist instruction. In *Minimalism Beyond the Nurnberg Funnel*, edited by J. M. Carroll, pp. 19–53. Cambridge, MA: The MIT Press.*

van Merriënboer, J. J. G. (1997). *Training Complex Cognitive Skills: A Four-Component Instructional Design Model for Technical Training*. Englewood Cliffs, NJ: Educational Technology Publications.*

van Merriënboer, J. J. G. and Kirschner, P. A. (2007). *Ten Steps to Complex Learning*. Mahwah, NJ: Lawrence Erlbaum Associates.*

---

* Indicates a core reference.

# Part III
# Technologies

This Technologies part of the *Handbook* was led by J. Michael Spector. The various chapters address both *upstream* technologies (analysis, planning, and design) and *downstream* technologies (development, deployment, and evaluation). This is the largest part of the *Handbook*, with sixteen chapters covering: (1) programmed technologies; (2) educational hyptertext; (3) computer-mediated technologies; (4) communications technologies; (5) media centers; (6) knowledge-based technologies; (7) flexible learning; (8) enabling time and place independence; (9) blended learning; (10) adaptive technologies; (11) technologies for generations Y and Z; (12) synthetic learning environments; (13) technologies linking learning, cognition, and instruction; (14) modeling technologies; (15) learning objects; and (16) open source and open standards. This part of the *Handbook* provides readers with a comprehensive review of recent research pertaining to a variety of instructional technologies that can be linked with Strategies in Part II, with Models in Part IV, and with Design and Development in Part V.

# 15

# Programmed Technologies

*Barbara B. Lockee, Miriam B. Larson, John K. Burton, and D. Michael Moore*
Virginia Polytechnic Institute and State University, Blacksburg, Virginia

## CONTENTS

## ABSTRACT

Programmed technologies of instruction have played an important role in the origins and development of the field of instructional design and technology (IDT). This chapter addresses the historical evolution of programmed technologies, their underlying psychological principals and characteristics, and the extensive research base that formed the early foundations of the IDT field. The most prominent models of programmed technologies are reviewed, including programmed instruction (PI), Personalized System of Instruction (PSI), and Precision Teaching (PT). Programmed technologies represent some of the most empirically investigated forms of instruction, with decades of studies that examined their effectiveness. The modified application of programmed technologies in current models of teaching and learning reflects the long-standing impact of these design approaches on instructional systems development.

# KEYWORD

*Programmed technologies:* Process-based methods and approaches to support learning and instruction, often represented in the form of algorithms and implemented in computer software.

# INTRODUCTION

Mention instructional technology to anyone outside the field and the term evokes mental pictures of computer hardware and software, cameras, projectors, and the like; however, instructional technology involves much more than the materials and equipment used in instruction. These are merely the products of instruction. Instructional technology (IT) is an applied field and, as such, implies a process, perhaps made more clear by talking about instructional design and technology (IDT). The applied field of accounting requires the application of pure mathematical theories. Cooking and baking require the application of chemical and physical theories to human nutrition; likewise, the applied field of instructional technology (referred to as IDT hereafter) requires the application of theories from educational psychology, computer science, management science, communications, and many other disciplines.

The process of instructional technology involves analyzing instructional problems and needs, selecting strategies to meet those needs, designing and developing materials to support those strategies, and evaluating the success of the design during and after implementation. Often, this process results in an instructional product, but occasionally it results in yet another process—an *instructional* process or technique. These instructional techniques can be simple or elaborate and are developed through the application of learning theories to a specific instructional problem. In this chapter, these process-based instructional techniques are referred to as *programmed technologies—programmed* because they are process based and do not necessarily require the use of electronic media for delivery (although many programmed technologies are capable of being conveyed via electronic media), and *technologies* in the sense that the user applies

scientific theory, or a systematic technique, method, or approach to solve a problem.

This chapter addresses several of the most well known of these programmed technologies, including programmed instruction, Keller's Personalized System of Instruction, and Precision Teaching. In each case, learning theories form the basis of the programmed technology, serving to justify its use and application to meet instructional needs and solve instructional problems. A study of these programmed technologies provides a valuable example of how to systematically apply learning theory to develop an instructional process *or* an instructional product.

# PROGRAMMED INSTRUCTION

Probably the best known programmed technology is programmed instruction (PI), considered by many to be a precursor to contemporary IDT (McDonald et al., 2005). A close examination of programmed instruction can build an insightful appreciation for IDT. Programmed instruction was an integral factor in the evolution of the instructional design process and served as the foundation for the procedures used currently to develop effective learning environments by instructional designers and performance technology professionals. The foundations of computer-mediated instruction are based on PI theory and research, and the term *programming* was applied to the production of print-based learning materials long before it was used to refer to computer-based learning materials. PI was the first empirically determined form of instruction; it played a prominent role in the convergence of science and education and represents a milestone in the legitimacy of the field. Equally important is its impact on the evolution of the instructional design and development process. Finally, many of the same design factors emphasized by those involved in the early development of PI are still valid for instructional designers today: presenting information in small steps, providing immediate knowledge of results, providing positive reinforcement, allowing self-pacing, and minimizing the rate of error (Deutsch, 1992).

## Historical Origins of Programmed Instruction

Although attempts at processes resembling programmed instruction date back to the 1920s (Pressey, 1926), the actual term is probably derived from B. F. Skinner's (1954) paper, "The Science of Learning and the Art of Teaching," presented at the University of Pittsburgh's conference of Current Trends in Psychology and the Behavioral Sciences on March 12, 1954. Skinner's remarks reflected his reaction to a 1953 visit to his daughter's fourth-grade arithmetic class (Vargas and Vargas, 1992). Skinner (1954, pp. 90–91) argued that schools were unable to accomplish the type of teaching that eventually leads to original thinking because:

- Schools relied on aversive stimulation or control; as Skinner described it, children worked to "avoid or escape punishment."
- Schools did not pay attention to the contingencies of reinforcement.
- Schools lacked a systematic plan for learning skills, or, in Skinner's words, "a skillful program which moves forward through a series of progressive approximations to the final complex behavior desired."
- Schools too infrequently provided reinforcement.

Skinner suggested a systematic plan—or programmed instruction—as the vehicle to accomplish the changes that needed to occur in classrooms, and in his description of that plan he made two statements that illustrate the importance of instructional design and its relationship to technology. He stated that "education is perhaps the most important branch of scientific technology" (1954, p. 93), and "in the present state of our knowledge of educational practices, scheduling [of behaviors and consequences] appears to be most effectively arranged through the *design* of the material to be learned" (p. 94, emphasis added). Skinner was at the forefront in articulating the need to accomplish this scheduling of behaviors and consequences and a program for effective and efficient learning through *operant conditioning*. Operant conditioning is a form of conditioning that reinforces desired behavior and it is this behaviorist theory that forms the basis for programmed instruction.

In his 1954 work, Skinner went on to discuss the potential for mechanical devices to provide feedback, feeling that the teacher's time was better spent in the design of the instruction and diagnosis of student progress. In his article "Teaching Machines," published in *Science* (1958a), Skinner pushed harder for the use of technology in education that could present instructional material prepared by programmers. In this work, he also emphasized that, if good programming was to become a scientific technology rather than an art, it would depend on the use of student performance data in making revisions. Again, he envisioned the powerful roll that machines could play in collecting these data.

A discussion of the history of programmed instruction is not complete without reference to its implementation in *teaching machines* designed to guide instructional events. Skinner (1958a) and others (e.g., Hartley and Davies, 1978) credited Sidney Pressey with developing the first teaching machine. Beginning in the 1920s, Pressey designed machines for administering tests. Hartley and Davies (1978) correctly pointed out that Pressey's devices were used *after* the instruction took place, but more important to Skinner was Pressey's (1926) understanding that not only could such machines test and score but they could also teach.

During the 1950s, educators and psychologists became concerned that the mass schooling precipitated by increasing demands on public education were not meeting an individual's needs for personal attention in the learning process, and they suggested that teaching machines could restore the "important features of personal instruction" (Skinner, 1986, p. 103). Additional teaching machines were introduced in the 1960s, largely as a result of the success of programmed instruction. A variety of simple machines were introduced, including Skinner's teaching machine, the Porter device, the Bell device, the punchboard, the Subject Matter Trainer by Briggs, the Arithmetic Machine by Skinner and Zeaman, and the Polymath by Rothkopf (Ysewijn, 1993).

The most notable teaching machine to implement programmed instruction was the first computer system completely devoted to computer-assisted instruction (CAI): PLATO (Programmed Logic for Automated Teaching Operations). As its name implies, PLATO was developed using PI in the 1960s and 1970s. Although extensively modified over time to incorporate instructional innovations and changing educational philosophies (Foshay, 1998), PLATO is still regarded as one of the most successful instructional software systems in the history of CAI and is used widely in American schools today.

## Psychological Principles of Programmed Instruction

Programmed Instruction is based on several principles from Skinner's operant conditioning theory, including *shaping*, *priming* and *prompting*, and *transfer of stimulus control*. The concept of *shaping* is based on the behavioral belief that the primary factor that determines a behavior is the learner's environment (physical, social, etc.). Shaping involves the use of positive reinforcement to reward successive approximations of the desired behavior, eventually creating a new response that did not previously exist in the learner's repertoire.

*Priming* and *prompting* are two terms that are occasionally confused. *Priming* is meant to elicit a behavior that is not likely to occur otherwise so it may be reinforced. Skinner (1968a) used imitation as an example of primed behavior. Like all behaviors that a teacher reinforces, to be sustained it would have to be naturally reinforced in the environment. Primes must be eliminated for the behavior to be learned. *Prompts* are stimulus-context cues that elicit a behavior so it can be reinforced (in the context of those stimuli). Skinner (1958a) discussed spelling as an example, where letters in a word are omitted from various locations and the user is required to fill in the missing letter or letters. The letters around the missing element serve as prompts. Prompts are gradually removed, or *faded*, until the desired response can be completed without any prompts (Skinner, 1958a).

*Transfer of stimulus control* refers to the practice of fading and delaying prompts to encourage the learner to respond to more naturally occurring stimuli; for example, at the beginning of a learning sequence, the learner is asked to make responses that are already familiar to him. As the learner proceeds to perform subsequent activities that build upon but are different from these, learning takes place. In the course of performing these intermediate activities, the student transfers his original responses to new subject matter content and also attaches newly learned responses to new subject matter.

## Research on Programmed Instruction

Literally thousands of studies have been conducted on the topic of programmed instruction. As such, many compendiums and substantive reviews of PI research are available, including Galanter (1959), Glaser (1965), Hartley (1974), Hughes (1963), Lockee et al. (2004), Lumsdaine and Glaser (1960), Ofiesh and Meirhenry (1964), Smith and Smith (1966), Stolurow (1961), and Taber et al. (1965), to name a few primary references. The following section provides an overview of the key research topics and studies related to PI.

### Effect of Learner Variables

Some of the general issues addressed in the PI research include how learner variables such as ability and attitudes affect learning from programmed materials. Several studies reported that there was little or no correlation between ability level and achievement on programmed materials (Detambel and Stolurow, 1956; Ferster and Sapon, 1958; Porter, 1957). Studies designed to gauge *learner attitudes* toward PI of learners at all levels and in a variety of settings found a very positive attitude toward this instructional approach (Eigen, 1963;

Engelmann, 1963; Jones and Sawyer, 1949; Smith, 1962; Smith and Smith, 1966; Stolurow, 1963).

### Elements of Programmed Instruction

Many studies compared elements of the PI model, such as the mode of presentation, the effects of overt vs. covert responding, prompting, sequencing of content and contingencies, step size (level of difficulty of content presented in a frame), error rate, and type of response options:

- *Mode of presentation*. Researchers found no significant difference in the amount of learning between linear and branching programs (Anderson, 1967; Coulson and Silberman, 1960; Holland, 1965; Leith, 1966; Roe, 1962; Silberman et al., 1961), with the exception of one study by Coulson et al. (1962), who found branching programs to be superior. In general, branching programs saved significantly more time in instruction than linear programs (Anderson, 1967; Coulson and Silberman, 1960; Holland, 1965; Leith, 1966).

- *Overt vs. covert responses*. Overt responses are those that require the student to *do* something (for example, writing or speaking an answer), whereas covert responses are those that involve thinking about or reading the material and are therefore not able to be observed. Holland and Porter's research (1961) indicated that if responses were not overt (public), they often ceased.

- *Prompting*. Holland (1965) defined a prompt as a cue given prior to an opportunity to give an overt response that can be reinforced (e.g., leaving blanks in a sentence to be filled in by the learner). A few studies that analyzed the advantages of prompting vs. non-prompting in a program sequence found no significant difference (Cook, 1961; Cook and Spitzer, 1960), but Angell and Lumsdaine (1961) found that programs should include both prompted and non-prompted components. This particular component of PI is evident in modern instructional techniques—for example, in the use of completion problems as guided problem-solving models (van Merriënboer and de Croock, 1992; van Merriënboer and Krammer, 1990). Such strategies assist learners in focusing on key features of the problem scenario and ease transfer of learning to real-world application.

- *Sequence*. One of Skinner's major tenets was the "construction of carefully arranged sequences of contingencies leading to the terminal performance" (1953, p. 169). Research comparing results on logical, ordered program sequences vs. nonlogical or random sequences provides mixed results. Many studies indicate that the effectiveness and efficiency of ordered sequences is significantly better than unordered (Gavurin and Donahue, 1960; Hickey and Newton, 1964; Miller, 1969). Other research studies comparing ordered and random program sequences do not support Skinner's principle of ordered sequences (Duncan, 1971; Miller, 1965; Neidermeyer et al., 1968; Wager and Broderick, 1974).
- *Size of step*. In studies comparing small step size (fewer concepts to a frame of instruction) to large step size (more concepts to a frame of instruction), the majority of research found that smaller step sizes produced significantly fewer learner errors (Evans et al., 1959; Gropper, 1966), especially for lower ability students. Results from several other studies, however, warned that programs using very small steps could introduce a "pall effect" (Rigney and Fry, 1961, p. 22) in which boredom was induced by the material, particularly with brighter students (Briggs et al., 1962; Feldhusen et al., 1962).
- *Error rate*. A major tenet of programmed instruction was to present a sequence of instruction that had a "high probability of eliciting desired performance" (Taber et al., 1965, p. 169); thus, care was to be taken in designing the difficulty of that sequence so as to avoid the possibility of errors. Many studies support the concept of low error rate (Holland and Porter, 1961; Keisler, 1959; Melaragno, 1960; Meyer, 1960). Gagné and Dick (1962), however, found low correlations between error rate and learning.

## PERSONALIZED SYSTEM OF INSTRUCTION

### Historical Origins of the Personalized System of Instruction

As programmed instruction became institutionalized practice, variations and derivative approaches evolved, maintaining the general theoretical underpinnings of behavioral teaching while altering specific facets of instruction to reflect the philosophical and psychological beliefs of their creators. One of the most effective models of teaching, the Personalized System of Instruction (PSI), was one such derivation. Created by Fred Keller, PSI was often referred to as the Keller Plan (Keller and Sherman, 1974).

In his seminal paper entitled, "Good-bye, Teacher...," Keller (1968) provided a brief history of the development of the PSI model, based on a practical need to establish a new department of psychology at the University of Brasilia and to create the first course by the given deadline. His colleagues were likeminded in their desire to try something new and were also interested in applying reinforcement theory as a means of instructional innovation. PSI courses were inherently different than traditional courses in that they were self-paced—there were no classes *per se*. Students engaged in instructional units, typically print-based, at a time and place of their choice. According to Keller (Keller, 1968), the distinguishing characteristics of the PSI model are:

- The go-at-your-own-pace feature, which permits a student to move through the course at a speed commensurate with his ability and other demands upon his time
- Unit perfection requirement for advance, which lets the student go ahead with new material only after demonstrating mastery of that which proceeded
- The use of lectures and demonstrations as vehicles of motivation rather than sources of critical information
- The related stress upon the written word in teacher–student communication
- The use of proctors which permits repeated testing, immediate scoring, almost unavoidable tutoring, and a marked enhancement of the personal–social aspect of the educational process

Keller himself noted the similarities between PSI and PI, particularly focusing on "analysis of the task, the same concern with terminal performance, the same opportunity for individualized progression, and so on" (Keller, 1977, p. 114). He indicated that the primary difference between the two instructional approaches were the larger "principle steps of advance" (p. 114), with PSI focusing on the broader understanding of a concept rather than discrete responses to individual prompts or questions. Features of PSI are evident in more recent models of customized, computer-based models of instruction, such as intelligent tutoring systems (ITS). Like PSI, ITS determines student knowledge of a particular domain or subject through strategic assessment approaches and provides a personalized curriculum based on the gap between the targeted learning outcomes and the learner's current knowledge of the content (Burns and Capps, 1988). However, ITS functions in a more "supportive" capacity, demonstrating the evolution of automated instruction from "strong systems" designed to replace human instructional tasks to "weak systems" that serve to extend human performance (Spector and Ohrazda, 2004).

## Psychological Principles of the Personalized System of Instruction

According to Sherman (1992, p. 59), instruction must support a "three-term contingency," including the provision of presentation, performance, and consequences, each constantly adjusted to meet the needs of every individual student. Keller (1968) advocated this individualized approach to instruction, the antithesis of lecture-driven models that left students behind if they were absent, confused, or somehow not able to accommodate the pace of the course curriculum. PSI was devised as a process that would not leave any contingency to chance—chance produces the normal curve (Sherman, 1974). Taveggia (1976) noted that the requirement of unit perfection provides a connection to classical learning theory. The notion of reinforcement through evaluation and feedback at the completion of each unit is a straightforward extension of Skinnerian theory.

## Research on the Personalized System of Instruction

### Student Achievement and Attitudes

Like programmed instruction, PSI is well grounded in empirical research, with thousands of studies supporting its effectiveness across a wide range of disciplines. Numerous meta-analyses have been conducted on PSI, including those by Hursh, 1976; Johnson and Ruskin, 1977; Kulik et al., 1976, 1979, 1990; Robin, 1976; Ryan, 1974; and Taveggia, 1976. Consistent across these reviews are performance gains of students engaged in PSI coursework. Kulik et al. (1979, p. 317) stated that "PSI final exams average about 8 points higher than exams in conventional classes, using Glass's index the effect size is .5. ... A somewhat larger PSI effect is found when achievement exams are administered several months after the end of a course, an improvement of about 14 percentage points." Differences in student ratings of PSI and control classes are also pronounced. Students rate PSI classes as more enjoyable, more demanding, and higher in overall quality and contribution to student learning than conventional classes (Hursh, 1978; Kulik et al., 1979).

### Research on Personalized System of Instruction Components

Various facets of the PSI approach have been investigated. Hursh (1976) provided a detailed overview of many PSI features, including the construction of units (unit size, unit format), the use of study questions (presence vs. absence, question format), quizzing (quizzing routine, question format, and mastery criterion), and student pacing. The use of proctors, another key characteristic of PSI, has also been widely investigated. Farmer et al. (1972) examined the effects of differing amounts of proctoring and found no difference in student performance with the exception of the absence of proctoring, which generated a negative impact on achievement; however, in their analysis of three PSI variables (learner pacing, the mastery requirement, and proctoring), Fernald et al. (1975) found that students learned best with a high amount of contact with a proctor. Mixed results possibly reflect some of the challenges of PSI research.

### Personalized System of Instruction Research Flaws

Hursh (1976, p. 92) pointed to sources of confounding in PSI effectiveness research, including differences in "instructors, curriculum materials, grading criteria, testing formats, student selection, and student expectations." Like much of the research on PI, varied interpretations and applications of the features of the PSI model may impact the quality and generalizability of some PSI studies.

## PRECISION TEACHING

### Historical Origins of Precision Teaching

Precision teaching is an approach to instruction that falls under the general behavioral notion of B. F. Skinner, with particular emphasis on the free operant, fluency, and rate of responding as a measure (standard celeration). PT is uniquely associated with Ogden Lindsley, a student of B. F. Skinner's at Harvard University in the mid-1950s. Like Skinner, Lindsley was influenced by Claude Bernard's (1865) argument that science proceeded from inductive (bottom up) reasoning rather than deductive. Certainly both men were influenced by Pavlov's (1927) terminology, and many of his notions of measurement.

In the 1950s, Lindsley began his career at the Harvard Medical School and Metropolitan State Hospital, where he founded the Harvard Behavioral Research Laboratory. In his laboratory, Lindsley became convinced that free-operant conditioning should focus on the frequency of responding rather than percentage correct. Free-operant conditioning refers to an environment where "students are free to respond at their own pace without having restraints placed on them by the limits of the materials or the instructional procedures" (Lindsley, 1950, p. 10). His advance in this regard was unusual. Skinner used controlled operants (discrete trials), rather than free operants. Lindsley (1966) did not agree with Skinner's work with teaching machines and programmed instruction for three reasons: (1) there was no opportunity to repeat a response in the presence of its stimulus—once a frame passed, it was passed; (2) the response measure was percentage of frames correct (as opposed to frequency of response); and (3) no provision was made for external reinforcement because teaching machine programs were designed on the premise that getting the answer correct was sufficient reinforcement. Lindsley argued that if that were true then all learners would demonstrate progress (but at different rates).

Lindsley (1990) became convinced him that education had to change and argued that teaching machines and PI did not work well enough: "I knew that the real power of learning enhanced by free-operant conditioning lay in frequency of responding (by allowing the student to be both accurate and fluent) and standard self-recording. When educators would not heed my caution and could not see my vision for dramatic learning opportunities, I decided the ethical thing to do was to close my hospital laboratory and devote myself to education" (pp. 10–11). In 1965, Lindsley became the Director of Educational Research at the University of Kansas Medical School, and in 1971 he became a Professor of Education working with preservice and in-service special education teachers. Precision teaching as a formal system emerged in 1964 and 1965.

## Psychological Principles of Precision Teaching

Precision teaching is about "basing educational decision on changes in continuously self-maintained performance frequencies display on standard celeration charts" (Lindsley, 1992, p. 51). As such, precision teaching does not prescribe what should be taught (curriculum) nor how to teach it (instruct); rather, it is "a precise and systematic method" (West and Young, 1992, p. 114) of evaluating curricula and instruction.

In a nutshell then, precision teaching was an individualized behavioral approach. It relied on the basic principles of operant conditioning in a free operant environment. Learning plans were written to address specific reinforcers for certain targeted behaviors, or pinpoints. Lindsley (1968) devised what he called the "dead-man test" to decide appropriate pinpoints. A good pinpoint involves observable actions and movements. A bad pinpoint lacks either movement or action, is completely internal and low level, or involves the sheer passage of time. In general, if a dead man can perform well on the pinpoint behavior, then it is a bad one. Terms such as *appreciate*, *know*, and *understand* are poor pinpoints because they reflect no actual measurable behavior.

Recording the frequency of behaviors is a hallmark of precision teaching; according to Skinner, "my major contributions are rate of response and the cumulating response records" (1968). Skinner felt that frequency was a "universal datum" that permitted comparison across individuals and behaviors; for example, one could compare "the acceleration in dressing produced by smiling at a retarded child with the slight change in the mathematics curriculum of a gifted teenager. And we can say that the rewarding smile for the retarded child was one half as accelerating as the curriculum change for the teenager" (Lindsley, 1972, p. 2). Lindsley also pointed out that the acceleration number could be used to determine cost–benefit ratios and could be used to replace test scores.

## Research on Precision Teaching

Much like PI and PSI, the effectiveness of the PT approach is demonstrated through empirical research and represents true data-based decision making regarding instructional design. Binder and Watkins (1990) contended that, despite the fact that PT may be one of the "most thoroughly validated and consistently effective methods yet developed in English speaking schools" (p. 74), educators and policymakers either lack awareness of the method or maintain political or philosophical objections to it. Although PT research was not as widely published as PI and PSI studies, a tremendous amount of student data was collected in the 1960s and 1970s that supports the efficacy of the PT method.

Lindsley (1991) noted a particularly impressive compilation of PT student data collected through a computerized database system established in 1967 by the Behavior Bank. Over 11,000 student records submitted by teachers were put into the database and accessed by scientists for research studies related to PT. The analysis of this extensive dataset indicated several major findings, the most notable of which is that "behavior frequencies celerate, bounce, and spread in multiples and should be charted on multiply scales" (Lindsley, 1991, p. 262). Also, another important finding is that many different stimuli and rewards were equally effective in producing the same behavior; none emerged as the "best" strategy for a given learning behavior.

An often-cited case study illustrating PT effectiveness is the Morningside Academy in Seattle. Beginning in 1980, the private institution targeted fluency by combining PT with Direct Instruction and the Tiemann–Markle instructional design strategy (Lindsley, 1992). Morningside guaranteed a tuition refund to students who did not progress two grade levels per year. As of 1989, no refunds had been given. The academy had similar success with an adult literacy program in support of the Job Training and Partnership Act, exceeding by over ten times the expected federal gains (Lindsley, 1992).

## CONCLUDING REMARKS

Although trends in educational philosophy and learning theory have shifted away from behavioral sciences to more cognitive and constructivist approaches, the influence of programmed technologies continues in the instructional design processes that serve as the standards for our field (Dick et al., 2000; Gagné et al., 1992; Gustafson and Branch, 2002; Kemp et al., 1998; Smith and Ragan, 1999). Trends in instructional design and technology indicate that, even though the systematic instructional design process has been embraced at varying levels across different venues (Reiser and Dempsey, 2002), its behavioral origins are still evident, and notions of programmed technologies are found in existing practice. The instructional innovations described herein served to transform several functions of instructional design into the cohesive process practiced today. These functions include the conduct of a needs assessment, the establishment of clearly defined and measurable objectives, the process of task analysis, the creation of assessment instruments and approaches that reflect the specified outcomes, the provision of opportunities for practice and feedback, and the evaluation of the instructional program or product. Perhaps the most prominent effect of the programmed technologies tradition on education as a whole is the convergence of the science of learning with the practice of teaching, a point originating from the first discussion of PI from Skinner (1954) himself in "The Science of Learning and the Art of Teaching."

Programmed technologies are still evident in the contemporary landscape of educational innovations. Features of the aforementioned instructional models are prominent in today's advanced learning systems, especially in the area of performance support. Electronic performance support systems, knowledge management systems, and expert systems are examples of current technologies that provide customized feedback and guidance based on user input — "weak systems" (Spector and Ohrazda, 2004, p. 686) specifically designed to enhance human performance. As educational researchers seek to assess the efficacy and value of more modern instructional approaches, revisiting the tremendous empirical base that demonstrates the effectiveness of programmed technologies for learning can provide insight and direction to IDT research designs and research plans for the 21st century.

## REFERENCES

Anderson, R. C. (1967). Educational psychology. *Annu. Rev. Psychol.*, 18, 129–164.

Angell, D. and Lumsdaine, A. A. (1961). Prompted and unprompted trials versus prompted trials only in paired associate learning. In *Student Response in Programmed Instruction*, edited by A. A. Lumsdaine, pp. 389–398. Washington, D.C.: National Research Council.

Bernard, C. (1865). *Introduction a l'etude de la medecine experimentale*. New York: Bailliere Bros.

Binder, C. and Watkins, C. L. (1990). Precision teaching and direct instruction: measurably superior instructional technology in schools. *Perform. Improve. Q.*, 3(4), 74–96.

Briggs, L. J. (1960). Two self-instructional devices. In *Teaching and Programmed Learning*, edited by A. A. Lumsdaine and R. Glaser, pp. 299–304. Washington, D.C.: National Education Association.

Briggs, L. J., Goldbeck, R. A., Campbell, V. N., and Nichols, D. G. (1962). Experimental results regarding form of response, size of step, and individual differences in automated programs. In *Programmed Learning and Computer-Based Instruction*, edited by J. E. Coulson, pp. 86–98. New York: Wiley.

Burns, H. L. and Capps, C. G. (1988). Foundations of intelligent tutoring systems: an introduction. In *Foundations of Intelligent Tutoring Systems*, edited by M. C. Polson and J. J. Richardson, pp. 1–19. Hillsdale, NJ: Lawrence Erlbaum Associates.

Carr, W. J. (1959). A functional analysis of self-instructional devices. In *Teaching Machines and Programmed Instruction*, edited by A. A. Lumsdaine and R. Glaser, pp. 540–562. Washington, D.C.: National Education Association.

Cook, J. O. (1961). From audience participation to paired-associate learning and response analysis in paired-associate learning experiments. In *Student Response in Programmed Instruction*, edited by A. A. Lumsdaine, pp. 351–373. Washington, D.C.: National Research Council.

Cook, J. O. and Spitzer, M. E. (1960). Supplementing report: prompting versus confirmation in paired-associate learning. *J. Exp. Psychol.*, 59, 257–276.

Coulson, J. E. and Silberman, H. F. (1960). Effects of three variables in a teaching machine. *J. Educ. Psychol.*, 51, 135–143.

Coulson, J. E., Estavan, D. P., Melaragno, R. J., and Silberman, H. F. (1962). Effects of branching in a computer controlled autoinstructional device. *J. Appl. Psychol.*, 46, 389–392.

Detambel, M. H. and Stolurow, L. M. (1956). Stimulus sequence and concept learning. *J. Exp. Psychol.*, 51, 34–40.

Deutsch, W. (1992). Teaching machines, programming, computers, and instructional technology: the roots of performance technology. *Perform. Instruct.*, 31(2), 14–20.

Dick, W., Carey, L., and Carey, J. O. (2000). *The Systematic Design of Instruction*, 5th ed. Reading, MA: Addison-Wesley.

Duncan, K. D. (1971). Fading of prompts in learning sequences. *Programmed Learn. Educ. Technol.*, 8(2), 111–115.

Eigen, L.D. (1963). High school student reactions to programmed instruction. *Phi Delta Kappan*, 44, 282–285.

Engelmann, M. D. (1963). Construction and evaluation of programmed materials in biology classroom use. *Am. Biol. Teacher*, 25, 212–214.

Evans, J. L., Glaser, R., and Homme, L. E. (1959). A Preliminary Investigation of Variation in Properties of Verbal Learning Sequences of the Teaching Machine Type. Paper presented at the Eastern Psychological Association Annual Meeting, Atlantic City, NJ.

Farmer, J., Lachter, G. D., Blaustein, J. J., and Cole, B. K. (1972). The role of proctoring in personalized instruction. *J. Appl. Behav. Anal.*, 5, 401–404.

Feldhusen, J. F., Ramharter, H., and Birt, A. T. (1962). The teacher versus programmed learning. *Wisconsin J. Educ.*, 95(3), 8–10.

Fernald, P. S., Chiseri, M. H., Lawson, D. W., Scroggs, G. F., and Riddell, J. C. (1975). Systematic manipulation of student pacing, the perfection requirement, and contact with a teaching assistant in an introductory psychology course. *Teach. Psychol.*, 2(4), 147–151.

Ferster, C. D. and Sapon, S. M. (1958). An application of recent developments in psychology to the teaching of German. *Harvard Educ. Rev.*, 28, 58–69.

Foshay, R. (1998). *Instructional Philosophy and Strategic Direction of the PLATO System*, ERIC Document Reproduction Service ED 464 603. Edina, MN: PLATO.

Gagné, R. M., Briggs, L. J., and Wager, W. W. (1992). *Principles of Instructional Design*, 4th ed. New York: Harper Collins.

Gagné, R. M. and Dick, W. (1962). Learning measures in a self-instructional program in solving equations. *Psychol. Rep.*, 10, 131–146.

Galanter, E. H. (1959). *Automatic Teaching: The State of the Art*. New York: John Wiley & Sons.

Gavurin, E. I. and Donahue, V. M. (1960). *Logical Sequence and Random Sequence Teaching–Machine Programs*. Burlington, MA: RCA.

Glaser, R., Ed., (1965). *Teaching Machines and Programmed Learning*, Vol. II. Washington, D.C.: National Education Association.

Gropper, G. L. (1966). *Programming Visual Presentations for Procedural Learning. Studies in Televised Instruction*. Pittsburgh, PA: American Institute for Research in Behavioral Sciences.

Gustafson, K. and Branch, R. M. (2002). What is instructional design? In *Trends and Issues in Instructional Design and Technology*, edited by R. A. Reiser and J. A. Dempsey, pp. 16–25. Upper Saddle River, NJ: Prentice Hall.

Hartley, J. (1974). Programmed Instruction 1954–1974: a review. *Programmed Learn. Educ. Technol.*, 11, 278–291.

Hartley, J. and Davies, I. (1978). Programmed learning and educational technology. In *Adult Learning: Psychological Research and Applications*, edited by M. Howe, pp. 161–183. New York: John Wiley & Sons.*

Hickey, A. E. and Newton, J. M. (1964). *The Logical Basis of Teaching: The Effect of Subconcept Sequence on Learning*. Newbury Port, MA: Entelek.

Holland, J. G. (1959). A teaching machine program in psychology. In *Automatic Teaching: The State of the Art*, edited by E. Galanter, pp. 69–82. New York: John Wiley & Sons.

Holland, J. G. (1960). Design and use of a teaching machine and program. *Teachers Coll. Rec.*, 63, 56–65.

Holland, J. G. (1965). Research on programming variables. In *Teaching Machines and Programmed Learning*, Vol. II, edited by R. Glaser, pp. 66–177. Washington, D.C.: National Education Association.

Holland, J. G., and Porter, D. (1961). The influence of repetition of incorrectly answered items in a teaching-machine program. *J. Exp. Anal. Behav.*, 4, 305–307.

Hughes, J. E., Ed., (1963). *Programmed Learning: A Critical Evaluation*. Chicago, IL: Educational Methods.

Hursh, D. E. (1976). Personalized systems of instruction: what do the data indicate? *J. Personalized Instruct.*, 1, 91–105.

Johnson, K. R. and Ruskin, R. S. (1977). *Behavioral Instruction: An Evaluative Review*. Washington, D.C.: American Psychological Association.

Jones, H. L. and Sawyer, M. O. (1949). A new evaluation instrument. *J. Educ. Res.*, 42, 381–385.

Joyce, B. and Moxley, R. A. (1988). August Dvorak (1894–1975): early expressions of applied behavior analysis and precision teaching. *Behav. Anal.*, 11(1), 33–40.

Keisler, E. R. (1959). The development of understanding in arithmetic by a teaching machine. *J. Educ. Psychol.*, 50, 247–253.

Keller, F. S. (1968). Good-bye, teacher.... *J. Appl. Behav. Anal.*, 1, 78–89.

Keller, F. S. (1977). *Summers and Sabbaticals: Selected Papers on Psychology and Education*. Champaign, IL: Research Press.*

Keller, F. S. and Sherman, J. G. (1974). *The Keller Plan Handbook: Essays on a Personalized System of Instruction*. Menlo Park, CA: W.A. Benjamin.*

Kemp, J., Morrison, G. R., and Ross, S. M. (1998). *Designing Effective Instruction*, 2nd ed. New York: Merrill.

Kulik, J. A., Kulik, C. L. C., and Smith, B. B. (1976). Research on the personalized system of instruction. *J. Programmed Learn. Educ. Technol.*, 13, 23–30.

Kulik, J. A., Kulik, C. L. C., and Cohen, P. A. (1979). A meta-analysis of outcome studies of Keller's personalized system of instruction. *Am. Psychol.*, 34(4), 307–318.*

Kulik, C. C., Kulik, J. A., and Bangert-Drowns, R. L. (1990). Effectiveness of mastery learning programs: a meta-analysis. *Rev. Educ. Res.*, 60(2), 269–299.

Leith, G. O. M. (1966). *A Handbook of Programmed Learning*, 2nd ed., Educational Review Occasional Publication Number 1. Birmingham, U.K.: University of Birmingham.

Lindsley, O. R. (1971). From Skinner to precision teaching: the child knows best. In *Let's Try Doing Something Else Kind of Thing*, edited by J. B. Jordan and L. S. Robbins, pp. 1–11. Arlington, VA: Council on Exceptional Children.

Lindsley, O. R. (1966). Is fluency free-operant response–response chaining? *Behav. Anal.*, 19, 211–224.

Lindsley, O. R. (1968). *Training Parents and Teachers to Precisely Manage Children's Behavior.* Address presented at the Mott Children's Health Center, Flint, MI.

Lindsley, O. R. (1990). Precision teaching: by teachers for children. *Teaching Exceptional Children*, Spring, 10–15.

Lindsley, O. R. (1991). Precision teaching's unique legacy from B. F. Skinner. *J. Behav. Educ.*, 1(2), 253–266.*

Lindsley, O. R. (1992). Precision teaching: discoveries and effects. *J. Appl. Behav. Anal.*, 25(1), 51–57.*

Lindsley, O. R. (1996). The four free-operant freedoms. *Behav. Anal.*, 19, 199–210.

Lockee, B. B., Moore, D. M., and Burton, J. K. (2004). Programmed instruction. In *Handbook for Research for Educational Communications and Technology*, 2nd ed., edited by D. Jonassen, pp. 545–569. Mahwah, NJ: Lawrence Erlbaum Associates.*

Lumsdaine, A. A. (1962). Experimental research on instructional devices and materials. In *Training Research and Education*, edited by R. Glaser, pp. 247–294. Pittsburgh, PA: University of Pittsburgh.

Lumsdaine, A. A. (1965). Assessing the effectiveness of instructional programs. In *Teaching Machines and Programmed Learning*. Vol. II. *Data and Directions*, edited by R. Glaser, pp. 267–320. Washington, D.C.: National Education Association.

Lumsdaine, A. A. and Glaser, R., Eds. (1960). *Teaching Machines and Programmed Learning*. Washington, D.C.: National Education Association.*

Lysaught, J. P. and Williams, C. M. (1963). *A Guide to Programmed Instruction*. New York: John Wiley & Sons.

Maccoby, N. and Sheffield, F. D. (1958). Theory and experimental research on the teaching of complex sequential procedures by alternative demonstration and practice. In *Symposium on Air Force Human Engineering*, *Personnel and Training Research*, edited by G. Finch and F. Cameron. Washington, D.C.: National Academy of Sciences, National Research Council.

MacDonald-Ross, M. (1973). Behavioral objectives: a critical review. *Instruct. Sci.*, 2, 1–52.

McDonald, J. K., Yanchar, S. C., and Osguthorpe, R. T. (2005). Learning from programmed instruction: examining implications for modern instructional technology. *Educ. Technol. Res. Dev.*, 53(2), 84–98.

Melaragno, R. J. (1960). Effect of negative reinforcement in an automated teaching setting. *Psychol. Rep.*, 7, 381–384.

Meyer, S. R. (1960). Report on the initial test of a junior high-school vocabulary program. In *Teaching Machines and Programmed Learning*, edited by A. A. Lumsdaine and R. Glaser, pp. 229–246. Washington, D.C.: National Education Association,

Miller, H. R. (1965). An Investigation into Sequencing and Prior Information Variables in a Programmed Evaluation Unit for Junior High School Mathematics. Paper presented at Department of Audiovisual Instruction Meeting, Milwaukee, WI.

Miller, H. R. (1969). Sequencing and prior information in linear programmed instruction. *AV Commun. Rev.*, 17(1), 63–76.

Neidermeyer, F., Brown, J., and Sulzen, R. (1968). The Effects of Logical, Scrambled and Reverse Order Sequences on the Learning of a Series of Mathematical Tasks at the Math Grade Level. Paper presented at the meeting of the California Educational Research Association, March, Oakland, CA.

Ofiesh, G. D. and Meirhenry, W. C., Eds. (1964). *Trends in Programmed Instruction*, Washington, D.C.: National Education Association.

Pavlov, I. P. (1965). Conditioned reflexes: an investigation of the physiological activity of the cerebral cortex (G. V. Anrep, trans.). London: Oxford University Press (original work published in 1927).

Porter, D. (1957). A critical review of a portion of the literature on teaching devices. *Harvard Educ. Rev.*, 27, 126–147.

Potts, L., Eshleman, J. W., and Cooper, J. O. (1993). Ogden R. Lindsley and the historical development of precision teaching. *Behav. Anal.*, 16, 177–189.

Pressey, S. L. (1926). A simple apparatus which gives tests and scores—and teaches. *School Society*, 23, 373–376.

Pressey, S. L. (1950). Development and appraisal of devices providing immediate automatic scoring of objective tests and concomitant self-instruction. *J. Psychol.*, 29, 417–447.

Reiser, R. A. (2001). A history of instructional design and technology. Part II. A history of instructional design. *Educ. Technol. Res. Dev.*, 49(2), 57–67.

Reiser, R. A. and Dempsey, J. V. (2002). *Trends and Issues in Instructional Design and Technology.* Upper Saddle River, NJ: Merrill Prentice Hall.

Rigney, J. W. and Fry, E. B. (1961). Current teaching-machine programs and programming techniques. *Audiovisual Commun. Rev.*, 9(3, Suppl. 3), 7–121.

Robin, A. R. (1976). Behavioral instruction in the college classroom. *Rev. Educ. Res.*, 46, 313–354.

Roe, A. A. (1962). A comparison of branching methods for programmed instruction. *J. Educ. Res.*, 55, 407–416.

Ryan, B. A. (1974). *Keller's Personalized System of Instruction: An Appraisal.* Washington, D.C.: American Psychological Association.

Severin, D. G. (1960). Appraisal of special tests and procedures used with self-scoring instructional testing devices. In *Teaching Machines and Programmed Learning*, edited by A. A. Lumsdaine and R. Glaser, pp. 678–680. Washington, D.C.: National Education Association.

Sherman, J. G. (1974). The theory behind PSI. In *PSI: Personalized System of Instruction*, edited by J. G. Sherman, pp. 223–225. Menlo Park, CA: W.A. Benjamin.

Sherman, J. G. (1992). Reflections on PSI: good news and bad. *J. Appl. Behav. Anal.*, 25(1), 59–64.

Silberman, H. F., Melaragno, R. J., Coulson, J. E., and Estavan, D. (1961). Fixed sequence versus branching auto-instructional methods. *J. Educ. Psychol.*, 52, 166–172.

Skinner, B. F. (1953). *Science and Human Behavior.* New York: Macmillan.

Skinner, B. F. (1954). The science of learning and the art of teaching. *Harvard Educ. Rev.*, 24, 86–97.*

Skinner, B. F. (1958a). Teaching machines. *Science*, 128, 969–977.*

Skinner, B. F. (1958b). Reinforcement today. *Am. Psychol.*, 13, 94–99.

Skinner, B. F. (1961). Why we need teaching machines. *Harvard Educ. Rev.*, 31, 377–398.

Skinner, B. F. (1968a). *The Technology of Teaching.* New York: Appleton Century Crofts.*

Skinner, B. F. (1968b). Reflections on a decade of teaching machines. In *Instructional Process and Media Innovation*, edited by R. A. Weisgerber, pp. 404–417. Chicago, IL: Rand McNally.

Skinner, B. F. (1986). Programmed instruction revisited. *Phi Delta Kappan*, 68(2), 103–110.

Smith, K. U. and Smith, M. F. (1966). *Cybernetic Principles of Learning and Educational Design.* New York: Holt, Rinehart and Winston.

Smith, N. H. (1962). The teaching of elementary statistics by the conventional classroom method versus the method of programmed instruction. *J. Educ. Res.*, 55, 417–420.

Smith, P. L. and Ragan, T. J. (1999). *Instructional Design*, 2nd ed. Upper Saddle River, NJ: Prentice Hall.

Spector, J. M. and Ohrazda, C. (2004). Automating instructional design: approaches and limitations. In *Handbook for Research for Educational Communications and Technology*, 2nd ed., edited by D. Jonassen, pp. 685–699. Mahwah, NJ: Lawrence Erlbaum Associates.

Stolurow, L. M. (1961). *Teaching by Machine*. Washington, D.C.: U.S. Department of Health, Education, and Welfare.

Stolurow, L. M. (1963). Programmed instruction for the mentally retarded. *Rev. Educ. Res.*, 33, 126–133.

Taber, J. I., Glaser, R., and Schaefer, H. H. (1965). *Learning and programmed Instruction*. Reading, MA: Addison Wesley.

Taveggia, T. C. (1976). Personalized instruction: a summary of comparative research 1967–1974. *Am. J. Physics*, 44, 1028–1033.

van Merriënboer, J. J. G. and de Croock, M. B. M. (1992). Strategies for computer-based programming instruction: program completion vs. program generation. *J. Educ. Comput. Res.*, 8, 365–394.

van Merriënboer, J. J. G. and Krammer, H. P. M. (1990). The 'completion strategy' in programming instruction: theoretical and empirical support. In *Research on Instruction*, edited by S. Dijkstra, B. H. M. van Hout-Wolters, and P. C. van der Sijde, pp. 45–61. Englewood Cliffs, NJ: Educational Technology Publications.

Vargas, E. A. and Vargas, J. (1992). Programmed instruction and teaching machines. In *Designs for Excellence in Education: The Legacy of B. F. Skinner*, edited by R. P. West and L. A. Hamerlynck, pp. 33–69. Longmont, CO: Sopris West.

Wager, W. W. and Broderick, W. A. (1974). Three objective rules of sequencing applied to programmed learning materials. *AV Commun. Rev.*, 22(4), 423–438.

West, R. P. and Young, K. R. (1992). Precision teaching. In *Designs for Excellence in Education: The Legacy of B. F. Skinner*, edited by R. P. West and L. A. Hamerlynck, pp. 113–146. Longmont, CO: Sopris West.

Ysewijn, P. (1993). A more or less subjective view on the history of CAI. *CBT Forum*, 2(3), 35–54 (http://www.mypage.bluewin.ch/Ysewijn/DOC/History_of_CAI.PDF).

* Indicates a core reference.

# 16

# Educational Hypertext

*Dale S. Niederhauser*
Iowa State University, Ames, Iowa

## CONTENTS

## ABSTRACT

The widespread development of digital, linked, text-based information repositories has prompted considerable research on learning from hypertext. The proliferation of the Internet has made the World Wide Web, with its hyperlinked Web pages, wikis, and blogs, the preferred information source for 21st-century world citizens. As we increasingly rely on hypertext-based information resources. It is critical that we focus on how reading hyperlinked text affects the learning process as we increasingly rely on hypertext-based informational resources. Grounded in cognitive flexibility theory and the construction–integration model, this chapter is focused on current empirical research that furthers our understanding of learning from hypertext. Clearly, one's goals for reading a given hypertext play an important role in determining what is learned from it. The degree to which these goals are self or externally imposed, the specificity of goals, and the interactions among goals, system structure, and individual characteristics of learners all influence what is learned when reading hypertext. Further, strategies readers use to navigate through hypertext content, and the inclusion of navigational scaffolds, also appear to influence learning. Finally, individual characteristics, such as prior knowledge and cognitive style, also appear to affect learning from hypertext, while metacognitive aspects such as active knowledge construction and self-regulated learning, coupled with coherence-promoting hypertext design elements, appear to hold great promise for future research.

## KEYWORDS

*Hierarchical hypertext:* A hypertext structure in which content is ordered relative to the concepts presented. The concepts presented on a screen link to superordinate (more general) concepts or subordinate (more specific) concepts.

*Hypertext:* Text-based informational screens that are presented using a computer; informational screens are connected to each other using links.

*Linear hypertext:* A hypertext structure in which links allow the reader to move forward and backward through the content, as if turning the pages of a book.

*Relational hypertext:* A hypertext structure with links that allow the reader to access information on other screens that have some logical, conceptual, or hierarchical connection to the content on the current screen.

*Self-regulated learning:* When learners set their own goals for learning, then attempt to plan, monitor, regulate, and control their cognition, motivation, behavior, and context.

*User control:* The degree to which the reader can determine the sequence and pacing of information accessed in a hypertext.

## INTRODUCTION

The development and widespread implementation of hypertext-based information presentation systems have prompted researchers to investigate how the use of such systems affects knowledge acquisition. Although the majority of research on hypertext is not specifically related to learning, a growing body of empirical research addresses learning with hypertext. This chapter provides a conceptual review of empirical research reported during the past 5 years and updates a previous *Handbook of Research on Educational Communications and Technology* chapter (Shapiro and Niederhauser, 2004).

Established theories that help explain reading and learning, such as the construction–integration model (Kintsch, 1988) and cognitive flexibility theory (Spiro et al., 1988, 1992), provide the theoretical underpinnings of the learning-from-hypertext process. According to Shapiro and Niederhauser (2004), the construction–integration model (CIM) of text processing suggests a three-stage process of text comprehension. The first two processes—character/word decoding and the construction of a *textbase* (a hierarchical propositional representation of the textual information)—are thought to be invariant across media. The third process, creation of a *situation model*, is central to our understanding of learning with hypertext.

Creating a situation model is the process whereby the learner constructs a conceptual representation of the content in the text by integrating new information from the text (textbase) with his or her prior knowledge. At its best, this active integration of the textbase with prior knowledge constitutes *meaning making*—a deep, complex, and coherent understanding of the material presented in the text. The active cognition inherent in this integrative process drives educators' and researchers' belief that hypertext can serve as a tool to promote high-level conceptual learning.

Cognitive flexibility theory (CFT) also contributes to our understanding of learning with hypertext. CFT suggests that a hypertext-based environment allows the reader to utilize the linking capabilities inherent in hypertext to construct his or her own unique pathway through the text (Jacobson and Spiro, 1995; Lawless and Kulikowich, 1996). Because the learner can access a given information screen from multiple other hyperlinked screens, he or she will encounter the same information from multiple perspectives depending on the paths taken. A rich understanding of *complex conceptual landscapes* will emerge when the learner has made numerous traversals of the domain from different perspectives (Jacobson and Spiro, 1995). Thus, the linked structure of hypertext allows the reader to access information from different paths—providing opportunities for learners to integrate new information from the text into their existing conceptions (create a situation model) and make connections among concepts that are not likely to occur when sequentially reading traditional text. This process of *criss-crossing the conceptual landscape* (Jacobson and Spiro, 1995; Spiro and Jehng, 1990; Spiro et al., 1987) requires the reader to engage in deeper levels of semantic processing to compare and contrast the linked information by analyzing the content in terms of meaningful properties.

The increased *learner control* associated with criss-crossing places additional demands on the reader's cognitive resources. Chief among these are the metacognitive demands associated with determining the structure of the textbase in the hypertext, integrating the textbase with prior knowledge, and navigating through the hypertext in a way that promotes the development of a complex and conceptually coherent representation of the content. To navigate effectively, the learner must monitor whether he or she understands what has been read, determine whether additional information is needed, and decide which of the available links might be useful for locating the needed information in the hypertext.

As noted in by Shapiro and Niederhauser (2004, pp. 606–607):

> CIM is informative to hypertext research because it offers an explanation of the relevance of user behavior. Specifically, it explains the research that points to user behaviors such as link choice, navigation patterns, and metacognitive practice as mediators of learning. CFT offers an explanation of meaningful learning on the part of advanced learners. It successfully explains why the exploration of identical texts can result in more flexible, transferable knowledge from a hypertext than a traditional text. It adds to our understanding of [hypertext-assisted learning] because it offers a unique explanation of how mental representations are constructed, reconstructed, and altered by exposure to dynamic information structures.

It is these *dynamic information structures* that make hypertext-based systems different from traditional print-based media. Hypertext supports nonlinear access to information through the use of navigational elements such as menus, concept maps, and *hotwords* embedded in the text. These features structure the content being presented and force the reader to choose his or her own path through the text. Requiring users to take this responsibility gives rise to issues concerning users' goals, motivations, and purposes for reading; their prior knowledge about the content; and the metacognitive strategies they use to monitor their understanding of the content and make decisions about the order of information access. Thus, essential hypertext-specific variables include the effects of: (1) reader goals, (2) navigation patterns, (3) learner characteristics, and (4) active cognitive engagement when learning with hypertext.

# READER GOALS

Goal-directed learning appears to have a powerful influence when learning with hypertext (Jonassen and Wang, 1993). When reading hypertext, a reader's learning goal may be influenced by several factors, including implicit and explicit teacher/researcher goals (e.g., to answer specific questions, for general meaning, to find certain information), features and information inherent in the hypertext itself (e.g., goal statements, embedded questions), and learner goals (e.g., interest, need to know). Gerjets and Scheiter (2003) reported a series of studies that demonstrated the effects on cognitive load of the interrelationships among teacher goals, learner goals, and learners' processing strategies—and the resulting influences on learning. They concluded that the relationship between instructional design (system structure) and pattern of extraneous and germane cognitive load is not as deterministic as many cognitive load researchers claim. Rather, the relation is moderated by instructional (teacher-imposed) goals, learner goals, and the learners' processing strategies. Differentiating goals and processing strategies appear to be important aspects of the development of our understanding of the processes associated with learning with hypertext.

## Specificity of Goals

Much of the hypertext-assisted learning research to date, however, has focused on the use of explicit teacher/researcher goals. Curry et al. (1999) conducted a study to examine the effect of providing a specific learning objective to guide the reading of a hypertext. Fifty university students read a 60-frame hierarchical hypertext on Lyme disease. Half of the students received a specific task to guide their learning. They were given a scenario about a man with physical symptoms and a probable diagnosis and were told to use the hypertext to determine the accuracy of the information in the scenario. The other half were told to read the text carefully, because they would be asked a series of questions at the end. Although no differences were found on recall measures, the concept maps that students drew did show differences. Students in the specific goal condition constructed more *relational* maps, which the authors felt demonstrated a more sophisticated conceptual representation of the content.

More recent research also examined the effects of specificity of goal-setting orientation on learning with hypertext (Gall, 2006; Moos and Azevedo, 2006; Zumbach and Reimann, 2002). Results indicated that goal orientation in these studies also influenced the type of learning that occurred. Gall (2006) examined the differential learning of Air Force Academy cadets who used a 200-article title-linked relational hypertext under three orienting conditions: browsing to learn the content, searching for factual information to answer specific questions, and looking for connections among articles to answer conceptual questions. Subjects who used the hypertext to find connections among concepts performed best on a measure of conceptual understanding. Cadets without a focused goal orientation (those in the browsing condition) learned the least.

Not all specific learning goals promote deep, meaningful learning, however. Azevedo and his colleagues (Azevedo et al., 2001, 2002) gave one group of subjects the explicit goal of answering specific questions about the human circulatory system, while other subjects were able to generate their own goals while reading a Microsoft Encarta-based relational hypermedia system. Some subjects in the question-answering groups increased the sophistication of their mental models of circulation, but many actually showed a decrease in sophistication. No subjects in the learner-generated goal condition showed a decrease in the quality of their mental models, and nearly all showed an increase. Moreover, those in the self-generated goal condition demonstrated more effective use of metacognitive strategies.

Results form other studies that examined reader-regulated goal structures, however, contradicted these results. Zumbach and Reimann (2002) presented students with either a seven-module, computer-based linear hypertext (an externally imposed explicit goal) or a relational hypertext that contained all of the content in the tutorial presented in a linked format. Subjects who received the hypertext treatment were given either strategy instruction in analyzing, comparing, and evaluating the causal relationships of facts and information (to prompt internally imposed goals) or a goal-based scenario that required them to role-play a newspaper editor who had to use the information in the hypertext to write a commentary (externally imposed general goal). Sixty adult participants were randomly assigned to one of the 3 treatment conditions (20 per treatment) and assessed on factual knowledge (multiple-choice test), structural knowledge (computerized concept-mapping tool), and application/inference/transfer of knowledge ("argumentation" task). Findings indicated that subjects in the tutorial condition performed best on the factual information task; subjects in the goal-based scenario condition performed best on the structural knowledge and application/inference/transfer task; and, contrary to results from Azevedo and colleagues' (2001, 2002) studies, subjects in the strategy group, despite explicit instructions, failed to apply the metacognitive strategy, yielding disappointing results for this group.

### Relationships among Goals, System Structure, and Learner Characteristics

Subjects in Curry and colleagues' (1999) and Gall's (2006) studies may have benefited from a specific goal because it capitalized on the features offered by hypertext. The specific fact-finding goal assigned in the studies by Azevedo et al. (2001, 2002) and Gall (2006) may be less compatible with hypertext-assisted learning. Early in the history of hypertext in educational settings, Landow (1992) considered the importance of matching learning goals to the uniqueness of the technology. He pointed out that hypertext and printed text have different advantages and that hypertext assignments should be written that complement hypertext, suggesting that goals such as fact retrieval squander the richness of hypertext because fact finding is not aided by multiple links.

Shapiro (1998b) examined the affects of matching system structure, goals, and prior knowledge when she matched specific learning goals with the use of a clear, conceptually based hypertext system. She found that the ability of low prior knowledge (PK) learners to meet their goals was mediated by a given structure's compatibility with the learning goal. Learning was enhanced for participants with low PK of the content domain who were specifically instructed to learn about that content and were provided with an advance organizer that represented the conceptual structure of the content presented in the hypertext. This result speaks to the potential of a well-defined, goal-appropriate structure for initial learning by novices.

## NAVIGATION PATTERNS

Several researchers have attempted to identify patterns of reader navigation as they read hypertext. In an early study of navigation patterns, researchers observed subjects reading hypertext and identified six distinct strategies: skimming, checking, reading, responding, studying, and reviewing (Horney and Anderson-Inman, 1994). In another effort, Castelli et al. (1998) examined the relationships among a battery of psychological factors and a series of navigation indices. Based on their examinations, the authors identified seven categories of hypertext users and related the kinds of cognitive characteristics associated with the various patterns. Such studies, however, simply addressed what readers did, not the relationship between reading patterns and learning.

Other investigations have examined how individual navigation patterns relate to learning. Lawless and her colleagues (Lawless et al., 2002) followed up on their previous research, which identified three distinct navigation patterns in hypertext users—knowledge seekers, feature explorers, and apathetic users—by examining whether these navigation patterns were age dependent (Lawless and Brown, 1997; Lawless and Kulikowich, 1996). They used hypertext with 60 fourth, fifth, and sixth graders and found similar navigation patterns to those identified in their previous studies with adults, but that the largest group of younger readers in the study were knowledge seekers, while the largest group of adult subjects were feature explorers (Lawless and Kulikowich, 1998). They hypothesized that the primary reason for this discrepancy was related to differing level of domain knowledge—the adult readers had lower prior knowledge and probably less interest in the content presented than did the younger readers.

## Navigational Scaffolding

Recent research has examined how incorporating support mechanisms that help users grasp the overall scope and structure of the content affects hypertext-assisted learning. Various factors have been examined, including the use of hierarchically structured overview navigation menus (Brinkerhoff et al., 2001); preview pop-up windows that gave a synopsis of linked information (Cress and Knabel, 2003); expanding hypertext, which allowed the reader to have more detailed information without losing the linear flow of information (Lee and Tedder, 2004); embedded annotations that provided additional information about the topic on the screen (Lee and Calandra, 2004); navigational prompts to direct reader through the content (Puntambekar and Stylianou, 2005); navigable concept maps (Puntambekar et al., 2003); and graphical overviews (de Jong and van der Hulst, 2002). Results from these studies typically provided support for the idea that scaffolding a user's understanding of scope and structure helped organize the content and orient the reader. As we will see later in this chapter, however, organization of the content interacts with other learning variables such as the reader's navigation strategies, goals, and prior knowledge; the complexity of the content; and the coherence of the information being linked.

## Active vs. Passive Navigation

Additional research has examined how the sequence in which the information is read affects learning of the content (Eveland et al., 2004; Niederhauser et al., 2000; Salmeron et al., 2005)—that is, the effects of reading in a sequential hierarchical fashion vs. more idiosyncratic jumping around in the hypertext. Su and Klein (2006) used a hypertext on the Internet and World Wide Web to examine learning of 354 undergraduate college students. Students were presented with one of three navigational forms of the hypertext program: (1) hierarchically structured content list, (2) concept map, and (3) embedded hyperlink. They determined that subjects who used the content list hypertext performed better on a test of factual knowledge than did subjects who used the embedded hyperlink hypertext.

Eveland and colleagues (2004) also demonstrated that users who read a more structured hypertext learned factual information but also showed that readers who read a nonlinear hypertext gained a better conceptual understanding of the textbase. They presented 172 college student and non-student adult subjects with a complex hypertext containing health information. One form of the hypertext allowed only hierarchical navigation; the other provided numerous relational hyperlinks among the information nodes. Results indicated that subjects in the hierarchical condition performed better on a factual knowledge measure than those in the relational condition, while subjects in the relational condition outperformed hierarchical condition subjects in terms of *knowledge structure density* (as measured with concept mapping).

Niederhauser and colleagues (2000) provided their subjects with a hypertext that allowed both hierarchical and relational navigation. Subjects were provided with navigational tools that supported both navigation options (a hierarchical map navigation tool and hotword links to conceptually related content). Subjects were allowed to read the hypertext, which described behaviorist and constructivist learning theories, using navigation options of their choice. Reading the 83-screen hypertext was part of a regular class assignment for 39 university students over a 2-week period, and students were tested on their learning of the content as a class assignment. Subjects' navigation pattern preferences were determined by examining server log files of the sequence of screen access.

Examination of navigation patterns showed that some students navigated in a passive manner. These students adopted a linear approach by systematically moving through each frame for the content on one theory, then moving through the content on the second theory in the same manner. Other students adopted a more active strategy as they read a screen on one theory, then used a link to compare that information with the other theory, proceeding through the text using this compare and contrast strategy. Results indicated that students who read the text in a more sequential fashion had higher scores on a combined measure (multiple-choice test of factual content and essay that required students to compare and contrast the major themes in the hypertext). Increased cognitive load was hypothesized as being the reason why students who used the linking features did not perform as well on the post-tests.

Zumbach et al. (2001) also examined the influence of active and passive navigation strategies in a yoke-controlled experimental design in which one group of 11 subjects was allowed to navigate freely through a 300-page relational hypertext about marine pollution accidents, and a yoked group of 11 students moved sequentially through the same screens as their counterparts. Results showed no significant difference on knowledge measures between the active and passive hypertext users and what appeared to be slightly better performance on the measure of conceptual understanding by the passive users. The authors concluded that "'active access' to [hyper]-text-based information does not always lead to better cognitive and metacognitive outcomes than a pre-sequenced presentation ('passive access')" (Zumbach et al., 2001, p. 316).

Finally, using a 24-node hierarchical hypertext on atmosphere pollution with 41 undergraduate students, Salmeron and colleagues (2005) demonstrated that, given a similar number of nodes read, subjects who read the contents in a high coherent order formed a better situation model of the text; that is, subjects tended to develop a better conceptual understanding of the content when they followed links that accessed information that had shared arguments and maintained the coherence of the text representation.

## The Role of Coherence

Navigation patterns that promote coherence appear to be an important aspect of learning with hypertext. McNamara and Shapiro (2005) addressed the importance of coherence when learning with hypertext by offering a series of guidelines for hypertext developers. Using the following guidelines may help learners recognize the relationships among ideas scattered across a hypertext: (1) provide ill-defined global structure for advanced learners, (2) provide well-defined, goal-appropriate global structure for domain novices, (3) create an environment that encourages a metacognitive approach to the content, and (4) highlight links that denote very important inter-document relationships.

In the study by Salmeron and colleagues (2005) described earlier, researchers also addressed the relationship between coherence of reading order and level of prior knowledge. They used their atmosphere pollution hypertext with 82 university students, this time including two different overviews of the content as navigation aids. The first overview contained a 6 × 4 matrix of nodes with high conceptual coherence reading right to left and top to bottom. The second had a similar array, except the nodes were arranged with low conceptual coherence. Subjects were required to read all screens but were not allowed to reread any screen. Findings revealed that participants with low domain knowledge tended to develop better situation models when reading the content in a high coherence order, while participants with high domain knowledge learned more from a low coherence order. Reading order did not, however, affect textbase construction.

In sum, the need to navigate through a hypertext is a defining feature that differentiates reading and learning in a hypertext environment from reading and learning with traditional printed text. Initial navigation strategies may be adopted due to interest, motivation, and intrinsic or extrinsic goals of the reader. Several authors (Niederhauser et. al., 2000; Shapiro, 1999; Tergan, 1997; Yang, 1997; Zumbach et al., 2001) have discussed issues of cognitive load when examining navigation patterns in hypertext-assisted learning. (For more about instructional issues associated with cognitive load, see Paas and van Merriënboer, 1994; Sweller, 1988; Sweller et al., 1998.) When users' navigation patterns do not support coherence, cognitive load associated with navigating through the text may interfere with a reader's ability to make sense of the content. The reader may then adopt compensatory strategies to simplify the learning task; thus, coherence may influence what the reader learns from the text and may be influenced by the navigational opportunities afforded by the hypertext.

## LEARNER CHARACTERISTICS

Individual characteristics, such as prior knowledge (Hofman and van Oostendorp, 1999; Potelle and Rouet, 2002; Shapiro, 1998a,b, 1999; Shin et al., 1994), metacognition (Azevedo, 2005; Graesser et al., 2005), and cognitive style (Dunser and Jirasko, 2005; Graff, 2003; 2005; Lin and Davidson-Shivers, 1996), play an important role in learning with hypertext.

## Prior Knowledge

Research on organizing tools and system structure indicates that low PK learners benefit from well-defined structures (such as hierarchies) when the learning goal is to achieve simple, factual knowledge (textbase). Nonhierarchical hypertext structures (e.g., alphabetically structured list or an unprincipled network of links) appear to confuse low PK learners and inhibit learning, even for factual information presented on individual screens (Potelle and Rouet, 2002). Caution is warranted in overgeneralizing these findings, especially as they relate to the use of use of complex conceptual maps. Evidence suggests that providing complex concept maps for low PK learners may overwhelm readers and hinder understanding if use of the map draws attention away from the content of the text and focuses learners on the macro structure (Hofman and van Oostendorp, 1999).

Simply providing hierarchical structure is probably not sufficient to ensure learning for low PK learners. The use of explicit pointers to conceptual relationships (an arrangement of thematic clusters) was related to an increase in problem-solving ability. Any device or structure that explicates the conceptual relationships between topics and increases text coherence can benefit learning for low-knowledge learners (McNamara and Shapiro, 2005; Shapiro, 1999).

Well-structured hypertexts may offer low PK learners an introduction to the ways in which topics relate to one another and an easy-to-follow introduction to a domain, especially when the structure is compatible with the learning goal. Well-defined structures may also help low-knowledge learners to stay oriented while exploring the information; however, as Spiro and colleagues (1987) noted, it is dangerous to oversimplify a topic for learners. Providing rigid structures, especially for ill-structured domains (such as history or psychology), can impose arbitrary delineations that may impede progress as a learner advances in knowledge. For this reason, ill-structured hypertexts may also offer advantages.

Demonstrating consistent benefits for ill-structured hypertext, however, has been challenging for several reasons. Reasonably sensitive, valid, and reliable measures for the types of gains that are likely promoted through the use of ill-structured hypertext (deep and connected conceptual learning) have only recently been developed and employed. Further, although many hypothesize that high PK users may be able to take advantage of ill-structured hypertexts and develop a high-level, interconnected conceptual understanding of the textbase, interactions among variables make it difficult to sort out the unique effects of system structure from numerous intervening, and potentially confounding, variables.

Providing less obvious organizational structures challenges learners to seek their own coherence within the system. The overall effect is to promote active cognitive engagement and improve learning; however, ill-structured systems may not always be effective for advanced learners. As pointed out in earlier sections, reader goals and motivation can affect whether learners actively attempt to integrate the textbase into their prior knowledge. A passive learner with unclear goals will likely learn little from any hypertext system, whereas the active cognitive engagement inherent in criss-crossing the conceptual landscape and creating a situation model may promote deep conceptual understanding of the content.

In keeping with prior research on traditional text-based learning, promoting active engagement with the content appears to be essential for developing a situation model. Providing a structure that is highly organized or simple to follow may cause readers to become passive. The task for hypertext designers is to create hypertext that sufficiently challenges beginning learners while not overburdening them to the point where learning is compromised.

## Cognitive Style

Early hypertext research literature on cognitive style failed to demonstrate much in the way of predictive or explanatory power (Dillon and Gabbard, 1998). These studies typically examined hypertext-based learning relative to concepts such as field dependence and independence (Lin and Davidson-Shivers, 1996). Recent work, however, has utilized style dimensions that show greater potential for predicting behavior and performance (Dunser and Jirasko, 2005; Graff, 2003, 2005).

Graff (2003) examined learning from three 64-node hypertexts—linear, hierarchical, and relational—relative to two measures of the users' learning styles. Ninety-six undergraduate university students were grouped according to scores on a wholist–analytic questionnaire (wholist/intermediate/analytic), which identified an individual's tendency to process information as an integrated whole or as discrete parts. Results indicated that the intermediate group in the relational condition tended to outperform all other group/condition configurations on measures of detail and number of words on a post-test essay. Using the same dataset, Graff then grouped students based on scores from a verbal–imager questionnaire (verbal/bimodal/imager), which identified an individual's tendency to process information either in words (working with verbal information) or in images (visual and spatial information). Subjects in the bimodal group in the hierarchical condition outperformed all other group/condition configurations on measures of detail and number of words on a post-test essay (although the verbal–relational group approached significance on both measures, as well).

Graff cautiously proposed support for the relationship between his two measures of cognitive style, the hypertext architectures he employed, and learning—indicating that subjects in the intermediate group possess both wholist and analytic characteristics and may have been more flexible in their processing of the relational hypertext. Further, he drew on Paivio's (1971) dual-coding model to suggest that bimodals were able to process information in verbal and imaginal subsystems simultaneously to incorporate the text-based media while maintaining their orientation in the hierarchically organized structure.

In a second study using the same materials and 55 undergraduate subjects (Graff, 2005), cognitive style was assessed using an intuitive–analytic cognitive style measure that was similar to the wholist–analytic measure described above. Dependent measures included scores on recall and concept map complexity and concept map density. For recall, a clear relationship between cognitive style and hypertext structure was found. Analysts scored highest in the hierarchical condition, intermediates in the relational condition, and intuitives in the linear condition. No significant effects were found for cognitive style on the concept map measures. It may be that there were no differences between groups on the conceptual models they developed, or perhaps concept maps do not assess conceptual learning in ways that effectively differentiate learners. Identifying and developing valid and reliable measures of conceptual knowledge are important and ongoing challenges for hypertext researchers.

## ACTIVE COGNITIVE ENGAGEMENT

Reading hypertext differs from reading traditional printed text in the degree to which the reader must make choices about how to proceed through the text, ostensibly increasing reader interest and engaging the reader in deeper processing of the information (Patterson, 2000). A fundamental shift in the reading process relates to the hypertext reader having to create his or her own path through the text. Actively engaged readers tend to feel a greater sense of control over what they read and how they read it. Results of their choices are instantaneous, and readers become part of the meaning construction as they create an individualized text that is not as tied to the author's intended message, as is the case with traditional printed text. Printed text tends to formalize the role of the author, while hypertext challenges our assumptions about the roles of the author and the reader; thus, the educational use of hypertext appears to have great potential because it forces the reader to actively participate in creating meaning from the text.

A critical variable influencing whether studying will lead to knowledge acquisition is the degree to which students become actively involved in trying to make sense of the material (Anderson-Inman and Tenny, 1989). This sense-making activity, which is inherent in constructing a situation model, relates to Piaget's (1985) notion of equilibration—an essential element in the learning process. In their study of traditional text-based learning, Mannes and Kintsch (1987, p. 93) noted that refraining from "providing readers with a suitable schema and thereby forcing them to create their own … might make learning from texts more efficient." This is a central principle in cognitive flexibility theory and provides a foundation for the use of complex, ill-structured hypertexts to promote deep and connected conceptual learning.

## Active Knowledge Construction

As mentioned earlier, Shapiro (1998a) compared hierarchical and unstructured systems in a study of American history learning. Participants in that study performed better on several measures when presented with the unstructured system. Subjects in the unstructured condition significantly outperformed those in the hierarchical condition on measures that included how well they integrated information from the hypertext into an essay that demonstrated their learning. It appeared that subjects in the hierarchical group were able to navigate more passively because the highly structured nature of the system kept them oriented in the information space. As a consequence, because a well-organized and structured model was presented, readers did not have to actively create conceptual connections within the content or integrate and reflect on the content to make decisions about which links to access. Those in the unstructured system condition, however, had to more carefully regulate their learning and be more principled in their movements through the information. Taken together, the essay and navigation results suggested that the less structured system forced readers to engage in more active processing and to systematically monitor and regulate their learning to develop a coherent situation model.

## Self-Regulated Learning

It should be clear by now that hypertext is a cognitively demanding mode of learning. As such, a users' ability to supervise his or her learning processes would seem to be essential in this context. Self-regulated learning (SRL) occurs when learners establish their own goals, then monitor, regulate, and control their thoughts and behaviors as they seek to achieve those goals (Graesser et al., 2005; Pintrich, 2000; Winne, 2001; Zimmerman, 2001). Relative to learning with hypertext, SRL models assume that learners (1) are active, constructive participants in the learning process; (2) are capable of monitoring, controlling, and regulating aspects of their own cognition, motivation, behavior, and context; (3) have a goal or criterion against which judgments are made about whether the learning process should continue or if some modification in strategy or metacognitive monitoring is needed; and (4) self-regulation of cognition, motivation, and behavior mediates personal characteristics, contextual characteristics, and learning (Azevedo, 2005; Pintrich, 2000; Zimmerman, 2001). A series of studies have examined the affects of SRL on learning with hypertext.

There is evidence that students who demonstrate more SRL behavior while learning with hypertext tend to develop more sophisticated mental models (Azevedo et al., 2004). Twenty-four undergraduate students spent 45 minutes studying the human circulatory system using a relational hypermedia encyclopedia. Gains from pre- to post-test were used to separate students into two groups (median split) based on the extent of conceptual change evidenced by their ability to identify parts of the heart and diagram the path of blood through the body, as well as by a free-recall measure. Results indicated that the group that made greater conceptual gains engaged in more self-regulated learning behavior—particularly in the areas of monitoring and their use of effective strategies. In terms of strategies, the group that made greater gains tended to use proportionally more effective strategies (e.g., summarizing, rereading, knowledge elaboration) than ineffective strategies (e.g., goal-free searching, copying information). Students who made little, or no, gains tended not to use SRL or used it ineffectively. These findings suggest that effective use of SRL is an important consideration when using hypertext to promote the development of high-level conceptual understandings. Additional research has examined ways to promote readers' use of SRL when learning with hypertext.

Azevedo and colleagues (2002) examined the affects of prompting SRL use. They used the same human circulatory hypermedia system that was described previously with 40 undergraduate students who were (1) trained in the use of SRL techniques themselves, (2) paired with a human tutor who was trained in SRL techniques (Winne, 1995, 2001) and who sat with the subject during the study session and prompted the use of SRL, (3) asked to self-generate and complete a personal goal, or (4) given a series of factual questions to answer. In the coregulation condition, the tutor encouraged metacognitive strategies by providing a variety of prompts; specifically, the tutor encouraged self-questioning, content evaluation, judgments of learning, planning, goal setting, prior knowledge activation, and other activities. In the SRL strategy instruction condition, subjects were trained to do the same thing as the tutor, but as independent learners. The other two conditions provided no metacognitive prompts, tutors, or training. Analyses revealed that the sophistication of learners' mental models shifted to a

significantly greater degree when provided with tutors or metacognitive training than when they were simply given learning goals and no training. Both the tutor group and the strategy instruction group demonstrated the greatest use of effective learning strategies and the least incidence of ineffective strategies; however, although *post hoc* tests were not reported, it did not appear that the tutor group significantly outperformed the strategy instruction group.

Given that having a one-on-one tutor to prompt SRL is not practical, an additional study singled out the effectiveness of SRL training and examined it more directly. In a study of 131 undergraduate students, Azevedo and Cromley (2004) had subjects in the treatment condition participate in a 30-minute training session on how to regulate learning of the circulatory system when using a hypermedia environment. Subjects in the control condition received no SRL training. All subjects were given a global learning goal: "Make sure you learn about the different parts and their purpose, how they work both individually and together, and how they support the human body" (p. 526). Results from this study supported findings from the previous study: (1) Students in the SRL training condition gained a deeper understanding of the content, (2) providing students with an overall learning goal and not SRL training did not promote increased conceptual understanding, and (3) students in the SRL training condition used SRL strategies more frequently and used them more effectively.

Explicit training in SRL techniques, however, is not the only way to encourage readers to monitor their learning in hypertext-based environments. Automated processes and tools that can be integrated into hypertext-based learning environments include learner-controlled question–answer facilities and artificial-intelligence-based animated conversational agents (Graesser et al., 2005; Kauffman, 2004). Kauffman (2004) developed a hypertext system that integrated questions designed to encourage metacognition. Subjects were presented with a hypertext on educational measurement. Half of the subjects were assigned to work with a system that presented automated self-monitoring prompts in the form of questions. The prompts appeared each time a reader moved from one node to another. If students were unable to correctly answer the question, they were encouraged to go back and review the page they had just read. The second group of subjects were able to click freely on link buttons and move to a new page without answering any questions about their understanding.

Both groups performed comparably on the declarative knowledge test; however, students in the metacognitive prompt condition outperformed their counterparts on a post-test that assessed their ability to apply what they learned to real-world problems (a measure of situation model learning). Interestingly, the groups did not differ in their awareness of meta-cognition. Thus, providing automated self-regulation prompts was an effective means of encouraging deep learning, even if subjects were unaware of how the prompts altered their thinking about their own learning. It should also be noted that, because of the small size of this hypertext, there were few link buttons and subjects received only three or four prompts during the learning period. That clear improvement in learning was observed after such a modest intervention speaks to the promise of using such prompts.

The active participation that takes place when reading hypertext clearly places additional cognitive demands on the reader. As in traditional reading of printed text, the learner must engage basic lower level processes (such as letter recognition and decoding words) and higher level processes (such as relating new information with prior knowledge). Further, reading hypertext requires additional metacognitive functioning such as choosing what to read and deciding on the sequence for reading information. As Niederhauser and colleagues (2000) pointed out, less proficient computer users must use cognitive resources simply to operate the computer (e.g., working the mouse, pressing keys, activating on screen buttons). Given these considerations and the cognitive load issues previously raised in this chapter, it is not surprising that explicit strategies for managing cognitive resources and regulating the learning process seem to be effective. Although Azevedo's work has been almost exclusively with low-prior-knowledge learners in hypermedia learning environments, there appears to be clear promise for the use of SRL techniques for enhancing learning with hypertext.

## CONCLUSION

Hypertext research continues to be a challenging but fruitful area. The numerous interacting and at times confounding variables contribute to the difficulty of building our knowledge base for learning with hypertext, and measures of learning for conceptual knowledge continue to pose challenges in this and many other areas. Yet, a core of rigorous and insightful research has emerged during the past 25 years since technological advances made computer-based hypertext possible. Current theoretically advanced work in coherence and self-regulated learning holds great promise for the future.

## REFERENCES

Anderson-Inman, L. and Tenny, J. (1989). Electronic studying: information organizers to help students to study 'better' not 'harder,' part II. *Comput. Teacher*, 17, 21–53.

Azevedo, R. (2005). Using hypermedia as a metacognitive tool for enhancing student learning? The role of self-regulated learning. *Educ. Psychol.*, 40(4), 199–209.*

Azevedo, R. and Cromley, J. (2004). Does training on self-regulated learning facilitate students' learning with hypermedia? *J. Educ. Psychol.*, 96(3), 523–535.

Azevedo, R., Guthrie, J., Wang, H., and Mulhern, J. (2001). Do Different Instructional Interventions Facilitate Students' Ability to Shift to More Sophisticated Mental Models of Complex Systems? Paper presented at the American Educational Research Association Annual Meeting, April 10–14, Seattle, WA.

Azevedo, R., Seibert, D., Guthrie, J., Cromley, J., Wang, H., and Tron, M. (2002). How Do Students Regulate Their Learning of Complex Systems with Hypermedia? Paper presented at the American Educational Research Association Annual Meeting, April 1–5, New Orleans, LA.

Azevedo, R., Guthrie, J. T., and Seibert, D. (2004). The role of self-regulated learning in fostering students' conceptual understanding of complex systems with hypermedia. *J. Educ. Comput. Res.*, 30(1–2), 87–111.

Brinkerhoff, J. D., Klein, J. D., and Koroghlanian, C. M. (2001). Effects of overviews and computer experience on learning from hypertext. *J. Educ. Comput. Res.*, 25(4), 427–440.

Castelli, C., Colazzo, L., and Molinari A. (1998). Cognitive variables and patterns of hypertext performances: lessons learned for educational hypermedia construction. *J. Educ. Multimedia Hypermedia*, 7(2–3), 177–206.

Cress, U. and Knabel, O. B. (2003). Previews in hypertexts: effects on navigation and knowledge acquisition. *J. Comput. Assist. Learn.*, 19(4), 517–527.

Curry, J., Haderlie, S., Lawless, K. A., Lemon, M., Ku T. W., and Wood, R. (1999). Specified learning goals and their effect on learners' representations of a hypertext reading environment. *Int. J. Instruct. Media*, 26(1), 43–51.

de Jong, T. and van der Hulst, A. (2002). The effects of graphical overviews on knowledge acquisition in hypertext. *J. Comput. Assist. Learn.*, 18(2), 219–231.

Dillon, A. and Gabbard, R. (1998). Hypermedia as an educational technology: a review of the quantitative research literature on learner comprehension, control, and style. *Rev. Educ. Res.*, 68(3), 322–349.*

Dunser, A. and Jirasko, M. (2005). Interaction of hypertext forms and global versus sequential learning styles. *J. Educ. Comput. Res.*, 32(1), 79–91.

Eveland, W. P., Cortese, J., Park, H., and Dunwoody, S. (2004). How Web site organization influences free recall, factual knowledge, and knowledge structure density. *Hum. Commun. Res.*, 30(2), 208–233.

Gall, J. (2006). Orienting tasks and their impact on learning and attitudes in the use of hypertext. *J. Educ. Multimedia Hypermedia*, 15(1), 5–29.*

Gerjets, P. and Scheiter, K. (2003). Goal configurations and processing strategies as moderators between design and cognitive load: evidence from hypertext-based instruction. *Educ. Psychol.*, 38(1), 33–41.*

Graesser, A. C., McNamara, D. S., and Van Lehn, K. (2005). Scaffolding deep comprehension strategies through Point&Query, AutoTutor, and iSTART. *Educ. Psychol.*, 40(4), 225–234.

Graff, M. (2003). Assessing learning from hypertext: an individual differences perspective. *J. Interact. Learn. Res.*, 14(4), 425–438.

Graff, M. (2005). Differences in concept mapping, hypertext architecture, and the analyst–intuition dimension of cognitive style. *Educ. Psychol.*, 25(4), 409–422.*

Hofman, R. and van Oostendorp, H. (1999). Cognitive effects of a structural overview in a hypertext. *Br. J. Educ. Technol.*, 30(2), 129–140.

Horney, M. A. and Anderson-Inman, L. (1994). The electro text project: hypertext reading patterns of middle school students. *J. Educ. Multimedia Hypermedia*, 3(1), 71–91.

Jacobson, M. J. and Spiro, R. J. (1995). Hypertext learning environments, cognitive flexibility, and the transfer of complex knowledge: an empirical investigation. *J. Educ. Comput. Res.*, 12(4), 301–333.

Jonassen, D. H. and Wang, S. (1993). Acquiring structural knowledge from semantically structured hypertext. *J. Comput.-Based Instruct.*, 20(1), 1–8.*

Kauffman, D. F. (2004). Self-regulated learning in Web-based environments: instructional tools designed to facilitate cognitive strategy use, metacognitive processing, and motivational beliefs. *J. Educ. Comput. Res.*, 30(1), 139–161.

Kintsch, W. (1988). The use of knowledge in discourse processing: a construction integration model. *Psychol. Rev.*, 95, 163–182.*

Landow, G. (1992). *Hypertext: The Convergence of Contemporary Critical Theory and Technology.* Baltimore, MD: The Johns Hopkins University Press.*

Lawless, K. and Brown, S. (1997). Multimedia learning environments: issues of learner control and navigation. *Instruct. Sci.*, 25(2), 117–131.

Lawless, K. and Kulikowich, J. (1996). Understanding hypertext navigation through cluster analysis. *J. Educ. Comput. Res.*, 14(4), 385–399.

Lawless, K. A. and Kulikowich, J. M. (1998). Domain knowledge, interest, and hypertext navigation: a study of individual differences. *J. Educ. Multimedia Hypermedia*, 7(1), 51–70.*

Lawless, K. A., Mills, R., and Brown, S. W. (2002). Children's hypertext navigation strategies. *J. Res. Technol. Educ.*, 34(3), 274–284.

Lee, J. K. and Calandra, B. (2004). Can embedded annotations help high school students perform problem solving tasks using a Web-based historical document? *J. Res. Technol. Educ.*, 37(1), 65–84.

Lee, M. J. and Tedder, M. C. (2004). Introducing expanding hypertext based on working memory capacity and the feeling of disorientation: tailored communication through effective hypertext design. *J. Educ. Comput. Res.*, 30(3), 171–195.

Lin, C. and Davidson-Shivers, G. (1996). Effects of linking structure and cognitive style on students' performance and attitude in a computer-based hypertext environment. *J. Educ. Comput. Res.*, 15(4), 317–329.

Mannes, B. and Kintsch, W. (1987). Knowledge organization and text organization. *Cognit. Instruct.*, 4, 91–115.*

McNamara, D. S. and Shapiro, A. M. (2005). Multimedia and hypermedia solutions for promoting metacognitive engagement, coherence, and learning. *J. Educ. Comput. Res.*, 33(1), 1–29.*

Moos, D. C. and Azevedo, R. (2006). The role of goal structure in undergraduates' use of self-regulatory processes in two hypermedia learning tasks. *J. Educ. Multimedia Hypermedia*, 15(1), 49–86.

Niederhauser, D. S., Reynolds, R. E., Salmen, D. J., and Skolmoski, P. (2000). The influence of cognitive load on learning from hypertext. *J. Educ. Comput. Res.*, 23(3), 237–255.*

Paas, F. and van Merriënboer, J. G. (1994). Instructional control of cognitive load in the training of complex cognitive tasks. *Educ. Psychol. Rev.*, 6, 351–371.

Paivio, A. (1971). *Imagery and Verbal Processes.* London: Holt, Rinehart and Winston.

Patterson, N. (2000). Hypertext and the changing roles of readers. *English J.*, 90(2), 74–80.

Piaget, J. (1985). *The Equilibration of Cognitive Structures: The Central Problem of Intellectual Development* (Brown, T. and Thampy, K. J., trans.). Chicago, IL: University of Chicago Press.

Pintrich, P. R. (2000). The role of goal orientation in self-regulating learning. In *Handbook of Self-Regulation*, edited by M. Boekaerts, P. Pintrich, and M. Zeidner, pp. 451–502. San Diego, CA: Academic Press.

Potelle, H. and Rouet, J. F. (2003). Effects of content representation and readers' prior knowledge on the comprehension of hypertext. *Int. J. Hum.–Comput. Stud.*, 58(3), 327–345.

Puntambekar, S. and Stylianou, A. (2005). Designing navigation support in hypertext systems based on navigation patterns. *Instruct. Sci.*, 33(5/6), 451–481.

Puntambekar, S., Stylianou, A., and Hubscher, R. (2003). Improving Navigation and Learning in Hypertext Environments with Navigable Concept Maps. *Hum.–Comput. Interact.*, 18(4), 395–428.

Salmeron, L., Canas, J. J., Kintsch, W., and Fajardo, I. (2005). Reading strategies and hypertext comprehension. *Discourse Processes*, 40(3), 171–191.

Shapiro, A. M. (1998a). Promoting active learning: the role of system structure in learning from hypertext. *Hum.–Comput. Interact.*, 13(1), 1–35.

Shapiro, A. M. (1998b). The relationship between prior knowledge and interactive organizers during hypermedia-aided learning. *J. Educ. Comput. Res.*, 20(2), 143–163.

Shapiro, A. M. (1999). The relevance of hierarchies to learning biology from hypertext. *J. Learn. Sci.*, 8(2), 215–243.*

Shapiro, A. M. and Niederhauser, D. (2004). Learning from hypertext: research issues and findings. In *Handbook of Research on Educational Communications and Technology*, 2nd ed., edited by D. H. Jonassen, pp. 605–620. Mahwah, NJ: Lawrence Erlbaum Associates.*

Shin, E. J., Schallert, D., and Savenye, W. (1994). Effects of learner control, advisement, and prior knowledge on young students' learning in a hypertext environment. *Educ. Technol., Res. Dev.*, 42(1), 33–46.

Spiro, R. J. and Jehng, J. C. (1990). Cognitive flexibility and hypertext: theory and technology for the nonlinear and multidimensional traversal of complex subject matter. In *Cognition, Education, and Multimedia: Exploring Ideas in High Technology*, edited by D. Nix and R. J. Spiro, pp. 163–205. Hillsdale, NJ: Lawrence Erlbaum Associates.

Spiro, R. J., Vispoel, W., Schmitz, J., Samarapungavan, A., and Boerger, A. (1987). Knowledge acquisition for application: cognitive flexibility and transfer in complex content domains. In *Executive Control Processes in Reading*, edited by B. Britton and S. Glynn, pp. 177–199. Hillsdale, NJ: Lawrence Erlbaum Associates.

Spiro, R. J., Coulson, R., Feltovich, P., and Anderson, D. (1988). Cognitive flexibility theory: advanced knowledge acquisition in ill-structured domains. In *Proceedings of the Tenth Annual Conference of the Cognitive Science Society*, pp. 375–383. Hillsdale, NJ: Lawrence Erlbaum Associates.

Spiro, R. J., Feltovitch, P., Jacobson, M., and Coulson, R. (1992). Cognitive flexibility, constructivism, and hypertext: random access instruction for advanced knowledge acquisition in ill-structured domains. In *Constructivism and the Technology of Instruction: A Conversation*, edited by T. Duffy and D. Jonassen, pp. 57–75. Hillsdale, NJ: Lawrence Erlbaum Associates.*

Su, Y. and Klein, J. D. (2006). Effects of navigation tools and computer confidence on performance and attitudes in a hypermedia learning environment. *J. Educ. Multimedia Hypermedia*, 15(1), 87–106.

Sweller, J. (1988). Cognitive load during problem solving: effects on learning. *Cognit. Sci.*, 12, 257–285.

Sweller, J., van Merriënboer, J. G., and Paas, F. G. (1998). Cognitive architecture and instructional design. *Educ. Psychol. Rev.*, 10(3), 251–296.

Tergan, S. O. (1997). Multiple views, contexts, and symbol systems in learning with hypertext/hypermedia: a critical review of research. *Educ. Technol.*, 37(4), 5–16.*

Winne, P. H. (1995). Inherent details in self-regulated learning. *J. Educ. Psychol.*, 87, 397–410.

Winne, P. (2001). Self-regulated learning viewed from models of information processing. In *Self-Regulated Learning and Academic Achievement: Theoretical Perspectives*, 2nd ed., edited by B. J. Zimmerman and D. Schunk, pp. 153–189. Mawah, NJ: Lawrence Erlbaum Associates.*

Yang, S. (1997). Information seeking as problem-solving using a qualitative approach to uncover the novice learners' information-seeking processes in a Perseus hypertext system. *Library Inform. Sci. Res.*, 19(1), 71–92.

Zimmerman, B. J. (2001). Theories of self-regulated learning and academic achievement: an overview and analysis. In *Self-Regulated Learning and Academic Achievement: Theoretical Perspectives*, edited by B. Zimmerman and D. Schunk, pp. 1–37. Mawah, NJ: Lawrence Erlbaum Associates.

Zumbach, J. and Reimann, P. (2002). Enhancing learning from hypertext by inducing a goal orientation: comparing different approaches. *Instruct. Sci.*, 30(4), 243–267.

Zumbach, J., Reimann, P., and Koch, S. (2001). Influence of passive versus active information access to hypertextual information resources on cognitive and emotional parameters. *J. Educ. Comput. Res.*, 25(3), 301–316.

---

* Indicates a core reference.

# 17

# Computer-Mediated Technologies

*Arthur C. Graesser, Patrick Chipman, and Brandon G. King*
University of Memphis, Memphis, Tennessee

## CONTENTS

## ABSTRACT

This chapter reviews research on the application of computer-mediated technologies to learning. This includes traditional computer-based training, multimedia, hypertext and hypermedia, interactive simulation, intelligent tutoring systems, inquiry-based information retrieval, animated pedagogical agents, virtual environments with agents, serious games, and collaborative learning environments. Most of these systems encourage active learning, knowledge construction, inquiry, and exploration on the part of the student, as opposed to being exposed to information delivery systems.

Unfortunately, the learning strategies of most students are extremely limited, so the systems must provide modeling of effective strategies, intelligent scaffolding, and accurate feedback. Available research has confirmed that students learn from most of these advanced learning environments compared to classroom lectures, reading textbooks, and noninteractive control conditions; however, empirical research on learning is conspicuously absent on some of these environments, such as virtual environments with agents and serious games. We advocate a research roadmap for the future that systematically investigates a broad landscape of learning technologies (T), pedagogical mechanisms (M), learning goals (G), and learner characteristics (L). A well-understood TMGL landscape will provide a principled foundation for assigning the right learning environment to the right learner at the right time. The costs of developing advanced learning environments are often high, so we encourage designers to follow standards for reusing learning objects, lessons, and systems developed by the research community. One major technical challenge will be to develop authoring tools to make it easy for designers, instructors, and students to develop new content that incorporates these advanced learning technologies.

## KEYWORDS

*Animated pedagogical agents:* Talking heads with speech, facial expressions, and gestures that implement pedagogical strategies.

*Hypertext/hypermedia:* Pages of text and other media with hot spots that users can click on to access other pages.

*Inquiry learning:* Students actively learn by asking questions and interpreting answers or by formulating and testing hypotheses.

*Intelligent tutoring systems:* Intelligent computer systems that model the learner's knowledge and skills at a fine-grained level and that adaptively respond.

*Interactive simulation:* Learners manipulate components and parameters of a complex system and observe what happens when system output is generated.

*Serious games:* Games that help students learn new content, strategies, and skills that are relevant to academic and practical subject matter.

## INTRODUCTION

A revolution in technology-based training has occurred since the advent of computers 50 years ago. In 1960, none of the following kinds of learning environments discussed in this chapter existed: adaptive computer-based training, dynamic multimedia, hypertext, hypermedia, interactive simulation, intelligent tutoring systems, inquiry-based information retrieval, animated pedagogical agents, virtual environments with agents, serious games, and collaborative learning environments. Most of these environments were not available 20 years ago and are still not mainstream technologies in schools today; however, the World Wide Web has exemplars or mature technologies for all these learning environments, so they are potentially available to all Web users.

The current revolution in technology-based training requires more research in the cognitive, learning, and social sciences. Most students do not know how to use advanced learning environments effectively, so modeling, scaffolding, and feedback on their optimal use are necessary. Indeed, students often do not even know how to get started. When researchers assess learning gains from these learning environments (LEs), the results are often disappointing because the developers of the systems have not had sufficient training in cognitive science, learning science, pedagogy, curriculum design, human–computer interaction, social interaction, discourse processing, and other relevant fields that are coordinated in interdisciplinary teams. Far too many LEs are launched without the required empirical testing on usability, engagement, and learning gains. The pace of new technologies hitting the market is so fast that there typically is not enough time to adequately test the systems. The only way to cope with the pace of technological innovations is to develop theoretical models and tools to forecast the quality of LE designs before or during their potential development.

The role of technology in education and training has always had its critics. Cuban (1986, 2001) documented that technology has historically had a negligible impact on improvements in education, pointing to the television and the radio as exemplar disappointments. Clark (1983) argued that it is the pedagogy underlying a LE, not the technology *per se*, that typically explains learning gains. That conclusion, of course, motivates the need to investigate how particular technologies are naturally aligned with particular pedagogical principles, theories, models, hypotheses, or intuitions; for example, a film on how to design a nuclear power plant would not be a technology that is naturally aligned with a pedagogical theory that emphasizes active discovery learning. Reading texts on the Web about negotiation strategies is not well aligned with a social learning theory that embraces modeling–scaffolding–fading. There somehow needs to be a systematic, principled foundation for creating technologies that mesh with theoretical learning mechanisms.

The first giant step is to map out a landscape of learning technologies and learning theories (Bransford et al., 2000; Jochems et al., 2004; Jonassen, 2004; Merrill, 2002; O'Neil and Perez, 2003). Any given technology (T) affords a number of cognitive, pedagogical, and social mechanisms (M) (Gee, 2003; Kozma, 1994; Norman, 1988). Examples of these mechanisms are mastery learning with presentation–test–feedback–branching, building on prerequisites, practice with problems and examples, multimedia learning, modeling–scaffolding–fading, reciprocal teaching, problem-based learning, inquiry learning, and collaborative knowledge construction. Nearly all of these mechanisms emphasize that the learner actively constructs knowledge and builds skills, as opposed to merely being exposed to information delivered by the LE. In addition to these TM mappings, it is essential to consider the goals (G) of the LE; that is, is the LE designed for quick training on shallow knowledge about an easy topic or for deep learning about explanations of a complex system? It is essential to consider the characteristics of the learners (L), such as whether they have high vs. low knowledge of the subject matter, high vs. low verbal ability, high vs. low prior experiences with technology, and so on. The resulting TMGL landscape of cells must be explored. Some cells are promising conditions for learning, others are impossible, and groups of cells give rise to interesting interactions. We advocate a long-term research roadmap that identifies an adequate TMGL landscape for education and training. This would provide a practical foundation for assigning the right LE to the right student at the right time.

The TMGL landscape would also allow researchers to select research projects that strategically cover cells that require attention; for example, not enough research has been done on learning gains from serious games that afford active discovery learning in adults with low reading ability. In contrast, a wealth of research exists with regard to learning gains from intelligent tutoring systems on algebra and physics, spanning the gamut of learner characteristics, pedagogical mechanisms, and learning goals (Anderson et al., 1995; Doignon and Falmagne, 1999; VanLehn et al., 2002). As another example, currently being debated are the conditions under which animated pedagogical agents are effective in improving learning and motivation, so the corresponding cells would need attention. An executive with high knowledge and high stress would probably not have the patience to learn from an embodied animated conversational agent, whereas such an environment might fit the bill for a child who has persistent motivational problems.

The LEs must be evaluated from the standpoint of learning gains, usage, engagement, and return on investment. Regarding learning gains, the outcome variables include tests of retention for shallow vs. deep knowledge, problem solving, and transfer of knowledge or skill to different but related contexts. Meta-analyses have revealed that computerized learning environments fare well compared to classroom instruction and other naturalistic control conditions (Corbett, 2001; Dodds and Fletcher, 2004; Wisher and Fletcher, 2004); these studies have reported effect sizes of .39 for computer-based training, .50 for multimedia, and

1.08 for intelligent tutoring systems. An effect size is defined as the difference in performance between the treatment and control conditions, measured in standard deviation units (called *sigmas*). Precious little data exist with regard to learning gains from most other classes of LEs, however, so research is needed in these arenas. Whereas learning gains are routinely reported in published studies, data are often incomplete with regard to usage (attrition), engagement (including how much the learners like the system), system development time, study time, instructor–student interaction time, and costs. The latter measures are needed for systematic and practical assessments of return on investment (Spector, 2005).

## CLASSES OF LEARNING TECHNOLOGIES

This section examines classes of computer-mediated learning technologies. For each, we will identify salient theoretical frameworks, empirical findings, and opportunities for future research.

### Adaptive Computer-Based Training

A prototypical computer-based training (CBT) system involves mastery learning. The learner (1) studies material presented in a lesson, (2) gets tested with a multiple-choice test or another objective test, (3) gets feedback on the test performance, (4) restudies the material if the performance in step 2 is below threshold, and (5) progresses to a new topic if performance exceeds threshold. The order of topics presented and tested can follow different pedagogical models, such as ordering on prerequisites (Gagné, 1985), a prestructured top-down hierarchical organization (Ausubel et al., 1978), a knowledge space model that attempts to fill learning deficits and correct misconceptions (Doignon and Falmagne, 1999), or other models that allow dynamic sequencing and navigation (O'Neil and Perez, 2003).

The materials presented in a lesson can vary considerably in CBT—organized texts with figures, tables, and diagrams (essentially books on the Web); multimedia; problems to solve; example problems with solutions worked out; and other classes of learning objects. CBT has been extensively studied over the last few decades and has evolved into a mature technology that is ripe for scaling up at an economical cost. As mentioned earlier, meta-analyses show effect sizes of .39 sigma compared to classrooms (Dodds and Fletcher, 2004). The amount of time that learners spend studying the material in CBT has a .35 correlation with learning performance (Taraban et al., 2001) and can be optimized by contingencies that distribute practice. Learning researchers have explored relations between learning activities and characteristics of the learners, such as subject-matter knowledge, cognitive abilities, learning style, age, gender, and so on. Such aptitude–treatment interactions underscore the importance of adapting the learning materials to the learner's cognitive and experiential profile.

The nature of the feedback in CBT merits careful attention (Kulhavy and Stock, 1989; Moreno and Mayer, 2005; Shute, 2006). Testing influences the course of learning in formative evaluation but simply scales a learner's mastery in summative evaluation (Hunt and Pellegrino, 2002; Shute, 2006). A test score alone is adequate feedback for informing the learner on how well they are doing but is not useful for clarifying specific deficits in knowledge or skill. We need a better understanding of the conditions under which the learner benefits from feedback in the form of correct answers, explanations of why correct answers are correct, identification of misconceptions, explanations of the misconceptions, and other forms of elaboration. Researchers also need to identify conditions in which it is best to withhold feedback so learners acquire self-regulated learning strategies.

The nature of the test format is an important determinant of the magnitude of learning gains. Most multiple-choice questions in actual courses, e-learning facilities, and commercial test banks tap shallow levels of comprehension rather than deep levels (Ozuru et al., 2006; Wisher and Graesser, 2007). Shallow questions quiz the learner on explicit information in the lessons, definitions of terms, properties of concepts, steps in procedures, and other forms of perception-based and memory-based processes that require little or no reasoning. Deep-level questions require the learner to understand causal mechanisms, logical justification of claims, explanations of complex systems, mental models, inferences, and applications (Bloom, 1956; Chi et al., 1994; Graesser and Person, 1994). An emphasis in training on shallow knowledge has the unfortunate consequence of learners settling for shallow standards of comprehension (Baker, 1985; Dwyer, 2005; Otero and Graesser, 2001). Experimental investigations need to manipulate the quality of questions affiliated with a course and measure the resulting impact on retention, problem solving, and transfer performance.

Conventional CBT has two potential disadvantages, both of which require confirmation with additional research. First, some populations of learners are not engaged in the learning process provided by CBT, particularly LEs that lack multimedia. Conventional electronic page-turning CBT is fine for motivated learners who desire training on moderate to easy material in the minimum amount of time but not for those who lack motivation and require more entertainment. Second, CBT seems more appropriate for acquiring inert knowledge than active application of knowledge (Bereiter and Scardamalia, 1985; Bransford et al., 2000) and for shallow knowledge rather than deep knowledge. Other types of LEs appear to be more appropriate for enhancing engagement, active application of knowledge and skills, and depth of mastery.

## Multimedia

Material can be delivered in different presentation modes (verbal, pictorial), sensory modalities (auditory, visual), and delivery media (text, video, simulations). The impact of different forms of multimedia has been extensively investigated by Mayer and his colleagues (Mayer, 2005). Meta-analyses reported by Dodds and Fletcher (2004) indicated an effect size of .50 sigma for multimedia learning, whereas it is considerably higher (1.00 sigma) in the meta-analyses reported by Mayer (2005). In many of these studies, retention, problem solving, and transfer of training are facilitated by multimedia because the separate modalities offer multiple representations (Paivio, 1986), conceptually richer and deeper representations (Craik and Lockhart, 1972), multiple retrieval routes, and more cognitive flexibility (Spiro et al., 1991). It is important, however, that the multimedia presentation does not present a large cognitive load and split the learner's attention (Kalyuga et al., 1999; Sweller and Chandler, 1994); for example, a picture on the screen with a voice that explains highlighted aspects of the picture provides multiple codes without overloading working memory. If text on the screen redundantly echoes the spoken explanations, then cognitive overload, interference, and a split attention effect (between print and the picture) may result. Inputs within the same sensory modality interfere with each other more than inputs from separate modalities.

Mayer (2005) has documented and empirically confirmed a number of principles that predict when different forms of multimedia will facilitate learning. Among these multimedia learning principles are the principles of modality, coherence, redundancy, and individual differences. These principles are based on a cognitive model that specifies the processes of selecting, organizing, and integrating information. Mayer's multimedia learning model attempts to predict when and how to highlight a text or diagram with arrows, lines, color, sound, spoken messages, and so on.

One counterintuitive result of research with multimedia is that noninteractive animations of a complex process often have no impact on learning (Lowe, 2004;

Rieber, 1996; Tversky et al., 2002). The animations run a number of risks: not being easy to understand, being transient, moving too quickly, presenting distracting material, placing demands on working memory, and depicting processes in a fashion other than what the learner would otherwise actively construct (Hegarty, 2004). In contrast, a static picture remains on the screen for inspection (off-loading working memory via an external memory), is available for active construction of interpretations at the learner's leisure, and potentially stimulates a mental construction of the dynamic process (Hegarty et al., 2003). Although some researchers have documented learning gains from animations, a persistent question is whether information equivalence between the simulation and control conditions exists.

A formal cognitive model is needed that predicts the impact of particular forms of multimedia on learning at varying levels of depth. What is desired, for example, is a GOMS (Goals, Operators, Methods, and Selection Rules) model (Card et al., 1983; Gray et al., 1993) of multimedia learning that has the theoretical scope, analytical precision, and predictive power that GOMS provided for the field of human–computer interaction in the 1980s and 1990s. A satisfactory model would consider the cognitive representations of the content, the processes needed to perceive and interpret the multimedia presentations, the knowledge of the learner, and the tasks the learner needs to perform. A fine-grained cognitive model appears to be needed to resolve some inconsistent findings in the literature and to make *a priori* predictions.

More research is needed to resolve a number of other questions about multimedia. How can learners be trained to interpret complex multimedia displays? What sort of semiotic theory is needed to explain how pictures/icons are interpreted and integrated with verbal input? How can cognitive theories inform graphic artists? How can multimedia presentations be tailored to the profile of the learners, including those with disabilities? How can different forms of content be represented with different types of multimedia? Given that most research on multimedia is based on experiments in which material is presented for less than an hour, how well does the existing multimedia research scale up to LEs that are used for several weeks? Will the razzle-dazzle of exotic multimedia end up being too exhausting to the learner over the long haul?

## Hypertext and Hypermedia

These systems provide a large space of Web pages with texts, pictures, animations, and other media. Each page has hot spots for the learner to click and explore. The learner has free rein to maneuver through the hypertext/hypermedia space, which of course is an ideal environment for active learning and inquiry. Unfortunately, most learners do not have the skills of self-regulation and metacognition to intelligently search through the space (Azevedo and Cromley, 2004; Conklin, 1987; Winne, 2001), so they get lost, get sidetracked by seductive details, and lose sight of the primary learning goals. These liabilities of this technology have resulted in mixed reports of learning gains from hypertext/hypermedia compared with a predesigned sequence of materials by an expert author (Azevedo and Cromley, 2004; Dillon and Gabbard, 1998; Rouet, 2006). Learners benefit from a navigational guide that trains, models, and scaffolds good inquiry strategies (Azevedo and Cromley, 2004). Another aid is an interface that shows learners an overview of the media space as well as the locations that they have visited; a graphical interface or labeled hierarchy may be suitable for providing this global context (Lee and Baylor, 2006). More research is necessary on training learners how to effectively use hypertext/hypermedia to achieve specific learning goals. We also need research that assesses and increases the likelihood that designers of these environments use principles of cognition, human factors, semiotics, and human–computer interaction. Many designers congest the Web pages with excessive options, clutter, and seductive details (i.e., feature bloat), which overload the cognitive system and distract learners with low ability.

## Interactive Simulation

Interactive simulation allegedly produces more learning than having students simply view simulations. In interactive simulation, the student can actively control input parameters and observe the results on the system. The learner can slow down animations to inspect the process in detail, zoom in on important subcomponents of a system during the course of a simulation, observe the system from multiple viewpoints, and systematically relate inputs to outputs (Kozma, 2000). Some studies have indeed shown advantages of interactive simulation on learning, whereas others have shown no gains of interactive simulation over various control conditions (Deimann and Keller, 2006; Jackson et al., 2006; Stern et al., 2006; van der Meij and de Jong, 2006a,b). The empirical results are therefore mixed and in need of a meta-analysis, assuming that a sufficient number of empirical studies have been conducted.

Unfortunately, simulations tend to have complex content and complex interfaces that are unfamiliar to learners. Students with low domain knowledge or computer expertise have trouble getting started and managing the human–computer interface. Students with more knowledge and expertise often do not understand how to strategically interact with the simulation to advance learning. Consequently, designers of these systems are sometimes disappointed in how little or ineffectively the simulations are used. Training, modeling, and scaffolding of the use of complex simulations must be provided before they can be used effectively. A game environment with points and feedback (as in the case of Flight Simulator; see http://www.microsoft.com/games/flightsimulator/) is presumably motivating and effective in promoting learning gains. Researchers need to investigate the cognitive and motivational mechanisms that encourage intelligent interactions with these simulations.

## Intelligent Tutoring Systems

Intelligent tutoring systems (ITSs) track the knowledge states of learners in fine detail and adaptively respond with activities that are sensitive to these knowledge states. The processes of tracking knowledge (called *user modeling*) and adaptively responding to the learner ideally incorporate computational models in artificial intelligence and cognitive science, such as production systems, case-based reasoning, Bayesian networks, theorem proving, and constraint satisfaction algorithms. Successful systems have been developed for mathematically well-formed topics, including algebra; geometry; programming languages (Cognitive Tutors) (Anderson et al., 1995; Koedinger et al., 1997); physics (Andes, Atlas, and Why/Atlas) (VanLehn et al., 2002, 2007); electronics (SHERLOCK) (Lesgold et al., 1992); and information technology (Mitrovic et al., 2004). These systems show impressive learning gains (1.00 sigma, approximately), particularly for deeper levels of comprehension. ITSs are expensive to build but are now in the phase of scaling up for widespread use. One challenge in getting more widespread use of these systems is that instructors do not know what systems are available, how to access and use them, and how to integrate the ITSs in course curricula. A second challenge lies in the authoring of new subject matter content in a timely fashion that keeps pace with the growth of knowledge.

Some of the recent ITSs have attempted to handle knowledge domains that are not mathematically precise and well formed. The Intelligent Essay Assessor (Foltz et al., 2000; Landauer et al., 2000) and e-Rater (Burstein, 2003) grades essays on science, history, and other topics as reliably as experts of English composition. Learners can get very quick feedback on the quality of their essays and on particular deficiencies.

Summary Street (Kintsch et al., 2000) helps the learner summarize texts by identifying idea gaps and irrelevant information. AutoTutor (Graesser et al., 2004b, 2005a) helps college students learn about computer literacy, physics, and critical thinking skills by holding conversations in natural language. AutoTutor shows learning gains of approximately .80 sigma compared with reading a textbook for an equivalent amount of time (Graesser et al., 2004b; VanLehn et al., 2007). These systems automatically analyze language and discourse by incorporating recent advances in computational linguistics (Jurafsky and Martin, 2000) and information retrieval, notably latent semantic analysis (Dumais, 2003; Landauer et al., 2007; Millis et al., 2004).

There are three major reasons for encouraging more research and development on ITSs with tutorial dialog in a natural language. The first is the need for intelligent training on subject matters that involve conceptualizations and verbal reasoning that are not mathematically well formed. Second, natural language dialog is a frequent form of communication, as in the case of chat rooms, multi-user domains (MUDs), object-oriented MUDs (MOOs), games, and instant messaging (Kinzie et al., 2005; Looi, 2005); indeed, the majority of teenagers in the United States use instant messaging every day. Third, the revolutionary advances in computational linguistics, corpus analyses, speech recognition, and discourse processing (Graesser et al., 2003a) have made it possible to make significant progress in developing natural language dialog systems. Two points of caution must be noted in this line of research and development. It is important to focus on making the conversational systems more responsive to the learner's ideas, threads of reasoning, and questions as opposed to merely coaching the learner in following the tutor's agenda. Second, it is necessary to have a fine-grained assessment of what aspects of natural language dialog facilitate learning, engagement, and motivation. Learners get irritated with conversation partners who do not seem to be listening at a sufficiently deep level (Mishra, 2006; Walker et al., 2003).

## Inquiry-Based Information Retrieval

One type of inquiry learning consists of asking questions and searching for answers in an information repository (Graesser et al., 2004a; Wisher and Graesser, 2007). High-knowledge individuals sometimes do not have the patience to wade through learning materials but prefer to actively ask questions and seek answers to achieve their goals. Query-based information retrieval occurs when Google is used to access information on the Web. The queries do not need to be well formed semantically and syntactically because the system uses keyword search algorithms. The responses are not direct answers to queries but rather are Web pages and documents that may contain the answers. More recently, advances in computational linguistics have made it possible for users to parse and interpret well-formed questions and for answers to the questions to be returned (Harabagiu et al., 2002; Voorhees, 2001). The information repositories have varied from focal topics (e.g., terrorism and finances in *The Wall Street Journal*) to open searches on the Web.

Formal evaluations of these question answering systems have been conducted with respect to their accuracy in accessing all of the desired information and, importantly, not returning irrelevant information (see informedia.cs.cmu.edu/aquaint/index.html). The performance of these query-based information retrieval systems has been quite impressive for short-answer questions (who, what, when, where) but not for questions that require lengthy answers (why, how). For the latter types of questions, the best that can be accomplished is returning a paragraph from the text that might contain the answer. What has been rare in these evaluations of question-and-answer systems is performance in the context of LEs. In one study, the accuracy of fetching paragraphs was quite respectable in an LE on research ethics; 95% of the paragraphs were judged by the learner as being relevant and 50% as being informative (Graesser et al., 2004a). More research is needed to assess the questions that students ask during learning and the fidelity of the answers delivered by the question-and-answer facilities in the learning environments.

One challenge that limits the utility of query-based retrieval systems is that most learners ask very few questions, and most of the questions they ask are shallow (Graesser et al., 2005b; Graesser and Person, 1994). Questions are typically asked when learners experience cognitive disequilibrium as a result of obstacles to goals, contradictions, anomalous information, difficult decisions, and salient knowledge gaps (Graesser and Olde, 2003). Even then, though, most learners need to be trained on how to ask good questions. Such training of question-asking skills does improve question quality and also comprehension (King, 1994; Rosenshine et al., 1996). Learners need to be exposed to good models of question asking, inquiry, and curiosity. A deep, curious learner is something rarely seen in classrooms and the real world.

A different sense of inquiry learning is manifested in LEs that stimulate hypothetical reasoning and the scientific method, such as Inquiry Island (White and Frederiksen, 2005). Learners are presented with authentic challenges that motivate them to generate hypotheses, plans on testing hypotheses, reports to colleagues, revisions of hypotheses, and so on. Ideally, the learners will be intrinsically motivated by the problem and the affordances of the LE to the point of engaging in the inquiry process; however, it is necessary to investigate the process of scaffolding effective inquiry for a wide range of learner profiles. Many LEs fail in stimulating genuine inquiry in most learners, so this is an area greatly in need of research. The time course of learning from these LEs involves weeks, months, or years (hardly one-hour training sessions), so the research is expensive and requires several months or years for adequate evaluations.

## Animated Pedagogical Agents (Agents)

Embodied animated conversational agents have become very popular in information and communication technologies, but the most serious applications have been in learning technologies (Atkinson, 2002; Baylor and Kim, 2005; Cole et al., 2003; Graesser et al., 2005a; Johnson et al., 2000; McNamara et al., 2004; Moreno and Mayer, 2004; Reeves and Nass, 1996). These agents speak, point, gesture, walk, and exhibit facial expressions. Some are built in the image of humans, whereas others are animals or cartoon characters. The potential power of these agents, from the standpoint of LEs, is that they can mimic face-to-face communication with human tutors, instructors, mentors, peers, or people who serve other roles. Ensembles of agents can model social interaction. Single agents can model individuals with different knowledge, personalities, physical features, and styles. Both single agents and ensembles of agents can be carefully choreographed to mimic virtually any social situation: curious learning, negotiation, interrogation, arguments, empathetic support, helping, and so on. As a result, agent technologies can potentially have a revolutionary impact on social science research.

Researchers have investigated the conditions in which single agents promote learning either alone or in the presence of other media (Mayer, 2005); for example, is it better to have information presented in print or spoken by agents? Are realistic agents better than cartoon agents? Does the attractiveness or conversational style of the agent matter? These and other similar questions can be related to the previous research on multimedia, discourse, and social psychology that was conducted before the onslaught of agent technologies. It is of course important to make sure that the agent does not create cognitive overload, a split attention effect, or a distraction from other information on the display that has higher importance (Moreno and Mayer, 2004). It is important to make sure that the agent is not so realistic that the learner has too high an expectation with regard to its intelligence (Norman, 1994; Shneiderman and Plaisant, 2005). Available research suggests that it is the content of what is expressed, rather than the aesthetic quality of the speech or face, that is most important in predicting learning (Graesser et al., 2003b). Research also suggests that it is possible to create social presence from facial icons with expressions, a minimalist form of the persona effect.

There are four directions that merit more attention in future research. First, ensembles of agents can model learning processes, so researchers can investigate how learning is systematically affected by different theories of social interaction; for example, dyads can exist between peer learners, between teacher and student, or between tutor and student, as well as triads among teachers, tutors, and peers (McNamara et al., 2004). Learners can learn vicariously from such interactions (Craig et al., 2000). The possibilities are endless. Second, researchers can explore the processes that designers and learners go through when they create agents with the tool kits that have been developed. In addition to understanding these design processes, researchers will accumulate a broader population of agents to test in their studies (i.e., beyond Microsoft agents), including those with diverse physical appearances, personalities, and styles that resonate with specific learner populations (Baylor and Kim, 2005). Third, researchers can develop agents that deeply interpret what learners express in tutorial dialog or other forms of human–computer interaction. This direction requires integration of advances from computational linguistics, cognitive science, and artificial intelligence. Fourth, researchers can investigate alternative ways that agents can be responsive to the learner as the learner makes contributions that vary in quality. This is already being done in AutoTutor (Graesser et al., 2005a), which holds a mixed initiative dialog with the learner. AutoTutor has dialog moves that are responsive to the learner's knowledge states: short feedback (positive, neutral, negative), pumps for information ("What else?"), hints, answers to learner questions, and corrections of student misconceptions. Similarly, McNamara's iSTART system has groups of agents that adaptively respond to learners who generate self-explanations while reading science texts (McNamara et al., 2004). These responsive agents require more intelligence than the preprepared choreographed agents.

## Virtual Environments with Agents

Virtual environments are getting progressively closer to real-world settings and therefore should have excellent transfer to the real world but at costs that can be much more economical than learning in field settings. The addition of agents to scaffold learners' interactions with these virtual realities has the potential to form an ideal meshing of technology and pedagogy (Winn, 2003). Outstanding examples of virtual environments with agents are those developed at the University of Southern California, namely Mission Rehearsal (Gratch et al., 2002) and Tactical Iraqi (Johnson and Beal, 2005). These virtual worlds are very close to authentic interactions in war scenarios or when soldiers interact with citizens in another culture with a different language. The learner holds a dialog in natural language, with speech recognition and multiple agents. These award-winning virtual environments are major milestones and have involved major investments by the military. Unfortunately, these learning environments are not currently on the Web, so the feasibility of transporting simpler versions on simpler platforms remains a question. More modest virtual environments with agents are available in MOOs (Slator et al., 2004). As mentioned earlier, there is a glaring deficit in the literature when it comes to evaluating the impact of these virtual environments on learners (Winn, 2003). More empirical evaluations of these systems on learning gains, usability, learner impressions, and the fidelity of specific computational modules are necessary.

## Serious Games

The game industry has certainly captured the imagination of this generation of young adults, with revenues larger than the movie industry. Serious teenage gamers play games approximately 20 hours per week (Yee, 2006). Nearly all of the rich taxonomy of games could be integrated with education and training (e.g., first-person shooter games, multiparty games, simulations of cities). A large-scale game such as America's Army is extremely appealing to both the young and old because it is engaging and simultaneously weaves in serious content about the Army. The challenge of combining entertainment and pedagogical content is the foundational question of serious games (Brody, 1993). Social scientists need to investigate the mechanisms necessary for this to succeed.

The components of games have been analyzed at considerable depth (Gee, 2003; Salen and Zimmerman, 2004), but more research is needed on the impact of these components on learning gains, engagement, and usability (Cameron and Dwyer, 2005; Conati, 2002; Lawrence, 2004; Malone and Lepper, 1987; Moreno and Mayer, 2005; Virvou et al., 2005). Presumably, the success of a game can be attributed to such factors as feedback, progress markers, engaging content, fantasy, competition, challenge, uncertainty, curiosity, control, and other factors that involve cognition, emotions, motivation, and art. Investigating the relationships between game features and outcome measures should be an important priority for future researchers because scientific data are sparse and the impact of games on society is enormous.

An adequate understanding of games requires research on the relations between emotions and learning. Connections between emotions and complex learning are receiving more attention in the fields of psychology (Dweck, 2002; Lepper and Henderlong, 2000), education (Meyer and Turner, 2006), neuroscience (Damasio, 2003), and computer science (Kort et al., 2001; Picard, 1997). Some of the recent intelligent tutoring systems automatically infer and track student emotions and motivational states on the basis of the tutorial interaction, facial expressions, speech intonation, posture, and other communication channels (De Vicente and Pain, 2002; D'Mello et al., 2005; Graesser et al., 2006; Litman and Forbes-Riley, 2004). Pervasive affective states during complex learning include confusion, boredom, flow/engagement, curiosity/interest, delight/eureka, and frustration from being stuck (Burleson and Picard, 2004; Craig et al., 2004; Csikszentmihalyi, 1990; Graesser et al., 2006; Kort et al., 2001).

Meyer and Turner (2006) identified three major theories that link emotions and learning, which they refer to as academic risk taking, flow theory, and goal theory. The academic risk theory contrasts students who like to be challenged with difficult tasks, take risks of failure, and manage negative emotions with those students who tackle easier tasks, take fewer risks, and minimize learning situations where they fail and experience negative emotions. According to flow theory, the learner is in a state of flow (Csikszentmihalyi, 1990) when the learner is so deeply engaged in learning the material that time and fatigue disappear. Metcalfe and Kornell (2005) predict that the flow experience is believed to occur when the learning rate is high and the learner has achieved a high level of mastery at the region of proximal learning. Goal theory emphasizes the role of goals in predicting emotions. Outcomes that achieve goals result in positive emotions, whereas outcomes that jeopardize goal accomplishment result in negative emotions (Dweck, 2002). Obstacles to goals are particularly diagnostic of both learning and emotions. The affective state of confusion correlates with learning gains perhaps because it is a direct reflection of deep thinking (Craig et al., 2004; Guhe et al., 2004). Confusion is diagnostic of cognitive disequilibrium, a state that occurs when learners face obstacles to goals, contradictions, incongruities, anomalies, uncertainty, and salient contrasts (Graesser et al., 2006). Cognitive equilibrium is restored after thought, reflection, problem solving, and other effortful deliberations.

An emotion-sensitive tutor would presumably enhance intelligent learning environments (D'Mello et al., 2005; Graesser et al., 2006; Lepper and Henderlong, 2000). If the learner is frustrated, for example, the tutor would generate hints to advance the learner in constructing knowledge or would make supportive empathetic comments to enhance motivation. If the learner is bored, the tutor would present more engaging or challenging problems for the learner to work on. Suitable adaptive moves of the tutor would be desired for learners who experience confusion, delight, surprise, and so on. One of the research frontiers of the future is to discover optimal links between student emotions and learning.

## Computer-Supported Collaborative Learning

In computer-supported collaborative learning (CSCL), groups of learners collaboratively construct knowledge on a topic in pursuit of project goals that typically are provided by instructors (Lee et al., 2006); for example, in Knowledge Forum (Bereiter, 2002; Scardamalia and Bereiter, 1994) students create messages that others can review, elaborate, critique, and build on. CSCL systems support threads of conversations that involve formulating arguments, problem solving, planning, report writing, and countless other tasks (Gunawardena et al., 1997). Because the length of most of these conversational threads is short (2.2 to 2.7 turns per thread) (Hewitt, 2005), attempts have been made to design these systems to lengthen the threads. Some evidence suggests that CSCL facilitates deeper learning, critical thinking, shared understanding, and long-term retention (Garrison et al., 2001; Johnson and Johnson, 1991), but the scale of these distributed learning environments makes it very difficult to perform systematic evaluations of them.

Social and behavioral scientists have the foundation necessary to step in and improve these CSCL systems in several ways (Clark and Brennan, 1991; Dillenbourg and Traum, 2006; Looi, 2005; Mazur, 2004; Soller et al., 1998; Wang, 2005). How do learners figure out how to use the complex interfaces on these multiparty computer-mediated communication systems? How does a potential contributor learn how and when to speak? How is knowledge grounded in these distributed systems? How can moderators guide the group of learners in productive directions? Research on CSCL is very much an open frontier.

## CONCLUDING REMARKS

Many are convinced that learning gains from technologies are best attributed to the underlying pedagogies rather than the technologies *per se*. At the same time, we all recognize that various technologies afford different pedagogies. One of the key challenges for the future is to explore how technologies and pedagogies can be effectively coordinated in a fashion that considers the learning goals and the learners' profiles. The TMGL landscape has a large space of empty cells that will potentially guide researchers for many decades. Progress will only be achieved when social, cognitive, and behavioral scientists are part of an interdisciplinary team of LE designers, developers, and deliverers.

The LEs significantly vary in development costs, of course. We have periodically been asked how expensive it is to develop and test these different types of learning technologies, so we have generated some ballpark estimates of such costs. Our estimates should be considered with caution because other experts may have very different viewpoints, and there is wide variance in these costs depending on detailed parameters of the relevant cells in the TMGL landscape. Approximate costs are $10,000 for an hour training session with conventional computer-based training; $100,000 for a 10-hour course with conventional computer-based training and rudimentary multimedia; $1,000,000 for an information-rich, hypertext/hypermedia system; $10,000,000 for an intelligent tutoring system without the benefit of a suite of authoring tools and utilities; and $100,000,000 for a serious game (not a frivolous commercial game) on the Web for thousands of users.

Given that training systems have costs and that some have nontrivial costs, one mission has been to find ways to cut the price, development time, and other resources associated with building these systems without sacrificing the quality of the learning experience. This mission has been pursued by the Advanced Distributed Learning initiative (for example, see www.adl-net.org; Dodds and Fletcher, 2004; Duval et al., 2004; Fletcher, 2003). Learning content is standardized by being decomposed, packaged, and organized into learning objects that have to conform to the standards of the Sharable Content Object Reference Model (SCORM). Each learning object has meta-tags that identify the relevant contexts of its application. A SCORM-conformant learning object can be used in most learning management systems, so the content is sharable, interoperable, reusable, and extendable. This represents a substantial savings in costs: Once content is created in a SCORM-conformant fashion, it can be used throughout the e-learning world. One of the chief challenges now is to get designers of courseware to reuse the SCORM-conformant learning objects (Brusilovsky and Nijhawan, 2002; Sampson and Karampiperis, 2006). This is accomplished by building and indexing large repositories of SCORM-conformant content, as in the case of CORDRA (Rehak, 2005; http://cordra.net), and to somehow market and encourage such repositories to be used. A second major challenge is to develop SCORM standards for the more advanced LEs now that SCORM is mainstream for computer-based training and most multimedia.

Other ways to reduce the costs of building LEs are available—for example, authoring tools for the easy preparation of course content for CBT and multimedia. Better authoring tools are necessary, however, to build new course content with the more advanced LEs (Murray et al., 2003). The existing authoring tools for advanced systems are very difficult to learn and use; these authoring tools are so complex that only the most advanced cognitive scientists and computer scientists can use them—often only the original designers of the systems. To allow these tools to be more widely used by individuals with varying backgrounds, it will be necessary to conduct systematic research on human factors and human–computer interaction that can be applied to developing course content with authoring tools; otherwise, it is difficult to see how these advanced systems will scale up to handle the large volume of training needs throughout the military, for example.

A salient side benefit of the authoring tools is that they can be viewed as LEs themselves; that is, learning a complex system at a deep level can be achieved by building an advanced LE on the system with an authoring tool. One of the exciting developments of the future is to explore the process of learning deep content and strategies by creating learning environments with these authoring tools. This not only will be engaging to many students but will also empower them for handling the technologies of the future.

## REFERENCES

Anderson, J. R., Corbett, A. T., Koedinger, K. R., and Pelletier, R. (1995). Cognitive tutors: lessons learned. *J. Learn. Sci.*, 4(2), 167–207.*

Atkinson, R. K. (2002). Optimizing learning from examples using animated pedagogical agents. *J. Educ. Psychol.*, 94(2), 416–427.

Ausubel, D., Novak, J., and Hanesian, H. (1978). *Educational Psychology: A Cognitive View*, 2nd ed. New York: Holt, Rinehart and Winston.

Azevedo, R. and Cromley, J. G. (2004). Does training on self-regulated learning facilitate students' learning with hypermedia? *J. Educ. Psychol.*, 96(3), 523–535.

Baker, L. (1985). Differences in standards used by college students to evaluate their comprehension of expository prose. *Reading Res. Q.*, 20, 298–313.

Baylor, A. L. and Kim, Y. (2005). Simulating instructional roles through pedagogical agents. *Int. J. Artif. Intell. Educ.*, 15, 95–115.

Bereiter, C. (2002). *Education and Mind in the Knowledge Age.* Mahwah, NJ: Lawrence Erlbaum Associates.

Bereiter, C. and Scardamalia, M. (1985). Cognitive coping strategies and the problem of 'inert knowledge.' In *Thinking and Learning Skills*. Vol. 2. *Current Research and Open Questions*, edited by S. F. Chipman, J. W. Segal, and R. Glaser, pp. 65–80. Hillsdale, NJ: Lawrence Erlbaum Associates.

Bloom, B. S., Ed. (1956). *Taxonomy of Educational Objectives: The Classification of Educational Goals: Handbook I, Cognitive Domain.* New York: Longmans, Green.

Bransford, J. D., Brown, A. L., and Cocking, R. R., Eds. (2000). *How People Learn*, expanded ed. Washington, D.C.: National Academy Press.

Brody, H. (1993). Video games that teach? *Technol. Rev.*, 96,(8), 50–58.

Brusilovsky, P. and Nijhawan, H. (2002) A framework for adaptive e-learning based on distributed re-usable learning activities. In *Proceedings of World Conference on E-Learning, E-Learn 2002: Montreal, Canada*, edited by M. Driscoll and T. C. Reeves, pp. 154–161. Chesapeake, VA: Association for the Advancement of Computing in Education.

Burleson, W. and Picard, R. W. (2004). Affective agents: sustaining motivation to learn through failure and a state of stuck. (2004). In *Proc. of the Intelligent Tutoring Systems 7th Int. Conf. (ITS 2004): Workshop on Social and Emotional Intelligence in Learning Environments*. August 30–September 4, Maceio-Alagoas, Brazil.

Burstein, J. (2003). The E-rater scoring engine: automated essay scoring with natural language processing. In *Automated Essay Scoring: A Cross-Disciplinary Perspective*, edited by M. D. Shermis and J. C. Burstein, pp. 133–122. Mahwah, NJ: Lawrence Erlbaum Associates.

Cameron, B. and Dwyer, F. (2005). The effect of online gaming, cognition and feedback type in facilitating delayed achievement of different learning objectives. *J. Interact. Learn. Res.*, 16(3), 243–258.

Card, S., Moran, T., and Newell, A. (1983). *The Psychology of Human–Computer Interaction*. Hillsdale, NJ: Lawrence Erlbaum Associates.*

Chi, M. T. H., de Leeuw, N., Chiu, M., and LaVancher, C. (1994). Eliciting self-explanations improves understanding. *Cognit. Sci.*, 18, 439–477.

Clark, H. H. and Brennan, S. E. (1991). Grounding in communication. In *Perspectives on Socially Shared Cognition*, edited by L. Resnick, J. Levine, and S. Teasely, pp. 127–149. Washington, D.C.: American Psychological Association.

Clark, R. E. (1983). Reconsidering research on learning from media. *Rev. Educ. Res.*, 53, 445–460.*

Cole, R., van Vuuren, S., Pellom, B., Hacioglu, K., Ma, J., Movellan, J., Schwartz, S., Wade-Stein, D., Ward, W., and Yan, J. (2003). Perceptive animated interfaces: first steps toward a new paradigm for human–computer interaction. *Proc. IEEE*, 91, 1391–1405.

Conati, C. (2002). Probabilistic assessment of user's emotions in educational games. *J. Appl. Artif. Intell.*, 16, 555–575.

Conklin, J. (1987). Hypertext: a survey and introduction. *IEEE Comput.*, 20(9), 17–41.

Corbett, A. T. (2001). Cognitive computer tutors: solving the two-sigma problem. In *User Modeling: Proceedings of the Eighth International Conference*, pp. 137–147. Berlin: Springer.

Craig, S. D., Gholson, B., Ventura, M., Graesser, A. C., and the Tutoring Research Group (2000). Overhearing dialogues and monologues in virtual tutoring sessions: effects on questioning and vicarious learning. *Int. J. Artif. Intell. Educ.*, 11, 242–253.

Craig, S. D., Graesser, A. C., Sullins, J., and Gholson, B. (2004). Affect and learning: an exploratory look into the role of affect in learning with AutoTutor. *J. Educ. Media*, 29, 241–250.

Craik, F. I. M. and Lockhart, R. S. (1972). Levels of processing: a framework for memory research. *J. Verbal Learn. Verbal Behav.*, 11, 671–684.

Csikszentmihalyi, M. (1990). *Flow: The Psychology of Optimal Experience.* New York: Harper-Row.

Cuban, L. (1986). *Teachers and Machines: The Classroom Use of Technology Since 1920.* New York: Teachers College.

Cuban, L. (2001). *Oversold and Underused: Computers in the Classroom.* Cambridge, MA: Harvard University Press.*

Damasio, A. R. (2003). *Looking for Spinoza: Joy, Sorrow, and the Feeling Brain.* Orlando, FL: Harcourt.

De Vicente, A. and Pain, H. (2002). Informing the detection of students' motivational state: an empirical study. In *Proceedings of the Sixth International Conference on Intelligent Tutoring Systems*, edited by S. A. Cerri, G. Gouarderes, and F. Paraguacu, pp. 933–943. Berlin: Springer.

Deimann, M. and Keller, J. M. (2006). Volitional aspects of multimedia learning. *J. Educ. Multimedia Hypermedia*, 15(2), 137–158.

Dillenbourg, P. and Traum, D. (2006). Sharing solutions: persistence and grounding in multimodal collaborative problem solving. *J. Learn. Sci.*, 15(1), 121–151.

Dillon, A. and Gabbard, R. (1998). Hypermedia as an educational technology: a review of the quantitative research literature on learner comprehension, control, and style. *Rev. Educ. Res.*, 68, 322–349.

D'Mello, S. K., Craig, S. D., Gholson, B., Franklin, S., Picard, R., and Graesser, A. C. (2005). Integrating affect sensors in an intelligent tutoring system. In *Affective Interactions: The Computer in the Affective Loop Workshop at the 2005 International Conference on Intelligent User Interfaces*, pp. 7–13. New York: AMC Press.

Dodds, P. and Fletcher, J. D. (2004). Opportunities for new 'smart' learning environments enabled by next-generation Web capabilities. *J. Educ. Multimedia Hypermedia*, 13(4), 391–404.

Doignon, J. P. and Falmagne, J. C. (1999). *Knowledge Spaces.* Berlin: Springer-Verlag.

Dumais, S. (2003). Data-driven approaches to information access. *Cognit. Sci.*, 27(3), 491–524.

Duval, E., Hodgins, W., Rehak, D., and Robson, R. (2004). Learning objects symposium special issue: guest editorial. *J. Educ. Multimedia Hypermedia*, 13(4), 331–342.

Dweck, C. S. (2002). Messages that motivate: how praise molds students' beliefs, motivation, and performance (in surprising ways). In *Improving Academic Achievement: Impact of Psychological Factors on Education*, edited by J. Aronson, pp. 61–87. Orlando, FL: Academic Press.

Dwyer, C. A., Ed. (2005). *Measurement and Research in the Accountability Era.* Mahwah, NJ: Lawrence Erlbaum Associates.

Fletcher, J. D. (2003). Evidence for learning from technology-assisted instruction. In *Technology Applications in Education: A Learning View*, edited by H. F. O'Neil, Jr., and R. S. Perez, pp. 79–99. Hillsdale, NJ: Lawrence Erlbaum Associates.*

Foltz, P. W., Gilliam, S., and Kendall, S. (2000). Supporting content-based feedback in on-line writing evaluation with LSA. *Interact. Learn. Environ.*, 8, 111–127.

Gagné, R. M. (1985). *The Conditions of Learning and Theory of Instruction*, 4th ed. New York: Holt, Rinehart and Winston.

Garrison, D. R., Anderson, T., and Archer, W. (2001). Critical thinking, cognitive presence, and computer conferencing in distance education. *Am. J. Distance Educ.*, 15(1), 7–23

Gee, J. (2003). *What Video Games Have to Teach Us About Learning and Literacy*. New York: Palgrave Macmillan.*

Graesser, A. C. and Olde, B. A. (2003). How does one know whether a person understands a device? The quality of the questions the person asks when the device breaks down. *J. Educ. Psychol.*, 95(3), 524–536.

Graesser, A. C. and Person, N. K. (1994). Question asking during tutoring. *Am. Educ. Res. J.*, 31, 104–137.

Graesser, A. C., Gernsbacher, M. A., and Goldman, S., Eds. (2003a). *Handbook of Discourse Processes*. Mahwah, NJ: Lawrence Erlbaum Associates.*

Graesser, A. C., Moreno, K., Marineau, J., Adcock, A., Olney, A., and Person, N. K. (2003b). AutoTutor improves deep learning of computer literacy: is it the dialog or the talking head? In *Proceedings of Artificial Intelligence in Education*, edited by U. Hoppe, F. Verdejo, and J. Kay, pp, 47–54. Amsterdam: IOS Press.

Graesser, A. C., Hu, X., Person, P., Jackson, T., and Toth, J. (2004a). Modules and information retrieval facilities of the Human Use Regulatory Affairs Advisor (HURAA). *Int. J. eLearn.*, 3(4), 29–39.

Graesser, A. C., Lu, S., Jackson, G. T., Mitchell, H., Ventura, M., Olney, A., and Louwerse, M. M. (2004b). AutoTutor: a tutor with dialogue in natural language. *Behav. Res. Methods Instrum. Comput.*, 36, 180–193.

Graesser, A. C., Chipman, P., Haynes, B. C., and Olney, A. (2005a). AutoTutor: an intelligent tutoring system with mixed-initiative dialogue. *IEEE Trans. Educ.*, 48, 612–618.

Graesser, A. C., McNamara, D. S., and VanLehn, K. (2005b). Scaffolding deep comprehension strategies through Point&Query, AutoTutor, and iSTART. *Educ. Psychol.*, 40, 225–234.

Graesser, A. C., McDaniel, B., Chipman, P., Witherspoon, A., D'Mello, S., and Gholson, B. (2006). Detection of emotions during learning with AutoTutor. In *Proceedings of the 28th Annual Meetings of the Cognitive Science Society*, edited by R. Son, pp. 285–290. Mahwah, NJ: Lawrence Erlbaum Associates.

Graesser, A. C., Jackson, G. T., and McDaniel, B. (2007). AutoTutor holds conversations with learners that are responsive to their cognitive and emotional states. *Educ. Technol.*, 47, 19-22.

Gratch, J., Rickel, J., Andre, E., Cassell, J., Petajan, E., and Badler, N. (2002). Creating interactive virtual humans: some assembly required. *IEEE Intell. Syst.*, 17, 54–63.

Gray, W. D., John, B. E., and Atwood, M. E. (1993). Project Ernestine: validating a GOMS analysis for predicting and explaining real-world performance. *Hum.–Comput. Interact.*, 8(3), 237–309.

Guhe, M., Gray, W. D., Schoelles, M. J., and Ji, Q. (2004). Towards an affective cognitive architecture. In *Proceedings of the 26th Annual Meeting of the Cognitive Science Society*, edited by K. D. Forbus, D. Gentner, and T. Regier, p. 1565. Hillsdale, NJ: Lawrence Erlbaum Associates.

Gunawardena, L., Lowe, C. A., and Anderson, T. (1997). Interaction analysis of a global on-line debate and the development of a constructivist interaction analysis model for computer conferencing. *J. Educ. Comput. Res.*, 17(4), 395–429.

Harabagiu, S. M., Maiorano, S. J., and Pasca, M. A. (2002). Open-domain question answering techniques. *Natural Language English*, 1, 1–38.

Hegarty, M. (2004). Dynamic visualizations and learning: getting to the difficult questions. *Learn. Instruct.*, 14(3), 343–351.*

Hegarty, M., Kriz, S., and Cate, C. (2003). The roles of mental animations and external animations in understanding mechanical systems. *Cognit. Instruct.*, 21, 325–360.

Hewitt, J. (2005). Toward an understanding of how threads die in asynchronous computer conferences. *J. Learn. Sci.*, 14(4), 567–589.

Hunt, E. and Pellegrino, J. W. (2002). Issues, examples, and challenges in formative assessment. *New Direct. Teaching Learn.*, 89, 73–85.

Jackson, G. T., Olney, A., Graesser, A. C., and Kim, H. J. (2006). AutoTutor 3-D simulations: analyzing user's actions and learning trends. In *Proceedings of the 28th Annual Meetings of the Cognitive Science Society*, edited by R. Son, pp. 1557–1562. Mahwah, NJ: Lawrence Erlbaum Associates.

Jochems, W., van Merrienboer, J. G., and Koper, R., Eds. (2004). *Integrated e-Learning: Implications for Pedagogy, Technology, and Organization*. London: Taylor & Francis.

Johnson, D. W. and Johnson, R. T. (1991). Classroom instruction and cooperative grouping. In *Effective Teaching: Current Research*, edited by H. C., Waxman and H. J. Walberg, pp. 277–294. Berkeley, CA: McCutchan.

Johnson, W. L. and Beal, C. (2005). Iterative evaluation of a large-scale intelligent game for language learning. In *Artificial Intelligence in Education: Supporting Learning Through Intelligent and Socially Informed Technology*, edited by C. Looi, G. McCalla, B. Bredeweg, and J. Breuker, pp. 290–297. Amsterdam: IOS Press.

Johnson, W. L., Rickel, J., and Lester, J. (2000). Animated pedagogical agents: face-to-face interaction in interactive learning environments. *Int. J. Artif. Intell. Educ.*, 11, 47–78.

Jonassen, D. H., Ed. (2004). *Handbook of Research on Educational Communications and Technology*, 2nd ed. Mahwah, NJ: Lawrence Erlbaum Associates.*

Jurafsky, D. and Martin, J. H. (2000). *Speech and Language Processing: An Introduction to Natural Language Processing, Computational Linguistics, and Speech Recognition*. Upper Saddle River, NJ: Prentice Hall.

Kalyuga, S., Chandler, P., and Sweller, J. (1999). Managing split-attention and redundancy in multimedia instruction. *Appl. Cognit. Psychol.*, 13, 351–371.

King, A. (1994). Guiding knowledge construction in the classroom: effects of teaching children how to question and how to explain. *Am. Educ. Res. J.*, 31(2), 338–368.

Kintsch, E., Steinhart, D., Stahl, G., and LSA Research Group. (2000). Developing summarization skills through the use of LSA-based feedback. *Interact. Learn. Environ.*, 8(2), 87–109.

Kinzie, M. B., Whitaker, S. D., and Hofer, M. J. (2005). Instructional uses of instant messaging (IM) during classroom lectures. *Educ. Technol. Soc.*, 8(2), 150–160.

Koedinger, K. R., Anderson, J., Hadley, W., and Mark, M. A. (1997). Intelligent tutoring goes to school in the big city. *Int. J. Artif. Intell. Educ.*, 8, 30–43.

Kort, B., Reilly, R., and Picard, R. (2001). An affective model of interplay between emotions and learning: reengineering educational pedagogy—building a learning companion. In *Proceedings IEEE International Conference on Advanced Learning Technology: Issues, Achievements, and Challenges*, edited by T. Okamoto, R. Hartley, Kinshuk, and J. P. Klus, pp. 43–48. Madison, WI: IEEE Computer Society.

Kozma, R. B. (1994). Will media influence learning? Reframing the debate. *Educ. Technol. Res. Dev.*, 42(2), 7–17.

Kozma, R. B. (2000). Reflections on the state of educational technology research and development. *Educ. Technol. Res. Dev.*, 48(1), 5–15.*

Kulhavy, R. W. and Stock, W. A. (1989). Feedback in written instruction: the place of response certitude. *Educ. Psychol. Rev.*, 1(4), 279–308.

Landauer, T. K., Laham, D., and Foltz, P. W. (2000). The Intelligent Essay Assessor. *IEEE Intell. Syst.*, 15, 27–31.

Landauer, T. K., McNamara, D., Dennis, S., and Kintsch, W., Eds. (2007). *Handbook of Latent Semantic Analysis*. Mahwah, NJ: Lawrence Erlbaum Associates.

Lawrence, R. (2004). Teaching data structures using competitive games. *IEEE Trans. Educ.*, 47(4), 459–466.

Lee, E. Y. C., Chan, C. K. K., and van Aalst, J. (2006). Students assessing their own collaborative knowledge building. *Int. J. Comput. Supported Collab. Learn.*, 1, 57–87

Lee, M. and Baylor, A. L. (2006). Designing metacognitive maps for Web-based learning. *Educ. Technol. Soc.*, 9(1), 344–348.

Lepper, M. R. and Henderlong, J. (2000). Turning 'play' into 'work' and 'work' into 'play': 25 years of research on intrinsic versus extrinsic motivation. In *Intrinsic and Extrinsic Motivation: The Search for Optimal Motivation and Performance*, edited by C. Sansone and J. M. Harackiewicz, pp. 257–307. San Diego, CA: Academic Press.

Lesgold, A., Lajoie, S. P., Bunzo, M., and Eggan, G. (1992). SHERLOCK: a coached practice environment for an electronics trouble-shooting job. In *Computer Assisted Instruction and Intelligent Tutoring Systems: Shared Goals and Complementary Approaches*, edited by J. H. Larkin and R. W. Chabay, pp. 201–238. Hillsdale, NJ: Lawrence Erlbaum Associates.

Litman, D. J. and Forbes-Riley, K. (2004). Predicting student emotions in computer-human tutoring dialogues. In *Proceedings of the 42nd Annual Meeting of the Association for Computational Linguistics*, pp. 352–359. East Stroudsburg, PA: Association for Computational Linguistics.

Looi, C. (2005). Exploring the affordances of online chat for learning. *Int. J. Learn. Technol.*, 1(3), 322–338.

Lowe, R. K. (2004). Interrogation of a dynamic visualization during learning. *Learn. Instruct.*, 14(3), 257–274.

Malone, T. and Lepper, M. (1987). Making learning fun: a taxonomy of intrinsic motivations of learning. In *Aptitude, Learning, and Instruction*. Vol. 3. *Conative and Affective Process Analyses*, edited by R. E. Snow and M. J. Farr, pp. 223–253. Hillsdale, NJ: Lawrence Erlbaum Associates.

Mayer, R. E. (2005). *Multimedia Learning*. Cambridge, MA: Cambridge University Press.*

Mazur, J. M. (2004). Conversation analysis for educational technologists: theoretical and methodological issues for researching the structures, processes and meaning of on-line talk. In *Handbook of Research on Educational Communications and Technology*, 2nd ed., edited by D. H. Jonassen, pp. 1073–1098. Mahwah, NJ: Lawrence Erlbaum Associates.

McNamara, D. S., Levenstein, I. B., and Boonthum, C. (2004). iSTART: interactive strategy trainer for active reading and thinking. *Behav. Res. Meth. Instrum. Comput.*, 36, 222–233.

Merrill, M. D. (2002). First principles of instruction. *Educ. Technol. Res. Dev.*, 50, 43–59.*

Metcalfe, J. and Kornell, N. (2005). A region or proximal of learning model of study time allocation. *J. Memory Language*, 52, 463–477.

Meyer, D. K. and Turner, J. C. (2006). Reconceptualizing emotion and motivation to learn in classroom contexts. *Educ. Psychology Rev.*, 18(4), 377–390.

Millis, K. K., Kim, H. J., Todaro, S., Magliano, J. P., Wiemer-Hastings, K., and McNamara, D. S. (2004). Identifying reading strategies using latent semantic analysis: comparing semantic benchmarks. *Behav. Res. Meth. Instrum. Comput.*, 36, 213–221.

Mishra, P. (2006). Affective feedback from computers and its effect on perceived ability and affect: a test of the computers as social actor hypothesis. *J. Educ. Multimedia Hypermedia*, 15(1), 107–131.

Mitrovic, A., Suraweera, P., Martin, B., and Weerasinghe, A. (2004). DB-Suite: experiences with three intelligent, Web-based database tutors. *J. Interact. Learn. Res.*, 15(4), 409–432.

Moreno, R. and Mayer, R. E. (2004). Personalized messages that promote science learning in virtual environments. *J. Educ. Psychol.*, 96(1), 165–173.

Moreno, R. and Mayer, R. E. (2005). Role of guidance, reflection, and interactivity in an agent-based multimedia game. *J. Educ. Psychol.*, 97(1), 117–128.*

Murray, T., Blessing, S., and Ainsworth, S., Eds. (2003). *Authoring Tools for Advanced Technology Learning Environments: Towards Cost-Effective Adaptive, Interactive and Intelligent Educational Software*. Dordrecht: Kluwer.

Norman, D. A. (1988). *The Psychology of Everyday Things*. New York: Basic Books.

Norman, D. A. (1994). How might people interact with agents? *Commun. ACM*, 37(7), 68–71.

O'Neil, H. F. and Perez, R. S., Eds. (2003). *Technology Applications in Education: A Learning View*. Hillsdale, NJ: Lawrence Erlbaum Associates.*

Otero, J. and Graesser, A. C. (2001). PREG: elements of a model of question asking. *Cognit. Instruct.*, 19, 143–175.

Ozuru, Y., Graesser, A. C., Rowe, M., and Floyd, R. G. (2006). Enhancing the landscape and quality of multiple choice questions. In *Spearman ETS Conference Proceedings*, edited by R. Roberts. Mahwah, NJ: Lawrence Erlbaum Associates.

Paivio, A. (1986). *Mental Representations*. New York: Oxford University Press.*

Picard, R. W. (1997). *Affective Computing*. Cambridge, MA: MIT Press.

Reeves, B. and Nass, C. I. (1996). *The Media Equation*. New York: Cambridge University Press.

Rehak, D. (2005). CORDRA: Content Object Repository Discovery and Registration/Resolution Architecture, http://cordra.net.

Rieber, L. P. (1996). Animation as feedback in a computer-based simulation: representation matters. *Educ. Technol. Res. Dev.*, 44(1), 5–22.

Rosenshine, B., Meister, C., and Chapman, S. (1996). Teaching students to generate questions: a review of the intervention studies. *Rev. Educ. Res.*, 66, 181–221.

Rouet, J.-F. (2006). *The Skills of Document Use: From Text Comprehension to Web-Based Learning*. Mahwah, NJ: Lawrence Erlbaum Associates.

Salen, K. and Zimmerman, E. (2004). *Rules of Play: Game Design Fundamentals*. Cambridge, MA: MIT Press.

Sampson, D. and Karampiperis, P. (2006). Towards next generation activity-based learning systems. *Int. J. E-Learn.*, 5(1), 129–149.

Scardamalia, M. and Bereiter, C. (1994). Computer support for knowledge-building communities. *J. Learn. Sci.*, 3(3), 265–283.

Shneiderman, B. and Plaisant, C. (2005). *Designing the User Interface: Strategies for Effective Human–Computer Interaction*, 4th ed. Reading, MA: Addison-Wesley.

Shute, V. J. (2006). *Focus on Formative Feedback*. Unpublished manuscript. Princeton, NJ: Educational Testing Service.

Slator, B. M., Hill, C., and Del Val, D. (2004). Teaching computer science with virtual worlds. *IEEE Trans. Educ.*, 47(2), 269–275.

Soller, A., Goodman, B., Linton, F., and Gaimari, R. (1998) Promoting effective peer interaction in an intelligent collaborative learning environment. In *Proceedings of the Fourth International Conference on Intelligent Tutoring Systems (ITS 98), San Antonio, TX*, pp. 186–195. Berlin: Springer-Verlag.

Spector, J. M. (2005). Time demands in online instruction. *Distance Educ.*, 26, 3–25.

Spiro, R. J., Feltovich, P. J., Jacobson, M. J., and Coulson, R. L. (1991). Cognitive flexibility, constructivism, and hypertext: random access instruction for advanced knowledge acquisition in ill-structured domains. *Educ. Technol.*, 31, 24–33.*

Stern, F., Xing, T., Muste, M., Yarbrough, D., Rothmayer, A., and Rajagopalan, G. et al. (2006). Integration of simulation technology into undergraduate engineering courses and laboratories. *Int. J. Learn. Technol.*, 2(1), 28–48.

Sweller, J. and Chandler, P. (1994). Why some material is difficult to learn. *Cognit. Instruct.*, 12, 185–233.

Taraban R., Rynearson, K., and Stalcup, K. A. (2001). Time as a variable in learning on the World Wide Web. *Behav. Res. Meth.*, 33(2), 217–225.

Tversky, B., Morrison, J. B., and Betrancourt, M. (2002). Animation: can it facilitate? *Int. J. Hum.–Comput. Stud.*, 57, 247–262.

van der Meij, J. and de Jong, T. (2006a). Supporting students' learning with multiple representations in a dynamic simulation-based learning environment. *Learn. Instruct.*, 16(3), 199–212.

van der Meij, J. and de Jong, T. (2006b). Learning with multiple representations: supporting students' learning with multiple representations in a dynamic simulation-based learning environment. *Learn. Instruct.*, 16, 199–212.

VanLehn, K., Lynch, C., Taylor, L., Weinstein, A., Shelby, R. H., Schulze, K. G. et al. (2002). Minimally invasive tutoring of complex physics problem solving. In *Intelligent Tutoring Systems 6th International Conference*, edited by S. A. Cerri, G. Gouarderes, and F. Paraguacu, pp. 367–376. Berlin: Springer.

VanLehn, K., Graesser, A. C., Jackson, G. T., Jordan, P., Olney, A., and Rose, C. P. (2007). When are tutorial dialogues more effective than reading? *Cognit. Sci.*, 31(1), 3–52.

Virvou, M., Katsionis, G., and Manos, K. (2005). Combining software games with education: evaluation of its educational effectiveness. *Educ. Technol. Soc.*, 8(2), 54–65.

Voorhees, E. (2001). The TREC question answering track. *Natural Language Eng.*, 7, 361–378.

Walker, M., Whittaker, S., Stent, A., Maloor, P., Moore, J. D., Johnson, M., and Vasireddy, G. (2003). Generation and evaluation of user tailored responses in multimodal dialogue. *Cognit. Sci.*, 28, 811–840.

Wang, C.-H. (2005). Questioning skills facilitate online synchronous discussions. *J. Comput. Assist. Learn.*, 21(4), 303–313.

White, B. and Frederiksen, J. (2005). A theoretical framework and approach for fostering metacognitive development. *Educ. Psychol.*, 40, 211–223.

Winn, W. D. (2003). Learning in artificial environments: embodiment, embeddedness and dynamic adaptation. *Technol. Instruct. Cognit. Learn.*, 1, 87–114.*

Winne, P. H. (2001). Self-regulated learning viewed from models of information processing. In *Self-Regulated Learning and Academic Achievement: Theoretical Perspectives*, edited by B. Zimmerman and D. Schunk, pp. 153–189. Mahwah, NJ: Lawrence Erlbaum Associates.

Wisher, R. A. and Fletcher, J. D. (2004). The case for advanced distributed learning. *Inform. Secur. Int. J.*, 14, 17–25.

Wisher, R. A. and Graesser, A. C. (2007). Question asking in advanced distributed learning environments. In *Toward a Science of Distributed Learning and Training*, edited by S. M. Fiore and E. Salas. Washington, D.C.: American Psychological Association.

Yee, N. (2006). The labor of fun: how video games blur the boundaries of work and play. *Games Culture*, 1(1), 68–71.

---

* Indicates a core reference.

# 18

# Computer-Mediated
# Communications Technologies

*Jay Pfaffman*
University of Tennessee, Knoxville, Tennessee

**CONTENTS**

## ABSTRACT

This chapter reports recent research on using text-based computer-mediated communication (CMC) in educational settings. CMC takes many forms, and the tools available are many. An outline of CMC features and their affordances is presented as a means to draw the attention of those designing, evaluating, or describing communication environments to the features—technical and social—that are the essence of the activity and away from the particular applications that provide them. The goals of research using CMC are widely varied. Some research focuses on how a particular activity is connected to a measure of learning. Other research focuses on the nature of CMC and how various forms differ from one another. With the tacit assumptions that people learn from thoughtful evaluation and respond to the ideas of others, some research looks at ways to increase participation or guide learners to communicate in particular ways. Because CMC is not affected by time or place, it is also used as a means for teacher training and reduction of the isolation that many educators feel.

## KEYWORDS

*Blog:* From the term "Web log"; originally a Web-based diary but often now used to refer to the software designed to support it which presents Web pages in a reverse chronological order.

*Computer-mediated communication (CMC):* Communication between two or more individuals with text-based tools such as e-mail, instant messaging, or computer-based conferencing systems.

*Learning management system (LMS):* A computer-based system to support or replace classroom-based learning; examples include Blackboard, Moodle, Sakai, and WebCT.

## INTRODUCTION AND SCOPE

A widening array of communications technologies can be found in education today. In addition to the ubiquitous Internet and its set of general-purpose communication tools, learning management systems (LMSs) such as Blackboard, Moodle, and Sakai are also increasingly prevalent, so the question educators ask is not whether or not to use these tools, but how. This chapter explores different types of communication technologies, their affordances, and their uses; the goals of research using these tools; and areas for further research.

## TECHNOLOGY AFFORDANCES

Historically, new media have first been used as a means to replace some other medium; for example, the most obvious educational use of motion pictures and later television was to allow more people to enjoy the benefits of attending high-quality lectures. A series of studies follows to determine whether the new medium is working as well as the one it has replaced (Cuban, 1986). One argument is that media are merely delivery vehicles, and it does not matter what kind of truck delivers your groceries; the other perspective is that we should look instead at the affordances of each medium and how to exploit them (Clark, 1983, 1994; Kozma, 1994). Russel (2001), and the companion website, provide an extensive annotated bibliography of media comparison studies as evidence that distance education can be as effective as face-to-face instruction. These

issues are further discussed in the second edition of this volume (Romiszowski and Mason, 2004). This section focuses on particular features of CMC and their affordances and is intended to help those designing or reporting CMC research to focus on the activity rather than the particular tools used. It is more informative to say, for example, that participants used threaded discussion than to list a specific tool that may have dozens of features unused in the activity reported.

### Text Handling

Computer-mediated communication text-handling features can be divided into synchrony, retrieval, and storage. Synchrony, whether the communication is real time or asynchronous, has a profound effect on the nature of a conversation. Honeycutt (2001) tested a theory of grounding proposed by Clark and Brennan (1991). Different media have different costs—for speakers, formulation and production; for addressees, reception and understanding; for both, delay, fault, and repair. As an example, the immediacy of feedback makes the costs to repair a faulty understanding in a face-to-face discussion relatively low. Honeycutt assigned students into groups of three; each group used chat to discuss writing revisions on one assignment and e-mail in another assignment in a 2-hour class. Content analysis showed that, when using e-mail, students made significantly more references to documents, their contents, and rhetorical contexts than when using chat. Using synchronous chats, students made greater reference to both writing and response tasks than when using e-mail.

In a similar design, Davidson-Shivers et al. (2001) randomly assigned groups of graduate students to communicate synchronously (chat) or asynchronously (threaded discussion) for one week; they then switched to the other tool in a subsequent week for a different topic. Though students reported liking both types of discussion, students especially liked the convenience of asynchronous threaded discussion. Results showed that students using chat were more likely to respond or react to other messages than during the threaded discussion.

Although infrequently studied explicitly, another significant feature in text handling is whether the information is pushed to the reader, as with e-mail, or must be sought out, as with threaded discussion. As the amount of electronic communication continues to expand, tools for managing its flow will become increasingly important.

What happens after the communication is received—how the application archives messages—not only affects how people communicate but is also critical to those who study communication. The need for archiving sometimes outweighs the type of communication researchers set out to study. Tidwell and Walther (2002) used e-mail to function as an instant messaging tool because e-mail facilitated recording the data that they wanted to analyze. Robust archival mechanisms can work to the advantage of both the discussant and the researcher; threaded discussion forums provide good support for those communicating and keep a complete record of the communication for researchers. Threaded discussion makes it easier for users to follow a conversation, and, because it can be calculated mechanically, for researchers thread length is a convenient variable to track. As the number of messages in an online conversation increases, especially for many speakers, it becomes more important to have a means to track which messages have been read already and to follow the thread of the conversation.

## Participant Selection

Another feature of CMC systems is how easily participants are selected and how easily these groupings are maintained. With e-mail, the writer must make a conscious decision regarding who to send a message to; with threaded discussion, the writer has no control or responsibility over the recipient list. When publishing on the Web, the writer typically cannot know who will read what is written. Barton (2005) argues that the open nature of blogs and other Web-based discussion environments are a means to help teach students the importance of public discussion to college composition courses. Richardson (2003) described how his high-school students used blogs to discuss a book not only with each other but also with the author. Public e-mail lists have been shown to reduce isolation among physical education educators, a finding that is likely replicable with many educators (Pennington and Graham, 2002).

An interesting result of the openness of chat rooms and discussions on the Internet is that they allow researchers access to groups that are otherwise difficult to study. A common methodology, especially among those interested in public health issues surrounding HIV/AIDS, is to survey members of online groups to learn more about their practices as a means of evaluating those forums as tools for public health education (Tikkanen and Ross, 2003; Wang and Ross, 2002).

Open groups are susceptible to unwanted communication. Whitney (2004) documents how jESSE, a discussion list for library and information science education, went from being a valuable resource to an unusable one as the percentage of unsolicited commer-

cial e-mail (spam) climbed from 13% to 75%. Perhaps even more insidious than spam are participants who join a group expressly to disrupt the conversation (Doostdar, 2004).

## Identity and Voice

Perhaps the most studied aspect of CMC is how it differs from face-to-face conversation. Communication patterns are also affected by whether participants' identities are known, anonymous, or pseudonymous. These variables have dramatic impacts on how people communicate but are sometimes not explicitly considered in research designs or their evaluation.

Subrahmanyam et al. (2004) were interested in studying developmental issues of sexuality and identity and found that anonymity allowed girls in an adult-monitored teen chat room to be sexually aggressive in ways that are uncommon in environments that are not anonymous. Panyametheekul and Herring (2003) reported similar findings regarding female empowerment in a Thai chat room. In both cases, the social mediator's anonymity, rather than the technical affordances of the medium, is what most affects the discussion. Group conversations in large classes where not all students know each other seem to maintain some of these characteristics of freer expression (Collins, 1996).

Studying how relationships are formed face to face vs. in CMC, Tidwell and Walther (2002) assigned mixed-gender pairs using either CMC or face-to-face discussion to either (1) get to know each other, or (2) work on a decision-making problem. Results showed that those in the CMC group were more likely to elicit and disclose personal information. Not explicitly discussed in the reporting is that, because they used e-mail accounts set up especially for the study, the CMC participants maintained their anonymity while those in the face-to-face condition did not. This additional variable likely not only contributed to the participants' sharing more personal information but also increased the need for requesting some personal information. As O'Connor and Ross (2004) pointed out, a common question in chat rooms is *a/s/l* (age, sex, location), but such a question is superfluous or rude in most face-to-face contexts. Anonymity is a major social factor affecting how we communicate.

In activities where anonymity is not an issue, online chat can provide affordances similar to those for face-to-face chat; for example, online dyads working collaboratively have been found to perform better than their counterparts working alone (Uribe et al., 2003), just as is the case in face-to-face dyads (Schwartz, 1995). Jensen et al. (2002) allowed students to chat while taking online tests. Another group who got random members' grades rather than their own was significantly more likely to use this tool to help see that everyone did well on the test.

## Group Text Production

A new type of communication that exists primarily online is the concept of group communication, made possible by *wikis*, which are Web-based applications that allow any user to edit any page (although more elaborate permission schemes exist). Wikipedia.org is an encyclopedia with over a million pages that is produced virtually anonymously from the perspective of most readers, who are interested primarily in the information presented, not in who produced it. A problem with group work is that it is difficult to know to whom to attribute various contributions. Because wikis can track who makes changes to a document, wikis might enable groups to work together on a project while still maintaining some ownership of their individual contributions; therefore, wikis are a tool that may be very useful in tracking how groups work together. The effects of wikis on group performance are a topic for further research. At least one case study suggests that wikis can support collaborative knowledge creation and sharing (Raman et al., 2005).

## GOALS OF RESEARCH

The goals of research in computer-mediated communication are varied. Arguably all educational media research is concerned with learning, but some research has focused more explicitly on measures of learning. Another goal is to study the effects of using the technology (e.g., a test or artifact) and analyze ways in which student communications change over time. Some research focuses on how to encourage participants to embrace a new technology—for example, a case study of how to increase the use of a learning management system (Bell and Bell, 2005). Another body of research covered here is concerned with teacher professional development. Because these communication tools are often used outside of the schools, they are sometimes used, especially by social scientists, as a source of data; chat rooms, for example, have been used to study the communities of practice of various intact groups.

## Learning

Research discussed in this section is focused explicitly on connecting some type of communication with evidence of learning—via changes in the nature of discussion itself or with regard to some other factor, such as a class grade or other measure of learning. Wang et al. (2001) looked at synchronous discussion in a statistical methods of psychology course and found that the number of comments correlated strongly with learning as measured by students' grades. Discourse analysis of a week of discussion indicated that the number of responses to questions about problems or examples given in lecture was also a predictor of the course grade.

Krentler and Willis-Flurry (2005) used asynchronous discussion with six sections of an undergraduate course in marketing. The number of posts that contained at least five sentences expressing a coherent thought based on theory rather than opinion was used as a measure of technology use, and the students' grades on three exams and a project were used as a measure of learning. Increased use of the discussion board was a reliable predictor of students' grades.

Weinberger et al. (2005) asked students to analyze a case involving attribution theory. Learning was measured by expert evaluation of students' case analyses. This experimental design crossed two independent variables: use of (1) an epistemic script and (2) a social script. Epistemic scripts are designed to prestructure the learning task to encourage knowledge construction activities; note starters are an example of epistemic scripts. Social scripts are those that prescribe a structure for interaction, perhaps by assigning roles for participation; a well-known example is reciprocal teaching (Brown and Palincsar, 1989). Learning was measured before and after the intervention by having students evaluate a case. Results showed that in the context of this threaded discussion social scripts resulted in better learning results and epistemic scripts did not.

Although millions of people blog regularly outside of classrooms, making a discussion tool available to a class of students is usually not enough to get them to use it. Sometimes online discussion must be a course requirement before students will take to it (Khan, 2005). Requiring participation is often not enough; instead, it is often more effective to model or prescribe how to participate (Bryant, 2005) and integrate the discussion into the pedagogical approach (Massimo, 2003). Using course grades as a measure of learning, Ellis and Calvo (2004) found that, regardless of medium, students interested in deep, as opposed to superficial, learning learned more. Cluster analysis of surveys of Australian engineering students identified two groups, one that used discussion to understand the subject more deeply (about a third of the participants) and another that engaged only superficially (the remaining two thirds). The deep-learning group also reported treating face-to-face discussion more meaningfully. Other techniques to better connect CMC with learning include an understanding of language and literacy (Mitchell and Erickson, 2004), mentoring and taxonomy (Brescia, 2003), and scaffolding cognitive engagement (Oriogun et al., 2005).

## The Nature of Communication

Many who study computer-mediated communication are interested in the nature of communication, so often they study the communication itself or are concerned with ways to make certain kinds of communication patterns more frequent. As an example, they might use CMC to improve relationships and foster closeness (O'Sullivan et al., 2004) or to encourage reflection (Greene, 2005; Maor, 2003; Nicholson and Bond, 2003). Others have studied the various patterns of communication that occur in CMC (Jeong, 2003).

## Guiding Discussion with CMC

An unstated assumption in some CMC research is that discussion is an indicator of learning; consequently, a common theme in this research is how to engender discussion, and how to encourage particular types of communication. Gilbert and Dabbagh (2005) found that providing exemplars for discussion to facilitators, posting discussion protocols, and offering evaluation rubrics all increased meaningful discourse with graduate students in education. Working with undergraduates in psychology, Nussbaum et al. (2004) found that conversation starters increased the frequency of disagreements (the authors assumed that disagreement is a positive indicator of deeper thinking) and encouraged students to consider alternative points of view. Correlating these data with a personality survey suggests that this technique is most effective with students who are less open to new ideas and are not highly anxious. Those interested in note starters should refer to Computer-Supported Intentional Learning Environment (CSILE) (Scardamalia and Bereiter, 1994), which later became the Knowledge Forum. When Moore and Marra (2005) investigated students' co-construction of knowledge, they set up two sections of instructional design graduate students who used asynchronous discussion. One group was instructed to use a constructive argumentation approach; the other was not. Content analysis showed that both groups co-constructed knowledge, but the group without the constraints attained a higher level of knowledge building.

Mazzolini and Maddison (2003) investigated how instructor participation affected the frequency of students' posting, lengths of threads, as well as self-report of satisfaction and other affective variables in an undergraduate course in astronomy. Results showed that more frequent instructor postings did not affect the frequency of student posts but did reduce the length of threads. Professors who posted more often were judged to be more enthusiastic and knowledgeable than those who posted less frequently.

## CMC as Change Agent

Some researchers use technology as a fulcrum to push reform. Sometimes merely adding online discussion to a face-to-face class is enough to redefine authority and voice (Merryfield, 2006), change classroom practices relating to honoring diverse cultural perspectives (Maher and Jacob, 2006), or change classroom discourse patterns (Wickstrom, 2003).

## Investigating Other Domains Using CMC

Increasingly, CMC is used by those who have not traditionally used or studied these tools. Woodruff et al. (2001) took advantage of the fact that many teenagers have access to computers and found that a virtual-reality chat room was a viable means to counsel a group of high-risk teenagers in smoking cessation. Others have investigated the psychological effects of using CMC. Morgan and Cotten (2003) surveyed 500 college freshmen and found that using communication tools such as e-mail and instant messaging was associated with decreased depression; however, students who spent more time using the Internet for other activities such as shopping, gaming, or research were more likely to exhibit depressive symptoms. Beebe et al. (2004), on the other hand, found a link between the chat-room use of high-school students and psychological distress and risky behaviors. Internet-based CMC tools can also provide public datasets that can provide insights regarding various groups of people. Mazur (2005) used blogs intended for teenagers in an undergraduate course on adolescence as a window into the lives of teenagers to help college students better understand adolescents. Surveys of students in the course suggested that using blogs in this way increased students' understanding of adolescent issues and was an effective pedagogical technique.

## Teacher Training and Professional Development

A frequent topic of educational communications research is teacher training. Asynchronous tools enable students to participate regardless of location, which makes them good for enabling teachers to have conversations about their practice (Geer and Hamill, 2003;

Jetton, 2003; Reynolds, 2002; Singer and Zeni, 2004). Devlin-Scherer and Daly (2001) asked student teachers to use asynchronous discussion to share their internship experiences outside the limited class time. Goldstein and Freedman (2003) used student journals to identify and resolve problems with how their student teachers were interacting with their students and their parents.

## SUMMARY

Computer-mediated communication (CMC) is becoming increasingly commonplace in education. This chapter began by pointing out which features a particular educational intervention is using to provide a means to better align the tool chosen with the activities that it must support. CMC environments are used for a variety of purposes in educational environments, from duplicating or supplementing classroom discourse to providing a broader audience for student work. CMC is a current subject of research that is looking into how CMC affects learning and evaluating whether or not discussion is evidence of learning. It is also being applied as a means for research when it can provide access to populations otherwise difficult to locate or can serve as a convenient means of collecting data.

## REFERENCES

Barton, M. D. (2005). The future of rational-critical debate in online public spheres. *Comput. Composition*, 22(2), 177–190.

Beebe, T. J., Asche, S. E., Harrison, P. A., and Quinlan, K. B. (2004). Heightened vulnerability and increased risk-taking among adolescent chat room users: results from a statewide school survey. *J. Adolesc. Health*, 35(2), 116–123.

Bell, M. and Bell, W. (2005). It's installed … now get on with it! Looking beyond the software to the cultural change. *Br. J. Educ. Technol.*, 36(4), 643–656.

Brescia, W. (2003). A support taxonomy for developing online discussions. *J. Public Affairs Educ.*, 9(4), 289–298.

Brown, A. L. and Palincsar, A. S. (1989). Guided, cooperative learning and individual knowledge acquisition. In *Knowing, Learning, and Instruction: Essays in Honor of Robert Glaser*, edited by L. B. Resnick, pp. 393–451. Hillsdale, NJ: Lawrence Erlbaum Associates.*

Bryant, B. K. (2005). Electronic discussion sections: a useful tool in teaching large university classes. *Teaching Psychol.*, 32(4), 271–275.

Clark, H. H. and Brennan, S. E. (1991). Grounding in communication. In *Perspectives on Socially Shared Cognition*, edited by J. M. Levine and S. D. Teasley, pp. 127–149. Washington, D.C.: American Psychological Association.

Clark, R. E. (1983). Reconsidering research on learning from media. *Rev. Educ. Res.*, 53(4), 445–459.

Clark, R. E. (1994). Media will never influence learning. *Educ. Technol. Res. Dev.*, 42(2), 21–29.*

Collins, A., Greeno, J. G., and Resnick, L. B. (1994). Learning environments. In *International Encyclopedia of Education*, 2nd ed., edited by T. Husen and T. N. Postlewaite, pp. 3297–3302. Oxford: Pergamon.*

Collins, M. (1996). A successful experiment with an electronic bulletin board in a large class. *J. Coll. Sci. Teaching*, 26, 189–191.

Cuban, L. (1986). *Teachers and Machines: The Classroom Use of Technology Since 1920*. New York: Teachers College Press.*

Davidson-Shivers, G. V., Muilenburg, L. Y., and Tanner, E. J. (2001). How do students participate in synchronous and asynchronous online discussions? *J. Educ. Comput. Res.*, 25(4), 351–366.

Devlin-Scherer, R. and Daly, J. (2001). Living in the present tense: student teaching telecommunications connect theory and practice. *J. Technol. Teacher Educ.*, 9(4), 617–634.

Doostdar, A. (2004). 'The vulgar spirit of blogging': on language, culture, and power in Persian Weblogestan. *Am. Anthropol.*, 106(4), 651–662.

Ellis, R. and Calvo, R. (2004). Learning through discussions in blended environments. *Educ. Media Int.*, 41(3), 263–274.

Geer, C. H. and Hamill, L. B. (2003). Using technology to enhance collaboration between special education and general education majors. *TechTrends*, 47(3), 26–29.

Gilbert, P. K. and Dabbagh, N. (2005). How to structure online discussions for meaningful discourse: a case study. *Br. J. Educ. Technol.*, 36(1), 5–18.

Goldstein, L. S. and Freedman, D. (2003). Challenges enacting caring teacher education. *J. Teacher Educ.*, 54(5), 441–454.

Greene, H. C. (2005). Theory Meets Practice in Teacher Education: A Case Study of a Computer-Mediated Community of Learners. Ph.D. dissertation. Blacksburg, VA: Virginia Polytechnic University.

Honeycutt, L. (2001). Comparing e-mail and synchronous conferencing in online peer response. *Written Commun.*, 18(1), 26–60.

Jensen, M., Johnson, D. W., and Johnson, R. T. (2002). Impact of positive interdependence during electronic quizzes on discourse and achievement. *J. Educ. Res.*, 95(3), 161–166.

Jeong, A. (2003). The sequential analysis of group interaction and critical thinking in online threaded discussions. *Am. J. Distance Educ.*, 17(1), 25–43.*

Jetton, T. L. (2003). Using computer-mediated discussion to facilitate preservice teachers' understanding of literacy assessment and instruction. *J. Res. Technol. Educ.*, 36(2), 171–191.

Khan, S. (2005). Listservs in the college science classroom: evaluating participation and 'richness' in computer-mediated discourse. *J. Technol. Teacher Educ.*, 13(2), 325–351.

Kozma, R. B. (1994). Will media influence learning? Reframing the debate. *Educ. Technol. Res. Dev.*, 42(2) 7–19.*

Krentler, K. A. and Willis-Flurry, L. A. (2005). Does technology enhance actual student learning? The case of online discussion boards. *J. Educ. Bus.*, 80(6), 316–321.

Maher, M. A. and Jacob, E. (2006). Peer computer conferencing to support teachers' reflection during action research. *J. Technol. Teacher Educ.*, 14(1), 127–150.

Maor, D. (2003). The teacher's role in developing interaction and reflection in an online learning community. *Educ. Media Int.*, 40(1/2), 127–137.

Massimo, V. S. (2003). Integrating the WebCT discussion feature into social work courses: an assessment focused on pedagogy and practicality. *J. Technol. Hum. Serv.*, 22(1), 49–64.

Mazur, E. (2005). Online and writing: teen blogs as mines of adolescent data. *Teaching Psychol.*, 32(3), 180–182.

Mazzolini, M. and Maddison, S. (2003). Sage, guide or ghost? The effect of instructor intervention on student participation in online discussion forums. *Comput. Educ.*, 40(3), 237–253.

Merryfield, M. M. (2006). WebCT, PDS, and democratic spaces in teacher education. *Int. J. Soc. Educ.*, 21(1), 73–94.

Mitchell, J. and Erickson, G. (2004). Constituting conventions of practice: an analysis of academic literacy and computer-mediated communication. *J. Educ. Thought*, 38(1), 19–42.

Moore, J. L. and Marra, R. M. (2005). A comparative analysis of online discussion participation protocols. *J. Res. Technol. Educ.*, 38(2), 191–212.

Morgan, C. and Cotten, S. (2003). The relationship between internet activities and depressive symptoms in a sample of college freshmen. *CyberPsychol. Behav.*, 6(2), 133–142.

Newhagen, J. and Rafaeli, S. (1996). Why communication researchers should study the internet: a dialogue. *J. Commun.*, 46(1), 4–13.

Nicholson, S. A. and Bond, N. (2003). Collaborative reflection and professional community building: an analysis of preservice teachers' use of an electronic discussion board. *J. Technol. Teacher Educ.*, 11(2), 259–279.

Nussbaum, E. M., Hartley, K., and Sinatra, G. M. (2004). Personality interactions and ECT3 27 scaffolding in on-line discussions. *J. Educ. Comput. Res.*, 30(1/2), 113–137.

O'Connor, S. and Ross, A. (2004). WebCT role-playing: immediacy versus e-mediacy in learning environments. *Learn. Environ. Res.*, 7(2), 183–201.

Oriogun, P. K., Ravenscroft, A., and Cook, J. (2005). Validating an approach to examining cognitive engagement within online groups. *Am. J. Distance Educ.*, 19(4), 197–214.

O'Sullivan, P. B., Hunt, S. K., and Lippert, L. R. (2004). Mediated immediacy: a language of affiliation in a technological age. *J. Lang. Soc. Psychol.*, 23(4), 464–490.

Panyametheekul, S. and Herring, S. C. (2003). Gender and turn allocation in a Thai chat room. *J. Comput. Mediated Commun.*, 9(1), 224–251.

Pennington, T. and Graham, G. (2002). Exploring the influence of a physical education listserv on K-12 physical educators. *J. Technol. Teacher Educ.*, 10(3), 383–405.

Raman, M., Ryan, T., and Olfman, L. (2005). Designing knowledge management systems for teaching and learning with wild technology. *J. Inform. Syst. Educ.*, 16(3), 311–320.

Reynolds, K. M. (2002). The effectiveness of a listserv for teacher preparation. *J. Educ. Technol. Syst.*, 31(1), 71–87.

Richardson, W. (2003). Blogging on. *Principal Leadership (High School Ed.)*, 4(3), 61–64.

Romiszowski, A. and Mason, R. (2004). Computer-mediated communication. In *Handbook of Research for Educational Communications and Technology*, 2nd ed., edited by D. H. Jonassen, pp. 397–432. Mahwah, NJ: Lawrence Erlbaum Associates.*

Russel, T. (2001). *The No Significant Difference Phenomenon*. Denver, CO: The International Distance Education Certification Center (http://www.nosignificantdifference.org).

Scardamalia, M. and Bereiter, C. (1994). Computer support for knowledge-building communities. *J. Learn. Sci.*, 3(3), 265–283.*

Schwartz, D. L. (1995). The emergence of abstract representations in dyad problem solving. *J. Learn. Sci.*, 4(3), 321–354.

Singer, N. R. and Zeni, J. (2004). Building bridges: creating an online conversation community for preservice teachers. *Engl. Educ.*, 37(1), 30–49.

Subrahmanyam, K., Greenfield, P. M., and Tynes, B. (2004). Constructing sexuality and identity in an online teen chat room. *J. Appl. Dev. Psychol.*, 25(6), 651–666.

Tidwell, L. C. and Walther, J. B. (2002). Computer-mediated communication effects on disclosure, impressions, and interpersonal evaluations: getting to know one another a bit at a time. *Hum. Commun. Res.*, 28(3), 317–348.

Tikkanen, R. and Ross, M. W. (2003). Technological tearoom trade: characteristics of Swedish men visiting gay Internet chat rooms. *AIDS Educ. Prev.*, 15(2), 122–132.

Uribe, D., Klein, J. D., and Sullivan, H. J. (2003). The effect of computer-mediated collaborative learning on solving ill-defined problems. *Educ. Technol. Res. Dev.*, 51(1), 5–19.*

Wang, A. Y., Newlin, M. H., and Tucker, T. L. (2001). A discourse analysis of online classroom chats: predictors of cyber-student performance. *Teaching Psychol.*, 28(3), 222–226.

Wang, Q. and Ross, M. W. (2002). Differences between chat room and e-mail sampling approaches in Chinese men who have sex with men. *AIDS Educ. Prev.*, 14(5), 361–366.

Weinberger, A., Ertl, B., and Fischer, F. (2005). Epistemic and social scripts in computer-supported collaborative learning. *Instruct. Sci.*, 33(1), 1–30.

Whitney, G. (2004). Messages not sent to jESSE: a study crushed by its own subject. *J. Educ. Library Inform. Sci.*, 45(4), 364–369.

Wickstrom, C. D. (2003). A 'funny' thing happened on the way to the forum. *J. Adolesc. Adult Literacy*, 46(5), 414–423.

Woodruff, S. I., Edwards, C. C., Conway, T. L., and Elliott, S. P. (2001). Pilot test of an internet virtual world chat room for rural teen smokers. *J. Adolesc. Health*, 29(4), 239–243.

* Indicates a core reference.

# 19

# K–12 Library Media Centers

*Delia Neuman*
University of Maryland, College Park, Maryland

## CONTENTS

## ABSTRACT

Since the early 20th century, public school library media centers in the United States have housed non-print educational materials. Since the middle of that century, K–12 library media specialists have designed learning experiences integrating these materials into classroom practice. For today's library media specialist, technology (both as materials and as process) is essential. Current American standards highlight instructional leadership, collaboration with teachers, and technology as the three integrating issues essential to the library media program (AASL and AECT, 1998). Much early research focused on developing and explaining the multifaceted role of the library media specialist. Until the 1990s, few studies looked at the relationship of K–12 library media programs to student learning. Since then, about two dozen studies have investigated that link. The political focus of much of this work is undeniable; concerns about the absence of library media from key national legislation related to American schooling have led to research designed to establish links between library media programs and student achievement. Similar pressures in the United Kingdom and Australia have led to comparable efforts there. Quantitative and qualitative approaches have been used to (1) demonstrate widespread correlations between high-quality library media programs and student learning, and (2) identify specific contributions of such programs. Various recent initiatives suggest an expansion of K–12 school library media research and a wider dissemination of its findings.

## KEYWORD

*Library media center:* A physical repository of instructional materials and technology resources found in most American public schools.

## INTRODUCTION

For almost 100 years, the library media center has been home to K–12 schools' emerging technology—from lantern slides to video editing equipment. For almost 50 years, the K–12 library media specialist has been expected to play a major role in helping students and teachers understand how to use the technology of the day to enhance learning. Today's library media specialist—through formally specified roles as teacher, as other teachers' partner in instructional design and delivery, as information specialist, and as administrator—is charged with "ensur[ing] that students and staff are effective users of ideas and information" (AASL and AECT, 1998, p. 6). The library media specialist achieves this mission not only through fulfilling these roles but also through promoting instructional and informational technologies as agents of learning.

In the United States, the library media specialist's dual focus on technology and instruction has been chronicled through successive editions of national standards and guidelines for the field—especially since the publication of *Standards for School Library Programs* (AASL, 1960), which first introduced both the term "audiovisual materials" and the library media specialist's role as an instructor in "library skills." *Standards for School Media Programs* (AASL and NEA, 1969), the first set of standards that saw the imprint of AECT (which was then DAVI), and *Media Programs: District and School* (AASL and AECT, 1975) promoted the role of the library media specialist as an instructional designer. *Information Power: Guidelines for School Library Media Programs* (AASL and AECT, 1988) brought the evolving responsibilities of the library media specialist into the electronic age, while the current national standards—*Information Power: Building Partnerships for Learning* (AASL and AECT, 1998)—highlight "leadership, [instructional] collaboration [with teachers], and technology" as the three integrating issues that "are integral to every aspect of the library media program and every component of the library media specialist's role" (p. 49). *School Library Guidelines* (IFLA/UNESCO, 2002) notes that "[t]eachers and librarians [should] work together in order to … develop, instruct, and evaluate pupils' learning across the curriculum" (p. 12) by using the resources of a library that "must provide access to all necessary electronic, computer, and audiovisual equipment" (p. 8).

The K–12 library media field has thus tried to position itself at the nexus of technology, information, and instructional design in the schools for almost 50 years. Small (1998) provided a brief overview of this history in the United States, and Neuman (2004) provided an extensive one—including an examination of the instructional design models developed specifically for library media specialists to use in collaborating with teachers. As society has increased its demands for accountability from the schools, the library media field has increasingly stressed its contributions to student learning and has sought to demonstrate that strong K–12 library media programs are essential not only to student learning but also to student achievement in the information age.

## THE RESEARCH CONTEXT

Much of the early research in the field of school library media focused on developing and delineating the role of the library media specialist. Before the 1990s, comparatively few studies looked at the contributions of library media programs to student learning. One landmark study published in 1963, however, addressed questions that resonate even today: Mary Gaver, who is still revered by library media researchers, investigated the effectiveness of centralized library services in 271 elementary schools in 13 states (Lance, 2006):

> She compared the test scores of students in schools with classroom libraries only, those with centralized libraries run by non-librarians, and those with centralized libraries run by librarians, with predictable results. Students in schools with centralized libraries managed by qualified librarians tended to score higher [on the Iowa Test of Basic Skills] than their counterparts in schools without centralized libraries or qualified librarians.

Although Gaver's findings are confounded by several methodological difficulties—for example, the students who scored higher "had [also] received sessions in learning about library use-skills similar to those on the [library-skills section] of the exam" (Callison, in Lance, 2006)—Gaver was clearly ahead of her time in her attempt to link strong library programs to student achievement. Some 20 years later, Didier reviewed the accumulated studies that had looked at the impact of K–12 library media programs on student learning—all 38 of them—and concluded that "overall, the findings show much evidence that school library media programs can be positively related to student achievement" (Didier, 1985, p. 33).

Throughout the 1990s and into the early part of this century, school library media researchers in North America investigated a number of aspects related to library media programs and learning: resource-based learning (Eisenberg and Small, 1995), learning as process (Kuhlthau, 1993; McGregor, 1994; Pitts, 1994; Todd, 1995), and learning in electronic environments (Bilal, 2001; Fidel et al., 1999; Large et al., 1998; Neuman, 1997; Solomon, 1994). Although the Library Power Project (1998–1991), the largest project to date in the history of the K–12 library media field, focused on the development and demonstration of effective library media programs rather than specifically on the learning such programs engendered, subsequent analysis of its data revealed some limited learning effects (Kuhlthau, 1999). The chapter on the library media center in the previous edition of this *Handbook* provides an extensive overview of the research and scholarly activities undertaken during these years (Neuman, 2004). Callison (2002) also provides a comprehensive review of the research conducted during this and earlier periods. Williams and Wavell (2001) and Williams et al. (2002) provide similar reviews from a British perspective, and Lonsdale (2003) offers insights from an Australian one.

# RECENT RESEARCH

The school library media field encompasses many facets, and its researchers continue to focus on all of them: the evolving role of the library media specialist, the nature and practice of collaboration, information literacy, information searching in electronic environments, policy issues, principals' perspectives on library media specialists and their programs, etc. A review of the contents of *School Library Media Research*—the research journal of the American Association of School Librarians (AASL)—for the past 5 years reveals a potpourri of topics and treatments. A similar review of the offerings of *School Libraries Worldwide*—the research journal of the International Association of School Librarians (IASL)—reveals a similarly eclectic mix. Within this broad array, however, the relationship of library media programs to learning has emerged in recent years as the single most important research topic within the field. As Neuman (2003, p. 517) noted in a special issue of a key journal devoted to research questions for the 21st century: "The question of student learning is at the crux of all the most significant research to be done in school library media in the next decade." Driven by such factors as "the emergence of electronic information resources that highlight the relationship between learning and information use as never before and the publication of statements of learning outcomes [in information literacy] related [directly] to information use" (Neuman, 2003, p. 503), today's most visible school library media researchers both in the United States and abroad concentrate on documenting the importance of strong K–12 library media programs and their impact on student learning and achievement. Since the 1990s, over two dozen studies have looked at this link.

## The Phenomenon of the Lance Studies

Many of these investigations are known as the "Lance Studies" because they represent efforts begun by Keith Curry Lance and his colleagues at the Colorado State Library and replicated by Lance's group and others. The first in the series, published in 1993, established the methodological parameters for all the subsequent research. Lance and his colleagues used statistical modeling to assess the impact of library factors on test scores while controlling for various school and community conditions (Lance, 2006). The researchers applied correlational analysis, followed by factor analysis, followed by regression analysis to determine the relationships of 23 independent variables to students' scores on either the Iowa Tests of Basic Skills or the Tests of Achievement and Proficiency. The scores came from a nonrandom but probably representative sample of 221 public elementary and secondary schools in Colorado that had responded to a 1989 survey of library media centers; Lance et al. used 1980 U.S. Census data about the schools' communities and building-level files from the Colorado Department of Education (where Lance directs the Library Research Service) to round out the dataset. The study produced a series of results (Lance, 1994)—including the dramatic finding that "the size of a library media program, as indicated by the size of its staff and collection, is the best school predictor of academic achievement" (p. 172). In other words, "The size of the school library staff and collection explained 21% of the variation in seventh-grade Iowa Tests of Basic Skills reading scores, while controlling for socioeconomic conditions" (Scholastic Library Publishing, 2006, p. 8).

Not surprisingly, the first of the Lance Studies, known as the "Colorado Study," dominated research discussions in the library media community. After a period of initial excitement, however, questions about its methodology—the small sample size, nonrandomness of the sample, nonexperimental design, and reliance on existing (rather than original) data—seemed to limit its influence for several years. By the end of the decade, however, political factors had intervened. No Child Left Behind, the landmark national educational legislation enacted in the United States in 2002, failed to mention school library media programs; many states failed to include information literacy in their standardized tests. Alarmed by this marginalization of key library media content and witnessing a concomitant drop in the number of library media programs in schools across the country, the field saw a pressing need to demonstrate the relationship of library media programs to student achievement. In at least 17 states, organizations of library media specialists and other interested stakeholders commissioned Lance's group and others to demonstrate that relationship. The earliest of the state reports was published in 1999. Interest crested in 2002 and again in 2003 with reports from four more states each year (Scholastic Library Publishing, 2006).

The sheer number of these reports as well as the widespread geographic distribution of the study sites captured the field's attention once again. Taken as a whole, these reports paint a compelling national picture of the relationship of strong K–12 school library media programs and student learning. Although some of the work is still in progress, the findings of the 14 reports released by March 2005 show that the relationship between school library programs and test scores cannot be explained away by non-library factors or conditions (Lance, 2006). Refinements of the original methodology by Lance's group and by various other researchers (e.g., greater numbers of schools, original as well as available data, more extensive and detailed questions, and even visits to school library media centers) provide even stronger evidence of the relationship. Lance (2006) argued strenuously against those who would dismiss all this evidence as merely correlational:

> The repeated identification of links between libraries and test scores that cannot be explained away by other school and community conditions seems to me to offer considerable evidence for a cause-and-effect argument. If the correlation is spurious, why has it been found in multiple states over time? If there are other school or community conditions that consistently explain away library–test score links, I am unaware of them.

Lance had become a celebrity in the school library media field, keynoting many conferences and presenting an overview of the findings at the White House Conference on School Libraries in 2002. By May 2005, a Web-based survey he had designed to determine the impact of the studies gathered information from 501 respondents from 36 states, who reported using the results to advocate for library media programs by sharing the research with principals (81%), teachers (66%), and others. Perhaps more importantly, respondents reported spending "more time collaborating with teachers, teaching information literacy skills to students (62%) … identifying materials for teachers (60%) … and spending more time teaching collaboratively with teachers (48%)" (Lance, 2006). Clearly, the phenomenon of the Lance research stream has had a major impact not only on documenting the value of strong K–12 library media programs but also on developing such programs.

## International Insights

The influence of the Lance Studies has extended well beyond the borders of North America to influence research in other parts of the world. For example, research reviews conducted for the Scottish Council for Museums, Archives, and Libraries on the impact of the school library resource center (SLRC) in both primary and secondary schools in England cited Lance's work (Williams and Wavell, 2001) and suggested that it can be applied to the English context (Williams et al., 2002). Similarly, a critical desktop review of research conducted in Australia noted that "the most influential body of research into the impact of school libraries on student achievement is that of Keith Curry Lance and his colleagues in the United States" (Lonsdale, 2003, p. 12).

Although these reviews cited the importance of Lance and his colleagues, they also staked out territory that is especially important in their own contexts. Williams and Wavell (2001) sought to gain an understanding of "the broader learning experience" (p. 4) in Scottish secondary schools by conducting focus groups and case studies designed to assess "teachers', students', and librarians' perceptions of how the [learning resource center] can contribute to learning," to identify "learning experiences related to the [resource center]," and to investigate "indicators to be used as evidence of learning and examine[d] the process of assessing the of the impact of the [learning resource center] on learning" (p. i). Through these focus groups, Williams and Wavell (2001) identified a number of perceptions of impact shared by all three groups—from the acquisition of information and information skills to the development of the ability to work both independently and interpersonally; from the case studies, they drew "learning themes of motivation, progression, independence, and interaction" (p. ii). Suggestions for moving ahead on the basis of their findings include a much more intense focus on the broader context they sought to address: "the need to look beyond the immediate SLRC for impact … across learning contexts, beyond the immediate situation, and over appropriate timescales" (p. 4).

The review by Williams et al. (2002) of research into the SLRC's role in primary schools built on ideas and methods used a decade earlier by Streatfield and

Markless (1994). The title of that early report to the British Library Research and Development Department set the context for the more recent study as well: *Invisible Learning? The Contribution of School Libraries to Teaching and Learning*. Both pieces argue that SLRCs do in fact contribute to student learning but in ways that are difficult to measure. They also suggest research into the impact of various models of library media service provision—for example, flexible or fixed scheduling, various levels and activities of staff, kinds of instructional and collaborative activities—on student learning. The question of scheduling has been an issue in the American K–12 library media field for years: Should library media programs be delivered through a fixed schedule, in which classes come to the facility for predetermined periods each week, or through a flexible schedule, in which individuals and groups come to the facility as needed for specific research projects collaboratively planned by the teacher and the library media specialist? By linking research on student achievement to the issue of scheduling, both reports suggest an important question for future research.

The Australian review, completed over a 4-week period for the Australian Library Association, included both Australian and international research conducted since 1990 and concluded that "existing research shows that school libraries can have a positive impact, whether measured in terms of reading scores, literacy or learning more generally, on student achievement" (Lonsdale, 2003, p. 30). Specific details related to that general conclusion echo insights provided by Didier (1985) and expanded more recently by Lance (Scholastic Library Publishing, 2005/2006). Lonsdale (2003, p. 2) suggested, further, that action research and evidence-based practice are critical to school libraries in the future:

> In general, the literature confirms the need for local, evidence-based practice if the roles of the school library and teacher librarian in student learning are to be valued in the way that the research suggests they should be valued. Such research is an important strategic tool for raising the profile and prestige of library professionals and for reinforcing in the minds of policy-makers and school communities the crucial contribution that school libraries can make to student achievement.

## The Ohio Study

Despite the influence of the Lance Studies, Lance himself noted that the Colorado model has been exhausted and that it is time to develop new directions for school library media impact research (Lance, 2006). Lance's personal concern is to devise research methods that will align school library media research with the experimental designs favored by the U.S. Department of Education, but the suggestions for contextual research noted above as well as the most prominent study in the United States today involve a qualitative rather than a quantitative approach. The Ohio Study, conducted under the auspices of Rutgers University's Center for International Scholarship in School Libraries (CISSL; pronounced "sizzle"), involved "39 effective school libraries across Ohio ... 13,123 students in grades 3 to 12 and 879 faculty. The research study sought to understand how students benefit from school libraries" (Todd, 2004, p. 1).

The focus, then, was to identify effective libraries and to ask those who use them to rate the dimensions of their effectiveness. Researchers received nominations for the schools to be included, and their choices were validated by an expert panel. They collected data through two Web-based surveys, one for students and one for faculty. Each survey included the same 48 items (adjusted to reflect the nature of the respondent) in seven blocks: (1) finding and getting information; (2) using information to complete school work; (3) supporting school work in general; (4) using computers in the library, elsewhere in the school, and at home; (5) supporting general reading interests; (6) helping with information tasks outside the school; and (7) supporting general school achievement. Respondents used a five-part Likert scale to rate how helpful the library was (most, quite, some, a little, and does not apply) with regard to each statement. Statements were a mix of the cognitive (e.g., "The school library has helped me find different opinions about my topics") and the affective (e.g., "The school library has helped me feel better about finding information"). Each survey also included an open-ended question designed to contextualize the responses provided through the surveys.

Not surprisingly, the results were overwhelmingly positive (Todd, 2004, p. 2):

> Statistically 99.44% of the sample (13,050 students) indicated that the school library and its services, including roles of school librarians, have helped them in some way, regardless of how much, with their learning as it relates to the 48 statements.

Faculty were even more positive than students: Their mean responses were higher than the student means in all seven blocks. Overall, the *helps* were most helpful at the elementary level, where students encounter information-literacy concepts for the first time and decreased in ranking as students moved through their school years. The *helps* that were "ranked highest by students" involved information technology and achieved high scores in whatever blocks they appeared

(Todd, 2004, p. 5). Two of them received higher percentages of "most helpful" ratings than any other items on the instrument: "Computers have helped me find information inside and outside of the school library" (49.0%) and "Computers in the school library have helped me do my school work better" (41.6%).

The Ohio study was responsive to the K–12 library media field's perceived need to demonstrate its relevance to student achievement, and it has corresponding limitations. It involved a dataset that was "very suburban with over 90% white population" and accepted "only positive testimony from teachers and students … so that conclusions would emphasize the constructive role the library could play in providing services with a staff of qualified librarians" (Callison, in Lance, 2006). In addition, it relied exclusively on self-reported data collected through a website—a methodology that might well present an irresistible temptation for mischief to middle- and high-school students, especially as they get to the end of a 49-item instrument. Nevertheless, the results of the study are informative about the specific ways in which high-quality library media programs can support student learning. Its widely publicized major conclusion "that an effective school library, led by a credentialed library media specialist who has a clearly defined role in information-centered pedagogy, plays a critical role in facilitating student learning for building knowledge" (Scholastic Library Publishing, 2006, p. 17) has evidentiary backing as well as political force.

## CURRENT ISSUES

Despite all the research suggesting that a comprehensive, integrated school library media program is closely associated with increased learning, many educators still think of school library media programs as a luxury—worthwhile but not integral to the curriculum or to student achievement—especially in the areas highlighted in the United States by federal legislation and covered by most states' standardized tests. Indeed, many jurisdictions classify school library media as a specialty area like music and physical education, making school library media programs especially vulnerable in an era of tightening budgets and increasing attention to standardized test scores. Anecdotal evidence abounds about library media centers being closed and positions either abolished or effectively cut in half as individual library media specialists are deployed to serve more than one school. The pressures in other parts of the world may be less immediate and less visible, but British and Australian researchers also cite the need for "demonstrating the value of, and

attaining appropriate recognition for, the work of the SLRC, an issue of concern to the Information and Library Science (ILS) profession world-wide" (Williams and Wavell, 2002, p. 4).

Facing a continuing threat of marginalization or elimination, the K–12 library media field continues to turn to research as the master key that will unlock the barriers to a full appreciation of the importance of library media programs and open the doors to fully realized, high-quality programs throughout the educational system. Scholastic Library Publishing has released two editions of a 20-page Research Foundation Paper entitled *School Libraries Work!* (2005/2006), drawing together findings from recent United States studies into a glossy public-relations brochure that has been widely circulated. A 2005 summit convened by *School Library Journal*, the major North American magazine for practitioners in the field, "ended with a loud call for more scholarly research into the impact of school libraries on learning" (Glick, 2005, p. 11) and expressed a yearning "for a way to demonstrate the complex ways in which school libraries contribute to student learning and growth, something beyond the grasp of standardized tests" (p. 12). Summiteers identified research into teacher–librarian collaboration and action research undertaken by practitioners as promising avenues for demonstrating school library media programs' contributions to student learning.

Attendees also recognized the importance of communicating their work to the broader educational world, noting that "a large body of research … already exists" (Glick, 2005, p. 12) but that it has not been available to or accepted by those outside the school library media field. This isolation has been a cause of concern for years, leading to repeated calls for school library media researchers to publish and present in allied fields. As Callison (2002, p. 362) noted, "Until research strands … move into a broader research framework, it is likely that findings, no matter how dramatic or significant, will remain dormant without causing change." Neuman (2004) discussed the situation in depth and suggested that a number of current educational trends—particularly the acceptance of the constructivist philosophy, the ubiquity of information and information technology, and the necessity for children to learn how to use information as a tool for learning in all the content areas—converge into a fruitful venue for advancing interest in and communication of school library media research.

Two current developments suggest that the field is indeed moving ahead, both in its research agenda and in its efforts to broaden its audience. CISSL, founded by prominent school library media researchers Carol Kuhlthau and Ross Todd in 2003, is committed to establishing a firm foundation for national and international research in the field. In 2005, CISSL hosted a research symposium (held at the headquarters of Scholastic Publishing) that brought together many of the field's premier researchers. In the spring of 2006, CISSL announced the formation of the CISSL Virtual Research Community, an open-source website at which five of those researchers lead online discussions around some of the major themes that emerged during the symposium held in 2005: collaboration, learning theory, the nature of research, organizational change, leadership, inquiry learning, and translating research into practice. CISSL plans to open the site to the K–12 school library media community at large and, eventually, to anyone who wants to participate.

Also in the spring of 2006, the American Educational Research Association voted to accept a new Special Interest Group (SIG) for school library media researchers. The new Research, Education, Information, and School Libraries SIG plans to bring school library media research to the programs and publications of the largest educational research association in the world. The effort is in its early stages, but it suggests a promising development in the expansion of the research and issues of the K–12 library media field into the broader realm of educational research and practice.

## CONCLUDING REMARKS

The political focus of much of the recent work in school library media—both in the United States and elsewhere—is undeniable: Concerns about the dwindling profile of the field have created a research agenda that often seems more about proving a foregone conclusion than about discovering new knowledge. Nevertheless, recent research has in fact produced compelling evidence that library media programs are related to various kinds of student achievement. In addition, a number of recent studies have resulted in a deeper understanding of the specific contributions of strong library media programs to student learning. Over the past decade, both quantitative and qualitative approaches have been used to gather this evidence.

The focus of this research reflects the culmination of the school library media field's evolution: No longer content to be seen as overseers of a collection and distribution point for materials—tucked away at the end of the hall—today's K–12 library media professionals have staked a claim to centrality in the schools' most important mission. Although the field still places a high priority on its traditional mission of promoting reading and a love of literature, years of research attention to its role in promoting learning through the use of technology and instructional design have led to an understanding that library media programs play an essential role in student learning in the information age. In the past decade, as the United States and other nations have increased their demands for accountability from schools—evidence that learning has actually occurred—the school library media field has increasingly recognized the importance of demonstrating to other educators, to parents, and to policymakers that strong library media programs are demonstrably essential to student achievement as well as to "the authentic [information-based] learning that modern education seeks to promote" (AASL and AECT, 1998, p. 2). Now looking at research as a political as well as an intellectual endeavor, the modern K–12 school library media field has indeed come of age.

## REFERENCES

American Association of School Librarians (AASL). (1960). *Standards for School Library Programs*. Chicago, IL: American Library Association.

American Association of School Librarians (AASL) and Association for Educational Communications and Technology (AECT). (1975). *Media Programs: District and School*. Chicago, IL, and Washington, D.C.: AASL and AECT.

American Association of School Librarians (AASL) and Association for Educational Communications and Technology (AECT). (1988). *Information Power: Guidelines for School Library Media Programs*. Chicago, IL, and Washington, D.C.: AASL and AECT.

American Association of School Librarians (AASL) and Association for Educational Communications and Technology (AECT). (1998). *Information Power: Building Partnerships for Learning*. Chicago, IL: American Library Association.*

American Association of School Librarians (AASL) and Department of Audiovisual Instruction, National Education Association (NEA). (1969). *Standards for School Media Programs*. Chicago, IL: American Library Association.

Bilal, D. (2001). Children's use of Yahooligans! Web search engine. II. Cognitive, physical, and affective behaviors on research tasks. *J. Am. Soc. Inform. Sci.*, 52(2), 118–136.

Callison, D. (2002). The twentieth-century school library media research record. In *Encyclopedia of Library and Information Science*, Vol. 71 (Suppl. 34), edited by A. Kent and C. M. Hall, pp. 339–369. New York: Marcel Dekker.*

Didier, E. K. (1985). An overview of research on the impact of school library media programs on student achievement. *School Library Media Q.*, 14(1), 33–36.*

Eisenberg, M. B. and Small, R. V. (1995). Information-based education: an investigation of the nature and role of information attributes in education. *Inform. Process. Manage.*, 29(2), 263–275.

Fidel, R., Davies, R. K., Douglass, M. H., Holder, J. K., Hopkins, C. J., Kushner, E. J., Miyagishima, B. K., and Toney, C. D. (1999). A visit to the information mall: Web searching behaviors of high school students. *J. Am. Soc. Inform. Sci.*, 50(1), 24–37.

Gaver, M. (1963). *Effectiveness of Centralized Library Service in Elementary Schools*. New Brunswick, NJ: Graduate Library School at Rutgers, The State University of New Jersey.

Glick, A. (2005). More research, please. *School Library J.*, 52(6), 11–12.

International Federation of Library Associations and Institutions (IFLA). (2002). *IFLA/UNESCO School Library Guidelines*, http://www.ifla/org/VII/s11/pubs/school-guidelines.htm.*

Kuhlthau, C. C. (1993). *Seeking Meaning: A Process Approach to Library and Information Services*. Norwood, NJ: Ablex.

Kuhlthau, C. C. (1999). Student learning in the library: what Library Power librarians say. *School Libraries Worldwide*, 5(2), 80–96.*

Lance, K. C. (1994). The impact of school library media centers on academic achievement. *School Library Media Q.*, 22(3), 167–170.*

Lance, K. C. (2006). Enough already? Blazing new trails for school library research: an interview [by D. Callison] with Keith Curry Lance. *School Library Media Research*, http://www.ala.org/ala/aasl/aaslpubsandjournals/slmrb.*

Large, A., Beheshti, J., and Breuleux, A. (1998). Information seeking in a multimedia environment by primary school students. *Library Inform. Sci. Res.*, 20(4), 343–376.

Lonsdale, M. (2003). *Impact of School Libraries on Student Achievement: A Review of the Research*. Victoria: Australian Council for Educational Research (http://www.asla.org.au/research).*

McGregor, J. H. (1994). Cognitive processes and the use of information: a qualitative study of higher-order thinking skills used in the research process by students in a gifted program. In *School Library Media Annual 1994*, edited by C. C. Kuhlthau, pp. 124–133. Englewood, CO: Libraries Unlimited.

Neuman, D. (1997). Learning and the digital library. *Library Trends*, 45(4), 687–707.

Neuman, D. (2003). Research in school library media for the next decade: polishing the diamond. *Library Trends*, 51(4), 508–524.*

Neuman, D. (2004). The library media center: touchstone for instructional design and technology in the schools. In *Handbook of Research on Educational Communications and Technology*, 2nd ed., edited by D. H. Jonassen, pp. 499–522. Mahwah, NJ: Lawrence Erlbaum Associates.*

Pitts, J. M. (1994). Personal Understandings and Mental Models of Information: A Qualitative Study of Factors Associated with the Information Seeking and Use of Adolescents. Ph.D. dissertation. Tallahassee: Florida State University.

Scholastic Library Publishing. (2005/2006). *School Libraries Work!* New York: Scholastic Library Publishing.*

Small, R. V. (1998). School librarianship and instructional design: a history intertwined. In *The Emerging School Library Media Center: Historical Issues and Perspectives*, edited by K. H. Latrobe, pp. 227–237. Englewood, CO: Libraries Unlimited.

Solomon, P. (1994). Children's information retrieval behavior: a case study of an OPAC. *J. Am. Soc. Inform. Sci.*, 44(5), 2245–2263.

Streatfield, D. and Markless, S. (1994). *Invisible Learning? The Contribution of School Libraries to Teaching and Learning*, Library and Information Research Report 98. London: British Library Research and Development Department.

Todd, R. J. (1995). Integrated information skills instruction: does it make a difference? *School Library Media Q.*, 23(2), 133–138.

Todd, R. J. (2004). *Student Learning through Ohio School Libraries*. Columbus, OH: Ohio Educational Library Media Association.*

Williams, D. and Wavell, C. (2001). *The Impact of the School Library Resource Centre on Learning*, Library and Information Commission Research Report 112. Aberdeen: Robert Gordon University (www.rgu.ac.uk/files/SLRCreport.pdf).*

Williams, D., Coles, L., and Wavell, C. (2002). *Impact of School Library Services on Achievement and Learning in Primary Schools: Critical Literature Review*. Aberdeen: Robert Gordon University (www.rgu.ac.uk/files/ACF1C8D.pdf).*

---

* Indicates a core reference.

# 20

# Technology-Based Knowledge Systems

*Ian Douglas*
Florida State University, Tallahassee, Florida

## CONTENTS

## ABSTRACT

Knowledge is collected and organized into technology-based systems in various ways to support learning and performance. Four main types of systems are identified under the general term of *knowledge systems*: (1) expert or knowledge-based, (2) knowledge management, (3) knowledge communities, and (4) hybrid systems that combine elements of the other types. Expert systems are computer programs that use knowledge derived from human experts to provide guidance to novices. A number of these systems have been adapted to assist in learning. Expert systems use captured knowledge to help a computer program provide assistance to a user. In knowledge management systems, the knowledge is captured and organized for direct access by the user. The third type of system is aimed at facilitating direct human-to-human communication of knowledge and includes research that comes under the categories of communities of practice or knowledge communities. This area also includes informal knowledge sharing networks that emerge through such technologies as instant messaging. This chapter highlights common research issues that cut across the three approaches, including how knowledge is derived from human sources; how knowledge is encoded in a machine readable form; how collections of digital knowledge are organized using taxonomies, metadata, and ontology; and, finally, knowledge quality assurance.

## KEYWORDS

*Knowledge-based system*: A computer program that can reason, based on a database of knowledge acquired from a human expert (also known as an expert system).

*Knowledge communities:* Technology focused on bringing communities of people together to both generate and share knowledge about a common interest.

*Knowledge management:* A collection of technologies and organizational processes aimed at capturing, disseminating, and archiving performance-related knowledge within an organization.

## INTRODUCTION

Before we begin to examine the area of knowledge systems, we need to establish what we mean by *knowledge*, and in particular how it is distinguished from data or information. A number of philosophical discussions on this distinction have been published—see, for example, Ackoff (1989), Davenport and Prusak (1998), Quigley and Debons (1999)—but they are beyond the scope of this chapter. As a basic working model, we can say that data are the basic elements of memory represented in symbols. Information is data that have been given meaning by way of a relational connection to other data. Knowledge arises from information that has been collected in such a way as to usefully inform action.

Knowledge is often broken down into further categories, such as: (1) *declarative* (knowledge about things) and *procedural* (knowledge of how to do something) (Kogut and Zander, 1992); (2) *explicit* (formally codified in documents and other formal communications) and *tacit* (personal intuitions and beliefs that are communicated informally by casual communications) (Nonaka, 1994); and (3) *general* (knowledge that is held by large numbers of individuals and easily transferred) and *specific* (knowledge that is possessed by a limited number of individuals and is difficult to transfer) (Jensen and Meckling, 1996). Specific knowledge is related to the concept of *expertise*, where someone has a recognized depth of knowledge in a specific area (Ericsson and Smith, 1991). Related to expert knowledge is *heuristic* knowledge, where decisions are made using general rules derived from experience. Experts tend to have a more developed set of heuristics than novices.

Much of the history of computing has involved developing more efficient data and information processing, leaving humans to derive the knowledge from the information and make decisions based on this knowledge (Campbell-Kelly and Aspray, 1996). What distinguishes knowledge systems is the desire to have software more actively assist in deriving knowledge and more directly facilitate decision making, or in some cases have the software make decisions (e.g., expert and agent-based systems).

Historically, three predominant areas of interest related to knowledge systems can be identified. The first of these was research directed toward computer systems that used expert-derived knowledge to guide novice users to solve a problem (Giarratano and Riley, 2004; Jackson, 1998). This research first became prevalent in the 1970s and 1980s. In the 1990s, interest developed more toward knowledge management systems (Awad and Ghaziri, 2003; Becerra-Fernandez et al., 2004). The emphasis shifted away from capturing and structuring knowledge for an intelligent program toward capturing and structuring knowledge for direct access by decision makers (a.k.a. knowledge workers). Another distinction of knowledge management is that it is interdisciplinary and not just about the technology. Knowledge management has gained impetus from the business and management fields, and it is very much concerned with the human and communication issues in the processing, collecting, and dissemination of knowledge. More recently, there has been a move toward supporting more dynamic knowledge creation and sharing communities through the use of collaborative technologies (Fuks et al., 2005). This chapter reviews technologies and research issues in these three areas, all of which share a number of underlying problems. In particular, how can we obtain and organize knowledge in such a way that it facilitates just-in-time learning and effective performance by individuals and organizations?

## KNOWLEDGE-BASED/ EXPERT SYSTEMS

Knowledge-based systems first emerged as an area of interest during the early development of the field of artificial intelligence (AI) (Russell and Norvig, 2002). In artificial intelligence, computer scientists attempted to come up with computer models for intelligence. They sought to move computer technology beyond number and data processing to knowledge processing, in which computers could make decisions similar to those made by humans. Initially, the interest was in language processing and general problem-solving algorithms, as reflected in the work of Newell and Simon (1963). The early work in AI hit on two of the enduring research questions in knowledge systems. First, how can we best represent knowledge within a computer system? Second, how can we efficiently search through represented knowledge to find the knowledge relevant to solving a particular problem? One way to confront these problems is to narrow the domain of interest in which we are trying to demonstrate some intelligence. This notion led toward an emergence in the 1970s of what were called *knowledge-based systems* or *expert systems*. Expert systems were constrained to solving problems in a narrow domain of interest, such as a particular area of medical diagnosis. Expert systems introduced another enduring research question for knowledge systems: How can we elicit from humans the knowledge they make use of to solve problem?

An expert system generally consists of a knowledge base and inference engine. A knowledge base is a store of recorded knowledge derived from interviewing experts. An inference engine is a computer program that, when given a particular problem, can identify which knowledge in the knowledge base is relevant and when it must ask questions of the user to obtain information relevant to the problem. Through interacting with the users, an inference engine can eventually propose a solution to the problem at hand. One of the best known of the early systems was MYCIN, which performed medical diagnosis (Shortliffe and Davis, 1975) and specified treatments for blood disorders. The software architecture of MYCIN became the basis for many subsequent expert systems. It used what was referred to as a *rule-based approach* to knowledge representation, which represented an expert's heuristic knowledge. The knowledge base consisted of a number of what were called *production rules*. These had the general form of "If A is true and B is true, then the diagnosis X is highly likely," where A and B represented a particular observation about a patient. Rules were derived from interviewing experts and were chained together. A and B in the previous example might be established by other rules, such as: "If the blood pressure is high and the patient is male, then A is true." Eventually the chaining of the rules would result in the generation of questions for the user—for example, "Is the patient's blood pressure 140/90 or higher?" If the system had enough rules for the domain and the user could provide the required information, the performance of the system could be tested against the real expert's performance.

It was recognized early that expert systems and the knowledge they contained not only had a role to play in assisting performance, such as supporting diagnoses, but could also have a role to play in education. In fact, GUIDON (Clancey, 1982), the first expert system to be built for educational purposes, was constructed from the MYCIN knowledge base. In addition to the knowledge base on the domain, it added a knowledge base of rules about how to teach. In GUIDON, users performed a diagnosis and asked questions (i.e., played the role of the expert system). The teaching rule determined how to answer requests for help or when to intervene and correct less than optimal performance by the user. A number of other systems and models for what became known as *intelligent tutoring systems* would later emerge (Beck et al., 1996; Wenger, 1987).

In addition to domain and instructional knowledge, another key defining feature of such systems is student models (Self, 1999). Representing knowledge of the student would allow the tailoring of instructional content and strategies to suit the needs of the individual student.

Despite a significant investment in expert systems technology throughout the 1970s and 1980s, interest had waned by the 1990s. Although the term *expert system* is now seldom used, research work related to it has not died out. It has instead formed a foundation for newer avenues of research. Expert systems technology is a key component of modern computer games (Laird, 2002), where it assists in creating more challenging computer-controlled opponents for human players. It is also an integral part of the currently popular area of research into intelligent agents (Agarwal et al., 2004; d'Inverno and Luck, 2003). Agents are computer programs that incorporate problem-solving abilities and act to assist users on some computer-based task. The work on agents builds upon the tradition of expert systems research but also integrates newer technology; for example, Baylor and Ryu (2003) investigated the use of human-like graphical interfaces (personas) on agents designed to assist learners and found them to have a positive effect on a learner's interactive experience.

## KNOWLEDGE MANAGEMENT

The area of knowledge management has arisen as an important area of study in the last 15 years. It has its roots in management thinking and the rising importance of what has been referred to as the *knowledge worker* (Drucker, 1959). Historically, organizations have consisted of large numbers of menial workers and relatively few decisions makers. Much of the decision making was done by the people at the top, and many people were employed to provide the information to those at the top; for example, in warehouses people were employed to perform manual inventories, and in production plants people were employed to walk around and check equipment gauges and operations. At the same time as much of this information gathering became automated through technologies such as bar-code readers and remote sensors, many businesses and markets underwent dramatic change. Decision making became more decentralized. Many more workers at all levels became required to deal with knowledge and make decisions. Organizations began to rely on knowledge and timely decision making to be flexible enough to survive in rapidly changing environments. New knowledge-dependent professions arose (e.g., marketing, software engineers), and traditionally knowledge-intensive professions (e.g., lawyers, researchers, and teachers) became more in demand.

On an organizational level, businesses became interested in how they could better support knowledge workers by providing them with processes and technology to efficiently develop, share, and use information and knowledge. From this change in business and associated developments in technology has emerged the need for what is now called *knowledge management*.

These changes do not just apply to businesses; they apply to all organizations, including political and military ones. Among the U.S. military is much discussion regarding force transformation. Rather than training based on preestablished doctrine in relation to known threats, it is now necessary to deal with what is called *asymmetric warfare*. In asymmetric warfare, threats come from adaptive, often unknown enemies who attack from many directions (Lovelace and Votel, 2004). Rigid centralized command and control are seen as too slow to respond to such threats. Another driver here is the fact that, as military technology is becoming more complex, the manpower and time available for training have been reduced; thus, traditional training practices (getting knowledge inside the head) must be complemented by systems that provide knowledge to decision makers on an as-needed basis.

Technology obviously plays a key role in supporting the knowledge worker; therefore, much of the emphasis in knowledge management is in the use of technology. Some would argue, however, this has tended to be overemphasized relative to the organizational and social factors involved, such as creating a knowledge sharing culture.

The Internet—in particular, the World Wide Web—is an important knowledge-management tool. Knowledge workers once had to spend much time in libraries sorting through catalogs, finding books and articles, and scanning through indexes. The Internet has provided an alternative source of information and knowledge that, due to the increasing sophistication of search engines, has allowed users to locate resources in minutes rather than hours. Despite the usefulness of the Web, there are deficiencies, and research is continually underway to make organizing, tagging, and searching for information and knowledge easier.

The problem is that a search engine cannot easily distinguish meaning. If you type the word "tank" into Google, you will get over 200 million hits, the top ones being for a space in a New York gallery, a children's cartoon character, and a military tank museum. Research by Bronander and colleagues (2004) revealed that many users take the path of least resistance rather than using effective search and retrieval methods. They will use few keywords and ignore the advanced functionality available.

The limitation of search technology stems from the fact that the language used to encode Web pages (HTML) is primarily designed to help a browser display the content. It is not designed to organize content according to its meaning. Much research is being carried out to move to what is called the *Semantic Web*, where the meaning of Web-based content is more readily apparent to automated systems and search engines. The vision of the Semantic Web is being promoted heavily by Tim Berners-Lee, the original inventor of the Web, who particularly emphasizes the potential of the Web as a knowledge-management environment (Berners-Lee et al., 2001). The development of the Semantic Web requires the use of computer-readable codes that designate the meaning of Web content. This includes embedded tags in text and metadata in digital resources (such as text, graphic video, and programs). Metadata are simply data that tell us something about other data; for example, the Dublin core (see http://dublincore.org/) is metadata that designate such things as the author and date of creation of a resource on the Internet. Metadata are an important part of the development of learning object technology (see Chapter 29 in this volume). Another important technology is Extended Markup Language (XML), which is a meta-language for creating systems of tags that add meaning to Web content.

## KNOWLEDGE COMMUNITIES

Some commentators have witnessed a move toward a second generation of knowledge-management systems (McElroy, 2003). In the first generation, the emphasis was mainly on using technology to capture, organize, and archive existing and primarily explicit knowledge. Traditional knowledge-management initiatives have often failed, and the reason most often cited for these failures is an overemphasis on technology and underemphasis on human and organizational issues, such as providing leadership and incentives for knowledge sharing (Ambrosio, 2000; Lesser et al., 2000; Ribière and Sitar, 2003). Second-generation knowledge management is more focused on connecting people to share their tacit knowledge and on the knowledge-generation process rather than the knowledge-archiving process. McElroy (2003) sees the work in knowledge management as converging with the concept of organizational learning developed by Senge (1990), in which learning and innovation are seen as social rather than administrative processes.

Other influences in this direction are a development of interest in virtual communities (Ellis et al., 2004) and communities of practice (Wenger and Snyder, 2000) and technologies that facilitative group work (Fuks et al., 2005). Virtual communities research is concerned with the development of relationships that occur exclusively through online interaction. The issues that researchers are considering include the nature of online identities (Boyd and Heer, 2006), their relationships to real communities (Wellman and Gulia, 1999), and the relative importance of social support to information support (Preece, 1999). Communities of practice relate to collections of people with the same goals, coming together to share knowledge about how best to achieve them. Learning and information sharing is situated in the context of work practices. There is particular interest in how communities of practice are facilitated through virtual communities (Davenport and Hall, 2002). Research into online communities of practice is often focused on their voluntary and self-sustaining nature (Wenger and Snyder, 2000).

Although most work in knowledge systems is built around knowledge within the organization, several technologies have had a particular effect on the way that people form networks, communicate, and share knowledge in everyday life. In particular, social networking websites such as myspace.com (Boyd and Heer, 2006) and instant messaging communications (Grinter and Palen, 2002) are having an increasing impact.

Expert systems, knowledge management, and knowledge communities are not necessarily exclusive approaches. It is possible to create hybrid systems. Communities can share tacit knowledge, commentary, and experience within the framework of more formal structures. Jubert (1999) described such a system in the context of business process innovation at Siemens Business Services (SBS) in France and highlighted the interplay of virtual communities, communities of practice, and traditional knowledge management. Weber and Kaplan (2003) described the interrelationships between knowledge-based systems and knowledge management. Douglas (2004) described how configurable software architecture enables hybrid knowledge systems. The software architecture was used to create a hybrid system that incorporated knowledge management and online communities using an organizational framework of performance roles and goals (Sasson and Douglas, 2006).

# CROSS-CUTTING ISSUES

Cross-cutting issues for knowledge systems include how knowledge is derived from human sources; how knowledge is encoded in a machine-readable form; how knowledge is organized using taxonomies, metadata, and ontology; and, finally, knowledge quality assurance.

## Populating a System with Knowledge

A knowledge system is only as useful as the knowledge it contains, so an important first step in creating any system is obtaining the knowledge from existing sources. The process of doing this is known as *knowledge elicitation*, and it has often been viewed as a bottleneck for the creation of usable systems. The issues involved will be familiar to instructional designers who also have to derive knowledge from subject-matter experts. The study of the effectiveness of different techniques is relevant. In addition to traditional techniques such as interviews and surveys, more sophisticated techniques are often required for knowledge-based systems given that they are focused on more depth of analysis and are more often required to extract tacit rather than explicit knowledge. Among the relevant techniques studied are cognitive task analysis (see Chapter 43 in this volume), protocol analysis (Ericsson and Simon, 1993), diagrammatic techniques (Cheng, 1996; see also Chapter 28 in this volume), and automated techniques (Shute et al., 1999; see also Chapter 24 in this volume).

Ethnographic studies are another way to learn about how knowledge workers both apply their knowledge and organize information to support their work. An example of this approach is the work of Gabbay and le May (2004), who spent 2 years observing primary-care clinicians in a medical practice and concluded that the clinicians rarely used explicit evidence from research or other sources but instead relied on collectively reinforced tacit guidelines which the authors termed *mindlines*. Reading played some part in the formation of mindlines, but they were mainly formed by interactions with patients, colleagues, and pharmaceutical representatives. Once formed, they were shared and negotiated into socially constructed knowledge within the practice.

In addition to studying humans and focusing on tacit knowledge, studies can be made of recorded online interactions and existing formal representations of knowledge such as documents. This can involve human study and coding of items such as e-mail messages, discussion boards, or instant messaging transcripts. It can also involve automated systems of analysis. One important technique in this regard is the use of latent semantic analysis (LSA) (Landauer et al., 1998), which extracts the contextual meaning of words by statistically analyzing large bodies of text within a particular domain.

In collaborative knowledge-sharing systems, a major issue is what motivates contributors to share when there is seldom a financial reward for contributing their knowledge. The development of online communities is seen as a mix of self-interest and altruism (Kollick, 1999), and various mechanisms have been adopted to encourage participation such as community recognition (Wellman and Gulia, 1999). Jeong (2006) performed an analysis of the language used in threaded discussions in an online class and found that the use of conversational language was an important factor in increasing responses within the dialog.

## Encoding Knowledge

Once knowledge is derived from a source, it must be encoded in the system in such a way as to be accessible by software such as inference engines, search engines, and knowledge-management classification schemes. In talking about expert systems, we introduced one form of knowledge representation: the production rule. This is a popular method of representing procedural knowledge. In addition to the procedural knowledge, we must also represent declarative knowledge or factual information about entities in the world. This is often represented in hierarchical or networked collections of nodes and links. In artificial intelligence, this knowledge is often encoded as semantic networks (Sowa, 1991), which have a close relationship with the idea of concept maps (see Chapter 29). Some knowledge encoding schemes can combine declarative and procedural knowledge. The idea behind object-oriented programming (Weisfeld, 2003) embodies this concept. An object embodies attributes (facts about the object) and methods (procedural code) that provide the behavior of the object within the system. Another important aspect of object-oriented knowledge systems is the hierarchical classification of objects. Knowledge classification schemes or knowledge ontologies have become a very important area of research, particularly for those interested in working toward the Semantic Web (Gomez-Perez et al., 2004). Ontology is a shared conceptualization of meaning, and several technologies exist for the construction of ontologies to assist in identifying the meaning of content on the Web (Warren, 2006). As many of these technologies are difficult to work with, higher level tools have also emerged to assist researchers in creating ontologies for different domains. A prominent example of this is Protégé (see http://protege.stanford.edu/), a free, open-source tool developed at Stanford University.

As the Internet and the World Wide Web are seen as the key platforms for knowledge management in the future, it is import that good tools and standards are developed to facilitate this. The main standards body behind the Web has been active in promoting knowledge representation and classification technologies (see http://www.w3.org/2001/sw).

## Ensuring Knowledge Quality

There has always been concern in ensuring the quality of the knowledge provided by knowledge systems. In the early expert systems, it was recognized that the user might not trust the conclusion provided by the system. Expert systems evolved systems of explanation by which they could show the reasoning behind their decision (Richards, 2003). The explanation was seen as providing confidence for the users that a conclusion was based on good reasoning. In early expert systems, explanation was merely a rule trace, but later systems evolved to provide more naturalistic explanations of decision making.

A pillar of conventional quality assurance of knowledge is peer review. This model features recognized outlets for the publication of knowledge, but before a contribution can be accepted for publication a number of peers must attest to the proposed contribution's correctness and worthiness. For logistical reasons, the number of reviewers is often limited, and the process of editing and review prior to publication can be time consuming. The Internet has made it possible for other models to emerge, particularly the move toward publication and review becoming an open, continuous, and collaborative process.

An interesting controversy has arisen recently over the development of Wikipedia (see http://en.wikipedia.org/wiki/Wikipedia), an online encyclopedia developed by a voluntary and self-regulated community. Some have argued that, without traditional expert-led and peer-review mechanisms, Wikipedia has the potential for disseminating false knowledge (Denning et al., 2005). Others have argued that such a system leads to more efficient and refined knowledge sources due to the openness of the process and the greater numbers of people involved. Surowiecki (2003) suggested that, under certain conditions, the collective wisdom of large groups can lead to more effective decision making than reliance on small groups of experts.

A number of mechanisms have emerged to assist people in gauging the quality of resources. Collectively, these have been termed *recommender systems* (Resnick and Varian, 1997). Any mechanism that allows a user to distinguish the quality or usefulness of a resource can be considered a recommender system. The most prominent type of recommender system is sometimes referred to as *collaborative filtering*, where users of resources review and rate them for the benefit of others. Automated approaches to recommending use knowledge of users' stated preferences or online behavior to construct recommendations for other resources to view. Burke (2000) provided a review of attempts to integrate knowledge-based system approaches into recommender systems. One example of such a system is Pandora (see www.pandora.com), a development of the music genome project. Pandora uses a knowledge base that classifies thousands of pieces of music based on hundreds of musical attributes. When a user enters the name of an artist or song, Pandora generates a radio station that plays a range of artists and songs that share similar attributes, thus allowing users to discover new music they might not otherwise have encountered.

## DISCUSSION

Many new technologies generate enthusiasm and interest when they first emerge and then seem to fade into the mainstream. Multimedia is a good example of this, and one of the reasons for highlighting expert systems in this chapter is that it also followed a similar trend. Since the initial enthusiasm and interest arose in the 1980s, work in this area has now merged into other interests in computing, such as agent technology. It is likely that a number of the technologies noted in this chapter will adapt and merge into hybrid systems that are part of the more general phenomenon of networked computer systems.

In addition to the enduring themes we have covered—how we can extract, codify, classify, and quality check knowledge within knowledge systems—some other trends are apparent. The first is a move from the document as the main unit of knowledge transfer to more granular digital units. Many readers will be familiar with learning objects. In other areas, the object concept is also being adapted. The technical data documentation community, which creates content that is often used by instructional designers, has adopted an object standard for making technical data documentation more granular (S1000D; see http:// www.s1000d. org/).

Object standards are the first step before creating digital repositories through which people can access and share such knowledge resources. The integration of collaboration and recommender systems with these repositories is the next step toward achieving knowledge systems that both serve and harness the efforts of entire communities rather than single organizations.

Network-centric ways of operating will have the most effect on human activities that currently use nondigital, document-based, or linear processes. One particularly prominent example of this is the recent U.S. National Science Foundation initiative to develop research into a cyber infrastructure for science and engineering (National Science Foundation, 2005). This program is intended to stimulate research in the use of the Internet to facilitate scientists and engineers in better sharing resources and better managing the development and archiving of knowledge. Central standards and repositories of scientific knowledge with data-sharing standards, open discussion, and mass peer review are seen as the future in this domain.

## CONCLUDING REMARKS

Individual knowledge systems in their various forms have experienced varying degrees of success and impact; however, the development of the ultimate knowledge system, the World Wide Web, has had an impact on the way people create, obtain, and share knowledge. The development of specific technologies for knowledge systems is likely to continue at a searing pace, despite understandable anxieties about the effect of these technologies on society. Underlying issues that researchers will have to address include: (1) eliciting, representing, structuring, accessing, and verifying the quality of knowledge, and (2) evaluating the effects of technology on individuals, organizations, and society. These issues overlap the traditional concerns of those in the field of instructional design who have a great deal to contribute to research in knowledge systems. Indeed, it is possible to argue that learning systems and knowledge systems should not be seen separately but as integral components of systems for supporting human performance and the development of human society.

## REFERENCES

Ackoff, R. L. (1989). From data to wisdom. *J. Appl. Syst. Anal.*, 16, 3–9.

Agarwal, R., Deo, A., and Das, S. (2004). Intelligent agents in e-learning. *ACM SIGSOFT Software Eng. Notes*, 29(2), 1–3.

Ambrosio, J. (2000). Knowledge management mistakes. *Computerworld.* 34, 27–44.

Awad, E. M. and Ghaziri H. M. (2003). *Knowledge Management.* Upper Saddle River, NJ: Pearson Education.

Baylor, A. L. and Ryu, J. (2003). Does the presence of image and animation enhance pedagogical agent persona? *J. Educ. Comput. Res.*, 28(4), 373–395.

Becerra-Fernandez, I., Gonzalez, A., and Sabherwal R. (2004). *Knowledge Management: Challenges, Solutions, and Technologies.* Upper Saddle River, NJ: Pearson Education.

Beck, J., Stern, M., and Haugsjaa, E. (1996). Applications of AI in education. *ACM Crossroads*, 3(1), 11–15.

Berners-Lee, T., Hendler., J., and Lassila, O. (2001). The Semantic Web. *Sci. Am.*, May, 28–37.

Boyd, D. and Heer, J. (2006). Profiles as conversation: networked identity performance on Friendster. In *Proceedings of the Hawaii International Conference on System Sciences (HICSS-39)*, January 7–10, Kauai, HI.

Bronander, K. A., Goodman, P. H., Inman, T. F., and Veach, T. L. (2004). Boolean search experience and abilities of medical students and practicing physicians. *Teaching Learn. Med.*, 16, 284–289.

Burke, R. (2000). Knowledge-based recommender systems. In *Encyclopedia of Library and Information Systems*, Vol. 69 (Suppl. 32), edited by A. Kent. New York: Marcel Dekker.

Campbell-Kelly, M. and Aspray, W. (1996). *Computer: A History of the Information Machine*, Sloan Technology Series. New York: Basic Books.

Cheng, P. C.-H. (1996). Diagrammatic knowledge acquisition: elicitation, analysis and issues. In *Advances in Knowledge Acquisition: 9th European Knowledge Acquisition Workshop (EKAW'96)*, edited by N. R. Shadbolt, H. O'Hara, and G. Schreiber, pp. 179–194. Berlin: Springer-Verlag.

Clancey, W. J. (1982). Overview of GUIDON. *J. Comput. Based Instruct.*, 10(1/2), 8–15.*

Davenport, E. and Hall, H. (2002). Organizational knowledge and communities of practice. In *Annual Review of Information Science and Technology*, Vol. 36, edited by B. Cronin, pp. 171–227. Medford, NJ: Information Today.

Davenport, T. H. and Prusak, L. (1998). *Working Knowledge: How Organizations Manage What They Know*. Boston, MA: Harvard Business School Press.*

Denning, P., Horning, J., Parnas, D., and Weinstein, L. (2005). Wikipedia risks. *Commun. ACM*, 48(12), 152.

d'Inverno, M. and Luck M. (2003). *Understanding Agent Systems*. New York: Springer-Verlag.*

Douglas, I. (2004). Net-centric performance improvement. In *Proceedings of the Sixth International Conference on Information Integration and Web-Based Applications and Services (iiWAS2004)*, September 27–29, Jakarta, Indonesia, pp. 713–718.

Drucker, P. F. (1959). *The Landmarks of Tomorrow*. New York: Harper.

Ellis, D., Oldridge, R., and Vasconcelos, A. (2004). Community and virtual community. In *Annual Review of Information Science and Technology*, Vol. 38, edited by B. Cronin, pp. 145–186. Medford, NJ: Information Today.

Ericsson, K. A. and Simon, H. A. (1993). *Protocol Analysis: Verbal Reports as Data*, rev. ed. Cambridge, MA: The MIT Press.

Ericsson, K. A. and Smith, J. (1991). *Toward a General Theory of Expertise: Prospects and Limits*. Cambridge, U.K.: Cambridge University Press.

Fuks, H., Lukosch, S., and Salgado, A. C., Eds. (2005). Groupware: design, implementation, and use. In *Proceedings of the 11th International Workshop on Groupware (CRIWG 2005)*, September 25–29, Porto de Galinhas, Brazil.

Gabbay, J. and le May, A. (2004). Evidence based guidelines or collectively constructed 'mindlines'? Ethnographic study of knowledge management in primary care. *Br. Med. J.*, 329(7473), 1013–1016A.

Giarratano, J. C. and Riley, G. D. (2004). *Expert Systems: Principles and Programming*, 4th ed. Boston, MA: PWS Publishing.

Gomez-Perez, A., Corcho, O., and Fernandez-Lopez, M. (2004). *Ontological Engineering: With Examples from the Areas of Knowledge Management, e-Commerce and the Semantic Web*. London: Springer-Verlag.

Grinter, R. E. and Palen, L. (2002). Instant messaging in teen life. In *Proceedings of Computer Supported Collaborative Work Conference (CSCW'02)*, pp. 21–30. New York: ACM Press.

Jackson, P. (1998). *Introduction to Expert Systems*, 3rd ed. New York: Addison-Wesley.

Jensen, M. C. and Meckling, W. H. (1996). Specific and general knowledge, and organizational structure. In *Knowledge Management and Organizational Design*, edited by P. S. Myers, pp. 17–38. Newton, MA: Butterworth-Heinemann.

Jeong, A. (2006). The effects of conversational styles of communication on group interaction patterns and argumentation in online discussions. *Instruct. Sci.*, 34(5), 367–397.

Jubert, A. (1999). Developing an infrastructure for communities of practice: the Siemens experience. In *Proceedings of the Third International Online Information Meeting*, December 7–9, London, pp. 165–168.

Kogut, B. and Zander, U. (1992). Knowledge of the firm, combinative capabilities and the replication of technology. *Organ. Sci.*, 3(3), 383–397.

Kollick, P. (1999). The economics of online cooperation. In *Communities in Cyberspace*, edited by M. A. Smith and P. Kollick, pp. 222–239. London: Routledge.

Laird, J. (2002). Research in human-level AI using computer games. *Commun. ACM*, 45(1), 32–35 (special issue on game engines in scientific research).

Landauer, T. K., Foltz, P. W., and Laham, D. (1998). Introduction to latent semantic analysis. *Discourse Process.*, 25, 259–284.

Lesser, E., Fontaine, M., and Slusher, J. (2000). *Knowledge and Communities: Resources for the Knowledge-Based Economy*. Woburn, MA: Butterworth-Heinemann.

Lovelace, J. J. and Votel, J. L. (2004). The asymmetric warfare group: closing the capability gaps. *Army Mag.*, March, 29–32.

McElroy, M. (2003). *The New Knowledge Management: Complexity, Learning, and Sustainable Innovation*. Burlington, MA: Elsevier Science.*

National Science Foundation. (2005). *Revolutionizing Science and Engineering Through Cyberinfrastructure*, Report of the National Science Foundation Blue-Ribbon Advisory Panel on Cyberinfrastructure (http://www.communitytechnology.org/nsf_ci_report/).

Newell, A. and Simon, H. A. (1963). GPS, a program that simulates human thought. In *Computers and Thought*, edited by E. Feigenbaum and J. Feldman, pp. 279–93. Cambridge, MA: MIT Press.*

Nonaka, I. (1994). A dynamic theory of organizational knowledge creation. *Organ. Sci.*, 5(1), 14–37.

Preece, J. (1999). Empathic communities: balancing emotional and factual communication. *Interact. Comput.*, 12, 63–77.

Quigley, E. J. and Debons, A. (1999). Interrogative theory of information and knowledge. In *Proceedings of Special Interest Group on Computer Personnel Research Annual Conference (SIGCPR'99)*, pp. 4–10. New York: ACM Press.

Resnick, P. and Varian, H. R. (1997). Recommender systems. *Commun. ACM*, 40(3), 56–58.

Ribière, V. M. and Sitar, A. (2003). Critical role of leadership in nurturing a knowledge-supporting culture. *Knowl. Manage. Res. Pract.*, 1(1), 39–48.

Richards, D. (2003). Knowledge-based system explanation: the ripple-down rules alternative. *Knowl. Inform. Syst.*, 5(1), 2–25.

Russell, S. J. and Norvig, P. (2002). *Artificial Intelligence: A Modern Approach*, 2nd ed. Upper Saddle River, NJ: Prentice Hall.

Sasson, J. and Douglas, I. (2006). A conceptual integration of performance analysis, knowledge management and technology: from concept to prototype. *J. Knowl. Manage.*, 10(6), 81–99.

Self, J. (1999). The defining characteristics of intelligent tutoring systems research: ITSs care, precisely. *Int. J. Artif. Intell. Educ.*, 10, 350–364.*

Senge, P. M. (1990). *The Fifth Discipline: The Art and Practice of the Learning Organization*. London: Random House.

Shortliffe, T. and Davis, R. (1975). Some considerations for the implementation of knowledge-based expert systems. *SIGART Bull.*, 55(Dec.), 9–12.

Shute, V. J., Torreano L. A., and Willis, R. E. (1999). Exploratory test of an automated knowledge elicitation and organization tool. *Int. J. Artif. Intell. Educ.*, 10, 365–384.

Sowa, J. F., Ed. (1991). *Principles of Semantic Networks: Explorations in the Representation of Knowledge*. San Mateo, CA: Morgan Kaufmann.

Surowiecki, J. (2003). *The Wisdom of Crowds*. New York: Doubleday.

Warren, P. (2006). Knowledge management and the Semantic Web: from scenario to technology. *IEEE Intell. Syst.*, 21(1), 53–59.

Weber, R. and Kaplan, R. (2003). Knowledge-based knowledge management. In *International Series on Advanced Intelligence*. Vol. 4. *Innovations in Knowledge Engineering*, edited by R. Jain, A. Abraham, C. Faucher, and B. van der Zwaag. Adelaide, South Australia: Advanced Knowledge International.

Weisfeld, M. (2003). *The Object-Oriented Thought Process*, 2nd ed. Indianapolis, IN: Sams.

Wellman, B. and Gulia, M. (1999). Net surfer's don't ride alone: virtual communities as communities. In *Communities in Cyberspace*, edited by M. Smith and P. Kollock, pp. 167–194. London: Routledge.

Wenger, E. (1987). *Artificial Intelligence and Tutoring Systems*. Los Altos, CA: Morgan Kaufmann.*

Wenger E. and Snyder, W. (2000). Communities of practice: the organizational frontier. *Harvard Bus. Rev.*, 78: 139–145.

---

* Indicates a core reference.

# 21

# Flexible Learning and the Architecture of Learning Places

*Peter Goodyear*
CoCo Research Centre, University of Sydney, Sydney, Australia

## CONTENTS

## ABSTRACT

The point of departure for this chapter is the idea that learning activity is becoming less constrained by time, space, and the organizational requirements of educational providers. As people take more control over their learning activity, there is a multiplication of the possible influences of time and space on their learning. If learning can take place anywhere, then we need to know more about the pedagogical affordances of the various *wheres* in which it is situated. This becomes a priority for the effective learner—needing to know how to select and configure appropriate *learnplaces*—as well as for researchers trying to understand the sometimes subtle connections between place and learning. The chapter offers a summary description of flexible learning and then moves on to consider the relations between learning and place. The account is structured, in part, by a distinction between weaker and stronger interpretations of what is meant by situated learning. The function of the weaker interpretation is to highlight the importance of the learning context, such that we can focus on the affordances of the learnplace and consider the ergonomics of supportive learning environments. The stronger interpretation of situated learning causes us to take seriously the idea that being a learner is first and foremost engagement in a cultural practice, that people have to learn to engage in such cultural practices, and that place has a distinctive role in cultural practice. Paradoxically, ideas about flexible learning and mobile learning help us put learning in its place.

## KEYWORDS

*Ergonomics of learning environments:* The applied science that helps illuminate the relationships between a learner and a *learnplace*.

*Flexible learning:* Learning that is relatively free of logistical and educational constraints.

*Learning places (or learnplaces):* The immediate physical setting for someone's learning activity, including the tools and artifacts, digital and material, that come to hand.

*Situated learning:* A perspective on learning that emphasizes its social and physical context.

## INTRODUCTION

Categorizations of instructional approaches and of the experience of learning are rarely symmetrical. A worldview that makes perfect sense to the teacher or instructional systems designer may well prove unrecognizable to the learner. This issue is particularly thorny when we talk about flexible learning, distance education, or blended learning. Who bends what in flexible learning? Where is the distance in distance education? What gets blended in blended learning?

This chapter is aimed at doing two things. At a substantive level, it introduces some key ideas and literature about flexible learning, the situated nature of learning, and the relations between learning and *learnplaces*. At a meta-level, the chapter tracks and combines some arguments for a richer conception of what is involved in being a learner. This is not an area with a rich base of empirical literature (Van Note Chism, 2002); consequently, many of the references are intended to help the reader explore better ways of conceptualizing the field. Some suggestions for promising lines of research can be found at the end of the chapter.

The term *learnplace* is used interchangeably with *learning place* in this chapter, depending on the flow of the text. The two mean the same. Learnplace, by analogy with workplace, is a place at which serious learning is done. Ford and colleagues (1996) and Slack and colleagues (1996) provided the earliest recorded usages of the term. *Place* is used deliberately as a way of indicating something more specific and concrete than space—something imbued with meaning and value (Auburn and Barnes, 2006; Jamieson et al., 2000; Sime, 1986).

*Flexible learning* connotes those learning situations in which the learner has substantial control over the logistics of learning, notably the location and timing of the learner's learning activity. It can also connote

situations in which learners have substantial control over what they set out to learn, how they go about learning it, and how their learning is assessed. In short, flexible learning involves the loosening of logistical or educational constraints (Boot and Hodgson, 1987). The focus on learning places reflects a growing acknowledgment of the importance of the physical environment in influencing how people learn and what they learn (Bliss et al., 1999; Poysa et al., 2005; Singleton, 1998). This is, in part, connected with trends toward more flexible arrangements for learning (Jamieson et al., 2000; Monahan, 2002). If one conceives of learning as that which takes place in a time-delimited lesson in a teacher's classroom, then the relations between learning and place seem bounded and obvious—part of what we take for granted in educational practice even though the physical layout of a classroom may impose strong constraints on pedagogy (Comber and Wall, 2001; Graetz and Goliber, 2002; Van Note Chism, 2002). Shifts toward anytime, anywhere, anyhow learning can be accompanied by two competing views about place: that place becomes irrelevant (the mobile fantasy) or that the qualities of place must be understood in a more nuanced way. The second main section of the chapter examines this through a consideration of ideas in the literature about weaker and stronger interpretations of what it means for learning to be situated. The implications of these two interpretations are drawn out in the third and fourth sections, which focus on physical contexts for learning and learning conceived as participation in cultural practice, where the culture provides physical and digital resources that influence the very nature of learning activity.

## FLEXIBLE LEARNING

...space and time are not just material constraints to be overcome or resources to be used; rather, they have different qualities depending on the historically specific discourse through which they are understood. Thus, new interpretive frames by which space and time are understood are integral to the creation of institutions which achieve new forms of control over the spacing and timing of human activity. (Friedland and Boden, 1994, p. 29)

The literature on flexible learning is of two kinds. One kind is essentially functional. In broad terms, it takes flexibility for granted as a good thing and aims to provide practical knowledge and advice about how to promote and support more flexible forms of learning activity (de Boer and Collis, 2005; Khan, 2006; Lockwood and Latchem, 1997; Mason, 1994; Van den

Brande, 1993; Wade et al., 1994). The other kind takes a more critical perspective. Much of it has the goal of demonstrating that intended benefits are not always achieved or that the liberationist discourse of flexibility conceals some hidden or unanticipated costs to students (Edwards, 1997; Edwards and Clark, 2002; Paechter et al., 2001; Willems, 2005). Both perspectives are necessary. Indeed, some of the practical guidance provided in the literature would be more useful if it took a less romantic or naïve view of the charms of flexibility. Lieve Van den Brande's (1993, p. 2) definition of flexible learning still serves us well: "Flexible learning is enabling learners to learn when they want (frequency, timing, duration), how they want (modes of learning), and what they want (that is, learners can define what constitutes learning to them)."

## Flexible Use of Time and Space

Temporal flexibility implies that learning is scheduled at times to suit the learner. This might include control over the deadline for achieving a learning objective, the duration and frequency of learning activities, and so on. At a macro-level (time spans measured in years), temporal flexibility includes such considerations as lifelong learning (i.e., that learning is not just restricted to the years of formal schooling). It refers to the freedom to learn when the need arises in the course of one's life, not just at the stages predetermined for the convenience of educational providers. Meso-level temporal flexibility operates on time spans of weeks and months. The ability to start a course of study at any time in the year, rather than (say) just at the beginning of a semester, would be an example of meso-level flexibility. Micro-level flexibility operates on a time scale of days down to seconds. Flexibility on this scale allows the learner detailed control over the scheduling and pace of their learning activity, allowing them, for example, to "harvest fragments of time" for learning in an otherwise hectic schedule (Roberts et al., 2003).

The spatial dimension of flexible learning refers to learning that takes place at locations that suit the learner. Flexible learning should minimize the disruption to the learner's other activities (at work, at home, etc.). Learning that involves the learner's absence from work or home may have the advantage of allowing the learner to concentrate fully on their learning activity, but it can also disadvantage those who are tied to the home or workplace and can be expensive for both the learner and their employer. Equally, enabling learners to study from their workplaces can help contextualize learning and dissolve unhelpful boundaries between work and learning (Goodyear, 2006; Van den Brande, 1993).

## Flexibility over Goals, Methods, and Assessment

Flexibility over learning goals means that learning activity can have its roots in the needs and interests of the learner and emerge from (or be inseparable from) their ongoing work and life. Much conventional learning activity is strongly shaped by the existence and nature of assessment systems or by the goals of teachers and educational institutions. Flexible learning may be relatively free from such influences.

The learner should take a lead in defining *what* it is they need to know. They may be helped in this by a teacher (or by other learners) who may have knowledge about good ways of refining and reaching the learner's objectives. Definition of needs can occur at a number of levels; the learner may define a high-level need and pass over to a teacher the lower level decisions about how this need can be met. Conversely, the higher level decisions may be made by a teacher or a competence-certifying institution, while control over the details of what is learned stays with the learner.

In a flexible learning regime, learners should exert a high level of control over *how* they study: whether reading texts or listening to lectures or through practical work. There is a strong impetus to recognize the learner's need for autonomy, but this is not to say that the unsupported learner is always able to make good decisions about their learning or that they should be dissuaded from asking for advice.

Flexible learning should make learning opportunities available to all those who wish to take advantage of them. This means doing away with entry qualifications. Less strongly, it means removing barriers that have no clearly demonstrable causal link with the learner's benefiting from the learning experience.

Use of self-study materials, such as books, articles, audio and video tapes, computer programs, and so on, is frequently associated with flexible learning. This is largely a byproduct of the economics and social organization of education—few people can afford on-demand access to teachers and other subject-matter experts. Nevertheless, there is no principled reason why flexible learning should involve the use of self-study materials.

Flexible learning is also often thought of as a solitary activity. In so far as this is true, it is a byproduct of distance-taught correspondence courses, models for flexible learning, and the costs (financial and other) of communication between dispersed learners. Flexible learning need not be a solitary activity. It often is so, because of the methods that institutions have adopted for supporting flexible learning or because the learner is learning without reference to an institution. A tension

253

also exists between individual flexibility and the circumstances most conducive to collaborative learning. Where individual learners choose to have a high level of control over the timing of their study, for example, it can be very difficult for them to engage in collaborative activities such as seminars (which may benefit from participants being at a common point in their learning). Resolving this tension between individual and group interests can be a difficult challenge.

## WEAK AND STRONG INTERPRETATIONS OF SITUATEDNESS

We now need to turn to *place*. Jean Lave and Etienne Wenger are to be credited for reminding us that learning is socially and physically situated (Lave, 1988; Lave and Wenger, 1991; Rogoff and Lave, 1984), although a number of other authors must also be acknowledged in considering the renaissance of this idea, such as Hutchins (1995), Scribner (1985), and Suchman (1987). The *force* of *situatedness* varies somewhat in different accounts, but Engestrom (1999) neatly arranges these into weaker and stronger interpretations. The weak version asserts that learning is situated in physical and social contexts so context must be taken into account when one studies learning. For examples of this position, see Greeno (1989) or Barab and Plucker (2002). The strong interpretation—exemplified in Lave and Wenger's work—is that learning is a byproduct of participation in a social practice, that such social practices do not have to be explicitly defined as practices of learning, and that one should focus on the practice rather than the context. Thinking about weak and strong interpretations of *physical* situatedness helps us partition the relevant literature on learning places. The weak (contextual) interpretation invokes notions of ergonomics and affordance. The stronger (social practice) interpretation raises deeper questions about being and becoming a learner and the role of place in knowledge practices. These two subthemes are reviewed in the next two sections.

## THE ERGONOMICS OF LEARNING ENVIRONMENTS

The work of John Sweller (this volume), Richard Mayer (2001), and others on the implications of cognitive load theory for learning from multimedia is a useful starting point for thinking about the design of resources that support efficient learning. This body of work represents the micro-level pole of a continuum for which the macro-level pole is the global environment within which a learner's activity is situated. A focus on learnplaces suggests the meso-level, but one must acknowledge straight away that learnplaces are constituted by artifacts of the micro-level and situated within influential, spatially more extensive contexts. The ways in which artifacts and tools (objects at the micro-level) exert influence upon learning is commonly conceptualized using notions of *affordance*. This construct originated in the ecological psychology of Gibson (1977) and was transplanted to educational technology via human–computer interaction (Norman, 1990, 1999), suffering some sleight of hand; it is now widely used to connote processes of influence rather than causation—as when one implies that the features of a tool or other artifact suggest one usage, or one course of action, rather than another (see Chapter 22 in this volume).

At the meso-level, where we can deal appropriately with the qualities of a learnplace, it may be more productive to focus on ergonomics rather than the logic of affordance. The case for an ergonomics of learning environments can be found in Goodyear (1997, 2000). The essence of this perspective is that the design of educational technologies is best informed by an understanding of the actuality of learners' work. One reason why educational technologies are ignored by learners is that they do not fit with the learners' actual work. They reflect teachers' views of the prescribed tasks rather than learners' real-world activity. An understanding of learnplace qualities can then be conceived as a kind of cognitive anthropology of situated learning.

## BEING A LEARNER: PUTTING LEARNING IN ITS PLACE

Flexible use of space (mobile learning) means that place cannot be used to delimit the social practices of learning: If one can learn anywhere, what does it mean to be a learner? Probing at this question reveals some interesting answers—not least, that most of the social practices we associate with learning are subtly influenced by place. As an example, take the work of Charles Crook and Paul Light on campus-based students' engagement in learning with information and communication technology (ICT) (Crook, 2002; Crook and Barrowcliff, 2001; Crook and Light, 1999, 2002). This program of research looked at differences and similarities in the study practices of undergraduate students from the same university, half of whom had computers with high-speed network connections in their study bedrooms and half of whom did not. Similarities in the study practices of the two groups help us identify some of the subtle influences of the material world and of the patterns of interaction and communication lodged in that material world (Crook and Light, 2002, p. 174):

> Deliberate learning involves engaging with exposition, orchestrated discussion, research, systematic annotation, the focused reading of text, and a variety of other directed activities that many students may not always find easy to mobilize and manage independently. Sites of formal education have evolved structures that sustain and coordinate such activities with a scaffold of cultural resources: timetables, curricula, designed spaces, discourse rituals and so on … making progress within this infrastructure amounts to a process of enculturation. Students are confronted with the various arenas of study as formalized versions of activities well rehearsed in their informal lives.

A good example is private study. An expectation of higher education is that engagement in private study will be focused and sustained. It is easy to miss the way in which the achievement of such study depends on the design and cultivation of various institutional spaces and practices (such as study bedrooms and quiet library spaces). ICT can break down some of the helpful insulation between the protecting spaces and orderly practices conducive to difficult study and the personal spaces and informal practices familiar from everyday life (Crook and Light, 2002).

Place matters in other ways. Places are home to artifacts, to a greater or lesser degree. From a sociocultural perspective, artifacts are embodiments of ideas, concepts, and methods. They are the "manufactured objects that silently impregnate the furniture of the world with human intelligence" (White, 1996, p. xiii). Not just books and computers but also rulers, watches, notepads, and Post-it notes enable some forms of knowledge work by "being to hand." The ability to offload memory to artifacts in the learnplace is a strong influence on what is cognitively possible, as well as a skill to be mastered (Perkins, 1993). To assert that one's PDA can do all these things is to trample roughshod over the subtle qualities of the learnplace (Crook and Barrowcliff, 2001).

## FURTHER RESEARCH

Three areas of research look particularly promising. First, we need more of the painstaking, anthropological studies that can help us understand the subtle influences of place on study practices and outcomes, along the lines of the work by Crook and colleagues (Crook, 2002; Crook and Barrowcliff, 2001; Crook and Light, 2002). A satisfactory program of study would embrace both familiar and emerging learnplaces and would

include study practices associated with new mobile technologies and ubiquitous intelligence (Benford, 2005; Sharples, 2000). Second, we need ways to capture, formalize, and share knowledge about recurring patterns in the physically situated activities associated with study and learning, such that we can help designers, teachers, and learners develop a better practical understanding of how to improve learnplaces. The people most closely involved in such matters do not have shared language or constructs to deal with phenomena that are of central importance to them, such as learning, study, the ergonomics and affordances of physical space, and digital tools. One promising line of work here is represented by a resurgence of interest in the analytic methods and writing of the architect Christopher Alexander on design patterns and pattern languages (see, for example, Alexander et al., 1977; Frizell and Hubscher, 2002; Goodyear, 2005). Third, we need to understand students' *experiences* of learning in situations where they are taking greater control over the time and location of their learning activity. Phenomenographical research methods are highly appropriate here (Marton, 1981; Prosser and Trigwell, 1999), as this research tradition has probably given us deeper insights into the nature and variation in students' experiences of learning than any comparable approach. Phenomenographic research is, however, remarkably quiet about the effects of place on student experience.

## CONCLUDING REMARKS

Technological change allows a shift in the expectations, practices and discourse around the location of activity in time and space. Although flexible learning, mobile learning, and their analogs are sometimes held to have conquered time and space, paradoxically they render time and space more important. This chapter has provided an entry point into some of the ideas and literature connecting learning to place and has suggested some points of departure for new research.

## REFERENCES

Alexander, C., Ishikawa, S., Silverstein, M., Jacobson, M., Fiksdahl-King, I., and Angel, S. (1977). *A Pattern Language: Towns, Buildings, Construction*. New York: Oxford University Press.

Auburn, T. and Barnes, R. (2006). Producing place: a neo-Schutzian perspective on the 'psychology of place.' *J. Environ. Psychol.*, 26, 38–50.

Barab, S. and Plucker, J. (2002). Smart people or smart contexts? Cognition, ability and talent development in an age of situated approaches to knowing and learning. *Educ. Psychol.*, 37, 165–182.*

Benford, S. (2005). *Future Location-Based Experiences*. London: U.K. Joint Information Systems Committee.

Bliss, J., Saljo, R., and Light, P., Eds. (1999). *Learning Sites: Social and Technological Resources for Learning*. Oxford: Elsevier.

Boot, R. and Hodgson, V. (1987). Open learning: meaning and experience. In *Beyond Distance Teaching: Towards Open Learning*, edited by V. Hodgson, S. Mann, and R. Snell, pp. 5–15. Buckingham: Open University Press.

Comber, C. and Wall, D. (2001). The classroom environments: a framework for learning. In *Learning, Space and Identity*, edited by C. Paechter, R. Edwards, R. Harrison, and P. Twining, pp. 87–101. London: Paul Chapman.

Crook, C. (2002). The campus experience of networked learning. In *Networked Learning: Perspectives and Issues*, edited by C. Steeples and C. Jones, pp. 293–308. London: Springer.*

Crook, C. and Barrowcliff, D. (2001). Ubiquitous computing on campus: patterns of engagement by university students. *Int. J. Hum.–Comput. Interact.*, 13, 245–258.

Crook, C. and Light, P. (1999). Information technology and the culture of student learning. In *Learning Sites: Social and Technological Resources for Learning*, edited by J. Bliss, R. Saljo, and P. Light, pp. 183–193. Oxford: Pergamon.

Crook, C. and Light, P. (2002). Virtualisation and the cultural practice of study. In *Virtual Society? Technology, Cyberbole, Reality*, edited by S. Woolgar, pp. 153–175. Oxford: Oxford University Press.

de Boer, W. and Collis, B. (2005). Becoming more systematic about flexible learning: beyond time and distance. *ALT-J Res. Learn. Technol.*, 13, 33–48.*

Edwards, R. (1997). *Changing Places? Flexibility, Lifelong Learning and a Learning Society*. London: Routledge.

Edwards, R. and Clarke, J. (2002). Flexible learning, spatiality and identity. *Stud. Contin. Educ.*, 24, 153–165.

Engestrom, Y. (1999). Situated learning at the threshold of the new millenium. In *Learning Sites: Social and Technological Resources for Learning*, edited by J. Bliss, R. Saljo, and P. Light, pp. 249–257. Oxford: Elsevier.

Ford, P., Goodyear, P., Heseltine, R., Lewis, R., Darby, J., Graves, J. et al. (1996). *Managing Change in Higher Education: A Learning Environment Architecture*. Buckingham, U.K.: SRHE/Open University Press.

Friedland, R. and Boden, D., Eds. (1994). *NowHere: Space, Time and Modernity*. Berkeley: University of California Press.

Frizell, S. and Hubscher, R. (2002). Aligning theory and Web-based instructional design practice with design patterns. In *Proceedings of e-Learn 2002 World Conference on e-Learning in Corporate, Government, Health, and Higher Education*, October 15–19, Montreal.

Gibson, J. (1977). The theory of affordances. In *Perceiving, Acting, and Knowing: Toward an Ecological Psychology*, edited by R. Shaw and J. Bransford, pp. 67–82. Hillsdale, NJ: Lawrence Erlbaum Associates.*

Goodyear, P. (1997). The ergonomics of learning environments: learner-managed learning and new technology. In *Creacion de materiales para la innovacion educativa con nuevas tecnologias*, pp. 7–17. Malaga: Instituto de Ciencias de la Educacion, Universidad de Malaga.

Goodyear, P. (2000). Environments for lifelong learning: ergonomics, architecture and educational design. In *Integrated and Holistic Perspectives on Learning, Instruction and Technology: Understanding Complexity*, edited by J. M. Spector and T. M. Anderson, pp. 1–18. Dordrecht: Kluwer.*

Goodyear, P. (2005). Educational design and networked learning: patterns, pattern languages and design practice. *Australasian J. Educ. Technol.*, 21(1), 82–101.

Goodyear, P. (2006). Technology and the articulation of vocational and academic interests: reflections on time, space and e-learning. *Stud. Contin. Educ.*, 28, 83–98.*

Graetz, K. and Goliber, M. (2002). Designing collaborative learning places: psychological foundations and new frontiers. *New Direct. Teaching Learn.*, 92, 13–22.

Greeno, J. (1989). A perspective on thinking. *Am. Psychol.*, 44, 134–141.

Hutchins, E. (1995). *Cognition in the Wild*. Cambridge, MA: MIT Press.*

Jamieson, P., Fisher, K., Gilding, T., Taylor, P., and Trevitt, A. (2000). Place and space in the design of new learning environments. *Higher Educ. Res. Dev.*, 19, 221–236.

Khan, B., Ed. (2006). *Flexible Learning in an Information Society*. Hershey, PA: Information Science Publishing.*

Lave, J. (1988). *Cognition in Practice*. Cambridge, U.K.: Cambridge University Press.

Lave, J. and Wenger, E. (1991). *Situated Learning: Legitimate Peripheral Participation*. Cambridge, U.K.: Cambridge University Press.*

Lockwood, F. and Latchem, C., Eds. (1997). *Staff Development in Open and Flexible Education*. London: Routledge.

Marton, F. (1981). Phenomenography: describing conceptions of the world around us. *Instruct. Sci.*, 10, 177–200.

Mason, R. (1994). *Using Communications Media in Open and Flexible Learning*. London: Kogan Page.

Mayer, R. E. (2001). *Multimedia Learning*. Cambridge, U.K.: Cambridge University Press.*

Monahan, T. (2002). Flexible space and built pedagogy: emerging IT embodiments, *Inventio*, 4(1), 1–19 (http://www.doit.gmu.edu/inventio/past/display_past.asp?pID=spring02&sID=monahan).

Norman, D. A. (1990). *The Psychology of Everyday Things*. New York: Basic Books.

Norman, D. (1999). Affordance, conventions, and design. *Interactions*, 6, 38–43.

Paechter, C., Edwards, R., Harrison, R., and Twining, P., Eds. (2001). *Learning, Space and Identity*. London: Paul Chapman.

Perkins, D. N. (1993). Person-plus: a distributed view of thinking and learning. In *Distributed Cognitions: Psychological and Educational Considerations*, edited by G. Salomon, pp. 88–110. Cambridge, U.K.: Cambridge University Press.*

Poysa, J., Lowyck, J., and Hakkinen, P. (2005). Learning together 'there'–hybrid 'place' as a conceptual vantage point for understanding virtual learning communities in higher education context. *PsychNol. J.*, 3(2), 162–180.

Prosser, M. and Trigwell, K. (1999). *Understanding Learning and Teaching: The Experience in Higher Education*. Buckingham, U.K.: SRHE/Open University Press.

Roberts, J., Beke, N., Janzen, K., Mercer, D., and Soetaert, E. (2003). *Harvesting Fragments of Time: Mobile Learning Pilot Project*. Toronto: McGraw-Hill (http://www.mcgrawhill.ca/college/mlearning/mlearn_report.pdf).

Rogoff, B., and Lave, J., Eds. (1984). *Everyday Cognition*. Cambridge MA: Harvard University Press.

Scribner, S. (1985). Knowledge at work. *Anthropol. Educ. Q.*, 16, 199–206.

Sharples, M. (2000). The design of personal mobile technologies for lifelong learning. *Comput. Educ.*, 34, 177–193.

Sime, J. (1986). Creating places or designing spaces? *J. Environ. Psychol.*, 6, 49–63.

Singleton, J., Ed. (1998). *Learning in Likely Places: Varieties of Apprenticeship in Japan*. Cambridge, U.K.: Cambridge University Press.

Slack, R., Tudhope, D., Beynon-Davies, P., and Mackay, H. (1996). *Working from the Learnplace, Learning from the Workplace: Some Thoughts on the Role of the Ethnographer in the Production of Ethnographic Account*s, No. CSRP 428. Brighton, U.K.: University of Sussex

Suchman, L. (1987). *Plans and Situated Actions: The Problem of Human–Machine Communication*. Cambridge, U.K.: Cambridge University Press.

Van den Brande, L. (1993). *Flexible and Distance Learning*. Chichester: Wiley

Van Note Chism, N. (2002). A tale of two classrooms. *New Direct. Teaching Learn.*, 92, 5–12.

Wade, W., Hodgkinson, K., Smith, A., and Arfield, J., Eds. (1994). *Flexible Learning in Higher Education*. London: Kogan Page.

White, S. (1996). Foreword. In *Cultural Psychology, A Once and Future Discipline*, edited by M. Cole. Cambridge, MA: Belknapp Press.

Willems, J. (2005). Flexible learning: implications of 'when-ever,' 'where-ever,' and 'what-ever.' *Distance Educ.*, 26, 429–435.*

* Indicates a core reference.

# 22

# Enabling Time, Pace, and Place Independence

*Som Naidu*
University of Melbourne, Australia

## CONTENTS

## ABSTRACT

This chapter examines technologies that enable time and place independence. Its particular focus is on the *affordances* of these technologies: their ability to support *self-paced learning*, offline or online, and *group-based learning*, asynchronously or synchronously. Self-paced learning *offline* is a mode of learning that enables individuals to study with the help of portable technologies in their own time, at their own pace, and in their own place. Technologies that support this mode of learning include printed books and a whole range of portable non-print media. Self-paced learning *online* is a mode of learning that enables individuals to study online and in their own time, at their own pace, and possibly from their own place. The most prominent technologies that support this model of learning include the Internet and various other computer-mediated communications technologies. Group-based learning *asynchronously* is a mode of learning that enables individuals to learn in groups with online technologies but in their own time, at their own pace, and from their own place. Technologies that support this mode of learning include online learning management systems, mailing lists, bulletin boards, Web logs, and wikis. Group-based learning *synchronously* is a mode of learning that enables individuals to learn in groups with online technologies at the same time and at the same pace as that of the group, but from different places. Commonly known technologies that allow this kind of flexibility are audio and video conferencing, broadcast radio and television, and newer technologies such as Internet telephony (VoIP), inter-relay chat, and online games and simulations.

## KEYWORDS

*Group-based learning asynchronously:* A mode of learning that enables individuals to learn in groups with online technologies in their own time, at their own pace, and from their own place.

*Group-based learning synchronously:* A mode of learning that enables individuals to learn in groups with online technologies at the same time and at the same pace as that of the group but from their own place.

*Self-paced learning offline:* A mode of learning that enables individuals to study with portable technologies in their own time, at their own pace, and from their own place.

*Self-paced learning online:* A mode of learning that enables individuals to study online in their own time, at their own pace, and from their own place.

## INTRODUCTION

The time and place of any educational activity are of significant importance to learners and teachers as well as the educational organization that is offering the activity. They are of interest to learners because of their implications for when and where they need to be to learn. Teachers are similarly affected by the implications of time and place in terms of when they must teach and where they need to be to teach. The time and place of learning and teaching activities also affect educational organizations in terms of what infrastructure and resources they must have and how to organize them to meet the requirements of where and when learning and teaching must take place.

Learning and teaching activities in campus-based educational settings have conventionally been regulated by time and place. Learners and teachers in these educational settings are expected to be present at designated places and times to engage in the educational activities. In so doing, this mode of learning and teaching imposes constraints on both learners and teachers who, for various reasons, are unable to be present in a required place and at the appointed time. This prevents a large number of learners from participating in their educational advancement because of their inability to be present at a particular place and time. The time and place of learning impose additional constraints on learners who are able to access campus-based educational provision but for various reasons are unable to complete their learning activities within a certain time frame.

## STRATEGIES

The constraints of the time and place of learning in campus-based educational settings potentially disadvantage a wide range of learners, such as those who are in regular employment or committed to other family care responsibilities, who are physically located too far away from the educational organization or source of the service, who are too poor to afford the various costs of campus-based education, or who lack the formal qualifications necessary to gain entry to this form of education.

### Correspondence Education

In most educational settings, the foregoing situation was found to be unacceptable, and something needed to be done about it. The growth of correspondence education was a direct result of an effort to address this problem. By capitalizing on two technological developments of the time—namely, the printing press and the postal services—correspondence education was able to offer education to those who were unable to access it in campus-based educational settings. Early initiatives with correspondence education involved individual teachers who were trying to reach small numbers of learners wherever they were. Notable instances included the teaching of shorthand, typing, and the English language. The successes of these early and solitary efforts with correspondence education led to established educational organizations rapidly adopting this approach alongside their campus-based educational programs.

As an alternative mode of learning and teaching, correspondence education developed rapidly and steadily in Europe, Canada, Australia, New Zealand, and South Africa and a little later in Asia and Africa. In the United Kingdom, for example, the growth of correspondence education was spearheaded by political will and with the establishment of the United Kingdom Open University by the Labor Government. In South Africa, the need for correspondence education was driven by the apartheid government's divisive policies of racial segregation that restricted certain racial groups from participating in mainstream educational provision leading to the establishment of the University of South Africa (UNISA). In Asia and Africa, the drivers of correspondence education were the very large numbers of people (both children and adults) who needed education and training, as well as the inability of many of them to afford the comparably high costs of campus-based education. Currently, numerous educational organizations all over the world use correspondence education to provide educational opportunities to many students. Many of these efforts, despite having access to other delivery technologies, continue to rely on little more than printed study materials to offer formal education to very large numbers of learners throughout the world via postal services (Daniel, 1996; Keegan and Rumble, 1982).

The essence of correspondence education was the asynchronous nature of the communication between the learners and their teachers or the educational organization (Holmberg, 1995, 2001; Moore, 1989; Peters, 1971). This model of learning allowed learners to study at a time, pace, and place that most suited them or their situation, regardless of where their teachers or the teaching organization may have been located. The acts of teaching included preparation of the study materials and assignments for the students and communication with them through feedback and comments on the assignments that they submitted.

Although correspondence education offered a viable solution for the constraints imposed by the time, place, and pace dependencies of campus-based education, it had many problems. The absence in such settings of various kinds of learning supports and services that are available to learners in campus-based educational settings caused many problems for learners as well as teachers. Some of these obvious learning supports included facilities for laboratory, tutorial, and small-group work and various forms of guidance and counseling services that students often need. The inability of correspondence education to provide a comparable level of such learner supports caused many learners to experience serious problems with their studies, often leading them to abandon their studies altogether (Amundsen and Bernard, 1989; Simpson, 2003; Sweet, 1986; Woodley and Parlett, 1983).

### Distance Education

To remain a viable educational alternative, correspondence education began to gradually incorporate in its armory increasingly more learner support strategies, ranging from local study center support to residential study sessions, usually during the summer breaks (Bernath and Szucs; 2004; Brindley et al., 2004; Sewart, 1993; Tait and Mills, 2003). It also included the use of a growing range of technologies to supplement the printed study materials to support the interaction between the learners and the teachers.

This shift in correspondence education from an exclusive reliance on the printed word and the postal services to the incorporation of a wider range of technologies for communication between learners and teachers made the term *correspondence education* increasingly unsuitable. With the growing use of non-print media in this mode of learning and teaching, much more than simply correspondence was taking place between the learners and the teachers or the teaching organization.

This led to a growing push for the adoption of the term *distance education* for this mode of learning and teaching. This new term was favored because it directed attention away from the mode of communication (i.e., print and postal services). The concept of distance in this mode of education focused attention on the nature of the separation of the learners from their teachers and the teaching organization and on the noncontiguous nature of the learning and teaching transaction (Keegan, 1990; Perraton, 1987; Rumble, 1989). Use of the term *distance education* for correspondence education grew due to the proliferation of newer technologies that were becoming available to support time, place, and pace independence. Although this shift has been a growing trend in the more developed and resource-rich economies, print and the postal services continue to be widely used for distance education in the less developed and resource-poor economies.

## TECHNOLOGIES

A meaningful way to cluster technologies that enable time, place, and pace independence is presented in Table 22.1 (Naidu, 2006; Romiszowski, 2004). The approach in this table helps to focus our attention on the key *affordances* of these technologies—that is, the opportunities that these technologies offer for individuals as well as groups of learners to work in their own time, at their own pace, and place, asynchronously or synchronously (see also Chapters 21 and 23 in this volume).

---

**TABLE 22.1**
**Clusters of Technology Affordances for Learning**

| | |
|---|---|
| Self-paced learning *offline* | Self-paced learning *online* |
| Group-based learning *asynchronously* | Group-based learning *synchronously* |

---

The concept of *affordance*, which was first developed by James Gibson in relation to his work on perception, refers to what an environment has, offers, or provides as clues or stimuli, either positive or negative, for perception or cognition to take place (Gibson, 1977, 1979). In relation to the use of educational technologies, the term *affordance* is being commonly used to refer to the *opportunities* that various *features* or *attributes* of technologies offer for various types of learning activities (Barnes, 2000; Gaver, 1991, 1992).

The review of research on the affordances of technology for learning adopts a consistent format. It starts off with a definition and description of the concept and mode of learning. This is followed by a description of attributes and affordances of the technologies that enable particular modes of learning. A review of key research directions on the mode of learning is then presented. This also includes key unanswered questions and some directions for further research.

## Self-Paced Learning Offline

The concept of self-paced learning implies freedom from the constraints of time and pace. In this mode of learning, individuals are able to carry out their learning activities within a time frame and at a pace that suits them, although some or all of these activities may have to be carried out at specific locations such as a library or a laboratory. Self-paced learning suits learners for different reasons. It is ideally suited for the independent learner who is pursing a hobby or who is learning something for very personal reasons and not necessarily for a formal credit (Brookfield, 1982). It is also suited to a learner who is studying for formal credit but who might need more or less time as well as a different pace from that of others.

A strong argument in the educational literature favors allowing the time and the pace that a learner needs to complete the required learning activities or to achieve his or her full potential (Carroll, 1963). Two models of learning that have been developed around the concepts of time and pace flexibility include Mastery Learning and the Personalized System of Instruction (Block and Anderson, 1975; Bloom, 1968; Keller, 1968). These models of learning are based on the premise that any learner is capable of achieving mastery if he or she has been allowed the time and the pace that he or she needs.

A technology that affords the greatest amount of flexibility in terms of the time, pace, and place of study is clearly the printed textbook. This can come in the form of commercially produced reference books, customized readers, and study guides. Carefully designed textual material makes judicious use of a range of design strategies to capture and communicate its message to the readers. These strategies include anything from introductions, in-text questions, and summaries to pictures and graphic illustrations. The printed textbook is a widely portable and relatively durable item that can be used by anyone who is able to read. It gives the reader the flexibility to read it when and where he or she needs or wishes to read it. Also, readers can vary the pace at which they might read different kinds of textual material; for example, students might read much of the daily newspaper a lot more quickly than they might read a journal article for their studies.

A wide range of non-print media also affords a considerable amount of flexibility in terms of time, pace, and place of study. The more conventional of the non-print technologies include the audiocassette, videocassette, CD-ROMs, and DVDs. These technologies are capable of capturing sound, animation, and the moving image which is crucial for representing various kinds of content. They are very durable and portable, and they offer users a good deal of flexibility in terms of the time, pace, and place of its use.

Contemporary non-print technologies include a growing list of portable devices, including mobile phones, a variety of personal digital assistants (PDAs), iPODs, laptop computers, and tablet PCs. Although the form and function of these portable technologies continue to change incessantly, their unique attribute is their ability to support time, place, and in many cases pace independence. Mobile phones, for example, in addition to serving as communication devices are able to support a range of other functions such as organizing and scheduling. Personal digital assistants that are now coming onto the market have similarly progressed from serving as simple calendars or schedulers to also supporting communication. The laptop computer is now the main working machine for many, as its power and speed have expanded to match those of the desktop machine. The increasing power and potential of these technologies afford substantially improved opportunities for individuals as well as groups to work and study at a time, pace, and place that is convenient for them.

There has been extensive research on the educational uses of the more conventional mobile technologies, such as printed study materials and other non-print mobile technologies (Bernard and Naidu, 1990, 1992; Bernard et al., 1991; Hackbarth, 1996; Heinich et al., 1993; Lockwood, 1998; Naidu, 1994; Naidu, and Bernard, 1992; Rigney, 1978). Research on the use of the more contemporary mobile technologies in learning and teaching, such as mobile phones and personal digital assistants, is only just beginning (Kukulska-Hulme and Traxler, 2005).

A growing body of research on the use of hand-held devices such as mobile phones in the classroom (Prensky, 2005) indicates that hand-held devices, and especially mobile phones, are becoming increasingly more affordable in both developed and developing countries. These are powerful tools that offer voice-based communication, text messaging, graphic displays, and Web browsing; however, their ubiquity has yet to be fully explored for learning and teaching purposes (Prensky, 2005).

The PDAs currently appearing on the market are able to serve several useful educational functions, including content delivery, organization, communication, and access to various types of educational guidance and support services (Kukulska-Hulme and Traxler, 2005). Preliminary reports are beginning to emerge on the use of various mobile technologies for a variety of educational purposes. These include the use of mobile phones in language learning (Levy and Kennedy, 2005) and the use of PDAs by medical staff and physicians for accessing critical information while they are away from their offices (Kneebone and Brenton, 2005; Smordell and Gregory, 2005). There are also reports on the use of handheld devices and wireless computers to improve assessment of learning and instruction (Moallem et al., 2005).

As the demand for greater flexibility in learning and teaching and just-in-time learning opportunities (i.e., learning at the time of need) increases, it is likely that greater use will be made of mobile technologies. No doubt, the mobile technologies of the future will have a lot more capacity than today's personal computers; however, their attraction will lie in their targeted use to support specific learning and teaching activities. Reports on their use should focus on the following types of questions:

- What are the ways in which mobile technologies can be used to support learning in both individualized and group-based educational settings? What are the impacts of such use of mobile technologies on various aspects of learning?
- What are the ways in which mobile technologies can be used to leverage various learning and teaching activities? What are the impacts of such use of mobile technologies on various aspects of learning?

To adequately answer these types of questions, great care should be taken to focus attention on the foregoing affordances of these technologies and especially on the ways in which they can support specific learning and teaching functions. These studies will have to use the full range of approaches on research and evaluation and draw upon the collective wisdom on research and evaluation of technology-enhanced learning (Abrami and Bernard, 2006; Taylor, 2003).

## Self-Paced Learning Online

Self-paced learning online is a mode of learning in which an individual is able to study at his or her own pace with a range of online technologies. A growing list of technologies is becoming widely available and also affordable to make time and pace independence online a considerably more pleasant experience. Perhaps the most prominent among the technologies supporting self-paced learning online are the Internet and the World Wide Web. The Internet refers to the network of computers that are connected to one another, thus enabling the sharing of data, information, communication, and other types of subject matter among its users via file-sharing protocols. Another set of technologies that is able to support self-paced learning is the variety of computer-mediated communications technologies, such as e-mail, mailing lists, and discussion forums (Naidu, 1989). This suite of technologies uses the electronic text to enable users to communicate with, and share information with individuals and groups in their own time and at their own pace, and from a place that is convenient to them (Naidu, 2006).

Also growing in popularity for supporting self-paced learning online in both campus-based and distance education systems are online learning management systems. These are software applications comprised of a collection of tools that can support a variety of learning and teaching activities, such as self-paced independent study as well as group-based learning activities; they provide the opportunity to access and work on a particular subject matter at the learner's own pace and time and from a place of his or her choice. They also allow communication with peers and teachers at the learner's own convenience (Naidu, 2006).

A critical enabler of self-paced online learning is access to electronic resources, which are becoming increasingly available to users online. These include various types of electronic databases, learning object repositories and archives, journals, and books (McGreal, 2004; Richards et al., 2004). They allow learners to search for and retrieve data and information from rich repositories at a time, pace, and from a place convenient to them. Publishers and promoters of these electronic resources are suggesting that these resources are the "building blocks of e-learning ... [and] the libraries of the e-learning era" (Richards et al., 2004, pp. 236, 242).

Despite its obvious advantages, self-paced learning online does have some limitations, particularly with relation to the loneliness and boredom that may set in due to the lack of *social presence*, which refers to the degree to which participants seem to be real in noncontiguous educational settings. Social learning theorists would argue that learning could be constrained by the lack of social presence (Bandura, 1977; Lave, 1991; Vygotsky, 1978; Wenger, 1998; Wertsch, 1991). This lack of social presence in self-paced online learning has been its major criticism and the subject of a great deal of research. The focus of that research is on the impacts and implications of the lack of social presence on learning (Gunawardena, 1995; Gunawardena and Zittle, 1997; Richardson and Swan, 2003; Swan and Shih, 2005) and on strategies that can be employed to reintegrate social presence in learning online (Conrad, 2005; Kreijns et al., 2002, 2003; Swan, 2002). A key premise of this line of research is that building social cohesiveness and community is essential to our learning and our learning capability (Kreijns et al., 2002, 2003).

## Group-Based Learning Asynchronously

Group-based learning is grounded in the principles of cooperative and collaborative learning and on the belief that the development of knowledge is a social process. It involves groups of people engaged in the negotiation of meaning and understanding (Slavin, 1990, 1994; Wenger, 1998). Although individuals can learn by themselves, proponents of group-based learning argue that group-based learning is a more powerful means for developing knowledge and understanding (Pea, 1993; Resnick et al., 1991).

Group-based learning asynchronously involves groups of learners working together without the need to be studying in the same place or at the same time. This is becoming increasingly possible with the availability of a range of technologies that can support asynchronous communication between individuals and groups who are not in the same location. Prominent among these is the suite of computer-mediated communications technologies, such as online learning management systems, mailing lists, Weblogs (blogs), wikis, and podcasts. Online learning management systems are software applications that allow learners to work together without the need to be at the same place or time. Students can log onto these systems at a time and from a place that suits them to carry out tasks that they have been assigned, and they are able to see what others have done. They can continue to work on these tasks for as long as they like or need to and as often as necessary until the group is satisfied

that the work is done. In this environment, teachers are able to monitor the contributions of individuals as well as the group.

Considerable research has been conducted on asynchronous group-based learning and the technologies that support it (Beldarrain, 2006; Mason, 1993; Mason and Kaye, 1989; Naidu, 1989; Rapaport, 1991). A predominant focus of much of this research is on the affordances of these technologies for collaborative learning (Koschmann, 1996; McConnell, 2000; Stahl, 2002), and building learning communities (Bernard and Lundgren-Cayrol, 2001; Hathorn and Ingram, 2002; Kanuka and Anderson, 1998; Paulus, 2004, 2005; Salmon, 2000; 2003).

Evidence and experience from this body of research suggest that, to achieve the best outcomes, asynchronous group-based learning requires the same level of rigor as any other mode of learning, including paying attention to structuring, managing, and moderating such activities. Although few would argue the benefits of asynchronous group-based learning, we must learn a great deal more about how to best assess learning outcomes within such educational settings. The affordances of the technology in this regard are still very primitive and underutilized. Future research on asynchronous group-based learning must focus on how learning achievement can be reliably and validly assessed in such educational settings.

## Group-Based Learning Synchronously

Group-based learning synchronously also enables groups of learners to work together; however, in this mode of learning, although the learners need not be in the same place, they must be present at the same time and progress pretty much at the same pace as the group. Commonly known technologies that offer this kind of flexibility include audio and video conferencing and broadcast radio and television. These technologies give learners who primarily study independently the rare opportunity to communicate and work with their peers for brief periods of intensive synchronous activities. These activities may include guest lectures, tutorials, and demonstrations. The use of these technologies is very popular in distance education settings, where they serve a critical role in complementing individualized self-paced study.

Audio and video conferencing, as well as radio and television, are widely known technologies that have demonstrated a great deal of opportunities for group-based synchronous learning (Hutton, 1984; Michel, 1987; Schramm, 1977; Thomas, 1987; Zuber-Skerritt, 1984). In distance education settings, widespread use of radio and television broadcasts enhances and supplements classroom and home schooling activities (Green, 2006; Potter and Naidoo, 2006).

Newer technologies that offer opportunities for synchronous activity include voice over IP (VoIP), inter-relay chat (IRC), and various types of games that can be played with MOOs and MUDs by multiple users on the Internet (MOO is an acronym for MUD, object-oriented, and MUD stands for multi-user domain).

The growth of online distance learning seems to be spearheading a growing interest in the newer collaborative learning technologies that promise group-based synchronous learning opportunities. Noteworthy work in this regard has attempted to integrate proven learning strategies such as role playing and problem solving with technologies to promote the concept that school learning should be more like life itself (Childress and Braswell, 2006; Doering, 2006; Naidu et al., 2000). This is encouraging and is the direction that research and development activity in synchronous group-based learning should be taking.

## DISCUSSION

Frequently asked questions about technology and education include (Clark and Solomon, 1986; Kozma, 1991): How does technology influence learning? Is this influence an improvement over face-to-face instruction? This line of inquiry is problematic, as it suggests that face-to-face education is an ideal form of learning and teaching and that it serves as a benchmark that must be met to establish success. Furthermore, it fails to define the meaning of the term *influence*, nor does it address how such influence is being ascertained and in relation to what specific attributes of face-to-face education.

Although the search for the influence of technology on learning is justified, much of the research in this regard is misguided (Clark, 1983, 1994; Kulik, 1985). Too many of these studies focus attention on the unique impacts of technology, which are almost impossible to delineate from how the technology is being used and for what purpose. Researchers have argued that with that kind of focus these studies run the risk of reporting results that cannot be attributed to the technology alone, as they are very likely to be due to the combined effects of both the technology and the teaching method (Clark, 1994; Kozma, 1991).

There is growing consensus around the view that research on the influence of technology on education should focus on the affordances of these technologies and not the technology itself (Clark, 1983, 1994). These affordances include the capabilities of tech-

nologies to capture and represent different types of content and messages, activate learning, provide opportunities for socialization, assess learning outcomes, and provide feedback and remediation to learners (Naidu, 2003). Although these are common educational activities, research should focus on how these activities are enhanced and supported by various technologies; for example, do time- and place-independent technologies have particular advantages for these learning and teaching activities? What are these advantages? How can these advantages be optimized with the use of various technologies? Research should focus on how technologies can be used to capture data and other types of information to make them accessible to users when and where they are needed. e-Books, for example, might be a great idea, but are they best delivered on a PDA or an iPOD? What types of information are best delivered on mobile technologies and to support what kind of learning and use?

## CONCLUDING REMARKS

Technologies that enable time, pace, and place independence are becoming widely available in both developed and developing societies. As these technologies become more accessible and affordable, they are likely to permeate all aspects of our daily lives; therefore, it would seem sensible to deploy them appropriately in learning and teaching rather than limit or ban them from these contexts. Inefficient use of these technologies will only lead to blaming the technology for ensuing problems, as we have done in the past. Technologies that enable time, pace, and place independence have particular advantages for various types of learning activities and different groups of learners. They allow learners and teachers to do things that are not possible within the parameters of campus-based educational settings. Many of these technologies can put a great deal of resources within easy reach of learners and in so doing can empower them in various ways and open up new opportunities for learning and teaching. These types of learning opportunities will require teachers as well as educational organizations to rethink their learning and teaching processes and how they may have been conducting their business in conventional campus-based educational settings (Herrington et al., 2006). This kind of reorientation to learning and teaching will have numerous implications for the design and development of such learning environments, and this is where research and development activities in the field ought to place much of their emphasis.

# REFERENCES

Abrami, P. and Bernard, R. M. (2006). Research on distance education: in defense of field experiments, *Distance Educ.*, 27(1), 5–26.

Amundsen, C. L. and Bernard, R. M. (1989). Institutional support for peer contact in distance education: an empirical investigation, *Distance Educ.*, 10(1), 7–27.

Bandura, A. (1977). *Social Learning Theory*. Englewood Cliffs, NJ: Prentice Hall.

Barnes, S. (2000). What does electronic conferencing afford distance education? *Distance Educ.*, 21(2), 236–247.

Beldarrain, Y. (2006). Distance education trends: integrating new technologies to foster student interaction and collaboration. *Distance Educ.*, 27(2), 139–153.

Bernard, R. M. and Lundgren-Cayrol, K. (2001). Computer conferencing: an environment for collaborative project-based learning in distance education. *Educ. Res. Eval.*, 7(2–3), 241–261.

Bernard, R. M. and Naidu, S. (1990). Enhancing interpersonal communication in distance education: can 'voice-mail' help? *Educ. Training Technol. Int.*, 27(3), 293–300.

Bernard, R. M. and Naidu, S. (1992). Post-questioning, concept mapping and feedback: A distance education field experiment. *Br. J. Educ. Technol.*, 23(1), 48–60.

Bernard, R. M., Naidu, S., and Amundsen, C. L. (1991). Choosing instructional variables to enhance learning in distance education, *Media Technol. Hum. Resource Dev. J. Educ. Technol.*, 4(1), 3–13.

Bernath, U. and Szucs, A., Eds. (2004). Supporting the learning in distance and e-learning. In *Proceedings of the Third European Distance Education and e-Learning Network (EDEN) Research Workshop*, March 4–6, Carl von Ossietzky University of Oldenburg, Germany.

Block, J. H. and Anderson, L. W. (1975). *Mastery Learning in Classroom Instruction*. New York: Macmillan.

Bloom, B. (1968). Learning for mastery (UCLA-CSEIP). *Eval. Comment*, 1(2), 1–12.

Brindley, J. E., Walti, C., and Zawacki-Richter, O. (2004). *Learner Support in Open, Distance and Online Learning Environments*. Oldenburg: Bibliotheks- und Informationssystem der Universität Oldenburg.

Brookfield, S. (1982). Independent learners and correspondence students, *Teaching Distance*, 22, 26–33.

Carroll, J. B. (1963). A model of school learning. *Teachers Coll. Rec.*, 64(8), 723–733.

Childress, M. D. and Braswell, R. (2006). Using massively multiplayer online role-playing games for online learning, *Distance Educ.*, 27(2), 187–196.

Clark, R. E. (1983). Reconsidering research on learning from media. *Rev. Educ. Res.*, 53(4), 445–460.*

Clark, R. E. (1994). Media will never influence learning. *Educ. Technol. Res. Dev.*, 53(2), 21–30.*

Clark, R. E. and Solomon, G. (1986). Media in teaching. In *Handbook of Research on Teaching*, 3rd ed., edited by M. Wittrock, New York: Macmillan.*

Conrad, D. (2005). Building and maintaining community in cohort-based online learning. *J. Distance Educ.*, 20 (1), 1–21.

Daniel, J. S. (1996). *Mega-Universities and Knowledge Media. Technology Strategies for Higher Education*. London: Kogan Page.

Doering, A. (2006). Adventure learning: transformative hybrid online education, *Distance Educ.*, 27(2), 197–215.

Gaver, W. W. (1991). Technology affordances. In *Proceedings of the SIGCHI Conference on Human Factors in Computing Systems: Reaching Through Technology*, edited by S. P. Robertson, G. M. Olson, and J. S. Ohlson, pp. 79–84. New York: ACM Press.

Gaver, W. W. (1992). The affordances of media spaces for collaboration. In *Proceedings of the 1992 ACM Conference on Computer-Supported Cooperative Work*, edited by M. Mantel and R. Baecker, pp. 17–24. New York: ACM Press.

Gibson, J. J. (1977). The theory of affordances. In *Perceiving, Acting, and Knowing: Toward an Ecological Psychology*, edited by R. Shaw and J. Bransford, pp. 67–82. Hillsdale, NJ: Lawrence Erlbaum Associates.*

Gibson, J. J. (1979). *The Ecological Approach to Visual Perception*. Boston: Houghton Mifflin.

Green, N. C. (2006). Everyday life in distance education: one family's home schooling experience. *Distance Educ.*, 27(1), 27–44.

Gunawardena, C. N. (1995). Social presence theory and implications for interaction and collaborative learning in computer conferences. *Int. J. Educ. Telecommun.*, 1(2/3), 147–166.

Gunawardena, C. N. and Zittle, F. (1997). Social presence as a predictor of satisfaction within a computer mediated conferencing environment. *Am. J. Distance Educ.*, 11(3), 8–26.

Hackbarth, S. (1996). *The Educational Technology Handbook: A Comprehensive Guide*. Englewood Cliffs, NJ: Educational Technology Publications.

Hathorn, L. G. and Ingram, A. L. (2002). Cooperation and collaboration using computer-mediated communication. *J. Educ. Comput. Res.*, 26(3), 325–347.

Heinich, R., Molenda, M., and Russell, J. D. (1993). *Instructional Media and the New Technologies of Instruction*. New York: Macmillan.

Herrington, J., Reeves, T., and Oliver, R. (2006). Authentic tasks online: a synergy among learner, task, and technology, *Distance Educ.*, 27(2), 233–247.

Holmberg, B. (1995). *Theory and Practice of Distance Education*. London: Routledge.

Holmberg, B. (2001). *Distance Education in Essence: An Overview of Theory and Practice in the Early 21st Century*. Oldenburg: Bibliotheks- und Informationssystem der Universitat Oldenburg.

Hutton, D. (1984). Video technology in higher education: the state of the art? In *Video in Higher Education*, edited by O. Zuber-Skerritt, pp. 11–25. London: Kogan Page.

Kanuka, H. and Anderson, T. (1998). Online social interchange, discord and knowledge construction. *J. Distance Educ.*, 13(1), 57–74.

Keegan, D. (1990). *Foundations of Distance Education*, 2nd ed. London: Routledge.

Keegan, D. and Rumble, G. (1982). Distance teaching at university level. In *The Distance Teaching Universities*, edited by G. Rumble and K. Harry, pp. 15–31. London: Croom Helm.

Keller, F. S. (1968). Good-bye, teacher…. *J. Appl. Behav. Anal.*, 1, 79–89.

Kneebone, R. and Brenton, H. (2005). Training perioperative specialist practitioners, In *Mobile Learning: A Handbook for Educators and Trainers*, edited by A. Kukulska-Hulme and J. Traxler, pp. 106–115. London: Routledge.

Koschmann, T., Ed. (1996). *CSCL: Theory and Practice of an Emerging Paradigm*. Mahwah, NJ: Lawrence Erlbaum Associates.

Kozma, R. B. (1991). Learning with media. *Rev. Educ. Res.*, 61(2), 179–211.*

Kreijns, K., Kirschner, P. A., and Jochems, W. (2002). The sociability of computer-supported collaborative learning environments. *J. Educ. Technol. Soc.*, 5(1), 8–22.*

Kreijns, K., Kirschner, P. A., and Jochems, W. (2003). Identifying the pitfalls for social interaction in computer-supported collaborative learning environments: a review of the research. *Comput. Hum. Behav.*, 19(3), 335–353.

Kukulska-Hulme, A. and Traxler, J. (2005). *Mobile Learning: A Handbook for Educators and Trainers*. London: Routledge.

Kulik, J. A. (1985). The importance of outcome studies: a reply to Clark. *Educ. Commun. Technol. J.*, 34(1), 381–386.*

Lave, J. (1991). Situating learning in communities of practice. In *Perspectives on Socially Shared Cognition*, edited by L. B. Resnick, J. M. Levine, and S. D. Teasley, pp. 63–82. Washington, D.C.: American Psychological Association.

Levy, M. and Kennedy, C. (2005). Learning Italian via mobile SMS. In *Mobile Learning: A Handbook for Educators and Trainers*, edited by A. Kukulska-Hulme and J. Traxler, pp. 76–83. London: Routledge.

Lockwood, F. (1998), *The Design and Production of Self-Instructional Materials*. London: Kogan Page.

Mason, R., Ed. (1993). *Computer Conferencing: The Last Word*. Victoria, B.C.: Beach Holme Publishers.

Mason, R. and Kaye, A., Eds. (1989). *Mindweave: Communication, Computers, and Distance Education*. Oxford: Pergamon Press.

McConnell, D. (2000). *Implementing Computer Supported Cooperative Learning*. London: Kogan Page.

McGreal, R., Ed. (2004). *Online Education Using Learning Objects*. London: Routledge.

Michel, C. (1987). Education radio and television: their transfer to developing societies, pages. In *Educational Technology: Its Creation, Development and Cross-Cultural Transfer*, edited by R. M. Thomas and V. N. Kobayashi, pp. 125–142. Oxford: Pergamon.

Moallem, M., Sue-Jen, C., and Kermani, H. (2005). Using handheld wireless computers to improve assessment of learning and instruction, *Educ. Technol.*, 45(6), 12–21.

Moore, M. G. (1989). Editorial: three types of transaction. *Am. J. Distance Educ.*, 3(2), 1–7.

Naidu, S. (1989). Computer conferencing in distance education, *Int. Counc. Distance Educ. Bull.*, 20, 39–46.

Naidu, S. (1994). Applying learning and instructional strategies in open and distance learning. *Distance Educ.*, 15(1), 23–41.*

Naidu, S., Ed. (2003). *Learning and Teaching with Technology: Principles and Practices*. London: Kogan Page.

Naidu, S. (2006). *E-Learning: A Guidebook of Principles, Procedures, and Practices*. New Delhi, India: Commonwealth Educational Media Center for Asia (CEMCA) and the Commonwealth of Learning.

Naidu, S. and Bernard, R. M. (1992). Enhancing academic achievement in distance education with concept mapping and inserted questions. *Distance Educ.*, 23(1), 218–233.

Naidu, S., Ip, A., and Linser, R. (2000) Dynamic goal-based role-play simulation on the Web: a case study. *Educ. Technol. Soc.*, 3(3), 190–202.

Paulus, T. (2004). Collaboration or cooperation? Small group interactions in a synchronous educational environment. In *Computer-Supported Collaborative Learning in Higher Education*, edited by T. S. Roberts, pp. 100–124. Hershey, PA: Idea Group.

Paulus, T. (2005). Collaborative and cooperative approaches to online group work: the impact of task type. *Distance Educ.*, 26(1), 111–125

Pea, R. D. (1993) Practices of distributed intelligence and design for education. In *Distributed Cognition: Psychological and Educational Considerations*, edited by G. Salomon, pp. 47–86. Cambridge, MA: Cambridge University Press.*

Perraton, H. (1987). Theories, generalizations and practice in distance education. *Open Learn.*, 2(3), 3–12.

Peters, O. (1971). Theoretical aspects of correspondence instruction. In *The Changing World of Correspondence Study: International Readings*, edited by O. Mackenzie and E. L. Christensen, pp. 223–228. University Park, PA: The Pennsylvania State University.

Potter, C. S. and Naidoo, G. (2006). Using interactive radio to enhance classroom learning and reach schools, classrooms, teachers, and learners, *Distance Educ.*, 27(1), 63–86.

Prensky, M. (2005). What can you learn from a cell phone? Almost anything! *Innovate*, 1(5), 1–7.

Rapaport, M. (1991). *Computer Mediated Communications: Bulletin Boards, Computer Conferencing, Electronic Mail and Information Retrieval*. London: John Wiley & Sons.

Resnick, L. B., Levine, J. M., and Teasley, S. D. (1991). *Perspectives on Socially Shared Cognition*. Washington, D.C.: American Psychological Association.

Richards, G., Hatala, M., and McGreal, R. (2004). POOL, POND, and SPLASH: portals for online objects for learning. In *Online Education Using Learning Objects*, edited by R. McGreal, p. 237. London: Routledge.

Richardson, J. C. and Swan, K. (2003). Examining social presence in online courses in relation to students' perceived learning and satisfaction. *J. Asynchronous Learn. Netw.*, 7(1), 68–88.

Rigney, J. W. (1978). Learning strategies: a theoretical perspective. In *Learnings Strategies*, edited by H. F. O'Neil, Jr., pp. 165–205. New York: Academic Press.

Romiszowski, A. (2004). How's the e-learning baby? Factors leading to success or failure of an educational technology innovation, *Educ. Technol.*, 44(1), 5–27.

Rumble, G. (1989). On defining distance education. *Am. J. Distance Educ.*, 3(2), 8–20.

Salmon, G. (2000). *E-Moderating: The Key to Teaching and Learning Online*. London: Kogan Page.

Salmon, G. (2003). *Etivities: The Key to Active Online Learning*. London: Routledge.

Schramm, W. (1977). *Big Media, Little Media: Tools and Technologies for Instruction*. Beverly Hills, CA: SAGE.

Sewart, D. (1993). Student support systems in distance education. *Open Learn.*, 8(3), 3–12.

Simpson, O. (2003). *Student Retention in Online, Open, and Distance Learning*. London: Kogan Page.

Slavin, R. E. (1990). *Cooperative Learning: Theory, Research, and Practice*. Englewood Cliffs, NJ: Prentice Hall.*

Slavin, R. E. (1994). Student teams achievement divisions. In *Handbook of Cooperative Learning*, edited by S. Sharan, pp. 3–19. Westport, CT: Greenwood Press.

Smordell, O. and Gregory, J. (2005). Knowmobile: mobile opportunities for medical students. In *Mobile Learning: A Handbook for Educators and Trainers*, edited by A. Kukulska-Hulme and J. Traxler, pp. 99–105. London: Routledge.

Stahl, G. (2002). Contributions to a theoretical framework for CSCL. In *Proceedings of the International Conference on Computer Supported Collaborative Learning (CSCL, 2002)*, pp. 62–71. Hillsdale, NJ: Lawrence Erlbaum Associates.

Swan, K. (2002). Building communities in online courses: the importance of interaction. *Educ. Commun. Inform.*, 2(1), 23–49.*

Swan, K. and Shih, L. (2005). On the nature and development of social presence in online course discussions. *J. Asynchronous Learn. Netw.*, 9 (3).

Sweet, R. (1986). Student dropout in distance education: an application of Tinto's model. *Distance Educ.*, 7(2), 201–203.

Tait, A. and Mills, R. (2003). *Rethinking Learner Support in Distance Education. Change and Continuity in an International Context*. London: Routledge.

Taylor, J. (2003). A task-centered approach to evaluating a mobile learning environment for pedagogical soundness. In *Learning with Mobile Devices: Research and Development*, edited by J. Attewell, and C. Savill-Smith, pp. 167–72. London: Learning and Skills Development Agency.

Thomas, R. M. (1987). Educational radio and television: their development in advanced industrial societies. In *Educational Technology: Its Creation, Development and Cross-Cultural Transfer*, edited by R. M. Thomas and V. N. Kobayashi, pp. 105–124. Oxford: Pergamon.

Vygotsky, L. S. (1978). *Mind and Society: The Development of Higher Psychological Processes*. Cambridge, MA: Harvard University Press.

Wenger, E. (1998). *Communities of Practice: Learning, Meaning and Identity*. Cambridge, U.K.: Cambridge University Press.

Wertsch, J. V. (1991). *Voices of the Mind: A Sociocultural Approach to Mediated Action*. Cambridge, MA: Harvard University Press.

Woodley, A. and Parlett, M. (1983). Student drop-out. *Teaching Distance*, 24, 2–23.

Zuber-Skerritt, O. (1984). *Video in Higher Education*. London: Kogan Page.

* Indicates a core reference.

# 23

# Blended Learning Environments

*Charles R. Graham*
Brigham Young University, Provo, Utah

*Charles Dziuban*
University of Central Florida, Orlando, Florida

## CONTENTS

## ABSTRACT

In recent decades, rapid technological innovation has facilitated a convergence between *traditional face-to-face* and *distributed* (or technology-mediated) learning environments. These *blended learning environments* try to take advantage of the strengths of both archetypal learning environments (Graham, 2006). The emergence of blended learning is highlighted in higher education and in industry training literature. The *Chronicle of*

269

*Higher Education* reports that the President of Pennsylvania State University regards the convergence between online and residential instruction as the "single greatest unrecognized trend in higher education today" (Young, 2002, p. A33). Similarly, the American Society for Training and Development identifies blended learning as one of the top ten emergent trends in the knowledge delivery industry (Finn, 2002). Yet, surprisingly, we understand little about the nature of blended learning systems. This chapter identifies core issues and research about blended learning using the Sloan Consortium's five pillars (learning effectiveness, student satisfaction, faculty satisfaction, cost effectiveness, and access) as an organizing framework (Lorenzo and Moore, 2002). The authors also discuss future directions in blended learning research.

## KEYWORDS

*Blended learning environment:* A learning environment that combines face-to-face instruction with technology-mediated instruction.
*Hybrid learning environment:* Alternative term for blended learning environment.

## INTRODUCTION

The term *blended learning* is relatively new in higher education and in corporate settings (the terms *hybrid* and *blended* can be used interchangeably). An ongoing discussion has ensued on the precise meaning of the term (Driscoll, 2002; Graham et al., 2003; Jones, 2006; Laster, 2004; Masie, 2006; Oliver and Trigwell, 2005; Osguthorpe and Graham, 2003), however, the most common position is that *blended learning environments combine face-to-face instruction with technology-mediated instruction* (Graham, 2006; Graham et al., 2003). Traditional face-to-face instruction involves interactions between instructors and learners who are in the same place, whereas technology-mediated instruction uses information and communication technologies (ICT) to mediate the learning experience and interactions without requiring that learners and instructors be located together.

Research suggests three primary reasons for adopting a blended approach to instruction: (1) improved learning effectiveness, (2) increased access and convenience, and (3) greater cost effectiveness (Graham, 2006). Most often, educators adopt blended learning approaches to explore gains and tradeoffs in comparison with strictly traditional settings or entirely distributed environments.

This chapter identifies core issues and research in the blended learning format using the Sloan Consortium's five pillars (learning effectiveness, student satisfaction, faculty satisfaction, cost effectiveness, and access) as an organizing framework (Lorenzo and Moore, 2002). We also provide some directions for future research. We have chosen to focus on blended learning environments in a higher education context, while acknowledging that significant innovations also occur in informal, military, and corporate contexts (Collis et al., 2005; Harris, 2005; Kirkley and Kirkley, 2005, 2006; Lewis and Orton, 2006; Newton and Ellis, 2005; Wenger and Ferguson, 2006; Wisher, 2006).

## LEARNING EFFECTIVENESS

Key questions with regard to the effectiveness of blended environments include:

- What are the affordances of face-to-face and technology-mediated contexts and how can the strengths of each be used to improve teaching and learning?
- How do short-term student learning outcomes interact with more systemic longer term student outcomes?
- What are the emerging models for assessing learning outcomes in the blended learning environment?
- What is the appropriate role for students becoming involved in the assessment of their own learning effectiveness?

### Transformational Potential

Researchers recognize the potential for transforming learning when combining both face-to-face and technology-mediated instruction (Garrison and Kanuta, 2004; Graham, 2006; Graham and Robison, 2007). Many allude to this potential when they state that blended learning capitalizes on the best of both worlds. The simple elegance of the blended learning concept can also be a weakness, however, if the focus is entirely on the mode of instruction rather than the holistic nature of the learning experience. For example, instructors commonly state that their course is a blend that consists of $x\%$ online and $y\%$ face-to-face, which is not informative without knowing the nature of the activities occurring in the distinct learning environments and how the course effectively uses the affordances of the two environments (Cross, 2006). For blended learning to reach its full transformational potential, the primary goal should be rethinking and redesigning the teaching and learning relationship (i.e., improved pedagogy) with efficiency and convenience as possible secondary benefits (Garrison and Kanuta, 2004, p. 99). Blended learning must capitalize on the strengths of both online and face-to-face modalities to create a more *active learning* environment (Graham and Robison, 2007).

## Completion Rates and Academic Performance

Current studies on learning effectiveness in blended courses and programs concentrate on measures such as grades and withdrawal rates that are highly sensitive to factors such as course level, college, and department. This instability suggests that using course mode as an effect in comparison studies is not a particularly viable line of inquiry; however, some studies have been directed toward learning effectiveness in blended environments. Rochester Institute of Technology's pilot program reported that completion rates were approximately 95% (Humbert and Vignare, 2004; Starenko et al., 2007), and Reasons and colleagues (Reasons, 2004; Reasons et al., 2005) found that fully online students succeed at rates higher than those in face-to-face or blended courses. Additional studies have shown comparable success in blended courses, yet others report them as superior regarding learning effectiveness (Boyle et al., 2003; Cottrell and Robinson, 2003; Dowling et al., 2003; O'Toole and Absalom, 2003; Riffell and Sibley, 2004). In larger data-mining studies of several thousand student registrations, researchers at the University of Central Florida found that blending learning courses produced comparable or superior success rates compared to face-to-face or fully online modes when college and gender contributions are removed (Dziuban et al., 2006).

## Assessment

At present, most assessment mechanisms in blended learning remain traditional, as they are objective, non-contextual, and inauthentic; however, as the initiative matures, student assessment will, by necessity, become interpretive, contextual, and authentic. Brown et al. (2007) identified several important student perceptions about the efficacy of assessment techniques in the blended environment. They found that novice learners believe that traditional measures such as multiple-choice tests better reflect their learning status than more interpretive measures. More experienced learners, however, report confidence in assessment activities that involve collaborative work and interactive feedback. These findings give credence to developing theories that incorporate the nexus of information literacy, technology literacy, and critical thinking into a broader concept of information fluency—a foundation for assessment in blended learning (University of Central Florida, 2005).

## ACCESS

Key questions with regard to access include:

- How does the enhanced accessibility afforded by blended learning impact completion rates in higher education?
- How does blended learning impact the educational opportunities for under-represented populations?
- How does accessibility interact with quality of learning?

The issue of learner access is fundamental to blended learning and includes access to institutions, access to programs, and access to courses (Mayadas, 2001). The issue of quality is critical when considering the goal of access. Shea (2007, pp. 19–20) asserts: "If quality suffers, increased access is of no benefit. Students don't want access to low quality programs, faculty do not wish to teach in such programs, and alumni do not wish to support such programs."

Three student populations appear to have particular needs with regard to access: those far from campus, those near campus, and those on campus. The issue for these populations hinges on determining the degree to which faculty and students need alternative instructional modalities (Otte, 2005). In addition, instructional modalities such as blending might facilitate access to educational opportunities for students with disabilities. Rochester Institute of Technology provides an excellent example of how blended courses can increase educational opportunities and learning effectiveness for hearing-impaired students (Starenko et al., 2007). Fundamentally, economic principles (e.g., reduced opportunity costs and comparative advantage) yield advantages for students who are either on or near campus.

## COST EFFECTIVENESS

Key questions regarding cost effectiveness include:

- What are some effective models for assessing cost effectiveness in blended learning?
- For which contexts (high enrollment courses, specific disciplines) is cost effectiveness accepted and valued by stakeholders?
- What relationships exist between cost effectiveness and student learning outcomes?

The Center for Academic Transformation (Twigg, 2003) developed the primary models for cost effectiveness in blended learning. Using these models, several institutions have demonstrated that it is possible to improve quality and reduce costs, typically through reduced dependence on human resources. Robinson (2005) demonstrated that, by adding technology to the instructional design, quality increases, and in most cases costs are comparable or somewhat lower than face-to-face offerings. The University of Central Florida has reported cost savings, improved facilities utilization, improved learning, and continued program growth (Dziuban et al., 2006); however, return on investment cannot be determined via a simple spreadsheet calculation. Many less tangible factors contribute, including increased success rates, reduced number of drop outs, and improved faculty and student skills. Depending on the institutional context and the model chosen, cost savings may or may not be realized. Blended learning, however, offers real potential for a positive return on investment.

## STUDENT SATISFACTION

Key research questions pertaining to student satisfaction include:

- What components in a blended learning environment contribute most to student satisfaction?
- In what contexts is student satisfaction a viable outcome measure for learning quality?
- How is student satisfaction impacted when students are given a range of options regarding the nature of the blend in a course?

Student issues in blended learning emerge from the traditional academy and from the burgeoning online environments in higher education. Prensky (2001a,b) suggested that *digital natives* (the millennial generation), who expect the immediacy of technology, collaborative learning opportunities, and active learning environments, force faculty and administrators to adopt more effective pedagogies. Oblinger and Oblinger (2005) claim that for these students computers and personal technologies are a way of life. The Internet is more important to them than television, and they learn primarily through the processes of trial and error (Bisoux, 2002; Oblinger and Oblinger, 2005). We should not be surprised, therefore, that some tension exists between the millennial generation's preferred learning styles and what higher education currently offers—even in blended courses (Aviles et al., 2005).

Several issues mediate student satisfaction with blended learning. Some studies report consistently high satisfaction levels for blended courses (Dziuban et al., 2004), while others indicate somewhat less positive attitudes (Utts et al., 2003). Some studies indicate that students with an intuitive cognitive style experience a lower sense of community in their blended courses than students with analytic approaches to learning (Graff, 2003). Conversely, studies such as those conducted by Rovai and Jordan (2004) have revealed a greater sense of community in blended courses when compared with face-to-face and fully online courses. Even though investigators report conflicting results about student satisfaction, most studies with substantial and stable samples have found predominately positive reactions; the majority indicate that convenience, flexibility, and the reduced opportunity costs involved in the learning process are the primary factors (Vignare, 2002). These elements tend to be independent of several potentially biasing factors, such as class size and discipline.

## FACULTY SATISFACTION

Key research questions with regard to faculty satisfaction with blended learning include:

- What factors lead to faculty satisfaction in blended learning?
- What models do we have for supporting faculty adoption of blended learning?
- How do faculty workloads relate to satisfaction with blended learning in the context of tenure and promotion?

Faculty satisfaction is an important element that supports or detracts from the adoption of blended learning. The University of Central Florida reported that 88% of the faculty who taught blended courses were satisfied with the course and would teach in a blended format again in the future, but only 41% of the faculty in the Rochester Institute of Technology Blended Learning Pilot Project expressed a similar interest (Dziuban et al., 2004; RIT Online Learning Department, 2005). Many documented factors influence faculty satisfaction (Hartman et al., 2000). Three major elements are (1) impact on learning, (2) impact on workload, and (3) recognition that faculty efforts are valued. Many faculty members adopt blended learning because they believe it will improve learning effectiveness; some also believe that it will add convenience and improve their efficiency.

Increasingly, faculty are acquiring new technological skills and assuming new role expectations associated with those skills (Dziuban et al., 2006; Kaleta et al., 2007). In blended learning, the faculty must master the skills of both the face-to-face instructor and the online facilitator; thus, most research reports that implementing blended learning requires additional faculty time and effort (Kaleta et al., 2007; Lee and Im, 2006; Lefoe and Hedberg, 2006). The faculty time investment can be reduced through properly designed professional development and instructional support services such as training opportunities and performance support systems. Many faculty members incur the additional workload costs because they see the benefits for student learning (Starenko et al., 2007) or because they view the extra workload as a cost that will diminish as they become more comfortable with the new technological tools. Although research cites faculty recognition and compensation as key elements in successful blended programs, only one fifth of higher education institutions report providing formal recognition and rewards for technology integration (Green, 2004).

# ORGANIZATIONAL CONSIDERATIONS

Key research questions with regard to organizational considerations and their impact on blended learning include:

- What organizational components should be in place for blended learning to become a systemic initiative?
- How will blended learning manifest itself in different organizational contexts such as community colleges, metropolitan research universities, and liberal arts colleges?
- What impact is blended learning having on the traditional academy?

Institutional support mechanisms play a vital role in the success of blended courses and programs. In considering an optimal institutional climate, Hartman (2005) suggested that the organizational foundation should be built on theories of practice where the academic units are able find a common ground for instructional development. He specified that the elements of those theories should address instructional models, faculty development issues, course development structures, and effective assessment designs, both institutional and at the course level. Further, an effective institutional model should undergo continuous refinement and development while the institution develops increased organizational capacity. Hartman argued that an effective institutional approach demands up-front executive buy-in and early infusion into the colleges and departments. Further prerequisites involve faculty- and student-centered approaches that make blended learning something the institution *is* rather than something it *does* (Hartman, 2005).

# RESEARCH DIRECTIONS

We now focus on two important areas for future research: institutional research and learning effectiveness research.

## Institutional Research

### Faculty Adoption

Ultimately, the success or failure of blended approaches hinges on widespread faculty adoption of effective practices. We know relatively little about why faculty adopt and implement a specific blended instructional model and how they are making the instructional choices involved in course redesign (Kaleta et al., 2007). Some course redesign efforts are systemic in nature, such as the 30 projects supported by the Center for Academic Transformation (Twigg, 2003). The majority of change, however, is occurring through a process that Collis and van der Wende (2002) refer to as *stretching the mold*. In a campus-wide survey of faculty, Graham and Robison (2007) found that over one third of the faculty reported having taught a blended course, but many of the blends only made small enhancements to practice and did not change teaching and learning in significant or transformative ways. We need to learn how to avoid some of the traps historically associated with the adoption of technology-rich solutions, such as embracing rigid practices, *status quo* adherence, or a tendency for educational systems to preserve themselves by domesticating new technologies to support old practices (Beckwith, 1988; Salomon, 2002).

### Models for Support and Training

Research supports the supposition that institutional support is necessary for mainstream faculty and students to adopt blended learning. Issues that require investigation include: (1) how to minimize increased demands on faculty and student time; (2) how to provide instructors and learners with the necessary skills to succeed, particularly in the technology-mediated environment; and (3) how to change the organizational culture into one willing to accept innovations such as blended learning. Other research might investigate models for faculty support and training in blended environments and what aspects of the models are transferable to other contexts.

## Learning Effectiveness Research

### Conceptual Frameworks and Models

Design problems, such as creating a blended environment, are highly context dependent, with an almost infinite number of possible solutions. Researchers should better articulate conceptual frameworks that will serve blended contexts (Shea, 2007). The *community of inquiry model* is one possible framework (Garrison et al., 2000; Garrison and Vaughan, 2007), but it would be more helpful to have a range of rich blended learning models so designers could design tradeoffs in their own specific contexts.

### Role of Live Interaction vs. Computer-Mediated Communication

Under what conditions is human interaction important to the learning outcomes and learner satisfaction with the experience? When and why should we be considering human interaction such as collaboration and learning communities (Alavi and Dufner, 2005)? How does live interaction vs. low-fidelity asynchronous interaction affect the learning experience? These questions are just a few that are directly relevant to deciding when to have face-to-face or technology-mediated interactions between participants or with a nonhuman instructional system. Some evidence indicates that learners in blended environments place greater value or emphasis on the face-to-face components, while other findings suggest that the face-to-face elements are unnecessary (Graham, 2006). Research related to better understanding the nature of human interaction in blended learning environments is a promising direction of inquiry (Shea, 2007).

### Role of Learner Choice and Self-Regulation

How are learners making choices about the kinds of blends in which they are participating? Are choices being made primarily on the basis of convenience and flexibility? How much information and guidance are being provided to learners to help them make decisions about how different blends will affect their learning experience? Online components are perceived as requiring a greater amount of discipline for learners to succeed (Allen and Seaman, 2005), so how can blended environments be designed to support increasing learner maturity and capabilities for self-regulation?

## CONCLUSIONS

Learning environments have affordances that facilitate or constrain different types of interactions and activities. Although much can be learned and synthesized from research in both distance and traditional learning environments, blended environments provide a paradigm that is different than just a linear combination of the two; for example, reactions to the use of computer-mediated discussions can be quite different in a course that also meets face-to-face vs. a completely online course (An and Frick, 2006; Schweizer et al., 2003; Yanes, 2004). In a completely online course, the computer-mediated discussion may be valued as the only means of human interaction, while in the blended context learners might perceive it as a low-fidelity, time-consuming channel for communication. Faculty and learners will take advantage of the opportunities in their learning environments based on their expectations, goals, and understanding of the learning possibilities within the environment. Currently, only a small (but growing) body of research is specifically related to blended environments. We need more research on the design of blended environments and how instructors and learners engage in the act of teaching and learning in these environments.

## REFERENCES

Alavi, M. and Dufner, D. (2005). Technology-mediated collaborative learning: a research perspective. In *Learning Together Online: Research on Asynchronous Learning Networks*, edited by S. R. Hiltz and R. Goldman, pp. 191–213. Mahwah, NJ: Lawrence Erlbaum Associates.

Allen, I. E. and Seaman, J. (2005). *Growing by Degrees: Online Education in the United States, 2005*. Needham, MA: Sloan Consortium.

An, Y.-J. and Frick, T. (2006). Student perceptions of asynchronous computer-mediated communication in face-to-face courses [electronic version]. *J. Comput.-Mediated Commun.*, 11, Article 5 (http://jcmc.indiana.edu/vol11/issue2/ an.html).

Aviles, K., Phillips, B., Rosenblatt, T., and Vargas, J. (2005). If higher education listened to me. *EDUCAUSE Rev.*, 40(5), 16–28.

Beckwith, D. (1988). The future of educational technology. *Can. J. Educ. Commun.*, 17(1), 3–20.

Bisoux, T. (2002). Rethinking IT. *BizEd*, Jan./Feb., 30–34.

Boyle, T., Bradley, C., Chalk, P., Jones, R., and Pickard, P. (2003). Using blended learning to improve student success in learning to program. *J. Educ. Media*, 28(2–3), 165–178.

Brown, G., Smith, T., and Henderson, T. (2007). Student perceptions of assessment efficacy in online and blended classes. In *Blended Learning: Research Perspectives*, edited by A. G. Picciano and C. D. Dziuban, pp. 145–160. Needham, MA: Sloan Consortium.

Collis, B. and van der Wende, M. (2002). *Models of Technology and Change in Higher Education: An International Comparative Survey on the Current and Future Use of ICT in Higher Education*. Enschede, the Netherlands: Center for Higher Education Policy Studies, University of Twente.

Collis, B., Bianco, M., Margaryan, A., and Waring, B. (2005). Putting blended learning to work: a case study from a multinational oil company. *Educ. Commun. Inform.*, 5(3), 233–250.*

Cottrell, D. M. and Robinson, R. A. (2003). Blended learning in an accounting course. *Q. Rev. Distance Educ.*, 4(3), 261–269.

Cross, J. (2006). Foreword. In *Handbook of Blended Learning: Global Perspectives, Local Designs*, edited by C. J. Bonk and C. R. Graham, pp. xvii–xxiii. San Francisco, CA: Pfeiffer Publishing.*

Dowling, C., Godfrey, J. M., and Gyles, N. (2003). Do hybrid flexible delivery teaching methods improve accounting students learning outcomes? *Account. Educ.*, 12(4), 373–391.

Driscoll, M. (2002). Blended learning: let's get beyond the hype [electronic version]. *e-Learning*, 54 (http://elearningmag.com/ltimagazine/article/articleDetail.jsp?id=11755).

Dziuban, C. D., Hartman, J., and Moskal, P. D. (2004). Blended learning. *EDUCAUSE Center for Applied Res. (ECAR) Res. Bull.*, 2004(7), 1–12.

Dziuban, C. D., Hartman, J., Juge, F., Moskal, P. D., and Sorg, S. (2006). Blended learning enters the mainstream. In *Handbook of Blended Learning: Global Perspectives, Local Designs*, edited by C. J. Bonk and C. R. Graham, pp. 195–208. San Francisco, CA: Pfeiffer Publishing.*

Dziuban, C., Shea, P., and Arbaugh, J. B. (2005). Faculty roles and satisfaction in asynchronous learning networks. In *Learning Together Online: Research on Asynchronous Learning Networks*, edited by S. R. Hiltz and R. Goldman, pp. 169–190. Mahwah, NJ: Lawrence Erlbaum Associates.

Finn, A. (2002). Trends in e-learning [electronic version]. *Learning Circuits*, 3 (http://www.learningcircuits.org/2002/nov2002/finn.htm).

Garrison, D. R. and Kanuta, H. (2004). Blended learning: uncovering its transformative potential in higher education. *Internet Higher Educ.*, 7(2), 95–105.*

Garrison, D. R. and Vaughan, N. (2007). *Blended Learning in Higher Education: Framework, Principles, and Guidelines.* San Francisco, CA: Jossey-Bass.

Garrison, D. R., Anderson, T., and Archer, W. (2000). Critical inquiry in a text-based environment: computer-conferencing in higher education. *Internet Higher Educ.*, 11(1), 1–14.

Graff, M. (2003). Individual differences in sense of classroom community in a blended learning environment. *J. Educ. Media*, 28(2–3), 203–210.

Graham, C. R. (2006). Blended learning systems: definition, current trends, and future directions. In *Handbook of Blended Learning: Global Perspectives, Local Designs*, edited by C. J. Bonk and C. R. Graham, pp. 3–21. San Francisco, CA: Pfeiffer Publishing.*

Graham, C. R. and Robison, R. (2007). Realizing the transformational potential of blended learning: comparing cases of transforming blends and enhancing blends in higher education. In *Blended Learning: Research Perspectives*, edited by A. G. Picciano and C. D. Dziuban, pp. 83–110. Needham, MA: Sloan Consortium.

Graham, C. R., Allen, S., and Ure, D. (2003). *Blended Learning Environments: A Review of the Research Literature*, http://msed.byu.edu/ipt/graham/vita/ble_litrev.pdf.

Green, K. C. (2004). *Campus Computing 2004: The 15th National Survey of Computing and Information Technology in American Higher Education*. Encino, CA: The Campus Computing Project.

Harris, P. (2005). Training's new wave. *Train. Dev.*, 59(8), 45–48.

Hartman, J. (2005). Online@UCF. Paper presented at the Sloan-C Workshop on Blended Learning, April 17–19, Chicago, IL.

Hartman, J., Dziuban, C., and Moskal, P. (2000). Faculty satisfaction in ALNs: a dependent or independent variable? *J. Asynchr. Learn. Netw.*, 4(3), 155–179.

Humbert, J. and Vignare, K. (2004). RIT introduces blended learning successfully. In *Engaging Communities: Wisdom from the Sloan Consortium*, edited by J. C. Moore, pp. 141–152. Needham, MA: Sloan Consortium.

Jones, N. (2006). e-College Wales, a case study of blended learning. In *Handbook of Blended Learning: Global Perspectives, Local Designs*, edited by C. J. Bonk and C. R. Graham, pp. 182–194. San Francisco, CA: Pfeiffer Publishing.

Kaleta, R., Skibba, K., and Joosten, T. (2007). Discovering, designing, and delivering hybrid courses. In *Blended Learning: Research Perspectives*, edited by A. G. Picciano and C. D. Dziuban, pp. 111–144. Needham, MA: Sloan Consortium.

Kirkley, S. E. and Kirkley, J. R. (2005). Creating next generation blended learning environments using mixed reality, video games and simulations. *TechTrends*, 49(3), 42–53.

Kirkley, J. R. and Kirkley, S. E. (2006). Expanding the boundaries of blended learning: transforming learning with mixed and virtual reality technologies. In *Handbook of Blended Learning: Global Perspectives, Local Designs*, edited by C. J. Bonk and C. R. Graham, pp. 533–549. San Francisco, CA: Pfeiffer Publishing.

Laster, S. (2004). Blended learning: driving forward without a definition. In *Engaging Communities: Wisdom from the Sloan Consortium*, edited by J. C. Moore. Needham, MA: Sloan Consortium.

Lee, O. and Im, Y. (2006). The emergence of the cyber-university and blended learning in Korea. In *Handbook of Blended Learning: Global Perspectives, Local Designs*, edited by C. J. Bonk and C. R. Graham, pp. 281–295. San Francisco, CA: Pfeiffer Publishing.

Lefoe, G. and Hedberg, J. G. (2006). Blending on and off campus: a tale of two cities. In *Handbook of Blended Learning: Global Perspectives, Local Designs*, edited by C. J. Bonk and C. R. Graham, pp. 325–337. San Francisco, CA: Pfeiffer Publishing.

Lewis, N. J. and Orton, P. Z. (2006). Blended learning for business impact. In *Handbook of Blended Learning: Global Perspectives, Local Designs*, edited by C. J. Bonk and C. R. Graham, pp. 61–75. San Francisco, CA: Pfeiffer Publishing.

Lorenzo, G. and Moore, J. C. (2002). *The Sloan Consortium Report to the Nation: Five Pillars of Quality Online Education* [electronic version], http://www.sloan-c.org/effective/pillarreport1.pdf.

Masie, E. (2006). The blended learning imperative. In *Handbook of Blended Learning: Global Perspectives, Local Designs*, edited by C. J. Bonk and C. R. Graham, pp. 22–26. San Francisco, CA: Pfeiffer Publishing.*

Mayadas, F. (2001). Testimony to the Kerrey Commission on Web-based education. *J. Asynchr. Learn. Netw.*, 5(1), 134–138.

Newton, D. and Ellis, A. (2005). Effective implementation of e-learning: a case study of the Australian army. *J. Workplace Learn.*, 17(5/6), 385–397.

Oblinger, D. G. and Oblinger, J. L. (2005). *Educating the Net Generation*, http://www.educause.edu/ir/library/pdf/pub7101.pdf.

Oliver, M. and Trigwell, K. (2005). Can 'blended learning' be redeemed? *E-learning*, 2(1), 17–26.

Osguthorpe, R. T. and Graham, C. R. (2003). Blended learning systems: definitions and directions. *Q. Rev. Distance Educ.*, 4(3), 227–234.*

O'Toole, J. M. and Absalom, D. J. (2003). The impact of blended learning on student outcomes: is there room on the horse for two? *J. Educ. Media*, 28(2–3), 179–190.

Otte, G. (2005). Using blended learning to drive faculty development (and visa versa). In *Elements of Quality Online Education: Engaging Communities*, Vol. 6, edited by J. Bourne and J. C. Moore, pp. 71–84. Needham, MA: Sloan Consortium.

Prensky, M. (2001a). Digital natives, digital immigrants. *On Horizon*, 9(5), 1–6.

Prensky, M. (2001b). Digital natives, digital immigrants. Part 2. Do they really think differently? *On Horizon*, 9(6), 1–6.

Reasons, S. G. (2004). Hybrid courses: hidden dangers? *Distance Educ. Rep.*, 8(7), 3–7.

Reasons, S. G., Valadares, K., and Slavkin, M. (2005). Questioning the hybrid model: student outcomes in different course formats. *J. Asynchr. Learn.*, 9(1), 83–94.

Riffell, S. K. and Sibley, D. F. (2004). Can hybrid course formats increase attendance in undergraduate environmental science courses? *J. Nat. Resour. Life Sci. Educ.*, 33, 1–5.

RIT Online Learning Department. (2005). *Blended Learning Pilot Project* [electronic version], http://online.rit.edu/faculty/instructional_design/blended/RITBlendedPilotFinalReport.pdf.

Robison, R. (2005). The business of online education: are we cost competitive? In *Elements of Quality Online Education: Engaging Communities*, edited by J. Bourne and J. C. Moore, pp. 173–181. Needham, MA: Sloan Consortium.

Rovai, A. P. and Jordan, H. M. (2004). Blended learning and sense of community: a comparative analysis with traditional and fully online graduate courses. *Int. Rev. Res. Open Dist. Learn.*, 5(2), 13.

Salomon, G. (2002). Technology and pedagogy: why don't we see the promised revolution? *Educ. Technol.*, 42(2), 71–75.

Schweizer, K., Paechter, M., and Weidenmann, B. (2003). Blended learning as a strategy to improve collaborative task performance. *J. Educ. Media*, 28(2–3), 211–224.

Shea, P. (2007). Towards a conceptual framework for learning in blended environments. In *Blended Learning: Research Perspectives*, edited by A. G. Picciano and C. D. Dziuban, pp. 19–36. Needham, MA: Sloan Consortium.

Starenko, M., Vignare, K., and Humbert, J. (2007). Enhancing student interaction and sustaining faculty instructional innovations through blended learning. In *Blended Learning: Research Perspectives*, edited by A. G. Picciano and C. D. Dziuban, pp. 161–178. Needham, MA: Sloan Consortium.

Twigg, C. (2003). Improving learning and reducing costs: new models for online learning. *EDUCAUSE Rev.*, 38(Sept./Oct.), 28–38.

University of Central Florida. (2005). *Quality Enhancement Program: Information Fluency Initiative*, http://www.if.ucf.edu/.

Utts, J., Sommer, B., Acredolo, M. W., Maher, M. W., and Matthews, H. R. (2003). A study comparing traditional and hybrid internet-based instruction in introductory statistics classes. *J. Stat. Educ.*, 11(3), 171–173.

Vignare, K. (2002). Longitudinal success measures of online learning students at the Rochester Institute of Technology. In *Elements of Quality Online Education: Practice and Direction*, Vol. 4, edited by J. Bourne and J. C. Moore, pp. 261–278. Needham, MA: Sloan Consortium.

Wenger, M. S. and Ferguson, C. (2006). A learning ecology model for blended learning from Sun Microsystems. In *Handbook of Blended Learning: Global Perspectives, Local Designs*, edited by C. J. Bonk and C. R. Graham, pp. 76–91. San Francisco, CA: Pfeiffer Publishing.

Wisher, R. A. (2006). Blended learning in military training. In *Handbook of Blended Learning: Global Perspectives, Local Designs*, edited by C. J. Bonk and C. R. Graham, pp. 519–532. San Francisco, CA: Pfeiffer Publishing.

Yanes, M. J. (2004). Distance education in traditional classes: a hybrid model. *Q. Rev. Distance Educ.*, 5(4), 265–276.

Young, J. R. (2002). 'Hybrid' teaching seeks to end the divide between traditional and online instruction. *Chron. High. Educ.*, March 22, A-33.

---

* Indicates a core reference.

# 24

# Adaptive Technologies

*Valerie J. Shute*
College of Education, Florida State University, Tallahassee, Florida

*Diego Zapata-Rivera*
Educational Testing Service, Princeton, New Jersey

## CONTENTS

## ABSTRACT

This chapter describes research and development efforts related to adaptive technologies, which can be combined with other technologies and processes to form an adaptive system. The goal of an adaptive system, in the context of this chapter, is to create an instructionally sound and flexible environment that supports learning for students with a range of abilities, disabilities, interests, backgrounds, and other characteristics. After defining key terms and establishing a rationale for adaptation, we present a general framework to organize adaptive technologies. We then describe experts' thoughts on what to adapt and how to adapt. We conclude with a summary of key challenges and potential futures of adaptive technologies.

## KEYWORDS

*Adaptivity:* The capability exhibited by an organic or an artificial organism to alter its behavior according to the environment. In the context of an instructional system, this capability allows the system to alter its behavior according to learner needs and other characteristics. This is typically represented within a learner model.

*Hard technologies:* These represent devices may be used in adaptive systems to capture learner information (e.g., eye-tracking devices) or to present content to a learner (e.g., tactile tablet). These devices can be used to detect and classify learners' performance data or affective states such as confusion, frustration, excitement, disappointment, boredom, confidence, contentment, and so on.

*Learner model:* A representation of the learner that is maintained by an adaptive system. Learner models can be used to provide personalized instruction to a particular individual, and may include cognitive and noncognitive aspects of the learner. Learner models have been used in many areas, such as adaptive educational and training systems, help systems, recommender systems, and others.

*Soft technologies:* These are usually algorithms, programs, or even environments that broaden the types of interaction between students and computers; for example, an adaptive algorithm may be employed in a program that selects an assessment task that provides the most information about a particular learner at a particular point in time.

# INTRODUCTION

Air-conditioning systems monitor and adjust room temperature; cruise-control systems monitor and adjust vehicle speed. Similarly, adaptive educational systems monitor important learner characteristics and make appropriate adjustments to the instructional milieu to support and enhance learning. In this chapter, we describe research and development related to adaptive technologies, which can be combined with other technologies and processes to form an adaptive system.

The goal of an adaptive system, in the context of this chapter, is to create an instructionally sound and flexible environment that supports learning for students with a range of abilities, disabilities, interests, backgrounds, and other characteristics. The challenge of accomplishing this goal depends largely on accurately identifying characteristics of a particular learner or group of learners—such as type and level of knowledge, skills, personality traits, affective states—and then determining how to leverage the information to improve student learning (Conati, 2002; Park and Lee, 2003; Shute et al., 2000; Snow, 1989, 1994).

After defining key terms and establishing a rationale for adaptation, we present a general framework to organize adaptive technologies. We then describe experts' thoughts on: (1) the variables to be taken into account when implementing an adaptive system (i.e., *what* to adapt), and (2) the best technologies and methods to accomplish adaptive goals (i.e., *how* to adapt). We conclude with a summary of key challenges and future applications of adaptive tools and technologies. Challenges include: (1) obtaining useful and accurate learner information on which to base adaptive decisions, (2) maximizing benefits to the learner while minimizing costs associated with adaptive technologies, (3) addressing issues of learner control and privacy, and (4) figuring out the bandwidth problem, which has to do with the amount of relevant learner data that can be acquired at any time.

## Definitions

Before we begin our discussion on adaptive technologies that support learners in educational settings, we will briefly define relevant terms. Most generally, to *adapt* means making an adjustment from one situation or condition to another (e.g., software programs and persons are capable of adaptation). *Technology* refers to the application of science (methods or materials, electronic or digital products or systems) to achieve a particular objective, such as the enhancement of learning. A *system* in this context refers to a network of related computer software, hardware, and data transmission devices.

An *adaptive system* adjusts itself to suit particular learner characteristics and needs of the learner. *Adaptive technologies* help achieve this goal and are typically controlled by the computational devices, adapting content for different learners' needs and sometimes preferences. Information is usually maintained within a *learner model*, which is a representation of the learner managed by an adaptive system. Learner models provide the basis for deciding how to provide personalized content to a particular individual and may include cognitive as well as noncognitive information. Learner models have been used in many areas, such as adaptive educational and training systems (e.g., intelligent tutoring systems), help systems, and recommender systems.

Adaptive systems may consist of *hard* or *soft* technologies (e.g., devices vs. algorithms). *Hard technologies* are devices used in adaptive systems to capture learner information (e.g., eye-tracking devices), thus they can be used to detect and classify learners' performance data or affective states such as confusion, frustration, excitement, and boredom. Hard technologies can also be used to present content in various formats (e.g., tactile tablet to accommodate visual disabilities). *Soft technologies* represent algorithms, programs, or environments that broaden the types of interaction between students and computers; for example, an adaptive algorithm may be employed in a program that selects an assessment task or learning object most appropriate for a learner at a particular point in time.

The effectiveness of adaptive technologies hinge on accurate and informative student or learner models. For the remainder of this chapter, we use the terms *student model* and *learner model* interchangeably, and abbreviate them as either SM or LM. Because this chapter focuses on the educational functions of adaptive systems, we limit our modeling discussion to the context of *students* or *learners*, rather than more broadly defined users.

## Rationale for Adapting Content

The attractiveness of adaptive technologies derives from the wide range of capabilities that these technologies afford. As discussed, one capability involves the real-time delivery of assessments and instructional content that adapt to learners' needs and preferences. Other technology interventions include simulations of dynamic events, extra practice opportunities on emergent skills, and alternative multimedia options, particularly those that allow greater access to individuals with disabilities. We now provide evidence that supports the importance of adapting content to students to improve learning. These arguments concern individual and group differences among students.

## Differences in Incoming Knowledge, Skills, and Abilities

The first reason for adapting content to the learner has to do with general individual differences in relation to incoming knowledge and skills among students. These differences are real, often large, and powerful; however, our educational system's traditional approach to teaching is not working well in relation to the diverse population of students in U.S. schools today (Shute, 2006). Many have argued that incoming knowledge is the *single* most important determinant of subsequent learning (Alexander and Judy, 1988; Glaser, 1984; Tobias, 1994). Thus, it makes sense to assess students' incoming knowledge and skills to provide a sound starting point for teaching. A second reason to adapt content to learners has to do with differences among learners in terms of relevant abilities and disabilities. The latter addresses issues of equity and accessibility. To illustrate, a student with visual disabilities will have great difficulty acquiring visually presented material, regardless of prior knowledge and skill in the subject area. Student abilities and disabilities can usually be readily identified and content adapted to accommodate the disability or leverage an ability to support learning (Shute et al., 2005).

## Differences in Demographic and Sociocultural Variables

Another reason to adapt content to learners relates to demographic and sociocultural differences among students, which can affect learning outcomes and ultimately achievement (Conchas, 2006; Desimone, 1999; Fan and Chen, 2001). Adaptive technologies can help reduce some major gaps that persist in the United States (e.g., differential access to information and other resources); for example, some researchers (see, for example, Snow and Biancarosa, 2003) have argued that the achievement gap in the United States is largely due to differential language proficiencies. In response to this need, adaptive technologies that support English language learners are being developed (Yang et al., 2006).

## Differences in Affective Variables

In addition to cognitive, physical, and sociocultural differences, students differ in relation to affective states—many of which influence learning—such as frustration, boredom, motivation, and confidence (Conati, 2002; Craig et al., 2004; Ekman, 2003; Kapoor and Picard, 2002; Litman and Forbes-Riley, 2004; Picard, 1997; Qu et al., 2005). Various noninvasive measures

infer learners' states and alter the instructional environment to suit different needs; for example, sensory input systems detect, classify, and analyze learners' facial expressions (Yeasin and Bullot, 2005), eye movements (Conati et al., 2005), head position (Seo et al., 2004), body posture and position (Chu and Cohen, 2005), gestures (Kettebekov et al., 2003), and speech (Potamianos et al., 2005). Bayesian networks and other statistical classifier systems can render inferences about states from a variety of inputs (e.g., excessive fidgeting implying inattention).

In summary, there are a number of compelling reasons to adapt content to learners. We now provide context and coherence for adaptive technologies by way of a general four-process model. This model has been extended from (1) a simpler two-process model that lies at the heart of adaptive technology (diagnosis and prescription), and (2) a process model to support assessment (Mislevy et al., 2003).

## Four-Process Adaptive Cycle

The success of any adaptive technology to promote learning requires accurate *diagnosis* of learner characteristics (e.g., knowledge, skill, motivation, persistence). The collection of learner information can then be used as the basis for the *prescription* of optimal content, such as hints, explanations, hypertext links, practice problems, encouragement, metacognitive support, and so forth. Our framework involves a *four-process cycle* connecting the learner to appropriate educational materials and resources (e.g., other learners, learning objects, applications, and pedagogical agents) through the use of a learner model (see Figure 24.1). The components of this four-process cycle include capture, analyze, select, and present.

### Capture

This process entails gathering personal information about the learner as the learner interacts with the environment (depicted in Figure 24.1 by the larger human figure). Relevant information can include cognitive as well as noncognitive aspects of the learner. This information is used to update internal models maintained by the system.

### Analyze

This process requires the creation and maintenance of a model of the learner in relation to the domain, typically representing information in terms of inferences on current states. In Figure 24.1, this is depicted as the smaller human figure (i.e., the SM).

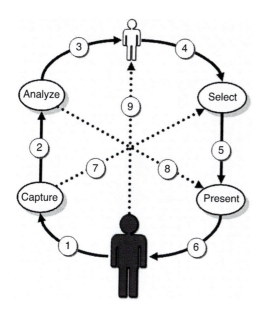

**Figure 24.1** Four-process adaptive cycle.

## Select

Information (i.e., content in the broadest sense) is selected according to the model of the learner maintained by the system and the goals of the system (e.g., next learning object or test item). This process is often required to determine how and when to intervene.

## Present

Based on results from the select process, specific content is presented to the learner. This entails appropriate use of different media, devices, and technologies to efficiently convey information to the learner. This model accommodates alternative scenarios. Table 24.1 describes some of these scenarios that involve different types of adaptation starting with a completely adaptive cycle and continuing to a nonadaptive presentation. Figure 24.2 illustrates the evolving nature of the four-process adaptive loop; that is, as time passes, the learner model becomes more refined and accurate, as represented in the figure by different degrees of saturation.

In general, the architecture of adaptive applications has evolved in a way that reflects the evolution of software systems architecture; for example, it is possible to find *stand-alone* adaptive applications where the complete adaptive system—including its student model—resides in a single machine. Also, adaptive applications have been implemented using a *distributed* architecture model. Some examples of distributed applications include: (1) client–server adaptive applications that make use of student modeling servers and shells (Fink and Kobsa, 2000); (2) distributed agent-based platforms (Azambuja Silveira et al., 2002; Vassileva et al., 2003); (3) hybrid approaches involving distributed agents and a student modeling server (Brusilovsky et al., 2005; Zapata-Rivera and Greer, 2004); (4) peer-to-peer architectures (Bretzke and Vassileva, 2003); and (5) service-oriented architectures (Fröschl, 2005; González et al., 2005; Kabassi and Virvou, 2003; Trella et al., 2005; Winter et al., 2005).

To illustrate how our four-process adaptive model can accommodate more distributed scenarios, Figure 24.3 depicts an extended version of our model, which includes a group of agents: application, personal, and pedagogical. Each agent maintains a personal view of

## TABLE 24.1
### Scenarios Represented in the Four-Process Adaptive Cycle

| Scenario | Description |
| --- | --- |
| A complete cycle (1, 2, 3, 4, 5, and 6) | All processes of the cycle are exercised: capturing relevant information, analyzing it, updating the variables, selecting appropriate resources and strategies that meet the current needs of the learner, and making them available to the student in an appropriate manner. This cycle will continue until the goals have been met. |
| Modifying the adaptive cycle (1, 2, 3, 4, 5, 6, and 9) | The learner is allowed to interact with the learner model. The nature of this interaction and the effects on the learner model can vary. Allowing human interaction with the model may reduce the complexity of the diagnostic and selection processes by decreasing uncertainty. It can also benefit the learner by increasing awareness and self-reflection. |
| Monitoring path (1, 2, and 3) | The learner is continuously monitored; information gathered is analyzed and used to update profiles (e.g., homeland security surveillance system, analyzing profiles of individuals for risk-analysis purposes). This path can be seen as a cycle that spins off to a third party instead of returning to the learner. |
| Short (or temporary) memory cycle (1, 7, 5, and 6) | The selection of content and educational resources is done by using the most recent information (e.g., current test results and navigation commands). No permanent learner model is maintained. Adaptation is performed using information gathered from the latest interaction between learner and the system. |
| Short (or temporary) memory, no selection cycle (1, 2, 8, and 6) | A predefined path on the curriculum structure is followed. No learner model is maintained. This predefined path dictates which educational resources and testing materials are presented to the learner. |

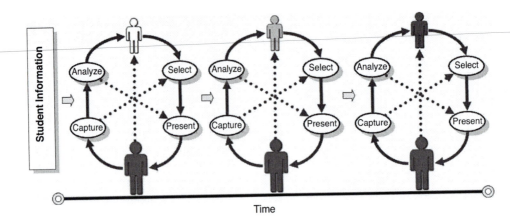

**Figure 24.2** Flow of diagnosis and adaptation over time.

the learner. Learner model information and educational resources can be distributed in different places. Agents communicate with each other directly or through an LM server to share information that can be used to help learners achieve their learning goals.

## SUMMARY OF CURRENT ADAPTIVE TECHNOLOGIES

This section describes adaptive technologies currently in use and relevant to the context of this chapter. The technologies have been divided into two main sections: soft and hard technologies. As described earlier, this distinction may be likened to *programs* vs. *devices*, respectively, and may be used across the array of processes described in the previous section (i.e., capturing student information, analyzing it, selecting content, and presenting it). The technologies selected for inclusion in this section are those that make use of, to some extent, a learner model in its formulation. Also, this listing is intended to be illustrative and not exhaustive. For a more thorough description of adaptive technologies in the context of e-learning systems, see Fröschl (2005), Kobsa (2006), Jameson (2006a), and Buxton (2006), the latter for a directory of sources for input technologies.

Figure 24.4 provides examples of both soft and hard technologies (in shaded boxes) operating within an adaptive learning environment in relation to our four-process adaptive cycle; for example, technologies for *analyzing* and *selecting* LM information include Bayesian networks and machine learning techniques. These technologies are examined in relation to both learner variables (cognitive and noncognitive) and modeling approaches (quantitative and qualitative). Similarly, examples of soft and hard technologies are provided for the processes of *capturing* and *presenting* information.

## Soft Technologies

Soft technologies represent programs or approaches that capture, analyze, select, or present information. Their primary goals are to create LMs (diagnostic function) and to utilize information from LMs (prescriptive function).

### Quantitative Modeling

In general, quantitative modeling of learners obtains estimates about the current state of some attribute. This involves models and datasets, as well as typically complex relationships and calculations. To begin modeling, relationships are established and tested, in line with a hypothesis that forms the basis of the model and its test. To quantify the relationships, one can use graphical models to create graphs of the relationships and statistical models that will define quantitative equations of expected relationships to model uncertainty (for more, see Jameson, 1995).

### Qualitative Modeling

Qualitative modeling supports learners by constructing conceptual models of systems and their behavior using qualitative formalisms. According to Bredeweg and Forbus (2003), qualitative modeling is a valuable technology because much of education is concerned with conceptual knowledge (e.g., causal theories of physical phenomena). Environments using qualitative models may use diagrammatic representations to facilitate understanding of important concepts and relationships. Evaluations in educational settings provide support for the hypothesis that qualitative modeling tools can be valuable aids for learning (Frederiksen and White, 2002; Leelawong et al., 2001).

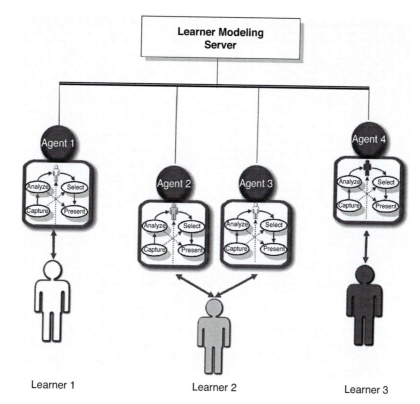

**Figure 24.3** Communication among agents and learners.

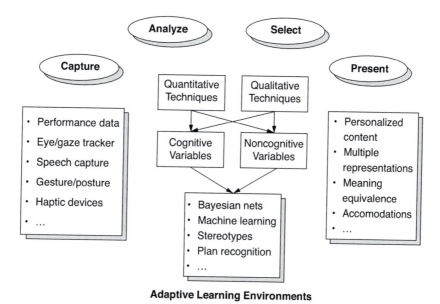

**Figure 24.4** Overview of technologies to support learner modeling.

### Cognitive Modeling

Cognitive models may be quantitative or qualitative. They help predict complex human behaviors, including skill learning, problem solving, and other types of cognitive activities. Generally, cognitive models may apply across various domains, serve different functions, and model well- or ill-defined knowledge (e.g., design problems). The range of cognitive modeling approaches includes, for example, symbolic, connectionist, hybrid, neural, probabilistic, and deterministic mathematical models. Probably the best known examples of cognitive models come from the cognitive tutoring research by John Anderson and colleagues (Anderson, 1993; Anderson and Lebiere, 1998; Anderson et al., 1990, 1995; Koedinger and Anderson, 1998; Koedinger et al., 1997; Matsuda et al., 2005).

## Machine Learning

Machine learning methods applicable for learner modeling include rule/tree (analogy) learning methods, probabilistic learning methods, and instance or case-based learning approaches. A learner model can take advantage of machine learning methods and thus increase accuracy, efficiency, and extensibility in areas not modeled before (Sison and Shimura, 1998). According to Webb and colleagues (2001), machine learning methods can be used to model: (1) cognitive processes underlying the learner's actions, (2) differences between the learner's skills and expert skills, (3) the learner's behavioral patterns or preferences, and (4) other characteristics of the learner.

## Bayesian Networks

Bayesian networks (Pearl, 1988) are related to the machine learning methods (see above) and are used within learner models to handle uncertainty by using probabilistic inference to update and improve belief values (e.g., regarding learner proficiencies). The inductive and deductive reasoning capabilities of Bayesian nets support "what if" scenarios by activating and observing evidence that describes a particular case or situation and then propagating that information through the network using the internal probability distributions that govern the behavior of the Bayesian net. Resulting probabilities inform decision making, as needed in, for example, our select process. Examples of Bayesian net implementations for LMs may be found in Conati et al. (2002), Shute et al. (2005), and VanLehn and colleagues (2005).

## Stereotype Methods

A stereotype is a collection of frequently occurring characteristics of users (e.g., physical characteristics, social background, computer experience). Adaptive methods are used to initially assign users to specific classes (stereotypes) so previously unknown characteristics can be inferred on the basis of the assumption that they will share characteristics with others in the same class (Kobsa, 2006). Creating stereotypes is a common approach to user modeling, whereby a small amount of initial information is used to assume a large number of default assumptions. When more information about individuals becomes available, the default assumptions may be altered (Rich, 1979). The two types of stereotyping are *fixed* and *default*. In fixed stereotyping, learners are classified according to their performance into a predefined stereotype that is determined by, for example, an academic level. Default stereotyping is a more flexible approach. At the beginning of a session, learners are stereotyped to default values, but, as the learning process proceeds and learner performance data is obtained, the settings of the initial stereotype are gradually replaced by more individualized settings (Kay, 2000).

## Overlay Methods

An overlay model is a novice–expert difference model representing missing conceptions, often implemented as either an expert model annotated for missing items or an expert model with weights assigned to each element in the expert knowledge base. One of the first uses of an overlay model was done with the WUSOR program (Stansfield et al., 1976). Current applications of this overlay approach can be found in a variety of research projects (Kay, 1999; Vassileva, 1998; Zapata-Rivera and Greer, 2000).

## Plan Recognition

A plan is a sequence of actions to achieve a certain goal, and it reflects the learner's intentions and desires. Plan recognition is based on observing the learner's input actions and the system then inferring all possible learner plans based on the observed actions. According to Kobsa (1993), two main techniques are used to recognize the learner's plan: (1) establishing a *plan library* containing all possible plans where the selection of the actual plan is based on the match between observed actions and a set of actions in the library, and (2) *plan construction*, where the system controls a library of all possible learner actions combined with the effects and the preconditions of these actions. Possible next actions may be calculated by comparing the effects of preceding actions with the preconditions of actions stored in the actions library. To read more about applying plan-recognition techniques in relation to instructional planning efforts, see Kobsa (1993) and Vassileva and Wasson (1992).

## Cumulative/Persistent Student Model

The cumulative student model represents the more traditional approach where the SM is analyzed and updated in response to the learner's activities. This involves building a student model that captures and represents emerging knowledge, skills, and other attributes of the learner, with the computer responding to updated observations with modified content that can be minutely adjusted. The selection and presentation of subsequent content are dependent on individual response histories (Shute and Psotka, 1996; VanLehn et al., 2005; Wenger, 1987).

### Temporary Student Model

Temporary student models usually do not persist in the system after the learner has logged out. In artificial intelligence, formalisms used to describe the world often face something called the *frame problem*, which is the problem of inferring whether something that was true is still true; for example, the accuracy of cumulative (or persistent) student models can degrade as students forget things. Brooks (1999) and others have circumvented the frame problem by using the world as its own model (e.g., if you want to know if a window is closed, check the actual window rather than consult an internal model). The same idea applies to student modeling; that is, if you want to know if a student can still multiply two fractions, ask the student to multiply two fractions. This is what human tutors do, and their one-time students yield a student model that is always up to date and corresponds to the short memory cycle scenario shown in Table 24.1.

### Pedagogical Agents

*Pedagogical* means that these programs are designed to teach, and *agent* suggests that the programs are semiautonomous, possessing their own goals and making decisions on what actions to take to achieve their goals (i.e., a programmer has not predefined every action for them). The current generation of pedagogical agents is interactive and sometimes animated; for example, students can speak to agents that can speak back, often have faces and bodies, use gestures, and can move around a computer screen. Some well-known agents include Steve (Johnson et al., 2000), AutoTutor (Graesser et al., 2001), AdeLE (Shaw et al., 1999), and the Tactical Language Training System (Johnson et al., 2004).

An interesting application of agent technologies is *teachable agents*, which have been successfully used to promote student learning of mathematics and science (Biswas et al., 2001). This computer-based environment involves a multi-agent system (Betty's Brain) that implements a learning by teaching paradigm. Students teach Betty by using concept map representations with a visual interface. Betty is intelligent, not because she learns on her own but because she can apply qualitative-reasoning techniques to answer questions that are directly related to what she has been taught. Another class of agents is *emotional agents* (affective computing), which have been employed to support student learning (Picard, 1997; Wright, 1997). Getting students motivated and sustaining their motivation have historically been major obstacles in education. Emotional (or affective) agents create a learning environment involving learners and interactive characters (or believable agents). Two important aspects of such characters are that they appear emotional and can engage in social interactions. This requires a broad agent architecture and some degree of modeling of other agents in the environment. Finally, pedagogical or virtual agents can collaborate with students, enabling new types of interactions and support for learning (Johnson et al., 2000).

## Hard Technologies

In this section, we review several hardware-based technologies. These are mainly used for input (i.e., data capture) and presentation purposes.

### Biologically Based Devices

Some biologically based devices were originally developed to support learners with disabilities (i.e., assistive technologies); however, many are being created or repurposed to support learner models for both cognitive and noncognitive student data. As an example, obtaining information about where on the computer the learner is looking during learning provides evidence about the learner's current state and attentiveness (for good reviews of eye-tracking research, see Conati et al., 2005; Merten and Conati, 2006). This information can inform the system about what is the next optimal path to take for this particular learner. In terms of eye-tracking technology, eye movements, scanning patterns, and pupil diameter are indicators of thought and mental processing that occurs during learning from visual sources (Rayner, 1998); consequently, eye-tracking data can be used as the basis for supporting and guiding learners during the learning process. To illustrate the approach, consider a novel application of this technology known as AdeLE (García-Barrios et al., 2004). This introduces a real-time, eye-tracking procedure for intelligent user profile deduction as well as the use of a dynamic background library to support learning.

### Speech-Capture Devices

These devices allow users to interact with the computer via speech, instead of relying on typing their input; consequently, this approach is valuable for individuals with physical disabilities that preclude typing, for young children who cannot yet type, and so on. One example project using speech-capture technology is Project LISTEN (Literacy Innovation that Speech Technology ENables), by Jack Mostow and colleagues. This is an automated reading tutor that displays stories on a computer screen and listens to children read aloud. It intervenes when the reader makes mistakes, gets stuck, clicks for help, or is likely to encounter difficulty (Project LISTEN, 2006).

### Head-Gesture Capture Devices

Many computers currently are equipped with video cameras. Processing the image provides a means to track head position and movement. Software by Visionics Corp., for example, provides this capability. Zelinsky and Heinzmann (1996) developed a system that can recognize 13 different head and face gestures. In addition, researchers in areas such as animated pedagogical and conversational agents have used sensors and a video camera for recognizing facial gestures. This information is used to facilitate human–agent interaction (Cassell et al., 2001).

### Assistive Technologies

Disabilities and non-native language status can be major obstacles to learning from a computer. Examining adaptations in light of a validity framework can be valuable if not essential for ensuring effectiveness (for more on this topic, see Hansen and Mislevy, 2005; Hansen et al., 2005). Currently, a growing number of sites on the Web provide information for persons with special needs. See the Special Needs Opportunity Window (SNOW, 2006) website for information about the different kinds of adaptive technologies for people with disabilities.

## Adaptive Environments

When several technologies (soft and hard) are integrated into a single environment or platform to accomplish the goal of enhancing student learning via adaptation, this is called an *adaptive environment*. We now examine several well-known types of adaptive environments.

### Adaptive Hypermedia Environment

Adaptive hypermedia environments or systems (AHSs) are extended from an intelligent tutoring system foundation and combine adaptive instructional systems and hypermedia-based systems (Brusilovsky, 1996). An AHS combines hypertext and hypermedia, utilizes features of the learner in the model, and applies the LM during adaptation of visible aspects of the system to the learner. Brusilovsky (2001) distinguished between two different types of AHS: (1) adapting the presentation of content (i.e., different media formats or orderings), and (2) adapting the navigation or learning path, via direct guidance; hiding, reordering, or annotating links; or even disabling or removing links (Kinshuk and Lin, 2004).

### Adaptive Educational Hypermedia Environment

A particular type of AHS is an adaptive educational hypermedia system (AEHS). The hyperspace of AEHS is kept relatively small given its focus on a specific topic; consequently, the focus of the LM is entirely on the domain knowledge of the learner (Brusilovsky, 1996). Henze and Nejdl (2003) have described AEHS as consisting of a document space, a learner model, observations, and an adaptation component. The document space belongs to the hypermedia system and is enriched with associated information (e.g., annotations, domain or knowledge graphs). The LM stores, describes, and infers information, knowledge, and preferences about a learner. Observations represent the information about the interaction between the learner and the AEHS and are used for updating the LM.

### Collaborative Learning Environment

An alternative approach to individualized learning is collaborative learning—that is, the notion that students, working together, can learn more than by themselves, especially when they bring complementary, rather than identical, contributions to the joint enterprise (Cumming and Self, 1989). Collaboration is a process by which "individuals negotiate and share meanings relevant to the problem-solving task at hand" (Teasley and Roschelle, 1993, p. 229). Research in this area examines methods to accurately capture and analyze student interactions in collaborative or distance learning environments; for example, Soller (2004) described various techniques (e.g., probabilistic machine learning) for modeling knowledge sharing interactions among different learners.

**TABLE 24.2**
**What to Adapt**

| Learner Variables | Instructional Variables |
|---|---|
| *Cognitive abilities* (e.g., math skills, reading skills, cognitive development stage, problem solving, analogical reasoning) | *Feedback* type (e.g., hints, explanations) and timing (e.g., immediate, delayed) |
| *Metacognitive skills* (e.g., self-explanation, self-assessment, reflection, planning) | *Content sequencing* (e.g., concepts, learning objects, tasks, items, and/or problems to solve) |
| *Affective states* (e.g., motivation, attention, engagement) | *Scaffolding* (e.g., support and fading as warranted, rewards) |
| *Additional variables* (e.g., personality, learner styles, social skills such as collaboration, and perceptual skills) | *View of material* (e.g., overview, preview, review, visualization of goal and/or solution structure) |

### *Simulation and Immersive Environment*

Although simulations and immersive environments (e.g., virtual reality) change in response to specific user actions, typically the change is not due to an underlying LM but rather is a function of a predefined set of rules. Some simulations and immersive environments, however, do maintain a learner model (Rickel and Johnson, 1997). Smithtown (Shute and Glaser, 1990; Shute et al., 1989) is a simulated environment where students change parameters in the hypothetical town—such as per-capita income, population, the price of gasoline—and see immediate changes in various markets, thus learning the laws of supply and demand. Smithtown actually maintains two learner models: one to model students' microeconomic knowledge and skills and the other to model their scientific inquiry skills.

As we have just shown, many different programs and devices are available to capture, analyze, select, or present information to a learner based on current or perceived needs or wants. We now turn our attention to what some experts in the field have to say about adaptive technologies. Our goal is to provide additional perspectives on relevant topics.

## EXPERTS' THOUGHTS ON ADAPTIVE TECHNOLOGIES

To supplement our literature review on adaptive technologies, we asked leading adaptive-technology experts to address two questions: (1) *what to adapt* (i.e., what variables should be taken into account when implementing an adaptive system?), and (2) *how to adapt* (i.e., what are the best technologies and methods that you use or recommend?). The experts who responded to our e-mail queries include Cristina Conati, Jim Greer, Tanja Mitrovic, Julita Vassileva, and Beverly Woolf.

### What to Adapt?

Our experts responded to the what-to-adapt question in two ways: (1) input data or *learner variables* to be measured and used as the basis for adaptation, and (2) output or *instructional variables* that adapt to learners' needs and occasionally to preferences. Table 24.2 summarizes their collective responses and illustrates a wide range of student variables and adaptive pedagogical responses.

### How to Adapt?

Responses to this question tended to focus on domain independent approaches and technologies based on analysis of student and pedagogical models. Table 24.3 lists the methods suggested by our experts which represent innovative implementations of the adaptive technologies discussed earlier.

In this section, we have presented a variety of learner traits and states that are judged relevant to modeling in educational contexts. In addition to these variables to be captured and analyzed in the learner model, new data-mining technologies permit the discovery of even more learning variables for a more refined just-in-time collection of student information. This will allow systems to discover new things about a learner based on multiple sources of information from a single learner as well as from different learners. This sets the stage for accomplishing more accurate individual, as well as distributed and collaborative learner modeling in the future. Challenges and envisioned futures are discussed next.

## CHALLENGES AND FUTURE OF ADAPTIVE TECHNOLOGIES

Several major obstacles must be overcome for the area of adaptive technologies to move forward. As in the previous section, we have augmented this section by

**TABLE 24.3**

**How to Adapt**

| Adaptive Approach | Rationale | Refs. |
|---|---|---|
| Probability and decision theory | Rule-based approaches are typically used in adaptive systems, but using probabilistic learner models provides formal theories of decision making for adaptation. Decision theory takes into account the uncertainty in both model assessment and adaptation action outcomes and combines it with a formal representation of system objectives to identify optimal actions. | Conati (2006) |
| Constraint-based tutoring | The domain model is represented as a set of constraints on correct solutions; the long-term student model contains constraint histories, and these can be used to generate the system's estimate of students' knowledge. Constraint histories can also be used to generate a population student model (e.g., probabilistic model), which can later be adapted with the student's data to provide adaptive actions (e.g., problem or feedback selection). | Mitrovic (2006) |
| Concept mapping | Content (e.g., sequences of concepts, learning objects, hints) is adapted to the student by employing a concept map with prerequisite relationships, an overlay model of the students' knowledge, and a reactive planning algorithm. | Vassileva (2006) |
| Unsupervised machine learning | Most existing student models are built by relying on expert knowledge, either for direct model definition or for labeling data to be used by supervised machine learning techniques. But, relying on expert knowledge can be very costly, and for some innovative applications it may be even impossible because the necessary knowledge does not exist. An alternative is to use unsupervised machine learning to build student models from unlabeled data using clustering techniques for defining classes of user behaviors during learning environment interactions. | Conati (2006) |
| Exploiting learning standards | Adapting around standardized content packages (e.g., IMS QTI, IEEE LOM) can make use (and reuse) of large quantities of high-quality content. This is done by extending the SCORM runtime environment specification to include user-modeling functionality. This permits content authors to take advantage of (and update) learner models in a content management system. Content recommendations to students are based on the learner model, and recommendation is done in a lightweight manner with minimal demands on content developers. | Greer and Brooks (2006) |
| Analyzing expert teachers | Studying expert teachers/tutors is an invaluable source of information on how to adapt instructional content, but it is not always possible. Moreover, for some innovative systems (e.g., educational games) human tutors may not know how provide effective pedagogical support. An alternative is to run so-called "Wizard of Oz" studies to test adaptation strategies defined via pedagogical or cognitive theories or through intuition. | Conati (2006) |
| Matching instructional support to cognitive ability | Adapting instructional support to match students' cognitive needs (i.e., developmental stage and different abilities) has been shown to promote better learning in a couple of experimental studies. The rationale is that if students receive instructional support that they are not cognitively ready to use it will be less effective in promoting learning. | Arroyo et al. (2004, 2006), Woolf (2006) |

directly asking leading researchers in the field of adaptive technologies to summarize their views on challenges and the future of adaptive technologies. Our experts include Anthony Jameson, Judy Kay, and Gord McCalla.

## Practical and Technical Challenges

The main barriers to moving ahead in the area of adaptive educational technologies are obtaining useful and accurate learner information on which to base adaptive decisions, maximizing benefits to learners while minimizing costs associated with adaptive technologies, addressing issues relating to learner control and privacy, and figuring out the bandwidth problem, relating to the scope of learner data. Each of these is now described.

### Developing Useful Learner Models

A core challenge of developing effective adaptive technologies is building useful LMs. According to Judy Kay (Kay, 2006), collecting meaningful learning traces (i.e., data obtained from records and student log files) should help overcome this challenge; that is, the large and increasing volume of learning trace data associated with individuals is generally trapped within logs of individual tools. As a consequence, these data represent a wasted, untapped resource that might be used to build rich LMs. To transform learning trace data into a LM, a process must interpret the data to infer relevant learner attributes, such as knowledge and preferences. This would require the addition of a knowledge layer that maps learner trace data (evidence) to a set of inferences about the learner's knowledge.

### Acquiring Valid Learner Data

A related barrier to overcome involves the acquisition of valid learner data, particularly when accomplished via self reports (Kay, 2006). Self-report information has at least two problems. First, learners may enter inaccurate data either purposefully (e.g., based on concerns about privacy or a desire to present themselves in a flattering light) or by accident (e.g., lack of knowledge about the characteristics they are providing). This problem may be solved by maintaining separate views of the LM (e.g., the learner's view) and providing mechanisms for reconciling different views into one LM. Second, when additional interactions are required during the learning process (e.g., completing online questionnaires), this increases the time imposition and can lead to frustration (Kay, 2006) as well as potentially invalid data from students simply trying to get

to the content quickly (Greer and Brooks, 2006). Gathering such information, however, can not only reduce the complexity of diagnosis but also encourage students to become more active participants in learning and assume greater responsibility for their own LMs.

### Maximizing Benefits

Currently, the cost of developing and employing adaptive technologies is often quite high while the return on investment is equivocal. This challenge is a practical one—how to maximize the benefit-to-cost ratio of adaptive technologies. Despite a growing number of adaptive technologies available today, there are too few controlled evaluations of the technologies and systems. According to Jameson (2006b), addressing this problem should begin with the identification of specific conditions that warrant adaptation. There are at least two standards of comparison for adaptivity: (1) fixed sequencing, and (2) learner control of content. The question is whether these comparison conditions accomplish the same goals that could be achieved via adaptation. Jameson (2006b) offered a strategy for finding appropriate adaptivity applications—look for cases where the learner is in a poor position to select content herself, such as: (1) the learner wants to choose an item from a very large set of items whose properties the learner is not familiar with, and (2) the learner is in a situation lacking in the resources that would be required for effective performance.

### Minimizing Costs

One straightforward way to minimize the technical costs associated with adaptivity involves the use of more or less off-the-shelf technology for user adaptivity (Fink and Kobsa, 2000; Jameson, 2006b). Another cost-minimizing option has been suggested by Greer and Brooks (2006) that involves leveraging existing content. They note that adaptive algorithms are often domain specific, requiring the hand coding of content to fit the specific form of adaptation. But, with the growing use of standardized content management systems and content available with descriptive metadata, the adaptive learning community has the opportunity to get in on the ground floor in creating standards for content adaptation. Their approach involves creating formal ontologies to capture content, context, and learning outcomes. Instances of these ontologies can be reasoned over by a learning environment to provide content (and peer help) recommendations. Formal ontologies may then be shared (e.g., via Semantic Web specifications) and provide a clear set of deduction rules as well as extensive tool support.

## Dealing with Learner Control Issues

Learners often want to control their learning environment. One strategy that addresses this desire is to allow them partial control of the process. According to Jameson (2006b), there are several ways to divide the job of making a learning-path decision by the system vs. the learner (see Wickens and Hollands, 2000, chap. 13). The system can (1) recommend several possibilities and allow the learner to choose from that list, (2) ask the learner for approval of a suggested action, or (3) proceed with a particular action but allow the learner to interrupt its execution of the action. Choosing the right point on this continuum can be just as important as ensuring high accuracy of the system's modeling and decision making.

## Addressing Privacy and Obtrusiveness Concerns

When a system has control of the learning environment and automatically adapts, its behavior may be viewed by learners as relatively unpredictable, incomprehensible, or uncontrollable (Jameson, 2006a). Moreover, the actions that the system performs to acquire information about the learner or to obtain confirmation for proposed actions may make the system seem obtrusive or threaten the learner's privacy (Kobsa, 2002). According to Kay (2006), one way to address this concern is to build all parts of the learner modeling system in a transparent manner to ensure that the learner can scrutinize the system's management of their data and the way in which those data are interpreted (Cook and Kay, 1994).

## Considering the Scope of the Learner Model

According to McCalla (2006), adapting to individual differences is essential to making adaptive systems more effective. Despite some support for this claim (Arroyo et al., 2004, 2006), significantly more experimental studies are needed. The traditional approach to achieving adaptivity has required the system to maintain a LM that captures certain characteristics of each learner and then use those data as the basis for adapting content (Greer and McCalla, 1994). One major problem concerns obtaining sufficient bandwidth of learner interactions to allow the capture of a sufficient range of characteristics to paint an accurate picture of the learner for appropriate adaptation. Bandwidth in this case refers to the amount of relevant learner data that can be passed along a communications channel in a given period of time. The bad news is that it is difficult to maintain a consistent model as learners' knowledge and motivations change over time, but the good news is that the bandwidth problem is diminishing as learners are currently spending more time interacting with technology (McCalla, 2006), and it is possible to gather a broad range of information about them. Moreover, learners' interactions can now be recorded at a fine enough grain size to produce more depth in the LM. The maintenance problem may be addressed by the simple expedient of not trying to maintain a persistent LM but instead making sense of a learner's interactions with an adaptive system just in time to achieve particular pedagogical goals.

Having summarized the main challenges surrounding adaptive technologies and possible ways to overcome them, we now present some visions of where the field may be heading in the future, through the eyes of our three experts.

# The Future of Adaptive Technology

## Judy Kay's Views

A long-term vision for adaptive technologies involves the design and development of life-long learner models under the control of each learner. This idea draws on the range of learning traces available from various tools and contexts. Learners could release relevant parts of their life-long LMs to new learning environments. Realizing such a vision requires that all aspects of the LM and its use are amenable to learner control. Part of the future for LMs of this type must include the aggregation of information across models. This relates back to two major challenges: privacy and user control of personal data, as well as its use and reuse. An important part of addressing these issues will be to build LMs and associated applications so learners can always access and control their LMs and their use. This approach must go beyond just making the LM more open and inspectable to ensuring that learners actually take control of its use.

## Gord McCalla's Views

The next envisioned future of adaptive technologies relates to the ecological approach. The learning environment is assumed to be a repository of known learning objects, but both learning object and repository are defined broadly to include a variety of learning environments. To further enhance flexibility, the repository may also include: (1) artificial agents representing learning objects, and (2) personal agents representing users (e.g., learners, tutors, and teachers). In this vision, each agent maintains models of other agents and users that help the agent achieve its goals. The models contain raw data tracked during interactions between the agents and users (and other agents), as well as inferences drawn from the raw data. Such inferences are only made as needed (and as resources allow) while an agent is trying to achieve a pedagogical goal. This is called *active modeling* (McCalla et al., 2000).

After a learner has interacted with a learning object, a copy of the model that her personal agent has been keeping can be attached to the learning object. This copy is called a *learner model instance* and represents the agent's view of the learner during this particular interaction, both what the personal agent inferred about the learner's characteristics and how the learner interacted with the system. Over time, each learning object slowly accumulates LM instances that collectively form a record of the experiences of many different learners as they have interacted with the learning object. To achieve various pedagogical goals, agents can *mine* LM instances—attached to one or more learning objects—for patterns about how learners interacted with the learning objects. The approach is called *ecological* because the agents and objects in the environment must continuously accumulate information, and there can be natural selection as to which objects are useful or not. Useless objects and agents can thus be pruned. Moreover, ecological niches may exist that are based on goals (e.g., certain agents and learning objects are useful for a given goal while others are not). Finally, the whole environment evolves and changes naturally through interaction among the agents and ongoing attachment of LM instances to learning objects. The ecological approach will require research into many issues (e.g., experimentation to discover algorithms that work for particular kinds of pedagogical goals).

### Anthony Jameson's Views

Although there are many improvements that can and should be made in terms of tools and techniques for adaptation, it is even more important to focus on the central problem of getting the benefits to exceed the costs. Adaptivity, like many other novel technologies, is a technology that is worthwhile, albeit within a restricted range of settings. It is thus critically important to clearly identify these settings and to solve the adaptation problems therein. The ultimate goal is to enhance (in the short or middle term) the usability and effectiveness of real systems in the real world.

## SUMMARY AND DISCUSSION

Adaptive systems have been evolving, and will continue to evolve, as new technologies appear in the field and old ones transform and become more established.

The future of the field is wide open in that it can evolve in different ways depending on factors such as the emergence of new technologies, new media, advances in learning, measurement, and artificial intelligence, and general policies and standards that take hold (or not) in relation to adaptive instruction and learning.

One shift that we see as critically important to the field, particularly in the near term, is toward conducting controlled evaluations of adaptive technologies and systems. This will enable the community to gauge the value-added of these often expensive technologies in relation to improving student learning or other valued proficiencies (e.g., self esteem, motivation). Our review has shed light on a range of technologies, but the bottom line has not yet been addressed: What works, for whom, and under which conditions and contexts?

Conati (2006) asserts and we agree that *learners' traits targeted for adaptation should clearly improve the pedagogical effectiveness of the system*. This depends on whether or not: (1) a given trait is relevant to achieve the system's pedagogical goals, (2) there is enough learner variability on the trait to justify the need for individualized interaction, and (3) there is sufficient knowledge on how to adapt to learner differences along this trait. Along the same lines, Jameson (2006b) argued that the benefits of adaptation should be weighed against the cost of modeling each candidate trait, to focus on traits that provide the highest benefit given the available resources.

A similar appeal for conducting controlled evaluations was made more than a decade ago, during the heyday of intelligent tutoring system development. Now, as then, the call for evaluations of adaptive technologies and systems is crucial for future development efforts to succeed in terms of promoting learning. Building adaptive systems and not evaluating them is like "building a boat and not taking it in the water" (Shute and Regian, 1993, p. 268). Evaluation is not only important to the future of the field but can also be as exciting as the process of developing the tools and systems. And, although the results may be surprising or humbling, they will always be informative.

## ACKNOWLEDGMENTS

We would like to acknowledge the various contributions to this chapter, including the editors of this *Handbook* as well as the experts cited herein who provided us with thoughtful and insightful responses to our adaptive technology queries: Chris Brooks, Cristina Conati, Jim Greer, Anthony Jameson, Judy Kay, Gord McCalla, Tanja Mitrovic, Julita Vassileva, and Beverly Woolf. We also thank Eric Hansen, Irvin Katz, and Don Powers for reviewing an earlier draft of the chapter.

# REFERENCES

Alexander, P. A. and Judy, J. E. (1988). The interaction of domain-specific and strategic knowledge in academic performance. *Rev. Educ. Res.*, 58(4), 375–404.

Anderson, J. R. (1993). *The Adaptive Character of Thought.* Hillsdale, NJ: Lawrence Erlbaum Associates.*

Anderson, J. R. and Lebiere, C. (1998). *The Atomic Components of Thought.* Mahwah, NJ: Lawrence Erlbaum Associates.

Anderson, J. R., Boyle, C. F., Corbett, A. T., and Lewis, M. (1990). Cognitive modeling and intelligent tutoring, *Artif. Intell.*, 42, 7–49.

Anderson, J. R., Corbett, A. T., Koedinger, K. R., and Pelletier, R. (1995). Cognitive tutors: lessons learned. *J. Learn. Sci.*, 4, 167–207.

Arroyo, I., Beal, C. R., Murray, T., Walles, R., and Woolf, B. P. (2004). Web-based intelligent multimedia tutoring for high stakes achievement tests. Proc. of ITS 2004: Intelligent Tutoring Systems, 7th Int. Conf., August 30–September 3, Maceiò, Alagoas, Brazil. *Lect. Notes Comput. Sci.*, 3220, 468–477.

Arroyo, I., Woolf, B. P., and Beal, C. R. (2006). Addressing cognitive differences and gender during problem solving, *Technol. Instruct. Cognit. Learn.*, 3(1), 31–63.

Azambuja Silveira, R. and Vicari, R. M. (2002). Developing distributed intelligent learning environment with JADE: Java Agents for Distance Education framework. *Intell. Tutoring Syst.*, 2363, 105–118.

Biswas, G., Schwartz, D. L., Bransford, J., and the Teachable Agent Group at Vanderbilt (TAG-V). (2001). Technology support for complex problem solving: from SAD environments to AI. In *Smart Machines in Education: The Coming Revolution in Educational Technology*, edited by K. D. Forbus and P. J. Feltovich, pp. 71–97. Menlo Park, CA: AAAI/ MIT Press.

Bredeweg, B. and Forbus, K. (2003). Qualitative modeling in education. *AI Mag.*, 24(4), 35–46.

Bretzke H. and Vassileva, J. (2003) Motivating cooperation in peer-to-peer networks. In *Proceedings from the User Modeling UM03 Conference*, pp. 218–227. Berlin: Springer Verlag.

Brooks, R. A. (1999). *Cambrian Intelligence: The Early History of the New AI.* Cambridge, MA: MIT Press.

Brusilovsky, P. (1996). Methods and techniques of adaptive hypermedia. *User Model. User-Adap. Interact.*, 6(2–3), 87–129.

Brusilovsky, P. (2001). Adaptive hypermedia. *User Model. User-Adap. Interact.*, 11(1/2), 87–110.*

Brusilovsky, P., Sosnovsky, S., and Shcherbinina, O. (2005). User modeling in a distributed e-learning architecture. In *Proceedings of the 10th International User Modeling Conference*, edited by L. Ardissono, P. Brna, and A. Mitrovic, pp. 387–391. Berlin: Springer-Verlag.

Buxton, W. (2006). *A Directory of Sources for Input Technologies.* (http://www.billbuxton.com/InputSources.html).

Cassell, J., Nakano, Y., Bickmore, T., Sidner, C., and Rich, C. (2001). Annotating and generating posture from discourse structure in embodied conversational agents. In *Proceedings of Workshop on Representing, Annotating, and Evaluating Non-Verbal and Verbal Communicative Acts to Achieve Contextual Embodied Agents, Autonomous Agents*, Montreal, Quebec.

Chu, C. and Cohen, I. (2005). Posture and gesture recognition using 3D body shapes decomposition. In *Proceedings of IEEE Workshop on Vision for Human–Computer Interaction (V4HCI)*, June 21, San Diego, CA (http://iris.usc.edu/~icohen/pdf/Wayne-v4hci05.pdf).

Conati, C. (2002). Probabilistic assessment of user's emotions in educational games. *J. Appl. Artif. Intell.*, 16(7–8), 555–575.

Conati, C. (2006). *What to Adapt, and How?* Personal communication, May 18, 2006.

Conati, C., Gertner, A., and VanLehn, K. (2002). Using Bayesian networks to manage uncertainty in student modeling. *User Model. User-Adap. Interact.*, 12(4), 371–417.*

Conati, C., Merten, C., Muldner, K., and Ternes, D. (2005). Exploring eye tracking to increase bandwidth in user modeling. *Lect. Notes Artif. Intell.*, 3538, 357–366.

Conchas, G. (2006). *The Color of Success: Race and High Achieving Urban Youth.* New York: Teachers College Press.

Cook, R. and Kay, J. (1994). The justified user model: a viewable, explained user model. In *Proceedings of the Fourth International Conference on User Modeling (UM94)*, edited by A. Kobsa, and D. Litman, pp. 145–150, Hyannis, MA: MITRE, UM Inc.

Craig, S. D., Graesser, A. C., Sullins, J., and Gholson, B. (2004). Affect and learning: an exploratory look into the role of affect in learning with AutoTutor. *J. Educ. Media*, 29(3), 241–250.

Cumming, G. and Self, J. (1989). Collaborative intelligent educational systems. In *Proceedings of Artificial Intelligence and Education*, edited by D. Bierman, J. Breuker, and J. Sandberg, pp. 73–80. Amsterdam: IOS.

Desimone, L. (1999). Linking parent involvement with student achievement: do race and income matter? *J. Educ. Res.*, 93(1), 11–30.

Ekman, P. (2003). *Emotions Revealed: Recognizing Faces and Feelings to Improve Communication and Emotional Life.* New York: Henry Holt.

Fan, X. and Chen, M. (2001). Parental involvement and students' academic achievement: a meta-analysis. *Educ. Psychol. Rev.*, 13(1), 1–22.

Fink, J. and Kobsa, A. (2000). A review and analysis of commercial user modeling servers for personalization on the World Wide Web. *User Model. User-Adap. Interact.*, 10, 209–249.

Frederiksen, J. and White, B. (2002). Conceptualizing and constructing linked models: creating coherence in complex knowledge systems. In *The Role of Communication in Learning to Model*, edited by P. Brna, M. Baker, K. Stenning, and A. Tiberghien, pp. 69–96. Mahwah, NJ: Lawrence Erlbaum Associates.*

Fröschl, C. (2005). User Modeling and User Profiling in Adaptive e-Learning Systems: An Approach for a Service-Based Personalization Solution for the Research Project AdeLE (Adaptive e-Learning with Eye-Tracking), Master's thesis. Graz, Austria: Graz University of Technology.

García-Barrios, V. M., Gütl, C., Preis, A., Andrews, K., Pivec, M., Mödritscher, F., and Trummer, C. (2004). AdeLE: a framework for adaptive e-learning through eye tracking. In *Proceedings of the International Conference on Knowledge Management (I-KNOW '04)*, June 30–July 1, Graz, Austria, pp. 609–616.

Glaser, R. (1984). Education and thinking: the role of knowledge. *Am. Psychol.*, 39(2), 93–104.*

González, G., Angulo, C., López, B., and de la Rosa, J. L. (2005). Smart user models: modelling the humans in ambient recommender systems. In *Proceedings of the Workshop on Decentralized, Agent Based and Social Approaches to User Modelling (DASUM 2005)*, July 25, Edinburgh, pp. 11–20.

Graesser, A. C., Person, N., Harter, D., and Tutoring Research Group (TRG). (2001). Teaching tactics and dialog in AutoTutor. *Int. J. Artif. Intell. Educ.*, 12, 257–279.

Greer, J. and Brooks, C. (2006). *What to Adapt, and How?* Personal communication, May 16, 2006.

Greer, J. E. and McCalla, G. I., Eds. (1994). *Student Modelling: The Key to Individualized Knowledge-Based Instruction*, Berlin: Springer Verlag.*

Hansen, E. G. and Mislevy, R. J. (2005). Accessibility of computer-based testing for individuals with disabilities and English language learners within a validity framework. In *Online Assessment and Measurement: Foundation, Challenges, and Issues*, edited by M. Hricko and S. Howell, pp. 212–259. Hershey, PA: Idea Group.

Hansen, E. G., Mislevy, R. J., Steinberg, L. S., Lee, M. J., and Forer, D. C. (2005). Accessibility of tests for individuals with disabilities within a validity framework. *Syst. Int. J. Educ. Technol. Appl. Linguist.*, 33(1), 107–133.

Henze, N. and Nejdl, W. (2003). Logically characterizing adaptive educational hypermedia systems. In *Proc. of Workshop on Adaptive Hypermedia and Adaptive Web-Based Systems (AH2003)*, May 20–24, Budapest, Hungary.

Jameson, A. (1995). Numerical uncertainty management in user and student modeling: an overview of systems and issues. *User Model. User-Adap. Interact.*, 5(3–4), 193–251

Jameson, A. (2006a). Adaptive interfaces and agents. In *Human–Computer Interaction Handbook*, 2nd ed., edited by J. A. Jacko and A. Sears, pp. 305–330. Mahwah, NJ: Lawrence Erlbaum Associates.

Jameson, A. (2006b). *Challenges and Future of Learner Modeling*. Personal communication, May 24, 2006.

Johnson, W. L. and Rickel, J. (1997). Steve: An animated pedagogical agent for procedural training in virtual environments. *ACM SIGART Bull.*, 8(1–4), 16–21.

Johnson, W. L., Rickel, J. W., and Lester, J. C. (2000). Animated pedagogical agents: face-to-face interaction in interactive learning environments. *Int. J. Artif. Intell. Educ.*, 11(1), 47–78.

Johnson, W. L., Beal, C., Fowles-Winkler, A., Narayanan, S., Papachristou, D., Marsella, S., and Vilhjálmsson, H. (2004). Tactical language training system: an interim report. *Lect. Notes Comput. Sci.*, 3220, 336–345.

Kabassi, K. and Virvou, M. (2003). Using Web services for personalised Web-based learning. *Educ. Technol. Soc.*, 6(3), 61–71.

Kapoor, A. and Picard, R. W. (2002). Real-Time, Fully Automatic Upper Facial Feature Tracking. Paper presented at the 5th IEEE International Conference on Automatic Face and Gesture Recognition, May 20–21, Washington, D.C.

Kay, J. (1999). A Scrutable User Modelling Shell for User-Adapted Interaction. Ph.D. thesis. Sydney, Australia: Basser Department of Computer Science, University of Sydney.

Kay, J. (2000). Stereotypes, student models and scrutability. *Lect. Notes Comput. Sci.*, 1839, 19–30.

Kay, J. (2006). *Challenges and Future of Learner Modeling*. Personal communication, June 6, 2006.

Kettebekov, S., Yeasin, M., and Sharma, R. (2003). Improving continuous gesture recognition with spoken prosody. In *Proc. of IEEE Computer Society Conference on Computer Vision and Pattern Recognition (CVPR)*, June 16–22, Madison, WI, pp. 565–570.

Kinshuk and Lin, T. (2004). Cognitive profiling towards formal adaptive technologies in Web-based learning communities. *Int. J. WWW-Based Communities*, 1(1), 103–108.

Kobsa, A. (1993). User modeling: recent work, prospects and hazards. In *Adaptive User Interfaces: Principles and Practice*, edited by T. K. M. Schneider-Hufschmidt and U. Malinowski, pp. 111–128. Amsterdam: North-Holland.

Kobsa, A. (2002). Personalization and international privacy. *Commun. ACM*, 45(5), 64–67.

Kobsa, A. (2006). Generic user modeling systems and servers. In *The Adaptive Web: Methods and Strategies of Web Personalization*, edited by P. Brusilovsky, A. Kobsa, and W. Neijdl. Berlin: Springer-Verlag.

Koedinger, K. R. and Anderson, J. R. (1998). Illustrating principled design: the early evolution of a cognitive tutor for algebra symbolization. *Interact. Learn. Environ.*, 5, 161–180.

Koedinger, K. R., Anderson, J. R., Hadley, W. H., and Mark, M. A. (1997). Intelligent tutoring goes to school in the big city. *Int. J. Artif. Intell. Educ.*, 8, 30–43.

Leelawong, K., Wang, Y., Biswas, G., Vye, N., and Bransford, J. (2001). Qualitative reasoning techniques to support learning by teaching: the teachable agents project. In *Proceedings of the Fifteenth International Workshop on Qualitative Reasoning*, May 17–18, St. Mary's University, San Antonio, TX.

Litman, D. J. and Forbes-Riley, K. (2004). Predicting student emotions in computer–human tutoring dialogues. In *Proceedings of the 42nd Annual Meeting of the Association for Computational Linguistics (ACL)*, July 21–26, Barcelona, pp. 351–358.

Matsuda, N., Cohen, W. W., and Koedinger, K. R. (2005). An intelligent authoring system with programming by demonstration. In *Proc. of the Japan National Conference on Information and Systems in Education*. Kanazawa, Japan.

McCalla. G. I. (2004). The ecological approach to the design of e-learning environments: purpose-based capture and use of information about learners. *J. Interact. Media Educ.*, 7, 1–23 (special issue on the educational Semantic Web; http://www-jime.open.ac.uk/2004/7/mccalla-2004-7.pdf).

McCalla, G. I. (2006). *Challenges and Future of Learner Modeling*. Personal communication, May 26, 2006.

McCalla, G. I., Vassileva, J., Greer, J. E., and Bull, S. (2000). Active learner modeling. In *Proceedings of ITS'2000*, edited by G. Gauthier, C. Frasson, and K. VanLehn, pp. 53–62. Berlin: Springer-Verlag.

Merten, C. and Conati, C. (2006). Eye-tracking to model and adapt to user meta-cognition in intelligent learning environments. In *Proc. of Int. Conf. on Intelligent User Interfaces (IUI'06)*, January 29–February 1, Sydney, Australia (http://www.cs.ubc.ca/~conati/my-papers/IUI06eyetrackingCamera.pdf).

Mislevy, R. J., Steinberg, L. S., and Almond, R. G. (2003). On the structure of educational assessments. *Meas. Interdisciplinary Res. Perspect.*, 1(1), 3–62.

Mitrovic, A. (2006). *What to Adapt, and How?* Personal communication, May 17, 2006.

Park, O. and Lee, J. (2003). Adaptive instructional systems. In *Handbook of Research for Educational Communications and Technology*, edited by D. H. Jonassen, pp. 651–685. Mahwah, NJ: Lawrence Erlbaum Associates.*

Pearl, J. (1988). *Probabilistic Reasoning in Intelligent Systems: Networks of Plausible Inference*. San Mateo, CA: Kaufmann.

Picard, R. W. (1997). *Affective Computing*. Cambridge, MA: MIT Press.

Potamianos, A., Narayanan, S., and Riccardi, G. (2005). Adaptive categorical understanding for spoken dialogue systems. *IEEE Trans. Speech Audio Process.*, 13, 321–329.

Project LISTEN. (2006). http://www.cs.cmu.edu/~listen/.

Qu, L., Wang, N., and Johnson, W. L. (2005). Detecting the learner's motivational states in an interactive learning environment. In *Artificial Intelligence in Education*, edited by C.-K. Looi et al., pp. 547–554, IOS Press.

Rayner, K. (1998). Eye movements in reading and information processing: 20 years of research. *Psychol. Bull.*, 124, 372–422.

Rich, E. (1979). User modeling via stereotypes. *Cognit. Sci.*, 3(4), 329–354.

Rickel, J. and Johnson, W. L. (1997). Intelligent tutoring in virtual reality. In *Proc. of Eighth World Conference on Artificial Intelligence in Education*, August 19–22, Kobe, Japan, pp. 294–301.

Seo, K., Cohen, I., You, S., and Neumann, U. (2004). Face pose estimation system by combining hybrid ICA-SVM learning and re-registration. In *Proc. of Asian Conference on Computer Vision (ACCV)*, January 27–30, Jeju Island, Korea.

Shaw, E., Johnson, W. L., and Ganeshan, R. (1999). Pedagogical agents on the Web. In *Proc. of the Third Int. Conf. on Autonomous Agents*, May 1–5, Seattle, WA, pp. 283–290.

Shute, V. J. (2006). *Tensions, Trends, Tools, and Technologies: Time for an Educational Sea Change*. Princeton, NJ: ETS.

Shute, V. J. and Glaser, R. (1990). Large-scale evaluation of an intelligent tutoring system: Smithtown. *Interact. Learn. Environ.*, 1, 51–76.

Shute, V. J. and Psotka, J. (1996). Intelligent tutoring systems: past, present, and future. In *Handbook of Research for Educational Communications and Technology*, edited by D. Jonassen, pp. 570–600. New York: Macmillan.*

Shute, V. J. and Regian, J. W. (1993). Principles for evaluating intelligent tutoring systems. *J. Artif. Intell. Educ.*, 4(3), 245–271.

Shute, V. J., Glaser, R., and Raghavan, K. (1989). Inference and discovery in an exploratory laboratory. In *Learning and Individual Differences*, edited by P. L. Ackerman, R. J. Sternberg, and R. Glaser, pp. 279–326. New York: W.H. Freeman.

Shute, V. J., Lajoie, S. P., and Gluck, K. A. (2000). Individualized and group approaches to training. In *Training and Retraining: A Handbook for Business, Industry, Government, and the Military*, edited by S. Tobias and J. D. Fletcher, pp. 171–207. New York: Macmillan.

Shute, V. J., Graf, E. A., and Hansen, E. (2005). Designing adaptive, diagnostic math assessments for individuals with and without visual disabilities. In *Technology-Based Education: Bringing Researchers and Practitioners Together*, edited by L. PytlikZillig, R. Bruning, and M. Bodvarsson, pp. 169–202. Greenwich, CT: Information Age Publishing.

Sison, R. and Shimura, M. (1998). Student modeling and machine learning. *Int. J. Artif. Intell. Educ.*, 9, 128–158.

SNOW. (2006). http://snow.utoronto.ca/technology/.

Snow, C. E. and Biancarosa, G. (2003). *Adolescent Literacy and the Achievement Gap: What Do We Know and Where Do We Go from Here?* New York: Carnegie.

Snow, R. E. (1989). Toward assessment of cognitive and conative structures in learning. *Educ. Res.*, 18(9), 8–14.

Snow, R. E. (1994). Abilities in academic tasks. In *Mind in Context: Interactionist Perspectives on Human Intelligence*, edited by R. J. Sternberg and R. K. Wagner, pp. 3–37. Cambridge, U.K.: Cambridge University Press.

Soller, A. (2004). Computational modeling and analysis of knowledge sharing in collaborative distance learning, *User Model. User-Adap. Interact.*, 14(4), 351–381.

Stansfield, J., Carr, B., and Goldstein, I. (1976). *Wumpus Advisor: A First Implementation of a Program That Tutors Logical and Probabilistic Reasoning Skills*, Technical Report 381. Cambridge, MA: Artificial Intelligence Laboratory, MIT.

Teasley, S. D. and Roschelle, J. (1993). Constructing a joint problem space: the computer as a tool for sharing knowledge. In *Computers as Cognitive Tools*, edited by S. P. Lajoie and S. J. Derry, pp. 229–258. Hillsdale, NJ: Lawrence Erlbaum Associates.

Tobias, S. (1994). Interest, prior knowledge, and learning. *Rev. Educ. Res.*, 64(1), 37–54.

Trella, M., Carmona, C., and Conejo, R. (2005). MEDEA: an open service-based learning platform for developing intelligent educational systems for the Web. In *Proc. of Workshop on Adaptive Systems for Web-Based Education at 12th Int. Conf. on Artificial Intelligence in Education (AIED 2005)*, July 18–22, Amsterdam, pp. 27–34.

VanLehn, K., Lynch, C., Schulze, K., Shapiro, J. A., Shelby, R., Taylor, L., Treacy, D., Weinstein, A., and Wintersgill, M. (2005). The Andes physics tutoring system: lessons learned. *Int. J. Artif. Intell. Educ.*, 15(3), 147–204.

Vassileva, J. (1998). DCG+GTE: dynamic courseware generation with teaching expertise. *Instruct. Sci.*, 26(3/4), 317–332.

Vassileva, J. (2006). *What to Adapt, and How?* Personal communication, May 15, 2006.

Vassileva, J. and Wasson, B. (1996). Instructional planning approaches: from tutoring towards free learning. In *Proc. of EuroAIED*, Sept. 30–Oct. 2, Lisbon, Portugal, pp. 1–8.

Vassileva, J., McCalla, G. I., and Greer, J. E. (2003). Multi-agent multi-user modeling in I-Help. *User Model. User-Adap. Interact.*, 13 (1–2), 179–210.

Webb, G., Pazzani, M. J., and Billsus, D. (2001). Machine learning for user modeling. *User Model. User-Adap. Interact.*, 11, 19–29.

Wenger, E. (1987). *Artificial Intelligence and Tutoring Systems*. Los Altos, CA: Morgan Kaufmann.

Wickens, C. D. and Hollands, J. G. (2000). *Engineering Psychology and Human Performance*, 3rd ed. Upper Saddle River, NJ: Prentice Hall.

Winter, M., Brooks, C., and Greer, J. (2005) Towards best practices for Semantic Web student modelling. In *Proc. of the 12th Int. Conf. on Artificial Intelligence in Education (AIED 2005)*, July 18–22, Amsterdam.

Woolf, B. (2006). *What to Adapt, and How?* Personal communication, May 22, 2006.

Wright, I. (1997). Emotional Agents. Ph.D. thesis. Birmingham, U.K.: University of Birmingham (http://citeseer.ist.psu.edu/wright97emotional.html).

Yang, M., Zapata-Rivera, D., and Bauer, M. (2006). E-grammar: an assessment-based learning environment for English grammar. In *Proc. of the Annual Conference of ED-Media*, June 26–30, Orlando, FL.

Yeasin, M. and Bullot, B. (2005). Comparison of linear and non-linear data projection techniques in recognizing universal facial expressions. *Proc. Int. Joint Conf. Neural Netw.*, 5, 3087–3092.

Zapata-Rivera, D. and Greer, J. (2000). Inspecting and visualizing distributed Bayesian student models. In *Proc. of the 5th Int. Conf. on Intelligent Tutoring Systems (ITS 2000)*, June 19–23, Montreal, Canada, pp. 544–553.

Zapata-Rivera, D. and Greer, J. (2004) Inspectable Bayesian student modelling servers in multi-agent tutoring systems, *Int. J. Hum.-Comput. Stud.*, 61(4), 535–563.

Zelinsky, A. and Heinzmann, J. (1996). Real-time visual recognition of facial gestures for human–computer interaction. In *Proc. of the Second Int. Conf. on Automatic Face and Gesture Recognition*, October 13–16, Killington, VT.

* Indicates a core reference.

# 25

# Generational Differences

*Thomas C. Reeves and Eunjung Oh*
University of Georgia, Athens, Georgia

## CONTENTS

## ABSTRACT

Generational differences are the subject of much popular speculation but relatively little substantive research. Among the speculations are suggestions that instructional designers should take generational differences into account when developing instruction and that games and simulations will be more effective learning environments with today's younger generation than they have been with earlier ones. This review examines the evidence in both the research and popular literature that supports (or fails to support) these speculations. Most of the popular literature on the subject of generational differences appears to rest on limited data, almost always conducted by survey methods characterized by a lack of reliability and validity data. The most recent research based on rigorous analysis of previous psychological studies does yield some evidence of substantive generational differences, especially between those generations born before and after 1970. Recommendations for further research in this area include examining generational differences across the whole spectrum of socioeconomic status and in international contexts, as well as implementing innovative design-based research approaches to accommodating generation differences in the process of instructional design.

## KEYWORDS

*Educational technology research:* Research focused on describing, predicting, understanding, and designing effective applications of technology to serve the goals of education, training, and performance support.
*Generational differences:* The theory that people born within an approximately 20-year time period share a common set of characteristics based on the historical experiences, economic and social conditions, technological advances, and other societal changes they have in common; the term first came into popularity in the 1960s when it was used to distinguish the rebellious Baby Boomer Generation from their parents.

*Instructional design:* The systematic process of analyzing, designing, developing, implementing, and evaluating instruction; also known as instructional systems design.

# INTRODUCTION

Generational differences, especially the differences between generations defined variously as the Baby Boom Generation, Generation X, and the Millennial Generation, are widely discussed in the popular press as well as in a few scholarly publications. Business entrepreneurs as well as social pundits have speculated that the various generations of students enrolled in today's higher education institutions as well as the different generations of employees in the corporate workplace require a different approach to education and training. Extensions of this speculation are that instructional designers should take generational differences into account when developing instruction and that generational differences represent a meaningful variable for research designed to examine the differential efficacy of various applications of educational technology. The purpose of this chapter is to review the research and popular literature that support (or fail to support) this speculation.

## Definitions of Generations

The nomenclature used to label various generations is not standardized because the different researchers and consultants exploring and writing about generational differences have come up with a variety of different names to label the specific generations. In addition, there is significant disagreement among the various authors about which span of years should be encompassed within any one generation. Table 25.1 presents a comparison of the different labels given to various generations as well as the different chronological schemes used to assign people born in any given year to one of the generations defined by the sources listed in the first column. As illustrated in the table, some authorities state that Generation Y workers were born as early as 1978 (Martin and Tulgan, 2002), whereas others (Howe and Strauss, 2000) have established a start date as late as 1982. Interestingly, both of these sources (Howe and Strauss, 2000; Martin and Tulgan, 2002) define the end date for Generation Y as 2000. The focus of this review is on the three middle generations (Boomer, X, and Millennial), because members of these three generations will be in higher education and the workforce over the next 15 years. For purposes of this review, the generations will be labeled and delineated as illustrated in Table 25.2; however, other synonymous terms for the three major generations are used in various sections of this review, especially when referring to specific literature resources that employ alternative terms.

## Do Generations Really Differ?

There is relatively little consensus of opinion and scholarship about whether generational differences exist that are worth taking into consideration in the workplace, colleges, and universities, and other con-

**TABLE 25.1**
**Generational Labels and Dates Reported in Different Sources**

| Source | Labels | | | | |
|---|---|---|---|---|---|
| Howe and Strauss (2000) | Silent Generation (1925–1943) | Boom Generation (1943–1960) | 13th Generation (1961–1981) | Millennial Generation (1982–2000) | — |
| Lancaster and Stillman (2002) | Traditionalists (1900–1945) | Baby Boomers (1946–1964) | Generation Xers (1965–1980) | Millennial Generation; Echo Boomer; Generation Y; Baby Busters; Generation Next (1981–1999) | — |
| Martin and Tulgan (2002) | Silent Generation (1925–1942) | Baby Boomers (1946–1960) | Generation X (1965–1977) | Millennials (1978–2000) | — |
| Oblinger and Oblinger (2005) | Matures (<1946) | Baby Boomers (1947–1964) | Gen-Xers (1965–1980) | Gen-Y; NetGen; Millennials (1981–1995) | Post-Millennials (1995–present) |
| Tapscott (1998) | — | Baby Boom Generation (1946–1964) | Generation X (1965–1975) | Digital Generation (1976–2000) | — |
| Zemke et al. (2000) | Veterans (1922–1943) | Baby Boomers (1943–1960) | Gen-Xers (1960–1980) | Nexters (1980–1999) | — |

**TABLE 25.2**
**Generational Labels and Dates**

| Label: | Mature Generation | Boom Generation | Generation X | Millennial Generation | Generation Z |
|---|---|---|---|---|---|
| Date: | 1925–1945 | 1946–1964 | 1965–1980 | 1981–2000 | 2001–present |

texts. For starters, as noted above, notable differences can be found in the labels used for the generations by different researchers and experts as well as across the spans of years used to delineate the different generations. In addition, Lancaster and Stillman (2002), among others, have made a distinction between people born on the edges of various generational spans and those caught between two generations by labeling them *cuspers*. Lancaster and Stillman (2002) maintained that the Traditionalist/Baby Boom cuspers were born between 1940 and 1945, Baby Boom/Generation X cuspers were born between 1960 and 1965, and the Generation X/Millennial cuspers were born between 1975 and 1980. The existence of cuspers further limits the generalization of generational traits to individuals based on their categorization with regard to generation.

Despite the lack of consistency in nomenclature and chronology, most authorities agree that a great deal of variance exists among the distinguishing characteristics within any given generation; thus, it is inadvisable to assume that if a person was born in 1985 then that person would have most of the characteristics of a Gen Y person or that someone born in 1960 (and thus a late Boomer) would be not as technologically sophisticated as a person born into Gen X or the Millennial Generation. In other words, it is definitely unjustified to make assumptions about any one individual based on that person's membership in a chronological generational cohort.

Indeed, birth years are only one factor to consider in distinguishing among generations, and a relatively minor one at that. Instead, most experts have argued that generations are shaped much more by history than by chronological dates. According to Howe and Strauss (2000), three attributes that more clearly identify the nature of a generation than years of birth are:

- *Perceived membership*—The self-perception of membership within a generation that begins during adolescence and coalesces during young adulthood
- *Common beliefs and behaviors*—The attitudes (toward family, career, personal life, politics, religion, etc.) and behaviors (choices made in regard to jobs, marriage, children, health, crime, sex, drugs, etc.) that characterize a generation

- *Common location in history*—The turning points in historical trends (e.g., from liberal to conservative politics) and significant events (e.g., the Vietnam War) that occur during a generation's formative years (adolescence and young adulthood)

Many of the theories and conclusions about generation differences reported in popular books such as those written by Howe and Strauss (2000) as well as the information found in research papers are based on survey data collected from young people from middle and upper middle socioeconomic groups. No national surveys related to generational differences that cut across the full range of socioeconomic status (SES) groups can be found in the literature. In addition, the majority of the research papers and other literature sources are focused on people who will enter colleges and universities and eventually pursue white-collar or knowledge-worker careers. Virtually no literature can be found that specifically addresses the generational differences among those who will not enter higher education or who are more likely to assume blue-collar jobs. In addition, the literature is remarkably ethnocentric, taking a perspective that ignores generational differences in cultures other than those associated with Western capitalism.

As an example, a survey conducted by Universum Communications (see http://www.universumusa.com/) involved 37,000 "soon-to-graduate college students of the millennial generation" (Stone, 2006, p. 1) from 207 colleges and universities in the United States. According to the survey conducted in the spring of 2006, the career goals of today's Net Gen college graduates are "to balance their personal and professional life (59 percent), pursue further education (46 percent), build a sound financial base (32 percent), and contribute to society (27 percent)." Whether these types of career ambitions would surface among non-college workers in the same Millennial cohort has not been addressed, nor have researchers investigated the ambitions of people in developing countries by generational membership.

The most frequently cited sources for issues related to generational differences are the works of Neil Howe and William Strauss, authors of a series of popular books that includes:

- *Generations: The History of America's Future, 1584 to 2069*
- *13th Gen: Abort, Retry, Ignore, Fail?*
- *The Fourth Turning, Millennials Rising: The Next Great Generation*
- *Millennials Go to College: Strategies for a New Generation on Campus*
- *Millennials and the Pop Culture*

Their most controversial projection is that the Millennial Generation will be the most successful generation since the so-called greatest generation that fought World War II. Howe and Strauss (2000, p. 4) predict a rosy future for Generation Y:

As a group, Millennials are unlike any other youth generation in living memory. They are more numerous, more affluent, better educated, and more ethnically diverse. More important, they are beginning to manifest a wide array of positive social habits that older Americans no longer associate with youth, including a new focus on teamwork, achievement, modesty, and good conduct.

Secondary sources such as Forrester Research, an independent technology and market research company, have extrapolated from Howe and Strauss and other pollsters to make optimistic conjectures about the work habits of Generation Y (Schooley, 2005, Executive Summary):

The "Millennials"—born between 1980 and 2000—have an innate ability to use technology, are comfortable multitasking while using a diverse range of digital media, and literally demand interactivity as they construct knowledge. Millennials lack the workaholic drive of their burned-out predecessors, but they compensate by using many technologies—often simultaneously—to get the job done quickly and have a personal life as well.

Of course, some critics take issue with such optimistic predictions, especially with the generalizations made from limited survey data by Howe and Strauss. Brooks (2000, p. 1), a reviewer for *The New York Times*, wrote:

Now if you're going to get through this book, you can't hurl it against the wall every time Howe and Strauss make a huge generalization about an entire age category, because you'll either knock down your house or tear your rotator cuff. This is not a good book, if by good you mean the kind of book in which the authors have rigorously sifted the evidence and carefully supported their assertions with data. But it is a very good bad book. It's stuffed with interesting nuggets. It's brightly written. And if you get away from the generational mumbo jumbo, it illuminates changes that really do seem to be taking place.

O'Neill (2000; see also http://www.millennialsrising.com and www.fourthturning.com) also criticized Howe and Strauss:

This latest book, like the others, mixes statistics from responsible data-collectors such as the Institute for Social Research with results from scientifically unrepresentative surveys of 200 high schoolers in Virginia and from postings on their websites.

Twenge (2006, pp. 6–7) criticized the optimistic conclusions drawn by Howe and Strauss:

My perspective on today's young generations differs from that of Neil Howe and William Strauss, who argue in their 2000 book, *Millennials Rising*, that those born since 1982 will usher in a return to duty, civic responsibility, and teamwork. Their book is subtitled *The Next Great Generation* and contends that today's young people will resemble the generation who won World War II. I agree that in an all-encompassing crisis today's young people would likely rise to the occasion – people usually do what needs to be done. But I see no evidence that today's young people feel much attachment to duty or to group cohesion. Instead, as you'll see in the following pages, young people have been consistently taught to put their own needs first and to focus on feeling good about themselves. This is not an attitude conducive to following social rules or favoring the group's needs over the individual's. ...Our childhood of constant praise, self-esteem boosting, and unrealistic expectations did not prepare us for an increasingly competitive workplace and the economic squeeze created by sky-high housing costs and rapidly accelerating health care costs. After a childhood of buoyancy, GenMe is working harder to get less.

It is difficult to find the details about the surveys upon which most of the popular books about generational differences are based. By contrast, Howe and Strauss (2000), authors of *Millennials Rising,* do provide information about their surveys on the companion website for their book at: http://www.millennialsrising.com/. They report that a total of 202 teachers and 655 students from the class of 2000 completed the surveys upon which their book is based. Some critics have suggested that the fact that all the surveys were conducted in Fairfax County, Virginia, an affluent suburban area just outside Washington, D.C., limits the generalizability of the optimistic conclusions that Howe and Strauss have drawn to less affluent areas of the country. Howe and Strauss have defended their results as follows (http://www.millennialsrising.com/survey.shtml):

Comprising the western suburbs of Washington, D.C., Fairfax County (with a total population of one million, including 170,000 school-age kids) has one of the largest

**TABLE 25.3**
**Generational Differences on 12 Criteria**

| Views toward | Boomers | Gen Xers | Millennials |
|---|---|---|---|
| Level of trust | Confident of self, not authority | Low toward authority | High toward authority |
| Loyalty to institutions | Cynical | Considered naive | Committed |
| Most admire | Taking charge | Creating enterprise | Following a hero of integrity |
| Career goals | Build a stellar career | Build a portable career | Build parallel careers |
| Rewards | Title and corner office | Freedom not to do | Meaningful work |
| Parent–child involvement | Receding | Distant | Intruding |
| Having children | Controlled | Doubtful | Definite |
| Family life | Indulged as children | Alienated as children | Protected as children |
| Education | Freedom of expression | Pragmatic | Structure of accountability |
| Evaluation | Once a year with documentation | "Sorry, but how am I doing?" | Feedback whenever I want it |
| Political orientation | Attack oppression | Apathetic, individual | Crave community |
| The big question | What does it mean? | Does it work? | How do we build it? |

*Source:* Debard, R.D., in *Serving the Millennial Generation: New Directions for Student Services*, Debard, R.D. and Coomes, M.D., Eds., Jossey-Bass, San Francisco, CA, 2004, pp. 33–45. With permission.

and most renowned school systems in the nation. Its student population is ethnically diverse—67 percent Caucasian, 13 percent Asian, 10 percent Hispanic, 8 percent African-American, and 3 percent other. Three of every ten students live in homes where a language other than English is spoken. Though Fairfax County is relatively well-to-do, with a median household income nearly twice the national average, eighteen percent of all students are eligible for free or reduced-price school lunches, nine percent live in households with annual incomes under $25,000, and five percent live beneath the official poverty line.

Whereas Howe and Strauss have focused on high-school students, others have focused their generational research on higher education students. In 2005, Diana G. Oblinger, Vice President of EDUCAUSE, a non-profit organization focused on improving the application of information technology in higher education, and James L. Oblinger, Chancellor of North Carolina State University, coedited a book titled *Educating the Net Gen* (see http://www.educause.edu/educatingthenetgen). The editors and the various authors of the chapters in this book argue that the current generation of students entering higher education has information technology skills that exceed those of the faculty members who will be teaching them, a trend that demands significant changes in the way that programs, courses, and learning environments are designed and implemented. Oblinger and Oblinger (2005, p. 2.5), however, admitted that the technological sophistication of today's Net Gen students may be somewhat superficial:

Having grown up with widespread access to technology, the New Gen is able to intuitively use a variety of IT devices and navigate the Internet. Although they are comfortable using technology without an instruction manual, their understanding of the technology or source quality may be shallow.

Debard (2004) has summarized the values of Boomers, Gen Xers, and Gen Yers that he thinks have implications for higher education administrators and faculty (see Table 25.3); for example, Debard maintained that members of the Millennial Generation have high trust in authority and are primarily rewarded by work they consider meaningful.

Although it is obvious that some in higher education are taking generational differences seriously, others view efforts to adjust teaching and other campus activities to the needs and preferences of the new generation of students with skepticism. Academic critics of optimistic predictions about the Millennial Generation may be closer to the realities of higher education challenges today than pollsters and pundits such as Howe and Strauss (2000). In 2006, *The Chronicle of Higher Education* published a special supplement focused on the relationship between school and college. The cover of the March 10, 2006, supplement reads as follows:

The facts are stunning. More than 40 percent of students arrive on college campuses needing remedial work. Only about half of the high school graduates who enter college have pursued a college-preparatory curriculum. Colleges and universities spend billions of dollars a year trying to bring those unprepared students up to speed. But most of those institutions play only a minor role in the movement to reform the schools. The whole nation is suffering as a result. America is fast losing its lead in critical fields.

A similarly dismal picture of the lack of preparation that America's students entering colleges and universities today exhibit was presented by Hersh and Merrow (2005) in a two-hour PBS television special and book that have the same title, *Declining by Degrees: Higher Education at Risk*. The book and video present interviews and extensive data that undermine the argument that the Millennial Generation is well prepared and motivated to succeed in higher education.

Taking an innovative approach to generational research, Twenge (2006) presented convincing evidence that most of today's American young people (which she labels Generation Me or GenMe) have been raised to think that they will be highly successful, even stars, although the reality is that they will find it more difficult than ever to get into and afford the best colleges, find a high-paying and personally rewarding job, and buy a decent home. Whereas most other generational researchers have taken a cross-sectional approach to their research wherein they distribute surveys to or conduct interviews with members of different generations at the same point in time, Twenge (2006) has painstakingly analyzed the results of studies that involved school children, adolescents, and college students completing well-designed, validated questionnaires in the 1950s, 1960s, 1970s, 1980s, 1990s, and today. This enabled her to compare, for example, the attitudes of the Baby Boomer Generation expressed when they were adolescents with the attitudes of GenMe expressed during their adolescence. A sample of her findings derived from data collected from 1.3 million young Americans since the 1950s include:

- In 2002, 74% of high-school students admitted to cheating whereas in 1969 only 34% admitted such a failing (p. 27).
- In 1967, 86% of incoming college students said that "developing a meaningful philosophy of life" was an essential life goal whereas in 2004 only 42% of GenMe freshmen agreed (p. 48).
- In 2004, 48% of American college freshmen reported earning an A average in high school, whereas in 1968 only 18% of freshmen reported being an A student in high school (p. 63).
- In the 1950s, only 12% of young teens agreed with the statement "I am an important person" whereas by the late 1980s, 80% claimed they were important (p. 69).
- In the 1960s, 42% of high-school students expected to work in professional jobs, whereas in the late 1990s 70% of high schoolers expected to work as professionals (p. 78).

- In a recent poll, 53% of GenMe mothers agreed with the statement that a person's main responsibility is to themselves and their children rather than making the world a better places, whereas only 28% of Boomer mothers agreed (p. 78).

Turning to the corporate world, a veritable cottage industry has sprung up around the theory that managers should attend to generational differences and make changes to their management styles and other business practices accordingly. Among the major providers of consulting services focused on generational differences are:

- Eric Chester (2002), author of *Employing Generation Why?* (http://www.generation-why.com/)
- Lynne Lancaster and David Stillman (2002), authors of *When Generations Collide* (http://www.generations.com/)
- Carolyn Martin and Bruce Tulgan (2002), authors of *Managing the Generational Mix* (http://www.rainmakerthinking.com/)
- Claire Raines (2003), author of *Connecting Generations: The Sourcebook for a New Workplace* (http://www.generationsatwork.com/)

Summing up generational differences at work and the implications for corporate business managers, Lancaster and Stillman (2002) also described a set of distinguishing characteristics among the three generations of interest in this review (see Table 25.4). Unfortunately, as with the predictions made by Howe and Strauss (2000), little substantive research backs up the generational distinctions that Lancaster and Stillman (2002), Chester (2002), Martin and Tulgan (2002), and Raines (2003) make for managers and trainers in the corporate world.

## DISCUSSION

One of the most frustrating aspects of the research focused on cognitive, affective, and psychomotor differences among the Boomer, X, and Millennial generations is that for the most part it is based on small, highly selective surveys rather than national datasets that cut across important variables such as socioeconomic status and level of education. Some critics have been especially critical of the data used by Howe and Strauss (2000) for making their optimistic predictions about the Millennials, maintaining that their data are

**TABLE 25.4**
**Lancaster and Stillman's Generational Differences**

| Factor | Baby Boomers | Generation Xers | Millennial Generation |
|---|---|---|---|
| Attitude | Optimistic | Skeptical | Realistic |
| Overview | They believe in possibilities, and often idealistically strive to make a positive difference in the world. They are also competitive and seek ways to change the system to get ahead. | The most misunderstood generation, they are very resourceful and independent and do not depend on others to help them out. | They appreciate diversity, prefer to collaborate instead of being ordered, and are very pragmatic when solving problems. |
| Description | Numbered at 80 million, the largest of the groups, Boomers were born between 1946 and 1964. They were influenced by Martin Luther King, JFK, Gloria Steinem, and The Beatles. Places such as the Hanoi Hilton, Woodstock, and Kent State resonate for this group. Television changed their world dramatically. In general, they can be described as optimistic. This was the generation that believed anything was possible—that they really could change the world. | Born between 1965 and 1980, this relatively small (46 million) segment of the workforce saw the likes of Bill Clinton, Al Bundy, Madonna, Beavis and Butthead, and Dennis Rodman make headlines during their formative years. Their world shape changed to include the former Soviet Union, Lockerbie, Scotland, and the Internet—in fact, this is the generation that, more than any other, is defined by media and technology. For Gen-Xers, the watchword is skepticism—this group puts more faith in the individual, in themselves, than in any institution, from marriage to their employer. | The youngest members of what will be the next Boomer wave, some 76 million Millennials were born between 1981 and 1999. Although they are just starting to trickle into the workforce, this group grew up with everybody from Prince William to Winky Tinky, Felicity, Marilyn Manson, Venus and Serena Williams, and Britney Spears. They have already lived through Columbine, the Columbia Space Shuttle disaster, and September 11. Stillman and Lancaster describe this group as realistic, confident, and pragmatic. Raised by optimistic Boomers, Millennials feel empowered to take positive action when things go wrong. |
| Work habits | They have an optimistic outlook. They are hard workers who want personal gratification from the work they do. They believe in self-improvement and growth. | They are aware of diversity and think globally. They want to balance work with other parts of life. They tend to be informal. They rely on themselves. They are practical in their approach to work. They want to have fun at work. They like to work with the latest technology. | They have an optimistic outlook. They are self-assured and achievement focused. They believe in strong morals and serving the community. They are aware of diversity. |

*Source:* Adapted from Lancaster, L.C. and Stillman, D., *When Generations Collide. Who They Are. Why They Clash. How to Solve the Generational Puzzle at Work*, Collins Business, New York, 2002 (excerpted from D'Addono, 2004).

primarily drawn from interviews and focus groups involving young people, conducted at times in the presence of their parents. Furthermore, they are criticized that their convenience samples have largely been drawn from wealthy suburbs in Northern Virginia near Washington, D.C., where the authors themselves live. Critics maintain that the research conducted by Howe and Strauss does not reflect regional differences sufficiently, much less issues related to socioeconomic status, race, culture, and other important factors.

Regardless of whether the survey samples are representative of the general population of the United States, it is important to remember that the data from these surveys are all based on self-reports rather than behavioral observations or other measures. In addition, the vast majority of the cases presented in the popular books about this topic are anecdotal in nature, frequently reflecting stereotypes reported in the news or represented in popular media. For example, television programs such as NBC's *Dateline*, CBS's *60 Minutes*, and ABC's *20-20* regularly feature stories about generational differences such as the impact of the Baby Boomers' pending retirement on younger generations or the phenomenon of "helicopter parents" who hover over their Millennial children.

Speaking about what would become known as the Baby Boomer Generation in 1959, Clark Kerr, President of the University of California at Berkeley said that "employers are going to love this generation. ...They are going to be easy to handle. There aren't going to be any riots" (quoted in Manchester, 1974). Kerr's naïve optimism about the Baby Boomers illustrates the danger of predicting the behavior of future generations. Many members of the Baby Boomer Generation protested, and even occasionally rioted, about civil rights, the Vietnam War, feminism, and the environment (Gillon, 2004). Arguably, the optimistic predictions made about the Millennials by Howe and Strauss (2000) and others may be just as mistaken as Kerr's errant prophecy.

Clearly, more rigorous research is needed to test whether the generational differences described by Howe and Strauss (2000), Lancaster and Stillman (2002), and others hold up when specifically looking at people living in the lower middle and lower socioeconomic groups, especially with respect to the more than 35 million American living below the poverty line. Race and gender are other individual differences that most of the researchers and self-professed authorities represented in the generational literature address inadequately. In addition, research about generational differences in other cultures, if it has been done at all, cannot be found in English language publications.

The best contemporary research on this topic comes from Twenge (2006), who devotes considerable attention to race and gender, although unfortunately she also largely ignores socioeconomic status. With respect to race, her analysis of numerous studies conducted between the 1950s and today led her to the conclusion that GenMe "will continue the shift toward equality across races" [and] "that race will become less important as a defining characteristic" (p. 214). With respect to gender, she predicted that women will soon be the majority of young professionals such as doctors and lawyers whereas engineering and physics "will remain majority male" (p. 215).

Generational differences are weak as a researchable variable in a manner similar to learning styles. A recent review of the learning styles literature conducted in England (Coffield et al., 2004) throws grave doubt on the validity and utility of employing learning styles as a basis for accommodating students of any generation. The reviewers found little rigorous scientific support for the very existence of the more than 70 learning styles models reported in hundreds of published studies from the educational and psychological research literature. According to Coffield et al. (2004), even the most widely studied models have not held up to scrutiny. The same can be said of the vast majority of scholarship focused on generational differences.

## CONCLUDING REMARKS

The bottom line on generational differences is that educational technology researchers should treat this variable as failing to meet the rigor of definition and measurement required for robust individual differences variables. The gross generalizations based on weak survey research and the speculations of profit-oriented consultants should be treated with extreme caution in a research and development context. Twenge's (2006) work appears to provide the most solid foundation for distinguishing between two major generations: the large Baby Boomer Generation that was born before 1970 and Generation Me that was born after 1970.

That said, there may be merit in examining the preferences of today generation of college students and workers for instructional designs that utilize video games, instant messaging, podcasts, and other cutting-edge technologies in higher education and the workplace; for example, there is growing evidence that video games do more good than bad with respect to cognitive outcomes (Gee, 2003), a finding that some still find heretical. Today's younger university students and workers have spent large amounts of their free time playing video games, and survey results indicate that today's students and workers alike prefer to be engaged in learning via games than by traditional classroom instruction. Nonetheless, similar to generational differences, this is an area in need of more substantive research for it to be assumed. It is recommended that design-based research approaches would be most amenable to future inquiry in this area because such approaches seek to solve real-world problems related to teaching, learning, and performance support as well as to identifying reusable design principles (van den Akker et al., 2006). Both are sorely needed at the intersection of generational differences and educational technology.

## REFERENCES

Brooks, D. (2000). What's the matter with kids today? Not a thing. *The New York Times*, Nov. 5 (http://query.nytimes.com/gst/fullpage.html?res=9B06E1D91E31F936A35752C1A9669C8B3&pagewanted=2).

Chester, E. (2002). *Employing Generation Why?: Understanding, Managing, and Motivating Your New Workforce*. Lakewood, CO: Tucker House Books.

Coffield, F., Moseley, D., Hall, E., and Ecclestone, K. (2004) *Learning Styles and Pedagogy in Post-16 Learning: A Systematic and Critical Review*. London: Learning and Skills Research Centre (http://www.lsda.org.uk/files/pdf/1543.pdf).

D'Addono, B. (2004). Bridging the generation gap. *Today's Officer*, http://www.moaa.org/TodaysOfficer/Careers/Generation_Gap.asp.

Debard, R. D. (2004). Millennials coming to college. In *Serving the Millennial Generation: New Directions for Student Services*, edited by R. D. Debard and M. D. Coomes, pp. 33–45. San Francisco, CA: Jossey-Bass.

Gee, J. P. (2003). *What Video Games Have to Teach Us About Learning and Literacy*. New York: Palgrave Macmillan.*

Gillon, S. M. (2004). *Boomer Nation: The Largest and Richest Generation Ever and How It Changed America*. New York: Free Press.

Hersh, R. H. and Merrow, J., Eds. (2005). *Declining by Degrees: Higher Education at Risk*. New York: Palgrave Macmillan.

Howe, N. and Strauss, W. (2000). *Millennials Rising: The Next Great Generation*. New York: Vintage Books.*

Lancaster, L. C. and Stillman, D. (2002). *When Generations Collide. Who They Are. Why They Clash. How to Solve the Generational Puzzle at Work*. New York: Collins Business.*

Manchester, W. (1974). *The Glory and the Dream: A Narrative History of America: 1932–1972*. Boston, MA: Little, Brown and Company.

Martin, C. A. and Tulgan, B. (2002). *Managing the Generational Mix*. Amherst, MA: HRD Press.*

Oblinger, D. and Oblinger, J., Eds. (2005). *Educating the Net Gen*. Washington, D.C.: EDUCAUSE.*

O'Neill, S. (2000). *Millennials Rising* by Neil Howe and William Strauss [review]. *Flak*, Sept. 23 (http://flakmag.com/books/mill.html).

Raines, C. (2003). *Connecting Generations: The Sourcebook for a New Workplace*. Menlo Park, CA: Crisp Publications.

Schooley, C. (2005). *Get Ready: The Millennials Are Coming! Changing Workforce*. Cambridge, MA: Forrester Research.

Stone, S. (2006, May). Millennials seek balance, continuing education. *Chief Learning Office (CLO) Online*, http://www.clomedia.com/.

Tapscott, D. (1998). *Growing Up Digital: The Rise of the Net Generation*. New York: McGraw-Hill.*

Twenge, J. M. (2006). *Generation Me: Why Today's Young Americans Are More Confident, Assertive, Entitled—and More Miserable Than Ever Before*. New York: Free Press.*

van den Akker, J., Gravemeijer, K., McKenney, S., and Nieveen, N., Eds. (2006). *Educational Design Research*. London: Routledge.

Zemke, R., Raines, C., and Filipczak, B. (2000). *Generations at Work: Managing the Class of Veterans, Boomers, X-ers, and Nexters in Your Workplace*. New York: Amacon.*

* Indicates a core reference.

# 26

# Technologies Linking Learning, Cognition, and Instruction

*Sabine Graf*
Vienna University of Technology, Vienna, Austria

*Kinshuk*
Athabasca University, Athabasca, Canada

## CONTENTS

Sabine Graf and Kinshuk

## ABSTRACT

People prefer to learn in many different ways. Furthermore, individuals have different cognitive abilities that influence the way effective learning takes place. Incorporating individual differences such as learning styles and cognitive abilities into education makes learning easier and increases the learner's performance. In contrast, learners whose needs are not supported by the learning environment experience problems in the learning process. In this chapter, we introduce some cognitive traits that are important for learning and also discuss how to incorporate different abilities in educational systems. In regard to learning styles, some major approaches as well as possible strategies for involving learning styles in online courses are presented. In the next section, recent research dealing with identifying learning styles and cognitive traits based on the behavior of students during a course is presented. This information is necessary to provide adaptive courses. Finally, the relationship between cognitive traits and learning styles is discussed. This relationship leads to additional information and therefore to a more reliable student model.

## KEYWORDS

*Cognitive abilities:* Abilities to perform any of the functions involved in cognition whereby cognition can be defined as the mental process of knowing, including aspects such as awareness, perception, reasoning, and judgment.

*Learning styles:* There is no single agreed definition of learning styles; a general definition is provided by Honey and Mumford (1992), who said that a learning style is a description of the attitudes and behaviors that determine an individual's preferred way of learning.

*Student modeling:* Student models store information about students, including domain competence and individual domain-independent characteristics. Student modeling is the process of building and updating the student model.

## INTRODUCTION

Individual learners play a central role in a technology-enhanced learning environment. Each learner has individual characteristics such as different cognitive abilities, learning style preferences, prior knowledge, motivation, and so on. These individual differences affect the learning process and are the reason why some students find it easy to learn in a particular course whereas others find the same course difficult (Jonassen and Grabowski, 1993).

The context in which learning takes place also plays an important role. This learning context includes learning objectives, learning activities, learning assessments, the technology or tools used, information resources, and teachers, tutors, or assistants. Learners with their individual differences as well as the mentioned aspects of the learning context can be seen as components of a learning system. Each of these components and especially the interactions among these components influence the learning process.

Gagné (1985), for example, argued that an interaction between the learning objectives and the learning activities exists and that different conditions on the structure and kind of learning activities are necessary for different types of learning objectives. He identified five categories of learning: verbal information, intellectual skills, cognitive strategies, motor skills, and attitudes. For learning attitudes, persuasive arguments or a kind of role model are necessary. In contrast, to learn motor skills an important condition of learning is to practice these skills. On the other hand, when learning verbal information, such as facts, no practices, arguments, or role models are necessary.

Another example is the interaction between information resources and individual differences in learning styles. The information resources can be presented in different forms, such as text, images, animations, simulations, graphs, and so on, and therefore match or mismatch each learner's preferred way of receiving information. The better these aspects match, the better the learning that can take place. Furthermore, the information might be comprised of concrete material such as facts and data or the information might deal with more abstract material such as concepts and theories. Again, matching or mismatching influences the learning process.

Many other links among the above-mentioned components are investigated in this chapter, and influences on learning are elaborated. We focus on research dealing with the links between aspects of individual learners—in particular, cognitive abilities and learning styles, how instruction can be designed to match or mismatch with these needs, and how these instructions can be supported by technology.

Concerning individual differences, much research has been done on prior knowledge and its influence on learning. Jonassen and Grabowski (1993) suggested that prior knowledge is one of the strongest and most consistent individual difference predictors of achievement. Although prior knowledge seems to account for more variance in learning than other individual differences, more recently educational researchers have focused on aspects of cognitive abilities and learning styles, their influence on learning, and how they can be incorporated in technology enhanced learning.

Cognitive abilities and learning styles play an important role in education; for example, cognitive overload may hinder the process of learning and yield to poor performance. With regard to learning styles, Felder (Felder and Silverman, 1988; Felder and Soloman, 1997) pointed out that learners with strong preference for a specific learning style may have difficulties in learning if the teaching style does not match their learning style. From a theoretical point of view, we can therefore argue that incorporating the cognitive abilities and learning style of students makes learning easier and increases the learning efficiency of the students. On the other hand, learners who are not supported by the learning environment may experience problems in the learning process.

Although these hypotheses seem to be intuitive and supported by educational theories, inconsistent results have been obtained by studies investigating the effects on achievement of matched and mismatched instruction for learners with different abilities and preferences. Jonassen and Grabowski (1993, p. 28) noted that several reasons for such inconsistent results are known in the field of aptitude–treatment interaction (ATI) research. Limitations might include "small samples size, abbreviated treatments, specialized aptitude constructs or standardized tests, and a lack of conceptual or theoretical linkage between aptitudes and the information-processing requirements of the treatment."

An example of a supporting study is the study performed by Bajraktarevic et al. (2003) showing that students attending an online course that matched their preferred learning style (either sequential or global) achieved significantly better results than those who completed a mismatched course. Another supporting example is the study by Ford and Chen (2001) where they investigated the performance of students attending courses that either matched or mismatched with their cognitive styles (field dependency or field independency). Also, in this case, students who undertook the matched courses achieved significantly better results than those who attended the mismatched courses. In contrast, a study by Brown et al. (2006) focused on the visual and verbal preference of learners. They concluded that, "It did not seem to matter whether a student was a visual or bimodal learner, nor if they were presented with visual, verbal or mixed representations of data" (Brown et al., 2006, p. 333). Another example of a study that did not yield significant results, described in Tillema (1982), dealt with the serial and holistic cognitive styles. These inconsistent results show that more future work is necessary.

Much recent research, however, has addressed aspects of incorporating cognitive abilities and learning styles in technology-enhanced learning systems. This chapter aims at providing an overview of these aspects. First, an introduction into cognitive traits and learning styles is provided, taking into account instructional strategies to support specific cognitive traits and learning styles of students in educational systems. The next section then discusses and gives examples of how cognitive traits and learning styles can be identified. Finally, the relationship between cognitive traits and learning style is discussed.

## COGNITIVE TRAITS

Humans typically have a number of cognitive abilities. In this section, we focus on cognitive abilities that are important for learning. For these abilities, we discuss how instruction is related with these cognitive abilities and how to support learners with low and high cognitive abilities in educational systems.

### Working Memory Capacity

Working memory allows us to keep active a limited amount of information (about five to nine items) for a brief period of time (Miller, 1956). In earlier times, working memory was also referred to as *short-term memory*. Despite varying views on the structure of the working memory, researchers now agree that it consists of both storage and operational subsystems (Richards-Ward, 1996). Deficiencies in working memory capacity result in different performances on a variety of tasks. Examples of affected tasks include natural language use (e.g., comprehension, production), recognition of declarative memory, skill acquisition, and so on (Byrne, 1996).

The dual-code hypothesis is based on the assumption that the working memory consists of two separate components, one concerned with verbal materials and one concerned with nonverbal materials (Clark and Paivio, 1991). According to this hypothesis, cognitive load is reduced when both channels (verbal and nonverbal) are attracted, thus better learning can take place. A supporting example is the study conducted by Moreno and Valdez (2005) where students were presented with diagrams (nonverbal information) and an explaining text (verbal information), with only diagrams, or with only the explaining text. Students who received both types of information achieved the best results in tests of retention as well as the transfer of knowledge. Another supporting study of the dual-code hypothesis was performed by Wey and Waugh (1993). They found that field-dependent learners, who tend to have low working memory capacity (Al Naeme, 1991; Bahar and Hansell, 2000), experienced difficulties in learning text-only material and benefited from material containing both text and graphics.

In some conditions, dual-code presentation has positive effects. According to Mayer (1997) and Kalyuga et al. (1999), information should not be redundant and should be integrated so students are not forced to split their attention. Presenting a text in written format as well as in audio format imposes an additional cognitive load and has a negative effect on learning. Furthermore, incorporating the domain experience of the learners seems to be important. Kalyuga et al. (2000) found in their study that the effectiveness of dual-code presentation of information decreases with the increasing learner experience. Although novice learners can achieve better results when learning from diagrams with audio text than with diagrams only, more experienced learners achieved better results from the diagrams-only situation due to the reduced cognitive load imposed by the diagram-only presentation.

Based on the exploration space control elements (Kashihara et al., 2000), different versions of courses can be created that suit different needs. These elements include the number and relevance of paths; the amount, concreteness, and structure of the content; and the number of information resources. The instructional design in learning systems should assist learners by considering their abilities and avoiding cognitive overload. For learners with low working memory capacity, this can be achieved by decreasing the number and increasing the relevance of paths in a course. Furthermore, less but more concrete content should be presented. Moreover, the number of available media resources should increase. In contrast, for learners with high working memory capacity, fewer relevant paths can be presented, and the amount of content and its abstractness can be increased (Kinshuk and Lin, 2003).

## Reasoning Ability

With respect to reasoning abilities, we can distinguish among inductive, deductive, and abductive reasoning. In the following discussion, we focus on inductive reasoning, as this ability is the most important one with regard to learning. We also address deductive reasoning.

Inductive reasoning skills relate to the ability to construct concepts from examples. Students who face complicated problems look for known patterns and use them to construct temporary internal hypotheses

or schema in which to work (Bower and Hilgard, 1981). It is easier for students who possess better inductive reasoning skill to recognize an already known pattern and generalize higher order rules. As a result, the load on working memory is reduced, and the learning process is more efficient. In other words, the higher the inductive reasoning ability, the easier it is to build up the mental model of the information learned. According to Harverty et al. (2000), inductive reasoning ability is the best predictor for academic performance.

For simulation-based discovery learning, students are asked to infer characteristics of a model through experimentations by using a computer simulation, thus they are being asked to use their inductive reasoning skills. According to Veermans and van Joolingen (1998), simulation-based discovery learning results in deeper rooting of the knowledge, enhanced transfer, the acquisition of regulatory skills, and thus better motivation; however, discovery learning does not always lead to better learning results. One reason is that students find it difficult to perform the required processes. To improve the learning progress and support learners with low inductive reasoning abilities, Veermans and van Joolingen designed a mechanism that provides advice based on the experiments performed in the simulation. This mechanism is integrated in SimQuest, an authoring system for simulation-based discovery (van Joolingen and de Jong, 2003).

Considering again exploratory learning and the exploration space control elements, many opportunities for observation should be provided to learners with low inductive reasoning skills. Learning systems can support these learners by providing a great amount of well-structured and concrete information with many paths. For learners with high inductive reasoning skills, the amount of information and number of paths should decrease to reduce the complexity of the hyperspace and enable the learners to grasp the concepts more quickly. Moreover, information can be presented in a more abstract way (Kinshuk and Lin, 2003).

Deduction is defined as drawing logical consequences from premises. An application for deductive reasoning is, for example, naturalistic decision making (Zsambok and Klein, 1997), or what people do in real-world situations. It has been observed that experienced decision makers recognize appropriate actions to take in various situations that might arise, whereas inexperienced decision makers perform an unorganized and almost random search of alternatives. When it comes to complex problems, humans often fail to find appropriate solutions. According to Dörner (1996), several reasons exist for such failures; for example, humans tend to oversimplify the mental model of the complex system, tend to be slow in thinking when it comes to conscious thoughts, or tend to ignore the possibility of side effects. Dörner's experiments, however, showed that leaders from business and industry tend to make more effective decisions in complex situations, and he argued that the necessary behavior and skills can be acquired and learned.

## Information Processing Speed

Information processing speed determines how quickly learners can acquire information correctly. Instructional designers should take into account a learner's information processing speed; for example, some learners have such slow reading speeds that they are unable to hold enough details in working memory to permit decoding of the overall meaning (Bell, 2001). Based on the exploration space control elements, learners with low information processing speed should be presented with only the important points. The number of paths and amount of information should decrease, and the relevance of the paths should increase. Additionally, the structure of the information should increase to speed up the learning process. In contrast, for learners with high information processing speed, the information space can be enlarged by providing a greater amount of information and number of paths (Kinshuk and Lin, 2003).

## Associative Learning Skills

The associative learning skills link new knowledge to existing knowledge. The association process requires pattern-matching to discover the space of existing information, analysis of the relationships between the existing and new knowledge, and retention of the new knowledge in long-term memory (or, more specifically, maintaining links to the new knowledge). To assist the association processes during a student's learning, the instruction must assist the recall (revisit) of learned information, clearly show the relationships of concepts (new to existing), and facilitate new or creative association or insight formation by providing information of the related domain area. A great amount of information, various media resources, and many relevant paths help a learner with low associative learning skills to associate one concept with another. Furthermore, well-structured information makes linkage between concepts easier. In contrast, for learners with high associative learning skills, providing less structured information allows them to navigate more freely and enhances learning speed. Additionally, the relevance of the paths should decrease to enlarge the information space (Kinshuk and Lin, 2003).

## Metacognition

The concept of metacognition was introduced by John Flavell (1976). Several definitions for metacognition exist; for example, according to Flavell (1976, p. 232), "Metacognition refers to one's knowledge concerning one's own cognitive processes and products or anything related to them." Panaoura and Philippou (2005) defined metacognition as the awareness and monitoring of one's own cognitive system and its functioning. Metacognition consists of several dimensions; however, self-representation (the knowledge about cognition) and self-regulation (the regulation of cognition) are the main ones. Recent research suggests that metacognition plays an important role in the learning process (Alexander et al., 2003; Mayer, 1998; Panaoura and Philippou, 2004); for example, it is known that learners with high metacognitive abilities perform better in problem-solving tasks (Lester et al., 1989; Mayer, 1998).

## LEARNING STYLES

Several different learning style models exist in the literature, each proposing different descriptions and classifications of learning types. To date, no single definition of learning style has been identified. Honey and Mumford (1992, p. 1) defined learning styles as "a description of the attitudes and behaviors which determine an individual's preferred way of learning." James and Gardner (1995, p. 20) defined it more precisely by suggesting that learning style is the "complex manner in which, and conditions under which, learners most efficiently and most effectively perceive, process, store, and recall what they are attempting to learn." Furthermore, researchers do not agree on whether learning styles are stable over time. In some studies, learning style changed quite quickly (see, for example, Clariana, 1997), whereas other researchers found learning styles to be stable over a long period of time (Felder and Spurlin, 2005; Keefe, 1979; Kolb, 1981).

In this section, we introduce some of the most common classifications of learning styles—namely, the Myers–Briggs Type Indicator (Briggs-Myers, 1962), Kolb's learning style model (Kolb, 1984), Honey and Mumford's learning style model (Honey and Mumford, 1982), and the Felder–Silverman learning style model (Felder and Silverman, 1988). Focusing on this last model, we also discuss possible teaching strategies that can be used to support learners with different learning styles in educational systems.

## Myers–Briggs Type Indicator

The Myers–Briggs Type Indicator (MBTI) (Briggs-Myers, 1962) is a personality test and is not focused specifically on learning; nevertheless, the personality of a learner influences how that person learns, so some learning style models are based on considerations of MBTI. Based on Jung's theory of psychological types (Jung, 1923), the MBTI distinguishes a person's type according to four dichotomies: extroversion/introversion, sensing/intuitive, thinking/feeling, and judging/perceiving. All possible combinations can occur, resulting in a total number of 16 types.

Extrovert and introvert refer to how a person orients and receives his or her energy. The preferred focus of people with an extrovert attitude is on their surroundings, such as other people and things, whereas introverts' preferred focus is on their own thoughts and ideas. Sensing and intuition deal with the way people prefer to perceive data. Whereas sensing people prefer to perceive data from their five senses, intuitive people use their intuition and prefer to perceive data from the unconscious. The judgment based on the perceived data can be distinguished between thinking and feeling. Thinking means that the judgment is based on logical connections, such as true–false or if–then, but feeling refers to more–less or better–worse evaluations; however, judgment and decisions are in both cases based on rational considerations. The last dichotomy describes whether a person is more extroverted in his or her stronger judgment function (thinking or feeling) or in the perceiving function (sensing or intuition). Judging people prefer step-by-step approaches and structure, as well as coming to a quick closure. Perceiving people have a preference for keeping all options open and tend to be more flexible and spontaneous. The four preferences interact with each other rather then being independent, and for a complete description of a person's type the combination of all four preferences must be considered.

## Kolb's Learning Style Model

The learning style theory proposed by Kolb (1984) is based on the experiential learning theory, which models the learning process and incorporates the important role of experience in this process. Following this theory, learning is conceived as a four-stage cycle. *Concrete experience* is the basis for *observations* and *reflections*. These observations are used to *form abstract concepts* and *generalizations*, which again act as basis for *testing implementations of concepts* in new situations. Testing implementations results in concrete experience, which closes the learning cycle. According to this theory, learners need four abilities for effective learning: (1) concrete experience abilities, (2) reflective observation abilities, (3) abstract conceptualization abilities, and (4) active experimentation abilities. On closer examination, there are two polar opposite dimensions: concrete/abstract and active/reflective. Kolb (1981) noted that, "as a result of our hereditary equipment, our particular past life experience, and the demands of our present environment, most of us develop learning styles that emphasize some learning abilities over others." Based on this assumption, Kolb identified four statistically prevalent types of learning styles.

*Convergers'* dominant abilities are abstract conceptualization and active experimentation; therefore, their strengths lie in the practical applications of ideas. The name "Convergers" is based on Hudson's theory of thinking styles (Hudson, 1966), where convergent thinkers are people who are good at gathering information and facts and putting them together to find a single correct answer to a specific problem. In contrast, *Divergers* excel at the opposite poles of the two dimensions—namely, concrete experimentation and reflective observation. They are good in viewing concrete situations in many different perspectives and in organizing relationships to a meaningful shape. According to Hudson, a dominant strength of Divergers is to generate ideas; therefore, Divergers tend to be more creative. *Assimilators* excel in abstract conceptualization and reflective observation. Their greatest strength lies in creating theoretical models. They are good in inductive reasoning and in assimilating disparate observations into an integrated explanation. *Accommodators'* strengths are opposite those of the Assimilators. Their dominant abilities are concrete experience and active experimentation. Their strengths lie in doing things actively, carrying out plans and experiments, and becoming involved in new experiences. They are also characterized as risk takers and as people who excel in situations that call for adaptation to specific immediate circumstances.

## Honey and Mumford's Learning Style Model

The learning style model by Honey and Mumford (1982) is based on Kolb's experiential learning theory and is developed further on the four types of Kolb's learning style model. The active/reflective and sensing/intuitive dimensions are strongly involved in the defined types as well. Furthermore, Honey and Mumford stated that the similarities between Kolb's model and theirs are more significant than the differences (Honey and Mumford, 1992). In Honey and Mumford's learning style model, the types are referred to as *Activist* (similar to Accommodator), *Theorist* (similar to Assimilator), *Pragmatist* (similar to Converger), and *Reflector* (similar to Diverger). Activists involve themselves fully in new experiences, are enthusiastic about anything new, and learn best by doing something actively. Theorists excel in adapting and integrating observations into theories; they need models, concepts, and facts to engage in the learning process. Pragmatists are interested in real-world applications of the learned material; they like to try out various ideas, theories, and techniques to see if they work in practice. Reflectors are people who like to observe other people and their experiences from many different perspectives and reflect about them thoroughly before coming to a conclusion; also, learning occurs for these people by observing and analyzing the observed experiences.

## Felder–Silverman Learning Style Model

Whereas Honey and Mumford's and Kolb's learning style models focus on a few statistically prevalent types, in the Felder–Silverman learning style model (Felder and Silverman, 1988), learners are characterized by values on four dimensions. These dimensions can be viewed independently, and they show how learners prefer to process (active/reflective), perceive (sensing/intuitive), receive (verbal/visual), and understand (sequential/global) information. Because the range of each dimension in the Felder–Silverman learning style model extends from +11 to −11, a balanced preference can also be expressed. These values represent tendencies, suggesting that even a learner with a strong positive or negative value sometimes can act differently.

The *active/reflective* dimension is analogous to the respective dimension in Kolb's model; active learners learn best by working actively with the learning material—for example, by working in groups, by discussing the material, or by applying it. To support these learners in technology-enhanced educational systems, exercises, interactive animations, and group work tasks can be provided to allow them to deal with the subject actively. In contrast, reflective learners prefer to think about and reflect the material, and they need enough time for doing so. Learning systems support this by allowing learners to learn in their own pace.

The *sensing/intuitive* dimension is taken from the Myers–Briggs Type Indicator and is similar to the sensing/intuitive dimension in Kolb's model. Learners who prefer a sensing learning style like to learn facts and concrete learning material. They tend to be more patient with details and also more practical than intuitive learners and like to relate the learned material to the real world. Intuitive learners prefer to learn abstract

learning material, such as theories and their underlying meanings. They like to discover possibilities and relationships and tend to be more innovative and creative than sensing learners; therefore, they score better in open-ended tests than in tests with a single answer to a problem. Whereas intuitive learners are good at learning abstract concepts and theories, sensing learners require a higher number of examples and various kinds of media resources that address their senses, such as audio or video objects, to support their learning process.

The *verbal/visual* dimension differentiates between learners who remember best what they have seen (e.g., pictures, diagrams, flow-charts) and learners who get more out of words, regardless of whether they are written or spoken. Accordingly, visual learners can be assisted by including visual elements such as pictures or diagrams in the learning material. For verbal learners, communication tools such as forum or chat are helpful.

The fourth dimension, *sequential/global*, distinguishes between sequential and global ways of understanding. Sequential learners learn in small incremental steps and have a linear learning progress. They tend to follow logical stepwise paths to find solutions. In contrast, global learners use a holistic thinking process and learn in large leaps. They tend to absorb learning material almost randomly without seeing connections, but after they have learned enough material they suddenly get the whole picture. They are then able to solve complex problems and put things together in novel ways; however, they find it difficult to explain how they did it. For sequential learners, it is important to provide a well-structured path through the course material and not overtax them by providing too many links. In contrast, global learners prefer to go their own way through the course. To help global learners gain an understanding of the whole picture of the course, overviews should be presented.

## IDENTIFYING COGNITIVE TRAITS AND LEARNING STYLES

To incorporate cognitive traits or learning styles in educational systems, information about cognitive traits and learning styles must first be collected. One approach is to let students perform comprehensive tests or questionnaires to reveal their cognitive traits or learning styles. Such an approach, however, has the potential to suffer from the biases and indecisiveness of the learners. A more meaningful approach is to track students' behavior and infer the required information from their behavior. The cognitive trait model

(Kinshuk and Lin, 2004; Lin and Kinshuk, 2005) uses this approach to profile learners according to their cognitive traits. To identify learning styles, approaches for detecting the various dimensions of the Felder–Silverman learning style model are used.

## Identification of Cognitive Traits

The cognitive trait model (CTM) is a student model that profiles learners according to their cognitive traits. Four cognitive traits—working memory capacity, inductive reasoning ability, processing speed, and associative learning skills—are addressed in the CTM. The CTM offers the role of *learning companion*, which can be consulted by and interact with a particular learner's learning environments. The CTM can still be valid after a long period of time due to the more or less persistent nature of cognitive traits of humans (Deary, 2004). When a student encounters a new learning environment, the learning environment can utilize the CTM of the particular student and does not need to reacquaint itself with the student. Identification of the cognitive traits is based on the behaviors of learners in the system. Various patterns—manifests of traits (MOTs)—are defined for each cognitive trait. Each MOT is a piece of an interaction pattern manifesting a learner's characteristics. A neural network (Lin and Kinshuk, 2004) is responsible for calculating the cognitive traits of the learners based on the information of the MOTs.

## Identification of Learning Styles

A number of adaptive systems are available in the literature that incorporate learning styles; for example, CS383 (Carver et al., 1999) was the first adaptive hypermedia system based on the Felder–Silverman learning style model (FSLSM). The course conducted in the system included the comprehensive collection of media objects. The system offered students the option to order these objects in accordance with how well they fit the learning styles of the students. Also based on FSLSM is MAS-PLANG (Peña et al., 2002), a multi-agent system that has been developed to enrich the intelligent tutoring system USD (Fabregat et al., 2000) with adaptivity with respect to learning styles. Another example is INSPIRE (Papanikolaou and Grigoriadou, 2003), which is based on Honey and Mumford's learning style theory. In all of these systems and in most other systems that incorporate learning styles, the learning style is identified based on a questionnaire that is filled out by learners before using the system. These questionnaires are based on the assumption that learners are aware of how they learn.

Jonassen and Grabowski (1993, p. 234) pointed out that, "because learning styles are based on self-reported measures, rather than ability tests, validity is one of their most significant problems."

García et al. (2007) studied the use of Bayesian networks (Jensen, 1996) to detect students' learning styles based on their behavior in the educational system SAVER. Based on the Felder–Silverman learning style model, they determined patterns of behavior representative of the respective dimensions, as well as the different states that these variables or patterns can take. Because SAVER does not incorporate the visual/verbal dimension, this dimension was not included in their investigations.

The above approaches were developed for specific systems, but Graf and Kinshuk (2006) proposed an approach to detecting learning styles in learning management systems in general. Similar to the approach of García et al. (2006), the Felder–Silverman learning style model is used as the basis, but in this case all four dimensions are incorporated. The patterns of behavior are derived from commonly used features in learning management systems, such as forums and exercises. The learning styles are determined by applying the index of learning styles (Felder and Soloman, 1997), a questionnaire used to identify learning styles according to the Felder–Silverman learning style model.

## THE RELATIONSHIP BETWEEN LEARNING STYLES AND COGNITIVE TRAITS

So far, cognitive traits and learning styles have been discussed separately. Consideration of their relationship with each other makes it possible to obtain additional information about a learner. In educational systems that consider either only learning styles or only cognitive traits, the relationship leads to more information. This additional information can be used to provide more adaptivity—namely, with regard to learning styles and cognitive traits. In systems that incorporate learning styles as well as cognitive traits, the interaction can be used to improve the detection process of the counterpart. This leads to a more reliable student model.

Graf et al. (2005) investigated the relationship between the Felder–Silverman learning style model and the cognitive trait of working memory capacity. Based on the literature, a relationship between high working memory capacity and a reflective, intuitive, and sequential learning style can be identified. Learners with low working memory capacity tend to prefer an active, sensing, and global learning style. With regard to the visual/verbal dimension, it can be concluded that learners with low working memory capacity tend to prefer a visual learning style, but learners with a visual learning style do not necessarily have low working memory capacity. To verify the proposed relationship, an exploratory study with 39 students was conducted (Graf et al., 2006). The results supported the existence of a relationship between working memory capacity and two of the four dimensions of the learning style model—the sensing/intuitive and the verbal/visual dimensions. For the two remaining dimensions, only tendencies but no significant correlations were found; therefore, a further study with a larger sample size is planned.

# CONCLUSION

Incorporating cognitive traits and learning styles in technology-enhanced educational systems supports learners and makes learning easier for them; nevertheless, only a few systems have considered these needs. Although at least some attention is paid to cognitive traits and learning styles in adaptive systems, learning management systems that are commonly used in e-education today do not incorporate such personal needs. This chapter has focused on three issues: (1) introducing cognitive traits that are important for learning and the major learning style theories, as well as strategies that incorporate both in educational systems; (2) approaches to identifying cognitive traits and learning style as a requirement to adapting to them; and (3) how the relationships between cognitive traits and learning styles can be used to improve student modeling. Linking learning styles and cognitive traits with instruction and incorporating them in educational systems is an important and beneficial issue for students. Obviously, more research on learning styles and especially on cognitive traits is necessary to further establish their importance in e-education.

# ACKNOWLEDGMENTS

This research has been partly funded by the Austrian Federal Ministry for Education, Science, and Culture, and the European Social Fund (ESF) under grant 31.963/46-VII/9/2002.

# REFERENCES

Al Naeme, F. F. A. (1991). The Influence of Various Learning Styles on Practical Problem-Solving in Chemistry in Scottish Secondary Schools. Ph.D. dissertation. Glasgow: University of Glasgow.

Alexander, J., Fabricius, W., Fleming, V., Zwahr, M., and Brown, S. (2003). The development of metacognitive causal explanations. *Learn. Individ. Diff.*, 13, 227–238.

Bahar, M. and Hansell, M. H. (2000). The relationship between some psychological factors and their effect on the performance of grid questions and word association tests. *Educ. Psychol.*, 20(3), 349–364.

Bajraktarevic, N., Hall, W., and Fullick, P. (2003). Incorporating learning styles in hypermedia environment: empirical evaluation. In *Proc. of the Workshop on Adaptive Hypermedia and Adaptive Web-Based Systems*, August 26–30, Nottingham, U.K., pp. 41–52.

Bell, T. (2001). Extensive reading: speed and comprehension. *Reading Matrix*, 1(1), 1–13.

Bower, G. H. and Hilgard, E. R. (1981). *Theories of Learning.* Englewood Cliffs, NJ: Prentice Hall.

Briggs-Myers, I. (1962). *Manual: The Myers-Briggs Type Indicator.* Palo Alto, CA: Consulting Psychologists Press.*

Brown, E., Brailsford, T., Fisher, T., Moore, A., and Ashman, H. (2006). Reappraising cognitive styles in adaptive Web applications. In *Proc. of the Int. World Wide Web Conf. (WWW2006)*, May 23–26, Edinburgh, U.K., pp. 327–335.

Byrne, M. D. (1996). A Computational Theory of Working Memory. Paper presented at the Doctoral Consortium of the Conference on Human Factors in Computing Systems (CHI 96), April 13–16, Vancouver, Canada, pp. 31–32 (http://www.acm.org/sigchi/chi96/proceedings/doctoral/Byrne/mdb_txt.htm).

Carver, C. A., Howard, R. A., and Lane, W. D. (1999). Addressing different learning styles through course hypermedia. *IEEE Trans. Educ.*, 42(1), 33–38.

Clariana, R. B. (1997). Colloquium: considering learning style in computer-assisted learning. *Br. J. Educ. Technol.*, 28(1), 66–68.

Clark, J. M. and Paivio, A. (1991). Dual coding theory and education. *Educ. Psychol. Rev.*, 3, 149–210.

Deary, I. J., Whiteman, M. C., Starr, J. M., Whalley, L. J., and Fox, H. C. (2004). The impact of childhood intelligence on later life: following up the Scottish mental surveys of 1932 and 1947. *J. Pers. Soc. Psychol.*, 86(1), 130–147.

Dörner, D. (1996). *The Logic of Failure: Why Things Go Wrong and What We Can Do to Make Them Right* (R. Kimber and R. Kimber, trans.). New York: Metropolitan Books.

Fabregat, R., Marzo, J. L., and Peña, C. I. (2000). Teaching support units. In *Computers and Education in the 21st Century*, edited by M. Ortega and J. Bravo, pp. 163–174. Dordrecht: Kluwer.

Felder, R. M. and Silverman, L. K. (1988). Learning and teaching styles in engineering education. *Eng. Educ.*, 78(7), 674–681 (preface added in 2002; http://www.ncsu.edu/felderpublic/Papers/LS-1988.pdf).*

Felder, R. M. and Soloman, B. A. (1997). *Index of Learning Styles Questionnaire*, http://www.engr.ncsu.edu/learning-styles/ilsweb.html.*

Felder, R. M. and Spurlin, J. (2005). Applications, reliability and validity of the Index of Learning Styles. *Int. J. Eng. Educ.*, 21(1), 103–112.

Flavell, J. (1976). Metacognitive aspects of problem solving. In *The Nature of Intelligence*, edited by L. B. Resnick, pp. 231–235. Hillsdale, NJ: Lawrence Erlbaum Associates.

Ford, N. and Chen, S. Y. (2001). Matching/mismatching revisited: an empirical study of learning and teaching styles. *Br. J. Educ. Technol.*, 32(1), 5–22.

Gagné, R. M. (1985). *The Conditions of Learning*, 4th ed. New York: Holt, Rinehart and Winston.

García, P., Amandi, A., Schiaffino, S., and Campo, M. (2007). Evaluating Bayesian networks' precision for detecting students' learning styles. *Comput. Educ.*, 49(3), 794–808.*

Graf, S. and Kinshuk. (2006). An approach for detecting learning styles in learning management systems. In *Proceedings of the International Conference on Advanced Learning Technologies*, pp. 161–163. Alamitos, CA: IEEE Computer Science.

Graf, S., Lin, T., and Kinshuk. (2005). Improving student modeling: the relationship between learning styles and cognitive traits. In *Proc. of the IADIS Int. Conf. on Cognition and Exploratory Learning in Digital Age (CELDA 2005)*, December 14–16, Lisbon, Portugal, pp. 37–44.*

Graf, S., Lin, T., Jeffrey, L., and Kinshuk. (2006). An exploratory study of the relationship between learning styles and cognitive traits. Proceedings of the European Conference of Technology Enhanced Learning. *Lect. Notes Comput. Sci.*, 4227, pp. 470–475.

Harverty, L. A., Koedinger, K. R., Klahr, D., and Alibali, M. W. (2000). Solving inductive reasoning problems in mathematics: not-so-trivial pursuit. *Cogn. Sci.*, 24(2), 249–298.

Honey, P. and Mumford, A. (1982). *The Manual of Learning Styles*, 1st ed. Maidenhead: Peter Honey.

Honey, P. and Mumford, A. (1992). *The Manual of Learning Styles*, 3rd ed. Maidenhead: Peter Honey.*

Hudson, L. (1966). *Contrary Imaginations*. London: Penguin.

James, W. B. and Gardner, D. L. (1995). Learning styles: implications for distance learning. *New Direct. Adult Contin. Educ.*, 67, 19–31.

Jensen, F. (1996). *An Introduction to Bayesian Networks*. New York: Springer-Verlag.

Jonassen, D. H. and Grabowski, B. L. (1993). *Handbook of Individual Differences, Learning, and Instruction*. Hillsdale, NJ: Lawrence Erlbaum Associates.*

Jung, C. (1923). *Psychological Types*. London: Pantheon Books.*

Kalyuga, S., Chandler, P., and Sweller, J. (1999). Managing split-attention and redundancy in multimedia instruction. *Appl. Cogn. Psychol.*, 13, 351–371.

Kalyuga, S., Chandler, P., and Sweller, J. (2000). Incorporating learner experience into the design of multimedia instruction. *J. Educ. Psychol.*, 92, 126–136.

Kashihara, A., Kinshuk, Oppermann, R., Rashev, R., and Simm, H. (2000). A cognitive load reduction approach to exploratory learning and its application to an interactive simulation-based learning system. *J. Educ. Multimedia Hypermedia*, 9(3), 253–276.

Keefe, J. W. (1979). Learning style: an overview. In *Student Learning Styles: Diagnosing and Prescribing Programs*, edited by J. W. Keefe, pp. 1–17. Reston, VA: National Association of Secondary School Principals.

Kinshuk and Lin, T. (2003). User exploration based adaptation in adaptive learning systems. *Int. J. Inform. Syst. Educ.*, 1(1), 22–31.*

Kinshuk and Lin, T. (2004). Cognitive profiling towards formal adaptive technologies in Web-based learning communities. *Int. J. WWW-Based Communities*, 1(1), 103–108.*

Kolb, D. A. (1981). Learning styles and disciplinary differences. In *The Modern American College: Responding to the New Realties of Diverse Students and a Changing Society*, edited by A. W. Chickering, pp. 232–255. San Francisco, CA: Jossey-Bass.

Kolb, D. A. (1984). *Experiential Learning: Experience as the Source of Learning and Development*. Englewood Cliffs, NJ: Prentice Hall.*

Lester, F., Garofalo, J., and Lambdin-Kroll, D. (1989). Self-confidence, interest, beliefs and metacognition: key influences on problem solving behaviour. In *Affect and Mathematical Problem Solving*, edited by D. B. McLeod and V. M. Adams, pp. 75–89. New York: Springer-Verlag.

Lin, T. and Kinshuk. (2004). Dichotomic node network and cognitive trait model. In *Proceedings of the Fourth IEEE International Conference on Advanced Learning Technologies*, edited by Kinshuk et al., pp. 702–704. Los Alamitos, CA: IEEE Computer Science.

Lin, T. and Kinshuk. (2005). Cognitive profiling in life-long learning. In *Encyclopedia of International Computer-Based Learning*, edited by C. Howard, J. V. Boettcher, L. Justice, K. Schenk, P. L. Rogers, and G. A. Berg, pp. 245–255. Hershey, PA: Idea Group.*

Mayer, R. E. (1997). Multimedia learning: are we asking the right questions? *Educ. Psychol.*, 32, 1–19.*

Mayer, R. E. (1998). Cognitive, metacognitive and motivational aspects of problem solving. *Instruct. Sci.*, 26, 49–64.*

Miller, G. A. (1956). The magic number seven, plus or minus two: some limit of our capacity for processing information. *Psychol. Rev.*, 63(2), 81–96.*

Moreno, R. and Valdez, A. (2005). Cognitive load and learning effects of having students organize pictures and words in multimedia environments: The role of student interactivity and feedback. *Educ. Technol. Res. Dev.*, 53(3), 35–45.*

Panaoura, A. and Philippou, G. (2004). Young pupil's metacognitive abilities in mathematics in relation to working memory and processing efficiency. In *Proc. of the Third Int. Biennial SELF Research Conf.*, July 4–7, Berlin (http://self.uws.edu.au/Conferences/2004_Panaoura_Philippou.pdf).

Panaoura, A. and Philippou, G. (2005). The Measurement of Young Pupils' Metacognitive Ability in Mathematics: The Case of Self-Representation and Self Evaluation. Paper presented at the Conference of European Society for Research in Mathematics Education. February 17–21, Sant Feliu de Guíxols, Spain (http://cerme4.crm.es/Papers%20definitius/2/panaoura.philippou.pdf).

Papanikolaou, K. A. and Grigoriadou, M. (2003). An instructional framework supporting personalized learning on the Web. In *Proceedings of the Third IEEE International Conference on Advanced Learning Technologies (ICALT'03)*, pp. 120–124. Los Alamitos, CA: IEEE Computer Society.

Peña, C. I., Marzo, J. L., and de la Rosa, J. L. (2002). Intelligent agents in a teaching and learning environment on the Web. In *Proc. of the Second Int. Conf. on Advanced Learning Technologies (ICALT 2002)*, September 9–12, Kazan, Russia.

Richards-Ward, L. A. (1996). Investigating the Relationship between Two Approaches to Verbal Information Processing in Working Memory: An Examination of the Construct of Working Memory Coupled with an Investigation of Meta-Working Memory. Ph.D. dissertation. Palmerston North, New Zealand: Massey University.

Tillema, H. (1982). Sequencing of text material in relation to information-processing strategies. *Br. J. Educ. Psychol.*, 32, 170–178.

van Joolingen, W. R. and de Jong, T. (2003). SimQuest, authoring educational simulations. In *Authoring Tools for Advanced Technology Learning Environments: Toward Cost-Effective Adaptive, Interactive, and Intelligent Educational Software*, edited by T. Murray, S. Blessing, and S. Ainsworth, pp. 1–31. Dordrecht: Kluwer.

Veermans, K. and van Joolingen, W. R. (1998). Using induction to generate feedback in simulation based discovery learning environments. Proceedings of the 4th International Conference on Intelligent Tutoring Systems. *Lect. Notes Comput. Sci.*, 1452, 196–205.

Wey, P. and Waugh, M. L. (1993). The Effects of Different Interface Presentation Modes and Users' Individual Differences on Users' Hypertext Information Access Performance. Paper presented at the Annual Meeting of the American Educational Research Association, April 12–16, Atlanta, GA.

Zsambok, C. E. and Klein, G. (1997). *Naturalistic Decision Making*. Mahwah, NJ: Lawrence Erlbaum Associates.

---

\* Indicates a core reference.

# 27

# Synthetic Learning Environments

*Janis A. Cannon-Bowers and Clint A. Bowers*
University of Central Florida, Orlando, Florida

## CONTENTS

## ABSTRACT

A variety of technology-based interventions have been proposed to accelerate learning. Although these technologies have enjoyed some success, we need a better understanding of the manner in which specific technologies affect the pedagogical factors associated with enhanced learning. In this chapter, we attempt to articulate a path forward for the development of synthetic learning environments by identifying variables that are important to their effectiveness. Further, we attempt to articulate the conditions under which such technologies are most likely to be successful.

## KEYWORDS

*Simulation:* A working representation of reality; used in training to represent devices and process and may be low or high in terms of physical or functional fidelity.

*Synthetic learning environments:* A learning environment characterized in terms of a particular technology, subject matter, learner characteristics, and pedagogical principles; a synthetic experience, as opposed to a real-world interaction with an actual device or process, is created for the learner through a simulation, game, or other technology.

## INTRODUCTION

The use of technology in education has received tremendous attention over the last 30 years, and its role is likely to increase even more as the demand for teaching students efficiently and effectively continues to grow. Indeed, a wide variety of computer-aided instructional packages, educational games, automated tutors, and other technologies have been developed to teach or aid in teaching. Although some of these development efforts have been successful, others have not, and still others (the majority perhaps) are of unknown value because they have never undergone rigorous empirical testing. Moreover, past technology-based education development efforts have too often been driven by the technology rather than the training needs or an attempt to make use of the newest gadget to come along (Gee, 2003). For all these reasons, we believe that the use of technology-based educational approaches is suboptimal.

To address this issue, it must be recognized that to create an optimal environment for learning we must consider the confluence of not only *technology* and *subject matter* but also *learner characteristics* and *pedagogical principles*. These are the ingredients of a true *synthetic learning environment* (SLE) (Dede et al., 1999). Such environments, we suggest, are an excellent opportunity to realize the benefits of technology-enabled education. In an effort to guide the development of SLEs, this chapter reviews areas of the scientific literature that are most pertinent, but often overlooked, in the development of technology-enhanced learning instruments.

### Definitions

Before we proceed, it is first important to define the key terms that we are using in this chapter: synthetic learning environments (SLEs), simulations, games, and virtual worlds. We define SLEs as tools that combine the key elements of learning theory and technology to create a context where optimal learning is achieved. Importantly, SLEs create a *synthetic experience* as the basis for learning; that is, they support learning by augmenting, replacing, creating, or managing a learner's actual experience with the world. Some of the technologies used to create synthetic experience include simulations and games, which are typically computer based.

The term *simulation* typically refers to a training device characterized by "a working representation of reality ... [that] may be an abstracted, simplified, or accelerated model of process" (Galvao et al., 2000, p. 1692). As such, simulations can vary from relatively low-fidelity representations of a process to elaborate, extremely realistic, full-motion platforms. *Simulation-based training*, therefore, is a type of training that depends on the simulation to provide essential cues to trigger appropriate behaviors. Whereas definitions of simulation have focused largely on the characteristics of the learning environment, definitions of *games* have more often focused on the nature of the learner's experiences; for example, Vogel and her colleagues (2006) have suggested that the essential characteristics of a computer game are goals, interactivity, and feedback. Galvao et al. (2000) include rules and competition as other important characteristics.

The constructs of *game* and *simulation* are not orthogonal; in fact, we view them as overlapping constructs. It is quite possible, for example, to have a simulation that has no gaming features (e.g., rules of play, competition, scorekeeping) or a game that is not based on a realistic simulation; however, a learning environment may have both simulation and gaming features. Because we are focusing on environments that provide synthetic experience in this chapter, we are most interested in training that is based on some type of simulation of the environment or relevant phenomenon. This does not mean that the system must be built on an accurate physical simulation, but it does mean that crucial aspects of the actual problem or domain are simulated (more will be said regarding the issue of simulation fidelity in subsequent sections). Suffice it to say here that our interest is in SLEs that promote development of expertise through synthetic experience (experience with simulated or artificial or virtual environments).

Advances in technology are also making more sophisticated types of SLEs possible; for example, interest is emerging in using *virtual worlds* as training environments. These environments typically involve a large number of geographically distributed players who all interact with and within a shared sestet of cues that comprise the virtual world. Many of these virtual worlds are *persistent*; that is, actions continue and the world changes whether or not any given player is involved. Interest in these worlds as synthetic learning environments is likely to increase in the coming years (Dickey, 2005).

It should be noted, however, that games, simulations, and so forth are not SLEs in and of themselves. Although it is possible to learn in these environments, reliable learning occurs when these technologies are used to present or practice new information in a manner that is pedagogically sound (Schmidt and Bjork, 1992).

## JUSTIFICATION FOR USING SLES

We should point out that there are very few, if any, *true* SLEs; that is, painfully few attempts have been made to systematically develop a learning environment that is not only well engineered from the technological standpoint but also built to be consistent with current learning science. Rather, SLEs are almost always built with an emphasis on technology, and pedagogy is often worked in as an afterthought. In fact, in several areas the science is currently not sufficient to give appropriate guidance, even if it were sought (Cannon-Bowers and Bowers, in press); however, a formidable literature does exist upon which to generate hypotheses about the likely components of SLEs that make them effective. This literature is reviewed briefly below.

### Why Should SLEs Work?

Theoretical justification for the proposition that SLEs can provide a viable context for instruction can be found in what is known about how expertise is developed through experience. Glaser (1989) argued that beginners' knowledge is spotty, consisting of isolated definitions and superficial understandings of central terms and concepts. With experience, these items of information become structured and are integrated with past organizations of knowledge. Research in expertise also suggests that experts may have "stored straightforward condition–action rules in which a specific pattern (the condition) will trigger a stereotypic" response (Chi et al., 1988, p. xvii). Through the acquisition of domain knowledge, it is argued that experts build up a repertoire of instances, indexing them in such a way that they are rapidly accessible when triggered by environmental cues (Gobet and Simon, 1996; Logan, 1988).

The notion that experts chunk information and recognize meaningful patterns in the problem space has been replicated across domains (DeGroot, 1965; Egan and Schwartz, 1979; Lesgold, 1988). It has also been

established that experts develop a well-organized set of schema around big ideas or concepts. According to Bransford et al. (2000, p. 26), "Experts appear to possess an efficient organization of knowledge with meaningful relations among related elements clustered into related units that are governed by underlying concepts and principles."

Related to this, learning researchers are increasingly making a distinction between rote memorization of knowledge and the more elusive goal of learning for understanding. Bransford et al. (2000) suggested that modern views of learning recognize that learning for understanding requires more than knowledge of a series of disconnected facts. They pointed to research that suggests that expert knowledge is "connected and organized around important concepts," that it is "conditionalized," and that it supports the ability to transfer to other areas or domains (Bransford et al., 2000, p. 9).

### The Potential of SLEs for Learning

These conclusions have several implications for the design of SLEs. One of the most pertinent is the notion that learning occurs best in a meaningful context; that is, effective learning leads people to recognize patterns that are used as the basis for knowledge organization, and this knowledge is conditionalized (i.e., specific to a context), suggesting that learning environments should provide realistic situations and problems for learners. New learning, in turn, can then be integrated into this past learning and world knowledge. Indeed, many lines of inquiry into the science of learning converge on the conclusion that *experiential learning* (i.e., learning through experience) is a fundamental human process (Kolb, 1984; Kolb et al., 2001; see also Chapter 4 in this volume).

The concepts of *anchored instruction* and *situated learning* are both consistent with the underlying assumptions of instruction based on experiential learning (Bransford et al., 1990; CTGV, 1992, 1997, 2000). These instructional approaches rest on the pedagogical principle that for learning to be effective it must be *anchored* in a meaningful context for learners. Anchoring instructions allows learners to understand how concepts are applied and why they are important and useful, thus enabling new learning to be more easily integrated into existing knowledge and mental models. According to the Cognition and Technology Group at Vanderbilt (CTGV, 2000), anchored instruction seeks to assist learners in understanding the types of problems and opportunities that real experts confront and how they use their knowledge to solve those problems. It also aids students in integrating their knowledge by employing multiple perspectives on the same problem.

In addition, anchored (situated) learning environments allow learners to understand how new information is connected to what they already know. These processes of accommodating ideas to the external world and assimilating experience into existing knowledge structures are critical driving forces underlying cognitive development (Kolb, 1984).

Synthetic learning environments provide a unique opportunity to achieve these objectives, in some cases even more effectively and less expensively than other forms of instruction. According to Cannon-Bowers and Bowers (in press), SLEs offer a number of advantages as compared to more traditional forms of training (especially in the workplace) because they:

- Can be used as practice environments for tasks that are too dangerous to be practiced in the real world
- Can provide increased opportunities for practice on tasks that occur infrequently (e.g., emergency procedures)
- Are available when actual equipment cannot be employed
- Can contain embedded instructional features (e.g., feedback) that enhance the instructional experience
- Can represent significant cost savings compared with training on operational equipment

Much popular attention has also recently been directed toward employing video and computer games as an opportunity to improve educational outcomes by capturing the motivational aspects of electronic gaming for educational purposes (Gee, 2003; Prensky, 2002). Considerable interest has been generated in electronic games for education, at least in part because of the obvious enthusiasm with which many children and adults currently play with them. Advocates suggest that gaming could increase trainee enthusiasm for educational material, which could in turn increase time on task and lead ultimately to improved student performance.

Moreover, the advent (and availability) of persistent virtual worlds for entertainment purposes is likely to grow considerably in the next few years; hence, the technology will exist and be ripe for application to training challenges. As noted, popular Web-based virtual worlds can attract millions of users (e.g., Second Life, World of Warcraft) even when a fee is associated with playing. It is not difficult to imagine using a similar approach to create realistic virtual organizations, markets, and economies that could provide employees with opportunities to explore, acquire, and

test important job-related skills (e.g., decision making, leader behavior, communication) in a safe, available, and engaging environment. Of course, the effectiveness of such an approach would hinge largely on its ability to embody sound principles of instructional design.

## EMPIRICAL LITERATURE REGARDING SLE EFFECTIVENESS

The potential effectiveness of components of SLEs for effective teaching has been demonstrated in many settings; for example, a recent meta-analysis has supported the efficacy of these environments (Vogel et al., 2006) in educational settings. In addition to the research cited by Vogel et al. regarding K–12 education and special education, other data suggest that similar gains can be obtained with college students. Green and Bavelier (2003), for example, described a series of studies that suggest that video game playing can improve visual attention skills in college students. Likewise, Emurian (2005) reported that a Web-based tutor was effective in improving college students' programming skills.

Using an immersive game, McClean and colleagues (2001) demonstrated improved learning outcomes. These researchers compared learning outcomes from a virtual-world-based geology game and a virtual-world-based biology game with outcomes from both Web-based presentation of the material and traditional classroom lectures. Lectures produced the lowest learning outcomes as measured by a graded test. The Web-presented information increased those outcomes by a margin that ranged from not statistically significant (geology) to 13 to 30% (cell biology). The games further increased learning outcomes either 15 to 40% (geology) or 30 to 63% (cell biology). These outcomes suggest that it is not merely the visual representation of material but also the active engagement that stimulates improved learning. This is consistent with findings from other researchers (Kearsley and Schneiderman, 1998).

Another set of data has been collected by Squire and colleagues (2004) on their game Supercharged!. In this study, a control group receiving interactive lectures improved their understanding by 15% over their pretest scores, while those who played with the game improved their understanding by 28%. These learning outcomes for Supercharged! are in line with those for the visual representations of the McClean et al. (2001) study, and this study also demonstrates that games are superior to lectures. Indeed, among girls, the control group (lecture only) improved on their pretest scores by only 5%, but in the simulation group this number was 23%; thus, at least in this one study, lectures alone did nothing for girls.

Low-fidelity simulations have also been demonstrated to be effective in workplace and occupational training; for example, several studies have supported the contention that management simulations can be effective training environments for graduate students and professionals (Gredler, 2004; Scherpereel, 2005). In addition, pilot training has relied successfully on simulators to train both technical and nontechnical skills (Goeters, 2002; Jentsch and Bowers, 1998; Roessingh, 2005). Some studies also suggest that SLEs can help train clinicians (Abell and Galinsky, 2002; Lane et al., 2001; Pederson, 2000), military personnel (Pleban et al., 2002; Ricci et al., 1996), firemen (Spagnolli et al., 2003), survey interviewers (Link et al., 2006), and elderly drivers (Roenker et al., 2003).

It should be noted, however, that SLEs have not been found to be universally effective. Dunn (2003) failed to find any change in knowledge of workplace diversity issues among trainees who used a computer game relative to a non-treatment control group. Cameron and Dwyer (2005) also failed to find an effect of computer games in reducing field dependence. Garg and colleagues (2002) did find a small advantage for virtual environments in teaching anatomy to medical students, but these differences disappeared after controlling for spatial ability. The mediating effects of spatial ability were also found in a laboratory study of virtual environments reported by Waller (2000). More generally, Ellis and colleagues (2005) found that an online case simulation system resulted in poorer performance and weaker knowledge structures among veterinary students relative to their traditionally trained peers.

# FACTORS THAT INFLUENCE SLE DESIGN

As noted, few attempts to develop and test full-scale SLEs have been accomplished. This is particularly true if one adopts a systems view of instructional design that includes not only technology but also characteristics of the learner, instructional features and strategies, and motivational factors. We contend that all of these factors must be considered in designing SLEs (see various chapters in Parts I and II in this volume for more on strategies and approaches). A brief review of variables in each of these areas that we believe are most crucial to sound SLE design is contained in the sections that follow.

## Learner Characteristics

Education and training scholars have long acknowledged that individual differences—that is, characteristics that trainees bring to the learning situation—influence learning outcomes (Jonassen and Grabowski, 1993). Among the variables studied are cognitive ability (with higher ability learners generally outperforming lower ones; see Mayer and Massa, 2003), prior knowledge and experience (with advantages for learners with more experience in a domain; see Shih et al., 2006), self-efficacy (with higher self-efficacy typically associated with enhanced learning; see Gist et al., 1991), and goal orientation (with learners who focus on their mastery of training content better able to transfer knowledge than learners who are more concerned with performing well in training; see Sideridis, 2005). It is likely the case that these characteristics will also have an influence on learning outcomes in SLEs; however, because the presentation of content is relatively flexible, it may be possible to develop SLEs that can be tailored to the individual needs of the trainee. This possibility could help mitigate the impact of lower ability or self-efficacy or the lack of prior experience.

Several other individual differences may also impact SLE effectiveness; for example, it has been noted that spatial ability appears to be an important potential moderator in determining SLE effectiveness. Evidence from studies by Garg and colleagues (2002) and Waller (2000) suggest that a learner's spatial ability may influence his or her ability to benefit from an SLE. It seems reasonable to suggest that the demands imposed on learners in an interactive, three-dimensional SLE are different than those associated with more passive forms of instruction (e.g., listening to a lecture or reading a book) or even other more static types of computer-based instruction.

Likewise, comfort with technology may be an important mediating factor in the effectiveness of SLEs. Past researchers have discussed knowledge- and skill-based constructs such as "digital/computer literacy" (Gee, 2003) and "technological fluency" (Baker and O'Neil, 2003). In this regard, it has been found that less comfortable participants tend to benefit less from these environments. Others have focused on self-efficacy as it relates to computers in general (Hasan, 2003) or specific software packages (Johnson, 2005). Still others have discussed negative emotions associated with computers, such as computer anxiety (McFarland and Hamilton, 2006) or technophobia (Brosnan, 1999), also indicating that these negative emotions might interfere with learning in technological environments.

Past researchers have also suggested that preconceived attitudes toward or expectations for training are effective predictors of subsequent learning outcomes (Smith-Jentsch et al., 1996; Tannenbaum et al., 1991). With respect to SLEs, it might be that the introduction of an SLE (especially a game, but even a simulation or virtual world) diverges so far from the learner's experience that it colors the learner's expectations for how effective it will be. In fact, some learners may not readily accept the use of a game to train serious knowledge and skill; for example, it is clear that some students are at least dubious about being educated in computer-based environments (Hunt and Bohlin, 1993). Similarly, even if the learner has positive expectations regarding the outcomes of this type of learning, negative attitudes of instructors or teachers who are part of the learning process may color the outcomes (MacArthur and Malouf, 1991).

Interestingly, the issue of expectations may be a double-edged sword. Specifically, the notion that training will include a video game could conjure up very specific expectations in learners who have experience playing popular entertainment games. If the educational game fails to meet trainee expectations (for reasons that have nothing to do with its efficacy as a learning device), its effectiveness could suffer; see Tannenbaum et al., 1991).

## Instructional Features and Strategies

Synthetic learning environments are complex learning systems that depend on a host of factors to be successful; in fact, SLEs can be developed in countless ways, and many variables must be taken into account. By the same token, it is this inherent flexibility that makes SLEs useful across a variety of settings and for a host of learning objectives. The sections that follow highlight some of the instructional features that must be considered in SLE design.

### Authenticity/Fidelity

One variable that has received attention in the educational design area is the authenticity of the learning experience. Authentic experiences are those for which students can make meaningful connections to their actual experience. This is an important feature of the learning environment according to the anchored-instruction view. Jonassen (2000), however, noted that authentic instruction does not necessarily have to be developed around specific, real-world tasks; rather, authenticity can best be described as the extent to which the learning environment causes learners to engage in cognitive processes that are similar to those in the real world (Honebein et al., 1993; Petraglia, 1998). Moreover, authentic learning environments provide learners with engaging, challenging problems that are similar to those confronted by experts (CTGV, 2000).

A related issue concerns model or simulation fidelity—that is, the degree to which underlying models or simulations faithfully represent the actual phenomenon or task it is meant to represent (Andrews and Bell, 2000). The question here typically concerns the ability to transfer specific knowledge and skill gained in training to the actual operational or job environment (Andrews and Bell, 2000). When trainees are learning how to apply a particular skill, then the training (simulated) environment must respond in a realistic manner or the trainee will receive incorrect feedback and perhaps experience negative transfer (i.e., applying skills incorrectly on the job). With respect to more traditional educational domains (i.e., even when there is no target environment to which learning is directly transferred), the issue is still important to ensure that what students are learning is actually correct.

### Model-Based Reasoning

The notion of model-based reasoning has gained attention in recent years. This line of work contends that students need to develop valid mental representations of the physical world and learn to create, revise, and use these models to reason about actual physical phenomena. This view characterizes scientific inquiry as sense making and contends that models and modeling can help bridge the gap between the concrete and the abstract (Raghavan et al., 1997). Lehrer and Schauble (2000) contend that model-based reasoning actually begins early in childhood, yet model-based instruction is typically not introduced until much later in education. Further, they proposed a taxonomy of models (including physical microcosms, representational systems, syntactic models, and hypothetical–deductive models) based on Gentner's (1983) syntactical theory of analogy.

Positive findings to support the use of model-based instruction come from evidence in genetics, evolutionary biology, near-Earth astronomy (Cartier and Stewart, 2000; Stewart et al., 2005), and scientific reasoning (Raghavan et al., 1997; Zimmerman et al., 2003). Taken together, these studies indicate that interacting with models as part of a formalized curriculum should contribute to the students' deep understanding of the domain, as well as problem-solving skills. Along these same lines, others argue that computer simulations afford the unique opportunity to engage learners in the study of abstract, complex physical phenomena (Dede et al., 1999) by making them more concrete.

## Scenario/Case Design

An important concern in designing effective SLEs is the design of scenarios or cases that provide the stimulus and context for instruction. According to Cannon-Bowers et al., in simulation-based training, the scenario is often the primary device by which instructional objectives are met. Recently, Cannon-Bowers, Salas, and colleagues (Cannon-Bowers and Salas, 1998; Fowlkes et al., 1998; Salas and Cannon-Bowers, 1997) developed a methodology where scenarios are designed by scripting and sequencing specific trigger events. Trigger events are designed to elicit targeted behavior, thereby allowing trainees to practice and receive feedback on targeted skills (Salas and Cannon-Bowers, 2001). This event-based approach to simulation-based training has been successfully demonstrated in several settings to date (Dwyer et al., 1999; Fowlkes et al., 1994; Johnston et al., 1995). In a similar vein, Schank et al. (1999) advocated a strategy for developing goal-based scenarios or cases that includes guidance for developing learning goals, missions, cover, role, scenario operations, resources, and feedback.

One of the problems with scenario or case design is that it is typically very time consuming and requires expertise from subject-matter experts and instructional designers. A possible solution to this challenge is to automate the development of scenarios by providing authoring tools for users (Jentsch et al., 2001). Developing such tools should be a priority in future work.

## Collaborative/Social Learning

The notion that collaboration can aid learning has gained traction with instructional researchers in recent years (CTGV, 2000; Clark and Wittrock, 2000). According to Nelson (1999), collaborative learning is effective because it takes advantage of learners' natural collaborative processes while fostering exchange in rich social contexts and allowing for multiple perspectives. Others advocate the creation of learning communities in classrooms (Bielaczyc and Collins, 1999) that emphasize development of mutual respect, diversity, and community growth. Examples of implementations of this type of approach include Brown and Campione's (1994, 1996) "fostering a community of learners" approach and Lampert's (1990) work in mathematics instruction. Indeed, a meta-analysis of some 122 studies of classroom instruction showed that, on average, cooperative modes of learning considerably outperformed competitive or solo approaches, and that the latter two were roughly comparable in terms of learning outcomes (Johnson, 1981).

These findings are particularly pertinent to the design of SLEs because technology affords the opportunity to develop multiplayer and team simulations (and games). In fact, many argue that online gaming is essentially a social phenomenon. Gaming occurs in distributed social groups that resemble communities of practice because they have their own language, practice, and norms. It has been argued that these communities are excellent potential learning environments (Squire, 2003).

## Motivational Factors

Many learning scholars acknowledge that motivation is paramount to learning (Clark and Wittrock, 2000); in fact, numerous variables appear to effect a student's motivation to learn, which in turn influences learning. It is important, then, to understand how SLE design can foster (or inhibit) motivation to learn. The follow sections briefly review some of the variables that are unique to SLEs in this regard.

## Goal Setting/Acceptance

In general, goal setting involves establishing a standard or objective for performance. In learning systems, goals help to focus learners on the task and help them to select or construct strategies for goal accomplishment; hence, they serve to direct attention (Locke and Latham, 1990). Goal commitment (i.e., the degree to which the learner is committed to the learning goal) is a determinant of how much the goal affects performance (Locke et al., 1981). In addition, goal setting has been linked to self-regulatory processes (Schunk and Ertmer, 1999), which are associated with effective learning. Research has also shown that, to be most effective in enhancing performance, goals must be specific and difficult but achievable and proximal (Locke and Latham, 1990).

With respect to SLEs (and specifically games), goal setting is particularly relevant because SLEs are often built to emphasize goal accomplishment. In many games, for example, players must reach a set of interim or subgoals in pursuit of overriding objectives. This mechanism may actually lend itself to goal setting in educational games because instruction can be nested naturally in an underlying goal hierarchy or structure. Exploiting this possibility warrants further attention.

## Engagement/Emotional Context

With the advent of virtual environments, researchers have begun to explore variables associated with engagement or immersion in learning. The notion of immersion is being hypothesized to be a psychological state resulting from a participant's intense feelings of "presence" in the virtual world (Gerhard et al., 2004). A related topic is the idea of *flow*. Csikszentmihalyi (1990) described flow as an experience where an individual becomes so engaged in an activity that time becomes distorted, self-consciousness is forgotten, and external rewards disappear. Instead, people engage in complex, goal-directed behavior because it is inherently motivating. From a pedagogical standpoint, it is not clear whether or how this notion of flow may affect the learning process; however, from a strictly time-on-task perspective (i.e., the amount of time engaging instructional content), it would follow that intense engagement should benefit learning.

Intensity of the learning experience may also impact the extent of transfer of learning, with the hope being that game play drives behavioral change long after the game is over. Limited evidence of this possibility is encouraging; for example, diabetic children presented with a diabetes management game had 77% fewer follow-up visits (emergency and urgent care) than a control group (Brown et al., 1997). Playing the game was not enforced. Children were simply given the game and allowed to take it home to play it as much or as little as they wished; yet, the strong rate of casual adoption for the game medium, combined with its unique learning paradigm, clearly had an impact.

### Reward and Social Status

Decades of research into motivation, especially intrinsic motivation, generally shows that externalizing the reward for engaging in a behavior can reduce a person's intrinsic motivation to engage in it (Deci et al., 1999; Ryan and Deci, 2000); however, researchers have also found that under certain conditions, externalized rewards and competition can increase intrinsic motivation (Reeve and Deci, 1996). In particular, an activity that is seen as challenging allows the user to gain feelings of competence and is not perceived as being controlling (i.e., forced on the user), and intrinsic motivation is enhanced. In addition, when the user places importance on doing well, competition generates affective involvement in the activity and increases personal meaningfulness (Epstein and Harackiewicz, 1992). It should be noted that in at least one study (with children), a gender difference was found with respect to public acknowledgment of achievement. In that case, boys were more likely to respond to such public recognition than girls (Nemeth, 1999).

### Embodiment, Personalization, and Engagement

The notion of *user embodiment* has gained attention of late as the development of collaborative computer systems and virtual worlds has increased. Embodiment refers to the mechanism of representation of the user in the virtual world. According to Gerhard et al. (2004), the notion of embodiment can be traced to philosophical writings about the meaning of the physical body. Avatars—graphical representations of the user in the world—help to establish the user's identity and provide a basis for conversation and social interaction (Gerhard et al., 2004; Slater et al., 2000). These factors, in turn, are predicted to increase the user's sense of engagement in the simulation.

Although far more empirical work is needed to better understand the impact of embodiment on both engagement and learning, some data suggest that personalizing the interaction with the student in a virtual environment can improve learning and retention of science content (Moreno and Mayer, 2004). Baylor's work on intelligent agents and mentors similarly indicates an impact of personalization and presentation style on learning outcomes (Baylor, 2001). Limited evidence suggests, then, that increasing a students' level of embodiment and personalization can increase engagement and learning.

## CONCLUSIONS

Clearly, many factors must be taken into account in the development of an environment optimized for the acquisition of new knowledge and skill. We have highlighted but a few of these here as they relate specifically to synthetic learning environment development. Gaining an adequate understanding of these factors and the manner in which they interact is obviously a formidable research challenge. This challenge is intensified by the fact that SLE research is typically expensive to conduct because it typically requires that a sufficiently developed SLE is available for study. It would seem, however, that the return on investment is this area stands to be huge, as the potential to improve the educational process is so vast. It is our hope that researchers will find ways to conduct viable SLE research—possibly by partnering in the development of viable testbeds and by sharing facilities. We are also hopeful that funding to support large-scale efforts becomes available. In the meantime, we encourage researchers to adopt a broad systems approach to SLE research so integration and generalization of findings can be achieved.

# REFERENCES

Abell, M. and Galinsky, M. (2002). Introducing students to computer-based group work practice. *J. Social Work Educ.*, 38(1), 39–54.

Andrews, D. H. and Bell, H. H. (2000). Simulation-based training. In *Training and Retraining: A Handbook for Business, Industry, Government, and the Military*, edited by S. Tobias and J. D. Fletcher, pp. 357–384. New York: Macmillan.*

Baker, E. L. and O'Neil, Jr., H. F. (2003). Technological fluency: needed skills for the future. In *Technology Applications in Education: A Learning View*, edited by H. F. O'Neil, Jr., and R. S. Perez, pp. 245–265. Mahwah, NJ: Lawrence Erlbaum Associates.*

Baylor, A.L. (2001). Agent-based learning environments for investigating teaching and learning. *J. Educ. Comput. Res.*, 26, 249–270.

Bielaczyc, K. and Collins, A. (1999). Learning communities in classrooms: a reconceptualization of educational practice. In *Instructional-Design Theories and Models: A New Paradigm of Instructional Theory*, Vol. II, edited by C. M. Reigeluth, pp. 269–292. Mahwah, NJ: Lawrence Erlbaum Associates.

Bransford, J. D., Sherwood, R. D., Hasselbring, T. S., Kinzer, C. K., and Williams, S. M. (1990). Anchored instruction: why we need it and how technology can help. In *Cognition, Education, and Multimedia: Exploring Ideas in High Technology*, edited by D. Nix and R. J. Spiro, pp. 115–141. Hillsdale, NJ: Lawrence Erlbaum Associates.

Bransford, J. D., Brown, A. L., and Cocking, R. R., Eds. (2000). *How People Learn: Brain, Mind, Experience, and School*. Washington, D.C.: National Academy Press.*

Brosnan, M. (1999). Modeling technophobia: a case for word processing. *Comput. Hum. Behav.*, 15(2), 105–121.

Brown, A. L. and Campione, J. C. (1994). Guided discovery in a community of learners. In *Classroom Lessons: Integrating Cognitive Theory and Classroom Instruction*, edited by K. McGilly, pp. 229–272. Cambridge, MA: MIT Press.

Brown, A. L. and Campione, J. C. (1996). Psychological theory and the design of innovative learning environments: on procedures, principles, and systems. In *Innovations in Learning: New Environments for Education*, edited by L. Schauble and R. Glaser, pp. 289–325. Mahwah, NJ: Lawrence Erlbaum Associates.

Brown, S. J., Lieberman, D. A., Gemeny, B. A., Fan, Y. D., Wilson, C. M., and Pasta, D. J. (1997). Education video game for juvenile diabetes: results of a controlled trial. *Med. Inform.*, 22(1), 77–79.

Cameron, B. and Dwyer, F. (2005). The effect of online gaming, cognition and feedback type in facilitating delayed achievement of different learning objectives. *J. Interact. Learn. Res.*, 16(3), 243–258.

Cannon-Bowers, J. A. and Bowers, C. (in press). Synthetic learning environments: on developing a science of simulation, games, and virtual worlds for training. In *Learning, Training, and Development in Organizations*, edited by S. Koslowski and E. Salas. Mahwah, NJ: Lawrence Erlbaum Associates.

Cannon-Bowers, J. A. and Salas, E. (1998). Team performance and training in complex environments: recent findings from applied research. *Curr. Dir. Psychol. Sci.*, 7, 83–87.

Cartier, J. L. and Stewart, J. (2000). Teaching the nature of inquiry: further development in a high school genetics curriculum. *Sci. Educ.*, 9, 247–267.

Chi, M. T. H., Glaser, R., and Farr, M. J., Eds. (1988). *The Nature of Expertise*. Hillsdale, NJ: Lawrence Erlbaum Associates.

Clark, R. and Wittrock, M. C. (2000). Psychological principles in training. In *Training and Retraining: A Handbook for Business, Industry, Government, and the Military*, edited by S. Tobias and J. D. Fletcher, pp. 51–84. New York: Macmillan.

Cognition and Technology Group at Vanderbilt (CTGV). (1992). Anchored instruction in science and mathematics: theoretical basis, developmental projects, and initial research findings. In *Philosophy of Science, Cognitive Psychology, and Educational Theory and Practice*, edited by R. A. Duschl and R. J. Hamilton, pp. 244–273. Albany, NY: State University of New York Press.*

Cognition and Technology Group at Vanderbilt (CTGV). (1997). *The Jasper Project: Lessons in Curriculum, Instruction, Assessment, and Professional Development*. Mahwah, NJ: Lawrence Erlbaum Associates.

Cognition and Technology Group at Vanderbilt (CTGV). (2000). Adventures in anchored instruction: lessons from beyond the ivory tower. In *Advances in Instructional Psychology: Educational Design and Cognitive Science*, Vol. 5, edited by R. Glaser, pp. 35–99. Mahwah, NJ: Lawrence Erlbaum Associates.

Csikszentmihalyi, M. (1990). *Flow: The Psychology of Optical Experience*. New York: Harper Perennial.

Deci, E. L., Koestner, R., and Ryan, R. M. (1999). A meta-analytic review of experiments examining the effects of extrinsic rewards on intrinsic motivation. *Psychol. Bull.*, 125, 627–668.

Dede, C., Salzman, M., Loftin, R. B., and Sprague, D. (1999). Multisensory immersion as a modeling environment for learning complex scientific concepts. In *Computer Modeling and Simulation in Science Education*, edited by N. Roberts, W. Feurzeig, and B. Hunter, pp. 282–319. New York: Springer-Verlag.*

DeGroot, A. (1965). *Thought and Choice in Chess*. The Hague: Mouton.

Dickey, M. (2005). Three-dimensional virtual worlds and distance learning: two case studies of active worlds as a medium for distance education. *Br. J. Educ. Technol.*, 36(3), 439–451.

Dunn, S. (2003). *Effects of a Simulation Game on Trainees' Knowledge and Attitudes About Age-Related Changes in Learning and Work Behaviors of Older Workers*. Ann Arbor, MI: University Microfilms International.

Dwyer, D. J., Oser, R. L., Salas, E., and Fowlkes, J. E. (1999). Performance measurement in distributed environments: initial results and implications for training. *Milit. Psychol.*, 11, 189–215.

Egan, D. E. and Schwartz, B. J. (1979). Chunking in recall of symbolic drawings. *Mem. Cogn.*, 7, 149–158.

Ellis, R., Marcus, G., and Taylor, R. (2005). Learning through inquiry: student difficulties with online course-based material. *J. Comput. Assist. Learn.*, 21(4), 239–252.

Emurian, H. (2005). Web-based programmed instruction: evidence of rule-governed learning. *Comput. Hum. Behav.*, 21(6), 893–915.

Epstein, J. A. and Harackiewicz, J. M. (1992). Winning is not enough: the effects of competition and achievement motivation on intrinsic interest. *Pers. Soc. Psychol. Bull.*, 18, 128–138.

Fowlkes, J., Lane, N., Salas, E., Franz, T., and Oser, R. (1994). Improving the measurement of team performance: the TARGETs methodology. *Milit. Psychol.*, 6(1), 47.

Fowlkes, J., Dwyer, D., and Oser, R. (1998). Event-based approach to training. *Int. J. Aviat. Psychol.*, 8, 209–22.

Galvao, J. R., Martins, P. G., and Gomes, M. R. (2000). Modeling realty with simulation games for a cooperative learning. In *Proc. of the 2000 Winter Simulation Conference (WSC 2000)*, December 10–13, Orlando, FL, pp. 1692–1698.

Garg, A., Norman, G. R., Eva, K., Spero, L., and Sharan, S. (2002). Is there any real virtue of virtual reality? The minor role of multiple orientations in learning anatomy from computers. *Acad. Med.*, 77, S97–S99.

Gee, J. P. (2003). *What Video Games Have to Teach Us About Learning and Literacy*. New York: Palgrave Macmillan.*

Gentner, D. (1983). Structure-mapping: a theoretical framework for analogy. *Cogn. Sci.*, 7, 155–170.

Gerhard, M., Moore, D. J., and Hobbs, D. (2004). Embodiment and copresence in collaborative interfaces. *Int. J. Hum.-Comput. Stud.*, 61, 453–480.

Gist, M. E., Stevens, C. K., and Baveta, E. G. (1991). Effects of self-efficacy and post-training intervention on the acquisition and maintenance of complex interpersonal skills. *Personnel Psychol.*, 44(4), 837–861.

Glaser, R. (1989). Expertise in learning: how do we think about instructional processes now that we have discovered knowledge structure? In *Complex Information Processing: The Impact of Herbert A. Simon*, edited by D. Klahr and D. Kotosfky, pp. 269–282. Hillsdale, NJ: Lawrence Erlbaum Associates.

Gobet, F. and Simon, H. A. (1996). Recall of random and distorted positions: implications for the theory of expertise. *Mem. Cogn.*, 24, 493–503.

Goeters, K. (2002). Evaluation of the effects of CRM training by the assessment of non-technical skills under LOFT. *Hum. Factors Aerospace Safety*, 2(1), 71–86.

Gredler, M. E. (2004). *Games and Simulations and Their Relationships to Learning*. Mahwah, NJ: Lawrence Erlbaum Associates.*

Green, C. and Bavelier, D. (2003). Action video game modifies visual selective attention. *Nature*, 423(6939), 534–537.

Hasan, B. (2003). The influence of specific computer experiences on computer self-efficacy beliefs. *Comput. Hum. Behav.*, 19(4), 443–450.

Honebein, P. C., Duffy, T. M., and Fishman, B. J. (1993). Constructivism and the design of learning environments: Context and authentic activities for learning. In *Designing Environments for Constructive Learning*, edited by T. M. Duffy, J. Lowyck, and D. H. Jonassen, pp. 87–108. New York: Springer-Verlag.

Hunt, N. and Bohlin, R. (1993). Teacher education students' attitudes toward using computers. *J. Res. Comput. Educ.*, 25(4), 487.

Jentsch, F. and Bowers, C. (1998). Evidence for the validity of PC-based simulations in studying aircrew coordination. *Int. J. Aviat. Psychol.*, 8(3), 243–260.

Jentsch, F., Bowers, C., Berry, D., Dougherty, W., and Hitt II, J. M. (2001). Generating line-oriented flight simulation scenarios with the RRLOE computerized tool set. In *Proc. of the Human Factors and Ergonomics Society 45th Annual Meeting*, October 8–12, Minneapolis, MN.

Johnson, D. (1981). Effects of cooperative, competitive, and individualistic goal structures on achievement: a meta-analysis. *Psychol. Bull.*, 89(1), 47–62.

Johnson, R. (2005). An empirical investigation of sources of application-specific computer-self-efficacy and mediators of the efficacy–performance relationship. *Int. J. Hum.-Comput. Stud.*, 62(6), 737–758

Johnston, J. H., Cannon-Bowers, J. A., and Smith-Jentsch, K. A. (1995). Event-based performance measurement system for shipboard command teams. In *Proceedings of the First International Symposium on Command and Control Research and Technology*, pp. 274–276. Washington, D.C.: The Center for Advanced Command and Technology.

Jonassen, D. H. (2000). Revisiting activity theory as a framework for designing student-centered learning environments. In *Theoretical Foundations of Learning Environments*, edited by D. H. Jonassen and S. M. Land, pp. 89–121. Mahwah, NJ: Lawrence Erlbaum Associates.*

Jonassen, D. H. and Grabowski, B. (1993). *Handbook of Individual Differences, Learning, and Instruction*. Mahwah, NJ: Lawrence Erlbaum Associates.*

Kearsley, G. and Schneiderman, B. (1998). Engagement theory: a framework for technology-based teaching and learning. *Educ. Technol.*, 38, 20–23.*

Kolb, D. A. (1984). *Experiential Learning: Experience as the Source of Learning and Development*. Englewood Cliffs, NJ: Prentice Hall.

Kolb, D. A., Boyatzis, R. E., and Mainemelis, C. (2001). Experiential learning theory: previous research and new directions. In *Perspectives on Thinking, Learning, and Cognitive Styles (The Educational Psychology Series)*, edited by R. J. Sternberg and L. Zhang, pp. 227–247. Mahwah, NJ: Lawrence Erlbaum Associates.

Lampert, M. (1990). When the problem is not the question and the solution is not the answer: mathematical knowing and teaching. *Am. Educ. Res. J.*, 27(1), 29–63.

Lane, J., Slavin, S., and Ziv, A. (2001). Simulation in medical education: a review. *Simul. Gaming*, 32(3), 297–314.*

Lehrer, R. and Schauble, L. (2000). Modeling in mathematics and science. In *Advances in Instructional Psychology: Educational Design and Cognitive Science*, Vol. 5, edited by R. Glaser, pp. 101–159. Mahwah, NJ: Lawrence Erlbaum Associates.

Lesgold, A. (1988). Toward a theory of curriculum for use in designing intelligent instructional systems. In *Learning Issues for Intelligent Tutoring Systems*, edited by H. Mandl and A. Lesgold, pp. 114–137. New York: Springer-Verlag.

Link, M., Armsby, P., Hubal, R., and Guinn, C. (2006). Accessibility and acceptance of responsive virtual human technology as a survey interviewer training tool. *Comput. Hum. Behav.*, 22(3), 412–426.

Locke, E. A. and Latham, G. P. (1990). Work motivation: the high performance cycle. In *Work Motivation*, edited by U. Kleinbeck and H. Quast, pp. 3–25. Hillsdale, NJ: Lawrence Erlbaum Associates.

Locke, E. A., Shaw, K. N., and Saari, L. M. (1981) Goal setting and task performance: 1969–1980. *Psychol. Bull.*, 90, 125–152

Logan, G. D. (1988). Toward an instance theory of automatization. *Psychol. Rev.*, 95, 492–527.

MacArthur, C. and Malouf, D. (1991). Teachers' beliefs, plans, and decisions about computer-based instruction. *J. Spec. Educ.*, 25(1), 44.

Mayer, R. E. and Massa, L. (2003). Three facets of visual and verbal learners: cognitive ability, cognitive style, and learning preference. *J. Educ. Psychol.*, 95(4), 833–846.

McClean, P., Saini-Eidukat, B., Schwert, D., Slator, B. M., and White, A. (2001). Virtual worlds in large enrollment science classes significantly improve authentic learning. In *Selected Papers from the 12th International Conference on College Teaching and Learning*, edited by J. A. Chambers, pp. 111–118. Jacksonville, FL: Center for the Advancement of Teaching and Learning.

McFarland, D. and Hamilton, D. (2006). Adding contextual specificity to the technology acceptance model. *Comput. Hum. Behav.*, 22(3), 427–447.

Moreno, R. and Mayer, R. E. (2004). Personalized messages that promote science learning in virtual environments. *J. Educ. Psychol.*, 96, 165–173.

Nelson, L. M. (1999). Collaborative problem solving. In *Instructional-Design Theories and Models: A New Paradigm of Instructional Theory*, Vol. II, edited by C. M. Reigeluth, pp. 241–267. Mahwah, NJ: Lawrence Erlbaum Associates.

Nemeth, E. (1999). Gender differences in reaction to public achievement feedback. *Educ. Stud.*, 25, 297–310.

Pederson, P. B. (2003) *"Walking the Talk": Simulations in Multicultural Training*. Alexandria, VA: Association for Multicultural Counseling and Development.

Petraglia, J. (1998). *Reality by Design: The Rhetoric and Technology of Authenticity in Education*. Mahwah, NJ: Lawrence Erlbaum Associates.

Pleban, R., Matthews, M., Salter, M., and Eakin, D. (2002). Training and assessing complex decision making in a virtual environment. *Percept. Motor Skills*, 94(3), 871–882.

Prensky, M. (2002). The motivation of gameplay or the real 21st century learning revolution. *On Horizon*, 10(1), 5–11.

Raghavan, K., Satoris, M. L., and Glaser, R. (1997). The impact of model-centered instruction on student learning: the area and volume units. *J. Comput. Math. Sci. Teaching*, 16, 363–404.

Reeve, J. and Deci, E. L. (1996). Elements within the competitive situation that affect intrinsic motivation. *Pers. Soc. Psychol. Bull.*, 22, 24–33.

Ricci, K., Salas, E., and Cannon-Bowers, J. (1996). Do computer-based games facilitate knowledge acquisition and retention? *Milit. Psychol.*, 8(4), 295–307.

Roenker, D., Cissell, G., Ball, K., Wadley, V., and Edwards, J. (2003). Speed-of-processing and driving simulator training result in improved driving performance. *Hum. Factors*, 45(2), 218–233.

Roessingh, J. (2005). Transfer of manual flying skills from PC-based simulation to actual flight: comparison of in-flight measured data and instructor ratings. *Int. J. Aviat. Psychol.*, 15(1), 67–90.

Ryan, R. M. and Deci, E. L. (2000). Self-determination theory and the facilitation of intrinsic motivation, social development and well-being. *Am. Psychol.*, 55, 68–78.

Salas, E. and Cannon-Bowers J. A. (1997). Methods, tools, and strategies for team training. In *Training for a Rapidly Changing Workplace: Applications of Psychological Research*, edited by M. A. Quinones and A. Ehrenstein, pp. 249–280. Washington, D.C.: APA.

Salas, E. and Cannon-Bowers, J. A. (2001). The science of training: a decade of progress. *Annu. Rev. Psychol.*, 52, 471–499.

Schank, R. C., Berman, T. R., and MacPherson, K. A. (1999). Learning by doing. In *Instructional-Design Theories and Models: A New Paradigm of Instructional Theory*, Vol. II, edited by C. M. Reigeluth, pp. 161–181. Mahwah, NJ: Lawrence Erlbaum Associates.

Scherpereel, C. (2005). Changing mental models: business simulation exercises. *Simul. Gaming*, 36(3), 388–403.

Schmidt, R. A. and Bjork, R. (1992). New conceptualizations of practice: common principles in three paradigms suggest new concepts for training. *Psychol. Sci.*, 3(4), 207–217.

Schunk, D. H. and Ertmer, P. A. (1999). Self-regulatory processes during computer skill acquisition: goal and self-evaluative influences. *J. Educ. Psychol.*, 91, 251–260.

Shih, P., Muñoz, D., and Sánchez, F. (2006). The effect of previous experience with information and communication technologies on performance in a Web-based learning program. *Comput. Hum. Behav.*, 22(6), 962–970.

Sideridis, G. (2005). Goal orientation, academic achievement, and depression: evidence in favor of a revised goal theory framework. *J. Educ. Psychol.*, 97(3), 366–375.

Slater, M., Sadagic, A., Usoh, M., and Schroeder, R. (2000). Small-group behaviour in a virtual and real environment: a comparative study. *Presence: Teleoperators Virtual Environ.*, 9, 37–15.

Smith-Jentsch, K. A., Jentsch, F. G., Payne, S. C., and Salas, E. (1996). Can pretraining experiences explain individual differences in learning? *J. Appl. Psychol.*, 81, 909–936.

Spagnolli, A., Varotto, D., and Mantovani, G. (2003). An ethnographic, action-based approach to human experience in virtual environments. *Int. J. Hum.-Comput. Stud.*, 59(6), 797–822.

Squire, K. (2003). Video games in education. *Int. J. Intell. Simul. Gaming*, (2), 1.

Squire, K., Barnett, M., Grant, J. M., and Higginbotham, T. (2004). Electromagnetism supercharged! Learning physics with digital simulation games. In *Proc. of the Sixth Int. Conf. of the Learning Sciences (ICLS)*. June 22–26, Los Angeles, CA.

Stewart, J., Cartier, J. L., and Passmore, C. M. (2005). Developing an understanding through model-based inquiry. In *How Students Learn: History, Mathematics, and Science Inquiry in the Classroom*, edited by M. S. Donovan and J. D. Bransford, pp. 515–565. Washington, D.C.: National Academies Press.

Tannenbaum, S. I., Mathieu, J. E., Salas, E., and Cannon-Bowers, J. (1991). Meeting trainees' expectations: the influence of training fulfillment on the development of commitment, self-efficacy, and motivation. *J. Appl. Psychol.*, 76(6), 759–769.

Vogel, J. J., Vogel, D. S., Cannon-Bowers, J. A., Bowers, C. A., Muse, K., and Wright, M. (2006). Computer gaming and interactive simulations for learning: a meta-analysis. *J. Educ. Comput. Res.*, 34(3), 229–243.

Waller, D. (2000). Individual differences in spatial learning from computer-simulated environments. *J. Exp. Psychol. Appl.*, 6(4), 307–321.

Zimmerman, C., Raghavan, K., and Sartoris, M. L. (2003). The impact of MARS curriculum on students' ability to coordinate theory and evidence. *Int. J. Sci. Educ.*, 25, 1247–1271.

* Indicates a core reference.

# 28

# Modeling Technologies

*Roy B. Clariana*
Pennsylvania State Great Valley, Malvern, Pennsylvania

*Johannes Strobel*
Concordia University, Montreal, Quebec, Canada

## CONTENTS

# ABSTRACT

Modeling technologies are a powerful tool for affecting learning. Although dynamic modeling is not an easy task, modeling technologies are maturing. As tools become easier to use, more people will build models, and this is likely to drive learning theory and practice in new directions (Hadwin et al., 2005). This chapter centers on one aspect of modeling: dynamic modeling with technology, where students build dynamic models that "run." This chapter particularly does not address other forms of modeling technologies such as concept mapping (as a form of modeling domain knowledge), expert systems (modeling of problems), and case databases (modeling experiences). The chapter begins with the conceptual framework for modeling with technology, describes extant dynamic modeling tools, reviews investigations of the factors associated with modeling technologies in the classroom, and points to future design and research.

# KEYWORDS

*Model:* An artifact representative of an object or of an internal interpretation, often represented on a computer screen.

*Simulation:* An executable (runnable) model; computer software that allows a learner to manipulate variables and processes and observe results.

# CONCEPTUAL FRAMEWORK OF MODELING TECHNOLOGIES

## Terms in Context

Modeling technologies are computer software that students use to build and run dynamic models. In this chapter *model* refers to the actual artifact represented on a computer screen, not the mental construct of an individual or the original that is being modeled. When students build models, there is an interplay between their current understanding of the original that is modeled (the original may be real or imagined) and the computer models they create. Simulations are computer software designed by others with their own views of the original to allow learners to manipulate variables or processes and observe the output results (Clariana, 1989). When students use simulations, there is interaction between their growing intuition and the underlying viewpoint of the simulation, with the simulation pressing a particular viewpoint on the learner; thus, there is a contrast between the two approaches. Using someone else's model (simulation) tends to be peremptory, while building one's own model tends to be dialectical.

The first executable models for learning (i.e., computer-based simulations) were created by highly skilled programmers at the advent of mainframe computers (Alessi, 2000; Riley, 1990). Today's modeling tools run on personal computers and do not require programming skills. The nature, methods, and limits of modeling with technology depend on the interrelationships between the person and the modeling technology. Model building is always constrained (and facilitated) by the technology. The malleability of the model artifact depends on the effort and ease required to amend or append the model, which depends on the modeling technology. Thus, the two most critical modeling design decisions are deciding what to show (the representations) and what actions the computer program should take under which conditions (Horwitz, 1999). If the model is intended to be used by other people, the activities in which they can engage have to be defined, too.

## The Relationship between What Is Modeled and the Model

The question of the nature of the relationship between the model and what is modeled (the original) is as old as modeling itself. The research literature falls in two camps. One camp stresses the representational character of models, meaning that models stand for reality (Tergan and Keller, 2005) or, as Korzybski (1958), the founder of general semantics, stated: "A map is not the territory it represents, but if correct, it has a similar structure to the territory, which accounts for its usefulness" (p. 58). The other camp argues for a footprint or inscriptional nature of the relationship (Pea, 1994), where the model is the shareable, tangible mental impression that is left behind. The model, the external representation or inscription, is second hand (i.e., not based directly on a phenomenon or system); in other words, a model is "denatured" (Gibbons, 2001, p. 514) because it is the interpretation of the modeler.

The question of the nature and validity of the relationship between model and modeled depends on one's philosophical standpoint and ontological and epistemological beliefs (see Lesh and Doerr, 2003, for an in-depth discussion). Empiricists or objectivists would stress the existence of an original and a way to capture the substance and consider how well their models represent the original. Pragmatist and neo-pragmatist would question structural relationships between theories and reality. Pragmatists would measure validity by how well a model is suited to solve a particular problem or function in a particular context (Strike and Posner, 1985). The postmodern camp would argue that the validity of the model is based on how well it aligns with the perceptions/thoughts/beliefs of the modeler without regard to any real original, because the original is either not detectable (skeptic position) or only a unique product of our construction (radical constructivism).

Numerous kinds of models can be used to represent phenomena in the world or the mental representations that learners construct to represent them. Harris (1999) described three kinds of models: theoretical models, experimental models, and data models. Giere (1999) described several kinds of models, including representational models, abstract models (mathematical models), hypotheses, and theoretical models (abstract models constructed with theoretical principles, such as Newton's laws). Lehrer and Schauble (2003) described a continuum of model types, including physical models, representational systems (grounded in resemblance between the model and the world), syntactic models (summarizing essential functioning of a system), and hypothetical–deductive models (formal abstractions). de Jong and van Joolingen (1998) distinguished between conceptual and operational models, where conceptual models hold principles, concepts, and facts that make up the system being modeled, and operational models include sequences of cognitive and noncognitive operations (e.g., procedures) that can be applied.

Different modeling technologies are built from and complement different views. These different views of the relationship between what is modeled and the model may require different inscriptional and visualization systems. The following section describes and classifies various modeling tools that support the construction of dynamic runnable models with visual outputs.

# DYNAMIC MODELING TOOLS

Dynamic and executable modeling tools generally have these attributes: (1) variables, rules, and mathematical equations embedded in the software can be executed; (2) the output and behavior of the model change over time; (3) changes are calculated and outputs are visually displayed; and (4) new variables can be added and relationships to existing variables defined, thereby changing the behavior of the system and the other variables within the system. Given these general attributes, which set dynamic modeling tools apart from, for example, concept mapping tools, drawing tools such as CAD, flow-chart, and other static representation tools, the remaining class of dynamic modeling tools can be still further classified.

## Classifications of Dynamic Modeling Tools with Examples

The following analytical categories of dynamic modeling builds upon and extends three learning-related classification approaches: (1) Jonassen and Reeves' (1996) *learning from computers* and *learning with computers* analogically becoming *learning from finished models* and *learning by modeling* (Jonassen and Strobel, 2005); (2) Maier and Größler's (2000) *modeling-oriented simulations* and *gaming-oriented simulations* (although their use of the term *simulation* remains unclear primarily because models are subsumed under simulation, where we would distinguish between simulation and models); and (3) Mellar and Bliss' (1994) *model expression* to *model exploration* continuum. Although using different terms, these classifications share as their main dimension the degree of student ownership and agency in the construction of the model and the visibility of the components, processes, and relationships within the model. Using Mellar and Bliss' (1994) modeling tools continuum as a foundation, Schwarz and White (2005) argued that modeling tools still differ on a variety of dimensions such as whether models focus on problem solving or theory building and so are more dependent on instructional context and the use of the models or modeling but are less applicable to define the tools themselves.

Other dimensions must also be included that provide additional analytical categories to classify dynamic modeling technologies. To better illustrate the various modeling technologies, Table 28.1 provides a summary of them.

### Model-Exploration vs. Model-Building Tools

- *Model exploration.* Simulations (as discussed by Cannon-Bowers in this *Handbook*) are *black boxes* that ask for input and display the output, but calculations are hidden in the system, and causal relationships between variables of the system can only be inferred. Input–output testing is a form of model exploration that stays on the visible surface of a model (Du Boulay et al., 1999). At the other end of the spectrum of model exploration tools are the so-called *glass-box* models (Resnick et al., 2000), where the mechanism and functions of the system's components are open for inspection and exploration.
- *Model building.* Unlike purely model-exploration tools (both black-box and glass-box approaches), where learners are able to change preselected variables as a form of

**TABLE 28.1**
**Modeling Technologies and Their Characteristics**

| Modeling Technology | Model Building | Glass-Box or Black-Box Exploration | Unit of Modeling | Purpose-Specific vs. Generic | Robotic Device External Data Sources | Embedded System; Web Interface | Embedded Support Structures | Individual or Collaborative | Language of Modeling | Other Tools |
|---|---|---|---|---|---|---|---|---|---|---|
| BioBLAST (NASA) | No | Black-box, some glass-box | Variables | Purpose-specific | No | N/A | Part of the simulation | Individual, collaboration in front of computer | Visual influence diagrams | Other simulations with glass-box features |
| NetLogo (Northwestern University) | Yes | Glass-box | Agents with properties | Generic | External input and output | Embedded in collaborative simulation space | Help system | Individual or collaborative (multimodeler); participatory modeling | Rule-based; if–then statements; variable-based | AgentSheets, Swarm |
| Tangible programming space | Yes | Glass-box | Agents with properties | Graphical blocks purpose-specific | External input by physical objects | N/A | N/A | Collaborative through physical input | Contextual signs | N/A |
| Vmodel (Northwestern University) | Yes | Glass-box | Variables | Generic | N/A | N/A | Active coaching support | Individual, collaboration in front of the computer | Qualitative process theory | ModelMaker, Model-It, Vensim, Berkeley Madonna, Extend, mystrategy, SimApp, others |

| | | | | | | | | | |
|---|---|---|---|---|---|---|---|---|---|
| CoolModes (University of Duisburg-Essen) | Yes | Glass-box | Variables | Generic | N/A | N/A | Peer annotation | Individual, collaborative | System dynamics; stochastics | N/A |
| STELLA (ISEE Systems) | Yes | Glass-box and black-box | Variables, building blocks | Generic finished model; purpose-specific | External input and output | Web interface | Storytelling mode; feedback on cyclical argument | Individual, collaboration in front of computer | Visual: system dynamics language; equations; visual loops | ModelMaker, Model-It, Vensim, Berkeley Madonna, Extend, mystrategy, SimApp, others |
| PowerSim | Yes | Glass-box and black-box | Variables, building blocks | Generic | External input and output | Embed with other authoring tools | N/A | Connected computer, network model | Visual: system dynamics language; equations; visual loops | ModelMaker, Model-It, Vensim, Berkeley Madonna, Extend, mystrategy, SimApp, others |
| Co-Lab (University of Twente) | Yes | Mixed glass-box and black-box | Variables | Generic | Reuse in other areas of environment | Embedded within learning environment | Help system; scaffolding | Individual collaborative within environment | System dynamics; visual influence | N/A |
| StageCast Creator | Yes | Mixed glass-box and black-box | Variables | Generic | N/A | Player mode | Guided creation | Individual, collaboration in front of computer | Graphical language | N/A |

input into the finished model and the software does not provide the option to alter the system, with model-building tools students are able to change aspects of the systems and attributes of variables and agents, as well as design different subsystems and functionalities of the system.

For both model exploration and model building, the degree of black-box to glass-box exploration and modeling becomes blurry. Some tools provide functions, subsystems, or layers that are not visible, not accessible, or are not manipulative by the user/modeler of the system (e.g., Model-It has a very limited mathematical equation level), whereas in other tools all functions and features allow manipulation by the learner (e.g., STELLA).

## Unit of Modeling

- *Variable-based.* Tools based on system dynamics such as STELLA, PowerSim, Vensim, and Model-It have their own formalized language for qualitative modeling (i.e., stocks, flow, converters) and underlying mathematical equations for the quantitative modeling emphasize the interrelationship and causal effects of variables on each other (Hannon and Ruth, 1999; Richmond, 1993). Variables can be anything from functions in mathematical models, such as elements in short-term memory in an information processing model, to the number of adults in a population model.
- *Agent/individual-based.* Agent-based (Axelrod, 1997; Reynolds, 1987) or individual-based (Grimm and Railsback, 2005) modeling tools build simulations based on consequences of local interactions of members (agents/individuals) of a population. In system dynamics models, variables do not possess attributes but behave dynamically over time based on the mathematical formulas that define the causal relationships of individual variables. But, in agent-based tools, agents carry different attributes, and their behavior changes according to a set of programmable rules to react to exposure to different contexts within an environment. The environments in which the agents interact most often contain a simulated or virtual environment with spatial dimensions in which the agents are acting, allowing models to simulate, for example,

the spread of a virus across a large population or to simulate players in a soccer game (for a comparison of agent-based modeling tools, see Railsback et al, 2006; see also Gilbert and Bankes, 2002; Tobias and Hofmann, 2004).

## Purpose/Domain-Specific vs. Generic Tools

- *Purpose/domain-specific.* Most all purpose/domain-specific tools are part of the model-exploration or simulation area and therefore will not be addressed in depth in this chapter. Exceptions include business process modeling tools such as ARIS, a real-time business process/flow modeling tool (Scheer, 2000), and decision support or intelligent support tools that can be modeled (Turban et al., 2005), which are not necessarily restricted to a particular purpose or domain. Due to some domain-specific embedded functions, their interfaces (i.e., to other software applications, to developers and designers, and to their growing user base) are primarily used in specific domains and so would be less efficient for other domains or purposes.
- *Generic.* Tools that allow learners to create, explore, and change models are generic tools when they are not restricted to modeling one domain area. Generic tools can accommodate a wide spectrum of phenomena and systems.

## Modeling Technologies That Combine Software and Hardware (Robotic-Controlled Devices)

The majority of computer-based modeling technologies are entirely software based with screen output only. Other modeling technologies, based on the constructionist paradigm, build on the idea that knowledge construction happens particularly well when the learner constructs something concrete (Papert, 1980). The LEGO Mindstorms (ROBOLAB) tools (Knudsen, 1999; Lego Group, 2003) are a combination of hardware and software technologies that allow learners to program robotic devices such as electronic hearts and dinosaurs with simple motor-driven features (described in an early childhood context by Bers et al., 2002; in a wider context, by Resnick, 1998). Other robotic devices with similar technologies were built for data collection and control of a greenhouse (see the spaceplanting project described by Milrad et al., 2003). As Thangiah and Joshi (1997) argued in their paper on programming robots in an undergraduate computer science class, working with robotics and the conditions under which the robots are operating especially "challenge the student to design programs that have the capability to deal with uncertainties" (p. 224) that otherwise would be difficult to simulate. So far, robotic device systems are almost exclusively based on rules and have been used to teach, for example, the creation of programming language to formalize these rules into systems (Gilder et al., 2003).

### Stand-Alone vs. Collaborative Tool vs. Model Embedded in a Larger Learning Environment

There is a substantial literature on collaborative or group modeling (see Rouwette et al., 2002, for a meta-analysis of 77 studies). Most software applications are stand-alone modeling tools, giving students only the option to collaborate when they share the physical environment in front of the computer screen. More recently, model building with runnable visualizations has been addressed in computer-supported collaborative learning environments (Pinkwart et al., 2001; van Joolingen, 2000). The Collide team (Pinkwart et al., 2001) developed CoolModes, a collaborative learning tool that contains a system modeling palette intended to extend the notion of mindtools to collaborative mindtools (Hoppe, 2001). A similar approach can be found in the collaborative system Co-Lab (van Joolingen et al., 2005) and ModellingSpace (Avouris et al., 2003). In the case of Co-Lab, the modeling tool is embedded in a larger learning environment that also provides remote experiments, contains task-specific simulations, and additional content structures (de Jong and van Joolingen, 1998). In ModellingSpace, the system contains a wide variety of different tools and utilizes a collaborative space metaphor (Dimitracopoulou and Komis, 2004).

### Embedded Teaching or Learning Support Structures within the Tool

Computerized modeling tools have a steep learning curve (Alessi, 2000; Mayer, 2004). Although many instructional strategies are available to facilitate modeling activities, some modeling tools already contain what can be classified as *hard support structures* (adapting a term from the literature on scaffolding). Brush and Saye (2002) distinguished between hard and soft scaffolds. Soft scaffolds are dynamic, situation-specific aids provided by a teacher or peer to support learning; they are often tailored responses to individual difficulties of a particular learner. Hard scaffolds are the static supports designed in anticipation of typical obstacles faced by learners. Vmodel, for example, contains feedback mechanisms that identify when structural elements of the model are inconsistent or causal relationships are flawed. Similarly, STELLA includes visual feedback to indicate violations of unit consistency or tautologies. The story-telling function of STELLA can be thought of as an embedded support of how to model when learning to model via modeling demonstrations. The thought processes including the conceptual and procedural knowledge in the expert's model are made visible, providing the learner with a task overview that serves as an advanced organizer for future performance. Additionally, learners can annotate their own models to provide a self-paced walk-through of the system they created.

### Different Modeling Languages or Building Blocks

Typically, a modeling technology representational system is textual, graphical, or mixed (e.g., STELLA stock-and-flow diagrams with text equations). The graphical representation tends to be more intuitive, while the textual representation (e.g., typing an equation to define a relationship) tends to be more precise and controlled. Further, the overall representation may be more or less an analog of the original (e.g., concrete vs. abstract, where the screen shows a drawing of a lake, river, and clouds vs. boxes with lake, river, or cloud labels), with the assumption that the least abstract is easier to apprehend.

Current modeling software typically has a graphical interface and describes relations in the model either quantitatively (i.e., with an equation; *high precision*) or qualitatively (i.e., with a set of predetermined visual notations; *intuitive*). This is important because different representation approaches have been shown to induce very different reasoning approaches (Löhner et al., 2005).

Real systems often can be described using a quantitative, axiomatic basis—for example, by using equations; however, "most of our mental models and verbal theories … do not talk about numbers and numerical values, but rather of properties which are categorical or, at best, ordinal" (Troitzsch, 2004, para. 7). If so, then an important part of model building is translating qualitative mental models into quantitative dynamic models. The representation scheme of a dynamic modeling system is constrained by the requirements of the underlying software code to be able to run the model—the machine-understandable ontology of modeling elements—and these constraints can make the modeling system more difficult to use.

## Programming Languages

Computer programming is probably the most abstract and perhaps most flexible approach for dynamic modeling with technology. The screen is a blank slate, and the programmer can make almost anything happen. Beyond knowing about the phenomenon or system being modeled, however, good modeling through computer programming requires considerable knowledge and skill of the programming language formalisms and system and of human–computer interactions, making this approach less accessible to a lay audience. Current modeling programs are easier to use than text-based programming, but there is always a trade-off between ease of use and depth and variety of functionality.

## Rule-Based Languages

A more accessible text-based computer language programming approach for modeling is rule-based programming. Logo (Papert, 1980) and StarLogo, for example, are rule-based programming languages where input by a user is interpreted using a set of rules and it is possible to use so-called *primitives*, self-defined or predefined functions. Through if–then–else conditions, rule-based models can be fairly sophisticated; although mostly used with agent-based modeling tools, they are perceived as not being sufficient to represent very complex problems (Repenning and Ioannidou, 2004). To remedy the shortcomings, tools are conceptualized in which the behavior (a response attribute or set of attributes) adapts to the context, and the tools are programmed to allow emerging modification of the rules based on self-measured performance to achieve certain goals, which become models that learn (e.g., when an avatar playing soccer in a virtual game adapts its shooting techniques based on the result of prior success of scoring a goal or passing the ball).

## Summary

Existing tools can be mapped on these and other dimensions; however, new developments in other areas such as social computing and scientific modeling software present challenges to our classification and to our model of what modeling technologies are. To sketch one of the challenges, one could argue that massively multiplayer online role-playing games (MMORPGs), such as Second Life with its 1.5 million players, could be classified as black-box, agent-based modeling tools in which the dynamic relationships between agents are partially visible (and can never be made fully visible because the agents are human beings) but personally controlled agents (avatars) are a mix of player-direct-manipulated and rule-based executed actions that are based on the affordances of the context in which the software application is supporting the automatization and mediation of the actions, and provides an historical record of the actions. Because this classification approach and examples were derived from the learning literature, they express some of the dimensions related to the complexity of using dynamic modeling in the classroom. What are some specific factors that have been studied?

# DYNAMIC MODELING IN THE CLASSROOM

The nature and complexity of dynamic modeling with technology present unique problems that can be ameliorated or exacerbated by the modeling technology. Hmelo-Silver and Azevedo (2006) noted that the complexity of modeling includes: (1) the amount of domain content to be modeled, (2) the granularity of the model depiction required by the modeling task, (3) the level of abstractness of the model representation, (4) the affordances available to the students, and (5) how difficult it is for students to perceive and to understand the model's output. These issues of complexity likely interact with students' individual differences, especially their beliefs about the nature of knowledge. The following sections look at these issues surrounding modeling complexity as each relates to modeling technologies.

## Complexity and Ill-Structuredness of the Modeling Task

### Amount of Domain Content

How much does the modeling technology limit the model's size? One aspect of modeling is determining where to start and end, but determining the model's boundary is a difficult task (Sterman, 2000). How do students know when the model they are building is done? Is the model done when the screen is full of stuff? How big is the screen, and how big should it be? Building small models seeks a pragmatic middle ground. Alessi (2000) advocated modeling small subsets of an original—for example, two or three variables at a time. As in traditional instruction, the instructional designer or instructor selects the content subset based on topic, task, student maturity, and so on. These smaller models can reflect, support, and refine students' mental models of that task and subset and later may be combined into larger models (Carney et al., 2002) but only if the modeling technology supports this.

## Granularity of the Model

Granularity is a form of abstraction that affects complexity. Level of aggregation or granularity refers to the level of resolution or scale of a model—for example, representing heat as vibrating molecules in motion vs. as a number on a thermometer (Spector et al., 2001). Grain size is a critical factor in dynamic modeling, so a modeling technology should allow representation at different levels of scale and allow the user to easily combine several models into one larger model; however, granularity is domain dependent, so the modeling technology must be purpose-built for such model building and representation (rather than generic).

## Level of Abstractness of the Model Representation

Dynamic modeling software employs structured representational formalisms (Carney, 2002) that include the way objects and the relationships between objects are displayed and the various ways output is depicted when the model is run. Löhner et al. (2003) listed four functions of a structured representational system: (1) support or extend working memory, thereby reducing cognitive load by simultaneously exhibiting all of the entities in the same space; (b) provide a layout of the problem space to include the relations between only the most necessary subset of entities; (3) determine cognitive behavior, as the syntax and semantics of the representations (what we call grammar) constrain some aspects and stimulate other aspects of cognitive behavior (see Smith and Olkun's, 2005, concept of *spatial priming*); and (4) provide a means for communication with self and with others.

Modeling technology formalisms strongly influence what is learned when building models. Vmodel (a visual representation language based on concept maps) was designed to lower the typical instructional overhead necessary to use dynamic modeling tools, referred to as a *low floor approach*. The underlying theory of Vmodel, qualitative process theory (Forbus, 1984), holds that process is central for explaining causality. In a descriptive study with seventh graders, Carney (2002) considered one aspect of the grammar of the Vmodel tool called the *process entity*. Findings show that students conflated (mixed up) process with other elements of the model—for example, labeling processes as things. Also, processes were seldom used, and most processes that were used had no influence on anything else in the model (i.e., they were dead ends). In this case the visual representation system may have led students to view process entities as represen-

tation elements to show structure rather than function of the original (Louca et al., 2003). In other words, every moveable thing on the screen became an object.

Löhner and colleagues (2003) considered the influence of graphical vs. text modeling representations (SimQuest) on the modeling process and product by having students make a model and then using it to generate output data to be compared to data from a preexisting hidden expert model. The authors anticipated a holistic vs. analytic outcome; that is, the graphic group would produce better models (i.e., as measured by congruence to the hidden original) because they could trial more relations in the time given, whereas the text group could trial fewer relations but would acquire a deeper understanding of those relations. As expected, the graphical groups ran more models with more total unique relations and with more average relations per model. The text group spent a lot of time trying to create equations. The graphical group obtained significantly greater modeling scores compared to the text group. Analyses of the spoken interactions revealed that the graphical and textual groups had similar spoken reasoning, and the model output data from both groups were used only minimally for testing the model. The authors recommended that these different representations should support different phases in the modeling process. Initially, a graphical approach is better for early generalized modeling, and then a text-based approach can be used for refinement of the general models—a transition from qualitative to quantitative modeling of this quantitative original.

In a follow-up investigation, Löhner and colleagues (2005) considered the influence of graphical vs. text modeling representations (SimQuest) on reasoning during modeling. As in the previous study, the students built a model that would generate output data to be compared with data from a preexisting expert model. As in the earlier study, students in the graphical condition produced better models than those in the textual condition. Process analysis revealed a considerable amount of off-task behavior by some groups (up to 50% of the time), contrary to some claims regarding the motivational affects of modeling, although most groups did stay on task more than 90% of the time. Students in the graphical modeling treatment spent significantly more time making evaluative comments about their model, and to a lesser degree talking about, planning, and carrying out the next iteration of their model. Generally, in both treatments, the inquiry process did not follow a systematic temporal order. Also, in both treatments there seemed to be a strong division or even chasm between building the model and using the model (i.e., to test the model), but this was most pronounced in the graphical treatment, where students repeated an orientation–hypothesis–build cycle without testing each model iteration. For both text and graphical treatments, students did most experiments (i.e., using the model to test the model) without expressing a hypothesis, and when a hypothesis was used it appeared out of the blue, especially with the text groups.

Louca and colleagues (2003) used a contextual inquiry qualitative analysis approach to determine how fifth graders communicated ideas while modeling relative motion (which is a quantitative, axiomatic original) using two computer modeling tools: MicroWorlds and Stagecast Creator. MicroWorlds models are built by writing a formal text-based script for each action (e.g., left, forward 10, wait 1), while Stagecast Creator models are built using a mouse-only, click-and-drag approach to develop visual scripts of each action. Note that the students used the software for ten 50-minute sessions over 2 weeks. The Stagecast Creator dyads, relative to the MicroWorlds dyads, spent more time in programming and program planning (both visual activities) and less time debugging but the same amount of time in testing and running the model. Students using the Stagecast Creator visual design approach focused more on holistically depicting relative motion through trial-and-error iteration, referred to as *explanatory ad hoc modeling* by Horwitz (1999); students using MicroWorlds were forced to examine the model primitives and functionally code each object (e.g., elegant programming using an axiomatic base) (Horwitz, 1999).

More remarkable is that these students used the modeling system's grammar to explain their ideas to each other, especially with Stagecast Creator. This suggests that learners internalize more than just domain concepts (Louca et al., 2003) but are also developing mental patterns of the modeling system's grammar (i.e., its ontology, terminology, and syntax). Internalizing the modeling system grammar may have profound long-term effects (Carney, 2002). Given enough exposure to a modeling system, acquiring the grammar of the software is a likely consequence that is a measurable and in some cases worthwhile outcome. But, this also means that the instructional designer must evaluate the modeling software's grammar to determining if it is worth learning.

### Interface of the Modeling Technology

Dynamic modeling software allows modelers to type, drag, click, or, most likely, all of these. Is the screen designed so these actions are obvious or not? Beyond interaction, dynamic modeling systems support other kinds of engagement and actions; for example, the screen layout can invite using an optimum number of components on the screen or the positioning of certain things in certain areas of the screen (see the previous discussion on graphical vs. textual layout).

A screen affordance also includes guiding, constraining, and determining physical action and cognitive behavior of the individual when using the modeling system (Zhang, 1997) and includes the cognitive residue that results from using it (Salomon, 1993). Each dynamic modeling tool provides different screen layouts and interactivity, so this begs the question of how much does a modeling affordance matter? Is there an important mental difference when using one layout vs. another, or are interactivity and layout simply a matter of ease of use, convenience, personal choice, and familiarity?

Does a mind–body connection bind screen affordance and mental representation? Smith and Olkun (2005) considered the affects of interactivity on mental rotation ability. Students observed objects rotating as a function of interactively dragging around it vs. just clicking once and observing an animation of rotation. The three investigations included a group of 9-year-old students, a second group of 9-year-olds, and a group of 20-year-olds. A computer-based post-test measured the accuracy and speed of the students' mental rotation ability. In all three investigations, the interactive treatment group's mental rotation ability was significantly more accurate than the animation group's. In terms of speed, the 9-year-olds in the interactive treatment group were generally faster than those in the animation treatment group; however, this pattern was reversed for the 20-year-olds, for whom the interactive group was significantly slower on the mental rotation post-test than the animation group. The authors suggested that the 9-year-old participants were visually primed by the lesson interactivity for the mental rotation post-test while the 20-year-old participants were disrupted by the interactive experience. Apparently, the lesson interactivity conflicted with the older students' already well-developed mental rotation approach (e.g., analytical pattern matching).

Extending this point, any learner may have a learned bias for one or another interaction approach, and a mismatch will likely affect those individuals negatively. A possible interactivity effect (Evans and Gibbons, 2006) should be exploited in modeling system software. Next-generation input devices (e.g., the Wii hand-held remotes) and sensor bars that detect three-dimensional hand motion, as well as click-type interactions that provide tactile (rumble) and audio feedback through the input device, will be learned and then subsumed by the next generation of learners through game play and so may become the expected way of interacting with modeling technologies.

### Output of the Model

When a dynamic model is run, the output usually includes some combination of text, numbers, graphics, pictures or others visuals, animations, videos, and audio. The combinations of multiple and different output representations mixed in with the model's representation are intended to complement each other; however, learners typically are not very good at attending to appropriate aspects on the screen, resulting in fragmentary and disjointed knowledge structures (Bodemer et al., 2004). Further, some types of output representations are more difficult than others for a novice to understand (e.g., vectors indicating force and direction, dot patterns indicating speed, graphs). So, increasing the amount and complexity of the output information on the screen increases cognitive load which, at some point, negatively affects understanding. What is the optimal model output format?

Bodemer and colleagues (2004) conducted two investigations that manipulated the cognitive load of visuals, specifically by separating the pictorial illustration from its labels (split representation), by directly labeling the illustration of a bicycle pump, or by having the learner interactively drag and drop the labels onto the illustration. Cognitive load was categorized as *intrinsic* (the complexity of the specific domain and related to previous familiarity), *extrinsic* (the interface), and *germane* (focus only on most important components). The experimental treatments were designed to both decrease extraneous cognitive load and increase germane cognitive load. Their findings suggest that an integrated screen is better than a split screen (experiment 1), which suggests that the model representation and model output should be spatially contiguous (Mayer, 1997). Further, in both experiments 1 and 2, drag-and-drop interactivity was better than the other pictorial conventions used.

Evans and Gibbons (2006) replicated Bodemer et al.'s (2004) investigation on the affects of interactivity on learning and coined the term *interactivity effect* to refer to the learning benefits gained from interacting with visual output vs. just observing the output, in this case on a transfer application test but not on the process description retention post-test. Rather than an interactivity effect, it can be argued that the drag-and-drop interactivity was more effective than the non-interactive treatment in this case because it forced the learners to slow down and pay attention to each individual component of the visual, relative to processing the visual as a whole at a glance.

If there is an interactivity effect, how can the learner interact with the model output? Typical output of a dynamic model consists of constant updating of numerical values in graphs showing quantity change over time, or values increasing and decreasing on model components, and so on. Placing charts and graphs contiguous to their most related model components makes sense. The most recent version of STELLA allows the learner to drag and drop a stock onto a graph to immediately see the output, a clear application of the interactivity effect. Also, the use of highlighting using color, size, and form to associate model components to model output may achieve a suitable level of attention to each of the output values.

## The Role of Individual Differences

Does individual difference influence modeling? If so, what role does the modeling technology play? Because of the cognitive load related to the complexity of dynamic modeling, higher ability students may be able to build better models and gain more from modeling than lower ability students (Gijlers and de Jong, 2005). Further research is needed in this area of individual differences.

Naïveté or lack of knowledge and experience with the domain content is important in modeling with technology. Overcoming commonly held but erroneous preconceptions is an issue that cuts across the research on using models for learning, especially in science education. An investigation by Tao and Gunstone (1999) considered the affects of 10 weeks of extensive use of models (simulations) in physics that intentionally used conceptual conflict—that is, scientific explanations that contradicted typical student preconceptions. They reported that students vacillated between their preconceptions and the scientific conceptions embodied in the simulations from one context to another during instruction. They maintained both mental conceptions at the same time (of two minds or vacillating) and relied on one or the other moment to moment, depending on context cues.

Learner preconceptions pose an even greater problem when building models. Unguided model building is likely to entrench naïve conceptions even more than using models, as students tend to build their naïveté into their models (Briggs, 1990). For this reason, the amount and type of guidance to provide during modeling are important. Some modeling technologies provide scaffolds, although the best guidance probably comes from the learning strategy, peers, and the instructor.

Possibly a critical factor in the instructional effectiveness of using and building models involves the student's belief about the nature, source, and extent of knowledge. Windschitl and Andre (1998) examined the affects of epistemological complexity when learning from a simulation of the human circulatory system under either confirmatory (guided discovery) or exploratory (free discovery) conditions. Among other findings, the treatment condition interacted significantly with epistemological beliefs. Individuals with more advanced epistemological beliefs learned relatively more in the exploratory treatment (as measured by a multiple-choice test), while individuals with less developmentally advanced beliefs learned more in the confirmatory treatment. Although a significant body of research has found that guided discovery is superior to free discovery when learning from using models (Bruner, 1961; Mayer, 2004), students' beliefs about the nature of knowledge may be a critical but overlooked variable that interacts with the amount of guidance, especially when building models. Also, it seems likely that extensive experience with dynamic modeling advances a learner's epistemological complexity.

## Scaffolding and Guidance during Model Building

Classroom activities that surround, direct, and support modeling activity are a critical part of the success of modeling; for example, guidance can include guiding questions and clear assignments, online tools (Bera and Liu, 2006), and, in particular, help in generating and testing hypothesis (Bodemer et al., 2004). Also, overarching design principles and model-building planning skills can be learned independently of the modeling software programming formalism (Fay and Mayer, 1994). These issues, however, are beyond the scope of this chapter (see Chapter 36 in this volume). Instead, our interest centers on guidance that can be provided directly or indirectly by the modeling technology.

As mentioned earlier, unguided model building may entrench naïve conceptions, as students will tend to build their naïve ideas into the model. An active coaching support system may provide one solution. Ureel and Carney (2003) determined the frequently asked questions that arise and the common mistakes that students make when they use Vmodel, and they included these in an active coaching support system. The system uses a rule-based system with model tracing or qualitative simulation to detect problems, and when a problem is detected—for example, when a model element is used incorrectly, a more appropriate component is available, or if there is a vague construction—then an onscreen avatar looks puzzled or frowns and the offending component of the model is highlighted. The student can click on either for help. To justify this level of model-building guidance, it is critical to know how much time and effort are required (cost vs. benefit) to build unique coaching solutions for the universe of models that might be built.

For most students, understanding the model representation and the model's output may require considerable support, depending on the student's familiarity with each form; for example, Smith et al. (1992) utilized a progression of simulations (i.e., Modeling with Dots, Archimedes, and Sink the Raft) to teach sixth graders the principles of weight and density. The instruction began with interactions with real objects of various weights and densities and then progressed to using a simulation depicting density as dots in same size boxes, then to a simulation of floating using liquids and objects using the same dot-box depiction of density, and then to an application simulation of density. The authors noted that these sixth graders developed concepts that have been shown to be quite difficult for seventh graders and are usually not attempted until ninth grade.

Simulations (using models) have the same issues regarding output complexity as does building models, but with a lower cognitive overhead. Perhaps using simulations can serve as a precursor to building models. In STELLA, a display page screen called the *interface level* can be used as a simulation by including output graphs and variable control knobs, while the map/model level remains hidden behind the interface screen. The student can learn the output formalisms and important variables from the simulation before trying to build a related model.

It is reasonable to have students build a progression of models beginning with foundational ideas and progressing to more advanced applications and interactions of these principles; however, the progression of models must be carefully planned and integrated and the modeling technology must be able to represent the various levels of abstraction required (both qualitative and quantitative), such as the SimQuest inquiry modeler (van Joolingen, 2004).

## DESIGN AND RESEARCH ISSUES

Dynamic modeling has positive and negative aspects. Dynamic modeling is time consuming, complex at many levels, difficult, may be especially dependent on students' beliefs about knowledge, is unfamiliar to most teachers, is unlike most classroom cultures, and may prematurely entrench inadequate ideas. On the other hand, dynamic modeling is unique and unlike all other instructional approaches, potentially encouraging authentic learning. Dynamic modeling certainly provides students (and teachers) with a new way to look at things, encouraging unique insight while establishing new mental competencies. The instructional effectiveness of building models is not yet established, and it is important to note that simulations (using models) are not very instructionally effective (de Jong and van Joolingen, 1998).

Students often have difficulty with: (1) understanding the effects of nonlinear relationships, (2) keeping the entire system original in mind when working on a component of the original, (3) appreciating (holistically) the full range of control and influence possible within a complex system, and (4) transferring principles learned in one context to a different situation (Milrad et al., 2002; van Eck and Dempsey, 2002). Add to this list the tendency to overgeneralize from a few examples (Feldman, 2003) or, put differently, the tendency to generalize from just a few examples (Tenenbaum, 1999); an inability to prioritize the functionally important components from the universe of possible model components, as evidenced by using fewer components and more irrelevant components (Spector et al., 2001); an inability to associate decisions with outcomes when the outcome is delayed; and perceptual myopia, where stubborn preconceptions veil or distort observations of the actual model output (Gunstone and Watts, 1985). Good model building forces learners to experience these issues but can serve as a mindtool to support areas of weakness.

Good modeling with technology, then, is about a distinctive kind of conceptual change in the modelers that requires attention to different kinds and levels of detail. Young or novice modelers often maintain a simple *copy epistemology* (Barowy and Roberts, 1999), holding the view that models are little more than mini copies of the original. A model can show surface features (descriptive), it can show function and behavior (i.e., relations and process; explanatory), and it can represent conceptual deep structure (i.e., structural knowledge; explanatory). Dynamic modeling requires managing the interconnections between a variety of structural and functional parts, and it especially depends on functional relations (Seel, 2003), but young students and novices will tend to represent visual structural features and confuse these with deeper functional relations (Hmelo et al., 2000).

Building and using models likely affects a broad range of learning outcomes not ordinarily measured by traditional measures of domain knowledge; for example, de Jong et al. (1999), in an investigation of several guided discovery approaches with a simulation, used three measures of learning: definitional knowledge of facts and concepts, speeded test of intuitive knowledge where both correctness and answer time were measured, and a concept sorting task measure of structural knowledge. No difference was found in definitional knowledge and structural knowledge measures for the three treatments, nor a difference in intuitive knowledge correctness for the three treatments; however, a significant difference was found for the "most guided" of the three for speed, as well as significant improvement in both correctness and speed from pretest to post-test. Future modeling research must focus on determining optimal modeling approaches for different learning outcomes.

Many science educators see modeling as fundamental to science and of great utility to scientists (Forbus et al., 2001; Jackson, 2006). Schwarz and White (2005) argued that learning about the nature and utility of scientific models and engaging students in the process of creating and testing models (called *model-based inquiry* or *meta-modeling*) should be a central focus of all science education. To support this, they developed a tool called Model-Enhanced Thinker Tools. In their pilot investigation in four seventh-grade classrooms in San Francisco over a three-month period, students gained physics knowledge, inquiry skills, scientific beliefs, and modeling knowledge. This was especially true for the high-ability students.

Place-based computing may become an important niche in dynamic modeling. Colella (2000) considered an approach called *immersive dynamic modeling*, where tenth-grade students acted as dynamic entities within a model of disease transmission by using wearable computers called *thinking tags* during a 3-week-long project. The students showed a persistent willingness to suspend their disbelief and behave as though the simulation activity was real and exhibited a remarkable level of ownership for the proposed experiments. Such place-based dynamic modeling may apply to some content areas that are not amenable to traditional screen-based modeling approaches due to requirements of actual social interaction.

It is increasingly common to use powerful models in everyday work settings. This begs some important questions: What is the optimal way to learn an underlying model used in the workplace? Are weather-predicting models objects to think with (Papert, 1980)? At what level does the weatherman need to understand the underlying model?—"Trying to learn meteorology from such a model would be like taking chess lessons from Deep Blue" (Horwitz, 1999, p. 181). The role of big models in learning is an open question.

As noted, the amount and kind of guidance provided during modeling are critically important research areas; however, further developments in the design of modeling software will occur. Strobel and Gottdenker (2002), for example, argued for tools that bridge static and dynamic modeling so variables, attributes, and relationships can be transformed with a click from, say, a concept map into to a dynamic system model.

In our opinion, one of the biggest unsolved problems in software development for distance or computer-supported collaborative learning is how to design pointing devices and features that allow the user to easily show another user aspects on the screen at a distance. Workplace and application sharing is still in its infancy.

Even though modeling with technology has been around for awhile, the recent availability of many new easier-to-use software modeling programs (and modeling system conferences) indicates a strong and growing interest in dynamic modeling. The empirical and theoretical basis for modeling, however, still requires substantial additional work.

## REFERENCES

Alessi, S. (2000). Building versus using simulations. In *Integrated and Holistic Perspectives on Learning, Instruction, and Technology*, edited by J. M Spector and T. M. Anderson, pp. 175–196. Boston, MA: Kluwer.*

Avouris, N., Margaritis, M., Komis, V., Saez, A., and Melendez, R. (2003). ModellingSpace: interaction design and architecture of a collaborative modelling environment. In *Proc. of the 6th Int. Conference on Computer-Based Learning in Science (CBLIS)*, July 5–10, Nicosia, Cyprus, pp. 993–1004.

Axelrod, R. (1997). *The Complexity of Cooperation: Agent-Based Models of Competition and Collaboration*. Princeton, NJ: Princeton University Press.*

Barowy, W. and Roberts, N. (1999). Modeling as inquiry activity in school science: what's the point? In *Modeling and Simulation in Science and Mathematics Education*, edited by W. Feurzeig and N. Roberts, pp. 197–225. New York: Springer.

Bera, S. and Liu, M. (2006). Cognitive tools, individual differences, and group processing as mediating factors in a hypermedia environment. *Comput. Hum. Behav.*, 22, 295–319.

Bers, M., Ponte, I., Juelich, C., Viera, A., and Schenker, J. (2002). Teachers as designers: integrating robotics in early childhood education. *Inform. Technol. Childhood Educ. Annu.*, 2002(1), 123–145.

Bodemer, D., Ploetzner, R., Feuerlein, I., and Spada, H. (2004). The active integration of information during learning with dynamic and interactive visualizations. *Learn. Instruct.*, 14, 325–341.

Briggs, P. (1990). The role of the user model in learning as an internally and externally directed activity. In *Mental Models and Human–Computer Interaction 1*, edited by D. Ackermann and M. J. Tauber, pp. 195–208. North-Holland: Elsevier.

Bruner, J. S. (1961). The act of discovery. *Harvard Educ. Rev.*, 31, 21–32.*

Brush, T. and Saye, J. W. (2002). A summary of research exploring hard and soft scaffolding for teachers and students using a multimedia supported learning environment. *J. Interact. Online Learn.*, 1(2), 1–12.

Carney, K. (2002). When is a tree a process? Influences on student representations of process in 'low floor' qualitative modeling tasks. In *Keeping Learning Complex: The Proceedings of the Fifth Annual International Conference of the Learning Sciences*, edited by P. Bell and T. Satwicz, pp. 49–56. Mahwah, NJ: Lawrence Erlbaum Associates (http://www.qrg.northwestern.edu/projects/NSF/Vmodel/papers/ICLS_02_final_carney.pdf).

Carney, K., Forbus, K., Ureel, L.C., and Sherin, B. (2002). Using Modeling to Support Integration and Reuse of Knowledge in School Science: Vmodel, a New Educational Technology. Paper presented at the annual meeting of the American Educational Research Association, April 1–5, New Orleans, LA. (http://www.qrg.northwestern.edu/people/ureel/papers/AERA02–vmodel-handout.doc).

Clariana, R. B. (1989). Computer simulations of science laboratory experiences. *J. Comput. Math. Sci. Teaching*, 8(2), 14–19.*

Colella, V. (2000). Participatory simulations: building collaborative understanding through immersive dynamic modeling. *J. Learn. Sci.*, 9(4), 471–500.

de Jong, T., Martin, E., Zamarro, J.-M., Esquembre, F., Swaak, J., and van Joolingen, W. R. (1999). The integration of computer simulation and learning support: an example from the physics domain of collisions. *J. Res. Sci. Teaching*, 36(5), 597–615.*

de Jong, T. and van Joolingen, W. (1998). Scientific discovery learning with computer simulations of conceptual domains. *Rev. Educ. Res.*, 68(2), 179–201.*

Dimitracopoulou, A. and Komis, V. (2004). Design principles for an open modeling environment for learning, modelling and collaboration in sciences. *Int. J. Contin. Eng. Educ. Life-Long Learning (IJCEELL)*, special issue on role of information and communication technology in science teaching and learning.

Du Boulay, B., O'Shea, T., and Monk, J. (1999). The black box inside the glass box: presenting computing concepts to novices. *Int. J. Hum.-Comput. Stud.*, 51(2), 265–277.*

Evans, C. and Gibbons, N. J. (2006). The interactivity effect in multimedia learning. *Comput. Educ.* (doi:10.1016/j.compedu.2006.01.008).

Fay, A. L. and Mayer, R. E. (1994). Benefits of teaching design skills before teaching LOGO computer programming: evidence for syntax independent learning. *J. Educ. Comput. Res.*, 11, 187–210.

Feldman, J. (2003). The simplicity principle in human concept learning. *Curr. Dir. Psychol. Sci.*, 12(6), 227–232.

Forbus, K. (1984). Qualitative process theory. *Artif. Intell.*, 24, 85–168.

Forbus, K., Carney, K., Harris, R., and Sherin, B. (2001). Modeling environment for middle-school students: a progress report. In *Papers from the 2001 Qualitative Reasoning Workshop*, edited by G. Biswas. Stoughton, WI: The Printing House (http://www.qrg.northwestern.edu/projects/NSF/Vmodel/papers/Vmodel_QR01_Final.pdf).

Gibbons, A. S. (2001). Model-centered instruction. *J. Struct. Learn. Intell. Syst.*, 14(4), 511–541.*

Giere, R. N. (1999). Using models to represent reality. In *Model-Based Reasoning in Scientific Discovery*, edited by L. Magnani, N. J. Nersessian, and P. Thagard, pp. 41–57. New York: Kluwer.

Gijlers, H. and de Jong, T. (2005). The relation between prior knowledge and students' collaborative discovery learning processes. *J. Res. Sci. Teaching*, 42(3), 264–282.

Gilbert, N. and Bankes, S. (2002). Platforms and methods for agent-based modeling. *Proc. Natl. Acad. Sci.*, 99(Suppl. 3), 7197–7198.

Gilder, J., Peterson, M., Wright, J., and Doom, T. (2003). A versatile tool for student projects: an ASM programming language for the LEGO Mindstorm. *ACM J. Educ. Resources Comput.*, 3(1), 1–14.

Grimm, V. and Railsback, S. F. (2005). *Individual-Based Modeling and Ecology.* Princeton, NJ: Princeton University Press.

Gunstone, R. F. and Watts, D. M. (1985). Force and motion. In *Children's Ideas in Science*, edited by R. Driver, E. Guesne, and A. Tiberghien, pp. 85–104. Philadelphia, PA: Open University Press.

Hadwin, A. F., Winne, P. H., and Nesbit, J. C. (2005). Roles for software technologies in advancing research and theory in educational psychology. *Br. J. Educ. Psychol.*, 75, 1–24.

Hannon, B. and Ruth, M., Eds. (1999). *Modeling Dynamic Biological Systems.* London: Springer.

Harris, T. (1999). A hierarchy of model and electron microscopy. In *Proceedings of the International Conference on Model-Based Reasoning in Scientific Discovery*, December 17–19, 1998, Pavia, Italy, edited by L. Magnani, N. J. Nersessian, and P. Thagard. New York: Kluwer.

Hmelo, C. E., Holton, D. L., and Kolodner, J. L. (2000). Designing to learn about complex systems. *J. Learn. Sci.*, 9(3), 247–298.*

Hmelo-Silver, C. E. and Azevedo, R. (2006). Understanding complex systems: some core challenges. *J. Learn. Sci.*, 15(1), 53–61.

Hoppe, H. U. (2001). Collaborative Mind Tools for the Classroom: Strategies for Pedagogical Innovation. Keynote at the International Conference for Computers in Education (ICCE), November 11–14, Incheon National University of Education, Seoul, Korea.

Horwitz, P. (1999). Designing computer models that teach. In *Modeling and Simulation in Science and Mathematics Education*, edited by W. Feurzeig and N. Roberts, pp. 179–196. New York: Springer.

Jackson, J. C. (2006). *Modeling Instruction in High School Physics*, http://www.ed.gov/pubs/edtechprograms/modeling-instruction.pdf.

Jonassen, D. H. and Reeves, T. C. (1996). Learning with technology: using computers as cognitive tools. In *Handbook of Research for Educational Communications and Technology*, edited by D. H. Jonassen, pp. 693–719. London: Macmillan.*

Jonassen, D. H. and Strobel, J. (2005). Modeling for meaningful learning. In *Engaged Learning with Emerging Technologies*, edited by Learning Sciences and Technologies Group, pp. 1–28. Dordrecht: Springer-Verlag.

Knudsen, J. (1999). *The Unofficial Guide to LEGO Mindstorms Robots.* Sebastopol, CA: O'Reilly and Associates.

Korzybski, A. (1958). *Science and Sanity: An Introduction to Non-Aristotelian Systems and General Semantics.* Lakeville, CN: The International Non-Aristotelian Library Publishing Company.

Kozma, R. B. (2000). The use of multiple representations and the social construction of understanding in chemistry. In *Innovations in Science and Mathematics Education: Advanced Designs for Technologies of Learning*, edited by M. Jacobson and R. Kozma, pp. 11–46. Mahwah, NJ: Erlbaum.

LEGO Group. (2003). LEGO Mindstorms home page, http://www.mindstorms.com.

Lehrer, R. and Schauble, L. (2003). Origins and evolution of model-based reasoning in mathematics and science. In *Beyond Constructivism: Models and Modeling Perspectives on Mathematics Problem Solving, Teaching, and Learning*, edited by R. Lesh and H. M. Doerr, pp. 59–70. Mahwah, NJ: Lawrence Erlbaum Associates.

Lesh, R. and Doerr, H. M. (2003). In what ways does a models and modeling perspective move beyond constructivism. In *Beyond Constructivism: Models and Modeling Perspectives on Mathematics Problem Solving, Learning, and Teaching*, edited by R. Lesh and H. M. Doerr, pp. 519–556. Mahwah, NJ: Lawrence Erlbaum Associates.*

Löhner, S., van Joolingen, W. R., and Savelsbergh, E. R. (2003). The effect of external representation on constructing computer models of complex phenomena. *Instruct. Sci.*, 31, 395–418.

Löhner, S., van Joolingen, W. R., Savelsbergh, E. R., and van Hout-Wolters, B. (2005). Students' reasoning during modeling in an inquiry learning environment. *Comput. Hum. Behav.*, 21, 441–461.

Louca, L., Druin, A., Hammer, D., and Dreher, D. (2003). Students' collaborative use of computer-based programming tools in science: a descriptive study. In *Designing for Change in Networked Learning Environments: Proceedings of the International Conference on Computer Support for Collaborative Learning (CSCL) 2003*, edited by B. Wasson, St. Ludvigsen, and U. Hoppe, pp. 109–118. Dordrecht: Kluwer.

Maier, F. and Größler, A. (2000). What are we talking about? A taxonomy of computer simulations to support learning. *Syst. Dynam. Rev.*, 16(2), 135–148.*

Mayer, R. E. (1997). Multimedia learning: are we asking the right questions? *Educ. Psychol.*, 32(1), 1–19.

Mayer, R. E. (2004). Should there be a three-strikes rule against pure discovery learning? The case for guided methods of instruction. *Am. Psychol.*, 59(1), 14–19.

Mellar, H. and Bliss, J. (1994). Introduction: modelling and education. In *Learning with Artificial Worlds: Computer-Based Modelling in the Curriculum*, edited by H. Mellar, R. Boohan, J. Bliss, J. Ogborn, and C. Tompsett, pp. 1–8. London: Falmer Press.

Milrad, M., Spector, J. M., and Davidsen, P. I. (2002). Model facilitated learning. In *eLearning: Technology and the Development of Teaching and Learning*, edited by S. Naidu, pp. 13–27. London: Kogan Page.*

Milrad, M., Gottdenker, J., Strobel, J., Björn, M., and Karlsson, M. (2003). Exploring Technologies and Activities to Support Authentic Scientific Inquiry Learning. Paper presented at the International Conference on Computers in Education (ICCE), December 2–5, Hong Kong.

Papert, S. (1980). *Mindstorms: Children, Computers, and Powerful Ideas.* New York: Basic Books.*

Pea, R. D. (1994). Seeing what we build together: distributed multimedia learning environments for transformative communications. *J. Learn. Sci.*, 3(3), 285–299.*

Pinkwart, N., Hoppe, U., and Gaßner, K. (2001). Integration of domain-specific elements into visual language based collaborative environments. In *Proc. of the Seventh Int. Workshop on Groupware (CRIWG 2001)*, September 6–8, Darmstadt, Germany, pp. 142–147.

Railsback, S. F., Lytinen, S. L., and Jackson, S. K. (2006). *Agent-Based Simulation Platforms: Review and Development Recommendations*, http://www.humboldt.edu/~ecomodel/documents/ABMPlatformReview.pdf.

Repenning, A. and Ioannidou, A. (2004). Agent-based end-user development. *Commun. ACM*, 47(9), 43–46.

Resnick, M. (1998). Technologies for lifelong kindergarten. *Educ. Technol. Res. Dev.*, 46(4), 43–55.

Resnick, M., Berg, R., and Eisenberg, M. (2000). Beyond black boxes: bringing transparency and aesthetics back to scientific investigation. *J. Learn. Sci.*, 9(1), 7–30.*

Reynolds, C. W. (1987). Flocks, herds, and schools: a distributed behavioral model. *Comput. Graphics*, 21(4), 25–34 (SIGGRAPH 1987 conference proceedings).

Richmond, B. (1993). Systems thinking: critical thinking skills for the 1990s and beyond. *Syst. Dynam. Rev.*, 9(2), 113–133.*

Riley, D. (1990). Learning about systems by making models. *Comput. Educ.*, 15(1–3), 255–263.

Rouwette, E. A. J. A., Vennix, J. A. M., and van Mullekom, T. (2002). Group model building effectiveness: a review of assessment studies. *Syst. Dynam. Rev.*, 18(1), 5–45.

Salomon, G. (1993). *Distributed Cognitions: Psychological and Educational Considerations*. Cambridge, U.K.: Cambridge University Press.*

Scheer, A. W. (2000). *ARIS: Business Process Modeling*. New York: Springer.

Schwarz, C. V. and White, B. (2005). Meta-modeling knowledge: developing students' understanding of scientific modeling. *Cogn. Instruct.*, 23(2), 165–205.

Seel, N. M. (2003). Model-centered learning and instruction. *Technol. Instruct. Cogn. Learn.*, 1, 59–85.*

Smith, C., Snir, J., and Grosslight, L. (1992). Using conceptual models to facilitate conceptual change: the case of weight-density differentiation. *Cogn. Instruct.*, 9(3), 221–283.

Smith, G. G. and Olkun, S. (2005). Why interactivity works: interactive priming of mental rotation. *J. Educ. Comput. Res.*, 32(2), 93–111.

Spector, J. M., Christensen, D. L., Sioutine, A. V., and McCormack, D. (2001). Models and simulations for learning in complex domains: using causal loop diagrams for assessment and evaluation. *Comput. Hum. Behav.*, 17, 517–545.*

Sterman, J. D. (2000). *Business Dynamics: Systems Thinking and Modeling for a Complex World*. Boston, MA: McGraw-Hill.*

Strike, K. A. and Posner, G. J. (1985). A conceptual change view of learning and understanding. In *Cognitive Structure and Conceptual Change*, edited by L. H. T. West and A. L. Pines, pp. 211–231. New York: Academic Press.

Strobel, J. and Gotttdenker, J. (2002). New Mindtool (Concept Mapping, System Modeling). Poster at ED-MEDIA—World Conference on Educational Multimedia, Hypermedia and Telecommunications, June 24–29, Denver, CO.

Tao, P.-K. and Gunstone, R. F. (1999). The process of conceptual change in force and motion during computer-supported physics instruction. *J. Res. Sci. Teaching*, 36(7), 859–882.

Tenenbaum, J. B. (1999). Bayesian modeling of human concept learning in *Advances in Neural Information Processing Systems*, Vol. 11, edited by M. S. Kearns, S. A. Solla, and D. A. Cohn, pp. 59–65. Cambridge, MA: MIT Press.

Tergan, S. O. and Keller, T., Eds. (2005). *Knowledge and Information Visualization, Searching for Synergies*, LNCS 3426. Heidelberg: Springer-Verlag.

Thangiah, S. and Joshi, S. (1997). Introducing robotics at the undergraduate level. *J. Comput. Math. Sci. Teaching*, 16(2), 223–237.

Tobias, R. and Hofmann, C. (2004). Evaluation of free Java-libraries for social-scientific agent based simulation. *J. Artif. Societies Soc. Simul.*, 7(1) (http://jasss.soc.surrey.ac.uk/7/1/6.html).

Troitzsch, K. G. (2004). Validating simulation models. In *Proc. of the 18th European Simulation Multiconference*, June 13–16, Magdeburg, Germany (http://www.econ.iastate.edu/tesfatsi/EmpValidABM.Troitzsch.pdf).

Turban, E., Aronson, J. E., and Liang, T. P. (2005). *Decision Support Systems and Intelligent Systems*, 7th ed. Upper Saddle River, NJ: Prentice Hall.

Ureel, L. C. and Carney, K. E. (2003). Design of computational supports for students in visual modeling tasks. In *Proceedings of the International Conference on Computer Support for Collaborative Learning, CSCL 2003, Community Events: Communication and Interaction*, edited by B. Wasson, R. Baggetun, U. Hoppe, and S. Ludvigsen, pp. 98–100. Bergen, Norway: University of Bergen Press.

van Eck, R. and Dempsey, J. (2002). The effect of competition and contextualized advisement on the transfer of mathematics skills in a computer-based instructional simulation game. *Educ. Technol. Res. Dev.*, 50(3), 23–41.

van Joolingen, W. R. (2000). Designing for collaborative discovery learning. In *Proc. of the 5th Int. Conf. on Intelligent Tutoring Systems (ITS 2000)*, June 19–23, Montreal, Canada, pp. 202–211.

van Joolingen, W. R. (2004). A tool for the support of qualitative inquiry modeling. In *Proc. of the IEEE Int. Conf. on Advanced Learning Technologies (ICALT'04)*, August 30–September 1, Joensuu, Finland (http://ieeexplore.ieee.org/iel5/9382/29792/01357382.pdf).

van Joolingen, W. R., de Jong, T., Lazonder, A. W., Savelsbergh, E. R., and Manlove, S. (2005). Co-Lab: research and development of an online learning environment for collaborative scientific discovery learning. *Comput. Hum. Behav.*, 21, 671–688.

Windschitl, M. and Andre, T. (1998). Using computer simulations to enhance conceptual change: the roles of constructivist instruction and student epistemological beliefs. *J. Res. Sci. Teaching*, 35, 145–160.

Zhang, J. (1997). The nature of external representations in problem solving. *Cogn. Sci.*, 21(2), 179–217.

---

* Indicates a core reference.

# 29

# The Learning Objects Literature*

*David A. Wiley*
Utah State University, Logan, Utah

## CONTENTS

## ABSTRACT

The learning objects literature is a collection of journal articles, book chapters, white papers, and blog entries that as a whole recognize few seminal works, share few common definitions of terms, and rarely reference or build upon one another. Learning objects research generally falls into one of two categories. The traditional approach to using learning objects focuses on enabling the just-in-time automated assembly of carefully structured learning objects to create personalized educational experiences. The permissive approach to using learning objects focuses on making the reuse and localization of all resources, regardless of their structure, as effective and efficient as possible. The field is subject to a large number of criticisms. Nascent work in open educational resources points to the likely future of the field.

---

\* The references used in this chapter, together with many that were collected but not used, are available online at http://www.citeulike.org/user/open-content; all websites referenced in this chapter were available February 1, 2007.

## KEYWORDS

*Learning object:* A digital resource that can be reused to mediate learning.

*Open educational resource:* A learning object that can be freely used, reused, adapted, and shared.

## INTRODUCTION

The learning objects literature is a collection of journal articles, book chapters, white papers, and blog entries that as a whole recognize few seminal works, share few common definitions of terms, and rarely reference or build upon one another. This lack of structure in the research makes it difficult to write an overview of the learning objects research literature. Rather than telling a compelling story that moves clearly and purposefully in a handful of directions, the best an author can do is cluster otherwise disconnected pieces by their underlying philosophies. This places an unusual amount of responsibility on the author. I have chosen the clustering of topics I felt most important, but I understand that others will have different views of what matters most.

## HISTORICAL OVERVIEW

The idea of reusing digital educational resources is almost as old as the computer itself. As early as the 1960s, researchers were describing how "curricular units can be made smaller and combined, like standardized Meccano [mechanical building set] parts, into a great variety of particular programs custom-made for each learner" (Gibbons et al., 2002, p. 28). Although the general notion of a learning object is at least 40 years old now, it was Ted Nelson (who coined the term *hypertext*) who developed the conceptual foundations of learning objects and modern content reuse in the description of his Xanadu (Nelson, 1982) and OSMIC (Nelson, 1996) systems beginning in the early 1960s. Nelson's work conceived and grapples with most of the major issues still facing learning object designers and reusers today.

The Xanadu design, which describes Nelson's ideal hypertext system, calls for all content to be archived in a fixed, uneditable manner. Whenever a user desires to make changes to a piece of content previously stored in the system, those changes are stored separately, and users have ongoing access to both versions of the document. The modern Connexions system developed at Rice University uses a similar system (see http://cnx.org/).

Because a specific version or historical view of a specific document is guaranteed to exist in a specific location in perpetuity, it is possible to reuse portions of documents in Xanadu by reference; for example, suppose an author wants to quote a portion of an existing document in a new document. Instead of cutting and pasting the text into the document, the author could reference the specific starting and stopping locations in the existing document, and the content from that existing document will be rendered dynamically in the new document whenever the new document is rendered. This functionality is currently available as the open-source Xanadu Transquoter (see http://transliterature.org/transquoter/).

Issues of granularity and context that plague current designers and reusers of learning objects are completely and elegantly sidestepped. Rather than requiring authors to design and build content with future reuse in mind, breaking their content into chunks, for example, as in the Xanadu approach, authors simply create and publish their content as they see fit. Other authors who desire to reuse portions of the content later on simply indicate the section of the existing document they wish to reuse, and this section is rendered dynamically within the new document later. Also, issues of context of learning objects are also completely avoided, as readers of the new document can always navigate back to the original document from which the snippet came to better understand the context of the learning object. (This functionality is currently approximated in the Purple system; see http://www.eekim.com/software/purple/purple.html.)

Nelson created a vocabulary and catalog of concepts and approaches relating to what would come to be called *learning objects*. Terms such as *primedia* (describing the primitive or primordial media bits that are reused within the system) and *transclusion* (describing the way in which primedia from one document are dynamically included in another) hold huge conceptual value for anyone desiring to learn more about the idea of reusable digital content. Unfortunately, these terms and concepts are all but absent from the current learning objects literature because the father of the modern concept grounded his thinking in another literature.

With the emergence of the World Wide Web in the early 1990s, the idea of reusable materials came to the forefront once more. In 1994, Wayne Hodgins coined these things *learning objects* (Hodgins, 2002). Perhaps because Nelson's Xanadu project had stalled and been largely forgotten by the time Hodgins was writing, Hodgins and other early writers (see, for example, Downes, 2000) located the conceptual roots of the learning objects approach in the reuse literature of object-oriented programming. This led researchers to say things like the following (Fernandez-Manjon and Sancho, 2002, p. 6):

> The idea behind learning objects is clearly grounded in the object-oriented paradigm: independent pieces of instruction that may be reused in multiple learning contexts and that fulfil [sic] the principles of encapsulation, abstraction and inheritance.

These statements place the development of learning objects within a computer science paradigm, asking instructional designers to speak about things in terms of encapsulation, abstraction, inheritance, and polymorphism (Morris, 2005). The popular connection of learning objects to software engineering has created a noticeably technical emphasis in the research. Had the learning objects notion been connected to Nelson's work instead of object-oriented programming, the research may well have been more focused on new media, creative writing, technical writing, and other fields more closely related to instructional design than computer science. This review of research is largely structured around this tension between differing views of the conceptual lineage and future trajectory of learning objects research.

## COMPETING DEFINITIONS AND RELATED TERMS

The learning objects notion is confusing in part because there are dozens of definitions of the term *learning object* (LO), as well as several phrases referring to the same notion of reusable digital educational resources. The most frequently cited definition of learning objects, and the most all-inclusive, is that put forth by the Institute of Electrical and Electronics Engineers' Learning Technology Standards Committee (IEEE, 2005): "Learning Objects are defined here as any entity, digital or non-digital, which can be used, re-used or referenced during technology supported learning. ...Examples of Learning Objects include:

- Multimedia content
- Instructional content
- Learning objectives
- Instructional software and software tools
- Persons, organizations, or events referenced during technology supported learning"

The reaction against this extremely broad definition has been very strong. Wiley struggled to constrain the definition somewhat with "any digital resource that can be reused to support learning" (Wiley, 2000a, p. 23),

but even this is still very broad. More colorfully, people have reacted by writing pieces such as *My Left Big Toe Is a Learning Object* (Levine, 2004) and *Urinal as a Learning Object* (Leinonen, 2005).

The problems created by so broad a definition are compounded by the sheer number of more specific definitions that appear in the literature. Indeed, almost every article written about learning objects provides its own unique definition of the term; for example, in reviewing papers from the 2004 ICALT conference, Rossano et al. (2005) found four separate definitions used within that single conference.

Whereas there are literally dozens of published definitions of *learning object*, a number of slightly different terms have similar meanings. Merrill (1998, p. 2) prefers the term *knowledge object* and defines it as something similar to a database schema: "A knowledge object consists of a set of fields (containers) for the components of knowledge required to implement a variety of instructional strategies." Gibbons et al. (2002, p. 27) prefer the term *instructional object*, describing it as any element "that can be independently drawn into a momentary assembly in order to create an instructional event." Other commonly used terms that describe similar concepts include the Department of Defense Advanced Distributed Learning Initiative's *sharable content objects* (ADL, 2004), Hannafin et al.'s (2002) *resources*, and Downes' different use of the term *resources* (Downes, 2004). Friesen (2004) decried the whole state of affairs regarding learning objects definitions and brought the discussion back to the ground by reminding us that, "innovations must be presented in terms that are meaningful for teaching practice."

## GUIDING METAPHORS

Learning objects researchers have used a variety of metaphors to describe learning objects and their appropriate use. The most common metaphors—including LEGOs, molecules, and bricks and mortar—provide an extremely interesting view into individuals' underlying beliefs about teaching and learning. The LEGO metaphor characterizes learning objects as small chunks of content which, through their adherence to standards, are each able to be combined with every other in a straightforward manner. This was the first popular metaphor, stressing ease of reuse, and was conceived by Hodgins (2002).

The molecular metaphor characterizes learning objects as small chunks of content which, according to their semantic and structural makeup, have stronger affinities for binding with some learning objects and weaker affinities for binding with others. This metaphor stresses the role of learning objects' contexts, emphasizing that not every object can fruitfully be combined with every other. This metaphor was also popular, showing up in Wiley (1999) and Norman (2004). Mejias (2003) applied for a patent relating to what he called learning molecules.

The brick-and-mortar metaphor characterizes learning objects as small chunks of content which, being a variety of shapes and sizes, are difficult to assemble in a meaningful way without some kind of contextual glue to hold them together and give the aggregation meaning. This metaphor stresses that learning objects are "bricks held together and made meaningful by a contextual mortar" and receives treatment in Wiley's (2005) discussion of learning object metaphors.

An important thing to note from this progression of metaphors is not that each one places more emphasis on the important role of context in the meaning making and learning process. The most important thing to notice is that each metaphor assumes that a learning object is a closed, uneditable unit—but unlike the primedia of Nelson's Xanadu, there is no mechanism for creating alternate versions of the objects. The prevailing metaphors make the assumption that learning objects can be aggregated but not adapted. This frequently unspoken assumption is discussed further below.

## DEGREES OF SPECIFICATION

Unsurprisingly, a wide variety of opinion exists regarding how learning objects should be structured internally, marked up for search, and reused in the context of learning. These differences of opinion are best characterized as lying along a continuum of specification. Some instructional design approaches demand adherence to exacting standards for the way learning objects are structured and tagged with metadata (e.g., the Sharable Content Object Reference Model, or SCORM), while others completely reject the notion that such decisions can be made ahead of time and forced upon the instructional design community. Both intellectual camps have important arguments to make in favor of their approach. Both approaches suffer from significant drawbacks as well.

### Highly Specified Approaches to Using Learning Objects

Merrill's (1999) instructional transaction theory provides a significant amount of instructional functionality to users of conforming systems. At a high level, a system implementing instructional transaction theory is a simulation environment with embedded facilities to both prompt learners to practice specific tasks and give personalized, intelligent feedback based on learner performance in the environment. All system content is represented as knowledge objects in a database, and system software operates on these knowledge objects to render the simulation, cue and respond to user actions in the simulation, and create and deliver feedback.

A system implementing instructional transactions is able to make such sophisticated use of knowledge objects because the format and structure of these data have been very precisely specified ahead of time, and system algorithms can depend on finding content structured and marked up in specified ways. Sophisticated, automated reuse is the strength of instructional transaction theory and other approaches that specify the manner in which learning objects should be structured and marked up. For additional highly specified approaches to using learning objects, see O'Keeffe et al. (2006), Duitama et al. (2005), and Colucci et al. (2005). The weakness of these approaches is that no learning objects occur "naturally" in the highly structured manner they specified—each existing chunk of content must be (paradoxically) specially prepared before it can be reused.

### Less Specified Approaches to Using Learning Objects

On the other hand, Wiley and colleagues' (2004) O2 model of using learning objects requires much less from the learning objects in terms of their structure. The O2 model centers on a sequence of increasingly difficult problems to be solved by learners. Instructional designers locate learning objects to be used by students and present them (perhaps with recommendations for the sequence in which learners should engage the materials) in the context of the problem whose solution they support. Extending the brick-and-mortar metaphor, learning objects are the bricks of this design model, and the problem statement (and optional learning object sequencing information) is the contextual mortar that gives the individual learning objects meaning.

The publicly accessible Internet contains literally thousands of terabytes of digital materials that can be reused to support learning without reformatting by models such as O2. The structure of this material varies greatly—some is video, some is audio, some is PDF (portable document format), some is HTML (hypertext markup language), and so on—but, because humans carry out the aggregation of these resources, the heterogeneous nature of the resources is not problematic. These resources may be amenable to semiautomated reuse via what Spector (1999) called *weak intelligent design support systems*—systems intended to supplement what a human does (whereas strong systems are intended to replace what a human does).

Immediate reuse is the strength of instructional design approaches that can use any kind digital resource. The weakness of these approaches is that only the most rudimentary, unsophisticated reuse of materials can be automated. Reuse in the context of less specified approaches almost always requires the involvement of human instructional designers (Wiley, 2000b).

## Highly Specified Approaches to Cataloging and Finding Learning Objects

Several technical specifications exist that describe the types of metadata that should be collected to enable the discovery of learning objects. As with the confusion regarding learning objects themselves, a large number of specifications or standards specify learning objects metadata. Metadata are data about data. A metadata record captures title, author, publication date, and other information to help people find learning objects, much as the cards in a card catalog help library patrons find books.

The five most important metadata standards or specifications for researchers of learning objects to know are the IEEE Learning Object Metadata standard (IEEE, 2005), the IMS Learning Resource Meta-Data Specification (IMS, 2006), the ARIADNE Educational Metadata Recommendation (ARIADNE, 1998), the Dublin Core metadata standard (DCMI, 2006), and the SCORM metadata specification (ADL, 2004). Briefly, the Dublin Core, IMS, and ARIADNE projects began their lives working independently, developing separate specifications for what metadata should be captured and how the data should be expressed. Eventually, the IMS and ARIADNE projects found out about each other (the IMS project was running in the United States and the ARIADNE project was running in the European Union), and it was agreed that they should harmonize their efforts under the auspices of a true international standards organization and guarantee that their work would interoperate. The IEEE Learning Object Metadata (LOM) Standard is the context in which they chose to carry out this work. Dublin Core later agreed to participate under similar terms. The ADL's SCORM work inherits the benefits of these interoperability agreements because SCORM is a best-of-breed package of existing specifications.

Practical efforts to create interoperability between these varying specifications and standards have been quite successful. Najjar and colleagues (2003) described how they transformed ARIADNE metadata into LOM metadata using XSLT. The authors are quick to point out that the work was not trivial. IMS (2006) has also released a best practice guide for using XSLT to transform IMS Learning Resource Meta-Data into IEEE LOM.

Given its status as an internationally recognized, accredited technical standard, the IEEE Learning Object Metadata standard is emerging as the primary standard. Perhaps more than any other metadata specification or standard, LOM belongs in a section on highly specified approaches. The LOM includes dozens of elements, many with their own controlled vocabularies. As an example, when describing the learning resource type of a learning object, creators of metadata must choose one of the following values: exercise, simulation, questionnaire, diagram, figure, graph, index, slide, table, narrative text, exam, experiment, problem statement, self-assessment, or lecture. In addition to using the list of elements and their possible values correctly, implementers of the LOM will also have to conform to the lengthy 54-page XML binding.

In addition to formal specifications and standards, several published research studies also describe highly specified approaches to cataloging learning objects using novel ontologies (see, for example, Qin and Hernandez, 2006). As with highly specified approaches to using learning objects, highly specified approaches to cataloging learning objects come with the strength of enabling sophisticated, automated uses of the metadata to support the location and use of learning objects. The weakness with following such a highly structured approach is the significant degree of time and technical expertise required to conform with the specified standards.

## Less Specified Approaches to Cataloging and Finding Learning Objects

In the mid-2000s, several Web-based services provided their users with a new way to catalog information. Both del.icio.us, a social bookmarking service, and flickr, a photo-sharing site, implemented functionality that has come to be called *tagging*. Tagging differs from the creation of traditional metadata in two significant ways. First, when librarians or educational content producers create metadata for learning objects, they create the metadata to support an unknown future user in finding resources. Conversely, when people tag bookmarks or photos in del.icio.us or flickr, they are creating metadata to help themselves find the materials sometime in the future. Second, when librarians or educational content producers create metadata they use terms from previously specified vocabulary lists, such as those provided by the Library of Congress or the

IEEE LOM standard. Conversely, when people tag bookmarks or photos in del.icio.us or flickr, they use any terms they like—whatever they think will best help them find the bookmark or photo later.

As opposed to the more complicated Open Archives Initiative metadata harvesting protocol employed by more structured approaches, services such as del.icio.us and flickr expose their metadata by means of Really Simple Syndication, or RSS. The idea of thinking about learning objects as syndicated resources rather than packaged resources was first described by Downes (2000) and then made explicit by a number of authors, most notably Downes (2002) and Lamb and Levine (2004).

The economics of the highly and less specified approaches are very different. In the first case, one works through lengthy, complicated standards to support the activities of an unknown future user. In the second case, people tag resources with whatever terms they think appropriate to support their own future uses. The combination of a simpler approach to creating metadata with clear personal incentives to create metadata has made tagging extremely popular. Although only large organizations or projects with trained staff can afford to create Library of Congress or LOM metadata, hundreds of thousands of people around the world have applied tens of millions of tags to millions of learning objects available online (understanding learning objects to be digital resources that can be reused to mediate learning). As of late 2006, most popular online services provided users with the ability to tag.

The strength of less specified approaches to cataloging learning objects is that the economics are such that hundreds of thousands of people now voluntarily create metadata. The weakness of the less specified approach is that the potential for problems related to polysemy in which a single tag may have many meanings (e.g., *Web* may refer to a spider's Web or the World Wide Web) and synonymy, in which a single concept may be tagged with different words (metadata vs. meta-data). Both problems can make it difficult for users to locate learning objects even when they have been tagged.

## Middle-Ground Approaches to Cataloging or Using Learning Objects

Some researchers have tried to walk a middle ground by blending some of the benefits of high degrees of specification with some of the benefits of lesser degrees of specification. Wang and Hsu (2006) developed an ontology-based system for cataloging materials that is not used to support an automated instructional design system. Their system supports human users in the discovery of learning objects, which humans then combine into courses by hand. They have reported an 80% mean savings in time to produce a new course across 30 users using either their blended system or traditional approaches.

Verbert and colleagues (2006) presented another approach they refer to as the *abstract learning object content model* (ALOCoM). ALOCoM includes an ontology that differentiates between content fragments, content objects, and learning objects. Content fragments are combined into content objects, which in turn are combined into learning objects. Content object types and their structures are defined with reference to IBM's Darwin Information Typing Architecture (DITA), a system for creating and managing reusable technical documentation. Verbert et al. (2006) defined types of learning objects only after analysis of what instructional content is actually already available to mediate the primary problem with highly specified approaches—the extensive retooling necessary for content to work in these systems. They therefore chose Slide as the first type of learning object to work with, and they built support for OpenOffice (Impress) and MS Office (PowerPoint) presentations into their system.

The system includes a disaggregator, into which users can upload presentations. The disaggregator pulls the slides apart into their constituent pieces (e.g., bullets of text, paragraphs of text, images) and maps these into the ALOCoM ontology, automatically creating metadata and storing metadata and content for future use. When building a new presentation, users search the repository from with PowerPoint itself (by means of a plug-in) for satisfactory bullets of text, paragraphs, images, or entire slides, and they can pull these directly into the presentations they are building.

## Criticisms of Learning Objects

Researchers have critiqued the entire learning objects way of thinking from a number of perspectives. Friesen (2004), in a well-known paper titled "Three Objections to Learning Objects and e-Learning Standards," clearly articulated some of the most popular criticisms. First, the community of interest seems incapable of reaching agreement on a common set of terms, a criticism echoed by Parrish (2004) and others. Second, specifications and standards related to learning objects are almost completely technical, focusing on things such as XML and controlled vocabularies. They fail to engage pedagogy directly and miss the opportunity to move the practice of teaching and learning forward. Third, the disproportionately large influence of large corporations and the American military on specifications and standards makes them all but irrelevant for public and higher education. Friesen (2004) summarized by suggesting that "objects and infrastructures for learning cannot simultaneously be both pedagogically neutral and pedagogically valuable."

Tompsett (2005) provided a mathematical, graph theoretic criticism of the purported capability of automated systems to assemble learning objects into instruction. Tompsett began by considering learning objects as nodes in a graph, where "mutually consistent" learning objects are connected by edges in the graph. He next modeled the problem of choosing learning objects for automated assembly as the search for a $k$-clique, in which at least $k$ nodes in the network are completely connected. Finally, he modeled the problem of sequencing these learning objects as a traveling salesman problem, in which a path must be found that traverses the collection of learning objects without visiting any learning object twice. Tompsett described these problems as being mathematically complex: "Each is almost trivial to solve on a small scale, but becomes unsolvable, within any practical terms, as the scale increases" (p. 443).

Wiley and colleagues (2004) identified a number of problems with learning objects regarding context. Instructional designers work to make learning objects as free from surrounding context as possible to increase their potential for reuse; however, in the current intellectual climate that emphasizes things such as social context, various aspects of settings, and situatedness, the move to decontexualize educational materials is troubling. Jonassen and Churchill (2004) viewed the entire learning object approach as supporting outdated instructivist ways of thinking about teaching and learning, and although Bannan-Ritland et al. (2002) agreed, they saw exciting opportunities for constructivists who are willing to work with learning objects. Wiley and colleagues summarized the context-related issue as the reusability paradox, in which the more reusable learning objects are, the less instructionally effective they are, and *vice versa*.

A final criticism relates to the anticipated emergence of an educational object economy in which individuals and corporations can buy and sell access to learning objects via micropayment systems—systems capable of selling digital goods for arbitrarily small amounts of money (e.g., access to an online news story for a penny or less). As Liber (2005) noted, the idea of micropayment systems has been around for a very long time (all the way back to Nelson's work in the 1960s!), but no viable micropayment has yet been implemented. Wiley and colleagues (2004) posited that the fear of pirated copies of learning objects being traded in Napster-like networks has prevented publishers from creating these systems. Wilhelm and Wilde (2005) reported that the burden of clearing copyright for learning objects to be used in the course production process can block the process altogether.

## OPEN EDUCATIONAL RESOURCES

Earlier in this chapter, I commented that the prevailing learning object metaphors make the assumption that learning objects can be aggregated but not adapted. Wilhelm and Wilde (2005, p. 69) made explicit the all-pervasive, fundamental barrier to repurposing or adapting learning objects: "While we contemplated modifying some learning material to construct part of our course, this task generally required obtaining permission from website owners."

Acquiring copyright-related permissions from a rights holder entails two kinds of costs. The first kind of cost is the license cost paid in exchange for the rights to reuse a learning object. The second kind of cost is the hidden transaction costs associated with determining who holds the rights to a specific learning object (which can be very time consuming), contacting the rights holder, and negotiating a contract under which you can acquire the right to reuse the learning object. The sum of the transaction and license costs can literally bury an instructional development process primarily dependent on learning objects, particularly when large numbers objects are being used. For this reason, most people assume that for all practical purposes learning objects can only be aggregated and not adapted to fit their specific contexts or meet the needs of their specific learners.

In the spring of 2002, the William and Flora Hewlett Foundation sponsored a forum at UNESCO related to this topic. The report of that meeting introduced the term *open educational resource* to the world (UNESCO, 2002):

> Open Educational Resources are defined as "technology-enabled, open provision of educational resources for consultation, use and adaptation by a community of users for non-commercial purposes." They are typically made freely available over the Web or the Internet. ...Open Educational Resources include learning objects such as lecture material, references and readings, simulations, experiments and demonstrations, as well as syllabi, curricula and teachers' guides.

Individuals who wish to reuse open educational resources bear neither the license costs nor the transaction costs associated with materials trapped within traditional copyrights due to the way in which these materials are licensed. Open educational resources are licensed with open-source-style licenses, such as the Creative Commons licenses (http://creativecommons.org/) or the GNU Free Documentation License (http://www.gnu.org/copyleft/fdl.html).

Although the idea of open educational resources sounds idealistic, according to Wiley (2006) over 2500 university courses (which are composed of individually addressable learning objects) are currently available as open educational resources, including over 1700 courses from U.S. universities, 450 from Chinese universities, 350 from Japanese universities, and 175 courses from French universities. As if to showcase the adaptability of the materials in these courses, many of them have already been translated into Spanish, Portuguese, Chinese, and Thai. The Connexions project at Rice currently hosts 3590 open learning objects; Textbook Revolution (http://textbookrevolution.org/) contains links to 260 freely available, copyright-clean textbooks.

Each of these millions of learning objects—everything from modules to textbooks to courses—is licensed in such as way that reusers can both aggregate and adapt the materials with neither license or transaction costs.

## CONCLUDING REMARKS

A review of the learning objects literature reveals a largely disconnected group of researchers united by an interest in reusing educational materials but little else. The research area is a conglomerate of competing terms, competing metaphors, competing technical standards, and competing ontologies. As implied by these many bifurcations, the research area itself is an uncomfortable amalgam of two competing philosophies.

First are the traditional learning objects researchers whose goal is to automate the just-in-time assembly of learning objects into personalized educational experiences. They rely on learning objects adhering to specific structural and content standards to leverage the power of intelligent systems to provide the learner exactly what she needs.

Second are the permissive learning objects researchers whose goal is to make the reuse and localization of all resources, regardless of their structure or adherence to other standards, as effective and efficient as possible. They assume that humans will be involved in the process of localizing learning objects, and they rely on learners to engage in selecting what they want.

Although the arguments of both parties have their strengths, neither has yet contributed the promised application or process that will revolutionize education and training. In such a young and leaderless field, great opportunities remain for researchers who can unify the field around practical, working responses to historic and emerging problems in education, training, informal, and lifelong learning.

Hybrid approaches that find creative ways to synthesize the seemingly contradictory agendas, prerequisites, and strengths of the traditional and permissive approaches to learning objects research are likely where the future of the field lies. Nascent work in open educational resources has revealed one assumption many seem to have looked past—namely, that when properly licensed learning objects can be adapted and adjusted in addition to being aggregated and aligned. As visionary people help the field identify and remove additional unspoken barriers we should eventually be able to bridge the gap between philosophical differences to better serve learners everywhere.

## REFERENCES

Advanced Distributed Learning (ADL®). (2004). Overview. In *Sharable Content Object Reference Model 2004*, 2nd ed., http://www.adlnet.gov/downloads/70.cfm.

ARIADNE. (1998). *ARIADNE Educational Metadata Recommendation V2.0*, http://web.archive.org/web/20041025023843/www.ariadne-eu.org/en/publications/metadata/ams_v20.html.

Bannan-Ritland, B., Dabbagh, N., and Murphy, K. (2002). Learning object systems as constructivist learning environments: related assumptions, theories, and applications. In *The Instructional Use of Learning Objects*, edited by D. A. Wiley, pp. 61–98. Bloomington, IN: AECT.*

Colucci, S., Di Noia, T., Di Sciascio, E., Donini, F. M., and Ragone, A. (2005). Semantic-based automated composition of distributed learning objects for personalized e-learning. In *The Semantic Web—Research and Applications: Second European Semantic Web Conference (ESWC 2005)*, LNCS 3532, edited by A. Gómez-Pérez and J. Euzenat, pp. 633–648. Berlin: Springer.

DCMI. (2006). DCMI metadata terms, http://dublincore.org/documents/dcmi-terms/.

Downes, S. (2000). Content syndication and online learning. *Educ. Dist.*, 14(11) (http://www.usdla.org/html/journal/NOV00_Issue/story02.htm).

Downes, S. (2002). *Design Principles for a Distributed Learning Object Repository Network*, http://www.downes.ca/cgi-bin/page.cgi?db=post&#38;q=crdate=1034188482&#38;format=full.

Downes, S. (2004). Resource profiles. *J. Interact. Media Educ.*, 5.

Duitama, F., Defude, B., Bouzeghoub, A., and Lecocq, C. (2005). A framework for the generation of adaptive courses based on semantic metadata. *Multimedia Tools Appl.*, 25(3), 377–390.

Fernandez-Manjon, B. and Sancho, P. (2002). Creating cost-effective adaptative educational hypermedia based on markup technologies and e-learning standards. *Interact. Educ. Multimedia*, 4, 1–11.

Friesen, N. (2004). Three objections to learning objects and e-learning standards. In *Online Education Using Learning Objects*, edited by R. McGreal, pp. 59–70. New York: Routledge (http://www.learningspaces.org/n/papers/objections.html).

Gibbons, A. S., Nelson, J., and Richards, R. (2002). The nature and origin of instructional objects. In *The Instructional Use of Learning Objects*, edited by D. A. Wiley, pp. 25–58. Bloomington, IN: AECT.*

Hannafin, M. J., Hill, J. R., and McCarthy, J. E. (2002). Designing resource-based learning and performance support systems. In *The Instructional Use of Learning Objects*, edited by D. A. Wiley, pp. 99–130. Bloomington, IN: AECT.*

Hodgins, W. (2002). The future of learning objects. In *The Instructional Use of Learning Objects*, edited by D. A. Wiley, 281–298. Bloomington, IN: AECT.*

IEEE. (2005). *The Learning Object Metadata Standard*. Piscataway, NJ: Institute of Electrical and Electronics Engineers (http://ieeeltsc.org/wg12LOM/lomDescription).*

IMS. (2006). *IMS Learning Resource Meta-Data Specification*. Lake Mary, FL: IMS (http://www.imsglobal.org/metadata/index.html).*

Jonassen, D. H. and Churchill, D. (2004). Is there a learning orientation in learning objects? *Int. J. E-Learn.*, 3(2), 32–41.*

Lamb, B. and Levine, A. (2004). *RSS for Objects*, http://careo.elearning.ubc.ca/wiki?action=browse&id=RSSForObjects.

Leinonen, T. (2005). *Urinal as a Learning Object*, http://flosse.dicole.org/?item=urinal-as-a-learning-object.

Levine, A. (2004). *My Left Big Toe Is a Learning Object*, http://cogdogblog.com/2004/01/23/my-left/.

Liber, O. (2005). Learning objects: conditions for viability. *J. Comput. Assist. Learn.*, 21(5), 366–373.

Mejias, U. A. (2003). *Learning Molecules* (white paper), http://ideant.typepad.com/ideant/2003/08/learning_molecu.html.

Merrill, M. D. (1998). Knowledge objects. *CBT Solutions*, March/April, 1–11.*

Merrill, M. D. (1999). Instructional transaction theory (ITT): instructional design based on knowledge objects. In *Instructional Design Theories and Models: A New Paradigm of Instructional Technology*, edited by C. M. Reigeluth, pp. 397–424. Mahwah, NJ: Lawrence Erlbaum Associates.*

Morris, E. (2005). Object oriented learning objects. *Australasian J. Educ. Technol.*, 21(1), 40–59.

Najjar, J., Duval, E., Ternier, S., and Neven, F. (2003). Towards interoperable learning object repositories: the ARIADNE experience. In *Proceedings of the IADIS International Conference WWW/Internet 2003*, pp. 219–226. Lisbon: IADIS Press.

Nelson, T. (1982). *Literary Machines*. Watertwon, MA: Eastgate.

Nelson, T. (1996). *OSMIC*, http://xanadu.com.au/ted/OSMIC/OSMICd1m.html.

Norman, D. A. (2004). *Learning Objects as Molecular Compounds*, http://www.darcynorman.net/2004/10/10/learning-objects-as-molecular-compounds/.

O'Keeffe, I., Brady, A., Conlan, O., and Wade, V. (2006). Just-in-time generation of pedagogically sound, context sensitive personalized learning experiences. *Int. J. E-Learn.*, 5(1), 113–127.

Parrish, P. (2004). The trouble with learning objects. *Educ. Technol. Res. Dev.*, 52(1), 49–67.

Qin, J. and Hernandez, N. (2006). Building interoperable vocabulary and structures for learning objects. *J. Am. Soc. Inform. Sci. Technol.*, 57(2), 280–292.

Rossano, V., Joy, M., Roselli, T., and Sutinen, E. (2005). A taxonomy for definitions and applications of LOs: a meta-analysis of ICALT papers. *Educ. Technol. Soc.*, 8(4), 148–160.

Spector, J. M. (1999). Intelligent support for instructional development: Approaches and limits. In *Design Methodology and Developmental Research in Education and Training*, edited by J. Akker, N. Nieveen, and T. Plomp, pp. 279–290. Berlin: Kluwer.*

Tompsett, C. (2005). Reconfigurability: creating new courses from existing learning objects will always be difficult! *J. Comput. Assist. Learn.*, 21(6), 440-448.

UNESCO. (2002). *UNESCO Promotes New Initiative for Free Educational Resources on the Internet*, http://www.unesco.org/education/news_en/080702_free_edu_ress.shtml.

Verbert, K., Duval, E., Meire, M., Jovanovic, J., and Gasevic, D. (2006). Ontology-based learning content repurposing: the ALOCoM framework. *Int. J. E-Learn.*, 5(1), 67-74.

Wang, H. and Hsu, C. (2006). Teaching-material design center: an ontology-based system for customizing reusable e-materials. *Comput. Educ.*, 46(4), 458–470.

Wiley, D. A. (1999). *The Post-LEGO Learning Object*, http://opencontent.org/docs/post-lego/.

Wiley, D. A. (2000a). *Getting Axiomatic about Learning Objects*, http://reusability.org/axiomatic.pdf.

Wiley, D. A. (2000b). Learning Object Design and Sequencing Theory. Ph.D. dissertation. Brigham Young University, Provo, Utah: Brigham Young University (http://opencontent.org/docs/dissertation.pdf).*

Wiley, D. A. (2005). *Learning Object Metaphors*, http://opencontent.org/wiki/index.php?title=Learning_Object_Metaphors.

Wiley, D. A. (2006). *On the Sustainability of Open Educational Resource Initiatives in Higher Education*, http://opencontent.org/docs/oecd-report-wiley-fall-2006.pdf.

Wiley, D. A., Waters, S., Dawson, D., Lambert, B., Barclay, M., Wade, D. et al. (2004). Overcoming the limitations of learning objects. *J. Educ. Multimedia Hypermedia*, 13(4), 507–521.*

Wilhelm, P. and Wilde, R. (2005). Developing a university course for online delivery based on learning objects: from ideals to compromises. *Open Learn.*, 20(1), 65–81.

---

* Indicates a core reference.

# 30

# Open Source and Open Standards

*Rob Koper*
Open University of the Netherlands, Heerlen, the Netherlands

## CONTENTS

## ABSTRACT

The objective of this chapter is to create an understanding of the importance of open source software and open standards (OSS/OS) for e-learning research. Open source is a fundamental new way to develop software, and open standards are needed to make software components work together. It is argued that OSS and OS can improve the convergence of knowledge in the e-learning field, improve the general quality and interoperability of e-learning applications, and improve collaboration between researchers and users. All of these are beneficial and necessary requirements for e-learning research. After a general introduction into basic OSS and OS concepts, the following questions will be answered: (1) How does OSS/OS facilitate the technological *activities* of the researchers in terms of methodology, collaboration, and dissemination of results? (2) How does

OSS/OS facilitate the development of technological *knowledge* in the field? (3) How does OSS/OS facilitate the development of technological *artifacts* in the field? The development and use of the open standard IMS Learning Design (a formal design language for online courses) and the open source applications that are developed to run and present IMS Learning Design courses are used as an example to demonstrate the use of OSS/OS in e-learning research. In the concluding section, we provide some practical information for researchers on how to get involved in OSS and OS and how to use them in e-learning research.

## KEYWORDS

*IMS Learning Design:* A formal instructional design language that is used to specify the design of a teaching and learning process in a machine interpretable way.

*Open source software (OSS):* Software that has one of the OSI Open Source Licenses attached. These licenses state that the source code of a program should always be available to everyone and that everyone can change the source code.

*Open standard (OS):* Commonly agreed upon and published specifications of the conventions used in a community to ensure the quality and interoperability of products and services.

*Technology-oriented research:* Research that aims to develop new technological knowledge, methods, and artifacts to change the world as it exists with the final aim of improving the way we live.

*Theory-oriented research:* Directed at the development of theories about the world as it exists, with the final aim of predicting or understanding events.

## INTRODUCTION

The objective of this chapter is to create an understanding of the importance of open source software and open standards (OSS/OS) for e-learning research. Open source is a fundamental new way to develop software, and open standards are required to make software components work together. Both stimulate exchange, collaboration, interoperability, and convergence of knowledge and these are beneficial requirements for future e-learning research.

e-Learning can be defined as the use of information and communication technologies (ICTs) to facilitate and enhance learning and teaching. e-Learning research is aimed at the development of new technol-

ogies to improve learning, training, and teaching in various ways:

- By making them more *accessible* to everyone at any place and at any time
- By making them more *effective* by facilitating the implementation of advanced pedagogical and organizational approaches
- By making them more *efficient* by providing advanced (partly automated) support mechanisms for learners and teachers to perform their various tasks
- By making them more *attractive* to users by providing adapted tasks and resources

e-Learning research is *technology oriented* instead of *theory oriented*. Technology-oriented research, also called *technology development* or *engineering*, differs in fundamental ways from theory-oriented research. These research approaches differ: (1) in how the problems are addressed, (2) in the ways in which research activities are performed, (3) in the notation and communication means that are used, and (4) in the results that are delivered (see, for example, Gibbons, 2000; Hannay and McGinn, 1980; McGinn, 1978; Rogers, 1995; Simon, 1969; Vincenti, 1990). Mitcham (1994, p. 116) stated that: "Virtually all historians … use the word 'technology' to refer to both ancient and modern, primitive and advanced making activities, or knowledge of how to make and use artifacts, or the artifacts themselves." A distinction can be made among (1) the technological *activities* of the researchers (methods for making an artifact), (2) the technological *knowledge* that is a result of these making activities (models and specifications), and (3) the technological *artifacts* that are the results of these activities. These distinctions have been used to structure this chapter when we discuss the use of OSS/OS in e-learning research. The following questions are answered:

- How does OSS/OS facilitate the technological *activities* of the researchers in terms of methodology, collaboration and dissemination of results?
- How does OSS/OS facilitate the development of technological *knowledge* in the field?
- How does OSS/OS facilitate the development of technological *artifacts* in the field?

Before going into these questions, the concepts of open source software (OSS) and open standards (OS) are discussed more in general with an emphasis on the use of OSS/OS as means to perform research on e-learning.

# OPEN SOURCE

## What Is Open Source?

Software is written in a computer language before it is compiled into binary code that computers can run. The human readable text originally written by the programmers in a computer language is the *source code* of a program. The source code, the derived binary code, and the documentation are protected by *intellectual property rights* (IPRs). Only the owner of the IPR is entitled to change the code or the documentation, and only the owner of the copyright is entitled to copy and distribute these.

This closed source software approach has been under attack by the free software and open source movement. The Free Software Foundation (FSF), founded by Richard Stallman in 1984, is the organization behind MIT's GNU project. One of the contributions of the FSF is the development of the General Public License (GPL, 2006) to protect the IPRs of contributors and prevent unwanted commercialization of the software. The FSF (FSF-DEF, 2006) defines free software as "the freedom of all users to run, copy, distribute, study, change and improve software. Source code is seen as a kind of scientific knowledge that should be published to facilitate innovation." It is worth noting that "free software" as used here does not coincide with the notion of software that is available without cost to the user. Some software that is freely available is not free software, and some free software may involve nominal costs to users.

The term *free software* has developed some negative connotations, especially in industry. This is the reason why a group of people, including Eric Steven Raymond, started in 1997 to promote the use of free software by stressing the technical superiority and low cost instead of its rather anti-business and ideological aspects. They used the term *open source software* instead of *free software* and founded the Open Source Initiative (OSI) in 1998 to provide a definition of OSS and a set of criteria for open source licenses (OSI-licenses, 2006). The GPL license is considered to be a valid OSI license, among many other licenses that are less restrictive for use in the commercial world.

## Open Source Development Model

Many OSS development projects are now underway. SourceForge, for example, supports more then a 100,000 projects, most for general use but many specifically developed for e-learning. One of the characteristics of OSS is that it is developed in a different way than commercial software. Raymond (1998, 2001) compared two development models: the cathedral (as a metaphor for traditional software development) and the bazaar (as a metaphor for OSS development) to ground the idea of higher quality and lower costs. Characteristics of the bazaar model for OSS development tend to include: (1) globally distributed communities of developers collaborating primarily through the Internet, (2) developers working in parallel, (3) developers exploiting the power of peer review for debugging and requirements analysis, (4) rapid, incremental release schedules, and (5) projects with pools of experienced and esteemed professional developers (Feller and Fitzgerald, 2002). OSS communities have developed some strong cultural norms that govern the mainly self-organized development system (Bergquist and Ljungberg, 2001; Jorgensen, 2001).

The success of the OSS development model has invoked many questions, especially in economics and organizational theory. Madey et al. (2002, p. 1807) formulated it this way:

> The OSS movement is a phenomenon that challenges many traditional theories in economics, software engineering, business strategy, and IT management. Thousands of software programmers are spending tremendous amounts of time and effort writing and debugging software, most often with no direct monetary compensation.

Empirical studies have been performed on the size and distribution of development teams (Crowston and Howison, 2005), comparisons of the organization of various OSS projects (Dempsey et al., 1999; Gallivan, 2001; Mockus et al., 2002), and the organization of social relationships and incentives in OSS communities (Bergquist and Ljungberg, 2001; Lerner and Triole, 2002).

Although an OSS development model is sometimes perceived as something new, the principle of sharing software and codeveloping has been a common practice among academics from the early days of computer programming. In the early 1960s, many fundamental software programs (operating systems, computer languages, etc.) were developed in universities such as the Massachusetts Institute of Technology and the University of California at Berkeley, and in company laboratories such as AT&T Bell Labs and Xerox's Palo Alto Research Center. Researchers shared their code so others could inspect, use, and improve it. This mode of working was rather similar to the way in which researchers have always shared ideas through publications, reports, notes, and conferences. This mode of sharing was rather informal, and as a result of this AT&T could begin to enforce its IPRs on UNIX in the beginning of the 1980s. This was one of the triggers for the development of the GNU license.

## General Open Source Applications

Many of the tools and services used in daily life are based on OSS, specifically on the server side (e.g., e-mail based on sendmail, websites based on Apache, servers running on Linux). For the client, many high-quality OSS alternatives are available for commercial software. Examples include Thunderbird (2006) as a mail client, Firefox (2006) as a browser, GIMP (2006) as an advanced drawing tool, FreeMind (2006) as a mind-mapping tool, Eclipse (2006) as an integrated software development environment, or OpenOffice.org (2006) as an office suite. Most of these tools are interoperable with commercial software through the use of import and export filters to different formats.

## Open Source in Learning, Education, and Training

Open source software is used in a variety of ways in learning, education, and training contexts. Many types of computer use involve some kind of informal learning, such as performing a search with Google, using Wikipedia, making and using podcasts, writing and reading blogs and wikis, and so on. The use of OSS in schools is being explored and applied in many regions in the world where cost savings and stimulating local industries are important issues. In these cases, the Linux operating system is often used as a base for an educational software package that contains a selection of general and specific open source applications that can be used in the schools (see, for example, Edubuntu, 2006). In the Spanish region of Extremadura, a Debian-based version of Linux (LiNex, 2006), is deployed on some 70,000 desktop PCs and 400 servers in the educational sector. In Norway, around 200 schools use Skolelinux (2006).

In addition to these products, many projects are delivering specific educational applications. The area of e-learning offers several open source learning management systems (LMSs), including Moodle (2006), Sakai (2006), .Learn (2006), Bodington (2006), ATutor (2006), and Dokeos (2006), among others. The development of these LMSs is at the moment challenged by the emergence of new generations of technologies, such as the use of:

- Web services for e-learning (Alonso et al., 2004; Vossen and Westerkamp, 2003)
- Semantic Web principles (Anderson and Whitelock, 2004; Berners-Lee et al., 2001)
- Adaptive learning principles (Berlanga and Garcia, 2005; Brusilovsky, 2001; De Bra et al., 2004)

- Learning-process-oriented systems (Dalziel, 2003; LAMS, 2006; Paquette et al., 2006)
- Social software (ELGG, 2006)
- Shared, self-created multimedia files (e.g., podcasts) (LionShare, 2006)
- Mobile technologies in learning (Jones et al., 2005)

BECTA (2005) has performed a study of the use of OSS in U.K. schools. The cases presented in the study show that OSS can be used as a server operating system, as a desktop operating system, and for applications used in the classroom or for administration. The study also mentions the reasons why schools moved to OSS:

- They liked its transparency and flexibility, which made it possible to alter the software according to their needs.
- There was an educational value to providing pupils with a broader experience of operating systems and software.
- It was a way to achieve value for the money spent and to extend the ICT network and facilities.
- They had access to appropriate knowledge, skills, and experience to support an OSS implementation.
- Most stakeholders (pupils, teachers, parents) also appreciated the use of OSS.

The disadvantages identified included a lack of curriculum-specific courseware, compatibility problems with some commercial software, and a lack of familiarity among teachers and pupils. The study has also found that the total costs for the use of OSS were lower compared to the use of proprietary software, but this is dependent largely on the way OSS is used and supported.

## OPEN STANDARDS

### What Are Open Standards?

Open standards are of enormous importance in our society to ensure that products and services are of sufficient quality and can work together—that is to say, they are interoperable. The term *open standard* has many interpretations. According to Krechmer (2005), this is due to the fact that creators, implementers, and users of OS each have a different set of requirements and as a result a different perspective on OS; for example, the creators, as represented by the standards organizations, will focus on the openness of the process of standard development, specifically a due process with open meetings and decisions made by consensus. The implementers will focus more on the free use of the standards and the compatibility with previous implementations. The end users will focus on such aspects as the number of implementations from different vendors and the compatibility with currently used systems. End users are often interested in *de facto* standards instead of OS—for example, when they say that they want to standardize on Blackboard.

The definition that I will use for OS (in e-learning) is as follows: "Open standards (in e-learning) are commonly agreed upon and published specifications of the conventions used in a community to ensure the quality and/or interoperability of (e-learning) products and services." Several remarks can be made about this definition. First of all, the definition contains the word *specification*, which means that an open standard is conceived as a document or set of documents and not as a specific product or service. These documents contain agreements about quality standards, data formats, and communication protocols. The idea is that e-learning products implement the different open standards to enable interoperability. Many products also advertise that they are compliant with certain standards, but this is difficult to test because of the lack of formal conformance procedures to test whether a product is truly compliant with a specific standard. The European TELCERT (2006) project has developed a first set of tools for such conformance testing.

Second, the definition defines two core functions of OS:

- To ensure the *quality* of e-learning products and services, including the quality of learning objects, the quality of a systems design, the usability of the software, and so on
- To ensure the *interoperability* of e-learning products and services; interoperability supports the collaboration between systems but also between humans who develop or use a system (for example, notation standards and standard vocabularies)

Furthermore, the definition points to the fact that standards are always agreed upon and used *within a certain community* of interest, such as a company, a consortium, a country, a specific technology, or a (worldwide) field of expertise. A standard has the status of a recommendation for the community members. This leaves open the possibility that different communities and different standards could exist in the same area, just as there are different power plug standards or railway systems in different countries. For metadata, we can use the IMS/IEEE Learning Object Metadata (LOM) (educational sector) or the Dublin Core metadata (library sector). Added to this, many countries, professional sectors, and companies have defined their own local standards which are not compatible with each other nor with international standards.

The ideal of the standards committees is to have one worldwide accepted standard that can be localized to fit the needs of different organizations. This ideal is, however, difficult to accomplish in practice, so we have to deal with the fact that there are still many different communities, each with its own incompatible standards. In that case, the interoperability question has to be solved when the two communities want to collaborate.

## How Are Open Standards Developed and Which e-Learning Standards Are Available?

International specifications are traditionally developed by three standards organizations: the International Organization or Standardization (ISO, founded in 1947), the International Electrotechnical Commission (IEC, founded in 1906), and the International Telecommunication Union (ITU, founded in 1865). Most countries and parts of the world have their own standards organizations that are directly associated with the international organizations (e.g., ANSI in the United States, CEN in Europe).

Besides these organizations being country or regionally specific, some standards organizations transcend country boundaries by adopting an expert model approach, such as the Institute of Electrical and Electronics Engineers (IEEE). Some well-known IEEE standards are the IEEE 802.3 Ethernet standard and the IEEE 802.11 Wireless Networking standard. The IEEE is also active in e-learning through the IEEE Learning Technologies Standards Committee (LTSC). This committee is working on topics such as a digital rights expression language, computer-managed instruction, learning objects metadata, and competency definitions.

The ISO formed a joint technical committee with the IEC (ISO/IEC JTC1) that has the objective to develop, maintain, promote, and facilitate ICT standards required by global markets meeting business and user requirements concerning the design and development of systems and tools, performance and quality of products and systems, security of systems and information, portability of application programs, interoperability of products and systems, unified tools and environments, and harmonized vocabulary and user-friendly and ergonomically designed user interfaces.

The JTC1 has several subcommittees, including SC36, which is responsible for Information Technology for Learning, Education, and Training. SC36 is working on standards for a collaborative workplace and agent/agent communication, as well as on a learner-to-learner interaction scheme. They are currently setting up many more groups.

Standards organizations that work according to a particular country's model (e.g., ISO) had a reputation in the 1990s of being too slow to keep up with the standardization needs of quickly changing areas such as ICT and e-learning. ISO had a large project, Open Systems Connect, that tried to develop a common computer networking standard. The project did not succeed and was stopped in 1996, at which point it was taken over by an organization called the Internet Engineering Task Force (IETF, founded in 1986). This task force had a less bureaucratic, open process and developed the basic protocol suites that were needed for the Internet to operate. Later, the IETF was also perceived as being too slow, and most industry vendors are currently working with specifications from more specialized consortia such as the World Wide Web Consortium (W3C). This consortium creates and maintains standards for the World Wide Web (HTTP, URL, Linking, XML, Semantic Web).

In the e-learning field, the dominant specialized consortium is IMS, a consortium of the major players, companies, and researchers in the e-learning field. IMS developed and maintains 17 specifications in the following fields: metadata, assessment, learning design, content packaging, sequencing, ePortfolio, learner information, digital repositories, competency definition, and interoperability of learning management systems with enterprise systems.

Most of the current e-learning standards concentrate on the syntax of the data format that should be used for the asynchronous exchange of learning resources or learner information. Less attention has been given to standardization of synchronous communication between systems and standardization of the semantics of the communication process. In the field of semantics, several exceptions can be found, including the work done by the International Board of Standards for Training, Performance, and Instruction (IBSTPI; http://www.ibstpi.org) on the definition of competencies for instructors, instructional design, training managers, and evaluators. These standards have not yet been defined in the technical formats provided by IMS, IEEE. or HR-XML.

## OSS/OS AS A MEANS TO FACILITATE E-LEARNING RESEARCH

How can OSS/OS facilitate e-learning research? As stated before, OSS/OS can facilitate e-learning research that results in both new technological knowledge and new technological artifacts. The next paragraphs discuss these possibilities of using an OSS/OS approach in e-learning research.

### OSS/OS to Facilitate Technological Activity in e-Learning

The major activity in e-learning research is to *develop* new e-learning technologies. This development process is facilitated by research methodologies based on the principles of systems engineering (Richey and Nelson, 1996). The use of OSS/OS can facilitate the development process in several ways: (1) by providing a standard notation system to foster communication and collaboration, (2) by facilitating the development of the systems by multiple distributed users using the OSS development model, (3) by facilitating the evaluation of the developed artifacts, and (4) by stimulating the dissemination of results.

During this development there is a need to communicate the design of the system among researchers and users within and outside the team. For communication purposes, a *notation system* is used to capture user requirements and to notate the design of the envisaged system. When such a notation system conforms to a widely known open standard, it facilitates the correct understanding of the design and thus the quality of the discussions among developers and users. The best example of such a notation system is the Unified Modeling Language (UML) (Booch et al., 1999; Fowler, 2000), an open standard developed by the Object Management Group (OMG). The use of UML is very common in ICT research today but is still a rather new phenomenon in e-learning research, although it is found more and more in e-learning publications (Zarraonandia et al., 2005).

Unified Modeling Language defines nine types of diagrams, each providing a different view of a system under development. Three types of diagrams in e-learning publications are most often used:

- Cases are used to model the (envisaged) user requirements and benefits of the system for (future) users (see Figure 2 of Asensio et al., 2004).
- Class Diagrams are used to model the core entities (concepts or classes) and their relationships in the problem domain; these dia-

grams can also be used to express a domain ontology or to design the data structures in an application (see Figure 2 of Koch and Wirsing, 2002).
- Activity Diagrams are used to model the processes or workflow in a system (see Figure 3 of Derntl and Motschnig-Pitrik, 2003).

The UML diagrams are shared among researchers in publications, and they support collaboration and communication during the process of analysis and design. They are also used in group communication to create a conceptual model that integrates different perspectives. An example is the UML that was developed to integrate the classical and modern views on assessment (Joosten-Ten Brinke et al., 2005).

Based on the UML models, OSS can be developed implementing OS. OSS/OS can be very beneficial to the project, as new systems can be built by reusing OSS code or by adapting the code of existing systems. The use of OS makes the inclusion of existing services or data possible. Another advantage of using OSS/OS is that it can facilitate the evaluation of the system in various ways. The bazaar methods of OSS can offer advantages with regard to the quality of the code. To paraphrase Raymond (2001), release early and often; involve the users; and remember that many eyeballs tame complexity and that, given enough eyeballs, all bugs are shallow. Furthermore, it offers advantages in the setup of the experiments themselves. When the software is made available and a user base is developing, these same users can be used for the evaluation research. This type of research can aim for high ecological validity (Gilbert and Troitzsch, 1999).

Another advantage of using OSS/OS in e-learning research is easy dissemination through channels such as SourceForge. This provides a natural means to attract new initiatives, to improve the software, and to use the software when it is at a certain quality. A basic requirement is that the product addresses a need perceived by a community of users.

## OSS/OS to Facilitate the Development of Technological Knowledge

One of the results of technological activities is the development of new technological knowledge. Technological knowledge is knowledge that describes how an artifact (or a system) can be made and how this artifact can be used. This knowledge is captured in:

- UML diagrams that are used to design the system
- Code of the system that has been developed

- Documentation of the system that provides a user perspective of the system
- Publications about the evaluation of the system

When using an OSS approach, this knowledge is available for all researchers to test, replicate, or elaborate. In closed source systems or in regular research approaches, the access to the design and the code of the system is restricted, so the knowledge is only partially available. The OSS approach can lead to more convergence of knowledge in the field when researchers adopt the habit of using and adapting what is already available, instead of building everything again from scratch.

The use and development of OS has another advantage in research. OS can be considered to be consolidated, agreed-upon knowledge about the data structure, functionality, or semantics of a system. Standards commissions provide a platform to converge divergent theories and models to the best possible abstraction of the current state of the art; for example, the IMS QTI specification summarizes the set of various test items that are frequently used in education. This process itself is a strong means in the field to come to an agreement and summary of some aspects in the field, especially when researchers are in the habit of contributing to the standards committees, use the standards that are released as much as possible, and test the specifications to identify strong and weak points.

## OSS/OS to Facilitate the Development of Technological Artifacts

Besides the creation of knowledge, the core result of technological activity is the development of the technological artifacts. In e-learning research, we produce the following types of artifacts: models and open standards, software, and documentation. In the previous paragraphs, many examples of the OSS/OS artifacts were mentioned—for example, specifications such as IMS QTI and IEEE LOM and software such as Moodle, LionShare, and Sakai.

## EXAMPLE

An example of the development and use of the open standard IMS Learning Design (IMSLD, 2003; Koper and Olivier, 2004; Koper and Tattersall, 2005) and the related OSS will demonstrate the use of OSS/OS in e-learning research.

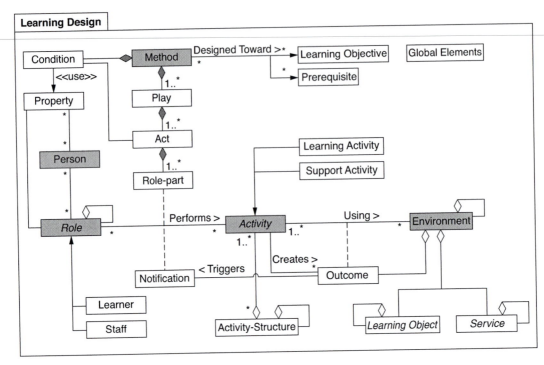

**Figure 30.1** The conceptual domain model of IMS learning design in UML.

## The IMS Learning Design Model (Technological Knowledge)

IMS Learning Design is an open standard that is used to specify the design of a teaching and learning process in a machine-interpretable way. LD can be seen as a formal instructional design language. The specification consists of a set of documents and an XML Schema Definition that supports the coding of the learning design of courses in XML format. At the base of the specification is the Conceptual Model as presented in Figure 30.1. This model is specified as a UML class model and is slightly adapted from the EML model that has been developed by studying and abstracting different instructional design approaches (Koper and Manderveld, 2004). It was tested, discussed, and adapted in different situations using different technologies (Tattersall et al., 2005; Van Es and Koper, 2005), and this process is continuing, although a first stable release of the open specification occurred after 5 years of work (1998–2002). The model itself can be seen as a technological theory that describes a large variety of instructional design approaches. In this way, it serves as a convergence mechanism in the field of instructional design. In essence, it should be possible to describe and implement most of the current instructional design models (Reigeluth, 1999) in LD. The fact that this is an open specification has invoked many different research initiatives in the area of ontologies

for learning design, patterns in learning design, runtime adaptations, and the design and development of a variety of authoring and runtime tools (Koper, 2005).

## IMS Learning Design Open Source Software

The availability of LD as an open standard has stimulated the development of many tools to support the specification. Most of these tools are developed as OSS in academic settings—for example, as part of doctorate study. Griffiths and colleagues (2005) have provided an overview of available tools and their classification. Major research issues are the development of more user-friendly and integrated authoring and runtime tools (Hernández-Leo et al., 2006), Authoring of adaptive learning designs (Van Rosmalen et al., 2005), the graphical representation of learning designs (Paquette et al., 2006), the integration of assessment in learning designs (Joosten-ten Brinke et al., 2005; Pacurar et al., 2004), and the use of Semantic Web tools with learning design (Amorim et al., 2006; Knight et al., 2006).

## CONCLUSION AND SOME PRACTICAL TIPS

The concepts of OSS and OS have been elaborated in this chapter. The discussion suggests that OSS and OS can improve the convergence of knowledge in the field, improve the general quality and interoperability of e-learning applications, and improve collaboration between researchers and users. How might one use OSS and OS in research? I conclude with this summary of key points in response to this question:

- Learn how to read and create UML diagrams to specify a system that solves some real problems in the fields of learning and teaching.
- Study the existing open standards in the e-learning field, specifically the ones from IMS and IEEE (and ISO as they become available). It is necessary to have some knowledge about XML (2003), RDF (2003), and standards organizations. Readers should refer to the references provided in this chapter.
- Download, install, test, and use a variety of open source programs and distributions. Consider the use of virtual machine software, such as VMware, which allows users to install various Linux distributions (e.g., Edubuntu) without affecting other programs on their computers.
- Learn to code and participate in an open source development project or start one on your own.
- Use existing OSS as much as possible in your work and be strict in the use of OS where possible to encourage convergence and collaboration.
- Participate in relevant communities; demonstrate your work in workshops; write conference papers and journal papers about your work; provide relevant feedback and input to standards committees.

## ACKNOWLEDGMENT

This chapter is sponsored by the TENCompetence Integrated Project, which is funded by the European Commission's 6th Framework Programme, priority IST/Technology Enhanced Learning, Contract 027087 (www.tencompetence.org).

### References

Alonso, G., Casati, F., Kuno, H., and Machiraju, V. (2004). *Web Services: Concepts, Architectures and Applications*. Heidelberg: Springer.

Amorim, R. R., Lama, M., Sánchez, E., Riera, A., and Vila, X. A. (2006). A learning design ontology based on the IMS specification. *Educ. Technol. Soc.*, 9(1), 38–57.

Anderson, T. and Whitelock, D. (2004). The educational Semantic Web: visioning and practicing the future of education. *J. Interact. Media Educ.*, 1 (http://www-jime.open.ac.uk/2004/1/editorial-2004-1-disc-paper.html#EditorialStart).

Asensio, J. I., Dimitriadis, Y. A., Heredia, M., Martinez, A., Alvarez, F. J., Blasco, M. T. et al. (2004). Collaborative Learning Patterns: Assisting the Development of Component-Based CSCL Applications. Paper presented at the 12th Euromicro Conference on Parallel, Distributed and Network-Based Processing, February 11–13, Coruña, Spain.

ATutor. (2006). *ATutor: Open Source Learning Management System*, http://www.atutor.ca/.

BECTA. (2005). *Open Source Software in Schools*, http://www.becta.org.uk/corporate/publications/documents/BEC5606_Full_report18.pdf.

Bergquist, M. and Ljungberg, J. (2001). The power of gifts: organising social relationships in open source communities. *Inform. Syst. J.*, 11(4), 305–320.

Berlanga, A. and Garcia, F. J. (2005). Learning technology specifications: semantic objects for adaptive learning environments. *Int. J. Learn. Technol.*, 1(4), 458–472.

Berners-Lee, T., Hendler, J., and Lassila, O. (2001). The Semantic Web: A new form of Web content that is meaningful to computers will unleash a revolution of new possibilities. *Sci. Am.*, 284(5), 34–43.

Bodington. (2006). *Bodington: Open Source Learning Management System*, http://bodington.org/.

Booch, G., Rumbaugh, J., and Jacobson, I. (1999). *The Unified Modeling Language User Guide*. Reading, PA: Addison-Wesley.

Brusilovsky, P. (2001). Adaptive hypermedia. *User Model. User Adapt. Interact.*, 11(1/2), 87–110.

Crowston, K. and Howison, J. (2005). The social structure of free and open source software development. *First Monday*, 10 (http://firstmonday.org/issues/issue10_2/crowston/index.html).

Dalziel, J. (2003). Implementing learning design: the learning activity management system. In *Interact, Integrate, Impact: Proceedings of the 20th Annual Conference of the Australasian Society for Computers in Learning in Tertiary Education*, December 7–13, Adelaide.

De Bra, P., Aroyo, L., and Chepegin, V. (2004). The next big thing: adaptive Web-based systems. *J. Digital Inform.*, 5 (http://jodi.tamu.edu/Articles/v05/i01/DeBra/).

Dempsey, B., Weiss, D., Jones, P., and Greenberg, J. (1999). *A Quantitative Profile of a Community of Open Source Linux Developers*, http://www.ibiblio.org/osrt/develpro.html.

Derntl, M. and Motschnig-Pitrik, R. (2003). Conceptual modeling of reusable learning scenarios for person-centered e-learning. In *Proc. of the International Workshop on Interactive Computer Aided Learning (ICL 2003)*, September 24–26, Villach, Austria.

Dokeos. (2006). *Dokeos: Open Source Learning Management System*, http://www.dokeos.com/.

DotLearn. (2006). *LRN: Open Source Learning Management System*, http://www.dotlrn.org/.

ECLIPSE. (2006). *Open Source Development Platform and Application Frameworks for Building Software*, http://www.eclipse.org/.

Edubuntu. (2006). *Edubuntu: Linux for Young Human Beings*, http://www.edubuntu.org/.

ELGG. (2006). *Open Source 'Learning Landscape,'* http://elgg.net.

Feller, J. and Fitzgerald, B. (2002). *Understanding Open Source Software Development*. London: Addison-Wesley.*

Firefox. (2006). *Firefox Open Source Web Browser*, http://www.mozilla.com/firefox/.

Fowler, M. (2000). *UML Distilled*, 2nd ed. Upper Saddle River, NJ: Addison-Wesley.

FreeMind. (2006). *FreeMind: Free Mind Mapping Software*, http://freemind.sourceforge.net/wiki/index.php/Main_Page.

FSF-DEF. (2006). Free Software Foundation, http://www.fsf.org/licensing/essays/free-sw.html.

Gallivan, M. J. (2001). Striking a balance between trust and control in a virtual organization: a content analysis of open source software case studies. *Inform. Syst. J.*, 11(4), 277–304.

Gibbons, A. (2000). The Practice of Instructional Technology. Paper presented at the annual meeting of the Association for Educational Communications and Technology (AECT), February 18, Long Beach, CA (http://www.aect.org/intranet/publications/index.asp).

Gilbert, N. and Troitzsch, K. G. (1999). *Simulation for the Social Scientist*. Buckingham, U.K.: Open University Press.

GIMP. (2006). GNU Image Manipulation Program, http://www.gimp.org/.

GPL. (2006). General Public License, http://www.gnu.org/copyleft/gpl.html.

Griffiths, D., Blat, J., Garcia, R., Vogten, H., and Kwong, K. (2005). Learning design tools. In *Learning Design: A Handbook on Modelling and Delivering Networked Education and Training*, edited by R. Koper and C. Tattersall, pp. 109–136. Heidelberg: Springer-Verlag.

Hannay, N. B. and McGinn, R. E. (1980). Anatomy of modern technology: prolegomenon to an improved public policy for the social management of technology. *Daedalus*, 109(1), 25–53.

Hernández-Leo, D., Asensio-Pérez, J. I., and Dimitriadis, Y. (2006). Computational representation of collaborative learning flow patterns using IMS learning design. *Educ. Technol. Soc.*, 8(4), 75–89.

IMSLD. (2003). IMS Learning Design Specification, http://www.imsglobal.org/learningdesign/index.cfm.

Jones, A., Kukulska-Hulme, A., and Mwanza, D. (2005). Portable learning: experiences with mobile devices. *J. Interact. Media Educ.* (http://www-jime.open.ac.uk/2005/21/).

Joosten-Ten Brinke, D., Van Bruggen, J., Hermans, H., Latour, I., and Koper, R. (2005). Conceptual Model for Assessment. Paper presented at the European Association for Research in Learning and Instruction, August 23–27, Nicosia, Cyprus.

Jorgensen, N. (2001). Putting it all in the trunk: incremental software development in the FreeBSD Open Source Project. *Inform. Syst. J.*, 11(4), 321–336.

Knight, C., Gasevic, D., and Richards, G. (2006). An ontology-based framework for bridging learning design and learning content. *Educ. Technol. Soc.*, 9(1), 23–37.

Koch, N. and Wirsing, M. (2002). The Munich reference model for adaptive hypermedia applications. In *Proceedings of the AH'02 Adaptive Hypermedia and Adaptive Web-Based Systems*, May 29–31, Malaga, Spain, LNCS 2347. Heidelberg: Springer-Verlag.

Koper, E. J. R. (2005). Current research in learning design. *Educ. Technol. Soc.*, 9(1), 13–22.*

Koper, E. J. R. and Manderveld, J. M. (2004). Educational modelling language: modelling reusable, interoperable, rich and personalised units of learning. *Br. J. Educ. Technol.*, 35(5), 537–552.*

Koper, E. J. R. and Olivier, B. (2004). Representing the learning design of units of learning. *Educ. Technol. Soc.*, 7(3), 97–111.

Koper, E. J. R. and Tattersall, C. (2005). *Learning Design: A Handbook on Modelling and Delivering Networked Education and Training*. Heidelberg: Springer-Verlag.*

Krechmer, K. (2005). The Meaning of Open Standards. Paper presented at the 38th Hawaii Int. Conf. on System Sciences (HICSS'05), January 3–6, Big Island, Hawaii.

LAMS. (2006). *LAMS: Open Source Activity Management System*, http://www.lamsfoundation.org.

Lerner, J. and Triole, J. (2002). Some simple economics of open source. *J. Industr. Econ.*, 50(2), 197–234.

LiNex. (2006). Linux version developed and used in the Spanish region of Extremadura, http://www.linex.org/.

LionShare. (2006). *LionShare: Secure Peer-to-Peer Environment for the Sharing of Educational Resources*, http://lionshare.its.psu.edu/main/.

Madey, G., Freeh, V., and Tynan, R. (2002). The Open Source Software Development Phenomenon: An Analysis Based on Social Software Theory. Paper presented at the Eighth Americas Conference on Information Systems, August 9–11, Dallas, TX.

McGinn, R. E. (1978). What is technology? *Res. Philos. Technol.*, 1, 179–197.

Mitcham, C. (1994). *Thinking Through Technology: The Path between Engineering and Philosophy*. Chicago, IL: The University of Chicago Press.

Mockus, A., Fielding, R. T., and Herbsleb, J. D. (2002). Two case studies of open source software development: Apache and Mozilla. *ACM Trans. Software Eng. Methodol.*, 11(3), 309–346.*

Moodle. (2006). *Moodle: Open Source Learning Management System*, http://moodle.org.

OpenOffice.org. (2006). Open source office package, http://openoffice.org.

OSI-licenses. (2006). Open source licenses, http://www.opensource.org/licenses/index.php.

Pacurar, E. G., Trigano, P., and Alupoaie, S. (2004). A QTI editor integrated into the netUniversité Web portal using IMS LD. *J. Interact. Media Educ.*, 9 (http://www-jime.open.ac.uk/2004/1/editorial-2004–1–disc-paper.html#EditorialStart).

Paquette, G., De la Teja, I., Léonard, M., Lundgren-Cayrol, K., and Marino, O. (2005). An instructional engineering model and tool for the design of units of learning. In *Learning Design: A Handbook on Modelling and Delivering Networked Education and Training*, edited by R. Koper and C. Tattersall, pp. 161–184. Heidelberg: Springer-Verlag.*

Raymond, E. S. (1998). The cathedral and the bazaar. *First Monday*, 3, 1–33 (http://www.firstmonday.org/issues/issue3_3/raymond/index.html).

Raymond, E. S. (2001). *The Cathedral and the Bazaar*. Sebastopol, CA: O'Reilly.

RDF. (2003). Resource Description Format (RDF), http://www.w3c.org/RDF/.

Reigeluth, C. E. (1999). *Instructional-Design Theories and Models: A New Paradigm of Instructional Theory*, Vol. II. Mahwah, NJ: Lawrence Erlbaum Associates.*

Richey, R. C. and Nelson, W. A. (1996). Developmental research. In *Educational Communications and Technology*, edited by D. H. Jonassen, pp. 1213–1245. New York: Macmillan.

Rogers, E. M. (1995). *Diffusion of Innovations*. New York: The Free Press.

Sakai. (2006). Sakai open source learning management system, http://sakaiproject.org/.

Simon, H. A. (1969). *The Sciences of the Artificial*, 2nd ed. Cambridge, MA: MIT Press.

Skolelinux. (2006). Skolelinux open source Linux for education, http://www.skolelinux.org.

Tattersall, C., Vogten, H., and Hermans, H. (2005). The Edubox Learning Design Player. In *Learning Design: A Handbook on Modelling and Delivering Networked Education and Training*, edited by R. Koper and C. Tattersall, pp. 303–310. Heidelberg: Springer-Verlag.

TELCERT. (2006). European Union research and development project aimed at conformance testing of open learning technology standards, http://www.opengroup.org/telcert/.

Thunderbird. (2006). Thunderbird open source mail client, http://www.mozilla.com/thunderbird/.

Van Es, R. and Koper, E. J. R. (2005). Testing the pedagogical expressiveness of LD. *Educ. Technol. Soc.*, 9(1), 229–249.

Van Rosmalen, P., Brouns, F. M. R., Tattersall, C., Vogten, H., van Bruggen, J., and Sloep, P. B. (2005). Towards an open framework for adaptive, agent-supported e-learning. *Int. J. Contin. Eng. Educ. Life-Long Learn.*, 15(3–6), 261–275.

Vincenti, W. G. (1990). *What Engineers Know and How They Know It: Analytical Studies from Aeronautical History*. Baltimore: The Johns Hopkins University Press.

Vossen, G. and Westerkamp, P. (2003). e-Learning as a Web Service. Paper presented at the Seventh International Database Engineering and Applications Symposium (IDEAS'03), July 16–18, Hong Kong.

XML. (2003). Extensible Markup Language (XML), http://www.w3c.org/XML/.

Zarraonandia, T., Dodero, J. M., and Fernández, C. (2005). Crosscutting runtime adaptations of LD execution. *Educ. Technol. Soc.*, 9(1), 123–137.

---

\* Indicates a core reference.

# Part IV
## Models

This fourth part of the *Handbook* was led by Jeroen J.G. van Merriënboer and focuses on issues concerned with various types of and approaches to learning. These models of learning clearly inform design and development and can be linked to various instructional strategies covered in Part II. This part includes general models directed toward learning in schools, general models directed toward learning outside schools and at the workplace, and models that focus on learning in specific domains such as medicine, science, and reading. This part of the *Handbook* consists of 11 chapters covering these topics: (1) human cognitive architecture; (2) outcomes-oriented models; (3) cooperative learning models; (4) cognitive apprenticeship approaches; (5) whole-task models; (6) model-facilitated learning; (7) adaptive instructional systems; (8) problem-based learning; (9) performance improvement approaches; (10) resource-based training; and (11) domain-specific approaches. The final chapter in this section is one of the chapters in this *Handbook* that consists of multiple sections with different authors (all authors are recognized as chapter coauthors and section authors are recognized where appropriate).

# 31

# Human Cognitive Architecture

*John Sweller*
University of New South Wales, Sydney, Australia

## CONTENTS

John Sweller

## ABSTRACT

Cognitive load theory integrates the origins of human cognition in evolutionary theory with the structures and functions of human cognitive architecture to provide effective instructional design principles. Many of those principles are directly relevant to instructional technology. This chapter outlines the evolutionary bases for human cognitive architecture, examines those aspects of human cognition that are directly relevant to instruction, and discusses the various instructional principles generated by cognitive load theory with specific reference to their applicability to instructional technology.

## KEYWORDS

*Cognitive load theory:* An instructional design theory based on our knowledge of human cognitive architecture.

*Human cognitive architecture:* The manner in which structures and functions required for human cognitive processes are organized.

*Long-term memory:* The store holding all knowledge acquired during the processes of learning.

*Natural information processing system:* The procedures by which natural systems such as human cognition and evolution by natural selection process information.

*Working memory:* The structure that processes information coming from either the environment or long-term memory and that transfers learned information for storage in long-term memory.

## INTRODUCTION

The extent to which any instruction is effective depends heavily on whether it takes the characteristics of human cognition into account. To determine the conditions that maximize learning, we need to closely study human cognition. Once we have established the mechanisms of human cognition, including why those mechanisms have their particular characteristics, we are in a position to design learning environments in accord with human cognitive architecture. Ideal learning environments in accord with human cognitive architecture are not always in accord with realistic learning environments that mimic the real world. Indeed, if human cognition was organized in a manner that always favored learning in realistic over artificial environments, there would never be a need for specialized instructional procedures or even for educational

institutions. Observing and interacting with the world would provide the best educational environment. Under such conditions, all instruction would have to be as realistic as possible and would only be required for economic or safety reasons rather than for educational reasons. In contrast, it is suggested in this chapter that, because of the characteristics of human cognition, in many conditions learning is best facilitated by instruction that does not accurately model reality.

Cognitive load theory can be used to determine some of the characteristics of effective instruction. This integrated theory is intended to provide a systematically organized hierarchy leading from evolutionary/ biological reasons for the characteristics of human cognitive architecture to the instructional consequences that flow from that architecture. Only some of the instructional procedures generated by cognitive load theory are relevant to educational technology, and those procedures are emphasized in this chapter. We begin by discussing human cognitive architecture within an evolutionary and biological framework.

## HUMAN COGNITIVE ARCHITECTURE

Human cognition has evolved to assimilate, process, and use information (or knowledge, used synonymously in this chapter when dealing with human cognition) to direct human action. It constitutes an example of a natural information processing system that is a class of information processing systems that can be found in nature. As a natural information processing system, human cognition is hardly likely to be unique and, indeed, evolution by natural selection can itself be classed as a natural information processing system (Sweller, 2003, 2004; Sweller and Sweller, 2006). The characteristics of such systems will vary depending on their functions, but all natural information processing systems share an identical basic structure or framework. That basic structure in turn can be used to determine how humans deal with information and what types of instructional procedures, including technology-dependent instruction, are likely to be effective.

The essential characteristics of a natural information processing system include: (1) a very large store of information that allows the system to function in the varied environments faced by natural information processing systems; (2) procedures for perpetuating the store of information by transferring information from one entity to another; (3) procedures for changing the store by creating new information to deal with a changing environment; (4) procedures to ensure that changes to the store do not destroy its effectiveness; and (5) procedures to relate information to the external world. These core characteristics as applied to human cognition are discussed here in terms of five principles (Sweller and Sweller, 2006).

## The Information Store Principle and Human Long-Term Memory

Human long-term memory provides the human cognitive system with the large store of information indispensable to a natural information system. A species' genome has a similar function in biological evolution. Our knowledge of the function of long-term memory has altered over time, and, arguably, specifying the role of long-term memory constitutes the primary finding of the cognitive science revolution. We no longer see long-term memory as a repository of isolated, unrelated facts that are occasionally stored and retrieved; instead, it is the central structure of human cognitive architecture.

### Origins, Evidence, and Implications

De Groot's (1946/1965) work on expertise in the game of chess can be seen as the initial work transforming our perception of the role of long-term memory. De Groot found that, if chess masters are shown a board configuration taken from a real game for about 5 seconds, they can reproduce it much more accurately than weekend players. Chase and Simon (1973) reproduced this finding but also found that masters and weekend players did not differ in their ability to reproduce random board configurations. This difference between experts and novices in memory for real configurations and situations has been replicated in a variety of fields (Egan and Schwartz, 1979; Jeffries et al., 1981; Sweller and Cooper, 1985). Furthermore, it is the only reliable difference that has been obtained differentiating novices and experts in problem-solving skill and is the only difference required to fully explain why an individual is an expert in solving particular classes of problems. A chess master has learned to recognize many thousands of board configurations. When faced with a configuration, he or she recognizes it and knows the best move to make given that configuration. We all have that skill in our own areas of expertise and, indeed, the ability to recognize situations and the appropriate actions that they require constitutes our skill base in a given area.

Several implications flow from these findings. First, problem-solving skill is domain specific. A brilliant mathematician has acquired mathematical problem-solving skills that are unlikely to transfer to, for example, financial or personal relationship skills. The skills allow a mathematician to recognize mathematical problem states and the best moves associated with

them. Such skills are only useful in a mathematical context. Second, the work on novice–expert differences explains why it takes so long to become an expert in a substantial field. It takes about 10 years of concentrated work for a person to become a chess grand master (Simon and Gilmartin, 1973). During that time, the person is not learning complicated, general problem-solving strategies. There is no evidence that learnable or teachable general problem-solving strategies exist; rather, the chess player is learning to recognize the huge number of board configurations required for chess expertise, just as all of us are required to learn the huge number of problem situations required to acquire problem-solving skill in a particular area. Third, data on novice–expert differences demonstrate the central importance of knowledge or information held in long-term memory to skill in any area (Chi et al., 1982). To be skillful, we must have a huge stock of knowledge available. Based on this conceptualization, long-term memory is critical to skilled performance. Knowledge held in long-term memory allows us to function in the variety of contexts in which we find ourselves in much the same way as a genome allows a species to function biologically. Accordingly, a major function of instruction, including technology-based instruction, is to ensure that appropriate knowledge is held in long-term memory.

## The Borrowing Principle and Transferring Knowledge

Once discovered, information held by natural information processing systems must be perpetuated, and a primary function of education is to ensure that knowledge is not lost because, as will be discussed below, there are structural reasons why the act of discovery is inordinately difficult. In genetics, the store of DNA-based information is perpetuated over long periods of time by sexual and asexual reproduction. Asexual reproduction includes precise copying from one generation to the next and appears to have no cognitive equivalent. In contrast, sexual reproduction is a constructive procedure designed to ensure that offspring differ from their parents. This process has an inevitable random component, with the precise combination of genetic material from male and female ancestors being intrinsically unpredictable.

Psychological mechanisms are required equally to preserve information held in long-term memory by its transmission from individual to individual. Accordingly, we have evolved to both efficiently transmit and receive information from other humans in either auditory or visual form. We imitate what others do, listen to what they say, and read what they write. That skill permits knowledge held in an individual's long-term memory to be perpetuated indefinitely. Nevertheless, as is the case with sexual reproduction, the process is constructive in nature. We combine new information with information previously stored in long-term memory (Bartlett, 1932). As is also the case with sexual reproduction, the process has a random component in that we cannot predict precisely how the two sources of information will be combined. This randomness has implications for the narrow limits of change principle discussed below.

### Origins, Evidence, and Implications

A major function of instruction is to organize efficient procedures that will permit knowledge to be transferred to the long-term memories of learners. Cognitive load theory has generated a variety of instructional procedures relevant to technology-based instruction (see below). All are dependent on the borrowing principle. The success of cognitive load theory in generating instructional procedures is, at least in part, due to its emphasis on learning from presented information. That success provides some of the evidence for the borrowing principle.

In earlier eras, the suggestion that a function of education is to transfer knowledge would have been considered self-evident. More recently, an emphasis on discovery and constructivist procedures encouraged learners to *discover* knowledge rather than to have instructors *transmit* knowledge. The impossibility of discovering even a tiny fraction of the huge amount of information required in the modern world was partially obscured by the field's ignorance of the massive size of long-term memory. That ignorance is being rectified and increasing numbers of investigators are reacting against the previous orthodoxy (Kirschner et al., 2006; Klahr and Nigam, 2004; Mayer, 2004).

Our increasing knowledge of the importance of imitation in human learning provides additional evidence for the borrowing principle. The discovery of mirror neurons that fire in the same manner when we take an action, observe someone else make the same action, or even listen to a sentence describing the action provides neuropsychological evidence for the importance of imitation as a learning mechanism (Tettamanti et al., 2005).

## Randomness as Genesis Principle and Creating Knowledge

The need to transfer knowledge should not obscure the fact that knowledge must first be created to have something to transfer. In addition, circumstances change and current knowledge may no longer be ade-

quate. The procedure for changing the store of information held by natural information processing systems is standard. All creative changes are random, but only effective changes are retained, and ineffective changes are jettisoned. In evolution by natural selection, this mechanism is well accepted. Random mutation is the initial source of all genetic variation with only successful mutations resulting in reproduction and continuation. In psychology, and especially instructional psychology, the suggestion requires further explanation.

Random generation followed by effectiveness testing is unavoidable in functioning, natural information-processing systems. Consider a person solving a novel problem, an activity intended to create a solution that is new for that person. When deciding on a problem-solving move or a series of moves, the two basic categories of move generators are random generation and generation based on previous knowledge. These two categories or a combination of these two categories are the only source of move generation. Previously acquired knowledge held in long-term memory can act as a central executive determining moves, but, of course, that knowledge is not always available. There is no general central executive that can determine moves in the absence of relevant knowledge. Random generation, either mentally or in the real world, is left as the only other alternative.

### Origins, Evidence, and Implications

The origin of this principle is largely logical rather than empirical. If knowledge to determine a problem-solving move is unavailable, random generation followed by tests for effectiveness is the only other option. We can see the impact of this logic in computer models of problem solving. Such models (Sweller, 1988) randomly generate moves if information is lacking.

Does random generation mean that whether or not a novel problem is solved is entirely due to chance? Random generation can only function properly when coupled with effectiveness testing, and the combination of random generation and effectiveness testing provides the knowledge- or information-creating process of natural information-processing systems. By only accepting effective alterations to an information store and rejecting ineffective alterations, the effectiveness of the store can increase incrementally over time. By transferring the information in a store to other entities that can continue the process of random generation followed by effectiveness testing indefinitely, very complex, sophisticated stores can by built by natural information-processing systems. Both evolution by natural selection and human cognition provide examples. Nevertheless, it must be recognized that random generation followed by effectiveness testing is a very slow way of generating knowledge (Cooper and Sweller, 1987; Sweller and Cooper, 1985) and should only be used when the alternative procedure of knowledge transfer is unavailable. Knowledge transfer is vastly more effective. Accordingly, technology-based instruction requiring problem solving (random generation followed by effectiveness testing) can be expected to be less effective than instruction providing demonstrations (knowledge transfer via the borrowing principle).

## The Narrow Limits of Change and Human Working Memory

There are limits to knowledge creation. In the initial instance, knowledge creation occurs using the randomness as genesis principle, which requires random generation followed by effectiveness testing. Knowledge may be altered using the borrowing principle but that also involves random generation when new information is combined with old information. Mechanisms are required to ensure that any alterations to the store of information in long-term memory maximize the probability that a particular change will be effective and minimize the probability that a change will destroy the functionality of the store. These conditions are met by the use of a series of small, incremental changes, each tested for effectiveness, rather than a single, very large change.

Assume that the effectiveness is being tested of adding a permutation of 4 elements to the store. Assume further that no knowledge is available to eliminate some of the possible permutations or select others for priority testing. Under these circumstances, there are $4! = 24$ possible permutations. In contrast, assume that rather than 4 elements being under consideration there are 10. The number of possible permutations is $10! = 3,628,800$. If only a limited number or perhaps only one permutation is actually effective, dealing with more than a very small number of elements that must be combined randomly and tested for effectiveness is futile because the presence of any more elements rapidly leads to a combinatorial explosion that no natural information processing system can possibly handle unless it has prior knowledge.

### Origins, Evidence, and Implications

This factor alone explains some of the major characteristics of human cognitive architecture. When dealing with novel information for which there is no or limited prior knowledge, human working memory is extremely limited in capacity (Miller, 1956). Although the precise nature of this limitation has provided a source of research and discussion (Cowan, 2005), few would dispute the existence of the limitation. The consequences of this limitation have profound consequences for instructional design. Instructional designs that ignore this limitation are likely to be ineffective.

## The Environment Organizing and Linking Principle

This principle pertains to how we use information to function in our environment. In contrast to the limitations of working memory, when dealing with familiar information that is already organized in long-term memory, there is no functional reason for working memory to be limited. Accordingly, huge amounts of organized information can be transferred from long-term memory to working memory without overloading working memory (Ericsson and Kintsch, 1995). That information can then be used to allow us to function in our complex environment; for example, if readers attempt to reproduce from memory the immensely complex set of squiggles that constitute the last sentence, most will be able to do so effortlessly. We are able to do so because of the organized, schematic information held in long-term memory that can be transferred and used in working memory. That information allows us to read, process, organize, and relate text to the external world. Similarly, whereas changes to a genome must be small and incremental, huge amounts of previously organized genetic information can be used simultaneously to produce the complex proteins required for biological survival in a complex environment.

### Origins, Evidence, and Implications

This principle has multiple origins. Miller's (1956) evidence that multiple elements could be "chunked" together to act as a single element in working memory, schema theorists demonstrating that the manner in which we process information depends on previous knowledge (Bartlett, 1932), and, more recently, Ericsson and Kintsch's (1995) concept of long-term working memory all contribute to the environment organizing and linking principle. Such lines of research demonstrate how we use our large store of information to impose order and meaning on our environment. The environment organizing and linking principle provides the ultimate justification for human cognition. The purpose of the previous four principles is to permit cognition to occur so we can function mentally in our environment.

# COGNITIVE LOAD THEORY

These characteristics of human cognitive architecture have direct implications for instructional design and hence the design and purpose of technology-based instruction. The preferred characteristics of technology-based instruction can be determined by using cognitive load theory (Clark et al., 2006; Paas et al., 2003, 2004; Sweller, 2005a; van Merriënboer and Sweller, 2005), as well as closely related theories such as Mayer's theory of multimedia learning (Mayer, 2005) or van Merriënboer's (1997) 4C/ID model, which use this architecture to determine general instructional design principles. As might be expected, all theories that use this architecture are compatible and make similar or identical predications.

Cognitive load theory specifies two sources of cognitive (or working memory) load that determine the effectiveness of instruction. Extraneous cognitive load is due to inappropriate instructional designs and so must be reduced. If working memory resources are being fully expended, a reduction in extraneous cognitive load is required to permit an increase in germane cognitive load, a form of cognitive load that can result in useful alterations to long-term memory. These two sources of cognitive load determine the effectiveness of instruction, but a third source of cognitive load, intrinsic cognitive load, cannot be manipulated without compromising understanding. Intrinsic cognitive load (Sweller, 1994) can be thought of as the intrinsic complexity of the material being studied. For learners at a given level of expertise, that complexity can be reduced (Pollock et al., 2002) but only by reducing learners' understanding of the subject matter. Intrinsic cognitive load can, of course, also be reduced by learning (i.e., by testing learners with more expertise).

These sources of cognitive load are additive and cannot exceed the available capacity of working memory. If intrinsic cognitive load is low, it may be possible for germane cognitive load to be high even with inappropriate instructional techniques causing a high extraneous cognitive load. The low intrinsic cognitive load is likely to leave sufficient working memory resources for students to learn even with a poor instructional design. In contrast, if intrinsic cognitive load is high due to high complexity material, unless the extraneous cognitive load is low there may be insufficient working memory capacity to permit a level of germane cognitive load that can result in learning. With a high intrinsic cognitive load, it is essential to keep the extraneous cognitive load low to permit a sufficient level of germane cognitive load. In other words, instructional design becomes critical with complex material.

Based on the cognitive architecture outlined above, extraneous cognitive load can be reduced and germane cognitive load increased by assisting learners to transfer information to long-term memory. Novel information coming from the senses is not organized and imposes a heavy load on working memory (the narrow limits of change principle). Information coming from long-term memory is organized and imposes a minimal load on working memory (the environment organising and linking principle). In other words, once learned, information no longer imposes a working memory load. How should we assist learners to transfer novel information to long-term memory? Wherever possible, that information should be in an organized form so learners do not have to expend working memory resources in imposing an organizational structure. Almost all information that learners must acquire has previously been laboriously organized over many generations using the randomness as genesis principle outlined above. Nothing is gained by requiring learners in an instructional setting to attempt to use random generation followed by tests of effectiveness rather than the borrowing principle.

Contrary to much current educational dogma (Kirschner et al., 2006; Mayer, 2004) and as indicated above, our cognitive architecture strongly facilitates learning through knowledge transfer via the borrowing principle rather than knowledge generation via the randomness as genesis principle. Not only should knowledge be presented to learners rather than have them engage in the impossible task of attempting to generate it themselves, but it should also be presented in a manner that reduces extraneous cognitive load and maximizes germane cognitive load. Cognitive load theory, making use of the borrowing principle, has generated a range of techniques intended to achieve this purpose. Most of those techniques are relevant to technology-based instruction and will be discussed next. Each technique has been studied as an experimental effect using randomized, controlled experiments in which an instructional technique generated by cognitive load theory is compared to an alternative, usually more traditional technique. These effects provide the instructional recommendations generated by cognitive load theory.

## Cognitive Load Theory Effects and Technology-Based Instruction

### Worked Example Effect

The worked example effect (Sweller and Cooper, 1985) occurs when novice learners studying worked solutions to problems perform better on a problem-solving test than learners who have been given the equivalent problems to solve during training. This effect flows directly from the cognitive architecture described above. When solving an unfamiliar problem, problem solvers have no choice but to use a random generation followed by effectiveness testing procedure at those choice points where they have insufficient knowledge to direct choice. The working memory load associated with using an effective problem-solving procedure will interfere with learning (Cooper and Sweller, 1987; Paas and van Merriënboer, 1994) and so constitutes an extraneous cognitive load. In contrast, using the borrowing rather than the randomness as genesis principle should enhance learning. Showing learners how to solve problems via worked examples by providing an organized structure rather than leaving learners to devise their own organization using their limited capacity working memory should minimize extraneous cognitive load. Findings from a large number of studies carried out by many researchers in the 1980s and 1990s provided strong support for these hypotheses.

There is every reason to suppose that the worked example effect should apply directly to technology-based instruction. Consider a computer-based simulation. A simulation should demonstrate a process or procedure. It should not require learners to solve novel problems even if problem solving is part of the process being simulated. The aim of a simulation demonstrating problem solving should be identical to the aim of any other instruction in problem solving, and that aim is to assist learners in acquiring knowledge in long-term memory concerning the problem-solving procedures relevant to that particular problem. Once that knowledge is acquired, learners will recognize the problem as belonging to a category requiring particular moves for solution (Chi et al., 1982). Searching for novel solutions using random generation followed by effectiveness testing as part of a simulation is no more likely to achieve this aim than searching for novel solutions in any other instructional context. Using the borrowing principle, a good simulation can eliminate randomness by precisely indicating the structure of what needs to be learned. (Practicing familiar problem solutions has a different function and is discussed below in the section on the expertise reversal effect.)

### Split-Attention Effect

Assume that the material being presented to learners consists of two or more sources of information. Assume further, that the sources of information are unintelligible in isolation and can only be understood in conjunction with each other. A geometry worked example provides an instance. The diagram tells novice learners little if anything of the problem solution, and the asso-

ciated statements are likely to be unintelligible without reference to the diagram. To understand the material, learners must mentally integrate the two sources of information. Mental integration requires working memory resources to be used to search for appropriate references between the multiple sources of information. That search process is indistinguishable from the random generation followed by effectiveness testing of problem solving. All searches not based on knowledge require the randomness as genesis principle. If a geometry solution includes the statement "angle ABC," then learners must randomly choose an angle and test whether it is angle ABC, with the process continuing until the angle is found. Little can be expected to be learned by this use of working memory resources. In contrast, borrowing other people's knowledge can reduce extraneous cognitive load. If the instructions are physically integrated so "angle ABC" is clearly associated with the appropriate angle, obviating the need to search for the angle, then extraneous cognitive load should be reduced and learning enhanced. That result also has been obtained on numerous occasions (Ayres and Sweller, 2005; Sweller et al., 1990). It must be emphasized that the split-attention effect *only* occurs when multiple sources of information must be integrated before they can be understood. Multiple sources of information that can be understood in isolation should not be physically integrated. Different instructional procedures are required when multiple sources of information can be understood in isolation and are discussed in the Redundancy Effect section.

Technology-based instruction that ignores the split-attention effect is likely to be less than effective; for example, a simulation demonstrating the functions of a mechanical device in which the function of a part of the device can only be understood in relation to the function of another part of the device runs the risk of split attention. Whenever possible, the simulation should be structured to clearly indicate the relation between the two parts. In addition, any written text should be formatted in a manner that reduces or eliminates a search for referents. Learners should not be left to work out relations between aspects of a simulation. Working memory resources can be better employed.

### Modality Effect

This effect occurs under the same conditions as the split-attention effect in that both effects occur under conditions with multiple sources of information that cannot be understood in isolation and so must be integrated (Low and Sweller, 2005). The effect relies on a particular characteristic of working memory. In the previous discussion of human cognition, working memory was treated as a unitary concept; in fact, it is best thought of as consisting of multiple channels or processors (Baddeley, 1992). A visual processor for dealing with two- or three-dimensional objects and an auditory processor for dealing with language are partially independent. As a consequence, the simultaneous use of both processors can expand the effective size of working memory, under some circumstances. One of those circumstances consists of the conditions leading to the split-attention effect—namely, multiple sources of information that must be integrated before they can be understood. Under those conditions, the use of both the auditory and visual processor can expand the effective size of working memory in an instructionally favorable manner.

Consider a geometry example again as discussed above. To understand a geometry worked example, the learner must simultaneously consider both the diagram and the text because neither conveys the required meaning in isolation. By presenting the verbal information in spoken rather than written form, working memory can be effectively expanded because information is shifted from the overloaded visual processor to be shared by both the visual (for the diagram) and auditory (for the text) processors. According to cognitive load theory, such an expansion of effective working memory should facilitate learning. Tindall-Ford et al. (1997) demonstrated the modality effect when learners presented with instructions in a visual, split-attention format learned less than learners presented with the same material but with all of the verbal information presented in spoken rather than written form.

The modality effect is directly applicable to technology-based instruction. Whereas an aspect of technology-based instruction requires verbal input to be intelligible, extraneous cognitive load can be reduced by using spoken rather than written text. The use of spoken text is particularly important during an animation. The expansion of effective working memory due to the use of both the auditory and visual processors can permit an animation to be viewed while simultaneously attending to speech that explains otherwise unintelligible aspects of the animation. The use of written rather than spoken text runs the risk of overloading the visual processor. In contrast, appropriate use of both visual and auditory information can maximize the potentially powerful effects of the borrowing principle.

### Redundancy Effect

The previous two effects discussed, the split-attention and modality effects, apply to multiple sources of information, each of which is unintelligible in isola-

tion. In contrast, the redundancy effect applies to multiple sources of information that are intelligible in isolation. That difference in the logical relation between sources of information results in quite different instructional consequences. The difference is important because frequently, on the surface, conditions that lead to the split-attention or redundancy effects can look identical. It is only by considering the relation between the multiple sources of information that the appropriate instructional recommendations can be provided.

In the current context, redundant information is defined as any information that is not relevant to learning. Most commonly, redundant information consists of the same information presented in different forms or media such as presenting the same verbal information in spoken and written form, but it can also consist of any unnecessary, additional information such as decorative pictures, background sound, or cartoons.

In instructional contexts, redundancy can frequently be found when textual information repeats information found in a diagram. A diagram indicating the flow of blood in the heart, lungs, and body along with a statement that "blood flows from the left ventricle to the aorta" provides an example of redundancy (Chandler and Sweller, 1991). Although a geometry diagram and its associated statements would appear, on the surface, to have the same properties and hence are governed by the same instructional principles as a blood flow diagram and its associated statements, they are structurally very different and require very different formatting. A geometry diagram tells us little of a problem solution and requires the statements for an intelligible solution to be communicated to learners. Those statements must be integrated with the diagram so a search for referents is reduced. In contrast, the blood flow diagram can be fully intelligible in its own right and provide a full explanation. The appropriate instructional procedure is not to integrate the statements with the diagram but rather to eliminate the least effective source of information, which, in this case, is the set of statements. Many experimental examples demonstrate that the elimination of redundancy facilitates learning (Chandler and Sweller, 1991).

Although the redundancy effect can be considered counter-intuitive, from a cognitive load theory perspective the reason why redundant information has negative consequences is straightforward. Attending to unnecessary information and attempting to integrate it with essential information requires working memory resources that consequently are unavailable for learning. Redundant information imposes an extraneous cognitive load. It is an ineffective use of the borrowing principle.

There are many forms of redundancy other than the diagram and text redundancy described above (for a detailed summary, see Sweller, 2005b). All forms of redundancy potentially apply to technology-based instruction; for example, a spoken commentary associated with a simulation should only be included if the visual material is unintelligible without the commentary. If visual material is intelligible in isolation, a spoken commentary will increase cognitive load as learners attempt to integrate the auditory and visual information. When devising a simulation, care must be taken to ensure that all information presented is essential and not simply an alternative way of presenting the same information. Equally damaging is additional information that bears little or no relation to the required information. It is a trap to assume that additional information will, at worst, be neutral in its effect and could be beneficial.

Increasing technical sophistication is permitting increasingly realistic simulations. By definition, the real world is realistic, but we developed instructional systems precisely because many aspects of the real world provide inadequate instruction. That inadequacy frequently is caused by redundancy. A realistic simulation that provides a depiction of a mechanical system may be indistinguishable from the real mechanical system, but that system may be almost useless as an instructional tool. When learning how the blood flows in the heart, lungs, and body, most of the structures, functions, and characteristics of the body are irrelevant, which is why it took so long to discover the processes of the circulatory system using the randomness as genesis principle. The "realistic" but irrelevant features served to conceal the critical features. Realistic features and processes should not be included in a simulation if the sole reason for inclusion is realism. To avoid redundancy and maximize the effect of the borrowing principle, there should be a clear instructional reason for including any information.

### Expertise Reversal Effect

Two related points must be made concerning the discussion of the previous effects. First, all of the above effects assume that learners are novices. It is novices who most frequently require instruction via the borrowing principle. Second, the previous explanation of the redundancy effect implicitly assumed that redundancy is purely a function of the materials being used; in fact, it is equally a function of levels of expertise. Information that is redundant for a more expert learner may be critically necessary for a less expert learner. A novice may need to borrow information from someone else, an expert may not. The expertise reversal effect was born from these considerations.

The effect occurs when an instructional procedure that is relatively effective for novices compared to a control procedure first loses its advantage as levels of expertise increase and then begins to be worse than the control procedure with further increases in expertise (Kalyuga et al., 2003). As an instance, studying worked examples is better than solving the equivalent problems for novices, but with increased expertise solving problems becomes better than studying examples (Kalyuga et al., 2001). As other instances, for novices, integrated format or dual-modality instruction is better than split-attention format instruction. With increasing expertise, rather than integrating, for example, diagrams and text or using dual-modality instruction, it is better to eliminate the text entirely (Kalyuga et al., 1998, 2000).

The expertise reversal effect is a complex effect that relies on redundancy. As expertise increases, previously essential information becomes redundant and so imposes an extraneous cognitive load. Studying worked examples may be essential for novices to reduce cognitive load, but such activity becomes redundant with increasing expertise and is better replaced by practice at solving problems which, at higher levels of expertise, no longer imposes a cognitive load. Similarly, explanatory text may be essential for novices and so should be physically integrated with diagrams or presented in spoken form to reduce extraneous cognitive load. With increasing expertise, the text becomes redundant and should be eliminated.

The expertise reversal effect suggests that the detail provided in technology-based instruction should be determined by the knowledge base of the learners. Details that are essential for novices may be redundant for more expert learners. Thus, technology-based instruction must be constructed so its specifications change with changes in expertise. Furthermore, if instructional materials are to change with changes in expertise, a method is required to rapidly determine levels of expertise. Kalyuga and Sweller (2004) provided a rapid test of knowledge based on the cognitive architecture described above. During instruction, learners were presented a partially completed problem and asked to indicate the next step required for solution. The extent to which a learner knows the next step to solution depends on the knowledge base held in long-term memory. That information can be used to determine subsequent instruction. It should similarly be possible to use this rapid assessment technique to determine the nature of any subsequent instruction.

### Guidance Fading Effect

The guidance fading effect (Renkl and Atkinson, 2003; Renkl et al., 2004) is closely related to the worked example and expertise reversal effects and is also a compound effect. It occurs when novices are initially presented with worked examples, but with increasing expertise those worked examples are replaced by completion problems (van Merriënboer et al., 2002) in which a partial solution is provided and the learner is required to complete the problem. With further increases in expertise, the completion problems should be replaced by full problems. Again, this sequence is predicated on the assumption that what constitutes an extraneous cognitive load depends not just on the nature of the instruction but on an interaction between the instructional procedures and learner characteristics in the form of levels of expertise. At low levels of expertise, the learner must make heavy use of other people's knowledge via the borrowing principle. With increasing expertise, the same information can be borrowed from the learner's own long-term memory and used for practice purposes.

Technology-based instruction should take account of the guidance fading effect by initially providing substantial guidance which should be gradually faded as expertise increases. As an example, initially, learners should be shown exactly what they need to do with minimal action required on their part. With increases in expertise, determined by rapid assessment techniques, learner activity should be increased and guidance decreased. Ultimately, it should be possible to remove all guidance with the learner simply practicing the skill.

## Imagination Effect

The imagination effect occurs when learners who are asked to imagine a procedure or concept learn more than learners who are asked to study the same procedure or concept (Cooper et al., 2001; Leahy and Sweller, 2005). Imagination instructions ask learners to turn away from the material and attempt to imagine the relevant procedures or concepts. Imagining involves running material through working memory which should assist in the transfer of the information to long-term memory. The technique is highly effective but only when used by learners with sufficient experience in the domain to be able to process all of the necessary information in working memory without assistance from the instructional material. For novices, attempts to run a procedure through working memory are likely to fail, so instructions to study material, which involves considering it while looking at it, are superior to imagination instructions. The switch from studying being superior to imagination being superior provides another example of the expertise reversal effect. Again, as was the case for the expertise reversal

and guidance fading effects, for novices information is best borrowed from another person's long-term memory, but as levels of expertise increase that information can be borrowed from one's own long-term memory for purposes of practice, in this case mental practice.

The imagination effect provides information on what mental activity learners should be engaged in when dealing with a simulation. Initially, they should simply study or interact with the simulation materials because due to working memory limitations they are unlikely to have sufficient knowledge to be able to effectively imagine the procedures and concepts. With increasing expertise, they should attempt to imagine the information covered by the instruction because that procedure seems to be the most rapid technique for transferring information to long-term memory and so increasing levels of expertise.

## Element Interactivity Effect

The expertise reversal effect discussed above places an emphasis on the cognitive load implications of individual differences in expertise. Differences in the structure of the information being considered are equally important. None of the above effects is obtainable using low-complexity material (Sweller, 1994) that has a low intrinsic cognitive load. Recall that total cognitive load is an addition of extraneous, intrinsic, and germane cognitive load. The above effects are primarily determined by an excessive extraneous cognitive load that reduces germane cognitive load because working memory capacity is exceeded. If intrinsic cognitive load is low, a high extraneous cognitive load may not matter a great deal. There may be sufficient working memory capacity available to enable germane cognitive load and its attendant rapid learning to occur.

What determines levels of intrinsic cognitive load? The only relevant factor within a cognitive load theory framework is element interactivity, which is determined by the number of interacting elements that must be considered simultaneously to understand the material. Some information is low in element interactivity in that the elements can be learned one element at a time without considering any other elements. Learning technical terminology provides an example. One can learn the name of a component without learning the names of any other components, so working memory load may be very low. Cognitive load effects are not likely to be relevant when intrinsic cognitive load is low. In contrast, learning how components interact in a machine has high element interactivity because it may be impossible to understand the function of one component without simultaneously considering the function of all of the components. High element interactivity results in a high intrinsic cognitive load, leaving little working memory capacity available for learning. Under these circumstances, levels of extraneous cognitive load become critical, and the cognitive load effects discussed above become relevant; thus, cognitive load effects become critical when technology-based instruction deals with complex, high element interactivity material.

### *Isolated Interacting Elements Effect*

When element interactivity is very high, it may be impossible for learners to understand the material because it may be impossible for them to simultaneously process all of the interacting elements in working memory. How should such material be presented? From a cognitive load theory perspective, the only way seems to be to initially present the material as individual elements ignoring their interactions. This procedure will permit the elements to be learned but without understanding. Once the individual elements have been learned, their interactions can be emphasized. It is only at that point that the material will be understood because it cannot be understood by simply considering individual elements. Empirical work has demonstrated that teaching individual elements first, at the expense of understanding, followed by teaching the interactions between elements results in more effective learning than attempting to have learners understand very high element interactivity material right from the beginning of instruction (Pollock et al., 2002).

The isolated, interacting elements effect may have considerable relevance to technology-based instruction such as instructional simulations. Material is difficult to understand because it is high in element interactivity. Presenting that material in a realistic fashion during a simulation may be condemning learners to attempting to understand information that vastly exceeds their working memory capacity because a realistic simulation may involve a huge number of interacting elements. A less realistic simulation with fewer interacting elements may be more readily understood and learned. Although a full understanding of the material is impossible by this technique, it is equally impossible to process a large number of interacting elements simultaneously. It may be better to provide simulations that result in limited understanding initially, followed by more complete versions that permit full understanding. In this manner, learners may be spared the need to attempt to understand material that is quite impossible for them to deal with.

## DISCUSSION

Cognitive load theory provides an integrated system dealing with the evolutionary origins of human cognition leading to an explanation of cognitive structures and processes. In turn, those structures and processes can be used to generate instructional principles. The generation of applications in the form of instructional principles provides some warrant for the validity of the original cognitive architecture. This unified system can provide a base for instructional design including the structure and function of technology-based instruction.

There are two aspects of technology-based education in general and of the work reported in this chapter that require emphasis. First, the use of technology in education should not be based merely on the availability of technology. There is a long history of new technological applications such as radio, films, television, mainframe computers attached to terminals, stand-alone microcomputers and now the Web being hailed as potentially revolutionizing education. Frequently, these technological advances have had minimal, long-term educational impact. While technology changes, human cognitive architecture does not. The introduction of educational technology without reference to its cognitive consequences is unlikely to be effective. The five natural information processing principles outlined above provide an initial guide. According to those principles, learning consists of changes to the long-term store, the most efficient method of bringing about those changes is by borrowing knowledge from knowledgeable educators, and that knowledge must be structured in a manner that reduces working memory load. I am not aware of any evidence that simply using technology will necessarily conform to any of the five principles. Instruction that ignores human cognitive architecture is likely to be ineffective whether or not it uses technology. In contrast, technology-based instruction that is explicitly structured to conform to what we know of human cognition has a much better chance of being effective.

All of the cognitive load effects discussed above were based on the assumption that the aim of instruction is the acquisition of knowledge in long-term memory and that the best way of achieving this aim is to make use of the borrowing principle by providing direct instructional guidance organized to reduce extraneous working memory load.

The second point that requires emphasis concerns how we determine whether technology-based education is effective. The instructional effects described above were not only based on our knowledge of human cognitive architecture but also were tested using controlled, randomized experimental designs. Experiments in which participants are randomly allocated to two or more experimental groups with different instructional procedures but identical test procedures are essential when determining effective instructional procedures in this field. Verification procedures in which instructors and learners are presented instruction using a new technology and simply asked if they think it is effective or if they enjoyed it have very limited utility.

While cognitive load theory indicates many conditions under which instruction may or may not be effective, those conditions are closely dependent on the cognitive architecture discussed and, specifically, on the characteristics of working and long-term memory. The theory is not intended as a general theory of cognition or of instruction, and so many important variables are not considered by the theory; for example, despite some discussion about including motivational variables in cognitive load theory and considering this issue in future research, at present it has not been incorporated into the theory. That incorporation will, in all probability, only occur if relations between cognitive architecture and motivation can be established.

In conclusion, advances in instructional technology have provided us with the ability to use instructional procedures that until recently were difficult or impossible to implement. Frequently, those procedures have been recommended purely because they are now possible rather than because there was evidence for their cognitive effectiveness or even desirability. Cognitive load theory is intended to provide a guide to the types of techniques that are likely to work. It has been tested using controlled, randomized experiments over many years by many investigators in a wide variety of technology-based environments. There is every reason to suppose that the use of our knowledge of human cognition will continue to generate technology-based instructional procedures.

## ACKNOWLEDGMENTS

The work reported here was supported under Office of Naval Research Award Number #N00014-04-1-0209, as administered by the Office of Naval Research. The findings and opinions expressed in this report do not necessarily reflect the positions or policies of the Office of Naval Research.

## REFERENCES

Ayres, P. and Sweller, J. (2005). The split-attention principle. In *Cambridge Handbook of Multimedia Learning*, edited by R. E. Mayer, pp. 135–136. Cambridge, U.K.: Cambridge University Press.*

Baddeley, A. (1992). Working memory. *Science*, 255, 556–559.*

Bartlett, F. (1932). *Remembering: A Study in Experimental and Social Psychology*. Cambridge, U.K.: Cambridge University Press.

Chandler, P. and Sweller, J. (1991). Cognitive load theory and the format of instruction. *Cogn. Instruct.*, 8, 293–332.

Chase, W. G. and Simon, H. A. (1973). Perception in chess. *Cogn. Psychol.*, 4, 55–81.

Chi, M., Glaser, R., and Rees, E. (1982). Expertise in problem solving. In *Advances in the Psychology of Human Intelligence*, edited by R. Sternberg, pp. 7–75. Hillsdale, NJ: Lawrence Erlbaum Associates.

Clark, R., Nguyen, F., and Sweller, J. (2006). *Efficiency in Learning: Evidence-Based Guidelines to Manage Cognitive Load*. San Francisco, CA: Pfeiffer.*

Cooper, G. and Sweller, J. (1987). The effects of schema acquisition and rule automation on mathematical problem-solving transfer. *J. Educ. Psychol.*, 79, 347–362.

Cooper, G., Tindall-Ford, S., Chandler, P., and Sweller, J. (2001). Learning by imagining. *J. Exp. Psychol. Appl.*, 7, 68–82.

Cowan, N. (2005). *Working Memory Capacity*. Oxford, U.K.: Psychology Press.*

De Groot, A. (1946/1965). *Thought and Choice in Chess*. The Hague: Mouton.

Egan, D. E. and Schwartz B. J. (1979). Chunking in recall of symbolic drawings. *Memory Cogn.*, 7, 149–158.

Ericsson, K. A. and Kintsch, W. (1995). Long-term working memory. *Psychol. Rev.*, 102, 211–245.*

Jeffries, R., Turner, A., Polson, P., and Atwood, M. (1981). Processes involved in designing software. In *Cognitive Skills and Their Acquisition*, edited by J. R. Anderson, pp. 255–283. Hillsdale, NJ: Lawrence Erlbaum Associates.

Kalyuga, S. and Sweller, J. (2004). Measuring knowledge to optimize cognitive load factors during instruction. *J. Educ. Psychol.*, 96, 558–568.

Kalyuga, S., Chandler, P., and Sweller, J. (1998). Levels of expertise and instructional design. *Hum. Factors*, 40, 1–17.

Kalyuga, S., Chandler, P., and Sweller, J. (2000). Incorporating learner experience into the design of multimedia instruction. *J. Educ. Psychol.*, 92, 126–136.

Kalyuga, S., Chandler, P., Tuovinen, J. E., and Sweller, J. (2001). When problem solving is superior to studying worked examples. *J. Educ. Psychol.*, 93, 579–588.

Kalyuga, S., Ayres, P., Chandler, P., and Sweller, J. (2003). Expertise reversal effect. *Educ. Psychol.*, 38, 23–31.

Kirschner, P., Sweller, J., and Clark, R. (2006). Why minimal guidance during instruction does not work: an analysis of the failure of constructivist, discovery, problem-based, experiential and inquiry-based teaching. *Educ. Psychol.*, 41, 75–86.

Klahr, D. and Nigam, M. (2004). The equivalence of learning paths in early science instruction: effects of direct instruction and discovery learning. *Psychol. Sci.*, 15, 661–667.

Leahy, W. and Sweller, J. (2005). Interactions among the imagination, expertise reversal and element interactivity effects. *J. Exp. Psychol. Appl.*, 11, 266–276.*

Low, R. and Sweller, J. (2005). The modality principle. In *Cambridge Handbook of Multimedia Learning*, edited by R. E. Mayer, pp. 147–158. Cambridge, U.K.: Cambridge University Press.

Mayer, R. E. (2004). Should there be a three-strikes rule against pure discovery learning? The case for guided methods of instruction. *Am. Psychol.*, 59, 14–19.

Mayer, R. E. (2005). Cognitive theory of multimedia learning. In *Cambridge Handbook of Multimedia Learning*, edited by R. E. Mayer, pp. 31–48. Cambridge, U.K.: Cambridge University Press.*

Miller, G. A. (1956). The magical number seven, plus or minus two: some limits on our capacity for processing information. *Psychol. Rev.*, 63, 81–97.

Paas, F. and van Merriënboer, J. J. G. (1994). Variability of worked examples and transfer of geometrical problem solving skills: a cognitive-load approach. *J. Educ. Psychol.*, 86, 122–133.

Paas, F., Renkl, A., and Sweller, J. (2003). Cognitive load theory and instructional design: recent developments. *Educ. Psychol.*, 38, 1–4.*

Paas, F., Renkl, A., and Sweller, J. (2004). Cognitive load theory: instructional implications of the interaction between information structures and cognitive architecture. *Instruct. Sci.*, 32, 1–8.

Pollock, E., Chandler, P., and Sweller, J. (2002). Assimilating complex information. *Learn. Instruct.*, 12, 61–86.

Renkl, A. and Atkinson, R. (2003). Structuring the transition from example study to problem solving in cognitive skill acquisition: a cognitive load perspective. *Educ. Psychol.*, 38, 15–22.

Renkl, A., Atkinson, R., and Große, C. (2004). How fading worked solution steps works: a cognitive load perspective. *Instruct. Sci.*, 32, 59–82.

Simon, H. A. and Gilmartin, K. (1973). A simulation of memory for chess positions. *Cogn. Psychol.*, 5, 29–46.

Sweller, J. (1988). Cognitive load during problem solving: effects on learning. *Cogn. Sci.*, 12, 257–285.*

Sweller, J. (1994). Cognitive load theory, learning difficulty and instructional design. *Learn. Instruct.*, 4, 295–312.*

Sweller, J. (2003). Evolution of human cognitive architecture. In *The Psychology of Learning and Motivation*, Vol. 43, edited by B. Ross, pp. 215–266. San Diego, CA: Academic Press.*

Sweller, J. (2004). Instructional design consequences of an analogy between evolution by natural selection and human cognitive architecture. *Instruct. Sci.*, 32, 9–31.

Sweller, J. (2005a). Implications of cognitive load theory for multimedia learning. In *Cambridge Handbook of Multimedia Learning*, edited by R. E. Mayer, pp. 19–30. Cambridge, U.K.: Cambridge University Press.

Sweller, J. (2005b). The redundancy principle. In *Cambridge Handbook of Multimedia Learning*, edited by R. E. Mayer, pp. 159–167. Cambridge, U.K.: Cambridge University Press.

Sweller, J. and Cooper, G. A. (1985). The use of worked examples as a substitute for problem solving in learning algebra. *Cogn. Instruct.*, 2, 59–89.

Sweller, J. and Sweller, S. (2006). Natural information processing systems. *Evol. Psychol.*, 4, 434–458.

Sweller, J., Chandler, P., Tierney, P., and Cooper, M. (1990). Cognitive load and selective attention as factors in the structuring of technical material. *J. Exp. Psychol. Gen.*, 119, 176–192.

Tettamanti, M., Buccino, G., Saccuman, M., Gallese, V., Danna, M., Scifo, P., Fazio, F., Rizzolatti, G., Cappa, S., and Perani, D. (2005). Listening to action-related sentences activates fronto-parietal motor circuits. *J. Cogn. Neurosci.*, 17, 273–281.

Tindall-Ford, S., Chandler, P., and Sweller, J. (1997). When two sensory modes are better than one. *J. Exp. Psychol. Appl.*, 3, 257–287.

Van Merriënboer, J. J. G. (1997). *Training Complex Cognitive Skills*. Englewood Cliffs, NJ: Educational Technology Publications.*

Van Merriënboer, J. J. G. and Sweller, J. (2005). Cognitive load theory and complex learning: recent developments and future directions. *Educ. Psychol. Rev.*, 17, 147–177.*

Van Merriënboer, J. J. G., Schuurman, J., de Croock, M., and Paas, F. (2002). Redirecting learner's attention during training: effects on cognitive load, transfer test performance and training efficiency. *Learn. Instruct.*, 12, 11–37.

---

* Indicates a core reference.

# 32

# Outcome-Referenced, Conditions-Based Theories and Models

*Tillman J. Ragan and Patricia L. Smith*
University of Oklahoma, Norman, Oklahoma

*L. K. Curda*
University of West Florida, Pensacola, Florida

## CONTENTS

Tillman J. Ragan, Patricia L. Smith, and L. K. Curda

## ABSTRACT

One of the most influential and pervasive theories underlying instructional design proposes that (1) there are identifiably different types of learning outcomes, and (2) the acquisition of these outcomes requires different internal and external conditions of learning. These propositions underlie an *outcome-referenced, conditions-based* paradigm of instructional design (ID). The outcome-referenced, conditions-based perspective is commonplace, if not universal, in current instructional psychology and instructional design thinking, even when the author's orientation and values are not based on the cognitive science that underlies this perspective. Whether or not individuals formally subscribe to or have an interest in these theories and models, it is part of the everyday work of instructional designers and scholars of instruction and learning environments. This chapter (1) presents the assumptions of the outcome-referenced, conditions-based perspective, (2) describes prevalent theories and models within this tradition, and (3) provides future directions for research and development.

## KEYWORDS

*Conditions-based instruction:* Described by Robert Gagné (1985) as (1) internal and external conditions of learning; (2) states possessed by the learner such as prior knowledge are internal conditions, and instructional supports that are designed to promote learning are external conditions.

*Learning hierarchy:* Description of successively achievable intellectual skills, each stated as a performance class in which achievement of a superordinate skill is in part dependent on the internal condition of having learned necessary subordinate skills.

*Outcome-referenced models:* Approaches to instructional design in which (1) consideration of the nature of the learning tasks and the conditions required to support them are central, and (2) learning outcomes are categorized to represent not only qualitative differences in the acquired capability (as a category of task or goal) but also external conditions that support learning and different learner states—the latter are referred to as *internal conditions*, which also facilitate learning.

## INTRODUCTION

One of the most influential and pervasive theories underlying instructional design proposes that (1) there are identifiably different types of learning outcomes, and (2) the acquisition of these outcomes requires different internal and external conditions of learning. In other words, this theory suggests that all learning is not qualitatively the same, that learning outcomes across contents, contexts, and learners have significant and identifiable similarities in their cognitive demands on the learner. Furthermore, each learning outcome category significantly differs from the other learning outcome categories in terms of its cognitive demands on the learner. Finally, as this family of theories is instructional in nature, they propose that these distinctive cognitive processing demands can be supported by equally distinctive instructional methods, strategies, tactics, or conditions.

These propositions underlie what Wilson and Cole (1991) term a *conditions-of-learning* paradigm of instructional design. Models of instructional design that follow an outcome-referenced, conditions-based theory are predicated upon the seminal principles of Robert Gagné (1965) that: (1) learning can be classified into categories that require similar cognitive activities for learning (Gagné termed these *internal conditions of learning*), and, therefore, (2) within these categories of learning, similar instructional supports are needed to facilitate learning (Gagné termed these *external conditions of learning*).

The influence of an outcome-referenced, conditions-based perspective can be found in the task analysis, strategy development, assessment, and evaluation procedures of conditions-based instructional design; however, the point at which the outcome-referenced, conditions-based perspective has the greatest influence and most unique contribution is in the development of instructional strategies. According to conditions-based theory, when designing instructional strategies, instructional designers must determine the goals of instruction, categorize these goals as to outcome, and select strategies that have been suggested as being effective for this category of learning outcome (or devise strategies consistent with the cognitive processing demands of the learning task).

The outcome-referenced, conditions-based assumption is commonplace, if not universal, in current instructional psychology and instructional design thinking, even when an author's orientation and values are not based on the cognitive science that underlies the conditions theory. For example, Nelson (1999, p. 242) took care to note that her prescriptions for collaborative problem solving "should only be used when those types of learning are paramount." This care in consideration of the nature of the learning task was remarkably absent before conditions theory was developed and is remarkably consistent in its application now. Whether or not individuals formally subscribe to or have an interest in the conditions theory, it is part of the everyday work of designers and scholars of instruction and learning environments.

## Alternatives to an Outcome-Referenced, Conditions-Based Perspective

To have a central concern with what is to be learned is not the only perspective that may be taken or has been taken by instructional theorists. Although the variety of viewpoints is myriad, brief consideration of four alternative views should help us put outcome-referenced thinking into perspective. The four views to be discussed here are (1) learner-centered, (2) experience-centered, (3) activity-centered, and (4) content-centered.

### Learner-Centered Instruction

Students of the history of educational thought are often struck with the popularity of learner-centered thinking in educational reforms since Rousseau's *Emile* (1773), which encouraged an education that would harmonize with the "natural conditions of a child's growth" (Ulich, 1950, p. 219). Pestalozzi (1746–1827) encouraged education that followed the "road of Nature" (Ulich, 1950, p. 260) in which children's individual personal paths were the essential guide to both what should be learned and how it should be taught. Herbart (1776–1841), although less romantic than Rousseau and Pestalozzi, was an important reformer in the early 19th century. He grounded his work in the study of children's learning and was guided in large measure by learners' personal interests.

### Experience-Centered Instruction

John Jacob Comenius, a 17th-century educational reformer, began to look at the experience of learners (rather than content) as guiding education. Although Froebel is part of the tradition of learner-centered educational reform of the 18th and 19th centuries along with Rosseau, Pestalozzi, and Herbart, we can see in his work an emphasis on experience: "The educator ought to lead the child through such situations as will help him to relate his experiences organically with one another" (Ulich, 1950, p. 288). Similar to outcome-referenced views, an experience-centered conception of instruction places more emphasis on instructional strategy than does a more conservative "content-centered" approach.

### Activity-Centered Instruction

John Dewey (1859–1952) has variously been characterized as both a learner-centered and experience-centered educational philosopher. Dewey provided enormous support for consideration of learner activity as a central concept. Ulich (1950, p. 319) noted that

Dewey "wants interest and activity to be more closely related to all the diverse features of community life, manual, intellectual, emotional, and social." Dewey was, at times, radical in his belief about the centrality of activity and experience, to the point of rejecting external goals altogether (Dewey, 1910, p. 13):

> … to set up any end outside of education, as furnishing its goal and standard, is to deprive the educational process of much of its meaning, and tends to make us rely upon false and external stimuli in dealing with the child.

Although it is possible to think of learning activities as contributors to *a priori* learning goals, it is also possible to think of activity as either an end in itself or as leading to outcomes not previously specified. With all due respect to Dewey's immense contributions to educational thought, the all-too-common practice of classroom activity for its own sake is not good practice, in our view. From our perspective, even when it is activity centered, good instruction is congruent with and facilitative of the goals for learning.

### Content-Centered Instruction

It is easy to mistake an outcome-referenced approach with a content-centered orientation. In comparison to learner-centered, experienced-centered, and activity-centered, both approaches seem hopelessly conservative to many people; however, in an outcome-referenced approach, content is only the context. In most cases, alternative contents may serve to facilitate the achievement of a learning goal. In contrast, with a content-centered view, the content is truly crucial. Perhaps the best example of a content-centered view is the *great books of the Western world curriculum* proposed by Robert Maynard Hutchins (1953), Mortimer Adler, and others. The perennialists, as they are described by Brameld (1955), have a particular body of content in mind, first and foremost.

### Integrated Perspectives for Design

Integration of the learner-centered, experience-centered, activity-centered, and content-centered perspectives in concert with an outcome-referenced, conditions-based approach is not out of the question. We believe, for example, that it is wholly appropriate for an instructional designer to determine what the intentions for learning are and then determine what sort of activities and experiences would best facilitate that learning, based on the structure and form of the content to be learned as well as the characteristics of the learner. These decisions are essentially strategic

(Smith and Ragan, 2005). Most designers are somewhat eclectic with regard to these alternative perspectives. Designers who first consider the learning outcome and who never lose consideration for it when identifying the instructional supports or strategies that facilitate the internal cognitive processes required for achieving the learning outcome are most aligned with an outcome-referenced, conditions-based perspective.

## Alternatives within an Outcome-Referenced, Conditions-Based Perspective

Concern with learning outcomes takes on a different shape depending on whether the context is at the *micro* level, as in designing instructional strategies for particular encounters, or is at the *macro* level, as with curriculum- and standards-based approaches. This chapter and the research it reports focus primarily on the micro level. Such a focus concentrates on the facilitation of learning of specific identified learning outcomes. The macro level, on the other hand, engages more frequently in policy issues such as the widely known and sometimes controversial *outcomes-based education* movement. Outcomes-based education, which is primarily about the nature and source of learning goals and the directions of school curricula, has little to do with how learning is facilitated, or about how instruction should proceed, or what conditions are required for efficient, effective, and appealing instruction. Generally speaking, only one element of instruction—assessment—is involved in outcomes-based education at the macro level. In contrast, outcome-referenced, conditions-based theories and models of instruction are fundamentally concerned with *ways to facilitate learning*. We believe it is important to maintain an awareness of the implications of these fundamental differences.

This chapter is not the only one in this handbook that posits theories and models within an outcome-referenced perspective. Within this chapter we have tried to minimize replication of models discussed in other chapters. We could have included a wide array of alternative ideas, ranging from philosophies to theories to models to particular strategies. As an example, whole task models that focus on multidimensional, complex cognitive skills as learning outcomes and the conditions that facilitate the attainment of highly integrated sets of various categories of outcomes fit within an outcome-referenced perspective. van Merriënboer and Dijkstra's (1997) four-component instructional design model is one example of such a model. Problem-based learning proceeds from an outcome-referenced perspective focusing on the conditions and strategies for problem solving and achieving related outcomes. Performance improvement models connect workplace outcomes and goals to specific interventions with the intent of closing gaps between existing and desired levels of performance. In addition, many of the instructional strategy chapters in this handbook provide discussions that link a specific strategy to the learning outcomes for which they are most appropriate.

Although it is possible to endlessly debate the categories, we find that many of the examples we provide have been described at many different levels—from philosophies to strategies. We think that all of these applications and interpretations of outcome-referenced thinking warrant consideration. In this chapter, we explore in depth a body of research-based instructional theory on a particular outcome-referenced approach, the *conditions-based theory*, and focus our examples on models and theories that most closely align themselves with this specific perspective.

## Utility of an Outcome-Referenced, Conditions-Based Perspective

The utilization of outcome-referenced, conditions-based theories and models of instructional design is evident across the various settings, domains, and application fields informed by instructional theory (Dijkstra et al., 1997). These include contexts, such as PreK–12 education (Podolskij, 1997; Wiggins and McTighe, 1998), higher education (Gagné and Merrill, 1990; Miles and Wilson, 2004; Terlouw, 1997), and business, military, and industry training (Clark and Blake, 1997; Pieters, 1997), as well as areas of application, such as instructional multimedia development (Deubel, 2003), distance learning (Bourdeau and Bates, 1997; Inglis, 1989), learning objects (Merrill, 1999), expert systems (Kasowitz, 1998), and performance support (Van Tiem et al., 2001). The pervasiveness of outcome-referenced, conditions-based thinking across many instructional design theories and models combined with the prevalence of its utilization across settings and areas of application make it among the most influential perspectives in the field of educational communications and technology. The purpose of this chapter is to (1) present the assumptions of the outcome-referenced, conditions-based perspective, (2) describe prevalent theories and models within this tradition, and (3) provide future directions for research and development.

## THE PROPOSITIONS OF A CONDITIONS-BASED THEORY

As noted in the chapter introduction, the primary propositions of conditions-based theory can be summarized by four main assertions: (1) Learning goals can be categorized as to learning outcome or knowledge type; (2) the acquisition of different outcome categories requires different internal conditions (alternatively phrased as "different internal conditions lead to different cognitive outcomes"); (3) learning outcomes can be represented in a predictable prerequisite relationship; and (4) different internal processes are supported by identifiably different instructional supports (or external conditions for learning). In this section, issues relating to each of the primary propositions are discussed.

## Learning Outcomes Can Be Categorized

To examine our first assertion, it is essential to understand what is meant by a *learning outcome*. The meaning we ascribe to outcomes differs depending on whether we perceive these outcomes as external (as a category of task or goal) or internal (as an acquired capability, perhaps supported by a unique memory system). Theories that have conveyed internal orientations include Gagné's (1985) classification system of outcomes as *acquired capabilities* and Landa's conceptualization of kinds of knowledge as *psychological phenomena*. In contrast, Reigeluth's categorization of types of content implies the categorization of an external referent. Merrill (1983) has described his outcome categories as *performances* and *learned capabilities*, representing a mix of internal and external connotations. Clearly, there is no consensus even within the models described in this chapter as to what the phrase *learning outcomes* denotes.

Instructional theorists have suggested a variety of category systems, most of which are compatible with the declarative/procedural classification (Anderson, 1990). Gagné added other categories to the schema: attitude, motor skill, and, perhaps, cognitive strategies. Tennyson and Rasch (1988) added a third class of learning—contextual knowledge. Given the variation within and across classification systems, there is also considerable variation in the type of evidence required to support the validity of each category system. The nature of the variation, which encompasses type and complexity of the evidence, depends on whether the phenomena are viewed as entities that are *outward* (i.e., they can be culled out and observed) or *within* (in which case we can only observe circumstantial evidence of their presence).

An examination of the assertion that learning outcomes can be categorized entails both a philosophical and a psychological view. Among the philosophers and psychologists who have posited ways of categorizing knowledge are Ryle (1949) and Anderson (1990), respectively, who proposed similar declarative or procedural classification systems. Depending on one's ori-

entation as a philosopher, psychologist, or instructional theorist, the evidence of the truth of the proposition would vary. For philosophers, the truth of the proposition would be an epistemological question, and the manner for determining its truth would depend on the philosophic school to which a particular philosopher subscribed. We do not pursue this approach for determining the validity of our assertion directly. Alternatively, Reigeluth (1983) suggested a utility criterion for determining whether a categorization system was appropriate. The psychologist would want empirical evidence that the categories are distinct, which leads to our second proposition.

## Different Outcome Categories Require Different Internal Conditions

Most of the models within outcome-referenced, conditions-based theories propose that learning categories are different in terms of cognitive processing demands and activities. All of the major design models described in this chapter appear to make this assumption to a greater or lesser degree. Whereas all of the models in this chapter suggest that general information processing occurs in learning, they also suggest that this processing is significantly and predictably different for each of the categories of learning identified by each model. For example, Gagné suggested that, in particular, the cognitive processes of retrieval of prior knowledge, encoding, and retrieval and transfer of new learning would differ significantly in nature, depending on the type of learning goal. Indeed, several of the model developers, including Gagné (1985), Merrill (1983), Smith and Ragan (2005), and Tennyson and Rasch (1988), postulated different memory structures for different types of learning outcomes.

A slightly different statement of the proposition allows for a closer relationship to the first proposition (that outcomes can be categorized): Different internal conditions lead to different cognitive outcomes. This assertion, which is more descriptive and less prescriptive, seems to be supported by additional educational theorists; for example, both Anderson (1990) and E. Gagné et al. (1993) proposed that different cognitive processes lead to declarative and procedural learning. They also proposed that these two types of learning have different memory systems–schemata for declarative knowledge and productions for procedural learning. Both theories provided some empirical evidence that these cognitive processes and storage systems were indeed unique to the two types of learning.

We must point out that even if connectionists (Bereiter, 1991; Hawkins and Blakeslee, 2004) are correct that there is only one memory system (neural

**TABLE 32.1**
**Results of Studies on Hierarchies**

| Author | Date | Learning Task | Results |
|---|---|---|---|
| Nicholas | 1970 | Not stated | Replicated Wiegand (1970) |
| Coleman and Gagné | 1970 | Exports comparison | Too much mastery by control group but better transfer to problem solving found |
| Eustace | 1969 | Concept "noun" | Hypothesized sequence better |
| Okey and Gagné | 1970 | Chemistry | Learning hierarchy revision better than original version |
| Resnick et al. | 1971 | Double classification | Successfully predicted outcomes |
| Caruso and Resnick | 1971 | Replication | Resnick et al. (1971) confirmed |
| Wang et al. | 1971 | Math curriculum | Several dependency sequences found |

networks) and only one basic cognitive process (pattern recognition, Bereiter; prediction, Hawkins), it does not necessarily preclude the possibility of different types of learning capabilities. It is possible, for example, that generalized activation patterns can represent certain types of learning.

## Outcomes Can Be Represented in a Prerequisite Relationship

Gagné's work on learning hierarchies has confirmed the assumption of prerequisite relationships. In 1973, Gagné described the idea of learning hierarchies and noted that learning hierarchies had the following characteristics: (1) They described "successively achievable intellectual skills, each of which is stated as a performance class"; (2) they did not include "verbal information, cognitive strategies, motivational factors, or performance sets"; and (3) each step in the hierarchy described "only those prerequisite skills that must be recalled at the moment of learning" to supply the necessary "internal" component of the total learning situation (pp. 21–22). Gagné also described several studies on the validation of learning hierarchies.

A fundamental way to approach validation was to look at differences in transfer between groups that attained and groups that did not attain hypothesized prerequisites. Gagné et al. (1962, p. 9, Table 3) was cited as an example providing positive evidence from such an approach. Other validation studies were reported, each investigating in one way or another the validity of a particular learning hierarchy—in other words, examining the extent to which the hierarchy was a true description of prerequisite relationships among hypothesized subtasks. As a set, these studies could be viewed as evidence of the validity of the concept of learning hierarchies. The studies are summarized in Table 32.1.

In addition to work done by Gagné and others working directly in his tradition, research by individuals working from entirely different frames of reference

has also solidly confirmed this assumption. Although early learning hierarchy research appeared to be highly confirmatory, White (1973) developed an important review of learning hierarchy research in the early 1970s. In his review, White sought studies validating the idea of learning hierarchies. Due to methodological weaknesses among the studies, though, White did not find any studies that validated a complete and precise fit between a proposed learning hierarchy and optimal learning and noted the weaknesses within the studies.

Research done subsequent to White's review, incorporated his recommendations to correct methodological weaknesses, and resulted in a series of published studies confirming the learning hierarchy formulation (Linke, 1973; White, 1974a,b,c). These results led Gagné to conclude, "The basic hypothesis of learning hierarchies is now well established, and sound practical methods for testing newly designed hierarchies exist" (White and Gagné, 1974, p. 363). Other research that may be considered within the Gagné tradition that appeared to confirm the learning hierarchy hypothesis includes studies by Merrill et al. (1970), Resnick (1967), Resnick and Wang (1969), and Yao (1989). Work on learning hierarchies outside the Gagné tradition (i.e., outside a conditions theory perspective) includes studies by Bergan et al. (1982, 1984), Kallison (1986), and Winkles (1986).

## Different Learning Outcomes Require Different External Conditions

In an effort to find evidence to support this basic assumption of conditions-based theory, we engaged in a survey of research, looking across a wide scope. For the interested reader, Table 32.2 presents representative topics and referenced studies that illustrate the breadth of evidence generally supporting this assumption of the outcome-referenced, conditions-based model. The sample of studies presented in the table lend support—in varying ways and from varying standpoints—to the theory that different instructional

**TABLE 32.2**
**Different Learning Outcomes Require Different External Conditions**

| Topic | Reviews and Studies |
|---|---|
| Interaction between usefulness of objectives and learning outcome | Hartley and Davies (1976); Yellon and Schmidt (1971) |
| Goal structure and learning task | Johnson and Johnson (1974) |
| Visual presentation mode and learning task | Dwyer and Dwyer (1987); Dwyer and Parkhurst (1982) |
| Evoked cognitive strategies and learning outcomes | Kiewra and Benton (1987); Levin (1986); Peper and Mayer (1978, 1986); Pressley et al. (1982); Shrager and Mayer (1989); |
| Expertise and learning hierarchies | Anderson (1990); Dunn and Taylor (1990, 1994) |
| Adjunct questions and type of learning | Hamilton (1985) |
| Practice | Hannafin and Calamaio (1987); Hannafin et al. (1986); Reiber (1989) |
| Feedback for different types of learning | Getsie et al. (1985); Schimmel (1983); Smith and Ragan (1993) |
| Provided vs. evoked instructional support for different types of learning | Husic et al. (1989) |

outcomes may best be achieved with differing types of instructional support. For further expansion and discussion of this basic tenet of conditions theory the reader should refer to Chapter 14 in this *Handbook* and Ragan and Smith (2004).

# EXAMPLES OF CONDITIONS-BASED THEORIES

Gagné provided the intellectual leadership for an outcome-referenced, conditions-based theory of instruction. This leadership was well explicated in a volume dedicated to Gagné's legacy (Richey, 2000). A number of scholars have followed in Gagné's tradition by developing more detailed prescriptions of the external conditions that support different types of learning. Three texts edited by Reigeluth (1983, 1987, 1999a), clearly delineated a number of models that we would describe as outcome-referenced, conditions-based models of design. Some of the models in these texts, such as the ones by Scandura, Collins, and Keller, we would not describe as full conditions-based models, as they do not describe the cognitive and instructional conditions for more than one learning type. Other models, particularly those presented in Volume II (Reigeluth, 1999a), that we did not consider to be conditions-based made few, if any, considerations of the learning task. We believe it is also likely that the theorists who developed these models would not be amenable to the label of outcome-referenced, conditions-based theory and the underlying cognitive science.

It is not the purpose of this chapter to replicate the thorough discussions of the conditions-based models presented by Reigeluth; however, we briefly discuss and compare some of these models, because it is through comparisons that many of the major issues regarding outcome-referenced, conditions-based mod-

els have been revealed and exemplified. We reference research and evaluation studies that have examined the effectiveness of the conditions-based model or theory as a whole or of an individual aspect of the theory. We also include in our discussion a few models that are not presented in Reigeluth's texts. Some of the examples we provide are arguably not *instructional design models* at all (such as the work of Horn, 1976; Resnick, 1967; and West et al., 1991), but they all employ, reflect, or extend the *conditions-based theory* propositions listed in the introduction to this chapter in one important way or another.

## Gagné and Gagné, Briggs, and Wager

The first full statement of a conditions-based theory of instruction appears to have been made by Gagné in the early 1960s; however, there was considerable conjecture within this paradigm by a variety of researchers prior to Gagné. In addition, Gagné and others have developed a conditions-based theory along a variety of lines of thinking through the present day. We direct the interested reader to Ragan and Smith (2004) for a more complete discussion of the evolution of the conditions-based theory and the contributions of Gagné. As Gagné is generally identified as the primary originator of a conditions-based model of instructional design, an understanding of his evolution of thought becomes foundational to understanding the theory that extends beyond his contribution. This theory was the basis of an instructional design model presented in *Instructional Design: Principles and Applications* (Briggs, 1977) and *Principles of Instructional Design* (Gagné and Briggs, 1979; Gagné et al., 1992).

Research examining the validity of Gagné's theory falls within one of two types: studies that have examined the validity of Gagné's instructional theory as a cluster of treatment variables and studies that have examined the individual propositions of the theory as separate variables (as discussed earlier). A few researchers have attempted to evaluate the overall value of specific instruction based on Gagné's theory or portions of Gagné's theory that were not central to the conditions-based theory. Goldberg (1987), Marshall (1986), Mengel (1986), and Stahl (1979) compared existing instruction to instruction designed according to Gagné's principles. These studies were across age groups and subject matters. Mengal and Stahl found significant differences in learning effects for the versions developed according to Gagné's principles, whereas Goldberg and Marshall found no significant difference in treatments. Although we believe such gross comparison studies to be essential to the development of research in an area, they suffered from some of the same threats to the validity of conclusions that have affected other comparison studies. In particular, it was unclear whether the *traditional* versions were completely devoid of features of Gagné's principles and whether the *Gagnétian* versions were fully consistent with his principles.

## Merrill's Component Display Theory and Instructional Transaction Theory

We consider Merrill's component display theory (CDT) (Merrill, 1983) and instructional transaction theory (ITT) (Merrill, 1999), which are extensions of Gagné's theory, to be outcome-referenced, conditions-based theories of instructional design, because they prescribe instructional conditions based on the types of desired learning outcomes. In CDT, Merrill classified learning objectives (or capabilities) along two dimensions: performance level (remember, use, or find) and content type (facts, concepts, principles, or procedures). Across the dimensions, his theory addressed 12 distinct categories of objectives. Instead of having an inclusive declarative knowledge category as Gagné did, though, CDT individually characterized remembering facts, concept definitions, rule statements, and procedural steps. Also, instead of having a single category for cognitive strategies as Gagné did, in CDT Merrill proposed *find* operations for each of the content types through his intersection of the two dimensions (e.g., find a fact, find a concept, find a rule, and find a procedure). In ITT, Merrill presented 13 types of learning with associated instructional strategies, which he identified as "transactions," grouped into three major categories: (1) component transactions, which involved identifying, executing, and interpreting; (2) abstraction transactions, which entailed judging, classifying, generalizing, deciding, and transferring; and (3) association transactions, which

involved propagating, analogizing, substituting, designing, and discovering (Merrill et al., 1992).

Merrill provided a rationale for his categorization scheme for CDT based on "some assumptions about the nature of subject matter" (Merrill, 1983, p. 298). The rationale for content type was based on five operations that he proposed could be conducted on subject matter: (1) identification (facts), (2) inclusion (concepts), (3) intersection (concepts), (4) ordering (procedures), and (5) causal operations (principles). He derived his performance levels from assumptions regarding differences in four memory structures: associative, episodic, image, and algorithmic. Merrill did not explicitly address the internal processes that accompanied the acquisition of each of these categories of learning types.

Merrill described instructional conditions as *presentation forms* in CDT and classified these forms as primary and secondary. Primary presentation forms had two dimensions: content (generality or instance) and approach (expository or inquisitory). Secondary presentation forms were types of elaborations that may have extended the primary presentations: context, prerequisite, mnemonic, mathemagenic help, representation or alternative representation, and feedback. Merrill's theory then further described for each category of capability "a unique combination of primary and secondary presentation forms that will most effectively promote acquisition of that type of objective" (Merrill, 1983, p. 283).

Researchers have examined CDT in two ways: evaluation in comparison to *traditional* approaches (Keller and Reigeluth, 1982; Robinson, 1984; Stein, 1982; Von Hurst, 1984) and examination of individual strategy variations within CDT (Chao, 1983; Keller, 1986; Sasayama, 1985). Many of the weaknesses of Merrill's theory were similar to those of Gagné's theory, such as the lack of an explicit and empirically validated connection between internal processes and external events. Merrill's theory, however, provided even less conjecture on internal processes. It was also less complete, as his theory (1) addressed only the cognitive domain, (2) did not fully delineate the instructional conditions for the *find* (cognitive strategies) category, and (3) did not have a category for complex learning reflected in what has often been called *problem solving*. On the other hand, a strength of CDT has been its evolution to fit the demands of designing intelligent CAI systems, as noted by Wilson (1987).

## Reigeluth: Elaboration Theory

Reigeluth and his associates (Reigeluth, 1999b; Reigeluth and Darwazeh, 1982; Reigeluth and Rogers, 1980; Reigeluth and Stein, 1983; Reigeluth et al., 1978) developed the elaboration theory as a guide for developing macro strategies for large segments of instruction, such as courses and units. The elaboration theory is conditions based in nature, as it describes "a) three models of instruction; and b) a system for prescribing those models on the basis of the goals for a whole course of instruction" (Reigeluth and Stein, 1983, p. 340). The theory specifies a general model of selecting, sequencing, synthesizing, and summarizing content in a simple to more complex structure. The major features of the general model include: (1) an epitome at the beginning of the instruction, (2) levels of elaboration of this epitome, (3) learning-prerequisite sequences within the levels of elaboration, (4) a learner-control format, and (5) use of analogies, summarizers, and synthesizers.

The conditions-based nature of the model stemmed from Reigeluth's specification of three differing structures—conceptual, procedural, and theoretical—which were selected based on the goals of the course. Reigeluth further suggested that conceptual structures were of three types: parts, kinds, and matrices (combinations of two or more conceptual structures). He described two kinds of procedural structures: procedural order and procedural decision. Finally, he subdivided theoretical structures into two types: those that described natural phenomena (descriptive structures) and those that affected a desired outcome (prescriptive structures).

The nature of the epitome, sequence, summarizers, prerequisites, synthesizers, and content of elaborations varied depending on the type of knowledge structure chosen, which was based on the goals of the course; for example, if the knowledge structure was conceptual, the epitome would contain a presentation of the most fundamental concepts for the entire course. If the structure was procedural, the epitome would present the procedure that was most fundamental or represented the shortest path. Reigeluth recommended using Merrill's CDT as the guideline for designing at the micro or lesson level within each elaboration cycle.

Increasingly, Reigeluth (1992) has placed more emphasis on the importance of using a simplifying-conditions method of sequencing instruction than on the sequencing and structuring of instruction based on one of the major knowledge structures. The simplifying-conditions method suggested that designers "work with experts to identify a simple case that is as representative as possible of the task as a whole" (p. 81). This task would serve as the epitome of the course, with succeeding levels of elaboration abating the simplifying conditions so that the task became increasingly complex. The theory still retains some of its conditions-based orientation, though, as Reigeluth has suggested, different simplifying-conditions structures must be developed for each of the kinds of knowledge structures he described (Reigeluth and Curtis, 1987; Reigeluth and Rogers, 1980). In recent years, Reigeluth's (1999b) discussions of elaboration theory have emphasized it as a holistic, learner-centered approach in an effort to distance it from analytic approaches centering on learning tasks or content.

As with the previous models, some research has evaluated the effectiveness of instruction based on the principles of elaboration theory in comparison to instruction based on other models. Examples of this type of research have included work done by Beukhof (1986) and Wedman and Smith (1989). Given that Reigeluth (1979) proposed that the elaboration theory was a macro-strategy theory effective for the design of units and courses and recommended CDT as a micro-design strategy for lessons, we are not surprised that researchers have not uniformly found positive effects of the elaboration theory designs on shorter instruction. Researchers have also examined design questions regarding individual variables within elaboration theory, such as synthesizers (McLean, 1983; Van Patten, 1984), summarizers (Tilden, 1985), non-examples in learning procedures (Marcone and Reigeluth, 1988), and sequencing (English and Reigeluth, 1994).

Elaboration theory is a macro-strategy design theory that was much needed in the field of instructional design as an alternative to designing instruction serially based on enabling objectives. Throughout the evolution of elaboration theory, Reigeluth has proposed design principles that have maintained a conditions-based orientation. Until Reigeluth's work, many designers had assumed that instruction should proceed from one enabling objective to another from the beginning of a course to the end, due to heavy emphasis on learning hierarchy analysis. Reigeluth suggested a theoretically sound alternative for designing large segments of instruction.

It is unfortunate that researchers in the field have not found it pragmatically possible to evaluate elaboration theory in comparison to alternatives with course-level instruction. In light of advances in cognitive theory, Wilson and Cole (1991) suggested a number of recommendations for revising the elaboration theory to which Reigeluth (1992) responded. We recommend these articles for further reading.

## Smith and Ragan

Rather than developing a new conditions-based model, Smith and Ragan (2005) sought to exemplify and elaborate Gagné's theory. To address what they perceived to be limitations in most conditions-based models, they focused on the cognitive process necessary for the acquisition of each of the different learning capabilities.

With regard to the external conditions of learning, Smith and Ragan suggested that the events of instruction as Gagné portrayed them insufficiently considered learner-generated and learner-initiated learning; therefore, Smith and Ragan restated the events in terms of being either learner supplied or instruction supported. Instruction, which predominated in learner-supplied or *generative* activities, characterized learning environments (Jonassen and Land, 2000) and new paradigms of instruction (Reigeluth, 1999a). In the case of learner-initiated events, instruction facilitated or prompted the learner to provide the cognitive processing necessary for an instructional event. As instruction provided increasing cognitive support for an instructional event, the event was considered to be more *supplantive* (or mathemagenic) in character.

Based on such findings that indicated that learners perform better on comprehension and recall tests if they generated associations for themselves rather than having the associations supplied, Smith and Ragan (2005) suggested that instructional strategies should be as generative as possible. Smith and Ragan acknowledged, however, that it was sometimes necessary to provide more external support "for learners to achieve learning in the time possible, with a limited and acceptable amount of frustration, anxiety, and danger" (pp. 145–146). The approach that Smith and Ragan recommended for instructional design was one of problem-solving, in which designers determined the amount of cognitive support required for the events of instruction based on careful consideration of context, learner, and learning task. Smith and Ragan also proposed a model for determining the optimal balance of generative strategies and supplantive strategies based on context, learner, and task variables. Many methods associated with constructivism, including guided discovery, coaching, and cognitive apprenticeship, were examples of learner-centered events involving external facilitation. As proposed by Dick (1997), these methods could be interpreted as micro theories that impacted the instructional strategy component of an outcome-referenced, conditions-based perspective.

Smith (1992) cited theoretical and empirical support for some of the learner–task–context–strategy relationships proposed in the comparison of generative and supplantive strategies (COGSS) model, which formed the basis of the suggested balance between instruction-supplied and learner-generated events. In Smith's presentation, she proposed an agenda for validation of the model. Smith and Ragan (2005) stated that the relative advantages afforded by generative or supplantive forms had not been thoroughly and empirically investigated; yet, "bodies of theory and research suggest that neither approach is universally superior but that many factors may influence the efficacy of one instructional approach over the other" (p. 143).

Smith and Ragan (2005) referenced several areas of research related to generative and supplantive strategies, such as research on generative vs. mathemagenic teaching methods (Jonassen, 1985; Osborne and Wittrock, 1985; Wittrock, 1974), learner control in computer-based instruction (Hannafin, 1984; Steinberg, 1977; Tennyson, 1984), discovery vs. expository learning (Herman, 1969; Ray, 1961), and cognitive capacity and allocation of mental resources (Britton et al., 1978; Burton et al., 1986; Craik and Lockhart, 1972; Duncan, 1980; Watkins, 1983). Additionally, Smith and Ragan (2005) proposed principles for making decisions regarding the optimal design position along the supplantive-generative continuum, based on variables within the learners, context, and task. They noted that the current state of theory and research allowed only hypothetical principles and suggested research to investigate the principles and interactions of the variables to determine what recommendations and overall principles could be proposed within this conditions-based perspective.

## Merrill, Li, and Jones: ID2

In reaction to a number of limitations that they perceived in existing instructional design theories and models (including Merrill's own models), Merrill, Li, and Jones (1990a,b) set out to construct a second generation theory of instructional design (ID2). One of the specific goals of its developers was to expedite the design of an automated ID system (ID Expert) and thereby expedite the instructional design process itself. Ultimately, the developers hoped that the system would provide both authoring and delivery environments that were increasingly grounded in a knowledge base and rule base. Of all the models we have described in this chapter, ID2 has reflected the highest ambition in the goal to thoroughly prescribe the instructional conditions for each type of learning. The ID2 model has been developed (1) to analyze, represent, and guide instruction to teach integrated sets of knowledge and skill; (2) to produce pedagogic prescriptions about selection and sequence; and (3) to be an open system capable of responding to new theory. As Merrill and his associates have elaborated on the relationships between outcomes and internal–external conditions, the ID2 model has retained its conditions-based orientation (Merrill et al., 1990, p. 8):

a) A given learned performance results from a given organized and elaborated cognitive structure, which we will call a mental model. Different learning outcomes require different types of mental models; b) the construction of a mental model by a learner is facilitated by instruction that explicitly organizes and elaborates the knowledge being taught, during the instruction; c) there are different organizations and elaborations of knowledge required to promote different learning outcomes.

Within ID2, outcomes of instruction were considered to be enterprises composed of entities, activities, or processes, which might loosely be interpreted as concepts, procedures, and principles, respectively. Merrill and his associates have spent a vast amount of effort describing the structure of knowledge relating to these types of knowledge and how these types of knowledge relate to each other.

Merrill and his colleagues have described a number of external conditions or instructional methods that could be controlled by either system or learner. These conditions were described as *transactions* of various classes, and evidence of Merrill's CDT could be found in the prescriptions for these transactions. To create this system based on his ID2 model, Merrill et al. (1991, 1992a,b, 1993) have attempted to identify the decisions that designers must make about the types of information in order to build them into the system and the methods by which this information could be made available to learners. They have conducted similar analyses of information that could be made available to learners when learning entities, activities, or processes. In addition to detailing the options for pedagogy and information that could be made available in instruction, the system developers could also establish the rules by which the system made choices for selecting options to present to learners.

Parts of the ID Expert system have been evaluated by Spector and Muraida (1991) and by Canfield and Spector (1991). As yet, there have been no comparison data with more conventional design processes. In their effort to carefully explicate the necessary knowledge for learning and instruction as well as the means by which these entities interacted with one another, the developers have created a model that is quite complex. One benefit of the model is it has reflected and made concrete much of the complexity of the instructional design process. Unfortunately, it seems that terminology has shifted during development. Among the criticisms that have frequently been leveled at ID2 are (1) its utility when used by novices, (2) the lack of evidence of theory base, (3) issues regarding sufficient agreement to generate strategies, and (4) the likelihood of sameness of results in multiple applications.

ID2 and its accompanying ID Expert are no longer alone in the development of ID expert systems (Kasowitz, 1998). Other expert systems that have been developed as part of the Advanced Instructional Design Advisor (AIDA) research project (Muraida and Spector, 1993; Spector et al., 1991) include the Guided Approach to Instructional Design Advising (GAIDA), which used tutorials and context-specific advice and examples, and the Experimental Advanced Instructional Design Advisor (XAIDA), which used the transactional theory framework to encapsulate context-specific knowledge. Additional advisory system models have also been proposed, such as Duchastel's (1990) Instructional Design Advanced Workbench. Some of these automated instructional design tools have operationalized instructional design theories and models by focusing on the cognitive aspects of instructional design, while other tools have highlighted the procedural steps of instructional design. Other tools have supported only the production phase of instructional design. Some of these tools have been within the framework of an outcome-referenced, conditions-based tradition, but others have not. Continued research on the efficiency and effectiveness of these models and tools, as well as comparisons across the tools, would be highly lucrative areas for further study.

## Other Applications of Conditions-Based Theory

The theories and models discussed in the previous sections represent the strongest body of development, research, and evaluation on outcome-referenced, conditions-based perspectives within instructional design. Mention of additional theories and models that have less extensive research and evaluation or represent somewhat incomplete instructional design models are important given that: (1) a number of notable scholars within and outside the instructional design field have utilized a conditions-based theory as a basis for much of their work, and (2) they illustrate how pervasive and influential the conditions-based theory has been. Six examples of such theories and models include: (1) Landa's (1983) algoheuristic theory of instruction, or *Landamatics*, which made a distinction between *knowledge* and *skills* seemingly equivalent to Gagné's notion of declarative and procedural knowledge; (2) Tennyson and Rasch's (1988) description of a model of how instructional prescriptions might be linked to cognitive learning theory; (3) Jonassen et al.'s (1991) decision model for selecting strategies and tactics of instruction based on three levels of decisions; (4) Horn's (1976) approach to text design which had many elements of a design model and clearly reflected a conditions-based set of assumptions; (5) West et al.'s (1991) work, which referred to three kinds of knowledge and described *cognitive strategies* that could support the acquisition of each of these learning types, and (6) E. Gagné's work (Gagné et al., 1993), which was primarily descriptive rather than prescriptive but utilized the conditions-based theory as she discussed the internal processes required in the acquisition of each of the types of knowledge and the instructional support that could promote this acquisition. For a review of each of these examples, see Ragan and Smith (2004).

## CONCLUSIONS

In its overview and analysis of the assumptions of the outcome-referenced, conditions-based perspective, the development and research on various theories and models, this chapter presented numerous areas for further research that would serve to improve the theories that guide the development of instruction. Despite the call made by various authors for continued rigorous, empirical evaluation of design practice and tools, very few models have validated answers such as whether a particular model has enhanced the quality of instruction (Botturi, 2005). Dick (1997) suggested that we improve our current theories through revision that reflected the outcomes that were being achieved with its current use and was exemplified by the work of English and Reigeluth (1996, p. 48):

> For example, when a design report has been critiqued and revised, why not use that information to determine how the process that led to the development of the design could be improved? If the design was not acceptable to the client, what went wrong and why? Was it a skills problem, or should the process, i.e., our theory, be improved?

This same directive was presented by Wang and Hannafin (2005) in their call for increased use of the design-based research paradigm. A thorough review of their identification of the underlying characteristics and goals of design-based research approaches and proposed principles for implementing design-based research is urged by all theorists and designers interested in furthering research aimed "to improve educational practices through iterative analysis, design, development, and implementation based on collaboration among researchers and practitioners in real-world setting, and leading to contextually-sensitive design principles and theories" (pp. 6–7).

Although Wang and Hannafin focused their principles on the application of design-based research to technology-enhanced learning environments, others have echoed their call across contexts and areas of application (Reigeluth and Frick, 1999; Richey et al., 2003; Richey and Nelson, 1996; van den Akker, 1999).

We believe that full engagement in design-based research approaches is the most likely category of future research that will serve to inform, improve, and advance outcome-referenced, conditions-based theories and models as well as advancing our knowledge in other perspectives on the design of instruction. Additionally, continued research in the direction of Merrill and associates (see Chapter 14 in this *Handbook*; see also Merrill, 2006) that proposes a framework for integrated research on instructional strategies that examines the interrelationships among instructional strategy principles would also serve to advance instructional thinking in the context of conditions-based theories and models.

We can draw some conclusions from this review. We reflected on the conclusions drawn in our chapter in the second edition of this volume (Ragan and Smith, 2004) and have modified them accordingly. Conditions models have a long history of interest in psychology, educational psychology, and instructional technology. This history illustrates work that may not be widely known among instructional technologists today: work that can be instructive as to the actual base and significance of the outcome-referenced, conditions-based approach. Perhaps we will see fewer erroneous statements in our literature about what is known regarding types of learning, learning hierarchies, and conditions of learning. We also envision a renewed interest in building on this research base with continued research examining the theoretical propositions as well as the application of theory to practical contexts.

We continue to see utility in thinking of learning as more than one kind of thing, especially for practitioners. It is too easy, in the heat of practitioners' struggles, to slip into the assumption that all knowledge is declarative (as is so often seen in the learning outcomes statements of large-scale instructional systems) or all problem solving (as is so often assumed in the pronouncements of pundits and critics of public education) and, as a result, fail to consider either the vast arena of application of declarative knowledge or the multitude of prerequisites for problem solving. It is unhelpful to develop new systems of types of learning for the mere purpose of naming. Improvements in categorization schemes should be based on known differences in cognitive processing and required differences in external conditions. Our field would benefit from research designed to provide evidence to support a current categorization scheme or with the potential to identify additional unique types of learning based on new evidence from cognition and instruction.

We have reached a conclusion about the work of Robert Gagné that we would like to share and suggest that readers examine their own conclusions from reading. We find Gagné's work, cast within so much that preceded and followed it, to remain both dominating in its appeal and utility and, paradoxically, somewhat limited and in need of improvement. The utility and appeal of this work appear to derive greatly from the solid scholarship and cogent writing that Gagné brought to bear, as well as his willingness to change the formulation to keep up with changing times and new knowledge. Many of the gaps and flaws, in keeping with the paradox, appear to be a product of the very changes that he made to keep up with current interests. We believe those changes to be beneficial in the main but see a clear need for systematic and rigorous scholarship on issues raised by those changes.

Conditions-based theory is characterized by a particular combination: on the one hand, its utility in helping specify instructional strategies, and, on the other hand, the sizable gaps and inconsistencies that exist in current formulations (although in an absolute sense these gaps are substantial, in a relative sense, compared to competing perspectives, the gaps are from within a well-tested framework). The combination of high utility and gaps in knowledge creates a need for more work. We have described in this chapter many fruitful areas for further research.

Substantial weakness exists in the tie between categories of learning and external conditions of learning. What is missing is the explication of the *internal* conditions involved in the acquisition and storage of different kinds of learning. Research on the transition from expert to novice and artificial intelligence research that attempts to describe the knowledge of experts should be particularly fruitful in helping us fill this void. Perhaps this void is a result of the failure to place sufficient emphasis on qualitative analysis of learners' actions and thoughts in our field.

Research supports the conclusion that different external events of instruction lead to different kinds of learning, especially looking at the declarative or procedural level. What appears to be lacking is any systematic body of research directly on the central tenet, not just of conditions-based theory but of practically anyone who would attempt to teach, much less design, instruction: What is the relationship between *internal* learner conditions and subsequent learning from instruction? This topic seems to be a far cry from studies that would directly inform designers about procedures and techniques, yet a very great deal seems to hinge on this one question. With more insight into it, many quibbles and debates may disappear and the work of translation into design principles may begin at a new level of efficacy.

# REFERENCES

Anderson, J. R. (1990). *Cognitive Psychology and Its Implications*, 3rd ed. New York: W.H. Freeman.

Bereiter, C. (1991). Implications of connectionism for thinking about rules. *Educ. Res.*, 20(3), 10–16.

Bergan, J. R., Towstopiat, O., Cancelli, A. A., and Karp, C. (1982). Replacement and component rules in hierarchically ordered mathematics rule learning tasks. *J. Educ. Psychol.*, 74(1), 39–50.

Bergan, J. R., Stone, C. A., and Feld, J. K. (1984). Rule replacement in the development of basic number skills. *J. Educ. Psychol.*, 76(2), 289–299.

Beukhof, G. (1986). Designing Instructional Texts: Interaction between Text and Learner. Paper presented at the Annual Meeting of the American Educational Research Association, April, San Francisco, CA (ERIC Document Reproduction Service No. ED 274 313).

Botturi, L. (2005). A framework for the evaluation of visual languages for instructional design: the case for EML. *J. Interact. Learn. Res.*, 16(4), 329–351.

Bourdeau, J. and Bates, A. (1997). Instructional design for distance learning. In *Instructional Design: International Perspectives*. Vol. 2. *Solving Instructional Design Problems*, edited by S. Dijkstra, N. M. Seel, F. Schott, and R. D. Tennyson, pp. 369–398. Mahwah, NJ: Lawrence Erlbaum Associates.

Brameld, T. (1955). *Philosophies of Education in Cultural Perspective*. New York: Dryden.

Briggs, L. J., Ed. (1977). *Instructional Design: Principles and Applications*. Englewood Cliffs, NJ: Educational Technology Publications.*

Britton, B. K., Westbrook, R. D., and Holdredge, T. S. (1978). Reading and cognitive capacity usage: effects of text difficulty. *J. Exp. Psychol. Hum. Learn. Mem.*, 4(6), 582–591.

Burton, J. K., Niles, J. A., and Lalik, R. M. (1986). Cognitive capacity engagement during and following intersperse math-emagenic questions. *J. Educ. Psychol.*, 78(2), 147–152.

Canfield, A. M. and Spector, J. M. (1991). *A Pilot Study of the Naming Transaction Shell*, AL-TP-1991-0006. Brooks AFB, TX: Armstrong Laboratory.

Caruso, J. L. and Resnick, L. B. (1971). Task Sequence and Overtraining in Children's Learning and Transfer of Double Classification Skills. Paper presented at the Annual Meeting of the American Psychological Association, Miami, FL.

Chao, C. I. (1983). *Effects of Four Instructional Sequences on Application and Transfer*, IDD&E Working Paper No. 12. Syracuse, NY: Syracuse University (ERIC Document Reproduction Service No. ED 289 461).

Clark, R. E. and Blake, S. B. (1997). Designing training for novel problem-solving transfer. In *Instructional Design: International Perspectives*. Vol. 1. *Theory, Research, and Models*, edited by R. D. Tennyson, F. Schott, N. M. Seel, and S. Dijkstra, pp. 183–214. Mahwah, NJ: Lawrence Erlbaum Associates.

Coleman, L. T. and Gagné, R. M. (1970). Transfer of learning in a social studies task of comparing-contrasting. In *Basic Studies of Learning Hierarchies in School Subjects*, Final Report, Contract No. OEC-4-062940-3066, U.S. Office of Education, edited by R. M. Gagné. Berkeley, CA: University of California.

Craik, F. I. and Lockhart, R. S. (1972). Levels of processing: a framework for memory research. *J. Verbal Learn. Verbal Behav.*, 11, 671–684.*

Deubel, P. (2003). An investigation of behaviorist and cognitive approaches to instructional multimedia design. *J. Educ. Multimedia Hypermedia*, 12(1), 63–90.

Dewey, J. (1910). *My Pedagogic Creed*. Chicago, IL: A. Flanagan.*

Dick, W. (1997). Better instructional design theory: process improvement or reengineering? *Educ. Technol.*, 37*I*(5), 47–50.*

Dijkstra, S., Seel, N. M., Schott, F., and Tennyson, R. D., Eds. (1997). *Instructional Design: International Perspectives*. Vol. 2. *Solving Instructional Design Problems*. Mahwah, NJ: Lawrence Erlbaum Associates.

Duchastel, P. C. (1990). Cognitive design for instructional design. *Instruct. Sci.*, 19(6), 437–444.

Duncan, J. (1980). The demonstration of capacity limitation. *Cogn. Psychol.*, 12, 75–96.

Dunn, T. G. and Taylor, C. A. (1990). Hierarchical structures in expert performance. *Educ. Technol. Res. Dev.*, 38(2), 5–18.

Dunn, T. G. and Taylor, C. A. (1994). Learning Analysis in Ill-Structured Knowledge Domains of Professional Practice. Paper presented at the Annual Meeting of the American Educational Research Association, April 4–8, New Orleans, LA.

Dwyer, C. A. and Dwyer, F. M. (1987). Effect of depth of information processing on students' ability to acquire and retrieve information related to different instructional objectives. *Programmed Learn. Educ. Technol.*, 24(4), 264–279.

Dwyer, F. M. and Parkhurst, P. E. (1982). A multifactor analysis of the instructional effectiveness of self-paced visualized instruction on different educational objectives. *Programmed Learn. Educ. Technol.*, 19(2), 108–118.

English, R. E. and Reigeluth, C. M. (1994). Formative Research on Sequencing Instruction with the Elaboration Theory. Paper presented at the Annual Meeting of the American Educational Research Association, April 4–8, New Orleans, LA.

English, R. E. and Reigeluth, C. M. (1996). Formative research on sequencing instruction with the elaboration theory. *Educ. Technol. Res. Dev.*, 44(1), 23–42.

Eustace, B. W. (1969). Learning a complex concept at differing hierarchical levels. *J. Educ. Psychol.*, 60, 449–452.

Gagné, E., Yekovich, C. W., and Yekovich, F. R. (1993). *The Cognitive Psychology of School Learning*, 2nd ed. New York: Harper Collins.

Gagné, R. M. (1965). *The Conditions of Learning*. New York: Holt, Rinehart and Winston.*

Gagné, R. M. (1973). Learning and instructional sequence. In *Review of Research in Education*, Vol. 1, edited by F. N. Kerlinger, pp. 3–33. Itasca, IL: Peacock.

Gagné, R. M. (1985). *The Conditions of Learning and Theory of Instruction*, 4th ed. New York: Holt, Rinehart and Winston.*

Gagné, R. M. and Briggs, L. J. (1979). *Principles of Instructional Design*, 2nd ed. Fort Worth, TX: Harcourt Brace Jovanovich.

Gagné, R. M. and Merrill, M. D. (1990). Integrative goals for instructional design. *Educ. Technol. Res. Dev.*, 38(1), 23–30.*

Gagné, R. M., Mayor, J. R., Garstens, H. L., and Paradise, N. E. (1962). Factors in acquiring knowledge of a mathematical task. *Psychol. Monogr.*, 76(7; whole no. 526) (in Gagné, R. M. (1989). *Studies of Learning*, pp. 197–227. Tallahassee, FL: Learning Systems Institute).

Gagné, R. M., Briggs, L. J., and Wager, W. W. (1992). *Principles of Instructional Design*, 4th ed. Fort Worth, TX: Harcourt Brace Jovanovich.*

Getsie, R. L., Langer, P., and Glass, G. V. (1985). Meta-analysis of the effects of type and combination of feedback on children's discrimination learning. *Rev. Educ. Res.*, 55(4), 49–22.

Goldberg, N. S. (1987). An evaluation of a Gagné–Briggs based course designed for college algebra remediation. *Diss. Abstr. Int.*, 47(12), 4313.

Hamilton, R. J. (1985). A framework for the evaluation of the effectiveness of adjunct questions and objectives. *Rev. Educ. Res.*, 55(4), 47–85.*

Hannafin, M. J. (1984). Guidelines for using locus of instructional control in the design of computer-assisted instruction. *J. Instruct. Dev.*, 7(3), 9–14.*

Hannafin, M. J. and Calamaio, M. E. (1987). The Effects of Locus of Instructional Control and Practice on Learning from Interactive Video. Paper presented at the Annual Meeting of the Association for Educational Communications and Technology, Atlanta, GA (published in Simonson, M. L. and Zvacek, S., Eds., *Proceedings of Selected Research Paper Presentations*, pp. 297–312. Ames, IA: Iowa State University).

Hannafin, M. J., Phillips, T. L., and Tripp, S. (1986). The effects of orienting, processing, and practicing activities on learning from interactive video. *J. Comput.-Based Instruct.*, 13(4), 134–139.

Hartley, J. and Davies, I. K. (1976). Preinstructional strategies: the role of pretests, behavioral objectives, overviews, and advance organizers. *Rev. Educ. Res.*, 46(2), 239–265.

Hawkins, J. and Blakeslee, S. (2004). *On Intelligence*. New York: Times Books.

Herman, G. (1969). Learning by discovery: a critical review of studies. *J. Exp. Educ.*, 38, 58–72.

Horn, R. E. (1976). *How to Write Information Mapping*. Lexington, MA: Information Resources.

Husic, F. T., Linn, M. C., and Sloane, K. D. (1989). Adapting instruction to the cognitive demands of learning to program. *J. Educ. Psychol.*, 81(4), 570–583.

Hutchins, R. M. (1953). *The Conflict in Education*. New York: Harper.

Inglis, A. (1989). Fifteen years of instructional design: a personal perspective. In *Development, Design and Distance Education*, 2nd ed., edited by M. Parer, pp. 259–277. Churchill Victoria, Australia: Center for Distance Learning, Monash University College, Gippsland.

Johnson, D. W. and Johnson, R. T. (1974). Instructional goal structure: cooperative, competitive, or individualistic. *Rev. Educ. Res.*, 44(2), 213–240.*

Jonassen, D. H. (1985). Generative learning vs. mathemagenic control of text processing. In *Technology of Text II*, edited by D. H. Jonassen, pp. 9–45. Englewood Cliffs, NJ: Educational Technology Publications.*

Jonassen, D. H. and Land, S. M., Eds. (2000). *Theoretical Foundations of Learning Environments*. Mahwah, NJ: Lawrence Erlbaum Associates.

Jonassen, D. H., Grabinger, R. S., and Harris, N. D. C. (1991). Analyzing and selecting instructional strategies and tactics. *Perform. Improve. Q.*, 4(2), 77–97.

Kallison, J. M. (1986). Effects of lesson organization on achievement. *Am. Educ. Res. J.*, 23(2), 337–347.

Kasowitz, A. (1998). *Tools for Automating Instructional Design*. Syracuse, NY: ERIC Clearinghouse on Information and Technology.

Keller, B. H. (1986). The effects of selected presentation forms using conceptual and procedural content from elementary mathematics (component display theory, concept learning and development model, best example). *Diss. Abstr. Int.*, 47(05), 1591.

Keller, B. and Reigeluth, C. H. (1982). *A Comparison of Three Instructional Presentation Formats*, IDD&E Working Paper No. 6. Syracuse, NY: Syracuse University, School of Education.

Kiewra, K. A. and Benton, S. L. (1987). Effects of notetaking, the instructor's notes, and higher-order practice questions on factual and higher order learning. *J. Instruct. Psychol.*, 14(4), 186–194.

Landa, L. N. (1983). The algo-heuristic theory of instruction. In *Instructional-Design Theories and Models*, edited by C. M. Reigeluth, pp. 163–211. Mahwah, NJ: Lawrence Erlbaum Associates.*

Levin, J. R. (1986). Four cognitive principles of learning strategy instruction. *Educ. Psychol.*, 2(1/2), 3–17.

Linke, R. D. (1973). The Effects of Certain Personal and Situation Variables on the Acquisition Sequence of Graphical Interpretation Skills. Ph.D. dissertation. Victoria, Australia: Monash University.

Marcone, S. and Reigeluth, C. M. (1988). Teaching common errors in applying a procedure. *Educ. Commun. Technol. J.*, 36(1), 23–32.

Marshall, J. M. (1986). A comparative study of two instructional methods employed in teaching nutrition among culturally diverse adolescents: teacher-oriented lecture and student-oriented instructional design. *Diss. Abstr. Int.*, 47(08), 2901.

McLean, L. (1983). *The Effects of Format of Synthesizer on Conceptual Learning*, IDD&E Working Paper No. 13. Syracuse, NY: Syracuse University.

Mengel, N. S. (1986). The acceptability and effectiveness of textbook materials revised using instructional design criteria. *J. Instruct. Dev.*, 9(2), 13–18.

Merrill, M. D. (1983). Component display theory. In *Instructional-Design Theories and Models*, edited by C. M. Reigeluth, pp. 279–333. Mahwah, NJ: Lawrence Erlbaum Associates.*

Merrill, M. D. (1999). Instructional transaction theory (ITT): instructional design based on knowledge objects. In *Instructional-Design Theories and Models*. Vol. II. *A New Paradigm of Instructional Theory*, edited by C. M Reigeluth, pp. 397–424. Mahwah, NJ: Lawrence Erlbaum Associates.*

Merrill, M. D. (2006). Hypothesized performance on complex tasks as a function of scaled instructional strategies. In *Dealing with Complexity in Learning Environments: Theory and Research*, edited by J. Elen and R. E. Clark, pp. 265–281. Amsterdam: Elsevier.

Merrill, M. D., Barton, K., and Wood, L. E. (1970). Specific review in learning a hierarchical imaginary science. *J. Educ. Psychol.*, 61, 102–109.

Merrill, M. D., Li, Z., and Jones, M. K. (1990a). Limitations of first generation instructional design. *Educ. Technol.*, 30(1), 7–11.

Merrill, M. D., Li, Z., and Jones, M. K. (1990b). Second generation instructional design. *Educ. Technol.*, 30(2), 7–14.

Merrill, M. D., Li, Z., and Jones, M. K. (1991). Instructional transaction theory: an introduction. *Educ. Technol.*, 31(6), 7–12.*

Merrill, M. D., Jones, M. K., and Li, Z. (1992a). Instructional transaction theory: classes of transactions. *Educ. Technol.*, 32(6), 12–26.

Merrill, M. D., Li, Z., and Jones, M. K. (1992b). Instructional transaction shells: responsibilities, methods, and parameters. *Educ. Technol.*, 32(2), 5–26.

Merrill, M. D., Li, Z., Jones, M. K., Chen-Troester, J., and Schwab, S. (1993). Instructional transaction theory: knowledge relationships among processes, entities, and activities. *Educ. Technol.*, 33(4), 5–16.

Miles, C. L. and Wilson, C. D. (2004). Learning outcomes for the twenty-first century: cultivating student success for college and the knowledge economy. *New Dir. Community Coll.*, 126, 87–100.

Muraida, D. J. and Spector, J. M. (1993). The advanced instructional design advisor. *Instruct. Sci.*, 21(4), 239–253.*

Nelson, L. M. (1999). Collaborative problem solving. In *Instructional-Design Theories and Models*. Vol. II. *A New Paradigm of Instructional Theory*, edited by C. M Reigeluth, pp. 241–267. Mahwah, NJ: Lawrence Erlbaum Associates.

Nicholas, J. R. (1970). Modality of Verbal Instructions for Problems and Transfer for a Science Hierarchy. Ph.D. dissertation. Berkeley, CA: University of California at Berkeley.

Okey, J. R. and Gagné, R. M. (1970). Revision of a science topic using evidence of performance on subordinate skills. *J. Res. Sci. Teaching*, 7, 321–325.

Osborne, R. and Wittrock, M. C. (1985). The generative learning model and its implications for science education. *Stud. Sci. Educ.*, 12, 59–87.

Peper, R. J. and Mayer, R. E. (1978). Notetaking as a generative activity. *J. Educ. Psychol.*, 70, 514–522.

Peper, R. J. and Mayer, R. E. (1986). Generative effects of notetaking during science lectures. *J. Educ. Psychol.*, 78, 34–38.

Pieters, J. M. (1997). Training for human resource development in industrial and professional organizations. In *Instructional Design: International Perspectives*, Vol. 2. *Solving Instructional Design Problems*, edited by S. Dijkstra, N. M. Seel, F. Schott, and R. D. Tennyson, pp. 315–340. Mahwah, NJ: Lawrence Erlbaum Associates.

Podolskij, A. I. (1997). Instructional design for schooling: developmental issues. In *Instructional Design: International Perspectives*, Vol. 2. *Solving Instructional Design Problems*, edited by S. Dijkstra, N. M. Seel, F. Schott, and R. D. Tennyson, pp. 289–314. Mahwah, NJ: Lawrence Erlbaum Associates.

Pressley, M., Levin, J. R., and Delaney, H. (1982). The mnemonic keyword method. *Review of Educational Research*, 52(1), 61–91.

Ragan, T. J. and Smith, P. L. (2004). Conditions theory and models for designing instruction. In *Handbook of Research on Educational Communications and Technology*, edited by D. H. Jonassen, pp. 623–649. Mahwah, NJ: Lawrence Erlbaum Associates.*

Ray, W. E. (1961). Pupil discovery vs. direct instruction. *J. Exp. Educ.*, 29(3), 271–280.

Reiber, L. P. (1989). The effects of computer animated elaboration strategies and practice on factual and application learning in an elementary science lesson. *J. Educ. Comput. Res.*, 54(4), 431–444.

Reigeluth, C. M. (1979). In search of a better way to organize instruction: the elaboration theory. *J. Instruct. Dev.*, 6, 40–46.

Reigeluth, C. M. (1983). Instructional design: what is it and why is it? In *Instructional-Design Theories and Models*, edited by C. M. Reigeluth, pp. 3–36. Mahwah, NJ: Lawrence Erlbaum Associates.*

Reigeluth, C. M., Ed. (1987). *Instructional Theories in Action: Lessons Illustrating Selected Theories and Models*. Hillsdale, NJ: Lawrence Erlbaum Associates.

Reigeluth, C. M. (1992). Elaborating the elaboration theory. *Educ. Technol. Res. Dev.*, 40(3), 80–86.

Reigeluth, C. M., Ed. (1999a). *Instructional-Design Theories and Models*. Vol. II. *A New Paradigm of Instructional Theory*. Mahwah, NJ: Lawrence Erlbaum Associates.*

Reigeluth, C. M. (1999b). The elaboration theory: guidance for scope and sequence decisions. In *Instructional-Design Theories and Models*. Vol. II. *A New Paradigm of Instructional Theory*, edited by C. M. Reigeluth, pp. 425–453. Mahwah, NJ: Lawrence Erlbaum Associates.*

Reigeluth, C. M. and Curtis, R. V. (1987). Learning situations and instructional models. In *Instructional Technology Foundations*, edited by R. M. Gagné, pp. 175–206. Mahwah, NJ: Lawrence Erlbaum Associates.

Reigeluth, C. M. and Darwazeh, A. N. (1982). The elaboration theory's procedures for designing instruction: a conceptual approach. *J. Instruct. Dev.*, 5, 22–32.

Reigeluth, C. M. and Frick, T. W. (1999). Formative research: a methodology for creating and improving design theories. In *Instructional-Design Theories and Models*. Vol. II. *A New Paradigm of Instructional Theory*, edited by C. M. Reigeluth, pp. 633–651. Mahwah, NJ: Lawrence Erlbaum Associates.

Reigeluth, C. M. and Rogers, C. A. (1980). The elaboration theory of instruction: prescriptions for task analysis and design. *NSPI J.*, 19, 16–26.

Reigeluth, C. M. and Stein, F. S. (1983). The elaboration theory of instruction. In *Instructional-Design Theories and Models*, edited by C. M. Reigeluth, pp. 335–382. Mahwah, NJ: Lawrence Erlbaum Associates.

Reigeluth, C. M., Merrill, M. D., Wilson, B. G., and Spiller, R. T. (1978). *Final Report on the Structural Strategy Diagnostic Profile Project*. San Diego, CA: Navy Personnel Research and Development Center.

Resnick, L. B. (1967). *Design of an Early Learning Curriculum*, Working Paper 16. Pittsburgh, PA: Learning Research and Development Center, University of Pittsburgh.

Resnick, L. B. and Wang, M. C. (1969). *Approaches to the Validation of Learning Hierarchies*. Pittsburgh, PA: Learning Research and Development Center, University of Pittsburgh.

Resnick, L. B., Siegel, A. W., and Kresh, E. (1971). Transfer and sequence in learning double classification skills. *J. Exp. Child Psychol.*, 11, 139–149.

Richey, R. C., Ed. (2000). *The Legacy of Robert M. Gagné*. Syracuse, NY: ERIC Clearinghouse on Information and Technology.*

Richey, R. C. and Nelson, W. A. (1996). Developmental research. In *Handbook of Research for Educational Communications and Technology*, edited by D. Jonassen, pp. 1213–1245. London: Macmillan.

Richey, R. C., Klein, J. D., and Nelson, W. A. (2003). Development research: studies of instructional design and development. In *Handbook of Research for Educational Communications and Technology*, 2nd ed., edited by D. H. Jonassen, pp. 1099–1130. Mahwah, NJ: Lawrence Erlbaum Associates.

Robinson, E. R. N. (1984). The relationship between the effects of four instructional formats and test scores of adult civilian and military personnel when learning to use a text editor. *Diss. Abstr. Int.*, 45, 3311.

Rousseau, J. J. (1773). *Emile, or a Treatise on Education*. Edinburgh, U.K.: Dickson and Elliot.

Ryle, G. (1949). *The Concept of Mind*. London: Hutchinson.*

Sasayama, G. M. D. (1985). Effects of rules, examples and practice on learning concept-classification, principle-using, and procedure using tasks: a cross-cultural study. *Diss. Abstr. Int.*, 46(01), 65.

Schimmel, B. J. (1983). A Meta-Analysis of Feedback to Learners in Computerized and Programmed Instruction. Paper presented at the Annual Meeting of the American Educational Research Association, April 11–15, Montreal.

Shrager, L. and Mayer, R. E. (1989). Note-taking fosters generative learning strategies in novices. *J. Educ. Psychol.*, 81(2), 263–264.

Smith, P. L. (1992). Walking the Tightrope: Selecting from Supplantive and Generative Instructional Strategies. Paper presented at the Annual Meeting of the Association for Educational Communications and Technology, February, Washington, D.C.

Smith, P. L. and Ragan, T. J. (1993). Designing instructional feedback for different learning outcomes. In *Interactive Instruction and Feedback*, edited by J. V. Dempsey and G. C. Sales, pp. 75–103. Englewood Cliffs, NJ: Educational Technology Publications.

Smith, P. L. and Ragan, T. J. (2005). *Instructional Design*, 3rd ed. Hoboken, NJ: Wiley.*

Spector, J. M. and Muraida, D. J. (1991). Evaluating instructional transaction theory. *Educ. Technol.*, 31(10), 29–35.

Spector, J. M., Muraida, D. J., and Marlino, M. R. (1991). Modeling User Interactions with Instructional Design Software. Paper presented at the Annual Meeting of the American Educational Research Association, April 3–7, Chicago, IL.

Stahl, R. J. (1979). Validating a Modified Gagnean Concept Acquisition Model: The Results of an Experimental Study Using Art-Related Content. Paper presented at the Annual Meeting of the American Educational Research Association, April, San Francisco, CA.

Stein, F. S. (1982). Beyond prose and adjunct questions: a comparison with a designed approach to instruction. *Diss. Abstr. Int.*, 43(09), 2880.

Steinberg, E. R. (1977). Review of student control in computer-assisted instruction. *J. Comput.-Based Instruct.*, 3, 84–90.

Tennyson, R. D. (1984). Application of artificial intelligence methods to computer-based instructional design: the Minnesota adaptive instructional system. *J. Instruct. Dev.*, 7, 17–22.

Tennyson, R. D. and Rasch, M. (1988). Linking cognitive learning theory to instructional prescriptions. *Instruct. Sci.*, 17, 369–385.

Terlouw, C. (1997). Instructional design in higher education. In *Instructional Design: International Perspectives*, Vol. 2. *Solving Instructional Design Problems*, edited by S. Dijkstra, N. M. Seel, F. Schott, and R. D. Tennyson, pp. 341–368. Mahwah, NJ: Lawrence Erlbaum Associates.

Tilden, D. V. (1985). The nature of review: components of a summarizer which may increase retention (instructional design). *Diss. Abstr. Int.*, 45(12), 159.

Ulich, R. (1950). *History of Educational Thought*. New York: American Book Company.

van den Akker, J. (1999). Principles and methods of development research. In *Design Methodology and Developmental Research in Education and Training*, edited by J. van den Akker, N. Nieveen, R. M. Branch, K. L. Gustafson, and T. Plomp, pp. 1–14. Dordrecht: Kluwer.

van Merriënboer, J. J. G. and Dijkstra, S. (1997). The four-component instructional design model for training complex cognitive skills. In *Instructional Design: International Perspectives*, Vol. 1. *Theory, Research, and Models*, edited by R. D. Tennyson, F. Schott, N. M. Seel, and S. Dijkstra, pp. 427–446. Mahwah, NJ: Lawrence Erlbaum Associates.*

Van Patten, J. E. (1984). The effects of conceptual and procedural sequences and synthesizers on selected outcomes of instruction. *Diss. Abstr. Int.*, 44(10), 2973.

Van Tiem, D. M., Moseley, J. L., and Dessinger, J. C. (2001). *Performance Improvement Interventions: Enhancing People, Processes, and Organizations Through Performance Technology*. Silver Spring, MD: International Society for Performance Improvement.

Von Hurst, E. M. (1984). The effectiveness of component display theory in the remediation of self-instructional materials for Japanese learners. *Diss. Abstr. Int.*, 45, 794.

Wang, F. and Hannafin, M. J. (2005). Design-based research and technology-enhanced learning environments. *Educ. Technol. Res. Dev.*, 53(4), 5–23.

Wang, M. C., Resnick, L. B., and Boozer, R. F. (1971). The sequence of development of some early mathematics behaviors. *Child Dev.*, 42, 1767–1778.

Watkins, D. (1983). Depth of processing and the quality of learning outcomes. *Instruct. Sci.*, 12, 49–58.

Wedman, J. F. and Smith, P. L. (1989). An examination of two approaches to organizing instruction. *Int. J. Instruct. Media*, 16(4), 293–303.

West, C. K., Farmer, J. A., and Wolf, P. M. (1991). *Instructional Design: Implications for Cognitive Science*. Upper Saddle River, NJ: Prentice Hall.

White, R. T. (1973). Research into learning hierarchies. *Rev. Educ. Res.*, 43(3), 361–375.*

White, R. T. (1974a). A model for validation of learning hierarchies. *J. Res. Sci. Teaching*, 11, 1–3.

White, R. T. (1974b). Indexes used in testing the validity of learning hierarchies. *J. Res. Sci. Teaching*, 11, 61–66.

White, R. T. (1974c). The validation of a learning hierarchy. *Am. Educ. Res. J.*, 11, 121–136.

White, R. T. and Gagné, R. M. (1974). Past and future research on learning hierarchies. *Educ. Psychol.*, 11, 19–28 (published in Gagné, R. M. (1989). *Studies of Learning*, pp. 361–373. Tallahassee, FL: Learning Systems Institute).

Wiegand, V. K. (1970). A study of subordinate skills in science problem solving. In R. M. Gagne (Ed.), *Basic Studies of Learning Hierarchies in School Subjects, Final Report*, edited by R. M. Gagné (ERIC Document Reproduction Service No. ED03964). Berkeley: University of California.

Wiggins, G. and McTighe, J. (1998). *Understanding by Design*. Upper Saddle River, NJ: Prentice Hall.

Wilson, B. G. (1987). Computers and instructional design: component display theory in transition. In *Proceedings of Selected Research Paper Presentations*, edited by M. L. Simonson and S. Zvacek, pp. 767–782. Ames, IA: Iowa State University.

Wilson, B. G. and Cole, P. (1991). A review of cognitive teaching models. *Educ. Technol. Res. Dev.*, 39(4), 47–64.*

Winkles, J. (1986). Achievement, understanding, and transfer in a learning hierarchy. *Am. Educ. Res. J.*, 23(2), 275–288.

Wittrock, M. C. (1974). Learning as a generative process. *Educ. Psychol.*, 11, 87–95.*

Yao, K. (1989). Factors related to the skipping of subordinate skills in Gagné's learning hierarchies. In *Proceedings of Selected Research Paper Presentations*, edited by M. L. Simonson and D. Frey, pp. 661–674. Ames, IA: Iowa State University.

Yellon, S. L. and Schmidt, W. H. (1971). The Effect of Objectives and Instructions on the Learning of a Complex Cognitive Task. Paper presented at the Annual Meeting of the American Educational Research Association, New York.

* Indicates a core reference.

# 33

# Cooperation and the Use of Technology

*David W. Johnson and Roger T. Johnson*
University of Minnesota, Minneapolis, Minnesota

## CONTENTS

David W. Johnson and Roger T. Johnson

## ABSTRACT

Technology may be more productively utilized when it is combined with cooperative learning. There are four types of cooperative learning: formal cooperative learning, informal cooperative learning, cooperative base groups, and academic controversy. Cooperative learning's worldwide use is based on a well-formulated theory (i.e., social interdependence theory) that has been validated by numerous research studies and operationalized into practical procedures that can be used at any level of education. Technology-supported cooperative learning tends to increase achievement (both academic achievement and learning how to use technology), positive attitudes (toward technology and cooperation), healthy development (cognitive development, learning control, social competencies), positive relationships with team members (including social presence), and innovation in groupware and hardware. Cooperative learning and technology-supported instruction have complementary strengths. The computer, for example, can control the flow of work, monitor accuracy, give electronic feedback, and do calculations. Cooperative learning provides a sense of belonging, the opportunity to explain and summarize what is being learned, shared mental models, social models, respect and approval for efforts to achieve, encouragement of divergent thinking, and interpersonal feedback on academic learning and the use of the technology. The use of cooperative learning with technology-assisted-instruction results in more positive attitudes toward technology (especially by females) and allows for argumentation (i.e., constructive controversy) to be part of lessons utilizing technology. Cooperative learning is an important part of enhancing the effectiveness of interacting around computers and interacting through computers (e.g., local networks, e-mail, videogames and simulations, adventure learning, and interacting with electronic pedagogical agents).

## KEYWORDS

*Collaborative learning:* Students working together to maximize their own and each other's learning (i.e., to achieve shared learning goals); synonymous with cooperative learning in this chapter.

*Competitive learning:* Students working individually to achieve a grade or recognition attainable by or restricted to only a few.

*Computer-supported cooperative learning:* The instructional use of technology combined with the use of cooperative learning.

*Constructive controversy:* Occurs when group members have different information, perceptions, opinions, reasoning processes, theories, and conclusions, and they must reach agreement in order to make progress or proceed.

*Cooperative learning:* Students working together to maximize their own and each other's learning (i.e., to achieve shared learning goals); synonymous with collaborative learning in this chapter.

*Positive interdependence:* Occurs when individuals perceive that they can reach their goals if and only if the other individuals with whom they are cooperatively linked also reach their goals.

## TECHNOLOGY IN THE CLASSROOM

We live in a historical period where knowledge is the most critical resource for social and economic development and people need to be able to participate in a networked, information-based society. Whereas previously people engaged in manufacturing-based work where they generally competed with or worked independently from each other, people now engage in information- and technological-rich work where they work in teams. People need to be able to work cooperatively designing, using, and maintaining the tools of technology. Technology and teamwork will continue to play a larger role in most people's lives. Children, adolescents, and young adults have no choice but to develop and increase their technological and teamwork literacy. There is no better place for them to begin than in school. Learning in cooperative groups (both face to face and online) while utilizing the tools of technology should occur in all grade levels and subject areas.

The failure of schools to adopt available instructional technologies and to maintain (let alone continuously improve) their use may be at least in part due to two barriers: (1) the individual assumption underlying most hardware and software development, and (2) the failure to utilize cooperative learning as an inherent part of using instructional technologies. Technology can either facilitate or obstruct learning, depending on the conditions under which it is used. The ways in which technology may enhance or interfere with learning have not been conceptualized, placed in a theoretical framework, researched, or applied in classrooms. The purpose of this chapter is to clarify the relationship between instructional technologies and cooperation among students. To understand how cooperative learning may be used with technology, the nature of cooperative learning must be defined, the theoretical foundations on which it is based must be clarified, the basic elements that make cooperation work must be defined, and the research validating its use must be reviewed. At that point, the interrelationships between cooperative learning and technology-supported instruction can be noted and their complementary strengths delineated. The future of technology supported cooperative learning can then be discussed.

## THE INDIVIDUAL ASSUMPTION

Before the 1990s, most of the research on computer-supported learning was based on the single-learner assumption. The *individual assumption* is that instruction should be tailored to each student's personal aptitude, learning style, personality characteristics, motivation, and needs. Computers were viewed as an important tool for individualizing learning experiences, especially for programmed learning programs and learning experiences derived from constructivist principles (Crook, 1994). Many hardware and software designers (as well as teachers) assumed that all technology-supported instruction should be structured individualistically (one student to a computer), and computer programs were written accordingly.

The ability of designers to adapt instruction sequences to the cognitive and affective needs of each learner, however, is limited by several factors. One is

the substantial variation that exists in types of learning styles and personality traits and, although many of them are sometimes correlated with achievement, few have been shown to predict achievement consistently. Another is that little agreement exists on how to translate differences in learning styles and personal traits into instructional prescriptions. The only design rule that is widely accepted is that students should control the flow of information. A third is that it is time consuming and expensive to create algorithms to adapt instruction to individual needs and design and produce multiple versions of lessons. Finally, each person has multiple characteristics and traits that interact in unknown and unpredictable ways. Instruction cannot truly adapt to the complex of characteristics and traits that make up one person.

More recently, Web courses have been developed with the assumption that each student will be taking the course individualistically. The individualistic assumption may be as strong today in Web courses as it was in the 1970s and 1980s in the instructional use of the computer. In addition to all of the problems noted above, such individualized instruction assumes that students will work in isolation (which may lower motivation by increasing boredom, frustration, anxiety, and the view that learning is impersonal), with only their own and the course-provided resources, thus they lack support and encouragement from their peers and cannot take advantage of the cognitive benefits associated with explaining to peers and developing shared mental models.

The omission of social interaction in technologically assisted learning experiences worried many educators in the 1980s (Baker, 1985; Cuban, 1986; Hawkins et al., 1982; Isenberg, 1992). Given the limitations and shortcomings of the individual assumption, technology may be more effective when it is combined with cooperative learning. The spontaneous cooperation often reported around technology, in addition, both casts doubt on the individual assumption and points toward the use of cooperative learning in technology-supported instruction (Dwyer, 1994). To use cooperative learning, however, educators must understand its nature.

## THE NATURE OF COOPERATIVE LEARNING

There are advantages to embedding technology-supported instruction in cooperative learning. Cooperative learning may be distinguished from traditional *direct transfer* models of instruction in which the instructor is assumed to be the distributor of knowledge and skills. To understand computer-supported cooperative learning, one must understand the nature of cooperative learning, the theoretical foundations on which it is based, the research validating its use, the distinctions between cooperative learning and other types of instructional groups, and the basic elements that make cooperation work.

## Cooperative Learning

*Cooperative learning* is students working together to maximize their own and each other's learning (i.e., achieve shared learning goals) (Johnson et al., 2002). Cooperative learning is usually contrasted with competitive and individualistic learning. *Competitive learning* is students working against each other to achieve an academic goal such as a grade that only one or a few students can attain. *Individualistic learning* is students working by themselves to accomplish learning goals unrelated to those of the other students. *Technology-supported cooperative learning* (TSCL), or *computer-supported cooperative learning* (CSCL), exists when the instructional use of technology is combined with the use of cooperative learning. Although the use of instructional technology has progressed beyond the computer, and it may be more accurate to discuss technology-supported cooperative learning in this chapter, for historical reasons the term *computer-supported cooperative learning* will be used in most cases in this chapter.

## Collaborative Learning

Cooperative learning is sometimes differentiated from *collaborative learning*, which has its roots in the work of Sir James Britton and others in England in the 1970s (Britton, 1990). Citing Vygotsky (1978), Britton noted that, just as the individual mind is derived from society, a student's learning is derived from the community of learners. Britton was quite critical of educators who wish to provide specific definitions of the teacher's role. He recommended placing students in groups and letting them generate their own culture, community, and procedures for learning. Britton believed in *natural learning* (learning something by making intuitive responses to whatever group members' efforts generate) rather than *training* (the application of explanations, instructions, structures, or recipes for action). The source of learning is interpersonal; learning is derived from dialogs and interactions with other students and sometimes the teacher. Britton viewed structure provided by teachers as manipulation that creates training, not learning; therefore, teachers should assign students to groups, provide no guidelines or instructions, and stay out of

their way until the class is over. As an educational procedure, therefore, collaborative learning has historically been much less structured and more student directed than cooperative learning, with only vague directions given to teachers about its use. The vagueness in the role of the teacher and students results in a vagueness of definition of the nature of collaborative learning.

Many of the current proponents of collaborative learning, however, have developed definitions beyond Britton's. Dillenbourg (1999), for example, stated that collaborative learning is a situation in which two or more people learn or attempt to learn something together. He noted that the terms "two or more," "learn something," and "together" are ambiguous. He then added that the concept of *collaboration* is in itself ambiguous, as the term may refer to the situation, interactions, learning mechanisms, or its effects. What seems to be lacking is a foundational theory of collaboration similar to Deutsch's (1949) theory of cooperation and competition that gives a single, unambiguous definition of collaboration. In breaking with Britton's (1990) position, furthermore, current proponents of collaborative learning recommend structures, procedures, and cognitive strategies to scaffold interaction among students and joint knowledge building. This more structured approach blurs the differences between cooperative and collaborative learning; therefore, the two terms (*cooperative learning* and *collaborative learning*) are increasingly interchangeable and synonymous. In this chapter, the two concepts are considered to be synonymous.

## Types of Cooperative Learning

The four types of cooperative learning that may be used in combination with instructional technology are (Johnson et al., 2002): (1) formal cooperative learning, (2) informal cooperative learning, (3) cooperative base groups, and (4) constructive controversy. *Formal cooperative learning* consists of students working together, for one class period to several weeks, to achieve shared learning goals and complete jointly specific tasks and assignments (such as problem solving, completing a curriculum unit, writing a report, conducting an experiment, or having a dialog about assigned text material). Any course requirement or assignment may be structured to be cooperative. In formal cooperative learning, teachers:

- *Make a number of preinstructional decisions*. A teacher has to decide on the objectives of the lesson (both academic and social skills objectives), size of groups, the method of assigning students to groups, the roles students will be assigned, the materials needed to conduct the lesson, and the way the room will be arranged.

- *Explain the task and the positive interdependence.* A teacher clearly defines the assignment, teaches the required concepts and strategies, specifies the positive interdependence and individual accountability, gives the criteria for success, and explains the expected social skills to be engaged in.

- *Monitor students' learning and intervene within the groups to provide task assistance or to increase students' interpersonal and group skills.* A teacher systematically observes and collects data on each group as it works. When necessary, the teacher intervenes to assist students in completing the task accurately and working together effectively.

- *Evaluate students' learning and help students process how well their groups functioned.* Students' learning is carefully assessed and their performances are evaluated. Members of the learning groups then process how effectively they have been working together.

*Informal cooperative learning* consists of having students work together to achieve a joint learning goal in temporary, *ad hoc* groups that last from a few minutes to one class period (Johnson et al., 2002, 2006). Students engage in quick dialogs or activities in temporary, *ad hoc* groups in response to a limited number of questions about what is being learned. The brief dialogs or activities may be used to focus student attention on the material to be learned, set a mood conducive to learning, help set expectations as to what will be covered in a class session, ensure that students cognitively process the material being taught, and provide closure to an instructional session. Informal cooperative learning groups are often organized so students engage in 3- to 5-minute *focused discussions* before and after a lecture and 2- to 3-minute *turn-to-your-partner* discussions interspersed every 10 to 15 minutes throughout a lecture.

*Cooperative base groups* are long-term, heterogeneous cooperative learning groups with stable membership whose primary responsibilities are to provide support, encouragement, and assistance to make academic progress and develop cognitively and socially in healthy ways as well as holding each other accountable for striving to learn (Johnson et al., 2002, 2006). Typically, cooperative base groups (1) are heterogeneous in membership, (2) meet regularly (for example, daily or biweekly), and (3) last for the duration of the

semester or year or until all members are graduated. Students are assigned to base groups of three to four members that meet at the beginning and end of each class session (or week) to complete academic tasks such as checking each members' homework, routine tasks such as taking attendance, and personal support tasks such as listening sympathetically to personal problems or providing guidance for writing a paper.

These three types of cooperative learning may be used together. A typical class session may begin with a base group meeting, which is followed by a short lecture in which informal cooperative learning is used. The lecture is followed by a formal cooperative learning lesson. Near the end of the class session another short lecture may be delivered with the use of informal cooperative learning. The class ends with a base group meeting.

*Constructive controversy* exists when one student's ideas, information, conclusions, theories, and opinions are incompatible with those of another, and the two seek to reach an agreement (Johnson and Johnson, 1979, 1995, 2003, 2006). Teachers structure academic controversies by choosing an academic issue, assigning students to groups of four, dividing the group into two pairs, and assigning one pair the pro position and the other pair a con position. Students then follow the five-step controversy procedure: (1) prepare the best case possible for their assigned position, (2) persuasively present the best case possible for their position to the opposing pair, (3) have an open discussion in which the two sides argue forcefully and persuasively for their position while subjecting the opposing position to critical analysis, (4) reverse perspectives, and (5) drop all advocacy and come to a consensus as to their best reasoned judgment about the issue. Controversies tend to be constructive when the situational context is cooperative, group members are heterogeneous, information and expertise are distributed within the group, members have the necessary conflict skills, and the canons of rational argumentation are followed.

## THEORETICAL FOUNDATIONS OF COOPERATIVE LEARNING

At least three general theoretical perspectives have guided research on cooperative learning: (1) cognitive–developmental, (2) behavioral, and (3) social interdependence. The *cognitive–developmental* or *constructivist* perspective is largely based on the theories of Piaget (1950) and Vygotsky (1978). The work of Piaget and related theorists is based on the premise that when individuals cooperate on the environment, sociocognitive conflict occurs that creates cognitive disequilibrium, which in turn stimulates perspective-taking ability and cognitive development. The work of Vygotsky and related theorists is based on the premise that knowledge is social, constructed from cooperative efforts to learn, understand, and solve problems. The *behavioral learning theory perspective* focuses on the impact of group reinforcers and rewards on learning. Skinner (1968) focused on group contingencies, Bandura (1977) focused on imitation and joint efficacy, and Homans (1961) as well as Kelley and Thibaut (1978) focused on the balance of rewards and costs in social exchange among interdependent individuals. Although the cognitive–developmental and behavioral theoretical orientations have their followers, by far the theory dealing with cooperation that has generated the most research is social interdependence theory.

## Social Interdependence Theory

*Social interdependence* exists when the accomplishment of each individual's goals is affected by the actions of others (Deutsch, 1949, 1962; Johnson, 1970, 2003; Johnson and Johnson, 1989, 2005). There are two types of social interdependence: positive (cooperation) and negative (competition). *Positive interdependence* exists when individuals perceive that they can reach their goals if and only if the other individuals with whom they are cooperatively linked also reach their goals. Participants, therefore, promote each other's efforts to achieve the goals. *Negative interdependence* exists when individuals perceive that they can obtain their goals if and only if the other individuals with whom they are competitively linked fail to obtain their goals. Participants, therefore, obstruct each other's efforts to achieve the goals. *No interdependence* results in a situation in which individuals perceive that they can reach their goal regardless of whether other individuals in the situation attain or do not attain their goals.

Each type of interdependence results in certain psychological processes. Positive interdependence tends to result in *substitutability* (i.e., the degree to which the actions of one person substitute for the actions of another person), *inducibility* (i.e., openness to being influenced and to influencing others), and *positive cathexis* (i.e., investment of positive psychological energy in objects outside of oneself) (Deutsch, 1949, 1962; Johnson, 2003; Johnson and Johnson, 1989, 2005). Negative interdependence tends to result in nonsubstitutability, resistance to being influenced by others, and negative cathexis. No interdependence detaches a person from others, thereby creating nonsubstitutability, no inducibility or resistance, and cathexis only to one's own actions.

The basic premise of social interdependence theory is that the way in which goals are structured determines how participants interact, and those interaction patterns determine the outcomes of the situation. Positive interdependence results in promotive interaction, negative interdependence results in oppositional or contrient interaction, and no interdependence results in the absence of interaction. *Promotive interaction* may be defined as individuals encouraging and facilitating each other's efforts to complete tasks, achieve, or produce to reach the group's goals. It consists of a number of variables, including mutual help and assistance, exchange of needed resources, effective communication, mutual influence, trust, and constructive management of conflict. *Oppositional interaction* may be defined as individuals discouraging and obstructing each other's efforts to complete tasks, achieve, or produce to reach their goals; individuals focus both on increasing their own productivity and on preventing any other person from producing more than they do. It consists of such variables as obstruction of each other's goal achievement efforts, tactics of threat and coercion, ineffective and misleading communication, distrust, and striving to win in conflicts. *No interaction* may be defined as individuals acting independently without any interchange with each other while they work to achieve their goals; individuals focus only on increasing their own productivity and achievement and ignore as irrelevant the efforts of others.

## The Basic Elements of Cooperation

### Potential Group Performance

Not all groups are cooperative (Johnson and Johnson, 2006). Placing people in the same room, seating them together, or telling them that they are a group does not mean they will cooperate effectively. To be cooperative, to reach the full potential of the group, five essential elements must be carefully structured into the situation: positive interdependence, individual and group accountability, promotive interaction, appropriate use of social skills, and group processing.

### Positive Interdependence: We Instead of Me

The heart of cooperation is positive interdependence. There are three major categories of interdependence: outcome, means, and boundary interdependence (Johnson, 2003; Johnson and Johnson, 2005). When persons are in a cooperative or competitive situation, they are oriented toward a desired outcome, end state, goal, or reward. If there is no outcome interdependence (goal and reward interdependence), there is no cooperation or competition. In addition, the means through which the mutual goals or rewards are to be accomplished specify the actions required on the part of group members. Means interdependence includes resource, role, and task interdependence (which are overlapping and not independent from each other). Finally, boundaries (i.e., discontinuities existing among individuals and groups) can define who is interdependent with whom (Koffka, 1935; Wertheimer, 1923). Discontinuity may be created by environmental factors (different parts of the room or different rooms), similarity (all wearing the same color shirt or jacket), proximity (seated together), past history together, expectations of being grouped together, and differentiation from other competing groups. Boundary interdependence thus includes outside enemy (i.e., negative interdependence with another group), identity (which binds them together as an entity), and environmental (such as a specific work area) interdependence (which are overlapping and not independent from each other).

The authors have conducted a series of studies investigating the nature of positive interdependence and the relative power of the different types of positive interdependence (Johnson, 2003; Johnson and Johnson, 2005). Our research indicates that positive interdependence provides the context within which promotive interaction takes place, that group membership and interpersonal interaction among students do not produce higher achievement unless positive interdependence is clearly structured, that the combination of goal and reward interdependence increases achievement over goal interdependence alone, and that resource interdependence does not increase achievement unless goal interdependence is present also.

### Individual Accountability/Personal Responsibility

*Individual accountability* exists when the performance of each individual member is assessed, the results are given back to the individual and the group to compare against a standard of performance, and the member is held responsible by groupmates for contributing his or her fair share to the group's success (Johnson, 2003; Johnson and Johnson, 2005). Individual accountability tends to increase achievement in cooperative learning, including computer-supported cooperative learning (Hooper et al., 1989; Johnson, 2003; Johnson and Johnson, 1989, 2005).

### Promotive Interaction

The greater the promotive interaction, the stronger the effects of cooperation (Johnson, 2003; Johnson and Johnson, 2005). Technology enables individuals to promote each other success all across the world, but

it does not always substitute for face-to-face interaction. Face-to-face communication has a richness that electronic communication may never match (Prusak and Cohen, 2001). Evidence suggests that up to 93% of people's intent is conveyed by facial expression and tone of voice, with the most important channel being facial expression (Druckman et al., 1982; Mehrabian, 1971). Harold Geneen, the former head of ITT, believed that his response to requests was different in face-to-face encounters than through electronic means, stating that it is easy to say "no" to an electronic request but face to face the answer may be "yes" because of the nonverbal cues attached to the request. He, therefore, made it company policy for problems to be solved face to face (cited in Trevino et al., 1987). Office spaces are increasingly built to maximize face-to-face interaction. The biggest complaint of students in a virtual high school was that interactions with online students just did not measure up to face-to-face context (Allen, 2001). On the other hand, Bonk and King (1998) suggested that promotive interaction in electronic environments has some advantages over live discussion in terms of engagement in learning, depth of discussion, time on task, and the promotion of higher-order thinking skills. Instructional programs, therefore, may be most effective when they include multiple ways for students to promote each other's success, both electronically and face to face whenever possible.

### Interpersonal and Small Group Skills

Cooperative learning is inherently more complex than competitive or individualistic learning because students have to simultaneously engage in taskwork and teamwork. The greater the members' teamwork skills, the higher will be the quality and quantity of their learning (Johnson, 1991, 2003, 2006; Johnson and Johnson, 2005, 2006). The combination of positive interdependence, an academic contingency for high performance by all group members, and a social skills contingency promoted tends to promote high levels of achievement and positive relationships among students.

### Group Processing

*Group processing* occurs when members discuss how well they are achieving their goals and maintaining effective working relationships among members (Johnson and Johnson, 1989, 2005). The purposes of group processing are to clarify and improve the effectiveness of members in contributing to the cooperative efforts to achieve the group's goals by: (1) enabling

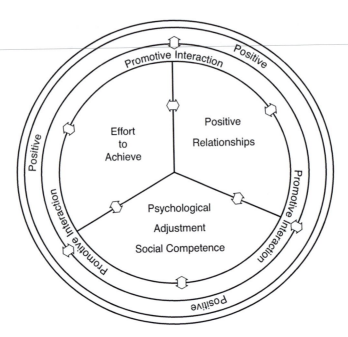

**Figure 33.1** Outcomes of cooperation. (From Johnson, D.W. and Johnson, R., *Cooperation and Competition: Theory and Research*, Interaction Book Company, Edina, MN, 1989. With permission.)

groups to improve continuously the quality of member's work, (2) facilitating the learning of teamwork skills, (3) ensuring that members receive feedback on their participation, and (4) enabling groups to focus on group maintenance. Groups that process how effectively members are working together tend to achieve higher than do groups that do not process or individuals working alone.

## RESEARCH ON COMPUTER-SUPPORTED COOPERATIVE LEARNING

Promotive, oppositional, and no interaction have differential effects on the outcomes of the situation (Johnson and Johnson, 1989, 2005). The research has focused on numerous outcomes, which may be subsumed within the broad and interrelated categories of effort to achieve, quality of relationships, and psychological health (Johnson and Johnson, 1989) (see Figure 33.1). Overall, the evidence is very strong that cooperation (compared with competitive and individualistic efforts) promotes (Johnson and Johnson, 1989, 2005):

- Greater effort exerted to achieve (e.g., higher achievement and greater productivity, more frequent use of higher-level reasoning, more frequent generation of new ideas and solutions, greater intrinsic and achievement

motivation, greater long-term retention, more on-task behavior, and greater transfer of what is learned within one situation to another)
- Higher quality of relationships among participants (e.g., greater interpersonal attraction, liking, cohesion or *esprit de corps*, appreciation for heterogeneity, and task-oriented and personal support)
- Greater psychological adjustment (e.g., greater psychological health, greater social competencies, higher self-esteem, a shared identity, and greater ability to cope with stress and adversity)

These outcomes have been discussed extensively elsewhere (Johnson and Johnson, 1989, 2005). This chapter focuses on the outcomes dealing with computer-supported cooperative learning.

### Computer-Supported Cooperative Learning and Achievement

Two large meta-analyses concluded that the use of technology markedly improved learning outcomes (Fletcher-Flinn and Gravatt, 1995; Khalili and Shashaani, 1994), but no differentiation was made among teaching practices and the ways technology was implemented in the classrooms. We conducted several studies examining the use of cooperative, competitive, and individualistic learning activities at the computer (Johnson et al., 1985, 1989, 1990, 1986a,b,c, 1987). The studies included students from the eighth grade through college freshmen and lasted from 3 to 30 instructional hours. The tasks were a computerized navigational and map-reading problem-solving task and word-processing assignments. Compared with competitive and individualistic efforts at the computer, computer-supported cooperative learning promoted: (1) higher quantity of daily achievement, (2) higher quality of daily achievement, (3) greater mastery of factual information, (4) greater ability to apply one's factual knowledge in test questions requiring application of facts, (5) greater ability to use factual information to answer problem-solving questions, and (6) greater success in problem solving. Cooperation at the computer promoted greater motivation to persist on problem-solving tasks. Students in the cooperative condition were more successful in operating computer programs. In terms of oral participation, students in the cooperative condition, compared with students in the competitive and individualistic conditions, made fewer statements to the teacher and more to each other, made more task-oriented statements and fewer social statements, and generally engaged in more positive, task-oriented interaction with each other (especially when the social skill responsibilities were specified and group processing was conducted). Finally, the studies provided evidence that females were perceived to be of higher status in the cooperative than in the competitive or individualistic conditions.

In addition to our work, a number of studies have found that students using a combination of cooperative learning and computer-based instruction learn better than do students using computer-based instruction while working individualistically (Anderson et al., 1995; Cockayne, 1991; Cox and Berger, 1985; Dalton, 1990a,b; Dalton et al., 1987; Dees, 1991; Fletcher, 1985; Hooper, 1992a,b; Hooper et al., 1993; Hythecker et al., 1985; Inkpen et al., 1995; King, 1989; Lin et al., 1999; Love, 1969; McInerney et al., 1997; Mevarech, 1993; Mevarech et al., 1991, 1987; Okey and Majer, 1976; Postthast, 1995; Regin, 1990; Repman, 1993; Rocklin et al., 1985; Shlechter, 1990; Stephenson, 1992; Underwood and McCaffrey, 1990; Webb, 1984; Weinberger et al., 2005; Whitelock et al., 1995; Yeuh and Alessi, 1988). In contrast, a number of studies have found no statistically significant differences in achievement between subjects who worked in groups and subjects who worked alone (Carrier and Sales, 1987; Cosen and English, 1987; Hooper and Hannafin, 1988; Trowbridge and Durnin, 1984). No study has reported significantly greater learning when students worked alone. Many of these studies, how-

ever, are short-term experiments focused on a small number of students. Several experiments provide evidence that the well-known CSCL programs such as CSILE and Belvedere have proved to be helpful for higher-order social interaction and, subsequently, for better learning in terms of deep understanding (Scardamalia et al., 1994; Suthers, 1998). What is still lacking is evidence that the same results could be found in normal classrooms. Some CSCL projects, such as CoVis, have been widely implemented (Pea et al., 1994), but few well-controlled follow-up evaluations have been published.

Hooper and his colleagues have conducted a series of studies on computer-supported cooperative learning involving fifth, sixth, seventh, and eighth graders and college students (Dyer, 1993; Hooper, 1992a,b; Hooper et al., 1988, 1991, 1989; Huang, 1993; McDonald, 1993). Their findings included the following:

- Cooperative group members achieved significantly higher than did students working under individualistic conditions.
- Cooperative learning groups in which individual accountability was carefully structured achieved higher than did cooperative learning groups in which no individual accountability was structured.
- The achievement of low-ability students in heterogeneous cooperative groups was consistently higher than the achievement of low-ability students in homogeneous groups.
- A positive and significant correlation was found between achievement and helping behaviors, and increases in achievement and cooperation were significantly related within heterogeneous groups.
- Cooperative (compared with individualistic) learning resulted in greater willingness to learn the material, options selection, time on task, perceived interdependence, and supportiveness for partners.

Carlson and Falk (1989) and Noell and Carnine (1989) found that students in cooperative groups performed higher than students working alone on learning tasks involving interactive videodiscs. Adams et al. (1990) suggested that cooperative learning can influence attention, motivation, and achievement when students use the medium of television. Finally, Ocker and Yaverbaum (1999) found that asynchronous cooperation is as effective as face-to-face cooperation in terms of learning, quality of solution, solution content, and satisfaction with the solution quality. Online learners, however, were significantly less satisfied with the asynchronous learning experience, both in terms of the group interaction process and the quality of group discussions. Hiltz (1998) argued that an online learning community structured cooperatively is more effective than working individually.

## Learning How to Use Technology

In addition to academic achievement, cooperative learning may reduce hardware and software problems that interfere with achievement when students work alone (Hativa, 1988). Students naturally form groups when learning how to use a new technology or software program (Becker, 1984). Generally, this evidence indicates that students will learn how to use hardware and software more quickly and effectively when they learn in cooperative groups rather than alone, especially when it involves new and complex procedures (Dwyer, 1994; Dyer, 1993; Hooper, 1992b; Hooper et al., 1993; Keeler and Anson, 1995; McDonald, 1993; Trowbridge and Durnin, 1984; Webb, 1984; Webb et al., 1986). When teachers wish to introduce new technology and new software programs of some complexity, they would be well-advised to use cooperative learning.

## Learner Control

Combining cooperative learning and computer-supported instruction results in students having more control over their learning. Hooper and his associates (Hooper, 1992b; Hooper et al., 1993) noted that three forms of lesson control are used in the design of technology-based instruction: learner, program, and adaptive control. *Learner control* involves delegating instructional decisions to learners so they can determine what help they need, what difficulty level or content density of material they wish to study, in what sequence they wish to learn material, and how much they want to learn. Learner-controlled environments include simulations, hypermedia, and online databases. *Program or linear control* prescribes an identical instructional sequence for all students regardless of interest or need. *Adaptive control* modifies lesson features according to student aptitude (Snow, 1980), prior performance (Tobias, 1987), or ongoing lesson needs (Tennyson et al., 1984). Linear or program control may impose an inappropriate lesson sequence on learners and thereby lower their motivation, and adaptive instruction may foster learner dependence (Hannafin and Rieber, 1989). As learner control increases so does instructional effectiveness and efficiency (Reigeluth and Stein, 1983), as well as learner independence, efficiency, mental effort, and motivation (Federico, 1980; Salomon, 1983, 1985; Steinberg, 1984).

Computer-supported cooperative learning tends to increase the effectiveness of learner control. When students work alone, in isolation from their peers, they tend not to control the learning situation productively, making ineffective instructional decisions and leaving instruction prematurely (Carrier, 1984; Hannafin, 1984; Milheim and Martin, 1991; Steinberg, 1977, 1989). Students working cooperatively tend to motivate each other to seek elaborative feedback for their responses to practice items during learning control and to seek a greater variety of feedback types more frequently than did those working alone (Carrier and Sales, 1987). Cooperative pairs spent longer times inspecting information on the computer screen as they discussed which level of feedback they needed and what the answers were to practice items. Students in the learner-controlled cooperative learning condition selected more options during the lesson and spent more time interacting with the tutorial than did students in the learner-controlled individual learning condition (McDonald, 1993). Hooper et al. (1993) found that students in the program-control conditions attempted more than four times as many examples and nearly twice as many practice questions as did the students in the learner-control conditions. The LOGO computer environment tends to promote more actual learner control over the task structure and the making of rules to govern it than does the CAI computer environment (Battista and Clements, 1986; Clements and Nastasi, 1985, 1988; Nastasi et al., 1990). Learner control seems to be most effective when prior knowledge is high or when students possess well-developed metacognitive abilities (Garhart and Hannafin, 1986). What these studies imply is that cooperative learning is an important variable in improving the effectiveness of learner-controlled environments.

## Computer-Supported Cooperative Learning and Relationships

The impact of cooperative efforts on relationships is as powerful for online relationships as it is for face-to-face relationships. Individuals who are widely separated geographically may develop positive relationships through cooperative efforts conducted through e-mail, chat rooms, bulletin boards, and conferences (Simon, 2003). Communication can be asynchronous and extremely fast in comparison with telephone conversations and interoffice mail. Participation may be more equalized and less affected by prestige and status (McGuire et al., 1987; Siegel et al., 1986). The egalitarian network structures may coexist with substantial hierarchy and centralization in patterns of communication (Ahuja and Carley, 1998). Digital conferencing, however, may make employees less risk averse and render group decision making less predictable, more time consuming, and more egalitarian (Sproull and Kiesler, 1991; Wellman et al., 1996), depending on the specific ways the technological systems are designed and implemented (O'Mahony and Barley, 1999; Sproull and Kiesler, 1991).

Significant differences may be found in relationships built electronically and those built face to face. In electronic communication, it is easy for a sender to be out of touch with the receiver and to be less constrained by conventional norms and rules for behavior in composing messages. Communicators can feel a greater sense of anonymity, detect less individuality in others, feel less empathy, feel less guilt, be less concerned over how they compare with others, and be less influenced by social conventions (Kiesler et al., 1984; Short et al., 1976). Such influences can lead both to more honesty and more *flaming* (name calling and epithets).

## Social Presence

Building relationships electronically may depend on the ability of individuals to create social presence. *Social presence* may be defined as the ability to project one's self and establish personal and purposeful relationships or the sense of being with another (Biocca, 2003). To reduce the drawbacks of distance learning, such as social isolation and decreased motivation, online individuals engaging in cooperative efforts need to develop a social presence to interact effectively. Just because a technology will allow participants to interact with each other does not mean that participants will (Kreijns, 2004). The instructional strategies used must require a consistent level of interaction and sustain the interaction in online learning environments (Muirhead, 2004). The lack of social presence can negatively affect the quality of interaction and cooperation among students (Kreijns et al., 2003; Rourke, 2000). Social presence is essential for online cooperation, as it encourages constructive discourse and builds a climate for exchanging ideas (Rourke et al., 1999) and impacts online learning (Tu and Corry, 2002; Tu and McIsaac, 2002). Social presence is also a predictor of online learners' satisfaction with their learning (Gunawardena and Zittle, 1997) and is crucial for building an online learning community (Hiltz, 1998). Ways to promote social presence include: (1) social interaction, (2) self-disclosure, (3) graphic representations of facial expressions, (4) ice breakers or discussion starters, and (5) development of group identity (e.g., group name or logo).

## Computer-Supported Cooperative Learning and Social Competencies

Numerous studies on computer-supported cooperative learning have demonstrated positive effects on the amount and quality of social interaction (Amigues and Agostinelli, 1992; Crook, 1994; Davis and Huttenlocher, 1995; Fishman and Gomez, 1997; McConnell, 1994; Rysavy and Sales, 1991). When teamwork procedures and skills are present, cooperative learning tends to result in higher achievement in computer-supported instructional lessons than individualistic learning (Hooper and Hannafin, 1988, 1991; Johnson et al., 1985, 1986c; Susman, 1998). In studies where teamwork procedures and skills were not emphasized, reliable differences in achievement in cooperative and individualistic technology supported instruction tended not to be found (McCaffrey, 1990; Mevarech et al., 1987; Susman, 1998; Underwood and Hooper et al., 1989).

Software designers may be able to facilitate the development of the interpersonal and small group skills required for teamwork by requiring initial tutorial activities on cooperative skills, suggesting roles for group members (keyboarder, recorder, checker for understanding, encourager of participation), providing students time for group processing to analyze and discuss how effectively they are working together and how they may work more effectively together in the future, giving reminders for students to monitor their own performance and to assist in optimizing group performance, and providing tangible prizes for individual successes and group achievement may increase motivation to succeed.

## Attitudes toward Technology-Based Instruction

Students tend to develop more positive attitudes toward the computer-based instructional lesson and learning with a computer when they work in cooperative learning groups than when they work individually (Hooper et al., 1993; Huang, 1993; McDonald, 1993; Sutton, 1996); they also tended to experience more enjoyment using the computer to engage in cooperative activities.

## Attitudes toward Cooperative Learning

Students involved in computer-based cooperative learning tend to have more positive towards cooperative learning and how it affects them personally than students who work individually (Hooper et al., 1993; Mevarech et al., 1987; Rocklin et al., 1985). Students participating in structured cooperative learning tend to develop more positive attitudes toward working cooperatively than students participating in unstructured cooperative learning or learning individualistically (Dyer, 1993; Hooper et al., 1993; Huang, 1993; McDonald, 1993).

## Preference for Using Technology Cooperatively

A natural partnership exists between technology and cooperation. The introduction of computers into classrooms tends to increase cooperative behavior and task-oriented verbal interaction (Chernick and White, 1981, 1983; Hawkins et al., 1982; Levin and Kareev, 1980; Rubin, 1983; Webb, 1984). Individuals tend to prefer to work cooperatively at the computer (Hawkins et al., 1982; Levin and Kareev, 1980; Muller and Perlmutter, 1985). Students are more likely to seek each other out at the computer than they normally would for other school work. Even when students play electronic games, they prefer to have partners and associates. Working at a computer cooperatively with classmates seems to be more fun and enjoyable as well as more effective to most students.

## Individual Differences

### Ability and Group Composition

A subject of considerable disagreement is whether the success of computer-supported cooperative learning is affected by the homogeneity or heterogeneity of the group composition. Students in heterogeneous ability groups tend to learn more than students in homogeneous ability groups (Yager et al., 1985, 1986), especially high-ability students (Beane and Lemke, 1971). The academic discussion and peer interaction in heterogeneous (as compared with homogeneous) groups promotes the discovery of more effective reasoning strategies (Berndt et al., 1988; Johnson and Johnson, 1979).

In a week-long study on the learning of LOGO, Webb (1984) investigated whether the higher ability students in cooperative groups of three would try to monopolize the computer. She found that: (1) student ability did not relate to contact time with the computer, and (2) student success in programming was predicted by different profiles of abilities and by group process variables such as verbal interaction. Yeuh and Alessi (1988) used group ability composition as one of their treatments for students utilizing the computer to learn three topics in algebra. They formed groups of medium-ability students and groups of mixed-ability students and found that group composition had no significant effect on achievement. Hooper and Hannafin (1988), in a study with 40 eighth grade students, found that on a computer task low-ability students

working with high-ability partners achieved higher than did low-ability students studying in homogeneous groups or alone, without lowering the achievement of high-ability students. In a subsequent study involving 125 sixth- and seventh-grade students, Hooper and Hannafin (1991) randomly assigned students to homogeneous or heterogeneous pairs and pairs to cooperative or individualistic conditions. The high-ability students interacted equally across treatments, but low-ability students interacted 30% more when placed in heterogeneous pairs. Students in the heterogeneous groups achieved and cooperated significantly more than did students in the homogeneous pairs (or the individualistic condition).

In an interactive videodisc science lesson, both high- and low-ability students spent more time on task and performed better on the post-test when they learned in cooperative groups (as well as developing more positive attitudes toward instruction, teamwork, and peers) than did students studying alone (Simsek and Hooper, 1992), and low-achieving students in heterogeneous cooperative groups tended to achieve higher and had more positive attitudes toward the experience than did their counterparts in homogeneous cooperative groups (Simsek and Tsai, 1992).

Hooper (1992a) compared individual and cooperative learning in an investigation of the effects of ability grouping on achievement, instructional efficacy, and discourse during computer-based mathematics instruction. Students completed the instruction more effectively in groups than alone. In groups, achievement and efficiency were highest for high-ability, homogeneously grouped students and lowest for average-ability, homogeneously grouped students. Generating and receiving help were significant predictors of achievement, and average-ability students generated and received significantly more help in heterogeneous groups than in homogeneous ones. Hooper et al. (1993) compared cooperative and individualistic learning on academically high and average or low performing students. They found that the students in the cooperative conditions performed higher on a computer-supported symbolic reasoning task than did the students in the individualistic conditions. Those who benefited most from the group learning experience appeared to be the highest performing students. Overall achievement increased by almost 20% for high-ability students, but only 4% for average- or low-ability students.

The results of these studies indicate that in technologically supported learning, cooperative learning may be used effectively with both homogeneous and heterogeneous groups, but that the greatest educational benefits may be derived when heterogeneous groups work with technology-supported instruction.

### *Gender*

The gender of group members has been hypothesized to be an important factor in determining the success of computer-supported cooperative learning. Johnson et al. (1986b) found that computer-supported cooperative learning, compared with competitive and individualistic computer-supported learning, increased the positiveness of female students' attitudes toward computers, equalized the status and respect among group members regardless of gender, and resulted in a more equal participation pattern between male and female members. Whereas females in cooperative groups liked working with the computer more than males did, there was no significant difference in oral interactions between males and females. Dalton et al. (1989) examined interactions between instructional method and gender and found that cooperative learning was rated more favorably by low-ability females than by low-ability males. Other studies noted no significant differences in performance between males and females in computer-based instruction cooperative learning settings (Mevarech et al., 1987; Webb, 1984). Carrier and Sales (1987) compared female pairs, male pairs, and mixed pairs among college juniors and noted that female pairs verbalized the most, while male pairs verbalized the least, and male–females pairs demonstrated the most off-task behavior. Lee (1993) found that males tended to become more verbally active and females tended to become less verbally active in equal-ratio, mixed-gender groups. Underwood and McCaffrey (1990) found that single-gender pairs completed more work with greater accuracy than did mixed gender pairs.

Evidence concerning the impact of computer-supported instruction on males and females is mixed. A conservative interpretation of the existing research is that there will be no performance differences between males and females on computer-supported cooperative learning, but females will have more positive attitudes toward using technology when they learn in cooperative groups.

## Constructive Controversy: Argumentation

*Constructive controversy* exists when group members have different information, perceptions, opinions, reasoning processes, theories, and conclusions, and they must reach agreement (Johnson and Johnson, 1979, 1989, 1995, 2003). Being confronted with an opposing point of view promotes uncertainty about the correctness of one's views, an active search for more information, a reconceptualization of one's knowledge and conclusions, and, consequently, greater mastery and retention of the material being studied and

a more reasoned judgment on the issue being considered. Individuals working alone in competitive and individualistic situations do not have the opportunity to experience such a process; therefore, their productivity, quality of decision making, and achievement suffer (Johnson and Johnson, 1979, 1995, 2003). In addition, compared with concurrence-seeking, debate, and individualistic efforts, controversy results in higher quality problem solving, greater creativity in thinking, greater motivation to learn more about the topic, more productive exchange of expertise among group members, greater task involvement, more positive relationships among group members, more accurate perspective taking, higher self-esteem, and greater enjoyment of the experience (Johnson and Johnson, 2003). Controversies tend to be constructive when the situational context is cooperative, group members are heterogeneous, information and expertise are distributed within the group, members have the necessary conflict skills, and the canons of rational argumentation are followed.

Clements and Nastasi conducted a series of studies on the occurrence of cooperation and controversy in computer-supported instruction (Battista and Clements, 1986; Clements and Nastasi, 1985, 1988; Nastasi and Clements, 1992; Nastasi et al., 1990). They found that both LOGO and CAI/CBI-W computer environments promoted considerable cooperative work and conflict (both social and cognitive). The LOGO environment (compared to CAI/CBI-W computer and traditional classroom tasks environments) promoted: (1) greater peer interaction focused on learning and problem solving, (2) self-directed problem-solving (i.e., learners solving problems they themselves have posed) with mutual *ownership* of the problem, (3) more frequent occurrence and resolution of cognitive conflicts, and (4) greater development of executive-level problem-solving skills (planning, monitoring, decision making), as well as higher levels of reasoning and cognitive development. The development of higher level cognitive processes seemed to be facilitated by the resolution of cognitive conflict that arises out of cooperating. They also found that the LOGO (compared with the CAI) computer environment resulted in greater learner satisfaction and expressions of pleasure at the discovery of new information and in their work, variables reflective of intrinsic and competence motivation.

More recently, Bell (2001) developed a program to create arguments to be used in discussions with other students (SenseMaker). It is designed to support a rhetorical construction of arguments by individuals by connecting evidence dots with claim frames. The intent is to teach students the nature of scientific inquiry by coordinating emerging evidence with an

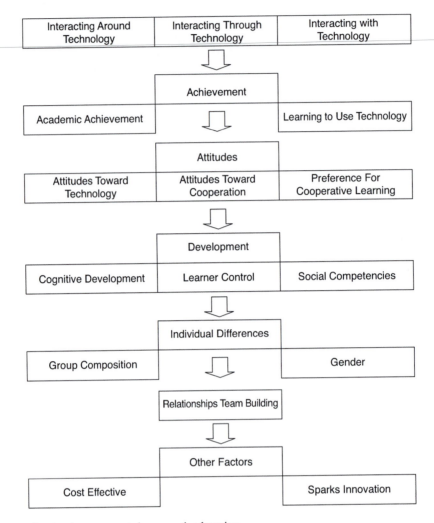

**Figure 33.2** Outcomes of technology-supported cooperative learning.

existing set of theories. McAlister et al. (2004) developed a tool called Academic Talk to support synchronous arguing among peers. Pilkington and Walker (2003) assigned online students roles (i.e., challenger, asker for clarification, provider of information) to structure their online arguments. Baker (2004) developed a program (CONNECT) that allows online students to agree or disagree with each statement made by other students. Suthers (2003) examined an argument map system (Belvedere 3.0) to help students engage in complex scientific argumentation. Studies of the Virtual Collaborative Research Institute (VCRI) tool (Jaspers and Erkens, 2002; Munneke et al., 2003) used argumentative diagrams to broaden students' arguments. Graphic representations can enhance the controversy process by forcing participants to be explicit and complete in presenting their ideas (Suthers and Hundhausen, 2003; van Bruggen et al., 2003), can be used to develop resources for discussion and reasoning (Baker, 2003; Suthers, 2003), can lead to a

shared focus (Veerman, 2000), and can organize students' thinking and maintain coherence during problem solving (Suthers, 2001).

## COOPERATIVE LEARNING AND TECHNOLOGY-SUPPORTED INSTRUCTION

Learning tends to be enhanced when technology promotes cooperation among students and creates a shared experience. In analyzing the relationship between technology and cooperative learning, a distinction can be made between (Crook, 1994) (see Figure 33.2):

- Interacting around computers; for example, computers may be used to facilitate face-to-face cooperation among students (e.g., by providing students with points of shared reference)

- Interacting through computers; for example, local-area networks (LANs) and wide-area networks (WANs) and the global version of the latter (the Internet) provide a variety of mediating tools for cooperation, such as e-mail and text messaging, chat rooms, bulletin boards, conferencing systems, Web pages, blogs, and specialized groupware.

Cooperating with computers (i.e., pedagogical agents) is a growing area of research.

## Cooperation and Computers

### Single-User Programs Reapplied to Cooperative Learning

Many computer programs were developed to tailor learning situations to individual students; however, applying these programs to cooperative learning among students offers several advantages (Crook, 1994; Hawkins et al., 1982). The technical extension of LOGO (Papert, 1980) to legoLOGO (LEGO-brick robots controlled by LOGO programs) has been an especially promising tool for creating cooperation among students (Eraut, 1995; Jarvela, 1996). Cooperative learning has been promoted by many different types of programs, such as databases, spreadsheets, math programs, programming languages, simulations, and multimedia authoring tools (Amigues and Agostinelli, 1992; Brush, 1997; Eraut, 1995; Lehtinen and Repo, 1996).

### Programs Developed to Promote Cooperation

For cooperation to take place, students must have a joint workspace. One of the promises of the computer is that it allows students to create shared spaces. Instead of sharing a blackboard or a worktable, students can share a computer screen. Such *groupware* (aimed at supporting group rather than individual work) has expanded dramatically the past 20 years. Numerous programs in a variety of subject areas have been developed to externalize the problem-solving process by displaying the student's solution or learning paths on the screen, and they generally tend to be helpful for both individual reflection and cooperative problem solving (Pauli and Reusser, 1997; Lehtinen et al., 1998). Technology and cooperative learning have been integrated in numerous ways—for example, in CSILE, the Belvedere system, and CoVis. CSILE (Computer-Supported Intentional Learning Environment), originally developed in the late 1980s (Scardamalia et al., 1989), uses a network to help students

build, articulate, explore, and structure knowledge. The system contains tools for text and chart processing and a communal database for producing, searching, classifying, and linking knowledge. The Belvedere system, developed by Lesgold et al. (1995), focuses and prompts students' cognitive activity by giving them a graphical language to express the steps of hypothesizing, data-gathering, and weighing of information. CoVis (Learning through Collaborative Visualization Project) focuses on cooperative project work in high-school science (Pea et al., 1994) by utilizing advanced networking technologies, collaborative software, and visualization tools to enable students and others to work together in classrooms and across the country at the same time (synchronously) or at different times (asynchronously). These and other groupware systems provide powerful opportunities for cooperative learning.

## Cooperation through Computers

The rapid expansion of computer network technology has allowed students all over the world to create powerful shared spaces on the computer screen. In a network-based environment, students and teachers can interact through the computer free of the limitations of time and place. The speed at which asynchronous and distance communication may be completed makes more intensive cooperation possible with out-of-school experts, brings students from different schools into contact with each other, and creates powerful tools for joint writing and knowledge sharing.

The network environment supports cooperation at different levels. From a series of studies, Bonk and King (1995) concluded that networks can (1) change the way students and instructors interact, (2) enhance cooperative learning opportunities, (3) facilitate class discussion, and (4) move writing from being a solitary to a more active type of social learning. The network tools include *LAN-based client–server systems*, which feature software programs based on local area networks and client–server architectures (e.g., CSILE, Belvedere, and CoVis). Another tool is e-mail, which is used to deliver information to students, supervise students, and support national and international communication between cooperative learning groups and schools located far away from each other. With the help of mailing lists, groups of students can use e-mail to share joint documents and comment on each other's work.

Also, the Internet and World Wide Web may be used for cooperative learning. Internet-based conferencing systems and e-mail systems are very similar. Developments in broad-bandwidth technology have resulted in synchronous shared workspaces and two-way audio-visual communication. Computer conferencing has existed since the first computer networks but has only recently been implemented as part of cooperative learning. Web-based cooperative learning is time independent and location independent, thus allowing a combination of synchronous and asynchronous discussions. Creating and using shared databases is especially helpful for network-based cooperative learning systems. Live video makes it easier for individuals and groups to conference with each other. Personal Web pages that link with those of friends and group members allow individuals to create networks of potential cooperators. Web logs (blogs) allow individuals to share their daily lives with others, exchange opinions and critiques of each other's work, carry on a dialog with others, and comment on current affairs. Personal Web pages and blogs make it easier for individuals to create a social presence and get to know each other on a personal level. Finally, courses and degree programs are offered on the Web through existing schools and through universities that primarily operate on the Web.

A fourth network tool is an immersive, interactive digital entertainment, or videogame playing, which has considerable economic, cultural, and social influence (Squire, 2006) and is often used for cooperative endeavors. Many children, adolescents, and young adults spend more time playing in digital worlds than they do watching television, reading, or watching films (Funk et al., 1999; Williams, 2003). These games are the leading edge of a culture of simulation. Simulations such as *Full Spectrum Warrior* and *America's Army* have changed the training of soldiers in the U.S. Army. Farming and town simulations such as *Animal Crossing* and *Harvest Moon* have make it possible for young children to plan and plant crops, pay off mortgages, and essentially run a farm. Disney's *Toontown* allows children from around the world to interact in a real-time, three-dimensional world where they meet and engage in cooperative quests.

Simulations can utilize cooperative efforts to engage participants in ideological systems, learning by performing, and designed experiences (Squire, 2006). First, ideologies are taught by games such as *Grand Theft Auto* (which teaches students how to survive in a crime-filled society) and *Civilization III* (which involves ruling a civilization from 4000 B.C. to the present, primarily teaching the ideologies of colonialization, economic growth, and democracy). The games immerse players in complex cooperative systems, allowing them to learn the points of view of those systems and develop identities within the systems; thus, organizations such as the U.S. military are using games to support their ideological agenda. Sec-

ond, a core characteristic of games is that they are organized for learning through doing or performance (Squire, 2006). Through recurring cycles of perceiving and acting, thinking and doing, players learn from their experiences, usually in cooperation with other players. In *Toontown*, for example, players band together in teams to play pranks on *cos*, evil cartoon villains who want to turn *Toontown* into a drab office environment. Finally, games provide designed experiences from which participants are active constructors of meaning with their own drives, goals, and motivations. In complex games such as *The Sims*, players form families and live in communities; in *World of Warcraft*, large numbers of players (over 7 million worldwide) form teams to solve puzzles, overcome challenges, and achieve tasks. Augmented reality simulation games (Klopfer and Squire, in press) place students in roles as investigators, scientists, or activists and have students work in cooperative teams to identify problems, pose data-gathering strategies, draw conclusions, and reframe their hypotheses as they work. Increasingly, immersive, interactive digital entertainment will become part of classroom experience, especially when it is coupled with cooperative learning.

The fifth network tool, and one of the most interesting uses of the Web utilizing cooperative learning, is adventure learning programs, such as GoNorth (a free adventure learning program for K–12 classes; www.PolarHusky.com) (Doering, 2006). From 2006 to 2010 a team of educators, scientists, and explorers will dogsled live to five circumpolar Arctic locations and share those experiences with students around the world. A curriculum and activity guide are provided for each trek. Activities on the trail are synched real time to the curriculum so students can engage in powerful cooperative experiences with the educators, scientists, and explorers as well with the huskies pulling the dogsleds (i.e., classes can adopt a dog and get involved in its feeding and care as well as its daily performance). Live field updates and field research findings are presented in collaboration with NASA and the National Science Foundation. The result is a community of over 3 million learners throughout the world acquiring knowledge from the expedition, the Arctic peoples, subject-matter experts, and each other (Doering, in press).

Adding technology to a lesson inherently increases the lesson's complexity. When students participate in technology-supported instruction, they have the dual tasks of learning how to use the technology (i.e., the hardware and software required by the lesson) and mastering the information, skills, procedures, and processes being presented within the technology. When cooperative learning groups are used, students have the additional task of learning teamwork procedures and skills; consequently, the initial use of technology-supported cooperative learning may take more time, but once students and teachers master the new systems the results will be worth the effort.

## Cooperation with Computers

The computer itself may be a member of a cooperative group. Pedagogical agents, human-like virtual characters employed in electronic learning environments (Baylor, 2002), can interact directly with students as if they themselves were human (Doering and Veletsianos, in press; Doering et al., in press; Veletsianos, 2006, 2007). Pedagogical agents have been utilized in a variety of subject areas (Veletsianos, 2006, 2007). Because humans tend to interact with computers and media as if they were human, social interactions between humans and computers may approximate social interactions among humans (Reeves and Nass, 1996; Veletsianos, 2006). If the computer is represented as a human-like character able to dynamically converse and interact in real time with the user, the distinction between human–human and human–computer interaction may blur, creating a situation in which the pedagogical agent and the student work together as a cooperatively pair. An interesting aspect of student–pedagogical agent interaction is that conflicts can arise when students become frustrated by the way the agent interacts or by the lack of agent response. Student anger at an agent indicates that pedagogical agents may soon be created that will be effective members of students' cooperative groups and will be interacted with similarly to interaction among human members. Some day further in the future, pedagogical agents may even exhibit emotions and a human-like intelligence (Veletsianos, 2006).

## Cost Effectiveness

The use of cooperative learning increases the cost effectiveness of technology. Although the range of technology that could be used in schools is increasing yearly, the cost of adopting new technologies is an inhibiting factor to its use. Giving cooperative learning groups access to the latest technology is usually more cost effective (not only for initial cost, but also for maintenance and upkeep) than giving each individual student access. An historical example is the adoption of computers by schools. By having groups work at computers (instead of individuals) schools have been able to significantly reduce the cost of obtaining and maintaining computers (Johnson and Johnson, 1986; Wizer, 1987).

## THE FUTURE OF TECHNOLOGY-SUPPORTED COOPERATIVE LEARNING

The future of technology-supported cooperative learning seems bright, yet it is built primary upon its rapid evolution and its great promise. The full promise of technology-supported cooperative learning will be realized when a number of factors are emphasized. Social interdependence theory provides a framework for understanding the relationship between the instructional use of technology and cooperative learning. When technology isolates students or places them in competition with each other, learning will tend to be obstructed. When technology is combined with cooperative learning, academic achievement is likely to be enhanced.

Research on technology-supported cooperative learning must be increased and should be more theoretically based. Almost all of the existing research has focused on the impact of specific software programs on achievement and related variables without testing theory. In the future, theoretically oriented research should be conducted, and the potential outcomes studied should be expanded. The unique strengths of technology-supported cooperative learning have not been documented.

The lack of theorizing and the narrowness of the research have created a corresponding limitation on the operational procedures for implementation. The implementation of technology-based cooperative learning has been driven by software development and by the traditional ways of structuring cooperation. As technology opens new avenues for cooperation, research should be conducted to provide better guidance as to how to structure technology-supported cooperative learning in ways that optimize its impact and how to train instructors and students in implementing new procedures.

It is clear from social interdependence theory and its validating research that the effective creation of operational procedures depends on the inclusion of five basic elements: positive interdependence, individual accountability, promotive interaction, appropriate use of social skills, and group processing. Groupware programs need to include these five elements more explicitly in their framework.

Longitudinal studies are necessary that track the use of technology-supported cooperative learning for at least one school year and ideally for several years. Although short-term studies of initial use can be quite helpful, investigating the long-term effects of using technology-supported cooperative learning is essential.

One might ask whether or not technology-supported instruction will increase inequality in educational outcomes (Becker and Sterling, 1987). Students who learn how to use technology in a cooperative effort will have an advantage over those who do not and will tend to have more learning opportunities involving technology.

Whereas advocates of technology see a revolution coming in instruction, historians point to the virtual absence of lasting or profound changes in classroom practice over the past 100 years. Lepper and Gurtner (1989) argued that the last technology to have had a major impact on the way schools are run is the blackboard. Most often new technologies are used in ways that do not disrupt regular classroom practices, which means that they can be ignored or dropped with no disruption to ongoing classroom life. Similarly, software selection is often conducted with the intention of supporting existing classroom practices rather than transforming them. Considerably more research is needed on the implementation process by which the combination of cooperative learning and learning technologies becomes integrated and institutionalized in classroom and schools.

## SUMMARY

We live in a networked, information-based society in which teams and technology must manage the complexity of learning, work, and living. For education to develop the technological and teamwork competencies of children, adolescents, and young adults, we must overcome the individualistic assumption that is historically connected with technology-supported instruction and should utilize cooperative learning as an inherent part of instruction. Technology may be more productively utilized when it is combined with cooperative learning. To be a cooperative group, five basic elements must be structured within the learning situation: positive interdependence, promotive interaction, individual accountability, social skills, and group processing. The four types of cooperative learning are formal cooperative learning, informal cooperative learning, cooperative base groups, and academic controversy. The worldwide use of cooperative learning is based on a well-formulated theory (i.e., social interdependence theory) that has been validated by numerous research studies and operationalized into practical procedures that can be used at any level of education. Technology-supported cooperative learning tends to encourage achievement (both academic achievement and learning how to use technology), positive attitudes (toward technology and cooperation), healthy development (cognitive development, learning control, social competencies), positive relationships with team members, positive effects on both high- and low-performing students and both male and female students, cost effectiveness, and innovation in groupware and hardware.

What this research illuminates is that cooperative learning and technology-supported instruction have complementary strengths. The more technology is used to teach, the more necessary is cooperative learning. The computer, for example, can control the flow of work, monitor accuracy, give electronic feedback, and do calculations. Cooperative learning provides a sense of belonging, the opportunity to explain and summarize what is being learned, shared mental models, social models, respect and approval for efforts to achieve, encouragement of divergent thinking, and interpersonal feedback on academic learning and the use of the technology.

There are few educational innovations that have the promise of technology-supported cooperative learning. The combination of cooperation and technology may change the way courses are being delivered, instruction is taking place, and the nature of classroom and school life. More theorizing, research, and refinement of practice are needed to help the field realize its possibilities.

## REFERENCES

Adams, D., Carson, H., and Hamm, M. (1990). *Cooperative Learning and Educational Media*. Englewood Cliffs, NJ: Educational Technology Publications.

Ahuja, M. K. and Carley, K. M. (1998). Network structure in virtual organizations. *J. Comput.-Mediated Commun.*, 3(4) (http://jcmc.indiana.edu/vol3/issue4/ahuja.html).

Allen, R. (2001). Technology and learning: how schools map routes to technology's promised land. *ASCD Curric. Update*, Fall, 1–3, 6–8.

Amigues, R. and Agostinelli, S. (1992). Collaborative problem-solving with computer: how can an interactive learning environment be designed? *Eur. J. Psychol. Educ.*, 7(4), 325–337.

Anderson, A., Mayes, T., and Kibby, M. (1995). Small group collaborative discovery learning from hypertext. In *Computer Supported Collaborative Learning*, edited by C. O'Malley, pp. 23–38. Heidelberg: Springer-Verlag.

Baker, C. (1985). The microcomputer and the curriculum: a critique. *J. Curric. Stud.*, 17, 449–451.

Baker, M. J. (2003). Computer-mediated argumentative interactions for the co-elaboration of scientific notions. In *Arguing to Learn: Confronting Cognitions in Computer-Supported Collaborative Learning Environments*, edited by J. Andriessen, M. Baker, and D. Suthers, pp. 47–78. Dordrecht: Kluwer.

Baker, M. J. (2004). Recherches sur l'elaboration de connaissances dans le dialogue [Research on knowledge elaboration in dialogues]. *Synthese pour l'habilitation a diriger les recherches*. Université Nancy 2.

Bandura, A. (1977). *Social Learning Theory*. Englewood Cliffs, NJ: Prentice Hall.

Battista, M. and Clements, D. (1986). The effects of LOGO and CAI problem-solving environments on problem-solving abilities and mathematics achievement. *Comput. Hum. Behav.*, 2, 183–193.

Baylor, A. L. (2002). Expanding preservice teachers' metacognitive awareness of instructional planning through pedagogical agents. *Educ. Technol. Res. Dev.*, 50(2), 5–22.

Beane, W. and Lemke, E. (1971). Group variables influencing the transfer of conceptual behavior. *J. Educ. Psychol.*, 62(3), 215–218.

Becker, H. (1984). *School Uses of Microcomputers: Reports from a National Survey*, Issue No. 6. Baltimore, MD: The Johns Hopkins University Press.

Becker, H. and Sterling, C. (1987). Equity in schools computer use: national data and neglected considerations. *J. Educ. Comput. Res.*, 3, 289–311.

Bell, P. (2001). Using argument map representations to make thinking visible in the classroom. In *CSCL2: Carrying Forward the Conversation*, edited by T. Koschmann, R. Hall, and N. Miyake, pp. 449–485. Mahwah, NJ: Lawrence Erlbaum Associates.

Berndt, T., Perry, T., and Miller, K. (1988). Friends' and classmates' interactions on academic tasks. *J. Educ. Psychol.*, 80, 506–513.

Biocca, F. (2003). Toward a more robust theory and measure of social presence: review and suggested criteria. *Presence*, 12(5), 456–480.

Bonk, C. and King, K. (1998a). Computer conferencing and collaborative writing tools: starting a dialogue about student dialogue. In *Electronic Collaborators: Learner-Centered Technologies for Literacy, Apprenticeship, and Discourse*, edited by C. Bonk and K. King, pp. 3–24. Mahwah, NJ: Lawrence Erlbaum Associates.

Bonk, C. and King, K., Eds. (1998b). *Electronic Collaborators: Learner-Centered Technologies for Literacy, Apprenticeship, and Discourse*. Hillsdale, NJ: Lawrence Erlbaum Associates.

Britton, J. (1990). Research currents: second thoughts on learning. In *Perspectives on Small Group Learning: Theory and Practice*, edited by M. Brubacher, R. Payne, and K. Richett, pp. 3–11. Oakville, Ontario: Rubicon.

Brush, T. (1997). The effects on student achievement and attitudes when using integrated learning systems with cooperative pairs. *Educ. Technol. Res. Dev.*, 45(1), 51–64.

Carlson, H. and Falk, D. (1989). Effective use of interactive videodisc instruction in understanding and implementing cooperative group learning with elementary pupils in social studies. *Theory Res. Soc. Educ.*, 17(3), 241–158.

Carrier, C. (1984). Do learners make good choices? A review of research on learner control in instruction. *Instruct. Innovator*, 29(2), 15–17.

Carrier, C. and Sales, G. (1987). Pair versus individual work on the acquisition of concepts in a computer-based instructional lesson. *J. Comput.-Based Instruct.*, 14(1), 11–17.

Chernick, R. and White, M. (1981). *Pupils' Interaction with Microcomputers vs. Interaction in Classroom Settings*. New York: Teachers College Press.

Chernick, R. and White, M. (1983). Pupil Cooperation in Computer Learning vs. Learning with Classroom Materials. Paper presented at New York State Psychological Association Meeting, May, Liberty, NY.

Clements, D. and Nastasi, B. (1985). Effects of computer environments on social-emotional development: LOGO and computer-assisted instruction. *Comput. Schools*, 2(2/3), 11–31.

Clements, D. and Nastasi, B. (1988). Social and cognitive interaction in educational computer environments. *Am. Educ. Res. J.*, 25, 87–106.

Cockayne, S. (1991). Effects of small group sizes on learning with interactive videodisc. *Educ. Technol.*, 31(2), 43–45.

Cosen, M. and English, J. (1987). The effects of grouping, self-esteem, and locus of control on microcomputer performance and help seeking by mildly handicapped students. *J. Educ. Comput. Res.*, 3, 443–460.

Cox, D. and Berger, C. (1985). The importance of group size in the use of problem-solving skills on a microcomputer. *J. Educ. Comput. Res.*, 1, 459–468.

Crook, C. (1994). *Computers and the Collaborative Experience of Learning*. London: Routledge.

Cuban, L. (1986). *Teachers and Machines: The Classroom Use of Technology Since 1920*. New York: Teachers College Press.

Dalton, D. (1990a). The effects of cooperative learning strategies on achievement and attitudes during interactive video. *J. Comput.-Based Instruct.*, 17, 8–16.

Dalton, D. (1990b). The Effects of Prior Learning on Learner Interaction and Achievement During Cooperative Computer-Based Instruction. Paper presented at the Annual Meeting of the American Educational Research Association, April 16–20, Boston, MA.

Dalton, D., Hannafin, J., and Hooper, S. (1987). Effects of individual and cooperative computer-assisted instruction on student performance and attitudes. *Educ. Technol. Res. Dev.*, 37(2), 15–24.

Dalton, D., Hannafin, M., and Hooper, S. (1989). Effects of individual and cooperative computer-assisted instruction on student performance and attitudes. *Educ. Technol. Res. Dev.*, 37(2), 15–24.

Davis, J. and Huttenlocher, D. (1995). Shared annotation for cooperative learning. In *Proceedings of CSCL95: First International Conference on Computer Support for Collaborative Learning*. Mahwah, NJ: Lawrence Erlbaum.

Dees, R. (1991). The role of cooperative learning in increasing problem-solving ability in a college remedial course. *J. Res. Math. Educ.*, 22(5), 409–421.

Deutsch, M. (1949). A theory of cooperation and competition. *Hum. Relat.*, 2, 129–152.

Deutsch, M. (1962). Cooperation and trust: some theoretical notes. In *Nebraska Symposium on Motivation*, edited by M. R. Jones, pp. 275–319. Lincoln, NE: University of Nebraska Press.

Dillenbourg, P. (1999). What do you mean by collaborative learning? In *Collaborative-Learning: Cognitive and Computational Approaches*, edited by P. Dillenbourg, pp. 1–19. Oxford: Elsevier.*

Doering, A. (2006). Adventure learning: transformative hybrid online education. *Dist. Educ.*, 27(2), 197–216.

Doering, A. (in press). Adventure learning: situating learning in an authentic context. *Innovate-J. Online Educ.*

Doering, A. and Veletsianos, G. (in press). Multi-scaffolding learning environment: an analysis of scaffolding and its impact on cognitive load and problem-solving ability. *J. Educ. Comput. Res.*

Doering, A., Veletsianos, G., and Yerasimou, T. (in press). Conversational agents and their longitudinal afffordances on communication and learning. *J. Interact. Learn. Res.*

Druckman, D., Rozelle, R., and Baxter, J. (1982). *Nonverbal Communication: Survey, Theory, and Research*. Beverly Hills, CA: Sage.

Dwyer, D. (1994). Apple classrooms of tomorrow: what we've learned. *Educ. Leadership*, 51(7), 4–10.

Dyer, L. (1993). An Investigation of the Effects of Cooperative Learning on Computer Monitored Problem Solving. Ph.D. dissertation. Minneapolis: University of Minnesota.

Eraut, M. (1995). Groupwork with computers in British primary schools. *J. Educ. Comput. Res.*, 13(1), 61–87.

Federico, P. (1980). Adaptive instruction: trends and issues. In *Aptitude, Learning, and Instruction*. Vol. 1. *Cognitive Process Analysis of Aptitude*, edited by R. Snow, P. Federico, and W. Montague, pp. 1–26. Hillsdale, NJ: Lawrence Erlbaum Associates.

Fishman, B. and Gomez, L. (1997). How activities foster CMC tool use in classrooms. In *Proceedings of the Second International Conference on Computer Support for Collaborative Learning (CSCL'97)*, December 10–14, Toronto, Canada, edited by R. Hall, N. Miyake, and N. Enyedy, pp. 37–44. Mahwah, NJ: Lawrence Erlbaum Associates.

Fletcher, B. (1985). Group and individual learning of junior high school children on a micro-computer-based task. *Educ. Rev.*, 37, 252–261.

Fletcher-Flinn, C. and Gravatt, B. (1995). The efficacy of computer assisted instruction (CAI): a meta-analysis. *J. Educ. Comput. Res.*, 12(3), 219–241.

Funk, J. B., Hagen, J. D., and Schimming, J. L. (1999). Children and electronic games: a comparison of parent and child perceptions of children's habits and preferences in a United States sample. *Psychol. Rep.*, 85, 883–888.

Garhart, C. and Hannafin, M. (1986). The accuracy of cognitive monitoring during computer-based instruction. *J. Comput.-Based Instruct.*, 13, 88–93.

Gunawardena, C. N. and Zittle, F. J. (1997). Social presence as a predictor of satisfaction within a computer-mediated conferencing environment. *Am. J. Dist. Educ.*, 11(3), 8–26.

Hannafin, M. (1984). Guidelines for using locus of instructional control in the design of computer-assisted instruction. *J. Instruct. Dev.*, 7(3), 6–10.

Hannafin, M. and Rieber, L. (1989). Psychological foundations of instructional design for emerging computer-based interactive technologies, Part II. *Educ. Technol. Res. Dev.*, 37(2), 102–114.

Hativa, A. (1988). Computer-based drill and practice in arithmetic: widening the gap between high- and low-achieving students. *Am. Educ. Res. J.*, 25(3), 366–397.

Hawkins, S., Sheingold, K., Gearhart, M., and Berger, C. (1982). Microcomputers in schools: impact on the social life of elementary classrooms. *J. Appl. Dev. Psychol.*, 3, 361–373.

Hiltz, S. R. (1998). *Collaborative Learning in Asynchronous Learning Networks: Building Learning*, http://web.njit.edu/~hiltz/collaborative_learning_in_asynch.htm.

Homans, G. C. (1961). *Social Behavior: Its Elementary Forms*. New York: Harcourt, Brace and World.

Hooper, S. (1992a). Effects of peer interaction during computer-based mathematics instruction. *J. Educ. Res.*, 85(3), 180–189.

Hooper, S. (1992b). Cooperation learning and computer-based instruction. *Educ. Technol. Res. Dev.*, 40(3), 21–38.

Hooper, S. (2003). The effects of persistence and small group interaction during computer-based instruction. *Comput. Hum. Behav.*, 19, 211–220.

Hooper, S. and Hannafin, M. (1988). Cooperative CBI: the effects of heterogeneous versus homogeneous groups on the learning of progressively complex concepts. *J. Educ. Comput. Res.*, 4(4), 413–424.

Hooper, S. and Hannafin, M. (1991). The effects of group composition on achievement, interaction, and learning efficiency during computer-based cooperative instruction. *Educ. Technol. Res. Dev.*, 39(3), 27–40.*

Hooper, S., Ward, T., Hannafin, M., and Clark, H. (1989). The effects of aptitude composition on achievement during small group learning. *J. Comput.-Based Instruct.*, 16, 102–109.

Hooper, S., Temiyakarn, C., and Williams, M. (1993). The effects of cooperative learning and learner control on high- and average-ability students. *Educ. Technol. Res. Dev.*, 41(2), 5–18.

Huang, C. (1993). The Effects of Feedback on Performance and Attitude in Cooperative and Individualized Computer-Based Instruction. Ph.D. dissertation, Minneapolis: University of Minnesota.

Hythecker, V., Rocklin, T., Dansereau, D., Lambiotte, J., Larson, C., and O'Donnell, A. M. (1985). A computer-based learning strategy training module: development and evaluation. *J. Educ. Comput. Res.*, 1(3), 275–283.

Inkpen, K., Booth, K., Klawe, M., and Upitis, R. (1995). Playing together beats playing apart, especially for girls. In *Proceedings of CSCL 1995: The First International Conference on Computer Support for Collaborative Learning*, edited by J. Schnase and E. Cunnius, pp. 177–181. Hillsdale, NJ: Lawrence Erlbaum Associates.

Isenberg, R. (1992). Social skills at the computer. *Cooperative Link*, 2(6), 1–2.

Jarvela, S. (1996). New models of teacher-student interaction: a critical review. *Eur. J. Psychol. Educ.*, 6(3), 246–268.

Jaspers, J. and Erkens, G. (2002). *VCRI: Virtual Collaborative Research Institute*, Version 1.0. Utrecht, the Netherlands: Utrecht University.

Johnson, D. W. (1970). *Social Psychology of Education*. New York: Holt, Rinehart and Winston.*

Johnson, D. W. (1991). *Human Relations and Your Career*. Englewood Cliffs, NJ: Prentice Hall.

Johnson, D. W. (2003). Social interdependence: the interrelationships among theory, research, and practice. *Am. Psychol.*, 58(11), 931–945.

Johnson, D. W. (2006). *Reaching Out: Interpersonal Effectiveness and Self-Actualization*, 9th ed. Boston, MA: Allyn & Bacon.

Johnson, D. W. and Johnson, F. (2006). *Joining Together: Group Theory and Group Skills*, 9th ed. Boston, MA: Allyn & Bacon.*

Johnson, D. W. and Johnson, R. (1979). Conflict in the classroom: controversy and learning. *Rev. Educ. Res.*, 49, 51–70.

Johnson, D. W. and Johnson, R. (1986). Computer-assisted cooperative learning. *Educ. Technol.*, 26(1), 12–18.*

Johnson, D. W. and Johnson, R. (1989). *Cooperation and Competition: Theory and Research*. Edina, MN: Interaction Book Company.*

Johnson, D. W. and Johnson, R. (1995). *Creative Controversy: Intellectual Challenge in the Classroom*, 3rd ed. Edina, MN: Interaction Book Company.

Johnson, D. W. and Johnson, R. (2003). Controversy and peace education. *J. Res. Educ.*, 13, 71–91.

Johnson, D. W. and Johnson, R. (2005). New developments in social interdependence theory: the interrelationships among theory, research, and practice. *Genet. Soc. Gen. Psychol. Monogr.*, 131(4), 285–358.

Johnson, D. W., Johnson, R., and Richards, P. (1986a). A scale for assessing student attitudes toward computers: preliminary findings. *Comput. Schools*, 3(2), 31–38.

Johnson, D. W., Johnson, R., Richards, S., and Buckman, L. (1986b). The effect of prolonged implementation of cooperative learning on social support within the classroom. *J. Psychol.*, 119, 405–411.*

Johnson, D. W., Johnson, R., and Stanne, M. (1989). Impact of goal and resource interdependence on problem-solving success. *J. Soc. Psychol.*, 129(5), 621–629.

Johnson, D. W., Johnson, R., Stanne, M., and Garibaldi, A. (1990). The impact of leader and member group processing on achievement in cooperative groups. *J. Soc. Psychol.*, 130, 507–516.

Johnson, D. W., Johnson, R., and Holubec, E. (2002). *Circles of Learning*, 5th ed. Edina, MN: Interaction Book Company.

Johnson, D. W., Johnson, R., and Smith, K. (2006). *Active Learning: Cooperation in the College Classroom*, 3rd ed. Edina, MN: Interaction Book Company.*

Johnson, R., Johnson, D. W., and Stanne, M. (1985). Effects of cooperative, competitive, and individualistic goal structures on computer-assisted instruction. *J. Educ. Psychol.*, 77, 668–677.

Johnson, R., Johnson, D. W., and Stanne, M. (1986c). A comparison of computer-assisted cooperative, competitive, and individualistic learning. *Am. Educ. Res. J.*, 23, 382–392.

Johnson, R., Johnson, D. W., Stanne, M., Smizak, B., and Avon, J. (1987). *Effect of Composition Pairs at the Word Processor on Quality of Writing and Ability to Use the Word Processor*. Minneapolis, MN: University of Minnesota.

Kelley, H. and Thibaut, J. (1978). *Interpersonal Relations: A Theory of Interdependence*. New York: Wiley.

Keeler, C. and Anson, R. (1995). An assessment of cooperative learning used for basic computer skills instruction in the college classroom. *J. Educ. Comput. Res.*, 19(4), 379–393.

Khalili, A. and Shashaani, L. (1994). The effectiveness of computer applications: a meta-analysis. *J. Res. Comput. Educ.*, 27(1), 48–62.

Kiesler, S., Siegel, J., and McGuire, T. (1984). Social psychological aspects of computer-mediated communication. *Am. Psychol.*, 39(10), 1123–1134.

King, A. (1989). Verbal interaction and problem solving within computer-assisted cooperative learning groups. *J. Educ. Comput. Res.*, 5(1), 1–15.

Klopfer, E. and Squire, K. (in press). Environmental detectives: the development of an augmented reality platform for environmental simulations. *Educ. Technol. Res. Dev.*

Koffka, K. (1935). *Principles of Gestalt Psychology*. New York: Harcourt, Brace.

Kreijns, K. (2004). Sociable CSCL Environments: Social Affordances, Sociability, and Social Presence. Ph.D. dissertation. Heerlen: Open University of the Netherlands.

Kreijns, K., Kirschner, P. A., and Jochems, W. (2003). Identifying the pitfalls for social interaction in computer-supported collaborative learning environments: a review of the research. *Comput. Hum. Behav.*, 19, 335–353.

Lee, M. (1993). Gender, group composition, and peer interaction in computer-based cooperative learning. *J. Educ. Comput. Res.*, 9(4), 549–577.

Lehtinen, E. and Repo, S. (1996). Activity, social interaction and reflective abstraction: learning advanced mathematics in a computer environment. In *International Perspectives on the Design of Technology Supported Learning Environments*, edited by S. Vosniadou, E. DeCorte, R. Glaser, and H. Mandl, pp. 105–128. Mahwah, NJ: Lawrence Erlbaum Associates.

Lehtinen, E., Hamalainen, S., and Malkonen, E. (1998). Learning Experimental Research Methodology and Statistical Inference in a Computer Environment. Paper presented at the Annual Meeting of the American Educational Research Association, April, San Diego, CA.

Lepper, M. and Gurtner J. (1989). Children and computers: approaching the twenty-first century. *Am. Psychol.*, 44(2), 170–178.

Lesgold, A., Weiner, A., and Suthers, D. (1995). Tools for Thinking About Complex Issues. Paper presented at the 6th European Conference for Research on Learning and Instruction, August 26–31, Nijmegen, the Netherlands.

Levin, J. and Kareev, Y. (1980). Problem-solving in everyday situations. *Q. Newslett. Lab. Compar. Hum. Cogn.*, 2, 47–51.

Lin, J., Wu, C., and Liu, H. (1999). Using SimCPU in cooperative learning laboratories. *J. Educ. Comput. Res.*, 20(3), 259–277.

Love, W. (1969). *Individual Versus Paired Learning of an Abstract Algebra Presented by Computer Assisted Instruction*. Tallahassee: Florida State University.

McAlister, S., Ravenscroft, A., and Scanlon, E. (2004). Combining interaction and context design to support collaborative argumentation using a tool for synchronous CMC. *J. Comput. Assist. Learn.*, 20(3), 194–204.

McConnell, D. (1994). Managing open learning in computer supported collaborative learning environments. *Stud. Higher Educ.*, 19(3), 175–191.

McDonald, C. (1993). Learner-Controlled Lesson in Cooperative Learning Groups During Computer-Based Instruction. Ph.D. dissertation. Minneapolis: University of Minnesota.

McGuire, T., Kiesler, S., and Siegel, J. (1987). Group and computer-mediated discussion effects in risk decision making. *J. Pers. Soc. Psychol.*, 52, 917–930.

McInerney, V., McInerney, D., and Marsh, H. (1997). Effects of metacognitive strategy training within a cooperative group learning context on computer achievement and anxiety: an aptitude-treatment interaction study. *J. Educ. Psychol.*, 89(4), 686–695.

Mehrabian, A. (1971). *Silent Messages*. Belmont, CA: Wadsworth.

Mevarech, Z. (1993). Who benefits from cooperative computer-assisted instruction? *J. Educ. Comput. Res.*, 9(4), 451–464.

Mevarech, Z., Stern, D., and Levita, I. (1987). To cooperate or not to cooperate in CAI: that is the question. *J. Educ. Res.*, 80(3), 164–167.

Mevarech, Z., Silber, O., and Fine, D. (1991). Learning with computers in small groups: cognitive and affective outcomes. *J. Educ. Comput. Res.*, 7(2), 233–243.

Milheim, W. and Martin, B. (1991). Theoretical bases for the use of learner control: three different perspectives. *J. Comput.-Based Instruct.*, 18(3), 99–105.

Muirhead, B. (2004). Encouraging interaction in online classes. *Int. J. Instruct. Technol. Dist. Learn.*, 1(6).

Muller, A. and Perlmutter, M. (1985). Preschool children's problem-solving interactions at computers and jigsaw puzzles. *J. Appl. Dev. Psychol.*, 6, 173–186.

Munneke, L., van Amelsvoort, M., and Andriessen, J. (2003). The role of diagrams in collaborative argumentation-based learning. *Int. J. Educ. Res.*, 39, 113–131.

Nastasi, B. and Clements, D. (1992). Social-cognitive behaviors and higher-order thinking in educational computer environments. *Learn. Instruct.*, 2, 215–238.

Nastasi, B., Clements, D., and Battista, M. (1990). Social-cognitive interactions, motivation, and cognitive growth in LOGO programming and CAI problem-solving environments. *J. Educ. Psychol.*, 82, 150–158.

Noell, J. and Carnine, D. (1989). Group and individual computer-based video instruction. *Educ. Technol.*, 29(1), 36–37.

Ocker, R. J. and Yaverbaum, G. (1999). Asynchronous computer-mediated communication versus face-to-face collaboration: results on student learning, quality, and satisfaction. *Group Decis. Negot.*, 8, 427–440.

Okey, J. R. and Majer, K. (1976). Individual and small-group learning with computer-assisted instruction. *AV Commun. Rev.*, 24(1), 79–86.

O'Mahony, S. and Barley, S. (1999). Do digital telecommunications affect work and organization? The state of our knowledge. *Res. Org. Behav.*, 21, 125–161.

Papert, S. (1980). *Mindstorms: Children, Computers, and Powerful Ideas*. New York: Basic Books.*

Pauli, C. and Reusser, K. (1997). Supporting collaborative problem solving: supporting collaboration and supporting problem solving. In *Proc. of Swiss Workshop on Collaborative and Distributed Systems*, May 2, Lausanne, Switzerland.

Pea, R. D., Edelson, E., and Gomez, L. (1994). The CoVis Collaboratory: High School Science Learning Supported by a Broadband Education Network with Scientific Visualization, Videoconferencing, and Collaborative Computing. Paper presented at the Annual Meeting of the American Educational Research Association, April 4–8, New Orleans, LA.

Piaget, J. (1950). *The Psychology of Intelligence*. New York: Harcourt.*

Pilkington, R. and Walker, A. (2003). Facilitating debate in networked learning: reflecting on online synchronous discussion in higher education. *Instruct. Sci.*, 31, 41–63.

Postthast, M. (1995). Cooperative Learning Experiences in Introductory Statistics. Paper presented at the Annual Meeting of the American Educational Research Association, April 18–22, San Francisco, CA.

Prusak, L. and Cohen, D. (2001). *In Good Company: How Social Capital Makes Organizations Work*. Cambridge, MA: Harvard Business School Press.

Reeves, B. and Nass, C. I. (1996). *The Media Equation: How People Treat Computers, Television, and New Media as Real People and Places*. Cambridge, U.K.: Cambridge University Press.

Regin, G. (1990). The effects of individualized and cooperative computer assisted instruction on mathematics achievement and mathematics anxiety for prospective teachers. *J. Res. Comput. Educ.*, 22, 404–412.

Reigeluth, C. M. and Stein, F. S. (1983). The elaborative theory of instruction. In *Instructional Design Theories and Models*, edited by C. M. Reigeluth, pp. 335–382. Hillsdale, NJ: Lawrence Erlbaum Associates.

Repman, J. (1993). Collaborative, computer-based learning: cognitive and affective outcomes. *J. Educ. Comput. Res.*, 9(2), 149–163.

Rocklin, T., O'Donnell, A., Dansereau, D., Lambiotte, J., Hythecker, V. I., and Larson, C. (1985). Training learning strategies with computer-aided cooperative learning. *Comput. Educ.*, 9(1), 67–71.

Rourke, L. (2000). Operationalizing social interaction in computer conferencing. In *Proc. of the 16th Annual Conf. of the Canadian Association for Distance Education*, http://www.ulaval.ca/aced2000cade/english/proceedings.html.

Rourke, L., Anderson, T., Garrison, D. R., and Archer, W. (1999). Assessing social presence in asynchronous text-based computer conferencing. *J. Dist. Educ.*, 14(3), 51–70.

Rubin, A. (1983). The computer confronts language arts: cans and shoulds for education. In *Classroom Computers and Cognitive Science*, edited by A. Wilkinson, pp. 201–218. San Diego, CA: Academic Press.

Rysavy, D. and Sales, G. (1991). Cooperative learning in computer-based instruction. *Educ. Technol., Res. Dev.*, 39(2), 70–79.

Salomon, G. (1983). The differential investment of mental effort in learning from different sources. *Educ. Psychol.*, 18(1), 42–50.

Salomon, G. (1985). Information technologies: what you see is not (always) what you get. *Educ. Psychol.*, 20(4), 207–216.*

Scardamalia, M., Bereiter, C., McLearn, R., Swallow, J., and Woodruff, D. (1989). Computer supported intentional learning environments. *J. Educ. Comput. Res.*, 5(1), 51–68.*

Scardamalia, M., Bereiter, K., and Lamon, M. (1994). The CSILE project: trying to bring the classroom into world 3. In *Classroom Lessons: Integrating Cognitive Theory and Classroom Practice*, edited by K. McGilly, pp. 201–228. Cambridge, MA: Bradford Books/MIT Press.

Shlechter, T. (1990). The relative instructional efficiency of small group computer-based training. *J. Educ. Comput. Res.*, 6, 329–341.*

Short, J., Williams, E., and Christie, B. (1976). *The Social Psychology of Telecommunications*. London: Wiley.

Siegel, J., Dubrovsky, V., Kiesler, S., and McGuire, T. (1986). Group processes in computer-mediated communication. *Organ. Behav. Hum. Dec. Proc.*, 37, 157–187.

Simsek, A. and Hooper, S. (1992). The effects of cooperative versus individual videodisc learning on student performance and attitudes. *Int. J. Instruct. Media*, 19(3), 209–218.

Simsek, A. and Tsai, B. (1992). The impact of cooperative group composition on student performance and attitudes during interactive videodisc instruction. *J. Comput.-Based Instruct.*, 19(3), 86–91.

Skinner, B. (1968). *The Technology of Teaching*. New York: Appleton-Century-Crofts.*

Snow, R. (1980). Aptitude, learner control, and adaptive instruction. *Educ. Psychol.*, 15, 151–158.*

Sproull, L. and Kiesler, S. (1991). Computers, networks and work. *Sci. Am.*, 65, 116–123.

Squire, K. (2006). From content to context: videogames as designed experience. *Educ. Res.*, 35(8), 19–29.

Steinberg, E. R. (1977). Review of student control in computer-assisted instruction. *J. Comput.-Based Instruct.*, 3(3), 84–90.

Steinberg, E. R. (1984). *Teaching Computers to Teach*. Hillsdale, NJ: Lawrence Erlbaum Associates.

Steinberg, E. R. (1989). Cognition and learner control: a literature review, 1977–1988. *J. Comput.-Based Instruct.*, 16(4), 117–124.*

Stephenson, S. (1992). Effects of student-instructor interaction and paired/individual study on achievement in computer-based training (CBT). *J. Comput.-Based Instruct.*, 19(1), 22–26.*

Susman, E. (1998). Cooperative learning: a review of factors that increase the effectiveness of cooperative computer-based instruction. *J. Educ. Comput. Res.*, 18(4), 303–332.

Suthers, D. D. (1998). *Computer Aided Education and Training Initiative*, Technical Report 12. Pittsburgh, PA: Learning and Research Development Center, University of Pittsburgh.

Suthers, D. D. (2001). Towards a systematic study of representational guidance for collaborative learning discourse. *J. Universal Comput. Sci.*, 7(3), 254–277.

Suthers, D. D. (2003). Studies of representational support for collaborative inquiry with Belvedere. In *Arguing to Learn: Confronting Cognitions in Computer-Supported Collaborative Learning Environments*, edited by J. Andriessen, M. Baker, and D. Suthers, pp. 27–46. Dordrecht: Kluwer.

Suthers, D. D. and Hundhausen, C. D. (2003). An experimental study of the effects of representational guidance on collaborative learning processes. *J. Learn. Sci.*, 12(2), 183–218.

Sutton, S. (1996). Planning for the twenty-first century: the California State University. *J. Am. Soc. Inform. Sci.*, 47(11), 821–825.

Tennyson, R. D., Christensen, D., and Park, O. (1984). The Minnesota Adaptive Instructional System: a review of its theory and research. *J. Comput.-Based Instruct.*, 11(1), 2–13.*

Tobias, S. (1987). Mandatory text review and interaction with student characteristics. *J. Educ. Psychol.*, 79, 154–161.

Trevino, L., Lengel, R., and Daft, R. (1987). Media symbolism, media richness, and media choice in organizations: a symbolic interactionist perspective. *Commun. Res.*, 14, 553–574.

Trowbridge, D. and Durnin, R. (1984). *Results from an Investigation of Groups Working at the Computer*. Washington, D.C.: National Science Foundation.

Tu, C. H. and Corry, M. (2002). The Relationships of Social Presence, Tasks, and Social Relationships in Online Learning Environment. Paper presented at the Annual Meeting of the American Educational Research Association, April 1–5, New Orleans, LA.

Tu, C. H. and McIsaac, M. S. (2002). An examination of social presence to increase interaction in online classes. *Am. J. Dist. Educ.*, 16(3), 131–150.

Underwood, G. and McCaffrey, M. (1990). Gender differences in a cooperative computer-based language task. *Educ. Res.*, 32, 44–49.

van Bruggen, J. M., Boshuizen, H. P. A., and Kirschner, P. A. (2003). A cognitive framework for cooperative problem solving with argument visualization. In *Visualizing Argumentation: Software Tools for Collaborative and Education Sense-Making*, edited by P. A. Kirschner, S. J. Buckinghan Shum, and C. S. Carr, pp. 25–47. London: Springer.

Veerman, A. L. (2000). Computer-Supported Collaborative Learning through Argumentation. Ph.D. dissertation. Utrecht, the Netherlands: Utrecht University.

Veletsianos, G. (2006). Contextual Pedagogical Agents: Stereotypes and First Impressions and their Impact on Student Learning and Perceptions of Agent Persona. Master's thesis. Minneapolis: University of Minnesota.

Veletsianos, G. (2007). Conversing with intelligent agents: a phenomenological exploration of communication with digital entities. Paper presented at the Annual Meeting of the American Educational Research Association, April 9–13, Chicago, IL.

Vygotsky, L. (1978) *Mind in Society.* Cambridge, MA: Harvard University Press.*

Webb, N. (1984). Microcomputer learning in small groups: cognitive requirements and group processes. *J. Educ. Psychol.*, 76, 1076–1088.

Webb, N., Ender, P., and Lewis, S. (1986). Problem solving strategies and group processes in small group learning computer programming. *Am. Educ. Res. J.*, 23(2), 243–261.

Weinberger, A., Etrl, B., Fischer, F., and Mandl, H. (2005). Epistemic and social scripts in computer-supported collaborative learning. *Instruct. Sci.*, 33, 1–30.

Wertheimer, M. (1923). Untersuchungen zur Lehre von der Gestalt: II. *Psychologische Forschung*, 4, 301–350.

Whitelock, D., Scanlon, E., Taylor, J., and O'Shea, T. (1995). Computer support for pupils collaborating: a case study on collisions. In *Proceedings of CSCL 1995: The First International Conference on Computer Support for Collaborative Learning,* edited by J. Schnase and E. Cunnius, pp. 380–384. Hillsdale, NJ: Lawrence Erlbaum Associates.

Wellman, B., Salaff, J., Dimitrova, D., Garton, L., Gulia, M., and Haythornwaite, C. (1996). Computer networks as social networks: collaborative work, telework, and virtual community. *Annu. Rev. Soc.*, 22, 213–238.

Williams, D. (2003). The video game lightning rod. *Inform. Commun. Soc.*, 6(4), 523–550.

Wizer, D. R. (1987). Cooperative learning with microcomputers. *Pointer*, 32, 31–33.

Yager, S., Johnson, D. W, and Johnson, R. (1985). Oral discussion, group-to-individual transfer, and achievement in cooperative learning groups. *J. Educ. Psychol.*, 77(1), 60–66.

Yager, S., Johnson, R., Johnson, D. W., and Snider, B. (1986). The impact of group processing on achievement in cooperative learning groups. *J. Social Psychol.*, 126, 389–397.

Yeuh, J. and Alessi, S. (1988). The effects of reward structure and group ability composition on cooperative computer-assisted instruction. *J. Comput.-Based Instruct.*, 15, 18–22.

---

* Indicates a core reference.

# 34

# The Cognitive Apprenticeship Model in Educational Practice

*Vanessa P. Dennen and Kerry J. Burner*
Florida State University, Tallahassee, Florida

## CONTENTS

Vanessa P. Dennen and Kerry J. Burner

## ABSTRACT

Cognitive apprenticeship is a process by which learners learn from a more experienced person by way of cognitive and metacognitive skills and processes. This chapter explores the elements of cognitive apprenticeship, first offering definitions and a historical context, then moving into a review of research. The research review is organized with a three-part focus: on studies that investigate a holistic approaches to educational applications of the process of cognitive apprenticeship; on studies that investigate portions of the process, such as scaffolding or mentoring; and on studies that investigate cognitive apprenticeship activities within communities of practice. Discussion about the intersection of technology and cognitive apprenticeship research is imbedded within each of the three areas of focus, reflecting the steady increase of systematically designed, computer-mediated instruction that is based in social learning theories, especially cognitive apprenticeship theories. Empirical studies have confirmed much of what theories have suggested: (1) that the cognitive apprenticeship model is an accurate description of how learning occurs, and (2) that the instructional strategies that have been extracted from these observations of everyday life can be designed into more formal learning contexts with positive effect. The chapter concludes with a call for more systematic and integrated program of studies working toward the development of guiding principles to support instructional design, teaching, and learning based on the cognitive apprenticeship model.

## KEYWORDS

*Apprenticeship:* A process through which a more experienced person assists a less experienced one by way of demonstration, support, and examples.

*Articulation:* In cognitive apprenticeship, verbalizing the results of reflective acts.

*Coaching:* In cognitive apprenticeship, assisting and supporting learners' cognitive activities.

*Cognitive apprenticeship:* An apprenticeship process that utilizes cognitive and metacognitve skills and processes to guide learning.

*Community of practice:* A group of people bound by participation in an activity common to them all; may be formal or informal.

*Exploration:* In cognitive apprenticeship, forming and testing a personal hypothesis in pursuit of learning.

*Modeling:* In cognitive apprenticeship, demonstrating thought processes.

*Reflection:* In cognitive apprenticeship, self-analysis and self-assessment.

*Scaffolding:* Support that is provided to assist learners in reaching skill levels beyond their current abilities; essential to scaffolding is fading the support inversely to the learners' acquisition of the skill that is being supported.

*Situatedness:* The context or constellation of influential events and elements that govern and shape human life.

*Zone of proximal development (ZPD):* A term coined by Vygotsky to describe the space between a learner's current skill level and the next skill level that the learner cannot reach without assistance.

## INTRODUCTION

Long before education was a field studied in universities—indeed, long before universities even existed—people were learning via apprenticeship. Most simply put, it is a process through which a more experienced person assists a less experienced one, providing support and examples, so the less experienced person gains new knowledge and skills. Apprenticeship is the process through which a parent may teach a child how to tie her shoes and the process through which a person may learn to become a chef or a tailor. In the first example, one would not expect the child to see a demonstration and be able to tie a shoe with no assistance on the first try. Similarly, it seems logical that a new chef starts out with simpler tasks, such as chopping ingredients or garnishing plates, and works his way up to preparing entire dishes and meals. Often larger skills are broken into smaller ones, and supports are provided so that tasks that are given to the apprenticing learner are within the reach of the learner's current ability level or zone of proximal development (ZPD) (Vygotsky, 1978). Also critical to apprenticeship is that tasks must be representative of authentic skills and not merely classroom-type exercises.

Apprenticeship programs have been formalized in many vocational education programs; for example, to become a journeyman electrician, one must work through various levels of apprenticeship. The educational value of apprenticeship, however, is not limited to the learning psychomotor skills or vocational trades. Apprenticeships can just as readily support cognitive and metacognitive learning processes and may appear in both formal and informal learning environments. This chapter first provides a brief description of concepts related to the cognitive apprenticeship model, followed by a description of the instructional strategies that comprise this model. Finally, it presents a summary of recent research related to the use of cognitive apprenticeship and its component instructional strategies.

# COGNITIVE APPRENTICESHIP DEFINED

The concept of a cognitive apprenticeship—defined as "learning through guided experience on cognitive and metacognitive, rather than physical, skills and processes" by Collins et al. (1989, p. 456)—has its roots in social learning theories. One cannot engage in a cognitive apprenticeship alone, but rather it is dependent on expert demonstration (modeling) and guidance (coaching) in the initial phases of learning. Learners are challenged with tasks slightly more difficult than they can accomplish on their own and must rely on assistance from and collaboration with others to achieve these tasks. In other words, learners must work with more experienced others and with time move from a position of observation to one of active practice. The learning tasks in cognitive apprenticeship are holistic in nature (see Chapter 35 on whole-task models in this *Handbook*) and increase in complexity and diversity over time as the learner becomes more experienced. A major advantage of learning by cognitive apprenticeship as opposed to traditional classroom-based methods is the opportunity to see the subtle, tacit elements of expert practice that may not otherwise be explicated in a lecture or knowledge-dissemination format.

## Instructional Strategies and Models Associated with Cognitive Apprenticeship

Although cognitive apprenticeships readily occur on their own, without intervention, certain instructional strategies are hallmarks of the theory and can be purposely implemented to support learning. Intentional teaching and learning through cognitive apprenticeship require making tacit processes visible to learners so they can observe and then practice them (Collins et al., 1989). The basic model consists of the following strategies:

- *Modeling*—Demonstrating the thinking process
- *Coaching*—Assisting and supporting student cognitive activities as needed (includes scaffolding)
- *Reflection*—Self-analysis and assessment
- *Articulation*—Verbalizing the results of reflection
- *Exploration*—Formation and testing of one's own hypotheses

Note that these strategies refer to the teacher's or expert's actions; the learners in cognitive apprenticeships (CAs) are engaged in acts of observation, practice, and reflection.

Collins and colleagues' (1989) model generally is considered the foundational one, but other slightly different versions have been proposed. Gallimore and Tharp (1990) identified six forms of scaffolded assistance: (1) instructing, (2) questioning, (3) modeling, (4) feeding back, (5) cognitive structuring, and (6) contingency management. Enkenberg (2001) added scaffolding and explanation as key strategies. LeGrand Brandt et al. (1993) presented a sequential model of modeling (both behavioral and cognitive), approximating, fading, self-directed learning, and generalizing. Liu (2005), who used a cognitive apprenticeship approach to support preservice education, offers instructional designers a three-phase Web-based CA model with a dynamic relationship between the initial modeling–observing phase and the second scaffolding–practice phase, which then is followed by the guiding–generalizing phase. The similarities across these models are their reliance on instructional strategies that provide learner guidance and engage learners in different types of practice until the guidance is no longer needed.

## Concepts Associated with Cognitive Apprenticeship

Four key concepts commonly discussed in the cognitive apprenticeship literature are (1) situatedness, (2) legitimate peripheral participation, (3) guided participation, and (4) membership in a community of practice.

### Situatedness

Situated learning is active learning that takes place via one's participation in an authentic task or setting (Lave and Wenger, 1991). Context, or situatedness, reflects the ways in which cultural, historical, and institutional factors influence the actions of our everyday lives (Brown et al., 1989; Rogoff, 1990; Wertsch, 1998). Learning that occurs within the context of application is considered more likely to result in improved practice; for example, would you prefer to receive medical treatment from someone who has classroom training only or someone who has trained on actual patients in a clinical setting? As Brown et al. (1998, p. 230) indicated, "The central issue in learning is becoming a practitioner, not learning about practice." Current educational systems, particularly universities, have been criticized for separating learning from practice, resulting in an education that does not sufficiently prepare students for job performance (Enkenberg, 2001); in other words, these systems are criticized when they lack situatedness and fail to engage learners in authentic practices with cultural tools and natural performance conditions.

## *Legitimate Peripheral Participation*

In cognitive apprenticeship, a newcomer who primarily observes is considered a legitimate peripheral participant. In essence, this label validates observation as a learning activity. It would be unreasonable to expect a newcomer to be a full participant in an activity. One must learn not only the whole tasks to be accomplished and their assessment criteria but also the smaller tasks that comprise them. An apprentice can gain initial experience through observing a holistic process from the periphery. Once the big picture is understood, participation can shift from peripheral to active, with the learner completing smaller, component parts of the larger task while receiving iterations of feedback from someone who is more experienced. At this point, the learner is no longer a legitimate peripheral participant, but instead is inbound, beginning to identify more with insiders of the community's practice.

## *Guided Participation*

Guided participation is the social element of cognitive apprenticeship. Often the guidance is provided tacitly, as one naturally participates in everyday life (Rogoff, 1990); there is an inherently situated component to guided participation. Guided participation, to be successful, must take place within a learner's zone of proximal development (ZPD). The ZPD, as originally defined by Vygotsky (1978), is a dynamic region that is just beyond the learner's current ability level; the ZPD of a learner gaining new skills and understanding moves with that learner's development. This space between actual and potential performance is assessed through social interaction between the learner and someone who is more experienced—potentially a teacher, parent, or even an advanced peer. Tharp and Gallimore (1988) used a four-stage model to describe the dynamic and recursive process through which learners work within their ZPDs and come to internalize knowledge, only to begin again with newly defined ZPDs. Rogoff (1990, p. 16) noted that cultural learning and development, in addition to individual cognitive development, occur as a result of teaching and learning in the ZPD:

> Interactions in the zone of proximal development are the crucible of development *and* of culture, in that they allow children to participate in activities that would be impossible for them alone, using cultural tools that themselves must be adapted to the specific practical activities at hand.

This observation again stresses the situated nature and social interconnectedness of learning through cognitive apprenticeship.

## Community of Practice

Although learning organizations and institutions have sought to implement elements of cognitive apprenticeships in formal learning situations, cognitive apprenticeships often naturally occur within a community of practice (CoP). A community of practice is a group of people—either formally or informally bound—who engage in and identify themselves with a common practice. Examples of a CoP might be educators within a given school district or members of a professional organization for clarinetists. What brings these people together as a CoP are three critical elements:

- *Mutual engagement*—A shared task or interest and a resulting identity
- *Joint enterprise*—A common set of community standards and expectations
- *Shared repertoire*—A common vocabulary that differentiates the CoP from others

Wenger (1998) suggested the following trajectories as a model of how membership within a community of practice occurs:

- *Peripheral*—One who may not become an insider to the community but who nevertheless takes part in community events (e.g., parents who volunteer in the classroom)
- *Inbound*—A person who is becoming a fully participating member of the community (e.g., a student teacher or brand new teacher)
- *Insider*—A person who has become a fully participating member of a community (e.g., a teacher)
- *Boundary*—A person who is not a fully participating member of the community but who participates by bringing a different set of skills or services to the community (e.g., a technology specialist)
- *Outbound*—A person who is preparing to leave the community (e.g., a teacher who is moving to an administrative position or preparing to retire)

Although one may enter a community on one trajectory point and move to other points (e.g., inbound to insider and eventually to outbound), such a path is not mandated. Learning need not occur through the interactions of participants on different levels of the trajectory; for example, teacher professional development may occur through peer reciprocal teaching (Glazer and Hannafin, 2006). Movement through the trajectories is fluid in many contexts, although some communities may have formal levels of membership that are aligned with these labels. The utility of the labels is that they support understanding of the different ways in which people might participate in a CoP or a cognitive apprenticeship.

# RESEARCH ON COGNITIVE APPRENTICESHIP

The body of research on cognitive apprenticeship has been growing steadily and in many ways overlaps with research on other constructivist learning theories and methods. For this chapter, we sought to include recent reports of empirical research on cognitive apprenticeship. Theoretical works or ones merely describing instructional projects, software, or elements of practice have not been included here. We have separated the research into studies focusing on (1) the whole CA model as enacted in instructional settings, (2) individual instructional strategies associated with CA (mentoring, scaffolding), and (3) cognitive apprenticeship within communities of practice. We note, however, that this separation is somewhat artificial given the interrelatedness of concepts and strategies. Additionally, we have limited this review to studies with a primary focus on *cognitive* apprenticeship and related strategies. Studies on trade and vocational apprenticeships were not included because they tend to focus on issues other than cognitive problem-solving skills. Similarly, studies that merely mention instructional strategies related to CA but do not focus explicitly on how those strategies relate to CA were not included. In excluding such studies, this chapter is not an exhaustive one, but it is representative of the types of research being done.

## Studying the Enactment of Cognitive Apprenticeship

Studies examining cognitive apprenticeship have researched both the parts and the whole. The parts are generally understood to be the instructional phases outlined by Collins et al. (1989), whereas the whole consists of the process of these events occurring at a specific time and place with unique individuals co-constructing the series of apprenticeship moments. These studies attempt to identify the critical elements of the CA episodes across settings and with varied populations. Cognitive apprenticeship is especially appealing to designers of Web-based learning environments who are embracing a more constructivist approach to learning and instruction. Similarly, CA has begun to find a home in both K–12 education and teacher education programs, both of which have been researched contexts.

## Cognitive Apprenticeship in Multimedia Environments

One dominant belief is that multimedia and Web-based environments can be programmed to support cognitive apprenticeship processes. Many such environments focus on one or two strategies related to cognitive apprenticeship and are discussed later in this chapter, but a few look at how to address the entire CA model. Wang and Bonk (2005) proposed using the CA model as the basis for constructing a groupware environment. Seel and Schenk (2003) used a CA model that sequences activities in the same order as Collins et al. (1989), with an interest in developing a multimedia-based system to support model-based learning. Their formative evaluation of five replication studies showed that CA may be effective as a guide for the design of multimedia learning environments, with scaffolding being the weakest spot. Their findings substantiated earlier studies on integrating CA and multimedia (Casey, 1996) on computer-based coaching (Lajoie and Lesgold, 1989). Generally, addressing individual learner needs in a programmed environment has proven challenging to do but promising for supporting learning; thus, researchers and developers continue to work on ways of implementing elements of cognitive apprenticeship in multimedia environments.

## Cognitive Apprenticeship in Higher Education

Many of the studies of cognitive apprenticeship in higher education are focused on teacher education programs. Two studies in particular exemplify the types of research being conducted on CA in the field of teacher education: de Jager et al. (2002) and Liu (2005) each looked at CA and teacher training. In the first, participants were trained in CA and in the second participants were trained using a CA approach.

Targeting the instructional design behavior of middle grade in-service teachers, de Jager and colleagues (2002) showed that, simply put, teacher training results in a change in teacher teaching behaviors. Specifically, their study offered teachers training in a CA approach or a directed instruction approach to reading comprehension then compared their behaviors with a control group of teachers who used the established curricular approach. Both experimental groups showed a change in teaching behaviors, according to their treatment group; however, the authors concluded that changing to a CA instructional approach is no more or less difficult than changing to a direct instruction approach. Because both approaches were founded in constructivist theory, the authors further concluded that their study shows that it is possible to "translate new theoretical insights in learning and instruction into regular school practices" (de Jager et al., 2002, p. 841).

Cognitive apprenticeship environments also may be used to help train preservice teachers. Liu (2005) studied the effects of a Web-based CA learning environment in preservice teaching education. Compared with a traditional classroom approach, the Web-based CA approach resulted in better performance and attitudes toward instructional planning.

Others have looked at using the CA model in fields such as instructional technology (Darabi, 2005), nursing (Cope et al., 2000), chemistry (Stewart and Lagowski, 2003), and engineering. Also studied is how CA impacts higher education teaching practices in general. Hendricks (2001) conducted an experimental study to determine whether CA was more likely to result in transferable knowledge than traditional instruction and found that the treatment group had greater post-test gains but did not perform significantly better on a transfer activity two weeks later.

### Cognitive Apprenticeship in K–12 Education

Teachers are being trained in and via CA learning environments and are conversely creating CA learning environments for their students. How do the students perceive these environments and do they benefit from them? Tsai (2005) developed and validated a questionnaire that was then used to determine student attitudes toward a computer-based science instruction; one of the scales asked about cognitive apprenticeship. Among other things, students who took the survey indicated that they preferred learning environments that connected concepts and reality. Considering student epistemological beliefs and learning preferences, Tsai pointed out, can be a useful and fundamental step when designing an instructional environment for a specific group of learners. Teong (2003) did not use information about learners' preferences in the intervention for his study; instead, the study examined the effect of metacognitive training using a word-problem-solving strategy, CRIME, on the experimental group's work with a CA-based instructional software, WordMath. The experimental group, which received metacognitive training, outperformed the other students in word-problem-solving skills in terms of both timing and quality of decisions.

## RESEARCH ON MENTORING

The word *mentoring* often brings to mind formal programs in which a more experienced practitioner is paired with a less experienced one to provide guidance in a new career or environment. Mentoring programs and tips on how to create and engage in them are fairly common, with published empirical reviews of them being much less common. The study of such programs and their effectiveness may well occur more often than is published, via internal or informal evaluations. Additionally, studies have been conducted to examine different mentoring practices or strategies as well as the use of technologies to support mentoring.

### Formal Mentoring Programs

The results of a review of ten evaluations of youth mentoring programs (Jekielek et al., 2002) found that their impact was felt in multiple areas, including academic achievement (in terms of attendance, attitudes, and continuing education, although not necessarily grades); health and safety (in terms of preventing and reducing negative behaviors); and social and emotional development. Productive mentoring practices were found to be structure, regular meetings, mentor training and preparation, and a focus on the mentees' needs rather than the mentors' expectations.

Lucas (2001) studied an after-school mentoring program for sixth-grade students. Mentors were college undergraduates who were enrolled in a for-credit course, and mentee participants were volunteers who were promised support for academic achievement. Lucas found that the relationship between mentor and mentee is heavily based on individual factors, including personal preferences, prior experiences, and goals and expectations; essentially, the nature of the experience transcends any traditional definition or training that may take place and is heavily shaped by the individuals who are involved in it. Lucas also found a much greater desire to engage in mentor–mentee interaction when it was focused around an activity that the mentee could not successfully complete alone.

Langer (2001), in his study of the nature of mandatory mentoring at SUNY Empire State College (ESC), found a gap between his results and the predominant views in the theoretical literature about mentoring. Although the literature base tends to place a heavy emphasis on the close interpersonal relationships developed between mentors and mentees, Langer in contrast observed a process that was almost exclusively focused on goal attainment. What Langer and ESC are referring to as mentoring might better fit the definition of coaching, which is more task focused than relationship focused.

Billet (2000) studied the learning process of mentees in a formal workplace mentoring program over a six-month period. This prolonged engagement allowed him to identify learning sources and strategies that were influential on the mentees' development. Mentors were trained in workshops that introduced guided learning strategies such as questioning, modeling, and coaching and helped them to identify ways in which these strategies might be used in their workplace. Engagement in everyday work was found to have the greatest influence on mentee development, supporting the concept of situated cognition, and Billet suggests that the guided learning strategies were used to enhance this engagement. Questioning, modeling, and coaching were perceived as most useful. Less used strategies, such as diagrams and analogies, were less valued.

Young and Perrewé (2000) looked at career and social support factors and their effects on participant perceptions of the success of a mentoring relationship, finding that mentors' expectations generally were met when a protégé (mentee) was involved in career support behavior. Conversely, protégés tended to measure the success of their mentoring relationship in terms of the amount of social support they received. Young and Perrewé hypothesized that this difference in perception may be due to the mentors' established status, which may have them focused on successes directly related to the mentoring goal (career enhancement), while their more novice protégés may not yet be able to predict the impact of particular career-related behaviors but will look for encouragement and friendship as indicators that they are performing as expected.

Bonnett et al. (2006) studied 20 mentor–protégé pairings of research scientists and university-level biology students who used an electronic mentoring program. The more effective pairs were found to have been more prolific and structured in their posting and to have focused more on topics than relationship management issues.

Hudson et al. (2005) created and validated an instrument based on the literature in primary science teaching by selecting five factors that seemed related to mentoring effectiveness (personal attributes, system requirements, pedagogical knowledge, modeling, and feedback). This instrument, called Mentoring for Effective Primary Science Teaching (MEPST), is intended to assess mentee perceptions of their mentors for their intern or practicum experiences.

The Internet has encouraged the exploration of mentoring in environments where mentors and learners are not colocated. A series of studies investigated the effects of online mentoring of preservice teachers in a project called Conference on the Web (COW), which spanned multiple years and involved collaborations from faculty and preservice teachers at other schools and universities internationally (Bonk et al., 2000, 2001a,b). Post-class surveys and interviews indicated that the students valued the mentoring they received

and felt that the computer-mediated forum was an appropriate outlet. The quality of student reflection was not as high as it might be, and further work is needed to develop better scaffolding and mentoring strategies for use in online environments.

## Mentoring Strategies

Integrative teaching is one mentor strategy that may be used. In this strategy, the mentor combines theory and practice in their explanation to the mentee. Hayward et al. (2001) found that most mentors provided far more information than the mentees had requested. A common strategy, used by one third of the mentors, was *expert push*, in which a mentor did not directly answer the mentee's question but instead returned questions intended to help the mentee find the correct answer.

In a qualitative study examining the effects of electronic peer mentoring in a university physical therapy class, it was found that both mentors and mentees learned through the process of reflection and articulation (Hayward et al., 2001). Mentees benefited from the mentors' stories and experiences which made the learning more concrete and authentic, and the mentors reinforced concepts already learned by connecting theory to practice. Also studying mentoring in a university setting, Beck (2004) found that linking a writing course to an engineering department's course could help students better learn how to write lab reports. In this instance, the writing instructor provided mentorship that carried over to the engineering curriculum.

Peers also may serve as mentors to each other, with learners in some instances identifying on their own both their knowledge gap (given their learning goals) and peers who can help them attain their learning goals. Engaging in study groups and asking for peer assistance is a common practice in many educational settings, as students realize that their peers can often supply the learning assistance that they need. Loong (1998) studied the peer apprenticeship that developed between two students engaged in a computer-mediated mathematical task. Initially, the students had different approaches and worked rather independently, with one student focused on mathematical rules and the other focused more on concepts. Over time, however, the rule-focused student noticed that the concept-focused student's expertise was needed, and he assigned himself to this peer in an apprentice role.

Pear and Crone-Todd (2002) examined ways of using computers to provide feedback to college-level students in a manner consistent with the tenets of social constructivism in a course that used a teaching system referred to as a *computer-aided personalized system of instruction* (CAPSI). Drawing on the concept of scaffolding, course material was arranged in manageable units. A peer–tutor model was developed in which more advanced learners provided feedback to their classmates in an open-ended question practice test environment. Although the findings of this study show that the method works to help ensure that students receive a high amount of feedback while keeping the process manageable on instructors, it neglects to comment on the impact of this intervention on the learning process for either the students who received the feedback or the peer tutors who provided it.

# RESEARCH ON SCAFFOLDING

Research on scaffolding has focused on how much is needed, what type is needed, and how to best provide it to both individuals and groups. The term *scaffold* appears in many studies, but it is not always well applied. Pea (2004) argued that the term has become a bit overused, to the point where it has lost its true meaning and significance. He traces the term back to its origins, first published in an article by Wood et al. (1976), which rather tightly tied it back to the concept of zone of proximal development. A scaffold was intended to be a tool to help children do something they could not do without assistance. Within this concept is the notion that the scaffold, when no longer needed (the ZPD has shifted with learning), could be faded. Pea (2004) rightly noted that in much of the published research we have shifted from discussing *scaffold with fading* to a different interpretation: *scaffold for performance*. In particular, Pea raised the issue that many so-called software-based scaffolds really are intended as performance supports that may never be removed from the learner; however, it is possible that some of the so-called scaffold-for-performance studies represent situations in which fading might be possible but was outside the scope of the study.

Good descriptions of fading can be found in the literature on reciprocal teaching (Brown and Palincsar, 1989; Palincsar and Brown, 1984; Palincsar et al., 1993; Rosenshine and Meister, 1994). Fading was studied explicitly by Roehler and Cantlon (1997). They examined the use of scaffolds in two social constructivist classrooms, exploring the types and characteristics of scaffolding in learning conversations taking place during elementary-school language instruction. Over time, students took more responsibility for learning in this environment, and the amount of scaffolding used by the instructor faded. Bean and Patel Stevens (2002) obtained somewhat contradictory results. In their study of how scaffolding affects the reflection process for teacher education students, they found that

students' written work followed the models given as a scaffold but did not extend in any substantial way beyond the scaffold. The authors concluded that, although scaffolding had a clear effect, it did not help achieve all of the instructional goals; this finding may represent an inherent issue with scaffolding (particularly a scaffold for performance), or it may be indicative of a scaffold that did not fully meet the learners' needs.

## Distributed Scaffolding and ZPD

A big challenge for classroom teachers is having to teach learners who all have different zones of proximal development. Within a class, the ZPD for many students may be similar, but there likely are some students whose zone is quite different. Some researchers have begun to examine how scaffolding can be flexibly designed to meet the needs of diverse students, recognizing that scaffolding should provide that extra support learners need to successfully complete a just out-of-reach task.

Savery (1998) found evidence that learners do not all need the same amount of scaffolding. He noted that instructors in a business writing course made use of all six of Gallimore and Tharp's (1990) forms of scaffolded assistance, although each occurred in different amounts based on student need. Instructing, questioning, modeling, and cognitive structuring were part of the teachers' interaction with the students. Feeding back occurred through grades and comments on assignments. Finally, contingency management was largely unspoken, although it had been designed into the course itself that students would face repercussions for unproductive behavior.

Puntambekar and Kolodner (2005) studied students learning science by design. They used a design diary with learners as a scaffold for their design-related activities. Their findings showed that one form of scaffolding may not be sufficient to meet all learners' needs at all times, and thus recommended the concept of distributed scaffolding. The basic concept behind distributed scaffolding is that offering more support and more types of it results in a greater chance of effectively scaffolding the learning process for each student in a meaningful way.

Building on this idea that scaffolds need not be limited to one kind per instructional intervention, Tabak (2004) discussed how distributed scaffolding can be synergistic in nature; for example, students might use software programs with built-in scaffolds but also rely on just-in-time scaffolding from their instructors. The two forms of scaffolds together are a more powerful learning support than either on its own.

## Teacher-Provided Scaffolding Strategies

Discourse-based scaffolding is one form of coaching that teachers tend to implicitly rely on in classroom settings as they respond to learning needs. To study discourse-based scaffolding, researchers typically examine the interactions that occur between teachers and learners and how they support the learning process on different types of projects. Teacher scaffolding may seem like a silent activity and thus not be immediately observed, but it is a constant for good teachers (Masters and Yelland, 2002). Through quiet monitoring, teachers are able to enter a group and ask questions or propose options at just the right time and withdraw such supports when they are no longer needed.

Determining student needs is a driving force for this research. Rasku-Puttonen et al. (2003) found that students need extensive scaffolding when working on long-term problem-based learning activities, as well as ample opportunity for reflection. Teacher flexibility in response to learner self-regulation also was considered important. Tabak and Baumgartner (2004) examined differences in the effectiveness of teacher modeling dependent on whether the teacher and students have a symmetric (*partnerlike*) or asymmetric (*mentorlike*) relationship. Symmetric and asymmetric relationships result in different discourse structures and impact mastery of cultural tools. They recommend a partner role for teachers helping to develop students identified as people who can work with scientific concepts. Meyer and Turner (2002) found that nonscaffolding classroom discourse (e.g., direct instruction or focus on objectives questions) is not as effective as scaffolded discourse at helping students become self-regulated math learners.

Another way in which students may need scaffolding assistance is task structuring (Tharp, 1993), which may include activities such as "chunking, sequencing, detailing, reviewing, or any other means to structure the task and its components so as to fit it into the learner's zone of proximal development" (Sugar and Bonk, 1998, p. 142). Supporting this theory, Dennen (2000) found that scaffolds in the form of chunking and sequencing tasks helped motivate students and enabled them to focus more on the content-based learning goals than on project management elements of the assignment. Although this study looked at a one-time project and thus fading did not occur, in the context of a larger classroom effort one might fade such scaffolds during successive projects.

Scaffolding is not limited to classroom situations; early interactions with one's parents ideally provide scaffolding as a child is guided through new experiences (Rogoff, 1990). Neitzel and Stright (2003) studied how mothers scaffolded their preschool children's performance on problem-solving tasks and then measured the children's self-regulatory abilities in the kindergarten classroom. They found that more highly educated mothers were more likely to scaffold their children's work and engage children in metacognitive discourse, and in turn these behaviors resulted in children who exhibited higher rates of task persistence and behavior control in the classroom.

## Software-Based Scaffolding

Software-based scaffolding has been a developing topic of interest as educational software becomes increasingly sophisticated. Reiser (2004) suggests that software-based scaffolding serves two major purposes. First, it can be used to help provide structure to the learning task, guiding them through the major stages or tasks and prompting them at appropriate times. Second, it can be used to create a problem space in which learners must explore the content. These two types of scaffolds may work harmoniously or may conflict with each other. Software-based scaffolds must be designed in consideration of various tradeoffs such as level of generality, learner control, and learner choice, with an attempt to support learners without stifling or over-directing them.

Shabo et al. (1997) designed scaffolding into Graphica, a computer-based environment focused on graphics learning. Graphica provides scaffolds that are built into learning exercises in the form of resources (hints, descriptions of expert processes), coaching (computer-based critiques of student work that are available on demand), and articulation (a newsgroup, the one form of human–human interaction built into the program). In a formative evaluation of Graphica, they found that many students were unsure of how to use its various components to support their learning processes. The practice exercises and visualization components were popular, but scaffolds such as the expert analyses and hints were not heavily used. The challenge for users of Graphica and similar programs is that they must have sufficient metacognitive development to identify their own learning needs, and their learning goals must be inline with the goals designed into the system.

Picking up on this issue of metacognitive development, Graesser et al. (2005) designed computer-based learning environments to support inquiry and metacognition. They have been able to develop pedagogical agents that both model self-explanation and coach students in metacognitive strategies, demonstrating that the computer is a viable tool for supporting development of deeper levels of metacognitive thinking and when explanatory reasoning is involved. Land and Zembal-Saul (2003) similarly found that software-based scaffolds are a useful support to articulation and reflection processes.

Davis and Linn (2000) and Davis (2003) studied the use of prompts to scaffold the reflection process for middle-school science students working within a computer-based system known as the Knowledge Integration Environment (KIE), developed by Bell et al. (1995). This system supports the scientific process by prompting students through related activities, such as identifying the needed evidence to support claims and determining whether presented evidence is adequate. Davis and Linn (2000) found in two related studies that reflective prompts in KIE promoted knowledge integration in students working on science projects. They suggested that the reflective articulation that is involved in responding to self-monitoring prompts helps students better self-assess their understanding and thus engages them in knowledge integration.

In Davis' 2003 study, students working in pairs received either generic prompts asking students to share their thoughts at that point in the activity or directed prompts. Learners who received the generic prompts were more likely to develop a coherent understanding of the overall project in which they were participating than those who received the more heavily scaffolded or controlled direct prompts. Learner autonomy was also a factor, with autonomous learners demonstrating the greatest comprehension benefits from the generic prompts.

It is possible that the directed prompts, which were prescribed and programmed into the KIE, were too limiting or narrow for these learners or did not challenge them enough. It will thus be interesting to see the results of recent research interests in scripting for online discourse (Choi et al., 2005; Jonassen and Remidez, 2005; Makitalo et al., 2005). Also, computers are unable to adjust to learners' unique needs in as subtle and personalized of a manner as a teacher might, making it difficult for a program to sufficiently and consistently identify each learner's zone of proximal development (Ainsworth et al., 1998). This research also indirectly supports the calls of Tabak (2004) and Puntambekar and Kolodner (2005) for the use of distributed scaffolding.

### Scaffolding and Computer-Supported Collaborative Learning

Scaffolding might be provided by human interactants mediated by computers. This form of scaffolding differs from software-based supports in that a live person uses computer-based tools to assist another's performance. Learner-centered strategies are important here (Bonk and Dennen, 2007), as we move from information-transmission models of learning which traditionally involve flat interactions with static content in an online environment. Scaffolding has been considered essential to the development of deep asynchronous discussion (Oliver and Herrington, 2000); however, in an online context the metaphor of scaffolding is not only appealing but also elusive and problematic (McLoughlin, 2002). Why is scaffolding in an online environment so challenging? In part because it raises the question of whether or not traditional roles of teacher and learner will be relied upon. McLoughlin suggested a variety of technology interventions that rely on scaffolding, including Computer-Supported Intentional Learning Environments (CSILEs), which are collaborative learning spaces in which the teacher is a facilitator and the student is tasked with communicating and creating knowledge objects (Scardamalia and Bereiter, 1994); intelligent tutoring systems (ITSs), which help break down and manage specific tasks; and goal-based scenarios (GBSs), which engage students in authentic tasks and provide computer-based resources and scaffolding in the form of task assistance and hints as needed (Schank et al., 1999). Other recent studies building on the CSILE foundation have looked at how Knowledge Forum, a program that offers knowledge-building scaffolds, impacts student learning (Bereiter and Scardamalia, 2003; Lax et al., 2004; Nason and Woodruff, 2003; Oshima et al., 2003). Studies in this area often use a design-based research method (see Chapter 54 in this *Handbook*).

Oshima and Oshima (2001) studied ways to improve learning for novices through the use of discourse scaffolding; specifically, the WebCSILE tool was used to support their interactions. A comparative analysis of two groups' discourse showed that, although students with a comprehension-oriented objective discussed content at the metacognitive level, those with a synthesis-oriented one did not. Further, the quality of writing did not improve in the group that also had a page of writing tips and a schedule as additional support. The researchers felt that the support in fact may have in some ways limited the interactions that took place. Learners in the second group used the provided scaffolding as a directive for what to do and followed its suggestions quite literally, like a task list.

Guzdial and Turns (2000) recommend the use of *anchors*, or topics that students wish to discuss to stimulate interest and motivation. Using a Collaborative and Multimedia Interactive Learning Environment (CaMILE), they compared anchored discussion to the use of a newsgroup tool lacking CaMILE's management, facilitation and anchoring features, hypothesizing that the anchored threads would be more effective (defined as having broad participation and being on-topic) than the unanchored ones. In an initial study, which looked at participation across multiple classes, findings indicated that discussion threads in CaMILE were longer than those in the newsgroup, with low variability of length in the newsgroups but high variability in CaMILE. No significant difference were observed between the two tools in terms of the number of active participants. A second study focused on discussion within a single class. Findings in this study indicated that the students who used CaMILE participated more extensively than their newsgroup counterparts and that teacher participation was greater in the number of messages but less in the percentage of messages.

# RESEARCH ON COMMUNITY OF PRACTICE

Cognitive apprenticeships are a natural occurrence within communities of practice, and the CoP model, as pioneered by Etienne Wenger (Wenger, 1998; Wenger et al., 2002), has been promoted as a way to support professional learning during the last decade. This movement toward thinking about professions as communities of practice has very much paralleled the rethinking of organizational knowledge and development of knowledge management strategies. Of particular interest to many researchers has been the experience of new employees as they get socialized into an organization. In other words, are new employees learning and assimilating by observing the practices of their more experienced peers? This research on people on peripheral and inbound trajectories helps examine how prior learning and initial learning within an organization tend to shape one's experience and overall path within a community.

## Cognitive Apprenticeship and Newcomer Adjustment

Socialization was found to be important to newcomer adjustment by Kammeyer-Mueller and Wanberg (2003). This study, situated within the organizational development discourse on proximal and distal indicators of newcomer adjustment, collected data from newcomers at seven different organizations four times during a 12-month period. In addition to socialization, both pre-entry knowledge and proactive personality were shown to be related to positive adjustment.

Also concerned with this critical point in one's membership in a community of practice, Klein et al. (2006) examined the impact of socialization experiences occurring prior to and immediately upon the hiring on 194 new employees at an educational institution. They found that two factors—realism of pre-entry knowledge and agent helpfulness—had a positive impact on job outcomes as measured through role clarity, satisfaction, and commitment to the organization.

Slaughter and Zickar (2006) found that role understanding, as indicated by the two variables of role conflict and role ambiguity, impacts how newcomers become involved in organizational activities. They concluded that the behavior of community insiders influences the attitudes of the newcomers, thus it matters with whom one interacts upon entry into a community. Their study was conducted within a university department, and they also found that graduate student activities or lack thereof in a department also may be indicative of different community alignments; in other words, some students may engage in activities that would show their commitment to their anticipated career more so than to their department, knowing that commitment to the department will not necessarily have career rewards.

In a study of a community of writers at an urban nonprofit organization, Beaufort (2000) explored the roles the writers played and how new writers were integrated into the community following an apprenticeship model. Fifteen roles were observed in this example, ranging from observer, reader/researcher, and clerical assistant on the novice end up to author, inventor, and coach on the expert end. New or less experienced writers learned the process through taking on roles such as the clerical assistant (a role reserved for new members), which allowed for extended observation of the expert writers at work. The results suggest that learning writing through a social process with authentic tasks is effective, and the researcher stated that a similar model may be useful in school settings, where writing has traditionally been an individual, general-skills learning activity.

## Research on Identity Development

Identity development—whether or not one immediately relates to a particular community of practice—also has been of interest to researchers. Identity issues were raised by Klein and colleagues (2006), as those who more readily understood the organization and were better able to identify their own role within it; however, communities of practice do not inherently transmit a sense of identity to those who are peripheral or on an inbound path. Davis (2006) found that the professional relationships one builds with others in the CoP and particularly with those in a supervisory capacity will impact trajectory and identity development among occupational therapists. Cope et al. (2000)

found that the nursing community of practice readily accepted student members into the community, but their professional acceptance was dependent on displayed competence. Thus, it seems that identity and acceptance are related, but other factors may be involved in becoming a successful practicing member of a profession.

Varelas et al. (2005) studied the relationship between identifying oneself as a scientist and as a science teacher in a population of new teachers. They found that these new teachers were identifying as scientists when engaging students in science learning activities and that they were drawing upon instructional strategies, such as mentoring, modeling, and articulation, that are part of the cognitive apprenticeship model. As time passed, these teachers identified more as science teachers and tried to create a community of scientists in their classrooms.

### Research on Community Interactions

Communities of practice also are often mentioned in relation to teachers and their professional development. New teachers tend to learn much from their interactions with more experienced teachers, including how to engage in teaching-related discourse (Smith, 2005); however, Smith found that, despite learning taking place, relationships between parties on different trajectories may not always be tension-free because of different personal needs and objectives.

Distributed scaffolding (also discussed in the Scaffolding Research section) is one way of addressing the different needs of a group of learners, but one also might bring the learners together as a community with a common goal, all working jointly within a ZPD. Goos et al. (2002) looked at how a collaborative ZPD might be developed among learners working on inquiry-based projects in a math community. They coded learners' interactions as reading, understanding, analysis, exploration, planning, implementation, or verification (for examples of the coding scheme, see Artzt and Armour-Thomas, 1992; Schoenfeld, 1992), as well as by metacognitive act. Their findings indicate that the social interactions of learners working together can lead to a collaborative ZPD.

Research on communities of practice need not be limited to work or school settings. Merriam et al. (2003) studied how informal learning takes place via social interactions in a community of practicing witches. Through talking to representatives of different covens, they found that membership in these groups very much fit Wenger's (1998) community of practice trajectory and that both formal and informal situated learning was prevalent.

## SUMMARY OF COGNITIVE APPRENTICESHIP RESEARCH

As can be seen in this review of theory and research on the cognitive apprenticeship model, the professional dialog spans diverse fields of study, learner groups, and settings. Empirical studies have confirmed much of what theories have suggested: (1) that the cognitive apprenticeship model is an accurate description of how learning occurs naturally as part of everyday life and social interactions, and (2) that the instructional strategies that have been extracted from these observations of everyday life can be designed into more formal learning contexts with positive effect. On the whole, however, the research is still fragmented, with bits and pieces situated in different subfields of educational research (e.g., teacher education, multimedia-based education, adult education). Although many of the studies point back to Collins et al. (1989) as a framework, few refer to each other. In part this may be due to the recency of this work and publication cycles.

## FUTURE STEPS IN RESEARCH AND PRACTICE

Two areas in which future research on cognitive apprenticeships may be particularly valuable are the design of communities of practice and technology-based learning programs. The growing popularity of situated learning and the desire to create learning communities to support professional development and organizational knowledge management have spurred the intentional design of communities of practice. Questions remain about how these communities are best designed and implemented or if they even can be purposely created as opposed to naturally evolved.

The potential impact of computer technologies on cognitive apprenticeships has been explored with two main purposes in mind: using computers to provide learning support and using computers to support learning-focused discourse. In the case of the former, the challenges to researchers and developers are twofold: (1) to develop guiding principles of providing computer-supported cognitive apprenticeships that will work across proprietary software products, and (2) to develop programs that are sufficiently able to address learners' individual needs and provide appropriate supports at the right moments. In the latter example, the literature on distance learning and online discourse, although not explicitly focused on cognitive apprenticeship, may provide a good start for examining how to engage in modeling and coaching and how to encourage articulation, reflection, and exploration in computer-mediated learning environments.

Finally, as research on the cognitive apprenticeship model matures, it would be helpful to see a more systematic and integrated program of studies working toward the development of guiding principles to support instructional design, teaching, and learning based on this model.

# REFERENCES

Ainsworth, S., Wood, D., and O'Malley, C. (1998). There is more than one way to solve a problem: evaluating a learning environment that supports the development of children's multiplication skills. *Learn. Instruct.*, 8(2), 141–157.

Artzt, A. F. and Armour-Thomas, E. (1992). Development of a cognitive-metacognitive framework for the study of interactions in the mathematics classroom. *Educ. Stud. Math.*, 41, 1–29.

Bean, T. W. and Patel Stevens, L. (2002). Scaffolding reflection for preservice and inservice teachers. *Reflect. Pract.*, 3(2), 205–218.

Beaufort, A. (2000). Learning the trade: a social apprenticeship model for gaining writing expertise. *Written Commun.*, 17(2), 185–223.

Beck, A. (2004). Collaborative teaching, genre analysis, and cognitive apprenticeship: engineering a linked writing course. *Teaching English Two-Year Coll.*, 31(4), 388–398.

Bell, P., Davis, E. A., and Linn, M. C. (1995). The Knowledge Integration Environment: Theory and Design. Paper presented at the Computer Supported Collaborative Learning Conference (CSCL'95), October 17–20, Bloomington, IN.

Bereiter, C. and Scardamalia, M. (2003). Learning to work creatively with knowledge. In *Powerful Learning Environments: Unravelling Basic Components and Dimensions*, edited by E. De Corte, L. Verschaffel, N. Entwistle, and J. van Merriënboer, pp. 55–68. New York, Pergamon Press.*

Billet, S. (2000). Guided learning at work. *J. Workplace Learn.*, 12(7), 272–285.

Bonk, C. J. and Dennen, V. P. (2007). Pedagogical frameworks for Web-based distance education. In *Handbook of Distance Education*, 2nd ed., edited by M. G. Moore, pp. 233–246. Mahwah, NJ: Lawrence Erlbaum Associates.

Bonk, C. J., Hara, N., Dennen, V. P., Malikowski, S., and Supplee, L. (2000). We're in TITLE to dream: envisioning a community of practice, 'The Intraplanetary Teacher Learning Exchange.' *CyberPsychol. Behav.*, 3(1), 25–39.

Bonk, C. J., Angeli, C., Malikowski, S., and Supplee, L. (2001a). Holy COW: Scaffolding case-based 'Conferencing on the Web' with preservice teachers. *Educ. Dist.*, 15(8) (http://www.usdla.org/html/journal/AUG01_Issue/article01.html).

Bonk, C. J., Daytner, K., Daytner, G., Dennen, V. P., and Malikowski, S. (2001b). Using Web-based cases to enhance, extend, and transform preservice teacher training: two years in review. *Comput. Schools*, 18(1), 189–211.

Bonnett, C., Wildemuth, B. M., and Sonnenwald, D. H. (2006). Interactivity between protégés and scientists in an electronic mentoring program*Instruct. Sci.*, 34, 21–61.

Brown, A. L. and Palincsar, A. S. (1989). Guided, cooperative learning and individual knowledge acquisition. In *Knowing, Learning, and Instruction: Essays in Honor of Robert Glaser*, edited by L. B. Resnick, pp. 393–451. Hillsdale, NJ: Lawrence Erlbaum Associates.*

Brown, J. S. (1998). Internet technology in support of the concept of 'communities-of-practice': the case of Xerox. *Account. Manage. Inform. Technol.*, 8, 227–236.

Brown, J. S., Collins, A., and Duguid, P. (1989). Situated cognition and the culture of learning. *Educ. Res.*, 18(1), 32–42.*

Casey, C. (1996). Incorporating cognitive apprenticeship in multi-media. *Educ. Technol. Res. Dev.*, 44(1), 71–84.

Choi, I., Land, S. M., and Turgeon, A. J. (2005). Scaffolding peer-questioning strategies to facilitate metacognition during online small group discussion. *Instruct. Sci.*, 33, 483–511.

Collins, A., Brown, J. S., and Newman, S. E. (1989). Cognitive apprenticeship: teaching the craft of reading, writing, and mathematics. In *Knowing, Learning, and Instruction: Essays in Honor of Robert Glaser*, edited by L. B. Resnick, pp. 453–494. Hillsdale, NJ: Lawrence Erlbaum Associates.*

Cope, P., Cuthbertson, P., and Stoddart, B. (2000). Situated learning in the practice placement. *J. Adv. Nurs.*, 31(4), 850–856.

Darabi, A. A. (2005). Application of cognitive apprenticeship model to a graduate course in performance systems analysis: a case study. *Educ. Technol. Res. Dev.*, 53(1), 49–61.

Davis, E. A. (2003). Prompting middle school science students for productive reflection: generic and directed prompts. *J. Learn. Sci.*, 12(1), 91–142.

Davis, E. A. and Linn, M. C. (2000). Scaffolding students' knowledge integration: prompts for reflection in KIE. *Int. J. Sci. Educ.*, 22(8), 819–837.*

Davis, J. (2006). The importance of community of practice in identity development. *Internet J. Allied Health Sci. Pract.*, 4(3), 1–8.

de Jager, B., Reezigt, G. J., and Creemers, B. P. M. (2002). The effects of teacher training on new instructional behaviour in reading comprehension. *Teaching Teacher Educ.*, 18(7), 831–842.

Dennen, V. P. (2000). Task structuring for online problem-based learning. *Educ. Technol. Soc.*, 3(3), 330–336.

Elliott, M. J., Stewart, K. K., and Lagowski, J. J. (2002). Teaching Future Scientists Laboratory Chemistry Using Cognitive Apprenticeship Theory. Paper presented at the National Meeting of the American Chemical Society (ACS'02), April 7–11, Orlando, FL.

Enkenberg, J. (2001). Instructional design and emerging teaching models in higher education. *Comput. Hum. Behav.*, 17(5–6), 495–506.

Gallimore, R. and Tharp, R. (1990). Teaching mind in society: teaching, schooling, and literate discourse. In *Vygotsky and Education: Instructional Implications and Applications of Sociohistorical Psychology*, edited by L. C. Moll, pp. 175–205. Cambridge, U.K.: Cambridge University Press.*

Glazer, E. M. and Hannafin, M. J. (2006). The collaborative apprenticeship model: situated professional development within school settings. *Teaching Teacher Educ.*, 22(2), 179–193.

Goos, M., Galbraith, P., and Renshaw, P. (2002). Socially mediated metacognition: creating collaborative zones of proximal development in small group problem solving. *Educ. Stud. Math.*, 49, 193–223.

Graesser, A. C., McNamara, D. S., and VanLehn, K. (2005). Scaffolding deep comprehension strategies through Point&Query, AutoTutor, and iStart. *Educ. Psychol.*, 40(4), 225–234.

Guzdial, M. and Turns, J. (2000). Effective discussion through a computer-mediated anchored forum. *J. Learn. Sci.*, 9(4), 437–469.

Hayward, L. M., DiMarco, R., Blackmer, B., Canali, A., Wong, K., and O'Brien, M. (2001). Curriculum-based electronic peer mentoring: an instructional strategy for integrative learning. *J. Phys. Ther. Educ.*, 15(4), 14–25.

Hendricks, C. C. (2001). Teaching causal reasoning through cognitive apprenticeship: what are results from situated learning? *J. Educ. Res.*, 94(5), 302–311.

Hudson, P., Skamp, K., and Brooks, L. (2005). Development of an instrument: mentoring for effective primary science teaching. *Sci. Educ.*, 89(4), 657–674.

Jekielek, S. M., Moore, K. A., Hair, E. C., and Scarupa, H. J. (2002). *Mentoring: A Promising Strategy for Youth Development* [research brief]. Washington, D.C.: Child Trends.

Jonassen, D. and Remidez, J. (2005). Mapping alternate discourse structures onto computer conferences. *Int. J. Knowl. Learn.*, 1(1/2), 113–129.*

Kammeyer-Mueller, J. D. and Wanberg, C. R. (2003). Unwrapping the organizational entry process: disentangling multiple antecedents and their pathways to adjustment. *J. Appl. Psychol.*, 88(5), 779–794.

Klein, H. J., Fan, J., and Preacher, K. J. (2006). The effects of early socialization experiences on content mastery and outcomes: a mediational approach. *J. Vocat. Behav.*, 68, 96–115.

Lajoie, S. P. and Lesgold, A. (1989). Apprenticeship training in the workplace: computer-coached practice environment as a new form of apprenticeship. *Machine-Mediated Learn.*, 3, 7–28.

Land, S. and Zembal-Saul, C. (2003). Scaffolding reflection and articulation of scientific explanations in a data-rich, project-based learning environment: an investigation of progress portfolio. *Educ. Technol. Res. Dev.*, 51(4), 65–84.

Langer, A. M. (2001). Confronting theory: the practice of mentoring non-traditional students at Empire State College. *Mentor. Tutor.*, 9(1), 49–62.

Lave, J. and Wenger, E. (1991). *Situated Learning: Legitimate Peripheral Participation*. Cambridge, U.K.: Cambridge University Press.*

Lax, L. R., Taylor, I., Wilson-Pauwels, L., and Scardamalia, M. (2004). Dynamic curriculum design in biomedical communications: integrating a knowledge building approach and a Knowledge Forum® learning environment in a medical legal visualization course. *J. Biocommun.*, 30(1) (http://www.jbiocommunication.org/30–1/BMC.html).

LeGrand Brandt, B., Farmer, J. A., and Buckmaster, A. (1993). A cognitive apprenticeship approach to helping adults learn. In *New Directions for Adult and Continuing Education*, edited by D. Flannery, pp. 69–78. San Francisco, CA: Jossey-Bass.

Liu, T. C. (2005). Web-based cognitive apprenticeship model for improving pre-service teachers' performances and attitudes towards instructional planning: design and field experiment. *Educ. Technol. Soc.*, 8(2), 136–149.

Loong, D. H. W. (1998). Epistemological change through peer apprenticeship learning: From rule-based to idea-based social constructivism. *Int. J. Comput. Math. Learn.*, 3(1), 45–80.

Lucas, K. F. (2001). The social construction of mentoring roles. *Mentor. Tutor.*, 9(1), 23–47.

Makitalo, K., Weinberger, A., Hakkinen, P., Jarvela, S., and Fischer, F. (2005). Epistemic cooperation scripts in online learning environments: fostering learning by reducing uncertainty in discourse? *Comput. Hum. Behav.*, 21, 603–622.

Masters, J. and Yelland, N. (2002). Teacher scaffolding: an exploration of exemplary practice. *Educ. Inform. Technol.*, 7(4), 313–321.

McLoughlin, C. (2002). Learn. support in distance and networked learning environments: ten dimensions for successful design. *Dist. Educ.*, 23(2), 149–162.

Merriam, S. B., Courtenay, B., and Baumgartner, L. (2003). On becoming a witch: learning in a marginalized community of practice. *Adult Educ. Q.*, 53(3), 170–188.

Meyer, D. K. and Turner, J. C. (2002). Using instructional discourse analysis to study the scaffolding of student self-regulation. *Educ. Psychol.*, 37(1), 17–25.

Nason, R. and Woodruff, E. (2003). Fostering authentic, sustained, and progressive mathematical knowledge-building activity in computer-supported collaborative learning (CSCL) communities. *J. Comput. Math. Sci. Teaching*, 22(4), 345–363.

Neitzel, C. and Stright, A. D. (2003). Mothers' scaffolding of children's problem solving: establishing a foundation of academic self-regulatory compliance. *J. Family Psychol.*, 17(1), 147–159.

Oliver, R. and Herrington, J. (2000). Using situated learning as a design strategy for Web-based learning. In *Instructional and Cognitive Aspects of Web-Based Education*, edited by B. Abbey, pp. 178–191. Hershey, PA: Idea Publishing Group.

Oshima, J. and Oshima, R. (2001). Next step in design experiments with networked collaborative learning environments: instructional interventions in the curriculum. In *CSCL 2: Carrying Forward the Conversation*, edited by T. Koschmann, R. Hall, and N. Miyake, pp. 99–109. Mahwah, NJ: Lawrence Erlbaum Associates.

Oshima, J., Oshima, R., Inagaki, S., Takenaka, M., Nakayama, H., Yamaguchi, E., and Murayama, I. (2003). Teachers and researchers as a design team: changes in their relationship through the design experiment approach with a CSCL technology. *Educ. Commun. Inform.*, 3(1), 105–127.

Palincsar, A. S. and Brown, A. L. (1984). Reciprocal teaching of comprehension-fostering and monitoring activities. *Cogn. Instruct.*, 1, 117–175.

Palincsar, A. S., Brown, A. L., and Campione, J. C. (1993). First-grade dialogue for knowledge acquisition and use. In *Contexts for Learning*, edited by E. A. Forman, N. Minick and C. A. Stone, pp. 43–57. New York: Oxford University Press.

Pea, R. D. (2004). The social and technological dimensions of scaffolding and related theoretical concepts for learning, education, and human activity. *J. Learn. Sci.*, 13(3), 423–451.

Pear, J. J. and Crone-Todd, D. E. (2002). A social constructivist approach to computer-mediated instruction. *Comput. Educ.*, 38(1–3), 221–231.

Puntambekar, S. and Kolodner, J. L. (2005). Toward implementing distributed scaffolding: helping students learn science from design. *J. Res. Sci. Teach.*, 42(2), 185–217.

Rasku-Puttonen, H., Etelapelto, A., Arvaja, M., and Hakkinen, P. (2003). Is successful scaffolding an illusion? Shifting patterns of responsibility and control in teacher-student interaction during a long-term learning project. *Instruct. Sci.*, 31, 377–393.

Reiser, B. J. (2004). Scaffolding complex learning: the mechanisms of structuring and problematizing student work. *J. Learn. Sci.*, 13(3), 273–304.

Roehler, L. R. and Cantlon, D. J. (1997). Scaffolding: a powerful tool in social constructivist classrooms. In *Scaffolding Student Learning: Instructional Approaches and Issues*, edited by K. Hogan and M. Pressley, pp. 6–42. Cambridge, MA: Brookline.

Rogoff, B. (1990). *Apprenticeship in Thinking: Cognitive Development in the Social Context*. New York: Oxford University Press.*

Rosenshine, B. and Meister, C. (1994). Reciprocal teaching: a review of the research. *Re. Educ. Res.*, 64(4), 479–487.

Savery, J. R. (1998). Fostering ownership for learning with computer-supported collaborative writing in an undergraduate business communication course. In *Electronic Collaborators: Learner-Centered Technologies for Literacy, Apprenticeship, and Discourse*, edited by C. J. Bonk and K. S. King, pp. 103–127. Mahwah, NJ: Lawrence Erlbaum Associates.

Scardamalia, M. and Bereiter, C. (1994). Computer support for knowledge-building communities. *J. Learn. Sci.*, 3(3), 265–283.*

Schank, R. C., Berman, T., and McPherson, J. (1999). Learn. by doing. In *Instructional Design Theories and Models: A New Paradigm of Instructional Theory*, edited by C. M. Reigeluth, pp. 161–181. Mahwah, NJ: Lawrence Erlbaum Associates.*

Schoenfeld, A. H. (1992). Learn. to think mathematically: problem solving, metacognition and sense making in mathematics. In *Handbook of Research on Mathematics Teaching and Learning*, edited by D. A. Grouws, pp. 334–370. New York: Macmillan.

Shabo, A., Guzdial, M., and Stasko, J. (1997). An apprenticeship-based multimedia courseware for computer graphics studies provided on the World Wide Web. *Computers and Education*, 29(2/3), 103–116.

Seel, N. M. and Schenk, K. (2003). An evaluation report of multimedia environments as cognitive learning tools. *Eval. Prog. Plan.*, 26(2), 215–224.

Slaughter, J. E. and Zickar, M. J. (2006). A new look at the role of insiders in the newcomer socialization process. *Group Org. Manage.*, 31(2), 264–290.

Smith, E. R. (2005). Learning to talk like a teacher: participation and negotiation in co-planning discourse. *Commun. Educ.*, 54(1), 52–71.

Stewart, K. K. and Lagowski, J. J. (2003). Cognitive apprenticeship theory and graduate chemistry education. *J. Chem. Educ.*, 80(12), 1362–1367.

Sugar, W. A. and Bonk, C. J. (1998). Student role play in the World Forum: analyses of an Arctic Adventure learning apprenticeship. In *Electronic Collaborators: Learner-Centered Technologies for Literacy, Apprenticeship, and Discourse*, edited by C. J. Bonk and K. S. King, pp. 131–155. Mahwah, NJ: Lawrence Erlbaum Associates.

Tabak, I. (2004). Synergy: A complement to emerging patterns of distributed scaffolding. *J. Learn. Sci.*, 13(3), 305–335.

Tabak, I. and Baumgartner, E. (2004). The teacher as partner: exploring participant structures, symmetry, and identity work in scaffolding. *Cogn. Instruct.*, 22(4), 393–429.

Teong, S. K. (2003). The effect of metacognitive training on mathematical word-problem solving. *J. Comput. Assist. Learn.*, 19(1), 46–55.

Tharp, R. (1993). Institutional and social context of educational reform: practice and reform. In *Contexts for Learning: Sociocultural Dynamics in Children's Development*, edited by E. A. Forman, N. Minnick, and C. A. Stone, pp. 269–282. Cambridge, U.K.: Cambridge University Press.

Tharp, R. and Gallimore, R. (1988). *Rousing Minds to Life: Teaching, Learning and Schooling in Social Context*. Cambridge, U.K.: Cambridge University Press.*

Tsai, C. C. (2005). Preferences toward internet-based learning environments: high school students' perspectives for science learning. *J. Educ. Technol. Soc.*, 8(2), 203–213.

Varelas, M., House, R., and Wenzel, S. (2005). Beginning teachers immersed into science: scientist and science teacher identities. *Sci. Educ.*, 89(3), 492–516.

Vygotsky, L. S. (1978). *Mind in Society: The Development of Higher Psychological Processes*. Cambridge, MA: Harvard University Press.*

Wang, F. K. and Bonk, C. J. (2005). A design framework for electronic cognitive apprenticeship. *J. Asynchr. Learn. Netw.*, 5(2) (http://www.sloan-c.org/publications/jaln/v5n2/v5n2_wang.asp).

Wenger, E. (1998). *Communities of Practice: Learning, Meaning, and Identity*. Cambridge, U.K.: Cambridge University Press.*

Wenger, E., McDermott, R., and Snyder, W. M. (2002). *Cultivating Communities of Practice: A Guide to Managing Knowledge*. Boston, MA: Harvard Business School Press.

Wertsch, J. V. (1998). *Mind as Action*. Oxford: Oxford University Press.*

Wood, D., Bruner, J., and Ross, G. (1976). The role of tutoring in problem solving. *J. Child Psychol. Psychiatry*, 17, 89–100.

Young, A. M. and Perrewé, P. L. (2000). What did you expect? An examination of career-related support and social support among mentors and protégés. *J. Manage.*, 26(4), 611–632.

---

* Indicates a core reference.

# 35

# Whole-Task Models in Education

*Jeroen J. G. van Merriënboer and Liesbeth Kester*
Open University of the Netherlands, Heerlen, the Netherlands

## CONTENTS

## ABSTRACT

Whole-task models support the development of educational programs for students who need to learn and transfer professional competences or complex cognitive skills to an increasingly varied set of real-world contexts and settings. They are a reaction to traditional atomistic approaches in which complex contents and tasks are reduced into increasingly simpler elements until reaching a level where the distinct elements can be transferred to the learners through presentation or practice. These approaches work well if there are few interactions between the elements, but they do not work well if the elements are interrelated because the whole is then more than the sum of its parts. Whole-task models basically try to deal with complexity without losing sight of the relationships between elements. This chapter briefly discusses the history of whole-task models. They are rooted in motor learning and sports, *andragogy* and adult learning, and Gestalt psychology. The characteristics of whole-task models in the field of educational communications and technology are also discussed. Elaboration theory, goal-based scenarios, and four-component instructional design are presented as three representative examples of whole-task models. We present empirical evidence for the effectiveness of the whole-task approach and the three example models. We conclude with a summary of findings and directions for future research on whole-task models.

## KEYWORDS

*Competence development:* A feature of the holistic approach, indicating that educational programs should be aimed at the development of competences rather than teaching different topics in different courses.

*Integrated curriculum:* A curriculum based on a whole-task approach aimed at the integration of supportive contents with whole tasks, knowledge, skills, and attitudes and at integrating first-order skills with higher-order skills.

*Mathemagenic methods:* Instructional methods that explicitly aim at the transfer of learning; these methods encourage learners to invest effort and time in the development of general or abstract cognitive schemas.

*Part-task models:* Instructional models that apply an atomistic approach in which complex contents and tasks are reduced into increasingly simpler elements until reaching a level where the distinct elements can be taught to the learners.

*Whole-task models:* Instructional models that apply a holistic approach in which complex contents and tasks are analyzed in coherence and taught from their simplest, yet still meaningful, version toward increasingly more complex versions.

There are contexts in which what is happening in the whole cannot be deduced from the characteristics of the separate pieces, but conversely what happens to a part of the whole is, in clearcut cases, determined by the laws of the inner structure of its whole. (Max Wertheimer, 1925)

## INTRODUCTION

In the 21st century, there has been a growing interest in whole-task models of learning and instructional design. In dealing with the learning of highly complex contents and tasks, whole-task models provide an alternative for atomistic, part-task models. To deal with complexity, atomistic models analyze a learning domain into smaller pieces and then teach the domain piece by piece. Whole-task models, in contrast, analyze a learning domain as a coherent, interconnected whole and then teach it from very simple, yet meaningful wholes that are representative for the whole domain to increasingly more complex wholes. They aim to solve three basic problems in education—namely, *fragmentation*, indicating that students are often not able to combine the many pieces they have learned into coherent wholes; *compartmentalization*, indicating that students have difficulties integrating acquired knowledge, skills, and attitudes; and low *transfer of learning*, indicating that learners are often not able to apply what they have learned to new problems and new situations (van Merriënboer, 2006).

The game of tennis may serve as an example to contrast a whole-task with a part-task approach (Gallwey, 1974). In a part-task approach, practice divides the activity into pieces that are not complete in themselves; the instructor focuses on teaching the student isolated components of good tennis playing such as the grip, the stance, and the swing. A holistic approach, in contrast, works with a complete pattern of activity; that is, practice takes place in the context of the whole task, starting simply and gradually growing in complexity toward the activity being trained. As described by Strauch (1984), it might start with the student on one side of the net holding a racket and the instructor on the other side of the net. The student's first task might be to say "toss" to signal the instructor to throw the ball and to say "bounce" when the ball bounces in the student's court. The second task might be to say "toss," after which the instructor begins a toss but does not complete it; the student says "toss … bounce" anyway, anticipating continuation of the past pattern. The third task might be to say "toss" to signal the instructor to throw the ball, to say "bounce" when the ball bounces, and to say "hit" when the student would hit the ball but without making an attempt to actually hit it, and so on.

This chapter first briefly discusses the history of whole-task models. They are rooted in motor learning and sports but also in andragogy and adult learning, as well as in Gestalt psychology. Second, the characteristics of whole-task models in the field of educational communications and technology, which only became popular in the early 1990s, are discussed. Third, elaboration theory, goal-based scenarios, and four-component instructional design are presented as three good examples of whole-task models. The fourth section provides empirical evidence for the effectiveness of the whole-task approach and three example models. In the fifth and final section, conclusions are made and directions for future research on whole-task models are suggested.

## BRIEF HISTORY OF WHOLE-TASK MODELS

In the field of educational communications and technology, interest in whole-task models only became evident in the late 1980s and early 1990s, but it has a much older history that is rooted, among others, in motor learning, andragogy, and psychology. In motor learning and sports, there is a history of comparing part-task and whole-task sequencing techniques for practice. In andragogy and adult learning, there is a history of holistic education and approaching the student as a whole person rather than as a learner *per se*. And, in psychology, an atomistic approach to the transfer of learning rooted in associationism has competed for a long time with a holistic approach rooted in German Gestalt psychology.

### Motor Learning and Sports

The field of (psycho)motor learning has a long-lasting tradition of comparing whole-task and part-task approaches to sequence training (for reviews, see Schmidt, 1991; Wightman and Lintern, 1985). In a whole-task sequence, the learner is taught whole meaningful tasks requiring the simultaneous coordination of component skills, and the tasks become more and more complex during the training. In a part-task sequence, in contrast, the learner is taught only one or a very limited number of isolated component skills simultaneously, and new component skills to practice are gradually added. If a skill consists of the component skills A, B, and C, a further distinction can be made between a part-task sequence with forward chaining (practice A, then B, then C); a part-task sequence with backward chaining (practice C given the results of AB, then B given the results of A, then A); a part-task sequence with forward chaining and snowballing (practice A, then AB, then ABC); and a part-task sequence with backward chaining and snowballing (practice C given the results of AB, then BC given the results of A, then ABC). For example, if A, B, and C refer to driving off, maneuvering, and park-

ing, the training schedules involve, in this order: (1) driving off, maneuvering, and parking; (2) parking after the instructor does the driving off and maneuvering, maneuvering after the instructor does the driving off, and driving off; (3) driving off, driving off and maneuvering, and driving off and maneuvering and parking; and, finally, (4) parking after the instructor does the driving off and maneuvering, maneuvering and parking after the instructor does the driving off, and, finally, driving off, maneuvering, and parking.

Furthermore, whole-task and part-task sequencing may be combined in two ways—namely, whole-part sequencing and part-whole sequencing. In whole-part sequencing, a sequence of simple to complex versions of whole tasks is developed first. If it turns out that the first whole task is still too difficult to start the training with, part-task sequencing techniques are used to divide this whole task and, if desired, subsequent whole tasks in parts. A whole-task sequence, for example, may pertain to driving a car in a training area, in a rural area, and in a city. If driving the car in the training area is still regarded as too difficult to start the training with, one might start with the component skill of *driving off* in the training area. In part-whole sequencing, a sequence of parts is developed first. If the first part is too difficult to start the training with, whole-task sequencing is used to sequence this part from simple to complex. For example, if the part-task sequence relates to driving off, maneuvering, and parking, and driving off is still regarded as too difficult to start the training with, one might start with driving off an automatic car and only then a stick-shift car.

Already in the 1960s, Briggs and Naylor (Briggs and Naylor, 1962; Naylor and Briggs, 1963) found that part-task and part-whole sequencing are most suitable for complex skills if little coordination of component skills is required (i.e., low task organization) and if each of the separate component skills is already complex of itself (i.e., high task complexity). But, for tasks with high task organization, whole-task and whole-part approaches are typically more effective. This finding is not only true for complex motor skills but also for many professional real-life tasks. Since the 1960s, overwhelming evidence has been obtained showing that breaking a complex task down into a set of distinct parts and then teaching or training those parts without taking their interactions and required coordination into account does not work because learners ultimately are not able to integrate and coordinate the separate parts in transfer situations (Clark and Estes, 1999; Perkins and Grotzer, 1997; Spector and Anderson, 2000). Performing a particular component skill in isolation is simply different from performing it in the context of a whole task. It seems to lead to different mental representations (Elio,

1986), and automaticity of a component skill that is developed as a function of extensive part-task practice is often not preserved in the context of whole-task performance (Schneider and Detweiler, 1988).

Whole-task models were developed in sports and in professions (Dreyfus, 1982; Feldenkrais, 1982; Strauch, 1984). One key issue in those models is how to deal with task complexity. Most holistic approaches introduce some notion of modeling to attack this problem. A powerful two-step approach to modeling first develops simple-to-complex models of reality or real-life tasks, and then models these models from a pedagogical perspective to ensure that they are presented in such a way that students can actually learn from them (Achtenhagen, 2001). Thus, in this view, instruction should ideally begin with a simplified but whole model of real-life task performance, which is then conveyed to the learners according to sound pedagogical principles, including, for example, the provision of learner guidance and support.

Concluding, part-task models have been found to be very effective to reduce task difficulty, but they hinder integration of knowledge, skills, and attitudes and limit the opportunities to learn to coordinate component skills. Whole-task models are better suited to learning to coordinate component skills and are preferred for tasks with a high level of organization. To deal with task complexity, simplification of the whole task and giving learners support and guidance are useful approaches.

## Andragogy and Adult Learning

Whereas researchers in the field of motor learning and sports stress the idea of the whole *task*, researchers in the field of andragogy and adult learning mainly emphasize the idea of the whole *person* in his or her context. Holistic education is defined as (Rinke, 1985, p. 67):

> A functional, integrated and generalized model of education that focuses on the whole teaching-learning situation, and varies the teaching-learning strategy to meet the needs of the learner, the teacher and the situation in an effort to attain educational outcomes greater than the sum of their parts.

This approach is rooted in Holism (Smuts, 1926) and related to, for example, the contingency approach in management, which maintains that managers should vary their leadership style in accordance with the situation to improve managerial effectiveness (Graen and Hui, 2001) and holistic medicine (Graham-Pole, 2001), which avoids the piecemeal treatment of isolated symptoms and regards the patient as a whole person who is co-responsible for his or her own health care.

A first characteristic of this holistic approach is the focus on the whole person and his or her meaningful, situated behaviors in real settings. To make this point clear, suppose you have to undergo surgery. Would you prefer a surgeon with great technical skills but with no knowledge of the human body? Or would you prefer a surgeon with great knowledge of the human body but with two left hands? Or, perhaps you would want a surgeon with great technical skills but who has a horrible bedside manner and a hostile attitude toward his patients? Or, finally, would you want a surgeon who has all of the knowledge, skills, and attitudes that he learned 35 years ago but has not kept them up to date? These questions clearly indicate that it makes little sense to distinguish domains of learning (e.g., conceptual knowledge, skills, attitudes), as is often done in formal educational programs. In a holistic approach, this compartmentalization of behaviors is replaced by a focus on whole and meaningful behaviors in realistic settings, and the learning of distinct pieces of knowledge is replaced by a model of personal development and growth.

A second characteristic pertains to the co-responsibility of the learner: The educator and the learner always work together to approach each learning task or learning opportunity with its unique characteristics (e.g., context, features of the task, personality characteristics) in the best possible way. Because no one knows a learner's desires, needs, and capabilities better than the learner, co-responsibility is a prerequisite to maximizing the effectiveness of the learning process. Furthermore, learners are also expected to assume responsibility for becoming lifelong learners who are able to realize their full potential. Thus, whereas the educator is responsible for diagnosing the learner's current level of competence, including readiness to learn and degree of dependence, and for making every effort to move the learner along the learning continuum, the holistic educator does not and cannot take full responsibility for the actual learning process. This view is currently found in several forms of on-demand education, in which learners select their own learning tasks (van Merriënboer and Kirschner, 2007), and in resource-based learning, in which learners are required to track their own learning resources (see Chapter 40 in this *Handbook*).

A third and last characteristic pertains to the systemic character of educational systems, meaning that the performance or function of each element directly or indirectly has an impact on, or is impacted by, one or more of the other elements in the system. To deal with that, a holistic approach takes an integrated perspective and repeatedly adds small increments of innovation and uses multiple strategies to capitalize on their synergy. Poindexter (2003) compared it to a weight-loss program: People who try one diet, one pill, or one exercise usually do not achieve their goals. Only when a holistic approach to health is taken, including incremental changes in eating, drinking, life style, and exercise, do weight loss and fitness occur. In educational systems, the best example of a failing nonholistic approach can be found in the use of new instructional methods that focus on deep processing, understanding, and higher-order skills without changing the assessment system. Such isolated changes are doomed to fail, because the test is at least as important to determine learning behaviors as the applied instructional methods (i.e., the tail wags the dog; see Pollio and Back, 2000). To reach desired results, there should be constructive alignment of changes throughout the whole educational system (Biggs, 1996).

To conclude, in the field of andragogy and adult learning, whole-task models are mostly found in a holistic approach. Apart from a focus on whole tasks, this approach stresses development and growth of the whole person, co-responsibility of the learner and the teacher, and an integrated approach to systemic change.

## Psychology and Transfer of Learning

In the field of experimental psychology, the distinction between part-task models and whole-task models becomes most evident in research on transfer of learning—that is, the ability to apply what has been learned to solving new problems in new situations (for reviews, see Adams, 1987; Annett, 1989; Annett and Sparrow, 1985; Ellis, 1965; Osgood, 1949; Royer, 1979). In the beginning of the 20th century, two approaches evolved that are still of importance to the issue of transfer of learning: the associationist approach, which is representative of a part-task model, and the Gestalt approach, which is representative of a whole-task model.

Within the associationist tradition, the identical elements theory of Thorndike and Woodworth (1901) claimed that transfer from one task to another task would only occur when both tasks shared the same parts, called *identical elements*. In general, it is assumed that the greater the number of identical parts, the greater the amount of transfer. This construction indicates that transfer is functionally related to the similarity and difference relationships between stimuli and responses in an original task and a transfer task. With respect to the transfer of learning, one current cognitive view tackles transfer problems by carefully analyzing the stimulus and response properties of the learning elements. These stimulus–response pairs are

subsumed in the concept of production systems, in which the productions may also be seen as the identical parts. Transfer is predicted in so far as the performance of two tasks can be described by identical productions (Singley and Anderson, 1985, 1988). This is clearly in the tradition of the associationist approach, because it is assumed that events that share the same parts will be recognized by the learner as being similar and that the responses learned for the first event can be transferred to the second event.

Unlike the associationists who consider the concept of identical elements as the determining factor for transfer of training, Gestalt psychologists rely on mental structures that act as a "gestalt"—a whole that is more than the sum of its parts. They consider the thinking process as reorganizing or relating one aspect of a problem situation to another, which may result in structural understanding (Ash, 1998; Mandler and Mandler, 1964). This involves restructuring the elements of a whole, meaningful problem situation in a new way so a problem can be solved. Gestalt psychologists hold that transfer from one task to another is achieved by arranging learning situations so a learner can gain insight into the problem to be solved. This type of learning is thought to be permanent, and reorganized knowledge may yield transfer to new situations. Some current cognitive views also make strong assumptions about the nature of underlying memory representations. The central assumption is that learners are conceptualized as active constructors of knowledge rather than as passive recipients of information; they actively seek to make sense of the environment by imposing structure and order on stimuli encountered through direct perception and experience. Memory is conceptualized as a highly structured storage system in which information is both stored and retrieved in a systematic manner. The critical step in transfer is then the retrieval and reorganization of a relevant cognitive schema when a particular problem is encountered.

It may seem impossible to reconcile a psychological whole-task model, which explains transfer of learning as a process of interpreting cognitive schemas to reorganize whole meaningful problem situations, with a part-task model, which explains transfer as a process of applying parts (i.e., identical elements or productions) that were acquired during learning tasks to new transfer tasks. But, the fundamental distinction between controlled and automatic cognitive processing (Schneider and Shiffrin, 1977; Shiffrin and Schneider, 1977) creates the opportunity to combine both approaches in a model that distinguishes two categories of learning processes: schema construction and schema automation. For task aspects related to problem solving and reasoning, the learner is then confronted with a varied sequence of whole-task situations promoting the construction of general cognitive schemas that allow for controlled processing, such as reorganizing a new situation in such a way that it can be understood in terms of the available schemas (whole-task practice). With regard to the to-be-automated task aspects, however, the learner may *in addition* be confronted with a repetitive sequence of practice items promoting the construction of stimulus–response pairs or productions that allow for automatic processing, such as performing routine aspects of new transfer tasks (part-task practice). The reader is referred to van Merriënboer (1997) for an elaborate discussion.

# WHOLE-TASK MODELS IN EDUCATIONAL COMMUNICATIONS AND TECHNOLOGY

Part-task models dominated the field of educational communications and technology until the late 1980s. From then on, constructivist views of learning and instruction have had a major impact on the thoughts and actions of many researchers in the instructional design field. Within this context, some researchers started to work on instructional design models building on the research traditions discussed in the previous section. These models share three characteristics. First, whole meaningful tasks are seen as the driving force for learning; easy-to-difficult sequencing techniques and learner support and guidance, which may be faded as learners acquire more expertise (i.e., scaffolded), are studied as methods to deal with task complexity. Second, there is a focus on the development of the whole person (i.e., learner-centered) rather than the acquisition of isolated pieces of knowledge, and the learner is co-responsible for a process of competence development. Third, there is a renewed interest in the study of instructional methods that explicitly aim at transfer of learning.

## The Integrated Curriculum

In the field of educational communications and technology, the traditional approach has for a long time been very similar to the atomistic part-task approach in motor learning and sports. Rather than breaking down a complex learning domain into component skills, it was described in terms of distinct learning goals or objectives. In a traditional objectives-driven approach (Gagné and Briggs, 1979; Landa, 1983; Scandura, 1983), the learner is taught only one or a very limited number of objectives at the same time. New objectives are gradually added to practice until all objectives have been treated. The basic assumption is that the teaching of different types of objectives (e.g., remembering a fact, applying a procedure, understanding a concept) requires different instructional methods, which is typical for outcomes-based models of instructional design (see Chapter 32 in this *Handbook*). To sequence the objectives, some kind of learning hierarchy is often used (Gagné, 1968, 1985). Such a hierarchy closely resembles a hierarchy of component skills; it has the most complex cognitive skill at its top and all of its prerequisite skills below it. Sequencing takes place from the base of the hierarchy to its top.

In the early 1990s, Gagné and Merrill (1990) identified the need to use learning goals that require an integration of multiple objectives. They proposed the term *enterprise* to denote a real-life learning activity (e.g., denoting, manifesting, discovering) in which the learner is engaged to reach such multiple objectives, and they stress the importance of enterprises to reach better transfer of learning. Their enterprises are good examples of what are referred to as *whole tasks* in this chapter, because they attempt to deal with complexity without losing sight of the separate elements and the interconnections between those elements. Van Merriënboer et al. (1992) discussed the requirements that had to be met when using whole learning tasks. They focus on the importance of sequencing whole, meaningful tasks from simple to complex and on the necessity to give learners support and guidance when they start to work on tasks at a higher level of difficulty.

## Competence Development

Atomistic instructional design models usually focus on one particular domain of learning, such as the cognitive, the affective, or the psychomotor domain. A further distinction (e.g., in the cognitive domain) is the differentiation between models for *declarative learning*, with an emphasis on instructional methods for the construction of conceptual knowledge, and models for *procedural learning*, with an emphasis on methods for the acquisition of procedural skills (Andrews and Goodson, 1980). In contrast, a holistic approach aims at the *integration* of declarative learning, procedural learning (including perceptual and psychomotor skills), and affective learning (including the predisposition to keep all of these aspects up to date) and so facilitates the development of an integrated knowledge base that increases the chance that transfer of learning occurs. Many superordinate terms that encompass knowledge, skills, and attitudes have been proposed in the literature, including *expertise*, *complex skills*, and (professional) *competences*.

In current whole-task models, final attainment levels are often described in terms of competences. On the basis of a comprehensive, analytical study on the concept of competence, van Merriënboer et al. (2002) concluded that three dimensions are basic to the use of this term. The first dimension, *integrativity*, indicates that competence always combines knowledge, skills, and attitudes as well as aptitudes of the task performer. The second dimension, *specificity*, indicates that a competence is always bound to a context that can be highly specific (e.g., a profession) or more general (e.g., a career). The third dimension, *durability*, indicates that a competence is more or less stable in spite of changes in tools, working methods, and technologies.

Whole-task educational programs or integrated curricula often aim at the simultaneous development of first-order, professional skills as well as higher order, general skills such as self-directed learning—including reflection on and assessment of one's own performance, self-monitoring of task performance, and planning one's own learning trajectories. In such programs, learners are able to select their own learning tasks, so each individual learner has his or her own curriculum rather than having a one-and-the-same curriculum for all learners. In such a form of on-demand education, support and guidance given by the teacher are not limited to performing the learning tasks but are also directed toward orienting, monitoring, assessing, and planning the learning tasks.

## Mathemagenic Methods

A logical result of using distinct learning objectives as the basis for instructional design is the application of instructional methods that minimize the number of practice items required, the time spent on the task, and the learners' investment of effort made to reach those objectives. Designing and producing practice items costs time and money, which are often scarce, and the learner does not have unlimited time or motivation to study. Consider the situation where students must learn to diagnose three different types of errors (e1, e2, and e3) in a complex technical system. If a minimum of three practice items is required to learn to diagnose each error, one may first train the students to diagnose error 1, then to diagnose error 2, and finally to diagnose error 3. This leads to the following training blueprint:

e1, e1, e1, e2, e2, e2, e3, e3, e3

Although this practice schedule will probably be most efficient for reaching the three objectives, thus minimizing the required time on task and student investment of effort, it also yields a *low* transfer of learning.

The reason for this is that the chosen instructional method invites students to construct highly specific knowledge for diagnosing each distinct error, which only allows them to perform in the way specified in the objectives but not to show performances that go *beyond* the given objectives. If a designer is aiming at a transfer of learning, and the objective is to train students to diagnose as many errors as possible in a technical system, it is far better to train the students to diagnose the three errors in a random order. This leads, for example, to the following training blueprint:

e3, e2, e2, e1, e3, e3, e1, e2, e1

This sequence is probably less efficient for reaching the three isolated objectives than the previous one because it may increase the necessary time on task or the investment of effort by the learners. It might even require four instead of three practice items to reach the same level of performance for each separate objective. But, in the end it yields *higher* transfer of learning! The reason for this increase of transfer is that this instructional method invites students to construct knowledge that is general and abstract rather than entirely bound to the three concrete, specific errors. This better allows them to diagnose new not earlier encountered errors. This phenomenon—where the methods that work the best for reaching isolated, specific objectives are often not the methods that work best for achieving integrated objectives and increasing the transfer of learning—is known as the *transfer paradox* (van Merriënboer et al., 1997, 2006). A whole-task approach takes this paradox into account and is always directed toward reaching multiple, integrated objectives that go beyond a limited list of highly specific objectives. Whole-task approaches are characterized by the use of mathemagenic instructional methods that are accompanied with a germane cognitive load (see Chapter 31 in this *Handbook*) and give rise to meaningful learning and transfer.

## EXAMPLES OF WHOLE-TASK MODELS

Based on a study of a variety of modern design theories and models, Merrill (2002a) suggested five *first principles of instruction*, stating that learning is promoted when: (1) learners are engaged in solving real-world problems, (2) new knowledge is applied by the learner, (3) new knowledge is integrated into the learner's world, (4) existing knowledge is activated as a foundation for new knowledge, and (5) new knowledge is demonstrated to the learner. The characteristics of whole-task models are clearly reflected in the first three principles.

**TABLE 35.1**
**Overview of Elaboration Sequences in Elaboration Theory**

| | Conceptual | Theoretical | Procedural |
|---|---|---|---|
| Learning goal: | Learning many related concepts | Learning many related principles | Learning procedural or heuristic tasks |
| Sequence: | Teach broader, inclusive concepts before narrow, detailed concepts | Teach broader, inclusive principles before narrow, detailed principles | Teach simpler versions of the whole task before complex versions |

| | All Sequences |
|---|---|
| Instructional approach: | Topical or spiral sequencing |
| | Integrate knowledge, skills, and attitudes |
| | Group wholes into learning episodes |
| | Give learners some control over contents/instructional method |

The first principle emphasizes that students learn better when they are involved in solving increasingly more complex real-world problems. This closely resembles a whole-task approach as well as the idea that tasks should be ordered from simple to complex, while the support and guidance given to learners decrease as they acquire more expertise. The second principle acknowledges the importance of applying newly acquired competences in real-life situations and reflects the importance of mathemagenic instructional methods that facilitate the transfer of learning. The third principle stresses the importance of integration. It is in agreement with the idea of competence growth in an integrated curriculum in which learners are co-responsible for their learning, as opposed to the one-way teaching of distinct pieces of knowledge, skills, and attitudes.

In this section, we briefly describe three example models. It is not our intention to provide an exhaustive overview of models but only to discuss a small number of models that are representative of the family of whole-task models. First, a description is given of *elaboration theory*. This forerunner of current whole-task models stresses the notion that working from simple to complex is a *sine qua non* for a whole-task approach. Second, a description is given of *goal-based scenarios*. This theory focuses on the importance of real-world applications and the transfer of learning. Finally, *four-component instructional design* is discussed as an example of a theory trying to implement all basic principles of the whole-task approach.

## Elaboration Theory

Reigeluth's elaboration theory (Reigeluth, 1987, 1999; Reigeluth and Stein, 1983; Reigeluth et al., 1980; Van Patten et al., 1986) can be seen as a forerunner of the whole-task approach in educational communications

and technology. The basic principle of this theory is that instruction should be organized from the simplest representation of the learning domain or task (i.e., the *epitome*, which contains the most fundamental and representative ideas at a concrete level) to increasingly more complex and elaborated representations. Originally, the theory focused on the sequencing of instructional content in conceptual and theoretical domains.

The conceptual elaboration sequence (see left column in Table 35.1) emphasizes the superordinate, coordinate, and subordinate relationships among concepts. The concept of *dog*, for example, is subordinate to *pet*, coordinate to *cat*, and superordinate to *poodle*. In a process of conceptual analysis, a conceptual knowledge structure or taxonomy is made of the learning content. This structure is translated to an elaboration sequence in which the broadest, most inclusive concepts are taught first, including the supporting content (i.e., relevant knowledge, skills, and attitudes) related to them, and subsequently the ever more narrow, detailed concepts are taught together with related supporting content. Typical approaches to sequencing are topical and spiral. In a topical approach, the content is presented in a vertical manner; for example, a student first studies the sequence pet–dog–poodle, then pet–cat–tabby, and so forth. A spiral approach, in contrast, reflects a horizontal method; for example, a student first studies the sequence pet–..., then dog–cat–..., then poodle–tabby–... and so on.

The theoretical elaboration sequence (see middle column in Table 35.1) focuses on interrelated sets of principles. An introductory course on psychology, for example, focuses on principles of human anatomy and physiology, elementary statistics, genetics, culture, and so forth. In a process of theoretical analysis, a structure is made of the learning content. Such a structure differs from a causal model because it shows principles that are elaborations of other principles, while a causal model shows principles that combine with other principles. The theoretical elaboration sequence that is derived from the theoretical structure first teaches, topically or spirally, the broadest, most inclusive and most general principles along with the supporting content, and then proceeds to teach ever more narrow, less inclusive, more detailed, and more precise principles and supporting content.

Elaboration theory clearly reflects some basic principles of whole-task models. The topical and spiral approach to sequencing works from simple to complex wholes. The combination of organizing content (conceptual, theoretical) and supporting contents aims at the integration of knowledge, skills, and attitudes. The concept of *learning episodes* is used to denote instructional units that allow for review and synthesis without breaking up the idea of a meaningful whole. And, finally, elaboration theory suggests giving learners some control over both content and instructional methods, which resembles the principle of shared responsibility. Later versions of the theory pay more attention to procedural organizing contents, with a focus on solution steps or heuristic tasks that focus on problem-solving principles, guidelines, and causal models. In a process of task analysis, a flowchart is made that depicts the steps (for a procedural task) or the principles, guidelines, and causal models (for a heuristic task) experts would use to decide what to do when. Based on this flowchart, a simplifying conditions sequence is built (see right column in Table 35.1). It begins with the simplest version of the task that is still representative of the *whole* task and ends with the most complex version of this task. This approach is also typical for the whole-task, learning-by-doing models discussed in the next two sections.

## Goal-Based Scenarios

Goal-based scenarios (Schank, 1993/1994; Schank et al., 1993/1994) are the backbone of learning in Schank's learning-by-doing paradigm (Schank et al., 1999). These goal-based scenarios represent "a learn-by-doing simulation in which students pursue a goal by practicing target skills and using relevant content knowledge to help them achieve their goal" (Schank et al., 1999, p. 165). A goal-based scenario consists of the following seven essential components:

- *Goal.* Two categories of learning goals are distinguished: process knowledge and content knowledge. Process knowledge reflects the skills and attitudes necessary to solve a problem, while content knowledge considers

the knowledge required to achieve the goal. A goal-based scenario best appeals to both categories.

- *Mission.* The mission of a goal-based scenario is closely related to the goal and represents the actual assignment the student has to carry out. The mission must be as realistic and motivating as possible for the students. It should resemble a real-life task that a real person would plausibly have to achieve for an important reason.
- *Cover story.* The cover story forms the incentive for the students to become engaged in practice. It should elicit students to practice the skills and attitudes and seek the information and construct the knowledge that are reflected in the learning goals.
- *Role.* The role defines the perspective the student will take in the cover story. This role should ensure that the student will achieve his or her learning goals, and it should be as realistic and appealing as possible to motivate them.
- *Scenario operations.* The scenario operations are the activities a student carries out to accomplish the learning goal. Each goal-based scenario should elicit numerous scenario operations that contain decision points so students can infer the consequences of their actions.
- *Resources.* Well-organized and easily accessible resources contain all the information (i.e., stories) that students need to achieve the learning goal.
- *Feedback.* The situated, just-in-time feedback can be derived from the consequences of certain actions, it could be given by coaches, or it can be found in the resources as domain experts' stories about similar experiences.

Elaboration theory and goal-based scenarios clearly resemble each other. Like the learning episodes in elaboration theory, goal-based scenarios provide an opportunity to integrate knowledge, skills, and attitudes in meaningful wholes. In addition, both theories stress the importance of some learner control over contents and strategies. In goal-based scenarios, teachers may design a diverse set of goals to help learners with different prior knowledge and interests acquire the same knowledge, skills, and attitudes, or learners may sometimes even be permitted to set their own subgoals. Compared to elaboration theory, however, goal-based scenarios pay far less attention to the sequencing of instruction. In contrast, there is a stronger focus on the

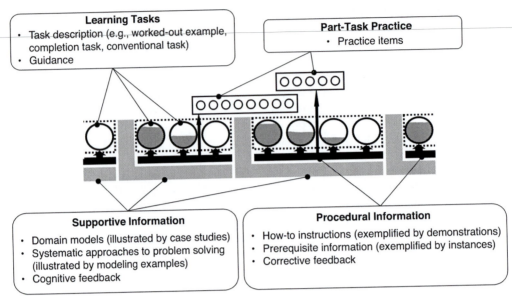

**Figure 35.1** A schematic overview of the 4C/ID model and its main elements.

performance of real-life tasks in authentic contexts to facilitate the transfer of learning. This fits the basic idea that more general goals (i.e., integrated objectives) should drive the learning process, because highly specific learning objectives invite learners to apply strategies that do not allow for the transfer of learning (for the role of goals in reaching the transfer of learning, see Machin, 2002).

## Four-Component Instructional Design

Van Merriënboer's four-component instructional design model (4C/ID model) (van Merriënboer, 1997; van Merriënboer et al., 2002, 2003) claims that whole-task environments for complex learning can always be described in four components:

- *Learning tasks*—Meaningful whole-task experiences that are based on real-life tasks. Ideally, the learning tasks ask the learners to integrate and coordinate many if not all aspects of real-life task performance, including problem solving and reasoning aspects, which are different across tasks, and routine aspects, which are consistent across tasks.
- *Supportive information*—Information that is supportive to the learning and performance of problem solving and reasoning for learning tasks. It describes how the task domain is organized and how problems in this domain can best be approached. It builds a bridge between what learners already know

and what may be helpful to know so they can work fruitfully on the learning tasks.
- *Procedural information*—Information that is prerequisite to the learning and performance of routine aspects of learning tasks. This information provides an algorithmic specification of how to perform those routine aspects. It is best organized in small information units and presented to learners precisely when they need it during their work on the learning tasks.
- *Part-task practice*. Additional exercises for routine aspects of learning tasks for which a very high level of automaticity is required after the instruction. Part-task practice is only necessary if the learning tasks do not provide enough repetition for a particular routine aspect to reach the required high level of automaticity.

The 4C/ID model shares it focus on authentic learning tasks with goal-based scenarios. The tasks are based on real-life tasks and ask learners to combine knowledge, skills, and attitudes. As in elaboration theory, ample attention is paid to sequencing the learning tasks. To do so, learning tasks are organized into so-called *task classes*, which are ordered from simple to complex (see Figure 35.1; task classes are the dotted rectangles around a set of learning tasks). The first task class contains the simplest learning tasks that an expert might encounter in the real world yet are still whole, meaningful tasks that allow the learners to quickly develop a holistic vision of the task. Subsequent task classes contain increasingly more complex and difficult learning tasks. Learning tasks within a particular task class are equivalent in the sense that they can be performed on the basis of the same body of knowledge; each subsequent, more complex task class requires more knowledge or more elaborated knowledge for effective performance than the preceding, simpler task classes.

An additional element in the 4C/ID model pertains to the support and guidance that are given to learners (in Figure 35.1, this is indicated by the filled-in circles). When learners begin to work on more difficult learning tasks in a new task class, they first receive sizeable support and guidance from the teacher or instructional materials. Support and guidance gradually decrease in a process of *scaffolding* as learners acquire more expertise. When learners are able to independently perform learning tasks without any support or guidance up to the given standards (empty circles in Figure 35.1), they are ready to continue to a next task class with more difficult tasks.

Also characteristic of the model is its focus on the transfer of learning. Supportive information (L-shaped, light-gray shapes in Figure 35.1) relates to the idea that transfer is explained by general or abstract information that may be interpreted by a task performer to solve a new problem situation (i.e., the Gestalt approach). Conceptual models (what is this?), structural models (how is this built?), causal models (how does this work?), and cognitive strategies (how should I approach this task?) provide this kind of information. Procedural information (dark-gray rectangles with upward-pointing arrows in Figure 35.1) and part-task practice (small series of circles in Figure 35.1) relate to the idea that transfer may be explained by the application of knowledge elements that are shared between the practice and the transfer situation (i.e., the associationist approach). Procedural information tells the learner, precisely when the information is needed, how to perform routine aspects of the learning tasks. Part-task practice may provide the additional practice required to develop knowledge elements that allow the learner to perform routine aspects at a high level of automaticity. Finally, like elaboration theory and goal-based scenarios, the 4C/ID model acknowledges the importance of a certain degree of learner control over and responsibility for the learning process. In new versions of the model (van Merriënboer and Kirschner, 2007), learners are able to select their own learning tasks, as well as the supportive information and the part-task practice relevant for those tasks.

# EMPIRICAL EVIDENCE FOR THE EFFECTIVENESS OF WHOLE-TASK MODELS

The previous sections presented a brief history of whole-task models, discussed the main characteristics of whole-task models in the field of educational communications and technology, and described three example models. The next sections discuss, in order, general research on the effectiveness of the whole-task approach and specific research on the effectiveness of elaboration theory, goal-based scenarios, and four-component instructional design.

## Whole-Task Practice

In a review study, Wightman and Lintern (1985) investigated the effectiveness of segmentation, fractionation, and simplification techniques for part-task training. They concluded that whole-task training was generally more beneficial for learning than part-task training. Only segmentation in the form of *backward chaining with snowballing* (i.e., first the final segment of a task is practiced and prior segments are successively added during training) was as beneficial for transfer performance as whole-task training. This conclusion was confirmed by the results of a study by Wightman and Sistrunk (1987) that showed that learners who received whole-task carrier-landing training outperformed learners who received part-task training using simplification, but they did not outperform learners who received part-task, backward-chaining training. Moreover, Goettl and Shute (1996) found that a segmentation with backward-chaining approach to training is only as efficient as whole-task training if it is composed of critical component tasks. Otherwise, whole-task training leads to higher transfer test performance.

In two laboratory experiments, Detweiler and Lundy (1995) studied the effects of single-task and dual-task practice of consistent word-category mapping and spatial-pattern visual search tasks on dual-task transfer test performance. They found that dual-task practice yielded higher transfer test performance than single-task practice. Based on their findings, they concluded that target tasks that must be performed together should also be practiced together. Peck and Detweiler (2000) compared four approaches to practicing concurrent tasks related to adjusting the navigation and peripheral systems of a fictitious submarine: (1) a part-task approach, (2) a part-task chaining approach (i.e., snowballing), (3) a concurrent-chaining approach, and (4) a whole-task approach. In this experiment, part-task practice consisted of single-task trials that required an adjustment of either the navigation system or the peripheral system. In part-task chaining practice, single-task practice gradually became multi-task practice. Concurrent-chaining practice referred to increasingly complex concurrent-task practice, and in whole-task practice concurrent-task practice was required from the start. The results of this study demonstrated the beneficial effects on transfer test performance of both the concurrent-chaining approach and the whole-task approach.

To summarize, whole-task training seems to be the preferred method of instruction when it comes to complex skill acquisition. Sometimes, however, it may be desirable to include some (additional) part-task practice in the training—for example, when the whole task is dangerous or highly demanding. Roessingh et al. (2002) developed and tested a model to determine the optimal training time schedule for such a combined training. They concluded that, if one part task has to be included in the training, then more than 50% of the total training time has to be devoted to whole-task practice to maximize performance. This indicates that even in cases where whole-task practice is not the only relevant type of training it still should take up the largest part of it. An example of the successful application of combined training can be found in an experiment of Pollock et al. (2002). They compared a mixed instructional approach (i.e., first part-task practice then whole-task practice) to a whole-task approach (i.e., only whole-task practice) to teach electrical safety tests and found that novices in the domain demonstrated superior performance on a knowledge test and practical task after receiving the mixed instruction. Such a combined approach, in which part-task practice is used to supplement preponderant whole-task practice, is also found in four-component instructional design. First, though, research on elaboration theory and goal-based scenarios are discussed.

## Elaboration Theory

Beissner and Reigeluth (1989, 1994) studied whether it was possible to design a course on physical-therapy treatment with combined sequencing techniques (i.e., multiple strands) as prescribed by elaboration theory. They carefully described the four-step design process. In the first step, a procedural elaboration sequence was designed using the simplifying conditions approach. Subsequently, and independent of the procedural sequence, a prescriptive theoretical elaboration sequence (i.e., understanding why principles work) and a descriptive theoretical elaboration sequence (i.e., understanding how principles work)

were designed as steps two and three. Finally, these three steps were integrated into a single course sequence. Beissner and Reigeluth concluded that it is possible to have parallel elaboration sequences in one course, yielding *learning episodes* (whole tasks) that integrate relevant knowledge, skills, and attitudes. The effectiveness of this multiple-strand technique, however, was not investigated.

English and Reigeluth (1996) conducted a study that used a mixed-method approach to determine the strengths and weaknesses of elaboration theory. They revised three chapters of a book on electrical circuit analysis according to multiple-strand sequencing (combining procedural and theoretical sequences). The qualitative data (i.e., impromptu and debriefing questions) obtained in this study indicated that the sequences could be improved in the following ways: (1) Every step in the elaboration sequence should highlight the important relationships and relate each step to previous steps and knowledge, (2) students should be informed that the first step is entry level and will be followed by steps that are more complex at the start of the sequence, and (3) learners should be given some learner control over the learning materials (note that this recommendation is incorporated in the 1999 version of elaboration theory discussed earlier). Furthermore, the quantitative data (pre- and post-test results) showed that the instructional material was effective for both low-ability and high-ability students. An explorative comparison of student performance after the experimental course and the regular course on this topic indicated that students who participated in the experimental course performed better than students in the regular course.

## Goal-Based Scenarios

Bell et al. (1993/1994) evaluated a goal-based scenario involving sickle cell disease known as the Sickle Cell Counselor. The Sickle Cell Counselor was installed in the Museum of Science and Industry in Chicago to evaluate its usefulness. The aim of the installation was to give museum visitors, in the course of a brief interaction, an understanding of sickle cell disease and the basic underlying inheritance mechanisms. Based on the fact that in a period of 25 days, 933 individuals spent on the average more than 7 minutes on the installation, the authors concluded that the Sickle Cell Counselor succeeded in attracting and holding onto the visitors' attention. The effectiveness of the Sickle Cell Counselor was evaluated in a subsequent study. Three groups were compared: a group that used the Sickle Cell Counselor, a group that read a pamphlet that conveyed the same information, and a control group. The group that used the Sickle Cell Counselor outperformed both the pamphlet group and the control group in role-playing performance and a paper-and-pencil test.

Another goal-based scenario, Architecting Business Change, developed for Andersen Consulting in St. Charles, Illinois, was evaluated by Kantor et al. (2000). This goal-based scenario addressed eight skills, and Kantor and colleagues conducted a needs assessment to find out the minimal proficiency level for each skill. The proficiency level ranged from *little/no ability* to *expert* and was based on ratings made by supervisors. The goal-based scenario was evaluated against those minimal proficiency levels. After working with the goal-based scenario, students were asked to rate their proficiency level before and after completing the scenario. A comparison of the minimal proficiency levels and those reported after completion indicated that students rated their proficiency level higher than minimally required for five out of eight of the trained skills. In addition, a comparison of the proficiency levels before and after completing the scenario indicated that all students rated their proficiency level higher after than before working with the goal-based scenario.

## Four-Component Instructional Design (4C/ID)

In two studies, Hoogveld et al. (2001, 2003) studied the effectiveness of the 4C/ID model as an instructional systems design (ISD) approach to designing competence-based education (for applications in the medical domain, see Janssen-Noordman et al., 2006). In the first study, two groups of teachers were compared: One group was trained to use the 4C/ID model to design instruction, and the other group was trained to optimize its own design approach. After the training phase, the design quality of their educational products was measured by experts, and it was found that teachers trained to use the 4C/ID model developed qualitatively better designs than the other teachers. The second study investigated whether teams or individuals benefited more from a 4C/ID approach to designing competence-based education. It was found that low achievers benefited more from the 4C/ID model when they were working in teams, but high achievers worked as well in teams as individually.

Other researchers studied the effectiveness of 4C/ID-based instruction from the learners' perspective. Nadolski et al. (2005) focused on segmenting complex whole learning tasks in the area of law into phases. They varied the number of phases (one, four, or nine) of the whole task to determine the optimal balance between the advantages of whole-task practice and the disadvantages of cognitive overload caused by

whole tasks that are too complex for learners. The results of this study showed that learners who carried out the learning task in four phases were most effective during practice as measured by the coherence and content of their practice products. Learners who carried out the learning tasks in one or four phases were most efficient during practice as measured by a combination of practice-product quality and invested mental effort. No effects were found on transfer test performance. These results were confirmed in a follow-up study (Nadolski et al., 2006) in which learners who received learning tasks that consisted of four phases outperformed learners who received tasks consisting of eight phases. The results indicate that whole learning tasks should only be segmented if this is the only possible way to diminish their complexity.

Using a model closely resembling the 4C/ID approach, Merrill (2002b) carried out a study at Thompson/NETg to validate his first principles of instruction. Three instructional scenarios for a course in Excel were developed: (1) a whole-task scenario group, (2) an e-learning group that received the existing commercial version of the NETg Excel course, and (3) a control group that only received three authentic test tasks. Statistical differences were found between the three groups on test task performance. The whole-task scenario group scored an average of 89%, the e-learning group scored an average of 68%, and the control group scored only an average of 34% correct on the test tasks. In addition, the whole-task scenario group required significantly less time to complete the three test tasks compared to the e-learning group.

A study by Lim and Reiser (2006) compared the effects of 4C/ID whole-task training and part-task training on the acquisition and transfer of a complex cognitive skill (preparing a grade book in Excel) for novices and advanced learners. They found that both novice and advanced learners achieved better whole-task performance and better transfer performance if they received the 4C/ID whole-task training. The superiority of a 4C/ID approach over other approaches was confirmed in another classroom study (Sarfo and Elen, 2005, 2006) that compared three groups who had to learn how to design a single building plan based on local conditions. The control group was taught according to an approach that was applied in technical schools in Ghana; the experimental groups were taught according to the 4C/ID approach, either with or without technology-enhanced learning. Although, the groups performed equally well on a pretest and both showed learning gains on a post-test, both experimental groups outperformed the control group on the post-test.

# DISCUSSION

This chapter has discussed the historical roots of whole-task models and the main features. It has also provided three examples of whole-task models in the field of educational communications and technology and has presented research findings concerning the effectiveness of whole-task models. Overall, research findings show that whole-task models are particularly effective to teach complex skills and professional competences; however, this research also highlights two limitations of whole-task models. First, whole-task models should only be used to teach content and tasks that are characterized by a high degree of coordination—that is, many interrelationships between knowledge elements and component skills. If coordination is low, part-task models may be equally effective or even more effective than whole-task models. Second, whole-task practice should not be seen as incompatible with part-task practice. Even in a dominant whole-task approach, it may be desirable to offer additional part-task practice for routine aspects of a complex task. Furthermore, if it proves to be impossible to develop a version of the whole task that is simple enough to begin the training with, it may be necessary to work from parts that are as large as possible within a whole-part approach. In a purely holistic model, however, this would be viewed as a very last resort.

Whole-task models are relatively new in the field of educational communications and technology, and there is a clear need for additional research. On the most basic level, much is still unknown regarding the design of optimal whole learning tasks, sequencing techniques, and ways to scaffold learners who are working on the tasks. Another set of research questions pertains to learner control and self-directed learning. In a whole-task model, self-directed learners should select their own learning tasks, based on self-assessments of their performance and information regarding the tasks (e.g., difficulty, available support and guidance). Future research should investigate how learners are best guided in their process of task selection (e.g., through the use of portfolios or coaching) and encouraged to develop their self-directed learning skills. Finally, the issue of transfer of learning is central to whole-task models. Here, an interesting line of research pertains to the importance of real-life, authentic whole tasks. Although some researchers argue that it is critical to perform those tasks in an authentic environment (see, for example, Brown et al., 1989), others claims that especially early in the learning process it is not the fidelity of the environment but the psychological fidelity of the task itself that is most important.

It is clear that whole-task models today hold a prominent position in the field of educational communications and technology and, at least in Western Europe, in vocational education and training and in higher professional education. In our opinion, this is an inevitable reaction to societal and technological developments as well as students' and employers' uncompromising views regarding the value of education. Due to new technologies, routine tasks have been taken over by machines and the complex cognitive tasks that must be performed by humans are becoming increasingly important. Moreover, both the nature of and the skills required for currently available jobs are rapidly changing while the information relevant to carrying out these jobs quickly becomes obsolete. This imposes higher demands on the workforce, as employers stress the importance of problem solving, reasoning, and self-directed learning to ensure that employees can and will flexibly adjust to rapid changes in their environment. Whole-task models in education aim to reach precisely those goals.

# REFERENCES

Achtenhagen, F. (2001). Criteria for the development of complex teaching-learning environments. *Instruct. Sci.*, 29(4–5), 361–380.

Adams, J. A. (1987). Historical review and appraisal of research on the learning, retention, and transfer of human motor skills. *Psychol. Bull.*, 101, 41–74.

Andrews, D. H. and Goodson, L. A. (1980). A comparative analysis of models of instructional design. *J. Instruct. Dev.*, 3(4), 2–16.*

Annett, J. (1989). *Training in Transferable Skills*. Sheffield, U.K.: The Training Agency.

Annett, J. and Sparrow, J. (1985). Transfer of training: a review of research and practical implications. *Programmed Learn. Educ. Technol.*, 22, 116–124.

Ash, M. G. (1998). *Gestalt Psychology in German Culture, 1890–1967: Holism and the Quest for Objectivity*. Cambridge, U.K.: Cambridge University Press.

Beissner, K. L. and Reigeluth, C. M. (1989). *Multiple Strand Sequencing Using the Elaboration Theory*, ERIC Document Reproduction Service No. ED 314025.

Beissner, K. L. and Reigeluth, C. M. (1994). A case study on course sequencing with multiple strands using elaboration theory. *Perform. Improve. Q.*, 7(2), 38–61.

Bell, B., Bareiss, R., and Beckwith, R. (1993/1994). Sickle cell counselor: a prototype goal-based scenario for instruction in a museum environment. *J. Learn. Sci.*, 3, 347–386.

Biggs, J. (1996). Enhancing teaching through constructive alignment. *Higher Educ.*, 32(3), 347–365.

Briggs, G. E. and Naylor, J. C. (1962). The relative efficiency of several training methods as a function of transfer task complexity. *J. Exp. Psychol.*, 64, 505–512.

Brown, J. S., Collins, A., and Duguid, S. (1989). Situated cognition and the culture of learning. *Educ. Res.*, 18(1), 32–42.*

Clark, R. E. and Estes, F. (1999). The development of authentic educational technologies. *Educ. Technol.*, 39(2), 5–16.

Detweiler, M. C. and Lundy, D. H. (1995). Effects of single- and dual-task practice on acquiring dual-task skill. *Hum. Factors*, 37, 193–211.

Dreyfus, S. E. (1982). Formal models vs. human situational understanding: Inherent limitations on the modeling of business expertise. *Office Technol. People*, 1, 133–165.

Elio, R. (1986). Representation of similar well-learned cognitive procedures. *Cogn. Sci.*, 10, 41–73.

Ellis, H. C. (1965). *The Transfer of Learning*. New York: Macmillan.

English, R. E. and Reigeluth, C. M. (1996). Formative research on sequencing instruction with the elaboration theory. *Educ. Technol. Res. Dev.*, 1, 23–42.

Feldenkrais, M. (1982). *The Illusive Obvious*. Cupertino, CA: Meta Publications.

Gagné, R. M. (1968). Learning hierarchies. *Educ. Psychol.*, 6, 1–9.

Gagné, R. M. (1985). *The Conditions of Learning*, 4th ed. New York: Holt, Rinehart and Winston.

Gagné, R. M. and Briggs, L. J. (1979). *Principles of Instructional Design*, 2nd ed. New York: Holt, Rinehart and Winston.

Gagné, R. M. and Merrill, M. D. (1990). Integrative goals for instructional design. *Educ. Technol., Res. Dev.*, 38(1), 23–30.*

Gallwey, W. T. (1974). *The Inner Game of Tennis*. New York: Random House.

Goettl, B. P. and Shute, V. J. (1996). Analysis of part-task training using the backward-transfer technique. *J. Exp. Psychol. Appl.*, 2, 227–249.*

Graen, G. B. and Hui, C. (2001). Approaches to leadership: toward a complete contingency model of face-to-face leadership. In *Work Motivation in the Context of a Globalizing Economy*, edited by M. Erez, U. Kleinbeck, and H. Thierry, pp. 211–225. Mahwah, NJ: Lawrence Erlbaum Associates.

Graham-Pole, J. (2001). 'Physician, heal thyself': how teaching holistic medicine differs from teaching CAM. *Acad. Med.*, 76, 662–664.

Hoogveld, A. W. M., Paas, F., and Jochems, W. M. G. (2001). The effects of a Web-based training in an instructional systems design approach on teachers' instructional design behavior. *Comput. Hum. Behav.*, 17, 363–371.

Hoogveld, A. W. M., Paas, F., and Jochems, W. M. G. (2003). Application of an instructional systems design approach by teachers in higher education: individual versus team design. *Teaching Teacher Educ.*, 19, 581–590.

Janssen-Noordman, A. M. B., van Merriënboer, J. J. G., Van der Vleuten, C. P. M., and Scherpbier, A. J. J. A. (2006). Design of integrated practice for learning professional competences. *Med. Teacher*, 28(5), 447–452.

Kantor, R. J., Waddington, T., and Osgood, R. E. (2000). Fostering the suspension of disbelief: the role of authenticity in goal-based scenarios. *Interact. Learn. Environ.*, 8, 211–227.

Landa, L. N. (1983). The algo-heuristic theory of instruction. In *Instructional-Design Theories and Models*, edited by C. M. Reigeluth, pp. 163–211. Hillsdale, NJ: Lawrence Erlbaum Associates.*

Lim, J. and Reiser, R. A. (2006). The Effects of Part-Task and Whole-Task Approaches on Acquisition and Transfer of a Complex Cognitive Skill. Paper presented at the Association for Educational Communications and Technology (AECT) Annual Convention, October 10–14, Dallas, TX.

Machin, M. A. (2002). Planning, managing, and optimizing transfer of training. In *Creating, Implementing, and Managing Effective Training and Development*, edited by K. Kraiger, pp. 263–301. San Francisco, CA: Jossey-Bass.

Mandler, J. M. and Mandler, G., Eds. (1964). *Thinking: From Association to Gestalt*. New York: Wiley (original work published in Germany, 1913).

Merrill, M. D. (2002a). First principles of instruction. *Educ. Technol. Res. Dev.*, 50, 43–59.*

Merrill, M. D. (2002b). A pebble-in-the-pond model for instructional design. *Perform. Improve. Q.*, 41(7), 39–51.*

Nadolski, R. J., Kirschner, P. A., and van Merriënboer, J. J. G. (2005). Optimizing the number of steps in learning tasks for complex skills. *Br. J. Educ. Psychol.*, 75, 223–237.*

Nadolski, R. J., Kirschner, P. A., and van Merriënboer, J. J. G. (2006). Process support in learning tasks for acquiring complex cognitive skills in the domain of law. *Learn. Instruct.*, 16, 266–278.

Naylor, J. C. and Briggs, G. E. (1963). Effects of task complexity and task organization on the relative efficiency of part and whole training methods. *J. Exp. Psychol.*, 65, 217–224.

Osgood, C. E. (1949). The similarity paradox in human learning: a resolution. *Psychol. Rev.*, 56, 132–154.

Peck, A. C. and Detweiler, M. C. (2000). Training concurrent multistep procedural tasks. *Hum. Factors*, 42, 379–389.

Perkins, D. N. and Grotzer, T. A. (1997). Teaching intelligence. *Am. Psychol.*, 52, 1125–1133.

Poindexter, S. (2003). The case for holistic learning. *Change*, 35(1), 25–30.

Pollio, H. R. and Back, H. P. (2000). When the tail wags the dog. *J. Higher Educ.*, 71(1), 84–102.

Pollock, E., Chandler, P., and Sweller, J. (2002). Assimilating complex information. *Learn. Instruct.*, 12, 61–86.

Reigeluth, C. M. (1987). Lesson blueprints based on the elaboration theory of instruction. In *Instructional Theories in Action: Lessons Illustrating Selected Theories and Models*, edited by C. M. Reigeluth, pp. 245–288. Hillsdale, NJ: Lawrence Erlbaum Associates.

Reigeluth, C. M. (1999). The elaboration theory: guidance for scope and sequence decisions. In *Instructional-Design Theories and Models. A New Paradigm of Instruction*, edited by C. M. Reigeluth, pp. 425–453. Mahwah, NJ: Lawrence Erlbaum Associates.*

Reigeluth, C. M. and Stein, F. S. (1983). The elaboration theory of instruction. In *Instructional-Design Theories and Models: An Overview of Their Current Status*, edited by C. M. Reigeluth, pp. 335–381. Hillsdale, NJ: Lawrence Erlbaum Associates.*

Reigeluth, C. M., Merrill, M. D., Wilson, B. G., and Spiller, R. T. (1980). The elaboration theory of instruction: a model for sequencing and synthesizing instruction. *Instruct. Sci.*, 9, 195–219.

Rinke, W. J. (1985). Holistic education: an answer? *Train. Dev. J.*, 39(8), 67–68.

Roessingh, J. J. M., Kappers, A. M. L., and Koenderink, J. J. (2002). *Transfer between Training of Part-Tasks in Complex Skill Training*, Technical Report No. NLR-TP-2002-646. Amsterdam: National Aerospace Laboratory.

Royer, J. M. (1979). Theories of the transfer of learning. *Educ. Psychol.*, 14, 53–69.

Sarfo, F. K. and Elen, J. (2005). Powerful learning environments and the development of technical expertise in Ghana: investigating the moderating effect of instructional conceptions. In *Proceedings of the 5th IEEE International Conference on Advanced Learning Technologies (ICALT'2005)*, July 5–8, Kaohsiung, Taiwan, edited by P. Goodyear, D. G. Sampson, D. J.-T. Yang Kinshuk, T. Okamoto, R. Hartley, and N.-S. Chen, pp. 1000–1004. Los Alamitos, CA: IEEE.

Sarfo, F. K. and Elen, J. (2006). The design of effective support for the acquisition of technical expertise. In *Avoiding Simplicity, Confronting Complexity*, edited by G. Clarebout and J. Elen, pp. 417–422. Rotterdam: Sense Publishers.

Scandura, J. M. (1983). Instructional strategies based on the structural learning theory. In *Instructional-Design Theories and Models*, edited by C. M. Reigeluth, pp. 213–246. Hillsdale, NJ: Lawrence Erlbaum.

Schank, R. C. (1993/1994). Goal-based scenarios: a radical look at education. *J. Learn. Sci.*, 3, 429–453.*

Schank, R. C., Fano, A., Bell, B., and Jona, M. (1993/1994). The design of goal-based scenarios. *J. Learn. Sci.*, 3, 305–345.

Schank, R. C., Berman, T. R., and Macpherson, K. A. (1999). Learning by doing. In *Instructional-Design Theories and Models. A New Paradigm of Instruction*, edited by C. M. Reigeluth, pp. 161–181. Mahwah, NJ: Lawrence Erlbaum Associates.*

Schmidt, R. A. (1991). *Motor Learning and Performance: From Principles to Practice*. Champaign, IL: Human Kinetics Books.

Schneider, W. and Detweiler, M. (1988). The role of practice in dual-task performance: toward workload modeling in a connectionist/control architecture. *Hum. Factors*, 30, 539–566.

Schneider, W. and Shiffrin, R. M. (1977). Controlled and automatic human information processing. I. Detection, search, and attention. *Psychol. Rev.*, 84, 1–66.*

Shiffrin, R. M. and Schneider, W. (1977). Controlled and automatic human information processing. II. Perceptual learning, automatic attending, and a general theory. *Psychol. Rev.*, 84, 127–190.*

Singley, M. K. and Anderson, J. R. (1985). The transfer of text-editing skill. *Int. J. Man–Machine Stud.*, 22, 403–423.

Singley, M. K. and Anderson, J. R. (1988). A keystroke analysis of learning and transfer in text editing. *Hum.-Comput. Interact.*, 3, 223–274.

Smuts, J. C. (1926). *Holism and Evolution*. New York: Macmillan.

Spector, J. M. and Anderson, T. M. (2000). *Holistic and Integrated Perspectives on Learning, Technology, and Instruction: Understanding Complexity*. Mahwah, NJ: Lawrence Erlbaum.*

Strauch, R. (1984). Training the whole person. *Train. Dev. J.*, 38(11), 82–86.*

Thorndike, E. L. and Woodworth, R. S. (1901). The influence of movement in one mental function upon the efficiency of other functions. *Psychol. Rev.*, 8, 247–261.

van Merriënboer, J. J. G. (1997). *Training Complex Cognitive Skills*. Englewood Cliffs, NJ: Educational Technology Publications.*

van Merriënboer, J. J. G. (2006). Alternate models of instructional design: holistic design approaches and complex learning. In *Trends and Issues in Instructional Design and Technology*, 2nd ed., edited by R. Reiser and J. Dempsey, pp. 72–81. Old Tappan, NJ: Prentice Hall.*

van Merriënboer, J. J. G. and Kirschner, P. A. (2007). *Ten Steps to Complex Learning*. Mahwah, NJ: Lawrence Erlbaum Associates.*

van Merriënboer, J. J. G., Jelsma, O., and Paas, F. (1992). Training for reflective expertise: a four-component instructional design model for training complex cognitive skills. *Educ. Technol. Res. Dev.*, 40(2), 23–43.

van Merriënboer, J. J. G., Clark, R. E., and de Croock, M. B. M. (1996). Blueprints for complex learning: the 4C-ID model. *Educ. Technol. Res. Dev.*, 50, 39–64.*

van Merriënboer, J. J. G., de Croock, M. B. M., and Jelsma, O. (1997). The transfer paradox: effects of contextual interference on retention and transfer performance of a complex cognitive skill. *Percept. Motor Skills*, 84, 784–786.

van Merriënboer, J. J. G., van der Klink, M. R., and Hendriks, M. (2002). *Competenties: Van complicaties tot compromis: Een studie in opdracht van de onderwijsraad* [Competences: from complications towards a compromise: a study for the National Educational Council]. The Hague: Onderwijsraad.

van Merriënboer, J. J. G., Kirschner, P. A., and Kester, L. (2003). Taking the load off a learners' mind: instructional design for complex learning. *Educ. Psychol.*, 38, 5–13.

van Merriënboer, J. J. G., Kester, L., and Paas, F. (2006). Teaching complex rather than simple tasks: balancing intrinsic and germane load to enhance transfer of learning. *Appl. Cogn. Psychol.*, 20, 343–352.*

Van Patten, J., Chao, C., and Reigeluth, C. M. (1986). A review of strategies for sequencing and synthesizing instruction. *Rev. Educ. Res.*, 56, 437–471.*

Wertheimer, M. (1925). Über Gestalttheorie [On Gestalt theory], *Philosophische Zeitschrift für Forschung und Aussprache*, 1, 39–60 (translation of lecture at the Kant Society, Berlin, 1924).

Wightman, D. C. and Lintern, G. (1985). Part-task training for tracking and manual control. *Hum. Factors*, 27, 267–284.

Wightman, D. C. and Sistrunk, F. (1987). Part-task training strategies in simulated carrier landing final-approach training. *Hum. Factors*, 29, 245–254.

* Indicates a core reference.

# 36

# Model-Facilitated Learning

*Ton de Jong and Wouter R. van Joolingen*
University of Twente, Enschede, the Netherlands

## CONTENTS

## ABSTRACT

In this chapter, we discuss the possible roles of models in learning, with computer models (simulations) as our focus. In *learning from models*, students' learning processes center around the exploration of a model by changing values of input variables and observing resulting values of output variables. In this process, they experience rules of the simulated domain or discover aspects of these rules. Models can also play a role in the learning process when we ask students to construct models. In *learning by modeling*, students are required to construct an external model that can be simulated to reproduce phenomena observed in a real system. Finally, both ways of using models can be combined in what we refer to as *model-based inquiry learning*. Here, students encounter a computer model that they can explore by changing values of the input variables and by observing values of the output variables and then they reconstruct the model, including its internal functioning, so both models will behave similarly.

## KEYWORDS

*Inquiry learning:* "An approach to learning that involves a process of exploring the natural or material world, and that leads to asking questions, making discoveries, and rigorously testing those discoveries in the search for new understanding" (NSF, 2000, p. 2).

*Model:* Structured representation of a system in terms of variables or concepts and their (quantitative or qualitative) relations that can be used for predicting system behavior by means of simulations.

*Modeling:* The process of creating simulations as a means for learning.

*Simulation:* Computer-based model of a natural process or phenomenon that reacts to changes in values of input variables by displaying the resulting values of output variables.

# INTRODUCTION

In many domains, especially in science, learning involves the acquisition and construction of models (Lehrer and Schauble, 2006). Models are defined as "a set of representations, rules, and reasoning structures that allow one to generate predictions and explanations" (Schwarz and White, 2005, p. 166). Models can be seen as structured representations of (parts of) domains in terms of variables or concepts and their interconnections. Each scientific domain has a set of externally represented *domain models* that are generally agreed upon by researchers working in these domains. Individuals have personal models that may be externally represented or that may be *mental models* (Gentner and Stevens, 1983). Scientific practice can be seen as a process of constantly adapting, refining, or changing models, under the influence of observations or of constraints set by the properties of the models themselves. In a similar vein, learning science consists of creating and adapting mental models with the aim of moving the mental model toward an expert or theoretical domain model (Clement, 2000; Snyder, 2000). Such adaptation of mental models may evolve with gradual modifications or involve more radical changes in the nature of the mental model (Chi, 1992).

In its influential report, the American Association for the Advancement of Science (AAAS, 1989) stated that students need time to explore, make observations, take wrong turns, test ideas, rework tasks, build things, calibrate instruments, collect things, construct physical and mathematical models, learn required mathematics and other relevant concepts, read materials, discuss and debate ideas, wrestle with unfamiliar and counterintuitive ideas, and explore alternative perspectives. According to this description, learning resembles creating and adapting mental models by using scientific inquiry. In 2000, the National Science Foundation defined inquiry learning as "an approach to learning that involves a process of exploring the natural or material world, and that leads to asking questions, making discoveries, and rigorously testing those discoveries in the search for new understanding" (NSF, 2000, p. 2).

In model-facilitated learning, the natural or material world in the above definition is replaced by a model. These models can take many forms (e.g., a simplified sketch or a concept map; see Gobert, 2000); however, in this chapter, we speak of *learning from models* only when students can interact with the model, which means that they can manipulate input to the model with a reaction of the model as a result. As a further specification, we focus on computer models (simulations) (de Jong, 1991) in this chapter. This restriction means that the models we discuss are executable; that is, they use some computational algorithm to generate output (i.e., a change in the values describing the model's state) on the basis of students' input (Hestenes, 1987). This process is called *simulation*. In *learning from models*, students' learning processes center around the exploration of a model by changing values of input variables and observing resulting values of output variables. In the process, they experience rules of the simulated domain or discover aspects of these rules (de Jong, 2006a). Models can also play a role in the learning process when we ask students to construct models. In this *learning by modeling*, students are required to construct an external model, with the objective of making the model behave as much like the real system as possible (Penner, 2001). Finally, both ways of using models can be combined in what we refer to as *model-based inquiry learning*. Here, students receive a model that they can explore by changing values of the input variables and observing values of the output variables. They then have to reconstruct this model, including its internal functioning, in such a way that both models will behave similarly (Löhner et al., 2005; van Joolingen et al., 2005).

In this chapter, we discuss three approaches to using models in education: one in which students try to grasp the properties of an existing model (*learning from models*), one in which students learn from creating models (*learning by modeling*), and a way of learning in which these two forms are combined. In doing so, we concentrate on learning in the science domains.

# LEARNING FROM COMPUTER MODELS

In learning from computer (simulation) models, students try to build a mental model based on the behavior of a given model with which they can experiment. There is a large variety of models and of possible ways to interact with them (van Joolingen and de Jong, 1991), but students basically interact with a computer model through a model interface that allows them to change values of variables in the model and that displays the computed results of their manipulations in one way or another.

Computer technology supporting learning from computer models began to be developed in the late 1970s and 1980s. Of course, many simulations existed that were used more or less directly in an educational context, but only a few systems were specifically geared toward education. Many of these systems primarily concerned either operational models or a combination of operational and conceptual models.

SOPHIE, for example, was an environment for teaching electronic troubleshooting skills, but it was also designed to give students insight into electronic laws, circuit causality, and the functional organization of particular devices (Brown et al., 1982). QUEST also focused on electronic circuit troubleshooting (White and Frederiksen, 1989). QUEST used model progression; circuits became increasingly more complex as students progressed through QUEST, and they could view circuits from different perspectives (e.g., a functional or a behavioral perspective). Another system that combined the learning of operational and conceptual knowledge was STEAMER. This system simulated a complex steam propulsion system for large ships (Hollan et al., 1984). Systems such as MACH-III for complex radar devices (Kurland and Tenney, 1988) and IMTS (Towne et al., 1990) also focused on troubleshooting. Smithtown was one of the first educational simulations that targeted a conceptual domain (economic laws) and that included several support mechanisms for students (Shute and Glaser, 1990). In Smithtown, students could explore simulated markets. They could change such variables as labor costs and population income and observe the effects on, for example, prices. A further example of early conceptual simulations for education was ARK (Alternate Reality Kit), a set of simulations on different physics topics (e.g., collisions) that provided students with direct manipulation interfaces (Scanlon and Smith, 1988; Smith, 1986).

Although scaffolds were already present to some degree in the systems cited here, research has emphasized the awareness that learning from models can only be successful if the student is sufficiently scaffolded. Unscaffolded inquiry is generally seen as not fruitful (Mayer, 2004). Cognitive scaffolds can be integrated with the simulation software and aim at one or more of the inquiry processes mentioned above. Overviews of systems that contain cognitive scaffolds have been presented by de Jong and van Joolingen (1998), Quintana et al. (2004), Linn et al. (2004), and recently de Jong (2006b).

Identifying the basis of adequate scaffolding requires a detailed insight into the learning processes associated with learning from models (de Jong and van Joolingen, 1998). The overall learning process that is associated with learning from models is a process of scientific discovery or inquiry. The National Research Council in 1996 defined inquiry as a multifaceted activity involving making observations, posing questions, examining various sources of information, planning investigations, reviewing what is known, using tools to gather and interpret data, proposing explanations and predictions, and communicating findings;

inquiry requires the identification of explicit assumptions, the use of critical and logical thinking, and the creation and consideration of alternative explanations (NRC, 1996). This description lists a large set of processes that constitute inquiry learning. De Jong (2006b) presented a number of processes that encompass the processes mentioned in the NRC definition: orientation, hypothesis generation, experimentation (i.e., experiment design, prediction, data interpretation), drawing a conclusion, and making an evaluation. In *orientation*, the general research issue is determined and the student makes a broad analysis of the domain; in *hypothesis generation*, a specific statement (or a set of statements, for example, in the form of a model) about the domain is chosen for consideration; in *experimentation*, a test to investigate the validity of this hypothesis or model is designed and performed, predictions are made, and outcomes of the experiments are interpreted; in *conclusion*, a conclusion about the validity of the hypothesis is drawn or new ideas are formed; and, finally, in *evaluation*, a reflection on the learning process and the domain knowledge acquired is made. A central and developing *product* in the inquiry learning process is the student's mental model of the domain (White and Frederiksen, 1998).

Figure 36.1 presents a diagrammatic attempt to depict the development of a student's mental model throughout the inquiry process. In this figure, the mental model in *orientation* has loose ends, relations are not yet defined, and variables are missing. When a student generates a *hypothesis*, a relation between variables is selected, and an idea (still uncertain) about this relation is formed. Of course, the ideas that are formed in the hypothesis phase are not necessarily constrained to single hypotheses but may refer to broader parts of a model (see the next section). In *experimentation*, a move to more manipulable variables is made. When *designing an experiment*, the conceptual variables are operationalized in variables that can be manipulated. In *prediction*, the hypothesis that was stated is translated into observable variables. In *data interpretation*, the outcomes of the experiment are known, and an understanding of the data must be reached. Stating a *conclusion* involves returning to a more theoretical level, in which the data that were interpreted are related to the hypothesis or mental model under consideration and decisions on the validity of the original ideas are made.

In Figure 36.1, the process of experimentation is at the level of manipulable (operationalized) variables, whereas the domain view in the processes of orientation, hypotheses, and conclusion is at the level of theory. Ideally, a student's view of the domain should go from orientation through hypotheses to conclusion,

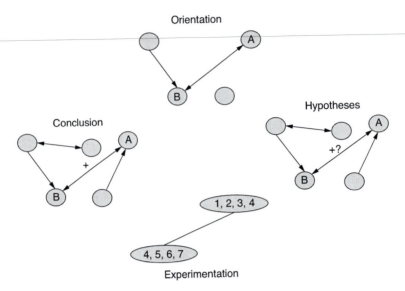

**Figure 36.1** An overview of the student's mental model of inquiry processes (ovals are variables, lines represent relations). (From de Jong, T., in *Dealing with Complexity in Learning Environments*, Elen, J. and Clark, R.E., Eds., Elsevier, London, 2006, pp. 107–128. With permission.)

resulting in a correct and complete mental model of the domain. In practice, however, after going through these learning processes a student's mental model will often still have some open ends (an orientation character), unresolved issues (a hypothesis aspect), and some firm ideas (conclusions, but still some of these may be faulty). This emphasizes the iterative character of the inquiry learning process.

The processes mentioned above directly yield knowledge (as is reflected in the developing view of the domain). de Jong and Njoo (1992) refer to these processes as *transformative* inquiry processes, reflecting the transformation of information into knowledge. Because inquiry learning is a complex endeavor with a number of activities and iterations, de Jong and Njoo (1992) added the concept of *regulation of learning*, comprised of processes aimed at planning and monitoring the learning process. Together, transformative and regulative processes form the main inquiry learning processes (de Jong and van Joolingen, 1998).

Evaluation takes a special place, located somewhere between transformative and regulative processes. In evaluation (or reflection), students examine the inquiry process and its results and try to take a step back to learn from their experiences. This reflection may concern the inquiry process itself (successful and less successful actions) as well as the domain under investigation (e.g., general domain characteristics). As is the case with all inquiry processes, evaluation activities can occur at any point in the cycle, not just during evaluation. Evaluation activities can influence the inquiry process itself and thus have a regulative character.

Smaller scale evaluations of inquiry learning often concentrate on assessing the effects of different types of scaffolding. This work shows that the effectiveness of inquiry learning can be greatly improved by offering students adequate scaffolds (de Jong, 2006a,b). Large-scale evaluations of technology-based inquiry environments comparing them to more traditional modes of instruction are not very frequent, but a few of these large-scale evaluations do exist. Smithtown, a supportive simulation environment in the area of economics, was evaluated in a pilot study with 30 students and in a large-scale evaluation with a total of 530 students. Results showed that after 5 hours of working with Smithtown, students reached a degree of micro-economics understanding that would have required approximately 11 hours of traditional teaching (Shute and Glaser, 1990). The *Jasper* project offers another classic example of a large-scale evaluation. The domain in this project is mathematics, and students learn in real contexts in an inquiry type of setting. Although *Jasper* is not a pure inquiry environment, the learning has many characteristics of inquiry, as students collect and try to interpret data. Evaluation data involving over 700 students showed that students who followed the *Jasper* series outperformed a control group that received traditional training on a series of assessments (Cognition and Technology Group at Vanderbilt, 1992).

White and Frederiksen (1998) described the ThinkerTools Inquiry Curriculum, a simulation-based learning environment on the physics topic of force and motion. The ThinkerTools software guides students through a number of inquiry stages that include experimenting with the simulation, constructing physics laws, critiquing each other's laws, and reflecting on the inquiry process. ThinkerTools was implemented in 12 classes with approximately 30 students each. Students worked daily with ThinkerTools over a period of a little more than 10 weeks. A comparison of the ThinkerTools students with students in a traditional curriculum showed that the ThinkerTools students performed significantly better on a (short) conceptual test (68% vs. 50% correct). Even the students who scored low on a test for general basic skills from the ThinkerTools curriculum had a higher average conceptual physics score (58%) than the students who followed the traditional curriculum.

Hickey et al. (2003) assessed the effects of the introduction of a simulation-based inquiry environment (GenScope) on the biology topic of genetics. In GenScope students can manipulate genetic information at different levels: DNA, chromosomes, cells, organisms, pedigrees, and populations. Students, for example, can change the chromosomes (e.g., for presence or absence of wings or horns) of virtual dragons, breed these dragons, and observe the effects on the genotype and phenotype of the offspring. A large-scale evaluation was conducted involving 31 classes (23 experimental, 8 comparison) taught by 13 teachers and a few hundred students in total. Overall, the evaluation results showed better performance by the GenScope classes compared to the traditional classes on tests measuring genetic reasoning. A follow-up study with two experimental classes and one comparison class also showed significantly higher gains for the two experimental classes on a reasoning test, with a higher gain for students from the one of these two groups in which more investigation exercises were offered.

Another recent example is the River City project. The River City project software is intended to teach biology topics and inquiry skills. It is a virtual environment in which students move around with avatars. River City contains simulations, databases, and multimedia information. Students have to perform a full investigation following all of the inquiry processes listed above and end their investigation by writing a letter to the mayor of the city. Preliminary results of a large evaluation (involving around 2000 students) of the River City project showed that, compared to a control group who followed a paper-based inquiry based curriculum, the technology-based approach led to a higher increase in biology knowledge (32 to 34% vs. 17%) and better achievement on tests for inquiry skills (Ketelhut et al., 2006). Linn et al. (2006) evaluated modules created in the Technology-Enhanced Learning in Science (TELS) center. These modules are inquiry

based and contain simulations (e.g., on the functioning of airbags). Over a sample of 4328 students and 6 different TELS modules, an overall effect size of 0.32 in favor of the TELS subjects over students following a traditional course was observed on items that measured how well students' knowledge was integrated.

## LEARNING BY CREATING COMPUTER MODELS

Apart from *observing* simulations based on formal models, students can also learn from *constructing* these models themselves (Alessi, 2000). This approach is in line with the basic ideas behind constructionism (Harel and Papert, 1991; Kafai, 2006; Kafai and Resnick, 1996), of which the main focus is "knowledge construction that takes place when students are engaged in building objects" (Kafai and Resnick, 1996, p. 2). Objects that are constructed can be physical objects and artifacts (Crismond, 2001), drawings (Hmelo et al., 2000), concept maps (Novak, 1990), computer programs (Mayer and Fay, 1987), instruction (Vreman-de Olde and de Jong, 2006), and more. In this section, we focus on constructing *executable models*, the same kind of models that are explored in the situations described in the previous section; instead of exploring these models, the students' task becomes one of constructing them.

Science has always used models to understand a domain. Simulation as a tool to predict a model's behavior was one of the first applications of computers as they became available shortly after World War II. The use of constructing models in the process of learning science goes back to the early 1980s, when Jon Ogborn created the Dynamical Modelling System (DMS) (Ogborn and Wong, 1984). In this system, students could create a model of a dynamical system by entering equations that described an initial state and the change of that state over time. Even before these attempts, Jay Forrester had developed his ideas on *system dynamics*, a way of representing processes in business organizations, which soon acquired a wider use as a versatile tool to model any kind of system (Forrester, 1961). An example of a system dynamics model is provided in Figure 36.2. This model uses the system dynamics notation introduced by Forrester (1961). The water level is represented by a *stock* (rectangle) and the outflow as a *flow* (the thick arrow pointing to the cloud. The thin arrows indicate relations between the variables.

At first, system dynamics models were created as drawings that were used as a tool for reasoning. Later these models were used as a guideline to create computer

461

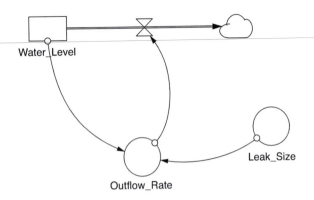

**Figure 36.2** System dynamics model of a leaking water bucket.

programs, and eventually systems such as STELLA (Steed, 1992) were introduced that allowed direct simulation of system dynamics models. The educational value of these systems was immediately recognized, and other systems following the same basic system dynamics ideas such as Model-It (Jackson et al., 1996) and Co-Lab (van Joolingen et al., 2005) were created. These newer systems improved on user-friendliness by offering alternative ways of specifying the model, but they adhere to the same basic principle: The student specifies a model drawn as a graphical structure that can be executed (simulated), yielding outcomes that are the consequences of the ideas expressed in the model. Through all of these developments we see an evolution toward tools that make it easier for students to create formal models.

A modeling activity starts from a scientific problem. Students generally find it very difficult to generate an adequate research question, and they often need help in arriving at a good research question (White and Frederiksen, 1998); therefore, students are often provided with an assignment that asks them to model a certain phenomenon (van Joolingen et al., 2005; White, 1993). The overall goal of a student is to create a model in such a way that the behavior of the model mimics the behavior of a theoretical model or the behavior of a real phenomenon. Hestenes (1987) described a (formal) model as a mathematical entity that consists of named *objects* and *agents*, *variables* to define the properties of these objects, *equations* that describe the development of variable values over time, and an *interpretation* that links the modeling concepts to objects in the real world. This characterizes the model as a computational (runnable, executable) entity that can be used for simulation. More recently, the modeling literature has also included *qualitative* models in which the development of variable values is defined in terms of (qualitative) relations rather than equations (Dimitracopoulou et al., 1999; Jackson et

al., 1996; Papaevripidou et al., 2007; Schwarz and White, 2005; van Joolingen et al., 2005), but this does not essentially change Hestenes' conceptualization.

Hestenes' (1987) conceptualization suggests that to construct a model students need to iterate through three types of processes: *orientation*, in which the objects and variables are identified and defined; *specification*, in which the relations and equations between variables are specified; and *evaluation*, in which the outcomes of the model are interpreted in terms of the real world and matched to expectations. In *orientation*, the student identifies objects and variables and makes an initial sketch of the model; in *specification*, the relations between the variables are specified in a qualitative or quantitative form that allows computation, and additional variables may be introduced. In *evaluation*, the model structure is assessed, model output is evaluated against outcome expectations, and the model output is compared with observations.

Initial evidence suggests that learning by modeling has positive effects on the understanding of dynamic systems. Kurtz dos Santos et al. (1997) reported transfer from a modeled domain to a new one. Schecker (1998) found that after a mechanics course using STELLA, five out of ten pairs of students were able to construct a qualitative causal reasoning chain on a new subject. Mandinach (1988) found that modeling led to better conceptual understanding of the content and the solution and an increase in problem-solving abilities. Mandinach and Cline (1996) noted a marked improvement in students' inquiry skills as an effect of modeling. Schwarz and White (2005) found that students who had received a modeling facility as part of a ThinkerTools (White and Frederiksen, 1998) environment improved on an inquiry post-test and on far transfer problems. Papaevripidou et al. (2007) found that students who used a modeling approach with a modeling tool acquired better modeling skills than students who used a more traditional worksheet and were also able to model the domain in an increasingly sophisticated way.

Apart from these first results, evidence to support these claims of learning by modeling is still scarce, especially when it comes to experimental studies (Löhner, 2005). Research is limited to qualitative studies that provide mainly anecdotal evidence, often with only two (Resnick, 1994; Wilensky and Reisman, 2006) or even one (Buckley, 2000; Ploger and Lay, 1992) subject. Spector (2001) attributes this lack of focus on quantitative evidence to the fact that most researchers in this field believe that the standard measures of learning outcomes are not adequate for a serious evaluation of learning in these environments. Although this may be true, it indicates a mission for the field to try to implement instruments that actually assess the knowledge that is acquired through learning by modeling.

An instrument to measure system dynamics thinking, operationalized as the ability to interpret data in terms of a model and to distinguish a value and its rate of change, has been developed by Booth Sweeney and Sterman (2000). The focus of this instrument is limited to some basic skills in system-dynamics-based modeling. Van Borkulo and van Joolingen have developed an instrument that aims to cover the complete range of knowledge types addressed by learning based on the creation of models. In their overview, the different learning outcomes are operationalized into four categories of test items, related to the kind of reasoning process for which the knowledge is used. *Reproducing* factual domain knowledge is the first category, relating to the idea that in modeling one acquires knowledge about the domain. Model-based reasoning appears as *applying* a model to given situations, more specifically as predicting and explaining model behavior, by performing a mental simulation of the model. Learning about modeling is reflected in two categories: *evaluating* a model—that is to say, determining its correctness or suitability for a given goal—and *creating* a model or parts of it. These four categories can be evaluated at two levels: the *node* level of individual relations in a model and the *structure* level, in which the effects of multiple interacting relations are at stake. Moreover, the categories of *apply*, *evaluate*, and *create* can be considered at both a domain-general and a domain-specific level. Initial tests with this instrument show that it can detect various aspects of model-based reasoning. Such instruments should eventually lead to systematically collected evidence of the benefits of learning by modeling as well as more detailed knowledge on supporting modeling processes.

# MODEL-BASED INQUIRY LEARNING

Much of the modeling literature sees modeling as a stand-alone activity. In most of the activities described, the modeling process takes place in the absence of data that are to be modeled. As such, modeling remains a purely theoretical activity. Löhner et al. (2003) as well as Schwarz and White (2005) presented work in which models are used to describe data generated from a given simulation. Modeling thus becomes an integrated part of the inquiry process. In this section, a short description of a specific learning environment, Co-Lab (van Joolingen et al., 2005), is presented. Co-Lab offers an environment in which students can work on scientific inquiry tasks collaboratively in small groups and in which they are offered a modeling tool. In Co-Lab, students have the opportunity to explore existing models, to create formal models with a dedicated modeling language based on system dynamics, and to compare their own model outcomes with the data generated by a given simulation or collected from an experiment.

A typical Co-Lab task is to construct a model of a phenomenon that is found within the environment, either as a simulation or as a remote laboratory that can be controlled from a distance. In one Co-Lab environment, for example, students can connect to a small greenhouse that contains a plant, along with sensors that measure the levels of $CO_2$, $O_2$, and $H_2O$, as well as the temperature and the intensity of the light. The goal for this environment is to construct a model that describes the rate of photosynthesis as a function of the amount of available light. To accomplish this, students can use the data obtained from the sensors and manipulate the intensity of light by repositioning a lamp (specially made for use in greenhouses) and determining when it should be on or off. They can thus create graphs that yield the photosynthesis rate for each level of lighting. Combining these results allows them to model the photosynthesis rate as a function of the light level.

A Co-Lab environment is divided into different buildings, with each building consisting of a number of floors. A building represents a domain (in this case, greenhouse effect), and a floor represents a subdomain (e.g., photosynthesis) or a specific level of difficulty, similar to the idea of model progression also found in SimQuest (van Joolingen and de Jong, 2003) and in earlier work by White and Frederiksen (1990). Each floor is composed of four rooms: the hall, a lab room, a theory room, and a meeting room. The photosynthesis scenario in this Co-Lab environment starts in the *hall*, the default entry room for all Co-Lab environments. In the hall, students meet each other and find a mission statement that explains the goal of the floor in the form of a research problem (e.g., creating a model that explains the photosynthesis rate); they also receive some background information they need to get started. After having read this mission statement, they can move to the *lab*, in which they find a remote connection to the greenhouse. They can see the greenhouse through a webcam, and they can control it and inspect the greenhouse parameters using a dedicated interface. They can start a measurement series and plot the development of the data in a graph. Data obtained this way can be stored as datasets in an object repository. In the *theory room*, students find a system dynamics modeling tool that

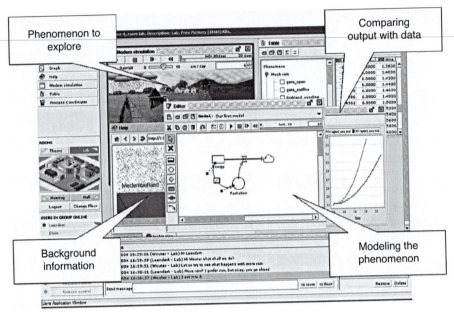

**Figure 36.3** Example of a modeling tool. (Courtesy of Co-Lab.)

allows for both qualitative (relations such as "if A increases then B increases") and quantitative (equations) modeling. In the theory room, students can inspect the datasets they have stored in the repository (which is shared across rooms) and use these as reference for their model. This can be done by plotting model output and observed data in one graph and comparing the two, or by using the observed data as an element in the model. Finally, students can plan and monitor their work in the *meeting room*. They can review important steps in the inquiry and modeling processes, such as planning experiments and evaluating models, using a process coordinator (Manlove et al., 2006). They can make notes that record the history of their learning process and can eventually be used as the basic ingredients for a report that they write to conclude the activity.

Co-Lab's main characteristic is that it combines learning from models and learning by modeling in one environment. These activities take place in the lab and theory room, respectively. In doing so, the environment offers opportunities to make the learning process more transparent. Hypotheses become visible as models or parts of models, their predictions can be made visible as model output, and the validity of models can be assessed with reference to the data collected from the domain model present in the lab. It is also possible to assess student's models based on a structural comparison of the model with a reference model (Bravo et al., 2006), indicating that the domain model may operate not only as a source of data but also as a resource for tutoring.

Figure 36.3 shows an example from the Co-Lab learning environment. The editor displays a model in the system dynamics formalism that is also used by STELLA and PowerSim. The graph shows the result of running this model (of warming of the Earth under the influence of solar radiation). In this example, the student has created a model of a physics topic (a black sphere problem) and has run the model to inspect its behavior. The model is expressed in terms of a graphic representation linking different kinds of variables, as well as equations or relations that detail the behavior of the model. The results can be expressed as graphs (as in Figure 36.3), tables, and animations.

Co-Lab has been evaluated in a number of experimental studies focusing on specific aspects of the environment. Sins et al. (2007) found that learners with task-oriented motivation performed more deep learning processes such as changing and running the model with a reference to prior knowledge, which in turn led to better models. They believe that the mode of communication between collaborators (online chat vs. face to face) influences the modeling process. Chatting learners used the modeling tool not only as a place to construct the model but also as a means of communication, resulting in many more small changes to the model they were constructing. Manlove et al. (2006) found that providing learners with regulative support in the form of a so-called *process coordinator* led to better performance on the modeling task. This finding highlights the need for instructional support in this kind of complex learning environment.

# CONCLUSIONS

In this chapter, we have discussed three modes of learning in which (computer) models play a pivotal role. One is learning from models in which students gather knowledge about a model underlying a simulation through inquiry learning. The second one is learning by modeling, in which students learn by creating models. Finally, we presented an example of a system in which both ways of learning are combined, yielding an integrated process of inquiry.

Learning from models and learning by modeling share a number of characteristics, but there are also differences. Both ways of learning generate knowledge of the domain that is involved in the model (e.g., a physics topic such as motion). Penner (2001) asserts that the main difference between learning from models in simulation-based environments and learning by modeling is that in the first case the underlying model stays hidden to the students (they have no direct access to this model), whereas in learning by modeling the exact characteristics of the model are central. As a consequence, a more intuitive type of knowledge is more likely to evolve in learning from models (Swaak et al., 1998), whereas in learning by modeling more explicit conceptual knowledge is likely to be acquired (White and Frederiksen, 2005). In both approaches, more general, process-directed knowledge is supposed to be acquired. Löhner (2005), for example, identified learning *about modeling and the modeling process* as an important learning outcome of learning by modeling. Learning about modeling is seen as important because science and technology have become increasingly important in society; reasoning with models, including model construction as well as awareness of the limitations of scientific models, is therefore seen as an important part of the science curriculum (Halloun, 1996). From modeling-based curricula, students should improve their modeling skills—that is, show effective modeling processes and also obtain a better understanding of the epistemology of modeling (Hogan, 1999; Hogan and Thomas, 2001). Model-based reasoning skills reflect the ability to use a model instrumentally to predict or explain behavior that can be observed in a modeled system. This means, for example, being able to predict the development of the temperature of the atmosphere under the influence of an increasing $CO_2$ concentration from a model of climate change (given or self-constructed). This requires mental simulation of the model—that is, reasoning from the relations given to projected values of variables or in the reverse direction, from observed values of variables to relations that explain these observations. Knowledge about performing sound scientific investigations is acquired in inquiry learning. This includes more general skills such as knowing how to follow an inquiry cycle (White and Frederiksen, 2005) as well as more specific knowledge of experimentation heuristics (Veermans et al., 2006) or strategies on how to cope with anomalous data (Lin, 2007). For a more complete overview, see Zachos et al. (2000). These inquiry skills are seen as important for students to become self-directed researchers.

The learning processes involved also show similarities. The processes of scientific inquiry as we have identified them (orientation, hypothesis generation, experimentation, and conclusion) strongly resemble the modeling processes (orientation, specification, and evaluation). There are, however, two basic differences. First, a hypothesis (or set of hypotheses) as present in *learning from models* does not have to form a runnable model. Second, in *learning by modeling* experimentation is not necessary to gather data for creating a model; instead, students can gather their information from many sources and use this as input for creating their model. One of the assumptions underlying the combination of learning from models and learning by modeling (as in the Co-Lab environment) is that both approaches can reinforce each other. Evidence for this claim can be found in Schwarz and White (2005). They found that students who received a modeling facility in ThinkerTools also improved on a test of inquiry skills. A comparison of the modeling-enhanced Thinker-Tools curriculum with a traditional Thinker-Tools curriculum showed no overall differences in an inquiry skills test except for a subscale measuring the students' ability to formulate conclusions. A correlational analysis of students who followed the Thinker-Tools curriculum with a modeling facility showed that at the pretest there were no significant correlations among knowledge of modeling, inquiry, and physics. At the post-test, however, these three tests correlated significantly, indicating that development in each of these three knowledge areas is mutually reinforcing.

Whatever approach is chosen, it is clear that students cannot perform inquiry, modeling, or a combination of the two without scaffolding (Klahr and Nigam, 2004; Mayer, 2004). In inquiry research, a large set of cognitive tools for inquiry has now been developed (for recent overviews, see de Jong, 2006a,b; Linn et al., 2004; Quintana et al., 2004). Comparable scaffolds for modeling are only now about to emerge (Bravo et al., 2006). Integrated environments such as Co-Lab, in which different approaches are combined and in which learning processes are scaffolded by collaboration and by an extensive set of cognitive tools, may provide students with learning opportunities that help them gain both (intuitive and formal) domain and general process knowledge.

# REFERENCES

Alessi, S. M. (2000). Building versus using simulations. In *Integrated and Holistic Perspectives on Learning, Instruction, and Technology*, edited by J. M. Spector and T. M. Anderson, pp. 175–196. Dordrecht: Kluwer.*

American Association for the Advancement of Science (AAAS). (1989). *Science for All Americans*. New York: Oxford University Press.*

Booth Sweeney, L. and Sterman, J. D. (2000). Bathtub dynamics: initial results of a systems thinking inventory. *Syst. Dynam. Rev.*, 16, 249–286.

Bravo, C., van Joolingen, W. R., and de Jong, T. (2006). Modeling and simulation in inquiry learning: checking solutions and giving intelligent advice. *Simul. Trans. Soc. Modeling Simul. Int.*, 82(11), 769–784.

Brown, J. S., Burton, R. R., and de Kleer, J. (1982). Pedagogical, natural language and knowledge engineering techniques in Sophie I, II, and III. In *Intelligent Tutoring Systems*, edited by D. Sleeman and J. S. Brown, pp. 227–282. London: Academic Press.*

Buckley, B. C. (2000). Interactive multimedia and model-based learning in biology. *Int. J. Sci. Educ.*, 22, 895–935.

Chi, M. T. H. (1992). Conceptual change within and across ontological categories: examples from learning and discovery in science. In *Cognitive Models of Science*, Vol. 15, edited by R. N. Giere, pp. 129–186. Minneapolis, MN: University of Minnesota Press.*

Clement, J. (2000). Model based learning as a key research area for science education. *Int. J. Sci. Educ.*, 22, 1041–1053.

Cognition and Technology Group at Vanderbilt (CTGV). (1992). The *Jasper* series as an example of anchored instruction: theory, program, description, and assessment data. *Educ. Psychol.*, 27, 291–315.*

Crismond, D. (2001). Learning and using science ideas when doing investigate-and-redesign tasks: a study of naive, novice, and expert designers doing constrained and scaffolded design work. *J. Res. Sci. Teaching*, 38(7), 791–820.

de Jong, T. (1991). Learning and instruction with computer simulations. *Educ. Comput.*, 6, 217–229.*

de Jong, T. (2006a). Computer simulations: technological advances in inquiry learning. *Science*, 312, 532–533.*

de Jong, T. (2006b). Scaffolds for computer simulation based scientific discovery learning. In *Dealing with Complexity in Learning Environments*, edited by J. Elen and R. E. Clark, pp. 107–128. London: Elsevier.

de Jong, T. and Njoo, M. (1992). Learning and instruction with computer simulations: learning processes involved. In *Computer-Based Learning Environments and Problem Solving*, edited by E. de Corte, M. Linn, H. Mandl, and L. Verschaffel, pp. 411–429. Heidelberg: Springer-Verlag.

de Jong, T. and van Joolingen, W. R. (1998). Scientific discovery learning with computer simulations of conceptual domains. *Rev. Educ. Res.*, 68, 179–202.

Dimitracopoulou, A., Komis, V., Apostolopoulos, P., and Politis, P. (1999). Design Principles of a New Modelling Environment for Young Students Supporting Various Types of Reasoning and Interdisciplinary Approaches. Paper presented at the 9th International Conference on Artificial Intelligence in Education: Open Learning Environments—New Computational Technologies to Support Learning, Exploration and Collaboration, July 19–23, Le Mans, France.

Forrester, J. W. (1961). *Industrial Dynamics*. Waltham, MA: Pegasus Communications.*

Gentner, D. and Stevens, A. L., Eds. (1983). *Mental Models*. Hillsdale, NJ: Lawrence Erlbaum Associates.

Gobert, J. D. (2000). A typology of causal models for plate tectonics: Inferential power and barriers to understanding *Int. J. Sci. Educ.*, 22, 937–977.

Halloun, I. (1996). Schematic modeling for meaningful learning of physics. *J. Res. Sci. Teaching*, 33, 1019–1041.

Harel, I. and Papert, S. (1991). *Constructionism*. Norwood, NJ: Ablex.

Hestenes, D. (1987). Towards a modeling theory of physics instruction. *Am. J. Phys.*, 55, 440–454.

Hickey, D. T., Kindfield, A. C. H., Horwitz, P., and Christie, M. A. (2003). Integrating curriculum, instruction, assessment, and evaluation in a technology-supported genetics environment. *Am. Educ. Res. J.*, 40, 495–538.

Hmelo, C. E., Holton, D. L., and Kolodner, J. L. (2000). Designing to learn about complex systems. *J. Learn. Sci.*, 9(3), 247–298.

Hogan, K. (1999). Relating students' personal frameworks for science learning to their cognition in collaborative contexts. *Sci. Educ.*, 83, 1–32.

Hogan, K. and Thomas, D. (2001). Cognitive comparisons of students' systems modeling in ecology. *J. Sci. Educ. Technol.*, 10, 319–344.

Hollan, J. D., Hutchins, E. L., and Weitzman, L. (1984). STEAMER: an interactive inspectable simulation-based training system. *AI Mag.*, 5, 15–27.

Jackson, S., Stratford, S. J., Krajcik, J., and Soloway, E. (1996). Making dynamic modeling accessible to pre-college science students. *Interact. Learn. Environ.*, 4, 233–257.

Kafai, Y. B. (2006). Constructionism. In *The Cambridge Handbook of the Learning Sciences*, edited by R. K. Sawyer, pp. 35–47. Cambridge, U.K.: Cambridge University Press.

Kafai, Y. B. and Resnick, M., Eds. (1996). *Constructionism in Practice: Designing, Thinking, and Learning in a Digital World*. Mahwah, NJ: Lawrence Erlbaum Associates.

Ketelhut, D. J., Dede, C., Clarke, J., and Nelson, B. (2006). A Multi-User Virtual Environment for Building Higher Order Inquiry Skills in Science. Paper presented at the Annual Meeting of the American Educational Research Association, April 8–12, San Francisco.

Klahr, D. and Nigam, M. (2004). The equivalence of learning paths in early science instruction: effects of direct instruction and discovery learning. *Psychol. Sci.*, 15, 661–668.*

Kurland, L. and Tenney, Y. (1988). Issues in developing an intelligent tutor for a real-world domain: training in radar mechanics. In *Intelligent Tutoring Systems: Lessons Learned*, edited by J. Psotka, L. D. Massey, and S. Mutter, pp. 59–85. Hillsdale, NJ: Lawrence Erlbaum Associates.*

Kurtz dos Santos, A., Thielo, M. R., and Kleer, A. A. (1997). Students modelling environmental issues. *J. Comput. Assist. Learn.*, 13, 35–47.

Lehrer, R. and Schauble, L. (2006). Cultivating model-based reasoning in science education. In *The Cambridge Handbook of the Learning Sciences*, edited by R. K. Sawyer, pp. 371–389. Cambridge, U.K.: Cambridge University Press.

Lin, J.-Y. (2007). Responses to anomalous data obtained from repeatable experiments in the laboratory. *J. Res. Sci. Teaching*, 44(3), 506–528.

Linn, M. C., Bell, P., and Davis, E. A. (2004). Specific design principles: elaborating the scaffolded knowledge integration framework. In *Internet Environments for Science Education*, edited by M. Linn, E. A. Davis, and P. Bell, pp. 315–341. Mahwah, NJ: Lawrence Erlbaum Associates.

Linn, M. C., Lee, H.-S., Tinker, R., Husic, F., and Chiu, J. L. (2006). Teaching and assessing knowledge integration in science. *Science*, 313, 1049–1050.

Löhner, S. (2005). *Computer Based Modelling Tasks: The Role of External Representation*. Amsterdam: University of Amsterdam.

Löhner, S., van Joolingen, W. R., and Savelsbergh, E. R. (2003). The effect of external representation on constructing computer models of complex phenomena. *Instruct. Sci.*, 31, 395–418.

Löhner, S., van Joolingen, W. R., Savelsbergh, E. R., and van Hout-Wolters, B. H. A. M. (2005). Students' reasoning during modeling in an inquiry learning environment. *Comput. Hum. Behav.*, 21, 441–461.

Mandinach, E. B. (1988). The Cognitive Effects of Simulation-Modeling Software and Systems Thinking on Learning and Achievement. Paper presented at the Annual Meeting of the American Educational Research Association, April, New Orleans.

Mandinach, E. B. and Cline, H. F. (1996). Classroom dynamics: the impact of a technology-based curriculum innovation on teaching and learning. *J. Educ. Comput. Res.*, 14, 83–102.*

Manlove, S., Lazonder, A. W., and de Jong, T. (2006). Regulative support for collaborative scientific inquiry learning. *J. Comput. Assist. Learn.*, 22, 87–98.

Mayer, R. E. (2004). Should there be a three-strikes rule against pure discovery learning? *Am. Psychol.*, 59, 14–19.*

Mayer, R. E. and Fay, A. L. (1987). A chain of cognitive changes with learning to program in Logo. *J. Educ. Psychol.*, 79(3), 269–279.

National Research Council (NRC). (1996). *National Science Education Standards*. Washington, D.C.: National Academies Press.

National Science Foundation (NSF). (2000). An introduction to inquiry. In *Inquiry: Thoughts, Views and Strategies for the K–5 Classroom*, Vol. 2, pp. 1–5. Washington, D.C.: National Science Foundation.*

Novak, J. D. (1990). Concept mapping: a useful tool for science education. *J. Res. Sci. Teaching*, 27, 937–949.*

Ogborn, J. and Wong, D. (1984). A microcomputer dynamical modelling system. *Phys. Educ.*, 19, 138–142.

Papaevripidou, M., Constantinou, C. P., and Zacharia, Z. C. (2007). Modelling complex marine ecosystems: an investigation of two teaching approaches with fifth graders. *J. Comput. Assist. Learn.*, 23(2), 145–157.

Penner, D. E. (2001). Cognition, computers, and synthetic science: Building knowledge and meaning through modelling. *Rev. Res. Educ.*, 25, 1–37.*

Ploger, D. and Lay, E. (1992). The structure of programs and molecules. *J. Educ. Comput. Res.*, 8, 347–364.

Quintana, C., Reiser, B. J., Davis, E. A., Krajcik, J., Fretz, E., Duncan, R. G. et al. (2004). A scaffolding design framework for software to support science inquiry. *J. Learn. Sci.*, 13, 337–387.

Resnick, M. (1994). *Turtles, Termites, and Traffic Jams*. Cambridge, MA: MIT Press.*

Scanlon, E. and Smith, R. B. (1988). A rational reconstruction of a bubble-chamber simulation using the alternate reality kit. *Comput. Educ.*, 12, 199–207.

Schecker, H. P. (1998). *Physik—Modellieren, Grafikorientierte Modellbildungssysteme im Physikunterricht*. Stuttgart, Germany: Ernst Klett Verlag GmbH.

Schwarz, C. V. and White, B. Y. (2005). Metamodeling knowledge: developing students' understanding of scientific modeling. *Cogn. Instruct.*, 23, 165–205.

Shute, V. J. and Glaser, R. (1990). A large-scale evaluation of an intelligent discovery world: Smithtown. *Interact. Learn. Environ.*, 1, 51–77.

Sins, P. H. M., van Joolingen, W. R., Savelsbergh, E., and van Hout-Wolters, B. H. A. M. (2007). Motivation and performance within a collaborative computer-based modeling task: relations between students' achievement goal orientation, self-efficacy, cognitive processing and achievement. *Contemp. Educ. Psychol.* (doi:10.1016/j.cedpsych.2006.12.004).

Smith, R. B. (1986). The Alternate Reality Kit: An Animated Environment for Creating Interactive Simulations. Paper presented at the IEEE Computer Society Workshop on Visual Languages, June 25–27, Dallas, TX.

Snyder, J. L. (2000). An investigation of the knowledge structures of experts, intermediates and novices in physics. *Int. J. Sci. Educ.*, 22, 979–992.

Spector, J. M. (2001). Tools and principles for the design of collaborative learning environments for complex domains. *J. Struct. Learn. Intell. Syst.*, 14, 484–510.*

Steed, M. (1992). STELLA, a simulation construction kit: cognitive process and educational implications. *J. Comput. Math. Sci. Teaching*, 11(1), 39–52.

Swaak, J., van Joolingen, W. R., and de Jong, T. (1998). Supporting simulation-based learning; the effects of model progression and assignments on definitional and intuitive knowledge. *Learn. Instruct.*, 8, 235–253.*

Towne, D. M., Munro, A., Pizzini, Q., Surmon, D., Coller, L., and Wogulis, J. (1990). Model-building tools for simulation-based training. *Interact. Learn. Environ.*, 1, 33–50.*

Van Borkulo, S. P. and van Joolingen, W. R. (2006). A Framework for the Assessment of Modeling Knowledge. Poster presented at the GIREP Conference, August 20–25, Amsterdam.

van Joolingen, W. R. and de Jong, T. (1991). Characteristics of simulations for instructional settings. *Education and Computing*, 6, 241–262.

van Joolingen, W. R. and de Jong, T. (2003). SimQuest: authoring educational simulations. In *Authoring Tools for Advanced Technology Educational Software: Toward Cost-Effective Production of Adaptive, Interactive, and Intelligent Educational Software*, edited by T. Murray, S. Blessing and S. Ainsworth, pp. 1–31. Dordrecht: Kluwer.*

van Joolingen, W. R., de Jong, T., Lazonder, A. W., Savelsbergh, E., and Manlove, S. (2005). Co-Lab: research and development of an on-line learning environment for collaborative scientific discovery learning. *Comput. Hum. Behav.*, 21, 671–688.

Veermans, K. H., van Joolingen, W. R., and de Jong, T. (2006). Using heuristics to facilitate scientific discovery learning in a simulation learning environment in a physics domain. *Int. J. Sci. Educ.*, 28, 341–361.*

Vreman-de Olde, C. and de Jong, T. (2006). Scaffolding the design of assignments for a computer simulation. *J. Comput. Assist. Learn.*, 22, 63–74.

White, B. Y. (1993). ThinkerTools: causal models, conceptual change, and science education. *Cogn. Instruct.*, 10, 1–100.*

White, B. Y. and Frederiksen, J. R. (1989). Causal models as intelligent learning environments for science and engineering education. *Appl. Artif. Intell.*, 3, 83–106.

White, B. Y. and Frederiksen, J. R. (1990). Causal model progressions as a foundation for intelligent learning environments. *Artif. Intell.*, 42, 99–57.

White, B. Y. and Frederiksen, J. R. (1998). Inquiry, modelling, and metacognition: making science accessible to all students. *Cogn. Instruct.*, 16, 3–118.*

White, B. Y. and Frederiksen, J. R. (2005). A theoretical framework and approach for fostering metacognitive development *Educ. Psychol.*, 40, 211–223.

Wilensky, U. and Reisman, K. (2006). Thinking like a wolf, a sheep, or a firefly: learning biology through constructing and testing computational theories—an embodied modeling approach. *Cogn. Instruct.*, 24, 171–209.

Zachos, P., Hick, T. L., Doane, W. E. J., and Sargent, C. (2000). Setting theoretical and empirical foundations for assessing scientific inquiry and discovery in educational programs. *J. Res. Sci. Teaching*, 37, 938–962.

---

\* Indicates a core reference.

# 37

# Adaptive Instructional Systems

*Jung Lee*
The Richard Stockton College of New Jersey, Pomona, New Jersey

*Ok-Choon Park*
Institute of Education Sciences, Washington, D.C.

## CONTENTS

Jung Lee and Ok-Choon Park

## ABSTRACT

Adaptive instruction embodies all instructional forms that accommodate the needs and abilities of different learners. This chapter summarizes five approaches to adaptive instruction: (1) macro-adaptive instruction; (2) aptitude–treatment interactions (ATI-based); (3) micro-adaptive instruction, including intelligent tutoring systems (ITSs); (4) the adaptive/adaptable hypermedia/Web-based system (AHS); and (5) specific pedagogy-centered systems. These approaches are presented in historical order, beginning with macro-adaptive systems. For each approach, its characteristics and representative systems are discussed. Although each has its own distinctive properties, some similarities can be found among the approaches. Due to the development of information and communication technology (ICT), the structural functions of recent adaptive systems are significantly more powerful than earlier ones. New Web-based systems have functions that simultaneously provide customized learning experiences to masses of individual learners. The challenges now facing researchers and developers are to optimally integrate many different theories, principles, and strategies of learning and instruction with system functions and to prove empirically the effects and value of these systems in real-world environments.

## KEYWORDS

*Adaptive hypermedia systems (AHSs):* Combining micro-adaptive systems and hypermedia systems to provide adaptive/adaptable, hybrid features by presenting learners with choices, along with guidance.
*Adaptive instructional systems:* Any forms of educational intervention aimed at accommodating individual learner differences.
*Aptitude–treatment interactions (ATIs):* Adapting specific instructional procedures and strategies to specific learner characteristics (or aptitudes).
*Macro-adaptive systems:* Allowing different alternatives for choosing instructional goals, curriculum content, and delivery systems, by grouping students.
*Micro-adaptive systems:* Diagnosing the learner's specific learning needs during instruction and providing instructional prescriptions for the needs.

## DEFINITION

A central and persistent issue in educational technology is the planning and provision of instructional environments and conditions that fit and support individu-
ally different educational goals and learning abilities (Park, 1996). In general, instructional approaches and techniques that are geared to meet the needs of individually different students in developing knowledge and skills required to learn a task are called *adaptive instruction* (Corno and Snow, 1986). Accordingly, any form of instruction is adaptive, whether it is delivered by teachers or in a technology-based format, if it accommodates different student learning needs and abilities.

Adaptive instruction has a long history and has been implemented in various forms and settings, from group-based, classroom instruction to Web-based, open space instruction. The development of computer technology has provided a powerful tool for developing and implementing sophisticated instructional systems from diagnostic assessment tools to tutoring systems generating individually tailored instructional prescription. Recent advances in information and communication technology (ICT) allow for the delivery of individually customized information and instruction to mass audiences simultaneously. This mass individualization has been increasingly popular and important in education and training communities (De Bra et al., 2004; Karagiannidis et al., 2001; van Merriënboer, 2005).

## HISTORY OF ADAPTIVE INSTRUCTIONAL SYSTEMS

The long history of efforts in adapting instruction to an individual student's needs and abilities has been documented by many researchers (Corno and Snow, 1986; Federico et al., 1980; Glaser, 1977; Reiser, 1987; Tobias, 1989; Wang and Lindvall, 1984). Since at least the fourth century B.C., adapting has been viewed as a primary requirement for successful instruction (Corno and Snow, 1986), and adaptive tutoring was the common instructional method until the mid-1800s (Reiser, 1987). Even after graded systems were adopted, the importance of adapting instruction to individual needs was continuously emphasized. Dewey, for example, in his 1902 essay, *Child and Curriculum*, deplored the then current emphasis on a single kind of curriculum development that produced a uniform, inflexible sequence of instruction (Dewey, 1902/1964). Thorndike (1911) argued for a specialization of instruction that acknowledged differences among pupils within a single class as well as specialization of the curriculum for different classes. Since then, various approaches and methods have been proposed to provide adaptive instruction to individually different students (for early systems, see Reiser, 1987).

Since Cronbach (1957) declared that a united discipline of psychology would be interested in not only organisms but also interactions between organisms and treatment variables, numerous studies have been conducted to investigate what kinds of student characteristics should be considered in adapting instruction and how instructional methods and procedures should be adapted to those characteristics (Cronbach, 1967; Cronbach and Snow, 1977; Federico et al., 1980; Snow and Swanson, 1992). Whereas early instructional systems considered only one or two variables, newer adaptive systems using computer technology implement models that have multiple layers, each with many variables. Each adaptive system lies along this complexity continuum, but they can be clustered into several types according to their approaches.

## DIFFERENT APPROACHES TO ADAPTIVE INSTRUCTIONAL SYSTEMS

Efforts to develop and implement adaptive instruction have taken five different approaches. Depending on available resources and constraints in the given situation, adaptive instruction can be designed using one or more of these approaches. The first approach is to adapt instruction on a macro-level by allowing alternatives in instructional goals, depth of curriculum content, delivery systems, etc. Most adaptive instructional systems developed as alternatives to the traditional lock-step group instruction in school environments have taken this approach. The second approach is to adapt specific instructional procedures and strategies to specific student characteristics. Because this approach requires the identification of the most relevant learner characteristics (or aptitudes) for instruction and the selection of instructional strategies that best facilitate the learning process of the students with those characteristics, it is based on aptitude–treatment interaction (ATI). The third approach is to adapt instruction on a micro-level by diagnosing the student's specific learning needs during instruction and providing instructional prescriptions for the needs. Intelligent tutoring systems (ITSs) are an example of this approach. The fourth approach is adaptive hypermedia and Web-based systems (AHSs). Although this approach can be considered as an extension of ITS, it has several new features. First, most AHSs apply adaptive/adaptable (hybrid) features by allowing users to initiate their choices, along with guidance (Cristea and Garzotto, 2004). Second, whereas previous adaptive systems are closed corpus systems confined to the program, most AHS applications are Web-based, open corpus systems which allows the possibility of utilizing other Web resources. The fifth is a group of systems that were developed based on specific pedagogical approaches. The pedagogical approaches applied in these systems include constructivism, motivation theory, social learning theory, and metacognition.

Although they are presented as five different approaches, some overlaps exist between categories. Further, an adaptive instructional system may contain characteristics of more than one approach. Also, although this review is intended to be comprehensive, it is certainly not complete. Several relevant endeavors in the field—for example, applications of cognitive load theory to adaptive instruction—are not included in this review because these systems are in the early stages of development.

## MACRO-ADAPTIVE INSTRUCTION

Initial attempts at homogeneous grouping had minimal effect because the groups seldom received different kinds of instructional treatments (Tennyson, 1975). In the early 1900s, a number of adaptive systems were developed to better accommodate different student abilities, such as the Burke plan, Dalton plan, and Winnetka plan (Reiser, 1987). The notion of mastery learning was also fostered in the Dalton and Winnetka plans.

Several macro-adaptive instructional systems were developed in the 1960s, 1970s, and 1980s (for a review, see Park and Lee, 2003). Examples of macro-adaptive instructional systems include Keller's Personalized System of Instruction (PSI) (Keller and Sherman, 1974), the Program for Learning in Accordance with Needs (PLAN) (Flanagan et al., 1975), Mastery Learning Systems developed by Bloom and his associates (Block, 1980), Individually Guided Education (IGE) (Klausmeier, 1975), and Individually Prescribed Instructional System (IPI) (Glaser, 1977). Although many macro-level systems have been criticized as being unsystematic, they were practiced in many school classrooms for a long time, and some systems are still used. The Adaptive Learning Environments Model (ALEM) developed by Wang and her associates (Wang, 1980; Wang and Lindvall, 1984; Wang et al., 1995; see also http://www.nwrel.org/scpd/catalog/ModelDetails.asp?ModelID=8) is still implemented in many schools. Another sample of macro-level approaches is the PLATO Learning Management (PLM) system; PLM was a computer-managed instructional (CMI) system with functions to diagnose student learning needs and prescribe instructional activities appropriate for those needs. The PLM could evaluate each student's performance on a test and provide specific instructional prescriptions (Hart, 1981).

As Glaser (1977) pointed out, the development and implementation of an adaptive instructional program in an existing system were complex and difficult. This problem may be the primary reason why most macro-adaptive instructional systems have not been used as successfully and widely as hoped. Computer technology, however, provides a powerful means to overcome at least some of the problems encountered in the development and implementation of adaptive instructional systems.

# APTITUDE–TREATMENT INTERACTIONS

Cronbach (1957) suggested that facilitating educational development for a wide range of students requires a wide range of environments suited to their optimal learning. He proposed prescribing one type of instructional sequence for a student with certain characteristics and another type for a student with different characteristics. This strategy has been based on aptitude–treatment interactions (ATIs). Cronbach and Snow (1977) defined *aptitude* as any individual characteristic that increases or impairs the student's probability of success in a given treatment, and they defined *treatment* as variations in the pace or style of instruction.

## An Eight-Step Model for Designing ATI-Based Courseware

Carrier and Jonassen (1988) proposed an eight-step model to provide practical guidance for applying the ATI-based model to the design of computer-based instructional (CBI) courseware. This model is basically a modified systems approach to instructional development (Dick and Carey, 1985; Gagné and Briggs, 1979): (1) Identify objectives for the courseware, (2) specify task characteristics, (3) identify an initial pool of learner characteristics, (4) select the most relevant learner characteristics, (5) analyze learners in the target population, (6) select final differences (in the learner characteristics), (7) determine how to adapt instruction, and (8) design alternative treatments. Carrier and Jonassen (1988) also listed important individual variables that influence learning, such as prior knowledge, cognitive styles, and personality variables. For instructional adaptation, they recommended several types of methods: (1) remedial,

(2) capitalization/ preferential, (3) compensatory, and (4) challenge. This model seemingly has practical value; however, without theoretically coherent and empirically traceable links among different learner variables and without clearly defined types and levels of learning requirements and instructional strategies for different tasks, the mere application of this model is not likely to produce better results than those of nonadaptive instructional systems.

## Limitations of ATI

Since Cronbach (1957) made his proposal, relatively few studies have found consistent results to support the paradigm. As shown in several reviews of ATI research (Berliner and Cahen, 1973; Corno and Snow, 1986; Cronbach and Snow, 1977; Tobias, 1976), intellectual abilities and other aptitude variables were used in many different studies to investigate their interactions with a variety of instructional treatments; however, no convincing evidence was found to suggest that such individual differences were useful variables for differentiating instructional treatments in a homogeneous age group (Glaser and Resnick, 1972; Tobias, 1987).

The inconsistent findings of ATI studies prompted researchers to reexamine the paradigm and propose alternative approaches. According to Tobias (1976, 1987, 1989), a number of limitations and problems in the ATI-based model have been proposed; for example:

- The abilities assumed to be most effective for a particular treatment may not be exclusive (Cronbach and Snow, 1977).
- Abilities required by a treatment may shift as the task progresses (Burns, 1980; Federico, 1983).
- ATIs validated for a particular task and subject area may not be generalizable to other areas (Peterson, 1977; Peterson and Janicki, 1979; Peterson et al., 1981).
- ATIs validated in laboratory experiments may not be applicable to actual classroom situations (Tobias, 1976, 1987, 1989).

Another criticism is that ATI research has tended to be overly concerned with exploration of simple input/output relations between measured traits and learning outcomes (DiVesta, 1975). Because individual difference variables are difficult to measure, the validity and reliability of the measures can be a problem in adapting instruction to the individual differences; however, research in ATI has continued.

Recently, several studies have been conducted to control learning environments using computers; for example, Maki and Maki (2002) examined the interactions of student comprehension skills with course format (online vs. lecture format). After examining the interactions among particular learning types, exploratory behavior, and two different learning environments (rule application vs. rule induction), Shute and Towle (2003) introduced an adaptive e-learning model utilizing ATI.

# MICRO-ADAPTIVE INSTRUCTION

Researchers have attempted to establish micro-adaptive instructional models using on-task measures rather than pre-task measures. On-task measures of student behavior and performance, such as response errors, response latencies, and emotional states, can be valuable sources for making adaptive instructional decisions during the instructional process. Such measures taken during the course of instruction can be applied to the manipulation and optimization of instructional treatments and sequences on a much more refined scale (Federico, 1983). Thus, micro-adaptive instructional models using on-task measures are likely to be more sensitive to the student's needs.

A typical example of micro-adaptive instruction is one-on-one tutoring. The tutor selects the most appropriate information and tutoring method for the student based on his or her judgment of the student's learning needs and abilities (Bloom, 1984; Kulik, 1982). As the one-on-one tutorial process suggests, two essential elements of micro-adaptive instruction are the ongoing diagnosis of the student's learning needs and the prescription of instructional treatments based on the diagnosis (Hansen et al., 1977; Holland, 1977; Landa, 1976; Rothen and Tennyson, 1978). Instructional researchers or developers have different views about the variables, indices, procedures, and actions that should be used in the diagnostic and the prescriptive processes (Atkinson, 1976; Rothen and Tennyson, 1977).

## Micro-Adaptive Instructional Models

Unlike macro-adaptive models, micro-adaptive models are dynamic and use the temporal nature of learner abilities and characteristics (e.g., current knowledge, motivation level) as a major source of diagnostic information on which instructional treatments are prescribed. By including more variables related to instruction, a typical micro-adaptive model provides a better control process than a macro-adaptive model or programmed instruction in responding to the student's

learning needs (Merrill and Boutwell, 1973). As described by Suppes et al. (1976), micro-adaptive models typically use a quantitative representation and trajectory methodology. An important feature of a micro-adaptive model is the timeliness and accuracy for determining and adjusting learning prescriptions during instruction.

Most micro-adaptive models are primarily developed to adapt two instructional variables: the amount of content to be presented and the presentation sequence of the content. Representative examples of micro-adaptive instructional models are mathematical models, multiple regression models, Bayesian probability models, and structural/algorithmic models (for a comprehensive review, see Park and Lee, 2003). The Bayesian probabilistic model and the multiple regression model are designed to select the amount of instruction required to learn a given task using both pre-task and on-task information (Hansen et al., 1977; Park and Tennyson, 1980, 1986; Ross and Anand, 1986; Ross and Morrison, 1986; Rothen and Tennyson, 1977). The structural/algorithmic approach emphasizes that the sequence of instruction should be decided by the content structure of the learning task as well as the student's performance history (Scandura, 1977a,b, 1983).

Regarding treatment variables, some studies (Hansen et al., 1977; Ross and Morrison, 1988) indicated that only prior achievement among pre-task measures (e.g., anxiety, locus of control) provides consistent and reliable information for prescribing the amount of instruction; however, subjects who received the amount of instruction selected based on both pre-task measures and on-task measures needed less time and showed higher test scores than subjects who received the amount of instruction based on only pre-task measures (Park and Tennyson, 1980). The results of the response-sensitive strategies studied by Park and Tennyson (1980, 1986) suggest that the predictive power of pre-task measures, including prior knowledge, decreases while that of on-task measures increases as the instruction progresses.

As reviewed above, a common characteristic of micro-adaptive instructional models is response sensitivity in diagnosing student learning needs and providing instructional prescriptions. Response-sensitive instruction has been used for a long time, from Crowder's simple branching program (1959) and Atkinson's mathematical model of adaptive instruction (1968) to intelligent tutoring systems. Until the late 1960s, technology was not readily available to implement the response-sensitive diagnostic and prescriptive procedures as a general practice outside the experimental laboratory (Hall, 1977).

## Intelligent Tutoring Systems

Intelligent tutoring systems (ITSs) were developed with the application of artificial intelligence (AI) techniques. Because the goal of ITSs is to provide adaptive instruction by intelligently diagnosing students' learning needs and progress in a response-sensitive manner, they are considered micro-level adaptive instructional systems. ITSs have three main components: a representation of the content to be taught (expert or domain model), an inherent teaching or instructional strategy (tutor or teaching model), and mechanisms for understanding what the student does and does not know (student model) (Akhras and Self, 2002; Shute and Psotka, 1996; Wenger, 1987). AI methods for the representation of knowledge (e.g., production rules, semantic networks, scripts frames) and problems make it possible for the ITS to generate and present knowledge to students based on their performance on the task rather than selecting the knowledge according to the predetermined branching rules. The capacity to make inferences about the cause of a student's misconceptions and his or her learning needs allows the ITS to make decisions based on qualitative data, unlike most micro-adaptive models based on solely quantitative data.

Furthermore, ITS techniques provide a powerful tool for effectively capturing human learning and teaching processes. It has apparently contributed to a better understanding of cognitive processes involved in learning specific skills and knowledge (Shute and Psotka, 1996). Some ITSs provided research environments for investigating specific instructional strategies and tools for modeling human tutors and simulating human learning and cognition (Koedinger and Anderson, 1998; Seidel and Park, 1994; Shute and Psotka, 1996). Recently, ITSs were expanded to enhance metacognition (Aleven et al., 2001; White et al., 1999); however, it has been noted that ITS developers have failed to incorporate many valuable learning principles and instructional strategies developed by instructional researchers and educators (Park et al., 1987). Ohlsson (1987, 1993) and others criticized ITS and other computer-based interactive learning systems for their limited range and adaptability of teaching actions compared to rich tactics and strategies employed by human expert teachers. Cooperative efforts among experts in different domains, including learning/instruction and artificial intelligence, are required to develop more powerful adaptive systems using the ITS methods and techniques (Park and Seidel, 1989; Seidel et al., 1989).

## Applying ATI to Micro-Level Adaptive Systems

To integrate the ATI-based approach in a micro-adaptive model, Tennyson and Christensen (1988; also see Tennyson and Park, 1987) proposed a two-level model of adaptive instruction based on the findings of their own research. First, this computer-based model allows the computer tutor to establish conditions of instruction based on learner aptitude variables (cognitive, affective, and memory structure) and context structure. Second, the computer tutor provides moment-to-moment adjustments of instructional conditions by adapting the amount of information, example formats, display time, sequence of instruction, instructional advisement, and embedded refreshment and remediation. The micro-level adaptation is based on the student's *on-task performance*, and the procedure is *response sensitive* (Park and Tennyson, 1980). The amount of information to be presented and the time to display the information on the computer screen are determined through the continuous decision-making process based on on-task performance data. The selection and presentation of other instructional strategies (sequence of examples, advisement, and embedded refreshment and remediation) are determined based on the evaluation of the on-task performance.

Evidence shows that some aptitude variables (e.g., prior knowledge, interest, intellectual ability) are important predictors in selecting instructional treatments (Tobias, 1994; Whitener, 1989); however, some studies (Park and Tennyson, 1980, 1986) suggest that the predictive value of aptitude variables decreases as the learning process continues. In contrast, the diagnostic power of on-task performance increases because it reflects the most updated and integrated reflection of aptitude and other variables involved in the learning. The decrease in the predictive power of the premeasured aptitude variables and the increase in that of on-task performance can be represented as shown in Figure 37.1.

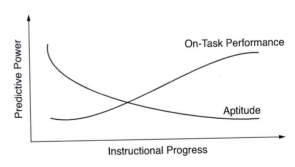

**Figure 37.1** Predictive power of aptitudes and on-task performance.

In the two-stage approach, the student is assigned initially to the best instructional alternative based on the aptitude measured prior to instruction, and then response-sensitive procedures are applied as the student's response patterns emerge to reflect his or her knowledge or skills on the given task. A representative example of this two-stage approach is the Bayesian adaptive instructional model. As the process for estimating student learning needs continues using a Bayesian probability model, the value of the pretest performance data becomes less important and recent performance data become more important. The effectiveness of the two-stage approach has been empirically supported (Park and Tennyson, 1980, 1986).

## ADAPTIVE HYPERMEDIA SYSTEMS

In the early 1990s, when researchers incorporated the concepts of hypermedia/hypertext with intelligent tutoring systems, adaptive hypermedia systems (AHSs) were born (Beaumont, 1994; Brusilovsky et al., 1996; De Bra et al., 2005; Fischer et al., 1990; Gonschorek and Herzog, 1995; Hohl et al., 1996; Kay and Kummerfeld, 1994). An AHS utilizes hyperlinks, and its technical approach, including a user-model-based interface, is similar to an ITS; however, AHSs differ from both micro-adaptive systems (including ITSs) and conventional hypermedia systems in terms of adaptability/adaptivity.

In general, computer-based instructional systems that allow the user to choose certain parameters and adapt the behavior of these systems are referred to as *learner-controlled instruction* (Williams, 1996) or *adaptable systems* (Cristea and Garzotto, 2004; Fink et al., 1998; Opperman, 1994), whereas adaptive systems in which behaviors are automatically based on the user's needs are referred to as *program-controlled (system-controlled) instruction*, or *adaptive systems.**

Conventional hypermedia learning environments are nonadaptive, as they provide the same content and the same set of links to all learners; however, they are adaptable because links or tasks to be presented next are determined by the learner's actions. Adaptability without adaptivity may lead the learner along a poor path (Steinberg, 1991; Williams, 1996). Unlike conventional hypermedia environments, an AHS is adaptive, providing content and links based on the individual user's needs and characteristics; for example, the

*next* button in an AHS may not be different in appearance but it will take different users to different pages (Schwarz et al., 1996).

Traditional micro-adaptive instructional systems are adaptive but not adaptable. They control the instructional process and activities based on an evaluation of student learning needs and abilities, but they do not allow students to control the process of adaptation. In contrast, most AHSs allow users to initiate their own choices; for example, an AHS might provide *a suggested set of most relevant links* based on the system's assessment of the user's needs and characteristics (Brusilovsky, 1994).

Because an AHS includes both learner and program control, it is also referred to as an *adaptive/adaptable* hybrid system (Cristea and Garzotto, 2004). Oppermann developed and tested the adaptive/adaptable system Flexcel. He concluded that adaptivity and adaptability should receive benefits from each other (Oppermann, 1994).

Another difference between AHSs and micro-adaptive systems is that, except for a few early AHSs developed before the advent of the Web, AHSs are Web based. As Brusilovsky (2003) pointed out, when using the Web platform course instructors or developers can use not only the *closed corpus* course material in the system but also *open corpus* Web sources. Open corpus Web sources were not available for previous adaptive systems.

Since the mid-1990s, with the advent of the Web, AHSs have grown rapidly (Brusilovsky, 2001). Now, the Web is the choice of all AHSs, and AHSs are now referred to as *adaptive Web-based hypermedia* or *Web-based adaptive hypermedia*. Due to its large variety of users, the Web is an ideal candidate for adaptivity and has served as a platform for AHS research and development (Brusilovsky, 2000). Many AHSs have been developed for education and training purposes, such as hypermedia, e-learning, virtual museums, and online information systems (Brusilovsky, 2003; Cristea, 2005). AHS research and development have been extended to the development of AHS authoring tools, such as Multibook (Steinacker et al., 1998), InterBook (Brusilovsky et al., 1998), ACE (Specht and Oppermann, 1998), KBS Hyperbook (Henze and Nejdl, 1999, 2001), AHA! (De Bra et al., 2003), ADAPTS (Brusilovsky and Cooper, 2002), WHURLE (Moore et al., 2004), and SmexWeb (Albrecht et al., 2000). Also, the functions of AHSs have been improved, from the application of simple one-layered, knowledge-based user models to sophisticated multiple-layered user models (Brown et al., 2005).

---

* These definitions of the words *adaptive* and *adaptable* are not employed universally; for example, Leutner (2004) referred to learning environments that are macro-adaptive as *adaptable* and those that are micro-adaptive as *adaptive*.

## AHS Taxonomies

In 1997, the Adaptive Hypertext and Hypermedia Discussion forum (Eklund and Sinclair, 2000) defined adaptive hypermedia systems as "all hypertext and hypermedia systems which reflect some features of the user in the user model and apply this model to adapt various visible and functional aspects of the system to the user." More specifically, an adaptive hypermedia system should: (1) be based on hypermedia or hypertext, (2) have a user model, (3) have a domain model, and (4) be modifiable (adaptive) based on information contained in the user-model (Eklund and Sinclair, 2000).

Brusilovsky (1996) developed the first taxonomy of AHSs which distinguishes two areas of adaptation: (1) adaptation of the content of the page, called *content-level adaptation* or *adaptive presentation*, and (2) behavior of the links, called *link-level adaptation* or *adaptive navigation support*. The goal of adaptive presentation is to adapt the content of a hypermedia page to the learner's goals, knowledge, and other information stored in the user model. The techniques of adaptive presentation are to adapt the content of a page accessed by a particular user to the user's current knowledge, goals, and other characteristics or to provide not only text but also a set of various multimedia items. The goal of adaptive navigation support is to assist learners in finding their optimal paths in hyperspace by adapting link presentation and functionality to the goals, knowledge, and other characteristics of individual learners. Direct guidance; sorting; annotation; link hiding, disabling, and removal; and link generation are ways to provide adaptive links to individual learners (Brusilovsky, 2000, 2003, 2004; Brusilovsky and Pesin, 1994, 1998; Brusilovsky and Rizzo, 2002; Brusilovsky and Vassileva, 1996; De Bra, 2000; Kayama and Okamoto, 1998).

Brusilovky's taxonomy was refined by others. Cristea and Calvi (2003) presented three layers of adaptation from direct adaptation techniques (low level), adaptation language (medium level), and adaptation strategies (high level). The low level is based on Brusilovky's taxonomy, the medium level refers primarily to goal- or domain-oriented adaptation techniques, and the high level refers to adaptation techniques for detecting learner's information-processing strategies and cognitive styles (Brown et al., 2005; Calvi and Cristea, 2002; Cristea and Calvi, 2003; Cristea and De Bra, 2002). My Online Teacher (MOT) is a representative sample of AHS authoring tools that have integrated the three layers of adaptation techniques (Brown et al., 2005; Cristea and Calvi, 2003).

## Limitations and Challenges

As reviewed earlier, two features distinguish AHSs from micro-adaptive systems: (1) adaptivity/adaptability and (2) open corpus learning environments. However, these features impose new challenges. Williams' comprehensive review (1996) of learner-controlled vs. program-controlled instruction revealed that learner-controlled (adaptable) systems and program-controlled (adaptive) systems have different strengths and weaknesses. According to Williams, each type of system is more effective than the other for some people and under certain conditions (for those conditions, see Williams, 1996). This finding suggests that a system with the combined functions of adaptability and adaptivity would be more effective than a system with only adaptable or adaptive functions. AHSs were developed to provide hybrid systems; however, decisions about how to design adaptive/adaptable systems are still made on an *ad hoc* basis without an adequate theoretical or empirical rationale for the design of these hybrid systems (Avgeriou et al., 2004; Cristea and De Bra, 2002). Adaptivity has risen to a new level; the question now is how to balance adaptivity and adaptability in a system.

A conceptual model for adaptable/adaptive systems can be found in Park's (1996) proposal of *on-task adaptive learner-control* (see Figure 37.1), in which learners have more freedom in choosing learning activities as the instruction progresses. In the beginning stage of learning, the student's familiarity with the subject knowledge and its learning requirements would be relatively low, and the student would not be able to choose the best strategies for learning. As the instruction and learning continue, however, the student's familiarity with the subject and ability to learn it would increase, thus enabling the student to make better decisions in selecting strategies for learning the subject. This argument is supported by research (Carrier, 1984; Ross and Rakow, 1981; Seidel et al., 1978; Snow, 1980). An on-task adaptive learner control system will decide not only when is the best time for giving the learner-control option but also what kind of control options (e.g., selection of contents, learning activities) should be given based on the student's on-task performance.

Cristea and Garzotto (2004) identified a set of *design variables* or *problem classes* to develop a taxonomy of adaptive/adaptable educational hypermedia: learner model, instructional strategy, instructional view, detection mechanism, and adaptation mechanism. Also, they provided typical problems that a developer might face and design guidelines for each of the problems. Although the guidelines are not yet complete, the taxonomy can be used as a starting point for establishing the design standards of adaptive/adaptable systems, including methods and procedures (Cristea and De Bra, 2002). Empirical study should be conducted to validate and refine these standards.

Web-based AHSs may or may not utilize open corpus resources in the Web; however, designing an AHS that utilizes the open corpus hyperspace is a challenging task. Brusilovsky (2003) pointed out that simply providing external links to multiple sources is not considered adaptive support for students. An important question is how the system provides *adaptive open resources* for students. Many systems and techniques have been developed to expose users to information relevant only to them (Hanani et al., 2001). Several Web-authoring tools, such as WHURLE (Moore et al., 2004) and KBS Hyperlink (Henze and Nejdl, 2001), generate hyperlinks not only inside of the lesson but also to external Web resources based on learners' previous activities. The adaptive Web recommendation (AWR) system is also another method for providing adaptive navigation support technologies for open corpus learning environments (Brusilovsky, 2004). Whereas typical AHSs attempt to adapt to various aspects of the users and provide a rich set of adaptive navigation support techniques in closed learning environments, AWRs focus on one aspect—user interest—and provide relevant external links. Web Knowledge Sea was developed utilizing AWR techniques (Brusilovsky, 2004; Brusilovsky and Rizzo, 2002). Providing adaptive navigational support is another important issue not only for the development of adaptive systems but also for the development of information and communication technology. With the steadily growing Semantic Web, which provides a generic structure for producing machine-processable Web content (see http://www.w3.org/2001/sw), adaptive navigational support will become more feasible.

Reusability, a long-standing problem in computer-based adaptive instructional systems, continues to plague those working with AHSs. Until recently, AHSs were domain-specific applications in particular systems only; therefore, it was difficult to reuse the technology in one system for the development of another system. Research is currently in progress to develop adaptation technology for establishing uniform standards (Brusilovsky, 2003; Cristea, 2004; de Assis et al., 2004). The Minerva project is an example. The goal of the project was to establish a European platform of standards, guidelines, techniques, and tools for user-model-based adaptability and adaptation (see http://wwwis.win.tue.nl/~acristea/HTML/Minerva/). This standardization effort is expected to address the reusability issue. Meta-adaptive models and adaptation standard techniques for AHSs have been tested (de Assis et al., 2004).

## ADAPTIVE SYSTEMS SUPPORTING SPECIFIC PEDAGOGICAL APPROACHES

Andriessen and Sandberg (1999) noted that adaptive computer-based instruction mainly focuses on the acquisition of conceptual and procedural knowledge, identification of common misconceptions in specific domains, and interactions between the program (or tutor) and students. As mentioned earlier, adaptive instructional systems were criticized for their limited range of teaching actions compared to human expert teachers. Researchers began to incorporate more complex pedagogical approaches, such as constructivist learning, contingent learning strategies, motivational competence, metacognitive strategies, and collaborative learning in adaptive instructional systems. These five adaptive approaches are not mutually exclusive, but they can be distinguished from one another in terms of their primary thrust. Although researchers are applying other pedagogical approaches to adaptive instructional systems, these five were selected to provide an overview of the impact of pedagogical approaches on the field.

### Constructivist Adaptive Systems

Constructivist learning theories emphasize active roles for learners to construct their own knowledge through experiences in a learning context in which the target domain is integrated. To implement constructivist principles into computer-based learning environments, researchers developed the concept of intelligent learning environments (ILEs), which emphasize the facilitatory role of the system as opposed to the tutoring role (Akhras, 2004; Brusilovsky, 1994).

Most adaptive instructional systems utilized representation of knowledge, inference of the learner's state of knowledge, and planning of instructional steps (Akhras and Self, 2000). Akhras and Self argued that "alternative views of learning, such as constructivism, may similarly benefit from a system intelligence in which the mechanisms of knowledge representation, reasoning, and decision making originate from a formal interpretation of the values of that view of learning" (p. 345). Constructivist intelligent systems shift the focus from a model of *what* is learned to a model of *how* knowledge is learned (Akhras and Self, 2000).

To model this facilitatory role, researchers (Akhras, 2004; Akhras and Self, 2000, 2002) proposed four important considerations when designing these systems: situation-based contexts, learning interactions in situation, time-extended processes of interaction, and affordances of learning situations. Their approach was implemented in INCENSE (INtelligent Constructivist ENvironment for Software Engineering learning). KBS Hyperbook is another example of constructivist AHS (Henze and Nejdl, 1999).

## Contingent Teaching Systems

According to Vygotsky's theory (1978), providing immediate and appropriately challenging activities and contingent teaching based on a learner's behavior is important for that learner to progress to the next level of learning. He believed minimal levels of guidance are the best for learners. Recently, this theory has been applied in several different ways to computer-based instruction. As compared to traditional adaptive instruction, a contingent teaching system has no global model of the learner. A learner's performance is local, and the situation is constrained by contingencies in the learner's current activity. Because the tutor's actions and reactions should be occurring in response to the learner's inputs, the theory promotes an active view of the learner and an account of learning as a collaborative and constructive process (Wood and Wood, 1996). Contingent tutoring systems generally provide two assessment methods: model tracing and knowledge tracing (du Boulay and Luckin, 2001). The purpose of model tracing is to keep track of all of the student's actions as the problem is solved and to flag errors as they occur. It also adapts the help feedback based on specific problem-solving contexts. The purpose of knowledge tracing is to choose the next problem that is *appropriately challenging* so the students can move in a timely but effective manner through the curriculum. Examples of contingent teaching systems include SHERLOCK (Lesgold, 2001; Lesgold et al., 1992), QUADRATIC tutor (Wood and Wood, 1999), DATA (Wood et al., 1998), Ecolab (Luckin and du Boulay, 1999), and M-Ecolab (Rebolledo Mendez et al., 2006).

## Motivation-Based Adaptive Systems

Some new adaptive instructional systems take into account student motivation. Proponents suggest that a comprehensive adaptive instructional plan should consist of a traditional instructional plan combined with a motivational plan (del Soldato and du Boulay, 1995; du Boulay and Luckin, 2001; Wasson, 1990). De Vicente and Pain (2002) have developed a model called the *motivation model*, which diagnoses a student's motivational state based on several variables (i.e., control, challenge, independence, fantasy, confidence, sensory interest, cognitive interest, effort, satisfaction). COSMO (Lester et al., 1999) supports a pedagogical agent that can incorporate nonverbal feedback and con-

versational signals such as its facial expression, its tone of voice, its gestures, and the structure of its utterances to indicate its own affective state and to increase students' motivation during its interactions with learners.

## Metacognition-Based Adaptive Systems

Metacognitive skills enable students to assess their own learning processes. As ICT-based individualized instruction, including online learning environments, becomes increasingly prevalent, metacognitive and self-regulatory processes are becoming more important in the design of systems (Azevedo, 2005a,b; Quintana et al., 2005; Zimmerman and Tsikalas, 2005). In contrast, most early tutoring systems did not promote students' metacognitive thinking (Carroll and McKendree, 1987).

White et al. (1999) argued that metacognitive processes can be easily understood and observed in a multi-agent social system that integrates cognitive and social aspects of cognition within a social framework. Based on this conceptual framework, they developed the SCI-WISE program, which houses a community of software agents, such as an Inventor, an Analyzer, and a Collaborator. The agents provide strategic advice and guidance to learners as they undertake research projects and as they reflect on and revise their inquiry; therefore, students express their metacognitive ideas as they undertake complex sociocognitive practices. Through this exercise, students develop explicit theories about the social and cognitive processes required for collaborative inquiry and reflective learning (White et al., 1999).

Another example focusing on improving metacognitive skills is the Geometry Explanation Tutor (GET) developed by Aleven et al. (2001). They argued that self-explanation is an effective metacognitive strategy. Having students explain examples or problem-solving steps helps them learn with greater understanding (Aleven et al., 2003a,b; Chi et al., 1989). Aleven and his associates conducted experimental studies to test the effects of GET. The results provided positive effects on learning outcomes.

The ability to pursue help effectively and efficiently when needed is an important metacognitive skill. Aleven and his associates (Aleven et al., 2003c, 2006) also developed Help-Seeking Tutor Agent, which helps students become better help seekers. They embedded it within their adaptive instructional system, Geometry Cognitive Tutor, and tested whether Help-Seeking Tutor Agent helped students to be better help seekers and to learn better as a result (Aleven et al., 2004). The results showed that the more help-seeking errors students made with the system, the less they learned. Other research (Roll et al., 2006) revealed that, although Help-Seeking Tutor Agent achieved positive effects because students followed its advice, students did not internalize the help-seeking principles.

## Collaborative Learning Systems

One of new pedagogical approaches incorporated in adaptive instructional systems is collaborative learning (Söller et al., 2005). Effective collaboration with peers is a powerful learning experience; however, simply placing students in a group and assigning a task to the group does not produce a valuable learning experience for them (Söller, 2001). Teachers (tutors in computer-based systems) should provide strategies for students to experience collaborative learning effectively and interestingly. Through the use of an intelligent collaborative system, Söller (2001) identified five characteristics of effective collaborative learning behaviors: (1) participation, (2) social grounding, (3) performance analysis and group processing, (4) application of active learning conversation skills, and (5) promotive interactions. Söller and her colleagues (2005) developed a conceptual framework, the Collaboration Management Cycle, represented by a feedback loop for the five-phased behaviors.

Although collaborative learning systems are still in development (Jermann et al., 2004; Or-Bach and van Joolingen, 2004; Söller et al., 2005), their contributions to adaptive instructional systems will be significant; they not only facilitate student group activities but also help educators and researchers better understand group interactions and determine how to support collaborative learning better. Appropriate combinations of sound pedagogical approaches such as the ones described above with the structural features and functions of adaptive/adaptable systems will further improve the technical capacity and instructional effectiveness of the systems.

## CONCLUSION

Adaptive instruction has a long history. Systematic efforts to develop adaptive instructional systems began in the early 1900s. Adaptive instructional systems have embodied different approaches: macro-adaptive, ATI-based, micro-adaptive (including ITS), and adaptive/adaptable hybrid systems, as well as other approaches that incorporate different pedagogical perspectives. Using interactive computer technology, a number of different micro-adaptive instructional systems have been developed; however, early applications were mostly in laboratory environments because of the limitations of their functional capabilities to handle complex learning and instructional processes.

Since the 1990s, with the advent of the Web and AHSs, adaptive instructional applications have moved out of the labs and into classrooms and workplaces. During the last decade, numerous AHS systems have been developed; however, the dearth of empirical evidence and weak theoretical foundations supporting their effectiveness (Shapiro and Niederhauser, 2004) remain as a hindrance for the wider use of the systems in school education and industry training. It is a difficult and challenging task to develop technically robust, theoretically sound, and empirically valid systems. Research and development on new pedagogical approaches in adaptive systems may provide stronger theoretical foundations for the development of future systems. AHS technology in collaboration with the Semantic Web may lead to standardized open adaptation technology for the development of future adaptive systems. If more theoretically sound and technically robust systems are developed, it becomes more likely that the effects of the systems will be supported in empirical evaluations.

## REFERENCES

Akhras, F. N. (2004). From Modelling Teaching Strategies to Modelling Affordances. Paper presented at Workshop on Modelling Human Teaching Tactics and Strategies, August 30, Maceio, Alagoas, Brazil (http://www.cenpra.gov.br/noticiaseeventos/its04workshop/akhras.pdf).

Akhras, F. N. and Self, A. J. (2000). System intelligence in constructivist learning. *Int. J. Artif. Intell. Educ.*, 11(4), 344–376.

Akhras, F. N. and Self, J. A. (2002). Beyond intelligent tutoring systems: situations, interactions, processes and affordances. *Instruct. Sci.*, 30(1), 1–30.

Albrecht, F., Koch, N., and Tiller, T. (2000). SmexWeb: An adaptive Web-based hypermedia teaching system. *J. Interact. Learn. Res.*, 11(3/4), 367–388.

Aleven, V., Popescu, O., and Koedinger, K. R. (2001). Towards tutorial dialog to support self-explanation: adding natural language understanding to a cognitive tutor. In *Artificial Intelligence in Education: AI-ED in the Wired and Wireless Future*, edited by J. Moore, L. Redfield, and W. Johnson, pp. 246–255. Amsterdam: IOS Press.

Aleven, V., Koedinger, K. R., and Popescu, O. (2003a). A tutorial dialog system to support self-explanation: evaluation and open questions. In *Proceedings of the 11th International Conference on Artificial Intelligence in Education, AI-ED 2003*, edited by U. Hoppe, F. Verdejo, and J. Kay, pp. 39–46. Amsterdam: IOS Press.

Aleven V., Popescu, O., Ogan, A., and Koedinger, K. R. (2003b). A formative classroom evaluation of a tutorial dialogue system that supports self-explanation. In *Supplemental Proceedings of the 11th International Conference on Artificial Intelligence in Education, AIED 2003*. Vol. VI. *Workshop on Tutorial Dialogue Systems: With a View toward the Classroom*, edited by V. Aleven, U. Hoppe, J. Kay, R. Mizoguchi, H. Pain, F. Verdejo, and K. Yacef, pp. 345–355. Sydney: School of Information Technologies, University of Sydney.

Aleven, V., Stahl, E., Schworm, S., Fischer, F., and Wallace, R. M. (2003c). Help seeking and help design in interactive learning environments. *Rev. Educ. Res.*, 73(2), 277–320.

Aleven, V., McLaren, B. M., Roll, I., and Koedinger, K. R. (2004). Toward tutoring help seeking: applying cognitive modeling to meta-cognitive skills. In *Proceedings of the Seventh International Conference on Intelligent Tutoring Systems (ITS-2004)*, edited by J. C. Lester, R. M. Vicari, and F. Paraguacu, pp. 227–239. Berlin: Springer-Verlag.

Aleven, V., McLaren, B. M., Roll, I., and Koedinger, K. R. (2006). Toward meta-cognitive tutoring: a model of help-seeking with a cognitive tutor. *Int. J. Artif. Intell. Educ.*, 16, 101–130.

Andriessen, J. and Sandberg, J. A. C. (1999) Where is education heading and how about AI? *Int. J. Artificial Intelligence in Education*, 10, 130–150.

Atkinson, C. R. (1968). Computerized instruction and the learning process. *Am. Psychol.*, 23, 225–239.*

Atkinson, C. R. (1976). Adaptive instructional systems: some attempts to optimize the learning process. In *Cognition and Instruction*, edited by D. Klahr, pp. 81–108. New York: Wiley.*

Avgeriou, P., Vogiatzis, D., Tzanavari, A., and Retalis, S. (2004). Design patterns in adaptive Web-based educational systems: an overview. In *Advanced Technology for Learning: Innovations in Advanced Technology for Learning: Authoring for Adaptive Educational Hypermedia*. Calgary, Canada: ACTA Press.

Azevedo, R. (2005a). Computer environments as metacognitive tools for enhancing learning. *Educ. Psychol.*, 40(4), 193–197.

Azevedo, R. (2005b). Using hypermedia as a metacognitive tool for enhancing student learning? The role of self-regulated learning. *Educ. Psychol.*, 40(4), 199–209.

Beaumont, I. (1994). User modeling in the interactive anatomy tutoring system NATOM-TUTOR. *User Model. User-Adapt. Interact.*, 4, 121–145.

Berliner, D. C. and Cahen, L. S. (1973). Trait-treatment interaction and learning. *Rev. Res. Educ.*, 1, 58–94.

Block, J. H. (1980). Promoting excellence through mastery learning. *Theory Pract.*, 19(1), 66–74.

Bloom, B. S. (1984). The 2 sigma problem: The search for methods of group instruction as effective as one-to-one tutoring. *Educ. Res.*, 13, 4–16.*

Brown, E., Cristea, A., Stewart, C., and Brailsford, T. (2005). Patterns in authoring of adaptive educational hypermedia: a taxonomy of learning styles. *Educ. Technol. Soc.*, 8(3), 77–90 (special issue on authoring of adaptive educational hypermedia).

Brusilovsky, P. (1994). Adaptive hypermedia: the state of the art. In *Proceedings of East–West International Conference on Multimedia, Hypermedia and Virtual Reality*, September 14–16, Moscow, edited by P. Brusilovsky, pp. 24–29. Moscow: ICSTI.*

Brusilovsky, P. (1996) Methods and techniques of adaptive hypermedia. *User Model. User-Adapt. Interact.*, 6(2–3), 87–129.*

Brusilovsky, P. (2000). Adaptive hypermedia: from intelligent tutoring systems to Web-based education. In *Intelligent Tutoring Systems*, LNCS 1839, edited by G. Gauthier, C. Frasson, and K. Van Lehn, pp. 1–7. Berlin: Springer.

Brusilovsky, P. (2001). Adaptive hypermedia. *User Model. User-Adapt. Interact.*, 11, 87–110.

Brusilovsky, P. (2003). Adaptive navigation support in educational hypermedia: the role of student knowledge level and the case for meta-adaptation. *Br. J. Educ. Technol.*, 34(4), 487–497.

Brusilovsky, P. (2004). Adaptive navigation support: from adaptive hypermedia to the adaptive Web and beyond. *PsychNology*, 2(1), 7–23.

Brusilovsky, P. and Cooper, D. W. (2002). Domain, task, and user models for an adaptive hypermedia performance support system. In *Proceedings of 2002 International Conference on Intelligent User Interfaces*, January 13–16, San Francisco, CA, edited by Y. Gil and D. B. Leake, pp. 23–30. Washington, D.C.: ACM Press.

Brusilovsky, P. and Pesin, L. (1994). An intelligent learning environment for CDS/ISIS users. In *Proceedings of the Interdisciplinary Workshop on Complex Learning in Computer Environments: Technology in School, University, Work and Life-Long Education (CLCE94)*, May 16–19, Joensuu, Finland, edited by J. J. Levonen and M. T. Tukianinen, pp. 29–33.

Brusilovsky, P. and Pesin, L. (1998). Adaptive navigation support in educational hypermedia: an evaluation of the ISIS-Tutor. *J. Comput. Inform. Technol.*, 6(1), 27–38.

Brusilovsky, P. and Rizzo, R. (2002). Map-based horizontal navigation in educational hypertext. *J. Digit. Inform.*, 3(1) (http://jodi.ecs.soton.ac.uk/Articles/v03/i01/Brusilovsky/).

Brusilovsky, P. and Vassileva, J. (1996). Preface. *User Model. User-Adapt. Interact.*, 6(2–3), v–vi.

Brusilovsky, P., Schwarz, E., and Weber, G. (1996). ELM-ART: an intelligent tutoring system on the World Wide Web. In *Intelligent Tutoring Systems*, LNCS 1086, edited by C. Frasson, G. Gauthier, and A. Lesgold, pp. 261–269. Berlin: Springer.

Brusilovsky, P., Eklund, J., and Schwarz, E. (1998). Web-based education for all: a tool for developing adaptive courseware. *Comput. Netw. ISDN Syst.*, 30(1–7), 291–300.

Burns, B. R. (1980). Relation of aptitude learning at different points in time during instruction. *J. Educ. Psychol.*, 72, 785–797.

Calvi, L. and Cristea, A. I. (2002). Towards generic adaptive systems: analysis of a case study. *Adaptive Hypermedia and Adaptive Web-Based Systems: Proceedings of AH'02*, edited by P. De Bra, pp. 79–89. Berlin: Springer-Verlag (http://wwwis.win.tue.nl/~acristea/Conferences/02/AH02/calvi-cristea-final-w-header-ah2002.pdf).

Carrier, C. (1984). Do learners make good choices? *Instruct. Innov.*, 29, 15–17, 48.

Carrier, C. and Jonassen, D. H. (1988). Adapting courseware to accommodate individual differences. In *Instructional Designs for Microcomputer Courseware*, edited by D. Jonassen, pp. 61–96. Mahwah, NJ: Lawrence Erlbaum Associates.

Carroll, J. and McKendree, J. (1987). Interface design issues for advice-giving expert systems. *Commun. ACM*, 30(1), 14–31.

Chi, M., Bassok, M., Lewis, M., Reimann, P., and Glaser, R. (1989). Self-explanations: how students study and use examples in learning to solve problems. *Cogn. Sci.*, 13, 145–182.

Corno, L. and Snow, R. E. (1986). Adapting teaching to individual differences among learners. In *Handbook of Research on Teaching*, edited by M. Wittrock, pp. 605–629. New York: Macmillan.*

Cristea, A. I. (2004). Is semi-automatic authoring of adaptive educational hypermedia possible? *Adv. Technol. Learn.*, 1(4), 227–236.

Cristea, A. I. (2005). Authoring of adaptive hypermedia; adaptive hypermedia and learning environments. In *Advances in Web-Based Education: Personalized Learning Environment*, edited by S. Y. Chen and G. D. Magoulas. Hershey: IDEA (http://wwwis.win.tue.nl/~acristea/Chen/AHChenBookChapt-camera Ready2. doc).

Cristea, A. I. and Calvi, L. (2003). *The Three Layers of Adaptation Granularity*, LNCS 2702, Berlin: Springer.

Cristea, A. I. and De Bra, P. (2002). ODL Education Environments Based on Adaptability and Adaptivity. Paper presented at E-Learn'2002 World Conference on E-Learning in Corporate, Government, Healthcare, and Higher Education, October 15–19, Montreal, (http://wwwis.win.tue.nl/~acristea/Conferences/02/ELEARN02/Cristea-Adaptation-Adaptability.pdf).

Cristea, A. I. and Garzotto, F. (2004). *Designing Patterns for Adaptive or Adaptable Educational Hypermedia: A Taxonomy*, Morgantown, WV: Association for the Advancement of Computing in Education (http://wwwis.win.tue.nl/~acristea/HTMP/Minerva/papers/Garzotto-Cristea-symposium-patterns-2give.doc).

Cronbach, J. L. (1957). The two disciplines of scientific psychology. *Am. Psychol.*, 12, 671–684.*

Cronbach, J. L. (1967) How can instruction be adapted to individual differences? In *Learning and Individual Differences*, edited by R. M. Gagné, Ed., pp. 353–379, Columbus, OH: Merrill.*

Cronbach, J. L. and Snow, E. R. (1977). *Aptitudes and Instructional Methods: A Handbook for Research on Interactions*. New York: Irvingston.*

Crowder, N. W. (1959). *Automatic Tutoring: The State of Art*. New York: Wiley.

de Assis, P., Schwabe, D., and Barbosa, S. (2004). Meta-models for adaptive hypermedia applications and meta-adaptation. In *Proceedings of ED-MEDIA 2004: World Conference on Educational Multimedia, Hypermedia, and Telecommunications*, edited by P. Kommers and G. Richards, pp. 1720–1727. Morgantown, WV: Association for the Advancement of Computing in Education.

De Bra, P. (2000). Pros and cons of adaptive hypermedia in Web-based education. *J. CyberPsychol. Behav.*, 3(1), 71–77.

De Bra, P., Aroyo, L., and Chepegin, V. (2004). The next big thing: adaptive Web-based systems, *J. Digit. Inform.*, 5(1), Article No. 247 (http://jodi.tamu.edu/Articles/v05/i01/ DeBra/).

De Bra, P., Santic, T., and Brusilovsky, P. (2003). AHA! meets Interbook, and more…. In *Proceedings of World Conference on the E-Learning, E-Learn 2003*, edited by A. Rossett, pp. 57–64. Morgantown, WV: Association for the Advancement of Computing in Education.

De Bra, P., Stash, N., and Smits, D. (2005). Creating Adaptive Web-Based Applications, tutorial at the 10th Int. Conf. on User Modeling, July 25, Edinburgh, Scotland (retrieved from htto://wwwis.win.tue.nl/~debra/um2005/tutorial.pdf).

De Vicente, A. and Pain, H. (2002) Informing the detection of the students' motivational state: an empirical study. In *Intelligent Tutoring Systems: Proceedings of the Sixth International Conference on Intelligent Tutoring Systems*, LCNS 2363, edited by S. A. Cerri, G. Gouarderes, and F. Paraguacu, pp. 933–943. Berlin: Springer.

del Soldato, T. and du Boulay, B. (1995). Implementation of motivational tactics in tutoring systems. *J. Artif. Intell. Educ.*, 6(4), 337–376.

Dewey, J. (1902/1964). The child and the curriculum. In *John Dewey on Education: Selected Writings*, edited by R. D. Archambault, pp. 339–358. New York: Modern Library.

Dick, W. and Carey, L. (1985). *The Systematic Design of Instruction*, 2nd ed. Glenview, IL: Scott, Foresman.

DiVesta, F. J. (1975). Trait-treatment interactions, cognitive processes, and research on communication media. *AV Commun. Rev.*, 23, 185–196.

du Boulay, B. and Luckin, R. (2001). Modeling human teaching tactics and strategies for tutoring systems. *Int. J. Artif. Intell. Educ.*, 12, 235–256.

Eklund, J. and Sinclair, K. (2000) An empirical appraisal of the effectiveness of adaptive interfaces for instructional systems. *Educ. Technol. Soc.*, 3(4), 165–177.

Federico, P. (1983). Changes in the cognitive components of achievement as students proceed through computer-managed instruction. *J. Comput.-Based Instruct.*, 9(4), 156–168.

Federico, P., Montague, E. W., and Snow, E. R. (1980). *Adaptive Instruction: Trends and Issues. Aptitude, Learning and Instruction, Cognitive Process Analyses of Aptitude*. Mahwah, NJ: Lawrence Erlbaum Associates.

Fink, J., Kobsa, A., and Nill, A. (1998). Adaptable and adaptive information provision for all users, including disabled and elderly people. *New Rev. Hypermedia Multimedia*, 4, 163–188.

Fischer, G., Mastaglio, T., Reeves, B., and Rieman, J. (1990). Minimalist explanations in knowledge-based systems. In *Proceedings of 23rd Annual Hawaii International Conference on System Sciences*, edited by L. W. Hoevel and V. Milutinovic, pp. 309–317. Los Alamitos, CA: IEEE.

Flanagan, J. C., Shanner, W. M., Brudner, H. J., and Marker, R. W. (1975). An individualized instructional system: PLAN. In *Systems of Individualized Education*, edited by H. Talmadge Berkeley, CA: McCutchan.

Gagné, R. M. and Briggs, L. J. (1979). *Principles of Instructional Design*, 2nd ed. New York: Holt.

Glaser, R. (1977). *Adaptive Education: Individual, Diversity and Learning*. New York: Holt.*

Glaser, R. and Resnick, L. B. (1972). Instructional psychology. *Annu. Rev. Psychol.*, 23, 207–276.

Gonschorek, M. and Herzog, C. (1995). Using hypertext for an adaptive help system in an intelligent tutoring system. In *Proceedings of AI-ED'95, 7th World Conference on Artificial Intelligence in Education*, edited by J. Greer, pp. 274–281. Morgantown, WV: Association for the Advancement of Computing in Education.

Hall, A. K. (1977). A research model for applying computer technology to the interactive instructional process. *J. Comput.-Based Instruct.*, 3, 68–75.

Hanani, U., Shapira, B., and Shoval, P. (2001). Information filtering: overview of issues, research and systems. *User Model. User-Adapt. Interact.*, 11(3), 203–259.

Hansen, D. N., Ross, M. S., and Rakow, E. (1977). *Adaptive Models for Computer-Based Training Systems*, Annual Report to Navy Personnel Research and Development Center. Memphis, TN: Memphis State University.

Hart, R. S. (1981). Language study and the PLATO IV System. *Studies Lang. Learn.*, 3, 1–24.

Henze, N. and Nejdl, W. (1999). Adaptivity in the KBS Hyperbook System. In *Proc. of the Second Workshop on Adaptive Systems and User Modeling on the World Wide Web (WWW)*, May 11–14, Toronto, Canada (http://www.kbs.uni-hannover.de/~henze/paperadaptivity/Henze.html).

Henze, N. and Nejdl, W. (2001) Adaptation in open corpus hypermedia. *Int. J. Artif. Intell. Educ.*, 12(4), 325–350.

Hohl, H., Boecker, D., and Gunzenhaeuser, R. (1996). Hyp-adapter: an adaptive hypertext system for exploratory learning and programming. *User Model. User-Adapt. Interact.*, 6(2–3), 131–156.

Holland, G. J. (1977). Variables in adaptive decisions in individualized instruction. *Educ. Psychol.*, 12, 146–161.*

Jermann, P., Soller, A., and Lesgold, A. (2004). Computer software support for CSCL. In *What We Know About CSCL … and Implementing It in Higher Education*, edited by P. Dillenbourg, J. W. Strijbos, P. A. Kirschner, and R. L. Martens pp. 141–166. Boston, MA: Kluwer.

Karagiannidis, C., Sampson, D., and Cardinali, F. (2001). Integrating adaptive educational content into different courses and curricula. *Educ. Technol. Soc.*, 4(3), 37–44

Kay, J. and Kummerfeld, J. R. (1994). An individualized course for the C programming language. In *Proceedings of the Second International WWW Conf.*, October 17–20, Chicago, IL (http://www.cs.usyd.edu.au/~bob/kay-kummerfeld.html).

Kayama, M. and Okamoto, T. (1998). A mechanism for knowledge navigation in hyperspace with neural networks to support exploring activities. In *Proceedings of Current Trends and Applications of Artificial Intelligence in Education Workshop at the 4th World Congress on Expert Systems*, edited by G. Ayala, pp. 41–48. Mexico City: ITESM.

Keller, F. S. and Sherman, J. G. (1974). *The Keller Plan Handbook*. Menlo Park, CA: W.A. Benjamin.

Klausmeier, H. J. (1975). IGE: an alternative form of schooling. In *Systems of Individualized Education*, edited by H. Talmage, pp. 48–83. Berkeley, CA: McCutchan.

Koedinger, K. R. and Anderson, J. R. (1998). Illustrating principled design: the early evolution of a cognitive tutor for algebra symbolization. *Interact. Learn. Environ.*, 5, 161–180.

Kulik, A. J. (1982). Individualized systems of instruction. In *Encyclopedia of Educational Research* 5th ed., edited by H. E. Mitzel, p. 2. New York: Macmillan.

Landa, L. N. (1976). *Instructional Regulation and Control*. Englewood Cliffs, NJ: Educational Technology Publications.*

Lesgold, A. (2001). The nature and methods of learning by doing. *Am. Psychol.*, 56(11), 964–973.*

Lesgold, A. M., Lajoie, S. P., Bunzo, M., and Eggan, G. (1992). SHERLOCK: a coached practice environment for an electronics troubleshooting job. In *Computer Assisted Instruction and Intelligent Tutoring Systems: Shared Issues and Complementary Approaches*, edited by J. Larkin and R. Chabay, pp. 201–238. Hillsdale, NJ: Lawrence Erlbaum Associates.

Lester, J. C., Towns, S. G., and Fitzgerald, P. J. (1999). Achieving affective impact: visual emotive communication in life-like pedagogical agents. *Int. J. Artif. Intell. Educ.*, 10(3–4), 278–291.

Leutner, D. (2004). Instructional design principles for adaptivity in open learning environments. In *Curriculum, Plans, and Processes in Instructional Design*, edited by N. M. Seel and S. Dijkstra, pp. 289–307. Mahwah, NJ: Lawrence Erlbaum Associates.*

Luckin R. and du Boulay B. (1999). Ecolab: the development and evaluation of a Vygotskian design framework. *Int. J. Artif. Intell. Educ.*, 10, 198–220.

Maki, H. R. and Maki, S. W. (2002). Multimedia comprehension skill predicts differential outcomes of Web-based and lecture courses. *J. Exp. Psychol. Appl.*, 8, 85–98.

Merrill, M. D. and Boutwell, R. C. (1973). Instructional development: methodology and research. In *Review of Research in Education*, edited by F. Kerlinger, pp. 95–131. Itasca, IL: Peacock.

Moore, A., Stewart, C. D., Martin, D., Brailsford, T. J., and Ashman, H. (2004). Links for Learning: Linking for an Adaptive Learning Environment. Paper presented at the Third IASTED Int. Conf. on Web-Based Education. February 16–18, Innsbruck, Austria (http://whurle.sourceforge.net/wbe04.pdf).

Ohlsson, S. (1987). Some principles of intelligent tutoring. In *Artificial Intelligence and Education*, edited by R. W. Lawler and M. Yazdani, pp. 203–237. Norwood, NJ: Ablex.

Ohlsson, S. (1993). Learning to do and learning to understand: a lesson and a challenge for cognitive modeling. In *Learning in Humans and Machines*, edited by P. Reimann and H. Spada, pp. 37–62. Oxford: Pergamon Press.*

Oppermann, R. (1994). Adaptively supported adaptability. *Int. J. Hum.-Comput. Stud.*, 40, 455–472.

Or-Bach, R. and van Joolingen, W. R. (2004). Designing adaptive interventions for online collaborative modeling. *Educ. Inform. Technol.*, 9, 355–375.

Park, O. (1996). Adaptive instructional systems. In *Handbook of Research on Educational Communications and Technology*, edited by D. H. Jonassen, pp. 634–664. New York: Macmillan.*

Park, O. and Lee, J. (2003). Adaptive instructional systems. In *Handbook of Research on Educational Communications and Technology*, 2nd ed., edited by D. H. Jonassen, pp. 651–684. Mahwah, NJ: Lawrence Erlbaum Associates.*

Park, O. and Seidel, R. J. (1989). A multidisciplinary model for development of intelligent computer-assisted instruction. *Educ. Technol. Res. Dev.*, 37, 72–80.

Park, O. and Tennyson, D. R. (1980). Adaptive design strategies for selecting number and presentation order of examples in coordinate concept acquisition. *J. Educ. Psychol.*, 72, 362–370.*

Park, O. and Tennyson, D. R. (1986). Computer-based response-sensitive design strategies for selecting presentation form and sequence of examples in learning of coordinate concepts. *J. Educ. Psychol.*, 78, 23–28.

Park, O., Perez, R. S., and Seidel, J. R. (1987). Intelligent CAI: old wine in new bottles or a new vintage? In *Artificial Intelligence and Instruction: Applications and Methods*, edited by G. Kearsley, pp. 11–45. Boston, MA: Addison-Wesley.

Peterson, L. P. (1977). Review of human characteristics and school learning. *Am. Educ. Res. J.*, 14, 73–79.

Peterson, P. L. and Janicki, T. C. (1979). Individual characteristics and children's learning in large-group and small-group approaches. *J. Educ. Psychol.*, 71, 677–687.

Peterson, P. L., Janicki, T. C., and Swing, S. (1981). Ability X treatment interaction effects on children's learning in large-group and small-group approaches. *Am. Educ. Res. J.*, 18, 453–473.

Quintana, C., Zhang, M., and Krajcik, J. (2005). A framework for supporting metacognitive aspects of online inquiry through software-based scaffolding. *Educ. Psychol.*, 40(4), 235–244.

Rebolledo Mendez, G., du Boulay, B., and Luckin, R. (2006). Motivating the Learner: An Empirical Evaluation. Paper presented at the 8th Int. Conf. on Intelligent Learning Systems, June 26–30, Jhongli, Taiwan (http://www.cogs.susx.ac.uk/users/bend/papers/ITS2006.pdf).

Reiser, A. R. (1987). Instructional technology: a history. In *Instructional Technology Foundations*, edited by R. M. Gagné, pp.11–48. Mahwah, NJ: Lawrence Erlbaum Associates.

Roll, I., Aleven, V., McLaren, B. M., Ryu, E., Baker, R., and Koedinger, K. R.(2006). The Help Tutor: Does Metacognitive Feedback Improve Students' Help-Seeking Actions, Skills and Learning? Paper presented at the 8th Int. Conf. on Intelligent Learning Systems, June 26–30, Jhongli, Taiwan (http://www.pitt.edu/~bmclaren/HelpTutor-ITS2006.pdf).

Ross, S. M. and Anand, F. (1986). Using Computer-Based Instruction to Personalize Math Learning Materials for Elementary School Children. Paper presented at the American Educational Research Association Annual Meeting, April, San Francisco, CA.

Ross, S. M. and Morrison, G. R. (1986). Adaptive instructional strategies for teaching rules in mathematics. *Educ. Commun. Technol. J.*, 30, 67–74.

Ross, S. M. and Morrison, G. R. (1988). Adapting instruction to learner performance and background variables. In *Instructional Designs for Microcomputer Courseware*, edited by D. H. Jonassen, pp. 227–243. Mahwah, NJ: Lawrence Erlbaum Associates.*

Ross, S. M. and Rakow, E. A. (1981). Learner control versus program control as adaptive strategies for selection of instructional support on math rules. *J. Educ. Psychol.*, 73, 745–753.

Rothen, W. and Tennyson, D. R. (1977). Pre-task and on-task adaptive design strategies for selecting number of instances in concept acquisition. *J. Educ. Psychol.*, 69, 586–592

Rothen, W. and Tennyson, D. R. (1978). Application of Bayes' theory in designing computer-based adaptive instructional strategies. *Educ. Psychol.*, 12, 317–323.

Scandura, J. M. (1977a). *Problem Solving: A Structural/Processes Approach with Instructional Implications*. New York: Academic Press.*

Scandura, J. M. (1977b). Structural approach to instructional problems. *Am. Psychol.*, 32, 33–53.

Scandura, J. M. (1983). Instructional strategies based on the structural learning theory. In *Instructional-Design Theories and Models: An Overview of Their Current Status*, edited by C. M. Reigeluth, pp. 213–249. Mahwah, NJ: Lawrence Erlbaum Associates.

Schwarz, E., Brusilovsky, P., and Weber, G. (1996). World Wide Intelligent Textbooks. Paper presented at the World Conference on Educational Telecommunications, June 1–22, Boston, MA (http://www.contrib.andrew.cmu.edu/~plb/ED-MEDIA-96.html).

Seidel, R. J. and Park, O. (1994). An historical perspective and a model for evaluation of intelligent tutoring systems. *J. Educ. Comput. Res.*, 10, 103–128.*

Seidel, R. J., Wagner, H., Rosenblatt, R. D., Hillelsohn, M. J., and Stelzer, J. (1978). Learner control of instructional sequencing within an adaptive tutorial CAI environment. *Instruct. Sci.*, 7, 37–80.

Seidel, R. J., Park, O., and Perez, R. (1989). Expertise of CAI: development requirements. *Comput. Hum. Behav.*, 4, 235–256.

Shapiro, A. M. and Niederhauser, D. (2004). Learning from hypertext: research issues and findings. In *Handbook of Research on Educational Communications and Technology*, 2nd ed., edited by D. H. Jonassen, pp. 605–620. Mahwah, NJ: Lawrence Erlbaum Associates.

Shute, V. J. and Psotka, J. (1996). Intelligent tutoring systems: past, present and future. In *Handbook of Research on Educational Communications and Technology*, edited by D. Jonassen, pp. 570–600. New York: Macmillan.*

Shute, V. J. and Towle, B. (2003). Adaptive e-learning. *Educ. Psychol.*, 38(2), 105–114.

Snow, E. R. (1980). Aptitude, learner control, and adaptive instruction. *Educ. Psychol.*, 15, 151–158.*

Snow, E. R. and Swanson, J. (1992). Instructional psychology: aptitude, adaptation, and assessment. *Annu. Rev. Psychol.*, 43, 583– 626.

Söller, A. L. (2001). Supporting social interaction in an intelligent collaborative learning system. *Int. J. Artif. Intell. Educ.*, 12, 40–62.

Söller, A. L., Martínez-Monés, A., Jermann, P., and Muehlenbrock, M. (2005). From mirroring to guiding: a review of state of the art technology for supporting collaborative learning. *Int. J. Artif. Intell. Educ.*, 15(4), 261–290.

Specht, M. and Oppermann, R. (1998). ACE: adaptive courseware environment. *New Rev. Hypermedia Multimedia*, 4, 141–161.

Steinacker, A., Seeberg, C., Rechenberger, K., Fischer, S., and Steinmetz, R. (1998). Dynamically Generated Tables of Contents as Guided Tours in Adaptive Hypermedia Systems. Paper presented at ED-MEDIA/EDTELECOM'99, 11th World Conf. on Educational Multimedia and Hypermedia and World Conf. on Educational Telecommunications, June 19–24, Seattle, WA (http://www.kom.e-technik.tu-darmstadt.de/publications/abstracts/SSR+99–1.html).

Steinberg, E. R. (1991). *Computer-Assisted Instruction: A Synthesis of Theory, Practice, and Technology*. Hillsdale, NJ: Lawrence Erlbaum Associates.

Suppes, P., Fletcher, J. D., and Zanottie, M. (1976). Models of individual trajectories in computer-assisted instruction for deaf students. *J. Educ. Psychol.*, 68, 117–127.

Tennyson, D. R. (1975). Adaptive instructional models for concept acquisition. *Educ. Technol.*, 15(4), 7–15.

Tennyson, R. D. and Christensen, D. L. (1988). MAIS: an intelligent learning system. In *Instructional Designs for Micro-Computer Courseware*, edited by D. Jonassen, pp. 247–274. Mahwah, NJ: Lawrence Erlbaum Associates.

Tennyson, R. D. and Park, O. (1987). Artificial intelligence and computer based learning. In *Instructional Technology: Foundations*, edited by R. M. Gagné, pp. 319–342. Mahwah, NJ: Lawrence Erlbaum Associates.

Thorndike, E. L. (1911). *Individuality*. Boston, MA: Houghton Mifflin.

Tobias, S. (1976). Achievement-treatment interactions. *Rev. Educ. Res.*, 46, 61–74.

Tobias, S. (1987). Learner characteristics. In *Instructional Technology: Foundations*, edited by R. M. Gagné, pp. 207–231. Mahwah, NJ: Lawrence Erlbaum Associates.

Tobias, S. (1989). Another look at research on the adaptation of instruction to students characteristics. *Educ. Psychol.*, 24(3), 213–227.*

Tobias, S. (1994). Interest, prior knowledge, and learning. *Rev. Educ. Res.*, 64, 37–54.

van Merriënboer, J. (2005). Learners in a Changing Learning Landscape: Reflections from an Instructional Design Perspective. Paper presented at the Presidential Workshop and Panel Session at the International Convention of the Association for Educational Communications and Technology (AECT), October 18–22, Orlando, FL (http://www.learndev.org/dl/ibstpi-AECT2005–Merrienboer.pdf#search=%22Merrienboer%20mass-individualization%22).*

Vygotsky, L. (1978). *Mind in Society: The Development of Higher Psychological Processes*. Cambridge, MA: Harvard University Press.

Wang, M. (1980). Adaptive instruction: building on diversity. *Theory Pract.*, 19, 122–128.*

Wang, M. and Lindvall, C. M. (1984). Individual differences and school learning environments. *Rev. Res. Educ.*, 11, 161–225.

Wang, M., Oates, J., and Whiteshew, N. (1995). Effective school responses to student diversity in inner-city schools: a coordinated approach. *Educ. Urban Soc.*, 27(4), 484–503.

Wasson, B. B. (1990). Determining the Focus of Instruction: Content Planning for Intelligent Tutoring Systems. Ph.D. thesis. Saskatchewan: Department of Computational Science, University of Saskatchewan.

Wenger, E. (1987). *Artificial Intelligence and Tutoring Systems: Computational and Cognitive Approaches to the Communication of Knowledge*. Los Altos, CA: Kaufmann.

White, B. Y., Shimoda, T. A., and Frederiksen, J. R. (1999). Enabling students to construct theories of collaborative inquiry and reflective learning: computer support for metacognitive development. *Int. J. Artif. Intell. Educ.*, 10, 151–182.

Whitener, E. M. (1989). A meta-analytic review of the effect on learning of the interaction between prior achievement and instructional support. *Rev. Educ. Res.*, 59, 65–86.

Williams, D. M. (1996). Learner-control and instructional technologies. In *Handbook of Research for Educational Communications and Technology*, edited by D.H. Jonassen, pp. 957–982. Mahwah, NJ: Lawrence Erlbaum Associates.

Wood, H. and Wood, D. J. (1996). Contingency in tutoring and learning. *Learn. Instruct.*, 6(4), 391–398.

Wood, H. and Wood, D. J. (1999). Help seeking, learning and contingent tutoring. *Comput. Educ.*, 33(2/3), 153–170.

Wood, H., Wood, D. J., and Marston, L. (1998). *A Computer-Based Assessment Approach to Whole Number Addition and Subtraction*, Technical Report No. 56. Nottingham, U.K.: Centre for Research in Development, Instruction and Training, University of Nottingham.

Zimmerman, B. J. and Tsikalas, K. E. (2005). Can computer-based learning environments (CBLEs) be used as self-regulatory tools to enhance learning? *Educ. Psychol.*, 40(4), 267–271.

---

* Indicates a core reference.

# 38

# Problem-Based Learning

*Woei Hung*
University of Arizona South, Sierra Vista, Arizona

*David H. Jonassen*
University of Missouri, Columbia, Missouri

*Rude Liu*
Beijing Normal University, Beijing, China

## CONTENTS

Woei Hung, David H. Jonassen, and Rude Liu

## ABSTRACT

Problem-based learning (PBL) is perhaps the most innovative instructional method conceived in the history of education. PBL was originally designed to respond to the criticism that traditional teaching and learning methods fail to prepare medical students for solving problems in clinical settings. Instead of requiring that students study content knowledge and then practice context-free problems, PBL embeds students' learning processes in real-life problems. After its successful implementation in various fields of medical education, PBL is now being implemented throughout higher education as well as in K–12 education. The purpose of this chapter is to inform researchers and practitioners about research findings and issues in PBL that may be used to inform future studies. In this chapter, we review PBL research from the past 30 years. We first describe the history of development and implementation of PBL in various educational settings and define the major characteristics of PBL. We then review the research on PBL. First, we examine the effectiveness of PBL in terms of student learning outcomes, including basic domain knowledge acquisition and applications, retention of content and problem-solving skills, higher order thinking, self-directed learning/lifelong learning, and self-perception. Second, we look at implementation issues, such as tutoring issues, curriculum design issues, and use of technology. Finally, we provide recommendations for future research.

## KEYWORDS

*Curriculum design:* A process of conceiving a plan to define a set of courses constituting an area of specialization that supports the specified learning goal.

*Problem-based learning:* An instructional method that initiates students' learning by creating a need to solve an authentic problem. During the problem-solving process, students construct content knowledge and develop problem-solving skills as well as self-directed learning skills while working toward a solution to the problem.

*Problem solving:* A process of understanding the discrepancy between current and goal states of a problem, generating and testing hypotheses for the causes of the problem, devising solutions to the problem, and executing the solution to satisfy the goal state of the problem.

## INTRODUCTION AND HISTORY

Problem-based learning (PBL) is perhaps the most innovative pedagogical method ever implemented in education. Its effectiveness in facilitating student problem-solving and self-directed learning skills has been widely reported in medical education (Barrows and Tamblyn, 1980; Schmidt, 1983). PBL has also become increasingly popular across disciplines in higher education and K–12 education settings (Barrows, 2000; Dochy et al., 2003; Gallagher et al., 1992; Hmelo-Silver, 2004; Hmelo et al., 2000; Torp and Sage, 2002; Williams and Hmelo, 1998). So, what is PBL? What are the theoretical bases for this instructional method? Why does it receive such attention from researchers and educators across disciplines and age levels? How does it work? And does it really work? We begin this chapter by introducing the origins of PBL and providing a brief history of PBL as background information, followed by a discussion of its conceptual assumptions. We then review research on the effectiveness of PBL and the various implementation issues emerging from PBL research over the past 30 years. Finally, we conclude the chapter with a series of proposed research issues in light of previous experience and empirical evidence from PBL research and implementation, as well as potential research topics for future studies.

### Brief History of PBL

#### *Problem-Based Learning in Medical Education*

Problem-based learning was first developed in medical education in the 1950s. The development of PBL is generally credited to the work of medical educators at McMasters University in Canada in the 1970s. Around the same time, other medical schools in various countries, such as Michigan State University in the United States, Maastricht University in the Netherlands, and Newcastle University in Australia were also developing problem-based learning curricula (Barrows, 1996). PBL was conceived and implemented in response to students' unsatisfactory clinical performance (Barrows, 1996; Barrows and Tamblyn, 1980) that resulted from an emphasis on memorization of fragmented biomedical knowledge in the traditional health science education. This emphasis was blamed for failing to equip students with clinical problem-solving and lifelong learning skills (Albanese and Mitchell, 1993; Barrows, 1996).

In the 1980s, the wider spread of PBL in the United States was accelerated by the GPEP report (Report of the Panel on the General Professional Education of the Physician and College Preparation for Medicine) sponsored by the Association of American Medical Colleges (Muller, 1984). This report made recommendations for changes in medical education, such as promoting independent learning and problem solving, reducing lecture hours, reducing scheduled time, and evaluating the ability to learn independently (Barrows, 1996). These recommendations strongly supported the implementation of PBL in medical education. During this period of time, some medical schools also began to develop alternative, parallel problem-based curricula (e.g., the Primary Care Curriculum at the University of New Mexico, the New Pathways Program in Medical School of Harvard University) for a subset of their students (Aspy et al., 1993; Barrows, 1996). Later, a number of medical schools, such as the University of Hawaii, Harvard University, and the University of Sherbrooke in Canada, assumed the more arduous tasks of converting their entire curriculum to PBL. In the 1990s, many more medical schools, such as Southern Illinois University, Rush, Bowman Gray, and Tufts, adopted PBL as their primary instructional method (Aspy et al., 1993; Barrows, 1994). Since its first implementation several decades ago, PBL has become a prominent pedagogical method in medical schools and health-science-related programs throughout the world, including North America, the Netherlands, England, Germany, Australia, New Zealand, and India.

### Problem-Based Learning Outside the Medical Field

#### Higher Education

The adoption of PBL in higher education outside of the medical field as well as K–12 settings gradually occurred throughout the 1990s. PBL has been applied globally in a variety of professional schools (Boud and Feletti, 1991; Gijselaers et al., 1995; Wilkerson and Gijselaers, 1996), such as architecture (Donaldson, 1989; Maitland, 1998), business administration (Merchand, 1995), chemical engineering (Woods, 1996), engineering studies (Cawley, 1989), law schools (Boud

and Feletti, 1991; Kurtz et al., 1990; Pletinckx and Segers, 2001), leadership education (Bridges and Hallinger, 1992, 1995, 1996; Cunningham and Cordeiro, 2003), nursing (Barnard et al., 2005; Higgins, 1994), social work (Bolzan and Heycox, 1998), and teacher education (Oberlander and Talbert-Johnson, 2004). Moreover, Moust et al. (2005) reported that PBL is also frequently integrated into a wider range of disciplines, such as biology (Szeberenyi, 2005), biochemistry (Osgood et al., 2005), calculus (Seltzer et al., 1996), chemistry (Barak and Dori, 2005), economics (Garland, 1995), geology (Smith and Hoersch, 1995), psychology (Reynolds, 1997), science courses (Allen et al., 1996), physics, art history, educational psychology, leadership education, criminal justice, nutrition and dietetics, and other domains of post-secondary education (Edens, 2000; Savin-Baden, 2000; Savin-Baden and Wilkie, 2004).

#### K–12 Education

In introducing PBL into K–12 education, Barrows and Kelson (1993) systematically developed PBL curricula and teacher-training programs for all high-school core subjects (see Illinois Math and Science Academy, http://www.imsa.edu). Since then, PBL has been promoted by a number of scholars and practitioners for use in basic education (Arends, 1997; Glasgow, 1997; Jones et al., 1997; Kain, 2003; Krynock and Robb, 1999; Savoie and Hughes, 1994; Stepien et al., 2000; Torp and Sage, 2002; Wiggins and McTighe, 1998). Various results of implementations of PBL in K–12 settings have been widely reported. First, PBL has been shown to be effective in conveying a variety of content areas—for example, mathematics (Cognition and Technology Group at Vanderbilt, 1993), science (Kolodner et al., 2003; Linn et al., 1999), literature (Jacobsen and Spiro, 1994), history (Wieseman and Cadwell, 2005), and microeconomics (Maxwell et al., 2005). Second, PBL has been implemented effectively in schools in urban, suburban, and rural communities (Delisle, 1997; Fogarty, 1997). Third, PBL can be used effectively in a wide variety of student populations—for example, gifted elementary-, middle-, and high-school students (Dods, 1997; Gallagher, 1997; Gallagher et al., 1995; Stepien and Gallagher, 1993; Stepien et al., 1993), as well as low-income students (Stepien and Gallagher, 1993).

Interest in PBL is increasing in higher education and K–12 education as evidenced by the widespread publication of books about PBL (such as Barrows, 2000; Duch et al., 2001; Evenson and Hmelo, 2000; Kain, 2003; Torp and Sage, 2002). As Internet servers concerned with PBL (see http://interact.bton.ac.uk/pbl/) reveal, many teachers around the world are using PBL, and the numbers are expected to grow. An increasing number of PBL literature reviews (Albanese and Mitchell, 1993; Dochy et al., 2003; Gijbels et al., 2005; Hmelo-Silver, 2004; Newman, 2003; Smits et al., 2002; Van den Bossche et al., 2000; Vernon and Blake, 1993) and PBL conferences (e.g., PUCP, 2006) also reflect the popularity of PBL.

## ASSUMPTIONS AND CHARACTERISTICS

### Assumptions

A primary assumption of PBL is that when we "solve the many problems we face everyday, learning occurs" (Barrows and Tamblyn, 1980, p. 1). Although such a statement may appear self-evident, this assumption is countered by the public assumption that learning occurs only in formal education settings, so once we leave school we cease to learn. Proponents of PBL believe, as did Karl Popper (1994), that "Alles leben ist Problemlösen [all life is problem solving]." If all life is problem solving, then all life is replete with learning opportunities. As we shall explain later, the most consistent finding from PBL research is the superiority of PBL-trained learners in life-long learning.

In addition to the importance of life-long learning, PBL proponents assume the primacy of problems in learning; that is, learning is initiated by an authentic, ill-structured problem. In PBL classes, students encounter the problem before learning, which is countered by centuries of formal education practice, where students are expected to master content before they ever encounter a problem and attempt to apply the content. Learning in PBL is bounded by problems.

Problem-based learning is based on constructivist assumptions about learning, such as:

- Knowledge is individually constructed and socially co-constructed from interactions with the environment; knowledge cannot be transmitted.
- There are necessarily multiple perspectives related to every phenomenon.
- Meaning and thinking are distributed among the culture and community in which we exist and the tools that we use.
- Knowledge is anchored in and indexed by relevant contexts.

Concomitantly, PBL is underpinned by theories of situated learning, which assume that learning is most effective when it is embedded in authentic tasks that are anchored in everyday contexts. In everyday and professional lives, people continuously solve ill-structured problems, those that have multiple or unknown goals, solution methods, and criteria for solving the problems. Because meaning is derived by learners from interactions with the contexts in which they are working or learning (ideas abstracted from contexts and presented as theories have little, if any, meaning to learners), knowledge that is anchored in specific contexts is more meaningful, more integrated, better retained, and more transferable. One reason for this phenomenon is the ontology that students use to represent their understanding (Jonassen, 2006). Knowledge constructed for solving problems results in epistemological (task-related procedural knowledge) and phenomenological (the world as we consciously experience it) knowledge types. These are richer, more meaningful and memorable representations.

In addition to supporting more meaning by anchoring learning in authentic problems, problems provide a purpose for learning. Without an intention to learn, which is provided by problems, meaningful learning seldom occurs. When studying course content, students who are unable to articulate a clear purpose or intention for learning seldom learn meaningfully. When knowledge is evaluated based on its similarity to an authority, students' epistemological development is retarded. They fail to understand or accommodate multiple perspectives and make no effort to construct their own culturally relevant understanding.

### Characteristics of PBL

Problem-based learning is an instructional methodology; that is, it is an instructional solution to learning problems. The primary goal of PBL is to enhance learning by requiring learners to solve problems. It is a methodology with the following characteristics:

- It is problem focused, such that learners begin learning by addressing simulations of an authentic, ill-structured problem. The content and skills to be learned are organized around problems, rather than as a hierarchical list of topics, so a reciprocal relationship exists between knowledge and the problem. Knowledge building is stimulated by the problem and applied back to the problem.
- It is student centered, because faculty cannot dictate learning.
- It is self-directed, such that students individually and collaboratively assume responsibility for generating learning issues and processes through self-assessment and peer

assessment and access their own learning materials. Required assignments are rarely made.

- It is self-reflective, such that learners monitor their understanding and learn to adjust strategies for learning.
- Tutors are facilitators (not knowledge disseminators) who support and model reasoning processes, facilitate group processes and interpersonal dynamics, probe students' knowledge deeply, and never interject content or provide direct answers to questions.

The PBL learning process normally involves the following steps:

- Students in groups of five to eight encounter and reason through the problem. They attempt to define and bound the problem and set learning goals by identifying what they know already, what hypotheses or conjectures they can think of, what they need to learn to better understand the dimensions of the problem, and what learning activities are required and who will perform them.
- During self-directed study, individual students complete their learning assignments. They collect and study resources and prepare reports to the group.
- Students share their learning with the group and revisit the problem, generating additional hypotheses and rejecting others based on their learning.
- At the end of the leaning period (usually one week), students summarize and integrate their learning.

In the following sections, we discuss PBL effectiveness and implementation issues from PBL research findings.

## RESEARCH RESULTS

Throughout the past several decades, a vast body of research on various aspects of PBL has contributed to our knowledge of PBL. Although PBL has gained popularity in K–12 and higher education, the majority of PBL research continues to be conducted in the medical education field. Within that body of research, some issues, such as the effects of PBL on student performance, have received more attention than others. In the following sections, we will review PBL studies in two major research areas: student learning outcomes and implementation issues.

## Learning Outcomes

### Basic Domain Knowledge Acquisition and Applications

Problem-based learning is often criticized for its emphasis on facilitating higher order thinking and problem-solving skills at the expense of lower level knowledge acquisition. This concern has been expressed not only by teachers (Angeli, 2002) but also by students (Dods, 1997; Lieux, 2001; Schultz-Ross and Kline, 1999). In some cases, the students believed that content was inadequately covered, even though they understood the content more thoroughly (Dods, 1997) and performed comparably to traditional students on assessments (Lieux, 2001).

### Higher Education and K–12 Education

Compared to PBL research conducted within the medical field, empirical studies conducted in nonmedical disciplines and K–12 settings are relatively scarce. Polanco et al. (2004) investigated the effect of PBL on engineering students' academic achievement. They found that, when compared to their counterparts, PBL curriculum significantly enhanced engineering students' performance on the Mechanics Baseline Test, in which the focus of the test was on understanding and application of the concepts rather than recall of factual knowledge. Also, to evaluate the validity of the criticism that PBL students tend to underperform on knowledge acquisition when being measured with standardized tests, Gallagher and Stepien (1996) embarked upon an investigation in which they devised a 65-item multiple-choice test intentionally imitating typical final exams on the topic of American studies. The results showed that no significant difference existed in the content acquisition between students who were in the PBL course and students who were in the non-PBL course; in fact, the PBL students' average gain was higher than the other three traditional classes.

Zumbach et al. (2004) also studied PBL effects on fourth graders in a German elementary school. They found no significant difference on domain knowledge acquisition between students who studied using PBL and traditional formats. Similar results were also found in student learning in a Quantity Food Production and Service course (Lieux, 2001) and diabetes-related learning among adolescents with diabetes (Schlundt et al., 1999). Yet, a significantly lower gain score in economic knowledge was found in PBL classes than in lecture- and discussion-based classes in high-school economics classes (Mergendoller et al., 2000).

## Medical Fields

Research from medical education, on the other hand, provides a rich body of empirical evidence for evaluating the effectiveness of PBL. Blake et al. (2000) reported a very successful implementation of PBL curriculum at the University of Missouri–Columbia. They compared the performance of six classes of medical students from 1995 to 2000 on the U.S. Medical Licensing Examination (USMLE, formerly NBME). They found that the PBL classes performed substantially better on both basic science and clinical science than did the classes under a traditional curriculum. More encouragingly, the mean scores of the PBL classes (1998 and 1999) were significantly higher than their respective national mean scores, and the mean scores of the traditional classes were lower than national mean scores. Especially, the 1996 class (traditional curriculum) scored significantly lower than the national mean score. Also, as measured by key feature problems (KFPs), Doucet et al. (1998) found PBL students performed significantly better on applying knowledge in clinical reasoning than did the traditional students in a headache diagnosis and management course. Similarly, PBL students performed significantly better than their counterparts in their clerkships (Distlehorst et al., 2005) and in podiatric medicine (Finch, 1999). Schwartz et al. (1997) compared PBL and traditional medical students at the University of Kentucky and found that PBL students performed equally well or better on factual knowledge tests and significantly better on the application of the knowledge in an essay exam and a standardized patient exam than did lecture-based students. Also, Shelton and Smith (1998) reported a better pass rate for the PBL biomedical students than their counterparts in both year 1 and year 2 in an undergraduate analytic science theory class.

To summarize existing empirical studies being conducted on PBL, a number of meta-analyses have been conducted. Albanese and Mitchell (1993) examined research from 1972 to 1992, and Vernon and Blake (1993) examined research from 1970 to 1992. Both meta-analyses concluded that, in general, the PBL research findings were mixed. The two meta-analyses agreed that traditional curriculum students perform better on basic science knowledge acquisition, but PBL students perform better on clinical knowledge acquisition and reasoning. Moreover, their finding that PBL students' knowledge acquisition was not robust was confirmed by another meta-analysis of 43 PBL studies conducted 10 years later by Dochy et al. (2003); however, when comparing students' performance on progress tests under PBL and traditional curriculum, Verhoeven et al.'s (1998) findings only partially agreed with the findings of Albanese and Mitchell and Vernon and Blake. They found that the traditional students obtained better scores on basic science, while PBL students performed better on social science; yet, to their surprise, the PBL students did not outperform traditional students on clinical science. Two other PBL literature reviews conducted by Berkson (1993) and Colliver (2000) did not agree with the two seminal meta-analyses and found no convincing evidence to support the superiority of PBL in the acquisition of either basic or clinical knowledge. Nevertheless, they concluded that PBL resulted in similar achievement as did traditional methods, which implied that PBL would not undermine students' acquisition of domain knowledge.

Even though there is consensus that PBL curricula result in better knowledge application and clinical reasoning skills but perform less well in basic or factual knowledge acquisition than traditional curriculum, McParland et al. (2004) demonstrated that undergraduate PBL psychiatry students significantly outperformed their counterparts in examinations, which consisted of multiple-choice questions. Equivalent performance on basic science knowledge acquisition (or USMLE step 1) and knowledge application and clinical reasoning (or USMLE step 2) between students learning under PBL curriculum and traditional curricula was reported in several studies (Alleyne et al., 2002; Antepohl and Herzig, 1999; Blue et al., 1998; Distlehorst et al., 2005; Prince et al., 2003; Tomczak, 1991; Verhoeven et al., 1998).

### Retention of Content

With respect to students' retention of content, PBL research revealed an interesting tendency. In terms of short-term retention, either no difference was found between PBL and traditional students (Gallagher and Stepien, 1996) or PBL students recalled slightly less (Dochy et al., 2003); yet, PBL students consistently outperformed traditional students on long-term retention assessments (Dochy et al., 2003; Mårtenson et al., 1985; Tans et al., 1986, as cited in Norman and Schmidt, 1992). In reviewing the studies that investigated the effects of PBL over time, Norman and Schmidt (1992) found some interesting results in several studies. Tans and associates found that PBL students' recall was up to five times greater on the concepts studied than traditional students 6 months after the course was completed. The study by Mårtenson et al. (1985) showed that no difference was found in the short-term retention of the content between PBL students and traditional students; however, the PBL students' long-term retention rate (average 25 points out of 40) was 60% higher than that of traditional students (average 16 points out of 40) 2 to 4-1/2 years after the course was completed. Also, the PBL students tended to remember more about principles, whereas the traditional students retained more rote-memorization types of knowledge. Similarly, Eisensteadt et al. (1990) discovered that PBL students retained less than traditional students in the immediate recall test. Nonetheless, their retention rate remained rather consistent 2 years later, while the traditional students' retention had declined significantly. Dochy et al.'s (2003) review of PBL studies also echoed Norman and Schmidt's observation. Norman and Schmidt (1992), therefore, concluded that PBL might not improve students' initial acquisition of knowledge; however, the deeper processing of information in PBL classes appears to foster better retention of knowledge over a longer period of time.

### Problem-Solving Skills

Improving problem-solving skills is one of the essential promises of PBL. The results of PBL research by and large support this assumption. Gallagher et al. (1992) conducted an experiment using an interdisciplinary PBL course called Science, Society and Future (SSF) on gifted high-school students with a comparison group of high-school students. They found that PBL students showed a significant increase in the use of the problem-finding step from pretest to post-test, which was a critical problem-solving technique. In contrast, in the post-test, the comparison group tended to skip the problem-finding step and move directly from the fact-finding step to the implementation step. The result suggested that PBL is effective in fostering students' development of appropriate problem-solving processes and skills.

Moreover, PBL has shown a positive impact on students' abilities to apply basic science knowledge and transfer problem-solving skills in real-world professional or personal situations. Lohman and Finkelstein (1999) found that the first-year dental education students in a 10-month PBL program improved significantly in their near transfer of problem-solving skills by an average of 31.3%, and their far transfer of problem-solving skills increased by an average of 23.1%. Based on their data, they suggested that repeated exposure to PBL was the key for facilitating the development of problem-solving skills. Several studies have shown that PBL has very positive effects on students' transfer of problem-solving skills to workplaces; for example, Woods (1996) reported that employers praised McMaster University's PBL chemical engineering graduates' outstanding problem-solving skills and job performance. Compared to other new employees who typically required 1 to 1-1/2 years of on-the-job training to be able to solve problems independently, " [the PBL graduates] think for themselves and solve problems upon graduation" (Woods, 1996, p. 97). Kuhn's (1998) study also illustrated the rapid development of expertise of first-year PBL residents in the emergency room. A superior ability to synthesize basic knowledge and clinical experience (Patel et al., 1991), in addition to applying and transferring the knowledge and skills into the workplace, may explain why PBL students outperformed traditional students in NBME/USMLE Part 2 while PBL students seemingly possessed slightly less basic science knowledge than traditional students as shown in their performance in NBME/USMLE Part 1. Clinical reasoning and solving problems on the job require more than mere memorization of factual knowledge. Norman and Schmidt (1992) pointed out that no evidence exists to confirm PBL advantages in general problem-solving skills that are content free, which, again, supports the effectiveness of authentic, contextualized learning in PBL.

### Higher Order Thinking

Higher order thinking is an important cognitive skill required for developing sophisticated problem-solving skills and executing complex ill-structured problem-solving processes. To be an effective problem solver, students need to possess analytical, critical thinking, and metacognitive skills. Articulating problem spaces requires analytical skills (Newell and Simon, 1972), evaluating information involves critical thinking skills, and reflecting on one's own problem-solving process requires metacognitive skills. Shepherd (1998) reported that fourth- and fifth-grade students gained a significantly greater increase in critical thinking skills measured by the Cornell Critical Thinking Test (CCTT) than did the comparison group after participating in a 9-week PBL course (the Probe Method). Schlundt et al. (1999) also observed an improvement of self-efficacy in insulin administration management, problem-solving skills, and flexibilities in choosing coping strategies to overcome the difficulty of dietary adherence among adolescent diabetic patients who received a 2-week PBL summer program. They concluded that, instead of just teaching the facts, the PBL course helped the patients rationalize the self-care guidelines and consider more alternatives to seek better solutions and strategies to cope with the difficult lifestyle. Furthermore, in a longitudinal study of the problem-solving performance of medical students using PBL and traditional methods, Hmelo (1998) observed that students' problem-solving skills and processes changed qualitatively over time. This change was certainly influenced by the type of curriculum. The students in the PBL curriculum, she noted, generated more accurate hypotheses and coherent explanations for their hypotheses, used hypothesis-driven reasoning, and also were more likely to explain their hypotheses and findings with science concepts as compared to traditional students.

### Self-Directed Learning/Life-Long Learning

The ultimate goal of PBL is to educate students to be self-directed, independent, life-long learners. Through actively executing problem-solving processes and observing tutors' modeling problem-solving, reasoning, and metacognitive processes, PBL students learn how to think and learn independently. Though their data did not support the superiority of PBL on knowledge or general problem-solving skills acquisition, Norman and Schmidt (1992) concluded that PBL appeared to enhance self-directed learning. This conclusion was supported by Woods' (1996) assessment of chemical engineering students' comfort level toward self-directed learning. Ryan (1993) also reported a significant increase in PBL students' perceptions of their abilities as self-directed learners at the end of the semester in a health-science-related course. Moreover, Blumberg and Michael (1992) used students' self-reports and library circulation statistics as measures of students' self-directed learning behaviors between a PBL class (partially teacher-directed) and a lecture-based class. They concurred that PBL promoted self-directed learning behaviors in students. Similar evidence was also found in a number of studies, such as those by Coulson and Osborne (1984), Dwyer (1993), Dolmans and Schmidt (1994), and van den Hurk et al. (1999).

The long-term effects of PBL on helping students develop self-directed/life-long learning skills and professional preparation was even more evident in other research results. Two studies revealed that PBL graduates rated themselves better prepared professionally than their counterparts in terms of interpersonal skills, cooperation skills, problem-solving skills, self-directed learning, information gathering, professional skills (e.g., running meetings), and the ability to work and plan efficiently and independently (Schmidt and van der Molen, 2001; Schmidt et al., 2006). Moreover, in Woods' (1996) study mentioned before, the PBL alumni and the employers who hired the PBL graduates gave highly positive comments regarding their self-directedness and independence in solving work-related problems and improving professional development. These studies provided strong evidence for the positive long-term effects of PBL on students' self-directed and life-long learning skills and attitudes.

Reflection is another essential element required for self-directed learning in PBL (Barrows and Myers, 1993). The reflective inquiry process used in the study by Chrispeels and Martin (1998) provided the students in an administrative credential program with a meta-cognitive framework. This reflective process helped the students become effective problem solvers by exercising higher order thinking skills to identify personal and organizational factors that constituted the administrative problems they faced in work settings.

### Self-Perception and Confidence

From students' perspectives, the effects of PBL have been positively perceived. Numerous studies have shown that students consider PBL to be effective in promoting their learning in dealing with complex problems (Martin et al., 1998), enhancing their confidence in judging alternatives for solving problems (Dean, 1999), acquiring social studies content (Shepherd, 1998), enriching their learning of basic science information (Caplow et al., 1997), developing thinking and problem-solving skills (Lieux, 2001), improving interpersonal and professional skills (Schmidt and van der Molen, 2001; Schmidt et al., 2006), and advancing self-directed learning, higher level thinking, and enhancement of information management skills (Kaufman and Mann, 1996).

In summary, PBL research results overall have clearly demonstrated advantages of PBL for preparing students for real-world challenges. The emphasis of PBL curricula on application of domain knowledge, problem solving, higher order thinking, and self-directed learning skills equips students with professional and life-long learning habits of mind, which are indispensable qualities of successful professionals. Although PBL students' performance in basic domain knowledge acquisition has been slightly inferior to traditional students, the format of the tests and the time-delay effects (PBL students have been found to retain information much longer and better than traditional students) may justify this result. This speculation may suggest further research issues and merit empirical evidence to shed deeper insight on these aspects of PBL.

## Implementation of PBL

Problem-based learning is considered by many researchers to be the most innovative instructional method to date. As indicted before, these beliefs are anchored in PBL's atypical instructional process and components. They include learning initiated by problems, self-directed learning, and collaborative learning in small groups. These components, which are radically different from traditional instructional methods, inevitably produce a considerable impact on the dynamics between instructors and students, among students, and on instructors and students' roles and responsibilities during the course of PBL.

### Student Roles, Tutor Roles, and Tutoring Issues

The students as well as instructors have encountered great challenges when transitioning from traditional instructional methods to PBL. These challenges might have evolved from students' as well as tutors' interpretations of self-directed learning. According to Miflin and associates (Miflin, 2004; Miflin et al., 1999, 2000), self-directed learning in PBL could range from preorganized teaching, student-initiated and -selected but instructor-guided learning, to completely self-taught learning. This wide spectrum of interpreting self-directed learning could have contributed to the confusion or unsettled feeling for the students while defining their roles in PBL courses. Similar uncertainty also occurred with the tutors when assuming their roles in the students' learning process. In the following sections, we discuss the perceptions of students as well as tutors in terms of their roles in the PBL processes, as well as the tutoring factors that influence student learning.

#### Students' Transition from Traditional Methods to PBL

In PBL, the students become the initiators of their own learning, the inquirers and problem solvers during the learning process, and they are no longer passive information receivers. The students not only are required to redefine their roles in the learning process but must also retune their learning habits. Woods (1994, 1996) speculated that uncertainty about their grades was one possibility accounting for students' uneasiness about a new instructional method, resulting in some resistance to change and making the initial transition from traditional curriculum to PBL curriculum more difficult. Schmidt et al. (1992) reported that students need at least 6 months to adapt to this new instructional method. The concern about the sufficiency of content coverage also partially contributed to students' anxiety during PBL (Lieux, 2001; Schultz-Ross and Kline, 1999). Jost et al. (1997) examined students' discomfort levels with PBL in the initial stage of instruction by analyzing the students' journals, self-evaluations, and a survey. They found that the students' anxiety mainly resulted from their uncertainty about their roles and responsibilities in the course and how they would be evaluated. The difficulty of assuming a more active role with more responsibility in the learning process

also results from the students' "learned" definition of roles in traditional methods (Dean, 1999; Jost et al., 1997, p. 90). Similar observations were also reported in studies by Fiddler and Knoll (1995), Dabbagh et al. (2000), and Lieux (2001). Furthermore, as Miflin and associates (1999, 2000) conjectured, the questionable presumption that adult learners are capable of conducting highly self-directed learning may also play a role in students' difficulties in transiting to PBL.

Although the sense of discomfort and anxiety is common among students during the initial stage of PBL implementation, Schultz-Ross and Kline (1999) found that the students' discomfort and dissatisfaction levels decreased significantly by the end of a PBL forensic psychiatry course. They reported that some students expressed uneasiness during the initial transition stage of PBL curriculum. Nonetheless, once the students adjusted to PBL environments and realized the merits of PBL, their perceived comfort levels about the learning issues of testimony, liability, and competence improved significantly, as did their perceptions regarding the subject matter (forensic psychiatry) learned in the course. Dabbagh et al. (2000) confirmed Schultz-Ross and Kline's observation.

#### Tutors' Roles in PBL

Barrows (1992) asserted that the two major responsibilities of tutors in PBL are facilitating the students' development of thinking or reasoning skills that promote problem solving, metacognition, and critical thinking, as well as helping them to become independent and self-directed learners. As Maudsley (1999) stated, the effectiveness of tutors is essential to the success of PBL. Maudsley suggested that PBL provides an opportunity for educators to redefine the nature of learning and, in turn, reposition their roles in teaching from a knowledge/information transmitter to a learning/thinking process facilitator. This shift requires PBL tutors to undergo a fundamental reconceptualization of their educational roles. Research showed that, after having gone through this reconceptualization process, a conceptual shift similar to that of the students also occurred among tutors.

Based on their data, Donaldson and Caplow (1996) described the PBL tutor's precarious position as a *dilemma*. Their research on the role expectations of PBL tutors revealed two major dilemmas perceived by PBL tutors: the conceptualization of facilitator and the tensions that arise as tutors tried to redefine their role in PBL as compared to their previous role as medical teacher. Naturally, PBL tutors' adjustments and perhaps some discomfort about their new roles were inevitable and anticipated. Margetson (1998) argued that this paradigm shift in instructional strategy could be threatening to teachers who need to maintain control of the learning environment and prefer passive students. In addition, teachers who conceive knowledge as a body of information that should be transmitted from the knowledgeable teacher to the unknowing student could also feel threatened by the PBL process; thus, Maudsley (1999) cautioned that the PBL tutor must balance a degree of participation in students' learning processes and refrain from the temptation to lecture. Aguiar (2000) conducted an exploratory qualitative case study that examined teachers' perceptions and experiences in their roles as PBL tutors. Five main themes emerged describing how tutors perceived their roles within PBL: (1) facilitating group work, (2) role modeling, (3) providing feedback, (4) imparting information, and (5) supporting students' professional development. Furthermore, Wilkerson and Hundert (1998) described the challenge of multiple roles experienced by PBL tutors and assigned the following names to the roles they identified in PBL tutors: information disseminator, evaluator, parent, professional consultant, confidant, learner, and mediator.

### Cognitive Congruence and Active Involvement

Schmidt and Moust (1995) introduced the concept of *cognitive congruence* as a necessary characteristic of an effective PBL tutor. Cognitive congruence is communication skills defined as "the ability to express oneself in the language of the students, using the concepts they use and explaining things in ways easily grasped by students" (Schmidt and Moust, 1995, p. 709). The effective communication skills are a premise for the other components of effective tutoring. Moreover, the authenticity of tutors' interactions is exhibited in their ability to communicate with students informally while maintaining an empathetic attitude. In addition, effective tutors must be willing to be actively involved with students. In the study by Martin et al. (1998), over 75% of the students felt that the faculty involved in the PBL course were passive and believed that their learning experiences would have been better if the faculty had more actively supported the students. The students' perceptions of tutors' passive involvement may have resulted from the tutors' misinterpretation of self-directed learning as self-taught learning discussed earlier.

### Modeling Metacognition Skills and Self-Directed Learning

Mayo et al. (1993) examined students' perceptions of tutor effectiveness in a PBL surgery clerkship, and their data indicated the importance of the tutor as a "metacognitive guide." As metacognitive guides, PBL tutors help promote students' development of clinical reasoning skills through actively modeling this process for the students. While not giving the answers, the tutors model what questions an expert physician would ask in a clinical setting and guide students to formulate questions as expert physicians would. Similar results were also obtained in Wilkerson's (1995) examination of students' perceptions of effective tutors. The results of a similar study conducted by Donaldson and Caplow (1996) echoed previous findings that effective tutors fell into three categories of role content: (1) facilitation expertise, (2) knowledge or cognitive expertise, and (3) clinical reasoning expertise. Students deemed tutors as effective and helpful when they encouraged students to critically evaluate the information gathered, questioned and probed the students' clinical reasoning processes, and, most importantly, allowed students to control the learning process. Questioning the students' clinical reasoning processes serves two functions: verifying the appropriateness of the students' reasoning and modeling expert physician's reasoning processes. Allowing self-control in the learning process is essential for students to develop self-directedness in their own learning.

### Group Processing

Collaborative learning is another essential element of PBL. A study by Martin et al. (1998) indicated that collaborative group processing in PBL was identified as an enhancer for the students' metacognitive skills. Utilization of collaborative learning in instruction is theoretically sound; however, it may not be as straightforward as it sounds in practice. Achilles and Hoover (1996) pointed out a major concern in their study of implementing PBL at grades 6 to 12 that students had difficulty working in groups. The need for effective guidance of group processing was perceived not only by K–12 students but also by the medical students. When Mayo et al. (1993) examined tutor effectiveness in facilitating group processing, they found that tutor skills differed significantly. When 44 students evaluated 16 tutors using 12 characteristics determined to be essential to tutor effectiveness, the results revealed four consequential facilitation skills: (1) helping the group be aware of how group processing works, (2) encouraging feedback within the group, (3) guiding the group to set appropriate learning issues, and (4) assisting the group to integrate learning issues.

Similarly, De Grave et al. (1999) used the Tutor Intervention Profile (TIP) to assess the effectiveness of PBL tutors and found that mastering the enhancement of the learning process in the tutorial group was one of the characteristics that the students valued. Thus, researchers have suggested that the skills and knowledge for creating productive collaboration relationships (Wilkerson, 1995) and an unthreatening working atmosphere (Schmidt and Moust, 1995) are critical. Furthermore, group size has also been found to be a factor that has potential effects on students' learning processes and outcomes. In studying the effects of group size on students' self-directedness, Lohman and Finkelstein (2000) found that the medium-sized group (six students) performed significantly better than the large group (nine students). Group processing is especially difficult when PBL is implemented in a large class. To address this issue, Shipman and Duch (2001) suggested that more structure of group processes is needed for facilitating large PBL classes. An interesting finding obtained by Elshafei (1998) was that, when students' higher level thinking in solving algebra problems was assessed, PBL did not show positive effects on students' performance when they were tested individually; yet, PBL appeared to be more effective when the students were tested in groups. This finding, whether PBL students' learning outcomes are collective or individual, seems worth pondering and pursuing further.

*Expert Knowledge*

The importance of expert knowledge is a relatively uncertain characteristic in facilitating group processing. When assessing the effectiveness of PBL tutors with TIP, De Grave et al. (1999) suggested that the occurrence of effective tutoring depended heavily on the use of expert knowledge. Also, Schmidt and Moust (1995) asserted that a suitable knowledge base with regard to the topic under study was imperative; yet, others (Davis et al., 1992; Silver and Wilkerson, 1991) have raised concerns that content experts tend to lecture and give explanations, which may undermine the intent of promoting students' self-directed learning. The majority of the research pertaining to this debate showed no significant differences in tutors' performance and students' perception about tutorial processes between content-experts and non-content-experts (Gilkison, 2003; Kaufman and Holmes, 1998; Regehr et al., 1995). Students generally rated expert tutors more effective than non-expert tutors, and in some of the studies (such as that by Eagle et al., 1992), students performed slightly better with expert tutors than with non-expert tutors. Yet, using students' perceptions and immediate learning outcomes as measures of effective tutoring could have masked what really happened; for example, Kaufman and Holmes (1998) observed that expert tutors have a more difficult time with the role of facilitator and tend to provide more explanations of case content. Similarly, Gilkison (2003) noted that the expert tutor initiated more topics

for discussion than the non-expert tutor (52% vs. 12.5%), and the non-expert tutor engaged more in facilitating group processes (55.9% vs. 38.5%) and less in directing learning (5.9% vs. 11.4%). These observations offered a plausible explanation for the expert tutors' better performance. Further examination of the interaction of expert and non-expert tutoring and students' development of self-directed learning skills would provide better insight on this issue. Also, the implications of these observations should be taken into account by PBL curriculum developers or designers when considering employing tutors who possess expert knowledge.

*Assessment Issues*

The assessment used in the early implementation of PBL largely relied on traditional U.S. board exams, which were standardized tests designed to assess students' factual knowledge (NBME step 1) and clinical reasoning (NBME step 2). Nendaz and Tekian (1999) criticized traditional assessment as not being in line with the principles of PBL; therefore, the PBL students' performance might have been at a disadvantage under traditional assessment. Fortunately, Blake et al. (2000) noted a shift in USMLE in more recent years such that the emphasis of assessment has moved from testing factual knowledge to assessing application of the knowledge. This change not only benefits the students who study under PBL curriculum but also signals an increasing attention to students' abilities to apply and transfer basic knowledge instead of focusing on factual knowledge acquisition. A number of different methodologies have been developed to assess students' problem-solving skills, reasoning skills, and personal progress; for example, according to the classification by Swanson et al. (1998), there are outcome-oriented instruments, such as the progress test (Van der Vleuten et al., 1996), essay exams, oral and structured oral examinations, patient-management problems, clinical reasoning exercises (Wood et al., 2000), problem-analysis questions (Des Marchais et al., 1993), and standardized patient-based tests, as well as process-oriented instruments, such as the triple-jump-based exercises (Smith, 1993), Medical Independent Learning Exercise (MILE) (Feletti et al., 1984), the four-step assessment test (4SAT) (Zimitat and Miflin, 2003), formative assessment (Neufeld et al., 1989), and tutor, peer, and self-assessment.

As Savin-Baden (2004) contended, assessment is probably one of the most controversial issues in PBL because it is probably the most important indicator for validating its effectiveness. The mixed results of PBL students' learning outcomes discussed earlier might have been largely due to incomparable assessment being used. In their meta-analysis of PBL research, Gijbels et al. (2005) found that the effects of PBL varied mostly depending on the focus of assessment instrument used. PBL had the most positive effects when the instrument focused on assessing the understanding of principles that link concepts. This may explain the pattern seen in PBL research that traditional students performed better in basic knowledge acquisition while PBL students did better in application of knowledge and clinical reasoning. Reviewing the assessment in the medical schools implementing PBL from 1966 to 1998, Nendaz and Tekian (1999) concluded that a lack of uniformity existed with regard to the assessment methodologies used in measuring PBL students' performance.

### Curriculum Design in PBL

A distinct characteristic of PBL is that learning is initiated by presenting a problem rather than teaching the content. If so, what is instruction in PBL? To this question, Barrows (1996, p. 8) stated that: "The curricular linchpin in PBL ... is the collection of problems in any given course or curriculum with each problem designed to stimulate student learning in areas relevant to the curriculum." This collection of problems is designed to fulfill four educational objectives in PBL: (1) structuring of knowledge for use in clinical contexts, (2) developing an effective clinical reasoning process, (3) developing effective self-directed learning skills, and (4) increasing motivation for learning (Barrows, 1986, pp. 481–482). Based on these educational objectives, Barrows developed a taxonomy for classifying PBL curricula into six categories using two variables with three levels each. The two variables include the degrees of self-directedness and problem structuredness. He further defined the three levels of the variable of self-directedness as teacher-directed, student-directed, and partially student and teacher directed. The three levels of the variable of problem structuredness were defined as complete case, partial-problem simulation, and full-problem simulation (free inquiry). The combination of the two variables and three levels creates a categorization of PBL curriculum design, which includes lecture-based cases, case-based lectures, case method, modified case-based, problem-based, and closed-loop problem-based. The decision regarding which category of PBL design a given PBL curriculum should take should be based on the degree of the educational objectives that must be reached and the characteristics of learners.

In more recent developments of PBL curriculum design, students were gradually being included in the curriculum design process to provide insights from students' perspectives. Chung and Chow (2004) reported that the students' workload and assessment methods designed in the curriculum were improved to better address students' capabilities and promoted learning when student representation was included in the curriculum design process. In medical schools, PBL curricula are usually designed by a team of faculty members and instructional designers; however, PBL in K–12 education and higher education, as Maxwell et al. (2001) indicated, is often adopted by a single teacher or implemented in a single course rather than as a departmental curriculum. It is much more challenging, therefore, for individual teachers to independently design PBL problems for their classes without resources and support from administration (Angeli, 2002). This may explain the considerably fewer implementations of PBL in K–12 and higher education settings than in medical-related fields.

### Problem Design

Given that a PBL curriculum consists of a collection of problems, there is no doubt that the problems themselves are crucial to the success of PBL (Duch, 2001; Trafton and Midgett, 2001). Perrenet et al. (2000) contended that students' learning could be enhanced by manipulating the quality of PBL problems because they in fact could influence students' activation of prior knowledge, their group processing, self-directed learning (Gijselaers and Schmidt, 1990), and generation of useful learning issues (Dolmans et al., 1993). Selecting and writing appropriate and effective PBL problems are very challenging and difficult tasks (Angeli, 2002); however, the issues of the effectiveness of problems and designing PBL problems have not been researched adequately.

### Effectiveness of Problems

The effectiveness of problems determines the effectiveness of PBL curriculum. The quality of PBL problems affects not only various aspects of student learning but also academic achievement. Ineffective problems could, as Dolmans et al. (1993) argued, cause students difficulty in generating learning issues that the problem is designed to cover and hence lead to insufficient content knowledge acquisition. To elucidate the effectiveness of PBL problems used in medical education, four studies set out to investigate this issue, and they yielded very similar results. According to Dolmans et al. (1993), the effectiveness of problems is defined as the degree of correspondence between student-generated learning issues and faculty objectives. When assessing how accurately the students identified learning issues that were specified by the faculty to a given problem, Coulson and Osborne (1984) found that on average students identified 24.0 learning issues out of 39.3 objectives (about 62%). Dolmans et al. (1993) analyzed the correspondence between the instructors' intended objectives and student-generated learning issues based on their interpretations of the PBL problems. They found that only 64% of intended content was identified in the student-generated learning issues. The degrees of correspondence between objectives specified by the faculty and the student-generated learning issues for the 12 problems ranged from 27.7 to 100%. Similarly, O'Neill (2000) reported a 62% correspondence rate between faculty objectives and student-generated learning issues. In the study by van Gessel et al. (2003), a 62% match between faculty and student objectives and learning issues was obtained. In these four studies, in addition to the student-generated learning issues that matched faculty objectives, irrelevant learning issues were generated by the students. These results showed that insufficient content coverage in PBL could in fact occur; hence, without assurance of the quality of problem or intended aims being met, the effects of PBL would be unpredictable and therefore questionable.

*Problem Design Models and Principles*

A number of researchers have discussed and provided suggestions and guidelines for designing PBL problems; for example, Duch (2001) suggested a process of five stages of writing PBL problems (choose a central idea, think of a real-world context for the concept, stage the problem to lead students' research, write a teacher's guide, and identify resources for students). Lee (1999) proposed a decision model for problem selection in which selection of the PBL problem is a function of learning objectives, prior knowledge, domain knowledge, problem structuredness and complexity, and time availability. Aiming at promoting higher order thinking, Weiss (2003) suggested several principles for designing PBL problems, including considering students' prior knowledge, using ill-structured and authentic problems, and promoting collaborative, life-long, and self-directed learning. Stinson and Milter (1996) also offered design guidelines that PBL problems should be holistic, ill-structured, and contemporary and should mirror professional practice. A step-by-step PBL problem development cycle was proposed by Drummond-Young and Mohide (2001). This eight-step design process was designed specifically for nursing education and includes the following steps: (1) review expected learning outcomes, (2) determine content, (3) select a priority health issue and develop the problem, (4) develop supplementary material, (5) seek

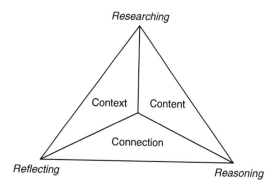

**Figure 38.1** The 3C3R problem-based learning (PBL) problem design model.

evaluative feedback, (6) pilot the problem, (7) revise and refine the problem, and (8) integrate the problem into the curriculum. These problem design guidelines, principles, and processes are very helpful yet overly general or excessively profession specific; therefore, they are inadequate for providing educators and practitioners with a complete conceptual framework and the systematic design process required for designing effective PBL problems for learners across disciplines and ages.

Compared to PBL research on student learning outcomes, tutor techniques, student perceptions, or group processing, research on PBL problem design is rather scarce and unsystematic. To provide PBL educators and practitioners with a systematic conceptual framework for designing effective and reliable PBL problems, Hung (2006a) introduced the 3C3R model as a conceptual framework for systematically designing optimal PBL problems. The 3C3R PBL problem design model is a systematic method specifically designed to guide instructional designers and educators to design effective PBL problems for all levels and across disciplines of learners by strengthening the characteristics of PBL and alleviating implementation issues revealed in previous research on PBL, such as dilemmas of depth vs. breadth of content and factual knowledge acquisition vs. problem-solving skills acquirement (Albanese and Mitchell, 1993; Gallagher and Stepien, 1996; Hung et al., 2003). The 3C3R model (see Figure 38.1) has two classes of components: core components and processing components. The core components—content, context, and connection—are primarily concerned with the issues of appropriateness and sufficiency of content knowledge, knowledge contextualization, and knowledge integration. The processing components—researching, reasoning, and reflecting—deal with students' acquisition of content knowledge and the development of problem-solving skills and self-directed learning skills.

Following the establishment of the 3C3R model, Hung (2006b) further developed a nine-step problem design process to operationalize the conceptual framework into a step-by-step process:

Step 1. Set goals and objectives.
Step 2. Conduct content/task analysis.
Step 3. Analyze context specification.
Step 4. Select/generate PBL problem.
Step 5. Conduct PBL problem affordance analysis.
Step 6. Conduct correspondence analysis.
Step 7. Conduct calibration processes.
Step 8. Construct reflection component.
Step 9. Examine inter-supporting relationships of 3C3R components.

## Use of Technology in PBL

The use of technology in PBL follows two major trajectories: distance learning and use of multimedia.

### Distance Learning and PBL

Most commonly, PBL takes place in a small group with intensive face-to-face discussions among students with guidance from tutors. With the development of technology and increasing popularity of the Internet, more and more online or distributed PBL (dPBL, defined as the use of PBL in an online environment; Cameron et al., 1999) curricula have been experimented with or implemented in the subject areas of, for example, social economy (Björck, 2002), education (Orrill, 2002), and science (Kim et al., 2001). To support PBL implementation at the University of Delaware, a Web-based technology system was utilized to help instructors organize courses (syllabi, groups, projects, and student reports) and to facilitate electronic communication (discussion sessions and between instructors and students), as well as provide online resources in support of PBL course development, such as ingredients for writing problems, inspiration for problem design, and information for solving problems (Watson, 2002).

In studying the effects of Internet technology on students' learning in PBL, Reznich and Werner (2001) observed a general positive effect, especially on the discussion process, in which the tutors played an important role in ensuring the success of the group sessions and guiding students to use electronic resources. In reviewing the literature of online PBL, we found that better access and retrieval of information are the main advantages of online PBL (Helokunnas and Herrala, 2001; Reznich and Werner, 2001; Watson, 2002); however, online environments seemed to fail to deliver the promise of fostering collaborative learning, which many online PBL advocates have claimed, due to unsophisticated and cumbersome technology (Barrows, 2002; Orrill, 2002).

### Use of Multimedia in PBL

Utilizing multimedia in constructing PBL environments is also gaining more attention as technology advances. The promise of using multimedia to enhance PBL is based on the assumption that PBL should take place in an authentic context (Albion and Gibson, 1998) to help students encode specificity of information, which is one of the necessary conditions for learning to occur (Schmidt, 1983). Some researchers (such as Hoffman and Ritchie, 1997) have argued that paper or oral presentation of PBL problems does not provide sufficient contextual or environmental information to prepare students to be able to recognize salient visual, auditory, or nonverbal cues that are crucial in some professions (Bridges, 1992). This implicit contextual information, such as social conventions or phenomenon and cultural/cross-cultural issues (Conway et al., 2002; Yamada and Maskarinec, 2004) or locality (Hays and Gupta, 2003), is lost in most conventional paper- or oral-based problem cases. This argument was confirmed by a study by Kamin et al. (2001) of the effects of different modalities on students' critical thinking abilities in a PBL course. They presented two groups of students with a problem in text format or video format. The results revealed that the video group did not identify as much of the information given in the problem as the text group. This performance of the video group in fact better resembled real-life situations; however, the video group examined the information more critically than the text group, who tended to accept the face value of the information given in the problem. Also, the video group had more active group processing than their counterparts. Bowdish et al. (2003) reported an experiment with a prototype of VPBL (virtual PBL). The VPBL incorporated multiple modalities, including digital video, images, text, questions, and text boxes, to present problem scenarios and facilitate the PBL process. This VPBL environment allowed the learners to observe the patient–doctor conversations and the doctor's bedside manner, to examine a chief complaint (for example, listening to heart and lung sounds), and to order and view diagnostic studies. To their surprise, no significant difference was found in the students' Teaching and Learning Environment Questionnaire (TLEQ) and achievement scores between the text-based group and the VPBL group. Similarly, William et al. (1998) reported that no difference existed in achievement scores when comparing computer-based and paper PBL with seventh graders in learning science concepts. Another case of using multimedia in PBL to promote situated learning was reported by Zumbach et al. (2004). Their results also showed no significant differences in elementary students' factual knowledge acquisition and problem-solving skills under the multimedia-enhanced PBL or traditional class; however, the multimedia-enhanced PBL class showed a significantly higher level of motivation to learn as well as retention of knowledge than did the traditional class.

# DIRECTIONS FOR FUTURE RESEARCH

As indicated earlier in this chapter, PBL is an instructional methodology. The PBL model calls for the construction of problem sets of authentic problems and the engagement of learning groups in negotiating learning issues to solve those problems. Although PBL has been shown to be successful in supporting deep levels of understanding, problem-solving skills, and lifelong learning, PBL research should pay more attention to the nature of the problems being solved. The PBL methodology assumes that all problems are solved in the same way and can be learned in the same way. We believe that this is a questionable assumption.

## Problem Types and PBL

Probably the most important research question is that of addressing the nature of problems that are amenable to PBL. PBL emerged in medical schools, where students learn to solve diagnosis–solution problems, which are moderately ill structured. The goal of diagnosis is to find the source of the physiological anomaly; however, numerous paths can lead to a diagnosis. In the treatment or management part of the process, the problem often becomes more ill structured because of multiple treatment options, patient beliefs and desires, insurance companies, and so on.

Problem-based learning has migrated in academic institutions to law schools, where students learn to construct arguments based on evidentiary reasoning, a complex form of rule-using problem. PBL is becoming increasingly popular in graduate business programs, where students primarily solve case analysis problems that are fairly ill structured. As PBL migrates to other academic programs, such as engineering, research must be focused on the nature of the problems being solved and how efficacious PBL methodologies are for those kinds of problems. Along the continuum from well-structured to ill-structured problems (Jonassen, 2000), which kinds of problems can be effectively supported using PBL? For example, can PBL be adapted to word problems in physics, despite the inau-

thentic nature of those problems? The kind of problem that engineers most commonly solve is the design problem, which typically tends to be the most complex and ill-structured kind of problem that can be solved. Given an initial statement of need, an infinite number of potential solutions exists. Can learners self-direct their ability to solve this kind of problem or is some form of studio course required to accommodate its complexity? What is the range of complexity and structuredness that can be effectively learned using PBL? When Jacobs et al. (2003) surveyed medical students with a questionnaire that was designed based on Jonassen's continuum of structuredness and complexity of problems, they found that students weighted problem structuredness more heavily than problem complexity, which indicated that students preferred some degree of structuredness to identify a solution more easily. Taking students' perceptions into account in addition to the nature of the subject matter, then, how well-structured or ill-structured can and should PBL problems be? This will require comparing successes and failures across domains.

Assuming that PBL is effective for a range of problems, a related question is whether the established PBL methodology is equally appropriate for all kinds of problems, or should the method be adapted to accommodate different kinds of problems? Jonassen (2004) has prescribed different models for designing learning environments for story problems, troubleshooting problems, and case-analysis problems. Models for additional kinds of problems (e.g., design, decision making) are under development, but we do not know how unique each model for each kind of problem will be. A number of instructional supports, such as case libraries, question ontologies, simulations, argumentation systems, and problem representation tools, may be effective across several kinds of problems. We simply do not know.

## Internal Factors and PBL

Problem-based learning was originally developed for training medical students. In those contexts, educators assume that students are cognitively ready for solving ill-structured problems and engaging in self-directed learning. As more PBL efforts are being implemented in K–12 schools, because of human development issues, younger students may not be ready to solve complex and ill-structured problems and self-direct their own learning. The question of learner characteristics (e.g., developmental level, epistemological beliefs, cognitive controls, maturity, reading ability) related to PBL has not been significantly addressed. Moreover, developing problem solving and self-directed learning skills is both a goal of the course of learning and at the same time a required ability to succeed in PBL classes. So, frustration or detrimental effects may be inevitable if the learners (younger students or even adult students) possess few problem-solving and self-directed learning skills when they begin a PBL course. How can we reconcile this circulative prerequisite and goal requirement in the PBL process?

## Designing Distributed PBL

With the emergence of online learning initiatives, researchers are working to implement PBL in online environments (Tan and Hung, 2007). This trend raises numerous implementation issues. How faithfully can PBL methodologies be applied online? An important element in PBL group processing and collaborative learning is building a sense of learning community. Barrows (2002) and Orrill (2002) showed that collaboration suffered in online PBL environments. Clearly, there is a distinct difference between conventional face-to-face and online PBL in the degree of social presence, which is defined by two factors: intimacy and immediacy (Wiener and Mehrabian, 1968). Given current technology, a low degree of intimacy and immediacy is inherent in online environments; thus, how do learning groups collaborate effectively to negotiate meaning? How can tutors effectively nurture and guide learning online? How can we support self-directed learning online? What compromises, if any, are required to engage learners in PBL online? Although the e-learning movement is not conceptually driven and the technology has not been as sophisticated as promised, it appears to be inevitable enough that these become important questions.

Multimedia can have a strong impact on the effectiveness of PBL when studying subjects for whom the ability to detect signs, symptoms, or behaviors through visual, audio, or tactile senses is crucial for solving problems. Appropriate modality of presentation of the problem could play a significant role in enhancing students' problem-solving skills in their fields. When training students, such abilities are one of the focuses of PBL curricula. Text-based problems would either give away the cues or be unable to afford the learning objectives of developing self-directed problem-solving skills; however, based on research results to date, the use of multimedia has seemed to fail to produce such effects. Thus, we might ask: Is it that the tutors did not take advantage of the technology and practice the same tutoring techniques as they did with text-based problems? What kind of facilitation should be given to guide students to the critical contextual information presented in the problem?

These issues that have emerged from experiences in implementing PBL in the past, as well as in response to new technology developments in the present, challenge PBL researchers and practitioners yet provide opportunities for new insights to be discovered in the future. Only continuing research will provide intellectual and scientific support to inform and improve the practice of PBL as well as education in general.

## REFERENCES

Achilles, C. M. and Hoover, S. P. (1996). Exploring Problem-Based Learning (PBL) in Grades 6–12. Paper presented at the Annual Meeting of the Mid-South Educational Research Association, November 6–8, Tuscaloosa, AL (ERIC Document Reproduction Service No. ED 406 406).

Aguiar, A. C. (2000). Consequences for Faculty of Changes in Medical Education: The Experience of Tutoring a Course About the Patient–Doctor Relationship. Ph.D. dissertation. Boston, MA: Harvard University (*Diss. Abstr. Int.*, 61, 1853B).

Albanese, M. A. and Mitchell, S. (1993). Problem-based learning: a review of literature on its outcomes and implementation issues. *Acad. Med.*, 68, 52–81.

Albion, P. R. and Gibson, I. W. (1998). Interactive multimedia and problem-based learning: challenge for instructional design. In *Proceedings of the 10th ED-MEDIA/ED-TELECOM 98 World Conference on Educational Multimedia and Hypermedia and World Conference on Educational Telecommunications*, June 20–25, Freiburg, Germany. Norfolk, WV: Association for the Advancement of Computing in Education (ERIC Document Reproduction Service No. 428 647).

Allen, D. E., Duch, B. J., and Groh, S. E. (1996). The power of problem-based learning in teaching introductory science course. In *Bringing Problem-Based Learning into Higher Education: Theory and Practice*, edited by L. Wilkerson and W. H. Gijselaers, pp. 43–52. San Francisco, CA: Jossey-Bass.

Alleyne, T., Shirley, A., Bennett, C., Addae, J., Walrond, E., West, S., and Pinto Pereira, L. (2002). Problem-based compared with traditional methods at the faculty of medical sciences, university of West India: a model study. *Med. Teacher*, 24(3), 273–279.

Angeli, C. (2002). Teachers' practical theories for the design and implementation of problem-based learning. *Sci. Educ. Int.*, 13(3), 9–15.

Antepohl, W. and Herzig, S. (1999). Problem-based learning versus lecture-based learning in a course of basic pharmacology: a controlled, randomized study. *Med. Educ.*, 33(2), 106–113.

Arends, R. I. (1997). *Classroom Instruction and Management*. New York: McGraw-Hill.

Aspy, D. N., Aspy, C. B., and Quinby, P. M. (1993). What doctors can teach teachers about problem-based learning. *Educ. Leadership*, 50(7), 22–24.

Barak, M. and Dori, Y. J. (2005). Enhancing undergraduate students' chemistry understanding through project-based learning in an IT environment. *Sci. Educ.*, 89(1), 117–139.

Barnard, A., Nash, R., and O'Brien, M. (2005). Information literacy: developing lifelong skills through nursing education. *J. Nurs. Educ.*, 44(11), 505–510.

Barrows, H. S. (1986). A taxonomy of problem-based learning methods. *Med. Educ.*, 20, 481–486.*

Barrows, H. S. (1992). *The Tutorial Process.* Springfield, IL: Southern Illinois University School of Medicine.

Barrows, H. S. (1994). *Practice-Based Learning: Problem-Based Learning Applied to Medical Education.* Springfield, IL: Southern Illinois University School of Medicine.

Barrows, H. S. (1996). Problem-based learning in medicine and beyond: a brief overview. In *Bringing Problem-Based Learning to Higher Education: Theory and Practice*, edited by L. Wilkerson and W. H. Gijselaers, pp. 3–12. San Francisco, CA: Jossey-Bass.

Barrows, H. S. (2000). *Problem-Based Learning Applied to Medical Education.* Springfield, IL: Southern Illinois University School of Medicine.

Barrows, H. S. (2002). Is it truly possible to have such a thing as dPBL? *Dist. Educ.*, 23(1), 119–122.

Barrows H. S. and Kelson, A. (1993). *Problem-Based Learning in Secondary Education and the Problem-Based Learning Institute* [monograph]. Springfield, IL: Southern Illinois University School of Medicine.

Barrows, H. S. and Myers, A. C. (1993). *Problem-Based Learning in Secondary Schools* [unpublished monograph]. Springfield, IL: Problem-Based Learning Institute, Lanphier High School, and Southern Illinois University Medical School.

Barrows, H. S. and Tamblyn, R. M. (1980). *Problem-Based Learning: An Approach to Medical Education.* New York: Springer.*

Berkson, L. (1993). Problem-based learning: have the expectations been met? *Acad. Med.*, 68, S79–S88.

Björck, U. (2002). Distributed problem-based learning in social economy: key issues in students' mastery of a structured method for education. *Dist. Educ.*, 23(1), 85–103.

Blake, R. L., Hosokawa, M. C., and Riley, S. L. (2000). Student performances on step 1 and step 2 of the United States Medical Licensing Examination following implementation of a problem-based learning curriculum. *Acad. Med.*, 75, 66–70.

Blue, A. V., Stratton, T. D., Donnelly, M. B., Nash, P. P., and Schwartz, R. W. (1998). Students' communication apprehension and its effects on PBL performance. *Med. Teacher*, 20(3), 217–221.

Blumberg, P. and Michael, J. A. (1992). Development of self-directed learning behaviors in a partially teacher-directed problem-based learning curriculum. *Teaching Learn. Med.*, 4(1), 3–8.

Bolzan, N. and Heycox, K. (1998). Use of an issue-based approach in social work education. In *The Challenge of Problem-Based Learning*, 2nd ed., edited by D. Boud and G. Feletti, pp. 194–202. London: Kogan Page.

Boud, D. and Feletti, G., Eds. (1991). *The Challenge of Problem-Based Learning.* New York: St. Martin's Press.

Bowdish, B. E., Chauvin, S. W., Kreisman, N., and Britt, M. (2003). Travels towards problem based learning in medical education (VPBL). *Instruct. Sci.*, 31, 231–253.

Bridges, E. M. and Hallinger, P. (1992). *Problem-Based Learning for Administrators.* Eugene, OR: ERIC Clearinghouse on Educational Management (ERIC Document Reproduction Service No. 347 617).

Bridges, E. M. and Hallinger, P. (1995). *Implementing Problem-Based Learning in Leadership Development.* Eugene, OR: ERIC Clearinghouse on Educational Management.

Bridges, E. M. and Hallinger, P. (1996). Problem-based learning in leadership education. In *Bringing Problem-Based Learning into Higher Education: Theory and Practice*, edited by L. Wilkerson and W. H. Gijselaers, pp. 53–61. San Francisco, CA: Jossey-Bass.

Cameron, T., Barrows, H. S., and Crooks, S. M. (1999). Distributed Problem-Based Learning at Southern Illinois University School of Medicine. Paper presented at the Computer Supported Collaborative Learning Conf. (CSCL'99), December 12–15, Stanford, CA.

Caplow, J. H., Donaldson, J. F., Kardash, C. A., and Hosokawa, M. (1997). Learning in a problem-based medical curriculum: students' conceptions. *Med. Educ.*, 31, 1–8.

Cawley, P. (1989). The introduction of a problem-based option into a conventional engineering degree course. *Stud. Higher Educ.*, 14, 83–95.

Chrispeels, J. H. and Martin, K. J. (1998). Becoming problem solvers: the case of three future administrators. *J. Sch. Leadersh.*, 8, 303–331.

Chung, J. C. C. and Chow, S. M. K. (2004). Promoting student learning through a student-centered problem-based learning subject curriculum. *Innov. Educ. Teaching Int.*, 41(2), 157–168.

Cognition and Technology Group at Vanderbilt (CTGV). (1993). Anchored instruction and situated cognition revisited. *Educ. Technol.*, 33(3), 52–70.*

Colliver, J. A. (2000). Effectiveness of problem-based learning curricula: research and theory. *Acad. Med.*, 75(3), 259–266.

Conway, J., Little, P., and McMillan, M. (2002). Congruence or conflict? Challenges in implementing problem-based learning across nursing cultures. *Int. J. Nurs. Pract.*, 8(5), 235–23

Coulson, R. L. and Osborne, C. E. (1984). Insuring curricular content in a student-directed problem-based learning program. In *Tutorial in Problem-Based Learning Program*, edited by H. G. Schmidt and M. L. de Volder, pp. 225–229. Assen, the Netherlands: Van Gorcum.

Cunningham, W. G. and Cordeiro, P. A. (2003). *Educational Leadership: A Problem-Based Approach.* Boston, MA: Pearson Education.

Dabbagh, N. H., Jonassen, D. H., Yueh, H.-P., and Samouilova, M. (2000). Assessing a problem-based learning approach to an introductory instructional design course: a case study. *Perform. Improv. Q.*, 13(3), 60–83.

Davis, W. K., Nairn, R., Paine, M. E., Anderson, R. M., and Oh, M. S. (1992). Effects of expert and non-expert facilitators on the small-group process and on student performance. *Acad. Med.*, 67, 407–474.

De Grave, W. S., Dolmans, D. H. J. M., and Van der Vleuten, C. P. M. (1999). Profiles of effective tutors in problem-based learning: scaffolding student learning. *Med. Educ.*, 33, 901–906.

Dean, C. D. (1999). Problem-Based Learning in Teacher Education. Paper presented at the Annual Meeting of American Educational Research Association, April 19–23, Montreal, Quebec (ERIC Document Reproduction Service No. ED 431 771).

Delisle, R. (1997). *How to Use Problem-Based Learning in the Classroom.* Alexandria, VA: Association for Supervision and Curriculum Development.

Des Marchais, J. E., Dumais, B., Jean, P., and Vu, N. V. (1993). An attempt at measuring student ability to analyze problems in the Sherbrooke problem-based curriculum: a preliminary study. In *Problem-Based Learning as an Educational Strategy*, edited by P. Bouhuijs, H. G. Schmidt, and H. J. M. van Berkel, pp. 239–248. Maastricht, the Netherlands: Network Publication.

Distlehorst, L. H., Dawson, E., Robbs, R. S., and Barrows, H. S. (2005). Problem-based learning outcomes: the glass half-full. *Acad. Med.*, 80(3), 294–299.

Dochy, F., Segers, M., van den Bossche, P., and Gijbels, D. (2003). Effects of problem-based learning: a meta-analysis. *Learn. Instruct.*, 13, 533–568.

Dods, R. F. (1997). An action research study of the effectiveness of problem-based learning in promoting the acquisition and retention of knowledge. *J. Educ. Gifted*, 20, 423–437.

Dolmans, D. H. J. M. and Schmidt, H. G. (1994). What drives the student in problem-based learning? *Med. Educ.*, 28, 372–380.

Dolmans, D. H. J. M., Gijselaers, W. H., Schmidt, H. G., and van der Meer, S. B. (1993). Problem effectiveness in a course using problem-based learning. *Acad. Med.*, 68(3), 207–213.

Donaldson, J. F. and Caplow, J. A. H. (1996). Role Expectations for the Tutor in Problem-Based Learning. Paper presented at the Annual Meeting of the American Educational Research Association, April 8–12, New York.

Donaldson, R. (1989). A good start in architecture. In *Problem-Based Learning: The Newcastle Workshop*, edited by B. Wallis, pp. 41–53. Newcastle, Australia: University of New-castle.

Doucet, M. D., Purdy, R. A., Kaufman, D. M., and Langille, D. B. (1998). Comparison of problem-based learning and lecture format in continuing medical education on headache diagnosis and management. *Med. Educ.*, 32, 590–596.

Drummond-Young, M. and Mohide, E. A. (2001). Developing problems for use in problem-based learning. In *Transforming Nursing Education Through Problem-Based Learning*, edited by E. Rideout, pp. 165–191. Boston, MA: Jones and Bartlett.

Duch, B. J. (2001). Writing problems for deeper understanding. In *The Power of Problem-Based Learning: A Practical 'How To' for Teaching Undergraduate Courses in Any Discipline*, edited by B. Duch, S. E. Groh, and D. E. Allen, pp. 47–53. Sterling, VA: Stylus Publishing.

Duch, B. J., Groh, S. E., and Allen, D. E., Eds. (2001). *The Power of Problem-Based Learning: A Practical 'How to' for Teaching Undergraduate Courses in Any Discipline*. Steer-ling, VA: Stylus Publishing.*

Dwyer, J. (1993). Predicting self-directed learning readiness: a problem or not? In *Research and Development in Problem-Based Learning*, edited by G. Ryan, pp. 219–232. Sydney, Australia: MacArthur.

Eagle, C. J., Harasym, P. H., and Mandin, H. (1992). Effects of tutors with case expertise on problem-based learning issues. *Acad. Med.*, 67, 465–469.

Edens, K. (2000). Preparing problem solvers for the 21st century through problem-based learning. *Coll. Teaching*, 48(2), 55–60.

Eisensteadt, R. S., Barry, W. E., and Glanz, K. (1990). Problem-based learning: cognitive retention and cohort traits of randomly selected participants and decliners. In *Research in Medical Education 1990: Proceedings of the Twenty-Ninth Annual Conference*, edited by B. Anderson, pp. S11–S12. Washington, D.C.: Association of American Medical Colleges.

Elshafei, D. L. (1998). A Comparison of Problem-Based and Traditional Learning in Algebra II. Ph.D. dissertation. Bloomington, IN: Indiana University.

Evenson, D. H. and Hmelo, C. E., Eds. (2000). *Problem-Based Learning: A Research Perspective on Learning Interactions*. Mahwah NJ: Lawrence Erlbaum Associates.

Feletti, G., Saunders, N., Smith, A. J., and Engel, C. (1984). Assessment of independent learning. *Med. Teacher*, 6, 70–73.

Fiddler, M. B. and Knoll, J. W. (1995). Problem-based learning in an adult liberal learning context: learner adaptations and feedback. *Contin. Higher Educ. Rev.*, 59(1/2), 13–24.

Finch, P. M. (1999). The effect of problem-based learning on the academic performance of students studying podiatric medicine in Ontario. *Med. Educ.*, 33, 411–417.

Fogarty, R. (1997). *Problem-Based Learning and Other Curriculum Models for the Multiple Intelligences Classroom*. Arlington Heights, IL: IRI Skylight Training and Publishing.

Gallagher, S. A. (1997). Problem-based learning: where did it come from, what does it do, and where is it going? *J. Educ. Gifted*, 20(4), 332–362.

Gallagher, S. A. and Stepien, W. J. (1996). Content acquisition in problem-based learning: depth versus breadth in American studies. *J. Educ. Gifted*, 19(3), 257–275.

Gallagher, S. A., Stepien, W. J., and Rosenthal, H. (1992). The effects of problem-based learning on problem solving. *Gifted Child Q.*, 36(4), 195–200.

Gallagher, S. A., Sher, B. T., Stepien, W. J., and Workman, D. (1995). Implementing problem-based learning in the science classroom. *Sch. Sci. Math.*, 95, 136–146.

Garland, N. J. (1995). Peer group support in economics: Innovations in problem-based learning. In *Educational Innovation in Economics and Business Administration: The Case of Problem-Based Learning*, edited by W. H. Gijselaers, D. Tempelaar, P. Keizer, E. Bernard, and H. Kasper, pp. 331–337. Dordrecht: Kluwer.

Gijbels, D., Dochy, F., van den Bossche, P., and Segers, M. (2005). Effects of problem-based learning: a meta-analysis from the angle of assessment. *Rev. Educ. Res.*, 75(1), 27–61.*

Gijselaers, W. H. and Schmidt, H. G. (1990). Development and evaluation of a causal model of problem-based learning. In *Innovation in Medical Education: An Evaluation of Its Present Status*, edited by Z. H. Nooman, H. G. Schmidt, and E. S. Ezzat, pp. 95–113. New York: Springer.

Gijselaers, W. H., Tempelaar, D. T., Keizer, P. K., Blommaert, J. M., Bernard, E. M., and Kasper, H., Eds. (1995). *Educational Innovation in Economics and Business Administration: The Case of Problem-Based Learning*. Norwell, MA: Kluwer.

Gilkison, A. (2003). Techniques used by 'expert' and 'non-expert' tutors to facilitate problem-based learning tutorials in an undergraduate medical curriculum. *Med. Educ.*, 37, 6–14.

Glasgow, N. A. (1997). *New Curriculum for New Times: A Guide to Student-Centered, Problem-Based Learning*. Thousand Oaks, CA: Corwin.*

Hays, R. and Gupta, T. S. (2003). Ruralising medical curricula: the importance of context in problem design. *Aust. J. Rural Health*, 11, 15–17.

Helokunnas, T. and Herrala, J. (2001). Knowledge searching and sharing on virtual networks. *Proc. ASIST 2001*, 38, 315–22.

Higgins, L. (1994). Integrating background nursing experience and study at the postgraduate level: an application of problem based learning. *Higher Educ. Res. Dev.*, 13, 23–33.

Hmelo, C. E. (1998). Problem-based learning: effects on the early acquisition of cognitive skill in medicine. *J. Learn. Sci.*, 7(2), 173–208.

Hmelo, C. E., Holton, D. L., and Kolodner, J. L. (2000). Designing to learning about complex systems. *J. Learn. Sci.*, 9, 247–298.

Hmelo-Silver, C. E. (2004). Problem-based learning: what and how do students learn? *Educ. Psychol. Rev.*, 16(3), 235–266.*

Hoffman, B. and Ritchie, D. (1997). Using multimedia to overcome the problems with problem based learning. *Instruct. Sci.*, 25, 97–115.

Hung, W. (2006a). The 3C3R model: a conceptual framework for designing problems in PBL. *Interdiscip. J. Problem-Based Learn.*, 1(1), 55–77.*

Hung, W. (2006b). A 9-Step PBL Problems Designing Process: Application of the 3C3R Model. Paper presented at the 2006 AERA Annual Meeting, April 8–12, San Francisco, CA.

Hung, W., Bailey, J. H., and Jonassen, D. H. (2003). Exploring the tensions of problem-based learning: insights from research. *In Problem-Based Learning in the Information Age*, edited by D. Knowlton and D. Sharp, pp. 13–23. San Francisco, CA: Jossey-Bass.*

Jacobs, A. E. J. P., Dolmans, D. H. J. M., Wolfhagen, I. H. A. P., and Scherpbier, A. J. J. A. (2003). Validation of a short questionnaire to assess the degree of complexity and structuredness of *PBL* problems. *Med. Educ.*, 37(11), 1001–1007.

Jacobsen, M. and Spiro, R. J. (1994). A framework for the contextual analysis of technology-based learning environments. *J. Comput. Higher Educ.*, 5(2), 3–32.

Jonassen, D. H. (2000). Toward a design theory of problem solving. *Educ. Technol. Res. Dev.*, 48(4), 63–85.*

Jonassen, D. H. (2004). *Learning to Solve Problems: An Instructional Design Guide*. San Francisco, CA: Jossey-Bass.*

Jonassen, D. H. (2006). Accommodating ways of human knowing in the design of information and instruction. *Int. J. Knowl. Learn.*, 2(3/4), 181–190.

Jones, B. F., Rasmussen, C. M., and Moffitt, M. C. (1997). *Real-Life Problem Solving: A Collaborative Approach to Interdisciplinary Learning*. Washington, D.C.: American Psychological Association.

Jost, K. L., Harvard, B. C., and Smith, A. J. (1997). A study of problem-based learning in a graduate education classroom. *In Proceedings of Selected Research and Development Presentations at the 1997 National Convention of the Association for Educational Communications and Technology*, February 14–18, Albuquerque, NM (ERIC Document Reproduction Service No. ED 409 840).

Kain, D. L. (2003). *Problem-Based Learning for Teachers, Grades K–8*. Boston, MA: Pearson Education.

Kamin, C. S., O'Sullivan, P. S., Younger, M., and Deterding, R. (2001). Measuring critical thinking in problem-based learning discourse. *Teaching Learn. Med.*, 13(1), 27–35.

Kaufman, D. M. and Holmes, D. B. (1998). The relationship of tutors' content expertise to interventions and perceptions in a PBL medical curriculum. *Med. Educ.*, 32, 255–261.

Kaufman, D. M. and Mann, K. V. (1996). Students' perceptions about their courses in problem-based learning and conventional curricula. *Acad. Med.*, 71(1), S52–S54.

Kim, H., Chung, J.-S., and Kim, Y. (2001). Problem-based learning in Web-based science classroom. *In Annual Proceedings of Selected Research and Development and Practice Papers Presented at the National Convention of the Association for Educational Communications and Technology*, November 8–12, Atlanta, GA (ERIC Document Reproduction Service No. ED 470 190).

Kolodner, J. L., Camp, P. J., Crismond, D., Fasse, B., Gray, J., Holbrook, J., Puntambekar, S., and Ryan, M. (2003). Problem-based learning meets case-based reasoning in the middle-school science classroom: putting Learning by Design™ into practice. *J. Learn. Sci.*, 12(4), 495–547.*

Krynock, K. and Robb, L. (1999). Problem solved: how to coach cognition. *Educ. Leadersh.*, 57(3), 29–32.

Kuhn, G. J. (1998). Designing Problem-Based Instruction to Foster Expertise in Emergency Medicine Residents. Ph.D. dissertation. Detroit, MI: Wayne State University (*Diss. Abstr. Int.*, 59, 0713A).

Kurtz, S., Wylie, M., and Gold, N. (1990). Problem-based learning: an alternative approach to legal education. *Dalhousie Law J.*, 13, 787–816.

Lee, J. (1999). Problem-based learning: a decision model for problem selection. *In Proceedings of Selected Research and Development Papers Presented at the National Convention of the Association for Educational Communications and Technology (AECT)*. February 10–14, Houston, TX (ERIC Document Reproduction Service No. ED 436 162).

Lieux, E. M. (2001). A skeptic's look at PBL. *In The Power of Problem-Based Learning: A Practical 'How To' for Teaching Undergraduate Courses in Any Discipline*, edited by B. Duch, S. E. Groh, and D. E. Allen, pp. 223–235. Sterling, VA: Stylus Publishing.

Linn, M. C., Shear, L., Bell, P., and Slotta, J. D. (1999). Organizing principles for science education partnerships: case studies of students learning about 'rats in space' and 'deformed frogs.' *Educ. Technol. Res. Dev.*, 47(2), 61–84.

Lohman, M. C. and Finkelstein, M. (1999). Segmenting Information in PBL Cases to Foster the Development of Problem-Solving Skill, Self-Directedness, and Technical Knowledge [unpublished manuscript]. Florida State University/University of Iowa.

Lohman, M. C. and Finkelstein, M. (2000). Designing groups in problem-based learning to promote problem-solving skill and self-directedness. *Instruct. Sci.*, 28, 291–307.

Maitland, B. (1998). Problem-based learning for an architecture degree. *In The Challenge of Problem-Based Learning*, 2nd ed., edited by D. Boud and G. Feletti, pp. 211–217. London: Kogan Page.

Margetson, D. (1998). Why is problem-based learning a challenge? *In The Challenge of Problem-Based Learning*, 2nd ed., edited by D. Boud and G. Feletti, pp. 36–44. London: Kogan Page.

Mårtenson, D., Eriksson, H., and Ingelman-Sundberg, M. (1985). Medical chemistry: evaluation of active and problem-oriented teaching methods. *Med. Educ.*, 19, 34–42.

Martin, K. J., Chrispeels, J. H., and D'eidio-Caston, M. (1998). Exploring the use of problem-based learning for developing collaborative leadership skills. *J. School Leadersh.*, 8, 470–500.

Maudsley, G. (1999). Roles and responsibilities of the problem-based learning tutor in the undergraduate medical curriculum. *Br. Med. J.*, 318, 657–660.

Maxwell, N. L., Bellisimo, Y., and Mergendoller, J. R. (2001). Problem-based learning: modifying the medical school model for teaching high school economics. *Soc. Stud.*, 92(2), 73–78.

Maxwell, N. L., Mergendoller, J. R., and Bellisimo, Y. (2005). Problem-based learning and high school macroeconomics: a comparative study of instructional methods. *J. Econ. Educ.*, 36(4), 315–331.

Mayo, P., Donnelly, M. B., Nash, P. P., and Schwartz, R. W. (1993). Student perceptions of tutor effectiveness in a problem-based surgery clerkship. *Teaching Learn. Med.*, 5(4), 227–233.

McParland, M., Noble, L., and Livingston, G. (2004). The effectiveness of problem-based learning compared to traditional teaching in undergraduate psychiatry. *Med. Educ.*, 38(8), 859–867.

Merchand, J. E. (1995). Problem-based learning in the business curriculum: an alternative to traditional approaches. In *Educational Innovation in Economics and Business Administration: The Case of Problem-Based Learning*, edited by W. Gijselaers, D. Tempelaar, P. Keizer, E. Bernard, and H. Kasper, pp. 261–267. Dordrecht: Kluwer.

Mergendoller, J. R., Maxwell, N. L., and Bellisimo, Y. (2000). Comparing problem-based learning and traditional instruction in high school economics. *J. Educ. Res.*, 93(6), 374–382.

Miflin, B. M. (2004). Adult learning, self-directed learning and problem-based learning: deconstructing the connections. *Teaching Higher Educ.*, 9(1), 43–53.

Miflin, B. M., Campbell, C. B., and Price, D. A. (1999). A lesson from the introduction of a problem-based, graduate entry course: the effects of different views of self-direction. *Med. Educ.*, 33, 801–807.

Miflin, B. M., Campbell, C. B., and Price, D. A. (2000). A conceptual framework to guide the development of self-directed, lifelong learning in problem-based medical curricula. *Med. Educ.*, 34, 299–306.

Moust, J. H. C., van Berkel, H. J. M., and Schmidt, H. G. (2005). Signs of erosion: reflections on three decades of problem-based learning at Maastricht University. *Higher Educ.*, 50(4), 665–683.

Muller, S. (1984). Physicians for the twenty-first century: report of the project panel on the general professional education of the physician and college preparation for medicine. *J. Med. Educ.*, 59(11, part 2), 1–208.

Nendaz, M. R. and Tekian, A. (1999). Assessment in problem-based learning medical schools: a literature review. *Teaching Learn. Med.*, 11(4), 232–243.

Neufeld, V. R., Woodward, C. A., and MacLeod, S. M. (1989). The McMaster MD program: a case study of renewal in medical education. *Acad. Med.*, 64, 423–432.

Newell, A. and Simon, H. A. (1972). *Human Problem Solving*. Englewood Cliffs, NJ: Prentice Hall.*

Newman, M. (2003). *A Pilot Systematic Review and Meta-Analysis on the Effectiveness of Problem-Based Learning*. Cambridge, U.K.: Teacher and Learning Research Program, Cambridge University (http://www.ltsn-01.ac.uk/resources/features/pbl).

Norman, G. R. and Schmidt, H. G. (1992). The psychological basis of problem-based learning: a review of the evidence. *Acad. Med.*, 67(9), 557–565.*

O'Neill, P. A. (2000). The role of basic sciences in a problem-based learning clinical curriculum. *Med. Educ.*, 34, 608–613.

Oberlander, J. and Talbert-Johnson, C. (2004). Using technology to support problem-based learning. *Action Teacher Educ.*, 25(4), 48–57.

Orrill, C. H. (2002). Supporting online PBL: design considerations for supporting distributed problem solving. *Dist. Educ.*, 23(1), 41–57.

Osgood, M. P., Mitchell, S. M., and Anderson, W. L. (2005). Teachers as learners in a cooperative learning biochemistry class. *Biochem. Mol. Biol. Educ.*, 33(6), 394–398.

Patel, V. K., Groen, G. J., and Norman, G. R. (1991). Effects of conventional and problem-based medical curricula on problem solving. *Acad. Med.*, 66, 380–389.

Perrenet, J. C., Bouhuijs, P. A. J., and Smits, J. G. M. M. (2000). The suitability of problem-based learning for engineering education: theory and practice. *Teaching Higher Educ.*, 5(3), 345–358.

Pletinckx, J. and Segers, M. (2001). Programme evaluation as an instrument for quality assurance in a student-oriented educational system. *Stud. Educ. Eval.*, 27, 355–372.

Polanco, R., Calderon, P., and Delgado, F. (2004). Effects of a problem-based learning program on engineering students' academic achievements in a Mexican university. *Innov. Educ. Teaching Int.*, 41(2), 145–155.

Pontificia Universidad Católica del Perú (PUCP). (2006). *Problem-Based Learning 2006 Conference*, http://www.pucp.edu.pe/eventos/congresos/pbl2006abp/.

Popper, K. (1994). *Alles leben ist problemlösen*. Munich, Germany: Piper Verlag.*

Prince, K. J. A. H., van Mameren, H., Hylkema, N., Drukker, J., Scherpbier, A. J. J. A., and Van der Vleuten, C. P. M. (2003). Does problem-based learning lead to deficiencies in basic science knowledge? An empirical case on anatomy. *Med. Educ.*, 37(1), 15–21.

Regehr, G., Martin, J., Hutchinson, C., Murnaghan, J., Cuisamano, M., and Reznick, R. (1995). The effect of tutors' content expertise on student learning, group process, and participant satisfaction in a problem-based learning curriculum. *Teaching Learn. Med.*, 7, 225–232.

Reynolds, F. (1997). Studying psychology at degree level: Would problem-based learning enhance students' experiences? *Stud. Higher Educ.*, 22(3), 263–275.

Reznich, C. B. and Werner, E. (2001). Integrating Technology into PBL Small Groups in a Medical Education Setting. Paper presented at the Annual Meeting of the American Educational Research Association, April 10–14, Seattle, WA (ERIC Document Reproduction Service No. ED 452 786).

Ryan, G. (1993). Student perceptions about self-directed learning in a professional course implementing problem-based learning. *Stud. Higher Educ.*, 18, 53–63.

Savin-Baden, M. (2000). *Problem-Based Learning in Higher Education: Untold Stories*. Buckingham, U.K.: Society for Research in Higher Education and Open University Press.

Savin-Baden, M. (2004). Understanding the impact of assessment on students in problem-based learning. *Innov. Educ. Teaching Int.*, 41(2), 223–233.

Savin-Baden, M. and Wilkie, K. (2004). *Challenging Research in Problem-Based Learning*. New York: Open University Press.

Savoie, J. M. and Hughes, A. S. (1994). Problem-based learning as classroom solution. *Educ. Leadersh.*, 52(3), 54–57.

Schlundt, D. G., Flannery, M. E., Davis, D. L., Kinzer, C. K., and Pichert, J. W. (1999). Evaluation of a multicomponent, behaviorally oriented, problem-based 'summer school' program for adolescents with diabetes. *Behav. Modif.*, 23(1), 79–105.

Schmidt, H. G. (1983). Problem-based learning: rationale and description. *Med. Educ.*, 17, 11–16.

Schmidt, H. G. and Moust, J. H. C. (1995). What makes a tutor effective? A structural-equations modeling approach to learning in problem-based curricula. *Acad. Med.*, 70(8), 708–714.

Schmidt, H. G. and van der Molen, H. T. (2001). Self-reported competency ratings of graduates of a problem-based medical curriculum. *Acad. Med.*, 76(5), 466–468.

Schmidt H. G., Boshuizen, H. P. A., and de Vries, M. (1992). Comparing problem-based with conventional education: a review of the University of Limburg medical school experiment. *Ann. Commun.-Oriented Educ.*, 5, 193–198.

Schmidt, H. G., Vermeulen, L., and van der Molen, H. T. (2006). Long-term effects of problem-based learning: a comparison of competencies acquired by graduates of a problem-based and a conventional medical school. *Med. Educ.*, 40(6), 562–567.

Schultz-Ross, R. A. and Kline, A. E. (1999). Using problem-based learning to teach forensic psychiatry. *Acad. Psychiatry*, 23, 37–41.

Schwartz, R. W., Burgett, J. E., Blue, A. V., Donnelly, M. B., and Sloan, D. A. (1997). Problem-based learning and performance-based testing: effective alternatives for undergraduate surgical education and assessment of student performance. *Med. Teacher*, 19(1), 19–24.

Seltzer, S., Hilbert, S., Maceli, J., Robinson, E., and Schwartz, D. L. (1996). An active approach to calculus. In *Bringing Problem-Based Learning into Higher Education: Theory and Practice*, edited by L. Wilkerson and W. H. Gijselaers, pp. 83–90. San Francisco, CA: Jossey-Bass.

Shelton, J. B. and Smith, R. F. (1998). Problem-based learning in analytical science undergraduate teaching. *Res. Sci. Technol. Educ.*, 16(1), 19–30.

Shepherd, N. G. (1998). The Probe Method: A Problem-Based Learning Model's Affect on Critical Thinking Skills of Fourth and Fifth Grade Social Studies Students. Ph.D. dissertation. Raleigh, NC: North Carolina State University (*Diss. Abstr. Int.*, 59, 779A).

Shipman, H. L. and Duch, B. J. (2001). Problem-based learning in large and very large classes. In *The Power of Problem-Based Learning: A Practical 'How To' for Teaching Undergraduate Courses in Any Discipline*, edited by B. Duch, S. E. Groh, and D. E. Allen, pp. 149–164. Sterling, VA: Stylus Publishing.

Silver, M. and Wilkerson, L. (1991). Effects of tutors with subject expertise on the problem-based tutorial process. *Acad. Med.*, 66(5), 98–300.

Smith, D. L. and Hoersch, A. L. (1995). Problem-based learning in the undergraduate geology classroom. *J. Geol. Educ.*, 43, 149–152.

Smith, R. M. (1993). The triple jump examination as an assessment tool in the problem-based medical curriculum at the University of Hawaii. *Acad. Med.*, 68, 366–71.

Smits, P. B. A., Verbeek, J. H. A. M., and de Buisonje, C. D. (2002). Problem-based learning in continuing medical education: a review of controlled evaluation studies. *Br. Med. J.*, 321, 153–156.

Stepien, W. J. and Gallagher, S. A. (1993). Problem-based learning: as authentic as it gets. *Educ. Leadersh.*, 50(7), 25–29.

Stepien, W. J., Gallagher, S. A., and Workman, D. (1993). Problem-based learning for traditional and interdisciplinary classrooms. *J. Educ. Gifted*, 16, 338–357.

Stepien, W. J., Senn, P. R., and Stepien, W. C. (2000). *The Internet and Problem-Based Learning: Developing Solutions Through the Web*. Tucson, AZ: Zephyr Press.

Stinson, J. E. and Milter, R. G. (1996). Problem-based learning in business education: curriculum design and implementation issues. In *Bringing Problem-Based Learning to Higher Education: Theory and Practice*, edited by L. Wilkerson and W. H. Gijselaers, pp. 33–42. San Francisco, CA: Jossey-Bass.

Swanson, D. B., Case, S. M., and Van der Vleuten, C. P. M. (1998). Strategies for student assessment. In *The Challenge of Problem-Based Learning*, 2nd ed., edited by D. Boud and G. Feletti, pp. 269–282. London: Kogan Page.

Szeberenyi, J. (2005). The biological activity of the large-T protein of SV40 virus. *Biochem. Mol. Biol. Educ.*, 33(1), 56–57.

Tan, O. S. and Hung, D. (2007). *Problem-Based Learning in E-Learning Breakthroughs*. Singapore: Thomson Learning.

Tomczak, R. L. (1991). The Effects of Problem-Based Learning on National Board Scores, Clinical Evaluations, and Residency Selection of Medical Students. Ph.D. dissertation. Des Moines, IA: Drake University (*Diss. Abstr. Int.*, 53, 2210A).

Torp, L. and Sage, S. (2002). *Problems as Possibilities: Problem-Based Learning for K–12 Education*, 2nd ed. Alexandria, VA: Association for Supervision and Curriculum Development.

Trafton, P. R. and Midgett, C. (2001). Learning through problems: a powerful approach to teaching mathematics. *Teaching Child. Math.*, 7(9), 532–536.

Van den Bossche, P., Gijbels, D., and Dochy, F. (2000). Does Problem-Based Learning Educate Problem Solvers? A Meta-Analysis on the Effects of Problem-Based Learning. Paper presented at the Seventh Annual EDINEB Int. Conf., June 21–23, Newport Beach, CA.

van den Hurk, M. M., Wolfhagen, I. H. A. P., Dolmans, D. H. J. M., and Van der Vleuten, C. P. M. (1999). The impact of student-generated learning issues on individual study time and academic achievement. *Med. Educ.*, 33, 808–814.

Van der Vleuten, C. P. M., Verwijnen, G. M., and Wijnen, W. F. H. W. (1996). Fifteen years of experience with Progress Testing in a problem-based learning curriculum. *Med. Teacher*, 18, 103–109.

van Gessel, E., Nendaz, M. R., Vermeulen, B., Junod, A., and Vu, N. V. (2003). Basic science development of clinical reasoning from the basic sciences to the clerkships: a longitudinal assessment of medical students' needs and self-perception after a transitional learning unit. *Med. Educ.*, 37, 966–974.

Verhoeven, B. H., Verwijnen, G. M., Scherpbier, A. J. J. A., Holdrinet, R. S. G., Oeseburg, B., Bulte, J. A., and Van der Vleuten, C. P. M. (1998). An analysis of progress test results of PBL and non-PBL students. *Med. Teacher*, 20(4), 310–316.

Vernon, D. T. A. and Blake, R. L. (1993). Does problem-based learning work: A meta-analysis of evaluative research. *Acad. Med.*, 68, 550–563.

Watson, G. (2002). Using technology to promote success in PBL courses. *Technol. Source*, May/June, http://technologysource.org/article/using_technology_to_promote_success_in_pbl_courses/.

Weiss, R. E. (2003). Designing problems to promote higher-order thinking. In *Problem-Based Learning in the Information Age*, edited by D. S. Knowlton and D. C. Sharp, pp. 25–31. San Francisco, CA: Jossey-Bass.

Wiener, M. and Mehrabian, A. (1968). *Language within Language: Immediacy, a Channel in Verbal Communication*. New York: Appleton-Century-Crofts.

Wieseman, K. C. and Cadwell, D. (2005). Local history and problem-based learning. *Soc. Stud. Young Learner*, 18(1), 11–14.

Wiggins, G. and McTighe, J. (1998). *Understanding by Design*. Alexandria, VA: Association for Supervision and Curriculum Development.

Wilkerson, L. (1995). Identification of skills for the problem-based tutor: student and faculty perspectives. *Instruct. Sci.*, 22, 303–315.

Wilkerson, L. and Gijselaers, W. H., Eds. (1996). *Bringing Problem-Based Learning to Higher Education: Theory and Practice*, New Directions for Teaching and Learning, No. 68. San Francisco, CA: Jossey-Bass.

Wilkerson, L. and Hundert, E. M. (1991). Becoming a problem-based tutor: increasing self-awareness through faculty development. In *The Challenge of Problem-Based Learning*, 2nd ed., edited by D. Boud and G. Feletti, pp. 160–172. London: Kogan Page.

William, D. C., Hemstreet, S., Liu, M., and Smith, V. D. (1998). Examining how middle school students use problem-based learning software. In *Proceedings of ED-MEDIA/ED-TELECOM 98 World Conference on Educational Multimedia and Hypermedia and World Conference on Educational Telecommunications*, June 20–25, Freiburg, Germany (ERIC Document Reproduction Service No. ED 428 738).

Williams, S. M. and Hmelo, C. E. (1998). Guest editors' introduction. *J. Learn. Sci.*, 7(3/4), 265–270.

Wood, T. J., Cunnington, J. P. W., and Norman, G. R. (2000). Assessing the measurement properties of a clinical reasoning exercise. *Teaching Learn. Med.*, 12(4), 196–200.

Woods, D. R. (1994). *Problem-Based Learning: How to Gain the Most from PBL*. Waterdown, Canada: Woods.

Woods, D. R. (1996). Problem-based learning for large classes in chemical engineering. In *Bringing Problem-Based Learning to Higher Education: Theory and Practice*, edited by L. Wilkerson and H. Gijselaers, pp. 91–99. San Francisco, CA: Jossey-Bass.

Yamada, S. and Maskarinec, G. G. (2004). Strengthening *PBL* through a discursive practices approach to case-writing. *Educ. Health: Change Learn. Pract.*, 17(1), 85–92.

Zimitat, C. and Miflin, B. (2003). Using assessment to induct students and staff into the PBL tutorial process. *Assess. Eval. Higher Educ.*, 28(1), 17–32.

Zumbach, J., Kumpf, D., and Koch, S. (2004). Using multimedia to enhance problem-based learning in elementary school. *Inform. Technol. Child. Educ. Annu.*, 16, 25–37.

* Indicates a core reference.

# 39

# Behavioral, Cognitive, and Technological Approaches to Performance Improvement

*Ruth Colvin Clark*
Clark Training and Consulting, Cortez, Colorado


*Frank Nguyen*
San Diego State University, San Diego, California

## CONTENTS

Ruth Colvin Clark and Frank Nguyen

## ABSTRACT

Often, training fails to improve organizational outcomes. Increasingly, practitioners are assuming a performance improvement perspective that takes a holistic and systemic perspective in analyzing causes of and solutions for gaps in organizational results. We review the models and evidence for three perspectives on performance improvement: behavioral engineering, cognitive–motivational, and technological. The behavioral engineering models prevalent among U.S. practitioner-oriented professional societies apply a pragmatic systemic approach that evaluates performance factors at the organizational, process, and individual worker or team levels. The cognitive–motivational approaches prevalent among industrial and organizational psychologists include guidelines for goal setting, feedback, and incentives. The cognitive models are based on empirical evidence and incorporate motivational and cognitive moderators of their interventions. Recent advances in computer technology offer opportunities to deliver performance support in new ways. In our discussion of technological approaches, we focus primarily on the evolution of and evidence for electronic performance support systems (EPSSs) in the workplace.

## KEYWORDS

*Electronic performance support system (EPSS):* Enabler of work tasks that are delivered by electronic technology provided to individuals or teams at the time of need on the job. Typical support includes procedural guidance or references to factual information needed to complete tasks.

*Feedback:* Information on goal attainment designed to help workers, teams, or functional units monitor and evaluate their progress in achievement of desired accomplishments. Feedback may be quantitative or qualitative; it may or may not include explanations to guide performance; it may be directed to individual, team, unit, or organizational levels; and it may be provided through personal communications or through impersonal channels such as charts and graphs posted in work areas or by computer.

*Goal-setting theory:* Guidelines for optimizing worker or team performance by setting specific and difficult goals; goal-setting theory considers the effects of self-efficacy, goal commitment, feedback, and incentives on goal effectiveness.

*Incentives:* Tangible and social rewards intended to optimize performance of individuals or teams; may include money, feedback, and social recognition.

*Performance improvement:* An approach to optimizing organizational outcomes that uses a systemic comprehensive methodology to define and resolve gaps at the organizational, process, and individual worker levels.

## INTRODUCTION

Imagine the following situations: (1) A large utility is the target of so many customer complaints of rude telephone service that the Public Utilities Commission directs the utility to remedy the problem or face fines. (2) A team of high-performing data entry clerks moves to a new facility, bringing along all of their existing furniture and computers; after a couple of weeks, management is distressed to see that online error rates have jumped. (3) A piece of equipment inexplicably shuts off, and the breakdown halts production in the factory and costs the company millions of dollars in lost productivity; the technician knows that this problem has happened before during another shift but does not know the procedure to repair the machine because it happens so infrequently. (4) Washington, D.C., gets federal funding to hire an extra 900 police officers to fight rising crime, but 3 years later 10 police officers hired during that time are arrested for abetting drug dealers. All of these real-life situations resulted in bottom-line negative consequences for the organizations involved, and in all cases the responsible managers requested a training program to solve the problem. Even after a well-designed training program was implemented, however, the problems remained. Why? The reasons for the performance gaps had nothing to do with lack of worker knowledge and skills. Frequent observations that well-designed training programs do not always translate into improved organizational outcomes have given rise to the principles and practice of performance improvement.

**TABLE 39.1**
**Definitions of Human Performance Technology**

| Term | Definition | Source |
|---|---|---|
| Human performance enhancement | The field focused on systematically and holistically improving present and future work results achieved by people in organizational settings | Rothwell (1996) |
| Human performance technology | The systematic and systemic identification and removal of barriers to individual and organizational performance | International Society of Performance Improvement (www.ispi.org) |
| Human performance technology | The process of selection, analysis, design, development, implementation, and evaluation of programs to most cost-effectively influence human behavior and accomplishment | Harless, cited in Geis (1986) |
| Human performance technology | The study and ethical practice of improving productivity in organizations by designing and developing effective interventions that are results oriented, comprehensive, and systemic | Pershing (2006) |
| Performance improvement | The process of identifying and analyzing important organizational and individual performance gaps, planning for future performance improvement, designing and developing cost-effective and ethically justifiable interventions to close performance gaps, implementing the interventions, and evaluating the financial and non-financial results | American Society for Training and Development (http://www.astd.org) |

Unlike many other chapters in this *Handbook* that discuss instructional interventions and issues, our chapter focuses on factors other than knowledge or skills that influence workforce performance in organizational settings.

## WHAT IS PERFORMANCE IMPROVEMENT?

In the past 20 years, scenarios like those summarized above have led to a professional practice called *human performance technology*. Table 39.1 lists some of the recent definitions for human performance technology. These definitions share the following two features:

- *A focus on desired organizational accomplishments*—Performance improvement initiatives are pragmatic: to improve outcomes that are linked to bottom-line goals of the organization. In the commercial sector, outcomes are typically related to metrics for sales, product quality, customer satisfaction, and work efficiency. In the government sector, outcomes are typically related to indicators of mission accomplishment, product or service quality, and efficiency.
- *Comprehensive and systemic perspectives*—Human performance analysis and interventions address the interrelated parts of an organization, including the individual worker, teams, departments, business processes, and organizational levels.

In 2006, in the United States about $56 billion was invested in workforce learning (*Training Magazine*, 2006). The actual investment was much greater because this figure does not take into account the most expensive element of any training program—the salary time of the training participants as well as the lost opportunity costs. While sales professionals are in training, they are earning a salary and they are not selling. Because training is an expensive intervention, a performance improvement perspective first defines the factors needed to attain desired outcomes and only recommends training when there is a gap in worker knowledge and skills. Managers often assume that training is the appropriate (and only) route to achieve performance goals. The challenge of the performance improvement professional is to partner with line clients to jointly assess the performance environment, define barriers to and enablers of those behaviors that lead to desired organizational accomplishments, and recommend interventions (solutions) that reduce or eliminate those barriers.

### How Is Performance Measured?

In this chapter, we examine three perspectives on performance improvement: behavioral, cognitive–motivational, and technological. All three perspectives have a similar goal—namely, the improvement of desired organizational end results. Unlike instructional-dependent variables, which usually rely on learning measures in the form of tests, the measures of performance improvement vary widely. In the commercial sector, bottom-line metrics are linked to profitability (e.g., sales, expenses, errors or rework, profit). In many cases, measures that are already in place in organizations, such as customer satisfaction, error rates, productivity measures, employee turnover, and sales volume, are used as dependent measures; for example, in a study on the effects of different incentives on performance in fast-food stores, the dependent measures included store profit, drive-through times, and employee turnover (Peterson and Luthans, 2006). In other organizations, such as nonprofits or government, the measures link to the organizational mission statement or goals. When organizations do not have clearly defined measurable goals, the first performance improvement intervention must engage responsible management to establish relevant goals and metrics.

## THREE APPROACHES TO PERFORMANCE IMPROVEMENT

There is nothing new about a focus on workplace performance. At the end of the 19th century, the Industrial Revolution spawned some of the first attempts to make workplace performance more efficient and effective. Frederick Taylor (1911) promoted *scientific management* based on time and motion studies to maximize work efficiency. His recommendation that rewards be linked to the level of performance is in line with contemporary evidence on the effect of compensation on performance. In the mid-1900s, Maslow's *theory of needs* and Vroom's *expectancy theory* both focused on motivational explanations of performance. At around the same time, *behaviorism* based on Thorndike's law of effect and extended by B.F. Skinner gave rise to a human engineering approach to performance. From these paradigms, two branches of performance improvement have evolved: one reflecting behaviorist roots tempered by systems theory and a second evolving from industrial/organizational (I/O) research and theory on motivation in the workplace. We refer to these two branches as *behavioral engineering* and *cognitive–motivational*. Recently, the evolution of computer-based technologies has prompted a third approach that we call *technological*. Our discussion of technological models focuses primarily on the use of computer technology to offer electronic performance support. Electronic performance support encompasses an eclectic array of digitally delivered interventions that may embody either behavioral or cognitive–motivational assumptions.

### The Evolution of the Behavioral Engineering Models

Around the mid-20th century, behaviorists applied the concept of contingencies to training through programmed instruction. A number of these behavioral scientists in the United States founded the National Society for Programmed Instruction in 1962. In the process of implementing and evaluating programmed instruction and instructional design models, several of these professionals discovered that even well-designed training did not result in the accomplishment of organizational goals. Thomas Gilbert, for example, stated: "I found that businesses had all kinds of performance problems and most had nothing to do with training. That really struck me. I realized that the world of work was really screwed up and that before I could make the world safe for instructional design I had to get all the other problems cleaned up. That's where the first ideas for performance technology came from" (Dean, 1994, p. 37).

The frequent failure of training to produce organizational results led to a focus on factors in addition to knowledge and skills that influence work place performance. Gilbert's book, *Human Competency: Engineering Worthy Performance*, published in 1978, and Joe Harless' *An Ounce of Analysis (Is Worth a Pound of Objectives)*, published in 1970, represent two milestones in the behavioral engineering approach to performance improvement. Over the past 40 years, as the behavioral engineering approach evolved, the National Society for Programmed Instruction refocused its mission and scope and today is called the International Society for Performance Improvement (www.ispi.org).

### The Evolution of the Cognitive–Motivational Models

At the same time, the cognitive–motivational branch of performance improvement scientists focused on managing work behaviors through motivational means, most notably through goal theory, recently integrated with social cognitive and self-efficacy theory. Based on 35 years of empirical research, Locke and Latham (2002) summarized their goal-setting model, which specifies the mechanisms and processes that link goal setting to performance improvement.

### The Evolution of the Technological Models

In her milestone book, *Electronic Performance Support Systems*, Gery (1991, p. 34) stated that:

> The goal of an EPSS is to provide whatever is necessary to generate performance and learning at the moment of need. We now have the means to model, represent, structure, and implement that support electronically—and to make it universally and consistently available on demand any time, any place and regardless of situation.

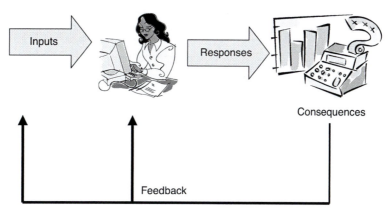

**Figure 39.1** A basic systems model of performance.

Performance support systems have evolved alongside advances in technology. Knowledge management systems allow employees to tap into the knowledge of experts. Learning content management systems now make it possible to link to learning objects originally developed for training as on-the-job support. Search engines and visual mapping systems make it increasingly easy for employees to locate support content. Mobile devices will allow employees to access content anytime, anywhere from their cell phones and iPods. Electronic performance support system (EPSS) approaches to performance improvement focus on the use of technology in various ways to help workers, teams, and functional units achieve organizational outcomes. EPSS interventions are varied and may reflect behavioral or cognitive–motivational perspectives.

In the next sections, we summarize the behavioral, cognitive, and technological approaches to performance improvement. Although we could have summarized many behaviorist performance models, we briefly describe three here that have played a significant role in the evolution of the International Society for Performance Improvement. These are the models of Gilbert, Rummler and Brache, and Pershing. We summarize the Gilbert model to describe one of the acknowledged foundational approaches to human performance technology. The Rummler–Brache model is included as one of the most influential recent performance improvement models that builds upon and extends Gilbert's pioneering work. Finally, we summarize the Pershing model as a very recent synthesis of behavioral approaches summarized in the 2006 *Handbook of Human Performance Technology*. Regarding cognitive–motivational approaches, we summarize goal setting and the high performance cycle from Locke and Latham (2002) as well as other recent research on goals, feedback, and incentives reflecting a cognitive perspective. To address the role of technology in per-

formance support, we will also look at research and practice in the use of electronic performance support systems (EPSSs) to improve workplace performance.

## BEHAVIORAL ENGINEERING MODELS OF PERFORMANCE IMPROVEMENT

Thomas Gilbert, who worked with B.F. Skinner, is considered one of the founding fathers of the behavioral performance improvement approach. Much of Gilbert's performance model, originally published in 1978, has been incorporated into more recent human performance models.

### Gilbert's Human Competence Model

As shown in Figure 39.1, Gilbert articulated a behavioral/systems model in which individual workers act on inputs (stimuli) in ways that produce results (responses) which in turn have consequences. Based on feedback, workers modify their performance to increase positive consequences. This systems perspective is a major feature of all behavioral engineering approaches to performance improvement. Gilbert defined specific performance factors in terms of information (inputs), instrumentation (inputs), and motivation (consequences) in a two-tier model with tier 1 focusing on the environmental factors and tier 2 focusing on the individual performer (Figure 39.2). Summarizing environmental performance factors, cell 1 includes the informational resources required to perform the job, including work standards, work documentation, and performance feedback. Cell 2 specifies environmental resources, including money, time, equipment, ergonomics, leadership support, and work processes. Cell 3 focuses on incentives including compensation, recognition, and developmental opportunities. The lower

511

|  | Information | Instrumentation | Motivation |
|---|---|---|---|
| Environment | Data | Instruments | Incentives |
|  | • Direction<br>• Feedback | • Tools<br>• Procedures<br>• Time | • Compensation |
| Person | Knowledge | Capacity | Motives |
|  | • Training<br>• Work aids | • Selection | • Individual<br>  motivators |

**Figure 39.2** Gilbert's six-cell performance factors. (Adapted from Gilbert, T., *Human Competence: Engineering Worthy Performance*, McGraw-Hill, New York, 1978.)

tier includes similar categories as they apply to the individual worker: Cell 4 includes knowledge and skills based on adequate training. Capability to do the job is the theme of cell 5, which includes the physical, mental, and emotional job prerequisites. Cell 6 addresses motives of the individual worker to invest effort and persist in response to the available incentives.

Many of the basic elements of human performance improvement are reflected in the Gilbert model, which has a focus on accomplishment—outcomes rather than events. He distinguished between environmental influences, such as tools and standards, and factors related to individual performers, such as working aids and selection. The Gilbert model is a behavioral systems approach that depicts workers as respondents to inputs adjusting outputs based on feedback and consequences of their actions. Aspects of the Gilbert model have been carried forward in all of the behavioral models that followed it.

## Rummler–Brache Three-Level Model

The Rummler–Brache (1995) model incorporates Gilbert's behavioral engineering concepts, adding a systems view of organizations and the opportunity for improvement through process alignment. In their 1995 book *Improving Performance: How to Manage the White Space on the Organization Chart*, they stated that: "In our experience, the greatest opportunities for performance improvement often lie in the functional interfaces—those points at which the baton is being passed from one department to another" (p. 9). As shown in Figure 39.3, the Rummler–Brache model focuses on planning and management at three levels of performance—the organizational level, the process level, and the individual job performer level. The job level performance factors are similar to those specified in the Gilbert model; however, the Rummler-Brache model emphasizes a holistic view of organizations and the need for alignment among the three main interfaces

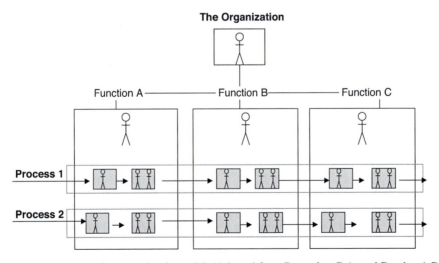

**Figure 39.3** Rummler–Brache three performance levels model. (Adapted from Rummler, G.A. and Brache, A.P., *Improving Performance: How to Manage the White Space on the Organization Chart*, 2nd ed., Jossey-Bass, San Francisco, CA, 1995.)

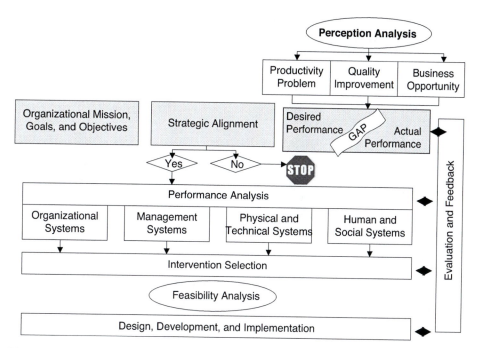

**Figure 39.4** Pershing performance improvement process model. (Adapted from Pershing, J.A., in *Handbook of Human Performance Technology*, 3rd ed., Pershing, J.A., Ed., Pfeiffer, San Francisco, CA, 2006, pp. 5–34.)

of organization, process, and individual performer. A Rummler–Brache analysis evaluates performance factors at all three levels: the strategies, goals, measures, structures, and resources at the organizational level; the flow of inputs and outputs through functional units at the process level; and the various individual worker factors described in the Gilbert model. One major underlying premise is that the three levels are interdependent and that planning and management must occur at all three levels. To address individual worker factors outside of the larger context will often be counterproductive. The Rummler–Brache model is widely used today as a guide for a comprehensive behavioral engineering approach to performance improvement.

## Pershing's Performance Improvement Process Model

We include the Pershing model (2006), summarized in Figure 39.4, because it focuses on the performance improvement process and thus adds a different quite recent perspective on human performance improvement. Typical initiators of a performance improvement project might be performance problems such as the ones we summarized in our opening paragraph, quality improvement initiatives or business opportunities such as acquisitions and mergers. The Pershing performance assessment process recommends initiating a performance improvement effort by identifying per-

ceptions or perceived needs. This process includes identifying the sponsors, champions and stakeholders of a performance improvement initiative, determining how the need originated and the importance of the initiative. An early step at this stage is to assess the alignment of any performance initiative with the operational objectives of the organization. If the problem is resolved or the goal is achieved, will the outcomes align with the values, culture, structure, and goals of the larger organizational environment? As Pershing (2006, p. 18) stated: "Organizations are often caught up in expending resources and time in solving problems or seizing opportunities with little or no payback or contribution to organizational goals."

Once an alignment is realized, the performance assessment examines factors in organizational, management, physical, and human systems. At the organizational level evaluating the structure, communication lines, divisions of labor, and methods of operation and decision making may offer avenues for improving organizational viability and effectiveness. Management system analysis assesses the quality of the key management functions to delegate, develop others, conduct performance appraisals, and set priorities. An assessment of physical and technical systems considers the adequacy of the technical processes as well as the equipment and tools that workers are using to accomplish their goals. This includes ergonomic issues, functionality of technical systems, process engineering, and job aids both traditional and electronic. Last, a review of the human systems focuses on selection processes, knowledge, and skills, along with rewards and incentives. As a result of the performance scan, gaps are identified related to one or more of these systems to be resolved by an appropriate intervention.

## Interventions in Behavioral Engineering Models

Interventions in the behavioral engineering approaches involve either a removal of barriers or the addition of enablers of performance within the organizational, management, physical, or human systems. Typical interventions can include process reengineering, management standards and training, ergonomic modifications, job aids (traditional and electronic), job standards, performance feedback, and incentives, as well as training, to name a few. Recall the performance problems we mentioned in our introduction. In all of these situations, management called for a training solution; for example, the utility management called for a telephone courtesy course to reduce customer complaints of rude service, the data entry clerks were given a refresher training course to reduce input errors, and so on. The performance problems did not wane after training, though. A closer look at the organizational, management, technical, and human systems found that the gaps were unrelated to knowledge and skills.

Structured observations of customer call simulations, for example, showed that most of the utility customer service representatives were capable of making courteous responses; however, their job standards, feedback, and incentives were set at 120 calls per day. There was a misalignment of job standards, feedback, and incentives with desired work accomplishments (e.g., courteous responses). As long as management demanded and rewarded quantitative outcomes only, quality would suffer.

With regard to the data entry clerks, analysis of error patterns showed that most were made in the later afternoon after 2:00 p.m. Interviews and observations of work conditions showed that sunlight coming through the large windows in the new facility created a glare on the computer screens that reduced the level of visibility on the screens in the afternoon hours. An inexpensive ergonomic solution was in order—good window shades (Addison and Haig, 2006).

In Washington, D.C., the $500 million in federal funds available to hire new police officers had to be spent within a 2-year period. As a result, there was no time for the usual psychological screening and background checks (Flaherty and Harrison, 1993). This

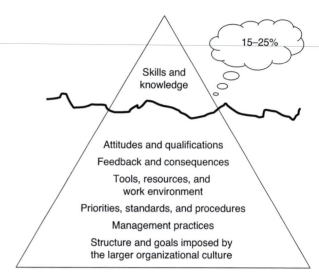

**Figure 39.5** The iceberg model of performance gaps. (From Addison, R.M. and Haig, C., in *Handbook of Human Performance Technology*, 3rd ed., Pershing, J.A., Ed., Pfeiffer, San Francisco, CA, 2006, pp. 35–54. With permission.)

performance problem had its roots in a failure to apply an effective selection system.

As shown in Figure 39.5, only a small proportion of performance gaps stem from lack of knowledge and skills and warrant a training solution. The vast majority require solutions that address the organizational, management, physical, or human systems. Rothwell and Kazanas (2004) identified five of the most frequent alternatives to instructional solutions: feedback, job performance aids, reward systems, employee selection practices, and organizational redesign.

## Features of the Behavioral Engineering Models

The strength of the behavioral perspective is its holistic and pragmatic approach that, when effectively applied, improves organizational results by aligning organizational efforts vertically, horizontally, and at the individual worker level. The knowledge base of the behavioral engineering community rests primarily on extensive case-study work and the articulation of models such as those summarized above. The behavioral engineering perspective lacks experimental evidence; for example, a review of articles published in the main ISPI research journal, *Performance Improvement Quarterly*, found that 36% of the articles in the period from 1997 to 2000 were based on data (Klein, 2002), a number that increased to 54% for the time period 2001 to 2005 (Marker et al., 2006). Of the reports based on data in the Marker et al. analysis, only 5% reflected experimental or quasi-experimental research studies.

As reflected in the models reviewed here, a diverse set of practitioner perspectives and skills is often needed to define and to implement a comprehensive performance solution. A second potential limitation of the behavioral models is the one-size-fits-all perspective. A basic assumption of the behavioral engineering orientation is that performance can be engineered by modifications to the environment with little consideration for how individual worker or task differences might interact with the modifications. This assumption may lead to recommendations that do not factor in critical differences in the nature of the work tasks or differences among individual worker motivations and skills.

# COGNITIVE–MOTIVATIONAL APPROACHES TO PERFORMANCE IMPROVEMENT

In the previous section, we reviewed the main tenets and assumptions of the behavioral engineering perspective on performance improvement. In contrast, industrial and organizational psychologists have relied to a large degree on experimental evidence as well as a cognitive perspective on workplace performance. In this section, we summarize the main findings from goal-setting theory as well as the effects of feedback and incentives on performance outcomes.

Similar to the behavioral engineering models summarized in the previous paragraphs, the cognitive–motivational performance models are designed to predict, explain, and positively influence organizational results. In addition, cognitive approaches address some of the same performance factors as the behavioral models—most notably, performance standards (goals), feedback, and incentives. Unlike the behavioral engineering models, however, cognitive–motivational guidelines are based on numerous experiments—both controlled laboratory experiments as well as field studies. In addition,

these models incorporate interactions between the workplace environment and internal psychological processes. Theories based on interactions between internal mental processes and external environmental factors are one of the features of cognitive models that distinguish them from behavioral approaches; for example, a behavioral perspective assumes that worker feedback will generally exert a positive effect on work outputs. In contrast, cognitive approaches show that sometimes feedback has a detrimental effect on performance because it directs attention to the self rather than the task (Kluger and DeNisi, 1996). For success, feedback must be designed and delivered in ways that direct attention to the task—not the self. When addressing performance factors such as goals, feedback, and incentives, cognitive models ask about how they exert their effects and how they should be implemented adaptively based on their mechanisms of action.

## Goal-Setting Theory

The core finding of goal theory is that there is a direct and positive relationship between goal difficulty and subsequent performance with effect sizes ranging from .52 to .82—in the moderate to high range. Locke and Latham (2002) have found that specific difficult goals consistently lead to higher performance than more general goals such as "do your best." When goal levels are held constant, higher levels of performance are realized from individuals with high self-efficacy who believe that with effort they can attain the goals.

### The High Performance Cycle Model

Goal-setting theory has studied both the mechanisms and modifiers of goals summarized in the high performance cycle model shown in Figure 39.6. Regarding mechanisms, goals are effective because they direct attention followed by effort toward goal-relevant activities and

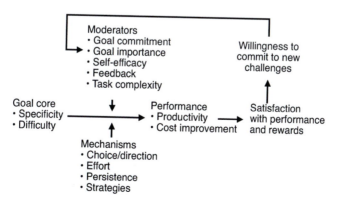

**Figure 39.6** The high performance cycle of goal setting theory. (From Locke, E.A. and Latham, G.P., *Am. Psychol.*, 57(9), 705–717, 2002. With permission.)

away from activities that do not achieve goals. In addition, goals energize performance, prolong effort and stimulate more effective approaches to job tasks.

Challenging specific goals may not always result in better performance, however, because there are some proven moderators of goal setting on performance. First, workers must make a personal commitment to achieving the goal. To ensure goal commitment, goal attainment should be positioned as important, and workers should be assured that they can attain the goal. Although there has been a popular belief that participative setting of goals results in greater goal commitment, research has not born this out; rather, an assigned goal is as effective as one set collaboratively provided the purpose or rationale for the goal is given. Meta-analysis of the effects of participation in decision making on performance has yielded a low effect size of .11 (Locke and Latham, 2002). Apparently, the greatest benefits derived from participative goal setting are cognitive in nature as a result of information exchange among the participants.

Goal commitment can be enhanced by monetary incentives, with more money leading to greater commitment; however, if the goal is very difficult and incentives are contingent on reaching the goal, workers will tend to abandon the goal once they sense they will not reach it. Instead, goals should be moderately difficult, or employers should pay for performance levels rather than goal attainment. To boost self-efficacy (e.g., to promote self-confidence in attaining the goal), adequate training must be provided to increase mastery, combined with role modeling or persuasive communications that express confidence in the workers' abilities.

A second moderator of goal-setting effects is feedback. For goals to be effective, workers benefit from feedback that shows their progress in relationship to the goals. Combining goals with feedback is more effective than goal setting alone; however, a recent meta-analysis on the effects of feedback on performance (Kluger and DeNisi, 1996), summarized in the next section, offers additional insights about how to use feedback most effectively to maximize performance.

Task complexity is a third moderator of goal-setting effectiveness. Most of the research has been conducted on tasks of relatively low complexity. As the complexity of the task increases, goal effects will increasingly depend on the ability of the worker to discover appropriate task strategies. Because some workers will be more successful than others, the effect of goals on complex tasks is smaller than on simple tasks. Meta-analysis shows an effect size of .48 for complex tasks compared to .67 for more simple tasks. On complex tasks, a learning goal might lead to better performance than a performance goal.

In summary, Locke and Latham (2002, p. 714) concluded that:

> ...the effects of goal setting are very reliable. ...With goal-setting theory, specific difficult goals have been shown to increase performance on well over 100 different tasks involving more than 40,000 participants in at least eight countries working in laboratory, simulation, and field settings.

## The Effects of Feedback on Performance

Providing feedback on goal attainment results in better performance than goal setting alone. Kluger and DeNisi (1996) summarize guidelines and a theory of feedback based on a meta-analysis of 607 effect sizes contained in 131 papers spanning 23,663 observations. A histogram of these effect sizes is shown in Figure 39.7. Although the average effect size was moderate

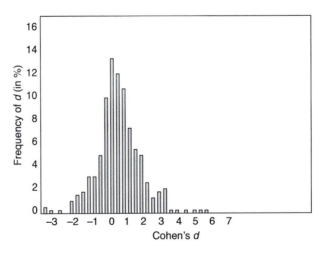

**Figure 39.7** Distribution of 607 effects of feedback intervention on performance. (From Kluger, A.N. and DeNisi, A., *Psychol. Bull.*, 119(2), 254–284, 1996. With permission.)

and positive (.4), over one third of the feedback interventions either had no effects or sometimes even depressed performance. Kluger and DeNisi (1996, p. 254) emphasized that "a considerable body of evidence suggesting that feedback intervention effects on performance are quite variable has been historically disregarded by most researchers. This disregard has led to a widely shared assumption that feedback interventions consistently improve performance."

To explain the variable effects of feedback on performance, Kluger and DeNisi proposed that feedback primarily refocuses the workers' attention to one of three levels: self, task, or task detail. A shift of attention to the task level or the task detail level usually will result in a positive effect; however, if attention is refocused to the self, performance suffers. The reason is that, for many, feedback that draws attention to the self is threatening and diverts limited cognitive resources from the productive task and task details level.

When Klugar and DeNisi evaluated the moderators of feedback, they found that cues that direct the workers' attention to self such as normative feedback (how you do compare to others?), feedback that is either discouraging or includes praise, and feedback from a person compared to feedback from a computer all attenuate the positive effects of feedback. That is because all of these cues direct mental resources to self goals rather than to task goals. In contrast, feedback that shows progress from previous attainments, emphasizes correct solutions, and comes from a less personal source such as a computer augments feedback effects by focusing attention on the task. These effects are moderated by self-esteem. Individuals low in self-esteem will direct negative feedback to the self more than individuals high in self-esteem; therefore, nega-tive feedback will have a more negative effect on the performance of those with low self-esteem. In addition, as summarized by Locke and Latham (2002), Kluger and DeNisi (1996) also reported that feedback improves performance more in the presence of goals.

## The Effects of Incentives on Performance

The role of consequences (rewards) is a key element of all performance improvement paradigms, but what do we know from research about the types of incentives that improve performance? Two meta-analyses published in 2003 offer some insights on the effects of incentives on performance. Stajkovic and Luthans (2003) reviewed the average individual and combined effects of three common incentives—money, feedback, and social recognition—on work performance. They hypothesized that the three reinforcers together would have a synergistic effect that was greater than the sum of the three used individually as a result of different and complimentary mechanisms. Money has high instrumental value and will likely lead to extra effort to increase performance; however, monetary rewards do not provide much information about the performance. Workers may not be sure what must be accomplished, where to get resources, or how to correct unproductive behaviors; therefore, a second reinforcer—feedback—derives its power from the information it provides. Finally, social recognition has positive effects on performance as a predictor of future positive consequences such as promotions and raises.

The data from the meta-analysis are summarized in Figure 39.8, which shows the percentage effects of various reinforcement interventions on performance both individually and in combination. The

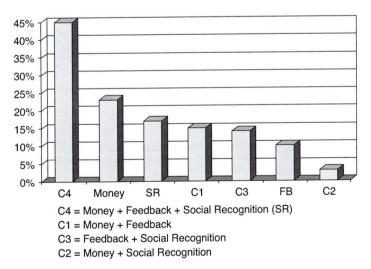

**Figure 39.8** Percentage effects of reinforcement interventions on employee performance. (From Stajkovic, A.D. and Luthans, F., *Pers. Psychol.*, 56(1), 155–194, 2003. With permission.)

three incentives combined (C4) clearly have a greater positive effect than any single incentive or the mathematical sum of the three effects measured individually. Of the individual incentives, money has the largest effect followed by social recognition. The studies that evaluated the effects of all three reinforcers showed a 45% impact on performance. The sum of the individual effect sizes equaled 1.48; however, the actual effect size from studies that combined all three equaled 1.88. This difference in actual and combined effect sizes suggests a synergistic effect of all three in concert. The authors reported an average effect size of 16% improvement in performance. Money improved performance 23%, social recognition 17%, and feedback 10%. Stajkovic and Luthans (2003) suggest that the impact of feedback will be even greater in more complex tasks where the information value of feedback will exert greater leverage than with less complex tasks.

A second meta-analysis on incentives by Condly et al. (2003) reported that all incentive programs in all work settings and on all work tasks resulted in a 22% gain in performance, a figure quite close to the 16% reported by Stajkovic and Luthans (2003). Condly et al. (2003) found that team-directed incentives had a markedly superior effect compared to individual-directed incentives and that monetary incentives resulted in higher performance gains than tangible incentives such as gifts and travel. They also found that long-term incentive programs led to greater performance gains than short-term programs.

A recent quasi-experimental control group study reported by Peterson and Luthans (2006) compared the effects of financial and nonfinancial incentives applied to fast-food franchise store teams on three outcome measures of performance over a 9-month time period. In their research, 21 fast-food stores were randomly assigned to two treatments or a control group. One treatment offered a monetary incentive to the entire team, the amount of which was contingent on the number of points earned by structured management observations of desired behaviors. The nonfinancial treatments involved feedback provided on charts and social recognition offered to the entire team by the managers. Peterson and Luthans (2006) compared the performance outcomes of store profit, drive-through times, and employee turnover at 3, 6, and 9 months.

With regard to profits, they found significant main effects for both interventions. At 3 months, both the financial and feedback-recognition groups outperformed the control stores, with the financial interventions outperforming the nonfinancial. By 6 and 9 months, however, both the financial and nonfinancial interventions had a similar positive impact on profits.

With regard to drive-through times, at all three time periods both the financial and nonfinancial groups improved performance equally compared to the control stores. Although both treatment groups experienced less turnover than the control groups, the financial incentive had significantly greater impact on turnover than the feedback-recognition incentives. Specifically, the study showed that average profits rose from 30% from pre-intervention to post-intervention over the 9 months for the financial condition and 36% for the nonfinancials; drive-through times decreased 19% for the financials and 25% for the nonfinancials; and turnover was reduced by 13% for the financials and by 10% for the nonfinancials. An interesting outcome of this study is the differential effects of the incentives on different performance outcomes; for example, turnover responded differently than profitability to monetary and feedback-recognition incentives. Consequently, we recommend that research studies use more than one performance metric as a dependent measure and evaluate results over a period of time.

In summary, the recent meta-analyses and experiments on incentives suggest that: (1) incentive programs in general will lead to about a 20% improvement in performance outcomes; (2) a coordinated program that uses a combination of incentives such as monetary rewards, feedback, and social recognition contingent on desired behaviors will exert the largest effects on performance; (3) team-administered incentives may yield greater performance outcomes than individual incentives; (4) there are likely to be different effects of various combinations of incentives for low- and high-complexity tasks and on different performance metrics; and (5) feedback on performance of complex tasks should incorporate explanatory or task-specific advice for maximum value.

## Features of the Cognitive–Motivational Models

In contrast to the behavioral engineering models reviewed previously, the cognitive motivational models rely to a greater extent on experimental evidence. These models are also more cognitive in that they incorporate internal personality factors, such as self-confidence, and cognitive factors, such as attention, to explain the diverse effects of various motivators on different performance outcomes. The cognitive–motivational approach considers interactions among diverse factors more than the behavioral perspectives, which assume a consistent effect of a given intervention. The behavioral engineering approach, for example, views feedback linked to desired behaviors as a consistently effective performance improvement

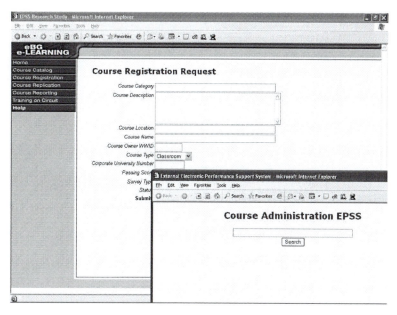

**Figure 39.9** An example of an external performance support system using a search engine. (From Nguyen, F. et al., *Perform. Improv. Q.*, 18(4), 71–86, 2005. With permission.)

mechanism. In contrast, the motivational perspective proposes that feedback may be more or less effective depending on how effectively feedback cues direct attention to tasks.

## TECHNOLOGICAL APPROACHES TO PERFORMANCE IMPROVEMENT

In the behavioral engineering models of performance improvement, we identified memory support in the form of job aids as one common intervention recommended in situations where it is not efficient or possible to train knowledge and skills required for job performance. Technical support personnel often encounter new issues and must quickly find or devise solutions. Sales representatives are often challenged to keep up with ever-evolving product lines and features. Finance controllers may be asked to conduct financial analyses that they learned months ago in training. Although training could be developed and delivered to address these situations, instructional interventions may not be timely or cost effective.

To address these issues, electronic performance support systems provide users with "individualized on-line access to the full range of ... systems to permit job performance" (Gery, 1995, p. 21). Unlike training, which requires participants to spend time away from their jobs, EPSS provides the information and tools that they need to do their job, on the job. Although much of the EPSS research summarized below assumed desktop-computer-delivered support, the evolution of mobile computing devices opens greater opportunities for EPSS in settings where computers have not been readily available; aircraft mechanics, factory workers, and sales agents will be able to access performance support content any time they have access to their cell phones, iPods, or other small form factor computing devices.

### Types of Performance Support

Among the models proposed to differentiate the types of performance support systems, Raybould (2000) argued that performance technologists should first employ *embedded* EPSS and then move to less powerful *linked* or *external* systems if embedded systems are not possible for a particular performance problem. Rossett and Schafer (2006, p. 67) pointed out that *planner* systems are used when a performer "gets ready to act and afterward, when [they] reflect on [their] efforts," while *sidekick* systems support performers while they are "in the work."

The most widely cited and discussed categorization of performance support was developed by Gery (1995), who proposed three categories of performance support systems: external, extrinsic, and intrinsic. External systems store content used to support task performance in an external database. This content is not integrated within a user's work interface; as a result, users are forced to manually locate relevant information in the external EPSS. Figure 39.9 illustrates a common form of external EPSS: a search engine. Other examples include frequently asked question pages and help indexes. External performance support also "may or

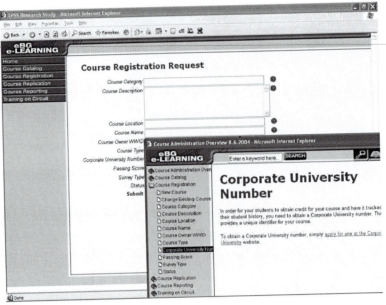

**Figure 39.10** An example of an extrinsic performance support system using context-sensitive help. (From Nguyen, F. et al., *Perform. Improv. Q.*, 18(4), 71–86, 2005. With permission.)

may not be computer mediated" (Gery, 1995, p. 53). Job aids or documentation are examples of non-computer-based performance support interventions.

Extrinsic "[p]erformance support … is integrated with the system but is not in the primary workspace" (Gery, 1995, p. 51). In other words, extrinsic systems integrate with the user's work interface in such a way that the EPSS can identify the user's location in a system or even the exact task they may be working on. With this contextual information, the extrinsic system can intelligently locate content that may be relevant to the task at hand. Figure 39.10 shows an extrinsic system that embeds help links in a software interface. These links enable the EPSS to intelligently locate the appropriate support content for a particular work context. Like external performance support systems, the content used to support the task is external to the work interface.

Intrinsic systems provide users with task support that is incorporated directly within their work interface. Due to this direct integration with the interface, Gery asserted that intrinsic EPSS provides "[p]erformance support that is inherent to the system itself. It's so well integrated that, to workers, it's part of the system" (Gery, 1995, p. 51). Under this rather broad definition, examples of intrinsic performance support systems can include tools that automate tasks and processes, user-centered design of work interfaces to reduce complexity and improve usability, or embedded knowledge that is displayed directly in the work interface, as illustrated in Figure 39.11.

## Applications of Performance Support

Case studies report the application of performance support systems to a wide range of settings and performance problems; for example, performance support systems have been used in educational settings. Brush et al. (1993) developed a performance support system to improve collaboration among teachers in rural communities. McCabe and Leighton (2002) created an EPSS to help master's students with analysis and instructional design. Darabi (2004) explained how a similar system was used to help graduate students with performance analysis.

Performance support systems have also been widely used in industry. Dorsey et al. (1993) and Cole et al. (1997) applied performance support systems to support local and remote sales employees. Huber et al. (1999) provided three examples of how intrinsic, extrinsic, and external EPSS were applied to automobile manufacturing, insurance, and civil engineering. Kasvi and Vartiainen (2000) demonstrated four different ways in which EPSS has been applied in factories. Gery (2003) cited examples of how performance support systems have been used in investment and financial planning, real estate, travel, and government applications. A survey conducted by McManus and Rossett (2006) showed that performance technologists had applied EPSS to problems ranging from vessel tracking by the U.S. Coast Guard to coaching restaurant managers.

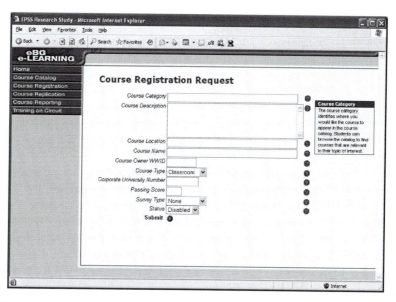

**Figure 39.11** An example of an intrinsic performance support system using tooltips. (From Nguyen, F. et al., *Perform. Improv. Q.*, 18(4), 71–86, 2005. With permission.)

The broad proliferation of performance support can be partially attributed to cost savings. Several authors have proposed methods to calculate returns on investment for performance support systems (Altalib, 2002; Chase, 1998; Desmarais et al., 1997; Hawkins et al., 1998). Desmarais et al. (1997) implemented an EPSS for support customer service representatives at a utility company and estimated a modest monetary savings realized through benefits such as reduced call time, improved productivity, and reduced training. Hawkins et al. (1998) reported that an EPSS developed for a government agency saved over $17.6 million over the lifetime of the system.

The benefits of performance support extend beyond dollars and cents. Hunt et al. (1998) conducted a meta-analysis on performance support systems in the medical field. The authors reviewed a total of 68 studies with systems that supported drug dosing, patient diagnoses, and preventive care. User performance improved in 42 of the studies reviewed, was not significantly changed in 19 cases, and decreased in only 7 instances. Although studies on EPSSs designed for diagnoses and certain types of drug dosing were inconsistent, the researchers noted that systems for other areas such as preventive care demonstrate positive results for these systems in ambulances, clinics, and hospitals. Villachica et al. (2006) reported the benefits of performer-centered design (PCD) winners from 1997 to 2004. The impact of these projects ranged from reductions in training time, increased user satisfaction, and improved productivity, among other factors.

## Research on Performance Support Systems

Research has also examined the most effective types of performance support systems. Bailey's (2003) meta-analysis found that linking, as one would do in an intrinsic or extrinsic performance support system, "tends to be more effective than searching to find content" as in an external system (Bailey, 2003, p. 1). Similarly, Spool (2001, p. 1) found that: "The more times users searched, the less likely they were to find what they wanted"; in fact, Spool observed that users were successful in finding the correct support information 55% of the time on the first try. On the second search attempt, only 38% were successful, and none was successful on the third attempt. Nielsen (2001) found similar results in another study where 51% were successful on the first search attempt, 32% on the second, and 18% on the third attempt.

A study by Nguyen et al. (2005) validated some of these results. The researchers tested three different types of performance support systems that aligned with Gery's intrinsic, extrinsic, and external EPSS categories. Results from the study indicated that users provided with intrinsic and extrinsic performance support systems performed significantly better on a software procedure compared to a control group with no EPSS. Also, all users provided with an EPSS had significantly more positive attitudes than the control group.

Research addressing other assumptions about performance support is currently lacking or inconclusive. One of the most widely held notions about EPSS, for example, is that implementing on-the-job support interventions can reduce or even eliminate the amount of training necessary to address a performance problem (Chase, 1998; Desmerais et al., 1997; Foster, 1997; Sleight, 1993). This notion of reducing training through EPSS and enabling "day-one performance" has been a major attraction for performance technologists. Bastiaens et al. (1997) examined this assumption by comparing the effectiveness of different combinations of computer-based and paper-based performance support with computer-based and instructor-led training. They found that users preferred paper-based forms over the electronic software tool as well as instructor-led training over computer-based training. They found no significant difference on test achievement scores, performance, or sales results for the other treatments over a 1-year period. Mao and Brown (2005) examined the effect of using an EPSS to support pre-task exercises and on-the-job performance as compared to an instructor-led training course. Users provided with the EPSS performed significantly better on an achievement test than those provided with training. They found no significant difference between the two groups on a procedural task. It should be noted that both of these studies suffered from potential validity problems, ranging from small sample sizes to procedural issues (such as using the EPSS for practice exercises—not an authentic use of on-the-job support).

## RESEARCH RECOMMENDATIONS FOR PERFORMANCE IMPROVEMENT MODELS

The advent of meta-analyses and effect sizes has in a short time period harvested useful performance improvement guidelines gleaned from many research studies. In this chapter, we have summarized findings from meta-analyses of research on goal setting, feedback, incentives, and EPSS. After gathering relevant studies, the research team reviews and selects only those studies that meet criteria to be included in the meta-analysis. Most meta-analyses are able to use only a small fraction of the available studies because many do not meet criteria for validity. We forward their call for research of higher quality that is either experimental or quasi-experimental with control groups to augment the many survey, case study, and anecdotal reports on performance improvement initiatives.

We cited the study by Peterson and Luthans (2006) of incentives in fast-food stores as an example of research that is useful because: (1) it was quasi-experimental in that it included a control group; (2) it compared two types of incentives—monetary vs. feedback with recognition; (3) it examined the effects of the incentives on three outcomes—profit, drive-through times, and turnover; (4) it evaluated the effects of incentives awarded to a team rather than to individuals; and (5) it evaluated outcomes over a 9-month period of time.

We recommend that the following issues or questions be addressed in future research:

- *How do task complexity and worker expertise affect performance interventions?* Many of the studies on goal setting, feedback, and incentives have focused on low-complexity tasks; however, the core strategic advantage for many organizations relies more on high-complexity work such as design, analysis, communication, and human interactions. The outputs of these tasks are more challenging to quantify, which may explain their scarcity in the literature to date. Task complexity is relative to the experience of the worker or team. We know from cognitive load theory (Clark et al., 2006) that instructional interventions that work well for novice learners not only do not help those with more experience but in many cases depress their performance. It is likely that the types of goals, feedback, incentives, and EPSSs that are appropriate for higher complexity work and less experienced workers will be different than those that best serve low-complexity tasks and new workers; for example, the research reports on the effects of feedback suggest that information cues in the feedback may have greater positive results on high than on low task complexity (Kluger and DeNisi, 1996).
- *How should performance support be deployed through new technology?* The research described previously on electronic performance improvement initiatives assumed delivery using a desktop computer. With the convergence of computing and telecommunications, small hand-held mobile devices offer the potential to deliver performance support to a new generation of technology. Research on feedback showed better results from computer-delivered feedback than from feedback provided by a person (Kluger and DeNisi, 1996). We need research to define what kinds of feedback, training, and EPSSs are best provided on devices such as cell phones, PDAs, and iPods.

- *Build explanatory models and taxonomies.* Performance improvement models that incorporate moderators of interventions offer opportunities for building performance theories and for adapting interventions to unique situations. The Kluger and DeNisi (1996) feedback model, for example, suggests that feedback will have its effects based on the types of cues embedded in the feedback with cues that direct attention to the task being most useful. This model can be tested and, if valid, offers practitioners guidelines for delivering feedback in ways that obtain the most benefit. Regarding EPSS, more robust taxonomies of the type of performance support needed would help practitioners define the best types of support systems to use for given tasks, workers, and devices.
- *Define the effects of combined interventions.* The majority of research reports focused primarily on a single intervention or perhaps on a combination of two such as goals and feedback. We could benefit from more studies that look at combinations of incentives, such as the Stajkovic and Luthans (2003) meta-analysis suggesting a synergistic effect among goals, feedback, and incentives. We need more data to understand the interactions among interventions such as EPSSs and training or incentives and goal setting.
- *Support and disseminate research.* In this chapter, we have briefly summarized a behavioral engineering, a cognitive–motivational, and a technological perspective on performance improvement. We suspect that these communities of practice often work independently and fail to leverage their potential combined strengths. In addition, practitioners rarely read the same publications and websites or attend the same conferences as the research community. We recommend a greater exchange of information among these communities initiated by professional associations involved in performance improvement.

## THE FUTURE OF PERFORMANCE IMPROVEMENT

We began our chapter by providing four vignettes of organizational failures that were not caused by a lack of knowledge and skills. We believe that a performance improvement perspective is an essential tool set to develop solution systems that do not rely on training alone to reach organizational objectives. The recent adoption of performance improvement certification programs by practitioner professional associations that formerly emphasized training only, such as the American Society for Training and Development and the International Society for Performance Improvement, along with increased mobility of electronic technologies, is advancing the opportunities for performance improvement initiatives. At the same time, the lack of experimental studies combined with failure to communicate the research results outside of the academic communities limit the full potential of performance improvement interventions. This is an opportune time to focus, improve, and disseminate research efforts to build a more evidence-based foundation for performance improvement initiatives. We hope this chapter and the *Handbook* contribute to that effort.

## REFERENCES

Addison, R. M. and Haig, C. (2006). The performance architect's essential guide to the performance technology landscape. In *Handbook of Human Performance Technology*, 3rd ed., edited by J. A. Pershing, pp. 35–54. San Francisco, CA: Pfeiffer.

Altalib, H. (2002). ROI calculations for electronic performance support systems. *Perform. Improv.*, 41(10), 12–22.

Bailey, B. (2003). *Linking vs. Searching: Guidelines for Use*, http://www.webusability.com/article_linking_vs_searching_2_2003.htm.

Bastiaens, Th. J., Nijhof, W. J., Streumer, J. N., and Abma, H. J. (1997). Working and learning with electronic performance support systems: an effectiveness study. *Int. J. Train. Dev.*, 1(1), 72–78.

Brush, T., Knapczyk, D., and Hubbard, L. (1993). Developing a collaborative performance support system for practicing teachers. *Educ. Technol.*, 33(11), 39–45.

Chase, N. (1998). Electronic support cuts training time. *Qual. Mag.*, http://openacademy.mindef.gov.sg/OpenAcademy/LearningResources/EPSS/c16.htm.

Clark, R. C., Nguyen, F., and Sweller, J. (2006). *Efficiency in Learning*. San Francisco, CA: Pfeiffer.*

Cole, K., Fischer, O., and Saltzman, P. (1997). Just-in-time knowledge delivery. *Commun. ACM*, 40(7), 49–53.

Condly, S. J., Clark, R. E., and Stolovitch, H. D. (2003). The effects of incentives on workplace performance: a meta-analytic review of research studies. *Perform. Improv. Q.*, 16(3), 46–63.

Darabi, A. (2004). Contributions of an electronic performance support system to learning a complex cognitive skill. In *The Internet Society: Advances in Learning, Commerce, and Security*, edited by K. Morgan and M. J. Spector, pp. 215–225. Billerica, MA: WIT Press.

Dean, P. J. (1994). *Performance Engineering at Work*. Batavia, IL: International Board of Standards for Training, Performance and Instruction.*

Desmarais, M. C., Leclair, R., Fiset, J. V., and Talbi, H. (1997). Cost-justifying electronic performance support systems. *Commun. ACM*, 40(7), 39–48.

Dorsey, L. T., Goodrum, D. A., and Schwen, T. M. (1993). Just-in-time knowledge performance support: a test of concept. *Educ. Technol.*, 33(11), 21–29.

Flaherty, P. and Harrison, K. A. (1993). City paying dearly for its 1989–90 rush to hire. *The Washington Post*, December 16.

Foster, E. (1997). Training when you need it. *InfoWorld*, February 24, pp. 51–42 (http://openacademy.mindef.gov.sg/OpenAcademy/Learning%20Resources/EPSS/c1.htm).

Geis, G. L. (1986). Human performance technology: an overview. In *Introduction to Performance Technology*, Vol. 2, edited by M. E. Smith, pp. 185–209. Washington, D.C.: National Society for Performance and Instruction.*

Gery, G. (1991). *Electronic Performance Support Systems*. Boston, MA: Weingarten Publications.*

Gery, G. (1995). Attributes and behaviors of performance-centered systems. *Perform. Improv. Q.*, 8(1), 47–93.

Gery, G. (2003). Ten years later: a new introduction to attributes and behaviors and the state of performance-centered systems. In *EPSS Revisited: A Lifecycle for Developing Performance-Centered Systems*, edited by G. J. Dickelman, pp. 1–3. Silver Spring, MD: International Society for Performance Improvement.

Gilbert, T. (1978). *Human Competence: Engineering Worthy Performance*. New York: McGraw-Hill.*

Harless, J. H. (1970). *An Ounce of Analysis (Is Worth a Pound of Objectives)*. Newnan, GA: Harless Performance Guild.

Hawkins, Jr., C. H., Gustafson, K. L., and Nielsen, T. (1998). Return on investment (ROI) for electronic performance support systems: a Web-based system. *Educ. Technol.*, 38, 15–22.

Huber, B., Lippincott, J., McMahon, C., and Witt, C. (1999). Teaming up for performance support: a model of roles, skills and competencies. *Perform. Improv. Q.*, 38(1), 10–14.

Hunt, D. L., Haynes, R. B., Hanna, S. E., and Smith, K. (1998). Effects of computer-based clinical decision support systems on physician performance and patient outcomes. *J. Am. Med. Assoc.*, 280(15), 1339–1346.

Kasvi, J. J. and Vartiainen, M. (2000). Performance support on the shop floor. *Perform. Improv.*, 39(6), 40–46.

Klein, J. D. (2002). Empirical research on performance improvement. *Perform. Improv. Q.*, 15(1), 99–110.*

Kluger, A. N. and DeNisi, A. (1996). The effects of feedback intervention on performance: a historical review, a meta-analysis, and a preliminary feedback intervention theory. *Psychol. Bull.*, 119(2), 254–284.

Locke, E. A. and Latham, G. P. (2002). Building a practically useful theory of goal setting and task motivation: a 35-year odyssey. *Am. Psychol.*, 57(9), 705–717.

Mao, J. and Brown, B. R. (2005). The effectiveness of online task support versus instructor-led training. *J. Org. End User Comput.*, 17(3), 27–46.

Marker, A., Huglin, L., and Johnsen, L. (2006). Empirical research on performance improvement: an update. *Perform. Improv. Q.*, 19(4), 7–22.

McCabe, C. and Leighton, C. (2002). Developing best practices for knowledge work: ISD plus KM, supported by software [electronic version]. *eLearning Dev. J.*, August 13, http://www.elearningguild.com.

McManus, P. and Rossett, A. (2006). Performance support tools delivering value when and where it is needed. *Perform. Improv.*, 45(2), 8–16.

Nguyen, F., Klein, J. D., and Sullivan, H. J. (2005). A comparative study of electronic performance support systems. *Perform. Improv. Q.*, 18(4), 71–86.

Nielsen, J. (2001). Search: visible and simple [electronic version]. *Alertbox*, May 13, http://www.useit.com/alertbox/20010513.html.

Pershing, J. A. (2006). Human performance technology fundamentals. In *Handbook of Human Performance Technology*, 3rd ed., edited by J. A. Pershing, pp. 5–34. San Francisco, CA: Pfeiffer.*

Peterson, S. J. and Luthans, F. (2006). The impact of financial and nonfinancial incentives on business-unit outcomes over time. *J. Appl. Psychol.*, 91(1), 156–165.

Raybould, B. (2000). Building performance-centered Web-based systems, information systems, and knowledge management systems in the 21st century. *Perform. Improv.*, 39(6), 69–79.

Rossett, A. and Schafer, L. (2006). *Job Aids and Performance Support*. San Francisco, CA: Wiley.*

Rothwell, W. J. (1996). *Beyond Training and Development: State-of-the-Art Strategies for Enhancing Human Performance*. New York: American Management Association.*

Rothwell, W. J. and Kazanas, H. C. (2004). *Mastering the Instructional Design Process*. San Francisco, CA: Wiley

Rummler, G. A. and Brache, A. P. (1995). *Improving Performance: How to Manage the White Space on the Organization Chart*, 2nd ed. San Francisco, CA: Jossey-Bass.*

Sleight, D. A. (1993). *Types of Electronic Performance Support Systems: Their Characteristics and Range of Designs* [electronic version], http://openacademy.mindef.gov.sg/OpenAcademy/Learning%20Resources/EPSS/c7.htm.

Spool, J. M. (2001). *Users Don't Learn to Search Better*. North Andover, MA: User Interface Engineering (http://www.uie.com/articles/learn_to_search).

Stajkovic, A. D. and Luthans, F. (2003). Behavioral management and task performance in organizations: conceptual background, meta-analysis, and test of alternative models. *Pers. Psychol.*, 56(1), 155–194.

Taylor, F. W. (1911). *The Principle of Scientific Management*. New York: Harper & Row.

*Training Magazine*. (2006). Industry reports. *Train. Mag.*, 38(12), 20–32 (www.Trainingmag.com).

Villachica, S. W., Stone, D. L., and Endicott, J. (2006). Performance support systems. In *Handbook of Human Performance Technology*, edited by J. A. Pershing, pp. 539–566. San Francisco, CA: Wiley.

---

* Indicates a core reference.

# 40

# Resource-Based Learning

*Michael J. Hannafin and Janette R. Hill*
University of Georgia, Athens, Georgia

## CONTENTS

## ABSTRACT

The nature of information has changed dramatically during the past 25 years. The digital age has redefined the nature of a resource and dramatically changed how resources are used to support learning. Media of often unknown origin and quality are now used across a wide range of learning systems to address diverse epistemological beliefs and associated learning goals. The number and types of resources have also grown exponentially.

Several factors increase the viability of resources for learning, including access to resources in contexts not previously available, increased flexibility in their use, and ready availability, manipulability, and sharability. The purposes of this chapter are to present a brief historical perspective on resource-based learning; describe components of resource-based learning; introduce the influence of underlying epistemology, foundations, and assumptions in grounding resource use; critically analyze related research; and identify implications for RBL.

## KEYWORDS

*Resource:* "Media, people, places or ideas that have the *potential* to support learning" (Hill and Hannafin, 2001, p. 38).

*Resource-based learning:* The use and application of available assets to support varied learning needs across contexts.

*Scaffolding:* Process through which individuals are supported in identifying, interpreting, or otherwise using resources.

*Tools:* Devices that aid individuals to engage and manipulate resources and ideas.

## INTRODUCTION

The digital age has both redefined the nature of information and transformed educational resources. Resources need no longer be intact and self-contained but can be readily repurposed as well as accessed, created, modified, and assembled from virtually anywhere to address individual goals and needs. The educational implications have only begun to emerge as homes, schools, classrooms, workplaces, and community centers become increasingly resource centered.

The potential and challenges of resource-based learning (RBL) are considerable. Increasingly, designers and learners must evaluate growing numbers of digital resources that are developed for purposes other than those being sought and used, that exist in ever-expanding and geographically dispersed repositories, and that are often of unknown quality, accuracy, and integrity. So, while technology has been lauded for potentially democratizing access to information (Kellner, 2003), educational use remains fraught with issues of literacy, misinterpretation, and propagandizing (Brooks, 2003) as well as problems with copyright and fair use (Kahle, 1997).

No singular, universally accepted definition exists as to what constitutes a resource or how resources should be used during learning. One distinction has focused on the extent to which resources embody pedagogical attributes. Wiley (2001) characterized a learning object as a digital resource that embodies pedagogical properties that can be reused to facilitate learning. Downes (2004) characterized a resource as being comprised of and supporting varied functions distributed across users and locations. Increased granularity may enable educators to utilize resources to address a wide variety of learning needs and to support a broad range of learning models, as well as to realize the potential of digital resources (Hodgins, 2001; Schatz, 2005).

Earlier, we characterized a resource as an information asset of broad applicability and defined resources as "media, people, places, or ideas that have the *potential* to support learning" (Hill and Hannafin, 2001, p. 38). Furthermore, we argued that the meaning of a given resource varies according to the epistemological, psychological, and pedagogical context of its use. Accordingly, we define *resource-based learning* as the use and application of available assets to support varied learning needs across contexts (Beswick, 1977; Doiron and Davies, 1998; Haycock, 1991).

Several factors increase the viability of resources for learning, including access in contexts not previously available, increased flexibility in their use, and ready availability, manipulability, and sharability across multiple contexts and purposes. The purposes of this chapter are to present a brief perspective on and describe components of resource-based learning, describe how resource definitions and use are mediated by the underlying beliefs and practices associated with different learning models, and identify implications for creating and using digital resources for varied learning purposes.

## THE EMERGENCE OF RESOURCE-BASED LEARNING

Although the use of resources for learning is not new (Beswick, 1977; Haycock, 1991), their creation and use were limited in predigital environments. Resources were typically static, created and published by companies, and used largely intact to address specific, well-defined needs and goals. In some instances, parts of an intact resource were used (e.g., chapter in a textbook), but it remained difficult to adapt resources to address individual needs. The digital age has changed the very nature of a resource. The resulting opportunities are considerable and range from increasing the number and availability through granularization, to repurposing component resources to address myriad individual needs, to providing multiple perspectives. We now have ready access to more traditional historic (e.g., books, articles) and contemporary (e.g., daily news) information sources (Maddux and Johnson, 1997), as well as emerging, dynamic information sources (e.g., blogs, wikis, podcasts) (Martindale and Wiley, 2005). Although the opportunities afforded through digitization are considerable, challenges remain. In this chapter, we describe the transformation of resources for educational purposes; introduce the foundations, assumptions, and components of resource-based learning; and describe a range of studies utilizing resource-based learning in varied teaching-learning models.

## Metamorphosis of Media

Media have become vastly easier to produce and access; for example, high-quality, sharable digital documents have become commonplace through word processing, movie making, and desktop publishing (Counts, 2006). It is no longer necessary for large design and production facilities to assemble or develop information resources, as individuals and small teams now have the ability to create—even customize—resources rapidly. Digitization has also reduced the need to warehouse resources at centralized repositories. According to Lyman and Varian (2003), the Web has become the leading technology for accessing and sharing information. Traditional publishing and production houses, although important, are no longer required to produce, store, and distribute information. Users must no longer wait for a book to arrive in a library or bookstore; many titles are now available directly from authors (see, for example, Stephen King's downloadable novels at http://www.stephen-king.com/). Likewise, television and movie titles are now downloaded directly or accessed on-demand—a trend that is projected to expand rapidly (Avery, 2004). Numerous online brokers and vendors (e.g., iTunes, Microsoft, Amazon.com) allow users to download digital music, computer software, books (.pdf documents or audiobooks), and video resources directly. Finally, public information, such as historical documents, weather information, and government reports, is increasingly digital in nature. Digital media are now available directly from a myriad of primary sources and brokers, democratizing availability and access across a vast array of hitherto centralized resources.

## Socially Constructed Resources

Blogs and wikis have become a primary source of information across a growing range of users. Blogs enable a wide distribution of ideas, and wikis enable broad distribution as well as the collaborative building of ideas (Engstrom and Jewett, 2005). Rainie (2005), in his work with the Pew Internet and American Life Project, documented a 58% rise in blog readership in 2004. Political blogs, such as Instapundit and Daily Kos (Harp and Tremayne, 2006), were among the top blogs visited, with 9% of respondents to the Pew Internet survey reporting regular or occasional readership (Rainie, 2005).

The increased use of political and news-related blogs provides an important indication of how socially constructed resources have democratized access to ideas and information (Bichard, 2006). Educators have used blogs and wikis both within their classes and to share ideas across a variety of disciplines and grade levels (Martindale and Wiley, 2005). (For a description of wikis in a graduate-level information systems course, see Raman et al., 2005; for a discussion of preservice teachers using blogs to facilitate learning in an instructional technology course, see West et al., 2006; for a discussion of the use of wikis with middle-grades students to engage the learners in the critical examination of an environmental challenge, see Engstrom and Jewett, 2005.)

Whereas interest in and the use of forums such as blogs and wikis appear to be increasing, some question their contributors, readers, and value of the integrity of their contents. Harp and Tremayne (2006) indicated that the majority of blogging in political contexts is male dominated. Likewise, upon examining bloggers in the Pew Internet project, Rainie (2005, p. 2) concluded that "like bloggers, blog readers are more likely to be young, male, well-educated, Internet veterans." This suggests that the presumably open-forum blogging available on the Internet may actually reflect rather narrow, rather than democratic and open, information resources. Other challenges discussed in the literature include variable reading level, unique communication styles, quality of information, and information literacy skills needed to generate, interpret, and use such resources (McPherson, 2006).

## Sophistication of Information Systems

During the past two decades, the amount of information available has increased exponentially; for example, Lawrence and Giles (1998) estimated that the indexable Web was comprised of approximately 320 million pages. More recently, DeKunder at Tilburg University estimated the total Web pages to be 14.3 billion, with a sustained growth rate of 2% per month (Tilburg University, 2006). With the extraordinary volume of available resources, problems have emerged, particularly with locating the "right" information. Mark-up technologies provide descriptive metatags where authors can specify unique search terms and categories for the end user (Hill et al., 2007), which provides fine-grained indexing previously unavailable by a resource's creator; however, some have suggested that the use of a given resource is continually redefined by subsequent users. Metadata may provide guidance in identifying media attributes but little insight into appropriateness for use in given contexts or for learning models (Mwanza and Engestrom, 2005).

## Affordability, Power, and Availability

Technologies have decreased in cost while growing exponentially in capability. According to recent estimates, the cycle processing rates of computer operating systems double every 18 to 20 months (Ekman et al., 2004). At the onset of the 21st century, a high percentage of households in Western countries reported at least one computer with Internet access (NTIA, 2000). Low-cost wireless computer technologies are now widely available and in use, enabling cost-effective access to almost anything, anytime, and anyplace (for a recent study exploring the promises and challenges of nomadic computing, see Cousins, 2004). Internet access has also improved exponentially. According to recent Federal Communication Commission statistics (FCC, 2006), access speeds range from telephone dial-up at 56 kilobits per second to broadband speeds of 200 kilobits per second to the home. T-1 access speeds (1.5 megabytes per second) are now commonplace in public and business facilities. For RBL, both traditional digital text and graphic resources, as well as streaming video and audio resources, can now be provided to the home as well as to education settings affording ready access to a wealth of basic and high-end media resources.

## Changing Nature of Resources

The emergence of learning objects (Northrup, 2007; Wiley, 2001) has stimulated alternative conceptions of resources. Traditional video content can be segmented into a series of scenes or clips that can be accessed individually or viewed in their entirety. Books need not be defined in their entirety but can be comprised of individual objects (e.g., words, tables, figures, and pictures) that can be used independently or in combinations. The meaning is continually redefined as audio recordings, video scenes, and Web resources are recontextualized. Individual resource components, thus, are malleable rather than fixed, affording infinite potential to redefine meanings, allow multiple literacies (Huot et al., 2004), and support different learning goals, contexts, and models.

## Economic and Practical Influences

According to the National Education Association (NEA, 2004), the past two decades have brought radical budgetary constraints to both formal and informal educational initiatives. Availability of resources is required across learning contexts and models to enable use for varied purposes. Resource-based learning, particularly in digital environments, offers promise for broad applicability across a variety of contexts to provide access to an expanding global library of digital resources.

## COMPONENTS

Resource-based learning involves establishing contexts for, tools for acting on and with, and scaffolds to guide the differentiated interpretation, use, and understanding of resources in ways that are consistent with the epistemology, foundations, and assumptions of a given learning model (Hill and Hannafin, 2001). RBL does not embody a particular epistemology but rather provides a process through which epistemologically different, but grounded, learning models are enacted. WebQuests, for example, are "inquiry-oriented activit[ies] in which some or all of the information that learners interact with comes from resources on the Internet" (Dodge, 1995, p. 12). In open-ended learning environments, resources are presumed to be epistemologically neutral until contextualized and designed to support unique learning goals (Hannafin et al., 1999). In the following sections, we describe how resource-based learning is enacted differentially to support different teaching-learning models.

## Context

*External contexts*—supplied situations or problems—are provided by an instructor or external agent to orient learners to a particular learning goal. Specific problem statements or questions, consistent with objectivist epistemology, direct expectations explicitly and guide the strategies and resources used by teachers and students (Hannafin et al., 1997). In *individual contexts*, learners establish learning contexts based on their unique circumstances or needs. Consistent with constructivist epistemology, individuals establish the learning context, define their knowledge and skill needs, identify resources to meet the needs, and situate the resource's meaning to address their needs. *Negotiated contexts* combine aspects of external and individual contexts. Typically, an external problem or issue is provided (e.g., social justice, civil rights), but the specific problems to be addressed (e.g., what led to nonviolent protests in the mid-20th century?) are unique to individual learners (Hill et al., 2007).

In problem-based learning models, the context typically enables multiple issues to be identified and studied using varied resources to support individual approaches. Iiyoshi (1999), for example, examined the effects of different orienting contexts on nursing students' search strategies, interpretation, and understanding using multimedia resources contained in a multimedia database, the Human Body. Students were provided tasks that explicitly directed them to specific resources, focused on relationships between two or more resources, or posed a problem requiring a synthesis of information across multiple resources. Participants tended to learn specific concepts using directed tasks but were only able to synthesize meaning across resources when oriented accordingly. Similarly, the *Jasper Woodbury* series establishes problem contexts using authentic video vignettes depicting dilemmas wherein different problems and subproblems can be identified to establish and implement a plan (Barron et al., 1995; Cognition and Technology Group at Vanderbilt, 1992).

## Tools

*Tools* enable learners to engage and manipulate both resources and ideas. Tool use varies with context and intention; the same tool can support different activities based on its alignment with given learning models. Numerous tool types (see, for example, Hill and Hannafin, 1997) and functions (Iiyoshi et al., 2005) have been identified. *Processing tools* help to manage cognitive demands associated with different RBL models. When embodying objectivist epistemology, spreadsheets enable learners to manipulate scenarios to test the limits within a simulation, extend their cognitive abilities, and reduce the extraneous cognitive load associated with tasks and mental manipulation (Hannafin et al., 2007). The same tools, in contrast, may embody constructivist epistemology when used to negotiate a resource's meaning in technology-enhanced, distance learning environments (Hill et al., 2007).

*Searching tools* can be used in directed as well as learner-centered environments. General-purpose Web-based search engines such as Google (www.google.com) identify the location of and direct access to a variety of electronic resources. Google Scholar, which seeks and generates Web-indexed links among published documents, and Apple Learning Interchange (http://ali.apple.com/ali_appleworks/templates.shtml), which supports searching for highly indexed pre–12

lesson planning resources, provide sophisticated function-specific searching tools. Domain-specific resources can be searched using the State of Georgia's GALILEO database (www.galileo.usg.edu), which contains a variety of subject-specific as well as general search engines, enabling direct access to associated electronic resources (e.g., journal articles, reports) as well as resources in libraries.

*Manipulation tools* are used to test or explore. Consistent with constructivist epistemology, applications such as SimCity or SimEarth empower learners to hypothesize, design, build, test, and rebuild cities and ecosystems to investigate relationships between and among objects and systems. Manipulation tools allow the testing of environmental scenarios and manipulation of systemic concepts such as global warming in ways otherwise impossible or impractical.

Finally, *communication tools* support the ability to exchange information and ideas. Asynchronous tools such as e-mail, podcasts, blogs, and wikis enable and sustain access among learners, instructors, and experts. Synchronous communication tools (e.g., instant messaging, videoconferencing) provide access to others in real time, whether they are located a few rooms away or around the globe.

## Scaffolds

*Scaffolding* is support provided initially and subsequently faded in a continuous cycle as knowledge and understanding develops. The amount and frequency of scaffolding vary with the individual learner, problems encountered, and the needs or demands of a specific context (Sharma and Hannafin, 2007). Procedural, conceptual, metacognitive, and strategic scaffolds are especially relevant for RBL. *Procedural scaffolds* emphasize how to use the features and functions of a given resource. Greene and Land (2000), for example, made extensive use of procedural scaffolds to support preservice teachers in their development of an Internet-based RBL lesson. Procedural scaffolds allow learners to focus cognitive resources for other learning activities (e.g., problem solving). *Conceptual scaffolds* guide learners in what to consider by assisting with the identification of knowledge related to a problem or by making connections between concepts more apparent. Resource-intense toolkits were created by the Open University to assist students with learning at a distance in a directed environment (Jelfs et al., 2004). *Metacognitive scaffolds*, common in inquiry-based environments, prompt reflection, comparison, and revision based on self-assessments of understanding. Checklists, for example, can assist the learner with reflecting upon decisions made or actions to take.

Cases also support reflection and comparison, presenting scenarios for learners to consider as well as confirmation points where learners reflect on their understanding to reveal what they do or do not understand (Kim and Hannafin, in press a; Kolodner et al., 2004). Finally, *strategic scaffolds* provide assistance in identifying ways to analyze, plan, and respond (e.g., identifying and selecting information, evaluating resources). Many models have been developed to guide learners in developing and applying information literacy skills (see, for example, Eisenberg et al., 2004). Several libraries have created websites to guide learners with evaluating print and electronic resources that can be used across learning contexts. The University of California–Berkeley (http://www.lib.berkeley.edu/TeachingLib/Guides/Evaluation.html) and Purdue University (http://owl.english.purdue.edu/handouts/research/r_evalsource.html) have established extensive websites for evaluating resources. Similarly, Trochim's (2004) social science research website provides strategic scaffolding to guide the research process.

# EPISTEMOLOGY, FOUNDATIONS, AND ASSUMPTIONS

In grounded design practice, epistemology, foundations, and assumptions are aligned to maximize their coincidence. Although isolated for clarity in the following, the extent to which activities are aligned with the associated foundations and assumptions determines how (or if) a given learning model is consistent with its espoused epistemology.

## Epistemology

We have advocated that learning systems be aligned with and grounded in underlying epistemological beliefs and associated foundations and embody the assumptions and practices underlying those beliefs and foundations (Hannafin and Hill, 2006; Hannafin et al., 2004). Objectivists' values and beliefs about the nature of knowledge and learning, for example, differ fundamentally from those of relativists (Jonassen, 1991). To ground design practices that reflect and manifest the values of objectivist epistemology, corresponding design foundations and practices are applied to support learning. Conversely, constructivists emphasize the uniquely individual construction of knowledge and the generation of meaning; accordingly, practices are designed to support unique rather than particular sense making (Hannafin et al., 1997). In effect, grounded design criteria require that the components, strategies, and activities of any learning environment reflect an alignment of associated foundations and assumptions underlying epistemological beliefs. The unique ways in which design practices are enacted vary according to the epistemology, foundations, and assumptions consistent with and extended from a given learning model (for a discussion of grounded design practices in case-based learning, see Kim and Hannafin, in press a).

## Foundations and Assumptions

### Psychological

Specific instantiations vary based on epistemological differences, but the importance of psychological foundations has been long recognized (Bednar et al., 1995; Brown and Campione, 1996; Gagné and Glaser, 1987). Beginning in the early 20th century, associationism dominated the psychological learning landscape. Operant behavioral theory and research, reflecting objectivist epistemology and influenced strongly by Skinner's research in operant conditioning, posit that learning involves an enduring change in behavior regulated by associations between a stimulus, a response, and a reinforcer: The more a desired behavior is reinforced in the presence of controlling stimuli, the greater the likelihood of repeating the response and the stronger the learning. Characteristically, behaviorists paid little attention to thinking or the organization of knowledge, tending instead to characterize learning in terms of complex stimulus–response–reinforcement associations—that is, observable phenomena deemed to influence learning (Burton et al., 2004).

Like behaviorism, cognitive psychology is largely rooted in objectivist epistemology; unlike behaviorists, cognitive psychologists emphasize the individual's processing of information and how knowledge is stored and retrieved (Winn, 2004). Cognitive theorists, for example, posit that mental processes mediate what is selected, remembered, recalled, and generalized based on individual background, needs, and interests. Information processing involves an exchange between external stimuli and internal mental processes such as sensory registers, selective perception, short-term memory (STM), and long-term memory (LTM) (Shuell, 1986). According to information-processing theory, sensory registers filter external stimuli, selectively isolating information and signals to be processed more deeply. This information is processed temporarily in working memory, where it is further filtered. Relevant information is encoded in permanent memory, and the remaining information is discarded. Learning, then, involves the transfer of information from working to permanent memory, while retrieval involves retrieving knowledge from permanent to working memory. The richer the initial and updated encoding, the more likely knowledge will be activated and retrieved under appropriate conditions, retrieved (decoded), and applied or transferred (Hannafin et al., 2007).

The psychological foundations of contemporary resource-based environments, such as inquiry-based learning and problem-based learning, are often rooted in constructivist epistemology. Kim and Hannafin (in press b), for example, described numerous examples of situated, constructivist-inspired inquiry learning. Situated cognition researchers and theorists consider knowledge and context to be inextricably intertwined; that is, meaning does not exist independent of context, but rather context shapes and defines meaning (Brown et al., 1989).

### Pedagogical

Psychological and pedagogical foundations are interdependent. Direct instruction, for example, typically emphasizes explicit identification of objective outcomes, hierarchical structures, and objective-based activities and assessment consistent with objectivist epistemology and behavioral psychology, whereas student-centered pedagogical approaches tend to be contextually based and epistemologically aligned with constructivism. Taken together, they reflect underlying beliefs about the nature of learning, the methods and strategies employed, and the ways in which domain information is organized and made available.

### Technological

Technological capabilities dictate the extent to which features *can* support learning, but pedagogical requirements dictate how and which capabilities *should be* integrated. Technological capabilities vary widely, but it is the manner in which they support or hamper efforts, not their mere availability, that influences learning. Some features are available but not appropriate given the pedagogical requirements of a given learning environment, while others may be desirable but inherently limited.

### Cultural

Cultural considerations reflect beliefs about education, the role of individuals in society, traditions in how different disciplines teach and learn, and the prevailing practices of a given community. They influence design by defining the values of a given setting. As an example, "back to basics" learning cultures tend to embrace objectivist epistemology, emphasize behavioral or cognitive psychological foundations, and apply direct instruction pedagogy. In effect, different learning models are both reflections and extensions of the cultures for which they are designed.

### Pragmatic

Each setting has unique situational constraints that affect how a learning model is implemented. Collins (1996), for example, described competing consequences involved in making practical tradeoffs, such as determining what should be taught, assessing costs and benefits, and evaluating activity alternatives. Issues such as hardware and software type and availability and costs routinely influence the adoption and diffusion of innovations. They establish, from a practical perspective, why a particular approach may or may not be feasible in a given learning environment.

## RESOURCE-BASED LEARNING RESEARCH

As noted previously, RBL-related approaches are commonly reflected in research on different learning models. We will not attempt to discuss research within different learning models; instead, we examine research involving the use of resources where no formal learning model was specified or apparent. Armatas et al. (2003) explored how individual characteristics (e.g., learning goals, study strategies, subject interest, computer attitudes) influenced learner engagement with course resources in an online environment involving 731 on- and off-campus students enrolled in a first-year psychology course in Australia. A learning management system (LMS) linked the course structures to a variety of prescribed and optional resources, ranging from a textbook to lectures to websites to discussion groups. A 165-item survey that assessed study habits, resources accessed, difficulties accessing, and perceived value of the resources was distributed toward the end of the term. In addition, computer attitudes, learning goals, study strategies, and interest in psychology were assessed.

Results indicated a significant influence for background factors, engagement with, and perceived value of RBL resources. Among enrollees, off-campus students reported spending more time studying than on-campus students. Off-campus students also indicated a preference for electronic resources and reported fewer problems with accessing the LMS than on-campus students and were more positive toward resource organization and usefulness. Overall, older students (more prevalent among off-campus enrollees) preferred working with the computer more than younger students, who reported less confidence in study strategies than older students. On-campus students, generally younger, preferred print-based resources.

Newnham et al. (1998) explored the use of Internet-based resources in an undergraduate geography course. The learning environment was largely externally directed, with the course instructor supplying extensive structure and explicit directions (for detailed discussions of directed distance learning environments, or DDLEs, see Sharma et al., 2007). Course resources were predetermined by the instructor and downloaded to a local network. In addition, students were encouraged to use bulletin boards related to topics under study (volcanic and earthquake activity). Student performance and student course evaluations were gathered over two academic years.

Results indicated significant improvements in student performance associated with externally directed use of Internet-based resources. According to the researchers, the standard of academic coursework was higher when students were provided directed access to Internet-based resources—particularly in the second year. Student perceptions related to the use of Internet resources were also positive, both for completing course assignments and for long-term employability.

Greene and Land's (2000) qualitative analysis of the use of resources in a college-level problem-focused RBL environment examined how learners used resources during project-based learning, how procedural scaffolds influenced project progress, and how interactions (student–student, student–instructor) shaped project quality. Participants were 18 undergraduate preservice teachers (16 female, 2 male) in an educational technology course. The activity involved students developing a project that integrated Web resources into the curriculum. Participants chose their own topics (e.g., trip planning for third graders) and elected to work in groups of two to four members or independently. Data collection focused on surveys, researcher observations, videotaped observations of Web use, and transcriptions of student verbalizations during Web use.

Results indicated that the ability to recognize and integrate specific Web resources into projects was influenced by knowledge of the Web, the topic under investigation, and a willingness to consider alternatives. Within-group student–student interactions and instructor–student interactions were reportedly valued and useful; across-group student–student interactions were successful only when the interaction was perceived to be of value. The dynamic questions and discussions between instructor and students promoted reflection on why students used Web resources. Greene and Land (2000) concluded that the contextualization and scaffolding supporting resource use influenced stu-

dents' perceived and actual usability, indicating that learners may need explicit guidance in selecting resources until they become sufficiently familiar with their topic or the context. They also noted that online information lacks adequate indexing to support educational purposes, and they underscored the need to structure and scaffold both search and use of Web resources.

Jelfs et al. (2004) explored resource "toolkits" for students in a directed, online learning environment at the British Open University. The researchers sought to determine which, when, and how to provide resources to assist distant undergraduate students during their online learning. Participants included 60 part-time undergraduates, and data included questionnaires and interviews. The questionnaires focused on students' perceptions of the resource scaffolding toolkits. Interviews were conducted by phone with students throughout the United Kingdom (England, Wales, Scotland, and Northern Ireland) to supplement questionnaire responses.

Overall, although the resource toolkits were effective in scaffolding resource use, students requested alternative formats (e.g., print, people) and the ability to access resources when needed. Some students preferred receiving the toolkits in print format, and others preferred retrieving materials from the Internet. Generally, students indicated a preference for fewer activities and for aesthetically attractive resources in the toolkits.

Macdonald et al. (2001) examined resource use in both an undergraduate and a graduate course taught over a 3-year period at the British Open University. Both courses included a variety of resources (electronic, human, Web-based) in multiple formats (print, video, animations) to support the learning process. The researchers examined the influence of information-handling skills and factors that influence the acquisition of those skills. Data sources included computer conferences, observations, interviews, and e-mail reflective follow-up; questionnaires were used to gather quantitative data. Undergraduates indicated that they enjoyed the resource-based learning approach; however, both time constraints for using the resources and information overload were cited as problems. Participants indicated that access to resources (primarily via CD-ROM) was relatively easy, although the skills needed to analyze and evaluate the information were not sufficiently developed.

Graduate participants also indicated that they favored the resource-based approach, but the researchers noted that they may have had greater prior experience and confidence in using multiple resources. Some participants indicated that RBL may be more applicable in some areas than in others (e.g., engineering) and that resource-based approaches may be more appropriate for upper-division undergraduate and graduate level study. The authors concluded that: (1) a variety of skills is needed to effectively use resources (e.g., IT skills, cognitive skills); (2) course complexity should inform how many and what resources are introduced; and (3) opportunities are needed for students to understand the benefits (as well as challenges) of RBL.

Although published research typically focuses on postsecondary environments, a few researchers have examined the use of resource-based approaches in elementary and secondary settings. In a seventh-grade project, "Children, Access, and Learning," McNichol et al. (2002) examined the RBL approaches of four U.K. schools. One class was selected from each school, and students were required to use information and communication technology (ICT) resources (e.g., Internet, CD-ROM) at school, at home, or in the community (e.g., public library). Participants represented a range of socioeconomic backgrounds (low socioeconomic to prosperous) and environmental settings (semi-rural, semi-urban, inner-city, rural). Student logs recorded resource use, summary logs documented reflection on the process, and individual follow-up interviews obtained student perceptions. Parent or guardian questionnaires and interviews provided independent data related to home resource usage.

Results indicated that ICT resource use in the home was high, even in poorer regions of the country (93%). While access varied (individual machine to a single shared computer in the house), the majority of the students had access to and made use of ICT resources. The perceived value of ICT resources differed between students and parents. Students expressed concern over the limited number of resources available, while parents expressed concerns related to laziness (i.e., too easy to find information), inadequate information literacy, access to inappropriate information, the cost of Internet access, the use of chatrooms, and inappropriate use of the ICT resources.

School-based ICT access varied widely from location to location. At one school, most resources were accessed in the classroom, library, and at home. Another school provided very limited and highly centralized access to ICT resources, housing most computers in the library. As a result of limited access, resources use was limited and the project teacher developed few skills.

## ISSUES AND IMPLICATIONS

One area of particular interest to RBL is literacy. As we have noted throughout the chapter, literacy concerns related to the multiple types and forms of resources include the rapid but largely unmanaged growth of resources, the presence of erroneous or misinformation, and the use of resources as propaganda. The largely unregulated generation, distribution, access, and use of digital resources pose both significant opportunities and challenges for resource-based learning.

Given the challenges associated with the identification of reliable and valid resources, developing literacy across media and multiple ways of knowing have become increasingly important (Mackey, 2002). Information literacy has a long history with both traditional text and electronic contexts. Barnard et al. (2005, p. 509) noted: "Individuals who are information literate can determine the extent of information needed, access information effectively, and critically evaluate information and its sources." Researchers in the United States and Western Europe have underscored the growing significance of information literacy; for example, in the study by McNichol et al. (2002), one participant stated: "They use [information literacy] in schools and businesses and this is the way things are going, so they need to have a good knowledge of computers. It's the future; if they don't know, they're stuck" (p. 399). Other researchers have advocated an expansion of our definitions and understandings of what it means to be *literate* in the information age. Mackey (2002) described the "ecologies of literacy" in a 1.5-year-long study exploring young students (age 10 and 13) using multiple resources. Huot et al. (2004), along with other scholars writing in their edited book, advocated that "literacy is not one thing and that time changes what we mean by literacy" (p. 1).

Despite widespread agreement as to the importance of information literacy, little is known about how recontextualized resources (as the raw materials of the information age) influence interpretation, meaning, and understanding during RBL. In externally imposed contexts, the range of intended interpretations and meaning is largely constrained by the tasks, activities, and goals to which their use is directed. The objectivist-inspired learning models typically convey common rather than unique meaning; however, in individual and negotiated learning models where individual selection and interpretation of a resource's meaning are expected, considerable variability has been reported in the resources used and their meaning.

Resource-based learning components are designed to instantiate individual resource selection and meaning making by providing the contexts and tools to explore and refine understanding and the scaffolds to guide and support reasoning. In some cases, unique sets of resources, tools, and scaffolds have been developed for specific learning models; see, for example, the description by Linn et al. (2003) of the Web-Based Inquiry Science Environment (WISE) program, as well as the summary of *Jasper*'s affordances by the Cognition and Technology Group at Vanderbilt (1992). In others, however, existing resources are recontextualized by the individual. Little evidence exists documenting their effectiveness in different, often distal, learning contexts. We need to further explore how literacy affects the use and interpretation of resources within these contexts.

Likewise, a great deal of literature has been published on orienting individuals to varied learning goals, activities that engage individuals with learning content, and guiding performance. Although this research provides some guidance for resource use, the epistemology, foundations, and assumptions embodied in the research often differ from those embodied in specific learning models. Findings related to providing prequestions may prove to be of value in designing directed learning models but of little utility in enabling contexts designed to induce unique learning goals. In addition, comparatively few researchers have examined interactions among contexts, tools, and scaffolds in learner-centered models. So, although a great deal of related research has been published, their relevance to learning models reflecting fundamentally different epistemologies has not been documented conclusively.

Finally, Wellington (2001) identified a host of issues related to resource use, including teacher control, worries about plagiarism, and perceived threats to teacher authority. Clearly, increased availability and quality have not tempered educators' concerns regarding the risks associated with everyday resource use. Significant barriers derive more from teaching–learning traditions than concerns over the inherent vs. malleable properties of a resource. These barriers are deeply engrained in education culture and may prove more formidable than quality, interpretive, and technical issues related to recontextualization.

## REFERENCES

Armatas, C., Holt, D., and Rice, M. (2003). Impacts of an online-supported, resource-based learning environment: Does one size fit all? *Dist. Educ.*, 24(2), 141–158.

Avery, S. (2004). *On-Demand Movies to Soar by 2010*, http://www.matrixstream.com/press_release/mediaweek. pdf#search=%22on-demand%20movies%20statistics%22.

Barnard, A., Nash, R., and O'Brien, M. (2005). Information literacy: developing lifelong skills through nursing education. *J. Nurs. Educ.*, 44(11), 505–510.

Barron, B., Vye, N. J., Zech, L., Schwartz, D. L., Bransford, J. D., Goldman, S. R., Pellegrino, J., Morris, J., Garrison, S., and Kantor, R. (1995). Creating contexts for community-based problem solving: the *Jasper* Challenge Series. In *Thinking and Literacy: The Mind at Work*, edited by P. A. C. Hedley, P. Antonacci, and M. Rabinowitz, pp. 47–72. Hillsdale, NJ: Lawrence Erlbaum Associates.

Bednar, A., Cunningham, D., Duffy, T., and Perry, J. D. (1995). Theory into practice: how do we link it? In *Instructional Technology: Past, Present, and Future*, 2nd ed., edited by G. Anglin, pp. 100–112. Englewood, CO: Libraries Unlimited.

Beswick, N. (1977). *Resource-Based Learning*. London: Heinemann Educational Books.*

Bichard, S. L. (2006). Building blogs: a multi-dimensional analyses of the distribution of frames on the 2004 presidential Web sites. *Journalism Mass Commun. Q.*, 83(2), 329–345.

Brooks, T. (2003). Web search: how the Web has changed information retrieval. *Inform. Res.*, 8(3), paper no. 154, http://informationr.net/ir/8-3/paper154.html.

Brown, A. and Campione, J. (1996). Psychological theory and the design of innovative learning environments: on procedures, principles, and systems. In *Innovations in Learning: New Environments for Education*, edited by L. Schauble and R. Glaser, pp. 289–325. Mahwah, NJ: Lawrence Erlbaum Associates.*

Brown, J. S., Collins, A., and Duguid, P. (1989). Situated cognition and the culture of learning. *Educ. Res.*, 18(1), 32–41.*

Burton, J., Moore, D. M., and Magliaro, S. G. (2004). Behaviorism and instructional technology. In *Handbook of Research in Educational Communication and Technology*, 2nd ed., edited by D. Jonassen, pp. 3–36. Mahwah, NJ: Lawrence Erlbaum Associates.

Cognition and Technology Group at Vanderbilt (CTGV). (1992). The *Jasper* experiment: an exploration of issues in learning and instructional design. *Educ. Technol.*, *Research and Development*, 40(1), 65–80.*

Collins, A. (1996). Design issues for learning environments. In *International Perspectives on the Design of Technology-Supported Learning Environments*, edited by S. Vosniadou, E. De Corte, R. Glaser, and H. Mandl, pp. 347–361. Mahwah, NJ: Lawrence Erlbaum Associates.*

Counts, E. (2006). From Gertie to gigabytes: revealing the world with digital media. *Int. J. Instruct. Media*, 33(1), 23–31.

Cousins, K. C. (2004). Access Anytime, Anyplace: An Empirical Investigation of Patterns of Technology Use within Nomadic Computing Environments. Ph.D. dissertation. Atlanta, GA: Georgia State University (http://etd.gsu.edu/theses/available/etd-12132004–144636/unrestricted/KCDiss.pdf).

Dodge, B. (1995). Some thoughts about WebQuests. *Dist. Educator*, 1(3), 12–15.*

Doiron, R. and Davies, J. (1998). *Partners in Learning: Students, Teachers, and the School Library*. Englewood, CO: Libraries Unlimited.

Downes, S. (2004). Resource profiles. *J. Interact. Media Educ.*, 5, 1–32.

Eisenberg, M. B., Lowe, C. A., and Spitzer, K. L. (2004). *Information Literacy: Essential Skills for the Information Age*, 2nd ed. Westport, CT: Libraries Unlimited.*

Ekman, M., Warg, F., and Nilsson, J. (2004). *An In-Depth Look at Computer Performance Growth*, http://www.ce.chalmers. se/research/group/hpcag/publ/2004/EWN04/performance-growth_tr-2004-9.pdf.

Engstrom, M. E. and Jewett, D. (2005). Collaborative learning the wiki way. *TechTrends*, 49(6), 12–15, 68.

FCC. (2006). *High-Speed Internet Access: Broadband*. Washington, D.C.: Federal Communications Commission (http://www.fcc.gov/cgb/consumerfacts/highspeedinternet.html).

Gagné, R. M. and Glaser, R. (1987). Foundations in learning research. In *Instructional Technology: Foundations*, edited by R. M. Gagné, pp. 49–84. Hillsdale, NJ: Lawrence Erlbaum Associates.*

Greene, B. A. and Land, S. M. (2000). A qualitative analysis of scaffolding use in a resource-based learning environment involving the World Wide Web. *J. Educ. Comput. Res.*, 23(2), 151–179.

Hannafin, M. J. and Hill, J. (2006). Epistemology and the design of learning environments. In *Trends and Issues in Instructional Design and Technology*, 2nd ed., edited by R. Reiser and J. Dempsey, pp. 53–61. Upper Saddle River, NJ: Prentice Hall.*

Hannafin, M. J., Hannafin, K. M., Land, S., and Oliver, K. (1997). Grounded practice and the design of constructivist learning environments. *Educ. Technol. Res. Dev.*, 45(3), 101–117.*

Hannafin, M. J., Land, S., and Oliver, K. (1999). Open learning environments: foundations and models. In *Instructional Design Theories and Models: A New Paradigm of Instructional Theory*, edited by C. M. Reigeluth, pp. 115–140. Mahwah, NJ: Lawrence Erlbaum Associates.*

Hannafin, M. J., Kim, M., and Kim, J. (2004). Reconciling research, theory and practice in Web-based teaching and learning. *J. Comput. Higher Educ.*, 15(2), 3–20.

Hannafin, M. J., Hill, J., Song, L., and West, R. E. (2007). Cognitive perspectives on technology-enhanced distance learning environments. In *Handbook of Distance Education*, 2nd ed., edited by M. Moore, pp. 123–136. Mahwah, NJ: Lawrence Erlbaum Associates.

Harp, D. and Tremayne, M. (2006). The gendered blogosphere: examining inequality using network and feminist theory. *Journalism Mass Commun. Q.*, 83(2), 247–264.

Haycock, C. A. (1991). Resource-based learning: a shift in the roles of teacher, learner. *NASSP Bull.*, 75(535), 15–22.

Hill, J. R. and Hannafin, M. J. (1997). Cognitive strategies and learning from the World Wide Web. *Educ. Technol. Res. Dev.*, 45(4), 37–64.*

Hill, J. R. and Hannafin, M. J. (2001). Teaching and learning in digital environments: the resurgence of resource-based learning. *Educ. Technol. Res. Dev.*, 49(3), 37–52.*

Hill, J. R., Domizi, D., Kim, M., Kim, H., and Hannafin, M. J. (2007). Teaching and learning in negotiated and informal environments. In *Handbook of Distance Education*, 2nd ed., edited by M. Moore, pp. 271–284. Mahwah, NJ: Lawrence Erlbaum Associates.

Hill, J. R., Hannafin, M. J., and Recesso, P. (2007). Creating a patchwork quilt for teaching and learning: the use of learning objects in teacher education. In *Learning Objects for Instruction: Design and Evaluation*, edited by P. Northrup, pp. 261–279. Hershey, PA: Idea Group.

Hodgins, H. W. (2001). The future of learning objects. In *Learning Objects*, edited by D. Wiley, pp. 281–298. Bloomington, IN: Association for Educational Communications and Technology.

Huot, B., Stroble, B., and Bazerman, C., Eds. (2004). *Multiple Literacies for the 21st Century*. Cresskill, NJ: Hampton Press.

Iiyoshi, T. (1999). Cognitive Processes Using Cognitive Tools in Open-Ended Hypermedia Learning Environments: A Case Study. Ph.D. dissertation. Tallahassee, FL: Florida State University.

Iiyoshi, T., Hannafin, M. J., and Wang, F. (2005) Cognitive tools and student-centered learning: rethinking tools, functions, and applications. *Educ. Media Int.*, 42(4), 281–296.

Jelfs, A., Nathan, R., and Barrett, C. (2004). Scaffolding students: suggestions on how to equip students with the necessary skills for studying in a blended learning environment. *J. Educ. Media*, 29(2), 85–96.

Jonassen, D. (1991). Objectivism versus constructivism: do we need a new philosophical paradigm? *Educ. Technol. Res. Dev.*, 39, 5–14.

Kahle, B. (1997). Preserving the Internet. *Sci. Am.*, 276(3), 82–83.

Kellner, D. (2003). Toward a critical theory of education. *Democracy Nat.*, 9(1), 51–64.

Kim, H. and Hannafin, M. J. (in press a). Grounded design and Web-enhanced, case-based reasoning. *Educ. Technol. Res. Dev.*

Kim, M. and Hannafin, M. J. (in press b). Foundations and practice for Web-enhanced science learning environments: grounded design perspectives. In *Trends in Distance Education*, 2nd ed., edited by R. Luppicini. Greenwich, CT: Information Age Publishing.

Kolodner, J. L., Owensby, J. N., and Guzdial, M. (2004). Case-based learning aids. In *Handbook of Research on Educational Communications and Technology*, 2nd ed., edited by D. H. Jonassen, pp. 829–861. Mahwah, NJ: Lawrence Erlbaum Associates.*

Lawrence, S. and Giles, C. L. (1998). Searching the World Wide Web. *Science*, 280, 98–100.

Linn, M. C., Clark, D., and Slotta, J. D. (2003). WISE design for knowledge integration. *Sci. Educ.*, 87(4), 517–538.

Lyman, P. and Varian, H. R. (2003). *How Much Information*, http://www.sims.berkeley.edu/how-much-info-2003.

Macdonald, J., Heap, N., and Mason, R. (2001). 'Have I learnt it?' Evaluating skills for resource-based study using electronic resources. *Br. J. Educ. Technol.*, 32(4), 419–433.

Mackey, M. (2002). *Literacies Across Media: Playing the Text*. New York: Routledge.

Maddux, C. and Johnson, D. L. (1997). The World Wide Web: history, cultural context, and a manual for developers of educational information-based Web sites. *Educ. Technol.*, 37(5), 5–12.

Martindale, T. and Wiley, D. A. (2005). Using Weblogs in scholarship and teaching. *TechTrends*, 49(2), 55–61.

McNichol, S., Nankivell, C., and Ghelani, T. (2002). ICT and resource-based learning: Implications for the future. *Br. J. Educ. Technol.*, 33(4), 393–401.

McPherson, K. (2006). Wikis and literacy development. *Teacher Librarian*, 34(1), 67–69.

Mwanza, D. and Engestrom, Y. (2005). Managing content in e-learning environments. *Br. J. Educ. Technol.*, 36(3), 453–463.

NEA. (2004). *No Child Left Behind?: The Funding Gap in ESEA and Other Federal Education Programs*. Washington, D.C.: National Education Association (http://www.nea.org/esea/images/funding-gap.pdf).

Newnham, R., Mather, A., Grattan, J., Holmes, A., and Gardner, A. (1998). An evaluation of the use of Internet sources as a basis for geography coursework. *J. Geogr. Higher Educ.*, 22(1), 19–34.

Northrup, P., Ed. (2007). *Learning Objects for Instruction: Design and Evaluation*. Hershey, PA: Idea Group.

NTIA. (2000). *Falling Through the Net: Toward Digital Inclusion*. Washington, D.C.: National Telecommunications and Information Administration (http://www.ntia.doc.gov/ntiahome/fttn00/chartscontents.html).

Rainie, L. (2005). *The State of Blogging*. Washington, D.C.: Pew Internet and American Life Project (http://www.pewinternet.org/pdfs/PIP_blogging_data.pdf).

Raman, M., Ryan, T., and Olfman, L. (2005). Designing knowledge management systems for teaching and learning with Wiki technology. *J. Inform. Syst. Educ.*, 16(3), 311–320.

Schatz, S. C. (2005). Unique metadata schemas: a model for user-centric design of a performance support system. *Educ. Technol. Res. Dev.*, 53(4), 69–84.

Sharma, P., Oliver, K., and Hannafin, M. (2007). Teaching and learning in directed environments. In *Handbook of Distance Education*, 2nd ed., edited by M. Moore, pp. 259–270. Mahwah, NJ: Lawrence Erlbaum Associates.*

Sharma, P. and Hannafin, M. J. (2007). Scaffolding in technology-enhanced learning environments. *Interact. Learn. Environ.*, 15(1), 27–46.

Shuell, T. J. (1986). Cognitive conceptions of learning. *Rev. Educ. Res.*, 56(4), 411–436.*

Tilburg University. (2006). *World Wide Web Has at Least 14 Billion Pages*, http://ilk.uvt.nl/events/dekunder.html.

Trochim, W. M. K. (2004). *The Web for the Center of Social Research Methods*, http://www.socialresearchmethods.net/.

Wellington, J. (2001). Exploring the secret garden: the growing importance of ICT in the home. *Br. J. Educ. Technol.*, 32(2), 233–244.

West, R. E., Wright, G., Gabbitas, B., and Graham, C. R. (2006). Reflections from the introduction of blogs and RSS feeds into a preservice instructional technology course. *TechTrends*, 50(4), 54–60.

Wiley, D. A., Ed. (2001). *The Instructional Use of Learning Objects*. Bloomington, IN: Association for Educational Communications and Technology.

Winn, W. (2004). Cognitive perspectives in psychology. In *Handbook of Research in Educational Communication and Technology*, 2nd ed., edited by D. H. Jonassen, pp. 79–112. Mahwah, NJ: Lawrence Erlbaum Associates.*

* Indicates a core reference.

# 41

# Instructional Models in Domains and Professions

*Henny P. A. Boshuizen\**
Open University of the Netherlands, Heerlen, the Netherlands

*Caroline Phythian-Sence and Richard K. Wagner*
Florida State University, Tallahassee, Florida

*Koeno Gravemeijer*
Utrecht University, Utrecht, the Netherlands

*Geerdina Maria van der Aalsvoort*
Leiden University, Leiden, the Netherlands

*Fleurie Nievelstein, Tamara van Gog and Frans J. Prins*
Open University of the Netherlands, Heerlen, the Netherlands

*Tim Dornan*
University of Manchester, Manchester, England

*Albert Scherpbier*
Maastricht University, Maastricht, the Netherlands

*John Spencer*
University of Newcastle, Newcastle, England

---

\* Henny P. A. Boshuizen was lead author for this chapter and coordinator for the domain-specific sections of this chapter.

## CONTENTS

## ABSTRACT

This chapter seeks to investigate grounds for the application and adaptation of general instructional models in specific domains and professions and for the generation of domain-specific instructional methods using the examples of reading, mathematics, science, law, and medicine. It does so by first investigating the specific teaching and learning difficulties of those domains by showing and analyzing domain- and profession-specific solutions to these problems. The chapter consists of a general analysis of the problems with general instructional design models that have to be solved before they can be used in specific domains, the requirements for the use of these models, and the effects of internal and external pressures for change. The chapter is completed by five contributions from these domains.

## KEYWORDS

*Abstract mathematical knowledge:* Mathematics as a body of knowledge that may be experienced as experientially real.

*Apprenticeship:* Learning a skilled practical trade through participation in practice.

*Clinical education:* Supervised acquisition of clinical skills.

*Conceptual model:* A theoretically based explanation of a natural phenomenon.

*Constructivism:* A point of view related to cognitive development; cognitive development depends upon a child's actions on his own surroundings to change and learn actively from those surroundings (Piaget) and on the strong relationship between a child's surroundings and his cognitive development (Vygotsky).

*Discovery learning environment:* Environment that provides students with a set of events or data that they can explore independently or in a prestructured way to discover the regularities in these data; a rich learning environment that facilitates children's own constructive endeavors to learning experiences.

*Domain-specific theories:* Theories on instruction that are tailored to a specific subject-matter domain.

*Embodiments:* Tactile or visual models that are meant to represent mathematical relationships and concepts in a ready apprehensible form.

*Emergent modeling:* A dynamic approach to modeling in mathematics education, in which the models that the students use develop from models of informal mathematical activity into models for more formal mathematical reasoning.

*Expertise development:* Acquisition of knowledge and skill in a domain.

*Gaming:* Taking part in open-ended activities that give opportunity to elicit conceptual learning.

*Ontology:* A shared and agreed upon explicit formal representation of a domain.

*Problem-based learning:* Acquiring knowledge as part of a learner group by analyzing a problem, studying privately, using various learning resources, and collectively synthesizing knowledge.

*Reasoning:* Formulating and substantiating conclusions based on given information.

*Science learning:* Understanding concepts related to biology, physics, chemistry, and astronomy.

## INTRODUCTION

*Henny P. A. Boshuizen*

The individual examples discussed in this chapter give the reader a view of how instructional-design models are developed, adapted, and used in specific domains. These examples are from diverse fields: reading, mathematics, science, law, and medicine. They cover both initial and advanced learning; they include knowledge and skills that everyone in Western societies are supposed to learn, as well as fields that are only taught at the university level; and they show a variety of methods and models that are being used in these domains. In this chapter, we move away from research into the models themselves and enter the world where instructional designers, pedagogues, and teachers work together to realize adequate instruction in a particular domain. The worlds of research and professional practice have different commitments, confront different problems, and work with different assumptions, principles, and expectations. Still, they build on each other. We will analyze the reasons for these differences in different domains and highlight problems that affect transfer of the insights and methods that have been described in previous chapters.

### Different Commitments

There are differences in focus and in research strategy between investigators and developers of instructional models on the one hand and domain-specific instructional designers on the other. Instructional designers and researchers whose first concern is to investigate and improve instructional models choose their topics and domains in such a way that the effectiveness of these models can be best examined. Discovery learning, for example, is primarily investigated using specific topics or laws in science (such as optical laws or electronics). Discovery learning environments provide students with a set of events or data that they can explore independently or in a prestructured way to discover the regularities in these data. Discovering these regularities is easiest when the relations under investigation are rather straightforward. From a research perspective, this is a wise approach that optimizes the chances for success. A particular domain and context provide a suitable venue for testing specific teaching methods while allowing variations in the model or the method that are required to test hypotheses about effectiveness and learning outcomes. Choosing the correct domain is a crucial part of a successful research project; however, the link between model or theory and the domain in which it is investigated has drawbacks. Investigators may not build up systematic knowledge of situations or parts of the domain where their methods and models do not apply.

The situation is different for instructional designers and teachers in specific domains and professions. For them, the specific domain comes first; they cannot select specific parts and leave out others. Their primary commitment is to solve specific teaching and learning problems. In this process, they may use and often adapt generic models and methods developed by researchers. Domain-specific instructional research has produced models that have later proven more generally applicable. An example is problem-based learning (PBL), first developed in medical education (Barrows, 1984) but now used in domains as diverse as engineering and economics. Emergent modeling, a method developed to teach mathematics and described in this chapter, may prove to be a significant contribution to other domains.

## Domain-Specific Problems

Using and adapting models and methods are not without problems. Many of these problems have to do with learning, but there are more. First, learning problems can be inherent to a domain. Much domain-specific instructional research is meant to uncover domain-specific learning challenges and determine the implications for instructional design; for example, researchers in medicine found out that the integration of different topic areas is a problem for students following a traditional medical curriculum. Often these topics are taught at different times by teachers who have little knowledge about what other teachers do and who emphasize the principles and idiosyncrasies of their own topic area rather than focus on an integrated application of knowledge in the context of clinical problems. Even in PBL approaches, integration has to be explicitly designed into the curriculum.

Problems and challenges in mathematics are different. Gravemeijer (this chapter) shows that the abstract view of mathematical knowledge that permeates mathematical teaching and textbooks makes it very difficult for high-school students to understand and apply mathematics. Gravemeijer and colleagues have resolved this difficulty by beginning with practical mathematical problems and gradually working toward higher levels of abstraction, building deeper insights based on naïve, procedural applications and directed knowledge and skills.

The problem with learning law has unique aspects (Nievelstein and colleagues, this chapter). The legal profession has explicitly defined concepts. These definitions only partially overlap with everyday use. The legal definitions cannot easily be changed. This strict ontology is something students must learn. Another problem is the adversarial argumentation style. Whereas medical education has a long tradition in instructional design research, legal education has been slow to embrace instructional design, partly because lawyers are used to considering nearly everything as contentious or arguable.

We present several examples of problems and how domain-specific instructional designers try to deal with them. Research in mathematics education has been most successful in terms of instructional procedures and methods. The strict ontology in law is at odds with the everyday use of the same words that students are accustomed to using. Learning difficulties in science may be linked to differences in parental style and verbalizations used at home. A better understanding of these and other difficulties is being sought, so instructional designers can directly address domain-specific difficulties.

A major instructional problem is the effect of socioeconomic status (SES). Several of the examples presented in this chapter report on this factor in several domains; however, without insight into how children and parents from high- and low-status groups might differ in terms of relevant experience, knowledge, skills, values, and expectations, SES will remain a formidable barrier.

A third problem area concerns the timing and sequencing of the constituent parts of the educational process. Instructional measures should be adapted to the level of mastery of the learner. Learning new knowledge and skills builds on previous learning. Failure to help learners establish meaningful links to existing knowledge typically leads to problems.

These problems relate to optimizing instruction in a domain to support the acquisition of knowledge and skill. There are other influences and problems to consider, including the stakeholders, the political climate, and developments within a profession and in society in general. The contribution on reading in this chapter shows how political change affects research. It also shows that choices made by external bodies can shape research agendas and strategies. Medicine provides another example of external influences on the content of the curriculum and the methods and models applied or under development.

## Problems with Models

Models do not automatically or perfectly fit specific domains, topics, skills, or competencies. Transfer from one domain to another will almost always require adaptations. Instructional models must be reinvented or significantly modified for a particular domain. None of the authors of the coming domain contributions raises this point. An interesting example of this phenomenon occurred at Maastricht University in the 1980s. At that time, the university was still under development and consisted of two faculties, medicine and health sciences, with two new ones planned. The university constitution prescribed an innovative, PBL curriculum. This had been a political decision; the university would never have come into existence without this commitment. In hindsight, designers and teachers could have foretold the problems that would emerge when they tried to get the two new faculties, law and economics, to embrace PBL. Two decades later, Nievelstein and colleagues (this chapter) can show that some factors that impede learning law and that affect adapting PBL to law education are still under investigation.

One reason why adopting PBL is so slow is related to the fact that introducing PBL methods and models to completely change a curriculum creates a significant departure from a traditional, teacher-centric, highly structured curriculum. In PBL curricula, the successful teacher not only communicates knowledge to students but also diagnoses individual problems and adjusts methods accordingly. Much of the required instructional knowledge in such cases is tacit. Making this tacit working knowledge explicit might be necessary to overcome this difficulty with the use and implementation of PBL instructional models in the domain of law education.

Another problem with instructional models is related to the representations and artifacts used. Three of the subsequent examples reveal that the use of unfamiliar or dissimilar representations is part of the problem (children in science education seem to grasp the conceptual meaning behind artifacts but are unable to express that verbally), but such variations in representations and artifacts can also be part of the solution. Phythian-Sence and Wagner (this chapter) refer to studies that show that multiple, transient, informal representations can help illiterate students bridge the gap between phonological decoding of words and the formal representation of English spelling. Similarly, Gravemeijer (this chapter) deliberately uses several different formal and informal representations familiar to students before introducing the canonical mathematical representation. This suggests that representations should be an integral part of an educational design.

A third problem revealed in the examples below is a consequence of dividing a curriculum into stages, such as junior and senior high school, bachelor and graduate education, and preclinical and clinical periods. These different stages often have different focuses. Roughly speaking, generic goals (such as in liberal arts and sciences or general skills programs) precede specific, profession-oriented goals. It seems obvious that methods and models should be adapted to these different goals.

## Requirements for Domain-Specific Use of Instructional Models

The general trend in society toward more transparency and accountability has also permeated the educational field. The international Programme for International Student Assessment (PISA; http://www.pisa.oecd.org) studies—begun in 2000 and including more than 40 countries—are an example of this trend. The PISA studies investigate how well 15-year-old students have reached educational goals in reading, mathematical, and scientific literacy. The tests cover not only mastery of school curricula but also important knowledge and skills needed in adult life (PISA, 2006). Other expressions of this trend are the call for evidence-based education in the United States or the treaties in the European Union on accreditation of higher education and student exchange that require more commonality in standards and criteria.

The call for accountability and transparency involves different aspects of education. In terms of *goals*, the questions raised are whether education reaches the desired goals and whether these goals are the right ones in the view of diverse stakeholders. In terms of *methods*, the question is whether the means used to reach goals are effective and efficient. The call for evidence-based education is an expression of the latter concern. Phythian-Sence and Wagner (this chapter) show that reading research in the United States is dominated by this concern. They also suggest that the investigation of important questions has come to a standstill due to the debate on allowable and acceptable methods. Similar problems have been reported from the domain of mathematics education.

Medicine struggles with a different problem. Dornan and colleagues (this chapter) show that the plea for accountability in medical education mainly concerns the content of the curriculum and the choice of appropriate methods as for the type of desired outcome—knowledge, skills, competencies, attitudes. The methods themselves are not under debate.

## Pressures for Change

What are the perils of exerting so much pressure on education to evaluate and change its methods and content? Societal pressure and pressure from professional organizations tend to focus on performance and the discrepancies between graduates' knowledge and skills and the requirements of the jobs for which they have been trained. Frustration about existing practices further complicates the pressure for changing professional education. The question is whether it is always wise to dramatically change practice and professional preparation, even assuming that job and task analyses have been done adequately. At least three aspects should be considered before deciding that a change in curriculum content and methods is a good solution. First, should a problem with the performance of graduates be addressed during the initial phase of education or is the workplace or continuing education preferred, or perhaps a combination? Different schools and professions provide different answers. Second, new entrants in a professional field are not likely change agents. They do not typically have sufficient influence to assume that role, although they may serve as a source of new knowledge and skills. If standing practices have to be changed, students can be prepared for it by a timely adaptation of training; however, changes in practices must be initiated and implemented by those who are accountable for these practices, such as the heads of departments. Finally, pleas for other content tend to overload the curriculum, not only with more content but also with more diversity in learning methods and places as well as in epistemologies, as Dornan and colleagues (this chapter) make evident. The question becomes one of how much diversity students and teachers can stand without ending up confused.

The use of instructional methods and models in domains and professions is affected by many factors that are internally and externally related to the instructional design process itself. Both types of factors must be carefully deliberated. Especially in case of major innovations, instructional design questions are affected by curriculum design questions. The next five sections of this chapter address these issues within the context of five different domains.

## LEARNING TO READ: AN ORIENTATION OF WHAT WORKS*

*Caroline Phythian-Sence and Richard K. Wagner*

### Introduction to Learning to Read

Experimental research on reading appears to have begun at Wundt's laboratory in the late 1800s. This work resulted in Huey's *The Psychology and Pedagogy of Reading* in 1908 (Rayner and Pollatsek, 1989). From the beginning, researchers were as concerned about pedagogy—instructional practices that made it possible to learn to read—as they were about the perceptual and cognitive processes upon which reading depends. Although interest in reading instruction has waxed and waned over the years, recent decades have witnessed a huge upswing in interest and activity motivated by the desire to improve reading performance.

Despite the fact that a number of children learn to read with seeming ease, for many children learning to read is a difficult, trying, and stressful ordeal. In the United States, the most recently published *Nation's Report Card* (Perie et al., 2005) finds that in a representative sample of fourth and eighth graders, less than a third of students were reading English at or above the proficient level. More striking still are the results for poor and minority children. For fourth and eighth graders eligible to receive free or reduced lunches, only 16% were reading at or above proficient level, with only 46% reading at or above basic level. Findings for minority children are equally bleak. Whereas 41% of Caucasian children read at or above proficient level, with 76% at or above basic level, only 13% of black children and 16% of Hispanic children were reading at proficient level, with 42% and 46%, respectively, reading at or above basic level.

We are still struggling with how to change poor readers' outcomes. Longitudinal evidence suggests that many children who fail to acquire adequate reading skills in early elementary school will never acquire the skills necessary to become proficient readers (Lonigan, 2006). Although historical efforts to improve reading ability focused on holistic approaches involving overall cognitive development, current efforts have honed in on identifying specific practices that will directly improve reading outcomes. With the passage of the No Child Left Behind (NLCB) Act in the United States and its academic cornerstone, *Reading First*, the demand for scientifically based, high-quality and effective reading

* This section was supported by NICHD Grant P50 HD052120 and by IES Grant R305G030104.

instruction has increased significantly. Consequently, the recent resurgence in educational research has sought to explicate better the underlying processes involved in learning to read, thereby identifying practices that are most effective in teaching children to read.

## Earlier Efforts: Compensatory Education

It has long been recognized that children from impoverished or minority families are at risk for academic failure (Ramey et al., 1983), particularly with regard to becoming proficient readers (Rauh et al., 2003). In the mid-19th century, religious and philanthropic groups provided daycare to children of immigrant workers founded on the presumption that the typical poor or immigrant family was not able to adequately provide for their young children (Ramey and Campbell, 1984). These same influences were seen again during the compensatory education movement, inspired by the civil rights movement of the 1960s and 1970s and seeking to *compensate* for social and economic inequalities (Kagan, 2002). Born of the movement were preschool programs such as the Perry Preschool Project and Project Head Start. It was hoped that these early childcare settings would replicate the environments that more affluent young children experienced before coming to school, thus providing the disadvantaged children with, among other things, social, language, and early literacy skills.

Although follow-up data of children enrolled in Head Start or similar programs suggest that early intervention influences children in educationally meaningful ways (Hebbeler, 1985), these effects all but disappear by the time children reach the middle elementary school years (Lee et al., 1990). Children at risk for academic failure (and, specifically, reading failure) need more than an enriching preschool environment to develop the skills necessary to become proficient readers. Children at risk for reading failure need rigorous and consistent support throughout elementary school to acquire the skills necessary to become proficient readers.

## Current Efforts: National Reading Panel, NCLB, and Reading First

In response to the National Assessment of Educational progress report of 1996, which showed that overall 40% of fourth graders in the United States did not demonstrate reading ability at even the basic level, Congress mandated the National Institute of Child and Human Development (NICHD) to establish the National Reading Panel (NRP). The main task of the NRP was to review current educational research and determine the most effective strategies and practices for teaching reading. In 2000, the NRP released its report, emphasizing the necessity of utilizing reading instruction with firm scientific grounding to improve reading outcomes. In 2002, in response to the NRP report, Congress passed the No Child Left Behind (NCLB) Act and the Reading First initiative, mandating exclusive use of reading curricula based on scientific research for those schools receiving federal grants. To develop scientifically grounded reading curricula, researchers have first sought to elucidate the components essential for reading proficiency: decoding, vocabulary, and comprehension.

## Current Understandings of Reading

Much of the existing instructional effort funded by Reading First has targeted basic reading skills, particularly word-level decoding, for children in kindergarten through third grade. Of serious concern is the identification of strategies for children with reading disabilities, particularly those children with dyslexia. For most individuals with dyslexia, the primary problem appears to be decoding rather than comprehension (Torgesen, 2002). Extensive research now suggests that dyslexia derives from phonological as opposed to visual difficulties (Schatschneider and Torgesen, 2004); consequently, one focus of current reading instruction, which now is a routine part of all major basic reading instruction, is promoting the development of phonological awareness.

Phonological awareness refers to an awareness of and access to the sound structure of one's oral language (Anthony and Francis, 2005; Jorm and Share, 1983; Wagner and Torgesen, 1987). The pronunciations of words can be represented as strings of phonemes. All spoken English words can be represented using a set of approximately 40 phonemes. Of the 10 trillion possible combinations of 40 phonemes, only a relatively small number actually occur in spoken language, and many of these combinations occur in multiple words (Wagner et al., 1997). Thus, *cat*, *rat*, and *hat* each consist of three phonemes; the first is different and the latter two are identical in the three words. These facts are represented by their spellings. Each has a different initial letter and identical medial and final letters. To a child with phonological awareness, the English writing system will appear to be a sensible way of representing spoken words in print. A child lacking such awareness will find the English writing system to be much more arbitrary.

Two streams of converging evidence support the view that phonological awareness plays a causal role in learning to read. First, causal modeling of longitudinal correlational data support such a role. Wagner and colleagues (1997) reported a 5-year longitudinal study of 216 children who were followed from kindergarten through fourth grade. The results supported a bidirectional model of causal relations: Phonological awareness plays a causal role in the development of beginning reading skills; conversely, the development of reading skills plays a causal role in the subsequent development of phonological awareness.

The second stream of support for reciprocal causal relations between phonological awareness and word-level reading comes from intervention studies and studies of illiterate adults and poor readers. Support for a causal influence of phonological awareness on subsequent word reading comes from studies that train phonological awareness and then look for effects on word-level reading (for a review of this literature, see the *Report of the National Reading Panel*, NICHD, 2000). In a longitudinal study by Torgesen and colleagues (1999) children with poor phonological processing skills were instructed in the Auditory Discrimination in Depth Program (Lindamood and Lindamood, 1984). The children were provided with explicit instruction in labeling the articulatory gestures associated with each phoneme, followed by phoneme tracking activities such as using colored blocks and letters to represent the phonemes in words. Results showed that when children with poor phonological processing skills were provided with intensive word-level instruction, their phonological processing, phonemic awareness, and word-level reading skills improved significantly more than those children provided with balanced text and word-level instruction and those children receiving instruction that mimicked normal classroom activities.

Attention now is turning to the relatively neglected topic of how to improve reading comprehension (Biemiller and Slonim, 2001). One approach that has been taken to improving comprehension has been to focus on improving vocabulary and other oral language skills. Oral language skills in general, and vocabulary in particular, are essential for effective reading comprehension; although decoding is essential because children need to be able to read the words they encounter, children also need to understand the words they have read.

Biemiller and Slonim (2001) estimate that children acquire as many as 2.2 new root words a day from age one through the second grade. Upon entry into school, children begin to learn words through either direct or indirect instruction (Graves, 1987). Direct or explicit instruction implies that students are taught information about words and word meanings. Although this method is effective in imparting word meanings essential for the successful reading of a particular story or understanding of a new concept, it is impossible for instructors to teach all the words children need to acquire to be competent readers overall (Sternberg, 1987). Indirect instruction implies that word meanings are acquired by students through reading; unknown word meanings are derived from contextual cues. Beck et al. (2002) have developed a robust approach to vocabulary instruction that provides students with rich, varied, contextual, and repeated experience with words (Beck et al., 2002, p. 2) by utilizing direct and explicit methods of vocabulary instruction in addition to indirect and contextual instruction. Rather than targeting words that most children will acquire without instruction (*clock*, *baby*, *walk*), this instruction targets words that are necessary for understanding higher level texts (words such as *coincidence*, *absurd*, *fortunate*). Although findings are mixed concerning the most effective means of vocabulary instruction, Beck and McKeown (1991, p. 805) summarized the general findings:

> First, all instructional methods produce better word learning than no instruction. Second, no one method has been shown to be consistently superior. Third, there is advantage for methods that use a variety of techniques. Fourth, there is advantage from repeated exposures to the words to be learned. The simple version of these findings is that people tend to learn what they are taught, and more attention to what is being taught is useful.

Stahl and Fairbanks (1986) conducted a meta-analysis on vocabulary instruction as it relates to reading comprehension and vocabulary scores. With regard to vocabulary, their analyses suggest that instruction has effect sizes of 1.37 (SD = .76, $N = 21$, $p < .01$) for word-specific contextual vocabulary measures, 1.70 (SD = 1.42, $N = 55$, $p < .01$) for definitional measures, and .26 (SD = .29, $N = 17$, $p < .01$) for global measures of vocabulary, with the greatest effect sizes being related to instruction that was mixed (direct and indirect).

More recently, the National Reading Panel (NICHD, 2000) attempted to conduct a meta-analytic review but did not find a sufficient number of studies that met the vocabulary subgroups' criteria for scientific rigor. In spite of its inability to perform a meta-analysis on vocabulary instruction, the National Reading Panel summarized several key trends for successful vocabulary instruction (NICHD, 2000), which are similar to those outlined by Beck and McKeown (1991). Successful vocabulary instruction should include both direct and indirect instruction and should involve multiple exposures in rich and varied context; the tasks should be restructured when necessary to ensure students' understanding. No single method of vocabulary instruction is recommended but rather a variety of techniques should be utilized to ensure that the students are actively engaged.

As previously stated, comprehension is the desired outcome of reading. Decoding allows children to read the words on the page and vocabulary knowledge allows children to understand the words they have read, but comprehension goes beyond these two skills and requires children to put together the words into strings of ideas and concepts. Although the connection between vocabulary and reading comprehension has long been accepted (correlations range from 0.3 to 0.8), researchers are continuing to define this relationship (Tannenbaum et al., 2006). Anderson and Freebody (1979) proposed three possible hypotheses. The general aptitude hypothesis suggests that the two are related because both are manifestations of general intelligence; the general knowledge hypothesis suggests that they are related because they are both manifestations of conceptual knowledge; and the instrumentalist hypothesis suggests that vocabulary and reading comprehension are causally related so improvements in vocabulary ability will positively influence reading comprehension. This last hypothesis is the most interesting to researchers because it suggests that it is possible to influence reading comprehension through vocabulary instruction (Stahl and Fairbanks, 1986).

Beck and colleagues have suggested that vocabulary instruction can influence reading comprehension (Beck and McKeown, 1991; Beck et al., 1987, 2002) when words are learned in varied, repeated, and meaningful ways (Tannenbaum et al., 2006). In the meta-analysis conducted by Stahl and Fairbanks (1986) in which they also analyzed vocabulary instruction, the results lend support to the instrumental hypothesis. The analyses yielded effect sizes of 0.97 (SD = .81, $N = 41$, $p < .01$, range 0–3.07) and 0.30 (SD = .22, $N = 15$, $p < .01$) for the influence of vocabulary instruction on global measures of comprehension.

In addition to indirectly influencing reading comprehension through vocabulary instruction, teaching methods have sought to enhance reading comprehension through direct instruction in cognitive strategies. The development of cognitive strategies by readers can be broken down into three stages: active awareness of processes involving comprehension, instruction in strategies useful for aiding comprehension, and practice and eventual independence in utilizing strategies for comprehension (NICHD, 2000). Among those strategies with support from empirical studies are mental imagery, graphic organizers, summarization, and most notably question generation. Interestingly, like vocabulary, no single strategy is the answer to the problem of comprehension. The National Reading Panel notes that mixed, or multiple strategies for comprehension have "considerable scientific support" (NICHD, 2000, p. 46).

## Concluding Remarks

In conclusion, a great deal of research has been carried out on models of instruction for development of reading and other language skills. Much of existing knowledge is limited to beginning reading, particularly word-level decoding, although developments are being made to better understand vocabulary ability, reading comprehension, and the relation between the two. As progress is made in explaining further the underlying processes of learning to read, corresponding improvements in developing effective reading instruction will follow.

## LEARNING MATHEMATICS: THE PROBLEM OF LEARNING ABSTRACT KNOWLEDGE

*Koeno Gravemeijer*

### Introduction to Learning Mathematics

Difficulty with learning mathematics is usually explained by referring to the gap between the student's personal knowledge and the abstract formal mathematical knowledge that has to be acquired. In this section, it will be argued that the problem is not simply in the gap that has to be bridged. The problem is that, for the student, there is nothing on the other side of the bridge. The abstract formal mathematical knowledge of the expert does not feature into the student's experiential reality. This point may be clarified by looking at the genesis of mathematical knowledge.

If one looks at the history of mathematics, one may discern a repeating pattern within which processes or procedures develop into objects. An example of such a development may be found in counting. Counting first emerges as a procedure to establish how many there are of something. Gradually, however, numbers get an independent quality, as objects in and of themselves. We may observe a similar shift with (algebraic) functions. Functions first come to the fore as prescriptions for how a given input is transformed into the corresponding output. Later, functions are defined as ordered number pairs and are conceived of as mathematical objects with certain characteristics; that is to say, mathematicians experience them as real objects that they can act upon and reason with—just as most adults experience numbers as real objects. With the construal of various mathematical objects, mathematicians create a body of knowledge that they experience as real.

Mathematics teachers, too, will have construed mathematics as an external body of knowledge that is experientially real for them. As a consequence, teachers and textbook authors may take their own abstract mathematical knowledge for an external body of knowledge that can be explained to students. The difference between the abstract knowledge of the teachers and the experiential knowledge of the students, however, constitutes a serious source of miscommunication.

## Different Frameworks of Reference

At a certain age, young children do not understand the question "How much is 4 plus 4?" even though they may very well understand that 4 apples and 4 apples equals 8 apples. The explanation for this phenomenon is that, for them, a number is still tied to countable objects as in "4 apples." In this case, "4" is more like an adjective than a noun for them. At a higher level, the number 4 will be associated with various number relations, such as: $4 = 2 + 2 = 3 + 1 = 5 - 1 = 8 \div 2$, and so on. At this higher level, numbers have become mathematical objects that derive their meaning form a network of number relations (Van Hiele, 1973).

When elementary-school teachers talk about numbers, they may very well be talking about mathematical objects that are not part of the students' experiential realities; thus, teachers and students speak different languages—without being aware of it. He or she talks about numbers as mathematical objects that exist within a network of numerical relations. The teacher may, for instance, reason that "7 + 6 equals 13 because 7 + 3 = 10, 6 = 3 + 3, and 10 + 3 equals 13". Students who have not yet construed the necessary network of numerical relations and think of numbers as adjectives cannot follow this line of reasoning and have to revert to copying and memorizing.

## Models

To accommodate the abstract character of mathematics, instructional designers try to devise tactile or visual models (embodiments) that represent mathematical relationships and concepts to students in a readily apprehensible form. The underlying idea is that these external representations will facilitate the process of making connections with the represented mathematical relationships and concepts. In this respect, the word *transparent* is used, which suggests that students can look through the models and see the mathematics. This would enable the students to construct internal mental representations that mirror those embodied in the external representations. The most well-known tactile models that fit this approach are the Dienes blocks, which are meant to concretize the decimal system (see Figure 41.1).

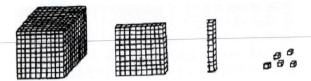

**Figure 41.1** Dienes blocks.

Students are expected to see one big block as consisting of 1000 tiny cubes, a flat slice as 100, and a rod as 10 tiny blocks. Research, however, shows that this interpretation is not self-evident (Labinowics, 1985). Cobb et al. (1992) argue that the problematic character of the Dienes blocks lies in its assumption that instructional representations are the primary source of the students' mathematical knowledge. For us as adults, it is self-evident what these instructional representations signify, but this is not the case for young students. The plausibility of the usefulness of representations such as those resides in the fact that mathematics educators experience mathematical constructs, such as tens, ones, and hundreds, as object-like entities that can be pointed to and spoken about. This feeling is due not only to their individual mathematical sophistication but also to their experience of being able to talk and reason about these objects unproblematically while interacting with others.

From the perspective of teachers and instructional designers, it makes perfect sense to try to develop transparent models; they see their knowledge of the decimal system reflected in the blocks. For students, however, the Dienes blocks are nothing but just wooden blocks. We cannot expect the students to see more sophisticated mathematics in the blocks than the mathematics they have already acquired. This problem is known as the *learning paradox* (Bereiter, 1985): How would it be possible for the students to recognize mathematical relationships that are developmentally more advanced than what they already know? The instructional consequence is that when students do not see what there is to be seen, the teacher does not have many options other than to spell out the correspondences between the blocks and the algorithm in detail.

## What Makes Mathematics Difficult?

In short, we may conclude that the difficulty of learning mathematics does not lie in the formal, abstract character of mathematics as such. The actual problem seems to reside in the fact that teachers and the textbook authors mistake their own more abstract mathematical knowledge for an external body of knowledge that can be explained to the students; however, the gap between the knowledge of the teachers and the experiential reality of the students is too big to make this work. We saw that instructional representations cannot bridge this gap, because what those materials signify depends on the eye of the beholder. We may conclude, therefore, that it is the tradition of ignoring where mathematics comes from that makes mathematics so difficult to learn. One might, of course, counter that reality shows that (at least some) people appear to have learned mathematics in spite of this form of instruction. We may reason, however, that their actual learning process will have been different from absorbing or memorizing an alien body of knowledge. According to Freudenthal (1991), they may have been able to reconstruct mathematics in a manner similar to a reinvention process. For these people the adage *learning first, understanding later* may be true; however, Freudenthal (1991) wondered whether that holds true for others who might be better served by what Freudenthal calls *guided reinvention*.

## Alternative

Freudenthal (1973, 1991) observed that the end product of the mathematical activity of many generations of mathematicians is taken as a starting point for the instruction of young students. He called this an *antididactical inversion*. An alternative is to create opportunities for students to reinvent mathematics. In relation to this, he spoke of "mathematics as a human activity." Just as the activity of mathematicians resulted in mathematics as we know it now, the activity of students can result in the construction of mathematics. This approach, therefore, offers an alternative for teaching students mathematics as a ready-made product.

We may elaborate Freudenthal's point further. For him—as a mathematician—mathematics is primarily an activity. An activity that he denoted as "mathematizing" or organizing. In relation to this, he spoke of the activity of organizing subject matter to make it more mathematical. This may concern both organizing matter from reality to make it accessible for mathematical means and organizing mathematical matter to make it more mathematical. We may relate "more mathematical" in this context to characteristics such as general, exact, brief, and sure, which suggests mathematical activities such as generalizing, formalizing, curtailing, and proving. Freudenthal (1973) argued that students can reinvent mathematics by mathematizing, although he also acknowledged that the students cannot simply reinvent the mathematics that took the brightest mathematicians eons to develop. This is why he proposes guided reinvention. Teachers and textbooks have to help the students along, while trying to

make sure that the students experience learning mathematics as a process of inventing mathematics for themselves. To accomplish this, a reinvention route has to be developed; therefore, teachers need the help of instructional designers, who in turn may be supported by researchers. Offering this kind of support has been the mission of the Freudenthal Institute in the Netherlands over the past decades. This has resulted in what is referred to as a domain-specific instruction theory for realistic mathematics education (RME).

## Emergent Modeling

According to this theory, guided reinvention may be supported by emergent modeling (Gravemeijer, 1999, 2004). The emergent modeling approach circumvents the learning paradox in a way that fits with Meira's (1995) historical analysis. On the basis of that historical analysis, he suggested a dialectic process of symbolizing and meaning making, in which both the symbolizations and the corresponding meaning co-evolve. Historically, symbols and models did not materialize out of thin air; they are the result of a long process of inventing, adjusting, and refining. So, one might conclude that, instead of trying to help students to make connections with ready-made mathematics, we should try to help students construe mathematics in a more bottom-up manner.

This recommendation fits with the idea of emergent modeling. The emergent modeling approach takes its point of departure in the activity of modeling. Modeling in this conception is an activity of the students, who are asked to solve a contextual problem. The students then model the problem to solve it with the help of that model. Such a modeling activity might involve making drawings, diagrams, or tables, or it could involve developing informal notations or using conventional mathematical notations. The conjecture is that acting with these models will help the students reinvent the more formal mathematics.

Initially, the models come to the fore as context-specific models. The models refer to concrete or paradigmatic situations that are experientially real for the students. Initial models should allow for informal strategies that correspond with situated solution strategies at the level of the situation that is defined in the contextual problem. Then, while the students gather more experience with similar problems, their attention may shift toward the mathematical relations and strategies. This helps them to further develop those mathematical relations which enables them to use the model in a different manner: The model becomes more important as a base for reasoning about these mathematical relations than as a way of representing a contextual problem. In this

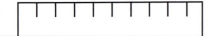

**Figure 41.2** Tenstrip.

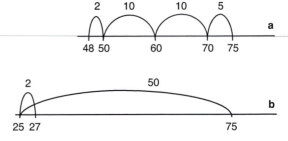

**Figure 41.3** (a) Jumps on the empty number line; (b) illustrating $75 - 48 = 75 - 50 + 2$.

manner, the model begins to become a referential base for more formal mathematics. In short, a model of informal mathematical activity develops into a model for more formal mathematical reasoning.

This approach has been elaborated successfully for a variety of topics, varying from data analysis (Cobb, 2002) and calculus (Doorman, 2005) to addition and subtraction up to 100 (Stephan et al., 2003). We will take the latter as an easily accessible example and briefly describe the instructional sequence that aims at developing a framework of number relations that students can use for flexible strategies for addition and subtraction up to 100. The starting point of that sequence is in measuring lengths by iterating a given measurement unit, quickly followed by iterating units of ten and one. While coordinating units of ten and one, the students begin to become aware of useful number relations, such as $48 = 50 - 2$, and $48 + 10 = 58$.

Next, a paper strip of ten units that can be used for both iterating units of ten and reading individual units is introduced as a measurement device (see Figure 41.2); subsequently, a ruler is construed by combining ten of the so-called *tenstrips*. Measuring with this ruler builds on the earlier activity of iterating units of ten and one. New activities follow that involve comparing, incrementing, and decrementing lengths. Students may begin using multiples of ten as benchmarks instead of counting individual units; for example, the difference between 48 and 75 can be found by using 50, 60, and 70 as benchmarks, while reasoning that $48 + 2 = 50$, $50 + 20 = 70$, $70 + 5 = 75$, thus the difference is $2 + 20 + 5 = 27$. Next, these arithmetical strategies are represented by jumps on an empty number line (see Figure 41.3a). Later on, when the students have become more flexible with number relations, they may reason: $75 - 48 = 75 - 50 + 2$, which they may elucidate with jumps on the number line (see Figure 41.3b).

The model then derives its meaning from the mathematical relations and has become a model for mathematical reasoning. In retrospect, we may observe a shift from numbers that initially are bound to measures (e.g., 37 inches) to numbers as entities in and of themselves that derive their meaning from a network of number relations (e.g., $37 = 30 + 7 = 40 - 3 = 20 + 17 = 47 - 10$). The sequence also gives a flavor of how the emergent modeling approach can be used in instructional design. First, the designer should try to describe the goals in terms of a framework of mathe-

matical relations; this informs the designer about the relations that have to be focused on. Second, the designer has to try to design a series of submodels that may support a "model of" to "model for" transition in such a manner that each new submodel builds on earlier experiences with preceding submodels.

## Conclusions

Abstract mathematical knowledge is difficult to transmit to students because it concerns knowledge on a different level of understanding. The actual problem, however, is that we tend to think of abstract mathematical knowledge as an external body of knowledge that can be explained to the students. Instead of trying to help students to make connections with a body of mathematical knowledge that "is not there" in the experiential realities the students, we may want to try to help them construct new mathematical knowledge by building on what they already know. Some of the strategies that realistic mathematics education offers for this alternative approach are guided reinvention and emergent modeling.

An important aspect of this approach is that it creates opportunities for students to develop mathematical knowledge that is grounded in their experiential reality. More importantly, it leaves the connection with those sources open which allows students to fold back to more concrete levels of understanding if they run into problems. The RME approach, however, does not offer an easy solution to the problem of how to teach abstract mathematics. First, realistic mathematics education requires instructional design. Teachers need instructional sequences or, better, the rationales or local instruction theories that underpin such sequences, together with resources that offer sets of potentially productive activities. Second, teacher development is necessary. Within the conception of teaching as helping students in making connections with mathematics as a ready-made body of knowledge, the central teaching activities will be those of giving directions and explaining. To change to the alternative approach, teachers will have to make a shift from giving directions and explanations to helping students to invent mathematics. This presents them with the difficult task of building on the input and ideas of the students while at the same time working toward given conventional goals.

Helping students invent implies that teachers will have to share some of their authority. The teacher, though, remains the authority in the classroom but in a different role. The teacher establishes the rules regarding what mathematics is and what it means to learn mathematics in his or her classroom. Moreover, the teacher decides on the choice of instructional activities, frames topics for discussion, and orchestrates whole-class discussions in such a manner that they contribute to the construction of the intended mathematics. In doing so, these teachers will have to strike a balance between guidance and invention or reinvention. In short, it is the teacher who is the one who shapes the curriculum innovation that is implied here.

# LEARNING SCIENCE: PROVOKING EXPLORATION OF PHENOMENA IN NATURE

*Geerdina Maria van der Aalsvoort*

## Introduction to Learning Science

Science learning suggests that students become more familiar with concepts related to biology, physics, chemistry, or astronomy and develop conceptual knowledge about the domains. Science learning is strongly dependent on science teaching. Although early exposures to natural phenomena supposedly trigger a child's interest in concepts related to science, a certain level of cognitive development is required for the child to notice natural phenomena, and this level of development is especially necessary for the child to be able to pose questions related to the underlying mechanisms of the phenomena.

From a constructivist point of view, growing understanding of concepts is part of the development of cognitive systems that take place over time. Piaget (DeLisi and Golbeck, 1999) evolved a constructivist theory of cognitive functioning and development that attempts to account for the growth and development of existing cognitive systems and application of already formed cognitive systems. Piaget found that children develop their concepts of natural phenomena through a process of finding a so-called equilibrium

between new skills that exert pressure on concepts already formed and those already established. In the child's struggle to relate those experiences, he or she may either fail to account for aspects of the environment or be overly influenced by environmental forces. The child's own activity, attention, and interest determine whether assimilation or accommodation takes place when constructing conceptual models.

Perret-Clermont et al. (2004), based on Vygotsky's point of view, emphasized the dependence of construction of knowledge on outside influences. They noted that a child learns when teachers bridge the gap between the child's available modes of thought and new ideas by working jointly in the zone of proximal development. In this way, the teacher, as "outside influence," guides the child toward more advanced forms of thought.

Especially in the case of science, learning is considered to be something that is transmitted in school (Nunes and Bryant, 2004). The development of scientific reasoning comes about when children learn to use the logical aspects of a concept, understand situations that give meaning to a concept, and become sensitive to the way a problem is represented. Conceptual mastery of scientific concepts requires being confronted with phenomena and finding solutions to understand a phenomenon by using logical thinking. The phenomena provide a means for cultivating or practicing the construction of explanations. Explanation generation is something that can be promoted in science classrooms. Whereas current theories recognize that there are general ways in which a child's intellect changes as the child grows older, accounting for the solution of specific problems requires an addition to or a change of currently available knowledge (Nunes and Bryant, 2004).

From a constructivist approach, new information is built upon existing knowledge structures. This approach defines conceptual change within a child's knowledge system as follows. Early in their lives, and over a period of time, children know a great deal about separate science issues. These disparate elements are all organized in complex ways. When new information is to be learned that comes into conflict with a learner's prior knowledge system, a major reorganization is required. Teachers can function as facilitators to guide the process of learning science and intentionally provoke such reorganization by the students in their classes (Ohlsson et al., 2000). There is no guarantee, however, that instruction and reorganization are immediately successful. Science learning is a construction process of new conceptual identities and is not merely a replacement of naïve knowledge with scientific knowledge (Kumpulainen et al., 2003). Students need to develop the appropriate cognitive structures before they can master scientific concepts, as there is a distinction between the child's initial exploratory framework prior to systematic instruction and misconceptions that may occur after instruction (Vosniadou and Verschaffel, 2004).

## Consequences for Learning Astronomy

Based on Piaget's theory of development of concepts, many studies have been undertaken that investigate the development of concepts of natural phenomena such as those related to astronomy (Vosniadou and Brewer, 1992, 1994; Vosniadou et al., 2005). The majority of the first-grade children included in these studies have been found to have formed initial models of the day and night cycle. Moreover, most of the participating children showed that they had discovered that the alternation of day and night constitutes a phenomenon that requires an explanation. They also showed that they had learned to form so-called *mental models* of natural phenomena such as the day and night cycle. A mental model refers to a particular kind of representation that is analogous to the states of the world it represents. It can be manipulated mentally, it allows predictions about the outcomes of causal states in the world, and it provides physical phenomena (Vosniadou and Brewer, 1994).

To investigate development concerning conceptual changes, an empirical approach can be sought that explores how young children develop science concepts after they are exposed to materials that evoke spontaneous discovery learning about natural phenomena. Information collected with respect to such learned concepts can then be used to rethink what could be successful elements of science teaching in formal education. We know, for example, from the study of Ohlsson et al. (2000) that kindergarten children (mean age 5 years) profited from being exposed to a game that included virtual traveling in space from an asteroid to Earth. They had significantly more correct answers on questions about the shape of the Earth immediately after exposure to the game. This result was maintained after a delay of 4 months, when the same questions were posed again. Findings like these suggest that discovery learning is a fruitful way to promote young children's learning of conceptual understanding of natural phenomena while at the same increasing their technology literacy (Cameron and Dwyer, 2005; Hertzog and Klein, 2005).

## A Field Study

Based on the findings of Ohlsson et al. (2000), we studied children's conceptual development by using PICCO, a computer program of particular natural phenomena (Kangassalo, 1997). PICCO offers virtual opportunities to explore the Earth, the planets in space, the meaning of time with respect to day and night, and the seasons. Seven actions can be activated on the screen: looking at a city in a virtual landscape; changing dates, which allows seasons to change; turning hands on the clock so day turns into night and *vice versa*; using a microscope or binoculars; using a dictionary; using a rocket that simulates travel into space; and using a compass that allows the user to change the angle of the landscape on the screen.

Because virtual traveling in space is possible by launching the rocket, children can study the position of the Earth in relationship to the moon, the sun, and other planets in space. This allows the child to see the Earth from outer space and to notice that the Earth is round. Moreover, the change of seasons can be elicited by manipulating the date, which causes the landscape to change from images related to spring, summer, autumn, or winter. Turning the hands on the clock can, for example, cause day to become night; as the landscape darkens, the birds stop singing. The visual experiences on the screen can be elicited any time the child activates the game. There are neither time limits nor rules for using the buttons that activate the elements on the screen. The children's mental models of the Earth and their ideas of the day and night cycle and the seasons may differ from the images presented on the screen. Actions that are allowed by PICCO are intended to evoke a cognitive conflict in the child's conceptual understanding of these phenomena of nature. As a consequence of this conflict, the child's understanding of a particular phenomenon is put under stress, which should evoke an imbalance in their conceptual knowledge related to the natural phenomenon. This imbalance in turn may promote deeper understanding of the phenomenon observed and elicit understanding of the phenomenon on a higher conceptual level.

### Results

We used PICCO to study the broader question of whether young students would profit from exposure to a program that allowed investigation of natural phenomena in a game-like environment (for details of the study, see Van der Aalsvoort et al., 2006). The program was installed on a computer in one classroom in each of two different schools and was available for use over 4 subsequent weeks. The teachers offered time and opportunity for their children to use the program at least once a week. After 4 weeks, PICCO was removed from the computer. The participants were interviewed both before and after their exposure to PICCO regarding their knowledge and understanding of the phenomena covered by the program. The sample involved 20 second-grade students from two regular education primary schools. Ten children from each class participated. They had been selected as the first ten on a list of students in their class. We collected intelligence scores as a child characteristic, as well as information about the socioeconomic status of the child's home. The mean scores on IQ were equal between the schools, but the scores related to socioeconomic status were remarkably higher in school 2 than in school 1. As a consequence, we tested the data for each school separately.

The methodology involved three steps that were designed to ensure that differences in the mental models of the children after the intervention could be interpreted as results of their exposure to the PICCO game. The first step was to compare the number of correct answers between the schools based on the interview with each student before and after the intervention. The children in school 2 only showed a significantly higher number of correct responses to the interview questions about natural phenomena after the exposure to the game.

The second step involved analyses of the answers of the children to the interview questions to reveal specific changes that may have resulted from their involvement in the gaming. Three levels of conceptual knowledge were distinguished with regard to the Earth, day and night cycle, and seasons by combining answers from the interview into those themes. The proportion of answers categorized as representing a scientific model of the shape of the Earth improved from 20 to 40% in the post-test responses of children in school 1, whereas the post-test responses of children in school 2 changed from 80 to 90%. Students from school 2 gave answers that were related to a scientific model of the day and night cycle in 20% of their answers after exposure to PICCO, whereas none of the students from school 1 reached that level. We attribute the huge differences between the pretest (maintained in the post-test) scores of the children in these groups to socioeconomic status, as the children from school 2 came from a significantly higher SES level. Thus, the children in school 2, despite IQ scores at a similar level as those in school 1, came from a higher SES level and obtained dramatically higher scores on their pre- and post-intervention interview responses.

In the final step, we analyzed the children's exploration pathways. The explorations pathways consist of the visual pattern reflected in the number of times and the order in which actions were undertaken during each PICCO session. We expected that the children would intentionally push buttons to achieve sequences in actions on the screen which would suggest that they were processing the information on a conceptual level. Three main sequences were anticipated. The first was related to the shape of the Earth: The child used buttons in a sequence of launching a rocket, viewing Earth from outer space as a round object, and then traveling back to earth. The second sequence referred to the day and night cycle: The child moved the hands of the clock and saw that the landscape changed from day into night and *vice versa*. The third sequence related to season: The child changed the date on the calendar so the landscape changed from one season into another and then changed the date once again. An example is a student we shall call William. William took part in ten sessions of PICCO. One sequence related to Earth was found. Moreover, three times sequences related to the day and night cycle and to the seasons were detected. His score on the interview after the intervention had improved on the theme of Earth only.

The final analysis showed a nonsignificant relationship between the higher order learning processes detected in the children's exploration paths and the answers they gave during the interviews. We, therefore, are not able to conclude that intentional actions with immediate feedback on the screen related to the deepening of the children's conceptual development. The results do allow us, however, to conclude that the students from school 1 profited mainly with respect to their knowledge of the shape of the Earth as a natural phenomenon, whereas the students from school 2 improved primarily with respect to their knowledge of the day and night cycle and the seasons.

In summary, the findings related to the use of PICCO in these second-grade classrooms revealed that the students profited from exposure to a program that allows investigation of natural phenomena in a game-like way; however, the children in each school made improvements in different content areas and at different levels. The students from school 1 improved with respect to their conceptual understanding of the shape of the Earth. In school 2, this knowledge was already present in most students. Among the school 2 students, the most improvement was found with regard to their understanding of the day and night cycle.

One main factor that seems to relate to these findings is that of SES; it seems that the higher the students' socioeconomic status and the more developed their conceptual knowledge about natural phenomena, the less they profited from a game that intends to allow discovery learning about these phenomena. The intervention findings also suggest, however, that although home environment may contribute to less developed conceptual developmental about natural phenomena improvement of the conceptual knowledge can be derived within a very short time.

## Discussion

The findings of the study have several implications. We present two that may improve our understanding of how the construction of mental models can be elicited by intervening in the child's surroundings (e.g., the classroom) and what this can mean for educational planning. The first implication concerns the relationship between socioeconomic status of the participants and exposure to materials that aim at eliciting development of conceptual models (Kohnstamm, 1967; Szechter and Liben, 2004). A study about solving scientific problems by 9- to 12-year-old children in proximity with their parents revealed that the parents of the children assumed the role of evidence interpretation but did not engage in collaborative discussions within which the child could develop scientific reasoning (Gleason and Schauble, 2000). The study alerts us with a concern that offering effective assistance appears to be related to verbalizations of scientific problem solving. If this is the case, then children less experienced in verbalizing their own explanations may be at a disadvantage in showing their understanding of natural phenomena. This concern cannot be accounted for in our findings, because when we interviewed the students we offered them paper and pencil and play dough so they could show the shape of the Earth and the position of the sun nonverbally as well as verbally. The children involved were not disadvantaged in showing their conceptual knowledge of natural phenomena. A second concern relates to the way the parents in the previous studies assisted their child in exploring natural phenomena. The differences between the schools in our study may have related to the parents' views about their activities with their children at home; this may have made it less interesting for the children to explore natural phenomena as they were too unfamiliar with the type of information provided by the screen.

The second implication of the results of this study relates to the use of artifacts. Vosniadou et al. (2005) discussed the specific meaning of artifacts for scientific reasoning. They stated that children need extensive instruction with the artifact to learn how to use it and to grasp the conceptual meaning behind it. Our experience with the PICCO materials revealed that the children could grasp concepts through reference to artifacts, such as the Earth in space being portrayed on a flat screen as a round shape. An alternative explanation of the results of the study is that adjusting to thoughts aimed at helping students grasp phenomena of nature while looking at the screen does not automatically teach the child to verbalize this conceptual knowledge. This raises an important question: What type of experience does a child need to have to develop an understanding of natural phenomena?

The third and final issue that we wish to raise with respect to discovery learning concerns the use of microgenetic analysis to gain insight into learning processes related to conceptual development within gaming. Although Hertzog and Klein (2005) suggested that the use of technology such as PICCO may be a good vehicle for channeling students' creativity and critical thinking, it is unclear which learning processes add to the formation of conceptual knowledge about natural phenomena. Another question is whether or not virtual discoveries overrule actual experiences, especially when parent involvement may be the mediating variable between exposure to gaming and learning from it. We suggest, therefore, that the microgenetic working method should be applied more often to attempt to interpret children's behavior during the course of gaming. Variations in the level or kind of pathways may provide insight into dynamic variations among children (Granott and Parziale, 2002; Steenbeek and Van Geert, 2002; Tunteler and Resing, 2004).

## Conclusions about Science Learning

What can we conclude from the findings with respect to science learning and science teaching? Our findings showed that the higher the socioeconomic status of students was, the more they profited from the opportunity to learn from a program that allowed investigation of natural phenomena. As a consequence a main message would be that schools need to offer a learning environment that favors the needs of children of families of low socioeconomic status. We suggest, however, first observing the children's everyday lives at home and deciding afterward which type of approaches or enrichment programs would best suit specific groups of children (Tudge and Hogan, 2005).

# LEARNING LAW: THE PROBLEMS WITH ONTOLOGY AND REASONING

*Fleurie Nievelstein, Tamara van Gog, and Frans J. Prins*

## Introduction to Learning Law

Before addressing the difficulties law students experience and describing research on effective instructional interventions and necessary future research in this area, we shortly describe both the common law (Anglo-Saxon) and the civil law (Continental) systems, along with providing a discussion of the cognitive processes the different law systems evoke and the teaching methods currently used.

## Common Law

Common law is largely uncodified; therefore, prior cases must be reviewed to determine the appropriate rules (Sinclair, 1971). It is characterized by the fact that judges utilize specific knowledge of previously experienced, concrete problem situations (cases) and the outcomes of those situations to build their judgments. This type of reasoning in common law is called *case-based reasoning*, which is inductive in nature. Law students and lawyers should be able to recognize structural similarities between the current and prior cases that are likely to differ on context-specific (surface) features and to make connections between those cases to infer a general solution. Case-based reasoning is a cyclic and integrated process of solving a problem, learning from this experience, and solving a new problem by analogy (Aamodt and Plaza, 1994).

The method of case-based teaching has become the primary mode of legal pedagogy in the United States and the United Kingdom. Thousands of legal cases are systematically organized and available for use by legal educators. Students have to construct meaning from facts that may at first seem simple but grow increasingly complex if they explore them at some depth when studying a particular case. Through case-based teaching, students develop skills in analytical thinking and reflective judgment by reading and discussing complex, real-world examples that are similar to situations earlier encountered in legal practice (Aamodt and Plaza, 1994; Carter and Unklesbay, 1989; Taylor, 2000).

## Civil Law

Civil law, in contrast, is codified and contains a whole set of rules that can be applied and interpreted by judges. The judge's task is to analyze the case, search for legal rules, and interpret these rules with the purpose to substantiate a solution for a particular case. Civil law relies more on *rule-based reasoning*, which is deductive in nature. Rather than working from specific pieces of information toward a general conclusion, one is working from general rules or assertions toward one specific conclusion (Chalmers, 1976; Maughan, 1996). Legal problems are analyzed in the light of generally accepted rules, from which a solution can be deduced.

A variation on the case-based teaching approach that is often used in common law is the problem-based method of teaching (Admiraal et al., 1999; Teich, 1986), in which students analyze and solve legal problems by finding and applying relevant principles of law. In the Netherlands, Crombag et al. (1977) developed a systematic approach to problem solving that aims at solving civil cases step by step. This didactic model represents an ideal, linear sequence of operations an experienced lawyer should consider to reason about a certain case. To solve a legal case, seven steps have to be taken: (1) formulation of the problem, (2) selection of legal facts, (3) selection of relevant law and rules, (4) analysis and interpretation of these rules, (5) application of the rules on the case, (6) evaluation of the construction, and (7) final formulation of a judgment. During case analysis, these phases are not strictly separated but form a cyclic process.

## Difficulties Learning Law

The differences between the two law systems as well as the corresponding reasoning approaches are obvious; however, for novice learners who have to solve law problems in either law system, similar difficulties arise. Difficulties arise, on the one hand, because a novice's knowledge base is not yet well developed and, on the other hand, because the domain entails some very complex concepts and skills that must be mastered.

### Knowledge Structure

To solve a legal problem, available information must be checked, legally interpreted, and completed, if necessary, and relevant legal information (previous cases or rules) must be selected. Facts of meager significance have to be distinguished from the ones that do matter. This is even more complicated because, depending on the perspective taken (e.g., lawyer of the plaintiff or defendant), different facts are of different importance. From research conducted on surface and structural problem features, it is known that novices are often distracted by surface features (contextual) and have problems identifying the structural features that play a crucial role in determining possible solutions (Holyoak and Koh, 1987). Effective legal reasoning requires identification and interpretation of structural features from a legal perspective. In other words, adequate determination of the significance of facts requires knowledge of rules of law and knowledge of the underlying policies of a case (Vandevelde, 1996).

Based on their experience, experts have formed scripts that help them to recognize and solve routine problems (Custers et al., 1998). Findings from research on expertise differences suggest that experts in a domain use mental frameworks or schemata that contain declarative knowledge (concepts and principles) to understand and frame a problem and procedural knowledge to apply principles to the problem (Chi,

2005; Dufresne et al., 1992; Schank and Abelson, 1977). Crombag et al. (1977) compared the knowledge structures of students and an expert with regard to one concept of private law, the tort. Participants had to order 29 different private law concepts around this main concept. They found that the expert's conceptual system of this legal concept consisted of specific clusters and elements, which could be interpreted as features of a tort script. In contrast, students' knowledge structures seemed incomplete, less organized, and less easily activated than the expert's script. Experts are also known to encapsulate lower level, detailed concepts under higher level concepts (i.e., they reach a higher level of abstraction) (Boshuizen and Schmidt, 1992). During work on routine problems, those abstract, higher level concepts are automatically activated; the lower level, detailed concepts are only activated if necessary for specific, nonroutine tasks. In sum, law students have to develop scripts and encapsulated concepts that will assist them in recognizing structural features and relevant facts in cases.

Alexander's (2003) model of domain learning (MDL) describes the quantitative and qualitative knowledge shifts that will take place during three stages of domain-specific expertise development: (1) acclimation, in which beginning students, who have limited and fragmented knowledge that cannot easily be activated, become familiar with the domain; (2) competence, in which fragmented knowledge changes into a more extensive, coherent, and principled whole; and (3) proficiency or expertise, which is characterized by a very extensive and well-structured expert knowledge base. In this final stage, individuals are able to contribute new knowledge to the domain, and as a result the domain keeps on growing (Alexander, 2003).

### Ontology

Apart from gaining knowledge of cases and rules and the development of scripts, novices in law must at the same time familiarize themselves with the official language of law (Lindahl, 2004). They need to master the ontology—that is, a shared and agreed upon, explicit, formal representation of the domain (Bench-Capon and Visser, 1997; Visser and Bench-Capon, 1998). This can be complicated, because many concepts that are routinely used in everyday informal life often have a very specific formal meaning that may only partially coincide with the everyday meaning (for a description of similar problems in the domain of science, see Chi, 2005; Chi and Roscoe, 2002). The following examples of an expert's and a novice's definition of the concept of *owner* illustrate this point. Asked for a definition of *owner*, the expert says: "Well, an owner has a subjec-

tive right of ownership on certain goods. It is the fullest right someone can have concerning goods and s/he is allowed to do everything s/he wants with regard to the good." A novice says: "An owner is someone who owns something; for example, if you have a dog, it is your dog" (Nievelstein et al., 2005).

### Intermediate Concepts

An additional problem for learners is that in the domain of law the function of certain concepts can vary depending on the described circumstances (Ashley and Aleven, 1991). Legal knowledge seems to be hierarchically ordered, and several concepts in such a hierarchical network function as intermediate concepts (Ashley and Brüninghaus, 2003). An intermediate concept determines the relationship between legal grounds, on the one hand, and legal consequences, on the other hand, and can have different functions depending on the described legal context (Lindahl, 2003). The term *ownership*, for example, can lead to a certain justification ground in one condition, whereas the same term can lead to another justification ground in another situation. Ownership regarding animals denotes other rights and responsibilities than ownership regarding a house, for example.

An example of a teaching tool making use of intermediate legal concepts is an artificial model for predicting and explaining case outcomes developed by Ashley and Brüninghaus (2003). The model relies on a large database of different cases. Every case represents a dispute between a plaintiff and a defendant and is represented by factors that either strengthen a plaintiff's claim or a defendant's response. The issue of every dispute is represented as an intermediate legal concept and is placed on top of a hierarchical tree. Depending on both the circumstances and the perspective taken (i.e., the role of the plaintiff or defendant), the intermediate concept fulfills a different role and leads to other legal consequences. The model compares a new case with cases contained in the database that share similar structural features (i.e., comparable issues). Whether a new case is won by the plaintiff or by the defendant is predicted and explained based on these comparisons

### Adversarial Reasoning

Legal argumentation plays a pivotal role in law and is therefore an important aspect of legal education (Carr, 2003). An argument can be defined as an assertion with an accompanying justification (Kuhn, 1991). One difficulty of argumentation in law is that reasoning is often adversarial—that is, performed in a context of debate and disagreement that requires that students learn to take multiple perspectives to place their own client in an optimal position. A legal argument that is acceptable in itself could be overturned by counterarguments and exceptions. The aim is to place oneself in an optimal position compared to an opponent by anticipating, understanding, and counteracting the opponent's actions (Thagard, 1992). Although rules, laws, and precedents are available, the adversarial context implies that their application is never a matter of straightforward verification.

## Supporting Law Students

The above section shows that, when learning law, difficulties arise related to knowledge development in general (acquiring domain-specific knowledge and scripts) and to the domain of law specifically (developing an ontology, understanding intermediate concepts, acquiring argumentation and perspective-taking skills). The question is how we can design law education in such a way that it will support law students, especially early on in their educational trajectory (novices), to overcome those difficulties.

### Research on Instructional
### Formats in Law

Much research on instructional design has been conducted in more structured domains than law; however, some instructional formats that have been found to be effective in those domains have also been investigated in law education. In this section, we discuss the following instructional formats: (1) worked-out examples, (2) a tutoring system that elicits adversarial reasoning, (3) a model for supporting argumentation, and (4) a method using cooperative learning.

The effectiveness of presenting students with worked-out examples and process worksheets has been theoretically argued for and has been studied in (specific phases of) learning how to prepare a plea (Hummel and Nadolski, 2002; Hummel et al., 2004, 2006; Nadolski et al., 2001). Hummel et al. (2004) found that students scored higher on a training plea (i.e., retention) after having studied worked-out examples but found no effect of worked-out examples on immediate and delayed transfer. Process worksheets positively affected delayed transfer.

Ashley and Aleven (1991) developed a tutoring system that provided practice and feedback opportunities for multiple perspective taking and the development of argumentation skills, which are both necessary for adversarial reasoning. This system teaches students how to make arguments by comparing and contrasting

cases. Each case is based on a dispute between a plaintiff and a defendant. By facing students with questions, alternative interpretations, rules, counter moves, and examples of the most effective or the best move, the system teaches them to distinguish structural case features and to reason in an adversarial context where they have to make and respond to arguments.

Carr (2003) compared arguments of two groups of second-year law students on a final exam. One group was trained to create arguments for legal problems with Toulmin's (1958) model of argument in a computer-supported setting, while the other group had to create arguments for the same problems without using this tool. The hypothesis that students trained with the model of argument would have higher scores on the final exam was not supported. One explanation for his findings could be that second-year students have not yet acquired enough domain knowledge to benefit from the tool, because to express an argument in a structured way knowledge of the domain is requisite (Kuhn, 1991). More advanced students, then, might have benefited from the tool.

Henderson and Martin (2002) studied cooperative learning in family law. Students had to work on a relatively general assignment: reviewing cases and writing a family law position paper. Their findings showed that, for this assignment, cooperative learning resulted in improved individual and group achievement, in more critical thinking about family law, and in better understanding of the problems in law.

### Suggestions for Further
### Educational Research in Law

The worked-out examples used by Hummel et al. (2004, 2006) can be called *product oriented* (van Gog et al. 2004), as they focused learners on solution steps to attain an end product (solution). These product-oriented, worked-out examples did not affect transfer. As Hummel et al. (2004) noted, process-oriented, worked-out examples might have improved transfer but were not investigated in that study. Process-oriented, worked-out examples provide both the solution steps and the strategic and domain-principled knowledge used in selecting the steps. In other words, the systematic approach to problem solving and the accompanying heuristics, as well as the principled domain knowledge that experts use in their reasoning process toward the solution, are explicated in combination with the worked-out solution steps provided (van Gog et al., 2004). Using such process-oriented worked-out examples in law might be very effective, as they essentially provide students with expert models of problem solving and reasoning.

An interesting question that Ashley and Brüning-haus (2003) did not address was whether people recognize intermediate concepts and structural features of a case more quickly and argue better when they are trained with the principles of the case-based prediction algorithm. Another technique that might assist in learning to argue and in learning to understand the different functions of intermediate concepts is the use of concept maps, which has proven effective for conceptual learning in science education (Roth, 1990; Van Boxtel et al., 2000). Students in this domain learned to assign meaning to concepts by making concept maps from different points of view. Using this technique in combination with cooperative learning might be effective in law. During group sessions, students could explain different concept arrangements to fellow students and challenge each other's opinions about their explanations.

Maughan (1996) contended that practice in authentic, real-life contexts is important, especially for the acquisition of argumentation and adversarial reasoning skills. Fully authentic training contexts are often difficult to achieve; however, authenticity can be conceived of as a multidimensional construct (Gulikers et al., 2004), and high authenticity on some of these dimensions might be more important for learning certain skills than others. A study of which dimensions should have a high degree of authenticity may generate guidelines for the construction of training situations (e.g., moot courts; see Taylor, 2000). Gulikers et al. have also shown that the importance of authenticity of different dimensions varies with expertise levels; hence, it may very well be that not so authentic cognitive tutors (Ashley and Aleven, 1991) are especially effective in the early stages of argumentation skill acquisition and that practice in contexts with a higher degree of authenticity becomes increasingly important with increasing skill development.

It may also be helpful to investigate ways to support law teachers, as they will in turn support students. Research on expert–laypeople communication has shown that experts often experience difficulties with accurately estimating novices' level of knowledge and adapting their explanations to that level (Bromme et al., 2001; Nückles et al., 2005). Although law teachers should be trained in recognizing students' knowledge levels and adapting to them, university teachers in particular are also domain experts, so expert–laypeople communication problems might also apply to law teachers. If this is the case, educational research should also be targeted toward improving teachers' understanding of development of ontology and conceptual understanding, on the one hand, and providing them with tools to accurately assess the level of development of their students, on the other hand.

## Discussion

This section has shown that, even though common law and civil law evoke somewhat different learning and teaching processes, students experience similar difficulties in learning law. Those difficulties are largely related to specific facets of this domain (ontology, intermediate concepts, and adversarial reasoning) that make knowledge and skill acquisition more complex than in other professional domains. A major challenge for educational researchers and instructional designers lies in identifying techniques that adequately support students' integrated knowledge and skill development at different stages in their educational trajectories. Surprisingly, compared to other complex professional domains such as medicine, research on learning and instruction in the domain of law is sparse. Some interesting previous studies have been described here, and an attempt has been made to identify promising directions for future research in this domain that will result in instructional formats and principles that will help students overcome the difficulties they encounter and foster their expertise development as much as possible during their formal education.

## LEARNING MEDICINE: A CONTINUUM FROM THEORY TO PRACTICE

*Tim Dornan, Albert Scherpbier, and John Spencer*

### Introduction to Learning Medicine

The medical profession is founded on a moral code. Its primary educational task is to encourage members of successive generations to uphold the code and to pass the code on to learners coming after them. Perpetuation of this value system gives education a central place in the profession which has been affirmed repeatedly from Hippocrates (Lyons and Petrucelli, 1987) to the present time (General Medical Council, 1999). That much is easy, but changes in the nature of clinical practice, educational practice, and the social order are making medical education an increasingly complex domain. This section concentrates on undergraduate medical education. It links special features of the domain to factors that are changing it and recently devised solutions. It uses examples from the United Kingdom to illustrate general points.

### Special Features of the Domain

#### General Description

Entrants come fresh from high school or as mature students with life experience and perhaps a prior

**TABLE 41.1**
**Disciplines Taught in Medical School**

More theoretical disciplines; for example:
  Physiology, anatomy, and chemistry of the body tissues and systems
  Chemistry of drugs and their actions
  Sciences of individual and social behavior
More applied disciplines; for example:
  Pathology
  Public health
Individual disciplines into which medicine is organized; for example:
  Internal medicine
  Surgery
  General practice

**TABLE 41.2**
**The Duties of a Doctor, as Defined by the U.K. General Medical Council**

*Doctors should:*

Make the care of their patient their first concern.

Treat every patient politely and considerately.

Respect patients' dignity and privacy.

Listen to patients and respect their views.

Give patients information in a way they can understand.

Respect the rights of patients to be fully involved in decisions about their care.

Keep their professional knowledge and skills up to date.

Recognize the limits of their professional competence.

Be honest and trustworthy.

Respect and protect confidential information.

Make sure their personal beliefs do not prejudice their patients' care.

Act quickly to protect patients from risk if they have good reason to believe that they or a colleague may not be fit to practice.

Avoid abusing their position as a doctor.

Work with colleagues in the ways that best serve patients' interests.

*Source:* General Medical Council, *Duties of a Doctor*, General Medical Council, London, 1993.

degree. Medical training takes 4 to 6 years, depending on the country and the student's previous education. High academic standards are required for admission, and students must be highly motivated because medical study is arduous. Entrants with no science background may be required to take an access course to ground them in the bioscientific vocabulary of medicine. In addition to being ambitious, medical students tend to be altruistically motivated. At the beginning, they learn biomedical science and perhaps behavioral and social science and humanities but have minimal workplace experience. In later years, the focus shifts from theory to practice, and they gain extensive clinical workplace experience. After graduating, new doctors take responsibility, under supervision, for the care of patients but have to undergo postgraduate training before they can practice unsupervised. The aim of undergraduate medical education, then, is to produce graduates who can enter the workforce and receive the postgraduate training that will make them independent practitioners.

### Subject Matter and Learning Outcomes

The wide, long, and deep competences (Hamilton, 1999) that underpin medical practice place a huge burden on learners. They are drawn from the disciplines listed in Table 41.1. The U.K. General Medical Council's definition of the duties of a doctor is shown in Table 41.2 (General Medical Council, 1993). It takes technical competence as a given and concentrates on the social responsibilities of a doctor; however, most of a medical student's education is taken up with acquiring technical rather than social competence, and knowledge acquisition takes pride of place.

The espoused knowledge of the domain and method of learning vary in character from one medical discipline to another. Anatomy, for example, is often

rote learned in preparation for tests of factual recall because the true science of human form is tied up in sciences of human embryology and evolution that students simply do not have time to study in any depth. Biochemistry and physiology are taught as experimental sciences, although it is left to students and curriculum planners to find clinical relevance in them because science teachers are not medical practitioners. In addition to the official curriculum (Coles, 1998), an unofficial curriculum covers a very different type of know-how, including such things as time management, how to behave in practice settings, role and hierarchy, and career development (Sinclair, 1997). Turning to the skills domain, medical students must acquire the study skills of a learner and the psychomotor and communication skills of practice. Table 41.3 shows a classification of clinical skills (Dornan et al., 2003). There is also a tacit curriculum of complex social skills required for success in the workplace. The term *attitudes* is used loosely to cover the several types of learning listed in Table 41.4 that sustain the learner during their studies and help them socialize professionally. These social and emotional aspects of medical education are further considered later in this section.

Doctors-in-waiting have to integrate all of this learning into safe, fluent, and spontaneous professional performance; a medical emergency could, for example,

---

**TABLE 41.3**
**A Classification of Clinical Skills**

| Type of Skill | Description |
|---|---|
| Consultation | Effective transaction with a patient to provide medical care |
| Physical examination | Examining a patient to make a diagnosis |
| Image interpretation | Examining a radiograph or electrocardiogram systematically, detecting abnormalities, and relating those findings to knowledge of health and disease |
| Procedure | Incrementing a patient's body for diagnostic or therapeutic purposes; for example, taking blood |
| Therapeutic | The procedural and/or intellectual act of safely administrating a complex treatment like a blood transfusion |
| Management | For example, coordinating the various services that will look after a patient when they are discharged from hospital |
| Laboratory | Handling specimens safely and conducting simple analyses on body fluids |
| Patient and staff safety | Hand washing and other ways of preventing transmission of communicable diseases |

---

**TABLE 41.4**
**Learning Outcomes Often Described as Attitudes**

*Knowledge of:*
  The professional value system
  How the legal and ethical frameworks of medicine have to be put into practice
*Personal qualities, such as:*
  Confidence
  Motivation
  Probity/integrity
  Sense of professional identity
  Self-awareness

---

call for knowledge of the different uniforms of the nursing hierarchy, knowledge of the biochemical effects of a patient's drugs, the intellectual skill of applying the information to analyze the problem, and the emotional and social skills of moderating interactions between the patient and nurse in the heat of the emergency.

### Educational Processes

Traditionally, medical students have acquired knowledge by attending lectures and practical classes and by learning from books. When the emphasis of their learning shifts from preclinical theory to clinical practice, they learn from practitioners in practice settings (Sinclair, 1997). Some attitudinal learning is projected onto medical students by didactic teachers, acquired as knowledge, or embedded in the skills they learn, but an important influence on attitudinal development is the process of role modeling (Elzubeir and Rizk, 2001; Tiberius et al., 2002). Research has consistently shown that medical students and young doctors identify as role models practitioners who are clinically excellent, behave compassionately toward patients, teach diligently, and focus on doctor–patient communication and patients' psychosocial problems (Wright et al., 1998). Skills such as conducting physiological experiments in the early curriculum are a means to the end of becoming knowledgeable. Skills learned later in workplaces, such as obtaining a complete history and conducting a full examination to replicate the behavior of a doctor, are both a means and an end. Practical skills are not just something doctors have to be able to perform but are a means for students to integrate into the practicing clinical team, which is vital to their clinical learning (Dornan, 2006).

**TABLE 41.5**
**Pressures toward Graduate Entry**

| | |
|---|---|
| Widened participation | To be equitable and balance the social mix of the medical profession, there is a wish to give disadvantaged teenagers the chance to enter the medical profession later in life. |
| Need for more doctors | There is pressure to admit students who can be turned quickly into the extra doctors society needs. |
| Personal attributes | Their greater life experience and the motivation that brought them into higher education at this late stage make them a particularly valued type of student for medical school. |
| Fitness for medical study | Evidence suggests that mature entrants make a smoother transition from classroom to workplace learning and grow in academic strength when nonmature entrants have reached a plateau. |

Today's medical education was conceived at a time when most practice was in hospitals, where patients were admitted for long periods of time, often with grossly apparent disease that medicine could not cure. The tradition was for medical students to be attached to a senior clinician and his postgraduate trainee doctors based in a single hospital ward. Traditional clinical apprentices functioned as the most junior members of medical teams, admitting patients to their teacher's ward, carrying out menial tasks, and providing an extra pair of hands for surgical operations. Medicine has a rich assessment tradition. Knowledge was traditionally assessed through essays, *viva voce* examinations, and cross-examination at the bedside. Practical competence was tested by asking questions about a patient the candidate had spent some time examining or by observing the candidate examining several patients with externally detectable evidence of disease (so-called long and short case exams, respectively). Such assessments were often adversarial in nature and confronted students with exotic manifestations of disease rather than commonplace situations they would have to deal with in practice.

### Special Themes in Medical Education

Medical education has to attend to medical students' social development as much as equip them with specific competences. It has to usher them through a process of moral development (Branch, 2000), when their idealism is challenged and they feel pressure to "adopt a ritualized professional identity" (Lempp and Seale, 2004). It must help them learn how to handle strong emotions stemming as much from the process of professional acculturation as from contact with disease and distress, sustain their motivation, build the confidence that enables them to interact with practitioners, and develop a sense of professional identity (Dornan, 2006). There are strong elements of risk in medical education. Junior medical students are painfully aware that blurting out the word "cancer" within a patient's hearing can do irrevocable harm to the object of their motivation, as could any failings in the practical tasks of medicine. Students could contract a potentially fatal communicable disease from a patient, fail in the competitive world of practice, or become the object of a lawsuit.

### Pressures for Change in Medical Education

The demand for more doctors is overcrowding medical schools and putting pressure on traditional clinical apprenticeship. Undergraduate entry systems are being pushed toward mature/graduate entry by the various factors listed in Table 41.5. Having more mature students, in its turn, pushes medical schools to adopt systems of education that are more respectful of learners' existing attributes. Medical practice in developed countries is changing in many ways that impact on medical education (see Table 41.6).

Medicine is caught in a more general tension between academia's traditional view of education as scholarship and the profession's increasing call for doctors who are fit for what Schön described as the "swampy lowlands" of uncertainty and real-world practice (Schön, 1983). It has also been strongly affected by the self-directed learning movement (Knowles, 1975), which challenged both traditional didacticism and the hierarchical relationship between clinical master and apprentice and resulted in widespread adoption of learner-centered methods. Medical education as it was practiced until very recently gave students a fairly pure grounding in science followed by opportunities to put theory into practice in

**TABLE 41.6**

**Changes in the Nature of Practice That Affect Medical Education**

| Change | Effect on Education |
|---|---|
| Shorter lengths of hospital stay and more care out of hospital | Favors community-based education and new methods and locations or settings for teaching in hospitals |
| Stronger emphasis on disease prevention and health promotion, as well as on long-term management of chronic disease | Changes the subject matter and focus of medical curricula |
| Strong emphasis on patient safety and mitigation of clinical risk | Eliminates learning by trial and error and makes it more difficult for learners to cross the threshold into practice |
| A change in medicine's traditionally privileged status with the rise of professions allied to medicine and more flexible use of skill mix | Changes the emphasis of medical education towards interprofessional and team learning; provides a rationale for interprofessional education |
| Empowerment of lay people | Shifts the subject matter from learning outcomes that matter primarily to pedagogues and calls for explicit training in patient-centered medical practice |
| Increasingly technical, specialized nature of practice and proliferation of clinical disciplines | Increases curriculum content; makes it more difficult to learn holistically and to cover a full breadth of curriculum content in any one discipline |
| Reappraisal of the nature of medical professionalism in the context of a new social compact between the profession and society | Increases curriculum content, particularly in areas such as ethics and communication, and the underpinning social and humanistic sciences |
| Advances in science such as the "new genetics" and molecular biology | Increases curriculum content |

apprenticeship attachments; however, the many forces listed in Table 41.7 are broadening and changing the epistemology of medical education.

As developed societies have become more egalitarian and lay people more empowered, doctors' privileged social position and sometimes insensitive or paternalistic behavior have been challenged. The result has been to restate medicine's value system within a new framework that emphasizes the subservient place of the medical profession (General Medical Council, 2002; Working Party of the Royal College of Physicians, 2005).

## Solutions and Unanswered Questions

While changes in practice have eroded the traditional relationship between master and apprentice, educational theory has shifted its focus from teachers to learners and the way they regulate their learning (Ten Cate et al., 2004). This new focus is a two-edged sword. The egalitarian relationship between a group of self-directed learners and a problem-based learning facilitator is an effective way of teaching the declarative knowledge of medicine (Prince et al., 2003); however, other types of learning depend on a relationship between learner and teacher that is "inherently asymmetrical" (Tiberius et al., 2002). To acquire psychomotor skills, medical students have to be trained by masters (Patrick, 1992). To acquire clinical expertise, they must socialize into communities of practice in which

their teachers are masters (Swanwick, 2005; Wenger, 1998). We found that a move toward self-directed learning in the workplace disenfranchised teachers and left learners confused and purposeless (Dornan et al., 2005a,b). Research is needed into the roles students should adopt within communities of clinical practice. Patients are increasingly recognized as active participants rather than passive recipients of medical care, so their role in contemporary medical education has also to be researched (Spencer et al., 2000).

### Outcome-Based Education and Subject Matter

Until recently, medical curricula would have been described in terms of the disciplines that taught them. Now, they have explicit learning outcomes, usually expressed as competences. Although it is self-evidently important to have clear goals, the supposition that medical expertise can be reduced to a set of competences is questionable. Experience and tacit knowledge have clearly defined places in clinical expertise (Schmidt et al., 1990; Wyatt, 2001) but are difficult to express as competences. Even separating educational process and product is questionable when students learn by forming relationships with practitioners. The current emphasis on professionalism ensures that the subject matter of medical curricula is expressed in wider terms than bioscience. Social awareness, ethical behavior, good communication, and effective resource management are all to be expected of 21st-century doctors. To

**TABLE 41.7**
**Epistemological Changes and Their Effect on Medical Education**

| Changes in the Epistemology of Medical Education | Effects |
| --- | --- |
| A state of maturity in science that changes the doctor from a pioneer of untested solutions to implementer, within social settings, of mature technology | Medical education must adapt to the role of doctor as a social rather than scientific agent of change |
| The demand in societies for doctors to show social qualities that are neither theoretically nor practically grounded in biomedical science | Medical education must choose to either provide an education that is not grounded in theory or adopt new foundation disciplines, including humanities |
| The rise of behavioral and social sciences that are theoretically coherent and have the power to explain and provide solutions to a variety of issues of health and disease | Provide new subject matter for a medical student's theoretical education |
| Entrant practitioners' experience of finding themselves poorly prepared for their professional roles by a theory-before-practice, science-based education | Shift at least in the sequence, and perhaps in the theoretical content, of medical curricula |
| Acknowledgment that modern medicine has many faces: medicine as science, medicine as humanity, medicine as practical know-how, and medicine as social *savoir faire* | Explicit adoption of a wide epistemology of practice rather than giving science preeminence and leaving other aspects of learning to the unofficial curriculum |

fulfill their social responsibilities, medical students must acquire emotional learning outcomes such as confidence, motivation, and a professional identity (Dornan, 2006). In addition, there are introspective qualities that are difficult to define because they are so individual yet are easy to recognize. One author coined the term *mindfulness* to describe the insight that allows a practitioner to generalize, tackle future challenges, incorporate new behaviors and attitudes, express compassion, and "be present" (Epstein, 1999). Mindfulness cannot be taught, but it can be developed through questioning, reflection, mentoring, and role modeling—literally, an education or a "bringing out." Better definition of the personal qualities of a doctor, the ways in which those qualities can be developed, and their relation to constructs such as emotional intelligence are important topics for future research.

### Curriculum Design

Integration is a dominant theme in contemporary medical education. Rather than a discontinuous sequence of educational experiences, each preparing for the next, contemporary medical education seeks progressively to shape the student entrant as a doctor. Abrupt transitions delay students' learning, including their moral development (Branch, 2000). Progressive exposure to workplaces alongside theoretical education helps them learn practically, cognitively, socially, and emotionally. Vertical integration, it can be argued, is a socially responsive curriculum design (Littlewood et al., 2005). There is also a call for curricula to be horizontally integrated—that is, cover a logical sequence of subject matter organized around body systems rather than individual disciplines. This works less well for workplace learning than for the theory of medicine. The expertise that teachers are keen to share with students is so bound up in their disciplinary practice that horizontal integration of workplace learning causes serious confusion (Patel et al., 2002). The relative merit of integrated vs. discipline-based workplace learning is an important topic for future research.

### Pedagogic Methods and Assessment

Problem-based learning has been one of medical education's most important contributions to higher education. Originally conceived as a way to teach transferable problem-solving skills (Barrows, 1984), it is a proven effective means of shifting regulation of education from teacher to learner (Schmidt, 1993). Critics have pointed out that problem-based learning does not make medical students more knowledgeable than traditional, didactic approaches (Berkson, 1993), overlooking evidence that it develops more appropriate learning skills, builds social skills, and is more enjoyable (Albanese and Mitchell, 1993; Vernon and Blake, 1993).

Concern for the safety of the student and patient led to the development of various simulation techniques and the widespread introduction of clinical skills laboratories. Interpersonal communication is trained and tested using simulated patients (Van Dalen et al., 1999). Psychomotor skills are taught using anatomical models, while more complex procedures use high-fidelity simulation technologies (Issenberg et al., 2005). How to promote the transfer of simulation education to practice settings is another important topic for future research.

Most research into clinical workplace learning is so contextually bound that there is a need for new, more generalizable conceptions. We have offered experience-based learning as one such conception. According to this model, the central condition for workplace learning is supported participation in practice. As learners become more experienced, they progress along a scale from observer to participant, culminating in performance for the patients' benefit. Supported participation results in emotional and practical learning, which reinforce one another. Learning is self-reinforcing because successful learning makes it easier for the learner to be a participant. The quality of supported participation is strongly influenced by qualities of the learning environment, predominant among which is the relationship between practitioners and learners. This theory provides a basis for continuing research into clinical workplace learning.

Much intensive research into assessment has been conducted. In the domain of medical knowledge, progress testing deserves special mention (Van der Vleuten et al., 1996). Introduced as a complement to problem-based learning and a way of discouraging students from "cramming and forgetting," this technique tests students' longitudinal growth of knowledge referenced to their peer group. Another form of assessment developed in medicine is the Objective Structured Clinical Examination (OSCE) (Harden et al., 1975). The OSCE assesses students on a variety of tasks, covering a wide range of subject matter. It has been widely adopted as a way of reducing bias and overcoming the problem of content specificity in practical examinations.

Evaluation—measuring the quality of education—is so closely linked to assessment that the two words are synonymous in U.S. English; however, the assumption that examination performance is a valid measure of the quality of a curriculum is questionable for two main reasons. First, students learn to the test. They strive to overcome the deficiencies of poor curricula by studying privately, very likely at the cost of learning outcomes that are not measured. Second, using assessment to measure curriculum quality supposes that the essential qualities of a curriculum are assessable. Because pass–fail decisions have to be made on reliable data, assessments have tended to focus on knowledge or skills that can be tested in highly controlled conditions. So, another important field of contemporary research is authentic assessment, which takes assessment into workplace settings.

## Conclusion

Medicine as a learning domain is characterized by risk to the learner and patient, a knowledge-rich education that has to prepare learners to handle complex problems immediately after qualification, strong emotional forces, and a close professional relationship between teacher and learner that gives education a high priority in the value system of the profession.

## REFERENCES

Aamodt, A. and Plaza, E. (1994). Case-based reasoning: foundational issues methodological variations, and system approaches. *AI Commun.*, 7, 39–59.

Admiraal, W., Wubbels, T., and Pilot, A. (1999). College teaching in legal education: teaching method, students' time on task, and achievement. *Res. Higher Educ.*, 40, 687–704.

Albanese, M. A. and Mitchell, S. (1993). Problem-based learning: a review of literature on its outcomes and implementation issues. *Acad. Med.*, 68, 52–81.

Alexander, P. A. (2003). The development of expertise: the journey from acclimation to proficiency. *Educ. Res.*, 32, 10–14.

Anderson, R. C. and Freebody, P. (1979). *Vocabulary Knowledge and Reading*. Reading Education Report no. 11. Urbana: University of Illinois.

Anthony, J. L. and Francis, D. J. (2005). Development of phonological awareness. *Curr. Direct. Psychol. Sci.*, 14(5), 255–259.

Ashley, K. D. and Aleven, V. (1991). Toward an intelligent tutoring system for teaching law students to argue with cases. In *Proceedings of the Third International Conference on Artificial Intelligence and Law*, pp. 42–52. New York: ACM Press.*

Ashley, K. D. and Brüninghaus, S. (2003). A predictive role for intermediate legal concepts. In *Legal Knowledge and Information Systems. Jurix 2003: The Sixteenth Annual Conference*, edited by D. Bourcier, pp. 153–162. Amsterdam: IOS Press.*

Barrows, H. S. (1984). A specific, problem-based, self-directed learning method designed to teach medical problem-solving skills, and enhance knowledge retention and recall. In *Tutorials in Problem-Based Learning*, edited by H. G. Schmidt and M. L. De Volder, pp. 16–32. Assen, the Netherlands: Van Gorcum.

Beck, I. L. and McKeown, M. G. (1991). Conditions of vocabulary acquisition. In *Handbook of Reading Research*, Vol. 2, edited by R. Barr, M. L. Kamil, P. Mosenthal, and P. Pearson, pp. 789–814. Hillsdale, NJ: Lawrence Erlbaum Associates.

Beck, I. L., McKeown, M. G., and Omanson, R. C. (1987). The effects and uses of diverse vocabulary instructional techniques. In *The Nature of Vocabulary Acquisition*, edited by M. McKeown and M. E. Curtis, pp. 147–163. Hillsdale, NJ: Lawrence Erlbaum Associates.

Beck, I. L., McKeown, M. G., and Kucan, L. (2002). *Bringing Words to Life: Robust Vocabulary Instruction. Solving Problems in the Teaching of Literacy*. New York: Guilford.*

Bench-Capon, T. J. M. and Visser, P. R. S. (1997). Ontologies in legal information systems: the need for explicit specifications of domain conceptualizations. In *Proceedings of the Sixth International Conference on Artificial Intelligence and Law*, pp. 132–141. New York: ACM Press.*

Bereiter, C. (1985). Towards a solution of the learning paradox. *Rev. Educ. Res.*, 55, 201–226.

Berkson, L. (1993). Problem-based learning: have the expectations been met? *Acad. Med.*, 68, S79–S88.

Biemiller, A. and Slonim, N. (2001). Estimating root word vocabulary growth in normative and advantaged populations: evidence for a common sequence of vocabulary acquisition. *J. Educ. Psychol.*, 93(3), 498–520.

Boshuizen, H. P. A. and Schmidt, H. G. (1992). On the role of biomedical knowledge in clinical reasoning by experts, intermediates and novices. *Cogn. Sci.*, 16, 153–184.

Branch, Jr., W. T. (2000). Supporting the moral development of medical students. *J. Gen. Intern. Med.*, 15, 503–508.

Bromme, R., Rambow, R., and Nückles, M. (2001). Expertise and estimating what other people know: the influence of professional experience and type of knowledge. *J. Exp. Psychol. Appl.*, 7, 317–330.

Cameron, B. and Dwyer, F. (2005). The effect of online gaming, cognition and feedback type in facilitating delayed achievement of different learning objectives. *J. Interact. Learn. Res.*, 16, 243–258.

Carr, C. S. (2003). Using computer supported argument visualization to teach legal argumentation. In *Visualizing Argumentation: Software Tools for Collaborative and Educational Sense-Making*, edited by P. A. Kirschner, S. J. Buckingham Shum, and C. S. Carr, pp. 75–96. London: Springer.*

Carter, K. and Unklesbay, R. (1989). Cases in teaching law. *J. Curric. Stud.*, 21, 527–536.

Chalmers, A. F. (1976). *What Is This Thing Called Science?* Oxford: University of Queensland Press.

Chi, M. T. H. (2005). Commonsense conceptions of emergent processes: why some misconceptions are robust. *J. Learn. Sci.*, 14, 161–199.

Chi, M. T. H. and Roscoe, R. D. (2002). The processes and challenges of conceptual change. In *Reconsidering Conceptual Change: Issues in Theory and Practice*, edited by M. Limón and L. Mason, pp. 3–27. Dordrecht: Kluwer.

Cobb, P. (2002) Mathematizing, symbolizing, and tool use in statistical data analysis. In *Symbolizing, Modeling and Tool Use in Mathematics Education*, edited by K. Gravemeijer, R. Lehrer, B. van Oers, and L. Verschaffel, pp. 171–195. Dordrecht: Kluwer.

Cobb, P., Yackel, E., and Wood, T. (1992). A constructivist alternative to the representational view of mind in mathematics education. *J. Res. Math. Educ.*, 23(1), 2–33.*

Coles, C. (1998). How students learn: the process of learning. In *Medical Education in the Millennium*, edited by B. Jolly and L. Rees, pp. 63–82. Oxford: Oxford University Press.

Crombag, H. F. M., de Wijkersloot, J. L., and Cohen, M. J. (1977). *Een theorie over rechterlijke beslissingen* [*A Theory of Judicial Decisions*]. Groningen, the Netherlands: H. D. Tjeenk Willink.*

Custers, E. J. F. M., Boshuizen, H. P. A., and Schmidt, H. G. (1998). The role of illness scripts in the development of medical diagnostic expertise: results from an interview study. *Cogn. Instruct.*, 16, 367–398.

DeLisi, R. and Golbeck, S. L. (1999). Implications of Piagetian theory for peer learning. In *Cognitive Perspectives on Peer Learning*, edited by A. M. O'Donnell and A. King, pp. 3–37. Mahwah, NJ: Lawrence Erlbaum Associates.

Doorman, L. M. (2005). *Modelling Motion: From Trace Graphs to Instantaneous Change*. Utrecht, the Netherlands: CD-Beta Press.

Dornan, T. L. (2006). *Experience Based Learning: Learning Clinical Medicine in Workplaces*. Maastricht, the Netherlands: Universitaire Pers Maastricht.

Dornan, T., Maredia, N., Hosie, L., Lee, C., and Stopford, A. (2003). A Web-based presentation of an undergraduate clinical skills curriculum. *Med. Educ.*, 37, 500–508.

Dornan, T., Hadfield, J., Brown, M., Boshuizen, H., and Scherpbier, A. (2005a). How can medical students learn in a self-directed way in the clinical environment? Design-based research. *Med. Educ.*, 39, 356–364.

Dornan, T., Scherpbier, A. J. J. A., King, N., and Boshuizen, H. (2005b). Clinical teachers and problem based learning: a phenomenological study. *Med. Educ.*, 39, 163–170.

Dufresne, R. J., Gerace, W. J., Thibodeau-Hardiman, P., and Mestre, J. P. (1992). Constraining novices to perform expert-like problem analyses: effects on schema acquisition. *J. Learn. Sci.*, 2, 307–331.

Elzubeir, M. A. and Rizk, D. E. E. (2001). Identifying characteristics that students, interns and residents look for in their role models. *Med. Educ.*, 35, 272–277.

Epstein, R. M. (1999). Mindful practice. *J. Am. Med. Assoc.*, 282, 833–839.

Freudenthal, H. (1973). *Mathematics as an Educational Task*. Dordrecht: Reidel.

Freudenthal, H. (1991). *Revisiting Mathematics Education*. Dordrecht: Kluwer.

General Medical Council. (1993). *Duties of a Doctor*. London: General Medical Council.

General Medical Council. (1999). *The Doctor as Teacher*. London: General Medical Council.

General Medical Council. (2002). *Tomorrow's Doctors*. London: General Medical Council.*

Gleason, M. E. and Schauble, L. (2000). Parents' assistance of their children's scientific reasoning. *Cogn. Instruct.*, 17, 343–378.

Granott, N. and Parziale, J. (2002). Microdevelopment: a process-oriented perspective for studying development and learning. In *Microdevelopment: Transition Processes in Development and Learning*, edited by N. Granott and J. Parziale, pp. 1–28. New York: Cambridge University Press.

Gravemeijer, K. (1999). How emergent models may foster the constitution of formal mathematics. *Math. Think. Learn.*, 1(2), 155–177.*

Gravemeijer, K. (2004). Learning trajectories and local instruction theories as means of support for teachers in reform mathematics education. *Math. Think. Learn.*, 6(2), 105–128.

Graves, M. F. (1987). The role of instruction in fostering vocabulary development. In *The Nature of Vocabulary Acquisition*, edited by M. McKeown and M. E. Curtis, pp. 165–184. Hillsdale, NJ: Lawrence Erlbaum Associates.

Gulikers, J. T. M., Bastiaens, T. J., and Kirschner, P. A. (2004). A five-dimensional framework for authentic assessment. *Educ. Technol. Res. Dev.*, 52, 67–86.

Hamilton, J. D. (1999). Outcomes in medical education must be wide, long and deep. *Med. Teacher*, 21, 125–126.

Harden, R. M., Stevenson, M., Wilson Downie, W., and Wilson, G. M. (1975). Assessment of clinical competence using objective structured examination. *Br. Med. J.*, 1, 447–451.

Hebbeler, K. (1985). An old and a new question on the effects of early education for children from low income families. *Educ. Eval. Policy Anal.*, 7(3), 207–216.

Henderson, T. L. and Martin, K. J. (2002). Cooperative learning as one approach to teaching family law. *Fam. Relat.*, 51, 351–360.

Hertzog, N. and Klein, M. (2005). Beyond gaming: a technology explosion in early childhood classrooms. *Gifted Child Today*, 28, 24–31.

Holyoak, K. J. and Koh, K. (1987). Surface and structural similarity in analogical transfer. *Mem. Cogn.*, 15, 332–340.

Hummel, H. G. K. and Nadolski, R. J. (2002). Cueing for schema construction: designing problem-solving multimedia practicals. *Contemp. Educ. Psychol.*, 27, 229–249.*

Hummel, H. G. K., Paas, F., and Koper, E. J. R. (2004). Cueing for transfer in multimedia programmes: process worksheets versus worked-out examples. *J. Comput. Assist. Learn.*, 20, 387–397.

Hummel, H. G. K., Paas, F., and Koper, E. J. R. (2006). Timing of cueing in complex problem-solving tasks: learner versus system control. *Comput. Hum. Behav.*, 22, 191–205.

Issenberg, S. B., McGaghie, W. C., Petrusa, E. R., Gordon, D. L., and Scalese, R. J. (2005). Features and uses of high-fidelity medical simulations that lead to effective learning: a BEME systematic review. *Med. Teacher*, 27, 10–28.

Jorm, A. F. and Share, D. L. (1983). Phonological recoding and reading acquisition. *Appl. Psycholinguist.*, 4(2), 103–147.

Kagan, J. (2002). Empowerment and education: civil rights, expert-advocates, and parent politics in Head Start, 1964–1980. *Teachers Coll. Rec.*, 104(3), 516–562.

Kangassalo, M. (1997). *The Formation of Children's Conceptual Models Concerning a Particular Natural Phenomenon Using PICCO, a Pictorial Computer Simulation*, Acta Universitatis Tamperensis 559. Tampere, Finland: University of Tampere.

Knowles, M. S. (1975). *Self-Directed Learning: A Guide for Learners and Teachers*. New York: Cambridge Book Co.

Kohnstamm, G. A. (1967). *Piaget's Analysis of Class Inclusion: Right or Wrong*. Paris: Mouton.

Kuhn, D. K. (1991). *The Skills of Argument*. New York: Cambridge University Press.

Kumpulainen, K., Vasama, S., and Kangassalo, M. (2003). The intertextuality of children's explanations in a technology-enriched early years' science classroom. *Int. J. Educ. Res.*, 39, 793–805.

Labinowics, E. (1985). *Learning from Children*. Amsterdam: Addison-Wesley.

Lee, V. E., Brooks-Gunn, J., Schnur, E., and Liaw, F.-R. (1990). Are Head Start effects sustained? A longitudinal follow-up comparison of disadvantaged children attending Head Start, no preschool, and other preschool programs. *Child Dev.*, 61(2), 495–507.

Lempp, H. and Seale, C. (2004). The hidden curriculum in undergraduate medical education: qualitative study of medical students' perceptions of teaching. *Br. Med. J.*, 329, 770–773.

Lindahl, L. (2003). Operative and justificatory grounds in legal argumentation. *Associations*, 7, 185–200.*

Lindahl, L. (2004). Deduction and justification in the law: the role of legal terms and concepts. *Ratio Juris*, 17, 182–202.

Lindamood, C. H. and Lindamood, P. C. (1984). *Auditory Discrimination in Depth*. Austin, TX: Pro-Ed.

Littlewood, S., Ypinazar, V., Margolis, S. A., Scherpbier, A. J. J. A., Spencer, J., and Dornan, T. (2005). Early practical experience and the social responsiveness of clinical education: systematic review. *Br. Med. J.*, 331, 387–391.

Lonigan, C. J. (2006). Development, assessment, and promotion of preliteracy skills. *Early Educ. Dev.*, 17(1), 91–114.*

Lyons, A. S. and Petrucelli, R. J. (1987). *Medicine: An Illustrated History*. New York: Abrams.

Maughan, C. (1996). Problem-solving through reflective practice: the oxygen of expertise or just swamp gas? *Web J. Curr. Legal Issues*, 6, http://webjcli.ncl.ac.uk.

Meira, L. (1995). The microevolution of mathematical representations in children's activities. *Cogn. Instruct.*, 13(2), 269–313.*

Nadolski, R. J., Kirschner, P. A., van Merriënboer, J. J. G., and Hummel, H. G. K. (2001). A model for optimizing step size of learning tasks in competency-based multimedia practicals. *Educ. Technol. Res. Dev.*, 49, 87–103.

NICHD. (2000). *Report of the National Reading Panel. Teaching Children to Read: An Evidence-Based Assessment of the Scientific Research Literature on Reading and Its Implications for Reading Instruction, Reports of the Subgroups*, NIH Publ. No. 00-4754. Washington, D.C.: National Institute of Child Health and Human Development.*

Nievelstein, F., Boshuizen, H. P. A., van Bruggen, J. M., and Prins, F. J. (2005). The Role of Knowledge Development and Ontological Change in the Development of Expertise in Legal Reasoning: Toward a Domain Model. Paper presented at the 11th Biannual Conference of the European Association for Research on Learning and Instruction (EARLI), August 23–27, Nicosia, Cyprus.*

Nückles, M., Wittwer, J., and Renkl, A. (2005). Information about a layperson's knowledge supports experts in giving effective and efficient online advice to laypersons. *J. Exp. Psychol. Appl.*, 11, 219–236.

Nunes, P. and Bryant, P. (2004). Mathematical and scientific thinking. In *Cognition and Language Development in Children*, edited by J. Oates and A. Grayson, pp. 261–301. Milton Keynes, U.K.: Blackwell.

Ohlsson, S., Moher, T. G., and Johnson, A. (2000). Deep learning in virtual reality: how to teach children that the Earth is round. In *Proceedings of the Twenty-Second Annual Conference of the Cognitive Science Society*, edited by L. R. Gleitman and A. K. Joshi, pp. 364–368. Mahwah, NJ: Lawrence Erlbaum Associates.

Patel, L., Buck, P., Dornan, T., and Sutton, A. (2002). Child health and obstetrics: gynaecology in a problem-based learning curriculum—accepting the limits of integration and the need for differentiation. *Med. Educ.*, 36, 261–271.

Patrick, J. (1992). *Training, Research and Practice*. London: Academic Press.

Perie, M., Grigg, W., and Donahue, P. (2005). *The Nation's Report Card: Reading 2005*. Washington, D.C.: Department of Education, National Center for Education Statistics.*

Perret-Clermont, A.-N., Carugati, F., and Oates, J. (2004). A socio-cognitive perspective on learning and cognitive development. In *Cognition and Language Development in Children*, edited by J. Oates and A. Grayson, pp. 305–332. Milton Keynes, U.K.: Blackwell.

PISA. (2006). *OECD Programme for International Student Assessment*. Paris: Organization for Economic Cooperation and Development (http://www.pisa.oecd.org/dataoecd/51/27/37474503.pdf).

Prince, K. J. A. H., Van Mameren, H., Hylkema, N., Drukker, J., Scherpbier, A. J. J. A., and Van der Vleuten, C. P. M. (2003). Does problem-based learning lead to deficiencies in basic science knowledge? An empirical case on anatomy. *Med. Educ.*, 37, 15–21.

Ramey, C. T. and Campbell, F. A. (1984). Preventive education for high-risk children: cognitive consequences of the Carolina Abecedarian Project. *Am. J. Ment. Defic.*, 88(5), 515–523.

Ramey, C. T., Dorval, B., and Baker-Ward, L. (1983). Group day care and socially disadvantaged families: effects on the child and the family. *Adv. Early Educ. Day Care*, 3, 69–106.

Rauh, V. A., Parker, F. L., Garfinkel, R. S., Perry, J. D., and Andrews, H. F. (2003). Biological, social, and community influences on third-grade reading levels of minority Head Start children: a multilevel approach. *J. Commun. Psychol.*, 31(3), 255–278.

Rayner, K. and Pollatsek, A. (1989). *The Psychology of Reading*. Hillsdale, NJ: Lawrence Erlbaum Associates.

Roth, K. J. (1990). Developing meaningful conceptual understanding in science. In *Dimensions of Thinking and Cognitive Instruction*, edited by B. F. Jones and L. Idol pp. 139–175. Hillsdale, NJ: Lawrence Erlbaum Associates.

Schank, R. C. and Abelson, R. A. (1977). *Scripts, Plans, Goals and Understanding: An Inquiry into Human Knowledge Structures*. Hillsdale, NJ: Lawrence Erlbaum Associates.

Schatschneider, C. and Torgesen, J. K. (2004). Using our current understanding of dyslexia to support early identification and intervention. *J. Child Neurol.*, 19(10), 759–765 (special issue on learning disabilities, attention-deficit hyperactivity disorder, and psychiatric comorbid conditions).

Schmidt, H. G. (1993). Foundations of problem-based learning: some explanatory notes. *Med. Educ.*, 27, 422–432.*

Schmidt, H. G., Norman, G. R., and Boshuizen, H. P. A. (1990). A cognitive perspective on medical expertise: theory and implications. *Acad. Med.*, 65, 611–621.

Schön, D. A. (1983). *The Reflective Practitioner*. New York: Basic Books.

Sinclair, K. (1971). Legal reasoning: in search of an adequate theory of argument. In *Legal Reasoning*, edited by A. Aarnio and D. N. MacCormick, pp. 3–40. Cambridge, U.K.: Dartmouth College.

Sinclair, S. (1997). *Making Doctors. An Institutional Apprenticeship*. Oxford: Berg.*

Spencer, J., Blackmore, D., Heard, S., McCrorie, P., McHaffie, D., Scherpbier, A. J. J. A. et al. (2000). Patient-oriented learning: a review of the role of the patient in the education of medical students. *Med. Educ.*, 34, 851–857.

Stahl, S. A. and Fairbanks, M. M. (1986). The effects of vocabulary instruction: a model-based meta-analysis. *Rev. Educ. Res.*, 56, 72–110.

Steenbeek, H. and Van Geert, P. (2002). Variations on dynamic variations. *Hum. Dev.*, 45, 167–173.

Stephan, M., Bowers, J., Cobb, P., and Gravemeijer, K., Eds. (2003). *Supporting Students' Development of Measuring Conceptions: Analyzing Students' Learning in Social Context*, JRME Monograph No. 12. Reston, VA: National Council of Teachers of Mathematics.

Sternberg, R. J. (1987). Most vocabulary is learned from context. In *The Nature of Vocabulary Acquisition*, edited by M. McKeown and M. E. Curtis, pp. 89–105. Hillsdale, NJ: Lawrence Erlbaum Associates.

Swanwick, T. (2005). Informal learning in postgraduate medical education: from cognitivism to 'culturism.' *Med. Educ.*, 39, 859–865.

Szechter, L. E. and Liben, L. S. (2004). Parental guidance in preschoolers' understanding of spatial-graphic representations. *Child Dev.*, 75, 869–885.

Tannenbaum, K. R., Torgesen, J. K., and Wagner, R. K. (2006). Relationships between word knowledge and reading comprehension in third-grade children. *Sci. Stud. Reading*, 10(4), 381–398.

Taylor, S. A. (2000). An experiment in reciprocal experiential learning: law students and lawyers learning from each other. *Active Learn. Higher Educ.*, 1, 60–78.*

Teich, P. (1986). Research on American law teaching: is there a case against the case system? *J. Legal Educ.*, 36, 167–188.

Ten Cate, O., Snell, L., Mann, K., and Vermunt, J. (2004). Orienting teaching towards the learning process. *Acad. Med.*, 79, 219–228.

Thagard, P. (1992). Adversarial problem solving: modeling an opponent using explanatory coherence. *Cogn. Sci.*, 16, 123–149.

Tiberius, R. G., Sinai, J., and Flak, E. A. (2002). The role of teacher-learner relationships in medical education. In *International Handbook of Research in Medical Education*, edited by G. R. Norman, C. P. M. Van der Vleuten, and D. I. Newble pp. 463–497. Dordrecht: Kluwer.

Torgesen, J. K. (2002). The prevention of reading difficulties. *J. School Psychol.*, 40(1), 7–26.

Torgesen, J. K., Wagner, R. K., Rashotte, C. A., Rose, E., Lindamood, P., Conway, T. et al. (1999). Preventing reading failure in young children with phonological processing disabilities: group and individual responses to instruction. *J. Educ. Psychol.*, 91(4), 579–593.

Toulmin, S. E. (1958). *The Uses of Argument*. Cambridge, U.K.: Cambridge University Press.

Tudge, J. and Hogan, D. (2005). An ecological approach to observations of children's everyday lives. In *Researching Children's Experience*, edited by S. Greene and D. Hogan, pp. 102–122. London: Sage.

Tunteler, E. and Resing, W. C. M. (2004). Age differences in patterns of strategy production for analogy problems among five- to eight-year-old children. *Educ. Child Psychol.*, 21, 74–88.

Van Boxtel, C., Van der Linden, J., and Kanselaar, G. (2000). Collaborative learning tasks and the elaboration of conceptual knowledge. *Learn. Instruct.*, 10, 311–330.

Van Dalen, J., Van Hout, J. C. H. M., Wolfhagen, H. A. P., Scherpbier, A. J. J. A., and Van der Vleuten, C. P. M. (1999). Factors influencing the effectiveness of communications skills training: programme contents outweigh teachers' skills. *Med. Teacher*, 21, 308–310.

Van der Aalsvoort, G. M., Baarda, M., and Bouwense, E. (2006). Conceptual Models of Phenomena in Nature: Exploratory Paths Underlying Development of These Models in Students from Dutch Kindergarten. Paper presented at the AERA 2006 Annual Meeting, April 8–12, San Francisco, CA.

Van der Vleuten, C. P. M., Verwijnen, G. M., and Wijnen, W. H. F. N. (1996). Fifteen years of experience with progress testing in a problem-based learning curriculum. *Med. Teacher*, 18, 103–108.

Vandevelde, K. J. (1996). *Thinking Like a Lawyer: An Introduction to Legal Reasoning*. Boulder, CO: Westview Press.

van Gog, T., Paas, F., and Van Merriënboer, J. J. G. (2004). Process-oriented worked examples: improving transfer performance through enhanced understanding. *Instruct. Sci.*, 32, 83–98.

Van Hiele, P. M. (1973). *Begrip en Inzicht [Understanding and Insight]*. Purmerend, the Netherlands: Muusses.

Vernon, D. T. A. and Blake, R. L. (1993). Does problem-based learning work? A meta-analysis of evaluative research. *Acad. Med.*, 68, 550–563.

Visser, P. R. S. and Bench-Capon, T. J. M. (1998). A comparison of four ontologies for the design of legal knowledge systems. *Artif. Intell. Law*, 6, 27–57.

Vosniadou, S. and Brewer, W. F. (1992). Mental models of the earth: a study of conceptual change in childhood. *Cogn. Psychol.*, 24, 535–585.

Vosniadou, S. and Brewer, W. F. (1994). Mental models of the day/night cycle. *Cogn. Sci.*, 18, 123–183.

Vosniadou, S. and Verschaffel, L. (2004). Extending the conceptual change approach to mathematics learning and teaching [editorial]. *Learn. Instruct.*, 14, 445–451.*

Vosniadou, S., Skopeliti, I., and Iokospentaki, K. (2005). Reconsidering the role of artifacts in reasoning: children's understanding of the globe as a model of the earth. *Learn. Instruct.*, 15, 333–351.

Wagner, R. K. and Torgesen, J. K. (1987). The nature of phonological processing and its causal role in the acquisition of reading skills. *Psychol. Bull.*, 101(2), 192–212.

Wagner, R. K., Torgesen, J. K., Rashotte, J. K., Hecht, S. A., Barker, T. A., Burgess, S. R. et al. (1997). Changing relations between phonological processing abilities and word-level reading as children develop from beginning to skills readers: a 5-year longitudinal study. *Dev. Psychol.*, 33(3), 468–479.

Wenger, E. (1998). *Communities of Practice. Learning, Meaning and Identity*. Cambridge, U.K.: Cambridge University Press.

Working Party of the Royal College of Physicians. (2005). *Doctors in Society. Medical Professionalism in a Changing World*. London: Royal College of Physicians.*

Wright, S. M., Kern, D. E., Kolodner, K., Howard, D. M., and Brancati, F. L. (1998). Attributes of excellent attending-physician role models. *New Engl. J. Med.*, 339, 1986–1993.

Wyatt, J. C. (2001). Management of explicit and tacit knowledge. *J. Roy. Soc. Med.*, 94, 6–9.

* Indicates a core reference.

# Part V
## Design and Development

This fifth part of the *Handbook* was led by M. David Merrill and focuses on research that pertains to professional practice. The emphasis in this part of the *Handbook* is on research that examines what instructional technologists do, how they work, and the tools they use. This part of the *Handbook* consists of 11 chapters covering these topics: (1) instructional design competencies, (2) task analysis, (3) performance assessment, (4) evaluation models and methods, (5) change agency, (6) design languages, (7) design and development teams, (8) user-centered design, (9) design and development tools, (10) design and development artifacts, and (11) systems design for change.

# 42

# Competencies for the New-Age Instructional Designer

*Roderick C. Sims*
Capella University, Woodburn, New South Wales, Australia

*Tiffany A. Koszalka*
Syracuse University, Syracuse, New York

## CONTENTS

## ABSTRACT

This chapter provides an analysis of current competencies (i.e., knowledge, skills, and attitudes) that are necessary to achieve effective instructional design and development outcomes with specific focus on contemporary technology-mediated educational applications. Referring to current competency standards and models, such as those devised by *ibstpi*®, this chapter elaborates on those competencies essential for supporting the integration of hardware and software technologies (mobile devices, personal blogs, multiplayer environments) into collaborative instructional networks. In addition, the analysis identifies recent models of design that provide a framework for educational professionals to ensure that they have the knowledge, skills, and attitudes to effectively manage the challenges and utilize the affordances of educational technology in today's complex social settings. By understanding these shifts, instructional designers will appreciate the expanding and changing nature of their role.

## KEYWORDS

*Competency:* A knowledge, skill, or attitude that enables one to effectively perform the activities of a given occupation or function to the standards expected in employment.

*Development model:* A recommended set of activities or tasks that defines a process for successful instructional design.

*Instructional design:* A purposeful activity that results in a combination of strategies, activities, and resources to facilitate learning.

*Instructional designer:* A person with the competencies to design instruction.

## INTRODUCTION

The field and practice of instructional design has a long and proud heritage. Through ongoing research and development, theories and models for best practice in the creation of instructional interventions have been established (Reigeluth, 1999) and supported by definitions and specifications of the knowledge, skills, and attitudes required to be an effective instructional designer (Richey et al., 2001). In fact, Reigeluth (1999, p. 5) stated that "an instructional design theory … offers explicit guidance on how to help people learn and develop." The competency standards articulated by Richey et al. (2001) provide a foundation from which individuals can effectively implement an instructional theory. It is important to note, however, that there are many permutations of instructional design and development teams. In terms of the players in the instructional design field, Richey and colleagues (2001, p. 108) argued that the field of instructional design has a number of established or emerging specialist roles. Four roles—analyst, evaluator, e-learning specialist, and project manager—have evolved and are common in many settings:

- The *analyst* specializes in performance analysis and training needs assessment.
- The *evaluator* specializes in various forms of evaluation and assessment, but especially transfer and impact evaluation.
- The *e-learning specialist* specializes in development of multimedia and electronic learning products, particularly Web-based learning.
- The *project manager* specializes in managing internal or external designers on one or several projects.

More recent writing has suggested that the teacher and the learner are considered integral to the overall design process (Sims and Jones, 2003; Sims and Hedberg, 2006). As course conceptualization and implementation change, we face a challenge to better understand the roles and skills required to establish effective learning environments for new generations of both teachers and learners. At the same time, we are consistently presented with alternatives to existing models of instructional design which impact on both the theoretical perspective and methods of implementation (Fox, 2006; Sims and Jones, 2003). We also face significant social and technological changes that, from the educational perspective, have been popularized by Prensky's (2001, 2006) notions of the digital immigrant and digital native, as well as changes in learners' behaviors due to access to online gaming and social networking technologies.

In this chapter, we consider the impact of these changes on the underlying skill sets for the instructional designer and also on where and when the instructional design role should be practiced. It is recognized that the practice of instructional design is not static (Irlbeck et al., 2006) and that it is essential to consistently reflect on best practices to meet contemporary learning environments and expectations. Understanding new perspectives of instructional design also means appreciating that interactions between elements in the system can lead to the emergence of highly complex, intelligent behavior (Kays, 2003); consequently, it is not merely a case of implementing an instructional design model but rather one of using behaviors and activities within the broader instructional design system as a means to allow complex and intelligent behaviors and higher level learning to occur. The application of emergence theory (Kays, 2003; Kays and Francis, 2003) to the design of online distance education derives from viewing the e-learning environment and the learning process itself as a problem in organized complexity. Kays innovatively linked emergence theory and instructional design (Kays, 2003; Kays and Francis, 2003), and as she argued in Irlbeck et al. (2006, pp. 177–178):

> The elements in it—students, instructor, resource materials, environment—interact spontaneously, even randomly, and are shaped by social processes of a natural alignment of the concepts for learning and dynamic group behaviour. …In the most pure application of emergence, the teacher or "pacemaker" would not exist in the traditional sense. Faculty in the emergent role will need a far different attitude from the conventional role and will become part of the collective rather than the controlling agent.

These perspectives on instructional design and the competencies required of the instructional designer gave rise to a range of challenges with regard to ensuring that individuals are well equipped with the necessary competencies to establish learning environments to meet the needs of today's learners. Consequently, it is imperative for current instructional designers to expand their skill set to meet these needs and challenges.

Reigeluth (1999) added the subtitle *A New Paradigm of Instructional Theory* to his text on instructional design, and since then we have witnessed radical shifts in the possibilities for educational delivery, predicated on the growth of online technologies. When examining the role and practice of instructional design, a key issue to emerge is the blurring between the activities of the designer and the user (teacher, learner, trainer, trainee). Whereas established models often assume that teaching strategies, learning activities, and resource materials are designed and developed independently from the delivery environment, current environments do allow those activities to be undertaken by all course participants (Sims and Jones, 2003). It is pertinent, therefore, to question who is the designer, what is his or her role, and what competencies are essential in the design and development context? It is also important to consider how instructional designers are gaining their skills and the extent to which certification programs are consistent with the current demands of society and the learner.

A second factor that confronts today's designers is to manage the balance between being knowledgeable (in creating environments and the expectations of the learner) and implementation (instructional and learning goals, timelines, and effective performance of outcomes). Effectively designed and implemented technology-enhanced collaborative learning systems and interactive learning objects can improve teaching and learning outcomes; however, building these environments may require more time than is allowed by development budgets or implementation timelines.

Another factor relates to the shifts and changes in the learner population, popularized by Prensky's (2001) differentiation of the digital native and the digital immigrant. Commentators are now referring to the millennial or new-age learner and the dynamic shift toward mobile and broadcast information access and the ability to learn constantly (Carmean, C., pers. commun.). The implication for instructional design is that the next generation of designers, instructors, and educators needs to develop competencies that expand upon or even replace those that have been considered essential (Richey et al., 2001). Certainly these competencies should emphasize that technologies are tools to think and learn with rather than objects to engage with and possibly learn from. Part of this newer understanding of learning with technology is its very social nature. The complexity of the world now requires learners to better understand content from multiple perspectives and to use tools such as communication networks, modeling, simulations, and hypertexts to access mul-

tiple perspectives of information that can enrich the instructional and learning experience. One question to consider is whether these networks will have the sophistication to enable learning without the intervention of the traditional instructional designer (Kays, 2003; Siemens, 2004).

These are the challenges of the new instructional designer: to understand what makes a powerful learning experience, what technologies can be integrated to foster learning in these environments, and how to do it effectively. The emerging social technologies (e.g., blogs) allow learners to collaborate and communicate informally, and hardware technologies are creating portable devices that facilitate the anytime, anywhere learning principle. So, the instructional designer is challenged with new technologies and with learners who are working with content and accessing content in quite different ways. Additionally, the ability of learners to source vast amounts of information necessitates a switch from content specification being solely the responsibility of a subject-matter expert. If we accept this development, we need to consider how content is contextualized within the learning environment and who the owner and responsible provider of that content is (Sims, 2006).

Finally, it is important to better understand how the established models of design and development can be effectively applied or modified to meet the ever-changing socioeconomic conditions and environments; for example, there is renewed interest in the use of games for education and training, and researchers are examining how podcasts and blogs might enhance the educational experience. More specific factors such as social capital and accessibility are having an impact on the instructional process, and designs catering to multicultural learners are in demand. Can current instructional design models meet these needs? Do instructional designers have the competencies to address these factors? Are existing competencies valid, or do they require repurposing?

To address these questions, this chapter uses the validated set of instructional designer competencies developed by the International Board of Standards for Training, Performance, and Instruction (*ibstpi*®; http://www.ibstpi.org/) to both emphasize the existing key competencies for the instructional designer as well as introduce those specific knowledge, skills, and attitudes we believe are necessary to meet the demands of 21st-century education and training. In developing this analysis, we use the definition of competency provided by Richey and colleagues (2001, p. 32): "a knowledge, skill, or attitude that enables one to effectively perform the activities of a given occupation or function to the standards expected in employment."

## COMPETENCY STANDARDS

The field of instructional design is well established. As such, a number of organizations have developed competency standards for those who wish to practice instructional design; for example, the International Society for Technology in Education (ISTE) standards, although not specifically directed at designers, provide relevant perspectives on technology competencies. Similarly, a recent project conducted by the United Nations Educational, Scientific, and Cultural Organization (UNESCO) recommended a series of competencies for training educators in information and communication technology (ICT). In contrast to the UNESCO standards, which focus on competencies of integrating educational technologies into teaching, and the ISTE competencies, which are educational technology standards and performance indicators for teachers, students, and administrators, *ibstpi®* provides a set of internationally validated competencies and performance indicators for instructional designers (Richey et al., 2001).

At the time of this writing, however, few organizations provide professional certification of individuals to perform instructional design tasks at an agreed-upon level. Numerous institutions offer instructional design programs, with the assumption that graduation will provide a form of certification. Even if formal certification of instructional designers were to become more prevalent, this would not preclude the need to continually investigate competency classifications to ensure their currency, relevance, and integrity. The questions of whether or not instructional designers should be certified and what the standards might be remain unanswered.

Given the rigorous validation procedures of the *ibstpi®* competencies and our association with *ibstpi®* as directors, we have selected this approach to reinforce established competencies for instructional designers and to highlight those areas where further work is required to address the shifting sands of the instructional designer's work. In terms of competency validation, a number of assumptions have been made, including: (1) instructional design is a process that is most commonly guided by systematic design models and principles, and (2) instructional design is most commonly aimed at the transfer of training and improved individual and organizational performance. These assumptions reinforce one perspective of the instructional designer—that of a person (or team) that operates separately in their endeavors from the implementation and delivery environment. The extent to which the *ibstpi®* competencies are relevant to the new-age instructional designer is the focus of the following section.

## The *ibstpi®* Standards

The *ibstpi®* standards are clearly significant in defining instructional designer competencies; yet, the opportunity remains to extend these to address the issues of blurred roles, efficiency, and the currency of design models. The *ibstpi®* competencies focus on four domains of skill: (1) professional foundations, (2) planning and analysis, (3) design and development, and (4) implementation and management. Within each of these groups, specific competency statements are defined. The following analysis identifies selected statements from these standards (italicized) and presents issues that must be addressed with respect to the way in which instructional designers approach the design of instructional materials and environments.

Within the professional foundations group, the first competency identified and considered essential for the instructional designer is the ability to *communicate effectively in visual, oral, and written form*. Although no one would dispute the importance of communication, when one interacts with design stakeholders who may exist within different time zones and geographic areas and whose communication is dependent on collaborative network tools, then certain forms of communication are often disabled (e.g., visual or oral), and the written form is the primary interactive element. What does this mean for the designer? The designer's communication skills must extend to combinations of asynchronous and synchronous interactions, and their ability to present instructional information must integrate key factors pertinent to the virtual environment. Even more frequently, instructional designers will have to rely on podcasts, wikis, and mobile phones to receive and respond to information; the traditional modes will be superceded by those underpinned by these emerging digital technologies.

A second competency states the importance to the instructional designer of being able to u*pdate and improve … knowledge, skills, and attitudes pertaining to instructional design and related fields*. One of the key issues emerging from current research and theory of instruction design is the importance of a multidisciplinary approach; for example, Kays (2003) emphasized the importance of emergence theory as a means to better understand the intricacies and dynamics of instructional design, while Irlbeck and colleagues (2006) argued the value of a multidisciplinary approach, extending the original concepts of Sims and Jones (2003). Design-based research is also being used to inform the development and revision cycles of technology-enhanced learning environments; this research methodology helps extend our knowledge of developing, implementing, and sustaining effective technology-enhanced learning environments and to create and test theoretical constructs of such designs. The intention of this research is to inquire into the nature of technology-enhanced learning and create frameworks for informing the use of design elements to enhance technology-based environments (Cobb, 2001; Collins, 1992; Design-Based Research Collective, 2003; Koszalka and Ganesan, 2004).

A third competency in this domain is to *identify and resolve ethical and legal implications of design in the workplace*. Although clearly important due to the growing issues of plagiarism, ownership, copyright, and intellectual property rights, the question remains as to how effectively this resolution can be achieved independently from the delivery environment. Not only must designers consider these issues when instructional materials are devised, but they must also allow for resolution within the actual delivery cycle. This reinforces the urgency of the role of the designer to shift from an external content focus to an internal dynamic focus. It also emphasizes the need to identify how all stakeholders might be involved in the design process (Sims and Hedberg, 2006).

With respect to the planning and analysis competencies, one of the key skills for the instructional designer is to *conduct a needs assessment* to determine the rationale and justification and outcomes for a proposed course. One of the shifting areas of the design framework is the input required from the many stakeholders who are integral to the success of technology-mediated projects (Sims and Hedberg, 2006). Needs assessment input is even more important now as complex technology-enhanced instructional environments emerge; determining what and who to engage in the needs analysis process is a critical competency that requires a set of performance activities that inform the design of effective instruction. Similarly, the competency to *design a curriculum or program* is not something that can be done in isolation from other key stakeholders (see Sims et al., 2002); therefore, the instructional designer has to shift from creator of a curriculum to one who conceptualizes environments where curricula can be dynamically created and modified. This extends to competencies such as *select and use a variety of techniques for determining instructional content*, as we must question whether this remains the role of the instructional designer or has content become too fragmented and complex to be predetermined (Sims et al., 2002).

Within the context of online learning, which is a key element of current educational technology, this argument extends to competencies such as *identify and*

*describe target population characteristics* and *analyze the characteristics of the environment*. Examining each of these leads to questions such as how easy is it to actually specify a target population and to what extent can we assume homogeneity in training groups? Certainly, there are what might be termed *closed* cohorts of learners (such as a new intake of Marines), but the same cannot be said of the classroom, where ethnic diversity and socioeconomic differences can result in vast differences in learner characteristics. Similarly, the environments in which people now learn cannot easily be predicted; for example, are they learning in the workplace, at home, or on the road? We argue that this may no longer be the instructional designer's role to define, but rather that role must be to enable the individual participants to adapt the learning environment to their individual and contextual needs. Although this would appear to be captured in the competency to *reflect upon the elements of a situation before finalizing design solutions and strategies*, we question how well an instructional designer can achieve this if they are separated from the teacher, learners, and delivery environment.

Considering the design and development competencies, there is an underlying assumption that the instructional designer is in a position to achieve certain outcomes and that instructional materials can be developed independently. As an example, s*elect and use a variety of techniques to define and sequence the instructional content and strategies* has a sense of predetermination of sequence, whereas current models of online learning argue for more dynamic and indeterminate or fuzzy aspects of content that may be relevant to a course of study. The ability of learners to take on this role, rather than the designers, cannot be underestimated (Sims et al., 2002). This also relates to defined competencies such as *develop instructional materials* and *design instruction that reflects an understanding of the diversity of learners and groups of learners*, where the question must again be raised as to how well the designer can predict the delivery environment and cater to that diversity effectively. Rather than predicting how learners will or should respond, designers have the responsibility to create environments where learners are empowered with such choices.

Given the above discussion, the set of competencies related to implementation and management of instructional environments takes on new meaning and importance; for example, the competency to *promote collaboration, partnerships, and relationships among the participants in a design project* has been emphasized, but it is argued the participants have been identified as having priority roles in the process.

## ENHANCED COMPETENCIES

In the current climate of education and training, practitioners are faced with competing theories of learning (Driscoll, 2005; McCarthy, 2000), debate and variation in instructional design theory (Fox, 2006; Jonassen, 2006; Reigeluth, 1999), shifting learning preferences and lifestyles of learners (Prensky, 2006), and continual technological change and development. Within this setting the way in which people engage in learning activities and the roles of those who devise those activities and associated teaching strategies are being challenged. The enhanced communications and connectivity afforded by digital technology enable a more immediate response to learning needs which in turn challenges the existing roles and competencies of instructional designers. In the following discussion, we present a set of enhanced competencies that are situated over and above those already deemed essential (Richey et al., 2001) and which demonstrate the need for those in the instructional design field to reflect on expanding their current skill sets.

We have presented a case that factors are emerging that require a reassessment of the competencies for those involved in instructional design. In fact, if we subscribe to the shift toward learner-centered environments as proposed by Reigeluth (1999) and integrate this shift with the critical factors impacting on learning environments, then we can propose that the overall role of the designer, in the context of institutional stakeholders, must be scrutinized and debated. As new models are established to support the growth of collaborative and networked learning (Crawford, 2004; Sims and Jones, 2003), it becomes imperative to reposition the roles and skill sets of instructional designers to the extent that the term *instructional design* might even be replaced by *learner/learning design* (Sims, 2006).

We propose that instructional design competencies be expanded to apply equally to learners, instructors, and technical support staff, rather than being identified solely with the instructional designer. To use a simple analogy, we are suggesting that the role of the instructional designer should shift toward that of an architect rather than a builder, with the latter skills being assigned to teachers and learners. Competency sets, such as those defined by *ibstpi*®, will form the basis for a new layer of competencies, and one question raised is whether they should continue to be referred to as instructional design competencies, as the potential shifts in skill requirements identified in this analysis could change the ways we perceive education and training.

This discussion also suggests that the control the instructional designer has on the overall educational process may be diminishing. Certainly, some would argue that social network environments allow the participants to create and develop the design (Siemens, 2004; Webb and Sims, 2006). Based on current technologies and social changes, it would appear that the designers of educational materials will no longer be creating predefined and complete courses but rather conceptualizing shells in which a multitude of activities and participants can interact in a dynamic and changing learning environment.

Another question is whether or not the word *instruction* best represents what is occurring in educational and workplace settings. Would it be preferable to think about an *interactive architect* or the *learning environment architect* rather than an instructional designer? For example, if massive multiuser online learning environments become established, it is feasible that the environment itself will become the teacher and that interactions between participants and the environment will define the learning experience. The competencies to achieve this are at a different level than those that currently apply to the established roles of *instructional designers*.

Following from this and considering the work of Kays (2003) and the relationship between emergence theory and instructional design, we face the potential of learning outcomes emerging from learning environments over which the instructional designer has no control—and the factors that govern the emergence of such occurrences are complex and uncertain. Thus, when considering existing sets of competencies for the instructional designer, we also must be very aware that significant social and technological changes are impacting the way we teach and the way we learn. As a consequence, it is essential that those who practice instructional design build new understandings of emergent learning environments to ensure that their practice is current and relevant.

## CONCLUDING REMARKS

In this chapter, we have posed key questions regarding who an instructional designer is and the key competencies required for him or her to perform their role effectively. *ibstpi*® (Richey et al., 2001) captures the key competencies of how we have traditionally defined the instructional design professional, and as technology is becoming more popular and easier to use this role is becoming less aligned to an individual and more distributed to those who facilitate technology-enhanced instruction and the learners who participate in such environments. The strength of the existing competencies are that they define how instruction must be tied to learning, regardless of who is designing, developing, implementing, or evaluating. And, although these competencies suggest a strong foundation for design professionals, questions are emerging in this new age around the explosive availability of new technologies and their integration into instruction and learning. We need to consider new aspects of learners, environments, technology features, and implementation coupled with emerging research. Although traditional learning and instructional theories can inform, shifts in learning and instructional paradigms help us to keep focused on the purpose of designing instruction: purposeful engagement, social interactions, and activities.

It is a time of change, when social and technological forces are redefining what it means to learn. It is a time of change, when learners come with a new set of skills that embrace mobile, digital, wireless technologies. It is a time of change, when the complexity of collaborative learning and the wealth of information accessible to individual learners can make predetermination of content almost impossible. Consequently, the extent to which the instructional designer can successfully work in and adapt to these conditions must be considered. Although the current sets of competencies remain important and the skills of practicing instructional designers remain critical to successful learning outcomes, we contend that the very nature of instructional design, as a role that exists separately from the delivery environment, is being challenged and that repurposing and modifying the core competencies are critical if the instructional design role is to be considered relevant to new modes of learning and teaching.

## REFERENCES

Cobb, P. (2001). Supporting the improvement of learning and teaching in social and institutional context. In *Cognition and Instruction: 25 Years of Progress*, edited by S. Carver and D. Klahr, pp. 455–478. Mahwah, NJ: Lawrence Erlbaum Associates.*

Collins, A. (1992). Toward a design science of education. In *New Directions in Educational Technology*, edited by E. Scanlon and T. O'Shea, pp. 15–20. New York: Springer-Verlag.

Crawford, C. (2004). Non-linear instructional design model: eternal, synergistic design and development, *Br. J. Educ. Technol.*, 35(4), 413–420.*

Design-Based Research Collective. (2003). Design-based research: an emerging paradigm for educational inquiry. *Educ. Res.*, 32(1), 5–8.

Driscoll, M. P. (2005). *Psychology of Learning for Instruction*, 3rd ed. Boston: Pearson.*

Fox, E. J. (2006). Constructing a pragmatic science of learning and instruction with functional contextualism. *Educ. Technol. Res. Dev.*, 54(1), 5–36.*

Irlbeck, S., Kays, E., Jones, D., and Sims, R. (2006). The Phoenix rising: emergent models of instructional design. *Dist. Educ.*, 27(2), 171–185.*

Jonassen, D. (2006). A constructivist's perspective on functional contextualism. *Educ. Technol. Res. Dev.*, 54(1), 43–47.

Kays, E. (2003). Creating emergent discourse: a critical ingredient in e-learning. In *Proceedings of E-Learn 2003: World Conference on E-Learning in Corporate, Government, Healthcare, and Higher Education*, pp. 252–256. Norfolk, VA: Association for the Advancement of Computing in Education.

Kays, E. and Francis, J. B. (2003). Emergence and e-learning: from artificial to natural selection. In *Proceedings of E-Learn 2003: World Conference on E-Learning in Corporate, Government, Healthcare, and Higher Education*, pp. 1286–1289. Norfolk, VA: Association for the Advancement of Computing in Education.

Koszalka, T. and Ganesan, R. (2004). Designing online courses: a taxonomy to guide strategic use of features available in course management systems (CMS) in distance education. *Dist. Educ.*, 25(2), 243–256.

McCarthy, B. (2000). *About Learning*. Wauconda, IL: About Learning.*

Prensky, M. (2001). Digital natives digital immigrants. *On the Horizon*, 9(5), http://www.marcprensky.com/writing/.

Prensky, M. (2006). *Don't Bother Me, Mom—I'm Learning! How Computer and Video Games Are Preparing Your Kids for 21st Century Success and How You Can Help!* St. Paul, MN: Paragon House.

Reigeluth, C. M., Ed. (1999). *Instructional-Design Theories and Models: A New Paradigm of Instructional Theory*, Vol. II. Mahwah, NJ: Lawrence Erlbaum Associates.

Richey, R. C., Fields, D. C., and Foxon, M. (2001). *Instructional Design Competencies: The Standards*, 3rd ed. Syracuse, NY: ERIC Clearinghouse.

Siemens, G. (2004). *Connectivism: A Learning Theory of the Digital Age*, http://www.elearnspace.org/Articles/connectivism.htm.

Sims, R. (2006). Beyond instructional design: making learning design a reality. *J. Learn. Des.*, 1(2), 1–8 (http://www.jld.qut.edu.au/).

Sims, R. and Hedberg, J. (2006). Encounter theory: a model to enhancing online communication, interaction and engagement, in *Interactions in Online Education: Implications for Theory and Practice*, edited by C. Jawah, pp. 27–45. London: Routledge.

Sims, R. and Jones, D. (2003). Where practice informs theory: reshaping instructional design for academic communities of practice in online teaching and learning. *Inform. Technol. Educ. Soc.*, 4(1), 3–20.

Sims, R., Dobbs, G., and Hand, T. (2002). Enhancing quality in online learning: scaffolding design and planning through proactive evaluation. *Dist. Educ.*, 23(2), 135–148.

Webb, R. and Sims, R. (2006). Online gaming and online gaming communities: ten reasons why they matter. In *AusWeb06: The Twelfth Australasian World Wide Web Conference: Making a Difference with Web Technologies: Proceedings of AusWeb06*, edited by A. Treloar and A. Ellis (http://ausweb.scu.edu.au/aw06/papers/refereed/webb/index.html).

---

* Indicates a core reference.

# 43

# Cognitive Task Analysis

*Richard E. Clark*
University of Southern California, Los Angeles, California

*David F. Feldon*
University of South Carolina, Columbia, South Carolina

*Jeroen J. G. van Merriënboer*
Open University of the Netherlands, Heerlen, the Netherlands

*Kenneth A. Yates*
University of Southern California, Los Angeles, California

*Sean Early*
University of Southern California, Los Angeles, California

## CONTENTS

Richard E. Clark, David F. Feldon, Jeroen J. G. van Merriënboer, Kenneth A. Yates, and Sean Early

## ABSTRACT

This chapter presents an overview of the current state of cognitive task analysis (CTA) in research and practice. CTA uses a variety of interview and observation strategies to capture a description of the explicit and implicit knowledge that experts use to perform complex tasks. The captured knowledge is most often transferred to training or the development of expert systems. The first section presents descriptions of a variety of CTA techniques, their common characteristics, and the typical strategies used to elicit knowledge from experts and other sources. The second section describes research on the impact of CTA and synthesizes a number of studies and reviews pertinent to issues underlying knowledge elicitation. In the third section, we discuss the integration of CTA with training design. Finally, in the fourth section, we present a number of recommendations for future research and conclude with general comments.

## KEYWORDS

*Automated knowledge:* About how to do something; with repetition, it operates outside of conscious awareness and executes much faster than conscious processes.

*Cognitive task analysis:* Interview and observation protocols for extracting implicit and explicit knowledge from experts for use in instruction and expert systems.

*Complex tasks:* Tasks where performance requires the integrated use of both controlled and automated knowledge to perform tasks that often extend over many hours or days.

*Declarative knowledge:* Knowledge about what or why; hierarchically structured; formatted as propositional, episodic, or visuospatial information that is accessible in long-term memory and consciously observable in working memory.

*Subject-matter expert (SME):* A person with extensive experience who is able to perform a class of tasks rapidly and successfully.

## INTRODUCTION

Cognitive task analysis is the extension of traditional task analysis techniques to yield information about the knowledge, thought processes and goal structures that underlie observable task performance. [It captures information about both] ... overt observable behavior and the covert cognitive functions behind it [to] form an integrated whole. (Chipman et al., 2000, p. 3)

Cognitive task analysis (CTA) uses a variety of interview and observation strategies to capture a description of the knowledge that experts use to perform complex tasks. Complex tasks are defined as those for which their performance requires the integrated use of both controlled (conscious, conceptual) and automated (unconscious, procedural, or strategic) knowledge to perform tasks that often extend over many hours or days (van Merriënboer et al., 2002). CTA is often only one of the strategies used to describe the knowledge required for performance. It is a valuable approach when advanced experts are available who reliably achieve a desired performance standard on a target task and the goal is to capture the cognitive knowledge used by them (Clark and Estes, 1999). Analysts use CTA to capture accurate and complete descriptions of cognitive processes and decisions. The outcome is most often a description of the performance objectives, equipment, conceptual knowledge, procedural knowledge, and performance standards used by experts as they perform a task. The descriptions are formatted so they can be used as records of task performance and to inform novices in a way that helps them achieve the performance goals in any context. CTA is most often performed before (or as an integral part of) the design of instruction, work, job aids, or tests. The descriptions are then used to develop expert systems, tests to certify job or task competence, and training for acquiring new and complex knowledge for attainment of performance goals (Chipman et al., 2000; Jonassen et al., 1999).

## TYPES OF COGNITIVE TASK ANALYSIS CURRENTLY IN USE

Researchers have identified over 100 types of CTA methods currently in use, which can make it difficult for the novice practitioner to choose the appropriate method (Cooke, 1994). The number and variety of CTA methods are due primarily to the diverse paths that the development of CTA has taken. It has origins in behavioral task analysis, early work in specifying computer system interfaces, and in military applications—each with its own demands, uses, and research base. Over the past 20 years, CTA has been increasingly informed by advances in cognitive science and has become an important component for the design of systems and training in many domains. The growing body of literature describing CTA methods, applications, and results mirrors the diverse application and development of CTA methods; however, reviews and classifications are available to guide those interested in exploring and applying CTA, including a comprehensive review of reviews provided by Schraagen et al. (2000).

## Cognitive Task Analysis Families

Cooke (1994) conducted one of the more extensive reviews of CTA. She identified three broad families of techniques: (1) observation and interviews, (2) process tracing, and (3) conceptual techniques. Observations and interviews involve watching experts and talking with them. Process tracing techniques typically capture an expert's performance of a specific task via either a think-aloud protocol or subsequent recall. In contrast, conceptual techniques produce structured, interrelated representations of relevant concepts within a domain.

Cooke's (1994) three families of techniques differ in terms of their specificity and formality. Generally, observations and interviews are informal and allow knowledge elicitors much flexibility during elicitation. Process tracing methods have more structure and specificity, although some analysis decisions are left to the elicitor. Conceptual techniques are well specified and formal, with few judgments on the part of the elicitor. As a further comparison, more formal methods require greater training on the mechanisms and produce more quantitative data compared to the informal methods, which focus on interview skills and generate qualitative output. Because different techniques may result in different aspects of the domain knowledge, Cooke recommends the use of multiple methods, a recommendation often echoed throughout the CTA literature (Ericsson and Simon, 1993; Russo et al., 1989; Vosniadou, 1994).

Wei and Salvendy's (2004) review of CTA methods introduced a fourth family—formal models—which uses simulations to model tasks in the cognitive domain. Their review further differs from others in that they provided practical guidelines on how to use the classifications of CTA methods to select appropriate techniques to accomplish various objectives. One guideline, for example, suggests that when tasks or jobs do not have a defined domain, observations and interviews are especially useful in the initial phase of CTA to generate a more explicit context and identify boundary conditions.

## VARIETIES OF CTA METHODS AND THEIR APPLICATIONS

These reviews provide a starting point to explore the numerous varieties of CTA methods and their applications. We examine the overall CTA process and describe in depth some methods that have particular application to instructional design. Although there are many varieties of CTA methods, most knowledge analysts follow a five-stage process (Chipman et al., 2000; Clark, 2007; Coffey and Hoffman, 2003; Cooke, 1994; Crandall et al., 2006; Hoffman et al., 1995; Jonassen et al., 1999). The five common steps in most of the dominant CTA methods are performed in the following sequence:

- Collect preliminary knowledge.
- Identify knowledge representations.
- Apply focused knowledge elicitation methods.
- Analyze and verify data acquired.
- Format results for the intended application.

The following sections contain descriptions of common CTA methods and brief explanations of each type as it is used during each stage of the general process.

## Collect Preliminary Knowledge

In this initial stage, the analyst identifies the sequence of tasks that will become the focus of the CTA. Analysts attempt to become generally familiar with the knowledge domain and identify experts to participate in the knowledge elicitation process. Although knowledge analysts and instructional developers do not need to become subject-matter experts (SMEs) themselves, they should be generally familiar with the content, system, or procedures being analyzed. If possible, two or more subject-matter experts should be selected to participate in the process (Chao and Salvendy, 1994; Lee and Reigeluth, 2003). Although specific criteria for identifying experts may change depending on circumstances,* all SMEs must have a solid record of successful performance at the tasks being analyzed. Experts are most often interviewed separately to avoid premature consensus regarding the knowledge and skills necessary for effective performance. Techniques typically used during this phase include document analysis, observation, and interviews (structured or unstructured). The analyst uses the results of this stage to identify the knowledge types and structures involved in performing the tasks.

### Document Analysis

Analysts often begin their reviews by collecting any available written resources describing the tasks and related subject matter. This can include a wide variety of documents, such as promotional literature, bro-

chures, manuals, employee handbooks, reports, glossaries, course texts, and existing training materials. These documents are analyzed for orientation on the tasks, preparation of the in-depth analysis, and confirmation of preliminary ideas (Jonassen et al., 1999). This orientation prepares analysts for subsequent task analysis activities; for example, the information elicited during structured interviews may be more robust when analysts are already familiar with experts' terminology. Documentation analysis also allows comparison of existing materials on a procedure with accounts of expert practitioners to identify any immediate discrepancies between doctrine and typical implementation.

### Observations

Observation is one of the most frequently used and most powerful tools of knowledge elicitation. It can be used to identify the tasks involved, possible limitations and constraints for subsequent analysis, and available information necessary to perform the task. It also allows analysts to compare an expert's description of the task with actual events. In many CTA systems, analysts will unobtrusively observe experts while they are performing the tasks under examination to expand their understanding of the domain. Analysts observe and record the natural conditions and actions during events that occur in the setting (Cooke, 1994). Although definitive identification of an expert's mental operations cannot be accomplished through observation, analysts may note the occasions on which it seems that experts must make decisions, assess situations, or engage in analysis.

### Unstructured Interviews

"The most direct way to find out what someone knows is to ask them" (Cooke, 1999, p. 487). In addition to observation, unstructured interviews are also common early in the CTA process to provide an overview of the domain and to raise issues and questions for exploration in subsequent structured interviews. In unstructured interviews, analysts may not dictate the content or sequence of conversation. In other instances, however, they may ask an expert to focus on a task, event, or case with instructions to "tell me everything you know about...."

## Identify Knowledge Representations

Using the information collected during the preliminary stage, analysts examine each task to identify subtasks and types of knowledge required to perform the task. Most CTA approaches are organized around knowledge

---

* See extensive discussions of appropriate definitions of expertise and criteria for identifying experts in Cooke (1992), Dawes (1994), Ericsson and Smith (1991), Glaser and Chi (1988), Mullin (1989), and Sternberg and Horvath (1998).

representations appropriate for the task, such as concept maps, flow charts, semantic nets, and so forth. These representations provide direction and order to latter stages in the CTA process because knowledge elicitation methods map directly to knowledge types. Some are best used to elicit procedural knowledge, while others are more successful for capturing declarative knowledge (Chipman et al., 2000). A learning hierarchy is one example of a method to organize the types of knowledge required to perform a task.

### Learning Hierarchy Analysis

A learning hierarchy analysis represents the content of skills ordered from more complex problem-solving skills at the top to simpler forms of learning (Gagné, 1962, 1968; Jonassen et al., 1999), so, for example, problem solving is followed by rule learning, which is followed by concepts. Thus, the basic idea is that people can only learn rules if they have already mastered the prerequisite concepts necessary to learn the rules. Analyzing a learning hierarchy begins by identifying the most complex (highest) learning outcome and then determining the underlying skills that must be mastered to achieve the target outcome. A hierarchy of skills is represented as a chart of tasks for each intellectual skill that is acquired to progress to increasingly complex skills. The learning hierarchy constructed at this stage of the CTA process provides the guide to structure the next stage of knowledge elicitation by identifying the information that must be captured from the SMEs. Thus, it reflects the reiterative nature of the CTA process, in which the details of the knowledge, skills, and cognitive strategies necessary for complex learning are revealed, refined, and confirmed.

### Apply Focused Knowledge Elicitation Methods

During knowledge elicitation, the analyst applies various techniques to collect the knowledge identified in the prior stage. Past research indicates that different elicitation methods yield different types of knowledge and that knowledge is rarely articulated without being the focus of elicitation (Crandall et al., 2006; Hoffman et al., 1998). Analysts attempt to choose methods appropriate to the targeted knowledge type as determined by the knowledge representations identified for each task; consequently, most elicitation efforts entail multiple techniques. Among the many types of knowledge elicitation methods, variations of structured and semi-structured interviews are most commonly involved in CTA because they are relatively easy to use and require less training than more formal methods such as protocol analysis (Ericsson and Simon, 1993)

or the use of repertory grids (Bradshaw et al., 1993). It is the variation in these specific techniques that defines the major differences between specific CTA models. Although the methods may differ in focus, they share a common purpose in capturing the conditions and cognitive processes necessary for complex problem solving. Following are descriptions of two CTA models that have been documented to effectively elicit experts' knowledge in a manner that is particularly effective for instruction (Crandall and Gretchell-Reiter, 1993; Velmahos et al., 2004).

### Concepts, Processes, and Principles

Gathering concepts, processes, and principles (CPPs) (Clark, 2004, 2007) involves a multi-stage interview technique that captures the automated and unconscious knowledge acquired by experts through experience and practice. Multiple SMEs describe the same procedure, followed by cycles of expert self-review and peer review. The initial, semi-structured interview begins with a description of the CTA process by the analyst. The SME is then asked to list or outline the performance sequence of all key subtasks necessary to perform the larger task being examined. SMEs are also asked to describe (or help the interviewer locate) at least five authentic problems that an expert should be able to solve if they have mastered the task. Problems should range from routine to highly complex whenever possible. The resulting sequence of tasks becomes the outline for the training to be designed or the job description produced after the CTA is completed. Starting with the first subtask in the sequence, the analyst asks a series of questions to collect:

- The sequence of actions (or steps) necessary to complete the subtask
- The decisions that have to be made to complete the subtask, when each must be made, the alternatives to consider, and the criteria used to decide among the alternatives
- All concepts, processes, and principles that are the conceptual basis for the experts' approach to the subtask
- The conditions or initiating events that must occur to start the correct procedure
- The equipment and materials required
- The sensory experiences required (e.g., the analyst asks if the expert must smell, taste, or touch something in addition to seeing or hearing cues in order to perform each subtask)
- The performance standards required, such as speed, accuracy, or quality indicators

The interview is repeated for each SME; each interview is recorded and transcribed verbatim for later analysis.

### *Critical Decision Method*

The critical decision method (CDM) (Klein et al., 1989) is a semi-structured interview method that uses a set of cognitive probes to determine the bases for situation assessment and decision making during critical (nonroutine) incidents (for a full procedural description, see Hoffman et al., 1998). CDM is based on the concept of expert decision making as the recognition of cue patterns in the task environment without conscious evaluation of alternatives; thus, situational awareness plays a dominant role in experts' selection of courses of action. The speed with which such decisions are made suggests that experts unconsciously assess feasible goals, important cues, situational dynamics, courses of action, and expectancies. To elicit this knowledge, CDM uses a retrospective, case-based approach with elicitation occurring in multiple sweeps to gather information in progressively deepening levels of detail.

The technique begins by selecting a critical incident from the expert's task experience that was unusual in some way. The experts involved provide unstructured accounts of the incident, from which a timeline is created. Next, the analyst and the experts identify specific points in the chronology at which decisions were made. These decision points are defined as instances when other reasonable alternative courses of action were possible. The decision points are then probed further using questions that elicit: (1) the perceptual cues used in making the decision, (2) prior knowledge that was applied, (3) the goals considered, (4) decision alternatives, and (5) other situation assessment factors. The reports are recorded and transcribed verbatim.

### Analyze and Verify Data Acquired

As noted above, CTA methods vary in structure, formality, and results. Because the knowledge elicitation techniques described here are less formal, they require that the analyst code and format the results for verification, validation, and applicability for use in their intended application. When conducting interviews with experts, practitioners recommend recording the interviews and transcribing them for review at a later time, rather than trying to take detailed notes during the interview, which may distract from the process. Transcripts may be coded to summarize, categorize, or synthesize the collected data.

Following coding, the formatted output is presented to the participating SMEs for verification, refinement, and revision to ensure that the representations of tasks and their underlying cognitive components are complete and accurate. Once the information in the formatted output has been verified or revised by the expert, the analyst should then compare it with the output of other experts to verify that the results accurately reflect the desired knowledge representation.

The analysis stage in CPP (Clark, 2004, 2007) begins with the analyst preparing a summary of the interview in a standard format that includes the task, a list of subtasks, and the conditions, standards, equipment, and materials required. For each subtask, the analyst then writes a procedure that includes each action step and decision step required to perform the task and gives the procedure to the SME to review. To verify the individual CTAs, the analyst gives each subject-matter expert's product to one of the other SMEs and asks that person to edit the document for accuracy and efficiency (that is, to determine the fewest steps necessary for a novice with appropriate prior knowledge to perform the task). In the final stage, the analyst edits the individual CTAs into one formatted description of how to accomplish all tasks. After final approval by the SMEs, this final, formatted document provides the information for the instructional design process. Clark (2007) provides the format of the protocol.

The critical decision method prescribes no single method for coding the transcripts that are transcribed verbatim from the recorded interviews, as each specific research question defines how the transcripts are coded (Klein et al., 1989). The coding scheme, however, should be domain relevant and have cognitive functionality; in other words, it should tag information that represents perceptual cues, decision points, and situational assessments. A sample of a coded protocol can be found in Hoffman and colleagues (1998).

### Format Results for the Intended Application

The results of some highly structured CTA methods (e.g., cognitive modeling) are readily applied to expert systems or computer-assisted tutoring applications. For less formal CTA methods, such as those described here, the results must be translated into models that reveal the underlying skills, mental models, and problem-solving strategies used by experts when performing highly complex tasks. Further, these models inform the instructional design of curriculum, training, and other performance applications. The concepts, processes, and principles (Clark, 2004, 2007) method generates a description of the conceptual knowledge, conditions, and a detailed list of the actions and decisions necessary to perform a task. These products can be incorporated into an instructional design system. Similarly, products resulting from the application of the critical decision method have been used for a variety of instructional applications, including building and evaluating expert systems and identifying training requirements. CDM can provide case studies and information regarding which aspects of a task depend on explicit knowledge and which depend on tacit knowledge (Klein et al., 1989).

## CURRENT RESEARCH EVIDENCE FOR THE IMPACT OF COGNITIVE TASK ANALYSIS

Modern CTA evolved from a behavioral approach to analyzing performance. As the understanding of occupational demands evolved from a focus on physical performance to a focus on cognitive performance, evidence suggested that key aspects of performance entailed knowledge that was not directly observable (Ryder and Redding, 1993; Schneider, 1985). Applications of behavioral task analysis to training resulted in incomplete descriptions that led to decision errors during job performance (Schraagen et al., 2000). Early versions of CTA were designed to capture the decisions and analyses that could not be directly observed as well as the deeper conceptual knowledge that served as the basis for analytical strategies and decisions (Clark and Estes, 1999). Thus, training shifted from the reinforcement of associations between perceptual stimuli and behaviors to the development of declarative and procedural knowledge.

Research evidence indicates that the accurate identification of experts' cognitive processes can be adapted into training materials that are substantially more effective than those developed through other means (Merrill, 2002; Schaafstal et al., 2000; Velmahos et al., 2004). When content is inaccurate or incomplete, any instruction based on that knowledge will be flawed (Clark and Estes, 1996; Jonassen et al., 1999). Such flaws interfere with performance and with the efficacy of future instruction (Lohman, 1986; Schwartz and Bransford, 1998). Resulting misconceptions resist correction, despite attempts at remediation (Bargh and Ferguson, 2000; Chinn and Brewer, 1993; Thorley and Stofflet, 1996).

### Declarative Knowledge and CTA

Declarative knowledge is hierarchically structured, propositional, episodic, visuospatial information that is accessible in long-term memory and consciously observable in working memory (Anderson, 1983; Anderson and Lebiere, 1998; Gagné et al., 1992). This type of knowledge supports performance through the conceptual understanding of processes and principles related to a task and the role that the task plays within its broader context (Gagné, 1982). SMEs possess extensive declarative knowledge of their domains in the form of principled frameworks of abstract, schema-based representations. These frameworks allow experts to analyze complex problems efficiently (Glaser and Chi, 1988; Zeitz, 1997). These elaborate schemas enable experts to retain and recall information, events, and problem states with a high degree of accuracy (Cooke et al., 1993; Dochy et al., 1999; Ericsson and Kintsch, 1995). Further, broad, principled understandings of their domains facilitate skill transfer to solve related novel and complex problems (Gagné and Medsker, 1996; Hall et al., 1995; van Merriënboer, 1997).

When communicated to novices, the organization of experts' knowledge also impacts training outcomes. In an examination of experts' instructions to novices, Hinds et al. (2001) found that trainees who received explanations from experts performed better on transfer tasks than trainees who received their explanations from non-experts. The experts provided explanations that were significantly more abstract and theoretically oriented than those of the non-experts, so learners in the expert-to-novice instructional condition were able to solve transfer problems more quickly and effectively than their counterparts in the non-expert-to-novice instructional condition.

Conceptual knowledge alone, however, is insufficient for generating effective performance. The non-expert instructors in the study provided more concrete, procedural explanations, which facilitated higher performance by trainees when they attempted to perform the original target task. The abstractions provided by the experts lacked key details and process information necessary for optimal performance. This finding is consistent with many others in the training literature, suggesting that the most effective learning occurs when all necessary information is available to the learner in the form of instruction and/or prior knowledge (for a review, see Kirschner et al., 2006).

Findings from a variety of studies indicate that without CTA to facilitate knowledge elicitation, experts in many fields unintentionally misrepresent the conceptual knowledge on which they base their performance. In a study by Cooke and Breedin (1994), for example, expert physicists attempted to predict the trajectories of various objects and provided written explanations of the methods by which they reached their conclusions; however, when the researchers attempted to replicate the physicists' predictions on the basis of the explanations provided, they were unable to attain the same results. The calculated trajectories were significantly different from those provided by the experts.

In a similar study, expert neuropsychologists evaluated hypothetical patient profiles to determine their theoretical levels of intelligence (Kareken and Williams, 1994). Participants first articulated the relationships between various predictor variables (e.g., education, occupation, gender, and age) and intelligence. They then estimated IQ scores on the basis of values for the predictor variables they identified; however, their estimates differed significantly from the correlations they provided in their explanations of the relationships among predictor variables. Many were completely uncorrelated. Clearly, the experts' performance relied on processes that were very different from their declarative knowledge of their practice.

## Procedural Knowledge and CTA

Procedural knowledge is required for all skilled performance. Skill acquisition often begins with learning declarative knowledge about discrete steps in a procedure; yet, the development of automaticity occurs as we practice those procedures. The automatization process involves learning to recognize important environmental cues that signal when the skill is to be applied and the association of the cues to the discrete covert (cognitive) and overt (action) steps required to attain a goal or subgoal (Neves and Anderson, 1981). Through practice, these associations and steps increase in reliability and speed of performance. Over time, the procedures require diminishing levels of mental effort or self-monitoring to perform until they utilize very few, if any, cognitive resources (Wheatley and Wegner, 2001). This consistent, repeated mapping of conditional cues and steps manifests as an integrated if–then decision rule between the cue (if) and the procedure (then) necessary to attain a goal from a particular problem state (Schneider and Shiffrin, 1977). This representation is a *production* within the ACT-R cognitive model of learning proposed by Anderson (Anderson, 1995; Anderson and Lebiere, 1998).

During complex tasks, multiple if–then productions are strung together to generate more sophisticated hierarchies of performances. Each individual production attains a subgoal that is a component of the overall goal. To move from one production to the next in a sequence, the new subgoal must be identified and an appropriate production selected. For novices, the identification and selection process for nearly every subgoal is a conscious, deliberate decision; however,

experts automate this process, so they cannot consciously identify many of these decision points (Blessing and Anderson, 1996).

Automaticity has two primary properties that limit the effectiveness of unassisted explanations by experts.* First, automated knowledge operates outside of conscious awareness, and executes much faster than conscious processes (Wheatley and Wegner, 2001). As such, it is not available for introspection or accurate self-monitoring. Second, automated processes are typically uninterruptible, so they cannot be effectively changed once they are acquired (Hermans et al., 2000); consequently, experts' unaided self-reports of their problem-solving processes are typically inaccurate or incomplete** (Chao and Salvendy, 1994; Feldon, 2004).

## Cues

Each element of an if–then production has great importance for effective training. For learners to develop effective procedures, they must attend to relevant cues to determine correctly which subgoals and procedures are appropriate. Thus, incorporating experts' knowledge of these cues is important for optimal instruction (Fisk and Eggemeier, 1988; Klein and Calderwood, 1991). Crandall and Gretchell-Reiter (1993), for example, investigated the procedural knowledge of expert nurses specializing in neonatal intensive care for newborn or premature babies. The participants were 17 registered nurses who averaged 13 years of overall experience and 8.1 years of specialization. Without a formal knowledge elicitation technique, they attempted to recall highly detailed accounts of critical incidents or measures they had implemented that they believed had positively influenced a baby's medical condition. After completing a free-recall phase, the researchers used CTA to identify additional relevant information that the nurses did not articulate. Analysis of the transcripts revealed that the CTA probes elicited significantly more indicators of medical distress in the babies than were otherwise reported. Before CTA, the nurses' explanations of the cues they used were either

---

* The literature on expertise has not reached a consensus on the role of automaticity; however, much empirical evidence suggests that it plays a defining role. See Feldon (in press) for an extensive review. Until the article reaches publication, it can be found on the SpringerLink website under digital object identifier (DOI) 10.1007/s10648-006-9009-0. A prepublication draft can also be located at http://www.cogtech.usc.edu/recent_publications.php.

** When experts attempt to solve novel problems, the elements of their decision-making processes that are newly generated are less likely to be reported inaccurately; however, preexisting processes that were applied to those problems will continue to be subject to self-report errors (Betsch et al., 1998).

omitted or articulated vaguely as "highly generalized constellations of cues" (Crandall and Gretchell-Reiter, 1993, p. 50).

Comparison of the elicited cues to those described in the available medical and nursing training literature of the time revealed that more than one third of the cues (25 out of 70) used by the expert nurses in the study to correctly diagnose infants were absent from that literature. These cues spanned seven previously unrecognized categories that were subsequently incorporated into standard training for novice nurses entering neonatal intensive care (Crandall and Gamblian, 1991).

## Decision Points

In addition to knowing which cues are important for decision making, it is also necessary to correctly identify the points at which those decisions must be made. Much of the research on decision making suggests that many decisions are made prior to awareness of the need to make a decision (Bargh et al., 2001; Wegner, 2002). Abreu (1999) found that practicing psychotherapists evaluated fictitious case studies more negatively when they were primed with material about African-American stereotypes than when they rated the same information without priming. Similarly, when Bargh et al. (2001) subconsciously primed participants with goals of either cooperation or high performance, the actions of the participants in a variety of tasks typically conformed to the subliminal goal despite their being completely unaware of either the content of the prime or the fact that they held the goal itself.

In professions, automaticity presents significant problems for training if experts are relied upon to explain the points at which decisions must be made. In medicine, for example, studies of the reliability of diagnoses by expert physicians for identical symptoms presented at different times only correlated between .40 and .50 (Einhorn, 1974; Hoffman et al., 1968). Despite self-reports suggesting that the participants considered extended lists of symptoms, analysis of the symptoms in the cases presented indicated that only one to four symptoms actually influenced diagnosis decisions (Einhorn, 1974).

Some experts freely acknowledge that they are unable to accurately recall aspects of their problem-solving strategies. Johnson (1983) observed significant discrepancies between an expert physician's actual diagnostic technique and the technique that he articulated to medical students. Later, he discussed with the physician why his practice and his explanation differed. The physician's explanation for the contradiction was, "Oh, I know that, but you see, I don't know how I do diagnosis, and yet I need things to teach students. I create what I think of as plausible means for doing tasks and hope students will be able to convert them into effective ones" (Johnson, 1983, p. 81).

## Cognitive Skills

Correctly identifying and explaining the sequences of cognitive and psychomotor actions that are triggered by cues at decision points are likewise crucial to effective instruction. Although psychomotor aspects of a task are relatively simple for learners to observe, cognitive operations require articulation for a learner to successfully replicate an expert's performance; however, automaticity often impairs this process. As an example, a team of engineers and technicians with expertise in the assembly of sophisticated research equipment attempted unsuccessfully to generate a complete set of assembly instructions, despite extensive and repeated efforts to include every relevant fact, process, and heuristic (Collins et al., 1985). When scientists who purchased the equipment attempted to assemble it according to the instructions, the equipment did not function. After many discussions with the engineers, the scientists eventually discovered that the expert team had accidentally omitted a necessary step from the instructions. The step turned out to be a universally implemented practice among the engineers and technicians that they had failed to articulate.

Chao and Salvendy (1994) systematically documented the rates at which experts omit cognitive skills from self-reports. Six expert programmers were asked to complete a series of challenging troubleshooting tasks, and all of their actions were recorded. The programmers were then asked to explain their procedures using a variety of different knowledge elicitation methods. No single expert was able to report more than 41% of their diagnostic actions, 53% of their debugging actions, or 29% of their interpretations, regardless of the knowledge elicitation method used; however, when the researchers began compiling the elicited explanations from different experts, they found that the percentage of actions explained increased. When explanations from all six experts were aggregated, the percentages of verbalization for each category of actions increased to 87%, 88%, and 62%, respectively. The improvement in information elicited reflects the experts' individual differences in which subgoal productions had been automated to greater and lesser extents. Thus, one promising practice for instruction based on expert knowledge is to employ CTA methods with multiple experts prior to developing instruction.

## Instructional Evidence

Several studies provide direct evidence for the efficacy of CTA-based instruction. In a study of medical school surgical instruction, an expert surgeon taught a procedure (central venous catheter placement and insertion) to first-year medical interns in a lecture/demonstration/practice sequence (Maupin, 2003; Velmahos et al., 2004). The treatment group's lecture was generated through a CTA of two experts in the procedure. The control group's lecture consisted of the expert instructor's explanation as a free recall, which is the traditional instructional practice in medical schools. Both conditions allotted equal time for questions, practice, and access to equipment. The students in each condition completed a written post-test and performed the procedure on multiple human patients during their internships. Students in the CTA condition showed significantly greater gains from pretest to post-test than those in the control condition. They also outperformed the control group when using the procedure on patients in every measure of performance, including an observational checklist of steps in the procedure, number of needle insertion attempts required to insert the catheter into patients' veins, frequency of required assistance from the attending physician, and time to completion for the procedure.

Similarly, Schaafstal et al. (2000) compared the effectiveness of a preexisting training course in radar system troubleshooting with a new version generated from cognitive task analyses. Participants in both versions of the course earned equivalent scores on knowledge pretests; however, after instruction, students in the CTA-based course solved more than twice as many malfunctions, in less time, as those in the traditional instruction group. In all subsequent implementations of the CTA-based training design, the performance of every student cohort replicated or exceeded the performance advantage over the scores of the original control group.

Merrill (2002) compared CTA-based direct instruction with a discovery learning (minimal guidance) format and a traditional direct instruction format in spreadsheet use. The CTA condition provided direct instruction based on strategies elicited from a spreadsheet expert. The discovery learning format provided authentic problems to be solved and made an instructor available to answer questions initiated by the learners. The traditional direct instruction format provided explicit information on skills and concepts and guided demonstrations taken from a commercially available spreadsheet training course. Scores on the post-test problems favored the CTA-based instruction group (89% vs. 64% for guided demonstration vs. 34% for the discovery condition). Further, the average times to completion also favored the CTA group. Participants

in the discovery condition required more than the allotted 60 minutes, the guided demonstration participants completed the problems in an average of 49 minutes, and the participants in the CTA-based condition required an average of only 29 minutes.

## Generalizability of CTA-Based Training Benefits

Lee (2004) conducted a meta-analysis to determine how generalizable CTA methods are for improving training outcomes across a broad spectrum of disciplines. A search of the literature in ten major academic databases (Dissertation Abstracts International, Article First, ERIC, ED Index, APA/PsycInfo, Applied Science Technology, INSPEC, CTA Resource, IEEE, Elsevier/AP/Science Direct) using keywords such as "cognitive task analysis," "knowledge elicitation," and "task analysis" yielded 318 studies. Seven studies qualified, based on the qualifications of (1) training based on CTA methods with an analyst, (2) conducted between 1985 and 2003, and (3) reported pre- and post-test measures of training performance. A total of 39 comparisons of mean effect size for pre- and post-test differences were computed from the seven studies. Analysis of the studies found effect sizes between .91 and 2.45, which are considered to be large (Cohen, 1992). The mean effect size was $d = +1.72$, and the overall percentage of post-training performance gain was 75.2%. Results of a chi-square test of independence on the outcome measures of the pre- and post-tests ($\chi^2 = 6.50$, $p < 0.01$) indicated that CTA most likely contributed to the performance gain.

## Cost–Benefit Studies of CTA

There are few published cost-effectiveness or cost–benefit studies that compare CTA with other task analysis approaches. One exception, reported by Clark and Estes (1996), described a field-based comparison of traditional task analysis and cognitive analysis by a large (10,000+ employees) European organization that redesigned a required training course in emergency and safety procedures for approximately 500 managers. The old and new versions of the course continued to be offered after the new version of the course was designed so the relative efficacy of the two approaches could be compared. All objectives and test items were similar in both the old and new versions. As Table 43.1 indicates, the use of CTA required a greater front-end investment of time (the organization refused to release salary data) both for the CTA itself and the training of instructors for the course (data on the time required to train instructors for the old course were not available). Yet, even with the approximately

**TABLE 43.1**
**Cost Comparison of Behavioral and Cognitive Task Analysis**

| Comparison Activities | Behavioral Task Analysis and Design Days[a] | Cognitive Task Analysis and Design Days |
|---|---|---|
| Task analysis and design | 7 | 38 |
| Training of presenters | 0 | 18 |
| Delivery by trainers | 80 | 34 |
| Subtotal | 87 | 90 |
| Total time for 500 trainers | 1000 | 500 |
| Total training days[b] | 1087 | 590 |

[a] Day = person work day to design and present safety course.
[b] Total savings with CTA: 1087 days — 590 days = 497 days, or 2.5 person years.

*Source:* Clark, R.E. and Estes, F., *Int. J. Educ. Res.*, 25, 403–417, 1996. With permission.

85% more front-end time invested in design, development, and instructor training, the new course resulted in 2.5 person-years of time savings, because it could be offered in 1 day (compared with 2 days for the previous course) with equal or greater scores on the performance post-test. Although these data are only suggestive, the time savings reported by Clark and Estes (1996) reflect similar time savings reported above by Velmahos et al. (2004) and Merrill (2002).

# INTEGRATING COGNITIVE TASK ANALYSIS AND TRAINING DESIGN

## Optimal Integration of CTA and Training Design

For optimal application to instruction, CTA methods should be fully integrated with a training design model to facilitate the alignment between learning objectives, knowledge (declarative and procedural) necessary for attaining the objectives, and instructional methods appropriate to the required knowledge. Currently, three major systems take this approach: the Integrated Task Analysis Model (ITAM) (Redding, 1995; Ryder and Redding, 1993), Guided Experiential Learning (GEL) (Clark, 2004, 2007), and the four-component instructional design (4C/ID) system (van Merriënboer, 1997; van Merriënboer and Kirschner, 2007; van Merriënboer et al., 2002). Of these, the 4C/ID model is the most extensively developed. It can be distinguished from other instructional design models in three ways. First, the emphasis of the model is on the integrated and coordinated performance of task-specific constituent skills rather than specific knowledge types or sequenced performance of tasks. Second, a distinction is made between supportive information, which helps

learners perform the nonrecurrent aspects of a complex skill, and procedural or just-in-time (JIT) information, which is presented to learners during practice and helps them to perform the recurrent aspects of a complex skill. Third, the 4C/ID model is based on learners performing increasingly complex skills as a whole task, with part-task practice only of the recurrent skills; in contrast, traditional design methods emphasize the deconstruction of a complex task into part tasks, which, once learned separately, are compiled as whole-task practice. The assumption of the 4C/ID model is that environments supporting complex skill learning can be described in terms of four interrelated components: learning tasks, supportive information, just-in-time information, and part-task practice.

### Learning Tasks

Learning tasks are concrete, authentic, whole-task experiences that are organized sequentially from easy to difficult. Learning tasks at the same level of difficulty comprise a *task class*, or group of tasks that draw upon the same body of knowledge. Learning tasks within a class initially employ scaffolding that fades gradually over subsequent tasks within the class. Learning tasks foster schema development to support nonrecurrent aspects of a task. They also facilitate the development of automaticity for schemata used during recurrent aspects of a task.

### Supportive Information

Supportive information assists the learner with interpreting, reasoning, and problem-solving activities that comprise the nonrecurrent aspects of learning tasks. It includes mental models demonstrated through case studies, cognitive strategies modeled in examples, and cognitive feedback. Through elaboration, supportive information helps learners to apply their prior knowledge when learning new information they need to perform the task.

### Just-in-Time Information

Just-in-time information consists of rules, procedures, declarative knowledge, and corrective feedback required by learners to perform recurrent aspects of the task. JIT information is presented in small units as "how-to" instruction, with demonstrations of procedures and definitions of concepts illustrated with examples. As learners perform the recurrent aspects of a task and acquire automaticity, the amount of JIT information provided diminishes.

### Part-Task Practice

Part-task practice opportunities are provided for repetitive performance of the recurrent aspects of a task when a high degree of automaticity is required. Part-task practice is repeated throughout instruction and mixed with other types of practice. Part-task practice includes items that vary from very familiar to completely novel.

## COGNITIVE TASK ANALYSIS AND 4C/ID MODEL

The 4C/ID model utilizes CTA to accomplish four tasks: (1) decomposing complex skills into skill hierarchies, (2) sequencing the training program within task classes, (3) analyzing nonrecurrent aspects of complex skills to identify cognitive strategies and mental models, and (4) analyzing recurrent aspects of the complex skill to identify rules or procedures and their prerequisite knowledge that generate effective performance. In general, these activities occur within the framework of the five-stage CTA process; however, because this process is highly integrated with the 4C/ID model, the instructional design model guides the CTA activities. This integration with the instructional design process tends to highlight the reiterative nature of the CTA process.

### Decomposition of the Complex Skill

In the first group of task analysis activities, complex skills are broken down into constituent skills, and their interrelationships are identified.* Performance objec-

tives are specified** for all constituent skills, and the objectives are classified as recurrent or nonrecurrent. Objectives are classified as nonrecurrent if the desired behavior varies from problem to problem and is guided by the use of cognitive strategies or mental models. Objectives are recurrent if the desired behavior is highly similar from problem to problem and is guided by rules or procedures. Sometimes recurrent constituent skills require a high degree of automaticity; these skills are identified for additional part-task practice.

Documentation analysis, observation, and unstructured interviews with SMEs provide the information for building a preliminary skills hierarchy to guide further knowledge elicitation efforts. Data collection, verification, and validation of the skills hierarchy require multiple iterations of knowledge elicitation using multiple SMEs. The verified skills hierarchy then serves as a guide for deeper CTA techniques, such as Clark's concepts, principles, and processes (Clark, 2004, 2007). The CPP data identify constituent skills and their interrelationships, performance objectives for each constituent skill, and the classification of the skill as recurrent or nonrecurrent. The CPP method also identifies problems ranging from easy to difficult to assist in sequencing task classes.

### Sequencing Task Classes

The second group of task analysis activities involves categorizing learning tasks into task classes. The skills hierarchy and classified performance objectives determine the sequence of training for individual constituent skills. The 4C/ID-model employs a whole-task approach, in which trainees learn all constituent skills at the same time. In the first task class, learners perform the simplest version of the whole task. As the conditions under which the task is performed become increasingly complex, the whole task scenarios become more authentic and reflective of those encountered by experts in the real world. CTA processes are used both to verify the skills hierarchy and to confirm the sequencing of task classes from simple to complex.

### Analyze the Nonrecurrent Aspects of the Complex Skill

The third set of analytic activities identifies the supportive information necessary for each task class in the form of mental models (how is the problem domain

---

* The three categories of interrelationships are *coordinate* (performed in temporal order), *simultaneous* (performed concurrently), and *transposable* (performed in any order).

** Performance objectives reflect the performance as a result of learning and include an action verb, a description of tools used, conditions, and standards for performance.

organized?) and cognitive strategies (how to approach problems in the domain?). Knowledge elicitation methods commonly used with SMEs to capture data for nonrecurrent aspects of a complex skill include interviews and think-aloud protocols. The CTA methods are repeated for both simple versions and complex versions of the task to capture the knowledge required for performing the nonrecurrent aspects of the task.

## Analyze the Recurrent Aspects of the Complex Skill

The final set of task analysis activities in the 4C/ID model is an in-depth analysis of the recurrent constituent skills. These are identified during the skill decomposition process to identify the JIT information required for the recurrent aspects of the learning tasks. Each constituent skill that enables the performance of another constituent skill is identified in a reiterative process, until the prerequisite knowledge already mastered by learners at the lowest level of ability is identified.

Analysts employ CTA techniques to identify task rules and generate highly specific, algorithmic descriptions of task performance. Next, the prerequisite knowledge required to apply the procedure is identified. The analysis of concepts occurs through the creation of feature lists that identify the characteristics of all instances of a concept. At a lower level, facts (which have no prerequisites) are identified. At a higher level, processes and principles are identified. When completed, the analyst incorporates these prerequisite knowledge components into the rules or procedures for performing the task.

In sum, the results of the four sets of CTA activities in the 4C/ID model provide detailed and in-depth information about the skills, sequence, cognitive strategies, mental models, rules, and prerequisite knowledge required for complex skill learning through the instructional design of its four interrelated components: (1) learning tasks, (2) supportive information, (3) JIT information, and (4) part-task practice. Combined, they form a fully integrated system for problem-based learning in complex domains. A complete description and procedure for implementing the 4C/ID model can be found in van Merriënboer and Kirschner (2007).

## THE NEXT GENERATION OF RESEARCH ON COGNITIVE TASK ANALYSIS

Although CTA appears to have significant potential to improve various kinds of performance, it shares many of the challenges reported in studies of instructional design theories and models (Glaser, 1976; Salas and Cannon-Bowers, 2001). We need many more well-designed studies that systematically compare the impact of different forms of CTA on similar outcome goals and measures. We also need to understand the efficacy of different CTA methods when used with different training design models and theories.

So many types of CTA have been used and reported, and variation in the application of methods is so overwhelming that it is doubtful that any generalization about CTA will satisfy basic standards of construct validity. Researchers are cautioned to look carefully at the description of the methods used to implement CTA to classify the family origin of the technique being replicated. We attempted to describe five common elements of most CTA methods in the first part of this chapter, but the specific strategies used to implement each of these elements varies across studies. The elements we described are focused on the common steps used to implement CTA. This is a *sequence model* and is similar to the analysis, design, development, implementation, and evaluation (ADDIE) model for instructional design. Schraagen et al. (2000) and Cooke (1994) have discussed this problem in detail and have attempted to organize the various methods into families based on the type of outcome being pursued (e.g., training, job design, and assessment). Wei and Salvendy (2004) have suggested 11 very useful guidelines for selecting the best CTA method to achieve a goal (see Table 43.2).

## First Principles of Cognitive Task Analysis

A different and equally valuable strategy for tackling the multiplicity of CTA methods would be to apply Merrill's (2002) first principles approach to a similar problem with instructional design models. Merrill classified what appeared to be the most psychologically active instructional methods in a group of popular, evidence-based instructional design models. One of the principles he suggested is that designs that help learners connect with prior knowledge are more successful. An attempt to identify first principles of CTA would be a benefit to researchers and practitioners by identifying the active ingredients in key CTA methods; for example, nearly all CTA methods seem to place a heavy premium on the identification of the environmental or contextual cues that indicate the need to implement a skill. The study of neonatal nurses by Crandall and Gretchell-Reiter (1993) involved generating more accurate diagnostic symptoms (cues) expressed by very sick babies. Because the recognition of conditional cues may be automated and unconscious for many SMEs, the need for accurate and exhaustive

Richard E. Clark, David F. Feldon, Jeroen J. G. van Merriënboer, Kenneth A. Yates, and Sean Early

**TABLE 43.2**
**Guidelines for Selecting CTA Methods**

| | Families of CTA Methods | | | |
|---|---|---|---|---|
| **When to Use Various CTA Methods** | **Observations and Interviews** | **Process Tracing** | **Conceptual Techniques** | **Formal Models** |
| Tasks and domain are not well defined in the initial stages. | X | | | |
| Procedures to perform a task are not well defined. | X | | | |
| Tasks are representative, and the process is clear. | | X | | |
| Task process and performance require tracking. | | X | | |
| Verbal data are easily captured without compromising performance. | | X | | |
| Domain knowledge and structures require defining. | | | X | |
| Multiple task analyzers are used, and task requires less verbalization. | | | X | |
| Task requires quantitative predication, and task models change little when the scenario changes. | | | | X |
| Task performance is affected or distracted by interference. | | X | X | X |
| Task analyzers lack significant knowledge and techniques. | X | X | X | |
| Tasks are: | | | | |
| Skill-based | X | X | | |
| Rule-based | | X | X | |
| Knowledge-based | | | X | X |

*Source:* Adapted from Wei, J. and Salvendy, G., *Behav. Inform. Technol.*, 23(4), 273–299, 2004.

identification of important cues may be one of the most important principles of CTA. In the case of the neonatal nursing studies, the cues captured during CTA have changed the textbook instructions for future neonatal nurses. Other principles may be associated with the identification of the sequence in which productions must be performed and the decisions that must be made (including the alternatives that must be considered and the criteria for selecting alternatives). Principles may also be related to the protocols that are used to observe and interview experts to capture the most accurate and exhaustive description of their task-based knowledge. It is also likely that a separate set of principles would be needed to characterize team or organizational CTAs (Schraagen et al., 2000).

## Research on Automated, Unconscious Expert Knowledge

Concerns about experts' awareness of their own expertise and the strategies used to capture unconscious knowledge are arguably the most important research issues associated with CTA. The body of research on unconscious, automated knowledge has yet to be widely integrated into instructional design or the practice of educational psychologists. Most of the research in this area has been conducted by those interested in psychotherapy and the dynamics of stereotypes and bias in decision making (Abreu, 1999; Bargh and Ferguson, 2000; Wheatley and Wegner, 2001) and motivation

(Clark et al., 2007). Yet, we have ample evidence of the importance of this issue in CTA and training from the results of current research by, for example, Velmahos et al. (2004) and Chao and Salvendy (1994). We need to know much more about how unconscious expertise influences the accuracy of task analysis. We also need to know much more about how to modify automated, unconscious knowledge when people must learn to modify skills. Clark and Elen (2006) have reviewed past research and made suggestions for further study.

## Cost Effectiveness and Cost–Benefit Research

Another promising area of future research is cost-effectiveness and cost–benefit analysis (Levin and McEwan, 2000). Existing studies have not explored this issue systematically, but very promising preliminary analyses indicate significant learner time savings and decreases in significant performance errors (Clark and Estes, 1996; Merrill, 2002; Schaafstal et al., 2000; Velmahos et al., 2004). These data are important in part because many key decision makers have the impression that CTA is an overly complex process that requires a great deal of time to conduct and should be avoided due to its cost (Cooke, 1994, 1999). It is accurate to state that CTA increases the time and effort required for front-end design—particularly when a number of experts who share the same skill must be observed and interviewed; yet, it is also possible that these costs may be offset by delivery-end savings due to increased learner accuracy and decreased learning time. People in formal school settings seldom consider decreased learning time as a benefit, but in business and government settings time is a valuable commodity. The conditions under which savings are, and are not, available would be a valuable adjunct to continued development of CTA. Many other suggestions are possible but are beyond the scope of this chapter.

## CONCLUSION

Cognitive task analysis is one of the major contributions to instructional technology that have resulted from the cognitive revolution in psychology and education beginning in the 1970s. CTA does not seek to replace behavioral task analysis (or the analysis of documents and research to support training) but instead adds to existing methods that help capture the covert mental processes that experts use to accomplish complex skills. The importance of CTA is based on compelling evidence that experts are not fully aware of about 70% of their own decisions and mental analysis of tasks (Clark and Elen, 2006; Feldon and Clark, 2006) and so are unable to explain them fully even when they intend to support the design of training, assessment, job aids, or work. CTA methods attempt to overcome this problem by specifying observational and interview strategies that permit designers to capture more accurate and complete descriptions of how experts succeed at complex tasks. Research evidence described in this chapter strongly suggests huge potential benefits for designers and learners when CTA-based performance descriptions are used in training and job aids.

Many designers are apparently not aware of or are not using CTA. In January 2007, we searched Google Scholar for the terms "task analysis" or "task analysis models" and then "cognitive task analysis" or "cognitive task analysis models." The former terms returned about nine to ten times more hits than the cognitive task analysis terms. We looked at a number of the texts used to teach instructional design and could not find any references to CTA.

Cognitive task analysis has been the subject of research more often than it has been applied in practice, so we suspect that few designers have been trained to conduct effective cognitive task analyses. It is also possible that the assumptions underlying CTA conflict with the assumptions that underlie some of the currently popular design theories such as constructivism and problem-based learning (Kirschner et al., 2006). Educators who avoid direct instruction in favor of expert-supported group problem solving or communities of practice would not be inclined to conduct CTA

to support a constructivist context for learning new skills or to teach CTA in graduate programs. Our review of the research evidence for CTA strongly indicates that if it is adopted it might make a huge contribution to learning and performance. It is also clear that many questions about CTA remain to be answered.

## REFERENCES

Abreu, J. M. (1999). Conscious and nonconscious African-American stereotypes: impact on first impression and diagnostic ratings by therapists. *J. Consult. Clin. Psychol.*, 67, 387–393.

Anderson, J. R. (1983). *The Architecture of Cognition*. Cambridge, MA: Harvard University Press.

Anderson, J. R. (1995) ACT: a simple theory of complex cognition. *Am. Psychol.*, 51, 355–365.

Anderson, J. R. and Lebiere, C. (1998). *The Atomic Components of Thought*. Mahwah, NJ: Lawrence Erlbaum Associates.*

Bargh, J. A. and Ferguson, M. J. (2000). Beyond behaviorism: on the automaticity of higher mental processes. *Psychol. Bull.*, 126, 925–945.*

Bargh, J. A., Gollwitzer, P. M., Lee-Chai, A., Barndollar, K., and Trötschel, R. (2001). The automated will: activation and pursuit of behavioral goals. *J. Pers. Soc. Psychol.*, 81, 1014–1027.

Betsch, T., Fiedler, K., and Brinkmann, J. (1998). Behavioral routines in decision making: the effects of novelty in task presentation and time pressure on routine maintenance and deviation. *Eur. J. Soc. Psychol.*, 28, 861–878.

Blessing, S. B. and Anderson, J. R. (1996). How people learn to skip steps. *J. Exp. Psychol. Learn. Mem. Cogn.*, 22, 576–598.

Bradshaw, J. M., Ford, K. M., Adams-Webber, J. R., and Agnew, N. M. (1993). Beyond the repertory grid: new approaches to constructivist knowledge acquisition tool development. In *Knowledge Acquisition as Modelling*, edited by K. M. Ford and J. M. Bradshaw, pp. 9–32. New York: John Wiley & Sons.

Chao, C.-J. and Salvendy, G. (1994). Percentage of procedural knowledge acquired as a function of the number of experts from whom knowledge is acquired for diagnosis, debugging and interpretation tasks. *Int. J. Hum.–Comput. Interact.*, 6, 221–233.*

Chinn, C. A. and Brewer, W. F. (1993). The role of anomalous data in knowledge acquisition: a theoretical framework and implications for science education. *Rev. Educ. Res.*, 63(1), 1–49.

Chipman, S. F., Schraagen, J. M., and Shalin, V. L. (2000) Introduction to cognitive task analysis. In *Cognitive Task Analysis*, edited by J. M Schraagen, S. F. Chipman, and V. J. Shute, pp. 3–23. Mahwah, NJ: Lawrence Erlbaum Associates.*

Clark, R. E. (2004). *Design Document for a Guided Experiential Learning Course*, Final Report on Contract DAAD 19-99-D-0046-0004 from TRADOC to the Institute for Creative Technology and the Rossier School of Education.

Clark, R. E. (2007). *The Use of Cognitive Task Analysis and Simulators for after Action Review of Medical Events in Iraq*. Technical Report produced under contract W81XWH-04-C-0093 from the U.S Army Medical Research and Materiel Command, Fort Detrick, MD.

Clark, R. E. and Elen, J. (2006). When less is more: research and theory insights about instruction for complex learning. In *Handling Complexity in Learning Environments: Research and Theory*, edited by J. Elen and R. E. Clark, pp. 283–297. Oxford: Elsevier.*

Clark, R. E. and Estes, F. (1996) Cognitive task analysis. *Int. J. Educ. Res.*, 25, 403–417.*

Clark, R. E., Howard, K., and Early, S. (2006). Motivational challenges experienced in highly complex learning environments. In *Handling Complexity in Learning Environments: Research and Theory*, edited by J. Elen and R. E. Clark, pp. 27–43. Oxford: Elsevier.

Coffey, J. W. and Hoffman, R. R. (2003). Knowledge modeling for the preservation of institutional memory. *J. Knowl. Manage.*, 7(3), 38–52.

Cohen, J. (1992). A power primer. *Psychol. Bull.*, 112, 155–159.

Collins, H. M., Green, R. H., and Draper, R. C. (1985). Where's the expertise? Expert systems as a medium of knowledge transfer. In *Proceedings of the Fifth Technical Conference of the British Computer Society Specialist Group on Expert Systems '85*, edited by M. Merry, pp. 323–334. New York: Cambridge University Press.

Cooke, N. J. (1992). Modeling human expertise in expert systems. In *The Psychology of Expertise: Cognitive Research and Empirical AI*, edited by R. R. Hoffman, pp. 29–60. Mahwah, NJ: Lawrence Erlbaum Associates.

Cooke, N. J. (1994). Varieties of knowledge elicitation techniques. *Int. J. Hum.–Comput. Stud.*, 41, 801–849.*

Cooke, N. J. (1999). Knowledge elicitation. In *Handbook of Applied Cognition*, edited by F. T. Durso, pp. 479–509. New York: Wiley.

Cooke, N. J. and Breedin, S. D. (1994). Constructing naive theories of motion on-the-fly. *Mem. Cogn.*, 22, 474–493.

Cooke, N. J., Atlas, R. S., Lane, D. M., and Berger, R. C. (1993). Role of high-level knowledge in memory for chess positions. *Am. J. Psychol.*, 106, 321–351.

Crandall, B. and Gamblian, V. (1991). *Guide to Early Sepsis Assessment in the NICU*. Fairborn, OH: Klein Associates.

Crandall, B. and Gretchell-Leiter, K. (1993). Critical decision method: a technique for eliciting concrete assessment indicators from the 'intuition' of NICU nurses. *Adv. Nurs. Sci.*, 16(1), 42–51.

Crandall, B., Klein, G., and Hoffman, R. R. (2006) *Working Minds: A Practitioner's Guide to Cognitive Task Analysis*. Cambridge, MA: MIT Press.*

Dawes, R. M. (1994). *House of Cards*. New York: Free Press.

Dochy, F., Segers, M., and Buehl, M. M. (1999). The relation between assessment practices and outcomes of studies: the case of research on prior knowledge. *Rev. Educ. Res.*, 69(2), 145–186.

Einhorn, H. (1974). Expert judgment: some necessary conditions and an example. *J. Appl. Psychol.*, 59, 562–571.

Ericsson, K. A. and Kintsch, W. (1995). Long-term working memory. *Psychol. Rev.*, 102, 211–245.*

Ericsson, K. A. and Simon, H. A. (1993). *Protocol Analysis: Verbal Reports as Data*, rev. ed. Cambridge, MA: Bradford.

Ericsson, K. A. and Smith, J. (1991). *Towards a General Theory of Expertise: Prospects and Limits*. New York: Cambridge University Press.

Feldon, D. F. (2004) Inaccuracies in Expert Self Report: Errors in the Description of Strategies for Designing Psychology Experiments. Ph.D. dissertation. Los Angeles, CA: Rossier School of Education, University of Southern California.

Feldon, D. F. (in press). Implications of research on expertise for curriculum and pedagogy. *Educ. Psychol. Rev.*

Feldon, D. F. and Clark, R. E. (2006). Instructional implications of cognitive task analysis as a method for improving the accuracy of experts' self-report. In *Avoiding Simplicity, Confronting Complexity: Advances in Studying and Designing (Computer-Based) Powerful Learning Environments*, edited by G. Clarebout and J. Elen, pp. 109–116. Rotterdam: Sense Publishers.*

Fisk, A. D. and Eggemeier, R. T. (1988). Application of automatic/controlled processing theory to training of tactical command and control skills: I. Background and task analytic methodology. In *Proceedings of the Human Factors Society 33rd Annual Meeting*, pp. 281–285. Santa Monica, CA: Human Factors Society.

Gagné, R. M. (1962). The acquisition of knowledge. *Psychol. Rev.*, 69, 355–365.

Gagné, R. M. (1968). Learning hierarchies. *Educ. Psychol.*, 6, 1–9.

Gagné, R. M. (1982). Developments in learning psychology: implications for instructional design and effects of computer technology on instructional design and development. *Educ. Technol.*, 22(6), 11–15.

Gagné, R. M. and Medsker, K. L. (1996). *The Conditions of Learning: Training Applications*. New York: Harcourt Brace.

Gagné, R. M., Briggs, L. J., and Wager, W. W. (1992). *Principles of Instructional Design*. Fort Worth, TX: Harcourt Brace Jovanovich.

Glaser, R. (1976). Components of a psychology of instruction: toward a science of design. *Rev. Educ. Res.*, 46(1), 1–24.

Glaser, R. and Chi, M. T. H. (1988). Overview. In *The Nature of Expertise*, edited by M. T. H. Chi, R. Glaser, and M. J. Farr, pp. xv–xxviii. Mahwah, NJ: Lawrence Erlbaum Associates.

Hall, E. M., Gott, S. P., and Pokorny, R. A. (1995). *A Procedural Guide to Cognitive Task Analysis: The PARI Methodology*. Brooks Air Force Base, TX: Manpower and Personnel Division, U.S. Air Force.

Hermans, D., Crombez, G., and Eelen, P. (2000). Automatic attitude activation and efficiency: the fourth horseman of automaticity. *Psychol. Belg.*, 40(1), 3–22.

Hinds, P. J., Patterson, M., and Pfeffer, J. (2001). Bothered by abstraction: the effect of expertise on knowledge transfer and subsequent novice performance. *J. Appl. Psychol.*, 86, 1232–1243.

Hoffman, P., Slovic, P., and Rorer, L. (1968). An analysis of variance model for the assessment of configural cue utilization in clinical judgment. *Psychol. Bull.*, 69, 338–349.

Hoffman, R. R., Shadbolt, N. R., Burton, A. M., and Klein, G. (1995). Eliciting knowledge from experts: a methodological analysis. *Org. Behav. Hum. Decis. Processes*, 62(2), 129–158.*

Hoffman, R. R., Crandall, B., and Shadbolt, N. (1998). Use of the critical decision method to elicit expert knowledge: a case study in the methodology of cognitive task analysis. *Hum. Factors*, 40, 254–277.*

Johnson, P. E. (1983). What kind of expert should a system be? *J. Med. Philos.*, 8, 77–97.

Jonassen, D. H., Tessmer, M., and Hannum, W. H. (1999). *Task Analysis Methods for Instructional Design*. Mahwah, NJ: Lawrence Erlbaum Associates.*

Kareken, D. A. and Williams, J. M. (1994). Human judgment and estimation of premorbid intellectual function. *Psychol. Assess.*, 6(2), 83–91.

Kirschner, P., Sweller, J., and Clark, R. E. (2006). Why minimally guided learning does not work: an analysis of the failure of discovery learning, problem-based learning, experiential learning and inquiry-based learning. *Educ. Psychol.*, 41(2), 75–86.*

Klein, G. A. and Calderwood, R. (1991). Decision models: some lessons from the field. *IEEE Trans. Syst. Man Cybernet.*, 21, 1018–1026.

Klein, G. A., Calderwood, R., and MacGregor, D. (1989). Critical decision method for eliciting knowledge. *IEEE Trans. Syst. Man Cybernet.*, 19, 462–472.*

Lee, J.-Y. and Reigeluth, C. M. (2003). Formative research on the heuristic task analysis process. *Educ. Technol. Res. Dev.*, 51(4), 5–24.

Lee, R. L. (2004). The Impact of Cognitive Task Analysis on Performance: A Meta Analysis of Comparative Studies. Ed.D. dissertation. Los Angeles, CA: Rossier School of Education, University of Southern California.

Levin, H. M. and McEwan, P. J. (2000). *Cost Effectiveness Analysis: Methods and Applications*, 2nd ed. Beverly Hills, CA: SAGE.

Lohman, D. F. (1986). Predicting mathemathantic effects in the teaching of higher-order thinking skills. *Educ. Psychol.*, 21(3), 191–208.

Maupin, F. (2003). Comparing Cognitive Task Analysis to Behavior Task Analysis in Training First Year Interns to Place Central Venous Catheters. Ph.D. dissertation. Los Angeles, CA: University of Southern California.

Merrill, M. D. (2002). A pebble-in-the-pond model for instructional design. *Perform. Improv.*, 41(7), 39–44.

Mullin, T. M. (1989). Experts estimation of uncertain quantities and its implications for knowledge acquisition. *IEEE Trans. Syst. Man Cybernet.*, 19, 616–625.

Neves, D. M. and Anderson, J. R. (1981). Knowledge compilation: mechanisms for the automatization of cognitive skills. In *Cognitive Skills and Their Acquisition*, edited by J. R. Anderson, pp. 335–359. Hillsdale, NJ: Lawrence Erlbaum Associates.

Redding, R. E. (1995). Cognitive task analysis for instructional design: applications in distance education. *Dist. Educ.*, 16, 88–106.

Russo, J. E., Johnson, E. J., and Stephens, D. L. (1989). The validity of verbal protocols. *Mem. Cogn.*, 17(6), 759–769.

Ryder, J. M. and Redding, R. E. (1993). Integrating cognitive task analysis into instructional systems development. *Educ. Technol. Res. Dev.*, 41, 75–96.

Salas, E. and Cannon-Bowers, J. A. (2001). The science of training: a decade of progress. *Annu. Rev. Psychol.*, 52, 471–497.

Schaafstal, A., Schraagen, J. M., and van Berlo, M. (2000). Cognitive task analysis and innovation of training: the case of the structured troubleshooting. *Hum. Factors* 42, 75–86.

Schneider, W. (1985). Training high-performance skills: fallacies and guidelines. *Hum. Factors*, 27, 285–300.

Schneider, W. and Shiffrin, R. M. (1977). Controlled and automatic human information processing. 1. Detection, search, and attention. *Psychol. Rev.*, 84, 1–66.

Schraagen, J. M., Chipman, S. F., and Shute, V. J. (2000) State-of-the-art review of cognitive task analysis techniques. In *Cognitive Task Analysis*, edited by J. M Schraagen, S. F. Chipman, and V. J. Shute, pp. 467–487. Mahwah, NJ: Lawrence Erlbaum Associates.

Schwartz, D. L. and Bransford, J. D. (1998). A time for telling. *Cogn. Instruct.*, 16, 475–522.

Sternberg, R. J. and Horvath, J. A. (1998). Cognitive conceptions of expertise and their relations to giftedness. In *Talent in Context*, edited by R. C. Friedman and K. B. Rogers, pp. 177–191. Washington, D.C.: American Psychological Association.*

Thorley, N. and Stofflet, R. (1996). Representation of the conceptual change model in science teacher education. *Sci. Educ.*, 80, 317–339.

van Merriënboer, J. J. G. (1997). *Training Complex Cognitive Skills: A Four-Component Instructional Design Model for Technical Training*. Englewood Cliffs, NJ: Educational Technology Publications.*

van Merriënboer, J. J. G. and Kirschner, P. A. (2007). *Ten Steps to Complex Learning: A Systematic Approach to Four-Component Instructional Design*. Mahwah, NJ: Lawrence Erlbaum Associates.

van Merriënboer, J. J. G., Clark, R. E., and de Croock, M. B. M. (2002). Blueprints for complex learning: the 4C/ID-model. *Educ. Technol. Res. Dev.*, 50(2), 39–64.*

Velmahos, G. C., Toutouzas, K. G., Sillin, L. F., Chan, L., Clark, R. E., Theodorou, D., and Maupin, F. (2004). Cognitive task analysis for teaching technical skills in an inanimate surgical skills laboratory. *Am. J. Surg.*, 18, 114–119.*

Vosniadou, S. (1994). Capturing and modeling the process of conceptual change. *Learn. Instruct.*, 4, 45–69 (special issue).

Wegner, D. M. (2002). *The Illusion of Conscious Will*. Cambridge, MA: MIT Press.

Wei, J. and Salvendy, G. (2004). The cognitive task analysis methods for job and task design: review and reappraisal. *Behav. Inform. Technol.*, 23(4), 273–299.*

Wheatley, T. and Wegner, D. M. (2001). Automaticity of action, psychology of. In *International Encyclopedia of the Social and Behavioral Sciences*, edited by N. J. Smelser and P. B. Baltes, pp. 991–993. Oxford: Elsevier.

Zeitz, C. M. (1997). Some concrete advantages of abstraction: how experts' representations facilitate reasoning. In *Expertise in Context*, edited by P. J. Feltovich, K. M. Ford, and R. R. Hoffman, pp. 43–65. Menlo Park, CA: American Association for Artificial Intelligence.

---

* Indicates a core reference.

# 44

# Design and Validation of Technology-Based Performance Assessments

*Eva L. Baker, Gregory K. W. K. Chung, and Girlie C. Delacruz*
UCLA/CRESST, Los Angeles, California

## CONTENTS

## ABSTRACT

This chapter describes approaches to the design and technical verification of assessments of performance. The chapter begins with a brief definition of performance measurement and describes a set of validity criteria that should be in place to guide the design of performance assessments that may serve multiple purposes. Design criteria include descriptions of families of cognitive demands, approaches to ensure content representation, and templates or objects to promote economic design and renewal. We then illustrate with multiple examples from K–12 education and from the training community. The context of most of the chapter is the use of technology tools for design, administration, and automated scoring. We conclude with future directions in performance measurement and its implications.

## KEYWORDS

*Assessment:* The systematic observation of achievement using any of a number of formats, including paper, technology, or live judgment.

*Performance:* Ability of student or trainee to demonstrate accomplishment in a very specific domain such as a formal examination, across domains and subject matters, or in realistic contexts.

*Validation (validity):* The process and outcome of collecting and interpreting results of assessments or measurement so that inferences from findings are warranted by evidence.

## INTRODUCTION

The design of outcome measures for instructional or learning interventions has become transformed as the promise of computer technology has begun to be realized. In this chapter, the characteristics of outcome measurement are described, validity and design criteria are offered and justified by research findings, and examples of applications and of the design and validation process are detailed. The chapter concludes with the likely and more speculative future of outcome measurement and the implications that this future will have for testing assessment practice and policy writ large.

### Performance Measurement

Although there are different interpretations by application context, such as military training, K–12 schooling, and the business community, we use *performance measurement* to mean the systematic sampling of domains of learning, skills, propensities, and accomplishments in constrained or standardized form. We use the term *performance* to mean a wide range of stimulus and response modes, including selected and constructed short answers, examples of multiple projects, and extended task performance under simulated or actual conditions. This use of performance can address individual or team, unit, or organizational performance. Its appropriate design requires the articulation of the set of cognitive demands, skills, and content domains to be assessed and the conditions and criteria used to judge the characteristics of performance to create a score or a category system. A further requirement is that the criteria or other schemes used to rate performance are replicable and, if human raters are used, the raters can be trained to reliably evaluate performance. The purpose of performance measurement is to develop results that can be used to draw an inference about ability or competence presumably developed or to be developed by an intervention. The inferences about students may involve ordering respondents by their scores, predicting future performance in other settings, or connecting outcomes to instructional attributes. A general use of performance measurement is in the evaluation process to determine the degree to which particular goals have been attained, retained, and generalized to different situations.

## VALIDITY

Just as outcome measures may be used for different purposes (e.g., certifying a trainee, certifying the instruction, or comparatively evaluating alternatives), so will the validity strategies be used for different purposes and situations. Of most importance is the notion that validity does not inhere in a measure or procedure, once and for all, but is moderated by the context and inferences of use. Rather than provide a single procedure, such as always correlating an existing set of scores with those of another measure, a validity argument is developed that marshals a wide range of data to make the case (AERA et al., 1999). Unfortunately, when a technical procedure such as validity seems to move away from a routinized or recipe base, both its application and its interpretation require greater expertise by the assessment designer and user. The former makes an argument based on theory and empirical results, and the latter must use his resources to determine if the argument is of sufficient relevance and merit for the purposes intended for the measure. Such an approach mitigates the checklist approach to ensuring assessment quality and may deter those charged with validity case making and interpretation. In current practice, a crusty subset of practitioners uses old models of validity, such as content (is what is being measured related to goals or domains?), face validity (does the test performance look like what is supposed to be measured?), predictive (do people with higher scores do better on a distal criterion measure?), and criterion (does performance on the new measure relate, or correlate, in predictable ways with an existing measure of known quality?).

Although all of these aspects may come into play in making a validity argument, there is no longer the notion that one sorts validation procedures into a four-way table and chooses one to use. It is also the case, unfortunately, that the validity of assessment is often seen as being separate from the learning and instructional goals of the measure. It may appear to be an add-on and as such simply encourages the designer to look for an existing, good-enough measure to use. This approach has the benefit of time and resource conservation. It also has the risk that the measure selected will not have validity evidence for the tasks, learners, situations, or purposes intended by the designer. As worrisome is that the measure may not be sufficiently related to the goals of the instruction—goal alignment—or be sensitive to the instructional intervention as delivered. Thus, the performance or scores obtained on the measure may be either irrelevant to the planned use of the measure or insensitive to the instructional or learning experiences of interest.

To understand the validity perspective presented below, it is important for the designer to adopt the notion that the outcome measure and its characteristics are an integral part of the instructional or learning vision that motivates the program design. Thus, attributes of validity should map to the range of expertise intended for the learner. The list below has been adapted from other statements about validity that are intended to evaluate the effects of instruction (Baker et al., 1993; Linn et al., 1991; Pellegrino et al., 2001).

## Validity Criteria

1. Cognitive demands in the measure represent the range, complexity, and subtasks required for success.
   *Comment.* Specifications used for instructional design should in essential respects correspond to the range of cognitive demands on the performance measure.
2. Content domains from which examples of situations and topics will be drawn explicate and represent the domain of interest rather than any arbitrary subset. A systematic procedure for sampling subject matter should be described and used.
   *Comment.* Various knowledge representations can be used to make explicit the domain representation and its boundaries, provide a common framework for task instantiation, and facilitate communication among developers and subject-matter experts.
3. Evidence should be provided about the stability of scores (over time) and consistency of scoring or marking to ensure dependable (reliable) results.
   *Comment.* Score reliability depends on interactions among the task, student, scoring scheme, and raters, if any. Computer-based algorithms used for scoring student responses should be described.
4. Evidence is used to set criterion performance standards or to create a set of performance categories, typically inferred from contrasts among performers with differing, established levels of expertise (i.e., expert-novice comparisons).
   *Comment.* Systematic experiments with criterion groups present one approach to this criterion. An alternative is one that documents the dependency relationships (both logically and empirically) of the tasks in different categories. A third method involves monitoring subsequent criterion performance and adjusting classifications to conform to empirical findings.
5. Evidence of the performer's ability to transfer and generalize to likely but directly uninstructed situations should be provided.
   *Comment.* Most instruction is directed to objectives, goals, or standards rather than to a particular subset of test items or tasks. Even in cases where procedures are the focus of instruction (e.g., troubleshooting or a particular surgical procedure), there are still numerous ways in which situations, time, or constraints can vary. Assessments should address both the class of illustrations given in instruction as well as some probable requirements to apply the knowledge or skill to a different setting or task.
6. It is essential to obtain routine evidence that the practice results in fair results—that is, outcomes that are indifferent to factors other than those intended to be measured.
   *Comment.* Such factors include background characteristics of learner's gender, language (for nonverbal tasks), the manner of communication (syntax, speed, usage, vocabulary) of the directions and the assessment, behavior by the test administrator, and interactions by the respondents if not in an individual setting. In simulation and other technology settings, familiarity with equipment, tasks, and contexts should not interact with group differences.

These criteria represent a minimum subset of validity concerns. Each requires analysis and may be strengthened by more than one empirical trial. In the process of system development of the task, it is desirable for these validity components to be assessed, even if only partially. The balance between the exigencies of time and schedule, on the one hand, and quality of the inferences presents a challenge that too often ends up with the quality of the measures lacking the basic warrants needed. Given that outcome measures are used for purposes of certifying competence, accountability, predicting readiness, evaluating training, and driving the revision of systems of learning and practice, the quality of the performance measures ought to be the last element compromised.

# DESIGN OF TECHNOLOGY-BASED PERFORMANCE ASSESSMENTS

In this section, we describe the design characteristics that flow from the validity criteria. Particularly important is the specification of the knowledge and cognitive skills required of a task—its cognitive demands—and how these demands influence the specification of the domain of interest, the task representation, and scoring.

## Cognitive Demands

The cognitive demand of a task refers to the domain-independent and domain-dependent set of knowledge and skills that an assessment should target (AERA et al., 1999; Baker, 1997; Baker and Mayer, 1999; Mislevy and Riconscente, 2006). When designing assessments of performance, it is important to be clear and explicit early in the design process about what the assessment is intended to measure. Baker's (1997) Model-Based Assessment (MBA) explicitly emphasizes this idea. MBA posits five areas that broadly capture the major learning outcomes of education and training: content understanding, problem solving, teamwork/collaboration, communication, and self-regulation. MBA begins with the specification of the type of learning outcomes to be measured, followed by attendant specifications of the content, task and materials, response modes, and scoring approaches. Only after designers have addressed the learning outcome their assessment is intended to measure should they make decisions about, for example, format, number of items, and the amount of testing time. The advantage of the MBA approach is that designers must be precise about the specific kind of cognitive outcome they are interested in (e.g., facts, declarative or procedural knowledge, conceptual knowledge, problem solving) and how other aspects of the assessment design can support the measurement of the cognitive outcome. For example, if the decision is made to measure factual knowledge, then a test format that is often suited for this purpose is multiple choice. Similarly, if the decision is made to measure students' conceptual understanding, then an essay or knowledge map may be useful for this purpose (Baker et al., 1991; Herl et al., 1996).

## Domain Representation

A domain representation is an explicit description of the content, knowledge, skills, abilities, interests, attitudes, and other properties of the construct that is intended to be assessed (AERA et al., 1999; Baker, 1997; Baker and Mayer, 1999; Baker and O'Neil, 1987). A domain representation is the basis for sampling test items, the referent against which to evaluate the relevance and representativeness of the test items, and reflects the universe to which performance on the test is being generalized.

An important function of a domain representation is to help assessment developers sample tasks over a domain so the tasks represent the important skills and knowledge of the domain. The tasks also should result in performance that differentiates between novices and experts. The general idea is that students' performance can be compared against a criterion performance, where the criterion performance represents a point on a continuum ranging from novice to expert performance (Baker, 1974; Glaser, 1963; Hively, 1974; Popham and Husek, 1969). A secondary function of these absolute (vs. normative) comparisons is to provide diagnostic information on what individuals can and cannot do; for example, if a domain is composed of different subdomains (e.g., addition and subtraction skills belonging to the larger domain of arithmetic), then items can be sampled from each subdomain and scales formed in a principled manner. Student performance on the scales can be used to infer the degree to which they have mastered those skills. The significance of such domain-referenced measurement is that performance is indexed to an explicit and precisely described definition of knowledge and skills. Because the items are conformant to the domain description, they are by definition relevant.

Several approaches have been used to develop domain representations. Hively et al. (1968), for example, described a technique in the area of arithmetic that precisely specified the math operations that were to be demonstrated by students. Canonical forms of problems were used to generate instances of math problems, thereby allowing a large number of items to be generated (or sampled) traceable to the domain definition. This general technique has been criticized as being applicable only to well-specified and constrained domains such as mathematics (for an in-depth discussion of domain-referenced testing issues, see Baker and O'Neil, 1987).

Variations of this basic approach have been developed subsequently. Tatsuoka's rule-space methodology (Birenbaum et al., 1993; Katz et al., 1998; Tatsuoka and Tatsuoka, 1983, 1997), like the method of

Hively et al. (1968), mapped items to well-defined skill attributes. Tatsuoka extended the work of Hively et al. by using a matrix to represent the item × skill mappings, from which a hierarchy of skills could be derived *a priori*. A third method to describing a domain is with the use of (external) knowledge representations. Bayesian networks can be used to model the dependencies among student skills, knowledge states, and other variables of interest in relation to observed student performance. These techniques underscore the idea that a domain representation should be explicit, precise, and externalized and should capture the essential elements of what is to be tested with respect to the target environment. Just as important, a good domain representation can support identification of student deficiencies, which could be used to guide remediation efforts.

Interestingly, artificial-intelligence-based knowledge representation techniques are gaining increased interest as a means for domain representation. Ironically, the strong representation techniques demonstrated by Hively et al. (1968), once criticized as being overly reductionist, are being revisited. An important difference today is that there are readily available tools that make practical the development of domain ontologies, which can be far more expressive than previous representations and include class hierarchies and nonlinear network associations (Gruber, 1995).

Examples of how knowledge representations are being used for assessment purposes can be seen in the use of ontologies for domain representation (Chung et al., 2003a,b) and constraint networks for assessment authoring support (Chung et al., in press; Niemi et al., in press; van der Linden, 2005). As these technologies, methods, and tools mature, rich multivariate descriptions of the domain become possible. As the domain representations increase in fidelity with respect to the target environment, students' performance on the assessment should be more representative of their future performance in the target environment.

## Task Representation

A task representation comprises the critical components of the assessment activity learners are expected to engage in, and it defines the testbed within which to observe and gather evidence about their performance, which is the basis for drawing inferences about their competence (AERA et al., 1999; Baker, 2002; Baker and Herman, 1983; Baker et al., 1991, 2005; Messick, 1995). The task representation includes the domain of interest (e.g., the set of knowledge, skills, behavior, attitudes, and other properties) that performance is being generalized to, the stimulus materials

(e.g., the prompt and materials learners are expected to interact with), the format of administration (e.g., paper- or computer-based), the set of measures and the format of students' responses (e.g., selected response, constructed response, clickstream), the administration details (e.g., setting, time limit), and the scoring method associated with the measures. Because the task representation defines the conditions under which student performance is interpreted, the higher the fidelity of the task to the target environment, the more likely the performance on the assessment task will generalize to the target environment (Kane et al., 1999; Messick, 1995). As alluded to in the discussion on domain representation, the substrate underlying task design is the domain representation. If the tasks are misaligned with the domain representation or the domain representation is not representative of the target environment, then inferences based on students' performance on these tasks will be suspect. When students are tested on content they have not been exposed to or are not tested on content they have been exposed to, the assessment results will not accurately reflect students' achievement (Baker et al., 1991).

Development in computer-based assessments has focused on creating tasks that allow observation of features of student behavior that could not be done feasibly in other ways (Baker and Mayer, 1999; Bennett, 1999; Chung and Baker, 2003a; Clauser, 2000; Huff and Sireci, 2001; Pellegrino et al., 2001; Scalise and Gifford, 2006; Yang et al., 2002). In addition to the examples described in this chapter, computer-based assessments have been developed for Web-searching skills (Schacter et al., 1999), math reasoning (Bennett et al., 2000), teamwork skills (Chung et al., 1999), design skills (Chung and Baker, 2003a; Katz and James, 1998), architecture design skills (Bejar, 1991), and writing skills (Attali and Burstein, 2006; Burstein, 2003; Landauer et al., 2003; Page and Petersen, 1995).

A common objective of computer-based assessments of performance is that they deliver tasks that require students to demonstrate the use of domain knowledge and problem solving strategies. A key issue underlying computer-based techniques is operationalizing how an activity would elicit the desired behaviors and cognitive demands from students and, assuming that is achieved, how to synthesize and interpret the observations. We discuss scoring in the Computer-Based Scoring Approaches section.

## Design Templates and Objects

The search for efficient and cost-effective means to simultaneously increase the throughput and quality of assessment development has been the driver behind efforts to create automated supports for task design (Baker, 2002; Chung et al., 2002, 2004, in press; Katz, 1998). The Assessment Design and Delivery System (ADDS) has been developed to provide teachers tools with which to create assessments. With ADDS, teachers have the capability to create assessment using assessment objects (e.g., new or preexisting prompts, information sources). Compared to non-ADDS teachers, ADDS users have been found to focus more on measuring conceptual knowledge and to create more appropriate rubrics and coherent prompts that address critical ideas (Niemi et al., in press; Vendlinski et al., 2005). A similar effort is attempting to operationalize Mislevy's evidence-centered design (ECD) approach in the Principled Assessment Designs for Inquiry (PADI) system (Mislevy and Riconscente, 2005; Mislevy et al., 2003; Riconscente et al., 2005). Although the PADI system is still under development, existing tasks of known structure and quality have been successfully reengineered using the PADI framework. This success suggests that a mature system will be able to impart the ECD approach into the design of assessments from scratch.

## COMPUTER-BASED SCORING APPROACHES

A scoring model refers to the method of translating observations of student performance into scores that represent a meaningful quantity about their performance. The scoring model includes an information measurement scale, scoring criteria, performance descriptions of each criteria at each point on the scale, and sample responses that illustrate the various levels of performance (AERA et al., 1999; Baker et al., 2005). Scoring issues in computer-based performance assessments are complex, as they offer the potential to yield a rich set of observations, particularly when the observations are fine grained, interrelated, and process oriented (Baker and Mayer, 1999; Bennett, 1999; Chung and Baker, 2003b; Clauser, 2000; Huff and Sireci, 2001; Pellegrino et al., 2001; Scalise and Gifford, 2006; Yang et al., 2002). In this case, it is important to define how the observations are combined and how they are scored and scaled. Evidence should be collected on how the measures relate to other measures of the construct and how the measures discriminate between high and low performers. Several classes of scoring techniques have been used for scoring: (1) expert-based scoring, (2) data-driven methods, and (3) domain-modeling methods.

## Expert Performance as the Criterion

The first approach is consistent with the idea that criterion performance is a point along a performance continuum. Expert *performance* is considered the referent or gold standard against which to compare student performance (Baker, 1997; Baker et al., 1991; Chi et al., 1988), not what experts say should be competent performance or experts' rating of student performance. This scoring approach has been used successfully to develop tasks for content understanding—for example, essays (Baker et al., 1991, 2005) and knowledge maps (Herl et al., 1996, 1999).

One example of how an expert referent has been used is in the area of scorable concept or knowledge maps (Herl et al., 1996, 1999). A knowledge map is a graphical way to show how concepts relate. Nodes represent concepts, and labeled links represent relations among concepts (Lambiotte et al., 1989; Novak and Gowin, 1984). To support automated scoring, domain experts define the set of terms and links for the mapping task. The task is then administered to one or more experts, and the set of expert maps is used as the scoring criteria for student maps. In numerous studies across age, content, and setting, scoring student knowledge maps using expert-based referents has been found to be sensitive to instruction, to discriminate between experts and novices, to discriminate between different levels of student performance, to relate moderately to external measures of the same construct, and to be sensitive to language proficiency, as well as showing reasonable technical properties (Chung et al., 2001, 2003a; Herl et al., 1996, 1999; Kim et al., 2004; Klein et al., 2002; Lee, 2000; Osmundson et al., 1999; Ruiz-Primo et al., 2001; Schacter et al., 1999; Yin and Shavelson, 2004).

## Modeling Expert Judgments

A second related approach is to model experts' rating of students' performance on various task variables. In this case, expert *judgment* is considered the gold standard against which to compare student performance. This scoring approach has been used successfully to model expert and rater judgments in a variety of applications (see, for example, Burstein, 2003; Clauser et al., 1999; Margolis and Clauser, 2006; Williamson et al., 1999).

Clauser and colleagues have developed a computer-based assessment of patient-management skills (Clauser et al., 1995, 1997, 1999, 2000; Margolis and Clauser, 2006). Medical students are presented with a description of the patient's appearance and location in the hospital, initial vital signs, and history. Students then choose from four categories of actions such as requesting more comprehensive information about the patient's history or advancing the case through simulated time. Students' choices are recorded for later scoring.

Scoring of students' performance was done by using a regression model that used students' actions to predict the students' score or by scoring the students' actions against a set of rules extracted from a policy capture procedure from a panel of experts. Both types of automated scoring procedures corresponded highly with human ratings of the same performance. Subsequent generalizability analyses demonstrated that these procedures were as generalizable across tasks as those produced by the expert raters (Clauser et al., 1995, 1997, 1999, 2000).

### Issues with Expert-Based Scoring Approaches

An issue with the use of experts is the selection of the expert (Baker and Schacter, 1996; Linn et al., 1991). When experts are used as the performance criterion, experts' biases may show up on their performance and the subsequent scoring model (Bennett, 2006; Bennett and Bejar, 1998). Similarly, experts' judgments may be affected by their content and world knowledge, linguistic competency, expectations of student competency, and instructional beliefs (Baker and O'Neil, 1996). Baker et al. (1995) found that low domain knowledge contributed to low reliability between raters' scoring written responses, and Burstein and Chodorow (1999) found a significant language by scoring method interaction in the scoring of essays using e-rater, which suggested encoding of biases (Powers et al., 2001).

## Data-Driven Techniques

A second class of scoring approaches is based on data-driven techniques. Student performance data are subjected to statistical analyses or machine learning (e.g., artificial neural network) analyses. Student performances are classified into different bins, where the within-bin similarity is maximized and the between-bin similarity is minimized. Raters examine the characteristics of student performances in each bin and an interpretation of what those performances represent is assigned to that bin. The performance interpretation is the score. Subsequent student performances categorized into a bin inherit that bin's performance description. Studies have demonstrated that this approach can generalize across tasks within a simulation and across simulations, differentiating between groups of students with presumed knowledge differences (Stevens and Casillas, 2006; Vendlinski and Stevens, 2002).

As with any data-driven approach, initial validation of the method is complicated because there is not an *a priori* expectation of what scores mean or an inherent meaning of the classification scheme. This situation requires *post hoc* interpretation (and the potential introduction of biases) of the categories after the categories have been formed. A second criticism is that machine learning techniques can be highly sample dependent, and the scoring process is driven by statistical rather than theoretical issues (Bennett, 2006). Thus, validity evidence is particularly important when using data-driven techniques to score student responses (Powers et al., 2000).

## Domain Modeling

A third class attempts to model the cognitive demands of the domain itself. The model attempts to specify how knowledge and skills influence each other and the task variables on which observations are being made. These approaches rely on *a priori* linking of student performance variables to hypothesized knowledge and skill states. Student knowledge and skills are then interpreted in light of the observed student performance. This approach has been used successfully in a variety of domains and modeling types, from the use by Hively et al. (1968) of canonical item types, to Tatsuoka's rule-space methodology (Birenbaum et al., 1993; Katz et al., 1998; Tatsuoka and Tatsuoka, 1997), to the use of Bayesian networks to model student understanding in numerous domains such as dental hygiene skills, hydraulic troubleshooting, network troubleshooting, Web searching, circuit analyses, and rifle marksmanship (Bennett et al., 2003; Chung et al., 2003b, 2006; Mislevy and Gitomer, 1995; Mislevy et al., 2002; Williamson et al., 2006). The most important issue in domain modeling is identifying the essential concepts and their interrelationships. This challenge is mitigated via thorough knowledge acquisition activities such as cognitive task analyses and direct observation of performance. Because of the importance of the domain model, it is critical to gather validity evidence, which is tantamount to validating the reasoning structure and inferences drawn by the Bayesian network. For examples of empirical validation techniques, see Chung (2003b, 2006) and Williamson et al. (2000).

## FUTURE DIRECTIONS

An obvious design need for assessment of outcomes is the automation or partial automation of the task design and performance measurement components. Various efforts have been undertaken to do some automated assessment design, some involving very specific topics (Koedinger and Nathan, 2004), some involving systems of training (Mislevy and Riconscente, 2005; Mislevy et al., 2003; Riconscente et al., 2005), and others focused on the cognition and content templates and objects to be used. In the future, it will be desirable to use complex modeling during instruction, post-instruction, retention trials, and generalization and transfer measurement to understand and locate the specific areas within the system where various learners lose their footing, as a combination of lack of knowledge, attention, motivation, or integration of content and skill. Using clickstream methods (Chung and Baker, 2003a; Schacter et al., 1999; Stevens and Casillas, 2006) some of these areas can be pinpointed now. Because of the growing sophistication of computationally supported data collection, and the importance of formative information about the trainee's process during learning, the future of outcome assessment will undoubtedly merge with process information to create learner profiles (rather than scores or classifications). We anticipate that these will have domain-independent components that may predict from learned responses (rather than from aptitude measures) learners' likely success in a range of other tasks. We further expect greater automation and verification of ontological approaches and see the study of experts as providing a continuing key to knowledge of performance measurement and its validity.

# REFERENCES

American Educational Research Association (AERA), American Psychological Association (APA), and National Council for Measurement in Education (NCME). (1999). *Standards for Educational and Psychological Testing*. Washington, D.C.: American Educational Research Association.*

Attali, Y. and Burstein, J. (2006). Automated essay scoring with e-rater® V.2. *J. Technol. Learn. Assess.*, 4(3) (available from http://www.jtla.org).

Baker, E. L. (1974). Beyond objectives: domain-referenced tests for evaluation and instructional improvement. *Educ. Technol.*, 14(6), 10–16.

Baker, E. L. (1997). Model-based performance assessment. *Theory Into Pract.*, 36(4), 247–254.*

Baker, E. L. (2002). Design of automated authoring systems for tests. In *Technology and Assessment: Thinking Ahead—Proceedings from a Workshop*, edited by Board on Testing and Assessment, National Research Council, pp. 79–89. Washington, D.C.: National Academy Press.

Baker, E. L. (2005). Technology and effective assessment systems. In *Uses and Misuses of Data for Educational Accountability and Improvement*, NSSE Yearbook, Vol. 104, Part 2, edited by J. L. Herman and E. H. Haertel, pp. 358–378. Chicago, IL: National Society for the Study of Education.

Baker, E. L. and Herman, J. L. (1983). Task structure design: beyond linkage. *J. Educ. Meas.*, 20, 149–164.

Baker, E. L. and Mayer, R. E. (1999). Computer-based assessment of problem solving. *Comput. Hum. Behav.*, 15, 269–282.*

Baker, E. L. and O'Neil, Jr., H. F. (1987). Assessing instructional outcomes. In *Instructional Technology*, edited by R. M. Gagné, pp. 343–377. Hillsdale, NJ: Lawrence Erlbaum Associates.

Baker, E. L. and O'Neil, Jr., H. F. (1996). Performance assessment and equity. In *Implementing Performance Assessment: Promises, Problems, and Challenges*, edited by M. B. Kane and R. Mitchell, pp. 183–199. Mahwah, NJ: Lawrence Erlbaum Associates.

Baker, E. L. and Schacter, J. (1996). Expert benchmarks for student academic performance: the case for gifted children. *Gifted Child Q.*, 40(2), 61–65.

Baker, E. L., Freeman, M., and Clayton, S. (1991). Cognitive assessment of history for large-scale testing. In *Testing and Cognition*, edited by M. C. Wittrock and E. L. Baker, pp. 131–153. Englewood Cliffs, NJ: Prentice Hall.*

Baker, E. L., O'Neil, Jr., H. F., and Linn, R. L. (1993). Policy and validity prospects for performance-based assessment. *Am. Psychol.*, 48, 1210–1218.*

Baker, E. L., Linn, R. L., Abedi, J., and Niemi, D. (1995). Dimensionality and generalizability of domain-independent performance assessments. *J. Educ. Res.*, 89, 197–205.

Baker, E. L., Aschbacher, P. R., Niemi, D., and Sato, E. (2005). *CRESST Performance Assessment Models: Assessing Content Area Explanation*, CSE Tech. Rep. No. 652. Los Angeles, CA: University of California/National Center for Research on Evaluation, Standards, and Student Testing (CRESST).

Bejar, I. I. (1991). A methodology for scoring open-ended architectural design problems. *J. Appl. Psychol.*, 76, 522–532.

Bennett, R. E. (1999). Using new technology to improve assessment. *Educ. Meas. Issues Pract.*, 18(3), 5–12.

Bennett, R. E. (2006). Moving the field forward: some thoughts on validity and automated scoring. In *Automated Scoring of Complex Tasks in Computer-Based Testing*, edited by D. M. Williamson, I. I. Behar, and R. J. Mislevy, pp. 403–412. Mahwah, NJ: Lawrence Erlbaum Associates.*

Bennett, R. E. and Bejar, I. I. (1998). Validity and automated scoring: it's not only the scoring. *Educ. Meas.*, 17(4), 9–17.

Bennett, R. E., Morley, M., and Quardt, D. (2000). Three response types for broadening the conception of mathematical problem solving in computerized tests. *Appl. Psychol. Meas.*, 24, 294–309.

Bennett, R. E., Jenkins, F., Persky, H., and Weiss, A. (2003). Assessing complex problem solving performances. *Assess. Educ. Princ. Policy Pract.*, 10, 347–359.

Birenbaum, M., Kelly, A. E., and Tatsuoka, K. K. (1993). Diagnosing knowledge states in algebra using the rule-space model. *J. Educ. Meas.*, 20, 221–230.

Burstein, J. C. (2003). The e-rater scoring engine: automated essay scoring with natural language processing. In *Automated Essay Scoring: A Cross-Disciplinary Perspective*, edited by M. D. Shermis and J. Burstein, pp. 113–122. Mahwah, NJ: Lawrence Erlbaum Associates.

Burstein, J. C. and Chodorow, M. (1999). Automated essay scoring for nonnative English speakers. In *Proceedings of Computer-Mediated Language Assessment and Evaluation of Natural Language Processing*, joint symposium of the Association of Computational Linguistics and the International Association of Language Learning Technologies, June 22, College Park, MD.

Chi, M. T. H., Glaser, R., and Farr, M., Eds. (1988). *The Nature of Expertise*. Hillsdale, NJ: Lawrence Erlbaum Associates.*

Chung, G. K. W. K. and Baker, E. L. (2003a). An exploratory study to examine the feasibility of measuring problem-solving processes using a click-through interface. *J. Technol. Learn. Assess.*, 2(2) (available from http://jtla.org).

Chung, G. K. W. K. and Baker, E. L. (2003b). Issues in the reliability and validity of automated scoring of constructed responses. In *Automated Essay Grading: A Cross-Disciplinary Approach*, edited by M. D. Shermis and J. E. Burstein, pp. 23–40. Mahwah, NJ: Lawrence Erlbaum Associates.*

Chung, G. K. W. K., O'Neil, Jr., H. F., and Herl, H. E. (1999). The use of computer-based collaborative knowledge mapping to measure team processes and team outcomes. *Comput. Hum. Behav.*, 15, 463–494.

Chung, G. K. W. K., Harmon, T. C., and Baker, E. L. (2001). The impact of a simulation-based learning design project on student learning. *IEEE Trans. Educ.*, 44, 390–398.

Chung, G. K. W. K., Baker, E. L., and Cheak, A. M. (2002). *Knowledge Mapper Authoring System Prototype*, CSE Tech. Rep. 575. Los Angeles, CA: University of California/National Center for Research on Evaluation, Standards, and Student Testing (CRESST).

Chung, G. K. W. K., Baker, E. L., Brill, D. G., Sinha, R., Saadat, F., and Bewley, W. L. (2003a). Automated assessment of domain knowledge with online knowledge mapping. *Proc. I/ITSEC*, 25, 1168–1179.

Chung, G. K. W. K., Delacruz, G. C., Dionne, G. B., and Bewley, W. L. (2003b). Linking assessment and instruction using ontologies. *Proc. I/ITSEC*, 25, 1811–1822.*

Chung, G. K. W. K., Sinha, R., de Souza e Silva, A. A., Michiuye, J. K., Cheak, A. M., Saadat, F. et al. (2004). *CRESST Human Performance Knowledge Mapping Tool Authoring System*, Deliverable to Office of Naval Research. Los Angeles, CA: University of California/National Center for Research on Evaluation, Standards, and Student Testing (CRESST).

Chung, G. K. W. K., Dionne, G. B., and Kaiser, W. J. (2006). An Exploratory Study Examining the Feasibility of Using Bayesian Networks to Predict Circuit Analysis Understanding. Paper presented at the Annual Meeting of the National Council on Measurement in Education, April 9–11, San Francisco, CA.

Chung, G. K. W. K., Baker, E. L., Delacruz, G. C., Bewley, W. L., Elmore, J., and Seely, B. (in press). An approach to authoring problem-solving assessments. In *Assessment of Problem Solving Using Simulations*, edited by E. L. Baker, J. Dickieson, W. Wulfeck, and H. F. O'Neil. Mahwah, NJ: Lawrence Erlbaum Associates.

Clauser, B. E. (2000). Recurrent issues and recent advances in scoring performance assessments. *Appl. Psychol. Meas.*, 24, 310–324.

Clauser, B. E., Subhiyah, R. G., Nungester, R. J., Ripkey, D. R., Clyman, S. G., and McKinley, D. (1995). Scoring a performance-based assessment by modeling the judgments of experts. *J. Educ. Meas.*, 32, 397–415.

Clauser, B. E., Margolis, M. J., Clyman, S. G., and Ross, L. P. (1997). Development of automated scoring algorithms for complex performance assessments: a comparison of two approaches. *J. Educ. Meas.*, 34, 141–161.

Clauser, B. E., Swanson, D. B., and Clyman, S. G. (1999). A comparison of the generalizability of scores produced by expert raters and automated scoring systems. *Appl. Meas. Educ.*, 12, 281–299.

Clauser, B. E., Harik, P., and Clyman, S. G. (2000). The generalizability of scores for a performance assessment scored with a computer-automated scoring system. *J. Educ. Meas.*, 37, 245–262.

Glaser, R. (1963). Instructional technology and the measurement of learning outcomes: some questions. *Am. Psychol.*, 18, 519–521.*

Gruber, T. R. (1995). Toward principles for the design of ontologies used for knowledge sharing. *Int. J. Hum.–Comput. Stud.*, 43, 907–928.*

Herl, H. E., Niemi, D., and Baker, E. L. (1996). Construct validation of an approach to modeling cognitive structure of U.S. history knowledge. *J. Educ. Res.*, 89, 206–218.

Herl, H. E., O'Neil, Jr., H. F., Chung, G. K. W. K., and Schacter, J. (1999). Reliability and validity of a computer-based knowledge mapping system to measure content understanding. *Comput. Hum. Behav.*, 15, 315–334.

Hively, W. (1974). Introduction to domain-referenced testing. *Educ. Technol.*, 14(6), 5–10.

Hively, W., Patterson, H. L., and Page, S. H. (1968). A 'universe defined' system of arithmetic achievement tests. *J. Educ. Meas.*, 5, 275–290.*

Huff, K. L. and Sireci, S. G. (2001). Validity issues in computer-based testing. *Educ. Meas. Issues Pract.*, 20(3), 16–25.*

Kane, M., Crooks, T., and Cohen, A. (1999). Validating measures of performance. *Educ. Meas. Issues Pract.*, 18(2), 5–17.*

Katz, I. R. (1998). *A Software Tool for Rapidly Prototyping New Forms of Computer-Based Assessments*, GRE Research Report 91-06aP. Princeton, NJ: ETS.

Katz, I. R. and James, C. M. (1998). *Toward Assessment of Design Skill in Engineering*, GRE Research Report 97-16. Princeton, NJ: ETS.

Katz, I. R., Martinez, M. E., Sheehan, K. M., and Tatsuoka, K. K. (1998). Extending the rule space methodology to a semantically rich domain: diagnostic assessment in architecture. *J. Educ. Behav. Stat.*, 24, 254–278.

Kim, J.-O., Chung, G. K. W. K., and Delacruz, G. C. (2004). Examining the sensitivity of knowledge maps using repeated measures: a growth modeling approach. In *Proceedings of Current Issues in Knowledge Mapping in Assessment and Instruction*, symposium conducted at the American Educational Research Association Annual Meeting, April 12–16, San Diego, CA.

Klein, D. C. D., Chung, G. K. W. K., Osmundson, E., and Herl, H. E. (2002). *Examining the Validity of Knowledge Mapping as a Measure of Elementary Students' Scientific Understanding*, CSE Technical Report No. 557. Los Angeles, CA: University of California/National Center for Research on Evaluation, Standards, and Student Testing (CRESST).

Koedinger, K. R. and Nathan, M. J. (2004). The real story behind story problems: effects of representations on quantitative reasoning. *J. Learn. Sci.*, 13, 129–164.

Lambiotte, J. G., Dansereau, D. F., Cross, D. R., and Reynolds, S. B. (1989). Multi-relational semantic maps. *Educ. Psychol. Rev.*, 1, 331–367.

Landauer, T. K., Laham, D., and Foltz, P. W. (2003). Automated scoring and annotation of essays with the Intelligent Essay Assessor. In *Automated Essay Scoring: A Cross-Disciplinary Perspective*, edited by M. D. Shermis and J. Burstein, pp. 87–112. Mahwah, NJ: Lawrence Erlbaum Associates.

Lee, J. J. (2000). The Impact of Korean Language Accommodations on Concept Mapping Tasks for Korean American English Language Learners. Ph.D. dissertation. Los Angeles, CA: University of California.

Linn, R. L., Baker, E. L., and Dunbar, S. B. (1991). Complex, performance-based assessment: Expectations and validation criteria. *Educ. Res.*, 20(8), 15–21.*

Margolis, M. J. and Clauser, B. E. (2006). A regression-based procedure for automated scoring of a complex medical performance assessment. In *Automated Scoring of Complex Tasks in Computer-Based testing*, edited by D. M. Williamson, I. I. Behar, and R. J. Mislevy, pp. 123–167. Mahwah, NJ: Lawrence Erlbaum Associates.

Messick, S. (1995). Standards of validity and the validity of standards in performance assessment. *Educ. Meas. Issues Pract.*, 14(4), 5–8.*

Mislevy, R. J. and Gitomer, D. H. (1995). The role of probability-based inference in an intelligent tutoring system. *User Model. User-Adapt. Interact.*, 5, 253–282.*

Mislevy, R. J. and Riconscente, M. M. (2005). *Evidence-Centered Assessment Design: Layers, Structures, and Terminology*, PADI Technical Report No. 9. Menlo Park, CA: SRI International.

Mislevy, R. J. and Riconscente, M. M. (2006). Evidence-centered assessment design: layers, concepts, and terminology. In *Handbook of Test Development*, edited by S. Downing and T. Haladyna, pp. 61–90. Mahwah, NJ: Lawrence Erlbaum Associates.*

Mislevy, R. J., Steinberg, L. S., Breyer, F. J., Almond, R. G., and Johnson, L. (2002). Making sense of data from complex assessments. *Appl. Meas. Educ.*, 15, 363–389.*

Mislevy, R., Hamel, L., Fried, R. G., Gaffney, T., Haertel, G., Hafter, A. et al. (2003). *Design Patterns for Assessing Science Inquiry*, PADI Technical Report No. 1. Menlo Park, CA: SRI International.

Niemi, D., Vendlinski, T. P., Baker, E. L., and Wang, J. (in press). On-line tools to improve formative assessment. *Br. J. Educ. Technol.*

Novak, J. D. and Gowin, D. B. (1984). *Learning How to Learn*. New York: Cambridge University Press.

Osmundson, E., Chung, G. K. W. K., Herl, H. E., and Klein, D. C. D. (1999). *Concept Mapping in the Classroom: A Tool for Examining the Development of Students' Conceptual Understandings*, CSE Technical Report No. 507). Los Angeles, CA: University of California/National Center for Research on Evaluation, Standards, and Student Testing (CRESST).

Page, E. B. and Petersen, N. S. (1995). The computer moves into essay grading: updating the ancient test. *Phi Delta Kappan*, 76, 561–565.

Pellegrino, J., Chudowsky, N., and Glaser, R., Eds. (2001). *Knowing What Students Know: The Science and Design of Educational Assessment*. Washington, D.C.: National Academy Press.*

Popham, W. J. and Husek, T. R. (1969). Implications for criterion-referenced measurement. *J. Educ. Meas.*, 6, 1–9.

Powers, D. E., Burstein, J. C., Chodorow, M., Fowles, M. E., and Kukich, K. (2000). *Comparing the Validity of Automated and Human Essay Scoring*, RR-00-10. Princeton, NJ: Educational Testing Service.

Powers, D. E., Burstein, J. C., Chodorow, M., Fowles, M. E., and Kukich, K. (2001). *Stumping e-rater: Challenging the Validity of Automated Essay Scoring*, RR-01-03. Princeton, NJ: Educational Testing Service.

Riconscente, M., Mislevy, R., Hamel, L., and PADI Research Group. (2005). *An Introduction to PADI Task Templates*, PADI Technical Report No. 3. Menlo Park, CA: SRI International.

Ruiz-Primo, M. A., Schultz, S. E., Li, M., and Shavelson, R. J. (2001). Comparison of the reliability and validity of scores from two concept-mapping techniques. *J. Res. Sci. Teaching*, 38, 260–278.

Scalise, K. and Gifford, B. (2006). Computer-based assessment in e-learning: a framework for constructing 'intermediate constraint' questions and tasks for technology platforms. *J. Technol. Learn. Assess.*, 4(6) (available from http://www.jtla.org).

Schacter, J., Herl, H. E., Chung, G. K. W. K., Dennis, R. A., and O'Neil, Jr., H. F. (1999). Computer-based performance assessments: a solution to the narrow measurement and reporting of problem-solving. *Comput. Hum. Behav.*, 15, 403–418.*

Stevens, R. H. and Casillas, A. (2006). Artificial neural networks. In *Automated Scoring of Complex Tasks in Computer-Based Testing*, edited by D. M. Williamson, I. I. Behar, and R. J. Mislevy, pp. 259–312. Mahwah, NJ: Lawrence Erlbaum Associates.

Tatsuoka, K. K. and Tatsuoka, M. M. (1983). Spotting erroneous rules of operation by the individual consistency index. *J. Educ. Meas.*, 20, 221–230.

Tatsuoka, K. K. and Tatsuoka, M. M. (1997). Computerized cognitive diagnostic adaptive testing: effect on remedial instruction as empirical validation. *J. Educ. Meas.*, 34, 3–20.

van der Linden, W. J. (2005). *Linear Models for Optimal Test Design*. New York: Springer-Verlag.

Vendlinski, T. and Stevens, R. (2002). Assessing student problem-solving skills with complex computer-based tasks. *J. Technol. Learn. Assess.*, 1(3) (available from http://www.jtla.org).

Vendlinski, T., Niemi, D., and Wang, J. (2005). Learning assessment by designing assessments: an on-line formative assessment design tool. In *Proceedings of the Society for Information Technology and Teacher Education International Conference 2005*, edited by C. Crawford, R. Carlsen, I. Gibson, K. McFerrin, J. Price, and R. Weber, pp. 228–240. Norfolk, VA: Association for the Advancement of Computing in Education.

Williamson, D. M., Bejar, I. I., and Hone, A. S. (1999). 'Mental model' comparison of automated and human scoring. *J. Educ. Meas.*, 36, 158–184.

Williamson, D. M., Almond, R. G., and Mislevy, R. J. (2000). Model criticism of Bayesian networks with latent variables. In *Uncertainty in Artificial Intelligence: Proceedings of the 16th Conference*, edited by C. Boutilier and M. Goldzmidt, pp. 634–643. San Francisco, CA: Morgan Kaufmann.

Williamson, D. M., Almond, R. G., Mislevy, R. J., and Levy, R. (2006). An application of Bayesian networks in automated scoring of computerized simulation tasks. In *Automated Scoring of Complex Tasks in Computer-Based Testing*, edited by D. M. Williamson, I. I. Behar, and R. J. Mislevy, pp. 201–257. Mahwah, NJ: Lawrence Erlbaum Associates.

Yang, Y., Buckendahl, C. W., Juszkiewicz, P. J., and Bhola, D. S. (2002). A review of strategies for validating computer-automated scoring. *Appl. Meas. Educ.*, 15, 391–412.

Yin, Y. and Shavelson, R. J. (2004). *Application of Generalizability Theory to Concept-Map Assessment Research*, CSE Technical Report No. 640. Los Angeles, CA: University of California/National Center for Research on Evaluation, Standards, and Student Testing (CRESST).

---

* Indicates a core reference.

# 45

# Models and Methods for Evaluation

*Ron Owston*
York University, Toronto, Canada

## CONTENTS

## ABSTRACT

This chapter situates the evaluation of technology-based programs in the context of the field of general educational program evaluation. It begins with an overview of the main evaluation approaches developed for general educational programs, including Tyler's early conception of assessing attainment of program objectives, decision-making approaches, naturalistic evaluation, and Kirkpatrick's four levels for evaluating program effectiveness. Following this is an overview of commonly used technology-specific program evaluation criteria and frameworks. Strategies distilled from these two fields are then suggested for evaluating technology-based learning programs. These strategies emphasize clarifying the goal or purpose of the evaluation and determining the information needs of the intended audiences of the evaluation at the beginning of the project. This, in turn, suggests the most appropriate evaluation methodology to be used. The chapter concludes with a description of tools that can be used for analysis of evaluative data, followed by a brief discussion of the dissemination of evaluation results.

## KEYWORDS

*Effect size:* A statistical measure of the difference between the mean of the control group and the mean of the experimental group in a quantitative research study.

*Evaluation:* The process of gathering information about the merit or worth of a program for the purpose of making decisions about its effectiveness or for program improvement.

*Naturalistic evaluation:* An evaluation approach that relies on qualitative methodology but gives evaluators freedom to choose the precise method used to collect, analyze, and interpret their data.

*Web log file:* A data file residing on a Web server that contains a record of all visitors to the site hosted by the server, where they came from, what links they clicked on, as well as other information.

## INTRODUCTION

New technologies that have potential implications for learning are being developed almost daily: blogs, wikis, podcasting, response clickers, interactive pads and whiteboards, advanced educational games and simulations, and social websites, to name a few. Although individual teachers are always willing to pioneer the use of these technologies in their classrooms, system administrators often face the challenge of having to make informed decisions on whether these technologies should be adopted on a wider scale or integrated into curricula. The main criterion for their adoption frequently is how effective they are at improving learning. Because of the newness of the technologies, seldom do we have any compelling evidence of their effectiveness apart from anecdotal accounts of early adopters. This inevitably leads to a call for a formal evaluation of programs that employ the technology.

The goal of this chapter is to provide guidance to those charged with the evaluation of technology-based programs on how to approach the task. What is very apparent from an examination of the literature on technology program evaluation is the large gap between it and the literature on the general field of program evaluation. As will be seen from the discussion that follows, program evaluation has become a mature field of study that offers a variety of approaches and perspectives from which the evaluator can draw. Those writing about technology evaluation tend either to ignore the field or to give it only cursory attention on the way to developing their own approaches, so another goal of this chapter is to bridge the gap between these two fields. I take the position that technology-based

program evaluation is a particular case of general program evaluation; therefore, the methods and tools in the program evaluation literature are equally applicable to technology evaluation. At the same time, the criteria that technology program evaluators offer can inform the more general evaluation approaches.

This chapter begins with a discussion of the field of general program evaluation and outlines some of the more influential evaluation approaches that have emerged. Following this is an overview of common technology program evaluation criteria and frameworks. Drawing from these two areas, I then suggest strategies that can be used to evaluate technology-based learning programs and describe several new data collection and analysis software tools that can help evaluators.

## GENERAL PROGRAM EVALUATION MODELS

### Evolution of Program Evaluation

Prior to the 1970s, educational program evaluators tended to concentrate on determining the extent to which a program met its stated objectives, a model first advocated by Tyler (1942) in a longitudinal study of schools in the 1930s. That model seemed sensible enough and served a generation or two of educators well, but during the 1960s and 1970s researchers began developing new evaluation models that went far beyond Tyler's original conception of evaluation.

The models that emerged were developed in response to the need to provide accountability for large U.S. government program expenditures in health, education, and welfare during this period. Scriven (1972) argued that evaluators must not be blinded by examining only the stated goals of a project as other program outcomes may be equally important. By implication, Scriven urged evaluators to cast a wide net in evaluating the results of a program by looking at both the intended and unintended outcomes. In fact, he went as far as advising evaluators to avoid the rhetoric around the program by not reading program brochures, proposals, or descriptions and to focus only on the actual outcomes. Scriven also popularized the terms *formative* and *summative evaluations* as a way of distinguishing two kinds of roles evaluators play: They can assess the merits of a program while it is still under development, or they can assess the outcomes of an already completed program. In practice, these two roles are not always as clearly demarcated as Scriven suggests; nonetheless, this distinction between the two purposes of evaluation is still widely drawn on today.

Suchman (1967) argued that evaluating the attainment of a program's goals is still essential, but more critical is to understand the intervening processes that led to those outcomes. He suggested that an evaluation should test a hypothesis such as: "Activity A will attain objective B because it is able to influence process C, which affects the occurrence of this objective" (p. 177). Following this reasoning, Weiss (1972) showed how a model could be developed and tested to explain how a chain of events in a teacher home visit program could lead to the ultimate objective of improving children's reading achievement. This early work led to the development of an approach known today as *theory-based evaluation*, *theory-driven evaluation*, or *program theory evaluation* (PTE). PTE consists of two basic elements: an explicit theory or model of how the program causes the intended or observed outcomes and an actual evaluation that is at least guided by the model (Rogers et al., 2000). The theory component is not a grand theory in the traditional social science sense, but rather it is a theory of change or plausible model of how a program is supposed to work (Bickman, 1987). The program model, often called a *logic model*, is typically developed by the evaluator in collaboration with the program developers, either before the evaluation takes place or afterwards. Evaluators then collect evidence to test the validity of the model. PTE does not suggest a methodology for testing the model, although it is often associated with qualitative methodology. Cook (2000) argues that program theory evaluators who use qualitative methods cannot establish that the observed program outcomes were caused by the program itself, as causality can only be established through experimental design. Generally speaking, the contribution of PTE is that it forces evaluators to move beyond treating the program as a black box and leads them to examining why observed changes arising from a program occurred.

## Decision-Making Evaluation Approaches

During the same period, other evaluators focused on how they could help educational decision makers. Best known is Stufflebeam (1973), who viewed evaluation as a process of providing meaningful and useful information for decision alternatives. Stufflebeam proposed his *context*, *input*, *process*, and *product* (CIPP) model, which describes four kinds of evaluative activities. Context evaluation assesses the problems, needs, and opportunities present in the educational program's setting. Input evaluation assesses competing strategies and the work plans and budgets. Process evaluation monitors, documents, and assesses program activities. Product evaluation examines the impact of the program on the target audience, the quality and significance of

outcomes, and the extent to which the program is sustainable and transferable. In essence, the CIPP model asks of a program: What needs to be done? How should it be done? Is it being done? Did it succeed? Stufflebeam also reconciled his model with Scriven's formative and summative evaluation by stating that formative evaluation focuses on decision making and summative evaluation on accountability.

Another popular approach that emerged was Patton's (1978) *utilization-focused evaluation*. Patton addressed the concern that evaluation findings are often ignored by decision makers. He probed evaluation program sponsors to attempt to understand why this is so and how the situation could be improved. From this study, he developed not so much an evaluation model as a general approach to evaluation that has only two fundamental requirements. First, he stated that relevant decision makers and evaluation report audiences must be clearly identified. Second, he maintained that evaluators must work actively with the decision makers to decide upon all other aspects of the evaluation, including such matters as the evaluation questions, research design, data analysis, interpretation, and dissemination. Patton admitted that the challenge of producing evaluation studies that are actually used is enormous but remained optimistic that it is possible and worth attempting.

Cronbach (1980), a student of Tyler, also focused on the decision-making process. His contribution was to emphasize the political context of decision making, saying that it is seldom a lone person who makes decisions about a program; rather, decisions are more likely to be made in a lively political setting by a policy-shaping community. Cronbach advocated that the evaluator should be a teacher, educating the client group throughout the evaluation process by helping them refine their evaluation questions and determine what technical and political actions are best for them. During this educative process, the evaluator is constantly giving feedback to the clients, and the final evaluation report is only one more vehicle for communicating with them. Unlike the other evaluation theorists mentioned above, Cronbach did not believe that the evaluator should determine the worthiness of a program nor provide recommended courses of action.

## Naturalistic Evaluation Approaches

At the same time these researchers were developing approaches that focused on how evaluation results are used, others concentrated their efforts on developing methods that place few, if any, constraints on the evaluator. Known as *naturalistic* or *qualitative*, these approaches give the evaluator freedom to choose the methods used to collect, analyze, and interpret their data. Stake's (1975) *responsive evaluation* is one such model. Stake was concerned that conventional approaches were not sufficiently receptive to the needs of the evaluation client. He advocated that evaluators must attend to actual program activities rather than intents, respond to the audience's needs for information, and present different value perspectives when reporting on the success and failure of a program. Stake believed that evaluators should use whatever data-gathering schemes seem appropriate; however, he did emphasize that they will likely rely heavily on human observers and judges. Rather than relying on methodologies of experimental psychology, as is often done in conventional evaluations, Stake saw evaluators drawing more from the traditions of anthropology and journalism in carrying out their studies.

Two other approaches are of interest in this discussion of naturalistic methods. First, is Eisner's (1979) *connoisseurship model*, which is rooted in the field of art criticism. His model relies on the evaluator's judgment to assess the quality of an educational program, just as the art critic appraises the complexity of a work of art. Two concepts are key to Eisner's model: *educational connoisseurship* and *educational criticism*. Educational connoisseurship involves the appreciation of the finer points of an educational program, a talent that derives from the evaluator's experience and background in the domain. Educational criticism relies on the evaluator's ability to verbalize the features of the program, so those who do not have the level of appreciation that the connoisseur has can fully understand the program's features.

The second approach is *ethnographic evaluation*, whose proponents believe can yield a more meaningful picture of an educational program than would be possible using traditional scientific methods (Guba, 1978). Ethnographic evaluators immerse themselves in the program they are studying by taking part in the day-to-day activities of the individuals being studied. Their data-gathering tools include field notes, key informant interviews, case histories, and surveys. Their goal is to produce a rich description of the program and to convey their appraisal of the program to the program stakeholders.

### Kirkpatrick's Four Levels

Although it is well established in the human resource development community, Kirkpatrick's (2001) *four-level model* is less known in educational evaluation circles because it focuses on the evaluation of corporate training programs. I have placed it in a category by itself because it has little in common with the other models discussed, as Kirkpatrick does not emphasize negotiation with the decision makers nor does he favor a naturalistic approach. Kirkpatrick's first writing on the model dates back to over 40 years ago, but it was not until more recently that he provided a detailed elaboration of its features. Even though it focuses on training program evaluation, the model is still relevant to general educational settings; for example, Guskey (2000) adapted it for the evaluation of teacher professional development programs.

Kirkpatrick proposed four levels that the evaluator must attend to: *reaction*, *learning*, *behavior*, and *results*. *Reaction* refers to the program participants' satisfaction with the program; the typical course evaluation survey measures reaction. *Learning* is the extent to which participants change attitudes, improve their knowledge, or increase their skills as a result of attending the program; course exams, tests, or surveys measure this kind of change. The next two levels are new to most educational evaluators and are increasingly more difficult to assess. *Behavior* refers to the extent to which participants' behavior changes as a result of attending the course; to assess this level, the evaluator must determine whether participants' new knowledge, skills, or attitudes transfer to the job or another situation such as a subsequent course. The fourth evaluation level, *results*, focuses on the lasting changes to the organization that occurred as a consequence of the course, such as increased productivity, improved management, or improved quality. In a formal educational setting, the fourth evaluation level could refer to assessing how students perform on the job after graduation. Kirkpatrick has recommended the use of control group comparisons to assess a program's effectiveness at these two higher levels, if at all possible.

## TECHNOLOGY EVALUATION APPROACHES

So far I have concentrated on models that are applicable to a wide range of educational programs, whether or not they might involve technology. Several frameworks have been proposed specifically to assess technology-based learning, although none has been employed much by researchers other than their developers. These frameworks tend to recommend areas in which evaluators should focus their data collection, provide criteria against which technology-based learning could be judged, or provide questions for the evaluator to ask. For example, Riel and Harasim (1994) proposed three areas on which data collection might focus for the evaluation of online discussion groups: the structure of network environment, social interaction that occurs

**TABLE 45.1**
**CIAO! Framework**

| | Context | Interactions | Outcomes |
|---|---|---|---|
| Rationale | To evaluate technology, we need to know about its aims and the context of its use. | Observing students and obtaining process data help us to understand why and how some element works in addition to whether or not it works. | Being able to attribute learning outcomes to technology when it is one part of a multifaceted course is very difficult. It is important to try to assess both cognitive and affective learning outcomes (e.g., changes in perceptions and attitudes). |
| Data | Designers' and course teams' aims. Policy documents and meeting records | Records of student interactions. Student diaries. Online logs | Measures of learning. Changes in students' attitudes and perceptions |
| Methods | Interviews with technology program designers and course team members. Analysis of policy documents | Observation. Diaries. Video/audio and computer recording | Interviews. Questionnaires. Tests |

*Source:* Adapted from Scanlon, E. et al., *Educ. Technol. Soc.*, 3(4), 101–107, 2000.

during the course or project, and the effects of the experience on individuals. Bates and Poole's (2003) SECTION model calls for the comparison of two or more online instructional delivery modes on the basis of the appropriateness of the technology for the targeted students, its ease of use and reliability, costs, teaching and learning factors, interactivity fostered by the technology, organizational issues, novelty of the technology, and how quickly courses can be mounted and updated. Ravitz (1998) suggested a framework that encourages the assessment of a project's evolution through interactive discussion, continual recordkeeping, and documentation. Mandinach (2005) has given evaluators a set of key questions to ask about an e-learning program in three general areas: student learning, pedagogical and intuitional issues, and broader policy issues. Finally, Baker and Herman (2003) have proposed an approach, which they call *distributed evaluation*, to deal with large-scale, longitudinal evaluation of technology. They emphasize clarifying evaluation goals across all stakeholders, using a variety of quantitative and qualitative measures ranging from questionnaires and informal classroom tests to standardized tests, designing lengthier studies so changes can be assessed over time, collecting data at the local level and entering them into a systemwide repository, and providing feedback targeted at various audiences.

Of particular note because of its origins and comprehensiveness is the context, interactions, attitudes, and outcomes (CIAO!) framework developed by Scanlon et al. (2000). The CIAO! framework represents a culmination of some 25 years of technology evaluation experience of the authors at the Open University in the United Kingdom. As shown in Table 45.1, the columns in the framework represent three dimensions of the technology-based learning program that must be eval-

uated: the *context* dimension concerns how the technology fits within the course and where and how it is used; *interactions* refers to how students interact with the technology and with each other; and *outcomes* deals with how students change as a result of using the technology. The first row of the framework provides a brief rationale for the need to evaluate each of the three dimensions. The second and third rows, respectively, highlight the kinds of data that should be collected for each dimension and the methods that should be employed for each. The authors point out that, while the framework has proven to be very valuable in highlighting areas in which evaluative data should be collected, caution should be exercised in not applying the framework in an overly prescriptive manner.

Perhaps the most widely used criteria for evaluating teaching with technology in higher education are the *Seven Principles for Good Practice in Undergraduate Education*, described in a seminal article by Chickering and Gamson (1987). Almost 10 years after this article was published, Chickering and Ehrmann (1996) illustrated how the criteria, which were distilled from decades of research on the undergraduate education experience, could be adapted for information and communication technologies. Briefly, the criteria suggest that faculty should:

- Encourage contact between students and the faculty.
- Develop reciprocity and cooperation among students.
- Encourage active learning.
- Give prompt feedback.
- Emphasize time on task.
- Communicate high expectations.
- Respect diverse talents and ways of learning.

Graham and colleagues applied the criteria to the evaluation of four online courses in a professional school of a large midwestern American university (Graham et al., 2000). The evaluation team developed a list of "lessons learned" for online instruction, aimed at improving the courses and which correspond to the seven principles. Similarly, Cook et al. (2003a) applied the criteria to the evaluation of a technology-enhanced undergraduate economics course. They used the principles as the basis of codes for the qualitative analysis of open-ended student survey responses and assessed the extent to which the criteria were exemplified in the course.

Although the *Seven Principles* describe effective teaching from the faculty member's perspective, the American Psychological Association has produced an often-cited list of 14 principles that pertain to the learner and the learning process (see http://www.apa.org/ed/lcp2/lcp14.html). The learner-centered principles are intended to deal holistically with learners in the context of real-world learning situations; thus, they are best understood as an organized set of principles that influence the learner and learning with no principle viewed in isolation. The 14 principles, which are grouped into four main categories, are as follows:

- *Cognitive and metacognitive* (six principles): Nature of the learning process; goals of the learning process; construction of knowledge; strategic thinking; thinking about thinking; context of learning
- *Motivational and affective* (three principles): Motivational and emotional influences on learning; intrinsic motivation to learn; effects of motivation on effort
- *Developmental and social* (two principles): Developmental influences on learning; social influences on learning
- *Individual difference factors* (three principles): Individual differences in learning; learning and diversity; standards and assessment

Bonk and Cummings (1998) discussed how these principles are relevant for the design of online courses from a learner-centered perspective and for providing a framework for the benefits, implications, problems, and solutions of online instruction. By implication, the APA principles could serve as criteria to guide the evaluation of the effectiveness of technology-based learning environments.

## IMPLICATIONS FOR THE EVALUATION OF TECHNOLOGY

What should be abundantly clear at this point is the surfeit of evaluation approaches, criteria, and models. Few experienced evaluators, however, pick one model and adhere to it for all of their work; they are more likely to draw upon different aspects of several models. Worthen and Saunders (1987, p. 151) expressed this well:

> The value of alternative approaches lies in their capacity to help us think, to present and provoke new ideas and techniques, and to serve as mental checklists of things we ought to consider, remember, or worry about. Their heuristic value is very high; their prescriptive value seems much less.

Several implications can be drawn from this discussion of models so far that will help in making decisions about the design of technology-based program evaluations. These are summarized in Figure 45.1. First, we must clarify why we are proposing an evaluation: Is it to assess a blended learning course developed by a faculty member who was given a course development grant? Is it to evaluate an elementary school laptop computer initiative? Is it being conducted because students are expressing dissatisfaction with an online course? Is it to see how an online professional learning community facilitates pedagogical change? The purpose of the evaluation will lead us to favor one approach over another; for example, in the case of the faculty member developing a course, the *Seven Principles* and/or the APA's learner-centered principles may be good criteria to judge the course. The *Seven Principles* may also be appropriate to guide the evaluation of the course where there is student dissatisfaction. On the other hand, in the case of the professional program, Kirkpatrick's model (or Guskey's extension of it) would direct us not only to examining teachers' perceptions of and learnings in the community but also to studying the impact of the program on the classroom practice. Table 45.2 provides additional guidance on selecting a model from among the most widely used ones for six common program evaluation purposes. Readers should exercise caution when interpreting the table, as there are no hard and fast rules about what model to use for a given purpose. Rarely is one model the only appropriate one to use in an evaluation; however, more often than not some models are better than others for a particular study.

We next have to give careful thought about who the intended audiences of the evaluation report are and should plan on providing those individuals with the

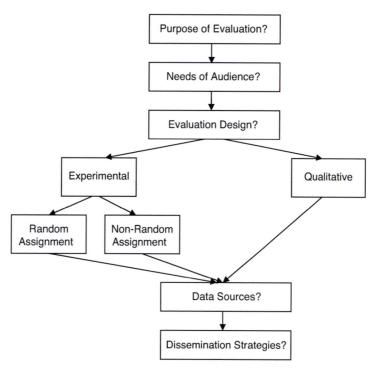

**Figure 45.1** Decisions for designing an evaluation study.

**TABLE 45.2**
**Evaluation Models Best Suited for Particular Evaluation Purposes**

| | Primary Purpose of Evaluation | | | | | |
|---|---|---|---|---|---|---|
| Evaluation Model | Attainment of the Program's Goals and Objectives | Program Improvement | Accreditation of the Program | Development of Theory about Intervention | Meeting Information Needs of Diverse Audiences | Overall Impact of Program |
| Goal-based (Tyler, 1942) | X | X | | | | |
| Goal-free evaluation (Scriven, 1972) | X | X | | | | X |
| Theory-based (Weiss, 1972) | X | X | | X | | X |
| Context, input, process, and product (CIPP) (Stufflebeam, 1973) | X | X | | | | X |
| Utilization-focused (Patton, 1978) | | | | | X | |
| Responsive (Stake, 1975) | X | X | | | X | |
| Connoisseurship (Eisner, 1979) | | | X | | | |
| Ethnographic (Guba, 1978) | X | X | | X | | X |
| Multilevel (Guskey, 2000; Kirkpatrick, 2001) | | X | X | | | X |
| CIAO! framework (Scanlon et al., 2000) | X | X | | | | X |
| Seven principles of good practice in undergraduate education (Chickering and Ehrmann, 1996) | | X | | | | X |

kinds of data needed to take appropriate action. Recall Stufflebeam's statement that the purpose of evaluation is to present options to decision makers. In a university setting, the decision makers or stakeholders might be a faculty member who is teaching an online course, a curriculum committee, a technology roundtable, a faculty council, or senior academic administrators. The stakeholders in a school setting could be a combination of parents, teachers, a school council, and the district superintendent. The challenge to the evaluator, therefore, is to identify these audiences and then find out what their expectations are for the evaluation and the kind of information they seek about the program. Patton, Cronback, and Stake all emphasized the critical importance of this stage. The process may involve face-to-face meetings with the different stakeholders, telephone interviews, or brief surveys. Because consensus in expectations is unlikely to be found, the evaluator will have to make judgments about the relative importance of each stakeholder and whose information should be given priority.

With the expectations and information needs in hand, the study now must be planned. We saw from Scriven's perspective that all program outcomes should be examined whether or not they are stated as objectives. My experience has taught me not only to assess the accomplishment of program objectives, as this is typically what stakeholders want done, but also to seek data on unintended outcomes, whether positive or negative, as they can lead to insights one might otherwise have missed.

## Design of Study

Next the evaluator must decide upon the actual design of the study. A major decision has to be made about whether to embark on an experimental design involving a comparison group or a non-experimental design. The information needs of the stakeholders should determine the path to follow (Patton, 1978; Stake, 1975). If the stakeholders seek *proof* that a technology-based program works, then an experimental design is what is likely required. The What Works Clearinghouse established by the U.S. Department of Education's Institute of Education Sciences holds experimental designs as the epitome of "scientific evidence" for determining the effectiveness of educational interventions (http://www.w-w-c.org). On the other hand, if the stakeholders seek information on how to improve a program, then non-experimental or qualitative approaches may be appropriate. Some even argue that defining a placebo and treatment does not make sense given the nature of education; hence, accumulation of evidence over time and qualitative studies are a more meaningful means of determining what works (Olson, 2004).

If a decision is made to conduct a randomized experimental study, Cook et al. (2003b) offer some helpful advice. They suggest that, rather than asking a broad question such as, "Do computers enhance learning?" (p. 18), the evaluator should formulate a more precise question that will address the incremental impact of technology within a more global experience of technology use. The authors illustrate, for example, how a study could be designed around a narrower question: "What effect does Internet research have on student learning?" (p. 19). Rather than simply comparing students who do research on the Internet with those who do not, they created a factorial design in which the presence or absence of Internet research is linked to whether teachers do or do not instruct students on best practices for Internet research. The result is four experimental conditions: best practice with Internet, best practice without Internet, typical Internet practice, and a control group whose teacher neither encourages nor discourages students from doing Internet research. The authors' recommendation echoes that offered by Carol Weiss some time ago when she made the point that the control group does not necessarily have to receive no treatment at all; it can receive a lesser version of the treatment program (Weiss, 1972). This advice is particularly relevant when speaking of technology, as it is commonly used by students today either in classrooms or outside of school, so to expect that the control group contains students who do not use technology would be unrealistic.

A problem that Cook et al. (2003b) mention only in passing is that of sample size and units of analysis—key considerations in an experimental study. In a report commissioned by the U.S. Institute of Education Sciences, Agodini et al. (2003) analyzed these issues when developing specifications for a national study on the effectiveness of technology applications on student achievement in mathematics and reading. The authors concluded that an effect size of 0.35 would be a reasonable minimum goal for such a study because previous studies of technology have detected effects of this size, and it was judged to be sufficiently large to close the achievement gaps between various segments of the student population. An effect size of 0.35 means that the effect of the treatment is 35% larger than the standard deviation of the outcome measure being considered. To achieve this effect size would require the following number of students under the given conditions of random assignment:

- *Students randomly assigned to treatments* would require 10 classrooms with 20 students in each (total of 200 students).
- *Classrooms randomly assigned to treatments* would require 30 classrooms with 20 students in each (total of 600 students) for a study of the effects of technology on reading achievement; however, 40 classrooms with 20 students (total of 800 students) would be

required for mathematics because of statistical considerations on the way mathematics scores cluster.

- *Schools randomly assigned to treatments* would require 29 schools with 20 students in each (total of 1160 students).

The first condition of random assignment of students to treatment is not likely a very feasible option in most schools, so the evaluator is left with the choice of random assignment to classrooms or to schools, both of which would require many more students. The result is that an evaluation of technology using an experimental design would likely be a fairly costly undertaking if these guidelines are followed.

Unfortunately, even random assignment to classrooms or schools may be problematic; therefore, the evaluator is left with having to compare intact classes, a design that is weak (Campbell et al., 1966). Finding teachers or students from an intact class to act as a comparison group is difficult. Even if their cooperation is obtained, so many possible competing hypotheses could explain any differences found between experimental and comparison groups (e.g., the comparison group may have an exceptional teacher or the students in the experimental group may be more motivated) that they undermine the validity of the findings.

When the goal of the study is program improvement rather than proving the program works, qualitative approaches such as those of Stake and of Guba described earlier in this chapter are particularly appropriate. Owston (2000) argued that the mixing of both qualitative and quantitative methods shows stronger potential for capturing and understanding the richness and complexity of e-learning environments than if either approach is used solely. Although some methodologists may argue against mixing research paradigms, I take a more pragmatic stance that stresses the importance and predominance of the research questions over the paradigm. This approach frees the evaluator to choose whatever methods are most appropriate to answer the questions once they are articulated. Ultimately, as Feuer et al. (2002) pointed out, "No method is good, bad, scientific, or unscientific in itself; rather, it is the appropriate application of method to a particular problem that enables judgments about scientific quality."

## Data Sources and Analysis

When the basic design of the study is developed, the next decision will be to determine the evaluation data sources. Generally, the best strategy is to use as many different sources as practical, such as test scores or scores on other dependent measures, individual and focus group interviews of students and teachers, Web-based survey data, relevant program documents, and classroom observation. The use of multiple data sources is standard practice in qualitative evaluation, as the need to triangulate observations is essential (Patton, 2002). In experimental studies, other qualitative and quantitative data sources may be used to help explain and interpret observed differences on dependent measures.

Log files generated by Web servers are a relatively new source of data that can be used to triangulate findings from surveys and interviews when the technology being evaluated is Web based. These files contain a record of communication between a Web browser and a Web server in text-based form. The files vary slightly depending on the type of server, but most Web servers record the following information:

- Address of the computer requesting a file
- Date and time of the request
- Web address of the file requested
- Method used for the requested file
- Return code from the Web server that specifies if the request was successful or failed and why
- Size of the file requested

Web server log files do not reveal or record the content of a Web browser request—only the fact that a request was made. Because each Web page has a distinct address, it is possible to determine that a user viewed a particular page. Log files grow to be exceedingly large and are often discarded by system administrators; however, evaluators can analyze the files using commercial tools such as WebTrends Log Analyzer (http://www.webtrends.com) or freeware tools such as AWStats (http://awstats.sourceforge.net). Output from the tools can be in tabular or graphical format (see Figure 45.2 for sample output). The tools can be used by the evaluator to answer questions such as what time of day or week users were accessing the system, how long they were logged into the system, what pages they viewed, and what paths they followed through the website. Figure 45.2 is typical of the graphical output that may be obtained on the average number of users visiting a website per day of the week.

The author and his colleagues have used log file analysis successfully in several technology evaluation studies. In one study, Wideman et al. (1998) found that students in a focus group said they made frequent use of a simulation routine in an online course, but the log files revealed that the routine was seldom used. In another study, Cook et al. (2003a)

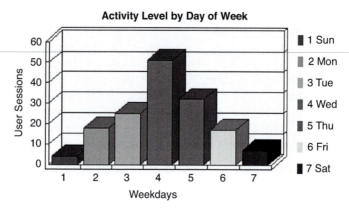

**Figure 45.2** Sample output from log file analysis.

were able to correlate student access to a university course website to final course grades to obtain an indicator of how helpful the site was to students. The researchers were able to obtain these data because the website required students to log in, and a record of each log-in appeared in the log file which could be matched to the student grades. Log-file analysis has some limitations (Haigh and Megarity, 1998), but we found that it provided more and better quality data than are generated by, for example, the course management system WebCT (http://www.webct.com).

Another tool developed by the author and his colleagues to aid in the evaluation of technology-based learning is the Virtual Usability Lab (VULab) (Owston et al., 2005). VULab was originally developed for educational game research, but it is applicable to any Web-based learning research where the learner's computer is connected to the Internet. The tool allows for the automated integration of a wide range of sources of data, ranging from user activity logs, online demographic questionnaire responses, and data from automatically triggered pop-up questions (see example in Figure 45.3) to the results of queries designed to automatically appear at key points when users interact with the application. Another feature of VULab is its capability to record the screens and voice conversations of remote users and store the files on the VULab server without the need to install special software on the users' computers. The data that are collected are stored in an integrated database system, allowing for subsequent data mining and *ad hoc* querying of the data by researchers. VULab also allows for ease of use for researchers in setting up the parameters for studies and automatically monitoring users whether they are interacting with computers locally or are scattered across the Internet. Owston et al. (2005) reported on how VULab was used to record student discussions when they were filling out an online questionnaire after play-

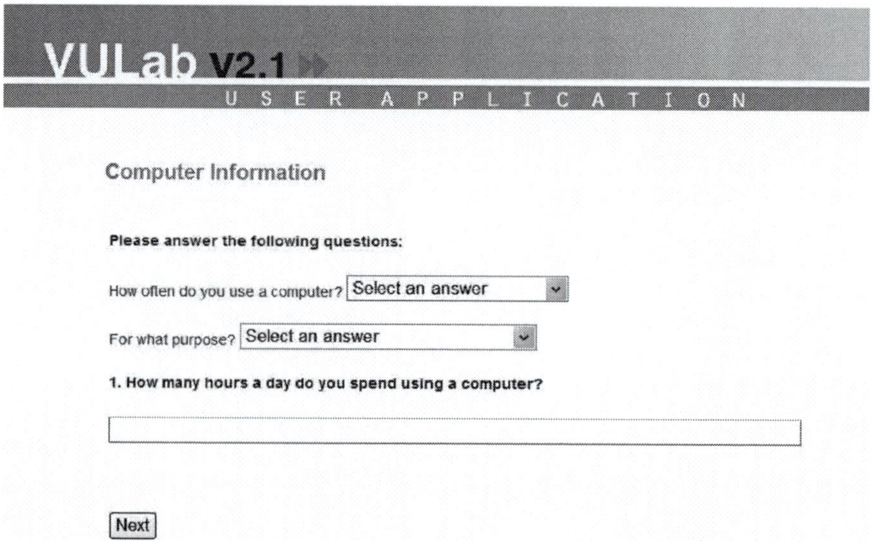

**Figure 45.3** Screen shot of VULab.

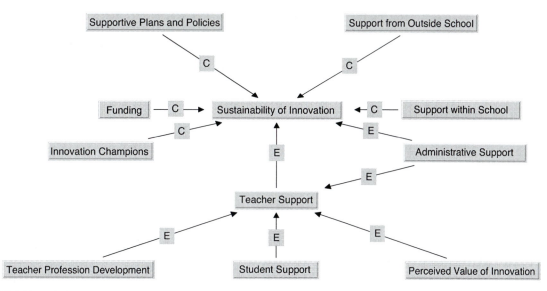

**Figure 45.4** Essential (E) and contributing (C) factors to the sustainability of innovative use of technology in the classroom. (Adapted from Owston, R.D., *J. Educ. Change*, 8(1), 61–77, 2007.)

ing an online game. The students were asked on the questionnaire whether or not they enjoyed playing the game, and a rich discussion of several minutes' duration ensued among a small group of students playing the game at one computer. When it came time to enter their responses into the questionnaire form, they simply entered "yes"; thus, valuable user feedback would have been lost if it had not been for the VULab recording. The tool also proved useful for identifying role playing among the groups of students playing the game, intra-group competition and collaboration, and pinpointing technical problems within the game itself.

Frequently, evaluations involve collecting large quantities of qualitative data, such as interview transcripts, open-ended responses to questionnaires, diaries, field notes, program documents, and minutes of meetings. Managing and analyzing these files can be simplified using qualitative data analysis (QDA) software tools. Two of the most popular QDA tools are Atlas.ti (http://atlasti.com/) and NVivo (http://www.qsrinternational.com/). These tools do not perform the analysis, but they help in the coding and interpretation of the data. Both of these tools also have a feature that allows researchers to visually map relationships between codes that may lead to theory development; for example, Owston (2007) studied factors that contribute to the sustainability of innovative classroom use of technology. Using Atlas.ti, he mapped the relationships among codes and developed a model (see Figure 45.4) that helps explain why teachers are likely to sustain innovative pedagogical practices using technology. Atlas.ti allows the importing of audio and video files as well as textual files, whereas NVivo does not.

In Atlas.ti, these files are coded the same way as textual files; in NVivo, the files cannot be directly imported but coding of external video and audio files can be done. If a project involves only audio or video, the best strategy may be to use Transana (http://transana.org) which is a free, open-source tool designed for the analysis of these kinds of files. A helpful feature of Transana is that while audio or video files are being played a typist can transcribe the voices directly into a separate window within the application.

An excellent website maintained by the Computer-Assisted Qualitative Data Analysis (CAQDAS) Networking Project (see http://caqdas.soc.surrey.ac.uk/) in the United Kingdom provides independent academic comparisons of popular qualitative data analysis tools and as well as other helpful resources and announcements. Those new to computerized analysis of qualitative data are well advised to visit this website for guidance in selecting the most appropriate tool to use in an evaluation.

## Dissemination

A final issue that needs addressing is the dissemination of evaluation findings. The American Evaluation Association's *Guiding Principles for Evaluators* (see http://www.eval.org/Publications/GuidingPrinciples. asp) provides valuable advice to evaluators who are disseminating their results. Evaluators should communicate their methods and approaches accurately and in sufficient detail to allow others to understand, interpret, and critique their work. They should make clear the limitations of an evaluation and its results.

Evaluators should discuss in a contextually appropriate way those values, assumptions, theories, methods, results, and analyses significantly affecting the interpretation of the evaluative findings. These statements apply to all aspects of the evaluation, from its initial conceptualization to the eventual use of findings.

Beyond this, the final report should contain no surprises for the stakeholders if evaluators are doing their job properly. That means that there should be an ongoing dialog between the evaluators and stakeholders, including formal and informal progress reports. This allows for the stakeholders to make adjustments to the program while it is in progress. At the same time, it is a way of gradually breaking news to the stakeholders if it looks as though serious problems are occurring with the program. Surprising stakeholders at the end of a project with bad news is one way to ensure that the evaluation report will be buried and never seen again! All the evaluation models reviewed in this chapter encourage, to varying degrees, continuous dialog between evaluators and stakeholders for these reasons. The end result should be that the evaluation report is used and its recommendations or implications are given due consideration.

## CONCLUSIONS

The challenge facing evaluators of technology-based programs is to design studies that can provide the feedback needed to enhance their design or to provide evidence on their effectiveness. Evaluators need to look broadly across the field of program evaluation theory to help discern the critical elements required for a successful evaluation undertaking. These include attention to aspects such as the audience of the report and their information needs, deciding to what extent the study will be influenced by stated objectives, whether a comparative design will be used, and if quantitative, qualitative, or a combination of methods will be brought into play. The study should also be guided by the criteria and approaches developed for or applicable to the evaluation of e-learning. When these steps are taken, evaluators will be well on their way to devising studies that will be able to answer some of the pressing issues facing teaching and learning with technology.

## REFERENCES

Agodini, R., Dynarski, M., Honey, M., and Levin, D. (2003). *The Effectiveness of Educational Technology: Issues and Recommendations for the National Study, Draft.* Washington, D.C.: U.S. Department of Education.

Baker, E. L. and Herman, J. L. (2003). Technology and evaluation. In *Evaluating Educational Technology: Effective Research Designs for Improving Learning*, edited by G. Haertel and B. Means, pp. 133–168. New York: Teachers College Press.*

Bates, A. and Poole, G. (2003). *Effective Teaching with Technology in Higher Education.* San Francisco, CA: Jossey-Bass.

Bickman, L. (1987). The functions of program theory. In *Using Program Theory in Evaluation: New Directions for Program Evaluation*, Vol. 33, edited by L. Bickman, pp. 5–18. San Francisco, CA: Jossey-Bass.*

Bonk, C. J. and Cummings, J. A. (1998). A dozen recommendations for placing the student at the centre of Web-based learning. *Educ. Media Int.*, 35(2), 82–89.

Bonk, C. J., Wisher, R. A., and Lee, J. (2003). Moderating learner-centered e-learning: problems and solutions, benefits and implications. In *Online Collaborative Learning: Theory and Practice*, edited by T. S. Roberts, pp. 54–85. Hershey, PA: Idea Group Publishing.

Campbell, D. T., Stanley, J. C., and Gage, N. L. (1966). *Experimental and Quasi-Experimental Designs for Research.* Chicago, IL: Rand McNally.*

Chickering, A. and Ehrmann, S. C. (1996). *Implementing the Seven Principles: Technology As Lever*, http://www.tltgroup.org/Seven/Home.htm.

Chickering, A. and Gamson, Z. (1987). Seven principles of good practice in undergraduate education. *AAHE Bull.*, 39, 3–7 (http://www.tltgroup.org/Seven/Home.htm).

Cook, K., Cohen, A. J., and Owston, R. D. (2003a). *If You Build It, Will They Come? Students' Use of and Attitudes towards Distributed Learning Enhancements in an Introductory Lecture Course*, Institute for Research on Learning Technologies Technical Report 2003-1. Toronto: York University (http://www.yorku.ca/irlt/reports.html).

Cook, T. D. (2000). The false choice between theory-based evaluation and experimentation. *New Direct. Eval. Challenges Oppor. Program Theory Eval.*, 87, 27–34.

Cook, T. D., Means, B., Haertel, G., and Michalchik, V. (2003b). The case for using randomized experiments in research on newer educational technologies: a critique of the objections raised and alternatives. In *Evaluating Educational Technology: Effective Research Designs for Improving Learning*, edited by G. Haertel and B. Means. New York: Teachers College Press.

Cronbach, L. J. (1980). *Toward Reform of Program Evaluation.* San Francisco, CA: Jossey-Bass.*

Eisner, E. W. (1979). *The Educational Imagination: On the Design and Evaluation of School Programs.* New York: Macmillan.*

Feuer, M. J., Towne, L., and Shavelson, R. J. (2002). Scientific culture and educational research. *Educ. Res.*, 31, 4–14.

Graham, C., Cagiltay, K., Craner, J., Lim, B., and Duffy, T. M. (2000). *Teaching in a Web-Based Distance Learning Environment: An Evaluation Summary Based on Four Courses*, Center for Research on Learning and Technology Technical Report No. 13-00. Bloomington: Indiana University (http://crlt.indiana.edu/publications/crlt00-13.pdf).

Guba, E. G. (1978). *Toward a Method of Naturalistic Inquiry in Educational Evaluation*, Center for the Study of Evaluation Monograph Series No. 8. Los Angeles: University of California at Los Angeles.*

Guskey, T. R. (2000). *Evaluating Professional Development.* Thousand Oaks, CA: Corwin Press.

Haigh, S. and Megarity, J. (1998). *Measuring Web Site Usage: Log File Analysis*. Ottawa, ON: National Library of Canada (http://www.collectionscanada.ca/9/1/p1-256-e.html).

Kirkpatrick, D. L. (2001). *Evaluating Training Programs: The Four Levels*, 2 ed. San Francisco, CA: Berrett-Koehler.*

Mandinach, E. B. (2005). The development of effective evaluation methods for e-learning: a concept paper and action plan. *Teachers Coll. Rec.*, 107(8), 1814–1835.

Olson, D. R. (2004). The triumph of hope over experience in the search for 'what works': a response to Slavin. *Educ. Res.*, 33(1), 24–26.

Owston, R. D. (2000). Evaluating Web-based learning environments: strategies and insights. *CyberPsychol. Behav.*, 3(1), 79–87.*

Owston, R. D. (2007). Contextual factors that sustain innovative pedagogical practice using technology: an international study. *J. Educ. Change*, 8(1), 61–77.

Owston, R. D. and Wideman, H. H. (1999). *Internet-Based Courses at Atkinson College: An Initial Assessment*, Centre for the Study of Computers in Education Technical Report No. 99-1. Toronto: York University (http://www.yorku.ca/irlt/reports.html).

Owston, R. D., Kushniruk, A., Ho, F., Pitts, K., and Wideman, H. (2005). Improving the design of Web-based games and simulations through usability research. In *Proceedings of the ED-MEDIA 2005: World Conference on Educational, Multimedia, Hypermedia, and Telecommunications*, June 29–July 1, Montreal, Canada, pp. 1162–1167.

Patton, M. Q. (1978). *Utilization-Focused Evaluation*. Beverly Hills, CA: SAGE.*

Patton, M. Q. (2002). *Qualitative Evaluation and Research Methods*, 3rd ed. Thousand Oaks, CA: SAGE.

Ravitz, J. (1998). Evaluating learning networks: a special challenge for Web-based instruction. In *Web-Based Instruction*, edited by B. Khan, pp. 361–368. Englewood Cliffs, NJ: Educational Technology Publications.

Riel, M. and Harasim, L. (1994). Research perspectives on network learning. *Machine-Mediated Learning*, 4(2/3), 91–113.

Rogers, P. J., Hacsi, T. A., Petrosino, A., and Huebner, T. A., Eds. (2000). *Program Theory in Evaluation Challenges and Opportunities: New Directions for Evaluation, No. 87*. San Francisco, CA: Jossey-Bass.

Scanlon, E., Jones, A., Barnard, J., Thompson, J., and Calder, J. (2000). Evaluating information and communication technologies for learning. *Educ. Technol. Soc.*, 3(4), 101–107.

Scriven, M. (1972). Pros and cons about goal free evaluation. *Eval. Comm.*, 3(4), 1–7.*

Stake, R. E. (1975). *Evaluating the Arts in Education: A Responsive Approach*. Columbus, OH: Merrill.*

Suchman, E. (1967). *Evaluative Research: Principles and Practice in Public Service and Social Action Programs*. New York: Russell Sage Foundation.

Stufflebeam, D. L. (1973). An introduction to the PDK book: educational evaluation and decision-making. In *Educational Evaluation: Theory and Practice*, edited by B. L. Worthern and J. R. Sanders, pp. 128–142. Belmont, CA: Wadsworth.*

Tyler, R. W. (1942). General statement on evaluation. *J. Educ. Res.*, 35, 492–501.

Weiss, C. H. (1972). *Evaluation Research: Methods for Assessing Program Effectiveness*. Englewood Cliffs, NJ: Prentice Hall.*

Wideman, H. H., Owston, R. D., and Quann, V. (1998). *A Formative Evaluation of the VITAL Tutorial 'Introduction to Computer Science,'* Centre for the Study of Computers in Education Technical Report No. 98-1. Toronto: York University (http://www.yorku.ca/irlt/reports.html).

Worthen, B. L. and Sanders, J. R. (1987). *Educational Evaluation: Alternative Approaches and Practical Guidelines*. New York: Longman.*

---

* Indicates a core reference.

# 46

# Change Agentry

*Brian Beabout and Alison A. Carr-Chellman*
Pennsylvania State University, University Park, Pennsylvania

## CONTENTS

## ABSTRACT

This chapter presents theoretical foundations and empirical findings of the construct of change agentry in order to aid change agents and scholars in effecting substantive organizational or educational change. Familiarity with this literature gives credibility to those of us in the educational communications and technology field seeking to effect significant change through collaborative efforts. We begin by defining change agentry and focusing on the theoretical foundations of change theories, agency theories, and diffusion theories. After this consideration of theoretical constructs, we turn to an examination of the empirical findings in research studies associated with K–12 school contexts, government organizations, corporations, and the healthcare industry. Our findings indicate three core ideas central to change agentry: (1) connecting an organization to its environment is important, (2) flexibly adaptive change may be a desired goal, and (3) local leaders as well as external supports are needed to support any successful change effort.

## KEYWORDS

*Change agentry:* The activity of facilitating change.

*Lethal adaptation:* An alteration to an innovation that undermines the expected benefits of the innovation.

*Loose coupling:* An organizational arrangement characterized by significant freedom between levels in the hierarchy.

*Mutual adaptation:* The coevolution of both an innovation and the environment in which it is implemented.

*Perturbances:* Events that cause a small disruption in organizational function; useful for encouraging reflection on an organization's purposes.

*Punctuated equilibrium:* A view of organizational change characterized by long periods of stasis and short periods of change.

*Reculturing:* Changes that involve examining the assumptions and purposes of an organization.

*Restructuring:* Changes that involve organizational structure, new work patterns, or new functions.

## DEFINING CHANGE AGENTRY

Suchan (2005, p. 17) defines change as "a planned activity whose goal is to realign the organization with its environment." Within instructional technology we keep hoping that whatever new or improved technologies we have to offer will revolutionize our classrooms and our organizations; yet, this has rarely been the case (Cuban, 1986). Instead, we have seen one wave after another of relatively incremental but minor changes with very little substantive impact of any technologies on the system of the school or organization. This has led the field of instructional technology to take very seriously the importance of understanding and facilitating change (Ellsworth, 2000; Ely, 1976). We have come to understand that to best create the effective *use* of our excellently designed human learning environments we must first figure out *how* to get people to use our designs rather than resisting, battling, refusing, or sabotaging our efforts. Although a good design is only as good as its actual implementation, we must recognize that our innovations exist in immensely complex webs of rela-

tionships and that *understanding*, not manipulation, must feature prominently in any discussion of change agentry. Indeed, we define change agentry as those activities of education and facilitation through which organizational stakeholders inhabit a new state *of their own design*. Now, this last, as we will see in this chapter, is not part of the traditional understanding of change agentry but more a part of user-design (Banathy, 1991; Carr-Chellman, 2007); however, we feel that true change agentry is, in fact, centered on facilitation of communities, organizations, and stakeholders.

## THEORETICAL FOUNDATIONS OF CHANGE AGENTRY

This facilitation process is grounded in a number of theoretical approaches to change. Van de Ven and Poole (1995) offered a typology of four change theories including life-cycle theories, teleological theories, dialectical theories, and evolutionary theories. Although we find this typology useful, a more process-oriented distinction is used here as we describe individual and organizational change theories, developmental change theories, and diffusion theories. Within this we include what little there is on agency theories that is relevant.

### Individual/Organizational Change Theories

Individual and organizational change theories are perhaps the most complicated set of theories associated with change agentry and surely the most relevant. Among these, one of the earliest is Lewin's (1951) planned change theories, which have given us the typically understood unfreeze–change–refreeze cycle. Lewin's work has been debated and criticized, in part due to the recent phenomenon of increasingly rapid cycles of freezing and unfreezing which leave organizations in a state of constant change.

A less cyclical theory of change was posited by Burke and Schmidt (1971), who argued that the group is the proper level of analysis for organizational change. Within such organizational change theories there are distinctions between episodic change (Abernathy and Utterback, 1978) and continuous change (Weick and Quinn, 1999). There is a traditional view of change in which longer periods of small, incremental changes are interrupted by brief periods of discontinuous and radical change (Brown and Eisenhardt, 1997). This episodic view of change has been termed *punctuated equilibrium* (Abernathy and Utterback, 1978) and produces the image of a rational organization that works according to plan unless dramatic external events (economic shifts, social conditions) force the organization to change. Change agents working in this episodic paradigm are primary actors in the overall change process as they generate responses to external events, build management support, and manage implementation (Weick and Quinn, 1999).

This view is contrasted with *continuous* change in which organizations act in unpredictable ways that are based on the actions of individual group members seeking to satisfy their social and professional needs. Weick and Quinn (1999, p. 375) described continuous change as that in which "small continuous adjustments, made continuously across units, can cumulate and create substantial change." This much more decentralized view of the change process, influenced by chaos and complexity theories and elements of complex system dynamics, requires a different role for change agents. Change agentry becomes more about responsiveness and facilitation as opposed to goal setting and motivating others. The differences between these two views of change, episodic and continuous, will have great implications on the role of change agents.

French and Raven (1959) described change with their social influence theory. According to the Evidenced-Based Intervention Work Group (EBIWG) at the University of Wisconsin–Madison, this theory focuses on "the power of one individual to change the beliefs, attitudes, or behaviors of another" (EBIWG, 2005, p. 476). Models of social influence have been developed that contain such components as physical attractiveness, position in the organizational hierarchy, interpersonal social history, and the perceived ability to distribute rewards or punishments (Cialdini, 2001; French and Raven, 1959; Yukl, 1994). Individuals who possess certain characteristics are more likely to be change agents than individuals without them. Social influence theory informs our discussion of change agency by emphasizing the importance of the *people* who introduce and implement reforms. This theoretical framework shows that if an unpopular leader presents a proposed change to an organization, the reform may be instantly undermined by the leader's lack of social influence. An approach that might minimize the negative effect of unpopular individuals is to create a social space in which *groups* of individuals can examine data about current organizational performance and participate in dialog about improving performance. Such a process would likely be more time consuming than management-driven change, but it would also be likely to increase stakeholder commitment and decrease resistance.

## Developmental Change Theories

Developmental change takes the traditional notions of change beyond the focus on individual pieces to a wider, broader notion of how change occurs across an entire system. Systemic change theories bring to the foreground the *ripple effects* that cause disruptions far from the site of the initial change, much like occurs in a pond when a stone is thrown into it. When change happens in one part of a system, interdependencies cause the rest of the system to react (Hutchins, 1996). The application of these ideas to K–12 schooling has been undertaken by Banathy (1991), Squire and Reigeluth (2000), and Jenlink et al. (1998).

Another theory that views change as a developmental process is the Concerns-Based Adoption Model (CBAM), for which Hall and Hord (1987) identified seven *stages of concern* that characterize the *attitudes* of potential adopters toward a given innovation. These stages range from no knowledge of the innovation to concerns about how the innovation might fit into existing structures to adapting the innovation to serve functions beyond its original intention. The focus here is on understanding the attitudes of stakeholders who, in their roles as *street-level bureaucrats* (Weatherly and Lipsky, 1977) ultimately decide the fate of a change effort.

The focus on the use of the innovation makes CBAM more appropriate with first-order (*morphostasis*) as opposed to second-order change (*morphogenesis*) (Mink et al., 1993). First-order changes that do not alter the core process of an organization (such as utilizing computers instead of textbooks for reading instruction) are easily observed with the "levels of use" checklist; however, second-order changes that more fundamentally alter practice (establishing a community relations office) are not quickly or easily measured by an outside observer. The need for dialog and overall mindset change required for second-order changes is not accommodated in CBAM; however, its utility for the implementation of first-order changes has been well established empirically (Ellsworth, 2000). Work in this area of special interest to educational technologists is that of Caffarella (2000).

## Diffusion Theory

Diffusion theory focuses on the rather unpredictable path that an innovation will follow from its conception to the divergent endpoints of implementation or rejection. Although theorists have sought to describe the many paths a given innovation might take along the way, it must be said that the number of forces at play in any social organization make prediction a nearly impossible task. In relation to the change theories discussed earlier, these diffusion theories keep the innovation at the center of the frame and deal with cultural, environmental, and individual forces as bumps along the road to adoption. Any serious discussion of diffusion begins with the seminal work of Rogers (2003) and his studies of the diffusion of hybrid corn among farmers in the United States. Based on his theories and research, he identified five perceived attributes of an innovation that influence its rate of adoption:

- *Relative advantage*—How well the innovation outperforms the current methods. The more potential adopters view the innovation as better than their current method, the more quickly diffusion will take place.
- *Compatibility*—How well the innovation can peacefully coexist with the work environment in which it is to be adopted. If the environment cannot accept the innovation, it will not diffuse widely.
- *Complexity*—Adopters are more likely to utilize an innovation that they understand and that does not take excessive effort to learn.
- *Trialability*—The extent to which an innovation can be test driven before a wholesale adoption takes place. Users are more likely to try out, and thus adopt, an innovation if it does not cost them anything to do so.
- *Observability*—An innovation is more likely to diffuse rapidly if the benefits to early adopters can be seen by those still hesitant about the innovation.

It has been long expressed that diffusion research is often biased toward successful innovation (Ellsworth, 2000; Rogers, 2003), and this point is not argued here nor is the point that Rogers original works were, relatively speaking, colonialist in nature. But, the frameworks for thinking about change and the vocabulary given to change research by Rogers are invaluable gifts.

## EMPIRICAL STUDIES OF CHANGE AGENTRY

### K–12 Change Agentry

Perhaps the largest body of empirical work is that of change agentry in K–12 (kindergarten to twelfth grade) schools. Empirical work focused on change agents in K–12 environments is fairly widespread and shows the difficulty of changing the deeply ingrained social institution of school. With regard to school change, Fullan (2000, p. 581) wrote that "there has been strong adoption and implementation, but not strong institutionalization." In other words, although school reforms have been dreamed up and tried out regularly, few of them seem to stick, and the result is little fundamental change in schooling practices. With several decades of mostly failed school reforms behind us (Fullan, 2001; Sarason, 1990), attention is being focused on what processes, actions, and mindsets are most helpful in getting meaningful changes to sustain themselves within schools. In this research, many things or people may serve as change agents: governmental policies (Borko et al., 2003), district leaders (Spillane, 2002), school principals (Avissar et al., 2003), classroom teachers (Olsen and Kirtman, 2002), student teachers (Lane et al., 2003), community groups (Arriaza, 2004), K–12 and university partnerships (Fishman et al., 2004; Rust and Freidus, 2001), K–12 and business partnerships (Corcoran and Lawrence, 2003), and even students themselves (Fielding, 2001). Despite this vast array of "stuff" that can fit under the title of change agent, there are some common characteristics that appear in the empirical research.

### Change Agents Connect Organizations to Their Environment

The first clear message from the research on K–12 change is that change agents must connect organizations to their environment. The people, resources, new ideas, feedback, and political support that school systems can receive from this reaching out process are vital to any successful change effort. Despite the many potential benefits to forging strong connections with the environment, however, there are risks as well. Fullan (2000) termed this phase of school change the *inside-out story*, in which, paradoxically, "most outside forces that have moved inside threaten schools in some way, but they are also necessary for success" (p. 582). In other words, these forces demand that schools take those uncomfortable glances in the mirror that often lead to positive change within the institution.

In their survey study of 110 Israeli elementary school principals, Avissar et al. (2003) examined the inclusion of Israeli special education students in regular education classes and found that the passage of a national law in 1998 had a significant impact on the number of principals who implemented the reform. This instance of policy as change agent demonstrates the influence a system's environment can have on how changes are implemented. While policies do not translate directly into predictable cause-and-effect responses in schools, they do exert considerable influence on the change process. Similarly, in an exploratory study of a local parent group organizing to put pressure on the school system to better accommodate the growing number of Spanish-speaking families, Arriaza (2004, p. 10) noted "that school reform initiatives have higher chances of becoming institutionalized when the community actively participates as an empowered change agent." Through analysis of historical documents, interviews with participants in the movement, and interviews with current educators, Arriaza traced one example of a community exerting tremendous force on schooling practices. Although the community as change agent featured in his study was not invited by the school to help facilitate the change process, they were nonetheless able to exert enough environmental pressure to create lasting changes in their school system.

Two-way lines of communication between a community and its schools undoubtedly lead to a healthier system in terms of getting community support and meeting community needs, but there is also a heightened state of uncertainty because changes in the economic, social, or political landscape can put unwanted pressure on schools. Reaching out into the environment presents some danger in that schools will be working with groups (parents, businesses, universities, funding agencies, etc.) who might have very different views of what education can, and should, be. Change agents will face difficulty in reconciling these diverse views in pursuit of a successful reform effort (EBIWG, 2005). Fishman et al. (2004, p. 67) described a project in Tennessee where "local politics created unforeseen challenges to a project that was otherwise successful." Change efforts are always subject to environmental pressures, so a wise reformer keeps a close eye on environmental trends that might impact an ongoing change. As Fullan (2000, p. 583) noted:

> Schools need the outside to get the job done. These external forces, however, do not come in helpful packages; they are an amalgam of complex and uncoordinated phenomena. The work of the school is to figure out how to make its relationship with them a productive one.

Schools that actively seek energy for change from their environment can turn a contentious relationship between a school and its community into a productive one. In her interpretive case study of a school considered a high implementer of information technology, Tearle (2003) concluded that schools that proactively search their surroundings for potential changes may be more likely to implement information technology reform than those schools who do not. She found that a "recognised

model commonly adopted in the school for implementation of a 'project' or curriculum development" (Tearle, 2003, p. 574) was a sign that a school was regularly interfacing with its environment and poised to take advantage of opportunities that came along.

The strength of the school–community relationship has led some to support the use of intermediary organizations to buffer specific change efforts from the constantly changing environment in which it exists. Corcoran and Lawrence (2003) described a K–12 and corporate partnership that worked with four school districts to improve science teaching. Their longitudinal evaluation study combined survey, interview, and observational data with student test scores in science. The authors were positive about the role of the external nonprofit organization that sponsored the program, saying that (Corcoran and Lawrence, 2003, p. 34):

> Reform support organizations can help school districts stay focused. They can legitimate strategies and policies, build public support, and buy the time to make them work... Intermediaries often are able to shape the stakeholders' definition of the "problem" and build a more stable reform agenda. Unlike schools and districts, they are not subject to direct political authority and are more focused in their aims.

Although change agentry should include connecting an organization with its environment as a top priority, there must also be an awareness that some protections, such as partnering with supportive organizations, must be created to prevent the reform effort from collapsing under the turbulence of daily life (Bodilly et al., 2004).

Additional research has also supported the use of external change facilitators to increase the success of a change effort (Goldenberg, 2003; Jenlink et al., 1998; Lane et al., 2003). In a unique case, Lane and colleagues (2003) describe the influences that change-oriented student teachers had on their mentor teachers while student teaching in the Los Angeles Unified School District. Their study analyzed written student teacher reflections as well as mentor teacher interviews to examine the impact that preservice teachers could have when trained to be critical practitioners. This case of student teacher as change-agent emphasizes the understanding that, whereas we generally view institutional power and the ability to cause change as being highly correlated, those with little official power are also able to create positive change. The external supports these student teachers received from the university (emotional support, critical dialog in courses, etc.) are shown to have been important parts of their ability to act as change agents in their placement schools.

An organization's environment is also an important source for well-designed theories of change. These theories can guide a facilitator along the process (Reigeluth, 2004). These theories can connect change facilitators with each other and lead to refinements in the reform process. Just a sampling of school change theories includes the Guidance System for Transforming Education (GSTE) (Jenlink et al., 1998), Step-Up-to-Excellence (Duffy, 2006), the professional development approach (Caine, 2006), user-design (Carr-Chellman and Almeida, 2006), and chaos theory (Reigeluth, 2004). When schools and change agents are cognizant of the theories that seek to describe and predict change, they have a scaffold that can support them toward seeing the process through to completion.

## K–12 Change Is Wholly Dependent on Teacher Change

Traditional planned change often seeks to take the scientifically validated "right" way to do schooling and transplant it uniformly into a diverse collection of schooling environments; however, current views of change tend to identify the source of change in the day-to-day teaching choices made by teachers in our classrooms, rather than the policy decisions made by reformers at a distance. Fullan (2001, p. 115) noted that "educational change depends on what teachers think and do—it's as simple and as complex as that." Similarly, it has been said that in effecting change, "challenging teachers' current thinking and guiding them toward new understandings was central" (Spillane, 2002, p. 396). If teachers and their thoughts and actions are the center of school change, then how can change agents work toward engaging these overworked and practice-oriented professionals in reform efforts? Strategies for centering change on teachers will guide this section.

It is now taken as fact that the "specificity of context (within which an innovation is tried out) plays a fundamental role for change to be embraced first by individuals, then groups and, eventually, large numbers of people" (Arriaza, 2004, p. 14). A study by Olsen and Kirtman (2002) involving interviews with a variety of stakeholders from 36 California schools showed that the importance of a teacher's context is ignored at the peril of any proposed change effort. Once classroom doors are closed, "regardless of a school's efforts, teachers *will* mediate school reforms in various—and identifiable—ways; schools may wish to appropriate this force for constructive means rather than observe its occurrence passively from the sidelines" (Olsen and Kirtman, 2002, p. 318). So, change agentry in this implementation-centered mindset must be informed by the classroom conditions in which a reform is to be implemented. If the change effort is the seed that will yield a better school, then we must pay as much attention to the soil as we do to the type of seed.

In the RAND change agent studies of the 1970s, the concept of *mutual adaptation* was developed to explain the process in which a school would alter an external reform idea to meet its own local needs (Berman and McLaughlin, 1975). In their examination of observational and survey data from 293 reform projects in U.S. schools, they concluded that both the reform *and* the school itself would change during the process of implementation. Given this idea, high fidelity with the original design did not necessarily contribute to a successful change effort. This notion "recognizes the importance of local re-invention of innovations in order to better match the norms (and capacity) of the adopting organization" (Fishman et al., 2004, p. 66). Given the rationalist roots of the study of change, the term *lethal adaptation* (Bron and Campione, 1994) entered our language to describe innovations that are altered locally in a way that their original purposes are not met. Researchers in the field have said that "we faced an inherent challenge of this [mutual adaptation] approach—variations that cause innovations to become very different than originally envisioned, potentially weakening the impact of the innovation" (Fishman et al., 2004, p. 66). As an example, Fishman and his colleagues (2004) found that experienced teachers were so comfortable in deviating from the planned technology innovation that they left out the technology component altogether, which, from the researcher's perspective, sabotaged the entire project.

Change agents must also recognize that teachers are socialized to take instructional ideas from others and adapt them to the needs of their students. In this sense, teachers have always been experts in mutual adaptation. If certain elements of an innovation are crucial to its success, teachers must be given a rationale, space to discuss it with colleagues, and time to experiment for themselves. Fostering the view of teachers "as active agents in their own learning" (Spillane, 2002, p. 391) is a central task of modern change agents. The example of student teacher as change agent given by Lane and colleagues (2003) is a good example of this mindset. Listening to training delivered by "experts" and reading memos drafted from administrators will rarely be sufficient to significantly change teacher practice (Cuban, 2001). For teachers to change their practice in the classroom, they must be given both autonomy and support.

This shift in focus from developing *good programs* to enacting *good implementations* has led to increased attention on the process of implementing reforms in particular schools. As the RAND change agent study concluded (Berman and McLaughlin, 1975, p. 83):

... many project evaluations focus on educational treatments in an attempt to relate them to student outcomes. These efforts may be misguided. Educational treatments, defined solely in terms of their technology or method, were only weakly related to implementation outcomes, because other elements of project design had stronger effects. The analysis showed that a project's implementation strategy affected implementation.

Change agents can influence mutual adaptation (and project success) by their choice of implementation strategy. One approach is through the involvement of teachers in a dialog with each other about a planned change effort. Professional development that allows for regular teacher–consultant contact and delves into the specific issues of classroom implementation were found to increase a project's success (Berman and McLaughlin, 1975).

Communicating reforms in ways that are meaningful to teachers' daily practice is also a relevant strategy. Borko et al. (2003) described this strategy in their case study of six schools considered exemplary models of standards-based reform in Washington state. Building on initial successes, focusing on implementable pieces of a larger reform, and "grafting of reform ideas onto familiar practices" (Knapp, 1997, as cited in Borko et al., 2003, p. 195) are suggested methods of implementing reforms in teacher-friendly ways. Another strategy to assist reform-weary teachers is to ensure that all reforms undertaken are "sustained, innovative efforts" (Borko et al., 2003, p. 199). This long-term commitment to a change effort can be reassuring to teachers who are unfortunately accustomed to losing support when funding cycles or leadership tenures are cut short (Fishman et al., 2004).

### Change Agents Are Vision Builders, Not Technicians

Organizational climate was one of three factors that heavily influenced change in the RAND change agent studies of the 1970s. As McLaughlin (1990, p. 12) later stated: "The local expertise, organizational routines, and resources available to support planned change efforts generate fundamental differences in the ability of practitioners to plan, execute, or sustain an innovative effort." Expertise and routines are deep structures that often implicitly guide the work of people in complex organizations such as schools. To address these deep structures, change agents must guide teachers to ask some fundamental questions of themselves: What is the purpose of our school? What are some unmet needs of our students? Is the community benefiting from our efforts? Change agents undertaking these types of questions are not merely working as techni-

cians, but are acting as facilitators in guiding teachers toward a dialog about where their organization needs to go.

Researchers have distinguished the differences between *restructuring* (Schlechty, 1990) and *reculturing* (Fullan, 2000). Restructuring involves creating new procedures or practices based on someone's new understanding of how schools should work, whereas reculturing involves digging slightly deeper to explicitly address the underlying assumptions that guide everyday teaching practices. Our conception of change agentry aligns more closely with the notion of reculturing. We find that "being a change agent includes both vision (driven by perceptions) and actions taken" (Avissar et al., 2003, p. 362). A "receptive school culture" (Newmann and Welhage, 1995, p. 57) is not one in which passive teachers do as they are told, but one in which professional learning is a value held in esteem. This is a value that is clearly not yet present in all schools, but Cochran-Smith (1991) found such a professional community among preservice teachers and certainly many school staffs exhibit similar characteristics. See the section on individual differences below for more of this discussion.

Change agents are also responsible for the cultivation of a common vision of reform amongst multiple stakeholders. Establishing this vision takes investments in time and capacity building (Jenlink et al., 1998), but change agents who do this will find that teachers will "persevere despite the vicissitudes of the change process" (Corcoran and Lawrence, 2003, p. 34). Vision development need not be the sole responsibility of administrators or outside consultants, however. In their study of school technology coordinators in New Zealand, Lai and Pratt (2004) found that important aspects of their job included visioning and planning to meet that vision. The most important aspect of creating a vision is not where it comes from but that it is communicated and accepted by a wide variety of stakeholders.

Although the creation of a vision is essential, one of the defining characteristics of a vision is that an individual or school can take multiple pathways to meet this vision. As an example of this loose coupling, Newmann and Welhage (1995, p. 37) studied schools in which "the mission for learning was powerful enough to guide instruction, but also flexible enough to encourage debate, discussion, and experimentation within the framework." Their meta-study of school reform research involving four separate studies and over 1000 U.S. schools concluded that reforms were likely to be successful when teachers were encouraged to find their own pathways while still adhering to an overarching vision.

### Get Leadership Approval and Participation

Another nearly universal characteristic of effective change is getting the support of leadership. Borko and colleagues (2003, p. 191) noted in their study of school change in Washington state that "the primary grade facilitator for literacy characterized her [the principal's] leadership as 'very strong' and noted that it was an 'extraordinarily important' factor in the school's success in attaining its reform goals." Although principal leadership and participation are important for the success of a reform effort, their study showed that teacher leadership is important as well (Borko et al., 2003, p.196):

> Leadership—both *principal leadership* and *distributed leadership*—was a key factor in the success of both schools' reform efforts. In fact, it was perhaps the most important factor because of its impact on the other five dimensions of school capacity. [italics in original]

Other researchers have described the benefits of the participation of teacher leaders in change (Fishman et al., 2004; Lai and Pratt, 2004; Olsen and Kirtman, 2002; Tearle, 2003), of principal participation in change (Goldenberg, 2003), and of central office participation in change (Corcoran and Lawrence, 2003). Strong leadership and the allocation of resources and time are likely signals to teachers that a particular reform effort is a legitimate one. Such leadership is clearly not yet present in all schools (Newmann and Welhage, 1995).

### Creation of Community and Individual Professional Development

It has been stated that classrooms of the 21st century look strikingly similar to classrooms of the late 19th century in terms of curriculum, pedagogy, and assessment and that this industrial-age paradigm of schooling based on sorting and ranking students does not meet the needs of our current information-age society (Reigeluth, 1999). If schools are to change to meet the demands of current society, then teachers must learn new ways of doing their work. Honing these new methods will require dialog and experimentation to find instructional practices that work for particular students in particular classrooms; therefore, the creation of a professional community that serves to build both individual and collective capacity is a key element of K–12 change agentry (Corcoran and Lawrence, 2003; Fullan, 2001). The importance of addressing local capacity has been identified as especially important in young reform efforts (Borko et al., 2003). Understandably, even extremely high levels of internal or external pressure for change will not be successful if the teachers do not know how to do what is being asked of them.

Delivering new teaching methods under the training paradigm of professional development has had a suspect history, but "what does make a difference is reculturing: the process of developing professional learning communities in the school. ... Structures can block or facilitate this process, but the development of a professional community must become the key driver of improvement" (Fullan, 2000, p. 582). Professional learning communities are groups of teachers and school leaders who critically examine their teaching practice and seek new ways to address unmet student needs. McLaughlin (1990) identified the Bay Area Writing Project, the Puget Sound Consortium, and the Urban Math Collaborative as groups that capitalized on existing teacher-led communities to foster change in teaching practice. The reculturing that fosters the growth of professional communities allows teachers, often dismissed as mere technicians in the change process, to have considerable influence on the design and implementation of classroom reforms. In their study of student teachers in Los Angeles area schools, Lane et al. (2003) found that the expertise that mentor teachers were accorded by their student teachers actually fostered the critical dialog that led to reflective practice and professional growth. Because the mentors were not threatened by their student teachers, they were perhaps more willing to enter into this important process. Corcoran and Lawrence (2003, p. 26) noted in their study of a science reform program in New Jersey and Pennsylvania schools:

> The increased respect shown for the clinical expertise of teachers and the expectation that they should be consulted in the design of policies and programs and changes in district leaders' perceptions of how teachers learn have contributed to these cultural changes. So too, have the collegial cultures of the summer workshops and the study groups fostered by MISE.

Many reforms have been upended by the fact that teachers are not supported (structurally or socially) in improving their practice with others. Changing this situation and creating the possibility for teachers to develop a professional community may have a positive effect on both the adoption rate of reforms and the quality of implementation.

Ignoring professional development can sidetrack a change effort (Lai and Pratt, 2004), as can doggedly pursuing the appearance of a professional community without allocating adequate time, physical space, and material resources (Fishman et al., 2004). Schools that wish to change should see the professional community as a key component in their preparation for change, for it can both weed out reforms that are unlikely to succeed as well as build support for those that have potential for improving teaching and learning in the local context.

In their study of restructuring in 36 California schools, Olsen and Kirtman (2002) found that the school-wide climate was a primary influence on whether or not individual teachers took reform ideas and used them to change their classroom practice. Supporting this view, Tearle (2003), in her case study of a school with high implementation of information technology, found that the existence of a professional community aided the adoption of the innovation. The school's professional community provided a framework for trying out experimental practices as well as a cadre of leaders who would take the innovation back to their departments and aid in diffusion.

### Individual Differences Matter

It is fitting that this discussion of K–12 change agentry ends with the admission that all of the general topics mentioned above, although supported by empirical evidence, are subject to the immense variety of individual characteristics that help to define a specific reform effort at a specific school. These unique characteristics have led research away from the fidelity perspective of systematic implementation to an "implementation perspective" (McLaughlin, 1990) that highlights the negotiation involved in any change process. As McLaughlin (1990, p. 13) stated, "variability … signals a healthy system, one that is shaping and integrating policy in ways best suited to local resources, traditions, and clientele" (p. 13). These individual quirks that define a local system are absolutely critical in the decisions made in the process of change. A brief examination of some of the individual differences that were uncovered in K–12 change research will illustrate this point.

In their study of Israeli school principals' views and practices concerning a state-mandated special education innovation, Avissar et al. (2003) found that the age of the school principal had an important influence in how this particular reform was interpreted and implemented. Their survey research of 110 elementary school principals found that the older a principal, the less likely he or she was to implement the full-inclusion practices mandated by the government. Fishman et al. (2004) identified comfort with technology and comfort level in deviating from a lesson plan as teacher characteristics that greatly influenced their technology-based change efforts. Also making reference to individual characteristics is the warning of Jenlink et al. (1998) that internal change facilitators, no matter how talented, may carry political baggage that can upset the reform process. Awareness of early adopters who generate interest and resistors who disagree with the goals of reform is an essential aspect of a successful K–12 reform.

## Change Agentry in Non-K–12 Contexts

Although the majority of the empirical work presented in this chapter is on K–12 change, valuable research from other fields has examined change agentry in areas such as government, business, and healthcare. A brief examination of this research both confirms findings from the K–12 research and adds additional insights into the discussion of change agentry which can be very enlightening for educational technologists and others interested in changing human learning.

### Government Change Agentry

In their case study involving a dozen U.K. civil servants working together over 15 months, Kakabadse and Kakabadse (2003) concluded that cultural change was more important than structural change when institutionalization is the goal. Their intensive work on the process of collaborative inquiry (CI) was initiated with the development of shared values that served as springboards for a critique of current practice. They also discussed the importance of perseverance in the difficult task of uncovering unexamined values and critiquing deeply held personal assumptions (Kakabadse and Kakabadse, 2003, p. 379):

> CI is a challenging experience as the process of inquiry confronts the underlying assumptions, values, power base and established ways of working within any situation. CI requires time, resources, social skills, and the ability to share personal experiential knowledge with the group.

As in the K–12 context, it is important to have these conversations and to allow for the appropriate amount of time and supports to complete the process.

In a large-scale survey study conducted by Simmons and Simmons (2004), it was concluded that governmental change is a complicated process that encompasses nearly every issue imaginable. The researchers found racial and educational differences to be at the heart of many of the differences, but they state that, "no single contextual, political, or institutional theory we considered explains all the conflict over government form" (p. 386). The complexities of change on the scale of city government are so great that no single theory can explain it all. The importance of individual differences and supporting open dialog are echoed here.

## *Corporate Change Agentry*

Since the early operations research work by Ackoff (1974), business environments have regularly utilized change agents, often referring to them as *external consultants* (Bennis, 1969, as cited in Kendra and Taplin, 2004). This definition of a consultant is narrower than our definition of change agentry described at the outset of this chapter, but a brief examination of these consultants should help in developing a fuller sense what a change agent is.

These external change agents have been valued for their "ability to affect the organization's power structure in ways that employees as change agents cannot and because they are less subject than employees to implicit and explicit organizational rewards and punishments" (Kendra and Taplin, 2004, p. 21). This view is very much influenced by the work of French and Raven (1959). External consultants have the ability to openly criticize people and practices without sacrificing their careers, potentially providing a less biased view of change efforts. Internal change agents, although likely to have better knowledge of the change context and the key stakeholders, may be influenced by their vested interests in the organization, leading to a corruption of the change process. This is a tradeoff that must be made by organizations when selecting people to act as change agents.

So, what are the qualities that researchers have found useful in these external consultants? There seems to be relative agreement from business research on three characteristics of successful change agents: excellent communication skills, the ability to function with loose coupling between management and employees, and the ability to cause perturbances in organizational practice.

Communications skills appear most often in the literature as an important characteristic of successful change consultants (Suchan, 1995; Weick and Quinn, 1999). Their work can be thought of as that of a translator who brings an idea of change into fruition. This requires that communication, both formal and informal, take place between the consultant and stakeholders. Sumner (1999), in her comparative case study of seven corporations implementing large-scale information technology systems, found that in five of the seven cases communication played a key role in the success of the innovation. Similarly, a survey study of cell phone adoption by Vishwanath and Goldhaber (2003) of 225 non-users of cell phones showed that, for late adopters, contact between customers and change agents (salespeople) was an important variable in the adoption process. The notion of speaking *differently*, not just arguing better, contributes to an understanding

of the complexities of communication for consultants (Rorty, 1989, as cited in Weick and Quinn, 1999). The communication between potential adopters and cell phone salespeople decreased the perceived complexity of the innovation, which, according to Rogers' diffusion theory (2003), increases the likelihood of adoption.

Business-oriented researchers have also noted the importance of a change agent's ability to foster loose coupling between management and employees (Orton and Weick, 1990; Weick, 1976). As described in the previous section on the creation of vision in K–12 schools, loose coupling is predicated on the creation of a shared organizational vision that guides the actions and intentions of all members. Under this umbrella of guidance, workers are given freedom to seek multiple pathways to pursue the organizational vision. In their study of the work relationships of Hollywood film actors, Faulkner and Anderson (1987) concluded that the loosely coupled organization of directors, producers, actors, and technicians led to the creation of small niches in which previously successful workers worked together repeatedly, ensuring future prosperity. The result is more movies that sell a lot of tickets and fewer flops.

In a multiple-case study of six companies in the information technology industry, Brown and Eisenhardt (1997) used interviews, observations, and environmental analysis to determine factors related to the success of multiple-product innovations. They concluded that loose coupling is one of three characteristics seen most often in companies successful in implementing multiple product innovations. By contrast, Dubois and Gadde (2002) argued, based on their previous research, that the loosely coupled nature of the construction business, although beneficial in terms of optimizing the time and costs of projects, may hurt innovation in the field. Loose coupling does encourage local experimentation and innovation, but without formal bonds by which successful innovations might be shared the construction field as a whole is slow to develop. The lesson from these conflicting viewpoints may be that change agents should encourage loose coupling between management and workers while insisting on regular communication so cross-pollination can occur.

A final characteristic of change agents/consultants in the literature on corporate change is the ability to cause perturbations in daily practice that can help initiate change. Suchan (2005, p. 18) gave a clear rationale for why this is an important change agent quality:

To overcome inertia, at least initially, a disruption is needed that can open a space to infuse new energy into the organizational system (Pfeifer, 1997). The source of that disruption could be a new technology, a major organizational opportunity (e.g., a merger or acquisition), an organizational crisis or potential crisis, or even the setting of goals that may be virtually impossible to attain.

Change agents are constantly bumping against the inertia of everyday activities within the organization. Successful change consultants are able to disrupt this hypnotic flow of events in ways that do not cause excessive stress on individual members but encourage a critical self-examination of daily practices. In a health study with implications for the disruption of habitual processes, Prochaska and Norcross (2001) examined smokers and weight-loss candidates. They found that individuals went through six phases during the behavior change process: precontemplation, contemplation, preparation, action, maintenance, and termination. It is noteworthy that only in one of the six phases are individuals actually engaged in behavioral change—and the rest is preparation and maintenance. Prochaska and Levesque (2001) expanded this line of inquiry to organizations by developing their Decisional Balance Inventory survey instrument. They reported over a dozen studies that have utilized this instrument, ranging from higher education to food service to retail sales and concluded that using their stage-based paradigm of change brings more people into the process and allows change agents to tailor change activities differently for different individuals or work groups who may be at varying levels of readiness for change.

The importance of perturbing everyday practice is also highlighted in Brown and Eisenhardt's (1997) finding that the six product development managers in their study "balanced between the rigidity of planning and the chaos of reacting by frequently probing the future using a variety of low-cost lenses ... experimental products, futurists, strategic partnerships, and frequent meetings" (p. 16). The results of these probes into the future might provide information to the group that would cause important shifts in their vision of the organization. Scholars have noted the importance of providing increased organizational performance data to employees as an early step in the change process (Dooley, 1997). Providing such data and providing for structured time in which people can talk about it are recommended tactics for jolting an organization out of its unquestioned routines. Change consultants working in corporate settings are skillful in disrupting the flow of everyday activities just enough to create some dissonance that will bring out the creative energies of the group.

### Healthcare Change Agentry

The importance of change agentry in the medical community is well stated by Redfern and Christian (2003, p. 236), who proposed that "a credible change agent who works with practitioners face-to-face to encourage enthusiastic involvement" is the most important factor in successful healthcare change efforts. Despite the rather rigid experimental traditions in medicine, research points to the oftentimes chaotic nature of change within complex healthcare organizations. A deep understanding of the organizational culture of the context in which any change agent works is essential.

Berman and McLaughlin's concept of mutual adaptation appears to apply to studies of change in the medical profession as well. Slater et al. (2005) studied a community-based mammography project, and their findings included the importance of an attitude that "permits the change agent organization to 'reinvent' it [the innovation] in a variety of settings and circumstances" (p. 465). The recognition of competing agendas (researchers vs. change agents vs. community) between different participants in the change effort underscores the need to allow for flexibility of implementation. To the contrary, a study of the dissemination of a sun safety program to zoological parks in the United States found that tailoring the way in which a sun safety program was communicated to zoos had little effect on the level of implementation (Lewis et al., 2005). This runs counter to much of the research that says that the more flexible an innovation is the more likely it is to be adopted (Berman and McLaughlin, 1975; Rogers, 2003). A possible explanation for this incongruence is that this innovation did not come through management first but was sent directly to disinterested implementers. These contradictory findings give rise to the notion that source of the innovation may be equally as important as its flexibility.

The authors in the zoo study also note that they did not facilitate communication between participating zoos in an effort to avoid contaminating the results of their study. They concede, however, that allowing for such communication would likely have improved adoption rates, and Rogers' (2003) notion of *observability* supports this conclusion. Allowing for communication between all participants in the change process appears to be a characteristic of successful medical change efforts. Slater et al. (2005) found that maximizing contact between collaborating agencies over the course of their 6-year project strengthened the change effort. In complex organizations such as these, where management, change agents, and adopters may not be regular collaborators, the change agent is wise to pay particular attention to facilitating communication among all participants.

# CONCLUSION

This discussion of change agentry has spanned contexts from schools to hospitals. We have described the current state of the theories surrounding change agentry with a particular emphasis on certain themes, including the importance of connecting organizations to their environments, the centrality of stakeholders in organizational change, the primacy of vision and culture, the necessity of leadership approval and buy-in, the usefulness of professional communities, and the recognition of individual differences among adopters. We have also looked at non-school contexts and found that culture is equally as important in organizations as it is in schools and that change agentry is a bit more well defined and delimited in the corporate sector. Change agents in non-school contexts have been shown to require heightened communication skills and a strong ability to function with loosely coupled management and employees. And, like the calls for school change that often result from sharing data related to school outcomes (Peck and Carr, 1997), corporate change agents must be able to show current failings in a way that generates positive momentum for change. The findings of most research seem to indicate that change agents are not always welcomed, supported, or given nearly sufficient time or human resources. In fact, most change agents in all contexts struggle mightily to effect and sustain substantive systemic organizational change. Indeed, it is within this struggle that those who tilt at windmills, as many instructional technologists are want to do, find their personal meaning. It is our hope that the research presented here will lighten your lances and sharpen your aim.

## REFERENCES

Abernathy, W. J. and Utterback, J., M. (1978). Patterns of industrial innovation. *Technol. Rev.*, 80, 40–47.

Ackoff, R. (1974). *Redesigning the Future.* New York: John Wiley & Sons.*

Arriaza, G. (2004). Making change that stay made: school reform and community involvement. *High School J.*, 87(4), 10–24.

Avissar, G., Reiter, S., and Leyser, Y. (2003). Principals' views and practices regarding inclusion: the case of Israeli elementary school principals. *Eur. J. Special Needs Educ.*, 18(3), 355–369.

Banathy, B. H. (1991). *Systems Design of Education: A Journey to Create the Future.* Englewood Cliffs, NJ: Educational Technology Publications.

Barabasi, A. L. (2002). *Linked: The New Science of Networks.* Cambridge, MA: Perseus.

Berman, P. and McLaughlin, M. (1975). *Federal Programs Supporting Educational Change.* Vol. 1. *A Model of Educational Change.* Santa Monica, CA: RAND.*

Bodilly, S. J., Chun, J., Ikemoto, G., and Stockly, S. (2004). *Challenges and Potential of a Collaborative Approach to Education Reform.* Santa Monica, CA: RAND.

Borko, H., Wolf, S. A., Simone, G., and Uchiyama, K. P. (2003). Schools in transition: reform efforts and school capacity in Washington state. *Educ. Eval. Policy Anal.*, 25(2), 171–201.

Bron, A. and Campione, J. (1994). Psychological theory and the design of innovative learning environments: on procedures, principles, and systems. In *Contributions of Instructional Innovation to Understanding Learning*, edited by L. Schauble and R. Glaser, pp. 289–325. Hillsdale, NJ: Lawrence Earlbaum Associates.

Brown, S. L. and Eisenhardt, K. M. (1997). The art of continuous change: linking complexity theory and time-paced evolution in relentlessly shifting organizations. *Admin. Sci. Q.*, 42, 1–34.

Burke, W. W. and Schmidt, W. H. (1971). In primary target for change: the manager or the organization? In *Social Intervention: A Behavioral Science Approach*, edited by H. A. Hornstein, B. B. Bunker, W. W. Burke, M. Gindes, and R. J. Lewicki, pp. 373–385. New York: Free Press.

Caffarella, E. P. (2000). Characteristics of Individuals Who Have Adopted an Innovation or Have Not Made a Decision to Adopt an Innovation. Paper presented at the Association for Educational Communications and Technology Conference, February 16–20, Long Beach, CA.

Caine, G. (2006). A professional development approach to systemic change. *TechTrends*, 50(2), 43–44.

Capra, F. (1982). *The Turning Point.* New York: Simon & Schuster.

Carr, A. A. (1997). User design in the creation of human learning systems. *Educ. Technol. Res. Dev.*, 45(3), 5–22.

Carr-Chellman, A. A. (2007). *User Design.* Mahwah, NJ: Lawrence Erlbaum Associates.

Carr-Chellman, A. A. and Almeida, L. C. (2006). User-design for systemic change. *TechTrends*, 50(2), 44–45.

Cialdini, R. B. (2001). *Influence: Science and Practice.* Boston: Allyn & Bacon.

Cochran-Smith, M. (1991). Learning to teach against the grain. *Harvard Educ. Rev.*, 51(3), 279–310.

Corcoran, T. and Lawrence, N. (2003). *Changing District Culture and Capacity: The Impact of the Merck Institute for Science Education Partnership.* Philadelphia, PA: Consortium for Policy Research in Education.

Cuban, L. (1986). *Teacher and Machines: The Classroom Use of Technology Since 1920.* New York: Teachers College Press.

Cuban, L. (2001). *Oversold and Underused: Computers in the Classroom.* Cambridge, MA: Harvard University Press.

Dirkx, J. M., Gilley, J. W., and Maycunich Gilley, A. (2004). Change theory in CPE and HRD: toward a holistic view of learning and change in work. *Adv. Dev. Hum. Res.*, 6(1), 35–51.

Dooley, K. (1997). A complex adaptive systems model of organizational change. *Nonlinear Dynamics Psychol. Life Sci.*, 1(1), 69–97.

Dubois, A. and Gadde, L. E. (2002). The construction industry as a loosely coupled system: implications for productivity and innovation. *Construct. Manage. Econ.*, 20, 621–631.

Duffy, F. M. (2006). Step-up-to-excellence: a protocol for navigating the whole-system change in school districts. *TechTrends*, 50(2), 41.

Ellsworth, J. B. (2000). *Surviving Change: A Survey of Educational Change Models.* Syracuse, NY: ERIC Clearinghouse on Information and Technology.

Ely, D. (1976). Creating the conditions for change. In *Changing Times: Changing Libraries*, edited by S. Faibisoff and G. Bonn, pp. 150–162. Champaign, IL: University of Illinois Graduate School of Library Science.

Evidence-Based Intervention Work Group (EBIWG). (2005). Theories of change and adoption of innovations: the evolving evidence-based intervention and practice movement in school psychology. *Psychol. School*, 42(5), 475–494.

Faulkner, R. R. and Anderson, A. B. (1987). Short-term projecting and emergent careers: evidence from Hollywood. *Am. J. Sociol.*, 92, 879–909.

Fielding, M. (2001). Students as radical agents of change. *J. Educ. Change*, 2(2), 123–141.

Fishman, B., Marx, R. W., Blumenfeld, P., Krajcik, J., and Soloway, E. (2004). Creating a framework for research on systemic technology innovations. *J. Learn. Sci.*, 13(1), 43–76.

French, J. R. P. and Raven, B. H. (1959). The bases of social power. In *Studies in Social Power*, edited by D. Cartwright, pp. 150–167. Ann Arbor, MI: Institute for Social Research.

Fullan, M. (2000). The three stories of education reform. *Phi Delta Kappan*, 81(8), 581–584.

Fullan, M. (2001). *The New Meaning of Educational Change*, 3rd ed. New York: Teachers College Press.*

Goldenberg, C. (2003). Settings for school improvement. *Int. J. Disab. Dev. Educ.*, 50(1), 7–16.

Hall, G. E. and Hord, S. M. (1987). *Change in Schools: Facilitating the Process*. Albany, NY: SUNY Press.*

Hutchins, C. L. (1996). *Systemic Thinking: Solving Complex Problems*. Aurora, CO: Professional Development Systems.

Jenlink, P. M., Reigeluth, C. M., Carr, A. A., and Nelson, L. M. (1998). Guidelines for facilitating systemic change in schools districts. *Syst. Res. Behav. Sci.*, 15, 217–233.

Kakabadse, N. K. and Kakabadse, A. (2003). Developing reflexive practitioners through collaborative inquiry: a case study of the U.K. civil service, *Int. Rev. Admin. Sci.*, 69(3), 365–383.

Kendra, K. A. and Taplin, L. J. (2004). Change agent competencies for information technology project managers. *Consult. Psychol. J. Pract. Res.*, 56(1), 20–34.

Kozol, J. (2006). Success for all: making an end run around inequality and segregation. *Phi Delta Kappan*, 87(8), 624.

Lai, K.-W. and Pratt, K. (2004). Information and communication technology (ICT) in secondary schools: the role of the computer coordinator. *Br. J. Educ. Technol.*, 35(4), 461–475.

Lane, S., Lacefield-Parachini, N., and Isken, J. (2003). Developing novice teachers as change agents: student teacher placements 'against the grain.' *Teacher Educ. Q.*, 30(2), 55–68.

Lewin, K. (1951). *Field Theory in Social Science*. New York: Harper & Row.*

Lewis, E., Mayer, J. A., Slymen, D., Belch, G., Engelberg, M., Walker, K. et al. (2005). Disseminating a sun safety program to zoological parks: the effects of tailoring. *Health Psychol.*, 24(5), 456–462.

McLaughlin, M. (1990). The RAND change agent study revisited: macro perspectives and micro realities. *Educ. Res.*, 19(9), 11–16.

Mink, O. G., Esterhuysen, P. W., Mink, B. P., and Owen, K. Q. (1993). *Change at Work: A Comprehensive Management Process for Transforming Organizations*. San Francisco, CA: Jossey-Bass.

Newmann, F. M. and Welhage, G. G. (1995). *Successful school restructuring*. Madison, WI: Center on Organization and Restructuring of Schools.*

Olsen, B. and Kirtman, L. (2002). Teacher as mediator of school reform: an examination of teacher practice in 36 California restructuring schools. *Teachers Coll. Rec.*, 104(2), 301–324.

Orton, J. D. and Weick, K. E. (1990). Loosely coupled systems: a reconceptualization. *Acad. Manage. Rev.*, 15(2), 203–223.

Oshry, B. (1996). *Seeing Systems: Unlocking the Mysteries of Organizational Life*. San Francisco, CA: Berrett-Koehler.

Peck, K. L. and Carr, A. A. (1997). Restoring public confidence in schools through systems thinking. *Int. J. Educ. Reform*, 6(3), 316–323.

Prochaska, J. O. and Levesque, D. O. (2001). A transtheoretical approach to changing organizations. *Admin. Policy Ment. Health*, 28(4), 247–261.

Prochaska, J. O. and Norcross, J. C. (2001). Stages of change. *Psychotherapy*, 38(4), 443–448.

Redfern, S. and Christian, S. (2003). Achieving change in health care practice. *J. Eval. Clin. Pract.*, 9(2), 225–238.

Reigeluth, C. M. (1999). What is instructional-design theory and how is it changing? In *Instructional-Design Theories and Models: A New Paradigm of Instructional Theory*, Vol. 2, edited by C. M. Reigeluth, pp. 5–30. Mahwah, NJ: Lawrence Earlbaum Associates.

Reigeluth, C. M. (2004). Chaos Theory and the Sciences of Complexity: Foundations for Transforming Education. Paper presented at the American Educational Research Association Annual Meeting, April 12–16, San Diego, CA.*

Rogers, E. M. (2003). *Diffusion of Innovations*, 5th ed. New York: Free Press.*

Rust, F. and Freidus, H., Eds. (2001). *Guiding School Change: The Role and Work of Change Agents*. New York: Teachers College Press.

Sarason, S. B. (1990). *The Predictable Failure of School Reform: Can We Change Course Before It's Too Late?* San Francisco, CA: Jossey-Bass.*

Schlechty, P. C. (1990). *Schools for the Twenty-First Century: Leadership Imperatives for Educational Reforms*. San Francisco, CA: Jossey-Bass.

Simmons, J. R. and Simmons, S. J. (2004). Structural conflict in contemporary cities. *Am. Rev. Public Admin.*, 34, 374–388.

Slater, J. S., Finnegan, Jr., J. R., and Madigan, S. D. (2005). Incorporation of a successful community-based mammography intervention: dissemination beyond a community trial. *Health Psychol.*, 24(5), 463–469.

Spillane, J. P. (2002). Local theories of teacher change: the pedagogy of district policies and programs. *Teachers Coll. Rec.*, 104(3), 377–420.

Squire, K. D. and Reigeluth, C. M. (2000). The many faces of systemic change. *Educ. Horizons*, 78(3), 143–152.

Suchan, J. (2006). Changing organizational communication practices and norms: a framework. *J. Bus. Tech. Commun.*, 20(1), 5–47.

Sumner, M. (1999). Critical Success Factors in Enterprise-Wide Information Management Systems Projects. Paper presented at the Association of Computing Machinery Special Interest Group on Computer Personnel Research (CPR) Annual Conference, April 8–10, New Orleans, LA.

Tearle, P. (2003). ICT implementation: what makes the difference? *Br. J. Educ. Technol.*, 34(5), 567–583.

Van de Ven, A. and Poole, M. (1995). Explaining development and change in organizations. *Acad. Manage. Rev.*, 20(3), 510–540.

Vishwanath, A. and Goldhaber, G. M. (2003). An examination of the factors contributing to adoption decisions among late-diffused technology products. *New Media Soc.*, 5(4), 547–572.

Weatherly, R. and Lipsky, M. (1977). Street-level bureaucrats and institutional innovation: implementing special-education reform. *Harvard Educ. Rev.*, 47(2), 171–191.

Weick, K. E. (1976). Educational organizations as loosely coupled systems. *Admin. Sci. Q.*, 21, 1–19.*

Weick, K. E. and Quinn, R. E. (1999). Organizational change and development. *Annu. Rev. Psychol.*, 50, 361–386.

Yukl, G. (1994). *Leadership in Organizations*. Englewood Cliffs, NJ: Prentice Hall.

* Indicates a core reference.

# 47

# Design Languages

*Andrew S. Gibbons*
Brigham Young University, Provo, Utah

*Luca Botturi*
NewMinE Lab, University of Lugano, Lugano, Switzerland

*Eddy Boot*
TNO Human Factors, Soesterberg, the Netherlands

*Jon Nelson*
Utah State University, Logan, Utah

## CONTENTS

## ABSTRACT

Design languages and notation systems hold great practical and theoretical significance for instructional design. Instructional designers use multiple design languages in the creation of designs. Notation systems make design languages visible and document those solutions. Design languages provide the building blocks of an evolving design. Design languages are used by individual designers; shared design languages and notation systems are necessary for multi-participant design teams to function, even at a basic level. Design languages for instructional design allow us to view instructional design, instructional theory, instructional design theory, and day-to-day practice in a new way that enhances our understanding of all of them.

## KEYWORDS

*Design language:* A set of abstractions used to give structure, properties, and texture to solutions of design problems; designs are expressed in terms of design languages.

*Design layer:* One aspect of a decomposed design problem that can be approached using one or more design languages; a subdomain of the larger problem to which one or more design languages pertain.

## INTRODUCTION

Design languages and notation systems hold great practical and theoretical significance for instructional design. In this chapter, we examine the evidence of the value of design languages, arguing that designers in many fields already realize significant benefits from conscious study and application of design languages. These benefits include:

- Improved design team communications
- Improved designer–producer communications
- Improved designer–client communications

- Promotion of design innovation
- More direction from theory and more applicable theory
- More nuanced theory integration with designs
- Improved design sharing and comparison of designs
- Improved designer education
- Design and production automation

## WHAT ARE DESIGN LANGUAGES?

As instructional designers, we all use multiple design languages. The very words that we use, such as *discussion*, *portfolio*, and *formative evaluation*, code special or professional concepts that help us explore an instructional problem space and identify, refine, and plan a solution (Goodwin, 1994). A design language is a set of abstractions used to give structure, properties, and texture to solutions of design problems. Design languages provide building blocks for designs. Design languages provide categories for thinking about design problems. Design languages provide an important link between technological theory and design practice. Design language terms signify objects to be acted upon, actors, actions, concepts, types of relation, composite objects, qualities, and properties.

One reviewer, a design theorist, commented that "whenever designers talk to members of their team they are using [the terms of] a design language" (private communication). Consider the following scenario illustrating a typical design situation: As an instructional designer, you are asked to support a communication specialist in the design of a *blended learning course* in effective communication skills for a company's workforce. At a meeting, you and the communication specialist are discussing *lectures*, *discussions*, *case studies*, *exercises*, *online discussion forums*, and other possible *activities*. As the discussion proceeds, you realize that the communication specialist does not recognize some of these terms. Further, you realize that the definitions of the terms that you do both recognize differ, sometimes in significant ways. You begin to find it difficult to discuss design details because you are not yet working from a common framework of meaning, and you do not have shared languages for communicating meaning.

The designer and the communications specialist need a shared set of terms for shaping their design that will be understood in roughly the same way by both. They will build one, drawing on personal and public design languages from their own training and experience, and new terms will be invented within the scope of the project. A shared local language will evolve through meaning negotiation (Winograd and Flores, 1987). Local notation systems that include drawings, symbols, and words will also evolve to publicly represent the design. This notational expression will be directed toward a specialized audience whose members know the language and its notation well enough to understand the implications of the design for manufacture. The design documentation will therefore be rich and dense and difficult for non-team members to interpret.

Schön (1987) described designing as a language-centered social phenomenon. Design languages are common to all fields of design (Gibbons and Brewer, 2005; Rheinfrank and Evenson, 1996; Waters and Gibbons, 2004; Winograd and Flores, 1987). We can discern features common to design languages in many fields.

## Design Layers and Design Languages

Numerous design languages are required in the creation of a single design, according to Schön (1987). He related design languages to *domains* of the design problem, and different problem domains represent subproblems to be solved during the completion of one design (Schön, 1987, p. 58):

> Elements of the language of designing can be grouped into clusters, of which I have identified twelve…. These design domains contain the names of elements, features, relations, and actions and of norms used to evaluate problems, consequences, and implications.

Schön's domains correspond roughly with the *design layers* described by Brand (1994) with respect to building designs. Brand identified six layers of a building's design: site, structure, skin, services, spaces, and stuff (furniture). He proposed that describing a design in layers allows the designer to change the design within one layer with minimal disruption to other layers. This results in design modularity, allowing individual layers to age independently. Separate layers can be designed

to *flow* past each other without disruption. Baldwin and Clark (2000) claimed that design modularization of this type governs the economics of the modern computer industry. This principle seems to apply to software design as well (Bass et al., 2003; Czarnecki et al., 2006; Rosenberg, 2007). Gray (2006) described how this principle supplies a major competitive advantage for the merchandiser Amazon. Layers are clearly defined in some Web design languages such as W2000 (Baresi et al., 2001) and IDM (Bolchini and Paolini, 2006). These examples suggest that design languages and their layered relationship frame a coherent theory of designing.

## Design Languages and Natural Languages

The term *design language* raises the question of the relationship between design languages and natural languages. To understand this relationship, we must consider the nature of natural languages. Contrary to our usual conception of languages as static lexicons and grammars, McWhorter (2003, p. 12) described how "everything about a language is eternally and inherently changeable." Words establish legitimacy. The word *language* itself connotes something bounded and settled. McWhorter said that instead "there is not even really such a thing as 'a language' at all. …It's the nature of language change that makes the concept of 'a language' logically impossible" and "most 'languages' are actually bundles of variations on a general theme, dialects" (McWhorter , 2003, pp. 52–53).

McWhorter's view of a single natural *language* as a multiplicity of dialects serves to situate the concept of design languages within natural languages. Design language expressions are made in a specialized dialect of a natural language. Design language expressions blend with natural language expressions in everyday use, being indistinguishable to a non-native listener. What makes a design language distinct from natural language is its unique semantics: one not shared by the general population of the language's users. To a mathematician speaking with another mathematician, for example, the term *code* might be most readily understood as the key to an encryption, but to a computer programmer speaking to another computer programmer the term *code* will more likely refer to a work product. Gibbons and Rogers (2007) characterized the differences between natural languages and design languages (see Table 47.1).

Design languages are a special case of natural languages in which a subpopulation of language users share terms, expression syntax, and semantics. Design language expressions mix specialized language elements with natural language elements, so design language users might appear to be speaking in code,

**TABLE 47.1**
**Natural Languages and Design Languages Compared in Terms of Primitives, Syntax, and Semantics**

| | Natural Language | Design Language |
|---|---|---|
| Primitive terms | Centered in everyday things and events; abstractions of experience; common to a wide range of users | Centered in specialized tools, processes, technologies, theories, or best practices |
| Syntax | Based on words as a medium of expression in which linear or positional order is critical | Dependent on the medium of problem solving and solution; sometimes spatial or view oriented |
| Semantics | Derived from the world as it is experienced and things that can be, or are desired to be, communicated | Derived from the problem domain and the context of problems in the domain |

*Source:* Adapted from Gibbons, A.S. and Rogers, P.C., in *Instructional-Design Theories and Models: A New Paradigm of Instructional Theory*, Vol. III, Reigeluth, C., Ed., Lawrence Erlbaum Associates, Mahwah, NJ, 2007.

which is in a sense what they are doing. It should be emphasized that the shared conceptual sets of the users are what allow the design language to make sense among users. These shared conceptual sets may find expression in diagrams, drawings, or other representational forms, so the syntax of design language expressions may include spatial and metaphorical dimensions also peculiar to the users (such as blueprint or schematic conventions).

Design languages exist along a continuum of formality. It is difficult to resist the temptation to treat design languages as a logical formalism, but design languages are at the same time a tool for and a byproduct of designing. They may be formalized for special purposes in the way in which computer languages are, and those formalisms may result in more precise and sophisticated designs, but overemphasis on formalism can replace the metaphoric uses of language and injure creativity. By far the most common use of design languages falls short of formalistic communication; instead, the more common use of design languages is joint problem solving and the negotiation of ever more precise meaning among designers and design team members.

## INSTRUCTIONAL DESIGN LANGUAGES

Design languages relate to instructional design architecture: the internal structure of an instructional artifact and its external structural relationships with its context. In this section we describe design languages for instructional design.

### Instructional Design Layers

Gibbons (2003) applied Brand's idea of layered designs to the architecture of instructional designs, describing instructional designs in terms of seven main layers, each with potentially many sublayers. Layer identities are based on a functional rather than process-oriented decomposition of the design problem. The main layers named are content, strategy, controls, message, representation, media-logic, and data management (Gibbons and Rogers, 2006). Within each layer, multiple instruction design languages now exist, implicit in the practices of instructional designers. Each language within each layer represents an approach to the design of a particular function. The multiplicity of usable design languages within a single layer shows how rapidly changing technologies, methods, processes, theories, tools, and styles are absorbed into languages.

### Example: Design Languages of the Content Layer

The design languages pertaining to the content layer of instructional designs have evolved and multiplied over the past 50 years. These languages identify possible partitionings of subject-matter elements. When behaviorist influence was strong, designers thought of subject matter in terms of *operants* and *operant chains* (Gagné, 1965). Over time, the prevailing view turned in the direction of information processing theories of learning, and new categories of learnable subject matter appeared (Gagné, 1985). New design languages or design language migrations occur frequently and can be stimulated by changes in theory, technique, tools, or conceptual systems. Viewing Gagné's learning categories as the terms of a design language for content description suggests we also consider the taxonomies of Bloom (1956), Miller (1971), Merrill (1994), and many others as content design languages. It also gives us a new perspective for considering the great variety of predesign analysis methodologies described by Jonassen and colleagues (1999), Gibbons (1977), and Gibbons and colleagues (2000). These attempts to understand the nature of analysis methodologies catalog languages for content description.

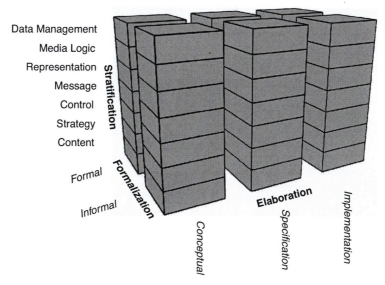

**Figure 47.1** The 3D model of design documentation. (From Boot, E.W., *Building Blocks for Developing Instructional Software*, Ph.D. dissertation, Open Universiteit of the Netherlands, Heerlen, 2005. With permission.)

New theoretical developments continue to spawn new content layer languages. Anderson's instructional designs (Anderson, 1993; Anderson et al., 1995) describe learnable subject matter in terms of productions (if–then rules) and working memory (semantic) elements. Anderson and his associates have applied this content design language to automated tutors in multiple subject-matter areas (Anderson et al., 1986, 1989; Koedinger and Anderson, 1998). This line of research continues (Koedinger and Corbett, 2006). Collins and colleagues (1989), in their description of the instructional theory of cognitive apprenticeship, defined four areas of design guidance, one of which they titled *content*, referring to four types of knowledge designers may use to perform subject-matter analyses. Situated learning theory, as described by Lave and Wenger (1991) and Wenger (1998), examines participation within communities of practice. This theory implicitly defines the *practices* of the *community* as the content structures.

### Practical Application: The 3D Model of Design Documentation

The Developing Design Documents (3D) model of design documentation (Boot et al., 2005) applies design layering and design language principles to the problem of design documentation. Design documents transfer information from instructional designers to producers to describe artifacts to be produced. Design documents may be difficult for producers to interpret for three reasons: (1) the artifact's instructional and technical description does not readily translate into the terms of the producer; (2) different levels of design detail may be mixed together from the producer's point of view; and (3) design expressions may be used in an inconsistent manner. The 3D model was introduced to guide designers in creating design documents that are better stratified, elaborated, and formalized. The model is illustrated in Figure 47.1.

- Dimension 1. *Stratification*—Stratification helps the producer determine the relationships between the functionally different instructional and technical structures while at the same time providing an orderly way of representing the integration of those structures within the complete design. The 3D model defines the seven design layers proposed by Gibbons (2003) for the stratification of the design document.
- Dimension 2. *Elaboration*—Fowler (2003) described three possible levels of elaboration in an instructional software design: (1) a conceptual perspective, which describes the structure of the major elements of the design with little technical detail; (2) a specification perspective, which provides sufficient detailed information for a skilled and experienced producer; and (3) an implementation perspective, which describes the design with a high degree of technical detail. The level of elaboration informs the level of detail in the design languages that must be used.
- Dimension 3. *Formalization*—Designers may determine the formalization of their design, making their choice of informal or formal

design languages explicit. Using the 3D model, designers can determine the level of documentation and the design languages used to communicate with different specialist groups taking part in design.

## Instructional Design Languages and Theories of Instruction

Gibbons and Rogers (2007) described a relationship between design languages and instructional theories:

> We propose that what an instructional theorist expresses in an instructional theory is a set of specialized, mutually-consistent design languages…that are distributed across multiple design layers. …[Layers] can be used by the same observer to analyze and compare different instructional theories. To the extent that different observers can agree upon a common definition of layers, they can jointly and publicly carry out such analyses and comparisons.

This relationship between design languages and theories—that one source of design languages is the terms introduced or given special meaning by theorists—answers the questions "Is there a best design language?" and "How can you tell whether one design language is better than another?" The answer to both questions is that it is not appropriate to declare a single language superior. A later section of this chapter describes how multiple instructional design languages (strategy languages, representation languages, control system languages, etc.) are required just to make a single instructional design. These languages interact in ways that bring out the strengths of language combinations. To say that one language is by itself superior is evidence of a misunderstanding of the composition of designs. Languages interacting with other languages can be judged on the basis of comparative effectiveness in use. A given combination of languages may be superior in a given context; the same combination may be inadequate to satisfy the needs of a different design problem within its context.

## Design Languages and Innovation

Polanyi (1958, p. 87) described the role of language in innovative thought where "symbolic operations … outrun our understanding and thus anticipate novel modes of thought." He suggested that we may use linguistic rules and linguistic symbols to create combinations that seem not to make sense at first but that on closer examination define a new path of innovative thought, either through: (1) a fumbling to be corrected later by our tacit understanding, or (2) a pioneering to be followed up later by our tacit understanding (Polanyi, 1958, p. 93):

> We should say we are referring … to a state of mental uneasiness due to the feeling that out tacit thoughts do not agree with our symbolic operations, so that we have to decide on which of the two we should rely and which we should correct in the light of the other.

Designers who consider design languages are accepting to a degree what Polanyi would term a "formalism [through language] of thought" (p. 94). Just as a child uses natural language, a design language user can form nonsense expressions using design language terms. This is a risk, he says, that comes with adopting any formal system for giving public form to what would otherwise remain *personal* or *tacit knowledge*, but he said there may also be benefits (Polanyi, 1958, p. 94):

> Remember how various new kinds of numbers—irrational, negative, imaginary, transfinite—were produced as a result of extending familiar mathematical operations into unexplored regions, and how these numbers after having been repudiated as meaningless, were eventually accepted as denoting important new mathematical conceptions. Such spectacular gains, achieved by the speculative use of mathematical notations for purposes not originally entertained, remind us that the major fruitfulness of a formalization may be revealed in its entirely uncovenanted functions, precisely at points where the peril seems greatest of drifting into absurdity.

The principle, then, of using design languages as a type of formalism for thinking about instructional designs might be stated (Polanyi, 1958, p. 95):

> Just as owing to the ultimately tacit character of all our knowledge, we remain ever unable to say all we know, so also, in view of the tacit character of meaning, we can never quite know what is implied in what we say.

In this spirit Botturi and colleagues (2006) proposed a two-dimensional classification of design languages according to their purposes for communication and creativity (see also Stubbs, 2006). These dimensions can be used to compare design languages in terms of the intentions of their creators to support particular aspects of the designer's activity. Figure 47.2 shows this kind of comparison among design languages for learning object design.

## THE RANGE OF INSTRUCTIONAL DESIGN LANGUAGES

Design languages vary across a range of characteristics, according to Gibbons and Brewer (2005, p. 113):

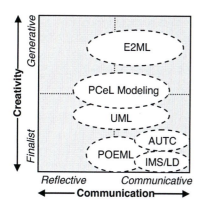

**Figure 47.2** An example of the use of the communication and creativity aspects of design languages for making comparisons among languages. (From Botturi, L. et al., A Classification Framework for Educational Modeling Languages in Instructional Design, paper presented at the International Conference on Advanced Learning Technologies, July 5–7, Kerkrade, the Netherlands, 2006. With permission.)

Some of our design languages, such as computer programming languages, are formal, and when we use them it is a conscious, deliberate design activity. Many of our design languages, however, are so subtle that we do not recognize them and realize that we use them to structure designs.

Gibbons and Brewer described several dimensions of design language variation:

- Complexity–simplicity
- Precision–nonprecision
- Formality–informality
- Personalization–sharedness
- Implicitness–explicitness
- Standardization–nonstandardization
- Computability–noncomputability

All of these characteristics can be seen in instructional design languages. The languages related to high-tech media design and production tend to be complex, precise, formal, shared, explicit, standard, and computable. Languages that describe instructional strategy structures tend to be relatively simple, nonprecise, informal, often personalized or stylized, implicit, nonstandard, and noncomputable.

## EXAMPLES OF SPECIALIZED INSTRUCTIONAL DESIGN LANGUAGES

Several research groups have pursued specialized design languages for use in designing learning objects (Botturi, 2006; Caeiro-Rodriguez et al., 2006; Derntl, 2007; Koper, 2002; Koper and Tattersall, 2005; Paquette, 2005). The boundaries for the application of

these languages are defined by: (1) a productivity-related instructional design concept (learning objects), (2) a programming paradigm (object-orientation), and (3) a programming tool concept (UML-like). Within this design space, these design language tools will grow over time, informing each other, migrating to new forms like natural languages, and producing dialects through processes described by McWhorter (2003).

## WHY STUDY INSTRUCTIONAL DESIGN LANGUAGES?

We identify four main reasons for the serious study of instructional design languages: (1) They encourage disciplined design practice, (2) they give organization to the growth of design fields, (3) their study gives historical context to evolving design fields, and (4) they connect practices of a design field to theoretical concepts.

### Design Languages Encourage Disciplined Design Practice

In many design fields, making design languages explicit has resulted in rapid advances in design productivity. Computer chip designs were originally recorded by hand in large and very detailed drawings. Over time, highly repetitive and detailed local design decisions were identified and ways were invented to express design problems in multiple, strictly bounded design languages. These languages could be translated into computer programming languages for solving. The end result has been a computer chip design process in which most low-level design decisions are made automatically. Chip design is now faster, and designs have increased exponentially in complexity and sophistication. A return to handmade and hand-drawn designs is unthinkable (Brayton and Darringer, 2003; Del Man and Rabaey, 2003; Kuh and Hsu, 2003; Sakallah et al., 2003).

Without the creation of design languages for problem expression, the computer would be irrelevant to designing. The earliest use of computers in computer-aided design was merely to record design decisions and eliminate drafting tables. Conscious attention to formal use of design languages has accelerated progress in many other design fields as well, including aviation, software, automotive, and architectural design, among others (Kuehlmann, 2003; Newsome et al., 1989; Saabagh, 1996). McDonald (McDonald, 2006; McDonald and Gibbons, in press) described how design practice can be disciplined through the explicit use of terms that describe the design practice itself.

## Study of Design Languages Gives Direction to the Growth of Design Fields

Design languages help organize the growing knowledge base of a technological field. Design usually involves the efforts of teams of specialists. Planning and coordination of their practice involve the use of specialized design languages. The use of the languages is most visible in the jargon of design team members. Families of languages needed to make coordinated action possible include:

- Artifact design and development languages
- Languages related to the design process
- Languages related to development processes
- Tool languages related to design and development tools
- Production specialty/specialist languages
- Artifact description languages
- Structure and dimension description languages
- Functional description languages
- Languages that describe artifact properties or qualities
- Artifact operation languages
- Languages describing artifacts and their contexts physically
- Languages describing modes of operation and use
- Measurement languages
- Instrument design languages
- Measurement process design languages
- Measurement concept and interpretation languages
- Status/state description languages
- Intervention planning languages
- Intervention pattern languages
- Intervention process languages

Design language terms support communication about specialized objects, dimensions, properties, qualities, and processes by design teams. Most instructional designers are not aware of their tacit use of a great variety of design languages in written and spoken communications, nor are they aware of the important function of those languages in making useful and increasingly subtle design distinctions (Stubbs, 2006).

## Evolution of Design Languages Gives Historical Context to Design Fields

The evolution of the design languages of a field reflects the changing questions of the field and their scope. By identifying the design languages of the past, research-

ers and students can: (1) chart trajectories that point to unsolved problems, (2) recognize the scope and limitations of past questions, and (3) extrapolate from past questions to form and set the scope of new questions. For example, successive attempts have been made to codify a definition for the instructional technology field and define its theoretical and practical issues (Dijkstra et al., 1997; Januszewski, 2001; Reigeluth, 1983, 1999; Richey, 1986; Seels and Richey, 1994; Snelbecker, 1985; Tennyson et al., 1997). Such publications give a snapshot of the implicit design languages of a period that can be used by researchers and students to understand their questions in a historical context.

## Design Languages Connect Practices of a Design Field to Theoretical Concepts

The study of design languages reveals avenues for the grounding of instructional design practices in the theories of related disciplines.

### Social Learning Theory and Sociolinguistics

Sociolinguistics is the study of the role of language in social interaction. The study of design languages within a sociolinguistic context is important to researching the inward conversations of designers and the outward conversations of design teams. Sociolinguistics allows the design theorist to consider the implications of research by studying discourse analysis (Barton and Tusting, 2005; Bazerman, 1999), conversation theory (Pask, 1976), conversation analysis (te Molder and Potter, 2005), and design as a social process (Bucciarelli, 1994).

Sociolinguists Barton and Tusting (2005) proposed that communities of practice cannot exist without a common language for communicating about the community's shared interest. Wenger's (1998) description of communities of practice anticipated the centrality of language to the function of communities using the concept of reification, which Wenger (1998, pp. 58–59) defined as:

> The process of giving form to our experience by producing objects that congeal this experience into 'thingness'. In so doing, we create points of focus around which the negotiation of meaning becomes organized. ...Any community of practice produces abstractions, tools, symbols, stories, terms and concepts that reify something of that practice in a congealed form.

Barton and Tusting (2005, p. 26) noted that "reification entails not only the negotiation of shared understandings but also enables particular forms of social relations to be shaped in the process of participation." In a community of designers, the formation of design languages is not just an interesting byproduct but an essential process that makes possible the existence of the community. The specialized communications of the community are carried out in the terms of these languages.

### Cognitive Semantics and Linguistics

Cognitive semantics (Jackendoff, 1993; Talmy, 2001) is the study of how humans develop and express meaning. Design languages are in some ways similar to other verbal, written, and symbolic languages; therefore, principles of cognitive semantics, linguistics, and semiotics may be used to study these specialized, local, and bounded languages. Semantically, design language terms take their meaning and interpretability from their context of use, from the intentions of the designer, and from the negotiation of meaning between designers (Winograd and Flores, 1987). This principle extends to the semantics of the design languages used by the many stakeholder communities that surround and support the use of a technology. Bazerman (1999, pp. 336–337) provided an account of the stabilization of the new technology of electrification and electrical lighting in the time of Thomas Edison:

> Technologists are tied into less obvious meaning systems for their development, appreciation, production, funding, operation, maintenance, social control, evaluation, and distribution. Moreover, these (and possibly other) functions are likely to be distributed among different groupings in the society, requiring differential distribution of representations to various social components that may not overlap. Papers must be filed with financial backers, government regulators, technical R&D departments, sales forces, material suppliers, production machinery producers, and shop floor designers.

In the future, descriptions like Bazerman's applied to the stabilization and mass application of instructional technologies of many kinds will become an important factor in establishing and maintaining them.

### Computer Science

Design languages can also be related to the special-purpose languages of the computer. The study of programming languages suggests possible connection points between computation and design languages. Early artificial intelligence research included experiments in intelligent tutoring. In many of these experiments, the goal was to generate some portion of the instructional experience in real time, taking into account a number of factors that included the structure of the subject matter and the history of recent actions of the learner. These experimental systems explored the real-time generation of many elements of the instructional experience, including generation of message (Carbonell, 1970; Drake et al., 1998; Stevens and Collins, 1977), generation of representations (Hollan et al., 1984), generation of strategy (Buchannan and Shortliffe, 1984; Clancey, 1984), and generation of control systems (Johnson et al., 2000), among others.

Design languages give designers a tool for discussing with greater precision which instantaneous design decisions can be shared with the computer; for example, *Exploring Emergence* (Resnick and Silverman, 2006) places side-by-side fixed traditional instructional forms and the computations of a dynamic graphical model, whose unpredictable variations no designer would think of creating and prestoring in graphic form.

Design languages are also related to the emerging study of ontologies for systematic semantics searches for patterns of relationship within databases (Nirenburg and Raskin, 2004; Noy and McGuinness, 2006). Ontologies will be pivotal in the development of a Semantic Web. Ontology-based searches will include finding resources with standard functional characteristics, such as those that contain specific modularized instructional functions.

## THE NATURAL HISTORY OF INSTRUCTIONAL DESIGN LANGUAGES

Design languages come into being in different ways. McWhorter (2003, pp. 11–12) described the natural history of natural languages in transformative terms:

> Language is ... analogous to cloud formations. We look at a cloud formation with full awareness of its inherently transitory nature: we know that if we look up again in an hour, the formation will almost certainly be different....

Most design languages are neither formalized nor standardized. Many of them enter widespread use with only the most vague specification and definition of terms. Even for languages whose terms are clearly defined, there is a danger that the terms may be appropriated by others or applied with modifications (McDonald, 2006). Those modifications may become a *de facto* alternative standard, and the originator of the design language must either live with the fuzziness or issue a correction reexpressing the original terms and definitions. This occurred when Barrows restated his definition of "problem-based learning" following many years of definition creep (Barrows, 1998; Barrows and Tamblyn, 1980). Design languages are in constant flux. As McWhorter (2003, p. 53) said of natural languages, "Dialects is all there is."

Primitive terms of design languages tend to be invented, and invention can take place suddenly with the introduction of a new process, tool, or theory. Most design language terms do not find their way into the lexicons of natural languages. Design languages may obey some of the rules of natural languages but tend to be separate from natural languages. Design languages are often promoted by the originators of the language, and language wars may occur. Sponsors may include theoreticians, special-interest groups, businesses, or business communities with connected interests, particularly in software tools or hardware they have created.

The syntactical rules of languages emerge slowly from usage. Syntax gives order to expressions of meaning. Through transformation, words and phrases can be placed in different surface arrangements that preserve meaning, but the surface form of the new arrangement is still linear. Design language syntax, on the other hand, is multidimensional. The primitive terms in a design language may be expressed as words, but expressions in a design must describe multiple relationships for every design element in adequate detail to support creation of an artifact. Relationships may be spatial (two- or three-dimensional), temporal (four-dimensional), or more complex (conditional). Design languages often require more complex notations to contain the amount of information requisite for a design. This can lead to three-dimensional drawing or models, four-dimensional animations, and even more complex modeling systems that involve multiple representation forms (Stubbs, 2006). Systems such as traditional architectural drawing have become so specialized that language notation standards are created to govern the representation of designs.

Natural language semantics is derived from patterns of cause and effect and states of being in real-world experience or by metaphorical processes operating on them (Talmy, 2001). The semantic of a design language is limited to a problem domain within which the design language is specified, such as Schön's architectural problem-solving domains or Brand's layers (Schön, 1987; Brand, 1994). Design language expressions have meanings bounded by the problem worlds for which they were created.

## DESIGN LANGUAGES AND NOTATION SYSTEMS

Waters and Gibbons (2004) made a distinction between a design language and public design representations through speech, writing, drawing, and ges-

tures. Private design languages exist that do not have corresponding symbolic forms and rules for sharing. Bucciarelli (1994, p. 159) described this:

> Shared vision is made explicit in documents, texts, and artifacts—in formal assembly and detail drawings, operation and service manuals, contractual disclaimers, production schedules, marketing copy, test plans, parts lists, procurement orders, mock-ups, and prototypes. But in the process of designing … each participant in the process has a personal collection of sketches, flow charts, cost estimates, spreadsheets, models, and above all stories—stories to tell about their particular vision of the object. The shared vision, as some synthetic representation of the artifact as a whole, is not in the documents or written plans. To the extent that it exists as a whole, it is a social construction.…

Design languages and notation systems support growth and improvement in each other. Once a consistent notation system is established, it can become: (1) a tool for remembering designs, (2) a structured problem-solving work space where designs can take form, and (3) a laboratory tool for sharpening and subdividing abstract design categories. Through a continuing cycle of refinement, both design language and notation system grow in parallel, and more sophisticated design ideas result.

## DESIGN LANGUAGE RESEARCH

Gibbons and Brewer (2005) proposed several directions for research in design languages and their potential uses:

- Identify, document, and study existing design languages.
- Extract principles in existing languages and learn to apply them deliberately.
- Obtain better language grounding through attachment to theory.
- Examine the generative principles of language that lead to new design languages.
- Generate better-defined languages and grammars.
- Create tools that emphasize the designer's languages rather than the computer's.
- Use design languages to redefine design processes.

This list can be supplemented with additional ideas described in this chapter:

- Explore the relationship between ontologies and design languages.

- Explore computable instructional design languages and their role in adaptive instructional experiences.
- Explore social dimensions of language use during designing.
- Explore positive economic benefits of design language use for design teams.
- Explore lessons learned in other design communities from design language application.
- Explore the use of design languages in educating new designers.
- Explore the role of design languages in securing new technologies and promoting their use among a range of stakeholders.

## ANTICIPATED BENEFITS

Several benefits may be expected from the above research:

- Improved tools for the support of all stages of instructional design, from initial conception to documentation of the completed design
- Clearer relationships between design decisions and structures, features, and qualities of designs
- Improved techniques for facilitating the formation of instructional design teams and their rapid movement toward productive activity
- Improved approaches for the training of new instructional designers
- A broader view of new designers with respect to the spectrum of design languages used by the many specialized members of their design teams
- New understanding of the nature of instructional designing and new processes that tailor the design process to the design problem

## CONCLUSION

Design languages supply primitives for private design and for public discourse about designs. In a complex technological world where designing can no longer be considered a single-person activity, increasing emphasis should be placed on the importance of design languages as a vehicle for sharing design processes. In addition to their use in creating designs, design languages supply a means by which theories used in designing can be examined, understood, compared, and implemented. In many design fields, attention to design languages and their use has produced enormous increases in productivity and creativity. Design languages are not an invention but the description of a new way of seeing what designers naturally do in every field of design. As such, it is a conceptual tool and not a truth, but as a conceptual tool we should explore the new possibilities design languages open to us for improving the range, precision, and sophistication of our designs. Consideration of the design languages of instructional design present us an opportunity to view instructional design, instructional theory, instructional design theory, and day-to-day practice in a new way that may advance our understandings of all of these.

## REFERENCES

Anderson, J. R. (1993). *Rules of the Mind*. Hillsdale, NJ: Lawrence Erlbaum Associates.

Anderson, J. R., Boyle, C. F., and Yost, G. (1986). The geometry tutor. *J. Math. Behav.*, 5–20.

Anderson, J. R., Conrad, F. G., and Corbett, A. T. (1989). Skill acquisition and the LISP tutor. *Cogn. Sci.*, 13, 467–506.

Anderson, J. R., Corbett, A. T., Koedinger, K. R., and Pelletier, R. (1995). Cognitive tutors: lessons learned. *J. Learn. Sci.*, 14(2), 167–207.

Baldwin, C. Y. and Clark, K. B. (2000). *Design Rules*, Vol. 1. *The Power of Modularity*. Cambridge, MA: MIT Press.*

Baresi, L., Garzotto, F., and Paolini, P. (2001). Extending UML for Modeling Web Applications. Paper presented at the 34th Annual Hawaii International Conference on System Sciences, January 3–6, Maui, HI.

Barrows, H. S. (1998). The essentials of problem-based learning. *J. Dent. Educ.*, 62(9), 630–633.

Barrows, H. S. and Tamblyn, R. M. (1980). *Problem-Based Learning: An Approach to Medical Education*. New York: Springer.

Barton, D. and Tusting, K. (2005). *Beyond Communities of Practice: Language, Power, and Social Context*. Cambridge, U.K.: Cambridge University Press.*

Bass, L., Clements, P., and Kazman, R. (2003). *Software Architecture in Practice*, 2nd ed. Reading, MA: Addison-Wesley.

Bazerman, C. (1999). *The Languages of Edison's Light*. Cambridge, MA: MIT Press.*

Bloom, B., Ed. (1956). *Taxonomy of Educational Objectives, Handbook I: Cognitive Domain*, Vol. I. New York: David McKay.

Bolchini, D. and Paolini, P. (2006). Interactive dialogue model: a design technique for multi-channel applications. *IEEE Trans. Multimedia*, 8(3), 529–541.

Boot, E. W., Nelson, J., van Merriënboer, J., and Gibbons, A. (2005). Stratification, elaboration, and formalization of design documents: effects on the production of instructional materials. In Building Blocks for Developing Instructional Software, edited by E. W. Boot. Ph.D. dissertation. Heerlen: Open Universiteit of the Netherlands.*

Botturi, L. (2006). E2ML: A visual language for the design of instruction. *Educ. Technol. Res. Dev.*, 54(3), 265–293.

Botturi, L., Derntl, M., Boot, E., and Figl, K. (2006). A Classification Framework for Educational Modeling Languages in Instructional Design. Paper presented at the International Conference on Advanced Learning Technologies, July 5–7, Kerkrade, the Netherlands.*

Brand, S. (1994). *How Buildings Learn: What Happens After They're Built*. New York: Penguin Books.*

Brayton, R. and Darringer, J. (2003). Logic synthesis overview. In *The Best of ICCAD: 20 Years of Excellence in Computer-Aided Design*, edited by A. Kuehlmann, pp. 181–190. Boston, MA: Kluwer.

Bucciarelli, L. L. (1994). *Designing Engineers*. Cambridge, MA: MIT Press.*

Buchannan, B. and Shortliffe, E. (1984). Intelligent computer-aided instruction. In *Rule-Based Expert Systems: The MYCIN Experiments of the Stanford Heuristic Programming Project*, edited by B. Buchannan and E. Shortliffe, pp. 455–463. Reading, MA: Addison-Wesley.

Caeiro-Rodriguez, M., Andino-Rifon, L., and Llamas-Nistal, M. (2006). POEML: A Perspective-Oriented Educational Modeling Language Meta-Model for Engineering e-Learning Practices. Paper presented at the 15th International World Wide Web Conference (WWW2006), May 23–26, Edinburgh, Scotland.

Carbonell, J. R. (1970). AI in CAI: an artificial intelligence approach to computer-aided instruction. *IEEE Trans. Man–Machine Syst.*, 11(4), 190–202.

Clancey, W. (1984). Use of MYCIN's rules for tutoring. In *Rule-Based Expert Systems: The MYCIN Experiments of the Stanford Heuristic Programming Project*, edited by B. Buchannan and E. Shortliffe, pp. 464–489. Reading, MA: Addison-Wesley.

Collins, A., Brown, J. S., and Newman, S. E. (1989). Cognitive apprenticeship: teaching the crafts of reading, writing, and mathematics. In *Knowing, Learning, and Instruction: Essays in Honor of Robert Glaser*, edited by L. Resnick, pp. 453–493. Hillsdale, NJ: Lawrence Erlbaum Associates.

Czarnecki, K., Antikiewicz, M., and Kim, C. H. (2006). Multi-level customization in application engineering: developing mechanisms for mapping features to analysis models. *Commun. ACM*, 49(12), 61–65.

Del Man, H. and Rabaey, J. (2003). System design and analysis overview. In *The Best of ICCAD: 20 Years of Excellence in Computer-Aided Design*, edited by A. Kuehlmann, pp. 93–106. Boston, MA: Kluwer.

Derntl, M. (2007). *Patterns for Person-Centered e-Learning*, Dissertations in Database and Information Systems–Infix Vol. 96. Amsterdam: IOS Press.

Dijkstra, S., Seel, N. M., Schott, F., and Tennyson, R. D., Eds. (1997). *Instructional Design: International Perspectives*. Vol. II. *Solving Instructional Design Problems*, Mahwah. NJ: Lawrence Erlbaum Associates.

Drake, L., Mills, R., Lawless, K., Curry, J., and Merrill, M. D. (1998). The Role of Explanations in Learning Environments. Paper presented at the Annual Meeting of the American Educational Research Association, April 13–17, San Diego, CA.

Fowler, M. (2003). *UML Distilled: A Brief Guide to the Standard Object Modeling Language*. Boston, MA: Addison-Wesley.

Gabriel, R. P. (1996). *Patterns of Software: Tales from the Software Community*. New York: Oxford University Press.

Gagné, R. M. (1965). *The Conditions of Learning*, 1st ed. New York: Holt, Rinehart and Winston.

Gagné, R. M. (1985). *The Conditions of Learning*, 4th ed. New York: Holt, Rinehart and Winston.

Gibbons, A. S. (1977). *A Review of Content and Task Analysis Methodology*, Technology Report No. 2. San Diego, CA: Courseware, Inc.

Gibbons, A. S. (2003). What and how do designers design? A theory of design structure. *TechTrends*, 47(5), 22–27.*

Gibbons, A. S. and Brewer, E. K. (2005). Elementary principles of design languages and notation systems for instructional design. In *Innovations in Instructional Technology: Essays in Honor of M. David Merrill*, edited by J. M. Spector, C. Ohrazda, A. Van Schaack, and D. Wiley, pp. 111–129. Mahwah, NJ: Lawrence Erlbaum Associates.*

Gibbons, A. S. and Rogers, P. C. (2006). Coming at Design from a Different Angle: Functional Design. Paper presented at the AECT Summer Research Symposium, June 22–25, Bloomington, IN.*

Gibbons, A. S. and Rogers, P.C. (2007). The architecture of instructional theory. In *Instructional-Design Theories and Models: A New Paradigm of Instructional Theory*, Vol. III, edited by C. Reigeluth, chap. 16. Mahwah, NJ: Lawrence Erlbaum Associates.*

Gibbons, A. S., Nelson, J., and Richards, R. (2000). *Theoretical and Practical Requirements for a System of Pre-Design Analysis: State of the Art of Pre-Design Analysis* (white paper). Idaho Falls, ID: Center for Human-Systems Simulation, Idaho National Engineering and Environmental Laboratory (DOE).

Goodwin, C. (1994). Professional vision. *Am. Anthropol.*, 96(3), 606–633.

Gray, J. (2006). A conversation with Werner Vogels: learning from the Amazon technology platform. *ACM Queue*, 4(4) (http://acmqueue.com/modules.php?name=Content&pa=showpage&pid=388).

Hollan, J., Hutchins, E., and Weitzman, L. (1984). STEAMER: an interactive inspectable simulation-based training system. *AI Mag.*, 5(2), 15–27.

Jackendoff, R. (1993). *Semantics and Cognition*. Cambridge, MA: MIT Press.

Januszewski, A. (2001). *Educational Technology: The Development of a Concept*. Englewood, CO: Libraries Unlimited.

Johnson, L., Rickel, J., and Lester, J. (2000). Animated pedagogical agents: face-to-face interaction in interactive learning environments. *Int. J. Artif. Intell. Educ.*, 11, 47–78.

Jonassen, D. H., Tessmer, M., and Hannum, W. H. (1999). *Task Analysis Methods for Instructional Design*. Mahwah, NJ: Lawrence Erlbaum Associates.

Koedinger, K. R. and Anderson, J. R. (1998). Illustrating principled design: the early evolution of a cognitive tutor for algebra symbolization. *Interact. Learn. Environ.*, 5, 161–180.

Koedinger, K. and Corbett, A. (2006). Cognitive tutors: technology bringing learning sciences to the classroom. In *The Cambridge Handbook of the Learning Sciences*, edited by R. K. Sawyer, pp. 61–78. Cambridge, U.K.: Cambridge University Press.

Koper, R. (2002). *Educational Modeling Language*, http://learningnetworks.org.

Koper, R. and Tattersall, C., Eds. (2005). *Learning Design: A Handbook on Modeling and Delivering Networked Education and Training*. Heidelberg: Springer-Verlag.

Kuehlmann, A., Ed. (2003). *The Best of ICCAD: 20 Years of Excellence in Computer-Aided Design*. Boston, MA: Kluwer.

Kuh, E. and Hsu, C. (2003). Physical design overview. In *The Best of ICCAD: 20 Years of Excellence in Computer-Aided Design*, edited by A. Kuehlmann, pp. 467–478. Boston. MA: Kluwer.

Lave, J. and Wenger, E. (1991). *Situated Learning: Legitimate Peripheral Practice*. Cambridge, U.K.: Cambridge University Press.

McDonald, J. K. (2006). Technology I, II, and III as Criteria to Better Understand How to Develop Scalable, Adaptive, and Generative Instruction. Ph.D. dissertation. Provo, UT: Brigham Young University.

McDonald, J. K. and Gibbons, A. S. (in press). Technology I, II, and III: criteria for understanding and improving the practice of instructional technology. *Educ. Technol. Res. Dev.*

McWhorter, J. (2003). *The Power of Babel: A Natural History of Languages*. New York: Times Books.*

Merrill, M. D. (1994). The descriptive component display theory. In *Instructional Design Theory*, edited by M. D. Merrill and D. G. Twitchell, pp. 111–157. Englewood Cliffs, NJ: Educational Technology Publications.

Miller, R. B. (1971). *Development of a Taxonomy of Human Performance*, Technical Report No. 11. Washington, D.C.: American Institutes for Research.

Newsome, S. L., Spillers, W. R., and Finger, S. (1989). *Design Theory '88: Proceedings of the NSF Grantee Workshop on Design Theory and Methodology*. New York: Springer-Verlag.

Nirenburg, S. and Raskin, V. (2004). *Ontological Semantics*. Cambridge, MA: MIT Press.

Noy, N. and McGuinness, D. (2006). *Ontology Development 101: A Guide to Creating Your First Ontology*, http://protege.stanford.edu/publications/ontology_development/ontology101-noy-mcguinness.html).

Paquette, G., Marino, O., De la Teja, I., Lundgren-Cayrol, K., Léonard, M., and Contamines, J. (2005). Implementation and deployment of the IMS learning design specification *Can. J. Learn. Technol.*, 31(2).

Pask, G. (1976). *Conversation Theory: Applications in Education and Epistemology*. New York: Elsevier.

Polanyi, M. (1958). *Personal Knowledge: Towards a Post-Critical Philosophy*. New York: Harper Torchbooks.

Reigeluth, C. M. (1983). *Instruction-Design Theories and Models: An Overview of Their Current Status*. Hillsdale, NJ: Lawrence Erlbaum Associates.

Reigeluth, C. M. (1999). *Instructional-Design Theories and Models: A New Paradigm of Instructional Theory*, Vol. II. Mahwah, NJ: Lawrence Erlbaum Associates.

Resnick, M. and Silverman, B. (2006). *Exploring Emergence*, http://llk.media.mit.edu/projects/emergence/contents.html.

Rheinfrank, J. and Evenson, S. (1996). Design languages. In *Bringing Design to Software*, edited by T. Winograd, pp. 63–79. New York: ACM Press/Addison-Wesley.

Richey, R. (1986). *The Theoretical and Conceptual Bases of Instructional Design*. New York: Kogan Page.

Rosenberg, S. (2007). Anything you can do I can do meta. *Technol. Rev.*, 110(1), 36–48.

Saabagh, K. (1996). *21st-Century Jet: The Making and Marketing of the Boeing 777*. New York: Scribner.

Sakallah, K., Walker, D., and Nassif, S. (2003). Timing, test, and manufacturing. In *The Best of ICCAD: 20 Years of Excellence in Computer-Aided Design*, edited by A. Kuehlmann, pp. 551–562. Boston, MA: Kluwer.

Schön, D. A. (1987). *Educating the Reflective Practitioner*. San Francisco, CA: Jossey-Bass.*

Seels, B. and Richey, R. (1994). *Instructional Technology: The Definition and Domains of the Field*. Bloomington, IN: Association for Educational Communications and Technology.

Snelbecker, G. E. (1985). *Learning Theory, Instructional Theory, and Psychoeducational Design*. Lanham, MD: University Press of America.

Stevens, A. L. and Collins, A. (1977). The Goal Structure of a Socratic Tutor. Paper presented at the 1977 ACM Annual Conference, October 17–21, Seattle, WA.

Stubbs, S. T. (2006). Design Drawing in Instructional Design at Brigham Young University's Center for Instructional Design: A Case Study. Ph.D. dissertation. Provo, UT: Brigham Young University.

Talmy, L. (2001). *Toward a Cognitive Semantics*. Cambridge, MA: MIT Press.

te Molder, H. and Potter, J., Eds. (2005). *Conversation and Cognition*. Cambridge, U.K.: Cambridge University Press.

Tennyson, R. D., Schott, F., Seel, N. M., and Dijkstra, S., Eds. (1997). *Instructional Design: International Perspectives*. Vol. I. *Theory, Research, and Models*. Mahwah. NJ: Lawrence Erlbaum Associates.

Waters, S. and Gibbons, A. S. (2004). Design languages, notation systems, and instructional technology: a case study. *Educ. Technol. Res. Dev.*, 52(2), 57–69.*

Wenger, E. (1998). *Communities of Practice: Learning, Meaning, and Identity*. Cambridge, U.K.: Cambridge University Press.*

Winograd, T. and Flores, F. (1987). *Understanding Computers and Cognition: A New Foundation for Design*. Reading, MA: Addison-Wesley.*

---

* Indicates a core reference.

# 48

# The Social Consequences of Design and Development Teams

*Laura Blasi and Stephen M. Fiore*
University of Central Florida, Orlando, Florida

*John Hedberg*
Macquarie University, North Ryde, New South Wales, Australia

*Richard F. Schmid*
Concordia University, Montreal, Quebec, Canada

## CONTENTS

## ABSTRACT

Providing a brief history of the work of design and development (D&D) teams grounded in the relevant literature, this chapter then offers several prominent examples from the past 65 years. These examples allow the comparison of the context for design and development focused on industry, government, and education. Although the implications for different approaches to teamwork for design and development are discussed, we highlight models for developing teams that are especially useful to those who are new to the field. We conclude with challenges faced by design and development teams specifically in regard to educational communications and technology. Design and development teams should: (1) organize in ways informed by the research, (2) access and apply research on teaching and learning, (3) conduct research for ongoing evaluation of technology in education, and (4) contribute to the research in the field from their own innovations, mindful of the social consequences of design and development.

## KEYWORDS

*Analytical science:* Within this perspective researchers aim to develop, test, and justify theories (D'Anjou, 2004; Hevner et al., 2004; Klabbers, 2003; Simon, 1996; van Aken, 2004); see design science and situated science.

*Design and development team:* The group of people and skill sets involved in the research-based development of artifacts and systems in education.

*Design science:* Within this perspective researchers aim to build and evaluate artifacts for well-defined contexts of use (D'Anjou, 2004; Hevner et al., 2004; Klabbers, 2003; Simon, 1996; van Aken, 2004); see analytical science and situated science.

*Design in the large (DIL):* Refers to the goal of changing existing situations into preferred ones (Klabbers, 2003); see design in the small (DIS).

*Design in the small (DIS):* Refers to the design of a specific innovation (Klabbers, 2003); see design in the large (DIL).

*Knowledge, skills, and abilities (KSAs):* Used in the traditional approach for specifying (team) competencies; recent research now expands the skills beyond those specifically attributed to the team task to include psychomotor and cognitive competencies (Cannon-Bowers et al., 1995).

*Shared mental models:* Crucial in the work of a team as members of the team need to share an accurate model of the problem to be addressed and the associated task to assess the problem, determine their own roles and responsibilities, and coordinate efforts over time (Cannon-Bowers et al., 1995).

*Situated science:* A perspective in which the scientific inquiry and attitude are carried into (instead of applied to) the field of the project and of practice, modifying each other over time as the project unfolds (Findeli, 2001; Simon, 1996); see analytical science and design science.

*Team Evolution and Maturation (TEAM) model:* Offers stages that have been observed in team performance that take into account time, experience, and training (Morgan et al., 1998).

*Transactional leader:* Exerts influence by setting goals, clarifying desired outcomes, providing feedback, and exchanging rewards and recognition for accomplishments; one of two leadership styles that hold the potential for more effective team performance, moving away from a traditional top-down directive approach (Bass, 1985; Sosik et al., 1997); see transformational leaders.

*Transformational leader:* Exerts influence by broadening and elevating followers' goals and providing them with the confidence to go beyond minimally acceptable expectations specified in the exchange; one of two leadership styles that hold the potential for more effective team performance, moving away from a traditional top-down directive approach (Bass, 1985; Sosik et al., 1997); see transactional leaders.

## INTRODUCTION

The challenges faced by design and development (D&D) teams in regard to developing information and communications technology in education begin with the ability to conceptualize needs, resources, and goals. At the very end of the D&D cycle, beyond the completion of individual tasks and products, impact is evident in the social consequences that unfold even after the project conclusion. Technology has an undeniable impact on all aspects of society, and yet the roles and responsibilities of designers and developers are not often discussed generally nor are they discussed specifically with regard to education.

This chapter is intended to offer discussion regarding the social consequences of design and development (Bowers, 1988, 2000; Ellul, 1964; Postman, 1992; Stoll, 1999) while outlining models of teamwork with three well-known projects alongside some of the most recent research in organizational theory and the development of technologies for teaching and learning. The uses of research findings and research methods are described in ways that can inform the development of individual projects in education, as designers and developers: (1) aim for optimal performance of the individual and the team informed by the research on organizational theory, (2) access and apply research on teaching and learning in the development of technologies for education, (3) conduct research for formative and summative evaluation of technology in education strengthened and aligned with a larger vision for education, and (4) contribute to the research in the field from their own individual innovation or artifact informing the larger efforts toward systemic change in education.

## DEFINING DESIGN AND DEVELOPMENT

Who are the designers and developers, and what is their relationship to the field of education? Finding them within a range disciplines, including education, D'Anjou (2004, p. 213) drew on the earlier writing of Simon (1996) and explained that:

> The science of design becomes the broader foundational paradigm for professional education, which includes any disciplines engaged in the intentional transformation of the world, from bridges to political programs ... they view the world as a project, whereas science, such as physics, biology, sociology, etc., views it as an object.

The distinction between the analytical sciences (developing, testing, and justifying theories) and the design sciences (building and evaluating artifacts for well-defined contexts of use) has been made by Klabbers (2003b) and others (Hevner et al., 2004; van Aken, 2004). As D&D teams work within the design sciences, they develop individual projects that are then implemented within a larger system.

Four elements are critical to D&D team members' ability to contribute to an individual project, as team members need to share an understanding of the: (1) information structure and its representation, (2) the instructional design and underlying beliefs about learning, (3) interaction possibilities and their design, and (4) interface mechanisms of their visual presentations (Hedberg and Sims, 2001). This definition draws upon the foundations of instructional design, which over time has placed increasing emphasis on the learner and on developing the interactive potential within innovations for teaching and learning (Dick et al., 2005; Ertmer and Quinn, 2003; Gagné and Briggs, 1974; Preece et al., 2002; Reigeluth, 1999; Schank and Jona, 1991). Drawing on Simon (1996) and the distinctions between science as applied and design as involved, Findeli (2001) cast the designer as a stakeholder who participates in the learning dimension of the project and ends up transformed.

As stakeholders within systems, designers and developers need to keep in mind the systemic perspective. In the case of education, this requires considering the needs and context in education at the beginning of a project as well as later, evaluating the value of the team work as a contribution to this field (Blasi and Alfonso, 2006). Not only does the work of D&D respond to larger questions and problems in society but it also has an impact on society. Ethicists are arguing that, unless those on the front lines become better able to appreciate the ethical dimensions of the issues they are addressing and become more adept at carrying out responsible solutions, "the power of science and technology will continue to accelerate [while] the ability of humans and their institutions to understand and respond to the changes wrought by science and technology will remain more or less the same" (Sarewitz, 2000, p. 14).

The work of designers and developers take place on two levels, which Klabbers has distinguished as design in the small (DIS), which refers to the design of a specific innovation, and design in the large (DIL), which refers to the goal of changing existing situations into preferred ones (2003a, p. 489). Individual D&D projects are part of an entire system in which the designer and the developer are stakeholders and have an impact in terms of both DIS and DIL. The following three examples offer a glimpse at the history and context for the unfolding work of D&D teams. These examples are followed by prevalent models and challenges from the research literature. Each example illustrates a specific instance in which the work within individual projects was then implemented within a larger system, with related social consequences.

Laura Blasi, Stephen M. Fiore, John Hedberg, and Richard F. Schmid

## THREE EXAMPLES OF DESIGN AND DEVELOPMENT

### The Manhattan Project (Government)

The Manhattan Engineer District included 37 installations in 19 states and employed at its peak some 150,000 workers (Williams, 1999). The Pulitzer Prize winning *The Making of the Atomic Bomb* (Rhodes, 1995) was followed by more analytical histories that described the context for the team work and criticized its authoritarian, antidemocratic, and coercive aspects (Goldberg, 1992; Hughes, 2004). Badash (2005) argued that the lack of a relevant tradition and the disparate nature of the project provided little basis for anticipating problems of social responsibility (Badash, 2005). The development and design tasks were divided and administered separately at the various sites of the project. Many involved, including Oppenheimer, later became active in the political discussions of nuclear issues (Badash, 2005). The beginning of the nuclear arms race, along with competition with the USSR for manned space flight, increased the demand for educational reform in the science, technology, engineering, and mathematics (STEM) fields, as well as for innovation in technology which included the advent of the personal computer.

### Apple (Industry)

The work of the D&D team that eventually led to today's Apple, Inc., is well-known for its humble beginnings in a family garage (Linzmayer, 1999). As an example of design and development, the Apple computer started out as a compelling example of self-managed teamwork: "The fascination of the story of Apple Computer is that Wozniak and Jobs broke all the rules. In many cases, they deliberately flaunted convention and they still succeeded, in conventional terms, beyond all expectation" (Elbinger, 1985, p. 90; see also Wolf, 1996). Unlike the Manhattan Project, with its time frame defined in terms of national defense, the development of the Apple computer was fueled by the developers' and their own interest in establishing a new market for personal computers. The advent of the personal computer paved the way for computers in the classroom and the design and development of specific applications of technology that were fun to play with and could work in schools.

### *The Adventures of Jasper Woodbury* (Education)

The *Adventures of Jasper Woodbury* was developed by the Cognition and Technology Group at Vanderbilt (CTGV, 1992; see also Bransford et al., 1990), which

was an interdisciplinary team focused on education. The CTGV was focused on developing a standards-based program linked to specific course content that could run on laserdisc technology while also drawing on computers and teleconferencing. The developers aligned their development of activities and their content with the National Council of Teachers of Mathematics (NCTM) Standards for School Mathematics (The Learning Technology Center, 1992), which are among several content standards in U.S. education. The *Jasper* program offers published examples of team development and design specific to education, as well as research on impact and implementation (Barron et al., 1998; Vye et al., 1997).

Certain characteristics of teamwork evident in these three examples are more systematically discussed in the text that follows in ways that can be applied in team development and performance, drawing on the published research regarding organizational theory (see Table 48.1).

## CURRENT RESEARCH ON TEAM FORMATION, DEVELOPMENT, AND PERFORMANCE

What is clear from these examples is the multidisciplinary nature of the problems that were addressed with teams that were diverse in terms of expertise and skills. Through strong leadership and a shared vision members of the teams were able to effectively collaborate. The three examples of innovation in design and development can be discussed in terms of their goals, specific to DIS and DIL (Klabbers, 2003a), as well as in terms of the conditions for team performance and the social consequences of the team products. A review of the research literature more fully presents some of the factors that challenge or contribute to effective team performance.

### Defining Teamwork

Teamwork is characterized by a well-designed development strategy, by clearly identified units of performance, and by a common purpose that can be translated into specific performance goals. Researchers have distinguished between *working groups* and *teams* and have documented the differences. Hoffman et al. (2001) have noted that deliberative team development strategies were seldom referenced throughout their 54 interviews and survey responses across 6 projects. Team development implies putting groups of people to work on common tasks. Hoffman and colleagues (2001) did not generally describe specific actions taken to strengthen the characteristics that they associated

**TABLE 48.1**
**Examples of Design and Development Teams and Questions**

| | The Manhattan Project (Government) | Apple Computer (Industry) | The Adventures of Jasper Woodbury (Education) |
|---|---|---|---|
| Question raised for design and development: | What are the responsibilities and the social consequences of design and development? | What factors need to be considered for team development and how do self-managed teams aim for success? | How can design and development teams contribute to the field of education? |

with the best or superior project teams: interdependence, cohesion, and commitment (Tanskanen et al., 1998). Katzenbach and Smith (1993), in their study of 50 different teams from over 30 companies, noted that groups emphasize individual products, individual accountability, delegating rather than doing tasks, and indirect measures of effectiveness (such as financial performance) rather than evaluating actual work of the group. In contrast, teams will share leadership roles and seek to fulfill a specialized purpose beyond the larger organization, with individual and mutual accountability focused on collective work products.

According to Salas et al. (1992, p. 4), teams can be defined as:

… a distinguishable set of two or more people who interact, dynamically, interdependently, and adaptively toward a common and valued goal/objective/mission, who have each been assigned specific roles or functions to perform, and who have a limited life-span of membership.

Distributed teams have emerged with individuals possessing complementary skills but separated by great distances and coordinating their actions using collaboration systems supporting teamwork over time and space (Fiore et al., 2003; Lipnack and Stamps, 2000).

In research regarding the formation and work of D&D teams, Hoffman et al. (2001, p. 2) noted that "rigorous definition and analysis of human variables have often been lacking. This lack has created a tendency to approach teams from a 'guru of the month' philosophy. Often the latest trend is applied to a project team, as opposed to a well-designed team development strategy based on research and experience" (p. 2). Katzenbach and Smith (1993, p. 112) suggested that teamwork requires a shift from thinking about the development and performance of teams in terms of positive values toward thinking about it in terms of discrete units of performance (see also Faraj and Sproull, 2000). Failed teams typically lack a common purpose, but the best teams "translate their common purpose into specific performance goals" (Katzenbach and Smith, 1993, p. 113).

## A Model for Team Development

The development of the team has been shown to follow patterns of activity rather than a linear, sequential process. The process of team formation was described by Tuckman (1965), who drew upon a review of 50 articles in group development to identify four stages: (1) orientation/testing/dependence, (2) conflict, (3) group cohesion, and (4) functional role relatedness. These stages are also referred to as *forming, storming, norming*, and *performing*. Building on Tuckman's work, Morgan et al. (1998) proposed the Team Evolution and Maturation (TEAM) model, which describes stages that have been observed in team performance that take into account time, experience, and training and "provides a framework for developing and evaluating instructional strategies, training methods, interventions, tools, procedures, and instructor behaviors that can be applied to the enhancement of team development" (p. 288).

## Approaches to Leadership

Individual leadership has been emphasized in the literature on organizational behavior. The leader may not necessarily be the manager of the team. Barak et al. (1999, p. 93) distinguished between the "external manager appointed by management" and the leader who emerges in a group who is less aligned with a managerial function and more closely associated with expertise and charisma. The roles of the leader in the development and performance of teams are complex. Individuals report higher levels of commitment and stronger satisfaction when they perceive they have some influence in the decisions made by their team leader (Morris et al., 2000). The effective sharing of information held by individuals can become part of the D&D process if the appropriate conditions are established within the team by a knowledgeable leader (Schittekatte, 1996; Stasser, 1992). Drawing on Bass (1985), Sosik et al. (1997, p. 90) suggested that "transactional leaders exert influence by setting goals … transformational leaders exert influence by broadening and elevating followers' goals." When teams are self-managed, however, they require collaborative leadership for optimal performance.

## Preparing for Participation in Self-Managed Teams

Barry (1991, p. 34) noted that within a self-managed team the "distributed leadership pattern that arises ... is necessarily an emergent one. It normally begins with different members initiating directions in areas they are naturally predisposed toward and that are needed by the team." Such teams have been described by Barry (1991, p. 32) as requiring "even more leadership than conventional organizational units. In addition to needing task-based leadership, they require leadership around group development processes," and "without the presence of formal authority, power struggles and conflict around both task and process issues surface more often, adding to the overall leadership burden that must be handled by the group." Stewart and Manz (1995) provided a typology and an integrative model of leadership for self-managing work teams based on Bandura's (1977) social learning theory and the continuum of leadership practices previously identified by Bass (1990). Stewart and Manz (1995, p. 752) presented four types of team-leader behavior: overpowering, powerless, power building, and empowered. In these four types of leader behaviors, goals influence each set of behaviors and elicit specific reactions and outcomes from the teams.

## Coordination of Process and Expertise Key to Team Performance

In their study of 69 software development teams, Faraj and Sproull (2000, p. 1554) reported that expertise coordination shows a strong relationship with team performance that remains significant over and above team input characteristics, presence of expertise, and administrative coordination; although expertise may be evident, the quality of performance relies on the team's ability to recognize and draw on that expertise. Barry (1991, p. 33) noted that "directive and socially centered support functions might vary as a group matures," with the need for direction being higher at the beginning of projects and later on the need for support, rather than direction, increasing.

Coordination approaches can include: (1) those in which most coordination happens at the end of the project, (2) the incremental approach where coordination takes place in cycles over time, and (3) the fault-driven approach where coordination takes place at the moments of highest instability (Chiang and Mookerjee, 2004). In educational projects, this coordination includes the educational and the technical expertise of other members of the development team, as they use formative evaluation data emphasizing the role of the learner as an actor in the interaction and how the user or learner will undertake the task, rather than focusing solely on the learning task (Hedberg and Sims, 2001). Ultimately, "proper process design is the key to better productivity" (Chiang and Mookerjee, 2004, p. 92).

## Stabilizing a Project Early in the Process

Observing that the coordination process within D&D teams is mostly *ad hoc*, Chiang and Mookerjee (2004, p. 967) noted that:

> ...project teams that can stabilize modules fairly quickly can afford to coordinate less frequently early on in the project. ...One trait of top-notch developers is their ability to acquire project-specific knowledge and avoid major rework—even in an unfamiliar project domain. Evidence of this learning process is the fact that the development team stabilizes (or "baselines") newly developed modules more efficiently as the project progresses.

Considering the role individuals play in the process of stabilization, it has been found that the preference for working in groups that individuals bring to the project and the positive perception of group capabilities that individuals develop within the project both predict group performance (Jung and Sosik, 1999). Looking at ways of improving team productivity, Chiang and Mookerjee (2004) suggested improving software-building technologies and refinement of the development process, but they also suggest strengthening individual competencies in addition to analyzing the roles individuals play within the team.

## Managing Individual Goals and Behaviors

Beyond the team leader, the individual decisions made within a team by designers and developers contribute to their own levels of commitment and satisfaction. The individuals on the team must be able to set individual goals while managing their own performance. Drawing on social learning theory (Bandura, 1977), Manz and Sims (1980, p. 361) emphasized that:

> ... individuals manage their own behaviors by setting personal standards, evaluating their performance in terms of these standards, and by self-administering consequences based on their self-evaluations. Specific techniques such as self-observation, goal specification, cueing strategies, incentive modification, and rehearsal can be used to exercise self-management behavior.

The leader of the team can facilitate individual self-management, modeling behaviors, and the development of self-management by subordinates by exerting external control and reinforcement while reducing the need for supervision.

Individual knowledge, skills, and abilities (KSAs) have an impact on team development and performance, specific to the context, the team, the task, or in some combination of these (Cannon-Bowers et al., 1995, p. 357). A broader conceptualization of what constitutes KSAs in a D&D team is needed to account for the ethical and societal dimensions and the need for multidisciplinary problem solving. Seldom are team members trained for awareness and responsiveness when faced with either of these challenges. At the same time, the ability to develop shared mental models and strategic consensus become part of this wider conceptualization of KSAs working alongside the diversity specific to the team and its leadership.

## Team Competencies and Training Requirements

Team development, training, and performance each have to be understood in terms of the context of the project—specifically, the tasks required and their associated environmental conditions. To determine training requirements, it is necessary to evaluate the competency requirements for the task at hand (Cannon-Bowers et al., 1995). Cannon-Bowers and her colleagues expanded the definition of skills in KSAs to include also psychomotor and cognitive competencies. Some competencies are task generic and other competencies are task specific, with team-specific competencies (e.g., perceived efficacy and compensation strategies) working alongside team-generic competencies (e.g., communications skills, leadership skills, and attitudes towards teamwork). With respect to understanding complex teamwork, the moderating influence of task complexity also must be examined. Component complexity describes the number of distinct acts associated with a task as well as the cues that must be processed (Wood, 1986). Here, the emphasis is on the importance of informational cues given that cue processing is increasingly recognized as a critical component of expert situation assessment. Coordinative complexity describes the degree to which task variables must be integrated for successful task completion. Awareness of such distinctions is necessary for coordination and participation in a complex teamwork situation.

## Understanding the Impact of Shared Mental Models for Strategic Consensus

Shared mental models also are crucial in the work of a team, as all members of the team need to share an accurate model of the problem to be addressed and the associated task to assess the problem, determine their own roles and responsibilities, and coordinate efforts over time (Cannon-Bowers et al., 1995). Researchers have investigated strategic consensus, or the degree to which mental models overlap without necessarily drawing on a deliberative consensus-seeking process. Measuring four demographic indicators of diversity, Knight et al. (1999) found that functional background and employment tenure were negatively related to consensus, with less evidence of impact evident for difference in age and level of education. The degree of consensus has an impact upon the strategic orientation of the larger organization and the process and products expected of individuals in design and development. At the same time, D&D teams can be strengthened by understanding that differences in functional background, employment tenure, age, and level of education will contribute to or challenge the team's ability to work within shared mental models, and subsequently it will impact their ability to develop strategic consensus. Diverse leadership styles are required, especially in teams that are self-managed, but as Barry (1991, p. 40) explained, using these differences effectively "entails developing genuine respect for the diverse styles and learning."

## Establishing the Optimal Context for Team Performance

Competencies within teams are mitigated by the context in which the team operates. Looking at distributed team performance, Fiore and his colleagues (2003, p. 343) drew on three inter-related constructs:

> (1) the socio-cognitive factors arising from the group dynamics inherent in team environments (e.g., team attitudes); (2) the artificial components consisting of the technology enabling the interaction among distributed team members (e.g., computer-mediated communication); and (3) the dynamic processes associated with distributed team interaction (e.g., coordination efforts occurring over time).

The types of collaboration supported by the development environment will have an impact on the process and the product of the D&D team. When they examined the effects of four modes of group communication on the outcomes of software requirements determination using 42 groups of graduates in computer and information services (CIS) or information services (IS) programs, Ocker et al. (1998) found that the combined group (face-to-face and asynchronous) demonstrated higher quality and creativity in their solutions while also reporting higher satisfaction with their solutions. With the increasing use of asynchronous communication technologies in the corporate environment, our research suggests that the use of a communication mode according to the type of group work at a given

Laura Blasi, Stephen M. Fiore, John Hedberg, and Richard F. Schmid

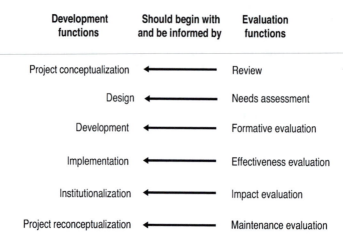

|Development<br>functions|Should begin with<br>and be informed by|Evaluation<br>functions|
|---|---|---|
|Project conceptualization|←|Review|
|Design|←|Needs assessment|
|Development|←|Formative evaluation|
|Implementation|←|Effectiveness evaluation|
|Institutionalization|←|Impact evaluation|
|Project reconceptualization|←|Maintenance evaluation|

**Figure 48.1** How designers and developers use research methods for evaluation. *Note:* The arrows indicate direction of information flow; they go from the evaluation function to the development stage. (Adapted from Reeves, T.C. and Hedberg, J.G., in *Flexible Learning in an Information Society*, Khan, B., Ed., Information Science Publishing, Hershey, PA, 2007, pp. 226–235.)

point in time can greatly affect the effectiveness of a group's work product (Ocker et al., 1998, p. 114; see also Linebarger et al., 2005).

## CHALLENGES FOR DESIGN AND DEVELOPMENT TEAMS

Design and development teams can aim for optimal performance drawing on the research literature in organizational theory. Their projects can grow out of their ability to access and apply the most up-to-date research on how and what students learn (Donovan et al., 1999; Kolodner, 1991; McGinn and Roth, 1999; Pellegrino, 2002), as well as on specific challenges in education such as the assessment of learning (Hunt and Pellegrino, 2002). It is, however, the team members' own use of research methods that will strengthen and align the development of technology for teaching and learning in relation to a larger vision for education. To align projects within a larger vision for education, evaluation is key throughout the project. The relationship between development and evaluation has been described by Reeves and Hedberg (2003) in Figure 48.1.

The development and design process across education, the government, and industry is often initiated on a project-basis; however, researchers have provided frameworks for addressing issues of scalability and sustainability that consider school capabilities, policy and management structures, and organizational culture (Blumenfeld et al., 2000). Researchers have also described the "incompatibilities between the demands of the innovations being introduced by the research community and the extant culture, capability, and management structures of schools" (Fishman et al., 2001).

After the project is complete, planning for scalability and sustainability must draw on evaluation data to align the project with an overarching vision for education. Here, the evaluation data for effectiveness, impact, and maintenance are key (Reeves and Hedberg, 2003). Four stages of evaluation within design and development begin with the educational goal for the artifact and then research methods are used by the D&D team to: (1) verify the artifact, (2) check the variation of the content, (3) verify its use in context, and, finally, (4) document its value in the wider field of education (Blasi and Alfonso, 2006).

Beyond applying research methods for the formative and summative evaluation of technologies for teaching and learning, researchers have developed a framework for research regarding innovation that calls for research in the context of systemic reform to address issues of usability, scalability, and sustainability across projects (Fishman et al., 2004). Although evaluation data can contribute to systematic change in education, the research and development process can also track the ways in which technologies for teaching and learning, as educative materials, actually have an impact on teacher learning as well as on student learning (Schneider and Krajcik, 1999).

### Team Purpose and Goals Informed by Research

The research literature on D&D teams offers a framework for optimal performance, but the research literature regarding teaching and learning can also be used by teams to inform projects developed for education (Quintana et al., 2004; Singer et al., 2000; Talsma and

Krajcik, 2002). When they use research in teaching and learning to inform decisions in D&D, designers and developers are transforming research findings into learning experiences. The extent to which teams are able to access and apply the research on teaching and learning will determine the extent to which larger, long-term social and economic goals are met by design and development in education.

A specific example of design and development that transforms the research on teaching and learning can be found in Alphie's Alley, which was developed by the Centre for the Study of Learning and Performance (CSLP, 2006). The Success for All Foundation (SFA) offers a comprehensive, schoolwide literacy program called Reading Roots, which emphasizes early intervention to anticipate and solve problems in reading (Slavin and Madden, 2001), and Alphie's Alley is the electronic performance support system (Gery, 2001) for Reading Roots. It was developed in collaboration with SFA to support the daily, one-on-one tutoring for the lowest performing 30% of first graders in this schoolwide literacy program throughout high-poverty Title I schools that serves more than 1 million children.

In Alphie's Alley, the software plays a supporting role by connecting the student and tutor through the computer, informed by the conviction that pedagogy must direct technology (Abrami et al., 2005; Clark, 2001; Hipps et al., 2005; Kozma, 1994a,b, 2000), and it was also developed out of the research on early literacy (Adams, 1990; Slavin and Madden, 2001). Built on a foundation of research in reading and evaluation using a randomized control group design, Alphie's Alley has yielded significant positive effects (Slavin et al., 2006) and positive tutor acceptance (Schmid et al., 2006), thus serving as just one example of a project that transforms the research in teaching and learning into an experience enabled through technology.

## CONCLUDING DISCUSSION AND SUMMARY

### The Social Consequences of Design and Development

As we have discussed, design and development teams occupy an important niche in our society. They are responsible for a form of creative problem solving that spans the development of educational software to the construction of the nuclear bomb. We need to understand the knowledge, skills, and abilities necessary for those making up D&D teams. On the one hand is the issue of leading such teams; on the other hand is the level of competency required by such teams, as discussed earlier. If we can understand how teams attempt

to understand task complexity within their work (DIS), we can better help them understand how this work more broadly has an impact on society (DIL).

Unfortunately, such teams often work to solve problems of such complexity that, without the requisite team training, they may not achieve their potential. Furthermore, research shows that when we attempt to understand complex problems, we often oversimplify the situation in our attempts to comprehend as much as possible. Indeed, understanding complex constructs represents an important challenge to the welfare of humankind given that misinterpretation of factors within a system or mismanagement of these factors can have devastating consequences. Scientific analysis of complex systems has identified a number of factors that make them particularly challenging to understand, including constant change coupled with high interdependence of multiple variables (Feltovich et al., 1997; Spiro et al., 1992). Problematically, these complexities are often overlooked because of our tendency to build simplified understandings and explanations that lead to misconceptions and possibly errors—a phenomenon termed the *reductive bias* (Feltovich et al., 2004).

Almost 20 years after an Association for Educational Communications and Technology (AECT) survey of 80 professors of instructional systems design and technology sought to assess the current thinking of association members toward ethics in the field (Nichols, 1987), there is a growing discussion about ethics in terms of social consequences. Twenty years ago most concluded that "they address ethical issues in a variety of ways, but that more needs to be done" (Nichols, 1987). At that time, most reported discussing technology impact "from the effects of technology on learners in general to the effects on whole cultures" rather than in regard to the designer role (Nichols, 1987). Findeli (2001, p. 14) illuminated the distinction between technicians (focused on the DIS) and designers (focused on the DIS and DIL):

> Within these complex systems, designers are expected to *act* rather than to *make* … In philosophical terms, one would say that design pertains to practical, not to instrumental, reason; or else that the frame of the design project is ethics, not technology. In existentialist terms, this could sound as follows: design responsibility means that designers always should be conscious of the fact that, each time they engage themselves in a design project, they somehow recreate the world. [emphasis original]

History offers clear examples of failed innovations that once held the promise of improved teaching and learning (Cuban, 1986, 2001). The documented process regarding change and the diffusion of innovations shows that success or failure relies in part on how and

Laura Blasi, Stephen M. Fiore, John Hedberg, and Richard F. Schmid

when the innovation is introduced and supported (Hall and Hord, 1987; McLaughlin, 1990; Rogers, 1995). Although designers and developers cannot control what happens to a product once it is released, it is possible to train for optimal team work, mindful of long-term social consequences. D&D teams can (1) organize in ways informed by the research from organizational theory, (2) access and apply the research regarding teaching and learning, and (3) conduct research toward formative and summative evaluation of technology in education. Through this process, they can also (4) contribute to the research in the field through their own innovations. In this way, D&D teams are co-creators within larger efforts toward systemic change in education, mindful of the social consequences of design and development.

## Summary

The work of designers and developers takes place on two levels, which Klabbers has distinguished as *design in the small* (DIS), which refers to the design of a specific innovation, and *design in the large* (DIL), which refers to the goal of changing existing situations into preferred ones (Klabbers, 2003a, p. 489). Designers and developers are stakeholders and have an impact in terms of both DIS and DIL. With the distinction made between individual projects and the entire system, a glimpse at the history and context for the unfolding work of design and development teams in three examples was then followed by prevalent models and challenges for teams from the research literature. Specifically, in this chapter, we began with a discussion of three examples of teamwork from the 20th century. Each example illustrates a specific instance in which the work within individual projects was then implemented within a larger system with related social consequences. Building on the questions raised by these examples, we discussed some of the lessons learned for team development and management drawn from the research literature, and we reviewed the core concepts necessary for effective design teams. These include the specification of performance factors, such as well-stated design purposes and goals; identification of the knowledge, skills, and abilities foundational to the team's purpose; and, last, a shared understanding of factors related to optimal teamwork. Our goals in this chapter were to (1) highlight the complexity inherent in design and development, (2) describe how design and development teams can draw from and contribute to research in the field of education, and (3) convey an appreciation of how theory and methods from differing disciplines can aid our understanding and improvement of this important process.

## ACKNOWLEDGMENTS

The authors wish to acknowledge the work of University of Central Florida graduate students Julia Berlin and Jennifer Grill for their assistance in conducting the literature review that contributed to this chapter.

## References

Abrami, P., Savage, R. S., Wade, A., and Hipps, G. (2005). Using Technology to Help Children to Learn to Read and Write. Keynote address to the Children's Learning in a Digital World Conference. August 19–20, Brock University, Ontario, Canada.

Adams, M. (1990). *Beginning to Read: Thinking and Learning About Print*. Cambridge, MA: MIT Press.

Badash, L. (2005). American physicists, nuclear weapons in World War II, and social responsibility. *Phys. Perspect.*, 7(2), 138–149.

Bandura, A. (1977). *Social Learning Theory*. Englewood Cliffs, NJ: Prentice Hall.

Barak, M., Maymon, T., and Harel, G. (1999). Teamwork in modern organizations: implications for technology education. *Int. J. Technol. Design Educ.*, 9. 85–101.*

Barron, L., Bransford, J., Goin, L., Goldman, E., Goldman, S., Hasselbring, T., Pellegrino, J., Rewey, K., Sherwood, R., and Vye, N. (1993). The *Jasper* experiment: using video to furnish real-world problem-solving contexts. *Arith. Teacher*, 40(8), 474–479.

Barron, B. J. S., Schwartz, D. L., Vye, N. J., Moore, A., Petrosino, A., Zech, L. et al. (1998). Doing with understanding: lessons from research on problem- and project-based learning. *J. Learn. Sci.*, 7(3), 271–311.

Barry, D. (1991). Managing the bossless team: lessons in distributed leadership. *Org. Dynam.*, 20(1), 31–47.*

Bass, B. M. (1985). *Leadership and Performance Beyond Expectations*. New York: Free Press.

Bass, B.M. (1990). *Bass and Stogdill's Handbook of Leadership: Theory, Research, and Managerial Applications*. New York: Free Press.

Blasi, L. and Alfonso, B. (2006). Increasing the transfer of simulation technology from R&D into school settings. *Simul. Gaming*, 37(2), 245–267.*

Blumenfeld, P., Fishman, B. J., Krajcik, J., Marx, R. W., and Soloway, E. (2000). Creating usable innovations in systemic reform: scaling up technology-embedded project-based science in urban schools. *Educ. Psychol.*, 35(3), 149–164.

Bowers, C. A. (1988). *The Cultural Dimensions of Educational Computing: Understanding the Non-Neutrality of Technology*. New York: Teachers College Press.*

Bowers, C. A. (2000). *Let Them Eat Data: How Computers Affect Education, Cultural Diversity, and the Prospects of Ecological Sustainability*. Athens, GA: The University of Georgia Press.

Bransford, J. D., Sherwood, R. D., Hasselbring, T. S., Kinzer, C. K., and Williams, S. M. (1990). Anchored instruction: why we need it and how technology can help. In *Cognition, Education, and Multimedia*, edited by D. Nix and R. Spiro, pp. 115–142. Hillsdale, NJ: Lawrence Erlbaum Associates.

Cannon-Bowers, J. A., Tannenbaum, S. I., Salas, E., and Volpe, C. E. (1995). Defining competencies and establishing team training requirements. In *Team Effectiveness and Decision Making in Organizations*, edited by R. Guzzo and E. Salas, pp. 333–380. San Francisco, CA: Jossey-Bass.*

Centre for the Study of Learning and Performance (CSLP). (2006). *Alphie's Alley*. Montreal: Department of Education, Concordia University (http://doe.concordia.ca/cslp/).

Chiang, I. R. and Mookerjee, V. S. (2004). Improving software team productivity. *Commun. ACM*, 47(5), 89–93.*

Clark, R. E., Ed. (2001). *Learning from Media*. Greenwich, CT: Information Age Publishing.

Cognition and Technology Group at Vanderbilt (CTGV). (1992). The *Jasper* series as an example of anchored instruction: theory, program description, and assessment data. *Educ. Psychol.*, 27(3), 291–315.

Cuban, L. (1986). *Teachers and Machines: The Classroom Use of Technology Since 1920*. New York: Teachers College Press.

Cuban, L. (2001). *Oversold and Underused: Computers in the Classroom*. Cambridge, MA: Harvard University Press.

D'Anjou, P. (2004). Theoretical and methodological elements for integrating ethics as a foundation into the education of professional and design disciplines. *Sci. Eng. Ethics*, 10(2), 211–218.

Dick, W., Carey, L., and Carey, J. O. (2005). *The Systematic Design of Instruction*, 6th ed. Boston, MA: Allyn & Bacon.

Donovan, M. S. E., Bransford, J. D. E., and Pellegrino, J. W. E. (1999). *How People Learn: Bridging Research and Practice*. Washington, D.C.: National Academy of Sciences.

Elbinger, L. (1985). WOZ and The Little Kingdom [book reviews]. *Bus. Soc. Rev.*, 52, 90.

Ellul, J. (1964). *The Technological Society*. New York: Vintage.

Ertmer, P. and Quinn, J. (2003). *The ID Case Book: Case Studies in Instructional Design*, 2nd ed. Upper Saddle River, NJ: Pearson Education.

Faraj, S. A. and Sproull, L. (2000). Coordinating expertise in software development teams. *Manage. Sci.*, 46, 1554–1568.

Feltovich, P. J., Spiro, R. J., and Coulson, R. L. (1997). Issues of expert flexibility in contexts characterized by complexity and change. In *Expertise in Context: Human and Machine*, edited by P. J. Feltovich, K. M. Ford, and R. R. Hoffman, pp. 125–146. Cambridge, MA: MIT Press.

Feltovich, P. J., Hoffman, R. R., Woods, D., and Roesler, A. (2004). Keeping it too simple: how the reductive tendency affects cognitive engineering. *IEEE Intell. Syst.*, 19(3), 90–94.

Findeli, A. (2001). Rethinking design education for the 21st century: theoretical, methodological, and ethical discussion. *Design Issues*, 17(1), 5–17.

Fiore, S. M., Salas, E., Cuevas, H. M., and Bowers, C. A. (2003). Distributed coordination space: toward a theory of distributed team process and performance. *Theor. Issues Ergon. Sci.*, 4(3/4), 340.*

Fishman, B., Soloway, E., Krajcik, J., Marx, R., and Blumenfeld, P. (2001). Creating Scalable and Systemic Technology Innovations for Urban Education. Paper presented at the American Educational Research Association Annual Meeting, April 10–14, Seattle, WA.

Fishman, B., Marx, R. W., Blumenfeld, P., Krajcik, J., and Soloway, E. (2004). Creating a framework for research on systemic technology innovations. *J. Learn. Sci.*, 13(1), 43–76.

Gagné, R. M. and Briggs L. J. (1974). *Principles of Instructional Design*. New York: Holt, Rinehart and Winston.

Gery, G. (2002). Achieving performance and learning through performance centered systems. *Adv. Dev. Hum. Resour.*, 4(4), 464–478.

Goldberg, S. (1992). Inventing a climate of opinion. *Isis*, 83(3), 429–452.

Hall, G. E. and Hord, S. M. (1987). *Change in Schools: Facilitating the Process*. New York: State University of New York Press.

Hedberg, J. and Sims, R. (2001). Speculations on design team interactions. *J. Interact. Learn. Res.*, 12(2/3), 193–208.*

Hevner, A. R., March, S. T., Park, J., and Ram, S. (2004). Design science in information systems research. *MIS Q.*, 28, 75–105.

Hipps, G., Abrami, P., Savage, R. S., Cerna, N., and Jorgensen, A. (2005). Abracadabra: research, design, and development of a Web-based early literacy software. In *Innovations et tendances en technologies de formation et d'apprentissage: Développement, intégration et évaluation des technologies de formation et d'apprentissage*, edited by S. Pierre, pp. 89–112. Quebec: Presses Internationales Polytechnique. Valeurisation de Researches de Quèbec (DIVA).

Hoffman, E. J., Kinlaw, C. S., and Kinlaw, D. C. (2001). *Developing Superior Project Teams: A Study of the Characteristics of High Performance in Project Teams*. Washington, D.C.: NASA (http://www.nasateammates.com/About/findings.pdf).

Hughes, J. (2004). Deconstructing the bomb: recent perspectives on nuclear history. *Br. J. Hist. Sci.*, 37(135), 455–464.

Hunt, E. and Pellegrino, J. W. (2002). Issues, examples, and challenges in formative assessment. *New Dir. Teaching Learn.*, (89), 73.

Jung, D. I. and Sosik, J. J. (1999). Effects of group characteristics on work group performance: a longitudinal investigation. *Group Dynam. Theory Res. Pract.*, 3(4), 279–290.

Katzenbach, J. R. and Smith, D. K. (1993). The discipline of teams. *Harvard Bus. Rev.*, 71(2), 111–120.*

Klabbers, J. H. G. (2003a). Simulation and gaming: introduction to the art and science of design. *Simul. Gaming*, 34, 488–494.

Klabbers, J. H. G. (2003b). Gaming and simulation: principles of a science of design. *Simul. Gaming*, 34, 569–591.*

Knight, D., Pearce, C. L., Smith, K. G., Olian, J. D., Sims, H. P., Smith, K. A. et al. (1999). Top management team diversity, group process, and strategic consensus. *Strat. Manage. J.*, 20, 445–465.

Kolodner, J. L. (1991). The Journal of the Learning Sciences: effecting changes in education. *J. Learn. Sci.*, 1(1), 1.

Kozma, R. B. (1994a). A reply: media and methods. *Educ. Technol. Res. Dev.*, 42(2), 11–14.

Kozma, R. B. (1994b). Will media influence learning? Reframing the debate. *Educ. Technol. Res. Dev.*, 42(2), 7–19.

Kozma, R. B. (2000). Reflections on the state of educational technology research and development. *Educ. Technol. Res. Dev.*, 48(1), 5–15.

Linebarger, J. M., Janneck, C. D., and Kessler, G. D. (2005). Leaving the world behind: supporting group collaboration patterns in a shared virtual environment for product design. *Presence: Teleoperators Virtual Environ.*, 14(6), 697–719.

Linzmayer, O. (1999). *Apple Confidential: The Real Story of Apple Computers*. San Francisco, CA: No Starch Press.

Lipnack, J. and Stamps, J. (2000). *Virtual Teams: People Working Across Boundaries with Technology*. New York: Wiley.*

Manz, C. and Sims, H. P. (1980). Self management as a substitute for leadership: a social learning theory perspective. *Acad. Manage. Rev.*, 5(3), 361–367.

McGinn, M. K. and Roth, W. M. (1999). Preparing students for competent scientific practice: implications of recent research in science and technology studies. *Educ. Res.*, 28(3), 14–24.

McLaughlin, M. (1990). The RAND change agent study revisited: macro perspectives and micro realities. *Educ. Res.*, 19(9), 11–16.

Morgan, Jr., B. B., Salas, E., and Glickman, A. S. (1998). An analysis of team evolution and maturation. *J. Gen. Psychol.*, 120(3), 277–291.*

Morris, L., Hulbert, L., and Abrams, D. (2000). An experimental investigation of group members' perceived influence over leader decisions. *Group Dynam. Theory Res. Pract.*, 4(2), 157–167.

Nichols, R. (1987). *Concern about Ethics and Ethical Issues among Professors of Instructional Systems Design and Technology*, Report Accession Number ED 304 099. Bloomington, IN: Association for Educational Communications and Technology.

Ocker, R., Fjermestad, J., Hiltz, S. R., and Johnson, K. (1998). Effects of four modes of group communication on the outcomes of software requirements determination. *J. Manage. Inform. Syst.*, 15(1), 99–118.

Pellegrino, J. W. (2002). Knowing what students know. *Issues Sci. Technol.*, 19(2), 48.

Postman, N. (1992). *Technopoly: The Surrender of Culture to Technology*. New York: Vintage Books.

Preece, J., Rogers, Y., and Sharp, H. (2002). *Interaction Design: Beyond Human–Computer Interaction*. New York: John Wiley & Sons.

Quintana, C., Reiser, B. J., Davis, E. A., Krajcik, J., Fretz, E., Duncan, R. G. et al. (2004). A scaffolding design framework for software to support science inquiry. *J. Learn. Sci.*, 13(3), 337–386.

Reeves, T. C. and Hedberg, J. G. (2003). *Interactive Learning Systems Evaluation*. Englewood Cliffs, NJ: Educational Technology Publications.

Reeves, T. C. and Hedberg, J. G. (2007). Evaluation strategies for open and distributed learning environments. In *Flexible Learning in an Information Society*, edited by B. Khan, pp. 226–235. Hershey, PA: Information Science Publishing.

Reigeluth, C. M., Ed. (1999). *Instructional-Design Theories and Models: A New Paradigm of Instructional Theory*. Mahwah, NJ: Lawrence Erlbaum Associates.

Rhodes, R. (1995). *The Making of the Atomic Bomb*. New York: Simon & Schuster.

Rogers, E. M. (1995). *The Diffusion of Innovations*. New York: The Free Press.

Salas, E., Dickinson, T. L., Converse, S. A., and Tannenbaum, S. I. (1992). Toward an understanding of team performance and training. In *Teams: Their Training and Performance*, edited by R. W. Swezey and E. Salas, pp. 3–29. Norwood, NJ: Albex.

Schank, R. C. and Jona, M. Y. (1991). Empowering the student: new perspectives on the design of teaching systems. *J. Learn. Sci.*, 1, 7–35.

Sarewitz, D. (2000). Science Policy Present: Where Is the Frontier? Paper presented at Gordon Research Conference, New Frontiers in Science and Technology Policy, August 20–25, Plymouth, NH.

Schittekatte, M. (1996). Facilitating information exchange in small decision-making groups. *Eur. J. Soc. Psychol.*, 26(4), 537–556.

Schmid, R. F., Tucker, B., Jorgensen, A., Abrami, P. C., Lacroix, G., and Nicolaidou, I. (2006). Tutor-Based Data on Implementation Fidelity of SFA Program Using Technology Versus No Technology. Paper presented at the American Educational Research Association Annual Meeting, April 8–12, San Francisco, CA.

Schneider, R. M. and Krajcik, J. (1999). *The Role of Educative Curriculum Materials in Reforming Science Education*. Arlington, VA: National Science Foundation.

Singer, J., Marx, R. W., Krajcik, J., and Chambers, J. C. (2000). *Designing Curriculum to Meet National Standards*. Arlington, VA: National Science Foundation.

Simon, H. A. (1996). *The Sciences of the Artificial*, 3rd ed. Cambridge, MA: MIT Press.

Slavin, R. E. and Madden, N. A., Eds. (2001). *One Million Children: Success for All*. Thousand Oaks, CA: Corwin.

Slavin, R. E., Chambers, B., Madden, N., Gifford, R., Abrami, P. C., Tucker, B., Therrien, M., and Cheung, A. (2006). Technology Infusion in Success for All: Reading Outcomes for Tutored and Nontutored First Graders. Paper presented at the American Educational Research Association Annual Meeting, April 8–12, San Francisco, CA.

Sosik, J. J., Avolio, B. J., and Kahai, S. S. (1997). Effects of leadership style and anonymity on group potency and effectiveness in a group decision support system environment. *J. Appl. Psychol.*, 82(1), 89–103.

Spiro, R. J., Feltovich, R. P., Jacobson, M. J., and Coulson, R. L. (1992). Cognitive flexibility, constructivism, and hypertext: random access instruction for advanced knowledge acquisition in ill-structured domains. In *Constructivism and the Technology of Instruction: A Conversation*, edited by T. M. Duffy and D. H. Jonassen, pp. 57–76. Hillsdale, NJ: Lawrence Erlbaum Associates.

Stasser, G. (1992). Pooling of unshared information during group discussion. In *Group Process and Productivity*, edited by S. Worchel, W. Wood, and J. A. Simpson, pp. 48–68. Newbury Park, CA: SAGE.*

Stewart, G. L. and Manz, C. C. (1995). Leadership for self-managing work teams: a typology and integrative model. *Hum. Relat.*, 48(7), 747–770.

Stoll, C. (1999). *High-Tech Heretic*. New York: Anchor Books.

Talsma, V. L. and Krajcik, J. S. (2002). Comparing Apples and Oranges: Using the National Science Education Standards as a Tool When Assessing Scientific Understandings. Paper presented at the National Association for Research in Science Teaching Annual Meeting, April 6–10, New Orleans, LA.

Tanskanen, T., Buhanist, P., and Kostama, H. (1998). Exploring the diversity of teams. *Int. J. Prod. Econ.*, 56–57, 611–619.

The Learning Technology Center. (1992). *What Is the Jasper Series?* Nashville, TN: Vanderbilt University (http://peabody.vanderbilt.edu/projects/funded/jasper/intro/Jasperintro.html).

Tuckman, B. (1965). Developmental sequence in small groups. *Psychol. Bull.*, 63, 384–399.

van Aken, J. E. (2004). Management research based on the paradigm of the design sciences: the quest for field-tested and grounded technological rules. *J. Manage. Stud.*, 41, 219–246.

Vye, N. J., Goldman, S. R., Voss, J. F., Hmelo, C., and Williams, S. (1997). Complex mathematical problem solving by individuals and dyads. *Cogn. Instruct.*, 15(4), 435–484.

Williams, R. H. (1999). Atomic spaces: living on the Manhattan Project. *J. Am. Hist.*, 85(4), 1653–1654.

Wolf, G. (1996). Steve Jobs: the next insanely great thing. *Wired Interview*, 4(2), http://www.wired.com/wired/archive/4.02/jobs_pr.html.

Wood, R. E. (1986). Task complexity: definition of the construct. *Org. Behav. Hum. Decis. Process.*, 37, 60–82.*

---

* Indicates a core reference.

# 49

# User-Centered Design and Development

*Eun-Ok Baek*
California State University, San Bernardino, California

*Kursat Cagiltay*
Middle East Technical University, Ankara, Turkey

*Elizabeth Boling and Theodore Frick*
Indiana University, Bloomington, Indiana

## CONTENTS

Eun-Ok Baek, Kursat Cagiltay, Elizabeth Boling, and Theodore Frick

## ABSTRACT

This chapter surveys methods, techniques, practices, and challenging issues in user-centered design and development (UCDD). The traditional instructional systems design (ISD) approach has been criticized for its bureaucratic and linear nature and its slow process. Two alternatives to that approach are discussed here: rapid prototyping and participatory design. These have been put forth as alternative models that address the many limitations of the conventional ISD model.

## KEYWORDS

*Participatory design:* A user-centered design approach in which users are actively involved in the design process of a system or product that addresses their specific needs.

*Rapid prototyping:* A user-centered design approach in which users participate in a rapid, iterative series of tryout and revision cycles during the design of a system or a product until an acceptable version is created.

*Usability:* The ease with which humans can use a system or a product to accomplish their goals efficiently, effectively, and with satisfaction.

*User-centered design:* A design philosophy and approach that places users at the center of the design process from the stages of planning and designing the system requirements to implementing and testing the product.

## INTRODUCTION

One of the most frequent and important challenges faced by instructional technologists is how to design and develop a product or program that both supports users' learning and performance in an effective and efficient manner and also generates user satisfaction. Recently, new approaches to the processes used in instructional design have been proposed and explored. Many researchers have pointed out that the traditional instructional systems design (ISD) approach is reductionist in nature and that it tends to solve a problem by fragmentation, one stage at a time (Finegan, 1994; Jonassen, 1990; You, 1993). In Gordon and Zemke (2000) and Zemke and Rossett (2002), several researchers and practitioners attacked the traditional ISD approach for its bureaucratic and linear nature, as well as its slow and clumsy processes.

The adoption of user-centered design and development (UCDD) into ISD is vital for designing systems

that better serve users' needs (Willis and Wright, 2000). If ISD does have to go through a paradigmatic transition, along with changes in the educational and socioeconomic environment, then the new paradigm of ISD must reflect these environmental changes. This would mean that the ISD process should become more user centered, more cost and time effective, and more performance focused.

The concept of UCDD is to place users at the center of the design process from the stages of planning and designing the system requirements to implementing and testing the product. UCDD appears in many different forms within design approaches. In this chapter, we have chosen a philosophical approach to object and systems design, participatory design (PD), and a particular process, rapid prototyping (RP), to elucidate the overall perspective of user-centered design. First, we review the big picture for UCDD, then we examine the participatory design approach—beginning with its historical background and then focusing on the different participation levels within this approach. This is followed by a description of rapid prototyping and a discussion of its challenges. Before concluding, the UCDD approach is reviewed in light of instructional design paradigms.

## THE BIG PICTURE FOR UCDD

### Key Elements of UCDD

What is UCDD? As Bannon (1991, p. 38) stated, "What the term user-centered system design means or how it can be achieved is far from clear." To begin sorting the issue out, we observe that there are two types of approaches to design and development: product-oriented and process-oriented. The product-oriented approach focuses mainly on the creation of a product. The utilization of the product can be a fixed and well understood idea; this means that design requirements can be determined in advance. The process-oriented approach requires designers to view their entire process of development in the context of human learning, work, and communication (i.e., use). The usage of the product in development takes place in an evolving world of changing needs. This involves certain advantages but also imposes various constraints. Because change is the norm in the process, prior specifications for an end-product are not predetermined completely. In UCDD, plans are just the beginning of the process, but the main mission is not conforming to the plan; rather, it is responding to changes throughout the life cycle of the project.

Our focus here is on process-oriented approaches, specifically those that fall under the sociotechnical umbrella. The sociotechnical perspective considers not only technical aspects of a system (tools, techniques, procedures) but also social aspects (people, network of roles, relationships, and tasks) (Goodrum et al., 1993; Mumford, 1983). To be able to implement the sociotechnical approach in system design, information must be extracted from the social context.

User-centered design and development can be considered a subcircle of the sociotechnical approach. UCDD and the sociotechnological perspective are guiding philosophies, not specific methods or processes for design. The idea is to approach design with knowledge of and the will to utilize social and cognitive analyses of human activities. These become the basis of the given project and direct its development; hence, the UCDD approach to design emphasizes user requirements and strives to keep those in mind. Designers are required to initiate early and continuous contact with prospective users to elicit what they need and how they will learn and perform. The approach also stresses that user-oriented technology in development must be tested for usability. These tests are done iteratively as opposed to using phased-stage or lock-step testing. These key elements of UCDD can be summarized as user participation (mutual learning), contextual inquiry, and iterative design. Each element is discussed below.

### User Participation

Users of technology are simply those who make use of the tools that designers create; however, this term should be further refined for our present purpose. Maguire (2001) and McCracken and Wolfe (2004) differentiated primary users from more broadly defined users. Primary users are those who will directly use and interact with the system to do tasks, and more broadly defined users are stakeholders—that is, anyone who will be influenced by primary users' capabilities to carry out their tasks or who affects the system requirements. The voices of both primary users and stakeholders should be respected in the design decision-making process.

User participation is vital in UCDD design, so users should be actively involved in the entire design process—not simply consulted at the beginning or at the testing stages of a product. Users can contribute important "folk knowledge" derived from their work contexts (Walenstein, 2002, p. 21). In this regard, designers should understand that users typically know more than what they can initially verbalize. If properly questioned, they may provide useful feedback on proposed design ideas (Nisbett and Wilson, 1977). This interactive process also potentially increases the users' accep-

tance of the product or system under development. Designers must take care to respect the users' various backgrounds and fields of expertise; this is a necessary condition for mutual learning (Muller, 2003).

The methods included under the UCDD perspective vary as to the timing and amount of user participation they include, from Carr-Chellman's (2007) insistence on users being fully franchised as design peers throughout the process to the sometimes minimal role played by test subjects in rote usability testing that occurs too late in the design cycle for changes to be made to a product (Krug, 2005). At the 1994 Participatory Design Conference, Tom Erickson of Apple Computer suggested four dimensions of user participation (Kuhn and Winograd, 1996). These include direct interaction with the designers, long-term involvement in the design process, broad participation in the overall system being designed, and maintaining a significant degree of control over design decisions.

### Contextual Analysis

Another key element in UCDD is considering the users' work needs in context. From the sociotechnical perspective, Goodrum et al. (1993) argued that designers must take into account the dynamics of people, environment, work practices, and technology to develop an *enriched learning and information environment*. Along the same lines, Read et al. (2002) suggested various contextual variables that influence users' participation in design activities. These include environment, knowledge, skills, and security. Read et al. (2002, p. 60) reported that:

- The cultural and physical environment in which a participatory design activity takes place will affect the activity.
- Each participant will bring to the design activity his or her own general knowledge, subject knowledge, and technical knowledge.
- The skills that will affect the ability of individuals to contribute to a participatory design activity include cognitive skills, motor skills, and articulatory skills. Different participants will bring different skills to any project, and it is likely that the balance of skills within a group will affect its functionality.
- Comfort factors, emotional stability, and stress also have an effect on how people contribute to a group activity. These factors can be quite individual and are difficult to predict. Feelings of security within a group will also be influenced by environment, knowledge, and skills.

## *Iterative Design*

In UCDD, designers are expected to initiate early contact with potential users and then focus continuously on what these users require of the technology to be designed. Testing must be done iteratively, in response to design questions and advances rather than being carried out on the basis of phases in a predetermined design process. The iterative process is one of reflection-in-action in which development stages are shaped in context to deal intelligently and creatively with "uncertainty, uniqueness, and value conflict" in a constantly changing world (Schön, 1987, p. 6).

Iterative design is closely related to the concept of *design space*, an idea borrowed from the fields of architecture and graphic design. As Beadouin-Lafon and Mackay (2003, p. 1011) explained design space:

> Designers are responsible for creating a design space specific to a particular design problem. They explore this design space, expanding and contracting it as they add and eliminate ideas. The process is iterative: more cyclic than reductionist. That is, the designer does not begin with a rough idea and successively add more precise details until the final solution is reached. Instead, she begins with a design problem, which imposes a set of constraints, and generates a set of ideas to form the initial design space. She then explores this design space, preferably with the user, and selects a particular design direction to pursue. This closes off part of the design space, but opens up new dimensions that can be explored. The designer generates additional ideas along these dimensions, explores the expanded design space, and then makes new design choices.

When designers expand the design space to generate ideas and contract it to select ideas, various design tools and techniques are used. Besides the most generally used techniques such as questionnaires, interviews (including individual interviews, focus groups, and workshops), and document analyses, other tools and techniques may be used to facilitate the iterative design process. These include task analysis, prototyping (Beadouin-Lafon and Mackay, 2003; Ehn and Kyng, 1991), role-playing activities (Ehn, 1992), site visitation and observation (Ehn, 1992), scenarios (Carroll, 1995, 2000), personas within design scenarios—virtual people who have jobs, hobbies, families, and educational accomplishments (Grudin and Pruitt, 2002)—and virtual reality (Davies, 2004).

## Process Approaches within the UCDD Perspective

Under UCDD we place multiple process approaches. These include *participatory design* (PD) (Bodker et

al., 1988), *rapid prototyping* (RP) (Goodrum et al., 1993; Frick et al., 2005), *user-friendly design* (Corry et al., 1997; Dumas and Redish, 1993; Norman, 1988; Sugar and Boling, 1995), *pluralistic walkthrough* (Bias, 1994), *contextual design* (Beyer and Holtzblatt, 1998; Tessmer and Wedman, 1995), *cooperative inquiry* (Druin, 1999), *situated design* (Greenbaum and Kyng, 1991), the *user-designer approach* (Reigeluth, 1996), *ID2 transaction shells* (Merrill et al., 1992), *R2D2 model* (Willis and Wright, 2000), *emancipatory design* (Carr-Chellman and Savoy, 2004), and *user design* (Carr-Chellman, 2007). Although these perspectives are not identical or equivalent, the common thread among them is that in all of them users actively participate to a greater or lesser degree in the design of a system or a product. To illuminate the overall perspective of user-centered design, we have chosen a philosophical approach to object and systems design (participatory design) and a particular process (rapid prototyping) to discuss in further detail.

## CHARACTERIZATION OF PARTICIPATORY DESIGN

### History of Participatory Design

Participatory design is both a set of theories for, and the practice of, using users' preferences to design products or systems. As explained by Greenbaum and Kyng (1991, p. 4) in participatory design, designers are required to take users' work practices and needs seriously; users are regarded as "human actors," not as cut-and-dried "human factors." Their work practices must be viewed within their own situated contexts. Observations of users' social interactions in the workplace are also employed by the designer, thus requiring continuous communication between users and designers.

The roots of systems and product-generating participatory design can be traced back to early Scandinavian systems design efforts in the 1970s (Ehn, 1988, 1993). It began with a political labor movement to bring democracy to work settings. Early projects usually took the form of collaborations between computer science researchers and union workers. Participatory design was pioneered by Kristen Nygaard, whose work involved collaboration with union leaders and members to create a Norwegian national agreement to ensure the rights of unions regarding the design and use of technology in the workplace (Ehn, 1988; Kuhn and Winograd, 1996). This triggered other, similar projects in Scandinavia. In Sweden, the DEMOS project involved an interdisciplinary team of researchers who collaborated with trade unions. With collaboration between

Swedish and Danish researchers and the Nordic Group Graphic Workers' Union, the UTOPIA project was created to design and develop a computerized desktop publishing system for newspaper graphic designers (Ehn, 1992).

The emphasis of this labor movement to empower users gradually changed in response to societal changes. After reviewing ten participatory design projects in the area of software development ranging from the 1970s to the 1980s, Clement and Van den Besselaar (1993) observed that the focus of this labor movement shifted from empowering workers in general to empowering specifically minority and female workers. This change reflected an increase in the population of women in the workplace. When participatory design was eventually applied in the United States, this political focus was deemphasized (Clement and Van den Besselaar, 1993). Now participatory design has widened to other fields such as engineering, architecture, and community design (Al-Kodmany, 1999; Carroll et al., 2000; Cohen, 2003).

## Different Levels of User Participation

As discussed earlier, there are varying degrees of user participation within participatory design. Although the definition of what constitutes participation varies in different projects, Kensing offered basic requirements for participation: "The employee must have access to relevant information; they must have the possibility for taking an independent position on the problems, and they must in some way participating in the process of decision making" (cited in Clement and Van den Besselaar, 1993, p. 31). According to Willis and Wright (2000, p. 7), there are "weak participatory design" and "strong participatory design" processes. In weak participatory design, design decision making is mainly undertaken by the designers themselves, even though user inputs are solicited using various tools and techniques. In strong participatory design, the users' full participation is utilized throughout the entire design process. Combining these interpretations with Erickson's user participation dimensions (Kuhn and Winograd, 1996), Table 49.1 summarizes the different levels of user participation.

With different combinations of these dimensions, user participation levels may range from minimal to full inclusion (Read et al., 2002) and to emancipatory design or *user design*—empowering stakeholders in the design (Carr-Chellman, 2007; Carr-Chellman and Savoy, 2004). At the minimal level, users may participate in the design process for a limited time or with a limited scope of influence. At the full inclusion level and the emancipatory level, users are empowered to

**TABLE 49.1**
**Levels of User Participation**

| | Weak Participation | Strong Participation |
|---|---|---|
| Interaction | Indirect | Direct |
| Length | Short | Long |
| Scope | Small | Large |
| Control | Very limited | Very broad |

participate in the design process by cooperating with researchers and developers or carrying out the design themselves with primarily facilitation provided by trained designers.

## Application of Participatory Design

In Clement and van den Besselaar's 1993 article, many successful cases of participatory design projects are surveyed. These are cases of projects in system design for work settings (e.g., computer center, human-centered office, local government) conducted since the 1970s, including architecture, urban planning, and community design (Al-Kodmany, 1999; Cohen, 2003), as well as recordkeeping in healthcare training (Carr-Chellman et al., 1998). It should be noted that participatory design projects in education are relatively under-researched (Carroll et al., 2000). In this section, we briefly illustrate one research and design project that has successfully integrated participatory design for computer system designs in the education field; however, we encourage the interested reader to refer also to the case examples above. We begin with a participatory design project of 5 years' duration which involved the design and development of a network-based collaborative learning system for middle-school physical science and high-school physics. The purpose of this example is to (1) illustrate how participatory design was carried out in a specific instance, including what methods were used and when, and (2) consider the effectiveness of, efficiency of, and participants' satisfaction with the participatory design methodology used as well as to consider the challenges encountered during the project.

### Case Studies

Carroll et al. (2000) presented an example of how participatory design was applied in the design of a virtual school to support collaborative learning in middle-school and high-school physical science. The case provides powerful insights into the transition of participants' roles over the course of the project. This 5-year project, called LiNC (Learning in Networked

Communities), began as a small-scale project involving teachers from one middle school and one high school physics class and was supported by a U.S. National Science Foundation grant.

The main players in the LiNC project were four middle and high school physics teachers and eight university research team members (four human–computer interaction specialists and four computer scientists). The project was a partnership between Virginia Tech University and the public schools of Montgomery County in Virginia to support collaborative science learning. During the project, physics classes were offered every other year to very small classes (three to five students). The purpose of the project was to bring systemic change to public education through a new computer networking infrastructure.

The project team observed developmental changes in participant teachers' roles as the project progressed, beginning with "practitioner–informant" and transforming along the way to "analyst," then "designer," and finally "coach." From the beginning, the university project team was mindful of employing participatory design in conceptualizing the project, foreseeing that the teachers' active participation must be continued even after the project ended to bring the sustainable systemic change to public education that the project originally set forth as its main purpose.

Although this project resulted in an enviable level of acceptance and use for the designed product, it is worth noting that Carroll et al. (2000) questioned whether it had to take 5 years to work effectively with teachers. In their view, some stages of the project could have been more efficient—for example, by assigning a lead teacher or by helping teachers attain prerequisite skills in design. They cautioned, however, that compressing the timeline for such a project would "compromise the coordination of participatory and ethnographically driven approaches to requirements development" (Carroll et al., 2000, p. 248) and noted that it takes time to build the trust and mutual understanding required to carry out effective design work. Indeed, participatory design is a philosophical perspective rather than a circumscribed set of methods. Within such a perspective, the inherent value of user participation and the presumed benefits resulting from that participation are held to be of greater ultimate importance than the efficiency of the method.

Perhaps with a different kind of preparation themselves, the trained designers on such a project could become more effective at facilitating the participation of users and designers in such a project, but this observation also requires us to step back from the case and consider what is necessary for such a shift in the training of designers. If the inherent worth of user partici-

pation in design is great enough, then overhauling the training provided to designers of educational systems might be seen as feasible.

One last aspect of this case to consider is that the users/participants appear to have been only the teachers who would incorporate the system into their classrooms. The students, who would presumably also be users of the system, were not included as participating designers, although they may have been included secondarily as part of the very small classes conducted during the development of the system. Although a case like this one describes a potentially effective, albeit costly, process approach for bringing about change in classroom teaching, it is important to discuss seriously the circumstances in which it is possible and desirable to apply this philosophy and the methods it requires.

A further example of participatory design is the work being done by Reigeluth and Duffy (2007) in the Decatur Township school district. The participants include school teachers, administrators, students, their parents, and community members, as well as the design leaders. Although this is an effort in systemic change, it is also a good example of participatory design in which the stakeholders play major roles throughout the process, the goal of which is the realization of their vision regarding what they want their school system to become. This process will occur over several years, as did the LiNC project described earlier.

# CHARACTERIZATION OF RAPID PROTOTYPING

## Background of Rapid Prototyping

Rapid prototyping, a methodology used in software design (and also in fabrication techniques in manufacturing via CAD/CAM) holds potential for addressing many of the limitations of the conventional ISD model. Since rapid prototyping was introduced as a design methodology in the ISD field (Tripp and Bichelmeyer, 1990), conflicting descriptions of how rapid prototyping applies to instructional development have appeared. This situation has resulted in an inconsistent view of this methodology in the literature.

Tessmer (1994) and Northrup (1995), in the field of instructional technology, argued that rapid prototyping should be considered as an alternative method of formative evaluation in the design and development phases. This is consistent with the role of prototyping described in many studies in human–computer interaction (HCI) and software design. Many people in the field of instructional technology, however, perceive rapid prototyping as a new paradigm of instructional design methodology (Dorsey et al., 1997; Jones and Richey, 2000; Rathbun et al., 1997; Tripp and Bichelmeyer, 1990). In this chapter, our position is the latter perspective, which views rapid prototyping as an alternative to the conventional ISD process. Note that, when rapid prototyping is practiced as an alternative to traditional ISD processes, it can also be characterized as a comparatively weak form of participatory design (Kuhn and Winograd, 1996; Willis and Wright, 2000). This does *not* imply that the rapid prototyping process is weak, but rather that the level of user participation in RP may be less than in other forms of PD.

Customizations of rapid prototyping methods to fit the instructional design field have been based on two perspectives on design. One is Simon's (1996) theoretical view that "artificial science" differs from natural science. Basically, the instructional design and software design arenas share the same design theory, which holds that design is a problem-solving process that uses optimization procedures. The other perspective is that of Schön (1987), who viewed the design process as an iterative process of *reflection in action*. Design plans are not to be predetermined so as to lead to a predefined goal, but should instead be a process that deals creatively with "uncertainty, uniqueness, and value conflict" (Schön, 1987, p. 6).

The purpose of rapid prototyping is to demonstrate possibilities quickly by building an inexpensive series of mock-ups so designers are able to obtain early feedback from which they may respond to user requirements This is particularly true in the following three types of situations: (1) cases that involve complex factors, which can make predictions difficult; (2) cases already examined by conventional methods without satisfactory results; and (3) new situations, which do not offer a lot of experience to draw from (Tripp and Bichelmeyer, 1990). Thus, rapid prototyping is appropriate for developing electronic performance support systems (Gery, 1995; Gustafson and Branch, 1997; Gustafson and Reeves, 1990; Law et al., 1995; Witt and Wager, 1994), conference video designs (Appelman et al., 1995), software designs (Dumas and Redish, 1993; Sugar and Boling, 1995), and computer-based instruction (Tripp and Bichelmeyer, 1990). It is also useful in Web design (Boling and Frick, 1997; Corry et al., 1997; Frick et al., 2005) and for collaborative learning (Goodrum et al., 1993; Tessmer, 1994).

As proponents of rapid prototyping have noted, however, it is not a panacea and can lead to an undisciplined design-by-repair approach that ignores initial analysis and planning. Although Sugar and Boling (1995) described conceptual prototyping for nonexistent technologies, rapid prototypes cannot easily be used to develop prototypes for many common instructional applications, such as lectures, workshops, and televised instruction sessions, because the prototyping effort may be prohibitive with regard to both time and cost (Tessmer, 1994; Tripp and Bichelmeyer, 1990). Tripp and Bichelmeyer (1990) pointed out further cautions in the use of rapid prototyping, including the need for tools that support building prototypes efficiently, choice of optimal methods for both design and evaluation of prototypes, and—most importantly—knowledgeable and experienced designers.

Frick et al. (2005) added important front and back ends to the rapid prototyping process. Their inquiry-based, iterative design process was developed and improved through formative research methods and includes needs assessment of the stakeholders, rapid prototyping on paper with usability testing, further rapid prototyping on computers with more usability evaluation, and creating and maintaining the product designed (Reigeluth and Frick, 1999, p. 21). Although their focus was on Web design, their work demonstrates that more than rapid prototyping itself is needed for designing products that work well with intended users.

## Definition of Rapid Prototyping

As Boling and Bichelmeyer (1998) have noted, rapid prototyping has been used in many different approaches to design and development. Examples include rapid prototyping (Tripp and Bichelmeyer, 1990), the participatory design process (Goodrum et al., 1993), rapid collaborative prototyping (Dorsey et al., 1997), user-centered design (Corry et al., 1997; Dumas and Redish, 1993; Sugar and Boling, 1995), context-sensitive design (Tessmer and Wedman, 1995), and ID2 transaction shells (Li and Merrill, 1990). All of these include a rapid series of iterative tests and revision cycles, coupled with the direct participation of users to result in a product that is shaped until an acceptable version is created (see Table 49.2).

Even though these various approaches share the use of rapid prototyping methodologies, the definition of what a prototype is differs somewhat from one approach to another. Tripp and Bichelmeyer (1990) asserted that a prototype should include a required database, the major program modules, screen displays, and input and output for interfacing systems. This definition emphasizes the availability of computer software that offers *modularity*, which allows for flexibility in adding, removing, or modifying a segment of the instruction without introducing severe interactions in the other segments. Modularity also provides *plasticity*, which refers to the ability to change aspects of a unit of instruction with only minimal time and cost (Tripp and Bichelmeyer, 1990, p. 38).

**TABLE 49.2**

**A Comparison of Instructional Systems Design (ISD) Approaches That Include Rapid Prototyping**

| | Tripp and Bichelmeyer (1990) | Jones et al. (1992) | Dorsey et al. (1997) | Tessmer and Wedman (1995) |
|---|---|---|---|---|
| Model name | Rapid prototyping | ID2 | Rapid collaborative prototyping | Context-sensitive ID model |
| Meaning of a prototype | A working model that includes a required database, the major program modules, screen displays, and input and output for interfacing systems | An incomplete but essentially executable version of the final product | Tangible solution ideas that have different amounts of fidelity | A working portion of the final product that is immediately implemented with a group of learners or is reviewed by experts |
| Processes | Assess needs and analyze content. Set objectives. Construct prototype. Utilize prototype. Install and maintain system. | Analyze knowledge. Analyze audience and environment. Analyze strategies. Specify transaction configurations. Develop transaction details. Implement. | Create visions. Explore conceptual prototypes. Experiment with mock-ups. Pilot test working prototypes. Implement product. | Analyze layers. Specify instructional scenarios. Develop alternative prototypes. Negotiate prototype. |
| ISD | New paradigm of ISD process model | Large-component prototype approach | Co-ownership of designers and users | New form of ISD |

Jones et al. (1992) argued that a prototype is an incomplete but essentially executable version of the final product. Tessmer and Wedman (1995) defined a prototype as a working portion of the final product that is immediately implemented with a group of learners or is reviewed by experts. Both definitions emphasize the aspect of a quick, working version of a final product; therefore, a prototype does not have to include everything that the final version will contain. Finally, Dorsey et al. (1997) and Sugar and Boling (1995) viewed a prototype as a tangible idea of possible solutions that have different range of fidelity from low to high. Their definition is very different from the others, in that even a conceptual version of a solution could be a prototype, and it is closest to that used in the software design community (Rudd et al., 1996).

## CHALLENGING ISSUES

Designers face many challenging issues when attempting to implement UCDD, such as effective incorporation of user participation in the design process, control issues over resources, and the practical implementation of the approach utilized. These issues are discussed below.

### Issue 1. Effective Incorporation of User Participation

One of the most difficult challenges of UCDD is the effective incorporation of user participation in the design process. Determination of which voices will be heard and how the users' preferences will be reflected in the design is a values-based decision and is rarely easy. This is especially true in large-sized commercial projects targeted at a range of users from different backgrounds and settings. Along with the issue of who gets to participate comes the issue of how to recruit users who will represent the potential target user groups appropriately when those groups are very large or very diverse. In addition, when user participation is limited only to a certain stage, the users' role will end up being that of information providers rather than codesigners of the project.

Even when the goal of UCDD is to place users at the center of the design process, in many situations the negotiation between the "designed for" approach, in which the designers assume leadership in the design process, and the "designed with" approach, in which the users assume ownership in the process, can become both a philosophical and a practical consideration. How much user participation is too much? Even for designers who consider active user participation throughout the entire process to be the ideal, some researchers have encountered practical difficulties with the process. In a participatory design project intended to build a community learning network using open source tools, Luke et al. (2004) observed that early group brainstorming heightened the users' expectations and demands, and these demands were furthermore unmoderated by any realistic conceptions of the time and costs they would require. When the first prototype was released (past its due date), these same heightened expectations turned into general disappointment. The authors attributed this problem to both the designers and the users, who were "too participatory and too open" (Luke et al., 2004, p. 11). They then warned that user participation in the early stages of a project can be disadvantageous if it is not balanced with realistic constraints. Processes can be developed to ameliorate or eliminate these kinds of problems, but the potential for them to arise remains.

Some researchers, however, have been able to elicit user participation positively, even in long-term, large-scale PD projects. Letondal and Mackay (2004) conducted participatory design activities with research biologists, bio-informaticians, and programmers at the Institut Pasteur in Paris over a period of 7 years. The focus of their project was the development of tools to support end-user programming. They did observe some tensions between different groups of participants; however, overall the participatory design worked in that context. The main reason for this success was attributed by the authors to maintaining a balance between "low-responsibility" and "useful results" (Letondal and Mackay, 2004, p. 39). Again, it appears that designs committed to the UCDD perspective require experience and skill to carry it out effectively.

## Issue 2. Control over Resources: Money, Time, Tools, and Space

Another challenging issue in UCDD is acquiring and maintaining control over enough resources to support a project—money, time, tools, and space. Acquiring and allocating these resources can cause a great deal of tension. Even after full members in the design team have been identified, the question still remains: How can the team elicit full user participation when the users may also have to fulfill their own full-time job duties? In their review of ten different participatory design projects, Clement and Van den Besselaar (1993) observed that, although some projects provided funds for the users to hire temporary staff to take their places while they were working with the design team, users in other projects had to perform their regular job duties while concurrently contributing to the project. Design teams seeking only intermittent and short-term involvement from users may face lower barriers but may still have trouble recruiting users who can afford to take the time necessary to participate in the test of a prototype—or repeating such sessions.

Sugar (2001) pointed out that one of the common misconceptions among researchers in UCDD is that designers should relinquish all of their authority and allow the participating users to make all of the design decisions. He warned that users are not expert design-ers, and designers should not expect users always to know exactly what they want to use. He pointed out that they may not be right all the time, either, and that even though users' opinions must be respected designers need to present the possibilities and limitations of proposed solutions properly. Although this is true for any design project, Sugar claimed that the governing responsibility of designers is certainly crucial in UCDD. To implement this approach effectively, designers must also delve beyond the surface of these issues and carefully consider each of them by means of in-depth analyses (Sugar, 2001). Carr-Chellman (2007) has offered multiple suggestions for carrying out user design activities in which users function as the primary designers and trained designers as facilitators but also pointed out that the process can be very difficult and is not suitable for every context or situation.

Raskin (2000), who played a major role in the design of the Macintosh computer interface at Apple Computer, emphasized that what users prefer in a design is not necessarily what is most efficient and effective. He cited several empirical studies where users actually performed more poorly with interface designs they preferred than they did with others they did not prefer. This illustrates the tension between what users want compared with what is best for them based on scientifically proven principles, similar to the problem with what people prefer to eat vs. what is good for them in terms of nutritional value and their long-term health.

## DISCUSSION

When designers select a design approach, their choice is influenced by their philosophies (Visscher-Voerman and Gustafson, 2004). In their attempt to understand how designers carry out instructional design projects in reality, Visscher-Voerman and Gustafson (2004) found that all 12 of their examined designers (from 6 different settings in the initial study) integrated a traditional ISD model into their work. The ways in which they incorporated this model, however, were diverse and varied. In their second study, Visscher-Voerman and Gustafson developed four alternative design paradigms (or conceptual frameworks) that are anchored in philosophy: instrumental, communicative, pragmatic, and artistic. Table 49.3 shows the characteristics of each of these paradigms. In general, the UCDD approach seems to be related to communicative and pragmatic paradigms in the sense that UCDD puts an emphasis on users as codevelopers in the design process. This is achieved by means of the nonlinear and iterative analysis/design/evaluation format of cooperation. Rapid

**TABLE 49.3**
**Four Alternative Design Paradigms**

| | Instrumental Paradigm | Communicative Paradigm | Pragmatic Paradigm | Artistic Paradigm |
|---|---|---|---|---|
| Emphasis | Aligned goals, learning situations, process, and outcome of the design | Communication between designers and users to reach consensus | Repeated testing and revision | Creative design |
| Designer's role | Expert (responsible for design) | Facilitator (shares responsibility with users) | Expert (responsible for design) | Artist (fully responsible for design) |
| User's role | Information provider and approval for action | Information provider; codesigner | Information provider; product user | Product user |
| Design process | Typically linear | Nonlinear and iterative | Nonlinear and iterative | Linear or nonlinear |

*Sources:* Adapted from Visscher-Voerman, I. and Gustafson, K.L., *Educ. Technol. Res. Technol.*, 52(2), 86, 2004.

prototyping, when used as the cornerstone of an alternative ISD model, may be closer in philosophy to the pragmatic paradigm. In either case, UCDD, in both strong and weak forms, represents some shift in philosophy for instructional designers who employ it. To the extent that UCDD gathers momentum in the teaching and practice of instructional design, we can expect to see changes in logistics, methods, and power dynamics in design projects within this field.

## REFERENCES

Al-Kodmany, K. (1999). Combining artistry and technology in participatory community planning. *Berkeley Plan. J.*, 13, 28–36.

Appelman, R., Pugh, R. C., and Siantz, J. E. (1995). Increasing the Efficacy of Informal Video Through Rapid Prototyping. Paper presented at the Midwestern Educational Research Association Annual Meeting, Chicago, IL.

Bannon, L. (1991) From human factors to human actors: the role of psychology and human–computer interaction studies in systems design. In *Design at Work: Cooperative Design of Computer Systems*, edited by J. Greenbaum and M. Kyng, pp. 25–44. Hillsdale, NJ: Lawrence Erlbaum Associates.

Beadouin-Lafon, M. and Mackay, W. (2003). Prototyping tools and techniques. In *The Human–Computer Interaction Handbook: Fundamentals, Evolving Technologies, and Emerging Applications*, edited by J. Jacko and A. Sears, pp. 1006–1031. Mahwah, NJ: Lawrence Erlbaum Associates.*

Beyer, H. and Holtzblatt, K. (1998). *Contextual Design: Defining Customer-Centered Systems*. San Francisco, CA: Morgan Kaufmann.

Bias, R. G. (1994). The pluralistic usability walkthrough: coordinated empathies. In *Usability Inspection Methods*, edited by J. Nielsen and R. L. Mack, pp. 63–76. New York: John Wiley & Sons.

Bodker, S., Ehn, P., Knudsen, J. L., Kyng, M., and Madsen, K. H. (1988). Computer support for cooperative design. In *Proceedings of CSCW 88: Second Conference on Computer-Supported Cooperative Work*, September 16–28, Portland, OR (http://citeseer.ist.psu.edu/bodker88computer.html).

Boling, E. and Bichelmeyer, B. (1998). Filling the Gap: Rapid Prototyping as Visualization in the ISD Process. Paper presented at Association for Educational Communications and Technology Annual Meeting, February 18–20, St. Louis, MO.*

Boling, E. and Frick, T. (1997). Holistic rapid prototyping for Web design: early usability testing is essential. In *Web-Based Instruction*, edited by B. H. Khan, pp. 319–328. Englewood Cliffs, NJ: Educational Technology Publications.*

Carr-Chellman, A. A. (2007). *User Design*. Mahwah, NJ: Lawrence Erlbaum Associates.

Carr-Chellman, A. A. and Savoy, M. (2004). User-design research. In *Handbook of Research for Education, Communications, and Technology*, 2nd ed., edited by D. H. Jonassen, pp. 701–716. Mahwah, NJ: Lawrence Erlbaum Associates.*

Carr-Chellman, A. A., Cuyar, C., and Breman, J. (1998). User-design: a case application in health care training. *Educ. Technol. Res. Dev.*, 46(4), 97–114.

Carroll, J. M. (1995). Introduction: the scenario perspective on system development. In *Scenario-Based Design: Envisioning Work and Technology in System Development*, edited by J. M. Carroll, pp. 1–17. New York: John Wiley & Sons.

Carroll, J. M. (2000). *Making Use: Scenario-Based Design of Human–Computer Interactions*. Cambridge, MA: MIT Press.

Carroll, J. M., Chin, G., Rosson, M. B., and Neale, D. C. (2000). The development of cooperation: five years of participatory design in the virtual school. In *Proc. of the Conference on Designing Interactive Systems: Processes, Practices, Methods, and Techniques*, June 25–28, London, pp. 239–251. New York: ACM Press.

Clement, A. and Van den Besselaar, P. (1993). A retrospective look at PD projects. *Commun. ACM*, 36(4), 29–37.*

Cohen, J. (2003). Participatory design with the Internet. *Architect. Rec.*, http://archrecord.construction.com/features/digital/archives/0308da-1.asp.

Corry, M. D., Frick, T., and Hansen, L. (1997). User-centered design and usability testing of a Web site: an illustrative case study. *Educ. Technol. Res. Dev.*, 45(4), 65–76.

Davies, R. C. (2004). Adapting virtual reality for the participatory design of work environments. *CSCW J.*, 13(1), 1–33.

Dorsey, L. T., Goodrum, D. A., and Schwen, T. M. (1997). Rapid collaborative prototyping as an instructional development paradigm. In *Instructional Development Paradigms*, edited by C. R. Dills and A. J. Romiszowski, pp. 445–465. Englewood Cliffs. NJ: Educational Technology Publications.

Druin A. (1999). Cooperative inquiry: developing new technologies for children with children. In *Proceedings of CHI'99*, May 15–20, Pittsburgh PA, pp. 529–599. New York: ACM Press.

Dumas, J. S. and Redish, J. C. (1993). *A Practical Guide to Usability Testing*. Norwood, NJ: Ablex Publishing.

Ehn, P. (1988). Playing the language games of design and use on skill and participation. In *Proceedings of the ACM SIGOIS and IEEECS TC-OA 1988 Conference on Office Information Systems*, edited by R. B. Allen, pp. 142–157. New York: ACM Press.

Ehn, P. (1992). Scandinavian design: on participation and skill. In *Usability: Turning Technologies into Tools*, edited by J. S. Brown and P. Duguid, pp. 96–132. New York: Oxford University Press.

Ehn, P. (1993). Scandinavian design: on participation and skill. In *Participatory Design: Principles and Practices*, edited by D. Schuler and A. Namioka, pp. 41–78. Hillsdale, NJ: Lawrence Erlbaum Associates.*

Ehn, P. and Kyng, M. (1991). Cardboard computers: mocking-it-up or hands-on the future. In *Design at Work: Cooperative Design of Computer Systems*, edited by J. Greenbaum and M. Kyng, pp. 169–195. Hillsdale, NJ: Lawrence Erlbaum Associates.*

Finegan, A. (1994). Soft systems methodology: an alternative approach to knowledge elicitation in complex and poorly defined systems. *Complex. Int.*, 1, http://www.csu.edu.au/ci/vol01/finega01/.

Flagg, B. N. (1990). *Formative Evaluation for Educational Technologies*. Hillsdale, NJ: Lawrence Erlbaum Associates.

Frick, T., Su, B., and An, Y. J. (2005). Building a large, successful website efficiently through inquiry-based design and content management tools. *TechTrends*, 49(4), 20–31 (http://education.indiana.edu/practical.html).

Gery, G. (1995). Attributes and behavior of performance-centered systems. *Perform. Improv. Q.*, 8(1), 47–93.

Goodrum, D. A., Dorsey, L. T., and Schwen, T. M. (1993). Defining and building an enriched learning and information environment. *Educ. Technol.*, 33(11), 10–20.*

Gordon, J. and Zemke, R. (2000). The attack on ISD. *Train. Mag.*, 37 (4), 42–49.

Greenbaum, J. and Kyng, M. (1991). Introduction: situated design. In *Design at Work: Cooperative Design of Computer Systems*, edited by J. Greenbaum and M. Kyng, pp. 1–24. Hillsdale: NJ: Lawrence Erlbaum Associates.*

Grudin, J. and Pruitt, J. (2002). Personas, Participatory Design and Product Development: An Infrastructure for Engagement. Paper presented at the Participatory Design Conference, June 23–25, Malmö University, Sweden.

Gustafson, J. L. and Branch, R. M. (1997). Revisioning model of instructional development. *Educ. Technol. Res. Dev.*, 45(3), 73–89.

Gustafson, K. L. and Reeves, T. C. (1990). IDioM: a platform for a course development expert system. *Educ. Technol.*, 30(3), 19–25.

Jonassen, D. H. (1990). Thinking technology: chaos in instructional design. *Educ. Technol.*, 30(2), 32–34.

Jones, M., Li, Z., and Merrill, M. (1992). Rapid prototyping in automated instructional design. *Educ. Technol. Res. Dev.*, 40(4), 95–100.*

Jones, T. S. and Richey, R. C. (2000). Rapid prototyping methodology in action: a developmental study. *Educ. Technol. Res. Dev.*, 48(2), 63–80.

Kuhn, S. and Winograd, T. (1996). Design for people at work. In *Bringing Design to Software*, edited by T. Winograd, pp. 290–294. New York: Addison-Wesley.

Krug, S. (2005). *Don't Make Me Think: A Common Sense Approach to Web Usability*, 2nd ed. Indianapolis, IN: Pearson Education.

Law, M. P., Okey, J .R., and Carter, B. J. (1995). Developing electronic performance support systems for professionals. In *Proceedings of the Annual Conference of the Association for Educational Communications and Technology*, February 8–12, Anaheim, CA.

Letondal, C. and Mackay, W. E. (2004). Participatory programming and the scope of mutual responsibility: balancing scientific, design and software commitment. In *Proceedings of PDC 2004: The Eighth Biennial Participatory Design Conference*, July 27–31, Toronto, Canada.

Luke, R., Clement, A., Terada, R., Bortolussi, D., Booth, C., Brooks, D., and Christ, D. (2004). The promise and perils of a participatory approach to developing an open source community learning network. In *Participatory Design Conference 2004*. Vol. 1. *Artful Integration: Interweaving Media, Materials and Practices*, edited by A. Clement, F. de Cindio, A. M. Oostveen, D. Schuler, and P. van den Besselaar, pp. 11–19. New York: ACM Press (http://trout.cpsr.org/conferences/pdc2004/proceedings/vol_1/p11_Luke.pdf).

Maguire, M. (2001). Context of use within usability activities. *Int. J. Hum.–Comput. Stud.*, 55, 453–483.

McCracken, D. D. and Wolfe, R. J. (2004). *User-Centered Website Development: A Human–Computer Interaction Approach*. Upper Saddle River, NJ: Prentice Hall.

Merrill, M. D., Li, Z., and Jones, M. K. (1992). Instructional transaction shells: responsibilities, methods, and parameters. *Educ. Technol.*, 32(2), 5–26.

Moonen, J. (1994). Prototyping as a design activity. In *Postlethwaiste: The International Encyclopedia of Education*, 2nd ed., edited by T. Husén and T. Neville. Oxford: Elsevier Science.

Mumford, E. (1983). *Designing Human Systems for New Technology: The ETHICS Method*. Manchester, U.K.: Manchester Business School.

Muller, M. J. (2003). Participatory design: the third space in human–computer interaction. In *The Human–Computer Interaction Handbook: Fundamentals, Evolving Technologies, and Emerging Applications*, edited by J. Jacko and A. Sears, pp. 1051–1068. Mahwah, NJ: Lawrence Erlbaum Associates.*

Nisbett, R. E. and Wilson, T. D. (1977). Telling more than we can know: verbal reports on mental processes. *Psychol. Rev.*, 84(3), 231–259.

Norman, D. A. (1988). *The Psychology of Everyday Things*. New York: Basic Books.

Northrup, P. T. (1995). Concurrent formative evaluation: guidelines and implications for multimedia designers. *Educ. Technol.*, 35(6), 24–31.

Raskin, J. (2000). *The Humane Interface: New Directions for Designing Interactive Systems*. Boston, MA: Addison-Wesley.

Rathbun, G. A., Saito, R. S., and Goodrum, D. A. (1997). Reconceiving ISD: Three Perspectives on Rapid Prototyping as a Paradigm Shift. Paper presented at the Association for Educational Communications and Technology Annual Meeting, February 12–16, Albuquerque, NM.

Read, J., Gregory, P., MacFarlane, S., McManus, B., Gray, P., and Patel, R. (2002). An investigation of participatory design with children: informed, balanced and facilitated design. In *Proceedings of Interaction Design and Children International Workshop*, pp. 53–64. Maastricht: Shaker Publishing.

Reigeluth, C. M. (1996). A new paradigm of ISD. *Educ. Technol.*, 36 (3), 13–20.

Reigeluth, C. M. and Duffy, F. M. (2007). Trends and issues in P-12 educational change. In *Trends and Issues in Instructional Design and Technology*, 2nd ed., edited by R. A. Reiser and J. V. Dempsey, pp. 209–220. Upper Saddle River, NJ: Prentice Hall.

Reigeluth, C. M. and Frick, T. (1999). Formative research: a methodology for creating and improving design theories. In *Instructional-Design Theories and Models*. Vol. II, edited by C. Reigeluth, pp. 633–652, Mahwah, NJ: Lawrence Erlbaum Associates.

Rudd, J., Stern, K., and Isensee, S. (1996). Low vs. high-fidelity prototyping debate. *Interactions*, 3(1), 76–85.

Schön, D. A. (1987). *Educating the Reflective Practitioner*. San Francisco, CA: Jossey-Bass.

Simon, H. A. (1996). *The Sciences of the Artificial*, 3rd ed. Cambridge, MA: MIT Press.

Sugar, W. A. (2001). What is a good about user-centered design? Documenting the effect of usability sessions on novice software designers. *J. Res. Comput. Educ.*, 3(3), 235–250.

Sugar, W. A. and Boling, E. (1995). User-Centered Innovation: A Model for Early Usability Testing. Paper presented at the Annual Conference of the Association for Educational Communications and Technology, February 8–12, Anaheim, CA.

Tessmer, M. (1994). Formative evaluation alternatives. *Perform. Improv. Q.*, 7(1), 3–18.

Tessmer, M. and Wedman, J. F. (1995). Context-sensitive instructional design models: a response to design research, studies, and criticism. *Perform. Improv. Q.*, 8(3), 38–54.

Tripp, S. and Bichelmeyer, B. (1990). Rapid prototyping: an alternative instructional design strategy. *Educ. Technol. Res. Dev.*, 38(1), 31–44.*

Visscher-Voerman, I. and Gustafson, K. L. (2004). Paradigms in the theory and practice of education and training design. *Educ. Technol. Res. Dev.*, 52(2), 69–89.*

Walenstein, A. (2002). Cognitive Support in Software Engineering Tools: A Distributed Cognition Framework. Ph.D. dissertation. Burnaby, B.C.: Simon Fraser University.

Willis, J. and Wright, K. E. (2000). A general set of procedures for constructivist instructional design: the new R2D2 model. *Educ. Technol.*, 40(2), 5–20.*

Witt, C. L. and Wager, W. (1994). A comparison of instructional systems design and electronic performance support systems design. *Educ. Technol.*, 34(6), 20–24.

You, Y. (1993). What can we learn from chaos theory? An alternative approach to instructional systems design. *Educ. Technol. Res. Technol.*, 41(3), 17–32.

Zemke, R. and Rossett, A. (2002). A hard look at ISD. *Train. Mag.*, 39(2), 26–35.

---

* Indicates a core reference.

# 50

# Tools for Design and Development of Online Instruction

*Bryan L. Chapman*
Brandon Hall Research/Chapman Alliance, Sunnyvale, California

## CONTENTS

## ABSTRACT

Today's instructional designers can choose from a wide variety of authoring and online learning development tools. With the evolution of learning technology, expectations from outside the learning and training discipline are looking to the technology to provide instructional design guidance and allow novice developers to create instructionally sound online learning. This chapter explores the tools that instructional designers and novice developers use most often to create online learning from both a design and development perspective, the types of instructional design support that can be found in different types of development tools, and how these tools may (or may not) impact the ability to meet instructional needs. A classification system is used to analyze tools as (1) standard authoring tools, (2) front-end design and automated instructional design (AID) tools, (3) simulation and gaming tools, or (4) team development or publishing tools such as learning content management systems (LCMSs) and groupware authoring. Although instructional design guidance, in some form or another, is now embedded inside several classifications of development tools, considerable innovation and research are still required to create holistic systems that negate or minimize the need for instructional design expertise, allowing nontrained designers to create online learning courseware without assistance.

## KEYWORDS

*Asynchronous learning:* Communication between learners and instructors that does not take place simultaneously or real time. An example of asynchronous learning is when a learner engages in a self-paced, self-service learning module without communicating with another person.

*Authoring tool:* A software application used by non-programmers to assemble digital media files into displays, presentations, and interactive exercises.

*Automated instructional design (AID):* Leveraging technology to automate the instructional design as part of the process of learning content development.

*Dynamic pretest:* A test delivered online that can literally adapt courseware to learner deficiencies identified through online testing and scale courseware to match specific learner needs.

*Groupware authoring:* Concurrent process of creating learning content in a team environment with multiple authors who often play different roles, such as writers, graphic artists, or instructional designers.

*Learning content management system (LCMS):* A multi-user software application in which learning developers can create, store, reuse, manage, and deliver digital learning content from a central object repository (database).

*Novice developer:* A person who has little or no training in instructional design yet has the responsibility of creating learning content using authoring tools.

*Soft-skills simulation:* Simulations designed for the specific purpose of teaching interpersonal skills such as leadership, coaching, facilitating, and so on.

*Storyboard:* A document that details and specifies on-screen text, narrative scripts, and interaction in a paper-based format before it is converted into an online course.

## INTRODUCTION

What if William Shakespeare would have had access to modern word-processing software? Would it have made him a better writer? This answer is likely an emphatic *no*. Taking the analogy one step further, what if the vendor who produced the word-processing software added an embedded wizard to assist Shakespeare in creating sonnets with perfect iambic pentameter? How much impact might this wizard have had on improving the quality and quantity of his work? Finally, what if a vendor touted new software that encapsulates the genius of Shakespeare such that anyone (even novice writers) who uses it could write classic material with the same style and effectiveness of Shakespeare himself? Like most people, you would likely be highly skeptical.

Seems like a series of ridiculous scenarios; yet, believe it or not, similar arguments still rage on about the role of software tools used by instructional designers to design and develop online learning courseware. In addition, many organizations have heightened expectations that relatively novice, nontechnical developers, and even subject-matter experts (SMEs) should be able to use such tools to create significant amounts of both traditional and online learning. In many cases, the developers have little or no instructional design training (Nantel and Vipond, 2006), relying instead on design and development tools to provide guidance throughout the process.

Software tools unquestionably play a valuable role in the process of instructional development, but what levels of instructional design support can we expect to come from the tools, and what part must still come from those who use the tools? The purpose of this chapter is to explore what tools instructional designers and novice developers most often use to create online learning from both design and development perspectives, what types of instructional design support can be found in different types of development tools, and how these tools may (or may not) impact the ability to meet instructional needs. This chapter focuses on four different tool classifications:

- Standard authoring tools
- Front-end design and automated instructional design (AID) tools
- Learning-activity, focused design tools, such as simulations and games
- Team development/publishing tools, such as learning content management systems (LCMSs) and groupware authoring tools

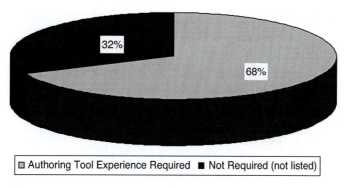

**Figure 50.1** Percentage of instructional design job postings requiring authoring tool experience.

## STANDARD AUTHORING TOOLS

Times have changed for instructional designers who work on online learning courses. In the early days of computer-based training (CBT) and through the early transition to Web-based delivery of asynchronous, self-paced learning, instructional development teams were most often organized with clear delineation between those who *designed* the instruction and those who programmed or *authored* course material. Instructional designers were responsible, primarily, for creating the specifications, such as design documents, scripts, storyboards, etc., while authoring specialist and programmers focused almost exclusively on assembling online learning materials to match the specifications. Over time, however, the lines between these roles continued to blur, with increased pressure on instructional designers to assume a more active role in the authoring stages of development.

To illustrate current demand for required authoring skills, a random sampling of instructional design job postings was taken from monster.com, Yahoo! hotjobs.com, and CareerBuilder.com from April to May 2006. Of the postings studied, 68% specifically listed the ability to use authoring tools as a requirement for the job, in most cases naming specific authoring tools, such as Adobe Flash, Dreamweaver, Authorware, and ToolBook (see Figure 50.1). The postings came from a wide array of organizations, both large and small, including The Johns Hopkins University, Becton Dickinson, OfficeMax, Fidelity Investments, Walgreen's, Sears, The Hartford, Merck, and the Federal Reserve Bank. In another study, organizations that create custom courseware for internal training reported on the tools they use to create self-paced learning materials. Table 50.1 shows the top ten authoring tools used most frequently, listed in order of the highest percentage of use (Chapman, 2006b). Many of these tools have existed in one form or another for over a decade, including Flash, Dreamweaver, Authorware, Director, Lectora, ToolBook, and Quest. Standard authoring tools really have not changed much since the early days of technology-based training (Foshay and Preese, 2005), even pre-dating the movement from hard-drive-delivered and CD-ROM courses to Web-based delivery.

Authoring tools were originally designed for the purpose of allowing nonprogrammers to easily assemble media objects and preconstructed scripting code to build instructional learning applications. Most standard authoring tools use the metaphor of a blank page, allowing authors (users of authoring tools) as much flexibility as possible to create visually appealing layouts and designs while also providing a scripting language for further extensibility in the creation of complex interactions. For the most part, authoring tools operated as advertised, although they still often required a steep learning curve in order to take advantage of their features (Merrill, 1997). In many ways,

**TABLE 50.1**

**Most Frequently Used Standard Authoring Tools for Online Courseware Development**

| Authoring Tool | Vendor | Companies Using Tool (%) |
|---|---|---|
| Flash | Adobe | 92 |
| Dreamweaver | Adobe | 67 |
| Authorware | Adobe | 34 |
| Director | Adobe | 27 |
| Lectora Publisher | Trivantis | 21 |
| Captivate | Adobe | 18 |
| ToolBook | SumTotal | 18 |
| Breeze | Adobe | 6 |
| Total LCMS | SumTotal | 4 |
| Quest | Allen Communication | 4 |

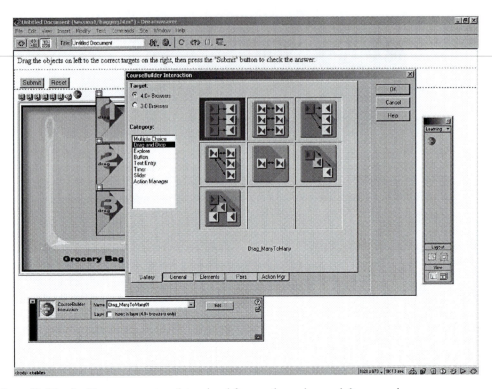

**Figure 50.2** CourseBuilder for Dreamweaver template wizard for creating a drag-and-drop exercise.

constructing courses with just an authoring tool is much like building an entire house stick by stick. Because of the open nature of authoring tools and the blank page metaphor, originally there was little or no instructional design guidance to assist novice developers in creating instructionally sound courseware.

The next evolutionary stage of authoring tools was the introduction of templates, designed for two primary purposes: (1) to facilitate rapid development of course content, and (2) to provide additional instructional design guidance for novice developers. As an example of the types of templates found in authoring tools, a set of templates named CourseBuilder was created as an add-on for Macromedia's Dreamweaver, which was initially designed for standard Webpage development and not for the creation of learning material. The learning templates are accessed from the menu bar as a wizard to walk novice developers through the process of creating complex learning interactions. The templates can be used to create a variety of test question formats, discovery exercises, and sophisticated drag-and-drop exercises (see Figure 50.2). The templates have built-in, automatic controls to record scoring information, answer judging, feedback, and remediation branching based on learner selection.

Templates also serve another valuable role in providing examples of good design and ideas for different types of instructional interventions; for example,

Articulate Presenter is a popular tool for converting PowerPoint presentations into e-learning courses. To expand on its core technology, Articulate released the Rapid E-Learning PowerPoint Template Kit, which includes dozens of professionally designed templates, including screen-layout templates and, even more importantly, examples of how the template may be applied to instruction (see Figure 50.3).

Although templates provide much needed additional design guidance to authors, desktop authoring tools still lack the core functionality to fully ensure adherence to sound instructional design principles, especially in the early stages of front-end analysis, objective writing, and designing appropriate interactions across an entire course. Bell (1998) concluded that authoring tools support many possible instructional applications, some of which may be well executed and some poorly executed, but none will be created with very much guidance from the tool.

Authoring tools, however, do play an important role in the overall instructional development process, as evidenced by the demand for authoring tool experience among posted instructional design job descriptions. Instructional designers, who also may use authoring tools, must apply their own design expertise in the early stages of instructional development, then use the authoring tools to carry out the design according to specifications.

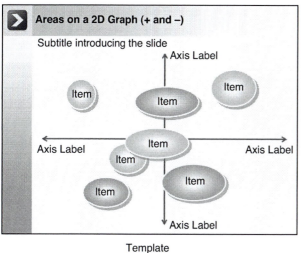

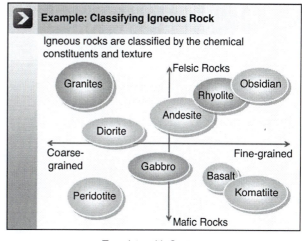

**Figure 50.3** Articulate instructional design template used for providing classification examples across multiple domains.

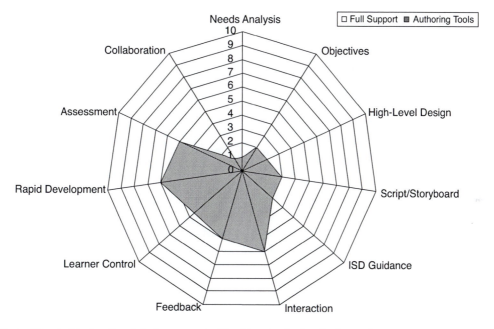

**Figure 50.4** Typical level of instructional design support offered by standard authoring tools.

Figure 50.4 illustrates the level of instructional design support one might expect from standard authoring tools. Most authoring tools provide little to no guidance in the areas of needs analysis, objective writing, high-level (course) design, script/storyboarding, and instructional design guidance; instead, they are more appropriately used during the development phases to create interaction, which provides feedback and opportunities for learners to control their own learning experience (learner control), rapid development of online course materials (as opposed to programming from scratch), and support for the creation of automated assessment. By understanding that standard authoring tools provide limited instructional design guidance, organizations can correctly position their use appropriately in the broader context of instructional development process by applying other methods and resources to the front-end design work. This discussion also suggests that standard authoring tools may not be best suited for novice development of learning content when expectations exist that the tool will provide guidance and structure through development.

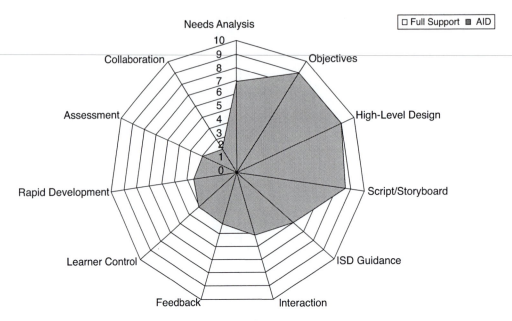

**Figure 50.5** Coverage of design guidance supported by automated instructional design tools (AIDs).

## FRONT-END DESIGN AND AUTOMATED INSTRUCTIONAL DESIGN TOOLS

Approaching the design and development task from the opposite end of the spectrum is a set of specialized software applications that provide guidance through the front-end of instructional development. None of these tools has achieved the same mass adoption rate experienced by standard authoring tools. Some were initially created as experimental projects, some as in-house development toolsets supporting custom development of CBT and online courseware, and still others simply as performance support tools designed to fill in the gap left by standard authoring tools. These applications also range significantly in scope of functionality and purpose. Some are designed to create high-level instructional design documents, while others span the entire development process from front-end design through the production phases of development. Holistic systems that also provide production of courseware are often referred to as *automated instructional design* (AID) tools. This moniker is what sets them apart from other design tools (Gros and Spector, 1994). As a classification of design and development tools, this category provides the most instructional design guidance targeting development by novice designers and subject matter experts and others responsible for developing instruction (Muraida and Spector, 1993). Information about the frequency of use of front-end design and AID solutions is difficult to obtain, because most studies of instructional design and devel-

opment tools focus on commercial products. Table 50.2 identifies some of the most high-profile projects and solutions in this area. The common thread among these tools is that they all serve a useful purpose for environments where instructional design expertise may be lacking or in short supply and for situations where subject matter experts and others are primarily responsible for developing instruction (Muraida and Spector, 1993). Figure 50.5 illustrates where front-end design and AID solutions provide the most support for instructional development, with strong emphasis on needs analysis, objective writing, high-level design, script/storyboarding, and ISD guidance.

A simple subclassification of front-end design and AID tools was presented by Kasowitz (1998): (1) those systems that focus on cognitive aspects of instructional design—in other words, systems that prescribe instructional interventions based on best practice theories (e.g., IDExpert, ADG), and (2) those systems that provide support and guidance for the procedural steps of instructional design (e.g., AIM II, The Designer's Edge, GAIDA, DesignWare, Coursewriter). As an example, IDExpert (ID2 Research Group, led by Dr. M. David Merrill) was based on instructional transaction theory (Cline and Merrill, 1995). Briefly, IDExpert included the intelligence to bring together elements of knowledge representation, best practice instructional strategies, and instructional design prescriptions, automatically producing all of the necessary interactions for a student to acquire a particular knowledge or skill (Merrill, 1999). IDExpert users followed

676

**TABLE 50.2**

**Some of the Most Recognized Front-End Design and Automated Instructional Design Tools**

| Design or AID Tool | Reason Created |
| --- | --- |
| AIM II | Created for the Navy to promote uniform instructional design practices and as a repository for course design specifications |
| The Designer's Edge (Allen Communication) | Created as a commercial application focusing on front-end analysis, objective writing, design specifications, storyboarding, and evaluation |
| GAIDA | Created by Armstrong Laboratories at Brooks Air Force Base for the purpose of providing instructional design guidance and examples during the front end of instructional development; based on Gagné's nine events of instruction |
| IDExpert | Created at Utah State University through grants and sponsorships to put into practice the theory of automated instructional design |
| ADG (acronym for "didactic engineering workbench" in French) | Created as joint project of research and academic institutions as an intelligent support system for course design |
| DesignWare (Langevin) | Created as a commercial, support tool to accompany Langevin's train-the-trainer workshops; focuses on guidance and organization course design specifications |
| CourseWriter (Darryl Sink and Associates) | Created as a commercial tool focused on, for example, front-end design, objective writing, and course organization |

steps provided by the system to enter appropriate content, and the system automatically generated and delivered the appropriate interactions until mastery was achieved by learners.

By contrast, The Designer's Edge (Allen Communication) uses a performance support approach by emulating the analyze, design, develop, implement,

and evaluate (ADDIE) model of instructional design as its primary interface (see Figure 50.6). Instead of prescribing specific design methodology, the system walks novice and expert designers through the common steps of instructional design, such as conducting a needs analysis, creating an audience profile, using an embedded wizard to create appropriately formatted

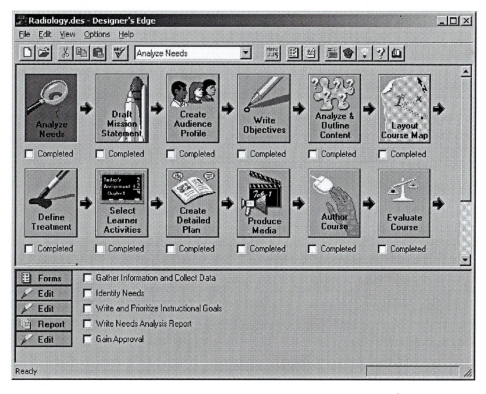

**Figure 50.6** The Designer's Edge interface based on the standard ADDIE model.

performance objectives, creating a master course map, and providing extensive tools for creating scripts and storyboards to be used by multimedia programmers when creating online learning.

To provide guidance beyond the ADDIE model interface, the system also serves up context-sensitive instructional design advice and guidance from leaders in the field, linked to tools that can be used to complete the task. Although Allen Communication has added tools to transmit the learning content from the storyboarding tool directly into standard authoring tools such as Authorware, ToolBook, and Dreamweaver, the primary focus of the system is on the front-end design tasks of instructional development.

Among the examples of successful front-end design developed by utilizing AID tools is GAIDA (Guided Approach to Instructional Design Advising), based on Gagné's nine events of instruction (Gagné, 1991). GAIDA was put through a series of tests where novices created course designs with only guidance from the support tool. The results concluded that the tool was "generally effective" in creating instructional sound learning content (Spector and Whitehead, 1994). The theory behind the tool, according to Gagné himself, was that it would "provide novices with easily understood, high-level guidance along with completely worked examples, and they will perform as if they were advanced apprentices" (Gagné, 1991). The tool is still available for a nominal fee from Cyberlearning (www.cyberlearning.com). The name of the product has been changed to GUIDE.

AIM (Authoring Instruction Materials) II has also proven to be a successful endeavor with the U.S. Navy; in fact, it is now the largest single database of training in the Navy (Arnone, 2001). In addition to providing instructional design guidance, it also serves as a primary content management system and monitors the workflow of instructional development projects. The Navy also uses the system to maintain design consistency for internal development and managing outsource course developers (Johnson, 2005).

With the promise and proven success (in part) of front-end design and AID solutions, it is a wonder why these systems have not garnered more widespread adoption, especially as more and more organizations look to novice developers and subject matter experts as course designers. This will continue to be an area of further research and study, and these early precursor projects will help set the stage for the next generation of front-end design and AID systems.

## LEARNING-ACTIVITY, FOCUSED DESIGN TOOLS (SIMULATIONS, GAMES)

Another classification of tools used by instructional designers consists of simulation and gaming tools, designed for a precise purpose and to achieve very specific instructional outcomes. From the very beginning of computer-facilitated instruction, simulations and games have been an important instructional intervention to support experiential learning and to reinforce higher level, cognitive learning methodologies. Early simulations and games were often custom programmed at the coding level or assembled through sophisticated use of standard authoring tools. Of course, simulations have been around for many years in a variety of forms, including large-scale flight simulators, role-playing simulations in the classroom, computer-delivered simulations, and, most recently, high-fidelity simulations that can be delivered through cyberspace.

In a recent study, organizations indicated that they would like to use simulations and games as part of a blended curriculum, but they feel that the barriers to entry (such as high development costs and difficulty of creating simulations on their own) are simply too prohibitive (Chapman, 2005). In fact, the study found that the average development time required to create 1 hour of simulation was 750 hours (ranging up to 1300:1), compared to an average ratio of 220:1 for standard e-learning courses. This explains why simulations and games are currently underutilized in online learning courses; however, this desire to utilize simulations has also resulted in an explosion of a whole new line of instructional design and development tools that focus on the development of simulations and games. The following taxonomy lists the major groupings of tools found on the market today (representing over 106 simulation tool providers):

- Software simulation
- Soft-skills simulations
- Role-playing (e.g., conversation with on-screen characters)
- Business skills (e.g., making decisions to play out a business scenario such as running a mock business)
- Business modeling/analytical (e.g., setting variable conditions and observing the outcome based on business rules; learning how to interpret data)
- Story-problem/scenario-based (e.g., setting up story problems and having learners make decisions to solve the problems)

- Sales process simulator (simulating mock sales scenarios)
- Hard skills/technical
- Troubleshooting/diagnostic (making decisions and observing the outcome of each action)
- Procedural walk-through (learner performs steps in a procedure)
- Simulating physical systems (e.g., simulating pieces of equipment or other objects, setting up a computer network)
- Simulating concepts (e.g., simulating a schematic diagram, simulating how weather patterns work using a diagram)
- Emergency response simulations (e.g., performing actions as a result of an emergency)
- Virtual worlds/spatial relationships (e.g., flight simulators or simulating an office environment, cockpit, or factory)

Some of the leading tools in each of these sectors are shown in Table 50.3.

## Software Simulation Tools

Software simulation tools allow novice developers to record screen interactions while walking through a procedure. The tool remembers each mouse click and keystroke for the purpose of later creating interactive simulations—for example, registering the coordinates and creating a click area for each mouse click. Simulation authors must simply clean up the recording and add feedback and remediation to complete the simulation. This is considerably quicker than using standard authoring tools to (1) capture screens, (2) manually add touch areas and text input fields, (3) create prompts and instructions for the learners, (4) wire each click or correct key entry into a branching pattern, etc. Software simulation tools have significantly reduced development time, while preserving a high degree of fidelity and interactivity in the learning event.

## Soft-Skills Simulation Tools

Soft-skills tools (Table 50.4) are usually based on a template model for quickly creating specific types of interactions such as developing a dialog, choosing on-screen characters, and creating a role-play simulation with graded responses and comparisons to expert paths through the simulation (how they may have handled the situation). The difficulty for makers of simulation tools is that they must try to provide the flexibility necessary to vary the simulation for different purposes while keeping focused on delivering high-fidelity,

**TABLE 50.3**
**Commercially Available Software Simulation Tools**

| Product | Company |
|---|---|
| Captivate | Adobe |
| OnDemand | Global Knowledge |
| Firefly | KnowledgePlanet |
| STT Trainer | Kaplan IT Learning |
| Assima | Assima |
| SoftSim | OutStart |
| RapidBuilder | XStream Software |

**TABLE 50.4**
**Commercially Available Soft-Skills Tools**

| Product | Company |
|---|---|
| Redwood development platform | Redwood e-Learning Systems |
| Forio simulation development software | Forio |
| KDSimStudio | Knowledge Dynamics |
| Experience Builder | ExperienceBuilders, LLC |
| RealCall | SIVOX |
| StarTrainer | Knowlagent |
| Simulated Role Play | SIMmersion, LLC |

workplace-relevant scenarios created in a very short amount of time. Figure 50.7 shows an example of a sophisticated simulation in which the learner makes decisions about how society may potential reverse the effects of global warming. The simulation, from Forio, is capable of simulating elapsed time as the learner may run the scenario over months or even years (compressed to an hour or less online).

## Hard-Skills/Technical Simulation Tools

The hard-skills/technical simulations category (Table 50.5) covers a broad range of skill areas. Think of systems in this category as being capable of modeling physical systems, such as a piece of machinery or an electronic measurement system. This category also covers task simulators designed to teach and measure a learner's ability to follow steps in a procedure with various levels of guidance. A good example of how this might work is the flight simulators often used in the aviation industry. Many airlines have figured out how to pass performance data from sessions in a flight simulator back to a central learning management system, which keeps performance records for classroom-based learning and e-learning courses.

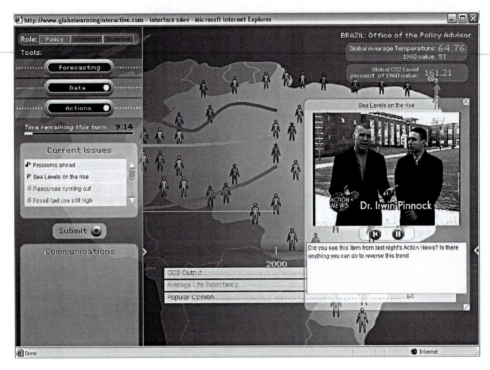

**Figure 50.7** Global warming simulation developed using Forio.

**TABLE 50.5**
**Hard-Skills/Technical Simulation Development Tools**

| Product | Company |
| --- | --- |
| Multigen Creator | Multigen-Paradigm |
| KDCalc | Knowledge Dynamics |
| NGRAIN Producer | NGRAIN |
| Visual Purple | Visual Purple |

**TABLE 50.6**
**Popular Development Tools for Instructional Games**

| Product | Company |
| --- | --- |
| Gameshow Pro (Web) | Learningware |
| Composica Enterprise | Composica |
| Games2Train | Games2Train |
| Game Development Environment | Galaxy Scientific |

## Gaming Tools

Games play a unique role in deploying an enterprise-wide learning strategy (Table 50.6). Although not primarily designed to deliver an entire training or teaching job alone (Kirk and Belovics, 2004), games provide a unique level of motivation in learning areas such as classification (matching games), reinforcing factual information (question and answer games), and rote learning (memorization games). In addition, as the new gaming generation enters the workforce, lecture-based training will likely be less effective (Kirk and Belovics, 2004). What makes simulation and gaming development tools unique is that instructional design guidance is not often obvious through the interface; rather, guidance comes from the intelligence and flexibility of the simulation or game designed to achieve a specific learning outcome. The primary instructional benefits

of using such tools is the depth of interaction and rich feedback available for learners, achievable through relative rapid development processes and minimizing the authoring savvy required on the part of instructional developers (see Figure 50.8).

## TEAM DEVELOPMENT/ PUBLISHING TOOLS

Since the beginning of 2000, a new classification of instructional development tools has evolved that is beginning to gain traction as commercially viable options for developing online learning. Many of the most popular traditional authoring tools available today are desktop applications, meaning that they typically can be used by only one instructional developer at a

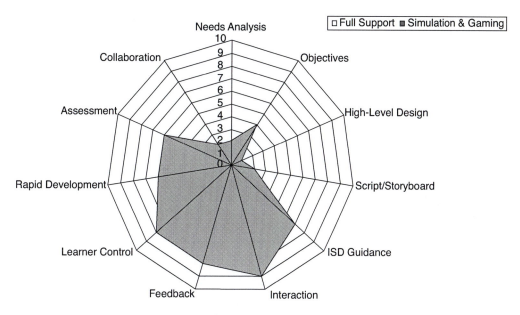

**Figure 50.8** Instructional design support offered by focused, learning-activity tools (such as simulation or gaming).

time to create interaction. In contrast, this new classification of tools is based on groupware projects based on a publishing model for online learning development, using multiple, concurrent content contributors, each working on learning content and interactive exercises that are part of a larger course or curriculum. To illustrate the point, consider the following question: Could the publishers of *The Los Angeles Times* use Microsoft Word to lay out and organize each daily newspaper? The answer is "yes." How efficiently could it be produced, though? The answer is "not very efficiently."

These groupware publishing systems are called *learning content management systems* (LCMSs). By definition, an LCMS is a multideveloper environment where developers can create, store, reuse, manage, and deliver learning content from a central object repository (Chapman, 2006a). Although many LCMS solutions have built-in authoring capabilities, most are also designed to assemble individual learning activities that may have been created using a variety of traditional authoring tools and storing the learning events as learning objects. A learning object is a reusable learning activity that can be (1) metadata tagged for easy retrieval, (2) standards that can communicate with other learning technologies, or (3) objects combined or clustered with other learning objects to create new, derivative learning structures such as lessons, units, or entire courses. Table 50.7 lists some of the most frequently used commercial LCMS solutions to date (Chapman, 2006b).

Beyond the rapid development capabilities offered by these systems, LCMS tools often also include a wide range of embedded instructional design guid-

**TABLE 50.7**
**Most Frequently Used**
**LCMS Solutions**

| Product | Company |
| --- | --- |
| Evolution | Outstart |
| TotalLCMS | SumTotal |
| ForceTen | Eedo |
| Saba LCMS | Saba |
| Learn.com | Learn.com |
| Generation 21 | Generation 21 |
| TopClass | WBT Systems |

ance, at times bordering on a hybrid between standard authoring and front-end design and automated instructional design (AID) tools. Following are some of the areas of instructional design guidance that can be found inside commercial LCMS solutions.

## Interactivity Templates

Learning content management system tools offer even more extensive capabilities for using and reusing design templates. One example would be a gaming template that is driven by a bank of test questions. The template provides the interface, look and feel, game show host, game boards, etc. Because all learning content in an LCMS is stored in a database, the test questions can be randomly and automatically extracted by the database each time a new version of the game is played; hence, the same template could yield thousands of variations of the same gaming

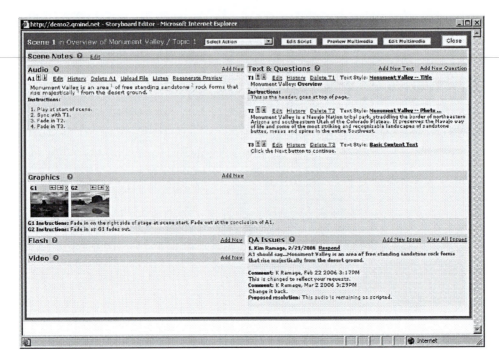

**Figure 50.9** Script/storyboarding tool available in QMIND.

template. Although most LCMS solutions are designed to be instructional-theory agnostic, there is evidence in most systems that they prescribe to certain aspects of instructional theory. Although this sounds like a weakness, it actually helps to create more focused design templates. Standardizing on a specific design theory is what allows template designers to create templates (Foshay and Preese, 2005). The flip side of this logic is that templated authoring tools are very restrictive, unless you happen to prescribe to that specific theory.

## Dynamic Pretesting

Most LCMS products use a dynamic pretesting model, meaning that individual test questions can be linked with learning content (stored as learning objects). Based on learner performance in the test, the LCMS can dynamically create a new version of the course based on demonstrated performance in the test, so learners do not receive instruction on content they have already mastered. When used correctly, dynamic pretest can dramatically shorten course contact time.

## Learning Objects

Although most references to learning objects focus on their reusability, there is a more significant instructional tie-in. Learning objects frequently are based on a single, enabling learning objective, thus providing focus and clarity on teaching and assessing learner performance against their mastery of the objective. Learning objects—with a one-to-one relationship with enabling objective—can be clustered with other enabling objectives to create new paths for working toward a broader terminal objective (the purpose of a lesson or entire course). Learning object design helps focus instructional designers on their ultimate goal.

## Storyboard Specifications

In the instructional development process, storyboards represent a detailed design specification for the course as an elaboration of high-level design documents. LCMS technology provides methods that allow learning objects to be based on objectives and then designed into delivery specifications via storyboarding in support of audio/video production, message design, and keeping track of complex details of interactivity. Figure 50.9 shows an example of an LCMS-generated storyboard interface for QMIND.

## Links between Assessment and Competencies

The makeup of LCMS technology makes it possible to create sophisticated links between test questions and competencies (skills, knowledge, and attitude).

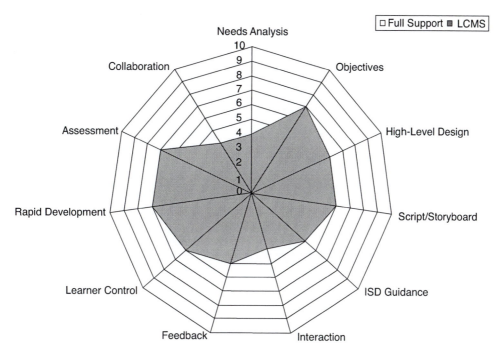

**Figure 50.10** Instructional design support offered by learning content management systems (LCMSs).

Programming numerous connections between learning performance and competencies is possible using standard authoring tools, but the complexity makes it a barrier to measuring learning performance in a meaningful way for novice developers. In general, LCMSs provide less guidance than front-end and automated design tools (see Figure 50.10). The structure of most systems is based on the notion that front-end analysis and high-level design have already previously been completed and that the purpose of the LCMS is to support the remaining development and delivery process. They do encourage developmental practices but still come up short in supporting the full range of instructional design guidance across the entire spectrum; however, of all the commercially viable learning technologies, LCMS technology appears to be evolving toward a platform that may show promise in providing both instructional design guidance and development system.

## CONCLUSIONS

At present, myriad online learning development tools cover a broad spectrum of choice and flexibility; yet, the shear number of these tools, plus new emerging technologies such as wikis, blogs, and podcasts, leaves organizations in a state of confusion when attempting to develop a cohesive authoring and development strategy. Although instructional design guidance, in some form or another, is now embedded inside several classifications of development tools, considerable innovation and research are still required to create holistic systems that negate or minimize the need for instructional design expertise, allowing nontrained designers to create online learning courseware without assistance.

Perhaps software developers will never create a wizard that allows writers to fully write like Shakespeare, and the same may be true for intelligent, instructional design software, but that does not mean that instructional design guidance and principles should not be embedded in the evolution of existing content development tools or future technologies. In the meantime, it is incumbent on every organization that creates online learning to find the appropriate balance and mix between internal expertise (people resources) and available tools and technology for designing instruction.

Great appreciation is extended to those who continually push the envelope and introduce instructional design savvy into the tools of the trade. They have laid a great foundation for future innovators to draw upon to create new methods, new tools, and new solutions, as long as they keep their vision clearly focused on the ultimate goal—namely, the design and creation of effective learning experience that result in optimal knowledge transfer.

# REFERENCES

Arnone, M. (2001). Navy rewrites its course-writing software to enhance online distance education. *Chronicle Higher Educ.*, December 5 (http://chronicle.com/free/2001/12/2001120501u.htm).

Bell, B. (1998). Investigate and decide learning environments: specializing task models for authoring tool design. *J. Learn. Sci.*, 7(1), 65–105.

Chapman, B. (1995). Accelerating the design process: a tool for instructional designers. *J. Interact. Instruct. Dev.*, 8(2), 8–15.

Chapman, B. (2005). *Online Simulations Knowledgebase.* San Jose: Brandon Hall Research.*

Chapman, B. (2006a). *LCMS Knowledge Base.* San Jose, CA: Brandon Hall Research.*

Chapman, B. (2006b). *Custom Content Developers: A Knowledge Base of 100+ Outsource Learning Providers.* San Jose, CA: Brandon Hall Research.

Clark, R. C. and Lyons, C. (1999). Using Web-based training wisely. *Training.* 36(7), 51–56.

Cline, R. W. and Merrill, M. D. (1995). Automated instructional design via instructional transactions. In *Automating Instructional Design: Computer-Based Development and Delivery Tools*, edited by R. D. Tennyson and A. E. Baron, pp. 317–353. New York: Springer-Verlag.*

Foshay, W. R. and Preese, F. (2005). Do we need authoring systems? A commercial perspective. *Technol. Instruct. Cogn. Learn.*, 2, 249–260.

Gagné, R. M. (1991). AIDA: concept of Operation. In *Designing an Advanced Instructional Design Advisor: Conceptual Frameworks*, Vol. 5, AL-TP-1991-0017, edited by R. M. Gagné, R. D. Tennyson, and D. J. Gettman. Brooks Air Force Base, TX: Armstrong Laboratory, Human Resource Directorate.*

Gros, B. and Spector, J. M. (1994). Evaluating automated instructional design systems: a complex problem. *Educ. Technol.*, 34(5), 37–46.*

Johnson, R. L. (2005). Authoring instructional materials (AIM). In *Encyclopedia of Educational Technology*, edited by B. Hoffman. San Diego, CA: San Diego State University.

Kasowitz, A. (1998). *Tools for Automating Instructional Design*, ED420304. Syracuse, NY: ERIC Clearinghouse on Information and Technology.

Kirk, J. J. and Belovics, R. (2004). An intro to online learning games. *Learn. Circuits*, April (www.learningcircuits.org).

Lewis, D. (2003). Automating Instructional Design with Automated Pedagogical Agent Systems: Will There Always Be a Need for Instructional Designers? Paper presented at the Association for Educational Communications and Technology Annual Meeting, October 22–26, Anaheim, CA (http://www.coedu.usf.edu/agents/aect2003/).

Merrill, M. D. (1997). Learning-oriented instructional development tools. *Perform. Improv.*, 36(3), 51–55.*

Merrill, M. D. (1999). Instructional transaction theory (ITT): instructional design based on knowledge objects. In *Instructional-Design Theories and Models: A New Paradigm of Instructional Theory*, Vol. II, edited by C. M. Reigeluth, pp. 397–424. Mahwah, NJ: Lawrence Erlbaum Associates.*

Muraida, D. J. and Spector, J. M. (1993). The advanced instructional design advisor. *Instruct. Sci.*, 21(4), 239–253.*

Nantel, R. and Vipond, S. (2006). *Authoring Tool Knowledgebase 2006: A Buyer's Guide to 100 of the Best E-Learning Content Development Applications.* San Jose, CA: Brandon Hall Research.*

Paquette, G., Aubin, C., and Crevier, F. (1994). An intelligent support system for course design. *Educ. Technol.*, 34(9), 50–57.*

Spector, J. M. and Whitehead, L. K. (1994). A Guided Approach to Instructional Design Advising. Paper presented at the Conference of the Association for the Development of Computer-Based Instructional Systems (ADCIS), February 15–19, Nashville, TN.*

Wiley, D. A., Ed. (2002). *The Instructional Use of Learning Objects.* Bloomington, IN: Association for Educational Communications and Technology/Agency for Instructional Technology (http://reusability.org/read/).

---

* Indicates a core reference.

# 51

# Artifacts as Tools in the Design Process

*Elizabeth Boling and Kennon M. Smith*
Indiana University, Bloomington, Indiana

## CONTENTS

## ABSTRACT

Both process and product artifacts are collected and disseminated in many fields of design as a source of design knowledge in the form of precedent, which includes both the artifacts themselves and the memories, or schema, retained as a result of interaction with or examination of the artifacts. The emergence of serious study into the practice of design in our field will extend beyond the study of process models and may be productively informed by understanding how artifacts are used as tools by designers.

## KEYWORDS

*Artifacts:* Designed objects or systems, including those created in the process of design and those resulting from the act of design.
*Precedent:* Artifacts and/or memory of designing them or examining them.

## INTRODUCTION

In recent years, there has been much discussion in the instructional design and technology literature regarding the ways we practice and teach design. Although the field has a significant history of developing process models to guide and structure design activities (such as those reviewed by Andrews and Goodson, 1980), recent criticisms of these sorts of models (Gordon and Zemke, 2000; Zemke and Rossett, 2002) have encouraged reconsideration of basic assumptions underlying practice in the field and have emphasized the need for more flexible approaches to complex design problems (Nelson and Stolterman, 2003). Authors have emphasized the importance of defining the field's value-added proposition in the face of rapidly changing academic and corporate settings (Hill et al., 2004), and for some years authors have openly wondered if the field could be strengthened by looking at processes and habits of thought in allied design fields (Bichelmeyer et al., 2006; Johnson, 2005; Murphy, 1992; Rowland et al., 1994).

In this environment of reflection, we anticipate the need for increased attention to research in the area of design science (Cross, 2001), with a view toward expanding what Bichelmeyer (2003) termed *instructional design theory*, which she said was required to systematically study the work of instructional design and the impact of such designs.

We propose to begin, in part, by examining the ways in which other design fields (such as art, architecture, and engineering) teach and practice design. We do not suggest that instructional design is entirely the same as other design fields, or that it should be; however, we do suggest that considering practices from related fields, both successful and unsuccessful, and pursuing the research questions generated by comparisons between their practices and those of instructional systems design (ISD) is a potentially fruitful avenue for expanding our own design science. This chapter examines one aspect of design practice in fields that share characteristics with ISD: the use of artifacts as tools for carrying out and teaching design.

## ARTIFACTS AS TOOLS

A striking feature of many design fields is the widespread use of, and attention given to, artifacts as tools in the design process. These artifacts fall into two primary categories: process artifacts and product artifacts. Process artifacts include sketches of several kinds (conceptual sketches, decision diagrams, formal or visualizing sketches, and so on) as well as documentation, generally written reports created at virtually any stage of the design process. Product artifacts are comprised of design work already completed, including instructional materials, final and end-user documentation, presentation materials, and episodic memories of reviewing or experiencing designed products. These two categories overlap, as the type of an artifact can depend on how it is being used by designers at a given time.

Some process artifacts and product artifacts are propositional; that is, they are largely verbal and largely abstract. Even when a design report describes the plans for an instructional experience, for example, such a description does not tend to be a concrete, or tangible, representation of that experience. It may be very detailed but does not as often take the form of a narrative, a symbolic/diagrammatic representation, or a spatial/verbal diagram—forms currently being explored by Parrish (2006), Appelman (2005), and Botturi (2006). In some of the related design fields under discussion, artifacts are more often descriptive and concrete, visual or constructed. They include sketches, concept diagrams, prototypes, and, to a greater degree than is publicly practiced in our field, finished artifacts (products) or published representations of such artifacts.

## Visual Process Artifacts as Cognitive Tools

One of the most ubiquitous forms taken by process artifacts in many fields of design is sketching. Fish and Scrivener (1990) detailed the visual cognition process involved in sketching. They described the interplay between the two modes of mental representation—propositional (largely symbolic) and analog ("quasi-pictorial, spatially depictive")—required for sketching (p. 121). As individuals sketch, the percept (what they are seeing) always undergoes mental manipulation before it is represented as marks; in turn, the marks "generate mental images that may in turn influence the sketch" (p. 120). Although they address sketching directly from life for the most part, they also state "there is objective evidence that spatially depictive images generated from memory have many of the properties needed to explain the ability of artists and designers to generate, manipulate, combine and inspect in imagination non-existent visual objects" (p. 122).

Goldschmidt (1991) built on the work of Fish and Scrivener to study the use of sketching in the design process, finding what she calls an *oscillation* between propositional thinking and descriptive thinking. She observed designers using two types of argumentation, based on these two types of thinking, during the process of design. The first is *seeing as* argumentation, which is depictive and sketch based. The second is *seeing that* argumentation, which is nonfigural. The use of these two types of argumentation oscillates, particularly in skilled designers, over many iterations. Goldschmidt stated that "the order in which arguments switch modalities is not important. What is significant is the fact that the shift occurs both ways. ...[It] helps translate the particulars of form into generic qualities, and generic rules into specific appearances" (pp. 138–139). In nonsketching protocols, Goldschmidt reported that "'seeing as' arguments are by far in the minority" (p. 140).

Fish and Scrivener examined direct sketching from reality, while Goldschmidt turned her attention to sketching from the internal eye during the process of architectural design. Laseau (1986) did not conduct formal studies but brought decades of observational and professional experience to bear on his discussions of visual artifacts that represent nonformal properties of a design space. His work makes it clear that visual artifacts are not produced solely for the sake of picturing an essentially visual product. Suwa and Tversky

(1996), in their study of sketching among architecture students and professionals, underscored Laseau's experiential insights. They concluded that study participants were able to use their sketches to explore not only visual relationships among parts but also to explore functional relationships (such as lighting or circulation). They noted that: "This analysis has revealed that sketches make apparent not only perceptual relations but also inherently non-visual functional relations to both advanced design students and practicing architects" (p. 192).

Goel (1995) offered an explanation for the mechanism whereby sketching supports cognition during the design process. He explained that sketches support design cognition by leaving options open because the elements of the symbol system used in sketching are *non-notational*. He drew on Goodman's (1976) taxonomy of symbol systems in which non-notational systems are defined as ambiguous with respect to what a given mark may stand for. As an example, a circle in a sketch may represent a sun, a wheel, a plate, or anything round. This ambiguity allows the designer to defer specific interpretation of the sketch (or diagram, as described by Laseau, 1986) and entertain or realize alternatives within the image that may not have been intended at the time of its creation. Fish and Scrivener (1990) labeled this same quality as *indeterminacy* and speculated, based on the visual theories of Kosslyn, a key proponent of the neurophysiologic view of representations in the brain as quasi-pictorial and manipulable, that "sketch indeterminacy may trigger innate recognition search mechanisms into generating a stream of imagery useful to invention" (pp. 121–123).

In his exhaustive discussion of the types of knowledge required for design engineers, Vincenti (1990, p. 220) pointed out that nonverbal thinking in the form of sketching, drawings, graphs, and models is a critical way of thinking that falls under the knowledge category *design instrumentalities*. In his discussion of how knowledge builds in the field of engineering, Vincenti also discussed *visible sketching and doodling*, which serve as *vicarious overt trials*. These trials are mechanisms for selecting variation in a larger model that includes generating blind variations of design solutions or components of solutions (blind in the sense that their outcomes cannot be known until they are actually built and tried), employing consistent processes for selecting variations, and preserving or propagating the variations that are selected. When discussing his hypothesis that "instruments, on a par with theory, bear knowledge," Baird (2004, p. xvii) criticized Vincenti for not going further in his exploration of engineering knowledge to accord artifacts themselves (including, presumably, sketches) the status of knowledge. Baird's work, however, focused primarily on scientific instruments, and more exploration of this area is needed to establish solid links between his detailed analysis and process artifacts.

## Use of Product Artifacts

In his discussion of the design knowledge used by architects, Lawson (1980) stressed designers' reliance on episodic memory rather than general principles or problem-solving algorithms (i.e., process models) to generate design solutions. Episodic memory includes direct experience with designed artifacts (designing them or experiencing the designs of others) and vicarious experience with descriptions and representations of designed artifacts. In more recent writing, Lawson (2004b, p. 443) explained that "precedent stored in the form of episodic memory," either of one's own design or of the designed artifacts of others, "is used by experts to recognize design situations for which gambits are available," where *gambits* are defined as "patterns known to have certain properties and to offer certain capabilities" (p. 449).

In his widely cited analysis of design science, or the study of design, Cross (2001, p. 54) listed experience in designing and manufacturing artifacts as two sources of design knowledge and the "knowledge inherent in the artifacts of the artificial world" as the third. Vincenti (1990, pp. 208) pointed to "fundamental design concepts" as the first category of design knowledge for engineers. These concepts include the operational principles underlying a device (how the device works) and "normal configuration" or the "general shape and arrangement that are commonly agreed to best embody the operational principle." These fundamental concepts are learned through experience even before students begin to study design and are also "learned deliberately by the design community." Episodic memory, knowledge inherent in artifacts, and fundamental design concepts are all derived in one way or another from the conscious examination of product artifacts. "Designers appear to be able to browse freely and associatively between multiple precedents [and] browsing enables the discovery of new, often unanticipated, concepts in precedents" (Oxman, 1994).

In much of design education, the use of product artifacts is considered to be critical. The authors conducted a simple analysis of published design class syllabi in graphic design and illustration (Heller, 1998; Heller and Arisman, 2000). Each syllabus was examined to determine whether or not there were explicit references to the use of artifacts in any one of three ways listed below:

**TABLE 51.1**

**Instances of Syllabi Explicitly Calling for Use of Artifacts in Graphic Design and Illustration Courses Surveyed**

| Type of Syllabus | Number of Syllabi Surveyed | Number of Syllabi Explicitly Calling for Use of Artifacts | | |
|---|---|---|---|---|
| | | Artifacts Created by Others | Artifacts Created by Students | Student Memory of Artifacts or Experiences |
| Illustration courses | 21 | 13/21 (62%) | 14/21 (67%) | 2/21 (10%) |
| Design courses | 8 | 3/8 (38%) | 1/8 (13%) | 0 |

- Students are instructed to use artifacts that have been created by others.
- Students participate in critiques of their own designs in process as represented by presentation artifacts.
- Students are expected to draw upon memories of artifacts or experiences.

Our findings are summarized in Table 51.1. In each collection of syllabi, courses covering professional issues (e.g., business skills for designers) and theoretical or philosophical issues (e.g., Green Design) appeared together with the studio courses focused on design practice; the former typically did not include the use of artifacts. Many other courses did, including over half the courses in the sample of syllabi from illustration programs that required students to use their own artifacts or those created by others as part of their design education. In the smaller sample of graphic design syllabi, almost 40% required the use by students of artifacts created by others. It may not be surprising to see few requirements for using memories of artifacts in design courses given the emphasis on hands-on experience in such courses and the possibility that instructors assume students will use episodic memory while designing as a matter of course.

Anthony's (1999) extended criticism of the design jury (a public form of critique often incorporating external reviewers or panels of reviewers to comment on students' work) in architecture education, which questions the forms that this pedagogical practice takes, also makes clear that explaining one's own artifacts and experiencing criticism of them is considered an integral, essential part of design education in her discipline. The most compelling evidence of her belief in the use of artifacts for design education is that the alternatives to the classic design jury that she proposes all include the consideration and critique of designed artifacts.

One of the most visible aspects of most design fields is their production of formal precedent: publications, juried competitions, design collections, case studies, and so on. *Precedent* in the sense we are using it here does not carry the connotation of restriction on future decision-making as it does when used as a legal term. It does include any and every designed artifact from which a designer might draw understanding of solutions in specific contexts or inspiration for *seeing as* argumentation that might apply to a current design situation. Episodic memory is a form of precedent individual to each designer, and it is informal in the sense that it is idiosyncratic to the experiences and focus of each designer. Episodic memory is greatly extended by the production of formal precedent which allows individual designers to examine the artifacts of many more peers than would be available in the absence of published and collected representations of design products. Vincenti (1990) took the existence of both formal and informal precedent and its role in disseminating design knowledge so much for granted that he said, "The methods of propagating and preservation of engineering knowledge (journals, handbooks, textbooks, engineering school teaching, design traditions, word of mouth, and so forth) are obvious in our cases and do not require elaboration" (p. 242).

A lot of time and money goes into disseminating precedent and maintaining adequate access to precedent for designers and design students in most fields of design. A brief search for design publications in well-stocked bookstores or online and a survey of these publications can make this point evident. To explore a fraction of the publications and competitions in one field of design, the reader may visit the website of the American Institute of Graphic Artists (AIGA; http://www.aiga.org/).

Rowe et al. (2005) reported on their visits to practicing designers from three fields (sculpture, editorial illustration, and graphic design) in their work spaces to observe the forms of precedent that they collect and used. These included annual publications featuring the works of designers who pay to be included; specialty journals featuring representations of product artifacts and process artifacts with commentary; books in which multiple samples of specific product types are collected, often with descriptions of the design situations and decisions made; collections of illustrated books and individual images from all kinds of sources; online image collections; and catalogs from competitive shows of work. Many of these sources of precedent clearly require widespread financial and logistical support for collecting, publishing, and distributing the materials as well as a strong commitment on the part of individual designers to contribute examples of their work and participate in competitions and shows of work. The designers in this small study reported using precedent materials specifically as sources of technical and conceptual learning, springboards for design inspiration, and vehicles for building fundamental skills.

## COLLECTING AND DISSEMINATING PRECEDENT IN ISD

Several noteworthy efforts at collecting and disseminating precedent exist in the field of instructional design. The St. Louis Educational Museum, founded in 1905 (eventually the Audiovisual Department of the St. Louis Public Schools and subsumed into other departments) was an early such effort. Allen (2005) reported that the museum first housed key educational exhibits from the St. Louis World's Fair of 1904 and subsequently collections of visuals, realia, and, in time, audio-visual materials and educational radio shows. Much of this material was donated in about 2003 to the Missouri Historical Society and the Academic Film Archive of North America. In 1946, Ole Larson at Indiana University started an instructional film library by purchasing materials from Encyclopedia Britannica and other sources. These were rented to schools and, in turn, funded the production of new audio-visual educational materials (Instructional Systems Technology Department, 2007). Although both of these collections still exist in archive form, neither was originally intended to serve as precedent material for designers, and neither is now readily available as such.

Hooper et al. (2002), of the University of Minnesota Curriculum and Instruction and Design, Housing, and Apparel programs, developed and coordinated the University of Minnesota Learning Software Design Competition, which ran from 2000 to 2002, the goals of which were to "promote innovative educational software design [and] developing resources for instructional design students and practitioners" (p. 5). Pacificorp and the Design and Development Division of the Association for Educational Communications and Technology (AECT) have collaborated on the Pacificorp Design and Development Award competition since 2004. The goals of this competition are to promote and recognize innovative design in adult instruction and to promote collaboration and mentoring between students, faculty and

practitioners of instructional design (AECT, 2007). There is not an explicit commitment to collection and dissemination of material from the competitions to serve as precedent in the field. Since the May/June 2004 issue, *TechTrends* (the membership journal of AECT) has published articles under the section heading "The Instructional Design Portfolio." The stated purposes of this feature are to "offer practitioners in the field of ID a chance to see the work of other designers" and to "provide for the sharing of design knowledge that is not always available in other formats" (AECT, 2004).

Apart from these efforts (not all of them yielding published precedent and some industry efforts not being available to designers outside the companies or design groups involved), the authors are not aware of a volume of relevant precedent materials, or discipline-wide efforts at disseminating such precedent, in the instructional design field comparable to those evidenced in the work spaces of the designers visited during our pilot study.

## IMPLICATIONS FOR ISD

We are a design field. Murphy (1992) came to this conclusion in reviewing Lawson's (1980) work on the thinking and knowledge of designers. Goel (1995), in studying the cognition of design, made the case that instructional design is a prototypical design activity, because its core activity—the design of instruction—shares high-level characteristics with other prototypical design endeavors. His analysis of prototypical design fields holds strong face validity for those who have practiced instructional design. He enumerated 12 characteristics of design-task environments and explained that the degree to which an environment exhibits these characteristics is the degree to which it resembles a prototypical design environment. These characteristics are (1) a lack of information exists about the start state, the goal state, and the transformation required to go from one to another; (2) constraints on the task, either natural or manmade, do not constitute or define the task; (3) problems are large and complex; (4) problems do not decompose into distinct units except as the designer or as custom dictate; (5) components of the problem are only connected by contingent interdependency; (6) there are no right and wrong answers; (7) informational inputs to and outputs from the problem conform to certain categories; (8) feedback loops need to be simulated before the designed artifact exists; (9) errors carry costs; (10) the artifact will have to function independent of the designer; (11) specification and delivery are distinct from each other; and (12) specification and delivery are separated in time (pp. 85–87). Using these characteristics, most instructional design problem spaces can be seen to be close to the prototypical design case, which places instructional design close to architecture, design engineering, graphic design, and other fields of design and allows us to ask whether their practices may have relevance for us.

If they do, much research lies ahead in multiple areas. In the area of artifacts as tools for design, research is needed to:

- Examine further how the use of sketching and precedent might be incorporated effectively into instructional design activities.
- Determine what might constitute rigor and applicability in representations of instructional designs for use as precedent.
- Explore the barriers and facilitating factors present in the field for investing in the production and use of precedent.
- Establish pedagogical guidelines for incorporating "designerly ways of knowing" (Cross, 2001) into ISD education.

## REFERENCES

Allen, J. (2005). St. Louis Educational Museum: a centennial commemoration. *TechTrends*, 49(2), 22–26, 65.

Andrews, D. H. and Goodson, L. A. (1980). A comparative analysis of models of instructional design. *J. Instruct. Dev.*, 3(4), 2–16.*

Anthony, K. (1999). *Design Juries on Trial: The Renaissance of the Design Studio*. Urbana-Champaign: University of Illinois.

Appelman, R. (2005). Designing experiential modes: a key focus for immersive learning environments. *TechTrends*, 49(3), 64–74.*

Association for Educational Communications and Technology (AECT). (2004). Call for proposals: *TechTrends* instructional design portfolio. *TechTrends*, 48(3), 71.

Association for Educational Communications and Technology (AECT). (2007). PacifiCorp Design and Development Award website, from http://www.aect.org/Pacificorp/.

Baird, D. (2004). Thing knowledge: a philosophy of scientific instruments. Berkeley, CA: University of California Press.

Bichelmeyer, B. (2003). Instructional theory and instructional design theory: what's the difference and why should we care? *IDT Rec.*, http://www.indiana.edu/%7Eidt/articles/documents/ID_theory.Bichelmeyer.html.

Bichelmeyer, B., Boling, E., and Gibbons, A. (2006). Instructional design and technology models: their impact on research and teaching in instructional design and technology. In *Educational Media and Technology Yearbook*, Vol. 29, edited by M. Orey, V. J. McClendon, and R. M. Branch, pp. 23–43. Westport, CN: Libraries Unlimited.*

Botturi, L. (2006). E2ML: a visual language for the design of instruction. *Educ. Technol. Res. Dev.*, 54(3), 265–293.*

Cross, N. (2001). Designerly ways of knowing: design discipline vs. design science. *Design Issues*, 77(3), 49–55.*

Fish, J. and Scrivener, S. (1990). Amplifying the mind's eye: sketching and visual cognition. *Leonardo*, 23, 177–126.

Goel, V. (1995). *Sketches of Thought*. Cambridge, MA: MIT Press.

Goldschmidt, B. (1991). The dialectics of sketching. *Creativity J.*, 4(2), 123–143.

Goodman, N. (1976). *Languages of Art: An Approach to a Theory of Symbols*, 2nd ed. Indianapolis, IN: Hackett.

Gordon, J. and Zemke, R. (2000). The attack on ISD. *Training*, 37(4), 43–53.

Heller, S., Ed. (1998). *Education of a Graphic Designer*. New York: Allworth Press.

Heller, S. and Arisman, M., Eds. (2000). *Education of an Illustrator*. New York: Allworth Press.

Hill, J. R., Bichelmeyer, B. A., Boling, E., Gibbons, A. S., Grabowski, B. L., Osguthorpe, R. T., Schwier, R. A., and Wager, W. (2004). Perspectives on significant issues facing instructional design and technology. In *Educational Media and Technology Yearbook*, Vol. 29, edited by M. Orey et al., pp. 23–43. Westport, CN: Libraries Unlimited.

Hooper, S., Hokansen, B., Bernhardt, P., and Johnson, M. (2002). A learning software design competition. *Educ. Technol.*, 42(5), 5–7.

Instructional Systems Technology Department. (2007). *The Larson to Sputnik Years: 1940–1957*, Bloomington: Indiana University, http://education.indiana.edu/~ist/students/history/larson.html.

Johnson, C. (2005). Pedagogical Patterns in Required Masters Level Instructional Design Courses with Reference to the IBSTPI Competencies of 1999. Ph.D. dissertation. Bloomington: Indiana University.

Laseau, P. (1986). *Graphic Problem Solving for Architects and Designers*, 2nd ed. New York: Van Nostrand Reinhold.

Lawson, B. (1980). *How Designers Think*. London: The Architectural Press, Ltd.*

Lawson, B. (2004a). Schemata, gambits and precedents: some factors in design expertise. *Design Stud.*, 25(5), 443–457.

Lawson, B. (2004b). *What Designers Know*. Amsterdam: Elsevier.*

Murphy, D. (1992). Is instructional design truly a design activity? *Educ. Train. Technol. Int.*, 29(4), 279–282.

Nelson, H. G. and Stolterman, E. (2003). *The Design Way: Intentional Change in an Unpredictable World: Foundations and Fundamentals of Design Competence*. Englewood Cliffs, NJ: Educational Technology Publications.*

Oxman, R. E. (1994). Precedents in design: a computational model for the organization of precedent knowledge. *Design Stud.*, 12(2), 141–157.

Parrish, P. (2006). Design as storytelling. *TechTrends*, 50(4), 72–82.*

Rowe, D., Smith, K. M., and Boling, E. (2005). In Defense of Picture Books: Design Artifacts as Sources of Knowledge for Instructional Designers. Paper presented at the Association for Educational Communications and Technology Annual Meeting, October 18–22, Orlando, FL.

Rowland, R., Parra, M., and Basnet, K. (1994). Educating instructional designers: different methods for different outcomes. *Educ. Technol.*, 34(6), 5–11.

Suwa, M. and Tversky, B. (1996). What architects see in their sketches: implications for design tools. In *Proceedings of CHI'96: Conference on Human Factors in Computing Systems*, pp. 191–192. New York: ACM Press.

Vincenti, W. G. (1990). *What Engineers Know and How They Know It: Analytical Studies from Aeronautical History*. Baltimore, MD: The Johns Hopkins University Press.

Zemke, R. and Rossett, A. (2002). A hard look at ISD. *Training*, 37(2), 27–35.

---

* Indicates a core reference.

# 52

# Systems Design for Change in Education and Training

*Sunnie Lee Watson and Charles M. Reigeluth*
Indiana University, Bloomington, Indiana

*William R. Watson*
Purdue University, West Lafayette, Indiana

## CONTENTS

## ABSTRACT

The purpose of this chapter is to introduce current research and theory on systems design for change, or systemic change, in the fields of education and training. Systems design is the process for determining what characteristics a new system should have, resulting in a model of the new system and a plan for creating it. Systemic change is the process of changing a system from one paradigm to another by applying systems thinking and systems theory. Repeated calls for massive reform of current educational and training practices have consistently been published over the last several decades. This has resulted in an increasing recognition of the need for systemic change in education as numerous structured, piecemeal approaches to education reform have been implemented and failed to significantly improve the state of education. This chapter first presents a description of design theory and systems theory as the foundations for systems design. Design theory is the concepts and principles that help to develop strategies and methods for designing. The term *system* has been defined in various ways by different researchers, but the core concept is one of relationships among components comprising the whole.

## KEYWORDS

*Design theory:* The concepts and principles that help to develop strategies and methods for designing.

*Systemic change:* The process of changing a system from one paradigm to another by applying systems thinking and systems theory.

*Systems design:* The process for determining what characteristics a new system should have.

*Systems theory:* An interdisciplinary field with applications in both the hard and soft sciences; it focuses on understanding relationships among components comprising the whole.

## INTRODUCTION

The purpose of this chapter is to introduce current research and theory on systems design for change, or systemic change, in the fields of education and training. Systems design is the process for determining what characteristics a new system should have, resulting in a model of the new system and a plan for creating it (Banathy, 1996). Systemic change is the process of changing a system from one paradigm to another by applying systems thinking and systems theory; however systemic change has different meanings for different people in education. Squire and Reigeluth (2000) identified four different meanings: statewide changes, districtwide changes, schoolwide changes, and ecological changes. Ecological systemic change is based on an understanding of interrelationships and interdependencies with the system and between the system and its systemic environment. This meaning more fully implements the concepts of systems theory and systems thinking by embracing the organic, interconnected nature of social systems, and it encompasses the other three meanings, so it will be the focus of this chapter.

A systems-thinking or systemic approach to design views problems and their solutions from the perspective of the whole system. A system is composed of many parts, all of which relate to each other. Systems design takes into account the interrelationships among these parts, rather than isolating individual problems and simplifying solutions by decomposing and fragmenting reality into an easier-to-understand but incomplete view.

The next section of this chapter presents the foundations of systems design by illustrating the need for systems design in education and training and summarizing the major literature in design theory and systems theory. The third section provides a synthesis of systems design principles. The fourth and final section presents a number of current systems design models in the literature.

# FOUNDATIONS OF SYSTEMS DESIGN

## Need for Systems Design and Systemic Change

Systemic change is concerned with the creation of a completely new system rather than a mere retooling of a current system. It entails a paradigm shift as opposed to piecemeal change. Repeated calls for massive reform of current educational and training practices have consistently been published over the last several decades. This has resulted in an increasing recognition of the need for systemic change in education as numerous piecemeal approaches to education reform have been implemented and failed to significantly improve the state of education. But, is a true paradigm shift needed to better meet the needs of today's learners?

Numerous publications have discussed the shift of society from the industrial age into what many call the information age (Reigeluth, 1994; Senge et al., 2000; Toffler, 1980). The current educational and training systems were built to fit the needs of an industrial-age society, where the focus was on sorting learners rather than on learning (Reigeluth, 1994). Learners in the industrial age were expected to learn the same amount of material in the same time, thereby forcing the slower students to accumulate learning deficits and eventually fail. In the industrial age, it was important to sort learners into management or worker roles, and the teacher-centered, standardized paradigm of education was well suited for this purpose (Joseph and Reigeluth, 2002).

In the current information age, however, the majority of jobs entail knowledge work that requires learners to master such skills as communication, problem-solving, critical thinking, and teamwork. Furthermore, employees are more and more expected to show initiative, manage themselves, and cooperate with others; therefore, training and education now must have a customized and learner-centered focus that the old paradigm does not offer. Systemic change seeks to shift from a paradigm in which time is held constant, thereby forcing achievement to vary, to one designed specifically to meet the needs of information-age learners and their communities by allowing students as much time as each needs to reach proficiency. Systems design focuses on creating a new system to meet the new educational and training needs of the information age.

The foundations of systems design are systems theory and design theory. The following two sections summarize these theories and their relation to systems design.

## Design Theory

One foundation of systemic change and systems design is design theory. Design theory is the concepts and principles that help to develop strategies and methods for designing. A number of different design theories in the literature provide insight on the complex and challenging task of designing organizations or educational systems. These include Nelson and Stolterman's (2003) *design way*, which is applicable to all kinds of organizations; Ackoff's (1999) *idealized design* for corporations; Banathy's (1996) *social systems* design for all kinds of organizations; and Reigeluth's (2006a) *leveraged emergent approach* for educational systems.

### *The Design Way*

Nelson and Stolterman (2003) noted that, fundamentally, design is a creative act, resulting in the creation of something that has not previously existed. It focuses on making choices to create the best design for a very specific system. As such, it examines a real, natural, complex world that requires systems thinking to take into account the interdependent relationships at work. Design is service oriented, a creative expression of what is desired, and it relies on relationships between formalized roles among the participants in a collaborative social system.

### *Idealized Design*

The key concept behind Ackoff's (1999) idealized design is the selection of ideals to create an ideal vision of what the new system should be. An idealized design should be technologically feasible, operationally viable, and capable of rapid learning and development. It is the most effective system of which the designers can conceive, and its vision should be shared by all participants.

### *Social Systems Design*

Banathy (1996) viewed design as a creative, iterative, holistic, decision-oriented process resulting in a model of a new system. It is key to understand that designers must transcend current approaches and solutions to design a completely new model of a system appropriate for the specific, unique context.

### *Leveraged Emergent Approach*

Reigeluth's (2006a) leveraged emergent approach posits that it is difficult to make the drastic changes to a new paradigm all at once, but piecemeal change is likely to be unsuccessful; therefore, high-leverage structural changes should be implemented that can resist the pull of the current system to return to the *status quo* and can exert leverage to change the rest of the system. These high-leverage changes will be guided by a few principles, and the remaining changes will emerge over time as the need for them becomes apparent and resources become available. This approach yields frequent visible progress to sustain momentum and win over skeptics.

## Systems Theory

Systems theory was established in the mid-20th century by a multidisciplinary group of researchers who shared the view that science had become increasingly reductionist and the various disciplines isolated. Bertalanffy (1968) was among the first to establish a general systems theory, which noted the existence of principles and laws that could be generalized across systems and their components regardless of the type of system or its relationship to other systems.

The term *system* has been defined in various ways by different researchers, but the core concept is one of relationships among components comprising the whole. Ultimately, systems theory is an interdisciplinary field with applications in both the hard and soft sciences. Hard systems thinking is appropriate for closed, engineered systems, while soft systems thinking is appropriate for the complexities of social systems (Checkland and Scholes, 1990). Nelson and Stolterman (2003) argued that there are no set types or categories of systems; instead, the view of a system is a matter of perspective and choice.

Flood (1990) took this viewpoint even further in his *liberating systems theory* (LST) by firmly focusing systems theory with a critical viewpoint. LST is related to critical systems theory, which draws from Habermas (1973) and seeks emancipation of humans in systems that promote subjugation and dominance (Flood, 1990). LST uses a post-positivist approach to analyze social conditions to liberate the oppressed while also seeking to liberate systems theory from tendencies such as self-imposed insularity, cases of internal localized subjugations in discourse, and liberation of system concepts from the inadequacies of objectivist and subjectivist approaches (Flood, 1990).

Banathy (1991) applies systems theory to social systems design by examining the design of educational systems. He suggested examining systems through three lenses: a "still picture lens," used to understand the components comprising the system and their relationships; a "motion picture lens," used to understand the processes and dynamics of the system; and a

"bird's-eye view lens," to understand the relationships between the system and its peer and suprasystems (Banathy, 1992).

Senge (1990) applied systems theory to organizational learning. Systems thinking is the fifth and most important of five disciplines of a learning organization, according to Senge. He suggested that learning organizations help their members to view the organization as a complex system of interrelated parts, rather than as isolated departments.

# PRINCIPLES OF SYSTEMS DESIGN

Of the many principles of systems design, the ones described in this section include systems thinking, design theory, idealized design, broad stakeholder involvement, mindset and culture, participatory leadership, shared vision, learning organization, and strange attractors and leverage.

## Systems Thinking

An important principle of systems design is a systems thinking approach to design. Systems thinking is a framework for seeing patterns and interrelationships in a complex organization or system. Banathy's (1992) three-lens view described earlier is a useful framework for examining the system through its components, its processes and relationships, and its peer systems and suprasystems. The complexity of systems can be overwhelming, but systems thinking makes these complex realities more manageable while still retaining a true view of reality, rather than the fragmented and inaccurate view of a systematic analysis.

## Design Theory

Also important is the recognition that systems design is about design, meaning the creation of a new system that has not previously existed (Banathy, 1996; Nelson and Stolterman, 2003). This is a shift to an entirely new paradigm, a transcendence of the current system rather than a piecemeal approach of modifying the existing system. Furthermore, the design process should be holistic and iterative, rather than sequential and systematic (Banathy, 1996; Nelson and Stolterman, 2003) by beginning with a "rough sketch" (Ackoff, 1999) or "fuzzy image" of the new system and proceeding to gradually work out more detail for the whole new system, one level at a time (Banathy, 1991). It is important to be able to generate feedback on the emerging vision or model of the new system through the development of artifacts and the implementation of accountability (Banathy, 1996; Nelson and Stolterman, 2003; Reigeluth, 2006a).

## Idealized Design

Related is the principle of idealized design. The result of the design process should be a model of the ideal system (Ackoff, 1981; Banathy, 1996). This ideal design should be the designer's best expression of what is desired by the clients or stakeholders, labeled "desiderata" by Nelson and Stolterman (2003). Design is driven by hope and vision, which motivates the participants to make the leap to a new paradigm, and the newly created system should meet the desired results as best as possible (Banathy, 1996; Nelson and Stolterman, 2003).

## Broad Stakeholder Involvement

An important principle to consider in systems design is the involvement of those who will be affected by any changes in the system. This is an ethical issue, but it is also a quality-of-design issue. The different stakeholders bring diverse perspectives to the process of systemic change. Different professions, cultures, understandings, and skills should come together to create a rich environment for design decisions in schools and other organizations. Hutchins (1996) pointed out that, because systems are complex, they usually serve multiple purposes—often changing over time and in conflict with each other. Because of the complex nature of any system, each stakeholder's perspective needs to be heard and addressed for more positive change in schools to occur.

The role of the community is extremely important in organizational change as well (Jenlink et al., 1998). A system does not exist in isolation, and the community impacts the schools and organizations within it. The roles of higher education institutions and community organizations and businesses are often overlooked but should be included when designing a new paradigm of education. Furthermore, rather than just involving stakeholders, it is important to create a collaborative social system (Nelson and Stolterman, 2003). This entails developing a design culture where participants become knowledgeable about design, develop design competence, and empower themselves (Banathy, 1996).

## Mindset and Culture

Mindsets or mental models are one of the most important things to consider in systemic change. One aspect of mindset is the nature of the change process. Edu-

cators are used to thinking in terms of piecemeal reforms imposed from the top down. A successful systemic change process requires a different mindset, one of empowerment, collaboration, consensus building, and trust. It is important to help stakeholders evolve their mindsets to participate effectively in the change process (Banathy, 1996; Nelson and Stolterman, 2003).

The other aspect of mindset entails helping participants to shift their mindsets from the standardized, time-based, industrial-age paradigm of training or education to the customized, attainment-based, information-age paradigm, and from piecemeal change to systemic change. Senge (1994) noted that good, new ideas rarely get put into practice, often because these new ideas conflict with participants' subconscious, internal images of the world. If stakeholders are operating on different mental models of what the designed system should be or how the process for creating that system should be enacted, then they will resist or oppose the changes and perpetuate the existing paradigm.

Culture for change can be viewed as the collective mindsets of participants in the change process. A culture of collaboration, consensus-building, empowerment, and trust among the stakeholders is crucial for true paradigm change to succeed in an organization. The roles of leaders (such as principals, school district administrators, or CEOs) are particularly important. To move forward in the beginning of a systemic change process, leaders must establish the culture of the system and set examples by taking the courageous first steps.

## Participatory Leadership

Leaders of the change process have big responsibilities in systemic change. They must not only evolve their own mindsets and guide the change process but also involve other stakeholders in the decision-making process and share responsibilities. Most leaders have experienced the authority-centered approach of leadership in systems; however, leaders in systemic change processes need a different paradigm of leadership. Leaders must be open to new ideas, be self aware, and pay individual attention to followers to empower them, help them grow, and stimulate their intellectual abilities (Duffy et al., 2000; Senge, 1994). Furthermore, it is important for leaders to be actively involved in the change process. A design team must have the full authority it needs to design and implement changes. Without the support of the top leaders in a system, design decisions will always run the risk of being overturned; it is therefore important to have the top leaders as members of the design team (Nelson and Stolterman, 2003). Moving beyond the traditional top-down approach of most organizations and the "principal-do-right" (Senge, 2000) leadership model in schools is important to achieve paradigm change in a system.

## Shared Vision

Shared vision is another vital notion in systemic change. There must be values and beliefs that individual stakeholders in the school system come to share to change the paradigm. Senge (1994) pointed out that no organization becomes great without goals, values, and a mission that become shared throughout the organization. A vision statement or the leader's charisma cannot be enough. Shared vision is fundamental for learning organizations that want to help their employees to fundamentally change their work. The overarching vision establishes not just commitment but also new ways of thinking and acting and consequently fosters risk taking and experimenting in the organization (Senge, 1994). This shared vision is related to the earlier discussion of a shared idealized design.

## Learning Organizations

Educational systems also must transform into learning organizations to succeed in systemic change. According to Senge (1994), a learning organization requires its members to acquire competency in five disciplines: systems thinking, personal mastery, mental models, shared vision, and team learning. These disciplines are provided to help the members and teams of the organization in shifting their mental models to understand their system as a whole rather than as parts and consequently to move toward a shared vision. Furthermore, they must become design knowledgeable and competent to fully participate in the design process (Banathy, 1996). These disciplines also consider all members as contributors to their own personal growth as well as the growth of their organization and team as a whole (Senge, 1994).

## Strange Attractors and Leverage Points

Fractals and strange attractors are another important notion in the systemic change process. Fractals are patterns that recur at all levels of a system (Wheatley, 1999), which in education are core ideas, values, and beliefs (Banathy, 1991; Reigeluth, 2006b, 2007). Strange attractors are a kind of fractal that has a powerful influence over the processes and structures

that emerge during transformation (Wheatley, 1999). These are similar to *memes*, which are the social counterpoints to genes in the physical organism and have the power to organize a system in a specific way (Caine and Caine, 1997). These strange attractors become essential in the mindsets or mental models held by a critical mass of participants; hence, they are an essential part of the culture of the organization (Reigeluth, 2007).

Leverage points are important in terms of the efficiency and effectiveness of the change process. They are related to Senge's (1994) notion of small changes being capable of producing big results. They are certain elements of the system that have a large impact in the entire organization (Reigeluth, 2006a). For the systemic change process to happen more quickly yet still effectively, it is important to identify the leverage points in the school system; however, Senge (1994) also talked about how the areas of highest leverage are often the least obvious. Investigating school systems and organizations to identify leverage points is a crucial step in systemic change.

## SYSTEMS DESIGN MODELS

This chapter has described systems theory and design theory as the foundations of systems design and presented systems design principles to guide the process of designing educational and training systems. This final section presents an overview of major systems design models in the literature. These models present specific, elaborate processes for designing education and training systems. These models include Jenlink et al.'s Guidance System for Transforming Education (GSTE), Duffy's Step-Up-to-Excellence, Schlechty's guidelines for leadership in school reform, Hammer and Champy's business process redesign/reengineering, and Ackoff's idealized systems design.

## Guidance System for Transforming Education

The Guidance System for Transforming Education (GSTE) (Jenlink et al., 1996, 1998) is a process model for facilitating systemic change. The GSTE was designed to provide process guidelines to a facilitator engaging in a K–12, districtwide systemic change effort. The GSTE does not provide any suggestion of what changes should be made in the school district; rather, it provides the facilitators with process guidelines to help the school district and its community make decisions about what changes should be made. The GSTE is comprised of:

- Core values about the change process
- Discrete events (a chronological series of activities for engaging throughout much or all of the change process)
- Continuous events (activities that must be addressed continuously throughout much or all of the change process)

The GSTE, originally developed by Jenlink et al. (1996, 1998), has undergone additional development based on Reigeluth's experience using it in the Metropolitan School District of Decatur Township in Indianapolis, Indiana. The discrete events listed in Table 52.1 reflect these tentative revisions of the GSTE. These events are guided by underlying principles and suggested activi-

**TABLE 52.1**
**Revised Discrete Events in the GSTE**

| | |
|---|---|
| Phase I. Initiate a systemic change effort | Facilitators assess and enhance their own readiness for the process and form a support team. |
| | Facilitators establish or redefine a relationship with a school district and discuss *per diem* payment for Event 3. |
| | Facilitators assess and enhance district readiness for change. |
| | Negotiate and sign a contract/agreement with the superintendent and board for Phase II. |
| Phase II. Develop starter team | Facilitators and superintendent form the starter team. |
| | Hold a retreat to develop the starter team dynamic. |
| | Develop starter team understanding of systems, design, mental models, systemic change process, dialog, and small-group facilitation. |
| | Assess and enhance district and community capacity for change (identify assets and barriers, and use community forums if needed). |
| | Develop an agreement/contract with the starter team and school board for Phase III, scope out resource needs, and plan a budget for internal funding and a proposal for external funding. |
| Phase III. Develop the districtwide framework and capacity for change | Starter team expands into the leadership team; starter team becomes facilitators; facilitator becomes an advisor and "critical friend." |
| | Hold a one-day retreat to develop the leadership team dynamic. |
| | Facilitators develop leadership team understanding of systems, design, mental models, systemic change process, dialog, and small-group facilitation (address throughout Events 13 to 17). |
| | Leadership team develops a district-wide framework with broad stakeholder participation (community forums). This includes identifying changes in the community's educational needs and using them to develop a mission, vision, and core values for an ideal school system. It takes this opportunity to assess and enhance district and community interest in, and culture for, systemic change. It develops pyramid groups for broad stakeholder involvement. |
| | Leadership team identifies current and recent change efforts and decides what relation those should have with this effort. |
| | Leadership team develops a change process strategy, including capacity building and funding; advisor's role is defined and funded for Phase IV. |
| Phase IV. Create ideal designs for a new educational system | Leadership team forms and capacitates building-level design teams and conducts a workshop on the framework. |
| | Design teams create building-level designs and systems for evaluating those designs with broad stakeholder involvement; leadership team supports and monitors the design teams. |
| | Leadership team forms and capacitates a district-level design team. |
| | Design team creates a design for ideal district administrative and governance systems and systems for evaluating that design, with broad stakeholder involvement; leadership team supports and monitors this design team. |
| Phase IV. Create ideal designs for a new educational system | Design teams create building-level processes for evolving as close as possible to their ideal designs; leadership team supports and monitors the design teams. |
| | Carry out implementation plans, formative evaluations, and revisions of the evolving designs and the implementation processes. |

*Source:* Reigeluth, C.M. and Duffy, F.M., in *Trends and Issues in Instructional Design and Technology*, 2nd ed., Reiser, R.A. and Dempsey, J.V., Eds., Prentice Hall, Upper Saddle River, NJ, 2007. With permission.

ties that help one to understand and engage in them. The core values underlying the GSTE are:

- Caring for children
- Co-evolution
- Collaboration
- Common language
- Community
- Context
- Conversation
- Culture
- Democracy
- Evolution of mindsets
- Facilitator
- Ideal vision
- Inclusiveness
- Participant commitment
- Process orientation
- Readiness
- Respect
- Responsibility
- Space
- Stakeholder empowerment
- Systemic thinking
- Time
- Wholeness

## Step-Up-to-Excellence

Step-Up-to-Excellence (SUTE) (Duffy, 2002, 2003, 2004, 2006) is a process methodology designed to help change leaders in school districts create and sustain whole-district improvement. This methodology combines effective tools for school system transformation. SUTE, a three-step process that is preceded by a *pre-launch preparation phase*, proceeds as follows.

Pre-launch preparation phase
Step 1: Redesign the entire school system
Step 2: Create strategic alignment
Step 3: Evaluate whole-system performance
Recycle to the next pre-launch preparation phase

### *Pre-Launch Preparation Phase*

The pre-launch preparation activities are carried out by the superintendent of schools and a couple of hand-picked subordinates. This small team is temporary, and it will not lead the transformation; its purpose is to prepare the system to engage in systemic change. If the decision is made that the transformation effort is to be launched, then the activities are transferred to a *strategic leadership team*, which is composed of the superintendent, teachers, and building administrators.

The team also appoints a *transformation coordinator*. The process then proceeds to Step 1.

### *Step 1. Redesign the Entire School System*

During Step 1, the district's core purpose, mission, values, and goals are defined. Educators then work in small teams within each cluster of schools (all those schools that feed into a single high school, plus that high school) to redesign their entire school district by improving three areas: their district's core and supporting work processes, its internal social architecture, and its relationship with its environment.

### *Step 2. Create Strategic Alignment*

After the redesign process of a district, change leaders invite educators to align their individual work with the goals of their teams, the work of teams with the goals of their schools, the work of schools with the goals of their clusters, and the work of clusters with the goals of the district. Creation of strategic alignment ensures everyone will work systemically toward the same goals and vision of the district. It also determines responsibilities for all stakeholders involved in a child's educational experience and frees the district from unnecessary bureaucratic hassles, dysfunctional policies, and obstructionist procedures that limit effectiveness.

### *Step 3. Evaluate Whole-System Performance*

During Step 3, change leaders evaluate the performance of the clusters, schools, and teams of the district. The purpose of this evaluation is to measure the success of the district's effort. Evaluation is reported to stakeholders and is used to sustain school district improvement by managing the district's performance.

### *Recycle to the Next Pre-Launch Preparation Phase*

After a predetermined period, the district steps up again by cycling back to the pre-launch preparation phase for further improvement and transformation.

## Schlechty Center's Guidelines for Leadership in School Reform

The Schlechty Center for Leadership in School Reform has been engaging in school district transformation processes from a comprehensive and systemic approach to school reform (Solomon, 2006). Theories and frameworks that provide guidelines for the activities of the school reform processes in the districts and schools with which the Schlechty Center works are provided below.

## Two Theories Underlying the Activities of the Schlechty Center

### The Theory of Change

The theory of change (Christensen, 1997) focuses on transforming schools from organizations based on the hypothesis that the central business of schools has to do with producing conformity and attendance to organizations where the central work focuses on nurturing attention and commitment towards students. The theory of change is the basis for the *Ten District Standards*, an underlying framework of the Schlechty Center which is described in the next section.

### The Theory of Engagement

The theory of engagement focuses on student motivation and the strategies that are needed to increase the perspective that schools and teachers will enlarge the presence of engaging tasks and activities in the everyday life of the schools. The theory of engagement is the basis of the *Working on the Work* framework (Schlechty, 2002), described below.

## Two Frameworks Underlying the Activities of the Schlechty Center

### Ten District Standards

The Ten District Standards framework helps leaders assess and build system capacity so the entire district is aligned and focused on the core purpose of schools by:

- Developing a shared understanding of the need for change
- Developing shared beliefs and vision
- Developing a focus on students and on the quality of work provided to students
- Developing structures for participatory leadership
- Developing structures for results-oriented decision making
- Developing structures for continuity
- Providing ongoing support
- Fostering innovation and flexibility
- Employing technology
- Fostering collaboration

### Working on the Work

The Working on the Work framework calls on everyone to provide challenging and engaging work for students that results in students learning what schools, parents, and the community want them to learn:

- Work that is challenging to students
- Work with which students persist when they experience difficulty
- Work from which students gain a sense of satisfaction

## Hammer and Champy's Business Process Redesign/Reengineering

Hammer and Champy (1993, 2003) defined the process of reengineering a corporation as the "fundamental rethinking and radical redesign of business processes to achieve dramatic improvements in critical, contemporary measures of performance, such as cost, quality, service and speed" (p. 32). They provided a systemic change design model for organizational transformation in corporate sectors with their *business process redesign/reengineering* (BPR) approach. BPR is a management approach that examines aspects of a corporation or business and its interactions and attempts to advance the competence of the underlying processes. It is a systemic and fundamental approach that redesigns the core work processes and either modifies or eliminates activities that are not producing value in the corporation. Hammer and Champy (1993, 2003) argued that far too much time is wasted by businesses that pass on tasks from one department to the other, and they claimed that it is much more important to build a team that can perform all tasks in the process. They identified four main themes that accompany reengineering:

- *Fundamentals*—Focusing on the fundamentals allows a look at tacit principles and assumptions; once these rules and assumptions are identified, they should be redesigned for an entirely new system.
- *Radical*—Organizational change must not engage in piecemeal changes; systemic change is needed.
- *Dramatic*—There should be big leaps in performance; reengineering is not for marginal changes.
- *Processes*—Organizational changes must be process oriented and must not be focused on individual tasks.

### Common Themes in Reengineering Efforts

Although reengineering processes take various forms, similarities exist. Hammer and Champy (1993, 2003) identified nine common themes to reengineering efforts:

- Steps in the process are simplified and several jobs are combined into one.
- Workers make decisions, which eliminates the hierarchy in decision making.
- Steps or processes are performed in a natural order.
- Processes are not standardized; they have multiple versions.
- Work occurs where it makes the most sense, sometimes by customers or suppliers.
- Checks and controls are reduced to reduce costs.
- Reconciliation is minimized to encourage consistency.
- A case manager provides a single point of contact with customers.
- Centralization and decentralization are one process.

### *The Change Process in Reengineering Efforts*

Hammer and Champy (1993, 2003) also provided change process guidelines for reengineering efforts:

- Identify and map the processes using process mapping.
- Identify the process requiring reengineering.
- Achieve high-level understanding of the current process from a customer perspective.
- Look outside the process to customer needs by observing performance.
- Look at the process itself by observing performance.
- Understand what is critical in the process.
- Consider feasibility, such as scope, cost, and commitment.
- Designate the process owner and form a process team.

## Ackoff's Idealized Systems Design

Based on the theoretical foundation of systems theory and the systems view of the world and organizations, Ackoff's (1999) *idealized systems design* approach identifies design strategies and implementation planning processes for organizational change and the recreation of business corporations. The process of creating the idealized systems design includes the following stages:

- Formulating the mess (sensing and making sense of the situation)
- Ends planning (where to go)
- Means planning (how to get there)

- Resource planning (what is needed to get there)
- Implementation and control (doing it and learning)

The design comes forth with situational analysis, which is a systemic understanding and detailed evaluation of the current state of the organization and its environment. Ackoff (1999) suggested that, upon achieving systemic comprehensive understanding of the current system, the system should progress to the idealized design stage.

The ends of an organization consist of ideals, objectives, and goals. Ends planning should be directed to make explicit exactly what is wanted in the organization. Ackoff (1999) emphasized that the vision of the ideal system of an organization must be a shared image among the stakeholders and that it should be created by all stakeholders in the system. The three characteristics of an idealized design are that it should be technologically feasible, operationally viable, and capable of being improved continuously.

Having a shared ideal vision of the system, system designers then engage in an implementation planning process. The means that the planning stage selects creates the means that will help achieve the ends. First, designers engage in the design of the means planning. Means planning determines the gaps between the current and ideal systems and constitutes a set of instructions that enable the possible realization of the vision. These means include acts, practices, processes, projects, programs, and policies of the system.

The means planning determines what kinds of resources are required for the implementation and further requires determining the allocation of these resources. In addition, appointing human resources is required in this phase: who is doing what, when, how, and where in the system. The next step is to plan the allocation of the resources that the means require. Money, capital goods, people, consumables, data, information, and knowledge are all involved. Finally, the designers formulate the design of a management learning and adaptation system that will aid in the realization of these requirements.

## CONCLUSION

This chapter reviewed the current research on systems design for change in education and training. It argued for the need for systemic change to create a completely new paradigm suitable for today's information age. It presented a description of design theory and systems theory as the foundations for systems design. Principles of systems design were offered, as well as several systems design models. Despite a history of systems design research and an increasing call for systemic change efforts over the last several decades, most change efforts continue to be piecemeal, tinkering with or revising the currently used yet horribly outdated paradigm of education and training. This chapter has summarized a foundation for better understanding systems design and how it can be applied to training and education.

# REFERENCES

Ackoff, R. L. (1999). *Recreating the Corporation: A Design of Organizations for the 21st Century.* New York: Oxford University Press.*

Banathy, B. H. (1991). *Systems Design of Education: A Journey to Create the Future.* Englewood Cliffs, NJ: Educational Technology Publications.*

Banathy, B. H. (1992). *A Systems View of Education: Concepts and Principles for Effective Practice.* Englewood Cliffs, NJ: Educational Technology Publications.

Banathy, B. H. (1996). *Designing Social Systems in a Changing World.* New York: Plenum Press.

Bertalanffy, L. V. (1968). *General Systems Theory.* New York: George Braziller.

Caine, R. N. and Caine, G. (1997). *Education on the Edge of Possibility.* Alexandria, VA: Association for Supervision and Curriculum Development.

Checkland, P. and Scholes, J. (1990). *Soft Systems Methodology in Action.* New York: Wiley.

Christensen, C. (1997). *Innovator's Dilemma: When New Technologies Cause Great Firms to Fail.* Boston, MA: Harvard Business School Press.

Duffy, F. M. (2002). *Step-Up-to-Excellence: An Innovative Approach to Managing and Rewarding Performance in School Systems.* Lanham, MD: Scarecrow Education.*

Duffy, F. M. (2003). *Courage, Passion and Vision: A Guide to Leading Systemic School Improvement.* Lanham, MD: Scarecrow Education and the American Association of School Administrators.

Duffy, F. M. (2004). *Moving Upward Together: Creating Strategic Alignment to Sustain Systemic School,* Vol. 1, Leading Systemic School Improvement Series. Lanham, MD: Scarecrow Education.

Duffy, F. M. (2006). *Step-Up-to-Excellence: A Change Navigation Protocol for Transforming School Systems,* Houston, TX: Connexions (http://cnx.org/content/m13656/latest/).

Duffy, F. M., Rogerson, L. G., and Blick, C. (2000). *Redesigning America's Schools: A Systems Approach to Improvement.* Norwood, MA: Christopher-Gordon Publishers.

Flood, R. L. (1990). Liberating systems theory: toward critical systems thinking. *Hum. Relat.,* 43(1), 49–75.

Habermas, J. (1973). *Theory and Practice* (J. Viertel, trans.). Boston, MA: Beacon.

Hammer, M. and Champy, J. (1993). *Reengineering the Corporation: A Manifesto for Business Revolution.* New York: HarperBusiness.*

Hammer, M. and Champy, J. (2003). *Reengineering the Corporation: A Manifesto for Business Revolution,* pbk. ed. New York: HarperBusiness Essentials.

Hutchins, C. L. (1996). *Systemic Thinking: Solving Complex Problems.* Aurora, CO: Professional Development Systems.

Jenlink, P. M., Reigeluth, C. M., Carr, A. A., and Nelson, L. M. (1996). An expedition for change. *TechTrends,* 41(1), 21–30.

Jenlink, P. M., Reigeluth, C. M., Carr, A. A., and Nelson, L. M. (1998). Guidelines for facilitating systemic change in school districts. *Syst. Res. Behav. Sci.,* 15(3), 217–233.*

Joseph, R. and Reigeluth, C. M. (2002). Beyond technology integration: the case for technology transformation. *Educ. Technol.,* 42(4), 9–13.

Nelson, H. G. and Stolterman, E. (2003). *The Design Way.* Englewood Cliffs, NJ: Educational Technology Publications.*

Reigeluth, C. M. (1994). The imperative for systemic change. In *Systemic Change in Education,* edited by C. M. Reigeluth and R. J. Garfinkle, pp. 3–11. Englewood Cliffs, NJ: Educational Technology Publications.*

Reigeluth, C. M. (2006a). A leveraged emergent approach to systemic transformation. *TechTrends,* 50(2), 46–47.

Reigeluth, C. M. (2006b). A chaos theory approach to systemic change. *TechTrends,* 50(2), 45–46.

Reigeluth, C. M. (2007). Chaos theory and the sciences of complexity: foundations for transforming education. In *Systems Thinkers in Action: A Field Guide for Effective Change Leadership in Education,* edited by B. Despres. New York: Rowman and Littlefield.

Reigeluth, C. M. and Duffy, F. M. (2007). Trends and issues in P–12 educational change. In *Trends and Issues in Instructional Design and Technology,* 2nd ed., edited by R. A. Reiser and J. V. Dempsey, pp. 209–220. Upper Saddle River, NJ: Prentice Hall.

Schlechty, P. C. (1997). *Inventing Better Schools: An Action Plan for Educational Reform.* San Francisco, CA: Jossey-Bass.

Schlechty, P. C. (2002). *Working on the Work: An Action Plan for Teachers, Principals, and Superintendents.* San Francisco, CA: Jossey-Bass.

Senge, P. M. (1990). *The Fifth Discipline.* New York: Doubleday.

Senge, P. M. (1994). *The Fifth Discipline: The Art and Practice of the Learning Organization.* New York: Doubleday.*

Senge, P. M., Cambron-McCabe, N., Lucas, T., Smith, B., Dutton, J., and Kleiner, A. (2000). *Schools That Learn: A Fifth Discipline Fieldbook for Educators, Parents, and Everyone Who Cares About Education.* Toronto: Currency.

Solomon, M. (2006). The Schlechty Center for leadership in school reform. *TechTrends,* 50(2), 43.

Squire, K. and Reigeluth, C. M. (2000). The many faces of systemic change. *Educ. Horiz.,* 78(3), 143–152.

Toffler, A. (1980). *The Third Wave.* New York: Bantam Books.

Wheatley, M. (1999). *In Leadership and the New Science.* San Francisco, CA: Berrett-Kohler.

* Indicates a core reference.

# Part VI
## Methodological Issues

This final part of the *Handbook* was led by Jeroen J.G. van Merriënboer and focuses on research issues. Rather than have separate and arbitrary chapters on quantitative, qualitative, and other research approaches, this part follows the research cycle through theory development, experimental design, and data collection and analysis. Design sections adhere to the main parts of the *Handbook* and treat research on strategies, technologies, models, and design and development. Analysis methods include the analysis of learning processes, interactions, and complex performances. This part ends with a provocative discussion that is intended to help our field build a strong scientific foundation for the future. This part of the *Handbook* consists of four chapters covering these topics: (1) theory development, (2) research design, (3) data collection and analysis, and (4) foundations for the future. Several of these chapters contain multiple sections by different authors. As before, all authors are recognized as chapter authors and individual contributions to specific sections are noted within the chapter.

# 53

# Theory Development

*Jan Elen and Geraldine Clarebout*
Katholieke Universiteit Leuven, Leuven, Belgium

## CONTENTS

## ABSTRACT

The field of educational technology is characterized by an abundance of sets of theoretical statements. These sets can be described from at least four perspectives. A first perspective pertains to the object or orientation of the (sets of) theoretical statements. Sets may address educational principles, features of interventions or tools, development procedures, or the nature of the field itself. The origin (theoretical or practical context) of these sets of statements is a second perspective from which they can be described. Theoretical statements can be clearly anchored in specific practical experiences, can be the result of a deductive effort to apply fundamental theoretical insights or theoretical perspectives, or can reflect a thoughtful interaction between a practical setting and a theoretical perspective. A third perspective relates to the level of theoretical sophistication of these (sets of) statements. Sets of theoretical statements can be collections of isolated theoretical expressions, descriptive or prescriptive models with respect to educational technological issues, or integrated, internally coherent sets of theoretical principles. The degree of justification of these (sets of) statements represents a fourth perspective. Some statements are purely explorative, whereas for others empirical evidence is readily available. Taking these differences into account, this chapter aims at discussing theory development. First, features of descriptive and prescriptive theories are elaborated by analyzing their commonalities and differences. Second, the development of theories itself is addressed by focusing on deductive, inductive, and mixed approaches. Third, theoretical levels of sophistication and justification are dealt with. In all this, the elaboration of instructional design models is focused upon.

## KEYWORDS

*Instructional design model:* A coherent set of mostly prescriptive theoretical statements on the appropriateness of particular instructional approaches or interventions.

*Theoretical statement:* Formal expression about the relationship between at least two variables or instantiations of variables.

*Theory:* An integrated and internally coherent set of theoretical statements that provides a sufficient basis for empirical research in which these statements can be tested.

*Theory development:* Systematic effort to generate (coherent sets of) theoretical statements.

## INTRODUCTION

Educational technology and more specifically instructional design are characterized by an abundance of sets of theoretical statements. Repeatedly overviews of the plethora of theoretical perspectives and insights have been presented (Dijkstra et al., 1997; Dills and Romiszowski, 1997; Jonassen, 1982, 1985, 1996a, 2004a; Reigeluth, 1983a, 1999; Seel and Dijkstra, 2003; Tennyson et al., 1997). Theoretical statements typically are formal expressions about the relationships between at least two variables or instantiations of variables. Theoretical statements in educational technology generally make such claims that are regarded to be relevant for educational technology or instructional design. A theory, then, is an integrated and internally coherent set of theoretical principles that provides a sufficient basis for empirical research in which these statements can be tested. For instance, a theoretical statement may explain how a learner-related variable in combination with an instructional goal is linked to an instructional strategy or how different activities are sequenced in a development procedure. An educational technological theory consists of a series of such statements that are mutually consistent and refer to one another.

In this chapter, differences between theoretical statements are addressed by presenting four perspectives from which such statements can be described. Taking

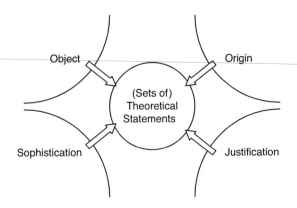

**Figure 55.1** Four perspectives to describe (sets of) theoretical statements.

these differences into account with respect to sets of theoretical statements, the remainder of this chapter discusses theory development with a focus on instructional design. Features of descriptive and prescriptive theories are elaborated by analyzing their commonalities and differences. The development of theories is addressed by focusing on deductive, inductive, and mixed approaches. Finally, levels of theoretical sophistication and empirical justification are dealt with.

## THEORETICAL STATEMENTS: FOUR PERSPECTIVES

Theoretical statements and sets of such statements differ in substantial ways. Their similarities and differences can be identified and described from at least four perspectives: object, origin, sophistication, and justification (see Figure 55.1). The absence of a clear and consolidated theoretical base in the field of educational technology can be shown by describing (sets of) theoretical statements from these four perspectives.

### The Object Perspective

Theoretical statements differ as to what the statements are all about. There are large variations in the object of (sets of) theoretical statements. A first series of sets addresses instruction-related principles. These statements bring forward what is regarded to be important or even essential for learning to occur in an instructional setting. A clear example is Ausubel's (1968, p. vi) statement: "If I had to reduce all of educational psychology to one principle, I would say this: the most important single factor influencing learning is what the learner already knows. Ascertain this and teach him accordingly." A more recent example comes from Merrill, who, in an attempt to consolidate the variety of theoretical statements in the educational technology field, postulated five *first principles of instruction*, such as "learning is promoted when learners are engaged in solving real-world problem" (Merrill, 2002, p. 45).

A second series addresses issues with respect to (technological) features of instructional interventions, tools, or devices. Traditionally, such statements mostly pertain to links between the format and outlook of information, on the one hand, and issues of accessibility and usability, on the other (Fleming and Levie, 1993). Examples are statements with respect to typographical cues in texts (Glynn et al., 1985), headings (Hartley and Jonassen, 1985), contents lists and indexes (Wright, 1985), or various features of Web-based materials (Brooks, 1997) that may facilitate access to information in printed or digital materials. More recently, and especially under the label of multimedia design, such statements also pertain to links between the format and outlook of information and cognitive issues directly related to learning. A clear example is the multimedia principle "students learn better from words and pictures than from words alone" (Mayer, 2001, p. 63). The *Cambridge Handbook of Multimedia Learning* (Mayer, 2005) compiled a large number of such principles. To this series also belong the large number of statements about how to use technological devices such as different types of information and communication technologies (Alessi and Trollip, 2001; Jonassen, 1996b; Morrison et al., 1999) to foster learning. Currently, e-learning (Clark and Mayer, 2003; Jochems et al., 2004) is generating a large number of such theoretical statements.

In a third series, the object of the statements is the design or development process. These statements discuss what procedures or instruments are best suited for what kind of design problem (task analysis procedures; see Jonassen et al., 1999) or specify how activities in a design or development process relate to one another (Andrews and Goodson, 1980; Dick et al., 2001; Gustafson and Branch, 1997; Kemp et al., 1994; Lee and Owens, 2000; Rothwell and Kazanas, 1998).

Finally, theoretical reflections also pertain to instructional design itself: the nature of educational technology or instructional design (Clark and Estes, 1998; Heinich, 1984; Van Patten, 1989; Wilson, 1997), their development (Clark and Estes, 1999; Reigeluth, 1983b; Schott and Driscoll, 1997), and the appropriateness of particular research approaches (Reeves, 2005; Ross and Morrison, 2004) are regularly discussed. Clark and Estes (1999), for example, pointed to the technological nature of instructional design, Schott and Driscoll (1997) stressed the need to focus on efficiency, and Reeves (2005) argued for the application of more design-based research approaches.

## The Origin Perspective

Theoretical statements can also be described by explicitly considering their origin. Three different origins can be easily distinguished. A first position is practice oriented and practice anchored. Theoretical statements are rooted in practice and result from a reflection on design and development practices. Examples are theoretical conclusions that are immediately linked to particular design or development projects (Elen and Clarebout, 2001; Hannafin and Land, 1997). Regularly, such theoretical statements are prescriptive. They specify how in a particular context an outcome can be realized by the application of a particular method. A second position is theory driven and theory oriented. Theoretical statements result from deliberate efforts to deduce design or development principles from more fundamental theories (e.g., learning theory, systems theory, activity theory) or specific theoretical perspectives (Gros, 2002; Jonassen and Rohrer-Murphy, 1999; Richey, 1986). A more general theory is applied to a specific problem or context to generate more specific theoretical statements. Whereas classical examples are contributions of Skinner (1968) and Gagné (1985), a more recent example is van Merriënboer's (1997) four-component instructional design (4C/ID) model. Most typical, however, is a third position in which a local instructional design theory is developed by applying a specific theoretical perspective to a specific instructional design issue. Using a specific instructional problem, intervention, or medium as an instructional design anchor point (Elen, 2004), an attempt is made to construct a consistent set of theoretical statements that directly apply to the selected problem, such as solving problems (Jonassen, 2004b). The statements may also pertain to the use of instructional interventions (Elen and Clarebout, 2006); interventions, such as problem-based learning (Schmidt, 1993) or metacognitive prompts (Bannert, 2006); or media, such as e-learning (Jochems et al., 2004) or learning objects (Wiley, 2002).

## The Sophistication Perspective

Theoretical statements also differ with respect to their theoretical sophistication and empirical justification. The level of theoretical sophistication and empirical justification of these (sets of) statements clearly differs. In a number of cases the (sets of) theoretical statements are simple collections of isolated theoretical expressions; for example, in the conclusion section of an empirical study a number of implications for instructional design are mentioned. Typical for instructional design, however, seems to be the abundance of descriptive or prescriptive models with respect to educational technology issues (Reigeluth, 1983a, 1999). Additionally, there is also a small set of attempts to really present an educational technological theory consisting of integrated, internally coherent sets of theoretical principles which provide a sufficient basis for empirical research in which these statements can be tested. The need for such integrated, internally coherent sets becomes very clear when attempts are made to automate instructional design (Spector et al., 1993). The need to formulate precise statements that are also mutually consistent and coherent helps them to become theoretically more explicit and sophisticated (Elen, 1998).

## The Justification Perspective

A different aspect relates to the empirical validation of the statements. Some statements are purely explorative or speculative, whereas for others empirical evidence is readily available. This empirical evidence may have been gathered through a variety of both quantitative and qualitative methods (e.g., experimental studies, usability and feasibility studies, design experiments, case studies, development research). Theoretical sophistication and empirical justification do not have to go along; for example, whereas Merrill (2002) claimed the theoretical soundness of his interrelated set of first principles of instruction, he also specified the need to test the empirical validity of these statements (Merrill, 2006).

## DESCRIPTIVE AND PRESCRIPTIVE THEORIES

The educational technology field and the instructional design field are areas of practice as well as areas of scientific inquiry. Research efforts in the field of instructional design are twofold. A first series of efforts and approaches aims at describing instructional phenomena. Why a particular intervention is suitable for a group of learners or how design processes are actually practiced is described and explained. When the object relates to how instructional interventions or approaches affect learning processes of particular groups of learners (for collaborative learning, see Littleton and Häkkinen, 1999), these endeavors may result in the specification of an instructional theory (Reigeluth, 1983b). When the process is focused upon, the descriptions mainly pertain to the very different context-specific ways in which design and development procedures and processes develop (Richey et al., 2004) and to the difficulties designers experience to implement well-defined and linear design procedures (Gibbons, 2003; Rowland, 1993).

A second series of research efforts aims at identifying what instructional interventions or approaches should look like in view of reaching an educational outcome within a specific context or what steps (in what order) are most indicated to generate a suitable instruction design. These theoretical attempts are prescriptive in nature (Reigeluth, 1983b). *Instructional design* (ID) is often the label used to refer to a prescriptive discipline that aims at optimizing decision-making for instruction (Elen, 1995). The label *instructional systems design* (ISD) refers to similar efforts that also include the actual development of instruction. How exactly ID and ISD relate to each other is an object of much discussion.

Although descriptive and prescriptive theories can be distinguished, they are highly interrelated. Descriptive theories evolve into more prescriptive indications (Clark and Mayer, 2003), and prescriptive theories generate research questions (Merrill, 2006), which in turn result in the elaboration or refinement of prescriptive theories.

## Descriptive Theories

Descriptive theories in the field of educational technology aim at modeling and explaining either the actual instructional processes and their learning effects or the actual way in which instruction is developed. By modeling these instructional and development processes, the theoretical statements identify which variables are relevant and how they relate to one another. Such (sets of) statements can have substantial predictive and explanatory power. They may help us to better understand what is happening in a concrete setting and to formulate expectations about probable effects and potential difficulties.

In modeling instructional processes, researchers are deeply influenced by the theoretical perspectives they adopt. The theoretical perspective greatly affects what is regarded to be important, what is considered, and what is discarded. With respect to instructional processes, for example, a clear evolution from behaviorist (Skinner, 1968), information-processing (Anderson, 1983; Andre, 1979; Kintsch and van Dijk, 1978), constructivist (von Glasersfeld, 1987; Wilson, 1996), and socioconstructivist (Lave and Wenger, 1991) can be observed. Each of these theoretical perspectives offers another set of glasses to look at instructional processes and hence results in the identification of different sets of variables and different interrelations between those variables.

After a period in which the constructivist nature of human learning was stressed, it seems that most recently a number of theoretical insights are more realistic with regard to instructional design. First of all, more and more studies strongly stress the need to systematically consider the limits of human cognition and more specifically the limited self-regulation skills in instructional settings (Kirschner et al., 2006; Mayer, 2004). Furthermore, warnings have been uttered that learners may be less compliant than expected (Goodyear, 2000), partly because their instructional conceptions do not match those of the designers (Elen and Lowyck, 2000).

With respect to the development of instruction, it seems that the systems approach and activity theory remain important. Continuously the models are being revised to ensure that all important design aspects are systematically considered (Dick et al., 2001; Tennyson, 2000). At the same time, cognitive research has clearly shown that designers, even expert designers, do not follow a linear procedure. The development is therefore better described as an iterative process. Affected by development approaches in informatics, rapid prototyping (Dorsey et al., 1996) has attracted attention as a valuable alternative to more linear procedures. Jonassen and Rohrer-Murphy (1999) have argued and illustrated that activity theory may provide a suitable framework when the design of constructivist learning environments is the goal.

## Prescriptive Theories

In contrast to descriptive theories, prescriptive theories discuss how things should be rather than how things are. Building on such prescriptive theories, various attempts have been made to automate instructional design by actually embedding the prescriptions in systems that support the automated development of instruction, such as the Advanced Instructional Design Advisor (Muraida and Spector, 1992) and ID Expert (Merrill, 1998); for a more in-depth discussion, see Spector and Ohrazda (2004).

The prescriptive orientation, as clearly outlined by Reigeluth (1983b), reveals the normative perspective and brings the goal issue immediately to the front. Prescriptive theories basically specify how instruction (in general or more specific) should look to enable specific groups of learners to reach an instructional goal or how the developmental process should look to increase the probability that adequate instruction is developed. Not surprisingly, then, changes in what are regarded to be important instructional outcomes affect the nature of prescriptive theoretical statements. Similarly, new target populations (distance education students) and, more specifically, different views on what are relevant learner characteristics result in differences between instructional design models. As an example,

the interest in motivational issues is growing and may result in changes to instructional design models (Clark et al., 2006). Finally, the diversity of instructional interventions considered as serious alternatives also affects the models. Goals, target populations, and instructional alternatives are heavily influenced by the context in which the instructional design model is elaborated; for example, some specific multimedia-based instructional design models have appeared (Lee and Owens, 2000) that differ from more general models as they consider only e-learning environments as the context in which the instructional interventions can be embedded.

The issue of goals has been especially influential in the last several decades with respect to the elaboration of instructional design models. Two interrelated observations can be made. First, the scope of instructional outcomes has been broadened (Reigeluth, 1999). Far more than in the past, attention is being paid to instructional goals such as the development of attitudes and the acquisition of complex problem-solving and learning skills. This reorientation in instructional goals has resulted in the emergence of more integrated and task-based instructional design models, whereas older models can be said to be more analytical and information-based. Immediately related to the broadening of instructional outcomes, some authors have pointed to the difficulties of specifying instructional outcomes in operational terms. Not surprisingly, the models that pertain to such more vague instructional outcomes are also more general and less specific. Typical examples are the cognitive apprenticeship model (Collins et al., 1989) and the notion of powerful learning environments (De Corte, 2003). In these cases, no direct prescriptions are formulated but general criteria for instruction are presented. Interest in models on automated skills is growing (Clark, 2006), and it is well recognized that solving complex, ill-structured, or wicked problems requires the use of a rich set of highly automated cognitive skills.

## DEVELOPING THEORIES

As already pointed out, theoretical statements—both descriptive and prescriptive ones—in the field of educational technology differ as to their origin. Some are generated through reflections on practical experiences, others are the outcome of deliberate deductions, and a last group results from interactions between theory-driven reflections and attempts to solve specific design issues. This section focuses on the development of instructional design models, as they constitute the bulk of more systematic sets of theoretical statements in the field. This also implies a focus on primarily prescriptive theoretical statements.

Given the applied nature of instructional design, the classical approach is a deductive one. An instructional design model is the result of a deductive approach when a theory, primarily a learning theory, is taken as the starting point for its elaboration. In developing the model, the instructional designer analyzes a learning theory and is especially interested in what the theory specifies to be important learner variables (internal conditions) and environmental features (external conditions). The elaboration of the instructional design model implies the application of the learning theory to a specific instructional context. The model specifies the instructional implications of the learning theory. A deductive approach necessarily implies that a transition from description to prescription is made. How the learning theory describes learning is used as the starting point to prescribe what the instruction should look like. Such a transition is intrinsically problematic, as *what is* may drastically differ from *what should be*. The consecutive models proposed by Gagné (1985) are typical examples of a deductive approach. The consecutive versions of the Gagné model also clearly show that models are adapted along with changes in the underlying learning theory. To assess the validity of these deductively constructed design models evaluation studies and experiments are regarded as being adequate research approaches (Tennyson and Cocchiarella, 1986).

When instructional design models emerge from a specific practical context, they are developed in line with an inductive approach. Within a specific context and often for a specific target group a number of instructional interventions, media, or approaches are explored. What outcomes can be reached by means of these instructional interventions, media, or approaches are investigated (for such an approach with regard to video games, see Gee, 2003; for WebQuests, see Dodge, 1995). In most situations, these endeavors begin with high expectations for the potential of the instructional interventions, media, or approaches at hand. The inductive elaboration of an instructional design model entails an abstraction. The model builder aims at generalizing the specific context and at broadening the application context of the instructional interventions, media, or approaches. In the absence of critical tests for these generalizations, there is an apparent danger of overgeneralization. Case studies and usability and feasibility studies may help to test inductively generated theoretical statements.

Although inductive and deductive approaches can logically be identified as clear alternatives, most instructional design models do result from a combination of inductive and deductive approaches. Elen (1995) suggested that differences between the theoretical statements in instructional design models can be explained by considering at the same time their knowledge base and their referent system. Whereas the knowledge base refers to the theoretical basis of the model, the reference system refers to the application context of the model. Any attempt therefore to build a model by only considering the knowledge base or the referent system is doomed to fail. It is not surprising that even when not explicitly mentioned and even when a general applicability is claimed, most models are clearly linked to a particular theoretical perspective and are rooted in a particular instructional context consisting of a set of highly valued instructional outcomes, potential target groups, or the instructional media being considered. As an example, programmed instruction (Skinner, 1968) and the notion of criss-crossing the landscape (Spiro et al., 1991) can only be well understood and compared when the specific outcomes, target groups, and instructional media are considered.

Assessing the validity of models based on a mixed approach remains a concern. Design experiments deeply rooted in both theory and practice and oriented toward both theory development and solving real problems are considered adequate (Reeves, 2005).

## THEORETICAL SOPHISTICATION AND JUSTIFICATION

Gordon (1968) formulated a number of criteria for theories of instruction. He argued that statements of an instructional theory should include a set of postulates and a definition of the terms involved in these postulates; each statement of an instructional theory or subtheory should make explicit the boundaries of its concern and the limitations under which it is proposed; any theoretical construction must have internal consistency; it must be a logical set of interrelationships. Furthermore, an instructional theory should be congruent with empirical data, be capable of generating hypotheses, contain generalizations that go beyond the data, be verifiable, and be stated in such a way that it is possible to collect data to disprove it; also, it not only must explain past events but must also be capable of predicting future events and may be expected to represent qualitative synthesis. These general criteria still apply today. A quick review of current (sets of) theoretical statements rapidly reveals that only a very limited number of such (sets of) theoretical statements actually meet these criteria. Instead of being theory based, the field is model based. The field is rather characterized by a plethora of models, which might be regarded to be the precursors of robust theories. Some of the most prominent problems are terminological confusion, an absence of specifications of the limits of the models, and a lack of empirical evidence to back up the claims embedded in the models. Although these models replace simple collections of *implications for instruction* at the end of research articles, it can also be observed that every time new media or technologies are introduced the field is tempted to reinvent the wheel. This suggests a need for (1) a consolidation of the theoretical approaches, and (2) a kind of classification of the various models so their relationships can be more clearly exemplified and more robust theories elaborated. Some (such as Duchastel, 1998) have argued for the need of such a consolidation, but not everybody is convinced of the relevance and the possibility of such an effort (see the discussion on ITFORUM, http://itech1.coe.uga.edu/itforum/paper27/index27.html).

## CONCLUSION

Educational technology, in general, and instructional design, in particular, are characterized by a diversity of efforts with respect to theory development. Despite these efforts, it is difficult to identify a generally accepted set of robust theories or even a widely accepted approach to develop such theories. From the perspective of theory development, the field is diverse and disparate. This diversity reflects both the complexity of the field in terms of the number of aspects that have to be dealt with and the diversity of theoretical perspectives that are brought to the field. More stability would require a greater consensus regarding these theoretical perspectives and the recognition of the need for a greater abstraction. Such an abstraction would, for example, require that new technological devices are not taken as the starting point for the elaboration of new models but as a challenge to apply what is known to that new device. Such attempts to apply the available models may in turn represent nice opportunities to actually validate the models and highlight their generalizability. A similar abstraction is indicated with regard to the formulation of instructional goals and target groups. Instructional goals and target groups must be described at a sufficient level of abstraction using the most relevant variables. As long as the field cannot make distinctions between relevant and superficial variables, theory development in the field of educational technology will remain a worthwhile but impossible endeavor. From this perspective, it could be argued that theory development is best helped by systematic efforts to automate instructional design.

Even when the actual product of such an endeavor may never be used in actual design work, the need for clarity with regard to the variables and the need for mutual consistency in attempts to automate may very well help to generate more coherent sets of theoretical statements and to develop an actual instructional design theory.

## REFERENCES

Alessi, S. M. and Trollip, S. R. (2001). *Multimedia for Learning. Methods and Development*, 3rd ed. Boston, MA: Allyn & Bacon.

Anderson, J. R. (1983). *The Architecture of Cognition*. Cambridge, MA: Harvard University Press.

Andre, T. (1979). Does answering higher-level questions while reading facilitate productive learning? *Rev. Educ. Res.*, 49, 280–318.

Andrews, D. H. and Goodson, L. A. (1980). A comparative analysis of methods of instructional design. *J. Instruct. Dev.*, 3(4), 2–16.

Ausubel, D. P. (1968). *Educational Psychology: A Cognitive View*. New York: Holt, Rinehart and Winston.*

Bannert, M. (2006). Effects of reflection prompts when learning with hypermedia. *J. Educ. Comput. Res.*, 4, 359–375.

Brooks, D. W. (1997). *Web-Teaching: A Guide to Designing Interactive Teaching for the World Wide Web*. New York: Plenum Press.

Clark, R. C. and Mayer, R. E. (2003). *e-Learning and the Science of Instruction: Proven Guidelines for Consumers and Designers of Multimedia Learning*. San Francisco, CA: Pfeiffer.

Clark, R. E. (2006). Not knowing what we don't know: reframing the importance of automated knowledge for educational research. In *Avoiding Simplicity, Confronting Complexity: Advances in Studying and Designing (Computer-Based) Powerful Learning Environments*, edited by G. Clarebout and J. Elen, pp. 3–14. Rotterdam: Sense Publishers.

Clark, R. E. and Estes, F. (1998). Technology or craft: what are we doing? *Educ. Technol.*, 38(5), 5–11.

Clark, R. E. and Estes, F. (1999). The development of authentic educational technologies. *Educ. Technol.*, 39(2), 5–16.*

Clark, R. E., Howard, K., and Early, S. (2006). Motivational challenges experienced in highly complex learning environments. In *Handling Complexity in Learning Environments: Theory and Research*, Advances in Learning and Instruction Series, edited by J. Elen and R. E. Clark, pp. 27–41. Amsterdam: Elsevier.

Collins, A., Brown, S. J., and Newman, S. E. (1989). Cognitive apprenticeship: teaching the craft of reading, writing, and mathematics. In *Knowing, Learning, and Instruction: Essays in Honor of Robert Glaser*, edited by L. B. Resnick, pp. 453–494. Hillsdale, NJ: Lawrence Erlbaum Associates.

De Corte, E. (2003). Designing learning environments that foster the productive use of acquired knowledge and skills. In *Powerful Learning Environments: Unravelling Basic Components and Dimensions*, Advances in Learning and Instruction Series, edited by E. De Corte, L. Verschaffel, N. Entwistle, and J. J. G. van Merriënboer, pp. 21–33. Amsterdam: Pergamon.

Dick, W., Carey, L., and Carey, J. O. (2001). *The Systematic Design of Instruction*, 5th ed. New York: Addison-Wesley.

Dijkstra, S., Seel, N. M., Schott, F., and Tennyson, R. D., Eds. (1997) *Instructional Design: International Perspective*, Vol. 2. Mahwah, NJ: Lawrence Erlbaum Associates.

Dills, C. R. and Romiszowski, A. J., Eds. (1997). *Instructional Development Paradigms*. Englewood Cliffs, NJ: Educational Technology Publications.*

Dodge, B. (1995). WebQuests: a technique for Internet-based learning. *Dist. Educator*, 1(2), 10–13.

Dorsey, L. T., Goodrum, D. A., and Schwen, T. M. (1996). Rapid collaborative prototyping as an instructional development paradigm. In *Instructional Development Paradigms*, edited by C. R. Dills and A. J. Romiszowski, pp. 445–465. Englewood Cliffs, NJ: Educational Technology Publications.

Duchastel, P. (1998) *Prolegomena to a Theory of Instructional Design*, http://itech1.coe.uga.edu/itforum/paper27/paper27.html.

Elen, J. (1995). *Blocks on the Road to Instructional Design Prescriptions: A Methodology for ID Research Exemplified*. Leuven, Belgium: Leuven University Press.

Elen, J. (1998). Automating ID: the impact of theoretical knowledge bases and referent systems. *Instruct. Sci.*, 26, 281–297

Elen, J. (2004). Electronic learning environments as instructional design anchor points. *Educ. Technol. Res. Dev.*, 52(4), 67–73.

Elen, J. and Clarebout, G. (2001). An invasion in the classroom: influence of an ill-structured innovation on instructional and epistemological beliefs. *Learn. Environ. Res.*, 4, 87–105.

Elen, J. and Clarebout, G. (2006). The use of instructional interventions: lean learning environments as a solution for a design problem. In: *Handling Complexity in Learning Environments: Research and Theory*, Advances in Learning and Instruction Series, edited by J. Elen and R. E. Clark, pp. 185–200. Oxford: Pergamon.

Elen, J. and Lowyck, J. (2000). Instructional metacognitive knowledge: a qualitative study of conceptions of freshmen about instruction. *J. Curric. Stud.*, 32(3), 421–444.

Fleming, M. and Levie, W. H., Eds. (1993). *Instructional Message Design. Principles from the Behavioral and Cognitive Sciences*, 2nd ed. Englewood Cliffs, NJ: Educational Technology Publications

Gagné, R. M. (1985). *The Conditions of Learning*, 4th ed. New York: Holt, Rinehart and Winston.*

Gee, J. P. (2003). *What Video Games Have to Teach Us about Learning and Literacy*. New York: Palgrave Macmillan.

Gibbons, A. S. (2003). What and how designers design: a theory of design structure. *TechTrends*, 47(5), 22–27.

Glynn, S. M., Britton, B. K., and Tillman, M. H. (1985). Typographical cues in text: management of reader's attention. In *The Technology of Text: Principles for Structuring, Designing, and Displaying Text*, Vol. 2, edited by D. H. Jonassen, pp. 192–209. Englewood Cliffs, NJ: Educational Technology Publications.

Goodyear, P. (2000). Environments for lifelong learning: ergonomics, architecture and educational design. In *Integrated and Holistic Perspectives on Learning, Instruction and Technology*, edited by J. M. Spector and T. M. Anderson, pp. 1–18. Dordrecht: Kluwer.

Gordon, I. J. (1968). *Criteria for Theories of Instruction*. Washington, D.C.: Association for Supervision and Curriculum Development, National Education Association.*

Gros, B. (2002). Knowledge construction and technology. *J. Educ. Multimedia Hypermedia*, 11(4), 323–343

Gustafson, K. L. and Branch, R. (1997). *Survey of Instructional Development Models*, 3rd ed. Syracuse, NY: ERIC Clearinghouse on Information and Technology.

Hannafin, M. J. and Land, S. M. (1997). The foundations and assumptions of technology enhanced student-centered learning environments. *Instruct. Sci.*, 25, 167–202.

Hartley, J. and Jonassen, D. H. (1985). The role of headings in printed and electronic text. In *The Technology of Text: Principles for Structuring, Designing, and Displaying Text*, Vol. 2, edited by D. H. Jonassen, pp. 237–263. Englewood Cliffs, NJ: Educational Technology Publications.

Heinich, R. (1984). The proper study of instructional technology. *Educ. Commun. Technol. J.*, 32(2), 67–87.*

Jochems, W., van Merriënboer, J. J. G., and Koper, R., Eds. (2004). *Integrated e-Learning: Implications for Pedagogy, Technology and Organization*. London: RoutledgeFalmer.

Jonassen, D. H., Ed. (1982). *The Technology of Text: Principles for Structuring, Designing, and Displaying Text*, Vol. 1. Englewood Cliffs, NJ: Educational Technology Publications.

Jonassen, D. H., Ed. (1985). *The Technology of Text: Principles for Structuring, Designing, and Displaying Text*, Vol. 2. Englewood Cliffs, NJ: Educational Technology Publications.

Jonassen, D. H., Ed. (1996a). *Handbook of Research for Educational Communications and Technology*. New York: Macmillan.*

Jonassen, D. H. (1996b). *Computers in the Classroom: Mindtools for Critical Thinking*. Englewood Cliffs, NJ: Merrill.

Jonassen, D. H., Ed. (2004a). *Handbook of Research for Educational Communications and Technology*, 2nd ed. Mahwah, NJ: Lawrence Erlbaum Associates.

Jonassen, D. H. (2004b). *Learning to Solve Problems: An Instructional Design Guide*. San Francisco, CA: Pfeiffer.

Jonassen, D. H. and Rohrer-Murphy, L. (1999). Activity theory as a framework for designing constructivist learning environments. *Educ. Technol. Res. Dev.*, 47(1), 61–79.

Jonassen, D. H., Tessmer, M., and Hannum, W. H. (1999). *Task Analysis Methods for Instructional Design*. Mahwah, NJ: Lawrence Erlbaum Associates.

Kemp, J. E., Morrison, G. R., and Ross, S. M. (1994). *Designing Effective Instruction*. New York: Merrill.

Kintsch, W. and van Dijk, T. (1978). Toward a model of text comprehension and production. *Psychol. Rev.*, 85, 363–394.

Kirschner, P. A., Sweller, J., and Clark, R. E. (2006). Why minimal guidance during instruction does not work: an analysis of the failure of constructivist, discovery, problem-based, experiential and inquiry-based teaching. *Educ. Psychol.*, 41(2), 75–86.

Lave, J. and Wenger, E. (1991). *Situated Learning: Legitimate Peripheral Participation*. Cambridge, U.K.: Cambridge University Press.

Lee, W. W. and Owens, D. L. (2000). *Multimedia-Based Instructional Design*. San Francisco, CA: Jossey-Bass.

Littleton, K. and Häkkinen, P. (1999). Learning together: understanding the processes of computer-based collaborative learning. In *Collaborative Learning: Cognitive and Computational Approaches*, Advances in Learning and Instruction Series, edited by P. Dillenbourg, pp. 20–30. Amsterdam: Pergamon.

Mayer, R. E. (2001). *Multimedia Learning*. Cambridge, U.K.: Cambridge University Press.*

Mayer, R. E. (2004). Should there be a three-strikes rule against pure discovery learning: the case for guided methods of instruction. *Am. Psychol.*, 59(1), 14–19.

Mayer, R. E., Ed. (2005). *The Cambridge Handbook of Multimedia Learning*. Cambridge, U.K.: Cambridge University Press.

Merrill, M. D. (1998). ID Expert: a second generation instructional development system. *Instruct. Sci.*, 26(3–4), 243–262.

Merrill, M. D. (2002). First principles of instruction. *Educ. Technol. Res. Dev.*, 50(3), 43–59.*

Merrill, M. D. (2006). Hypothesized performance on complex tasks as a function of scaled instructional strategies. In *Handling Complexity in Learning Environments: Research and Theory*, Advances in Learning and Instruction Series, edited by J. Elen and R. E. Clark, pp. 265–281. Amsterdam: Pergamon.

Morrison, G. R., Lowther, D. L., and DeMeulle, L. (1999). *Integrating Computer Technology into the Classroom*. Upper Saddle River, NJ: Merrill.

Muraida, D. J. and Spector, J. M. (1992). The advanced instructional design advisor. *Instruct. Sci.*, 21(4), 239–253.

Reeves, T. C. (2005). Design-based research in educational technology: progress made, challenges remain. *Educ. Technol.*, 45(1), 18–52.

Reigeluth, C. M., Ed. (1983a). *Instructional Design Theories and Models: An Overview of Their Current Status*. Hillsdale, NJ: Lawrence Erlbaum Associates.*

Reigeluth, C. M. (1983b). Instructional design: what is it and why is it? In *Instructional Design Theories and Models: An Overview of Their Current Status*, edited by C. M. Reigeluth, pp. 3–36. Hillsdale, NJ: Lawrence Erlbaum Associates.*

Reigeluth, C. M., Ed. (1999). *Instructional-Design Theories and Models. A New Paradigm of Instructional Theory*, Vol. II. Mahwah, NJ: Lawrence Erlbaum Associates.*

Richey, R. C. (1986). *The Theoretical and Conceptual Bases of Instructional Design*. London: Kogan Page.*

Richey, R. C., Klein, J. D., and Nelson, W. A. (2004). Development research: studies of instructional design and development. In *Handbook of Research for Educational Communications and Technology*, 2nd ed., edited by D. H. Jonassen, pp. 1099–1130. Mahwah, NJ: Lawrence Erlbaum Associates.*

Ross, S. M. and Morrison, G. R. (2004). Experimental research methods. In *Handbook of Research for Educational Communications and Technology*, 2nd ed., edited by D. H. Jonassen, pp. 1021–1043. Mahwah, NJ: Lawrence Erlbaum Associates.

Rothwell, W. J. and Kazanas, H. C. (1998). *Mastering the Instructional Design Process: A Systematic Approach*, 2nd ed. San Francisco, CA: Jossey-Bass.

Rowland, G. (1993). Designing and instructional design. *Educ. Technol. Res. Dev.*, 41(1), 79–91.

Schmidt, H. G. (1993). Foundations of problem-based learning: some explanatory notes. *Med. Educ.*, 27, 422–432.

Schott, F. and Driscoll, M. P. (1997). On the architectonics of instructional theory. In *Instructional Design: International Perspective*, Vol. 1, edited by R. D. Tennyson, F., Schott, N. Seel, and S. Dijkstra, pp. 135–173. Mahwah, NJ: Lawrence Erlbaum Associates.

Seel, N. M. and Dijkstra, S., Eds. (2003). *Curriculum, Plans and Processes of Instructional Design: International Perspectives*. Mahwah, NJ: Lawrence Erlbaum Associates.

Skinner, B. F. (1968). *The Technology of Teaching*. New York: Appleton-Century-Crofts.

Spector, J. M. and Ohrazda, C. (2004). Automating instructional design: approaches and limitations. In *Handbook of Research for Educational Communications and Technology*, 2nd ed., edited by D. H. Jonassen, pp. 685–699. Mahwah, NJ: Lawrence Erlbaum Associates.*

Spector, J. M., Polson, M. C., and Muraida, D. J., Eds. (1993). *Automating Instructional Design: Concepts and Issues*. Englewood Cliffs, NJ: Educational Technology Publications.*

Spiro, R. A., Feltovich, P. J., Jacobson, M. J., and Coulson, R. L. (1991). Cognitive flexibility, constructivism, and hypertext: random access instruction for advanced knowledge acquisition in ill-structured domains. *Educ. Technol.*, 31(5), 24–33.

Tennyson, R. D. (2000). Fourth generation instructional systems development: A problem solving approach. *J. Struct. Learn. Intell. Syst.*, 14, 114–128.

Tennyson, R. D. and Cocchiarella, M. J. (1986). An empirically based instructional design theory for teaching concepts. *Rev. Educ. Res.*, 56(1), 40–71.

Tennyson, R. D., Schott, F., Seel, N. M., and Dijkstra, S., Eds. (1997). *Instructional Design: International Perspective*, Vol. 1. Mahwah, NJ: Lawrence Erlbaum Associates.

van Merriënboer, J. J. G. (1997). *Training Complex Cognitive Skills: A Four-Component Instructional Design Model for Technical Training*. Englewood Cliffs, NJ: Educational Technology Publications.*

Van Patten, J. (1989). What is instructional design? In *Instructional Design: New Alternatives for Effective Education and Training*, edited by K. A. Johnson and L. K. Foa, pp. 16–31. New York: Macmillan.*

von Glasersfeld, E. (1987). *The Construction of Knowledge*. Seaside: Intersystems Publications.

Wiley, D. A., Ed. (2002). *The Instructional Use of Learning Objects*. Bloomington, IN: Agency for Instructional Technology, Association for Educational Communications and Technology.

Wilson, B. G. (1996). Reflections on constructivism and instructional design. In *Instructional Development Paradigms*, edited by C. R. Dills and A. J. Romiszowski, pp. 63–80. Englewood Cliffs, NJ: Educational Technology Publications.

Wilson, B. G. (1997). Thoughts on theory in educational technology. *Educ. Technol.*, 37(1), 2–26.*

Wright, K. C. (1985). Designing contents lists and indexes for access. In *The Technology of Text: Principles for Structuring, Designing, and Displaying Text*, Vol. 2, edited by D. H. Jonassen, pp. 264–286. Englewood Cliffs, NJ: Educational Technology Publications.

---

* Indicates a core reference.

# 54

# Research Designs

*Steven M. Ross\**
University of Memphis, Memphis, Tennessee

*Gary R. Morrison*
Old Dominion University, Norfolk, Virginia

*Robert D. Hannafin and Michael Young*
University of Connecticut, Storrs, Connecticut

*Jan van den Akker and Wilmad Kuiper*
University of Twente, Enschede, the Netherlands

*Rita C. Richey*
Wayne State University, Detroit, Michigan

*James D. Klein*
Arizona State University, Tempe, Arizona

## CONTENTS

---

\* Steven M. Ross was lead author for this chapter and coordinator for the various sections.

# ABSTRACT

This chapter examines the types of designs and methodological approaches used by educational technology and instructional design researchers to investigate: (1) instructional strategies, (2) educational technologies, (3) instructional design models, and (4) design and development of instruction. These four approaches correspond to the four main parts of the *Handbook*. In the opening section, Ross and Morrison discuss how experimental methods have been predominantly used in determining the effectiveness of instructional strategies used to teach specific content, affect the design of a course, or improve message design. In the second chapter section, Hannafin and Young examine how research on instructional technologies has been influenced by the manner in which *technology* has been conceptualized as a *treatment* or intervention. When it is regarded as simply a medium for learning (e.g., computer-assisted instruction), usage of highly controlled experimental designs is most common; when conceived more broadly as a *technology-enhanced learning environment* (TELE), use of design-based research is favored. In the third section, van den Akker and Kuiper examine design and development research focusing on models for instructional design. Specific attention is directed to analyzing the trends that are most visible in model development and validation and exploring how research on models can be redirected to foster blending of theory and practice. In the final section, Richey and Klein focus on methods and issues related to conducting research on the *design and development* of instruction. Studies in this area, although highly diverse, most frequently rely on qualitative techniques, including case studies, interviews, document reviews, and observations.

# KEYWORDS

*Component investigation:* The identification or confirmation through research of steps (procedural models) and factors (conceptual models) critical to the instructional design process.

*Design and development research:* Research that seeks to create knowledge grounded in data systematically derived from practice and based upon a systematic analysis of specific cases.

*Experiment:* A design that involves the comparison of one treatment to another, using two or more different groups.

*External validity:* The degree to which the results of an experiment can be generalized to other settings.

*In-program learner behaviors:* Measures of learner activities and outcomes while engaged in an instructional task.

*Instructional strategies:* The prescribed sequences and methods of instruction to achieve a learning objective.

*Internal validity:* The degree to which the results of a study can be attributed to the treatment rather than extraneous or confounding variables.

*Log files:* A sequence of behavioral data stored in a permanent file, offering time- or location-stamped records of human choices made through computer interfaces with learning environments.

*Mixed-methods research:* Studies that combine qualitative and quantitative data collection methods.

*Model research:* Research that addresses the validity or effectiveness of an existing or newly constructed development model, process, or technique.

*Model validation:* Experiments, quasi-experiments, interviews, and expert reviews that are used for verification and evaluation of a particular design and development technique.

*Open-ended learning environment:* Instructional projects based, to varying degrees, on constructivist principles in which learners self-discover concepts and principles while engaged in authentic learning tasks.

*Qualitative research:* Research that emphasizes verbal descriptions or narrative accounts of observed or recorded events.

*Quasi-experiment:* An experimental design in which participants are not randomly assigned to treatments.

*Technology-enhanced learning environments:* Technology-based learning and instructional systems through which students acquire skills or knowledge, usually with the help of teachers or facilitators, learning support tools, and technological resources.

*Tool research:* The research-based design and development of products and tools to enhance learning.

# INTRODUCTION

*Steven M. Ross*

Research in educational technology and communications has had a long history, extending well over half a century. Throughout most of the 1900s, influenced most strongly by the paradigms of behaviorism and the physical sciences, researchers relied predominately on experimental methods both to derive principles and laws and empirically identify more effective ways of designing and delivering instruction. As the field matured and conceptualizations of instructional design and technology have broadened, a need has arisen for diverse research methodologies that focus not only on the culminating outcomes of technology-based interventions but also on the learning and developmental processes that interventions engender through interactions with learning contexts, individual differences, and instructional design approaches.

Based on this rationale, this chapter examines the types of designs and methodological approaches used by contemporary instructional design and educational technology researchers to investigate: (1) instructional strategies, (2) educational technologies, (3) instructional design models, and (4) design and development of instruction. In the opening chapter section, Ross and Morrison describe how experimental methods have been predominantly used in determining the effectiveness of instructional strategies used to teach specific content, affect the design of a course, or improve message design. They further examine the tensions cultivated by current national trends that emphasize strong rigor in research methods (and therefore favor randomized experiments) with needs by educational practitioners and researchers to learn (through qualitative and quantitative methods) how interventions work in more complex field-based applied contexts.

In the second chapter section, Hannafin and Young examine how research on instructional technologies has been influenced by the manner in which *technology* (referred to as IT) has been conceptualized as a *treatment* or intervention. When IT is regarded as simply a medium for learning (e.g., computer-assisted instruction), use of highly controlled experimental designs is most common, but, when IT is conceived more broadly as a *technology-enhanced learning environment* (TELE), use of design-based research is favored. Aside from identifying the variable or cluster of variables that constitute effective application in instruction, a key issue and challenge for researchers is identifying and operationally defining meaningful dependent measures to determine technology's complex potential impacts on learners.

In the third section, van den Akker and Kuiper examine design and development research focusing on models for instructional design. Specific attention is directed to analyzing the trends that are most visible in model development and validation and exploring how research on models can be redirected to foster blending of theory and practice. Given the complexity and conceptual nature of design models, studies in this area use highly diverse methodologies but predominantly draw on qualitative designs (case studies, document, analyses, and surveys) in investigating *model uses* and on experimental-type methods in conducting *model validations*.

In the fourth and final section, Richey and Klein focus on methods and issues related to conducting research on the *design and development* of instruction. Such research can involve studying the design and development work of others or studying one's own development and design activities as they occur. Accordingly, although diverse research methodologies have been employed (including experimental-type approaches), design and development studies most frequently rely on qualitative techniques conducted in actual work settings, including case studies, interviews, document reviews, and observations. Methodological issues for increasing validity, such as avoiding researcher bias and over-relying on recall data, are also discussed.

These sections support the theme that the research methods in the field of instructional design and technology are continually evolving to investigate more fully and meaningfully the impacts of contemporary technology applications and technology-supported learning environments. Researchers, therefore, can benefit from being knowledgeable about how and where to apply diverse methodologies ranging from case studies and document reviews to randomized experiments.

# RESEARCH ON INSTRUCTIONAL STRATEGIES

*Steven M. Ross and Gary R. Morrison*

In this chapter section, we examine research methods used to investigate *instructional strategies* in educational technology. As will be discussed, such strategies entail methods for improving instructional delivery, design, and ultimately learning performance. Although the full gamut of research methodologies, ranging from formative evaluation and design-based research (see Richey and Klein in this chapter; Wang and Hannafin, 2005) to qualitative and case studies to true (randomized) experiments, has been used to investigate strategy effects, the predominant approach in the research literature has been *experimental designs* to increase objectivity and rigor. In the process, a frequent and often natural trade-off has occurred between internal validity—the ability to infer causation from strategy effects—and external validity—the ability to generalize results to real-world educational settings. We will revisit these issues in later sections.

That research on instructional strategies in educational technology has relied so extensively on experimental methods should not come as a surprise. Experimental designs have had a long tradition in psychology and education. When psychology emerged as an infant science during the 1900s, it modeled its research methods on the established paradigms of the physical sciences, which for centuries relied on experimentation to derive principals and laws. Subsequent reliance on experimental approaches was strengthened by behavioral approaches to psychology and education that predominated during the first half of the 20th century. Thus, usage of experimentation in educational technology over the past 60 years has been influenced by developments in theory and research practices within its parent disciplines.

In the following pages, we examine practices, issues, and trends related to the application of experimental research methods in educational technology, with particular focus on instructional strategies research. Respecting the scope and desired length of this chapter section, our examination of experimental research issues and methodology necessarily is brief. Interested readers can find a more detailed discussion in Ross et al. (2005) and in any mainstream educational research textbook (such as Creswell, 2002). In subsequent sections, we examine through explanation and concrete examples research on instructional strategies usage in education, including micro-strategy, macro-strategy, and message design research methods. Next,

we present an analysis of the prevalence over time of experimental studies in published research. Factors affecting the rigor of experiments on instructional strategies, such as internal and external validity concerns, are examined in a final major section, followed by a summary of key ideas emerging from the preceding topics.

## Research on Instructional Strategies Usage in Educational Technology

### The Rise, Fall, and Likely Resurgence of Experimentation on Instructional Strategies

Experiments comprise the highest proportion of studies on instructional strategies published in the research section of *Educational Technology Research and Development (ETR&D)*; however, a noticeable trend over the past two decades both in *ETR&D* and in leading educational psychology journals (Hsieh et al., 2005; Levin, 2004) has been a steady decline in the quantity of experimental studies performed on educational interventions. The rise, however, occurred first.

What gave experimental designs initial impetus for researching instructional strategies? Two decades ago, Hannafin (1986) posited four reasons. One is the obvious influence of the field's behavioral roots. A second reason is that experimentation has been traditionally viewed as the definition of *acceptable* research in the field. Positivist views have reinforced beliefs about the importance of scientific rigor, control, statistical verification, and hypothesis testing and their being the *correct* approaches to research in the field. Qualitative researchers have challenged this way of thinking, but until recently acceptance of alternative paradigms has been reluctant and of minimal consequence (Guba, 1981; Savenye and Robinson, 2004). Third, promotion and tenure criteria at colleges and universities have been strongly biased toward experimental studies. Fourth, the research journals have published proportionately more experimental studies than alternative types. As a result, a self-perpetuating situation is created, in which increased exposure to experimental studies increases the likelihood that beginning researchers will also favor the experimental method in their research.

To borrow from music legend, Bob Dylan (with apologies to our past English teachers), "the times, they have been a changing" and appear to be changing still. In the recent Hsieh et al. (2005) study, articles published in four empirical educational psychology journals in 1983 and from 1995 to 2004 were reviewed. Findings indicated that the percentage of randomized intervention studies published in these journals declined from 47% in 1983 to only 34% in 1995 and 26% in 2004 (Hsieh et al., 2005, p. 524). To what factors can this trend be attributed? Ironically, one potential cause might be the very promotion of such studies as the *gold standard* of scientifically credible research. Confronted with more explicit and complex standards for rigor (Shavelson et al., 2002), combined with the intrinsic challenges of randomizing interventions in actual classrooms, researchers might view the randomized experiment as exceeding their available resources and time. A second factor, as noted above, might be the increased interest in and acceptance of qualitative studies over the years.

The tide seems to be shifting once again, however, but too late for the new wave of randomized and highly rigorous quasi-experimental studies to have been detectable in the reviews by Hsieh et al. in 2005 or Levin in 2004. The impetus is the strong advocacy by the No Child Left Behind (2001) legislation for using rigorous scientific research to determine *what works* in education. Guidance for judging the quality of research has recently been proposed by national organizations, such as the National Research Council (NRC) (Eisenhart and Towne, 2003; Feuer et al., 2002; Shavelson et al., 2002) and the What Works Clearing-house (http://w-w-c.org/standards.html). In the hierarchy of rigorous studies, randomized experiments hold the highest position, followed by rigorous regression discontinuity designs and rigorous quasi-experiments. Of note, the 2005 national recompetition for Regional Educational Laboratories (RELs) by the Institute for Educational Sciences was shifted from the traditionally emphasized capacity to use research evidence to provide technical assistance to practitioners to *generating* scientifically based research evidence on important educational interventions *using randomized field trials*. Today, in 2007, many of the federal grant competitions specifically encourage or require randomized or rigorous quasi-experimental designs for the evaluation component of the project. We therefore predict increased publication of such studies in the research journals within the next few years.

### Types of Experimental Designs

The purpose of an experiment is to determine the degree to which outcomes of interest are caused by the treatment (intervention) as opposed to extraneous factors. The *true* or randomized experiment generally is considered best equipped to provide such evidence due to its control over possible sampling bias. An advantage over less rigorous designs is the elimination, through random assignment, of any systematic error

that might be associated with using intact groups; thus, differences in learning outcomes should be solely attributable to treatment effects.

Oftentimes in educational studies, it is neither practical nor feasible to randomly assign participants to treatments. Such constraints are likely to occur in school-based research, due to principals and teachers understandably being resistant to changing students' class assignments or subject themselves to having to use different programs based on luck. In such instances, rigorous quasi-experimental (matched treatment-control group) designs are typically far more practical to implement across broad and diverse application sites (Borman et al., 2003). A common application in educational technology would be to expose to similar classes or groups of students alternative instructional strategies and compare them on designated dependent measures (e.g., learning, attitude, classroom behavior) during the year.

An important component of the quasi-experimental study is the use of pretesting or analysis of prior achievement to establish group equivalence. In the true experiment, randomization makes it improbable that one group will be significantly superior in ability to another, but systematic bias can easily be introduced in the quasi-experiment; for example, although the first- and third-period algebra classes may have the same teacher and identical lessons, it may be the case that honors English is offered third period only, thus restricting those honors students to taking first-period algebra.

To determine the effectiveness of instructional strategies, educational technology researchers have relied extensively on randomized and rigorous quasi-experiments to establish high levels of *internal validity*—the ability to isolate treatment effects from extraneous variables. Because instructional strategies research represents our focus, we next establish a clearer definition of "instructional strategies" and then examine exemplary studies used to test theories and hypotheses about their effectiveness for learning.

### Instructional Strategies and Heuristics

Instructional strategies can be defined as the prescribed "sequences and methods of instruction to achieve an objective" (Morrison et al., 2007, p. 150). The particular prescriptions are not only determined by the content and performance specified in the learning objectives, but also by underlying learning theory; for example, behavioral learning theory promotes strategies that use reinforcement and active responding (practice) to build strong connections between stimuli and responses. Cognitive theory shifts the emphasis to fostering meaningful learning by associating new material with the learner's prior knowledge.

Given these factors—type of content, desired performance, theoretical paradigm—coupled with constraints imposed by learning contexts (e.g., student characteristics, resources, allotted time), decisions involving which instructional strategies to choose are usually quite complex. As described by Morrison and colleagues (2007), however, practical and scientifically grounded *heuristics* can be derived to guide the identification of strategies for teaching certain types of content, such as facts, concepts, principles and rules, procedures, interpersonal skills, and attitudes. Research-supported heuristics for teaching facts, for example, prescribe such strategies as rehearsal practice, mnemonics, and usage of concrete representations.

An application of such heuristics in a more restricted domain is illustrated in a recent paper by Morrison and Anglin (2005). In reviewing a collection of experimental studies on cognitive load theory, published in a special issue of *ETR&D*, the authors created heuristics for e-learning based on the research findings. To illustrate, their initial two examples are:

- For teaching learners with limited technology skills, a strategy requiring initial learning of the relevant technology skills, *then* the particular content area concepts, will enhance learning (Morrison and Anglin, 2005, p. 95; based on Clarke et al., 2005).
- Exploratory practice results in greater involvement than do worked examples for experienced students (Morrison and Anglin, 2005, p. 96; based on Paas et al., 2005).

The above examples illustrate how the instructional design process is informed directly from educational technology research on instructional strategies. Specifically, research findings are interpreted into heuristics that guide strategy identification, development, and usage for certain types of educational contexts and learning objectives. Central to this chapter section is the historical and current reliance on *experimental* research to provide the scientific evidence on the effects of such strategies.

## Research and Instructional Methods

In this section, we first describe research methods used to investigate *micro-instructional strategies* that focus on teaching specific content information such as facts and concepts. Second, we examine methods used to investigate *macro-instructional* strategies such as

cooperative learning, problem-based learning, and feedback that affect the design of a course. Third, we discuss research methodologies used to investigate message design strategies.

### Micro-Instructional Strategy Research Methods

Research that focuses on component (or *micro*) strategies to help students learn specific content such as facts, concepts, and principles is a rich area of exploration and experimentation for researchers and a critical knowledge base for the development of heuristics by practitioners. The most common research approach is a true experiment that contrasts two or more strategies. The following examples are representative of the types of studies used to investigate micro-instructional strategies. The first two studies focus on fact learning and the third focuses on concept learning.

### Example 1. Rummel, Levin, and Woodward (2003)

Rummel et al. (2003) compared usage of a visual mnemonic to free study of a list of theorists' names and accomplishments. Participants were randomly assigned to either a visual mnemonic or a free study treatment. The visual mnemonic showed an image of one or more individuals with objects to provide the mnemonic device to aid recall. Dependent variables included an immediate and delayed post-test and a measure of attitude toward the effectiveness of the method. The research design resulted in a 2 (study strategy) × 2 (subtopic order) analysis of variance (ANOVA). Results showed that participants in the mnemonic group remembered more of the targeted information (i.e., information in the mnemonic) than the free study group. For designers, this suggests that visual mnemonics are beneficial in helping learners recall important information.

### Example 2. Woloshyn, Paivio, and Pressley (1994)

Woloshyn et al. (1994) presented participants with 32 factual statements, 16 of which were consistent and 16 of which were inconsistent with their beliefs. The control group was told to read the facts for understanding, whereas the elaboration (experimental) group was told to explain why the fact was true. The facts were written in three formats: traditional ("All fire trucks are not red."), refutational ("Some people think all fire trucks are red; they are not."), and inverted refutational, where the inaccurate belief was presented second ("Not all fire trucks are red, although some people think they are."). Participants completed an immediate and 14-day delayed test. The data were analyzed via a 2 (strategy) × 2 (fact) × 3 (sentence format) ANOVA. Findings indicated that the use of elaboration enhanced the recall of factual information regardless of consistency with prior beliefs; thus, an alternative strategy to rehearsal of factual information is the use of an elaboration strategy.

### Example 3. Park and Tennyson (1986)

This experiment was designed to investigate the effectiveness of different strategies for learning concepts (Park and Tennyson, 1986). The four treatments included two variations in presentation form (adaptive or fixed selection) and two sequences (generalization or discrimination rule). The result was a $2 \times 2$ factorial design using a multiple analysis of variance (MANOVA), followed by separate univariate tests (ANOVAs). This design allowed the researchers to identify significant interactions between the presentation format and sequence that provided useful heuristics for designers based on the intended outcomes; that is, the design indicated one approach for developing conceptual knowledge and another for developing procedural knowledge.

### Macro-Instructional Strategy Research Methods

Macro-strategies have a wider focus and affect a broader aspect of a course than do micro strategies. As illustrations of macro strategies, we will describe below experimental research methodologies used to investigate broader strategies domains such as personalization, feedback, pedagogical agents, problem-based learning, cooperative learning, and distance education.

### Example 1. Ku and Sullivan (2000)

Ku and Sullivan (2000) described a study in which they used personal information about each participant to personalize word problems (Anand and Ross, 1987). Participants were grouped by ability (high or low) and assigned to either a personalized or nonpersonalized treatment. Data included a nonpersonalized pretest, a post-test of personalized and nonpersonalized items, and an attitude survey. Two different analyses were performed. The first was a 2 (treatment) $\times$ 2 (ability) $\times$ 2 (test occasion: pretest vs. post-test) ANOVA. This analysis used treatment and ability as between-subject variables and test occasion as a within-subjects variable. The second analysis was a 2 (treatment) $\times$ 2 (ability) $\times$ 2 (problem type: personalized vs. nonpersonalized) ANOVA used to compare post-test performance on the two problem types. Similar to the Park and Tennyson (1986) study described above, this design allowed the investigators to identify significant interactions as well as significant main effects. The study did not find an advantage for personalized prob-

lems but did find that personalized problems were preferred by the participants. While these results are inconsistent with other studies on personalized strategies, the results support the idea that personalization may enhance motivation when solving math story problems.

### Example 2. Kim, Baylor, and Group (2006)

Another example of a macro strategy is the use of pedagogical agents (Kim et al., 2006). Participants classified as low or high competency were assigned to a proactive (initiated by agent) or responsive (initiated by participant) interaction, resulting in four treatments. Data collected included participants' self-efficiency rating, attitude toward the agent, and an achievement test that assessed recall and application. The resulting design was a 2 (competency) $\times$ 2 (interaction) between-subjects factorial design using multiple analysis of covariance (MANCOVA). The findings suggest that designers create highly competent *pedagogical agents as learning companions* (PALs) when the objectives focus on knowledge and skill acquisition; however, if the learner has low self-efficacy, he or she might be threatened by this type of expert PAL. The designer, therefore, might consider providing a less competent, more peer-like PAL.

### Example 3. Clariana and Lee (2001)

Feedback in instruction is an example of a well-researched macro strategy. Clariana and Lee (2001) examined the comparative effectiveness of five different feedback treatments. Four included multiple-choice questions paired with (1) a single try, (2) multiple try and feedback, (3) a single try and overt typing of correct response, and (4) multiple try with overt typing of the response. The fifth treatment was constructed-response questions with feedback. Data collected included immediate post-test, time-on-task data and learner responses to two interview questions. A 5 (treatment) $\times$ 7 (post-test question level) post-test-only design with repeated measures, using a mixed ANOVA, was employed. A second 5 (treatment) $\times$ 2 (time in lesson and time in test) mixed ANOVA was also used. The study found that feedback following an incorrect response plus entering the correct answer was the most effective and efficient strategy for recognition-type learning.

### Example 4. Cavalier, Klein, and Cavalier (1995)

Research on classroom-oriented strategies such as cooperative learning and problem-based learning have commonly employed true experimental and quasi-experimental designs. The study by Cavalier et al. (1995) of cooperative learning in a technical training course used a quasi-experimental design. Intact groups were assigned to either a cooperative learning treatment or control (conventional instruction) treatment, both of which were taught by the same instructor. Assessments included a post-test, attitude survey, and group interaction behaviors. ANOVA was used to compare the post-test scores of the two groups, and MANOVA was used to analyze group differences between social and cognitive interaction behaviors. Findings showed that practice in a cooperative group environment produced superior achievement as well as higher levels of social and cognitive interactions.

### Message Design Research Methods

Much of the message design research has focused on perception issues such as pictures, colors, and legibility (Fleming and Levie, 1978). More recently, the work on cognitive load theory also has been classified within the message design category (Anglin and Morrison, 2001).

### Example 1. Lamberski and Dwyer (1983)

Lamberski and Dwyer (1983) investigated the effect of color vs. black-and-white illustrations on learning. Participants read a 21-page instructional unit on the human heart that included either color or black-and-white illustrations on each page. An 80-item criterion test consisting of terminology, ability to draw a heart, identification of parts, and comprehension of heart functions was administered immediately after completing the instruction and 6 weeks later. One version of the multiple-choice items had the distracters printed in the same color as they appeared in the drawings. Participants were randomly assigned to one of four treatment groups: (1) color-coded instruction, color-coded test; (2) color-coded instruction, black-and-white test; (3) black-and-white instruction, color-coded test; and (4) black-and-white instruction, black-and-white test. The data were analyzed using ANOVA with repeated measures. The results showed that the color instruction was superior to black-and-white instruction for this task, but the color-coded tests were of no benefit.

### Example 2. Chandler and Sweller (1992)

A more recent study focused on the split-attention effect identified by Sweller and his colleagues. In a traditional textbook, readers must split their attention between the narrative explanation in the text and a table or graphic. In the current study (Chandler and Sweller, 1992), a revised version of the text that integrated the explanatory text with the graphic information was created. A t-test was used to assess the differences between the split-attention and integrated

groups' scores on each item of the post-test. The authors concluded from the findings that an integrated design used to reduce split attention resulted in both improved performance and more efficient learning.

The above discussion has illustrated the types of research methods used to investigate the effectiveness of micro, macro, and message design strategies. All examples were of true or rigorous quasi-experiments, thus reflecting the strong historical preference in the educational technology field for investigating instructional strategies via experimentation. But, have these preferences of educational technology researchers diminished over the years? In the following section, we examine the trends through an analysis of published articles in a leading educational technology research journal, *ETR&D*.

## The Prevalence of Experimentation in Intervention Research in Educational Technology: A Trend Analysis of *ETR&D*

As described in an earlier section, Hsieh et al. (2005) recently asked if educational intervention research is on the decline. They defined intervention research as strategies for affecting cognitive, affective, and behavioral outcomes. The analysis of four educational psychology journals revealed a drop in the percentage of intervention studies published. In 1983, 55% of the articles were intervention studies, but in 1995 and 2004 the percentages fell to 47% and 35%, respectively. For this chapter section, we conducted a similar analysis on the Research section of *ETR&D* for the same years.

### Method

Included in the analyses were articles published in 1983* in the *Educational Communications and Technology Journal* (*ECTJ*; the predecessor of *ETR&D*) and from the Research section of *ETR&D* (1994–2005). Excluded from the analyses were studies, whether experiments or other designs, included as part of special issues from the Development section of the journal. The included articles were classified as "true experiments" or "other," with the latter category further classified as survey, case study, qualitative, theoretical, literature review, or other. For the true experimental studies only, participants were classified as K–12 students, college students, or adults (i.e., not enrolled in a college-level course). The type of assessments (achievement/performance and attitude) were noted if there were multiple forms of achievement; for example, a post-test that assessed both recall and application of

---

\* 1983 is used as a benchmark as in the study by Hsieh et al. (2005).

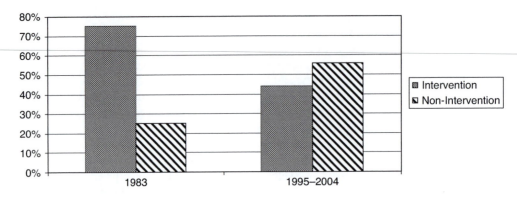

**Figure 54.1** Percentage of intervention studies published in *ERT&D*.

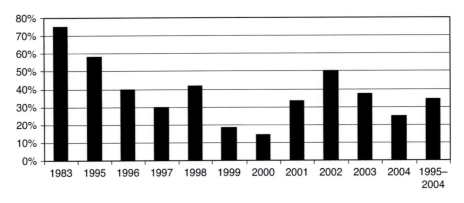

**Figure 54.2** Percentage of true experiments published in *ERT&D*.

the content was considered a multiple assessment. Time of testing was classified as immediate, delayed, or immediate and delayed. The length of the intervention (e.g., treatment) was classified as less than 3 hours, 1 day or less, 1 week or less, and more than 1 week. Last, the technology of interest in the study was classified as computer, print, television, audio, or other.

### Results and Implications

Consistent with Hsieh et al. (2005), the data show (see Figure 54.1) a declining trend for intervention studies during the 1995–2004 period. In 1983, 75% of the articles published were intervention studies. For the 1995–2004 time period, however, intervention studies accounted for only 44% of the published papers. Figure 54.2 shows the number of intervention studies that used a true experimental (e.g., random assignment of participants) design. Following the pattern for intervention studies in general, there is a decreasing trend in the usage of true experiments in the published *ETR&D* research.

An analysis of the non-intervention studies (see Figure 54.3) provides some insights into the type of articles published by the Research section. In 1983,

non-intervention studies accounted for only 25% of published articles. The non-intervention studies were equally distributed between theoretical and literature reviews and qualitative studies. Theoretical papers are the most frequent type of non-intervention study published, and qualitative studies account for the second most frequent type in the 1994–2004 time frame. Our findings regarding the drop in the prevalence of intervention studies in educational technology thus mirror those of Hsieh and colleagues (2005) for educational psychology in general.

K–12 students were used as participants in 49% of the studies in the 1995–2004 articles, followed by college students (43%). The majority (64%) of the interventions lasted 3 hours or less; in contrast, 20% lasted more than a week. These intervention times may be the result of the number of studies conducted in a K–12 classroom. This bimodal distribution suggests that the studies are either a one-time investigation of a micro-instructional strategy or a longer examination of a macro strategy such as cooperative learning. Given the large number of instructional designers employed in business, military, government, and healthcare settings, these data suggest an opportunity for collaborative partnerships between practitioners and researchers

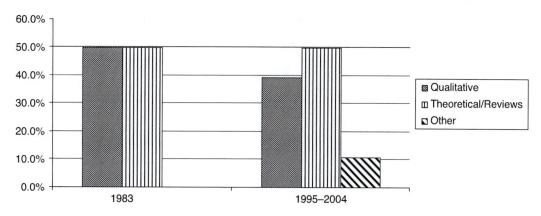

**Figure 54.3** Other studies published in *ETR&D*.

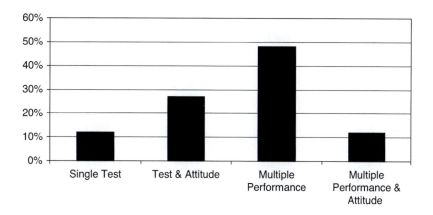

**Figure 54.4** Types of outcome data.

to conduct studies in workplace settings using realistic materials with participants who have a need and possible motivation for learning the content. Such studies might provide the field with an additional perspective and data on micro- and macro-instructional strategies.

A total of 86% of the studies from 1995 to 2004 used only an immediate achievement or performance measure. Further, 14% used both an immediate and delayed assessment. As shown in Figure 54.4, almost 50% of the studies used multiple achievement/performance measures; however, only 27% of the studies employing a single assessment collected attitude data, and only 12% employing multiple forms of assessment collected attitude data. Although almost half of the studies used multiple achievement assessments, the data suggest that newer studies should consider richer data collections that add not only instruments to assess higher levels of learning but also collection of data on time on task and individual use of the materials (e.g., instructional path/selections), as well as attitudinal data.

Our final analysis focuses on the type of technology used in the intervention studies. Figure 54.5 shows the primary technology of interest used. The

data for 1983 illustrate a usage of varied types of technology, whereas in the 1995–2004 articles computer technology was dominant in the intervention studies analyzed.

Have educational technology researchers become less active in using experimental designs? Although our data do show an increase in qualitative studies, the more prominent gain actually is reflected in the writing of theoretical articles and literature reviews. The latter trend may be indicative of Hsieh and colleagues' (2005) concern about the cost and complexity for the typical academician of creating the stimulus materials and implementing experiments on meaningful instructional strategies. In 1983, it was relatively easy to create television, print, audio, and projected materials, such as 35-mm slides for stimulus materials. Similarly, it was fairly straightforward to create simple computer programs on a microcomputer to serve as the instructional presentation for experiments. The trend for the 1995–2004 period, however, has been to focus on computer technology for delivery of the intervention treatment. The complexity and cost of producing multimedia materials

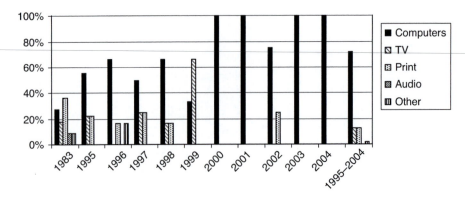

**Figure 54.5** Types of technology used in studies.

may have significantly limited the number of individual researchers with either the expertise or resources required to develop the individual treatments. The complexity and cost of technology, however, have always been an issue in the field of educational technology; for example, compare the cost and complexity of Hoban's (1953) study that used an existing U.S. Army 16-mm training film to that of Levonian's (1963) study in which a specific film was created for the study. Although the use of technology to deliver a treatment has costs, additional benefits are derived, such as the automated collection and scoring of data. If the cost and complexity of technology are major barriers to conducting intervention research, then researchers might want to consider using print as the primary technology and focusing on the instructional strategy as suggested by Clark (1983, 1994). Nonetheless, the current era of scientifically based research is placing more emphasis than ever before on determining the effects of real-world interventions (programs, models, strategies) in raising learner achievement (Shavelson et al., 2002; Slavin, 2006). From an external validity standpoint, receptivity to *basic* research performed with artificial, simplified lesson material or delivery systems is likely to be much lower than was the case several decades ago.

## Factors Impacting the Rigor of Experiments on Instructional Strategies

Thus far, we have examined varied experimental designs, their application to instructional strategies research, and trends in educational technology strategies research over time. In this concluding section, we briefly overview, for the benefit of researchers and consumers of research, major factors that impact the rigor of experiments on instructional strategies.

### Types of Validity Threats

Rigorous experiments are valued for being high in *internal validity*, defined as the degree to which the design controls the effects extraneous variables (Borg et al., 1993). Common examples of the latter include the control and experimental groups differing in abilities, one group receiving more time to learn or exposure to a better teacher than the other, or an historical event (e.g., an after-school program) impacting the fidelity of the treatment-control manipulation. In 1963, Campbell and Stanley identified different classes of such threats. Researchers interested in conducting experiments on instructional design and technology topics should be familiar with these factors.

*Validity threat* means only that a factor has the *potential* to bias results. Knowing about validity threats gives the experimenter a framework for evaluating the particular situation and making a judgment about its severity. Such knowledge may also permit actions to be taken to limit the influences of the validity threat in question. Examples are as follows:

- Concern that a pretest may bias post-test results leads to the decision by the experimenter not to use a pretest.
- Concern that two intact groups to be used for treatment comparisons (quasi-experimental design) may not be equal in ability leads to the decision to pretest participants on ability and employ a statistical adjustment (analysis of covariance) if the groups significantly differ.
- Concern that participants may mature or drop out during the experiment leads to the decision to shorten the length of the treatment period, use different types of participants, or introduce incentives to fulfill all participation requirements.

- Concern that the post-test may differ in difficulty from the pretest leads to the decision to use each test form as the pretest for half the students and the post-test for the other half.

Even after all reasonable actions have been taken to eliminate the operation of one or more validity threats, the experimenter must still make a judgment about the internal validity of the experiment overall. Where internal validity is seriously compromised, the experiment needs to be redone. In cases less severe, experimenters have the obligation to note the validity threats and qualify their interpretations of results accordingly.

## Balancing Internal and External Validity

The quest for high internal validity orients researchers to design experiments in which treatment manipulations can be tightly controlled. In the process, using naturalistic conditions (e.g., real classrooms) can prove challenging, given the many extraneous sources of variance that are likely to operate in those contexts; for example, the extensive research conducted on verbal learning in the 1960s and 1970s largely involved instructional strategies for increasing associative learning of simple words and nonsense syllables (Underwood, 1966). With simplicity and artificiality come greater opportunity for control.

This orientation directly supports the objectives of the basic learning or educational psychology researcher whose interests lie in testing the generalizable principles and laws associated with treatment strategies, independent of the specific delivery methods and contextual conditions (e.g., teacher preparation and attitude, classroom structure and resources) involved in their implementation (Ross, 2003). Educational technology researchers, however, are directly interested in the interaction of medium and method (Kozma, 1991, 1994; Ullmer, 1994). To learn about this interaction, realistic media applications rather than artificial ones need to be established. In other words, external validity becomes as important a concern as internal validity.

## Basic-Applied Design Replications

Once a principle has been thoroughly tested in highly controlled experiments, the natural progression is to evaluate its use in a real-world application. Making the leap to a real-life application, however, runs the risk of clouding the underlying causes of obtained treatment effects due to their confounding with extraneous variables (Ross, 2005).

### Levin's Stage Model

In discussing these issues, Levin (2004) proposed a model of educational intervention research (Levin and O'Donnell, 1999). Stages 1 and 2 consist of formulating ideas and hypotheses and conducting initial observations and pilot work. Stage 2 encompasses controlled laboratory experiments (high internal validity) on the strategies of interest, along with classroom-based demonstrations and design experiments. *Demonstration experiments* involve implementing the instructional strategy in a single classroom or outside a classroom with a particular group of students. Although realism may be high, internal validity will likely be quite low due to the failure to control the effects of extraneous factors that are intrinsically part of the single classroom, and, because there is only one classroom, generalizability to other settings, and thus external validity, likewise may be low. The *design experiment*, as described by Levin (2004), is comparable to popular forms of research in instructional technology, such as design-based research, developmental research, design research, and formative research (Wang and Hannafin, 2005; also see Richey and Klein in this chapter). Such studies are also conducted in authentic learning environments, but unlike traditional experiments the implementation of the instructional strategies is not fixed but modified over time based on formative evaluation data and associated instructional design decisions. Stage 3 consists of *randomized field trials* (RFTs) whereby the intervention is implemented under realistic conditions with randomly selected participants. Outcomes are then compared to those for participants the randomly selected control group.

### Units of Random Assignment

In conducting RFTs, what options exist for the units of randomization? As the first author has described (Ross, 2005), the most powerful approach is to randomize at the *student level* within classes. Half of the students in each participating classroom are assigned to the experimental program and the other half to the control program. Classroom teachers and conditions are thus identical for both groups, thereby eliminating major validity threats. A further benefit is increasing the potential for large sample sizes (and greater statistical power) because the units of analysis will be individual students rather than whole classes or schools. Unfortunately, unless the control and experimental interventions can be administered individually and unobtrusively by computers or self-paced manuals, they may be mutually interfering or create unreasonable delivery demands on teachers (Ross, 2005).

If student-level assignment is not feasible, researchers may next consider randomizing at the *classroom level*; for example, half of the fourth-grade classes at participating schools would be designated to use Program A and the other half to use Program B. The major advantage is that each classroom (and teacher) is exposed to only one program. A downside, however, is reducing sample size and statistical power by treating whole classrooms rather than students as the randomized observation units. Researchers might also encounter resistance from principals and teachers concerned about creating a schism in the school's academic program. Actualizing what researchers sometimes call the *John Henry effect*, control group teachers might attempt to outperform the experimental group by emulating their strategies or simply trying harder.

A third approach is to randomize at the *school level*; for example, half of the schools eligible to use the experimental program in a district would be randomly selected to implement it and the other half to serve as control schools. Although this design keeps instructional activities consistent within each school, its major disadvantage is drastically reduced sample size due to schools being the units of randomization. Much happens in a school separate from program effects. Only by comparing the experimental and control programs at a sufficiently large number of schools (say, 20–30 for each) can we gain confidence that program effects (not school variables) are the primary cause of achievement differences.

### Replication Experiments

Levin's model just reviewed encompasses a progression from nonexperimental, demonstration, and design studies to RFTs. A complementary model proposed by the present authors (Ross and Morrison, 1989) promotes a replication of a highly controlled, experimental design with an applied design examining a comparable instructional strategy. Specifically, Experiment 1, the basic research part, would examine the instructional strategies of interest by establishing a relatively high degree of control and high internal validity. Experiment 2, the applied component, would then reexamine the same learning variables by establishing more realistic conditions and high external validity. Consistency of findings across experiments would provide strong convergent evidence supporting the obtained effects and underlying theoretical principles. Inconsistent findings, however, would suggest influences of intervening variables that alter the effects of the variables of interest when converted from their pure form to realistic applications. Such contamination may often represent *media effects*, as might occur, for example, when strategies used with print material are natu-

rally made more powerful and effectual via interactive computer-mediated communications (Lou et al., 2006) and adaptive computer-based instruction (CBI). In the latter case, for example, a learner who confuses, say, discovery learning with inquiry learning in response to an inserted lesson question may be branched immediately to a remedial CBI frame that differentiates between the two approaches, whereas his or her counterpart in a parallel print lesson might experience the same type of feedback by having to reference the response selected on an answer page and manually locate the appropriate response-sensitive feedback in another section of the lesson. The next implied step of a replication design would be further experimentation on the nature and locus of any unique effects associated with the applied context.

As an example of basic-applied replication studies, Morrison and colleagues (1995) examined uses of different feedback strategies in learning from CBI. Built into the experimental design was a factor representing the conditions under which college students participated in the experiment—simulated or realistic. Interestingly, the results showed similar relative effects of the different feedback conditions. Examination of learning *process* variables, however, further revealed that students in the realistic conditions performed better, while making greater and more appropriate use of instructional support options provided in association with the feedback. Although the experimentation on the simulated condition was valuable as a basic and purer test of theoretical assumptions, the field experiment provided more valid insights into how the different forms of feedback likely would be used in combination with other learning resources on an actual learning task.

## Are Media Instructional Strategies?

A popular focus of past research on instructional strategies in educational technology was comparing different types of media-based instruction to one another or to teacher-based instruction to determine which approach was "best." The fallacy or, at least, unreasonableness of this orientation, now known as *media comparison studies*, was forcibly explicated by Clark (1983) in his now classic article (see also Hagler and Knowlton, 1987; Petkovich and Tennyson, 1984; Ross and Morrison, 1989; Salomon and Clark, 1977). Clark argued that media were analogous to grocery trucks that carry food but do not in themselves provide nourishment (i.e., instruction).

For present purposes, these considerations present a strong case against experimentation that simply compares media. This traditional type of media comparison study still remains prevalent today and, in fact, may have been rejuvenated from the current emphasis, spurred by No Child Left Behind, on conducting rigorous intervention research to determine what works in education (Berliner, 2002; Slavin, 2002). As an example, a study currently completing its third and final year is using a large-scale randomized field trial to determine the efficacy of technology applications designed to improve student learning in math and reading (http://edtech.mathematica-mpr.com/). The basic design involves random assignment of teachers within schools to treatments using commercial tutorial software programs in these subjects and to control (no software) treatments. Students taught by the two groups of teachers are then compared according to how they perform on standardized tests. As of this writing, the results have not been released, but it seems fair to speculate that, if the control teachers used equivalent time to provide quality supplementary instruction (using workbooks or cooperative learning), then the two comparison groups might perform the same. Is the effectiveness of *technology* really being tested here or is it the efficacy of the types of instructional strategies the software developers chose to incorporate in their programs? A more meaningful focus, it would seem, is to analyze how unique attributes of the technology enable specialized or improved usage of specific instructional strategies (e.g., remedial branching) that work effectively for certain types of learners and contexts.

A second type of inappropriate media comparison experiment is to create artificially comparable alternative media presentations, such that both variations contain identical attributes but use different modes of delivery. So, for example, if a researcher wants to explore the effects of the computer as a medium for distance education (DE) learning in algebra (Lou et al., 2006), it makes little sense to develop a course that is an exact replica (90-minute lectures and all) of the traditional algebra course used at the same schools. In fact, the first author is currently part of a team conducting a randomized field trial of a hybrid algebra course that combines DE with in-class teacher coaching. For both educational and scientific purposes, the primary interest is making the hybrid course as powerful as possible given the unique capabilities of the combined DE and teacher-based interventions. The instructional strategies embedded in the hybrid and traditional courses will necessarily differ but represent realistic and ecologically valid interventions.

One recommended alternative to media comparisons is to test *a priori* hypotheses of differences between the two media presentations based directly on analyses of their different attributes (Kozma, 1991, 1994). It might be hypothesized, for example, that for teaching an instructional unit on a cardiac surgery pro-

cedure, a conventional lecture presentation might be superior to an interactive video presentation for facilitating retention of factual information, whereas the converse would be true for facilitating meaningful understanding of concepts. The rationale for these hypotheses would be based on analyses of the special capabilities (embedded instructional strategies) of each medium in relation to type of material taught. Findings would be used to support or refute these assumptions.

A second recommended study, which we have called *media replications* (Ross and Morrison, 1989), examines the consistency of effects of given instructional strategies delivered by alternative media. Consistent findings, if obtained, are treated as corroborative evidence to strengthen theoretical understanding of the instructional variables in question as well as claims concerning the associated strategy's effectiveness for learning. If inconsistent outcomes are obtained, methods and theoretical assumptions are reexamined and the target strategy subjected to further empirical tests using diverse learners and conditions. Thus, media replications provide valuable tests of the generalizability of the effects of particular instructional strategies.

## Summary

The focus of this chapter section is research on instructional strategies involving applications of educational technology. Major concepts and points addressed included the following:

- Experimental studies have been the preferred choice of researchers for investigating instructional strategies.
- Usage of experimental designs in educational technology and in educational psychology research in general has declined over the past several decades. A primary reason seems to be the increased logistical demands of conducting experiments on meaningful interventions; another reason has been the growing popularity of qualitative and correlational research. The current emphasis on scientifically based research, however, spurred by the No Child Left Behind legislation, is creating a resurgence in the popularity and status of experimental studies.
- True or randomized experiments involve randomly assigning participants to treatment conditions. Quasi-experiments, however, use preexisting groups or convenience samples that are not randomly composed. By reducing sampling bias as a validity threat, true experiments typically have greater internal validity—

the ability to attribute outcomes to the treatment alone—than do quasi-experiments.

- Instructional strategies are the prescribed sequences and methods of instruction to achieve an objective. The particular prescriptions are not only determined by the content and performance specified in the learning objectives but also by underlying learning theory. Practical and scientifically grounded *heuristics* can be derived to guide the identification of strategies for teaching certain types of content, such as facts, concepts, principles and rules, procedures, interpersonal skills, and attitudes.

- *Micro-instructional* strategies focus on teaching specific content information such as facts and concepts. *Macro-instructional* strategies such as cooperative learning, problem-based learning, and feedback represent broader, more complex instructional strategies that affect the design of a course. Message design research has focused on perception issues such as pictures, colors, and legibility. More recently, the work on cognitive load theory also has been classified within the message design category.

- In examining research design trends in articles published over several decades in *Educational Technology Research and Development* (*ETR&D*), we found a decline in experiments on instructional strategies and an increase in qualitative studies. The complexity and cost of producing multimedia materials may have significantly limited the number of individual researchers with either the expertise or resources needed to develop the individual treatments.

- Researchers interested in conducting rigorous experiments on instructional strategies need to be aware of potential validity threats such as history, maturation, testing, instrumentation, statistical regression, selection, mortality, and diffusion of treatments. Achieving balance between internal validity (control) and external validity, and between basic vs. applied research (generalizability) is also important.

- Comparing media is less important scientifically and practically than well-designed experiments investigating: (1) which instructional strategies are most effectual and practical using different media, and (2) how the effects of instructional strategies are replicated or mitigated by media characteristics.

# RESEARCH ON EDUCATIONAL TECHNOLOGIES

*Robert D. Hannafin and Michael Young*

*Technology ... Does it work?* There is probably not a more frequently asked question of, and by, educational technology researchers. It is asked by teachers, now expected to wisely integrate new tools; by parents shopping for a new home computer that will help their children in school; by school boards, who need to justify expensive network improvements; and by the taxpayers, who suffer a higher mil rate to pay for them. It is a fair, and on the face of it, simple question, one that so-called experts should be able to answer; however, despite a substantial research effort, the answer has not come and if anything has led to more questions. In this section, we use the question of *Does it work?* to frame the discussion of research in technology.

Germane to answering this simple question are issues of research methodology, contemporary understanding of how people think and learn, and consensus among educational researchers as to what constitutes evidence of improved learning and enhanced thinking abilities; for example, some would argue that learning occurs only in the heads of the users and thus would accept a test of facts and procedures retrieved from memory as evidence of learning. Such constructivists contend that knowledge is accumulated and stored by the brain, much as a computer stores and retrieves information. Others, however, would argue that knowledge and practice are deeply intertwined in the situations and context in which they occur. They would argue that we do not want students who know disembodied facts and cannot apply them to solve problems, nor do we want robots who act without reflection or understanding of the procedures they are doing. So, from this perspective, knowing must be enacted and is referred to, variously, as situated, embedded, and embodied cognition. For this group, test performance is not enough. They seek evidence that students can use their knowledge in context, in the lived-in world, to address problems that matter. Such differences in perspective lead to very different conceptions for "it" and "works" when asking *Does it work?*

In this section, we discuss what *it* is and how the definition has evolved over the past 30 years. We briefly examine a sample of studies over this period to provide examples of that evolution. The blurring of the boundaries between design and research is then discussed in the context of several recent technology-enhanced learning environments (Wang and Hannafin, 2005). Finally, we describe several of the data analysis and research design challenges presented by these new environments and the reconception of *it*. In this section, we do not hope to cover all types of research relevant to this discussion; rather we hope to stimulate discussion and to provide a framework for that discussion.

## When "It" Was Simple

### What Is "It"?

*It* can be defined for our purposes as any treatment that uses technology to affect a predetermined outcome. The question asked over the years by stakeholders and researchers alike has often taken the form: *Do computers improve learning?* Hopes were high in the 1970s and 1980s that the computer alone would positively impact learning, this despite the fact that previous media innovations (e.g., film, radio, television) had consistently failed to have the expected effect (Cuban, 1986). The computer generation of media comparison studies was exclusively experimental and quasi-experimental and examined whether one delivery medium (computer) was favored over another (book or worksheet). In a typical media comparison study, all other variables were controlled in an attempt to prove that instruction delivered by computers was more effective than the same instruction delivered via traditional means (for a summary, see Clark, 1983). To prove causality, it was necessary to keep constant all other instructional noise like instructional strategies and methods; thus, these studies, when well designed, enabled researchers to answer the question *Does it work?*, where *it* was simply the computer, and *work* was performance on a post-test or some other learning outcome.

The value of this line of inquiry was questioned by several researchers, most notably Clark (1983) in his seminal work, "Reconsidering Research on Learning from Media." Clark argued that efforts to privilege the role of any medium in learning should stop altogether. He pointed out that many of the studies attributing learning gains to media either had unexplored alternative explanations or had unintentionally attributed the impact of the instructional methods to the delivery medium, with *methods* defined as "the conditions which can be implemented to foster the acquisition of competence" (Glaser, 1976, p. 1, as cited in Clark, 1983).

### Technology as Conveyances: The CAI Era

The majority of the empirical technology research from the late 1970s through the 1990s would fall under what Salomon and Clark (1977) and later Clark (1983) termed learning *with* media. These studies used technology (usually computers) as conveyances of the treatment (e.g., computer-assisted instruction, or CAI)

to examine and isolate other variables of interest (Clark, 1983), but, although computers were not the variable of study, the research goal of both categories was the same—that is, to experimentally isolate variables to prove a causal relationship with learning. For educational technology research to be taken seriously and to empirically prove causality, studies must have treatment fidelity. This need can be traced, according to Ross and Morrison (1989; this chapter), to the field's roots in educational psychology and the inherent value placed on studies with high internal validity. We identified three types of studies that used technology (mainly computers) as conveyances: aptitude–treatment interaction, learner control, and in-program learner behaviors studies. We discuss each in turn.

### Aptitude–Treatment Interactions

Some of the work where computers were conveyances of the treatment include aptitude–treatment interaction (ATI) research (Cronbach and Snow, 1981; DiVesta, 1975) where *aptitude* is a learner's incoming knowledge, skills, and personality traits and *treatment* is the condition or environment that supports learning (Shute, 1993). ATI research began before computers became popular, but many researchers took advantage of the computer's ability to customize instructional treatments (e.g., adapting questions to prior performance or skipping presentations based on pretest performance) to renew the effort to find elusive interactions with learner aptitudes (Cronbach and Snow, 1981). Unfortunately, despite the design flexibility the computers afforded researchers, identifying stable ATIs that could prescribe instructional programs remained elusive.

### Learner Control

Learner control studies represent another line of inquiry in the computer-as-conveyance category. In these studies, computers were typically used to allow learners some control over elements of their instruction and to track learner choices and options use during an instructional program. Kinzie et al. (1988), for example, found that students given control over content review scored higher on a post-test than students without that control. Gray (1987) reported that students controlling the sequence of their instruction scored higher on one of two achievement measures than learners under program control. Ross et al. (1989) found that college students granted choice of presentation medium (print vs. computer) for their instruction achieved more than students with no choice. Tennyson and associates noted that college students benefited from controlling elements of their own instruction, but only when advised on their performance relative to program criteria (Tennyson and Buttrey, 1980; Tennyson and Rothen, 1979). On the other hand, students did not always make wise instructional choices. Pollock and Sullivan (1990) reported that learners receiving required practice scored higher on a post-test than learners who could bypass the practice. Tennyson and Rothen (1979) cautioned that students tend to make poor instructional choices more frequently in complex instructional tasks, and Carrier (1984) reported that this was also true when they lack sufficient prior knowledge. Researchers have also noted that learners given guidance by their instructional program seem to make better choices and achieve more than learners given no guidance (Ross and Rakow, 1981; Tennyson, 1980).

A great many studies also examined student ability, with and without learner control. The hope here was that because the computer was infinitely patient and because of its ability to deliver large amounts of practice and feedback and to adapt instruction dynamically to adjust to learner needs, low-ability learners in particular would benefit. On balance, there is some evidence that lower ability students benefit more from program control than when they are afforded some control (Goetzfried and Hannafin, 1985; Ross and Rakow, 1981). Hativa (1988) found that high-ability students in a learner-control treatment spent more time on task than low-ability students. Others have concluded that low-ability learners lack the metacognitive skills to manage their own instruction (Chung and Reigeluth, 1992; Hannafin, 1984). Thus, ceding control to learners is effective in certain circumstances but not in others (for a summary, see Hannafin, 1984).

### In-Program Learner Behaviors

Many studies have used the computer to track learner en route behaviors such as option-selection patterns and time on task during CAI programs (Hannafin and Sullivan, 1995; Hicken et al., 1992). In studies by Carrier and her associates, sixth graders were found to select more options earlier in a program on advertising than they did toward the end of the program (Carrier et al., 1984, 1986), a pattern also detected by Hannafin and Sullivan (1996) among high-school students working in a geometry CAI program. Kinzie and associates (Kinzie and Sullivan, 1989; Kinzie et al., 1988) reported that students in a learner-control group, despite bypassing instances of content review, spent a similar amount of time overall on the instructional program as did learners who were required to see the review. Tennyson (1980) found that college students given control over the amount and sequence of elements of an instructional program spent less time on the program and chose fewer options than students who were advised by the program. According to Carrier and colleagues (1986), tracking on-task behaviors

is important to understanding why some learners make more prudent choices than others.

These experimental and quasi-experimental studies sought to control conditions and isolate the independent variable (*it*) to prove an impact on learning. *It* was simple, or pure. We do not mean to suggest, however, that the research was simple, or simplistic. It is arguably more difficult to design and conduct an experimental study with high internal validity than any other research design (see Ross and Morrison in this chapter), but the value of tightly controlled laboratory studies and the separation of media and methods began to be questioned by educational technology researchers in the late 1980s.

## Then "It" Got Complicated

### "It" and the Great Media Debate

Kozma (1991, 1994) agreed with most of Clark's (1983, 1994) arguments but took exception to the somewhat circular nature of part of Clark's logic. Kozma argued that if, as he believed, powerful learning opportunities reside in the interactions between method and medium and if researchers were not allowed to look at those in the name of design integrity, then how could they ever be detected? Thus, in the context of this discussion, Kozma was calling for a broader, more inclusive definition of *it*, conceding the inability to know exactly what part of a treatment caused learning to occur; whereas, Clark argued for a definition of *it* as media alone, insisting that was the only way we can prove causality. In many ways, this great media debate exemplifies the tension described by Ross and Morrison between the need for rigorous research design (internal validity) and the need to build realistic, ecologically valid instructional environments (external validity).

The impact of Clark's work was profound. It caused many researchers to rethink their designs, be more cautious about causality claims, and to acknowledge limitations at work when confounding factors are suspected, but his most lasting contribution is perhaps prompting a lively discussion that eventually led to many clarifications. Together, Clark and Kozma sparked a conversation that eventually led to more accurate definitions and clearer vocabulary for a generation of researchers. One merely needs to cite the phrase "grocery truck analogy" to be universally understood as referring to the separation of media and method. The great media debate in a sense was all about the question *Does it work*? Though the great debate focused on just the delivery medium, it raised issues that related quite directly to how the field perceived *it*, what was considered good research, and what was worth investigating.

Before Kozma's (1991) response to Clark, Ross and Morrison (1989) argued that, because educational technology researchers tend to have a genuine interest in the technology aspect of the treatments they investigate, it was reasonable to value the interaction of medium and method, rather than viewing it as an unwanted source of error variance. Thus, they argued, external validity—or the extent to which results can be applied to real-life settings—should be an important design consideration. They also said that separating media from methods may not always be desirable, in a sense giving the field permission to consider a broader definition of *it*.

### OLEs and TELEs

About the same time Ross and Morrison (1989) were making this case to education technology researchers from a methodological point of view, a powerful instructional movement emerged, with competing theoretical assumptions that unapologetically broke many conventions that caused earlier debate. The phrase "open learning environments" (OLEs) has been used to describe a wide array of instructional projects based, to varying degrees, on constructivist principles. Constructivism as a theory of how people learn had been around for a number of years, but little attempt was made to instantiate any of its tenets into an instructional model or product that would enable researchers to test the theory. In other words, constructivist learning remained a theoretical proposition—one could experience it in real-life situations, but no one knew how constructivist learning could be proactively applied toward the design of instruction in schools. Advances in technology changed that by allowing problem situations to be enacted in realistic and engaging contexts. In this section, we use the term *technology-enhanced learning environments* (TELEs), which was used by Wang and Hannafin* (2005, p. 5) to describe "technology based learning and instructional systems through which students acquire skills or knowledge, usually with the help of teachers or facilitators, learning support tools, and technological resources."

## Then "It" Became a "Cloud of Correlated Variables"

Another pivot point in the evolution of *it* was the Salomon et al. (1991) essay in *Educational Researcher* where they argued that learning effects were possible for learners who mindfully engaged with intelligent

technologies such as TELEs. One example the authors cited was where students who used the computer program STELLA (Richmond, 1985) to construct mathematical models of, say, ecological systems were able to manipulate variables, values, and generate and test hypotheses *without* needing to first memorize discrete facts. The tool, they argued, allowed learners to organize ideas according to deep rather than surface criteria, an ability more typical of the expert than novice learner. They asserted that such mindful partnerships in TELEs support the notion that computers can be used as what Pea (1985) called *cognitive tools*. Further, they argued that the tools (Salomon et al., 1991, p. 4):

> … potentially allow a learner to function at a level that transcends the limitations of his cognitive systems. …Indeed it can be argued that work with specific computer tools might accomplish more than just enabling the beginner to do the same thing, faster and with less effort. These tools might redefine and restructure the learning or performance task much as the pencil has qualitatively restructured the act of remembering. …In sum, the intellectual partnership with such tools can change the ratio between accessing prior knowledge and construction of new knowledge in favor of the latter. …A partnership between a human and technology could be far more "intelligent" than the performance of the human alone.

They then made the case that the impact of technology is cultural, and cannot be measured in isolation (Salomon et al., 1991, p. 8):

> … profound effects of intelligent technology on minds can take place only when major changes in the culture take place as well. No important impact can be expected when the same old activity is carried out with a technology that makes it a bit faster or easier; the activity itself has to change, and such a change cannot take place in a cultural vacuum. …But this means that it is not the technology alone affecting minds but the whole "cloud of correlated variables"**—technology, activity, goal, setting, teacher's role, culture—exerting their combined effects.

### Jasper Woodbury Series

One of the earliest and best known examples of a TELE was the *Jasper Woodbury* series developed by the Cognition and Technology Group at Vanderbilt (CTGV, 1990, 1993). The work by the CTGV took seriously the idea that learning, in this case middle-school mathematics concepts such as distance–rate–time, are "situated" and that the best situations are those that have many attributes of realism, those that "ring true" for

---

* Wang and Hannafin based this description on work by Aleven et al. (2003), Land (2000), and Shapiro et al. (1995).

---

** The authors credit Scarr (1985) with this analogy.

everyday cognition (Rogoff and Lave, 1999) and engage one's "cognition in the wild" (Hutchins, 1995). This perspective led to very different research questions, specifically different conceptions of what *it* should be. And, by instantiating a theory of situated learning that takes as a working premise the nonlinear multidimensional interactive nature of learning, simple static (pre–post) assessments of its success were not enough. To detect if the *Jasper Woodbury* series *worked* required as a starting premise that assessment itself also had to be situated, inherently the result of student–environment interactions, in the service of both student learning and effective teaching, and different in each new circumstance.

### Design-Based Research

Struggling with similar issues, Brown (1992) proposed a hybrid cycle of prototyping, classroom field testing, and laboratory study that drew from the work of engineering research, and she called this approach *design research*. Design research combines qualitative and quantitative analysis and rejects the call for educational research to make scientific, controlled studies that prove causality the *sine qua non* of scholarly work in education. Using mixed methods optimizes both internal and external validity simultaneously while acknowledging other forms of test validity such as ecological and systemic validity (Messick, 1995). Design-based research tends to theoretically align with the situated cognition tradition, which suggests that assessments should be seamless because they themselves are the result of embedded and embodied cognition. In sum, the techniques of design research seek a dialectic between theory and practice that contributes in a scholarly way to both activities.

This approach continues to be controversial (see the special issue of *Educational Researcher*, 32(1), 2003) but has ignited a dialog among researchers as to the value of seeking only causal results that rarely generalize to school setting, or descriptions of settings that fail to inform theoretical model-building. Iterative techniques that use both qualitative and quantitative analyses for multilevel descriptions of learning provide quite a challenge to most existing research frameworks, because they reject the standard linear model and instead propose nonlinear multidimensional complex systems that are at the very least emergent from student and environment interactions across time. Such effects are not available for averaging across participants and require the unit of analysis focus on the agent–environment interactions rather than either the student's performance or the environment alone (Kulikowich and Young, 2001).

In the spring 2006,* we had the privilege to interview developers of seven renowned TELEs who have been trying to answer *Does it work?* by conducting design research (in some form) as advocated by Brown (1992). We next discuss three of those: *Model-It*, *Alien Rescue*, and *River City*. Each TELE is different, to be sure, with distinct learning assumptions and radically different design considerations; however, like the CTGV, they share the premise that learning is situated, inextricably linked to the environment, including the medium (CTGV, 1990; Kozma, 1994). Also driving the development of these robust and student-centered TELEs was the reconception of what constitutes learning, or, again in the context of our super ordinate question, what is meant by *work* when asking *Does it work?* These programs sought to support deep understanding and elicit performances as evidence of that understanding.

### Model-It

The designers of Model-It sought to create a *cognitive tool* that was flexible and adaptive, that would allow for the building and testing of systems models with varying degrees of complexity, and that would facilitate a learner's transition to more expert-like modeling practices and reasoning (Metcalf et al., 2000). The designers believed that the computer could amplify the range of activities possible to learners, and they argued that computer-based learning environments in which the learner actively constructs an artifact have strong potential for promoting cognitive growth (Jackson et al., 1995). Citing Salomon (1990), Jackson and colleagues argued that cognitive capacities are extended while using visualization technology; not only do learners accomplish more with the computer than would be possible without, but they also engage in much more mindful learning with computers than without computers. During the first implementation phase of Model-It, eighth-grade students built a model of a pond's ecosystem after systematically taking measurements of the different chemicals found in the pond over time. The researchers found that, when students were able to collect and analyze authentic data and represent those data in a working model that accurately portrayed the interrelationships among the elements in the ecosystem, they were also able to test and refine their mental representations and understandings of that system (Metcalf et al., 2000).

---

* As part of a graduate course in interactive learning environments, the authors interviewed Dr. Elliot Soloway (Model-It), Dr. Janet Kolodner (Learning by Design), Dr. James Slotta (WISE), Dr. Chris Dede (River City), Dr. Sasha Barab (Quest Atlantis), Drs. Min Liu and Susan Pederson (Alien Rescue), and Drs. Thomas Brush and John Saye (Persistent Issues in History).

## *Alien Rescue*

Alien Rescue is a simulation that opens with a video news report that six species of alien life forms are on spaceships orbiting Earth. Students learn that, because the home worlds of the aliens have been destroyed, the aliens have come to Earth to ask for help in finding new homes in our solar system. To add a sense of urgency, before they can establish contact with Earth their spaceship is damaged, forcing them to enter a suspended state of animation. The student scientists are sent to the newly operational international space station orbiting Earth to participate in a multinational rescue operation to save the aliens. Their task is to use a variety of tools at their disposal to learn about the aliens and to explore the solar system to find a suitable habitat to match the unique characteristic of each alien species. One of the challenging research questions in this environment involves finding which of the tools are most helpful in solving the problem (Liu and Bera, 2005; Liu et al., 2002). Alien Rescue contains an amalgam of strategies, scaffolds, and technologies that make it difficult, if not impossible, to separate medium from methods.

## *River City*

Three-dimensional multi-user virtual environments (MUVEs) such as River City illustrate the complexity of understanding and analyzing the interactions between learner and environment. River City is a classroom-based situated-learning experience to support problem solving in biology and ecology (Dede, 2003). Students explore a three-dimensional virtual 19th-century town to discover why its citizens (represented as non-player agents) are getting sick. Three strands of illness (waterborne, airborne, and insect-borne) are integrated with historical, social, and geographical content to allow students to tackle multicausal problems embedded within a complex environment. A river runs through the city, and the landscape has different terrains that influence water runoff. The students also inhabit the city as avatars and interact with other computer-based characters in the city. Students acquire clues by interacting with the computer-based agents and by overhearing residents' conversations with one another where they disclose indirect clues about what is going on in River City.

River City generates a personal history of each student in the form of extensive log files. The logs show exactly where each student went, with whom they communicated, what they said, what artifacts they activated, and how long each of these activities took. According to Dede (2006, personal communication), the challenge for researchers is to relate the rich log

file data with the more familiar quantitative performance measures (test scores on content knowledge and the quality of letters to the mayor) and qualitative measures (in-class observations interviews). Dede conceded in the 2006 interview that the sheer volume of data in the log files made it very challenging to make sense of them:

> It is not like you can form a query that can be answered by an automated process. It depends on the type of questions we are asking. The log files cannot explain why something happened. Log files need human inspection or interviews to be fully interpretable. Currently, we are in the process of exploring the range of questions the log files can answer.

## Parts of "It" Look Strangely Familiar

We believe that a large body of literature from earlier CAI studies (noted earlier) with a rich library of findings about learners and their behaviors has not been adequately exploited by designers of TELEs. Some of the problems encountered by TELE developers (e.g., persistent underuse of program scaffolds) might have been anticipated; for example, the work by Tennyson and his associates on program advisement in a CAI program seems to have implications for the design of effective scaffolds, but this work is not frequently cited in the scaffolding literature (Tennyson, 1980; Tennyson and Buttrey, 1980; Tennyson and Rothen, 1979). Also, the work by Carrier and associates on option usage patterns would seem to be helpful in designing ways to sustain leaner interest and curiosity (Carrier et al., 1984, 1986). There seems to be an unnecessary schism between the new guard (expanded view of *it*) and the old (experimental purists), which perhaps results in a tendency to focus on the differences while overlooking valuable similarities that could create synergy between both views.

## Where Is "It" Going?

As noted by Ross and Morrison earlier in this chapter, the 2006 trend in research design is toward an increase in empirical studies, with fewer qualitative investigations. They suggest that this is due, in part, to political forces that establish research priorities and the types of research that will be supported by government grant programs. This trend was also recognized by the TELE designers we interviewed. In response to the question "How much attention did you pay to the content standards in your design?" most answered that they simply had no choice but to align content with relevant state and national standards. Even if they disagreed philosophically with imposed standards, however, they did not believe this detracted from the effectiveness of their programs. Some were quite forthcoming that they had to play by the rules if they wanted to find support, but here, too, they saw it as not seriously compromising the overall goals of the product. Most thought they could do both, but if Ross and Morrison are right then what are the long-term implications for the development of such rich TELEs?

The future of efforts to define educational technology may go beyond hardware and software, or even pedagogy, to include individual and group human–computer interactions, as well as rich three-dimensional avatar-based virtual worlds and *multiverse* environments that create a sociocultural context for thinking and learning. We might extend Friedman's (2005) view that "the world is flat" to suggest that learning technology might enable any learner, anywhere in the world, to collaborate and learn with any other learner who has shared interests by meeting in virtual space. The added advantage for educational researchers is that server log files can record every action taken by learners, including time and location, so learners' behaviors can be calibrated to when, where, and how they interact with each other and reproducible contextual factors within the learning environment to produce knowledge and understanding.

There is also a trend to extend our understanding of technology and learning into the realm of literacy (Leu et al., 2004). As technology becomes ubiquitous in schools, instead of writing a book report, students may create a multimedia production, complete with movies, photos, animations, simulations, music, voice recordings, and, of course, prudently used text. Also, the format for communication may expand beyond the book report format to include presentation slides, digital movies, Web pages, and hyperlinked documents, both individual (blogs) and collaborative (wikis). It seems clear to many that reading and writing in these formats require new literacies beyond those required to craft and comprehend a book report; for example, the results of a Google Internet search do not present the same challenges to comprehension as those of the chapters of a novel or a Shakespeare play. Similarly, one would not expect students to apply the same organizational principles they learned for writing a good essay (opening sentence, elaboration, closing argument), for example, when they are composing a menu bar for a website. Future research on educational technology may involve its impact on curriculum and the broader view of what it means to be literate, a good reader and writer. So, in addition to operationally defining a particular technology, as it is used in a particular classroom, toward particular pedagogical goals, researchers in the near future may have to address the systemwide impact of the use of a technology and the extent to which its associated new literacies become ingrained into the teaching and learning environment.

If, as we have suggested here, research on the effects of technology requires a complex understanding of learner–, technology–, physical–, and social–environment interactions, then simple statistical analyses that work for highly controlled experimental laboratory environments may prove inadequate. Such an understanding requires huge datasets from log files of massively multiplayer environment interactions through time, in which case new experimental designs and statistical methods, including data visualization, complex systems modeling, and simulations, may prove useful in educational technology research, as they have in physics, climatology, meteorology, and other fields dealing with applied and messy phenomena and large dynamic datasets.

These assumptions suggest that the randomized designs of true experiments may fatally trade internal validity for all applied value, yielding no generalizations, and they may be antithetical to assumptions that learning is highly contextual, individual, social, and interactive. That is, although the results of a true experiment may be true, they may only be so for the completely artificial controlled conditions of the laboratory which eliminate the interactions of interest to ensure that only one variable is causing changes. If the more situated, embedded, and embodied views of cognition are correct, there may never be a real-world occasion on which only a single variable is affecting thinking, learning, perceiving, and acting in context—learners may never step in the same river twice. Thus, scholarly methods for addressing the nature of complex interactions must be developed and applied, including those successfully used in other complex fields, such as modeling, simulating, and data visualization of what is occurring in context. Techniques such as these may be useful in interpreting and making sense of log files in the spirit of design research to simultaneously advance theory and the practice of instructional design.

Log files, such as those generated in River City, are a sequence of behavioral data stored in a permanent file (Hulshof, 2004). They offer time-stamped (sometimes location-stamped) records of human choices made through computer interfaces with learning environments. Figure 54.6 is an example of a log file, showing a text summary of user actions. Figure 54.7 and Figure 54.8 are visualizations of log files that graphically present the log data across time and space in a TELE. Such files result from online Internet navigation (stored at the server side or as *cookies* at the client side), online and console-based game play, the

```
Student:    Young    Mike
Starting 9/18/98
Time in: 11:43:59 AM
 Startup 11:43:59 AM
Instructions 11:44:01 AM

...
Facts 3:33:38 PM
  Add Fact: CC at 156.6 3:33:51 PM
  Add Fact: home at 132.6 3:33:59 PM
Calculating 3:34:02 PM
  Calc: 156.6  -  132.6  =  24
  ANSWER: How far is it from Cedar Creek to home? = 24 miles
...
Facts 3:38:39 PM
  Add Fact: has 12 gallons 3:38:53 PM
  Add Fact: burns 5 gal/hr 3:39:08 PM
Calculating 3:39:10 PM
  Calc: 5  *  3  =  15
  ANSWER: How much fuel is needed? = 15 gals.
...
Survey Data:
P Q F C V, So, Ma, Sc, St, Ba, Cma, Comp, R, H, Sol
101, 78, 1012, 170, 27, 0, 0, 0, 0, 0, 87, 99, 46, 98, 0,
Time out:    3:56:47 PM
```

**Figure 54.6** Sample log file.

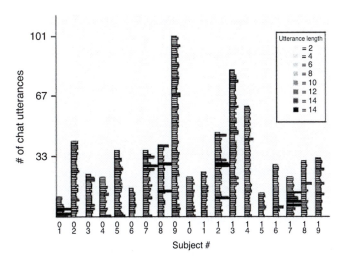

**Figure 54.7** Visualization of log file data. (Based on Börner, K. et al., in *Proceedings of the Sixth International Conference on Information Visualization (IV'02)*, July 10–12, 2002, London, pp. 25–31; http://vw.indiana.edu/cive02/004_borner_ VisSpatialTemporal.pdf.)

use of computer-based modeling and writing tools, and avatar-based communication and interactions. Log files retain a record of process and thus afford researchers a rich source for assessment and design research decision making. It bears repeating that advocates would argue that in design-based research, unlike tightly controlled experimental studies, *a priori* hypotheses are not possible or even particularly useful. *Warrants* based on theory can be made for both design changes and classroom activities in concert with observation of a

panoply of variables available through data visualization in the log files. See particularly Shavelson et al. (2003) in the special issue of *Educational Researcher* on the role of design in educational research.

Log files are used for market research (as when Amazon.com selects other book choices to present to users based on their log files of book-buying choices) and for customization of advertising in many e-commerce settings. Educational research is just starting to tap into this potential. Log file data can include both

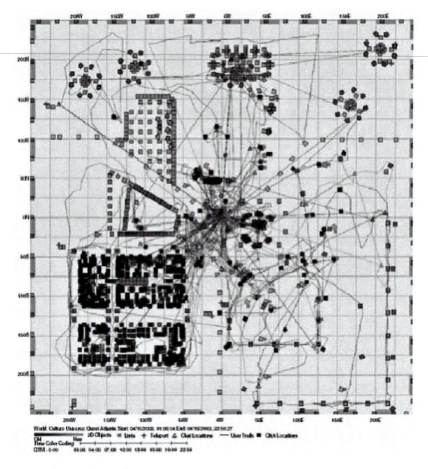

**Figure 54.8** Another visualization of log file data.

time and spatial data associated with each online behavior. As shown in Figure 54.8, both files can display where information is found or where each type of chat occurs within an avatar-based virtual environment.

Parallel to these new data analysis challenges, hybrid methodologies that combine the causal elements of true experiments with correlational and observational techniques of qualitative research must be sought. Iterative cycles of design, analysis, theory, and redesign may yield scholarly and scientific information that addresses causality while honoring the complex interactions that constitute learning.

## Wrapping "It" Up

Educational research is naturally driven by funding and the political agenda that influences what schools do and the metrics to which students, teachers, schools, and districts are held accountable. As a final observation about the nature and future of educational technology research, it is important to point out that policymakers set the agenda for what is investigated and what counts as a convincing argument for what works concerning the wise use of technology in instruction. This suggests that, like all of science, we must acknowledge that educational technology research is a human endeavor and, as such, draws upon an ever-emerging social interaction that defines how technology should *work* and what is accepted as evidence of its working. To the extent that this is true, we must accept that if we find that technology is working today that it might not be working tomorrow, and *vice versa*, as new expectations for education and new testing criteria are adopted. For our purposes, we just want to go on record as stating that, to be true to contemporary learning theory, our description of educational technology research must itself be seen as situated in the context of today's educational practices and learning environments that are currently hot among researchers and educators.

If this section had been written by researchers in the teacher education community, or the learning sciences, or the corporate or military training community, the emphasis would look and feel different. We believe, however, that the central arguments proposed here—namely, the proposition that all research in technology can be boiled down to the central question of *Does it work?*—still apply. The tools have gotten more powerful, the environments more complex and realistic, the data collection more multivariate and dynamic, but researchers and stakeholders still want to know if the intervention is having its intended effect, any ill effects, or any effect at all for that matter, with the ultimate purpose of safe, effective, and efficient learning.

## Summary

We discussed research on technology presented in the context of the question *Does it work*? Major concepts and points addressed include the following:

- Technology has been used in educational research as the variable under study (e.g., media comparison studies), as the conveyor of instructional treatments, and to support complex learning environments.
- The research community valued experimental research with high internal validity that could identify causal relationships, which gave rise to a necessarily narrow conception of what was studied (*it*).
- As human learning was increasingly viewed as embedded and embodied, TELEs emerged to create complex and realistic environments.
- Research on TELEs is largely design based, with an emphasis on external validity, and it conceives of *it* as a "cloud of correlated variables," with the unit of analysis being the learner–environment interaction.
- Some of the findings from design-based research might have been predicted by a better understanding of previous research on technology.
- Vast amounts of user data recorded in the log files of TELEs hold great potential to advance the understanding of how students learn in open environments, but effective analysis techniques are complex, multidimensional, and multivariate.

We addressed two key issues: (1) what variables constitute the wise application of technology to instruction, and (2) how do we operationally define the dependent measures used to determine how technology–pedagogy–environment interactions affect knowledge, attitudes, and behaviors. The variables we select will emerge from the dialectic among theories such as situated cognition, environments that can generate large

log files concerning the dynamics of student–computer interaction, and learners who perceive and act according to their own goals and constructed understandings. In the introduction, we cited the question *Does it work?* as the organizer for our discussion. As we look forward, we see promising trends that can advance our understanding of what *it* is and help us reliably measure more fully how it *works*.

## RESEARCH ON MODELS FOR INSTRUCTIONAL DESIGN

*Jan van den Akker and Wilmad Kuiper*

This chapter section deals with research on models for instructional design. The literature on instructional design is abundantly supplied with models. Many of these models claim to be unique and deserving of attention, but most have the limitation of being too abstract to inspire and support designers in their professional practice. With the ultimate aim to try to strengthen the weak link between theory and practice in instructional design models, we raise two main questions. First, which trends are visible in research on model development, use, and validation so far? Second, how can research on instructional design be redirected to foster blending of theory and practice? In answering the second question, we take the position that *instructional* design can become more productive if its perspective is broadened to *educational* design. This conception includes incorporating multiple levels and components of learning and instruction (for example, not only the individual student or a group of students but also the teacher who operates within a curricular framework) as well as embedding design work in systemic educational development approaches. A *design research* approach is therefore implied.

In using the term *research on models* we build on Richey and Klein (in this chapter), who divide studies of instructional design and development into two general types of design and developmental research: *product and tool research* and *model research*. The two types have been previously called, respectively, Type 1 and Type 2 (Richey et al., 2004) or *formative research* and *reconstructive studies* (van den Akker, 1999). The first type of research pertains primarily to research-based design and development of products and tools. A typical example of product and tool research is McKenney's (2002) report on CASCADE-SEA, a computer-based tool to support curriculum materials development in the context of secondary science and mathematics education in southern Africa. The second type of research—as stated, the focus of this chapter section—deals with the development, validation, and use of design and development models, such as Jones and Richey's (2000) in-depth examination of the use of rapid prototyping methods in two instructional design projects in natural work settings. These studies focus on the models and processes themselves, rather than their demonstration. Although it is possible to conduct model research in conjunction with the development of a product or program, most model studies concentrate on previously developed instruction and consequently are not project specific. Model research may address the validity or effectiveness of an existing or newly constructed development model, process, or technique. In addition, these studies often seek to identify and describe the conditions that facilitate successful design and development (see Richey and Klein in this chapter).

## Research on Instructional Design Models: Trends and Reflections

### Instructional Design Models as Conceptual, Communication, and Procedural Tools

Over the years, there have been many attempts, including efforts by the Association for Educational Communications and Technology (AECT), to label and define the field of instructional design or technology. A representative AECT definition is the one published in *Instructional Technology: The Definitions and Domains of the Field* (Seels and Richey, 1994). In that volume, *instructional technology* is concisely defined as the "theory and practice of design, development, utilization, management, and evaluation of processes and resources for learning" (p. 1). In this chapter section, we take this definition and the term *instructional design* as a starting point. Later on, the instructional design perspective will be broadened to *systematic educational engineering*. Rather than adopting the terms *processes* and *resources* from the Seels and Richey (1994) definition, we prefer to use the more generic term *interventions*, which serves as a common denominator for products, programs, materials, procedures, scenarios, processes, and the like (van den Akker, 1999).

The literature is well supplied with definitions (Reiser and Dempsey, 2002) and with alternative instructional design models. These models serve as conceptual, communication, and procedural tools for analyzing, designing, creating, and evaluating broad educational environments as well as narrow training applications (Gustafson and Branch, 2002b). Most models assume that the use of systematic procedures can make interventions more effective. Design and development may be conceived as a single linear pro-

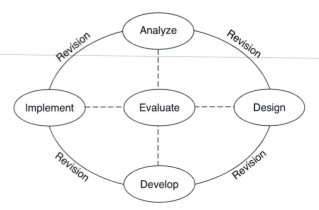

**Figure 54.9** Core elements of instructional design.

cess or—more realistically and preferably—as a set of concurrent iterative or recursive engineering procedures with integrated research activities to feed the process forward and backward. Most model descriptions include the core elements of analysis, design, development, implementation, and evaluation (ADDIE). The five core elements each inform the other as development takes place, and revision continues at least until the instruction is implemented (Gustafson and Branch, 2002a,b). Figure 54.9 depicts the relationship among these so-called ADDIE elements.

### Characterization of Research on Instructional Design Models

In reviewing model research studies, Richey and colleagues (2004; see also Richey and Klein in this chapter) analyzed 58 examples published between 1984 and 2002 in terms of, among other things, range of research methodologies used and nature of research conclusions. From their analysis, it appears that quite a diversity of research methods is employed in model research. As regards *model development*, common research methods are literature reviews, surveys (based on interviews), case studies (employed, but far less prominently than in product and tool research), Delphi techniques (aimed at reaching consensus of experts' opinions), and think-aloud protocols. For research on *model use*, surveys (based on interviews), case studies (interviews and field observations), document analyses, and think-aloud methods are employed. Research methods commonly applied in the context of *model validation* are experiments and quasi-experiments (critical to the verification and evaluation of a particular design and development technique), interviews, and expert reviews. Model research studies are unique in that they are ultimately directed toward general principles, which are applicable in a wide range of design and development projects. The issues addressed in the conclusions are the following (Richey et al., 2004): evidence of validity or effectiveness of a particular technique or model, conditions and procedures that facilitate the successful use of a particular technique or model, explanations of the successes or failures encountered in using a particular technique or model, a synthesis of events or opinions related to the use of a particular technique or model, and a new or enhanced model.

We next illustrate some typical model research studies in more detail and begin with four examples of examples of *research on model development*. From the beginning of the 1970s to the present, several literature reviews of instructional design models have been published, including the review by Andrews and Goodson (1980) of 40 models in the *Journal for Instructional Development*. Of more recent date are the reviews by Gustafson (1981, 1991) and Gustafson and Branch (1997, 2002a) of instructional development models. To help clarify the underlying assumptions of each model and identify the conditions under which each might be appropriately applied, Gustafson and Branch (2002a) classified up to 15 ADDIE models according to the primary type of instruction they were designed to produce. Their taxonomy of instructional development models has three categories, indicating whether a given model is best applied for designing and developing: (1) instruction to be delivered in a *classroom* by a teacher, with little time and resources for the teacher to devote to the comprehensive development of instructional materials (four models); (2) instructional *products* for implementation by users others than the designers, such as computer-based modules designed for wide distribution, with considerable emphasis on tryout and revision (five models); and (3) large-scale instructional *systems* directed at an organization's problems or goals, such as a distance learning course or a curriculum encompassing an entire degree program (six models). Gustafson and Branch categorized the ADDIE models according to the following nine characteristics: (1) typical output in terms of amount of instruction prepared, (2) resources committed to the development effort, (3) whether it is a team or individual effort, (4) expected instructional design skill and experience of the individual or team, (5) whether instructional materials will be selected from existing courses or represent original design and development, (6) amount of preliminary analysis conducted, (7) anticipated technological complexity of the development and delivery environments, (8) amount of tryout and revision conducted, and (9) amount of dissemination and follow-up occurring after development. For a characterization of the models selected as well as their underlying assumptions, we refer to Gustafson and Branch (2002b).

Other authors have created different classification schemes for instructional design models and processes. Richey (2005) distinguished two major types of instructional design models. One type, labeled *conceptual models*, identifies variables that impact the design process and shows their interrelationships; the second type, *procedural models*, represents the recommended steps to follow in a design process. Most instructional design models can be visualized in diagrams and are procedural in nature. Most procedural models pertain to comprehensive design projects. Others address more specific aspects of the design, development, and evaluation processes.

Another example of model development research is the already-mentioned study by Jones and Richey (2000), a study that also has been referred to and summarized by Richey and colleagues (2004) and by Richey and Klein (this chapter). Jones and Richey conducted an in-depth qualitative examination of the use of rapid prototyping methods in two instructional design projects in natural settings. Data were collected from structured personal interviews, activity logs, and a review of extant data. Participants included two experienced instructional designers who employed rapid prototyping in the design and development of two projects in the automotive industry and in the healthcare industry. In addition, one client was interviewed to obtain perceptions of product quality and usability, cycle-time reduction, and customer satisfaction. After discussing how rapid prototyping was successfully used in the context of the study, the authors provided general conclusions and suggested a revised model of instructional design that includes rapid prototyping.

An example of *research on model use* is an investigation by Rowland (1992) of what expert instructional designers actually do. Four expert and four novice designers were asked to think aloud as they solved a design problem. The resulting protocols were analyzed and compared. Important differences were identified between experts and novices, including the following:

- Experts interpreted the problem they were faced with as poorly defined by the given information. They challenged givens and added much information through inference. Novices interpreted the problem as well defined by the given information and did little elaboration.
- Experts thought of possible solutions immediately but delayed commitment pending a deeper understanding of the problem. Novices moved quickly to solution generation after a brief examination of the materials.

- Experts represented the problem as a deep and rich causal network of many links. Novices split the problem (and therefore the solution) into parts based on surface differences.
- Experts considered many global (system-wide) and local (immediate) factors in making decisions. Novices considered few factors, only local factors, and only one factor at a time.

Rowland also discussed the implications of these differences for assisting and training instructional designers.

Another example of research on model use is Visscher-Voerman's (1999) reconstructive study of how instructional designers actually conduct projects in various training and education contexts (design of textbooks, curriculum development, multimedia, human resource development programs, and distance education). This researcher collected case study data from 24 professional designers by means of interviews and document analysis. Results showed that scientific design models differed from design approaches applied in practice by experienced designers in the sense that experienced educational designers worked much more heterogeneously and diversely than models suggest. Specific practices of experienced educational designers included: (1) conducting only a restricted problem and context analysis at the start, generally resulting in a further specification of a potential solution rather than a specification of the problem; (2) minimally generating and weighing alternative solutions, while instead exploring alternatives within a given solution; (3) not distinguishing between design and development; and (4) generally interweaving formative evaluation activities with design activities rather than conducting formative evaluation activities in a distinct phase. Based on the extensive research findings, Visscher-Voerman created a classification framework consisting of four design paradigms (Visscher-Voerman and Gustafson, 2004; Visscher-Voerman et al., 1999): (1) instrumental (planning by objectives), (2) communicative (communication to reach consensus), (3) pragmatic (interactive and repeated tryout and revision), and (4) artistic (creation of products based on educational connoisseurship). Rather than focusing on the context of the development and use of instruction as done by Gustafson and Branch, Visscher-Voerman characterized the underlying philosophy and values of each design paradigm.

A third example of research on model use is a study conducted by Kirschner et al. (2002). First, they reviewed the following eight studies describing actual instructional design practices: Kerr (1983), Le Maistre

(1998), Perez and Emery (1995), Pieters and Bergman (1995), Rowland (1992), Visscher-Voerman (1999), Wedman and Tessmer (1993), and Winer and Vasquez-Abad (1995). From their review they concluded that instructional designers, among other things, should thoroughly explore and interpret the problem; consider a wide range of possible solutions and a wide range of factors, combining them and using context knowledge; take more time for prototyping and evaluation; and use a highly interactive and collaborative design approach. Second, they carried out two experiments with expert educational designers from a university setting and a business setting to find out what the designers actually did and which priorities they employed when designing competence-based learning environments. From the two experiments it appeared that designers in a university context and in a business context agreed almost completely on what design principles are important, the most important being that one should start a design enterprise from the needs of the learners, instead of the content structure of the learning domain. The main difference between the two groups is that university designers find it extremely important to consider alternative solutions during the entire design process, something that is considerably less important by business designers. University designers also tend to focus on the project plan and the desired characteristics of the instructional blueprint whereas business designers were much more client oriented and stressed the importance of gaining client buy-in early in the process.

An example of research on model validation is Tracey's (2002; also see Richey and Klein in this chapter) comparison between the use of the Dick and Carey (1996) model and an instructional design model enhanced with a consideration of multiple intelligences (MI). Tracey established two design teams, each with two novice designers. One team worked with the Dick and Carey model, and the second used the MI model. Both teams were instructed to design a 2-hour, instructor-led, classroom-based, team-building course for a nonprofit organization. The resulting programs were implemented and their impact compared in terms of learner knowledge and attitudes. Instrumentation used during the study included designer logs giving reactions to their tasks and the models used, learner knowledge post-tests, and surveys addressing participant reactions to the instruction.

### Reflections on Research on Instructional Design Models

Many of the instructional design models described in the literature claim to be unique and deserving of attention; however, in almost all instances, the authors have assumed that their models are worthwhile or rely on user testimonials as proof of their effectiveness but present no evidence to substantiate their positions. There is a disturbingly small volume of literature describing any testing of the models. Many have never been systematically applied, not to mention rigorously evaluated and empirically validated (Gustafson and Branch, 2002a; Richey, 2005). That there is a need for doing so can, among other things, be derived from Visscher-Voerman's (1999) retrospective study (see also Visscher-Voerman and Gustafson, 2004) from which it appeared that design approaches applied by experienced educational designers differ from design approaches reflected in scientific design models. Also, Kirschner and colleagues (2002) found a clear gap between instructional design processes as described in prescriptive instructional design models and the design process as it is performed in the real world.

As already stated, research also shows that design models are interpreted differently by expert designers and novice designers (Perez and Emery, 1995; Rowland, 1992, 1993). Although the key tasks are still completed by experts, experts tend to treat design problems as ill defined. They consider a wide variety of situational factors in combination, as well as both instructional and non-instructional solutions but delay making design decisions as long as possible (Richey, 2005). Experts *interpret* design problems, whereas novices *identify* them (Perez and Emery, 1995). The developmental study of rapid prototyping in action (Jones and Richey, 2000) showed that some approaches to design, especially interactive, cyclic, and spiral procedures such as rapid or evolutionary prototyping, also appeal to a greater ability of judgment and larger repertoire of design skills. Expert designers basically use a general instructional design model, but the design process tends to be more iterative, and the sequencing of design steps varies to meet the demands of the individual design project. Design tasks are often performed concurrently, a finding that has also been confirmed by Visscher-Voerman.

Richey (2005) noted the paucity of model validation studies and attributed such to time constraints and ill-defined model validation procedures rather than to a lack of the fundamental need for validation. She viewed instructional design model validation as a carefully planned process of collecting and analyzing empirical data to demonstrate the effectiveness of a model's use in the workplace (external validation) or to provide support for the various components of the model itself (internal validation). Richey distinguished the following five approaches to validation:

- Internal validation procedures (emphasizing formative evaluation of the model):

  *Expert review*, a process whereby instructional design experts (often representing both design practitioners and design theorists) critique a given model in terms of its components, overall structure, and future use

  *Usability documentation*, the systematic documentation of designers using a particular model

  *Component investigation*, the identification or confirmation through research of steps (procedural models) and factors (conceptual models) critical to the instructional design process

- External validation procedures (emphasizing summative or confirmative evaluation of the model):

  *Field evaluation*, involving the actual use of the model to produce instruction

  *Controlled testing*, establishing experiments that isolate the effects of the given instructional design model as compared to the use of another model or approach

## Major Challenges to Research on Instructional Design Models

It is difficult to find fault with Richey's underlying message that "as a field we should be validating our many instructional design models as well as developing them, and that validation should become a natural part of the model development process" (2005, p. 183). Nevertheless, some major challenges arise when addressing this issue.

As can be inferred from the retrospective study conducted by Visscher-Voerman (1999), there is a strong need for a better correspondence between, on the one hand, the rather abstract instructional design models and, on the other hand, the real and messy world of professional design and development practices. This issue has two sides. Acknowledging that most of the deviations of design practice from design theory (as reflected from the Visscher-Voerman study) seem to be realistic, the models need to be improved to better match actual processes. At the same time, there seems to be ample room for improvement of existing, often ineffective practices.

How can we conceptualize models that fit better to the real-world challenges of practitioners, while also stimulating and supporting approaches that seem more valid from a theoretical perspective? In other words, how can we strengthen the links between theory and

---

**TABLE 54.1**
**Curriculum Components**

| | |
|---|---|
| Rationale: | Why are they learning? |
| Aims and objectives: | Toward which goals are they learning? |
| Content: | What are they learning? |
| Learning activities: | How are they learning? |
| Teacher role: | How is the teacher facilitating learning? |
| Materials and resources: | With what are they learning? |
| Grouping: | With whom are they learning? |
| Location: | Where are they learning? |
| Time: | When and for how long are they learning? |
| Assessment: | How should their learning progress be assessed? |

---

practice in instructional design models, making them more relevant for the improvement of learning? For that purpose, in the authors' opinion, more productive instructional design models should:

- Be highly relevant to realistic circumstances.
- Take into account the wider environment of design and development challenges, with more deliberate anticipation on implementation processes in user contexts.
- Be comprehensive, considering a more systemic view on educational improvement.
- Address learning processes and outcomes from multiple perspectives and include a wide range of influential variables.

We elaborate on these issues in the next section.

## Broadening the Instructional Design Perspective

### Addressing Multiple Levels of Learning and Instruction

The improvement of learning should, of course, always be the ultimate aim of instructional design, but successful approaches require a broadening to *educational* design. An essential insight is that individual learning occurs in educational contexts that influence the aims, processes, and outcomes of learning in distinctive ways. In most instructional situations, teachers (or educators or trainers) still have a dominant role in arranging the learning trajectories and environments of their students. Also, teachers usually do not operate in isolation or complete autonomy, but within curriculum frameworks. Those curricula (in essence, plans for learning) can be found at various levels, ranging from the *macro* level (system, society, nation, state) via the *meso* level of the school or institution, to the *micro*

level of the classroom or group, and ultimately to the *nano* level of the individual person (van den Akker, 2003). Student learning is usually influenced by curricular representations at higher levels; for example, schools are usually not neutral institutions with regard to what and how students learn within their environment. Despite this, the repertoire of teachers within their respective curricular framework at the micro level (textbooks, instructional materials) is most influential on the daily learning activities of students. Thus, the design of individual student learning is almost always embedded in educational planning and implementation at other levels, and that perspective deserves to be incorporated in design approaches (McKenney et al., 2006).

### Incorporating Multiple Components of Learning and Instruction

The relevance and meaningfulness of instructional design would also be improved if the scope of design would be broadened and elaborated. Educational design is not only about learning activities. Many other related questions about learning design are usually at stake. From a broader curriculum perspective, it makes sense to pay attention to a coherent set of ten components that address ten specific questions about the planning of student learning (Table 54.1) (McKenney et al., 2006; van den Akker, 2003).

Our preferential visualization of the ten components is to arrange them as a spider web (Figure 54.10), which not only illustrates their many interconnections but also underlines the vulnerability of the curriculum as a whole, especially during implementation. At the hub of the model is the rationale, which connects all the other components: aims and objectives, content, learning activities, teacher role, materials and resources, grouping, location, time, and assessment. The spider web metaphor emphasizes that, within one

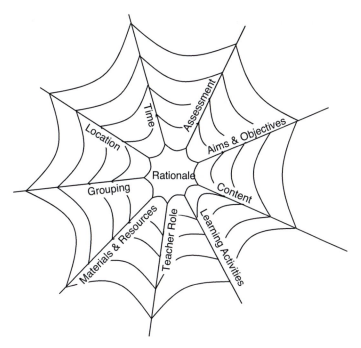

**Figure 54.10** Curricular spider web.

curriculum, component accents may vary over time but any dramatic shift in balance will pull the entirety out of alignment. Though the system may endure the stress for a while, prolonged imbalance will cause it to break. Efforts directed toward curriculum reform, (re)design, development, and implementation must therefore devote attention to the balance and linkages among the ten components. A striking example is the trend toward integration of ICT in the curriculum, usually with initial attention to changes in materials and resources. Many implementation studies have revealed the need for a more comprehensive approach and systematic attention to the other components before one can expect robust changes. The spider web also illustrates a familiar expression: Every chain is as strong as its weakest link. That seems another very appropriate metaphor for a curriculum, pointing to the complexity of efforts to improve the curriculum in a balanced, consistent, and sustainable manner.

### Strengthening the Relevance and Scope of Design Approaches

In addition to addressing more levels and components of learning, instructional design also can become more productive by linking its efforts to other educational development activities. If instructional design focuses on exemplary trajectories for learning that cover many of the aforementioned components of the spider web, then it has already strengthened its curricular rele-

vance. To increase its scope and potential impact at a larger scale, however, it is also recommended that the design work be connected to other systemic activities in the domains of teacher education, school development, and examinations/assessment (McKenney et al., 2006). Such interconnections definitely contribute to system coherence, which appears to be a vital condition to sustainability of innovations. As expressed by Hargreaves and Fink (2006, p. 1): "Change in education is easy to propose, hard to implement, and extraordinarily difficult to sustain." Integrating instructional design in systemic (and usually long-term) approaches of educational development can further the sustainability of its results.

### Implications for Research Approaches

#### Design Research

Although the validation studies on instructional design models, as suggested by Richey (2005), are certainly worthwhile to apply, the previous section has already underlined various characteristics of (more) productive research approaches. They all refer to broadening the scope of instructional design, embedding it within integrated educational development. Moreover, there is a need for more interactive and developmental approaches to research on instructional design models. Although other labels also are used, such research approaches are often labeled as *design-based research* (Design-Based Research Collective, 2003) or as *design* research (van den Akker et al., 2006a). The following generic definition, which encompasses most variations of educational design research, is offered by Barab and Squire (2004, p. 2): "a series of approaches with the intent of producing new theories, artifacts, and practices that account for and potentially impact learning and teaching in naturalistic settings." According to van den Akker et al. (2006a), various interests in conducting such design research include: (1) increasing the relevance of research for educational policy and practice, (2) developing empirically grounded theories, and (3) increasing the robustness of design practice. The edited book *Educational Design Research* (van den Akker et al., 2006b) contains a series of chapters providing examples of and reflections on design research from a variety of perspectives (e.g., learning design, technology, curriculum, philosophy, engineering). Some common characteristics of design research appear to be (Cobb et al., 2003; Design-Based Research Collective, 2003; Kelly, 2003; Reeves et al., 2005; van den Akker, 1999; van den Akker et al., 2006a):

- *Interventionist*—The research aims at developing an intervention in the real world.
- *Iterative*—The research incorporates a cyclic approach of design, evaluation, and revision.
- *Process oriented*—A black box model of input–output measurement is avoided; the focus is on understanding and improving interventions.
- *Utility oriented*—The merit of the design is measured, in part, by its practicality for users in real contexts.
- *Theory oriented*—The design is (at least partly) based on theoretical propositions, and field testing of the design contributes to theory building.

Moreover, it should be noted that design research does not emphasize isolated variables. Although design researchers do focus on specific objects and processes in specific contexts, they try to study those as integral and meaningful phenomena. The context-bound nature of much design research (conducted with often rather small and purposive samples) also explains why researchers usually do not strive for context-free generalizations from sample to population, based on statistical techniques. Investments are needed in analytical forms of generalization; readers need to be supported in their own attempts to explore the potential transfer of research findings to theoretical propositions in relation to their own contexts. Reports on design research can facilitate that task of analogy reasoning

by a clear articulation of the design principles applied and by a careful description of both the evaluation procedures and the implementation contexts (van den Akker, 1999).

### Research-Based Educational Engineering

Within design research, one may want to distinguish between *validation studies* (primarily aiming to prove or disprove learning theories) and *development studies* (aiming to solve an educational problem using relevant theoretical knowledge). The latter typically includes the following stages (Nieveen et al., 2006; van den Akker, 1999):

- *Preliminary research* includes thorough context and problem analysis along with development of a conceptual framework based on literature review. Some typical activities include literature review, consultation of experts, analysis of available promising examples for related purposes and contexts, and case studies of existing practices to specify and better understand needs and problems in intended user contexts. This stage should result in the formulation of design principles for subsequent design activities.
- *Prototyping stage* sets out substantive design specifications and procedural guidelines and optimizes prototypes through iterative cycles of design, formative evaluation, and revision (Nieveen, 1999).
- *Summative evaluation* of the effectiveness preferably also includes an exploration of transferability and scaling (Burkhardt, 2006; Burkhardt and Schoenfeld, 2003).
- *Systematic reflection and documentation* portrays the entire study to support retrospective analysis, followed by specification of design principles and articulation of their links to the conceptual framework.

The whole cycle of research-based *educational engineering* departs from a sound theoretical base by validation studies, develops through practical understanding from development studies, and is eventually tested by (large-scale) effectiveness research. The cycle also shows a gradual shift from exploratory to confirmatory approaches (Nieveen et al., 2006). The increasing call for more evidence-based learning and teaching approaches also implies that educational design and development activities themselves have a stronger theoretical and empirical base that underpins the claims for evidence. Research-based educational engineering as described above can contribute to this challenge.

Obviously, these more comprehensive tasks cannot be addressed by instructional designers or educational researchers only. Such challenges require thorough interaction and collaboration between designers, researchers, practitioners, and policymakers alike. Moreover, these interactions preferably go beyond the short-term time horizon that is often available for design and research activities. They would be supported by a programmatic framework that can connect and sustain a series of separate studies.

## Summary

The focus of this chapter section is research on instructional design model development, use, and validation. Major concepts and point addressed included the following:

- Common research methods as regards model development are literature reviews, surveys (based on interviews), case studies, Delphi techniques, and think-aloud protocols. For research on model use, surveys (based on interviews), case studies (interviews and field observations), document analyses, and think-aloud methods are employed. Research methods commonly applied in the context of model validation are experiments and quasi-experiments, interviews, and expert reviews. Examples of studies in these three categories of model research have been described.
- Apparent from several studies is the strong need for a better correspondence between, on the one hand, the rather abstract instructional design models and, on the other hand, the real and messy world of professional design and development practices. Acknowledging that most of the deviations of design practice from design theory seem to be realistic, the models need to be improved to better match actual processes. At the same time, there seems to be ample room for improvement of existing, often ineffective practices.
- To foster the blending of theory and practice and to make the models more relevant for the improvement of learning (the ultimate aim of instructional design), more productive instructional design models should address learning processes and outcomes from multiple perspectives (not only a focus

on students but also on teachers who operate within curriculum frameworks at various levels) and include a wide range of influential variables. Basically, this requires a broadening to *educational* design.

- The relevance and meaningfulness of instructional design would also be improved if the scope of design would be broadened and elaborated. Educational design is not only about learning activities. Many other related questions about learning design are usually at stake. From a broader curriculum perspective, it makes sense to pay attention to a coherent set of ten components that address ten specific questions about the planning of student learning: rationale, aims and objectives, content, learning activities, teacher role, materials and resources, grouping, location, time, and assessment.
- Besides addressing more levels and components of learning, instructional design also can become more productive by linking its efforts to other educational development activities. To increase its scope and potential impact at a larger scale, it is recommended that the design work also be connected to other systemic activities in the domains of teacher education, school development, and examinations and assessment.
- Moreover, more interactive and developmental approaches to research on instructional design models are needed. Such research approaches are often labeled as *design-based research* or *design research*. Educational design research is defined as "a series of approaches with the intent of producing new theories, artifacts, and practices that account for and potentially impact learning and teaching in naturalistic settings." Interests in conducting design research include: (1) increasing the relevance of research for educational policy and practice, (2) developing empirically grounded theories, and (3) increasing the robustness of design practice. Characteristic to design research is that it is interventionist, iterative, process oriented, utility oriented, and theory oriented.
- Within design research, one may want to distinguish between validation studies (primarily aiming to prove or disprove learning theories) and development studies (aiming to solve an educational problem using relevant theoretical knowledge). The latter typically

includes the following stages: (1) a thorough context and problem analysis along with development of a conceptual framework based on literature review (preliminary research); (2) setting out substantive design specifications and procedural guidelines and optimizing prototypes through iterative cycles of design, formative evaluation, and revision (prototyping); (3) summative evaluation of effectiveness and preferably also an exploration of transferability and scaling; and (4) systematic reflection and documentation.

- The whole cycle of research-based educational engineering departs from a sound theoretical base by validation studies, develops through practical understanding from development studies, and is eventually tested by (large-scale) effectiveness research.

# RESEARCH ON DESIGN AND DEVELOPMENT

*Rita C. Richey and James D. Klein*

This section of the chapter examines design and development research. This type of research offers a way to test theory and to validate practice that has been perpetuated essentially through unchallenged tradition. In addition, it is a way to empirically establish new procedures, techniques, and tools based on a methodical analysis of specific cases.

The practice of design and development is empirical by nature. Most design models parallel the scientific problem-solving processes; therefore, it would be reasonable to assume that design and development processes themselves have robust empirical support, but historically little research has been directed toward our design processes and products. Design and development research is an empirical approach to address this problem.

In the following pages, we examine methods, strategies, and issues related to conducting design and development research. Its definition and scope are discussed, and the two major types of design and development research—product and tool research and model research—are explored. Three main sources for locating design and development research problems are provided. The methods and strategies commonly used in design and development studies including qualitative, quantitative, and mixed-methods approaches are examined. Examples from the literature are provided to demonstrate how these approaches

have been successfully used by researchers. Methodological concerns that design and development researchers commonly face are addressed, including the constraints of conducting research in natural work settings and issues of researcher–participant dual roles. Recent trends in design and development research are also discussed as is the future of this type of scholarly endeavor. This examination of design and development research is necessarily concise. Readers who are interested in learning more can find a detailed discussion in Richey and Klein (2007).

## The Definition and Scope of Design and Development Research

### The Evolving Nature of Design and Development Research

Design and development research seeks to create knowledge grounded in data systematically derived from practice. Many examples of design and development research can be found in the literature spanning up to four decades. In recent years, however, there has been renewed interest in this research orientation and the benefits it offers the field. Furthermore, notions of design and development research continue to evolve. Design and development research* can be defined as the systematic study of design, development, and evaluation processes with the aim of establishing an empirical basis for the creation of instructional and noninstructional products and tools and new or enhanced models that govern their development (Richey and Klein, 2007).

Design and development research covers a wide spectrum of activities and interests. In its simplest form, it can be either (1) the study of the process and impact of specific design and development efforts, or (2) the study of the design and development process as a whole, or of particular process components. Such research can involve a situation in which someone is studying the design and development work of others; however, it can also involve a situation in which someone is performing design and development activities and studying the process at the same time. In either case, a distinction is made between *doing* design and

---

* The term *developmental research* has been used previously to describe this approach (Richey and Klein, 2005; Richey and Nelson, 1996; Richey et al., 2004; Seels and Richey, 1994). Over the years the term *development* has been ambiguous to many in the instructional design and technology field and has generated considerable discussion regarding its meaning. It refers to many other areas of study, such as human development, international development, organizational development, and staff development. A more complete rationale for this terminology change is presented in Richey and Klein (2007).

**TABLE 54.2**
**Types of Design and Development Research**

| | Product and Tool Research | Model Research |
|---|---|---|
| Emphasis | Study of specific product or tool design and development projects | Study of model development, validation or use |
| Outcome | Lessons learned from developing specific products and analyzing the conditions that facilitate their use | New design and development procedures or models and conditions that facilitate their use |
| | **Context-Specific Conclusions** $\rightarrow$ | **Generalized Conclusions** |

development and *studying* the processes. Design and development studies often involve collaboration between researchers and practitioners using a wide range of qualitative and quantitative techniques. Together they work to add to the instructional design knowledge base by studying the nature of the designer and the design processes, often using projects from natural work environments.

### Types of Design and Development Research

The two major types of design and development research are (1) product and tool research and (2) model research. The two categories of design and development research have been previously called *Type 1* and *Type 2* (Richey et al., 2004), but it may be easier to grasp the breadth of these types by looking at their general outcomes. The first type of research pertains primarily to studies of the design and development of products and tools, such as Preese and Foshay's (1999) research on the development and impact of a set of object-oriented authoring tools. Often the entire design and development process is documented. Some research, however, concentrates on one aspect of design and development only (such as production) or de-emphasizes some phases (such as needs assessment). Many recent studies focus on the design and development of technology-based instruction. This type of research has a tendency to combine the task of doing design and development and studying the processes.

The second type of design and development research pertains to studies of the development, validation, and use of design and development models, such as Adamski's (1998) research on models for designing job aids used in high-risk situations. These studies focus on the models and processes themselves, rather than their demonstration. Although it is possible to conduct model research in conjunction with the development of a product or program, most model studies concentrate on previously developed instruction and consequently are not project specific. Model

research may address the validity or effectiveness of an existing or newly constructed development model, process, or technique. In addition, these studies often seek to identify and describe the conditions that facilitate successful design and development.

### Generalized and Context-Specific Conclusions

In the contemporary orientation toward research, most accept the premise that research can have a broader function than the creation of generalizable statements of law; context-specific studies also are valued. Design and development research encompasses studies with conclusions that are both generalizable and contextually specific. This reflects the fact that product and tool research typically involves studies that describe and analyze the design and development processes used in *particular* projects and are thus to a great extent context bound. Model research studies, on the other hand, are oriented toward a general analysis of design and development processes. These studies tend to be more generalizable than product studies. Table 54.2 portrays the relationships between the two major types of design and development research.

### Sources of Design and Development Research Problems

Although the idiosyncratic interests of individual researchers guide much research, other common sources of design and development research problems include:

- Actual workplace settings and projects
- New technology
- Theoretical questions prompted by the literature

The workplace and practitioners are primary sources of research problems. Those problems that are typically viewed as researchable reflect situations that are recurring and common to many settings, are considered to be basically solvable, and reflect areas of current interest in the field. One example of problems generated by the workplace can be found in the research by Sullivan et al. (2000), who were involved in the development and implementation of a comprehensive, K–12 energy education curriculum over a 20-year period that was used by more than 12 million students in the United States. In this case, the workplace is K–12 educational settings across the country. Their research report described the components of the program itself, including instructional objectives, test items, and instructional materials and provided guidelines for long-term instructional development projects. The problems addressed by Sullivan et al. (2000) were important because the curriculum in question is commonly used by many school districts. Moreover, the scope of the program implementation is so large that the results are viable for many school districts, and the long-term nature of the project provides an opportunity to examine retrospective data collected on many students from grades K–12.

Today, many of the cutting-edge research topics relate to the development and use of emerging technologies. In general, these studies focus on how we can best take advantage of the potential of the new technologies. The questions that people have with respect to technology-based design and development are often simple—How do you do it? What are the problems I can expect? How can I avoid them? What resources are needed? Problems such as these tend to lend themselves to research on product development in which an actual project is documented and studied. Corry et al. (1997) conducted a study that involved the design and usability of a university website. The object was to identify ways of maximizing the usability of informational websites. They conducted a case study of the design processes and strategies implemented to ensure usability. The topic of this study is important because website design is a topic of great interest today and one in which many developers are currently involved.

Instructional design (ID) models continue to serve as an important part of the theory base of the field, and as such provide direction for identifying design and development research problems. These problems tend to focus upon a validation of ID models themselves and the study of particular elements and phases of the ID process. They are important to the substantiation of the design process. ID model validation can be viewed as either an internal validation of the components and process of the model or the external validation of the impact of the products of a model's use (Richey, 2005).

Another category of theory-based problems attuned to design and development research techniques concerns the nature of designer thinking and decision making. The study by Perez and Emery (1995) is an example of this type of research. They sought to identify the differences in cognitive processing and problem-solving paths of expert and novice designers. The design task for each participant was controlled; each was presented with the same design task and was given a standard time limit. This study's problem was important because it attempted to determine the actual design processes used, understand the different thinking tactics used by persons of varying levels of design expertise, and relate the cognitive psychology research literature to the ID process.

## The Characteristics of Design and Development Research Methodology

*Design and development research* is an umbrella term for the study of design and development using a broad collection of traditional methods and strategies, both quantitative and qualitative. Which methods are selected and how these methods are employed depend not only on the nature of the research problem and questions but also on whether the study involves product and tool research or model research. The following section examines three aspects of design and development research:

- Common research methodologies
- The use of mixed and multiple methods research techniques
- Typical participants and settings employed

### Commonly Used Design and Development Methods and Strategies

Design and development research uses a wide variety of methodologies. Much design and development research—both product and tool research and model research—relies on a variety of qualitative techniques, including case studies, interviews, document reviews, and observations. Evaluation research techniques (both qualitative and quantitative) are also included in many studies that focus on product and tool development. Model development and use studies often employ survey research techniques, while model validation studies frequently use traditional experimental designs. Some of the most commonly used design and development research methods are shown in Table 54.3. Design and development research tends to rely more on qualitative techniques than on quantitative techniques. Perhaps this is because this research often demands the use of exploratory procedures, rather than employing the controls required by many quantitative

**TABLE 54.3**
**Common Methods Used in Design and Development Research**

| Type of Research | Project Emphasis | Research Methods Employed |
|---|---|---|
| Product and tool research | Comprehensive design and development projects | Case study, content analysis, evaluation, field observation, in-depth interview |
| | Phases of design and development | Case study, content analysis, expert review, field observation, in-depth interview, survey |
| | Tool development and use | Evaluation, expert review, in-depth interview, survey |
| Model research | Model development | Case study, Delphi, in-depth interview, literature review, survey, think-aloud methods |
| | Model validation | Experimental, expert review, in-depth interview |
| | Model use | Case study, content analysis, field observation, in-depth interview, survey, think-aloud methods |

methods. Perhaps it is because these studies tend to deal more with real-life projects than with simulated or contrived projects. In any case, design and development research is always applied research and related to the practice of ID, rather than an examination of isolated variables.

### Common Use of Mixed and Multiple Methods Research

Design and development research tends to be complex methodologically. This is typically because of the complexities of real-life situations and of the design and development processes themselves. As a result, this research tends to employ either a mixed-methods or multiple methods approach. The term *mixed-methods research* describes those studies that combine qualitative and quantitative methods. An example of a mixed-method approach is a study by Plummer et al. (1992), who used two research methodologies—case study and experimental—in conjunction with an ID task. This project involved the development of a job aid for use by military personnel operating a complicated piece of communications equipment. The experimental phase involved an evaluation of the effectiveness of the job aid and compared three different types of uses of the job aid. This study provided impact information, as well as information relating to the best conditions for developing and using the product.

Many design and development studies, however, that employ multiple research methods are not mixing the quantitative and qualitative orientations. They are simply making use of a variety of similar strategies; for example, Corry and colleagues (1997) used several qualitative methods when they studied product development by conducting in-depth interviews, as well as conducting field observations.

### Typical Participants and Settings

Design and development research is often context bound, and the nature of the conditions in which people work is critical to the processes and outcomes of a particular project; consequently, the setting of a study is typically as important as are the people participating in the study. Each design and development setting has a unique culture and set of conditions that can have a profound impact on the activities occurring there. This impact is most critical when the study is being conducted in a natural work environment. The researcher's most crucial decision with respect to setting is whether it includes the conditions and elements addressed in the research questions; however, additional concerns include feasibility (i.e., how practical is it to conduct a study in that setting?), access (i.e., will the organization allow all needed personnel to participate in the research?), and proprietary rights (i.e., will key documents be available to the researcher and will the data be publishable?).

Participants involved in design and development research may or may not be selected because of their association with a particular organization; however, they are almost always selected because of their particular role in the design and development process. Studies documenting and analyzing the development of an instructional product would obviously include those persons involved in designing the actual product—designers, developers, and perhaps clients and evaluators. At times, the design team as a whole participates in such research. Studies of the impact of an innovative product or tool would include those who are affected by its use—clients, learners, instructors, and perhaps supervisors. Participants in model development and model use studies often parallel those in product development and use. Model validation studies can include persons in all of these roles. Participants in design and development research tend to be (not surprisingly) designers and developers, rather than learners and instructors. This is a key distinction between design and development research and traditional teaching-learning research. Even so, a wide variety of people serving in many roles are critical to design and development research.

What is rather unique to design and development studies are the non-human entities that serve as research participants; for example, it is not unusual for the project itself to serve as a type of participant. In these situations, the project characteristics become a key focus of the research. For example, as projects can differ in terms of the types of products they create, with possible delivery system variations or content variations. These differences often become key rationales for the inclusion of a given project in a study. In these studies, the project becomes a key unit of analysis.

In some design and development studies, the participants are organizations themselves. Types of organizations may be selected to provide a systematic distribution of setting constraints within a particular study. In this way, environmental effects may be identified. The organization's size in terms of personnel or budget, its focus, its philosophy—all can be factors in selecting particular organizations to participate in a study. Some studies, for example, may seek to determine the differences among the design and development practices in educational, corporate, or military settings.

# Product and Tool Research: Methods and Strategies

## Methods for Research on Product Development

The classic product development study is descriptive research using case study methods. Many of these studies describe the entire life span of the product development process in detail. Research by Visser et al. (2002) is an example of a product development study, from an initial pilot study to a year-long try-out to evaluation of the product. The entire product development effort was an empirical process. The research culminated in an instructional product that addresses learner motivation and, in turn, is intended to reduce the drop-out and noncompletion rates of distance education programs.

The pilot study was designed to identify the characteristics of effective motivational messages and to develop a prototype of such a message. Participants were 17 international students enrolled in one distance education course. Data were collected from student records, interviews with program staff, and end-of-course questionnaires.

The main study was extended to 81 students enrolled in 5 distance education courses, of which 2 used personalized motivational messages, 2 collective motivational messages, and 1 no motivational messages. Each course was considered as a separate year-long case study. Instructors developed the motivational messages for their own courses according to a structured plan devised by the researcher. A variety of data collection instruments were used in addition to those used in the pilot study. Student-related data were collected with pre- and post-course questionnaires and telephone interviews. Instructors provided existing course completion records, questionnaires, course logbooks, and time monitoring sheets and also had in-depth interviews with the researcher. These data enabled the researchers to determine if motivational messages were effective and efficient and which types of messages were superior.

## Methods for Research on Tool Development and Use

Recently, some researchers have been concentrating on studying the development and use of tools that either make design and development itself easier or support the teaching/learning process. Not surprisingly, the bulk of these have been computer-based tools, and research has been directed toward automating design and development through their use. Below is a representative example of a tool use study.

Nieveen and van den Akker's (1999) tool research focused on a computer system that served as a performance support tool for designers during the formative evaluation phase of an ID project. This particular study concentrated on the use of the tool, seeking to assess not only the effectiveness of the tool but also its practicality. In Phase 1, 65 designers and developers with varied experience and expertise participated in a workshop on the use of the tool and then had an hour to use it to develop a formative evaluation plan. The computer system tracked participant actions and time-on-screen data. The workshop leader and assistant noted comments and the support they provided to designers during the exercise. The contents of the evaluation plans constructed during the workshop were collected for analysis, and a post-workshop questionnaire was used to gather perceptions of practicality, and other reactions to the tool.

Phase 2 involved a try-out with four ID projects currently underway in two different work settings. Three of the designers were experienced and one was a novice. Data collected included: (1) two or three interviews per designer after completion of significant parts of the formative evaluation task, and (2) documentation of the evaluation activities completed (evaluation plan, instruments, final report, log book of activities). Using a synthesis of the data collected, a detailed report of each try-out project was written. Summaries of these project reports were also written. Participating designers then reviewed these summaries and recommended minor changes. The findings of this research led to changes in the tool, confirmation of the assumption that the tool was appropriate for both novice and experienced designers, and identification of the constraints of daily practice that impacted the use and effectiveness of the tool.

Like many other examples of design and development research, this tool use study used a mixed-methods design. In Phase 1, the methods employed were survey research techniques and content analysis. In Phase 2, the methods were in-depth interviews and content analysis.

## Model Research: Methods and Strategies

### Methods for Research on Model Development

In spite of the widespread use of models in the field, there is a lack of research on model formation. Many ID models are constructed by conducting a literature review of theory and research and then synthesizing the findings; however, some research does specifically address model construction procedures. A study by Jones and Richey (2000) is an example of model development research using multiple qualitative methods. The outcome of the study was a revised rapid prototyping ID model that describes designer tasks performed, the concurrent processing of those tasks, and the nature of customer involvement. Data were obtained from a natural design and development work setting. Designers and clients from two contrasting projects participated in the study. The projects varied in terms of size, product, and industry. Both projects had been completed at the time of the research.

The designers constructed task logs in which they identified the tasks they had completed, when they were completed, and the time it took to do each job. As part of the logging process, designers reviewed extant data, including the project proposal, time sheets, design memos, prototype specifications, and the final product. Next, a structured hour-long interview was conducted with each designer to determine the impact of the rapid prototyping methodologies on the ID process and on product quality. Telephone interviews were conducted with the customer. All interviews were tape-recorded.

After coding and synthesizing the data, the researchers could determine which design and devel-

opment tasks were performed by whom and when. The time expended on each task was determined and an ID rapid prototyping procedural model was devised. The primary methods used in this model development research were content analysis of extant data and newly constructed diaries, as well as in-depth interviews.

### Methods for Research on Model Validation

Design models can be externally validated by isolating the effects of the given model as compared to the use of another model or approach. A study by Tracey (2002) is an example of controlled testing validation. Tracey compared use of the Dick and Carey (1996) model with an instructional systems design (ISD) model enhanced with a consideration of multiple intelligences. This served as an external validation of the newly constructed multiple intelligences (MI) design model. She established two design teams, each with two novice designers. One team worked with the Dick and Carey model, and the second used the MI model. Both teams were instructed to design a 2-hour, instructor-led classroom-based team building course for a nonprofit organization. The teams each received: (1) materials regarding the organization; (2) written content on team building; (3) audience, environment, and gap analysis information; and (4) an ISD model.

All four instructional designers met as a group to assess the needs, identify the goals of the team building training, and review the content. The teams then separated to conduct their own learner and environmental analyses based on the information given and their assigned model. Both teams worked individually to create their performance objectives based on the results of their analyses and the steps of the design model they were using. The teams reconvened to review their objectives to ensure that each met the same team-building goals, and together they wrote the post-test questions. The teams then separated again and worked simultaneously in the same location in two different offices during the remainder of the design and development process. Each group was provided computers, an office, any desired training materials, and a desktop publisher to create the instructor guide, participant guide templates, and all finished products.

The resulting programs were implemented and their impact compared in terms of learner knowledge and attitudes. Instrumentation used during the study included designer logs giving reactions to their tasks and the models used, learner knowledge post-tests, and surveys addressing participant reactions to the instruction.

## Methods for Research on Model Use

Design and development research that focuses on model use addresses ID processes as they occur naturally or concentrates on the use of a particular model. A study by Visscher-Voerman and Gustafson (2004) provides an example of how in-depth interviews can allow design and development researchers to explore the intricacies of the ID process as it actually occurs. Twenty-four different designers, including those with and without formal design training, were selected according to pre-determined criteria. These designers represented six different design settings. The study had two phases. In the first phase, 12 designers, 2 per setting, were interviewed for about 1-1/2 hours. The first interview included discussions of their backgrounds and their projects. They were asked about the strategies they had used in a recent project and were encouraged to give concrete examples, to explain why they worked in a given manner, and why they deviated from general plans. These interviews were audiotaped and transcribed. Interview data were corroborated through an examination of related project documents. A report was then generated based on the interviews that covered each designer's profile, a project summary, and a project description. The report was revised after the designer reviewed and reacted to it. This process of verifying the accuracy of one's data is called *member checking* (Creswell, 2002). The revised reports, rather than the interviews, were used as the basis for the preliminary analysis.

The preliminary analysis began by labeling each design activity described using analysis, design, development, implementation, and evaluation (ADDIE) terminology. Next, there was a more detailed analysis of each major activity as described by each designer. These analyses were then synthesized and interpreted in light of the literature to produce four different general design paradigms (not models), each of which represents a unique philosophical orientation.

In the second round of in-depth interviews, two designers from each setting were interviewed following the same procedures as had been previously used, and data were initially analyzed in the same manner. All data were then combined and analyzed to determine the underlying rationales for designer actions. Detailed descriptions of designer activities and their underlying paradigms resulted.

## Unique Design and Development Research Methodology Concerns

Methodological issues that tend to be more problematic for design and development researchers than for scholars dealing with other topics include:

- Avoiding biases when researchers assume participant roles
- Difficulties working with recall data
- Constraints on research in natural work environments

### Researcher–Participant Dual Roles

In most research, it is unusual for the researcher to be a part of the observations. In design and development research, especially in product and tool development studies, researchers often *are* the designers and developers. In other words, by design the researchers are observing themselves. This is a far different matter than the participant observation that is common in ethnographic and field research and invites the possibility of serious flaws in the data. Any time that researchers assume dual roles in a project, the research design of the study must delineate specific strategies for ensuring unbiased data. The most common techniques of doing this are by using carefully structured data collection instruments and by triangulating multiple sources of data.

In an illustrative study, McKenney and van den Akker (2005) assumed the multiple roles of not only researchers and designers but also developers, programmers, and evaluators. They used the following strategies to avoid interjecting personal biases into the dataset:

- Establish procedures to segregate data and subjective inferences.
- Triangulate data by collecting data of different types and data from different sources.
- Use different investigators to collect data.
- Conduct data analysis and interpretation with a larger group of colleagues and research assistants.

These are reasonable procedures that could also be applied in other studies in which the researcher assumes the role of the designer or developer.

If researchers do assume participant roles in product and tool research, it is more likely to be that of the designer, but not always. It is not unusual for instructors to be involved, especially in the try-out of a product. Once again, procedures must be established to prevent the researcher from unintentionally interjecting biases into the dataset.

### Working with Recall Data

Although it is always preferred that design and development research be conducted while the project is underway, this is not always possible, especially if one is dealing with the time constraints of real projects occurring in natural work settings. The dangers of using recall data are obvious—people may forget project details. When it is necessary to use recall data, provisions should be made for: (1) using systematic procedures to prompt and stimulate participants' memories, and (2) verifying the accuracy of the data that are provided. Many techniques for accomplishing these goals are available, including:

- Having participants construct project task logs and using extant data to verify these project recollections
- Requiring participants to complete a pre-interview activity form to stimulate recall
- Triangulating data from multiple sources
- Allowing participants to verify the accuracy of their reports

Research designs using recall data should also provide for multiple sources of data to help ensure the reliability of a dataset.

### Research in Natural Work Environments

Design and development research is by nature an applied type of research. Most studies seek to collect data from realistic design and development situations, be they simulated or naturally occurring. Product and tool research is almost exclusively the study of actual design and development efforts. When studying ID processes that occur in real-world settings, one is blessed with authenticity and cursed with a myriad of contextual factors, some of which are relevant and others that are not. By and large, such studies recognize the influence of the work environments through full descriptions; for example, design and development studies have addressed the following aspects of work and instructional contexts:

- Characteristics and backgrounds of the learners for whom the product, program, or tool was designed
- Characteristics and backgrounds of the designer/developers for whom the tool was designed
- Structure of the design and development team
- Facilities used for product implementation
- Resources and procedures utilized in the distribution and implementation of the product, tool or program

In addition to including contextual variables in case studies, some studies also address such factors in quantitative analyses. Typically, this occurs in a product or program evaluation phase; for example, Sullivan et al. (2000) measured school administrator attitudes, an organizational climate characteristic, and considered their impact on the success of their energy curriculum.

### Trends in Design and Development Research

Design and development research is expanding (Richey and Klein, 2007; Wang and Hannafin, 2005) with more persons tackling design problems from this relatively new research perspective. New products and programs are being empirically studied. New models are being devised and validated. In this section, we provide a brief overview of these trends and speculate on the future role of design and development research in our field.

### Trends in Product and Tool Research

The design and development of instructional products and programs are considered by many to be the heart of our field. Product and tool studies most frequently concern the use of instructional interventions in schools or in employee training situations. Recent research has also focused on non-instructional products and tools; for example, Nguyen (2005) described a needs assessment conducted to determine the types of electronic performance support systems (EPSSs) that training professionals and end users think are valuable to facilitate performance. In addition, Nguyen et al. (2005) conducted an experiment in which employees at a manufacturing company completed a procedural task and either received support from an intrinsic, extrinsic, or external EPSS or received no support. Recent trends in the study of non-instructional interventions have caused us to expand our definition of design and development research (see above). This is in keeping with expanded definitions of the field that encompass notions of performance improvement and non-instructional interventions (Reiser, 2007).

Another trend in product and tool research reflects the evolution of media and technology use in the field; for example, early product research with an audiovisual emphasis is exemplified by Greenhill's (1955) description of producing low-cost motion pictures with sound for instructional purposes and by Cambre's (1979) study of the development of formative evaluation procedures for instructional television. With the increased computer-based instruction in schools and training settings, research studies focusing on the design, development and evaluation of these products and tools also increased (Buch, 1989; Kearsley, 1986; Lewis et al., 1993; Munro and Towne, 1992). Trends in distance learning products and Web-based tools have provided another stimulus for design and development researchers (Chou and Sun, 1996; Corry et al., 1997; Koszalka, 2001; Visser et al., 2002).

### Trends in Model Research

Although design and development models will undoubtedly continue to proliferate as they have in the past, research on these models is in its infancy; nonetheless, a growing amount of empirical work supports the model development process. Much of this work concerns the development of instruction using newer models and procedures of instructional design that reflect the influence of cognitive science and constructivism. Cronjé (2006), for example, has constructed and tested a new model that integrates objectivist and constructivist design orientations, and Schatz (2005) developed and tested a model for developing learning-object tags for use by K–12 educators. In many cases, newer model development research is being blended with model validation efforts, such as in a study by Tracey and Richey (2007).

Model use research, on the other hand, has been an important research genre for some time, especially in an array of studies on designer decision making (Goel and Pirolli, 1988; Nelson, 1990). This line of research continues with a new emphasis on the impact of specific designer characteristics on the design process. Most notable are the studies of the nature of designer expertise and the differences between novice and expert designers (Kirschner et al., 2002; Perez and Emery, 1995; Rowland, 1992; Tennyson, 1998). Other characteristics, however, have been studied to determine their impact on the use of design models; for example, Chase (2003) studied the effects of gender and gender-related thinking processes on the use of design models. Model research is growing and is open to the exploration of a very broad array of theoretical orientations, work settings, and variables of interest.

### The Future of Design and Development Research

In addition to the traditional design and development research discussed here, other researchers are using alternative approaches to address many of the same problems. The most prominent of these approaches is design-based research. Design-based research is the study of learning in context (Design-Based Research Collective, 2003; also see van den Akker and Kuiper in this chapter). Using this approach (Winn, 2004, p. 104):

> ...designers build tools that they test in real classrooms and gather data that contribute both to the construction of theory and to the improvement of the tools. This process proceeds iteratively, over a period of time, until the tool is proven to be effective and our knowledge of why it is effective has been acquired and assimilated in theory.

It seeks to clarify the nature of the process by which people learn, typically through their interactions with instructional materials and other learners. This type of research design has been extensively used in the study of technology-based instructional materials. It is typically context specific. Although there are similarities to design and development research (especially to product and tool studies), this is a somewhat different orientation compared to the techniques discussed here which concentrate on the design and development procedures themselves.

These various research methods, however, all reflect the preponderance of scholars turning to research designs and methodologies that rely on real-life and complex design and instructional environments rather than controlled settings. These studies also speak to the needs of practitioners as well as the development of theory. Ultimately, the expansion of design and development research will depend more on the pressure exerted by critical disciplinary and workplace problems than the voices of advocates of this type of research.

The sources of problems that have generated our current design and development research—emerging technology, the workplace, and theory—are likely to be the same problem areas that will continue to stimulate this research in the future, probably in this order of magnitude. Technology is a fairly straightforward impetus for design and development research, and this research is often prompted by clear-cut practitioner problems. Similarly, workplace problems demand resolution and researchers respond. This is typically not the case with theory-related research. Ultimately, the particular interests of individual scholars generate theory-based research. Future research, however, is likely to address non-instructional as well as instructional problems and products.

### Summary

This chapter section focused on design and development research. Major concepts and points addressed included the following:

- Design and development research seeks to create knowledge grounded in data systematically derived from practice. It provides a way to test theory, validate practice, and establish new procedures, techniques, and tools based on a systematic analysis of specific cases.

- Such research can involve a situation in which someone is studying the design and development work of others or in which someone is performing design and development activities and studying the process at the same time. In either case, a distinction is made between *doing* design and development and *studying* the processes.
- The two major types of design and development research are product and tool research and model research. Product and tool research usually involves studies that describe and analyze the design and development processes used in a particular project; conclusions are context bound. Model research studies are oriented toward a general analysis of design and development processes and tend to be more generalizable than product studies.
- The entire design and development process is often documented in product and tool research; however, some product and tool studies concentrate on one phase of design and development only or de-emphasize some phases.
- Model research encompasses studies of model development, model validation, and model use.
- The most common sources of design and development research problems are actual workplace settings and projects, new technology, and theoretical questions prompted by the literature.
- Although design and development researchers use a wide variety of methods, these studies tend to rely more on qualitative approaches than on quantitative approaches. Qualitative data-gathering techniques, including case studies, interviews, document reviews, and observations, are frequently used. Evaluation research techniques are also included in many studies that focus on product and tool development. Model development and use studies often employ survey research techniques, while model validation studies often use traditional experimental designs.
- Due to the complexity of studying design and development processes in actual work settings, many studies employ mixed-methods research that combine qualitative and quantitative methods or multiple research methods that make use of a variety of similar approaches.

- Design and development researcher should address the following methodological issues when conducting their studies: avoiding bias when assuming a participant role, the danger in relying on recall data, and the constraints on research in natural work environments.

## REFERENCES

Adamski, A. J. (1998). The Development of a Systems Design Model for Job Performance Aids: A Qualitative Developmental Study, Ph.D. dissertation, Wayne State University, 1998. *Dissert. Abstr. Int. A*, 59(03), 789.

Aleven, V., Stahl, E., Schworm, S., Fischer, F., and Wallace, R. (2003). Help seeking and help design in interactive learning environments, *Rev. Educ. Res.*, 73, 277–320.

Anand, P. G. and Ross, S. M. (1987). Using computer-assisted instruction to personalize arithmetic materials for elementary school children. *J. Educ. Psychol.*, 79, 72–78.

Andrews, D. H. and Goodson, L. A. (1980). A comparative analysis of models of instructional design. *J. Instruct. Dev.*, 3(4), 2–16.

Anglin, G. J. and Morrison, G. R. (2001). Cognitive Load Theory: Implications for Instructional Design Research and Practice. Paper presented at the Association for Educational Communications and Technology Annual Meeting, Atlanta, GA.

Barab, S. and Squire, K. (2004). Design-based research: putting a stake in the ground. *J. Learn. Sci.*, 13(1), 1–14.*

Berliner, D. C. (2002). Educational research: the hardest science of all. *Educ. Res.*, 31(8), 18–20.

Borg, W. R., Gall, J. P., and Gall, M. D. (1993). *Applying Educational Research*, 3rd ed. New York: Longman.

Borman, G. D., Hewes, G., Overman, L. T., and Brown, S. (2003). Comprehensive school reform and achievement: a meta-analysis. *Rev. Educ. Res.*, 73(2), 125–230.

Börner, K., Hazlewood, W. R., and Sy-Miaw, L. (2002) Visualizing the spatial and temporal distribution of user interaction data collected in three-dimensional virtual worlds. In *Proceedings of the Sixth International Conference on Information Visualization (IV'02)*, July 10–12, London, pp. 25–31 (http://vw.indiana.edu/cive02/004_borner_ VisSpatialTemporal.pdf).

Brown, A. L. (1992). Design experiments: theoretical and methodological challenges in creating complex interventions in classroom settings. *J. Learn. Sci.*, 2(2), 141–178.

Buch, E. E. (1989). A systematically developed training program for microcomputer users in an industrial setting, Ph.D. dissertation, University of Pittsburgh, 1988. *Dissert. Abstr. Int. A*, 49(4), 750.

Burkhardt, H. (2006). From design research to large-scale impact: engineering research in education. In *Educational Design Research*, edited by J. van den Akker, K. Gravemeijer, S. McKenney, and N. Nieveen, pp. 121–150. London: Routledge.

Burkhardt, H. and Schoenfeld, A. H. (2003). Improving educational research: towards a more useful, more influential and better funded enterprise. *Educ. Res.*, 32(9), 3–14.

Cambre, M. A. (1979). The development of formative evaluation procedures for instructional film and television: the first fifty years, Ph.D. dissertation, Indiana University, 1978. *Dissert. Abstr. Int. A*, 39(7), 3995

Campbell, D. T. and Stanley, J. C. (1963). Experimental and quasi-experimental designs for research on teaching. In *Handbook of Research on Teaching*, edited by N. L. Gage, pp. 171–246. Chicago, IL: Rand McNally.*

Carrier, C. A. (1984). Do learners make good choices? *Instruct. Innov.*, 29(2), 15–17.

Carrier, C. A., Davidson, G. V., Higson, V., and Williams, M. D. (1984). Selection of options by field independent and field dependent children in a computer-based coordinate concept lesson. *J. Comput.-Based Instruct.*, 11(2), 49–54.

Carrier, C. A., Davidson, G. V., Williams, M. D., and Kalweit, C. M. (1986). Instructional options and encouragement effects in a microcomputer-delivered concept lesson. *J. Educ. Res.*, 79, 222–229.

Cavalier, J. C., Klein, J. D., and Cavalier, F. J. (1995). Effects of cooperative learning on performance, attitude, and group behaviors in a technical team environment. *Educ. Technol. Res. Dev.*, 43(3), 61–71.

Chandler, P. and Sweller, J. (1992). The split-attention effect as a factor in the design of instruction. *Br. J. Educ. Psychol.*, 62, 233–246.

Chase, C. A. (2003). The effects of gender differences and levels of expertise on instructional design, Ph.D. dissertation, Wayne State University, 2002. *Dissert. Abstr. Int. A*, 63(11), 3815.

Chou, C. and Sun, C. (1996). Constructing a cooperative distance learning system: the CORAL experience. *Educ. Technol. Res. Dev.*, 44(4), 71–84.

Chung J. and Reigeluth, C. M. (1992). Instructional prescriptions for learner control, *Educ. Technol.*, 32(10), 14–20.

Clariana, R. B. and Lee, D. (2001). The effects of recognition and recall study tasks with feedback in a computer-based vocabulary lesson. *Educ. Technol. Res. Dev.*, 49(3), 23–36.

Clark, R. E. (1983). Reconsidering the research on learning from media. *Rev. Educ. Res.*, 53(4), 445–459.*

Clark, R. E. (1994). Media will never influence learning. *Educ. Technol. Res. Dev.*, 42(2), 21–29.

Clarke, T., Ayres, P., and Sweller, J. (2005). The impact of sequencing and prior knowledge on learning mathematics through spreadsheet applications. *Educ. Technol. Res. Dev.*, 53(3), 15–24.

Cobb, P., Confrey, J., diSessa, A., Lehrer, R., and Schauble, L. (2003). Design experiments in educational research. *Educ. Res.*, 32(1), 9–13.

Cognition and Technology Group at Vanderbilt (CTGV). (1990). Anchored instruction and its relationship to situated cognition. *Educ. Res.*, 19(6), 2–10.

Cognition and Technology Group at Vanderbilt (CTGV). (1993). Anchored instruction and situated cognition revisited. *Educ. Technol.*, 33(3), 52–70.

Corry, M. D., Frick, T. W., and Hansen, L. (1997). User-centered design and usability testing of a Web site: an illustrative case study. *Educ. Technol. Res. Dev.*, 45(4), 65–76.

Creswell, J. W. (2002). *Educational Research: Planning, Conducting, and Evaluating Quantitative and Qualitative Research*. Upper Saddle River, NJ: Pearson Education.

Cronbach, L. J. and Snow, R. E. (1981). *Aptitudes and Instructional Methods: A Handbook for Research on Interactions*. New York: Irvington.

Cronjé, J. (2006). Paradigms regained: toward integrating objectivism and constructivism in instructional design and the learning sciences. *Educ. Technol. Res. Dev.*, 54(4), 387–416.

Cuban, L. (1986). *Teachers and Machines: The Classroom Use of Technology Since 1920*. New York: Teachers College Press.

Dede, C. (2003). MUVEES project, http://vista.uconn.edu/webct/cobaltMainFrame.dowebct.

Dede, C. (2006). *River City*, videoconference interview presented to students and faculty at the University of Connecticut, Storrs, CT.

Design-Based Research Collective. (2003). Design based research: an emerging paradigm for educational inquiry. *Educ. Res.*, 32(1), 5–8.

Dick, W. and Carey, L. (1996). *The Systematic Design of Instruction*, 4th ed. New York: HarperCollins.

DiVesta, F. J. (1975). Trait-treatment interactions, cognitive processes, and research on communication media. *AV Commun. Rev.*, 23, 183–196.

Eisenhart, M. and Towne, L. (2003). Contestation and change in national policy on 'scientifically based' education research. *Educ. Res.*, 32(7), 31–38.

Feuer, M. J., Towne, L., and Shavelson, R. J. (2002). Scientific culture and educational research. *Educ. Res.*, 31(8), 4–14.

Fleming, M. and Levie, W. H. (1978). *Instructional Message Design: Principles from the Behavioral Sciences*. Englewood Cliffs, NJ: Educational Technology Publications.

Friedman, T. L. (2005). *The World Is Flat: A Brief History of the Twenty-First Century*. New York: Farrar, Straus and Giroux.

Glaser, R. (1976). Components of a psychology of instruction: towards a science of design. *Rev. Educ. Res.*, 46, 1–24.

Goel, V. and Pirolli, P. (1988). *Motivating the Notion of Generic Design within Information Processing Theory: The Design Problem Space*, Report No. DPS-1. Washington, D.C.: Office of Naval Research (ERIC Document Reproduction Service No. ED 315 041).

Goetzfried, L. and Hannafin, M. J. (1985). The effect of the locus of CAI control strategies on the learning of mathematics rules. *Am. Educ. Res. J.*, 22(2), 273–278.

Gray, S. H. (1987). The effect of sequence control on computer assisted learning. *J. Comput.-Based Instruct.*, 14(2), 54–56.

Greenhill, L. P. (1955). *A Study of the Feasibility of Local Production of Minimum Cost Sound Motion Pictures*, Technical Report No. SDC 269-7-48, Pennsylvania State University Instructional Film Research Program. Port Washington, NY: U.S. Naval Training Device Center, Office of Naval Research.

Guba, E. G. (1981). Criteria for assessing the trustworthiness of naturalistic inquiries. *Educ. Commun. Technol. J.*, 29, 75–92.

Gustafson, K. L. (1981). *Survey of Instructional Development Models*. Syracuse, NY: ERIC Clearinghouse on Information and Technology, Syracuse University.

Gustafson, K. L. (1991). *Survey of Instructional Development Models*, 2nd ed. Syracuse, NY: ERIC Clearinghouse on Information and Technology, Syracuse University.

Gustafson, K. L. and Branch, R. M. (1997). *Survey of Instructional Development Models*, 3rd ed. Syracuse, NY: ERIC Clearinghouse on Information and Technology.

Gustafson, K. L. and Branch, R. M. (2002a). *Survey of Instructional Development Models*, 4th ed. Syracuse, NY: ERIC Clearinghouse on Information and Technology.

Gustafson, K. L. and Branch, R. M. (2002b). What is instructional design? In *Trends and Issues in Instructional Design and Technology*, edited by R. A. Reiser and J. V. Dempsey, pp. 16–25. Upper Saddle River, NJ: Merrill/Prentice Hall.*

Hagler, P. and Knowlton, J. (1987). Invalid implicit assumption in CBI comparison research. *J. Comput.-Based Instruct.*, 14, 84–88.

Hannafin, M. J. (1984), Guidelines for using locus of instructional control in the design of computer-assisted instruction. *J. Instruct. Dev.*, 7(2), 6–10.

Hannafin, M. J. (1986). The status and future of research in instructional design and technology. *J. Instruct. Dev.*, 8, 24–30.

Hannafin, R. D. and Sullivan, H. J. (1995). Learner control in full and lean CAI programs. *Educ. Technol. Res. Dev.*, 43(1), 7–19.

Hannafin, R. D. and Sullivan, H. J. (1996). Learner preferences and learner control over amount of instruction. *J. Educ. Psychol.*, 88, 162–173.

Hargreaves, A. and Fink, D. (2006). *Sustainable Leadership*. San Francisco, CA: Jossey-Bass.

Hativa, N. (1988). Differential characteristics and methods of operation underlying CAI/CMI drill and practice systems. *J. Res. Comput. Educ.*, 20, 258–270.

Hicken, S., Sullivan, H. J., and Klein, J. P. (1992). Learner control modes and incentive variations in computer-delivered instruction, *Educ. Technol. Res. Dev.*, 40(4), 15–26.

Hoban, C. F. (1953). Determinants of audience reaction to a training film. *Audio Visual Commun. Rev.*, 1(1), 30–52.

Hsieh, P., Acee, T., Chung, W., Hsieh, Y., Kim, H., Thomas, G., Levin, J. R., and Robinson, D. H. (2005). Is educational intervention research on the decline? *J. Educ. Psychol.*, 97(4), 523–529.

Hulshof, C. D. (2004). Log file analysis. In *Encyclopedia of Social Measurement*, edited by K. Kempf-Leonard. New York: Academic Press.

Hutchins, E. (1995). *Cognition in the Wild*. Boston, MA: MIT Press.

Jackson, S., Stratford, S. J., Krajcik, J., and Soloway, E. (1995). Making System Dynamics Modeling Accessible to Pre-College Science Students. Paper presented at the Annual Meeting of the National Association for Research in Science Teaching, April 3–6, San Francisco, CA.

Jones, T. S. and Richey, R. C. (2000). Rapid prototyping in action: a developmental study. *Educ. Technol. Res. Dev.*, 48(2), 63–80.

Kearsley, G. (1986). Automated instructional development using personal computers: research issues. *J. Instruct. Dev.*, 9(1), 9–15.

Kelly, A. (2003). Research as design. *Educ. Res.*, 32(1), 3–4.

Kerr, S. T. (1983). Inside the black box: making design decisions for instruction. *Br. J. Educ. Technol.*, 14, 45–58.

Kim, Y., Baylor, A. L., and Group, P. (2006). Pedagogical agents as learning comparisons: the role of agent competency and type of interaction. *Educ. Technol. Res. Dev.*, 54(3), 223–243.

Kinzie, M. B. and Sullivan, H. J. (1989). Continuing motivation, learner control, and CIA. *Educ. Technol. Res. Dev.*, 37(2), 5–14.

Kinzie, M. B., Sullivan, H. J., and Berdel, R. L. (1988). Learner control and achievement in science computer-assisted instruction. *J. Educ. Psychol.*, 80, 299–303.

Kirschner, P. A., Carr, C., van Merriënboer, J. J. G., and Sloep, P. (2002). How expert designers design. *Perform. Improv. Q.*, 15(4), 86–104.

Koszalka, T. A. (2001). Designing synchronous distance education: a demonstration project. *Q. Rev. Dist. Educ.*, 2(4), 333–345.

Kozma, R. B. (1991). Learning with media. *Rev. Educ. Res.*, 61, 179–212.*

Kozma, R. B. (1994). Will media influence learning? Reframing the debate. *Educ. Technol. Res. Dev.*, 42, 7–19.

Ku, H. and Sullivan, H. J. (2000). Personalization of mathematics word problems in Taiwan. *Educ. Technol. Res. Dev.*, 48(3), 49–59.

Kulikowich, J. M. and Young, M. F. (2001). Locating an ecological psychology methodology for situated action. *J. Learn. Sci.*, 10(1/2), 165–202.

Lamberski, R. J. and Dwyer, F. M. (1983). The instructional effect of coding (color and black and white) on information acquisition and retrieval. *Educ. Commun. Technol.*, 31(1), 9–21.

Land, S. M. (2000). Cognitive requirements for learning with open-ended learning environments, *Educ. Technol. Res. Dev.*, 48(3), 61–78.

Le Maistre, C. (1998). What is an expert instructional designer? Evidence of expert performance during formative evaluation. *Educ. Technol. Res. Dev.*, 46, 21–36.

Leu, Jr., D. J., Kinzer, C. K., Coiro, J., and Cammack, D. (2004). Toward a theory of new literacies emerging from the Internet and other information and communication technologies. In *Theoretical Models and Processes of Reading*, 5th ed., edited by R. B. Ruddell and N. Unrau, pp. 1568–1611. Newark, DE: International Reading Association (http://www.readingonline.org/newliteracies/lit_index.asp?HREF=/newliteracies/leu).

Levin, J. R. (2004). Random thoughts on the (in)credibility of educational–psychological intervention research. *Educ. Psychol.*, 39(3), 173–184.*

Levin, J. R. and O'Donnell, A. M. (1999). What to do about educational psychology's credibility gaps? *Issues Educ. Contrib. Educ. Psychol.*, 5, 177–229.

Levonian, E. (1963). Opinion change as mediated by an audience-tailored film. *Audio Visual Commun. Rev.*, 11(4), 104–113.

Lewis, E. L., Stern, J. L., and Linn, M. C. (1993). The effect of computer simulations on introductory thermodynamics understanding. *Educ. Technol.*, 33(1), 45–58.

Liu, M. and Bera, S. (2005). An analysis of cognitive tool use patterns in a hypermedia learning environment, *Educ. Technol. Res. Dev.*, 53(1), 5–21.

Liu, M., Williams, D., and Pedersen, S. (2002). Alien Rescue: a problem-based hypermedia learning environment for middle school science, *J. Educ. Technol. Syst.*, 30(3), 255–270.

Lou, Y., Bernard, R. M., and Abrami, P. C. (2006). Media and pedagogy in undergraduate distance education: a theory-based meta-analysis of empirical literature. *Educ. Technol. Res. Dev.*, 54(2), 141–176.

McKenney, S. (2002). Computer-Based Support for Science Education Materials Developers in Africa: Exploring Potentials, Ph.D. dissertation. Enschede: University of Twente.

McKenney, S. and van den Akker, J. (2005). Computer-based support for curriculum designers: a case of developmental research. *Educ. Technol. Res. Dev.*, 53(2), 41–66.*

McKenney, S., Nieveen, N., and van den Akker, J. (2006). Design research from a curriculum perspective. In *Educational Design Research*, edited by J. van den Akker, K. Gravemeijer, S. McKenney, and N. Nieveen, pp. 67–90. London: Routledge.

Messick, S. (1995). Standards of validity and the validity of standards in performance assessment. *Educ. Meas. Issues Pract.*, 14(4), 5–8.

Metcalf, S. J., Krajcik, J., and Soloway, E. (2000). Model-It: a design retrospective. In *Innovations in Science and Mathematics Education: Advanced Design for Technologies of Learning*, edited by M. J. Jacobson and R. B. Kozma, pp. 77–115. Mahwah, NJ: Lawrence Erlbaum Associates.

Morrison, G. R. and Anglin, G. J. (2005). Research on cognitive load theory: application to e-learning. *Educ. Technol. Res. Dev.*, 53(3), 94–104.

Morrison, G. R., Ross, S. M., Gopalakrishnan, M., and Casey, J. (1995). The effects of incentives and feedback on achievement in computer-based instruction. *Contemp. Educ. Psychol.*, 20, 32–50.

Morrison, G. R., Ross, S. M., and Kemp, J. E. (2007). *Designing Effective Instruction*, 5th ed. Hoboken, NJ: Jossey-Bass.

Munro, A. and Towne, D. M. (1992). Productivity tools for simulation-centered training development. *Educ. Technol. Res. Dev.*, 40(4), 65–80.

Nelson, W. A. (1990). Selection and utilization of problem information by instructional designers, Ph.D. dissertation, Virginia Polytechnic Institute and State University, 1988. *Dissert. Abstr. Int. A*, 50(4), 866.

Nguyen, F. (2005). EPSS needs assessment: oops, I forgot how to do that! *Perform. Improv.*, 44(9), 33–39.

Nguyen, F., Klein, J. D., and Sullivan, H. J. (2005). A comparative study of electronic performance support systems. *Perform. Improv. Q.*, 18(4), 71–86.

Nieveen, N. (1999). Computer Support for Curriculum Developers. A Study on the Potential of Computer Support in the Domain of Formative Curriculum Evaluation, Ph.D. dissertation. Enschede: University of Twente.

Nieveen, N. and van den Akker, J. (1999). Exploring the potential of a computer tool for instructional developers. *Educ. Technol. Res. Dev.*, 47(3), 77–98.

Nieveen, N., McKenney, S., and van den Akker, J. (2006). Educational design research: the value of variety. In *Educational Design Research*, edited by J. van den Akker, K. Gravemeijer, S. McKenney, and N. Nieveen, pp. 151–158. London: Routledge.*

No Child Left Behind Act. (2001). Pub. L. No. 107-110, 107th Congress.

Paas, F., Tuovinen, J. E., van Merriënboer, J. J. G., and Darabi, A. A. (2005). A motivational perspective on the relation between mental effort and performance. *Educ. Technol. Res. Dev.*, 53(3), 25–34.

Park, O. and Tennyson, R. D. (1986). Computer-based response-sensitive design strategies for selecting presentation form and sequence of examples in learning of coordinate concepts. *J. Educ. Psychol.*, 78, 153–158.

Pea, R. D. (1985). Beyond amplification: using the computer to reorganize mental functioning. *Educ. Psychol.*, 20, 167–182.

Perez, R. S. and Emery, C. D. (1995). Designer thinking: how novices and experts think about instructional design. *Perform. Improv. Q.*, 8(3), 80–95.

Petkovich, M. D. and Tennyson, R. D. (1984). Clark's 'Learning from media': a critique. *Educ. Commun. Technol. J.*, 32, 233–241.

Pieters, J. M. and Bergman, R. (1995). The empirical basis of designing instruction. *Perform. Improv. Q.*, 8(3), 118–129.

Plummer, K. H., Gillis, P. D., Legree, P. J., and Sanders, M. G. (1992). The development and evaluation of a job aid to support mobile subscriber radio-telephone terminal (MSRT). *Perform. Improv. Q.*, 5(1), 90–105.

Pollock, J. C. and Sullivan, H. J. (1990). Practice mode and learner control in computer-based instruction. *Contemp. Educ. Psychol.*, 15, 251–260.

Preese, F. and Foshay, W. (1999). The PLATO courseware development environment. In *Design Approaches and Tools in Education and Training*, edited by J. van den Akker et al., pp. 195–204. Dordrecht: Kluwer.

Reeves, T., Herrington, J., and Oliver, R. (2005). Design research: a socially responsible approach to instructional technology research in higher education. *J. Comput. Higher Educ.*, 16(2), 97–116.*

Reiser, R. A. (2007). What field did you say you were in? Defining and naming our field. In *Trends and Issues in Instructional Design and Technology*, 2nd ed., edited by R. A. Reiser and J. V. Dempsey, pp. 2–9. Upper Saddle River, NJ: Prentice Hall.

Reiser, R. A. and Dempsey, J. V. (2002). What field did you say you were in? Defining and naming our field. In *Trends and Issues in Instructional Design and Technology*, edited by R. A. Reiser and J. V. Dempsey, pp. 5–15. Upper Saddle River, NJ: Prentice Hall.

Richey, R. C. (2005). Validating instructional design and development models. In *Innovations in Instructional Technology: Essays in Honour of David Merrill*, edited by J. M. Spector, C. Ohrazda, A. van Schaack, and D. A. Wiley, pp. 171–185. Mahwah, NJ: Lawrence Erlbaum Associates.*

Richey, R. C. and Klein, J. D. (2005). Developmental research methods: creating knowledge from instructional design and development practice. *J. Comput. Higher Educ.*, 16(2), 23–38.

Richey, R. C. and Klein, J. D. (2007). *Design and Development Research: Methods, Strategies, and Issues*. Mahwah, NJ: Lawrence Erlbaum Associates.

Richey, R. C. and Nelson, W. A. (1996). Developmental research. In *Handbook of Research for Educational Communications and Technology*, edited by D. Jonassen, pp. 1213–1245. New York: Simon & Schuster.

Richey, R. C., Klein, J. D., and Nelson, W. A. (2004). Developmental research: studies of instructional design and development. In *Handbook of Research on Educational Communications and Technology*, 2nd ed., edited by D. H. Jonassen, pp. 1099–1130. Mahwah, NJ: Lawrence Erlbaum Associates.

Richmond, B. (1985). *STELLA*. Lyme, NH: High Performance Systems.

Rogoff, B. and Lave, J. (1999). *Everyday Cognition: Its Development in Social Context*. New York: iUniverse.

Ross, S. M. (2003). Effective schools correlates as indicators of educational improvement: an examination of three urban reform initiatives. *J. Effective Schools*, 2(2), 67–81.

Ross, S. M. (2005). Randomized field trials: challenges and strategies. *TransFormation*, Spring/Summer, p. 7.

Ross, S. M. and Morrison, G. R. (1989). In search of a happy medium in instructional technology research: issues concerning external validity, media replications, and learner control. *Educ. Technol. Res. Dev.*, 37, 19–24.*

Ross, S. M. and Rakow, E. A. (1981). Learner control versus program control as adaptive strategies for selection of instructional support on math rules. *J. Educ. Psychol.*, 73, 745–753.

Ross, S. M., Morrison, G. R., and O'Dell, J. K. (1989). Uses and effects of learner control of context and instructional support in computer-based instruction, *Educ. Technol. Res. Dev.*, 37(4), 29–39.

Ross, S. M., Morrison, G. R., and Lowther, D. (2005). Using experimental methods in higher education. *J. Comput. Higher Educ.*, 16(2), 39–64.*

Rowland, G. (1992). What do instructional designers actually do? An initial investigation of expert practice. *Perform. Improv. Q.*, 5(2), 65–86.

Rowland, G. (1993). Designing and instructional design. *Educ. Technol. Res. Dev.*, 41(1), 79–91.

Rummel, N., Levin, J. R., and Woodward, M. M. (2003). Do pictorial mnemonic text-learning aids give students something worth writing about? *J. Educ. Psychol.*, 95, 327–334.

Salomon, G. and Clark, R. W. (1977). Reexamining the methodology of research on media and technology in education. *Rev. Educ. Res.*, 47, 99–120.

Salomon, G., Perkins, D. N., and Globerson, T. (1991). Partners in cognition: extending human intelligence with intelligent technologies. *Educ. Res.*, 20(3), 2–9.

Savenye, W. C. and Robinson, R. S. (2004). Qualitative research issues and methods. In *Handbook for Educational Communications and Technology*, 2nd ed., edited by D. H. Jonassen, pp. 1045–1071. Mahwah, NJ: Lawrence Erlbaum Associates.

Scarr, S. (1985). Constructing psychology: making facts and fables of our times. *Am. Psychol.*, 40, 449–512.

Schatz, S. C. (2005). Unique metadata schemas: a model for user-centric design of a performance support system. *Educ. Technol. Res. Dev.*, 53(4), 69–84.

Seels, B. and Richey, R. (1994). *Instructional Technology: The Definitions and Domains of the Field*. Washington, D.C.: Association for Educational Communications and Technology.

Shapiro, W. L., Roskos, K., and Cartwright, G. P. (1995). Technology-enhanced learning environments, *Change*, 27(6), 67–69.

Shavelson, R. J., Phillips, D. C., Towne, L., and Feuer, M. J. (2003). On the science of education design studies, *Educ. Res.*, 32(1), 25–28.

Shavelson, R. J., Towne, L., and the Committee on Scientific Principles for Education Research, Eds. (2002). *Scientific Research in Education*. Washington, D.C.: National Academy Press.

Shute, V. J. (1993). A macroadaptive approach to tutoring. *J. Artif. Intell. Educ.*, 4(1), 61–93.

Slavin, R. E. (2002). Evidence-based educational policies: transforming educational practice and research. *Educ. Res.*, 31(7), 15–21.

Slavin, R. (2006). *Educational Psychology: Theory and Practice*, pp. 133–162. Boston, MA: Pearson.

Sullivan, H. J., Ice, K., and Niedermeyer, F. (2000). Long-term instructional development: a 20-year ID and implementation project. *Educ. Technol. Res. Dev.*, 48(4), 87–99.

Tennyson, R. D. (1980). Instructional control strategies and content structures as design variables in concept acquisition using computer-based instruction. *J. Educ. Psychol.*, 72, 525–532.

Tennyson, R. D. (1998). Defining the core competencies of an instructional developer. *J. Courseware Eng.*, 1, 31–36.

Tennyson, R. D. and Buttrey, T. (1980). Advisement and management strategies as design variables in computer-assisted instruction. *Educ. Commun. Technol. J.*, 28, 169–176.

Tennyson, R. D. and Rothen, W. (1979). Management of computer-based instruction: design of an adaptive control strategy. *J. Comput.-Based Instruct.*, 5, 63–71.

Tracey, M. W. (2002). The construction and validation of an instructional design model for incorporating multiple intelligences, Ph.D. dissertation, Wayne State University 2001. *Dissert. Abstr. Int. A*, 62(12), 4135.

Tracey, M. W. and Richey, R. C. (2007). ID model construction and validation: a multiple intelligences case. *Educ. Technol. Res. Dev.*, 55(4), 369–390.

Ullmer, E. J. (1994). Media and learning: are there two kinds of truth? *Educ. Technol. Res. Dev.*, 42, 21–32.

Underwood, B. J. (1966). *Experimental Psychology*. New York: Appleton-Century-Crofts.

van den Akker, J. (1999). Principles and methods of development research. In *Design Approaches and Tools in Education and Training*, edited by J. van den Akker, R. M. Branch, K. Gustafson, N. Nieveen, and T. Plomp, pp. 1–14. Dordrecht: Kluwer.

van den Akker, J. (2003). Curriculum perspectives: an introduction. In *Curriculum Landscapes and Trends*, edited by J. van den Akker, W. Kuiper, and U. Hameyer, pp. 1–10. Dordrecht: Kluwer.*

van den Akker, J, Gravemeijer, K., McKenney, S., and Nieveen, N. (2006a). Introducing educational design research. In *Educational Design Research*, edited by J. van den Akker, K. Gravemeijer, S. McKenney, and N. Nieveen, pp. 1–8. London: Routledge.

van den Akker, J., Gravemeijer, K., McKenney, S., and Nieveen, N., Eds. (2006b), *Educational Design Research*. London: Routledge.

Visscher-Voerman, I. (1999). Design Approaches in Training and Education. A Reconstructive Study, Ph.D. dissertation. Enschede: University of Twente.

Visscher-Voerman, I. and Gustafson, K. L. (2004). Paradigms in the theory and practice of education and training design. *Educ. Technol. Res. Dev.*, 52(2), 69–89.

Visscher-Voerman, I., Gustafson, K., and Plomp, T. (1999). Educational design and development: an overview of paradigms. In *Design Approaches and Tools in Education and Training*, edited by J. van den Akker, R. M. Branch, K. Gustafson, N. Nieveen, and T. Plomp, pp. 15–28. Dordrecht: Kluwer.

Visser, L., Plomp, T., Amirault, R. J., and Kuiper, W. (2002). Motivating students at a distance: the case of an international audience. *Educ. Technol. Res. Dev.*, 50(2), 94–110.

Wang, F. and Hannafin, M. J. (2005). Design-based research and technology-enhanced learning environments. *Educ. Technol. Res. Dev.*, 53(4), 5–24.*

Wedman, J. F. and Tessmer, M. (1993). Instructional designers' decisions and priorities. a survey of design practice. *Perform. Improv. Q.*, 8, 43–57.

Winer, L. R. and Vasquez-Abad, J. (1995). The present and future of ID practice. *Perform. Improv. Q.*, 8(3), 55–67.

Winn, W. (2004). Cognitive perspectives in psychology. In *Handbook of Research for Educational Communications and Technology*, 2nd ed., edited by D. Jonassen, pp. 79–112. Mahwah, NJ: Lawrence Erlbaum Associates.

Woloshyn, V. E., Paivio, A., and Pressley, M. (1994). Use of elaborative interrogation to help students acquire information consistent with prior knowledge and information inconsistent with prior knowledge. *J. Educ. Psychol.*, 86(1), 79–90.

---

\* Indicates a core reference.

# 55

# Data Collection and Analysis

*Tamara van Gog and Fred Paas\**
Open University of the Netherlands, Heerlen, the Netherlands

*Wilhelmina Savenye*
Arizona State University-Tempe, Tempe, Arizona

*Rhonda Robinson*
Northern Illinois University, DeKalb, Illinois

*Mary Niemczyk*
Arizona State University-Polytechnic, Mesa, Arizona

*Robert Atkinson*
Arizona State University-Tempe, Tempe, Arizona

*Tristan E. Johnson*
Florida State University, Tallahassee, Florida

*Debra L. O'Connor*
Intelligent Decision Systems, Inc., Williamsburg, Virginia

*Remy M. J. P. Rikers*
Erasmus University Rotterdam, Rotterdam, the Netherlands

*Paul Ayres*
University of New South Wales, Sydney, Australia

*Aaron R. Duley*
National Aeronautics and Space Administration, Ames Research Center, Moffett Field, California

*Paul Ward*
Florida State University, Tallahassee, Florida

*Peter A. Hancock*
University of Central Florida, Orlando, Florida

---

\* Tamara van Gog and Fred Paas were lead authors for this chapter and coordinated the various sections comprising this chapter.

# CONTENTS

# ABSTRACT

The focus of this chapter is on methods of data collection and analysis for the assessment of learning processes and complex performance, the last part of the empirical cycle after theory development and experimental design. In the introduction (van Gog and Paas), the general background and the relation between the chapter sections are briefly described. The section by Savenye, Robinson, Niemczyk, and Atkinson focuses on methods of data collection and analysis for assessment of individual learning processes, whereas the section by Johnson and O'Connor is concerned with methods for assessment of group learning processes. The chapter section by van Gog, Rikers, and Ayres discusses the assessment of complex performance, and the final chapter section by Duley, Ward, Szalma, and Hancock is concerned with setting up laboratories to measure learning and complex performance.

# KEYWORDS

*Assessment criteria:* Describe the aspects of performance that will be assessed.

*Assessment of learning:* Measuring learning achievement, performance, outcomes, and processes by many means.

*Assessment standards:* Describe the quality of performance on each of the criteria that can be expected of participants at different stages (e.g., age, grade) based on a participant's past performance (self-referenced), peer group performance (norm-referenced), or an objective standard (criterion-referenced).

*Collective data collection:* Obtaining data from individual group members; data are later aggregated or manipulated into a representation of the group as a whole.

*Complex performance:* Refers to real-world activities that require the integration of disparate measurement instrumentation as well as the need for time-critical experimental control.

*Direct process measure:* Continuous elicitation of data from beginning to end of the (group) process; direct process measures involve videotaping, audiotaping, direct researcher observation, or a combination of these methods.

*Group:* Two or more individuals working together to achieve a common goal.

*Group learning process:* Actions and interactions performed by group members during the group learning task.

*Holistic data collection:* Obtaining data from the group as a whole; as this type of data collection results in a representation of the group rather than individual group member, it is not necessary to aggregate or manipulate data.

*Indirect process measure:* Discrete measure at a specific point in time during the (group) process; often involves multiple points of data collection; indirect process measures may measure processes, outcomes, products, or other factors related to group process.

*Instrumentation:* Hardware devices used to assist with the process of data acquisition and measurement.

*Mixed-methods research:* Studies that rely on quantitative and qualitative as well as other methods for formulating research questions, collecting and analyzing data, and interpreting findings.

*Online/offline measures:* Online measures are recorded during task performance, offline measures are recorded after task performance.

*Process-tracing techniques:* Records performance process data such as verbal reports, eye movements, and actions that can be used to make inferences about the cognitive processes or knowledge underlying task performance.

*Qualitative research:* Sometimes called naturalistic; research on human systems whose hallmarks include researcher as instrument, natural settings, and little manipulation.

*Quantitative research:* Often conceived of as more traditional or positivistic; typified by experimental or correlational studies. Data and findings are usually represented through numbers and results of statistical tests.

*Task complexity:* Can be defined subjectively (individual characteristics, such as expertise or perception), objectively (task characteristics, such as multiple solution paths or goals), or as an interaction (individual and task characteristics).

# INTRODUCTION

*Tamara van Gog and Fred Paas*

The most important rule concerning data collection and analysis is *do not attempt to collect or analyze all possible kinds of data.* Unless you are conducting a truly explorative study (which is hardly ever necessary nowadays, considering the abundance of literature on most topics), the first part of the empirical cycle—the process of theory development—should result in clear research questions or hypotheses that will allow you to choose an appropriate design to study these. These hypotheses should also indicate the kind of data you will need to collect—that is, the data you have hypotheses about and some necessary control data (e.g., time on task), and together with the design provide some indications as to how to analyze those data (e.g., $2 \times 2$ factorial design, $2 \times 2$ MANCOVA). But, these are just indications, and many decisions remain to be made. To name just a few issues regarding data collection (for an elaboration on those questions, see, for example, Christensen, 2006; Sapsford and Jupp, 1996): Which participants (human/nonhuman, age, educational background, gender) and how many to use? What and how many tasks or stimuli to present and on what apparatus? What (control) measures to take? What instructions to give? What procedure to use? When to schedule the sessions?

Making those decisions is not an easy task, and unfortunately strict guidelines cannot be given because acceptable answers are highly dependent on the exact nature, background, goals, and context of the study. To give you some direction, it might help to have a look at how these questions have been dealt with in high-quality studies in your domain (which are generally published in peer-reviewed, high-impact journals). Because of the importance and difficulty of finding correct operationalizations of these issues, it is gener-

ally advisable to conduct a pilot study to test your data collection and analysis procedures.

In educational research many studies share the common goal of assessing learning or performance, and the chapter sections in this chapter provide information on methods for collecting and analyzing learning and performance data. Even though learning and performance are conceptually different, many of the data collection and analysis techniques can be used to assess both; therefore, we first discuss the differences between the assessment of learning and the assessment of performance before giving a brief overview of the content of the chapter sections.

## Assessment of Learning vs. Performance

The definitions of learning and performance have an important similarity, in that they can be used to refer both to an outcome or product and to a process. The term *learning* is used to refer to the knowledge or skill acquired through instruction or study (note that this dictionary definition ignores the possibility of informal learning, unless this is encompassed by study), as well as the process of acquiring knowledge or skill through instruction or study. The term *performance* is used to refer to things accomplished (outcome or product) and to the accomplishment of things (process). Performance implies the *use* of knowledge rather than merely *possessing* it. It seems that performance is more closely related to skill than to knowledge acquisition (i.e., learning), but an important difference between the definitions of learning and performance is that performance can be, but is not defined as, a result of instruction or study.

The similarities and differences between these terms have some important implications for educational research. First of all, the fact that both learning and performance can refer to a product and a process enables the use of many different kinds of measures or combinations of measures to assess learning or performance. This can make it quite difficult to compare results of different studies on learning or performance, as they might have assessed different aspects of the same concept and come to very different conclusions.

Second, collection and analysis of data about the knowledge an individual possesses can be used to assess their learning but not their performance. That possessing knowledge does not guarantee the ability to use it has been shown in many studies (see, for example, Ericsson and Lehmann, 1996). Nonetheless, for a long time, educational certification practices were based on this assumption: Students received their diplomas after completing a series of courses successfully, and success was usually measured by the amount of knowledge a student possessed. Given that this measure has no one-to-one mapping with successful performance, this practice posed many problems, both for students and employers, when students went to work after their educational trajectory. Hence, in the field of education it is recognized now that knowledge is a necessary but not sufficient condition for performance, and the field is gradually making a shift from a knowledge-based testing culture to a performance-based assessment culture (Birenbaum and Dochy, 1996).

Finally, because performance is not defined as a result of instruction or study, it can be assessed in all kinds of situations, and when applied in instructional or study settings it may be assessed before, during, and after instruction or study phases. Note though, that in that case, only the difference between performance assessed before and after instruction or study is indicative for learning. One should be careful not to interpret gains in performance during instruction or study as indicators for learning, as these may be artifacts of instructional methods (Bjork, 1999).

## Brief Overview of the Chapter Sections

The first chapter section, Assessment of Individual Learning Processes by Savenye, Robinson, Niemczyk, and Atkinson, introduces educational technology researchers to the conceptual basis and methods of data collection and analysis for investigating individual learning processes. They discuss the quantitative and qualitative research paradigms and the associated approaches to data collection and analysis. They also point out the benefits of combining quantitative and qualitative approaches by conducting mixed-methods studies.

The second chapter section, Assessment of Group Learning Processes by Johnson and O'Connor, focuses on the study of group learning processes, which is more complex than the study of individual learning processes. They discuss several issues that need to be considered prior to setting up a study of group learning processes, such as holistic vs. collective data collection, direct vs. indirect methods of data collection, aggregation or manipulation of individual data into group level data, and special considerations for setting up a study of group learning processes.

The third chapter section, Assessment of Complex Performance by van Gog, Rikers, and Ayres, discusses data collection and analysis methods for assessment of complex performance. In line with the two-edged definition of performance as a thing accomplished or accomplishing a thing, they distinguish product and process measures and subdivide the process measures further into online (while working on a task) vs. offline (after task completion) measures. They also discuss

the opportunities to combine several different measures and the benefits of doing so.

The fourth and final chapter section, Setting Up a Laboratory for Measurement of Complex Performances by Duley, Ward, Szalma, and Hancock, provides insight into the technical setup of laboratories for the assessment of learning processes and complex performance. Rather than providing a list of available hardware, software, and instruments, they have chosen to take the more sensible approach of familiarizing the reader with setting up configurations for stimulus presentation, control options, and response recording, which are relevant for many laboratory studies.

## ASSESSMENT OF INDIVIDUAL LEARNING PROCESSES

*Wilhelmina Savenye, Rhonda Robinson,*
*Mary Niemczyk, and Robert Atkinson*

It is the goal of this section to introduce educational technology researchers to the conceptual basis and methods of data collection and analysis for investigating individual learning processes, including both quantitative and qualitative research techniques. Learning processes, of course, may involve both individual and group efforts of learners in the form of strategies and activities designed to facilitate their learning. Though this section focuses on individual processes and performances, using a variety of methods, these may be adapted for group use (see the chapter section by Johnson and O'Connor).

Several assumptions guide this work. Although methods can be suggested here, the researcher must be responsible for understanding the foundational ideas of any study. He or she will want to conduct the study with the utmost attention to quality and therefore will want to turn to specific and detailed texts to learn more deeply how to apply research methods. This section will point the researcher to such references and resources.

The objectives of this section are listed below. It is hoped that after reading this chapter, educational technology researchers will be able to:

- Describe methods and techniques for conducting research on individual learning, and compare qualitative and quantitative methods.
- Describe common problems in conducting and evaluating quantitative and qualitative research methods to examine learning processes.
- Consider issues that contribute to the quality of studies using mixed methods.

## Rationale for Using Mixed Methods

The terms *quantitative* and *qualitative* are commonly used to describe contrasting research approaches. Typically, quantitative research is considered to be more numbers driven, positivistic, and traditional (Borg and Gall, 1989), while qualitative research is often used interchangeably with terms such as *naturalistic*, *ethnographic* (Goetz and LeCompte, 1984), *subjective*, or *post-positivistic*. We define qualitative research in this section as research that is devoted to developing an understanding of human systems, be they small, such as a technology-using teacher and his or her students and classroom, or large, such as a cultural system. Quantitative and qualitative methods for data collection derive in some measure from a difference in the way one sees the world, which results in what some consider a paradigm debate; however, in assessing learning processes, both approaches to data collection have importance, and using elements from both approaches can be very helpful. Driscoll (1995) suggested that educational technologists select research paradigms based on what they perceive to be the most critical questions. Robinson (1995) and Reigeluth (1989) concurred, noting the considerable debate within the field regarding suitable research questions and methods. Learning processes are complex and individual. Lowyck and Elen (2004) argued that learning processes are active, constructive, self-regulated, goal oriented, and contextualized. In addition, digital technologies are changing the nature of knowledge and of teaching and learning (Cornu, 2004). It is clear then that the methods required to collect and analyze how learning processes work, when they work, and why they work can be drawn from a mixed-method approach. Thus, researchers can investigate carefully and creatively any questions they choose and derive valid data to help understand learning processes using a combination of methods from both perspectives. Although not the main focus of this chapter, it is assumed that researchers will submit all procedures, protocols, instruments, and participation forms to the appropriate human-subjects or ethics review unit within their organizations. In any case, researchers should be specific about how they define the assumptions of the study and why what was done was done—in short, they should be able to enter into the current and upcoming discussions as thoughtful, critical, and creative researchers.

## Analyzing Learning Using Quantitative Methods and Techniques

Learning achievement or performance in educational technology research is often the primary outcome measure or dependent variable of concern to the researcher.

Learning is often therefore studied using more quantitative measures, including what researchers may call tests, assessments, examinations, or quizzes. These measures may be administered in paper-and-pencil form or may be technology based. If they are technology based, they may be administered at a testing center, with tutors or proctors, or completed on the student's own. In either format, they may be scored by an instructor or tutor or may be automatically scored by the computer (Savenye, 2004a,b). Issues of concern in selecting and developing tests and test items also are relevant when learning is measured *en route* as performance on practice items. Completion time, often in conjunction with testing, is another learning process variable that can efficiently be examined using quantitative methods.

Learning achievement on complex tasks may also be measured more quantitatively using numerically based rubrics and checklists to evaluate products and performances or to evaluate essays or learner-created portfolios. Rubrics and checklists are also often used to derive quantitative data for measuring learning in online discussions or to build frequencies of behaviors from observations of learning processes, often used in conjunction with more qualitative methods (discussed later in this section). Many computer-based course management systems now routinely collect course statistics that may be examined to determine how learners proceed through instruction and what choices they make as they go. Self-evaluations and other aspects of learning, such as learner attitudes, are more commonly measured using questionnaires. Selected types of quantitative methods for examining learning are discussed in turn:

- Tests, examinations, quizzes (administered via paper or technology, including self-evaluations)
- Rubrics or checklists to measure learner performance
- Measuring learning processes in technology-mediated communications
- Technology-based course statistics
- Attitude measures such as questionnaires using Likert-type items

## Selecting Tests

Educational researchers frequently select existing tests to assess how individual learning processes are impacted by a novel educational intervention. During this process, the researchers must be conversant with a number of important concepts, including validity and reliability. In the following sections, these concepts are described in greater detail with a specific focus on what researchers need to know when selecting tests.

## Validity

Arguably, the most critical aspect of a test is its quality or validity. Simply put, a test is considered valid if it measures what it was created to measure (Borg and Gall, 1989). A test is generally considered valid if the scores it produces help individuals administering the test make accurate inferences about a particular characteristic, trait, or attribute intrinsic to the test taker. As an example, researchers exploring the relative impact of several learning environments would consider a test valid to the extent to which it helps them make an accurate determination of the relative quality and quantity of learning displayed by the students exposed to the respective learning environments.

Validity is not a unitary concept; in fact, test developers use several widely accepted procedures to document the level of validity of their test, including content-related, criterion-related, and construct-related validity. *Content-related validity* represents the extent to which the content of a test is a representative sample of the total subject matter content provided in the learning environment. Another type of validity is *criterion-related validity*, which depicts how closely scores on a given test correspond to or predict performance on a criterion measure that exists outside the test. Unlike content validity, this type of validity yields a numeric value that is the correlation coefficient reported on a scale of −1 (perfect, negative relationship) to +1 (perfect, positive relationship). The third type of validity is *construct-related validity*, which refers to the extent to which the scores on a test correspond with a particular construct or hypothetical concept originating from a theory.

Also worth mentioning is a relatively unsophisticated type of validity known as *face validity*, which is based on the outward appearance of the test. Although this is considered a rather rudimentary approach to establishing validity, it is considered important because of its potential impact on the test taker's motivation. In particular, respondents may be reluctant to complete a test without any apparent face validity.

## Reliability

Another important concept involved in test selection is reliability. Simply put, reliability refers to the consistency with which a test yields the same results for a respondent across repeated administrations (Borg and Gall, 1989). Assuming that the focus of the test—a particular attribute or characteristic—remains unchanged between test administrations for a given individual, reliability sheds light on the following question: Does the test always yield the same score for an individual when it is administered on several occasions?

### Determining and Judging Reliability

The three basic approaches to determining the reliability of a test are test–retest, alternate forms, and internal consistency (Borg and Gall, 1989; Morris et al., 1987). Perhaps the simplest technique for estimating reliability is the *test–retest method*. With this approach, a test developer simply administers the test twice to the same group of respondents and then calculates the correlation between the two sets of scores. As a general rule, researchers select tests displaying the highest reliability coefficient because values approaching +1.00 are indicative of a strong relationship between the two sets of respondents' scores; that is, the respondents' relative performance has remained similar across the two testing occasions. Specifically, values above .80 are preferable (Chase, 1999).

Another approach to determining reliability is the *alternate forms method*, in which two equivalent forms of a test are administered to a group of respondents on two separate occasions and the resulting scores correlated. As with the test–retest method, the higher the reliability coefficient, the more confidence a test administer can place in the ability of a test to consistently measure what it was designed to measure.

The final method for estimating the reliability of a test is referred to as *internal consistency*. Unlike the two previous methods, it does not rely on testing the same group of respondents twice to estimate the internal consistency of a test. Instead, the reliability of a test is estimated based on a single test administration, which can be accomplished in two ways—either using the *split halves* method or using one of the Kuder–Richardson methods, which do not require splitting a test in half.

### Limits of Reliability

A number of caveats are associated with reliability. First, it is important to recognize that high reliability does not guarantee validity; in other words, a test can consistently measure what it was intended to measure while still lacking validity. Knowing that a test is reliable does not permit someone to make judgments about its validity. Reliability is, however, necessary for validity, as it impacts the accuracy with which one can draw inferences about a particular characteristic or attribute intrinsic to the test taker. The reliability is impacted by several factors. Test length is the first. All things being equal, shorter tests tend to be less reliable than longer tests because the latter afford the test developer more opportunities to accurately measure the trait or characteristic under examination. The reliability of a test is also impacted by the format of its items. A general heuristic to remember is that tests constructed with select-type items tend to be more reliable than tests with supply-type or other subjectively scored items.

## Evaluating and Developing Tests and Test Items

The construction of learning assessments is one of the most important responsibilities of instructors and researchers. Tests should be comprised of items that represent important and clearly stated objectives and that adequately sample subject matter from all of the learning objectives. The most effective way to ensure adequate representation of items across content, cognitive processes, and objectives is to develop a test blueprint or table of specifications (Sax, 1980). Multiple types of performance measures allow students an opportunity to demonstrate their particular skills in defined areas and to receive varied feedback on their performances; this is particularly important in self-instructional settings, such as online courses (Savenye, 2004a,b). Multiple learning measures in online settings also offer security advantages (Ko and Rossen, 2001).

Tests should also give students the opportunity to respond to different types of item formats that assess different levels of cognition, such as comprehension, application, analysis, and synthesis (Popham, 1991). Different approaches and formats can yield different diagnostic information to instructors, as well; for example, well-developed multiple-choice items contain alternatives that represent common student misconceptions or errors. Short-answer item responses can give the instructor information about the student's thinking underlying the answer (Mehrens et al., 1998).

Because the test item is the essential building block of any test, it is critical to determine the validity of the test item before determining the validity of the test itself. Commercial test publishers typically conduct pilot studies (called *item tryouts*) to get empirical evidence concerning item quality. For these tryouts, several forms of the test are prepared with different subsets of items, so each item appears with every other item. Each form may be given to several hundred examinees. Item analysis data are then calculated, followed by assessment of the performance characteristics of the items, such as item difficulty and item discrimination (i.e., how well the item separates, or discriminates, between those who do well on the test and those who do poorly). The developers discard items that fail to display proper statistical properties (Downing and Haladyna, 1997; Nitko, 2001; Thorndike, 1997).

## Scores on Numerically Based Rubrics and Checklists

Assessing performance can be done by utilizing numerically based rubrics and checklists. Typically, two aspects of a learner's performance can be assessed: the product the learner produces and the process a learner uses to complete the product. Either or both of these elements may be evaluated. Because performance tasks are usually complex, each task provides an opportunity to assess students on several learning goals (Nitko, 2001). Performance criteria are the specific behaviors a student should perform to properly carry out a performance or produce a product. The key to identifying performance criteria is to break down the overall performance or product into its component parts. It is important that performance criteria be specific, observable, and clearly stated (Airasian, 1996).

Scoring rubrics are brief, written descriptions of different levels of performance. They can be used to summarize both performances and products. Scoring rubrics summarize performance in a general way, whereas checklists and rating scales can provide specific diagnostic information about student strengths and weaknesses (Airasian, 1996). Checklists usually contain lists of behaviors, traits, or characteristics that are either present or absent, to be checked off by an observer (Sax, 1980). Although they are similar to checklists, rating scales allow the observer to judge performance along a continuum rather than as a dichotomy (Airasian, 1996).

## Measuring Learning Processes in Technology-Mediated Communications

Tiffin and Rajasingham (1995) suggested that education is based on communication. Online technologies, therefore, provide tremendous opportunities for learning and allow us to measure learning in new ways; for example, interactions in online discussions within Internet-based courses may be used to assess students' learning processes. Paulsen (2003) delineated many types of learning activities, including online interviews, online interest groups, role plays, brainstorming, and project groups. These activities, generally involving digital records, will also yield online communication data for research purposes, provided the appropriate ethics and subject guidelines have been followed.

The postings learners create and share may also be evaluated using the types of rubrics and checklists discussed earlier. These are of particular value to learners when they receive the assessment tools early in the course and use them to self-evaluate or to conduct peer evaluations to improve the quality of their work

(Savenye, 2006, 2007). Goodyear (2000) reminded us that digital technologies add to the research and development enterprise the capability for multimedia communications.

Another aspect of online discussions of value to researchers is that the types of postings students make and the ideas they discuss can be quantified to illuminate students' learning processes. Chen (2005), in an online course activity conducted with groups of six students who did not know each other, found that learners under a less-structured forum condition posted many more socially oriented postings, although their performance on the task was not less than that of the students who did not post as many social postings. She also found that the more interactions a group made, the more positive students' attitudes were toward the course.

### Using Technology-Based Course Statistics To Examine Learning Processes

In addition to recording learners' performance on quizzes, tests, and other assignments, most online course management systems automatically collect numerous types of data, which may be used to investigate learning processes. Such data may include information about exactly which components of the course a learner has completed, on which days, and for how much time. Compilations of these data can indicate patterns of use of course components and features (Savenye, 2004a).

### Measuring Attitudes Using Questionnaires That Use Likert-Type Items

Several techniques have been used to assess attitudes and feelings of learners in research studies and as part of instruction. Of these methods, Likert-type scales are the most common. Typically, respondents are asked to indicate their strength of feeling toward a series of statements, often in terms of the degree to which they agree or disagree with the position being described. Previous research has found that responding to a Likert-type item is an easier task and provides more information than ranking and paired comparisons. The advantage of a Likert-type item scale is that an absolute level of an individual's responses can be obtained to determine the strength of the attitude (O'Neal and Chissom, 1993).

Thorndike (1997) suggested several factors to consider in developing a Likert-type scale, including the number of steps, odd or even number of steps, and types of anchors. The number of steps in the scale is important as it relates to reliability—the more steps, the greater the reliability. The increase is noticeable up to about seven steps; after this, the reliability begins to diminish, as it becomes difficult to develop meaningful anchors. Five-point scales tend to be the most common. Increasing the number of items can also increase reliability. Although there is considerable debate about this, many researchers hold that better results can be obtained by using an odd number of steps, which provides for a neutral response. The anchors used should fit the meaning of the statements and the goal of the measurement. Common examples include continua such as agree–disagree, effective–ineffective, important–unimportant, and like me–not like me.

## Analyzing Learning Using More Qualitative Methods and Techniques

Although learning outcomes and processes can be productively examined using the quantitative methods discussed earlier, in a mixed-methods approach many qualitative methods are used to build a deeper understanding of what, why, and how learners learn. With the increasing use of interactive and distance technologies in education and industry, opportunities and at times the responsibility to explore new questions about the processes of learning and instruction have evolved. New technologies also enable researchers to study learners and learning processes in new ways and to expand our views of what we should investigate and how; for example, a qualitative view of how instructors and their students learn through a new technology may yield a view of what is really happening when the technology is used.

As in any research project, the actual research questions guide the selection of appropriate methods of data collection. Once a question or issue has been selected, the choice of qualitative methods falls roughly into the categories of observations, interviews, and document and artifact analysis, although others have conceptualized the methods somewhat differently (Bogdan and Biklen, 1992; Goetz and LeCompte, 1984; Lincoln and Guba, 1985). Qualitative researchers have basically agreed that the human investigator is the primary research instrument (Pelto and Pelto, 1978).

In this section, we begin with one approach to conducting qualitative research: grounded theory. We then discuss specific methods that may be called *observations, interviews, and document and artifact analysis*. As in all qualitative research, it is also assumed that educational technology researchers will use and refine methods with the view that these methods vary in their degree of interactiveness with participants. The following qualitative methods, along with several research perspectives, are examined next:

- Grounded theory
- Participant observations
- Nonparticipant observations
- Interviews, including group and individual
- Document, artifact, and online communications and activities analysis

### Grounded Theory

In their overview of grounded theory, Strauss and Corbin (1994, p. 273) noted that it is "a general methodology for developing theory that is grounded in data systematically gathered and analyzed," adding that it is sometimes referred to as the *constant comparative method* and that it is applicable as well to quantitative research. In grounded theory, the data may come from observations, interviews, and video or document analysis, and, as in other qualitative research, these data may be considered strictly qualitative or may be quantitative. The purpose of the methodology is to develop theory, through an iterative process of data analysis and theoretical analysis, with verification of hypotheses ongoing throughout the study. The researcher begins a study without completely preconceived notions about what the research questions should be and collects and analyzes extensive data with an open mind. As the study progresses, he or she continually examines the data for patterns, and the patterns lead the researcher to build the theory. The researcher continues collecting and examining data until the patterns continue to repeat and few new patterns emerge. The researcher builds the theory from the data, and the theory is thus built on, or *grounded* in, the phenomena.

### Participant Observation

In participant observation, the observer becomes part of the environment, or the cultural context. The hallmark of participant observation is continual interaction between the researcher and the participants; for example, the study may involve periodic interviews interspersed with observations so the researcher can question the participants and verify perceptions and patterns. Results of these interviews may then determine what will initially be recorded during observations. Later, after patterns begin to appear in the observational data, the researcher may conduct interviews asking the participants about these patterns and why they think they are occurring.

As the researcher cannot observe and record everything, in most educational research studies the investigator determines ahead of time what will be observed and recorded, guided but not limited by the research questions. Participant observation is often successfully used to describe what is happening in a context and why it happens. These are questions that cannot be answered in the standard experiment.

Many researchers have utilized participant observation methods to examine learning processes. Robinson (1994) observed classes using Channel One in a Midwestern middle school; she focused her observations on the use of the televised news show and the reaction to it from students, teachers, administrators, and parents. Reilly (1994) analyzed video recordings of both the researcher and students in a project that involved defining a new type of literacy that combined print, video, and computer technologies. Higgins and Rice (1991) investigated teachers' perceptions of testing. They used triangulation and a variety of methods to collect data; however, a key feature of the study was participant observation. Researchers observed 6 teachers for a sample of 10 hours each and recorded instances of classroom behaviors that could be classified as assessment. Similarly, Moallem (1994) used multiple methods to build an experienced teacher's model of teaching and thinking by conducting a series of observations and interviews over a 7-month period.

### Nonparticipant Observation

Nonparticipant observation is one of several methods for collecting data considered to be relatively unobtrusive. Many recent authors cite the early work of Webb et al. (1966) as laying the groundwork for use of all types of unobtrusive measures. Several types of nonparticipant observation have been identified by Goetz and LeCompte (1984). These include stream-of-behavior chronicles recorded in written narratives or using video or audio recordings, proxemics and kinesics (i.e., the study of uses of social space and movement), and interaction analysis protocols, typically in the form of observations of particular types of behaviors that are categorized and coded for analysis of patterns. In nonparticipant observation, observers do not interact to a great degree with those they are observing. The researchers primarily observe and record, using observational forms developed for the study or in the form of extensive field notes; they have no specific roles as participants.

Examples of studies in which observations were conducted that could be considered relatively nonparticipant observation include Savenye and Strand (1989) in the initial pilot test and Savenye (1989) in the subsequent larger field test of a multimedia-based science curriculum. Of most concern during implementation was how teachers used the curriculum. A careful sample of classroom lessons was recorded using video, and the data were coded; for example, teacher questions were coded, and the results indicated that teachers typically used the system pauses to ask recall-level rather than higher-level questions. Analysis of the coded behaviors for what teachers added indicated that most of the teachers in the sample added examples to the lessons that would provide relevance for their own learners. Of particular value to the developers was the finding that teachers had a great degree of freedom in using the curriculum and the students' learning achievement was still high.

In a mixed-methods study, nonparticipant observations may be used along with more quantitative methods to answer focused research questions about what learners do while learning. In a mixed-methods study investigating the effects and use of multimedia learning materials, the researchers collected learning outcome data using periodic tests. They also observed learners as they worked together. These observations were video recorded and the records analyzed to examine many learning processes, including students' level of cognitive processing, exploratory talk, and collaborative processing (Olkinuora et al., 2004). Researchers may also be interested in using observations to study what types of choices learners make while they proceed through a lesson. Klein and colleagues, for instance, developed an observational instrument used to examine cooperative learning behaviors in technology-based lessons (Crooks et al., 1995; Jones et al., 1995; Klein and Pridemore, 1994).

A variation on nonparticipant observations represents a blend with trace-behavior, artifact, or document analysis. This technique, known as *read-think-aloud protocols*, asks learners to describe what they do and why they do it (i.e., their thoughts about their processes) as they proceed through an activity, such as a lesson. Smith and Wedman (1988) used this technique to analyze learner tracking and choices. Techniques for coding are described by Spradley (1980); however, protocol analysis (Ericsson and Simon, 1984) techniques could be used on the resulting verbal data.

### Issues Related to Conducting Observations

Savenye and Robinson (2004, 2005) have suggested several issues that are critical to using observations to studying learning. These issues include those related to scope, biases and the observer's role, sampling, and the use of multiple observers. They caution that a researcher can become lost in the multitudes of observational data that can be collected, both in person and when using audio or video. They recommend limiting

the scope of the study specifically to answering the questions at hand. Observers must be careful not to influence the results of the study; that is, they must not make things happen that they want to happen. Potential bias may be handled by simply describing the researcher's role in the research report, but investigators will want to examine periodically what their role is and what type of influences may result from it. In observational research, sampling becomes not random but purposive (Borg and Gall, 1989). For the study to be valid, the reader should be able to believe that a representative sample of involved individuals was observed. The multiple realities of any cultural context should be represented. If several observers will be used to collect the data, and their data will be compared or aggregated, problems with reliability of data may occur. Observers tend to see and subsequently interpret the same phenomena in many different ways. It becomes necessary to train the observers and to ensure that observers are recording the same phenomena in the same ways. When multiple observers are used and behaviors counted or categorized and tallied, it is desirable to calculate and report inter-rater reliability.

### Interviews

In contrast with the relatively non-interactive, nonparticipant observation methods described earlier, interviews represent a classic qualitative research method that is directly interactive. Interviews may be structured or unstructured and may be conducted in groups or individually. In an information and communication technologies (ICT) study to investigate how ICT can be introduced into the context of a traditional school, Demetriadis et al. (2005) conducted a series of semistructured interviews over 2 years with 15 teachers/mentors who offered technology training to other teachers.

The cornerstone for conducting good interviews is to be sure one truly listens to respondents and records what they say rather than the researcher's perceptions or interpretations. This is a good rule of thumb in qualitative research in general. It is best to maintain the integrity of the raw data and to make liberal use of the respondents' own words, including quotes. Most researchers, as a study progresses, also maintain field notes that contain interpretations of patterns to be refined and investigated on an ongoing basis.

Many old, adapted, and exciting techniques for structured interviewing are evolving. One example of such a use of interviews is in the Higgins and Rice (1991) study mentioned earlier. In this study, teachers sorted the types of assessment they had named previously in interviews into sets of assessments that were most alike; subsequently, multidimensional scaling was used to analyze these data, yielding a picture of how these teachers' viewed testing. Another type of structured interview, mentioned by Goetz and LeCompte (1984), is the interview using projective techniques. Photographs, drawings, and other visuals or objects may be used to elicit individuals' opinions or feelings.

Instructional planning and design processes have long been of interest to educational technology researchers; for example, using a case-study approach, Reiser and Mory (1991) employed interviews to examine two teachers' instructional design and planning techniques. One of the models proposed for the design of complex learning is that of van Merriënboer et al. (1992), who developed the four-component model, which subsequently was further developed as the 4C/ID model (van Merriënboer, 1997). Such design models have been effectively studied using mixed methods, including interviews, particularly when those processes relate to complex learning. How expert designers go about complex design tasks has been investigated using both interviews and examination of the designers products (Kirschner et al., 2002).

Problem-based instructional design, blending many aspects of curriculum, instruction, and media options (Dijkstra, 2004), could also be productively studied using interviews. Interviews to examine learning processes may be conducted individually or in groups. A specialized group interview method is the focus group (Morgan, 1996), which is typically conducted with relatively similar participants using a structured or semi-structured protocol to examine overall patterns in learning behaviors, attitudes, or interests.

Suggestions for heightening the quality of interviews include employing careful listening and recording techniques; taking care to ask probing questions when needed; keeping the data in their original form, even after they have been analyzed; being respectful of participants; and debriefing participants after the interviews (Savenye and Robinson, 2005).

### Document, Artifact, and Online Communications and Activities Analysis

Beyond nonparticipant observation, many unobtrusive methods exist for collecting information about human behaviors. These fall roughly into the categories of document and artifact analyses but overlap with other methods; for example, verbal or nonverbal behavior streams produced during video observations may be subjected to intense microanalysis to answer an almost unlimited number of research questions. Content analysis, as one example, may be done on these narratives. In the Moallem (1994), Higgins and Rice (1991), and Reiser and Mory (1991) studies of teachers' planning, thinking, behaviors, and conceptions of testing, documents developed by the teachers, such as instructional plans and actual tests, were collected and analyzed.

Goetz and LeCompte (1984) defined artifacts of interest to researchers as things that people make and do. The artifacts of interest to educational technologists are often written, but computer and online trails of behavior are the objects of analysis as well. Examples of artifacts that may help to illuminate research questions include textbooks and other instructional materials, such as media materials; memos, letters, and now e-mail records, as well as logs of meetings and activities; demographic information, such as enrollment, attendance, and detailed information about participants; and personal logs participants may keep.

In studies in educational technology, researchers often analyze the patterns of learner pathways, decisions, and choices they make as they proceed through computer-based lessons (Savenye et al., 1996; Shin et al., 1994). Content analysis of prose in any form may also be considered to fall into this artifact-and-document category of qualitative methodology. Lawless (1994) used concept maps developed by students in the Open University to check for student understanding. Entries in students' journals were analyzed by Perez-Prado and Thirunarayanan (2002) to learn about students' perceptions of online and on-ground versions of the same college course. Espey (2000) studied the content of a school district technology plan.

### Methods for Analyzing Qualitative Data

One of the major hallmarks of conducting qualitative research is that data are analyzed continually, throughout the study, from conceptualization through the entire data collection phase and into the interpretation and writing phases. In fact, Goetz and LeCompte (1984) described the processes of analyzing and writing together in what they called analysis and interpretation.

### Data Reduction

Goetz and LeCompte (1994) described the conceptual basis for reducing and condensing data in an ongoing style as the study progresses. Researchers theorize as the study begins and build and continually test theories based on observed patterns in data. Goetz and LeCompte described the analytic procedures researchers use to determine what the data mean. These procedures involve looking for patterns, links, and relationships. In contrast to experimental research, the qualitative researcher engages in speculation while looking for meaning in data; this speculation will lead the researcher to make new observations, conduct new interviews, and look more deeply for new patterns in this recursive process. It is advisable to collect data in its raw, detailed form and then record patterns. This enables the researcher later to analyze the original data in different ways, perhaps to answer deeper questions than originally conceived. It should be noted that virtually all researchers who use an ethnographic approach advocate writing up field notes immediately after leaving the research site each day. If researchers have collected documents from participants, such as logs, journals, diaries, memos, and letters, these can also be analyzed as raw data. Similarly, official documents of an organization can be subjected to analysis. Collecting data in the form of photographs, films, and videos, either produced by participants or the researcher, has a long tradition in anthropology and education. These data, too, can be analyzed for meaning. (Bellman and Jules-Rosette, 1977; Bogaart and Ketelaar, 1983; Bogdan and Biklen, 1992; Collier and Collier, 1986; Heider, 1976; Hockings, 1975).

### Coding Data

Early in the study, the researcher will begin to scan recorded data and to develop categories of phenomena. These categories are usually called *codes*. They enable the researcher to manage data by labeling, storing, and retrieving it according to the codes. Miles and Huberman (1994) suggested that data can be coded descriptively or interpretively. Bogdan and Biklen (1992) recommended reading data over at least several times to begin to develop a coding scheme. In one of the many examples he provided, Spradley (1979) described in extensive detail how to code and analyze interview data, which are semantic data as are most qualitative data. He also described how to construct domain, structural, taxonomic, and componential analyses.

### Data Management

Analysis of data requires continually examining, sorting, and reexamining data. Qualitative researchers use many means to organize, retrieve, and analyze their data. To code data, many researchers simply use notebooks and boxes of paper, which can then be resorted and analyzed on an ongoing basis. Computers have long been used for managing and analyzing qualitative data. Several resources exist to aid the researcher in finding and using software for data analysis and management, including books (Weitzman and Miles, 1995) and websites that discuss and evaluate research software (American Evaluation Association, 2007; Cuneo, 2000; Horber, 2006).

### Writing the Research Report

In some respects, writing a report of a study that uses mixed-methods may not differ greatly from writing a report summarizing a more traditional experimental study; for example, a standard format for preparing a research report includes an introduction, literature review, description of methods, and presentation of findings, completed by a summary and discussion (Borg and Gall, 1989). A mixed-methods study, however, allows the researcher the opportunity to create sections of the report that may expand on the traditional. The quantitative findings may be reported in the manner of an experimental study (Ross and Morrison, 2004). The qualitative components of research reports typically will be woven around a theme or central message and will include an introduction, core material, and conclusion (Bogdan and Biklen, 1992). Qualitative findings may take the form of a series of themes from interview data or the form of a case study, as in the Reiser and Mory (1991) study. For a case study, the report may include considerable quantification and tables of enumerated data, or it may take a strictly narrative form. Recent studies have been reported in more nontraditional forms, such as stories, plays, and poems that show participants' views. Suggestions for writing up qualitative research are many (Meloy, 1994; Van Maanen, 1988; Wolcott, 1990).

In addition to the studies mentioned earlier, many excellent examples of mixed-methods studies may be examined to see the various ways in which the results of these studies have been written. Seel and colleagues (2000), in an investigation of mental models and model-centered learning environments, used quantitative learning measures that included pretests, posttests, and a measure of the stability of learning four months after the instruction. They also used a receptive interview technique they called *causal explanations* to investigate learners' mental models and learning processes. In this and subsequent studies, Seel (2004) also investigated learners' mental models of dynamic systems using causal diagrams that learners developed and teach-back procedures, in which a student explains a model to another student and this epistemic discourse is then examined.

### Conclusion

The challenges to educational technology researchers who choose to use multiple methods to answer their questions are many, but the outcome of choosing mixed methods has great potential. Issues of validity, reliability, and generalizability are central to experimental research (Ross and Morrison, 2004) and mixed-methods research; however, these concerns are addressed quite differently when using qualitative methods and techniques. Suggestions and criteria for evaluating the quality of mixed-methods studies and research activities may be adapted from those suggested by Savenye and Robinson (2005):

- Learn as much as possible about the context of the study, and build in enough time to conduct the study well.
- Learn more about the methods to be used, and train yourself in these methods.
- Conduct pilot studies whenever possible.
- Use *triangulation* (simply put, use multiple data sources to yield deeper, more true views of the findings).
- Be ethical in all ways when conducting research.
- Listen carefully to participants, and carefully record what they say and do.
- Keep good records, including audit trails.
- Analyze data continually throughout the study, and consider having other researchers and participants review your themes, patterns, and findings to verify them.
- Describe well all methods, decisions, assumptions, and biases.
- Using the appropriate methods (and balance of methods when using mixed methods) is the key to successful educational research.

## ASSESSMENT OF GROUP LEARNING PROCESSES

*Tristan E. Johnson and Debra L. O'Connor*

Similar to organizations that rely on groups of workers to address a variety of difficult and challenging tasks (Salas and Fiore, 2004), groups are formed in various learning settings to meet instructional needs as well as to exploit the pedagogical, learning, and pragmatic benefits associated with group learning (Stahl, 2006). In educational settings, small groups have been typically used to promote participation and enhance learning. One of the main reasons for creating learning groups is to facilitate the development of professional skills that are promoted from group learning, such as communication, teamwork, decision making, leadership, valuing others, problem solving, negotiation, thinking creatively, and working as a member of a group (Carnevale et al., 1989).

Group learning processes are the interactions of two or more individuals with themselves and their

environment with the intent to change knowledge, skill, or attitude. We use the term *group* to refer to the notion of small groups and not large groups characterized as large organizations (Levine and Moreland, 1990; Woods et al., 2000). Interest in group learning processes can be found not only in traditional educational settings such as elementary and secondary schools but also in workplace settings, including the military, industry, business, and even sports (Guzzo and Shea, 1992; Levine and Moreland, 1990).

There are several reasons to assess group learning processes. These include the need to measure group learning as a process outcome and to capture the learning process to provide feedback to the group with the intent to improve team interactions and thereby improve overall team performance. Studies looking at group processes have led to improved understanding about what groups do and how and why they do what they do (Salas and Cannon-Bowers, 2000). Another reason to assess group learning processes is to capture highly successful group process behaviors to develop an interaction framework that could then be used to inform the design and development of group instructional strategies. Further, because the roles and use of groups in supporting and facilitating learning have increased, the interest in studying the underlying group mechanisms has increased.

Many different types of data collection and analysis methods can be used to assess group learning processes. The purpose of this section is to describe these methods by: (1) clarifying how these methods are similar to and different from single learner methods, (2) describing a framework of data collection and analysis techniques, and (3) presenting analysis considerations specific to studying group learning processes along with several examples of existing methodologies.

### Group Learning Processes Compared with Individual Learning Processes and Group Performance

Traditional research on learning processes has focused on psychological perspectives using traditional psychological methods. The unit of analysis for these methods emphasizes the behavior or mental activity of an individual concentrating on learning, instructional outcomes, meaning making, or cognition, all at an individual level (Koschmann, 1996; Stahl, 2006). In contrast, the framework for group research focuses on research traditions of multiple disciplines, such as communication, information, sociology, linguistics, military, human factors, and medicine, as well as fields of applied psychology such as instructional, educational, social, industrial, and organization psychology.

As a whole, these disciplines extend the traditional psychological perspectives and seek understanding related to interaction, spoken language, written language, culture, and other aspects related to social situations. Stahl (2006) pointed out that individuals often think and learn apart from others, but learning and thinking in isolation are still conditioned and mediated by important social considerations.

Group research considers various social dimensions but primarily focuses on either group performance or group learning. Group learning research is focused in typical learning settings. We often see children and youth engaged in group learning in a school setting. Adult group learning is found in post-secondary education, professional schools, vocational schools, colleges and universities, and training sessions, as well as in on-the-job training environments. A number of learning methods have been used in all of these settings. A few specific strategies that use groups to facilitate learning include cooperative learning, collaborative learning (Johnson et al., 2000; Salomon and Perkins, 1998), computer-supported collaborative learning (Stahl, 2006), and team-based learning (Michaelsen, 2004). General terms used to refer to the use of multiple person learning activities include *learning groups*, *team learning*, and *group learning*. Often, these terms and specific strategies are used interchangeably and sometimes not in the ways just described.

In addition to learning groups, adults engage in groups activities in performance (workplace) settings. Although a distinction is made between learning and performance, the processes are similar for groups whose primary intent is to learn and for those focused on performing. The literature on workplace groups (whose primary focus is on completing a task) offers a number of techniques that can be used to study group learning processes much like the literature on individual learning. Group learning process methods include the various methods typically found when studying individuals and also have additional methodologies unique to studying groups.

## Methodological Framework: Direct and Indirect Process Measures

When studying group learning processes, three general categories of measures can be employed: (1) the process or action of a group (direct process measures), (2) a state or a point in time of a group (indirect process measure), and (3) an outcome or performance of a group (indirect non-process measure). Direct process measures are techniques that directly capture the process of a group. These measures are continuous in nature and capture data across time by recording the sound and sight of the group interactions. Examples of these measures include recording the spoken language, written language, and visible interactions. These recording can be video or audio recordings, as well as observation notes.

Indirect process measures use techniques that indirectly capture group processes. These measures are discrete and capture a state or condition of the group processes at a particular point in time, either during or after group activity. These measures involve capturing group member or observer perceptions and reactions that focus on group processes. Examples of these measures involve interviews, surveys, and questionnaires that focus on explicating the nature of a group learning process at a given point in time. These measures focus on collecting group member responses about the process and are specifically not a direct observation of the process.

Indirect non-process measures capture group learning data relating to outcomes, products, performance. These are not measures of the actual process but are measures that might be related to group processes. They may include group characteristics such as demographics, beliefs, efficacy, preferences, size, background, experience, diversity, and trust (Mathieu et al., 2000). These types of measures have the potential to explicate and support the nature of group learning processes. These measures are focused on collecting products or performance scores as well as soliciting group member responses about group characteristics. These measures are not a direct observation of the group learning process. Examples of these measures include performance scores, product evaluations, surveys, questionnaires, interview transcripts, and group member knowledge structures. These measures focus on explicating the nature of a given group's non-process characteristics.

When considering how to assess group learning processes, many of the techniques are very similar or the same as those used to study individuals. Group learning process measures can be collected at both the individual and group levels (O'Neil et al., 2000; Webb, 1982). Because the techniques can be similar or identical for individuals and groups, some confusion may arise when it is realized that individual-level data are not in a form that can be analyzed; the data must be group-level data (group dataset; see Figure 55.1) for analysis.

When designing a study on group learning processes, various measurement techniques can be used depending on the type of questions being asked. Although numerous possibilities are associated with the assessment of group learning processes, three

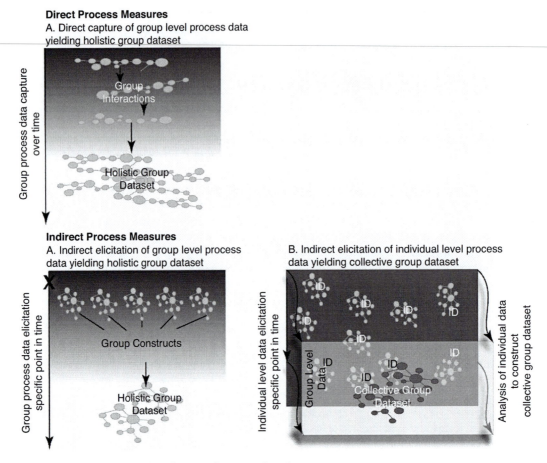

**Figure 55.1** Alternative process measures for assessing group learning processes.

elements must be considered when deciding on what techniques to use: data collection, data manipulation, or data analysis.

Data collection techniques involve capturing or eliciting data related to group learning processes at an individual or group level. Data collected at the group level (capturing group interactions or eliciting group data) yield holistic group datasets (Figure 55.1). When the collected data are in this format, it is not necessary to manipulate the data. In this form, the data are ready to be analyzed. If, however, data are collected at the individual level, then the data must be manipulated, typically via aggregation (Stahl, 2006), to create a dataset that represents the group (collective group dataset) prior to data analysis (Figure 55.1). Collecting data at the individual level involves collecting individual group members' data and then transforming the individual data to an appropriate form (collective group dataset) for analysis (see Figure 55.1). This technique of creating a collective group dataset from individual data is similar to a process referred to as *analysis constructed dataset creation* (O'Connor and Johnson, 2004). In this form, the data are ready to be analyzed.

## Data Collection and Analysis Techniques

When considering the different group learning process assessment techniques, they can be classified based on the type of measure (continuous or discrete). The corresponding analytical techniques that can be used are dependent on the collected data. Many techniques have been used to assess groups. The following section presents the major categories of techniques based on their ability to measure group processes directly (continuous measures) or indirectly (discrete measures). Table 55.1 summarizes the nature of data collection, manipulation, and analysis for the three major grouping of measurement techniques: direct process measures and the two variations of indirect process measures.

### Direct Process Data Collection and Analysis

Direct process measurement techniques focus specifically on capturing the continuous process interactions in groups (O'Neil et al., 2000). These techniques include measures of auditory and visual interactions. Several data collection and data analysis techniques

**TABLE 55.1**

**Summary of Measurement Techniques Used to Assess Group Learning Processes**

*Direct Process Measure Techniques—Holistic Group Dataset*

| | |
|---|---|
| Data collection | Directly capturing group learning processes involves techniques that are used by all group members at the same time. |
| Data manipulation | Data manipulation not needed because data is captured at group level (holistic group dataset). |
| Data analysis | Continuous process techniques focus on interactions of group members generating qualitative and quantitative findings associated with continuous measures. |

*Indirect Process Measure Techniques—Holistic Group Dataset*

| | |
|---|---|
| Data collection | Indirectly eliciting group learning processes involves techniques that are used by all group members at the same time. |
| Data manipulation | Data manipulation not needed because data is captured at group level (holistic group dataset). |
| Data analysis | Discrete process techniques are dependent on dataset characteristics (focus on process or performance). They can include qualitative and quantitative data analysis techniques associated with discrete measures. |

*Indirect Process Measure Techniques—Collective Group Dataset*

| | |
|---|---|
| Data collection | Indirectly eliciting group learning processes involves techniques that are used by each group member separately. |
| Data manipulation | Individual data is then aggregated to create a dataset that represents the group data (analysis constructed). |
| Data analysis | Discrete process techniques are dependent on dataset characteristics (focus on process or performance). They can include qualitative and quantitative data analysis techniques associated with discrete measures. |

are related to measuring the group learning processes directly. The two key techniques for capturing actions and language are (1) technology and (2) observation. Using technology to capture group processes can provide researchers with data different from the observation data. Researchers can combine the use of technology and observation simultaneously to capture group processes (O'Neil et al., 2000; Paterson et al., 2003). These data can be analyzed in the captured form or transcribed into a text form.

## Use of Technology to Capture Group Process

### Spoken Language Processes

Techniques to capture a group's spoken language involve either audio recording or video recording (Schweiger, 1986; Willis, 2002) the spoken language that occurs during group interactions (Pavitt, 1998). It can also include the spoken language of group members as they explain their thinking during group processes in the form of a think-aloud protocol (Ericsson and Simon, 1993).

### Written Language Processes

Group learning processes are typically thought of as using spoken language, but new communication tools are available that allow groups to communicate and interact using written language. Examples include chat boards, whiteboards (although these are not limited to written language), and discussion boards. Also, computer-supported collaborative learning (CSCL) is a computer-based network system that supports group learning interactions (Stahl, 2006).

### Visible Processes

Techniques to capture a group's visible interactions include video recording of the behaviors and actions that occur in group interactions (Losada, 1990; Prichard, 2006; Schweiger, 1986; Sy, 2005; Willis et al., 2002).

## Use of Observations to Capture Group Process

Although the use of technology may capture data with a high level of realism, some group events can be better captured by humans because of their ability to observe more than what can be captured by technology. Observations ideally are carried out with a set of carefully developed observation protocols to help focus the observers and to teach them how to describe key process events. Observers are a good source for capturing various types of information (Patton, 2001), such as settings, human and social environments, group activities, style and types of language used, nonverbal communication, and events that are not ordinary. Observational data, for example, are important for studying group learning process (Battistich et al., 1993; Lingard, 2002; Sy, 2005; Webb, 1982; Willis et al., 2002). The type of information typically captured includes location, organization, activities, and behaviors (Battistich et al., 1993; Losada, 1990), as well as the frequency and quality of interactions (Battistich, 1993).

## Direct Process Data Analysis

Data that are a direct measure of group processes are captured in a holistic format that is ready to be analyzed (Figure 55.1 and Table 55.1). Several analytical techniques are available that can be used for analyzing group data, particularly direct process data. The following list is a representative sample of the analysis techniques applied to spoken or written language, visible interaction, and observational data: sequential analysis of group interactions (Bowers, 2006; Jeong, 2003; Rourke et al., 2001), analysis of interaction communication (Bales, 1950; Qureshi, 1995), communication analysis (Bowers et al., 1998), anticipation ratio (Eccles and Tenenbaum, 2004), in-process coordination (Eccles and Tenenbaum, 2004), discourse analysis (Aviv, 2003; Hara et al., 2000), content analysis (Aviv, 2003; Hara et al., 2000), cohesion analysis (Aviv, 2003), and protocol analysis (Ericsson and Simon, 1980, 1993). Visible interactions techniques also include using a behavior time series analysis (Losada, 1990). This analysis involves looking at dominate vs. submissive, friendly vs. unfriendly, or task-oriented vs. emotionally expressive behavior. For observational data, researchers focus on various qualitative techniques associated with naturalistic observations (Adler and Adler, 1994; Patton, 2001). Some common tasks associated with this type of analysis include group and character sequence analysis and assertion evaluation (Garfinkel, 1967; Jorgensen, 1989).

### Indirect Process Data Collection and Analysis

Many data collection techniques are related to measuring the group learning processes indirectly. Indirect group process, characteristic, and product measurement techniques elicit group information at a specific point in time. These discrete measures do not capture group processes directly but elicit data that describe group processes or process-related data such as group characteristics or group outcomes (things that may have a relation to the group processes). The three key types of data related to group learning processes are *indirect group process data*, *group characteristic data*, and *group product data*, within which specific factors can be measured. Indirect group process data describe group processes and can include factors such as group communication (verbal/nonverbal), group actions, group behaviors, group performance, and group processes. Group characteristic data, relating to group processes, include factors such as group knowledge, group skills, group efficacy, group attitudes, group member roles, group environment, and group leadership. The key elicitation techniques for both of these types of indirect data include interviews, questionnaires, and conceptual methods (Cooke et al., 2000). Each technique can be focused on group process or group characteristics. After reviewing methods to analyze group processes, we discuss methods for analyzing group products.

### Interviews

Interviews are a good technique for collecting general data about a group. The various types of interviewing techniques include unstructured interviews (Lingard, 2002) and more structured interviews, which are guided by a predetermined format that can provide either a rigid or loosely constrained format. Structured interviews require more time to develop but are more systematic (Cooke et al., 2000). Interviews are typically conducted with a single person at a time; however, is not uncommon to conduct a focus group, where the entire group is simultaneously interviewed. In a focus group, a facilitator interviews by leading a free and open group discussion (Myllyaho et al., 2004). The analysis of interview data requires basic qualitative data analysis techniques (Adler and Adler, 1994; Patton, 2001). Conducting interviews can be straightforward, but the analysis of the data relies tremendously on the interviewer's interpretations (Langan-Fox, 2000). Key steps to analyzing interviews are coding the data for themes (Lingard, 2002) and then studying the codes for meaning. Each phrase is closely examined to discover important concepts and reveal overall relationships. For a more holistic approach to analysis, a group interview technique can be used to discuss findings and to generate collective meaning given specific questions (Myllyaho et al., 2004). Content analysis is commonly used to analyze written statements (Langan-Fox and Tan, 1997). Other key analysis techniques focus on process analysis (Fussell et al., 1998; Prichard, 2006), specifically looking at discussion topics, group coordination, group cognitive overload, and analysis of task process. Other group characteristic analysis techniques could include role analysis and power analysis (Aviv, 2003).

### Questionnaires

Questionnaires are a commonly used technique to collect data about group processes (O'Neil et al., 2000; Sy, 2005; Webb, 1982; Willis et al., 2002). Similar to highly structured interviews, questionnaires can also look at relationship-oriented processes and task-oriented processes (Urch Druskat and Kayes, 2000). Questionnaires can be either closed ended or open ended (Alavi, 1994). Open-ended questionnaires are more closely related to a structured interview; the data collected using this format can be focused on group processes as well as group characteristics. Closed-ended questionnaires offer a limited set of responses. The limited responses involve some form of scale that could be nominal, ordinal, interval, or ratio. Data from this format have a limited ability to capture group process data, but this is the typical format for collecting data associated with group characteristics such as social space, group efficacy scales, group skills, group efficacy, group attitudes, group member roles, leadership, and group knowledge. Data from questionnaires can be analyzed much like interview data if the items are open ended. If the questionnaire is closed ended, then the instrument must be scrutinized for reliability prior to data analysis. Assuming sufficient evidence of reliability, analyzing data from closed-ended questionnaires involves interpreting a measurement based on a particular theoretical construct. The types of data analysis techniques that are appropriate depend on the type of scale used in a questionnaire (nominal, ordinal, interval, or ratio).

### Conceptual Methods

Conceptual methods involve assessing individual or group understanding about a given topic. Several data collection techniques are utilized to elicit knowledge structures. A review of the literature by Langan-Fox et al. (2000) found that knowledge in teams has been investigated by several qualitative and quantitative methods, including various elicitation techniques (e.g., cognitive interviewing, observation, card sorting, causal mapping, pairwise ratings) and representation techniques (e.g., MDS, distance ratio formulas, Pathfinder) that utilize aggregate methods.

One of the most common methods for assessing group knowledge is the use of concept maps (Herl et al., 1999; Ifenthaler, 2005; O'Connor and Johnson, 2004; O'Neil et al., 2000). Through concept mapping, similarity of group mental models can be measured in terms of the proportion of nodes and links shared between one concept map (mental model) and another (Rowe and Cooke, 1995). Several researchers believe that group knowledge and group processes are linked. Research has shown that specific group interactions such as communication and coordination mediate the development of group knowledge and thus mediate group performance (Mathieu et al., 2000). Group interactions coupled with group shared knowledge are a predominate force in the construct of group cognition. As teammates interact, they begin to share knowledge, thus enabling them to interpret cues in similar ways, make compatible decisions, and take proper actions (Klimoski and Mohammed, 1994). Group shared knowledge can help group members explain other members' actions, understand what is occurring with the task, develop accurate expectations about future member actions and task states, and communicate meanings efficiently.

Analyzing knowledge data can certainly involve qualitative methods. These methods tend to offer more detail and depth of information than might be found through statistical analyses (Miles and Huberman, 1994; Patton, 2001). Using qualitative analysis, we obtain greater understanding about the relationships between concepts within the context of the individual mental model. We also gain better insight into the sharedness of understanding between group members. Quantitative data analysis techniques provide researchers with tools to draw inferences on the change in group knowledge as well as statistically proving a change or variation in knowledge structures.

Several methods have been developed to analyze data regarding group knowledge. Most of them include an elicitation and analysis component. Some techniques use mixed methods such as the analysis-constructed shared mental model (ACSMM) (O'Connor and Johnson, 2004), DEEP (Spector and Koszalka, 2004), and social network analysis (Qureshi, 1995). Other methods are quantitative in nature, such as the Stanford Microarray Database (SMD) (Ifenthaler, 2005), Model Inspection Trace of Concepts of Relations (MITOCAR) (Pirnay-Dummer, 2006), multidimensional scaling (MDS), distance ratio formula, and Pathfinder (Cooke et al., 2000).

*Group product data* are the artifacts created from a group interaction. Group products typically do not capture the process that a group undertook to create the product but is evidence of the group's abilities. Many research studies that claim to study group processes only capture group product data. This is due in part to the claim that is made regarding the link between group products and group processes and characteristics (Cooke et al., 2000; Lesh and Dorr, 2003; Mathieu et al., 2000; Salas and Cannon-Bowers, 2001; Schweiger, 1986). Although some evidence suggests this relationship in a few areas, more research is required to substantiate this claim.

Analysis of the group product data involves techniques used when analyzing individual products. Analyzing the quality of a product can be facilitated by the use of specified criteria. These criteria are used to create a product rating scale. Rating scales can include numerical scales, descriptive scales, or checklists. Numerical scales present a range of numbers (usually sequential) that are defined by a label on either end. Each item in the questionnaire is rated according to the numerical scale. There is no specific definition of what the various numbers mean, except for the indicators at the ends of the scale; for example, a scale from 1 (very weak) to 5 (very strong) is very subjective but relatively easy to create. Descriptive scales are similar, but focus on verbal statements. Numbers can be assigned to each statement. Statements are typically in a logical order. A common example of a descriptive scale is "strongly disagree (1), disagree (2), neutral (3), agree (4), and strongly agree (5)." A checklist can be developed to delineate specific qualities for a given criterion. This can provide a high level of reliability because a specific quality is presented and the rater simply indicates whether an item is present or not. The validity of a checklist requires a careful task analysis to ensure scale validity.

## General Considerations for Group Learning Process Assessment

In assessment of group learning processes, researchers should consider several issues. These issues fall into four categories: (1) group setting, (2) variance in group member participation, (3) overall approach to data collection and analysis, and (4) thresholds.

### Group Setting

To a somewhat lesser degree than the other three issues, group settings should be considered when determining the best approach and methods for a particular study. Finalizing which techniques to use may depend on whether the groups will be working in a group learning setting or individually and then coming together as a group at various points. Some groups may meet in face-to-face settings or other settings that allow for synchronous interactions; however, distributed groups have technology-enabled synchronous and asynchronous tools or asynchronous interactions only. These variations in group setting can influence the selection of specific group learning process assessment methods.

### Variance in Group Member Participation

When collecting multiple sets of data over time, researchers should consider how they will deal with a variance in group member participation (group members absent during data collection or new members joining the group midstream). There are benefits and consequences for any decision made, but it is necessary to determine whether or not all data collected will be used, regardless of the group members present at the time of data collection. Researchers who choose not to use all data might consider using only those data submitted by group members who were present during all data collection sessions (O'Connor and Johnson, 2004). If data analysis will be based on a consistent number of group members, it will be necessary to consider how to handle data from groups that may not have the same group members present in each measure

point. Also, with fluctuations in group compositions, it is important to consider the overall group demographics and possible influences of individual group members on the group as a whole.

### Overall Approach to Data Collection and Analysis

In a holistic approach, individual group members work together and one dataset represents the group as a whole; however, the processes of group interaction naturally changes how individual group members think. The alternative is to capture individual measures and perform some type of aggregate analysis methods to represent the group; however, researchers should consider whether or not the aggregate would be a true representation of the group itself.

### Thresholds

When using indirect measures that require an aggregation or manipulation of data prior to analysis, researchers will have to consider such issues as similarity scores. These scores define the parameters for deciding if responses from one individual group member are similar to the responses from other group members (O'Connor and Johnson, 2004; Rentsch and Hall, 1994; Rentsch et al., in press); for example, will the rating of 3.5 on a 5-point scale be considered similar to a rating of 4.0 or a rating of 3.0? When aggregating individual data into a representation of the group, will the study look only at groups where a certain percentage of the group responded to measures (Ancona and Caldwell, 1991)? How will what is similar or shared across individual group members be determined? Will the analysis use counts ($x$ number of group members) or percentage of the group (e.g., 50%)? What level of similarity or sensitivity will be used to compare across groups (O'Connor and Johnson, 2004) — 50%? 75%? What about the level of mean responses in questionnaires (Urch Druskat and Kayes, 2000)? Many different thresholds that must be considered when assessing group learning processes and analyzing group data are not concerns when studying individuals.

## Conclusion

Assessment of group learning processes is more complex than assessment of individual learning processes because of the additional considerations necessary for selecting data collection and analysis methods. As in most research, the "very type of experiment set up by researchers will determine the type of data and therefore what can be done with such data in analysis and interpretation" (Langan-Fox et al., 2004, p. 348).

Indeed, it is logical to allow the specific research questions to drive the identification of data collection methods. The selection of research questions and subsequent identification of data collection methods will naturally place limitations on suitable data analysis methods. Careful planning for the study of group learning processes, from the selection of direct or indirect assessment measures to considering the possible influences group characteristics may have on group learning processes, is essential.

Because of the many possible combinations of methods and techniques available for studying group learning processes, some feel that research has not yet done enough to determine the best methods for studying groups (Langan-Fox et al., 2000). Many group learning process studies consider only outcome measures and do not directly study group learning processes (Worchel et al., 1992). Others look only at portions of the group process or attempt to assess group learning processes through a comparison of discrete measures of the group over time. Still other methods for data collection and analysis of group data are being developed as we speak (Seel, 1999). No one best method has been identified for analyzing group learning process data, so we suggest that studies should consider utilizing multiple methods to obtain a more comprehensive picture of group learning processes. If we are to better understand the notion of group learning processes and utilize that understanding in design, implementation, and management of learning groups in the future, then we must address the basic issues that are related with conceptualization and measurement (Langan-Fox et al., 2004).

## ASSESSMENT OF COMPLEX PERFORMANCE

*Tamara van Gog, Remy M. J. P. Rikers, and Paul Ayres*

This chapter section discusses assessment of complex performance from an educational *research* perspective, in terms of data collection and analysis. It begins with a short introduction on complex performance and a discussion on the various issues related to selecting and defining appropriate assessment tasks, criteria, and standards that give meaning to the assessment. Although many of the issues discussed here are also important for performance assessment in educational *practice*, readers particularly interested in this topic might want to refer, for example, to Chapter 44 in this *Handbook* or the edited books by Birenbaum and Dochy (1996) and Segers et al. (2003). For a discussion of laboratory setups for data collection, see the section by Duley et al. in this chapter.

Complex performance can be defined as performance on complex tasks; however, definitions of task complexity differ: Campbell (1988), in a review of the literature, categorized complexity as primarily subjective (psychological) or objective (function of objective task characteristics), or as an interaction between objective and subjective (individual) characteristics. Campbell reported that the subjective perspective emphasized psychological dimensions such as task significance and identity. On the other hand, objective definitions consider the degree of structuredness of a task or of the possibility of multiple solution paths (Byström and Järvelin, 1995; Campbell, 1988). When the process of task performance can be described in detail *a priori* (very structured), a task is considered less complex; in contrast, when there is a great deal of uncertainty, it is considered highly complex. Similarly, complexity can vary according to the number of solutions paths possible. When there is just one correct solution path, a task is considered less complex than when multiple paths can lead to a correct solution or when multiple solutions are possible.

For the interaction category, Campbell (1988) argued that both the problem solver and the task are important. By defining task complexity in terms of cognitive load (Chandler and Sweller, 1991; Sweller, 1988; Sweller et al., 1998) an example of this interaction can readily be shown. From a cognitive load perspective, complexity is defined by the number of interacting information elements a task contains, which have to be simultaneously handled in working memory. As such, complexity is influenced by expertise (i.e., subjective, individual characteristic); what may be a complex task for a novice may be a simple task for an expert, because a number of elements have been combined into a cognitive schema that can be handled as a single element in the expert's working memory. Tasks that are highly complex according to the objective definition (i.e., lack of structuredness and multiple possible solution paths) will also be complex in the interaction definition; however, according to the latter definition, even tasks with a high degree of structuredness or one correct solution path can be considered complex, given a high number of interacting information elements or low performer expertise.

In this chapter section, we limit our discussion to methods of assessment of complex performance on *cognitive* tasks. What is important to note throughout this discussion is that the methods described here can be used to assess (improvements in) complex performance both during training and after training, depending on the research questions one seeks to address. After training, performance assessment usually has the goal to assess learning, which is a goal of many studies in education and instructional design. If one seeks to assess learning, one must be careful not to conclude that participants have learned because their performance improved during training. As Bjork (1999) points out, depending on the training conditions, high performance gains during training may not be associated with learning, whereas low performance gains may be. It is important, therefore, to assess learning on retention or transfer tasks, instead of on practice tasks. Selection of appropriate assessment tasks is an important issue, which is addressed in the next section.

## Assessment Tasks

An essential step in the assessment of performance is the identification of a collection of representative tasks that capture those aspects of the participant's knowledge and skills that a study seeks to address (Ericsson, 2002). Important factors for representativeness of the collection of assessment tasks are authenticity, number, and duration of tasks, all of which are highly influenced by the characteristics of the domain of study.

Selecting tasks that adequately capture performance often turns out to be very difficult. Selecting atypical or artificial tasks may even impede learners in demonstrating their true level of understanding. Traditional means to evaluate the learners' knowledge or skills have been criticized because they often fail to demonstrate that the learner can actually do something in real life or in their future workplace with their knowledge and skills they have acquired during their training (see, for example, Anderson et al., 1996; Shepard, 2000; Thompson, 2001).

The argument for the use of authentic tasks to assess the learners' understanding has a long tradition. It started in the days of John Dewey (1916) and continues to the present day (Merrill, 2002; van Merriënboer, 1997); however, complete authenticity of assessment tasks may be difficult to realize in research settings, because the structuredness of the domain plays a role here. For structured domains such as chess and bridge, the same conditions can be reproduced in a research laboratory as those under which performance normally takes place; for less or ill-structured domains, this is difficult or even impossible to do (Ericsson and Lehmann, 1996). Nonetheless, one can always strive for a high degree of authenticity. Gulikers et al. (2004) defined authentic assessment as a five-dimensional construct (i.e., task, social context, physical context, form/result, and criteria) that can vary from low to high on each of the dimensions.

The number of tasks in the collection and the duration are important factors influencing the reliability and generalizability of a study. Choosing too few tasks or tasks of too short duration will negatively affect reliability and generalizability. On the other hand, choosing a large number of tasks or tasks of a very long duration will lead to many practical problems and might exhaust both participants and researchers. In many complex domains (e.g., medical diagnosis), it is quite common and often inevitable to use a very small set of cases because of practical circumstances and because detailed analysis of the learners' responses to these complex problems is very difficult and time consuming (Ericsson, 2004; Ericsson and Smith, 1991). Unfortunately, however, there are no golden rules for determining the adequate number of tasks to use or their duration, because important factors are highly dependent upon the domain and specific context (Van der Vleuten and Schuwirth, 2005). It is often easier to identify a small collection of representative tasks that capture the relevant aspects of performance in highly structured domains (e.g., physics, mathematics, chess) than in ill-structured domains (e.g., political science, medicine), where a number of interacting complex skills are required.

## Assessment Criteria and Standards

The term *assessment criteria* refers to a description of the elements or aspects of performance that will be assessed, and the term *assessment standards* refers to a description of the quality of performance (e.g., excellent/good/average/poor) on each of those aspects that can be expected of participants at different stages (e.g., age, grade) (Arter and Spandel, 1992). As Woolf (2004) pointed out, however, the term *assessment criteria* is often used in the definition of standards as well. Depending on the question one seeks to answer, different standards can be used, such as a participant's past performance (self-referenced), peer group performance (norm-referenced), or an objective standard (criterion-referenced), and there are different methods for setting standards (Cascallar and Cascallar, 2003). Much of the research on criteria and standard setting has been conducted in the context of educational practice for national (or statewide) school tests (Hambleton et al., 2000) and for highly skilled professions, such as medicine, where the stakes of setting appropriate standards are very high (Hobma et al., 2004; Van der Vleuten and Schuwirth, 2005). Although formulation of good criteria and standards is extremely important in educational practice, where certification is the prime goal, it is no less important in educational research settings. What aspects of performance are measured and what standards are set have a major impact on the generalizability and value of a study.

The degree to which the domain is well structured influences not only the creation of a collection of representative tasks but also the definition of criteria, setting of standards, and interpretation of performance in relation to standards. In highly structured domains, such as mathematics or chess, assessing the quality of the learner's response is often fairly straightforward and unproblematic. In less structured domains, however, it is often much more difficult to identify clear standards; for example, a music student's interpretation of a piano concerto is more difficult to assess than the student's technical performance on the piece. The former contains many more subjective elements (e.g., taste) or cultural differences than the latter.

## Collecting Performance Data

No one best method for complex performance assessment exists, and it is often advisable to use multiple measures or methods in combination to obtain as complete a picture as possible of the performance. A number of methods are described here for collecting performance outcome (product) and performance process data. Methods are classified as online (during task performance) or offline (after task performance). Which method or combination of methods is the most useful depends on the particular research question, the possible constraints of the research context, and the domain. In ill-structured domains, for example, the added value of process measures may be much higher than in highly structured domains.

### Collecting Performance Outcome (Product) Data

Collecting performance outcome data is quite straightforward. One takes the product of performance (e.g., an electrical circuit that was malfunctioning but is now repaired) and scores it along the defined criteria (e.g., do all the components function as they should, individually and as a whole?). Instead of assigning points for correct aspects, one can count the number of errors, and analyze the types of errors made; however, especially for assessment of complex performance, collecting performance product data alone is not very informative. Taking into account the process leading up to the product and the cognitive costs at which it was obtained provides equally if not more important information.

### Collecting Performance Process Data

#### Time on Task or Speed

An important indication of the level of mastery of a particular task is the time needed to complete a task. According to the *power law of practice* (Newell and

Rosenbloom, 1981; VanLehn, 1996), the time needed to complete a task decreases in proportion to the time spent in practice, raised to some power. Newell and Rosenbloom (1981) found that this law operates across a broad range of tasks, from solving geometry problems to keyboard typing. To account for the power law of practice, several theories have been put forward. Anderson's ACT-R explains the speed-up by assuming that slow declarative knowledge is transformed into fast procedural knowledge (Anderson, 1993; Anderson and Lebiere, 1998). Another explanation suggested that speed-up is the result of repeated encounters with meaningful patterns (Ericsson and Staszewski, 1989); that is, as a result of frequent encounters with similar elements, these elements will no longer be perceived as individual units but will be perceived as a meaningful whole (i.e., chunk). In addition to chunking, automation processes (Schneider and Shiffrin, 1977; Shiffrin and Schneider, 1977) occur with practice that allow for faster and more effortless performance. In summary, as expertise develops equal performance can be attained in less time; therefore, it is important to collect time-on-task data to assess improvements in complex performance.

### Cognitive Load

The same processes of chunking and automation that are associated with decreases in the time required to perform a task are also responsible for decreases in the cognitive load imposed by performing the task (Paas and van Merriënboer, 1993; Yeo and Neal, 2004). Cognitive load can be measured using both online and offline techniques. The cognitive capacity that is allocated to performing the task is defined as *mental effort*, which is considered to reflect the actual cognitive load a task imposes (Paas and van Merriënboer, 1994a; Paas et al., 2003). A subjective but reliable technique for measuring mental effort is having individuals provide self-ratings of the amount of mental effort invested. A single-scale subjective rating instrument can be used, such as the nine-point rating scale developed by Paas (1992), or a multiple-scale instrument, such as the NASA Task Load Index (TLX), which was used, for example by Gerjets et al. (2004, 2006). As subjective cognitive load measures are usually recorded after each task or after a series of tasks has been completed they are usually considered to be offline measurements, although there are some exceptions; for example, Ayres (2006) required participants to rate cognitive load at specific points within tasks.

Objective online measures include physiological measures such as heart-rate variability (Paas and van Merriënboer, 1994b), eye-movement data, and secondary-task procedures (Brünken et al., 2003). Because they are taken during task performance, those online measures can show fluctuations in cognitive load during task performance. It is notable, however, that Paas and van Merriënboer (1994b) found the heart-rate variability measure to be quite intrusive as well as insensitive to subtle fluctuations in cognitive load. The subjective offline data are often easier to collect and analyze and provide a good indication of the overall cognitive load a task imposed (Paas et al., 2003).

### Actions: Observation and Video Records

Process-tracing techniques are very well suited to assessing the different types of actions taken during task performance, some of which are purely cognitive, whereas others result in physical actions, because the "data that are recorded are of a pre-specified type (e.g., verbal reports, eye movements, actions) and are used to make inferences about the cognitive processes or knowledge underlying task performance" (Cooke, 1994, p. 814). Ways to record data that allow the inference of cognitive actions are addressed in the following sections. The following options are available for recording the physical actions taken during task performance: (1) trained observers can write down the actions taken or check them off on an *a priori* constructed list (use multiple observers), (2) a (digital) video record of the participants' performance can be made, or (3) for computer-based tasks, an action record can be made using screen recording software or software that logs key presses and coordinates of mouse clicks.

### Attention and Cognitive Actions: Eye-Movement Records

Eye tracking (Duchowski, 2003)—that is, recording eye-movement data while a participant is working on a (usually, but not necessarily computer-based) task—can also be used to gather online performance process data but is much less used in educational research than the above methods. Eye-movement data give insights into the allocation of attention and provide a researcher with detailed information of what a participant is looking at, for how long, and in what order. Such data allow inferences to be made about cognitive processes (Rayner, 1998), albeit cautious inferences, as the data do not provide information on *why* a participant was looking at something for a certain amount of time or in a certain order. Attention can shift in response to exogenous or endogenous cues (Rayner, 1998; Stelmach et al., 1997). Exogenous shifts of attention occur mainly in response to environmental features or changes in the environment (e.g., if something brightly colored would start flashing in the corner of a computer screen, your attention

would be drawn to it). Endogenous shifts are driven by knowledge of the task, of the environment, and of the importance of available information sources (i.e., influenced by expertise level) (Underwood et al., 2003). In chess, for example, it was found that experts fixated proportionally more on relevant pieces than non-expert players (Charness et al., 2001). In electrical circuits troubleshooting, van Gog et al. (2005a) also found that participants with higher expertise fixated more on a fault-related component during problem orientation than participants with lower expertise.* Please note that this is not an exhaustive overview and that we have no commercial or other interest in any of the programs mentioned here. Haider and Frensch (1999) used eye-movement data to corroborate their information-reduction hypothesis, which states that with practice people learn to ignore task-redundant information and limit their processing to task-relevant information.

On tasks with many visual performance aspects (e.g., troubleshooting technical systems), eye-movement records may therefore provide much more information than video records. Some important problem-solving actions may be purely visual or cognitive, but those will show up in an eye-movement record, whereas a video record will only allow inferences of visual or cognitive actions that resulted in manual or physical actions (van Gog et al., 2005b). In addition to providing information on the allocation of attention, eye-movement data can also give information about the cognitive load that particular aspects of task performance impose; for example, whereas pupil dilation (Van Gerven et al., 2004) and fixation duration (Underwood et al., 2004) are known to increase with increased processing demands, the length of saccades (i.e., rapid eye movements from one location to another; see Duchowski, 2003) is known to decrease. (For an in-depth discussion of eye-movement data and cognitive processes, see Rayner, 1998.)

### Thought Processes and Cognitive Actions: Verbal Reports

Probably the most widely used verbal reporting techniques are concurrent and retrospective reporting (Ericsson and Simon, 1993). As their names imply, concurrent reporting is an online technique, whereas retrospective reporting is an offline technique. Concurrent reporting, or *thinking aloud*, requires participants to verbalize all thoughts that come to mind during task

---

* Note that the expertise differences between groups were relatively small (i.e., this was not an expert–novice study), suggesting that eye-movement data may be a useful tool in investigating relatively subtle expertise differences or expertise development.

performance. Retrospective reporting requires participants to report the thoughts they had during task performance immediately after completing it. Although there has been considerable debate over the use of verbal reports as data, both methods are considered to allow valid inferences to be made about the cognitive processes underlying task performance, provided that verbalization instructions and prompts are carefully worded (Ericsson and Simon, 1993).

Instructions and prompts should be worded in such a way that the evoked responses will not interfere with the cognitive processes as they occur during task performance; for example, instructions for concurrent reporting should tell participants to think aloud and verbalize everything that comes to mind but should not ask them to explain any thoughts. Prompts should be as unobtrusive as possible. Prompting participants to "keep thinking aloud" is preferable over asking them "what are you thinking?" because this would likely evoke self-reflection and, hence, interfere with the cognitive processes. Deviations from these instructional and prompting techniques can change either the actual cognitive processes involved or the processes that were reported, thereby compromising the validity of the reports (Boren and Ramey, 2000; Ericsson and Simon, 1993). Magliano et al. (1999), for example, found that instructions to explain, predict, associate, or understand during reading influenced the inferences from the text that participants generated while thinking aloud. Although the effect of instructions on cognitive processes is an interesting topic of study, when the intention is to elicit reports of the actual cognitive processes as they would occur without intervention, Ericsson and Simon's (1993) guidelines for wording instructions and prompts should be adhered to.

Both reporting methods can result in verbal protocols that allow for valid inferences about cognitive processes; however, the potential for differences in the information they contain must be considered when choosing an appropriate method for answering a particular research question. According to Taylor and Dionne (2000), concurrent protocols mostly seem to provide information on actions and outcomes, whereas retrospective protocols seem to provide more information about "strategies that control the problem solving process" and "conditions that elicited a particular response" (p. 414). Kuusela and Paul (2000) reported that concurrent protocols contained more information than retrospective protocols, because the latter often contained only references to the effective actions that led to the solution. van Gog et al. (2005b) investigated whether the technique of cued retrospective reporting, in which a retrospective report is cued by a replay of

a record of eye movements and mouse/keyboard operations made during the task, would combine the advantages of concurrent (i.e., more action information) and retrospective (i.e., more strategic and conditional information) reporting. They found that both concurrent and cued retrospective reporting resulted in more action information, as well as in more strategic and conditional information, than retrospective reporting without a cue.

Contrary to expectations, concurrent reporting resulted in more strategic and conditional information than retrospective reporting. This may (1) reflect a genuine difference from Taylor and Dionne's results, (2) have been due to different operationalizations of the information types in the coding scheme used, or (3) have been due to the use of a different segmentation method than those used by Taylor and Dionne (2000).

An explanation for the finding that concurrent reports result in more information on actions than retrospective reports may be that concurrent reporting occurs online rather than offline. Whereas concurrent reports capture information available in short-term memory during the process, retrospective reports reflect memory traces of the process retrieved from short-term memory when tasks are of very short duration or from long-term memory when tasks are of longer duration (Camps, 2003; Ericsson and Simon, 1993). It is likely that only the correct steps that have led to attainment of the goal are stored in long-term memory, because only these steps are relevant for future use. This is why having participants report retrospectively based on a record of observations or intermediate products of their problem-solving process is known to lead to better results (due to fewer omissions) than retrospective reporting without a cue (van Gog et al., 2005b; Van Someren et al., 1994). Possibly, the involvement of different memory systems might also explain Taylor and Dionne's (2000) finding that retrospective protocols seem to contain more conditional and strategic information. This knowledge might have been used during the process but may have been omitted in concurrent reporting as a result of the greater processing demands this method places on short-term memory (Russo et al., 1989). Although this explanation is tentative, there are indications that concurrent reporting may become difficult to maintain under high cognitive load conditions (Ericsson and Simon, 1993). Indeed, participants in van Gog et al.'s study who experienced a higher cognitive load (i.e., reported investment of more mental effort) in performing the tasks indicated during a debriefing after the experiment that they disliked concurrent reporting and preferred cued retrospective reporting (van Gog, 2006).

Tamara van Gog, Fred Paas et al.

## Neuroscientific Data

An emerging and promising area of educational research is the use of neuroscience methodologies to study (changes in) brain functions and structures directly, which can provide detailed data on learning processes, memory processes, and cognitive development (see, for example, Goswami, 2004; Katzir and Paré-Blagoev, 2006). Methods such as magnetic resonance imaging (MRI), functional magnetic resonance imaging (fMRI), electroencephalography (EEG), magnetoencephalography (MEG), positron-emission tomography (PET), and single-photon emission computed tomography (SPECT) provide (indirect) measures of neuronal activity. The reader is referred to Katzir and Paré-Blagoev (2006) for a discussion of these methods and examples of their use in educational research.

## Data Analysis

Analyzing performance product, time on task, and mental effort data (at least when the subjective rating scales are used) is a very straightforward process, so it is not discussed here. In this section, analysis of observation, eye movement, and verbal protocol data is discussed, as well as the analysis of combined methods/measures.

### Analysis of Observation, Eye Movement, and Verbal Protocol Data

#### Observation Data

Coding and analysis of observation data can take many different forms, again depending on the research question. Coding schemes are developed based on the performance aspects (criteria) one wishes to assess and sometimes may incorporate evaluation of performance aspects. Whether coding is done online (during performance by observers) or offline (after performance based on video, screen capture, or mouse-keyboard records), the use of multiple observers or raters is important for determining reliability of the coding. Quantitative analysis on the coded data can take the form of comparison of frequencies, appropriateness (e.g., number of errors), or sequences of actions (e.g., compared to an ideal or expert sequence) and interpreting the outcome in relation to the set standard.

Several commercial and noncommercial software programs have been developed to assist in the analysis of action data;* for example, Observer (Noldus et al.,

2000) is commercial software for coding and analysis of digital video records; NVivo (Bazeley and Richards, 2000) is commercial software for accessing, shaping, managing, and analyzing non-numerical qualitative data; Multiple Episode Protocol Analysis (MEPA) (Erkens, 2002) is free software for annotating, coding, and analyzing both nonverbal and verbal protocols; and ACT Pro (Fu, 2001) can be used for sequential analysis of protocols of discrete user actions such as mouse clicks and key presses.

#### Eye-Movement Data

For analysis of fixation data it is important to identify the gaze data points that together represent fixations. This is necessary because during fixation the eyes are not entirely motionless; small tremors and drifts may occur (Duchowski, 2003). According to Salvucci (1999), the three categories of fixation identification methods are based on velocity, dispersion, or region. Most eye-tracking software allows for defining values for the dispersion-based method, which identifies fixation points as a minimum number of data points that are grouped closely together (i.e., fall within a certain dispersion, defined by pixels) and last a minimum amount of time (duration threshold). Once fixations have been defined, defining *areas of interest* (AoIs) in the stimulus materials will make analysis of the huge data files more manageable by allowing summaries of fixation data to be made for each AoI, such as the number of fixations, the mean fixation duration, and the total time spent fixating. Furthermore, a chronological listing of fixations on AoIs can be sequentially analyzed to detect patterns in viewing behavior.

#### Verbal Protocol Data

When verbal protocols have been transcribed, they can be segmented and coded. Segmentation based on utterances is highly reliable because it uses pauses in natural speech (Ericsson and Simon, 1993); however, many researchers apply segmentation based on meaning (Taylor and Dionne, 2000). In this case, segmentation and coding become intertwined, and the reliability of both should be evaluated. It is, again, important to use multiple raters (at least on a substantial subset of data) and determine the reliability of the coding scheme. The standard work by Ericsson and Simon (1993) provides a wealth of information on verbal protocol coding and analysis techniques. The software program MEPA (Erkens, 2002) can assist in the development of a coding scheme for verbal data, as well as in analysis of coded data with a variety of quantitative or qualitative methods.

---

* Please note that this is not an exhaustive overview and that we have no commercial or other interest in any of the programs mentioned here.

## Combining Methods and Measures

As mentioned before, there is not a preferred single method for the assessment of complex performances. By combining different methods and measures, a more complete or a more detailed picture of performance will be obtained; for example, various process-tracing techniques such as eye tracking and verbal reporting can be collected and analyzed in combination with other methods of assessment (van Gog et al., 2005a). Different product and process measures can easily be combined, and it can be argued that some of them *should* be combined because a simple performance score* ignores the fact that, with expertise development, time on task and cognitive load decrease, whereas performance increases.

Consider the example of a student who attains the same performance score on two comparable tasks that are spread over time, where cognitive load measures indicate that the learner had to invest a lot of mental effort to complete the task the first time and little the second. Looking only at the performance score, one might erroneously conclude that no progress was made, whereas the learner actually made a subtle step forward, because reduced cognitive load means that more capacity can be devoted to further learning.

The mental efficiency measure developed by Paas and van Merriënboer (1993) reflects this relation: Higher performance with less mental effort invested to attain that performance results in higher efficiency. This measure is obtained by standardizing performance and mental effort scores, and then subtracting the mean standardized mental effort score ($zE$) from the mean standardized performance score ($zP$) and dividing the outcome by the square root of 2:

$$\frac{zP - zE}{\sqrt{2}}$$

When tasks are performed under time constraints, the combination of mental effort and performance measures will suffice; however, when time on task is self-paced, it is useful to include the additional time parameter in the efficiency measure (making it three-dimensional) (Paas et al., 2003; Tuovinen and Paas, 2004):

$$\frac{zP - zE - zT}{\sqrt{3}}$$

---

* This term is somewhat ambiguous, as we have previously classified mental effort and time-on-task data as performance process data. We feel they should be regarded as such; however, in the literature *performance score* is often used to refer to the grade assigned to a solution or solution procedure, which is the sense in which the term is used in this subsection.

## Discussion

Much of the research into learning and instruction involves assessment of complex performances of cognitive tasks. The focus of this chapter section was on data collection and analysis methods that can be used for such assessments. First, the important issues related to selecting an appropriate collection of assessment tasks and defining appropriate assessment criteria and standards were discussed. Then, different ways for collecting performance product and process data, using online (during task performance) or offline (after task performance) measurements, were described. Analysis techniques were discussed and, given the lack of a single preferred method for complex performance assessment, ways to combine measures were suggested that will foster a more complete or more detailed understanding of complex performance.

This chapter section aimed to provide an overview of the important issues in assessment of complex performance on cognitive tasks and of available data collection and analysis techniques for such assessments, rather than any definite guidelines. The latter would be impossible when writing for a broad audience, because what constitutes an appropriate collection of tasks, appropriate criteria and standards, and appropriate data collection and analysis techniques is highly dependent on the research question one seeks to address and on the domain in which one wishes to do so. We hope that this overview, along with other chapter sections, provides the reader with a starting point for further development of rewarding and informative studies.

# SETTING UP A LABORATORY FOR MEASUREMENT OF COMPLEX PERFORMANCES

*Aaron R. Duley, Paul Ward, and Peter A. Hancock*

This chapter section describes how to set up laboratories for the measurement of complex performance. *Complex performance* in this context does not exclusively refer to tasks that are inherently difficult to perform; rather, the term is used here in a broader sense to refer to the measurement of real-world activities that require the integration of disparate measurement instrumentation as well as the need for time-critical experimental control. We have assumed that our primary readership is comprised of graduate students and research faculty, although the chapter addresses issues relevant to all who seek a better understanding of behavioral response.

The central theme of this section relates to laboratory instrumentation. Because instrumentation is a requisite element for complex performance measurement, a common problem encountered by researchers is how to overcome the various technical hurdles that often discourage the pursuit of difficult research objectives. Thus, creating a testing environment suitable to address research questions is a major issue when planning any research program; however, searching the literature for resources relating to laboratory instrumentation configurations yields a surprisingly scant number of references and resources that address these issues. Having made just such an attempt for the purposes of this section, the ability to articulate a general-purpose exposition on laboratory setup is indeed a challenging endeavor. This pursuit is made more difficult by addressing a naturally ambiguous topic such as complex performance; nevertheless, our section looks to provide the bearings needed to resolve such questions. In particular, we cover stimulus presentation and control alternatives, as well as hardware choices for signal routing and triggering, while offering solutions for commonly encountered problems when attempting to assemble such a laboratory. Some portions of this section are moderately technical, but every attempt has been made to ensure that the content is appropriate for our target audience.

## Instrumentation and Common Configurations

Psychology has a long legacy of employing tools and instrumentation to support scientific inquiry. The online Museum of the History of Psychological Instrumentation, for example, has illustrations of over 150 devices used by early researchers to visualize organ function and systematically investigate human psychological processes and behavior (see http://www.chss.montclair.edu/psychology/museum/museum.htm). At this museum, one can view such devices as an early Wundt-style tachistiscope or the *Rotationsapparatus für Komplikations-Versuche* (rotary apparatus for complication studies). Titchener, a student of Wundt, continued this tradition in his own laboratory at Cornell University and described the building requirements and the costs associated with items needed for establishing the ideal psychological laboratory (Titchener, 1900, pp. 252–253):

> For optics, there should be two rooms, light and dark, facing south and north respectively, and the later divided into antechamber and inner room. For acoustics, there should be one large room, connected directly with a small, dark, and (so far as is possible without special construction) sound-proof chamber. For haptics, there should be a moderately sized room, devoted to work on cutaneous pressure, temperature, and pain, and a larger room for investigations of movement perceptions. Taste and smell should each have a small room, the latter tiled or glazed, and so situated that ventilation is easy and so does not involve the opening of doors or transom-windows into the building. There should, further, be a clock-room, for the time-registering instruments and their controls; and a large room for the investigations of the bodily processes and changes underlying affective consciousness.

Instrumentation is a central component of complex performance measurement; however, the process by which one orchestrates several devices in the broader context of addressing an experimental question is indeed challenging. Modern-day approaches reflect a paradigm shift with respect to early psychological procedures. Traditionally, a single instrument would be used for an entire experiment. Complex performance evaluation, however, often entails situations where the presentation of a stimulus is controlled by one computer, while supplementary instrumentation collects a stream of other data on a second or perhaps yet a third computer. Certainly, an ideal testing solution would allow one to minimize the time needed to set up an experiment and maximize the experimental degree of automation, thus minimizing investigator intervention, without compromising the scientific integrity of the experiment. Nevertheless, the measurement of complex performance is often in conflict with this idyllic vision. It is not sufficient for contemporary researchers simply to design experiments. They are also required to have access to the manpower and the monetary or computational resources necessary to translate a scientific question into a tenable methodological test bed.

## Design Patterns for Laboratory Instrumentation

Design patterns represent structured solutions for such recurring assessment problems (Gamma et al., 1995). The formal application of design patterns as abstract blueprints for common challenges has relevance for laboratory instrumentation configuration and equipment purchasing decisions. Although research questions vary, experiments will regularly share a comparable solution. These commonalities are important to identify, as the ability to employ a single set of tools has distinct advantages compared to solutions tailored for only one particular problem. Such advantages include cost savings, instrumentation sharing, instrumentation longevity, and laboratory scalability (e.g., the capacity to run multiple experiments simultaneously).

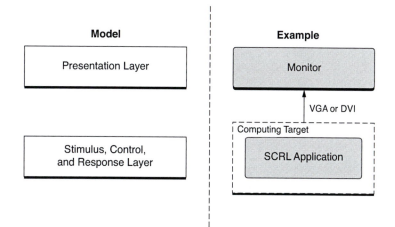

**Figure 55.2** Stimulus and presentation control model.

The purpose of the following section is to provide a level of abstraction for instrumentation configurations commonly encountered in the design of experiments related to complex performance. This approach is favored beyond simply providing a list of items and products that every laboratory should own. We acknowledge the considerable between-laboratory variability regarding research direction, instrumentation, and expertise; therefore, we focus primarily on instrumentation configuration and architecture as represented by design patterns common to a broad array of complex performance manipulations.

Given that an experiment will often require the manipulation of stimuli in a structured way and seeing the impracticality in comprehensively covering all research design scenarios, the following assumptions are made: (1) Stimuli are physically presented to participants, (2) some stimulus properties are required to be under experimental control (e.g., presentation length), (3) measurable responses by the participant are required, and (4) control or communication of secondary instrumentation may also be necessary. These assumptions accommodate a broad spectrum of possible designs and from these assumptions several frameworks can be outlined.

### Stimulus Presentation and Control Model

Figure 55.2 depicts the simplest of the design patterns, which we term the *stimulus presentation and control* (SPC) model. The SPC model is a building block for more complex configurations. The basic framework of the SPC model includes the *presentation layer* and the *stimulus, control, and response layer*. The presentation layer represents the medium used to physically display a stimulus to a participant (e.g., monitor, projector,

speaker, headphones). The stimulus, control, and response layer (SCRL) encapsulates a number of inter-related functions central to complex performance experimentation, such as the experimental protocol logic, and is the agent that coordinates and controls experimental flow and, potentially, participant response. Broadly speaking, SCRL-type roles include stimulus manipulation and timing, instrument logging and coordination, and response logging, in addition to experiment procedure management.

As the SCRL often contains the logic necessary to execute the experimental paradigm, it is almost always implemented in software; thus, the SCRL application is assumed to operate on a computing target (e.g., desktop, portable digital assistant), which is represented by the dashed box in Figure 55.2. As an example implementation of the SPC model, consider a hypothetical experiment in which participants are exposed to a number of visual stimuli for 6 sec each. Each visual stimulus occurs after a fixed *foreperiod* of 1 sec and a subsequent *fixation cross* (i.e., the point at which participants are required to direct their gaze) presented for 500 msec. Each visual stimulus is followed by a 2-sec inter-trial interval (ITI). The only requirement of the participant is to view the visual stimuli for the duration of its presentation. How do we implement this experiment?

This problem has several possible solutions. A monitor (presentation layer) and Microsoft PowerPoint (SCRL) would easily accomplish the task; however, the SPC model is suitable to handle an extensive arrangement of experimental designs, so additional procedural requirements increase the need for added SCRL functionality. Consider an experiment where both a monitor and speakers are required to present the stimuli. This basic pattern still reflects an SPC

**TABLE 55.2**
**SCRL-Type Applications**

| Name | Description | Type | Platform |
|---|---|---|---|
| Cogent 2000/ Cogent Graphics | Complete PC-based software environment for functional brain mapping experiments; contains commands useful for presenting scanner-synchronized visual stimuli (Cogent Graphics), auditory stimuli, mechanical stimuli, and taste and smell stimuli. It is also used in monitoring key presses and other physiological recordings from the subject. | Freeware | Windows |
| DMDX | Win 32-based display system used in psychology laboratories around the world to measure reaction times to visual and auditory stimuli. | Freeware | Windows |
| E-Prime | Suite of applications to design, generate, run, collect data, edit, and analyze the data; includes: (1) a graphical environment that allows visual selection and specification of experimental functions; (2) a comprehensive scripting language; (3) data management and analysis tools. | Commercial | Windows |
| Flashdot | Program for generating and presenting visual perceptual experiments that require a high temporal precision. It is controlled by a simple experiment building language and allows experiment generation with either a text or a graphical editor. | Freeware | Windows, Linux |
| FLXLab | Program for running psychology experiments; capabilities include presenting text and graphics, playing and recording sounds, and recording reaction times via the keyboard or a voice key. | Freeware | Windows, Linux |
| PEBL (Psychology Experiment Building Language) | New language specifically designed to be used to create psychology experiments. | Freeware | Linux, Windows, Mac |
| PsychoPy | Psychology stimulus software for Python; combines the graphical strengths of OpenGL with the easy Python syntax to give psychophysics a free and simple stimulus presentation and control package. | Freeware | Linux, Mac |
| PsyScope | Interactive graphic system for experimental design and control on the Macintosh. | Freeware | Mac |
| PsyScript | Application for scripting psychology experiments, similar to SuperLab, MEL, or E-Prime | Freeware | Linux, Mac |
| PyEPL (Python Experiment-Programming Library) | Library for coding psychology experiments in Python; supports presentation of both visual and auditory stimuli, as well as both manual (keyboard/joystick) and sound (microphone) input as responses. | Freeware | Linux, Mac |
| Realtime Experiment Interface | Extensible hard real-time platform for the development of novel experiment control and signal-processing applications. | Freeware | Linux |
| SuperLab | Stimulus presentation software with features that support the presentation of multiple types of media as well as rapid serial visual presentation paradigms and eye tracking integration, among other features. | Commercial | Windows, Mac |

model and PowerPoint could be configured to present auditory and visual stimuli within a strict set of parameters. On the other hand, a real experiment would likely require that the foreperiod, fixations cross, and ITI appear with variable and not fixed timing. Presentation applications like PowerPoint, however, are not specifically designed for experimentation. As such, limitations are introduced as experimental designs become more elaborate. One solution to this problem is to use the Visual Basic for Applications (VBA) functionality embedded in Microsoft Office; however, requiring features such as variable timing, timing determinism (i.e., executing a task in the exact amount of time specified), support for randomization and

counterbalancing, response acquisition, and logging illustrates the advantages for obtaining a flexible SCRL application equipped for research pursuits.

A number of commercial and freeware applications have been created over the past several decades to assist researchers with SCRL-type functions. The choice to select one application over the other may have much to do with programming requirements, the operating system platform, protocol requirements, or all of the above. Table 55.2 provides a list of some of the SCRL applications that are available for psychological and psychophysical experiments. Additional information for these and other SCRL applications can be found in Florer (2007). The description column is

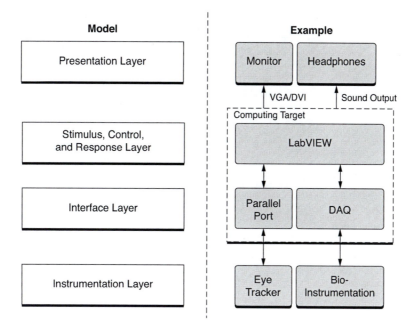

**Figure 55.3** SPC model with external hardware.

text taken directly from narrative about the product provided by Florer (2007). A conventional programming language is best equipped for SCRL functionality. This alternative to the applications listed in Table 55.2 may be necessary for experiments where communication with external hardware, interfacing with external code, querying databases, or program performance requirements are a priority, although some of the SCRL applications listed in Table 55.2 provide some varying degrees of these capabilities (e.g., E-Prime, SuperLab).

The prospect of laboratory productivity can outweigh the flexibility and functionality afforded by a programming language; for example, from a laboratory management perspective, it is reasonable for all laboratory members to have a single platform from which they create experiments. Given the investment required to familiarize oneself with a programming language, the single platform option can indeed be challenging to implement in practice. Formulating a laboratory in this manner does allow members to share and reuse previous testing applications or utilize knowledge about the use and idiosyncrasies of an SCRL application.

Despite the learning curve, a programming language has potential benefits that cannot be realized by turnkey SCRL applications. As mentioned, high-level programming languages offer inherently greater flexibility. Although it is important to consider whether the SCRL application can be used to generate a particular test bed, one must also consider the analysis

requirements following initial data collection. The flexibility of a programming language can be very helpful in this regard. One might also consider the large support base in the form of books, forums, and websites dedicated to a particular language which can mitigate the problems that may arise during the learning process.

### Stimulus Presentation and Control Model with External Hardware

Communicating with external hardware is essential to complex performance design. Building upon the basic SPC framework, Figure 55.3 depicts the SPC model with support for external hardware (SPCxh). Figure 55.3 illustrates a scenario where the SCRL controls both monitor and headphone output. The SCRL also interfaces with an eye tracker and a bio-instrumentation device via the parallel port and a data acquisition device (DAQ), respectively. DAQ devices are an important conduit for signal routing and acquisition, and we discuss them in greater detail later. Extensions of the SPCxh and the SPC model are the interface and instrumentation layers. A good argument can be made for another interface layer to exist between the presentation layer and the SCRL, but for our purposes the interface layer specifically refers to the physical connection that exists between the SCRL and the instrumentation layer. Figure 55.3 depicts the stimulus presentation and control model with external hardware support (SPCxh). The SPCxh is derived from the basic

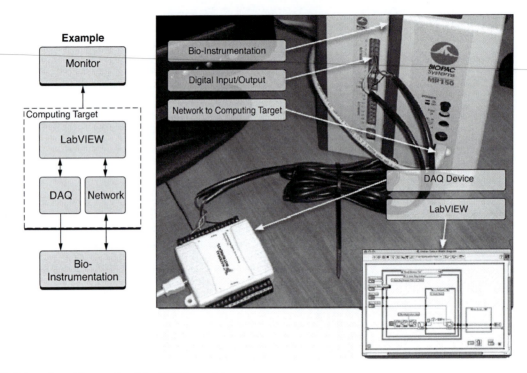

**Figure 55.4** A real-world example of the SPCxh model.

SPC model, with two additional layers: one to represent the external hardware, the second to interface that hardware with the SCRL.

It is important to emphasize that the SPC and SPCxh models are only examples. We recognize that an actual implementation of any one model will most certainly differ among laboratories. The main purpose of illustrating the various arrangements in this manner is to address the major question of how complex performance design paradigms are arranged in an abstract sense. When the necessary components are identified for their specific research objective, then comes the process of determining the specific hardware and software to realize that goal.

It is imperative to understand the connection between a given model (abstraction) and its real-world counterpart. Using the example described above, consider an experiment that requires the additional collection of electrocortical activity in response to the appearance of the visual stimulus. This type of physiological data collection is termed *event-related potential*, as we are evaluating brain potentials time-locked to some event (i.e., appearance of the visual stimulus in this example). Thus, we need to mark in the physiological record where this event appears for offline analysis. Figure 55.4 depicts one method to implement this requirement. On the left, the SPCxh model diagram is illustrated for the current scenario. A monitor is used to display the stimulus. A programming lan-

guage called LabVIEW provides the SCRL functionality. Because the bio-instrumentation supports digital input/output (i.e., hardware that allows one to send and receive digital signals), LabVIEW utilizes the DAQ device to output digital markers to the digital input ports of the bio-instrumentation while also connecting to the instrument to collect the physiological data over the network. We are using the term *bio-instrumentation* here to refer to the hardware used for the collection and assessment of physiological data. The picture on the right portrays the instantiation of the diagram. It should be observed that the diagram is meant to represent tangible software and hardware entities. Although LabVIEW is used in this example as our SCRL application, any number of alternatives could have also been employed to provide the linkage between the software used in our SCRL and the instrumentation.

A number of derivations can also be organized from the SPCxh model; for example, in many cases, the SCRL may contain only the logic needed to execute the experiment but not the application program interfaces (APIs) required to directly control a vendor's hardware. In these situations, it may be necessary to run the SCRL application alongside (e.g., on another machine) the vendor-specific hardware application. Figure 55.5 depicts this alternative, where the vendor-specific hardware executes its procedures at the same time as the SCRL application. Because the layers for

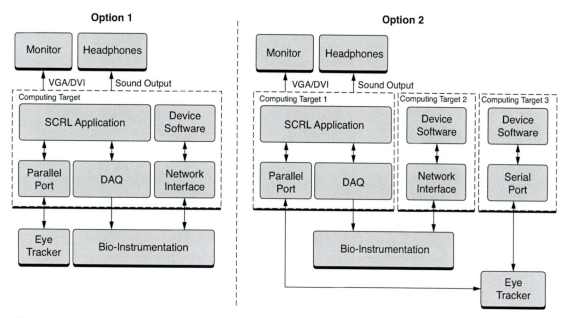

**Figure 55.5** SCLEs application operating concurrently with software.

the SPCxh are the same as in Figure 55.3, Figure 55.5 depicts only the example instantiation of the model and not the layers for the SPCxh model. The SPCxh example in Figure 55.5 is a common configuration because hardware vendors do not always supply software interfaces that can be used by an external application. The major difference between the two options, as shown, is that the second option would require a total of three computing targets: one to execute the SCRL application and for stimulus presentation, one to execute the bio-instrumentation device software, and a third to execute the eye tracker device software.

A very common question is how to synchronize the SCRL application and the device instrumentation. As with the previous example, the method of choice for the example is via the DAQ device for communication with the bio-instrumentation and through the parallel port for the eye tracker; however, the option for event marking and synchronization is only applicable if it is supported by the particular piece of instrumentation. Furthermore, the specific interface (e.g., digital input/output, serial/parallel) is dependent on what the manufacturer has made available for the end-user. Given this information, one should ask themselves the following questions prior to investing resources in any one instrument or SCRL alternative. First, what type of limitations will be encountered when attempting to interface a particular instrument with my current resources? That is, does the manufacturer provide support for external communication with other instruments or applications? Second, does my SCRL application of choice support a method to com-

municate with my external hardware if this option is available? Third, does the device manufacturer provide or sell programming libraries or application program interfaces if data collection has to be curtailed in some particular way? Fourth, what are the computational requirements to run the instrumentation software? Will the software be so processor intensive that it requires a sole execution on one dedicated machine?

### Common Paradigms and Configurations

A number of common paradigms exist in psychological research, from recall and recognition paradigms to interruption-type paradigms. Although it is beyond the scope of this section to provide an example configuration for each, we have selected one example that is commonly used by many of contemporary researchers; this is the *secondary task paradigm*. Both the SPC and SPCxh models are sufficient for experiments employing this paradigm; however, a common problem can occur when the logic for the primary and secondary tasks is implemented as mutually exclusive entities. An experiment that employs a simulator for the primary task environment can be viewed as a self-contained SPCxh model containing a simulation presentation environment (presentation layer), simulation control software (SCRL application), and simulation-specific hardware (interface and instrumentation layers). The question now is how can we interface the primary task (operated by the simulator in this example) with another SPRL application that contains the logic for the secondary task?

795

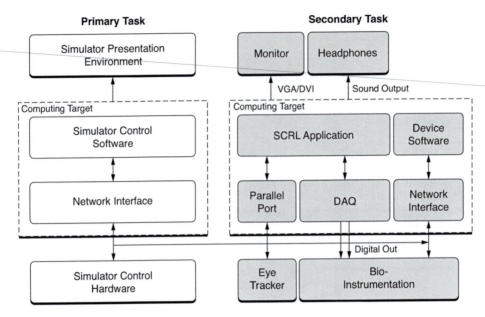

**Figure 55.6** Secondary task paradigm.

Figure 55.6 contains a graphical representation of a possible configuration: an SPCxh model for the simulator communicating via a network interface that is monitored from the SCRL application on the secondary task side. On the left side of Figure 55.6 is the primary task configuration, and on the right side is the secondary task configuration. It should be noted that the simulator control software, our SCRL application, or the device-specific software does not necessarily need to be executed on separate computers; however, depending on the primary or secondary task, one may find that the processor and memory requirements necessitate multiple computers. On the secondary task side, the diagram represents a fairly complex role for the SCRL application. As shown, the SCRL application has output responsibilities to a monitor and headphones while also interfacing with an eye tracker via the serial port, interfacing the simulator via the network, and sending two lines of digital output information via the DAQ device.

Numerous complex performance test beds require that a primary and secondary task paradigm be used to explicate the relationship among any number of processes. In the field of human factors, in particular, it is not uncommon for an experiment to employ simulation for the primary task and then connect a secondary task to events that may occur during the primary task. A major problem often encountered in simulation research is that the simulators are often closed-systems; nevertheless, most simulators can be viewed as SPCxh arrangements with a presentation layer of some kind, an application that provides SCRL

function, and the simulator control hardware itself. If one wishes to generate secondary task events based on the occurrence of specific events in the simulation, the question then becomes one of how we might go about configuring such a solution when there is no ready-made entry point between the two systems (i.e., primary task system and secondary task system). The diagram on the left shows the SPCxh model for the secondary task, which is responsible for interacting with a number of additional instruments. The diagram shows a connecting line between the secondary systems network interface and the network interface of the primary task as controlled by the simulation. Because simulation manufacturers will often make technotes available that specify how the simulator may communicate with other computers or hardware, one can often ascertain this information for integration with the secondary tasks SCRL.

### Summary of Design Configurations

The above examples have been elaborated in limited detail. Primarily, information pertaining to how one would configure a SCRL application for external software and hardware communication has been excluded. This specification is not practical with the sheer number of SCRL options available to researchers. As well, the diagrams do not inform the role that the SCRL application plays when interfacing with instrumentation. It may be the case that the SCRL application plays a minimal role in starting and stopping the instrument and does not command full control of the instrument via a program interface; nevertheless, one should attempt to understand the various configurations because they do appear with great regularity in complex performance designs. Finally, it is particularly important to consider some of the issues raised when making purchasing decisions about a given instrument, interface, or application.

## General-Purpose Hardware

It is evident when walking through a home improvement store that countless tools have proved their effectiveness for an almost limitless number of tasks (e.g., a hammer). An analog to this apparent fact is that various tools are also exceedingly useful for complex performance research; thus, the purpose of the following sections is to discuss some of these tools and their role in complex performance evaluation.

### Data Acquisition Devices

Given the ubiquity of DAQ hardware in the examples above, it is critical that one has a general idea of the functionality that a DAQ device can provide. DAQ devices are the research scientist's Swiss Army knife and are indispensable tools in the laboratory. DAQ hardware completes the bridge between the SCRL and the array of instrumentation implemented in an experiment; that is, the DAQ hardware gives a properly supported SCRL application a number of useful functions for complex performance measurement. To name a few examples, DAQ devices offer a means of transmitting important data between instruments, supports mechanisms to coordinate complex actions or event sequences, provides deterministic timing via a hardware clock, and provides methods to synchronize independently operating devices.

A common use for DAQ devices is to send and receive digital signals; however, to frame this application within the context of complex performance design, it is important that one be familiar with a few terms. An *event* refers to any information as it occurs within an experiment; for example, an event may mark the onset or offset of a stimulus, a participant's response, or the beginning or end of a trial. A common design obstacle requires that we know an event's temporal appearance for the purpose of subsequent analyses or, alternatively, to *trigger* supplementary instrumentation. The term *trigger* is often paired with *event* to describe an action associated with an the occurrence of an event. In some cases, event triggers may be completely internal to a single SCRL application, but in other instances event triggers may include external communications between devices or systems.

Data acquisition devices have traditionally been referred to as A/D boards (analog-to-digital boards) because of their frequent use in signal acquisition. A signal, in this context, loosely refers to any measurable physical phenomenon. Signals can be divided into two primary classes. Analog signals can vary continuously over an infinite range of values, whereas digital signals contain information in discrete states. To remember the difference between these two signals, visualize two graphs, one where someone's voice is recorded (analog) and another plotting when a light is switched on or off (digital).

The traditional role of a DAQ device was to acquire and translate measured phenomena into binary units that can be represented by a digital device (e.g., computer, oscilloscope). Suppose we need to record the force exerted on a force plate. A DAQ device could be configured such that we could sample the data derived from a force plate at a rate of 1 msec per sample and subsequently record that data to a computer or logging instrument.

One should note that the moniker *device* as a replacement for *board* is more appropriate given that modern DAQ alternatives are not always self-contained boards but may connect to a computing target in a few different ways. DAQ devices are available for a number of bus types. A *bus*, in computing vernacular, refers to a method of transmission for digital data (e.g., USB, FireWire, PCI). The DAQ device pictured in Figure 55.4, for example, is designed to connect to the USB port of a computer.

Despite their traditional role in signal acquisition (e.g., analog input), most DAQ devices contain an analog output option. Analog output reverses the process of an A/D conversion and can be used to convert digital data into analog data (D/A conversion). Analog output capabilities are useful for a variety of reasons; for example, an analog output signal can be used to produce auditory stimuli, control external hardware, or output analog data to supplementary instrumentation. The primary and secondary task example above illustrates one application for analog output. Recall that in the SPCxh model described earlier the simulator was a closed-system interfaced with the SCRL application via a network interface. Suppose that it was necessary to proxy events as they occurred in the simulation to secondary hardware. A reason for this approach might be as simple as collapsing data to a single measurement file; for example, suppose we want to evaluate aiming variability in a weapons simulation in tandem with a physiological measure. One strategy would require that we merge the separate streams of data after all events have been recorded, but, by using another strategy employing the analog output option,

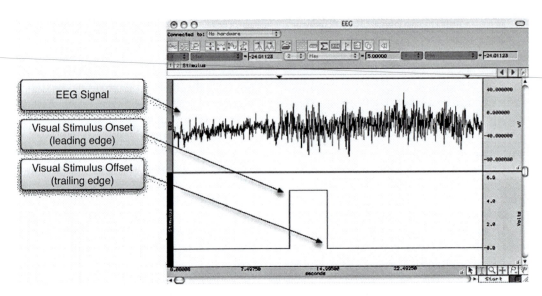

**Figure 55.7** Event triggering and recording.

we could route data from the simulator and proxy it via the SCRL application controlling the DAQ device connected to our physiological recording device.

In addition to analog output, DAQ functionality for digital input/output is a critical feature to solving various complex performance measurement issues. Recall the example above where an experiment required that the SCRL application tell the physiological control software when the visual stimulus was displayed. This was accomplished by the SCRL application sending a digital output from the DAQ device to the digital input port on the bio-instrument. Figure 55.7 depicts this occurrence from the control software for the bio-instrument. The figure shows one channel of data recorded from a participant's scalp (i.e., EEG); another digital channel represents the onset and offset of the visual stimulus.

When configuring digital signals, it is also important that one understand that the event can be defined in terms of the leading or trailing edge of the digital signal. As depicted in Figure 55.7, the leading edge (also called the *rising edge*) refers to the first positive deflection of the digital waveform, while the trailing edge (also called the *falling edge*) refers to the negative going portion of the waveform. This distinction is important, because in many cases secondary instrumentation will provide an option to begin or end recording from the leading or trailing edge; that is, if we mistakenly begin recording on the trailing edge when the critical event occurs on the leading edge, then the secondary instrument may be triggered late or not at all. Another term native to digital events is *transistor–transistor logic* (TTL), which is often used to express digital triggering that operates within spe-

cific parameters. TTL refers to a standard where a given instrument's digital line will change state (e.g., on to off) if the incoming input is within a given voltage range. If the voltage supplied to the digital line is 0 then it is off, and if the digital line is supplied 5 volts then it is on.

Event triggering is an extremely important constituent of complex performance experimentation. Knowing when an event occurs may be vital for data analysis or for triggering subsequent events. The example here depicts a scenario where we are interested in knowing the onset occurrence of a visual stimulus so we can analyze our EEG signal for event-related changes. The channel with the square wave is the event that tells when the event occurred, with the leading edge representing the onset of the visual stimuli (5 volts) and the falling edge reflecting its offset (0 volts). A setup similar to that demonstrated in Figure 55.4 could easily be configured to produce such an example. Although this example only shows two channels, a real-world testing scenario may have several hundred to indicate when certain events occur. One strategy is to define different events as different channels. One channel may represent the visibility of a stimuli (on or off), another may represent a change in its color, and yet another may indicate any other number of events. An alternative solution is to configure the SCRL application to send data to a single channel and then create a coding scheme to reflect different events (e.g., 0 volts, stimulus hidden; 2 volts, stimulus visible; 3 volts, color changed to black; 4 volts, color changed to white). This approach reduces the number of channels and maximizes the number of digital channels that one can control.

The utility of digital event triggering cannot be overstated. Although its application for measurement of complex performance requires a small degree of technical expertise, the ability to implement event triggering affords a great degree of experimental flexibility. Under certain circumstances, however, analog triggering may also be appropriate. Consider an experiment where the threshold of a participant's voice serves as the eliciting event for a secondary stimulus. In this case, it is necessary to determine whether or not the SCRL application and DAQ interface might support this type of triggering, because such an approach offers greater flexibility for some design configurations.

*Purchasing a DAQ Device*

The following questions are relevant to purchasing a DAQ device for complex performance research. First, is the DAQ device going to be used to collect physiological or other data? If the answer is yes, one should understand that the price of a DAQ device is primarily a function of its resolution, speed, form factor, and the number of input/output channels supported. Although a discussion of unipolar vs. bipolar data acquisition is beyond the scope of this chapter, the reader should consult Olansen and Rosow (2002) and Stevenson and Soejima (2005) for additional information on how this may effect the final device choice.

Device resolution, on the other hand, refers to the fidelity of a DAQ device to resolve analog signals; that is, what is the smallest detectable change that the device can discriminate? When choosing a board, resolution is described in terms of bits. A 16-bit board can resolve signals with greater fidelity than a 12-bit board. By taking the board resolution as an exponent of 2, one can see why. A 12-bit board has $2^{12}$ or 4096 possible values, while a 16-bit has a $2^{16}$ or 65,536 possible values. The answer to this question is also a function of a few other factors (e.g., signal range, amplification). A complete understanding of these two major issues should be established prior to deciding on any one device. As well, prior to investing in a higher resolution board, which will cost more money than a lower resolution counterpart, one should evaluate what is the appropriate resolution for the application. If the primary application of the DAQ device is for digital event triggering, then it is important to purchase a device that is suitable for handling as many digital channels as are necessary for a particular research design.

Third, does the design require analog output capabilities? Unlike digital channels, which are generally reconfigurable for input or output, analog channels are not, so it is important to know in advance the number of analog channels that a DAQ device supports. Fourth, does the testing environment require a level of timing

determinism that cannot be provided by software in less than 1 msec? For these scenarios, researchers might want to consider a DAQ device that supports hardware timing. For additional information about A/D board specifications and other factors that may affect purchasing decisions, see Staller (2005).

## Computers as Instrumentation

Computers are essential to the modern laboratory. Their value is evident when one considers their versatile role in the research process; consequently, the computer's ubiquity in the science can account for significant costs. Because academic institutions will often hold contracts with large original equipment manufactures, computing systems are competitively priced and warranties ensure maintenance for several years. Building a system from the ground up is also a viable option that will often provide a cost-effective alternative to purchasing through an original equipment manufacturer. Although the prospect of assembling a computer may sound daunting, the process is really quite simple, and numerous books and websites are dedicated to the topic (see, for example, Hardwidge, 2006). Customization is one of the greatest advantages to building a machine, and because only necessary components are purchased overall cost is usually reduced. On the other hand, a major disadvantage to this approach is the time associated with reviewing the components, assembling the hardware, and installing the necessary software.

Most new computers will likely be capable of handling a good majority of laboratory tasks; however, one should have a basic understanding of its major components to make an informed purchasing decision when planning complex performance test beds. This is important given that one can potentially save considerable resources that can be allocated for other equipment and be assured that the computer is adequate for a given experimental paradigm.

The following questions should be considered whether building or buying a complete computing system. First, does the number of expansion ports accommodate input boards that may be needed to interface instrumentation? For example, if an instrument interfaced an application via a network port and we wanted to maintain the ability to network with other computers or access the Internet, it would be important to confirm that the motherboard of the computer had a sufficient number of slots to accommodate this addition. Furthermore, because DAQ devices are often sold as input boards this same logic would apply.

Computers have evolved from general-purpose machines to machines with specific aptitudes for particular tasks. A recent development is that vendors now market a particular computing system for gaming vs. video-editing vs. home entertainment purposes. To understand the reasons behind these configurations, we strongly advocate developing a basic understanding of how certain components facilitate particular tasks. Although space prevents us from accomplishing this within this chapter, it is important to realize that computing performance can alter timing determinism, particularly in complex performance environments.

## Discussion

The challenge of understanding the various technical facets of laboratory setup and configuration represents a major hurdle when the assessment of some complex performance is a central objective. This section has discussed the common problems and design configurations that one may encounter when setting up such a laboratory. This approach, abstract in some respects, was not intended to illustrate the full range of design configurations available for complex performance evaluation; rather, the common configurations discussed here should only be viewed as general-purpose architectures, independent of new technologies that may emerge. After developing an understanding of the various design configurations, one must determine the specific hardware and software that are required to address the research question. The purpose of providing a few design configurations here was to emphasize that, in many complex performance testing environments, one must specify what equipment or software will fill the roles of presentation, stimulus control and response, instrumentation, and their interfaces.

## CONCLUDING REMARKS

Setting up laboratories for the measurement of complex performances can indeed be a challenging pursuit; however, becoming knowledgeable about the solutions and tools available to aid in achieving the research objectives is rewarding on a number of levels. The ability to identify and manipulate multiple software and hardware components allows quick and effective transitioning from a research question into a tenable methodological test bed.

## REFERENCES

Adler, P. A. and Adler, P. (1994). Observational techniques. In *Handbook of Qualitative Research*, edited by N. K. Denzin and Y. S. Lincoln, pp. 377–392. Thousand Oaks, CA: Sage.*

Airasian, P. W. (1996). *Assessment in the Classroom*. New York: McGraw-Hill.

Alavi, M. (1994). Computer-mediated collaborative learning: an empirical evaluation. *MIS Q.*, 18, 159–174.

American Evaluation Association. (2007). Qualitative software, www.eval.org/Resources/QDA.htm.

Ancona, D. G. and Caldwell, D. F. (1991). *Demography and Design: Predictors of New Product Team Performance*, No. 3236-91. Cambridge, MA: MIT Press.

Anderson, J. R. (1993). *Rules of the Mind*. Hillsdale, NJ: Lawrence Erlbaum Associates.

Anderson, J. R. and Lebiere, C. (1998). *The Atomic Components of Thought*. Mahwah, NJ: Lawrence Erlbaum Associates.

Anderson, J. R., Reder, L. M., and Simon, H. A. (1996). Situated learning and education. *Educ. Res.*, 25(4), 5–11.

Arter, J. A. and Spandel, V. (1992). An NCME instructional module on: using portfolios of student work in instruction and assessment. *Educ. Meas. Issues Pract.*, 11, 36–45.

Aviv, R. (2003). Network analysis of knowledge construction in asynchronous learning networks. *J. Asynch. Learn. Netw.*, 7(3), 1–23.

Ayres, P. (2006). Using subjective measures to detect variations of intrinsic cognitive load within problems. *Learn. Instruct.*, 16, 389–400.*

Bales, R. F. (1950). *Interaction Process Analysis: A Method for the Study of Small Groups*. Cambridge, MA: Addison-Wesley.

Battistich, V., Solomon, D., and Delucchi, K. (1993). Interaction processes and student outcomes in cooperative learning groups. *Element. School J.*, 94(1), 19–32.

Bazeley, P. and Richards, L. (2000). *The NVivo Qualitative Project Book*. London: SAGE.

Bellman, B. L. and Jules-Rosette, B. (1977). *A Paradigm for Looking: Cross-Cultural Research with Visual Media*. Norwood, NJ: Ablex Publishing.

Birenbaum, M. and Dochy, F. (1996). *Alternatives in assessment of achievements, learning processes and prior knowledge*. Boston, MA: Kluwer.

Bjork, R. A. (1999). Assessing our own competence: heuristics and illusions. In *Attention and Performance*. Vol. XVII. *Cognitive Regulation of Performance: Interaction of Theory and Application*, edited by D. Gopher and A. Koriat, pp. 435–459. Cambridge, MA: MIT Press.

Bogaart, N. C. R. and Ketelaar, H. W. E. R., Eds. (1983). *Methodology in Anthropological Filmmaking: Papers of the IUAES Intercongress, Amsterdam, 1981*. Gottingen, Germany: Edition Herodot.

Bogdan, R. C. and Biklen, S. K. (1992). *Qualitative Research for Education: An Introduction to Theory and Methods*, 2nd ed. Boston, MA: Allyn & Bacon.*

Boren, M. T. and Ramey, J. (2000). Thinking aloud: reconciling theory and practice. *IEEE Trans. Prof. Commun.*, 43, 261–278.

Borg, W. R. and Gall, M. D. (1989). *Educational Research: An Introduction*, 5th ed. New York: Longman.

Bowers, C. A. (2006). Analyzing communication sequences for team training needs assessment. *Hum. Factors*, 40, 672–678.*

Bowers, C. A., Jentsch, F., Salas, E., and Braun, C. C. (1998). Analyzing communication sequences for team training needs assessment. *Hum. Factors*, 40, 672–678.*

Bridgeman, B., Cline, F., and Hessinger, J. (2004). Effect of extra time on verbal and quantitative GRE scores. *Appl. Meas. Educ.*, 17(1), 25–37.

Brünken, R., Plass, J. L., and Leutner, D. (2003). Direct measurement of cognitive load in multimedia learning. *Educ. Psychol.*, 38, 53–61.

Byström, K. and Järvelin, K. (1995). Task complexity affects information seeking and use. *Inform. Process. Manage.*, 31, 191–213.

Campbell, D. J. (1988). Task complexity: a review and analysis. *Acad. Manage. Rev.*, 13, 40–52.*

Camps, J. (2003). Concurrent and retrospective verbal reports as tools to better understand the role of attention in second language tasks. *Int. J. Appl. Linguist.*, 13, 201–221.

Carnevale, A., Gainer, L., and Meltzer, A. (1989). *Workplace Basics: The Skills Employers Want*. Alexandria, VA: American Society for Training and Development.

Cascallar, A. and Cascallar, E. (2003). Setting standards in the assessment of complex performances: the optimised extended-response standard setting method. In *Optimising New Modes of Assessment: In Search of Qualities and Standards*, edited by M. Segers, F. Dochy, and E. Cascallar, pp. 247–266. Dordrecht: Kluwer.

Chandler, P. and Sweller, J. (1991). Cognitive load theory and the format of instruction. *Cogn. Instruct.*, 8, 293–332.*

Charness, N., Reingold, E. M., Pomplun, M., and Stampe, D. M. (2001). The perceptual aspect of skilled performance in chess: evidence from eye movements. *Mem. Cogn.*, 29, 1146–1152.*

Chase, C. I. (1999). *Contemporary Assessment for Educators*. New York: Longman.

Chen, H. (2005). The Effect of Type of Threading and Level of Self-Efficacy on Achievement and Attitudes in Online Course Discussion, Ph.D. dissertation. Tempe: Arizona State University.

Christensen, L. B. (2006). *Experimental Methodology*, 10th ed. Boston, MA: Allyn & Bacon.

Collier, J. and Collier, M. (1986). *Visual Anthropology: Photography as a Research Method*. Albuquerque, NM: University of New Mexico Press.

Cooke, N. J. (1994). Varieties of knowledge elicitation techniques. *Int. J. Hum.–Comput. Stud.*, 41, 801–849.

Cooke, N. J., Salas E., Cannon-Bowers, J. A., and Stout R. J. (2000). Measuring team knowledge. *Hum. Factors*, 42, 151–173.*

Cornu, B. (2004). Information and communication technology transforming the teaching profession. In *Instructional Design: Addressing the Challenges of Learning Through Technology and Curriculum*, edited by N. Seel and S. Dijkstra, pp. 227–238. Mahwah, NJ: Lawrence Erlbaum Associates.*

Crooks, S. M., Klein, J. D., Jones, E. K., and Dwyer, H. (1995). Effects of Cooperative Learning and Learner Control Modes in Computer-Based Instruction. Paper presented at the Association for Communications and Technology Annual Meeting, February 8–12, Anaheim, CA.

Cuneo, C. (2000). *WWW Virtual Library: Sociology Software*, http://socserv.mcmaster.ca/w3virtsoclib/software.htm

Demetriadis, S., Barbas, A., Psillos, D., and Pombortsis, A. (2005). Introducing ICT in the learning context of traditional school. In *Preparing Teachers to Teach with Technology*, edited by C. Vrasidas and G. V. Glass, pp. 99–116. Greenwich, CO: Information Age Publishers.

Dewey, J. (1916/1966). *Democracy and Education: An Introduction to the Philosophy of Education*. New York: Free Press.

Dijkstra, S. (2004). The integration of curriculum design, instructional design, and media choice. In *Instructional Design: Addressing the Challenges of Learning Through Technology and Curriculum*, edited by N. Seel and S. Dijkstra, pp. 145–170. Mahwah, NJ: Lawrence Erlbaum Associates.*

Downing, S. M. and Haladyna, T. M. (1997). Test item development: validity evidence from quality assurance procedures. *Appl. Meas. Educ.*, 10(1), 61–82.

Driscoll, M. P. (1995). Paradigms for research in instructional systems. In *Instructional Technology: Past, Present and Future*, 2nd ed., edited by G. J. Anglin, pp. 322–329. Englewood, CO: Libraries Unlimited.*

Duchowski, A. T. (2003). *Eye Tracking Methodology: Theory and Practice*. London: Springer.

Eccles, D. W. and Tenenbaum, G. (2004). Why an expert team is more than a team of experts: a social-cognitive conceptualization of team coordination and communication in sport. *J. Sport Exer. Psychol.*, 26, 542–560.

Ericsson, K. A. (2002). Attaining excellence through deliberate practice: insights from the study of expert performance. In *The Pursuit of Excellence Through Education*, edited by M. Ferrari, pp. 21–55. Hillsdale, NJ: Lawrence Erlbaum Associates.

Ericsson, K. A. (2004). Deliberate practice and the acquisition and maintenance of expert performance in medicine and related domains. *Acad. Med.*, 79(10), 70–81.*

Ericsson, K. A. and Lehmann, A. C. (1996). Expert and exceptional performance: evidence for maximal adaptation to task constraints. *Annu. Rev. Psychol.*, 47, 273–305.

Ericsson, K. A. and Simon, H. A. (1980). Verbal reports as data. *Psychol. Rev.*, 87, 215–251.*

Ericsson, K. A. and Simon, H. A. (1984). *Protocol Analysis: Verbal Reports as Data*. Cambridge, MA: MIT Press.*

Ericsson, K. A. and Simon, H. A. (1993). *Protocol Analysis: Verbal Reports as Data*, rev. ed. Cambridge, MA: MIT Press.

Ericsson, K. A. and Smith, J., Eds. (1991). *Toward a General Theory of Expertise: Prospects and Limits*. Cambridge, U.K.: Cambridge University Press.

Ericsson, K. A. and Staszewski, J. J. (1989). Skilled memory and expertise: mechanisms of exceptional performance. In *Complex Information Processing: The Impact of Herbert A. Simon*, edited by D. Klahr and K. Kotovsky, pp. 235–267. Hillsdale, NJ: Lawrence Erlbaum Associates.

Erkens, G. (2002). *MEPA: Multiple Episode Protocol Analysis, Version 4.8*, http://edugate.fss.uu.nl/mepa/index.htm

Espey, L. (2000). Technology planning and technology integration: a case study. In *Proceedings of Society for Information Technology and Teacher Education International Conference 2000*, edited by C. Crawford et al., pp. 95–100. Chesapeake, VA: Association for the Advancement of Computing in Education.

Florer, F. (2007). *Software for Psychophysics*, http://vision.nyu.edu/Tips/FaithsSoftwareReview.html.

Fu, W.-T. (2001). ACT-PRO action protocol analyzer: a tool for analyzing discrete action protocols. *Behav. Res. Methods Instrum. Comput.*, 33, 149–158.

Fussell, S. R., Kraut, R. E., Lerch, F. J., Shcerlis, W. L., McNally, M. M., and Cadiz, J. J. (1998). Coordination, Overload and Team Performance: Effects of Team Communication Strategies. Paper presented at the Association for Computing Machinery Conference on Computer Supported Cooperative Work, November 14–18, Seattle, WA.

Gamma, E., Helm, R., Johnson, R., and Vlissides, J. (2005). *Design Patterns: Elements of Reusable Object-Oriented Software*. Addison-Wesley: Reading, MA.

Garfinkel, H. (1967). *Studies in Ethnomethodology: A Return to the Origins of Ethnomethodology*. Englewood Cliffs, NJ: Prentice Hall.

Gerjets, P., Scheiter, K., and Catrambone, R. (2004). Designing instructional examples to reduce cognitive load: molar versus modular presentation of solution procedures. *Instruct. Sci.*, 32, 33–58.*

Gerjets, P., Scheiter, K., and Catrambone, R. (2006). Can learning from molar and modular worked examples be enhanced by providing instructional explanations and prompting self-explanations? *Learn. Instruct.*, 16, 104–121.

Goetz, J. P. and LeCompte, M. D. (1984). *Ethnography and Qualitative Design in Educational Research*. Orlando, FL: Academic Press.*

Goodyear, P. (2000). Environments for lifelong learning: ergonomics, architecture and educational design. In *Integrated and Holistic Perspectives on Learning, Instruction, and Technology: Understanding Complexity*, edited by J. M. Spector and T. M. Anderson, pp. 1–18. Dordrecht: Kluwer.*

Goswami, U. (2004). Neuroscience and education. *Br. J. Educ. Psychol.*, 74, 1–14.

Gulikers, J. T. M., Bastiaens, T. J., and Kirschner, P. A. (2004). A five-dimensional framework for authentic assessment. *Educ. Technol. Res. Dev.*, 52(3), 67–86.*

Guzzo, R. A. and Shea, G. P. (1992). Group performance and intergroup relations in organizations. In *Handbook of Industrial and Organizational Psychology* Vol. 3, 2nd ed., edited by M. D. Dunnette and L. M. Hough, pp. 269–313. Palo Alto, CA: Consulting Psychologists Press.

Haider, H. and Frensch, P. A. (1999). Eye movement during skill acquisition: more evidence for the information reduction hypothesis. *J. Exp. Psychol. Learn. Mem. Cogn.*, 25, 172–190.

Hambleton, R. K., Jaegar, R. M., Plake, B. S., and Mills, C. (2000). Setting performance standards on complex educational assessments. *Appl. Psychol. Meas.*, 24, 355–366.

Hara, N., Bonk, C. J., and Angeli, C. (2000). Content analysis of online discussion in an applied educational psychology course. *Instruct. Sci.*, 28, 115–152.

Hardwidge, B. (2006) *Building Extreme PCs: The Complete Guide to Computer Modding*. Cambridge, MA: O'Reilly Media.

Heider, K. G. (1976). *Ethnographic Film*. Austin, TX: The University of Texas Press.

Herl, H. E., O'Neil, H. F., Chung, G. K. W. K., and Schacter, J. (1999). Reliability and validity of a computer-based knowledge mapping system to measure content understanding. *Comput. Hum. Behav.*, 15, 315–333.

Higgins, N. and Rice, E. (1991). Teachers' perspectives on competency-based testing. *Educ. Technol. Res. Dev.*, 39(3), 59–69.

Hobma, S. O., Ram, P. M., Muijtjens, A. M. M., Grol, R. P. T. M., and Van der Vleuten, C. P. M. (2004). Setting a standard for performance assessment of doctor–patient communication in general practice. *Med. Educ.*, 38, 1244–1252.

Hockings, P., Ed. (1975). *Principles of Visual Anthropology*. The Hague: Mouton Publishers.

Horber, E. (2006). *Qualitative Data Analysis Links*, http://www.unige.ch/ses/sococ/qual/qual.html.

Ifenthaler, D. (2005). The measurement of change: learning-dependent progression of mental models. *Technol. Instruct. Cogn. Learn.*, 2, 317–336.*

Jeong, A. C. (2003). The sequential analysis of group interaction and critical thinking in online threaded discussions. *Am. J. Distance Educ.*, 17(1), 25–43.*

Johnson, D. W., Johnson, R. T., and Stanne, M. B. (2000). *Cooperative Learning Methods: A Meta-Analysis*, http://www.co-operation.org/pages/cl-methods.html.*

Jones, E. K., Crooks, S., and Klein, J. (1995). Development of a Cooperative Learning Observational Instrument. Paper presented at the Association for Educational Communications and Technology Annual Meeting, February 8–12, Anaheim, CA.

Jorgensen, D. L. (1989). *Participant Observation: A Methodology for Human Studies*. London: SAGE.*

Katzir, T. and Paré-Blagoev, J. (2006). Applying cognitive neuroscience research to education: the case of literacy. *Educ. Psychol.*, 41, 53–74.

Kirschner, P., Carr, C., van Merrienboer, J., and Sloep, P. (2002). How expert designers design. *Perform. Improv. Q.*, 15(4), 86–104.

Klein, J. D. and Pridemore, D. R. (1994). Effects of orienting activities and practice on achievement, continuing motivation, and student behaviors in a cooperative learning environment. *Educ. Technol. Res. Dev.*, 41(4), 41–54.*

Klimoski, R. and Mohammed, S. (1994). Team mental model: construct or metaphor. *J. Manage.*, 20, 403–437.

Ko, S. and Rossen, S. (2001). *Teaching Online: A Practical Guide*. Boston, MA: Houghton Mifflin.

Koschmann, T. (1996). Paradigm shifts and instructional technology. In *Computer Supportive Collaborative Learning: Theory and Practice of an Emerging Paradigm*, edited by T. Koschmann, pp. 1–23. Mahwah, NJ: Lawrence Erlbaum Associates.*

Kuusela, H. and Paul, P. (2000). A comparison of concurrent and retrospective verbal protocol analysis. *Am. J. Psychol.*, 113, 387–404.

Langan-Fox, J. (2000). Team mental models: techniques, methods, and analytic approaches. *Hum. Factors*, 42, 242–271.*

Langan-Fox, J. and Tan, P. (1997). Images of a culture in transition: personal constructs of organizational stability and change. *J. Occup. Org. Psychol.*, 70, 273–293.

Langan-Fox, J., Code, S., and Langfield-Smith, K. (2000). Team mental models: techniques, methods, and analytic approaches. *Hum. Factors*, 42, 242–271.

Langan-Fox, J., Anglim, J., and Wilson, J. R. (2004). Mental models, team mental models, and performance: process, development, and future directions. *Hum. Factors Ergon. Manuf.*, 14, 331–352.

Lawless, C. J. (1994). Investigating the cognitive structure of students studying quantum theory in an Open University history of science course: a pilot study. *Br. J. Educ. Technol.*, 25, 198–216.

Lesh, R. and Dorr, H. (2003). *A Models and Modeling Perspective on Mathematics Problem Solving, Learning, and Teaching*. Mahwah, NJ: Lawrence Erlbaum Associates.*

Levine, J. M. and Moreland, R. L. (1990). Progress in small group research. *Annu. Rev. Psychol.*, 41, 585–634.

Lincoln, Y. S. and Guba, E. G. (1985). *Naturalistic Inquiry*. Beverly Hills, CA: SAGE.

Lingard, L. (2002). Team communications in the operating room: talk patterns, sites of tension, and implications for novices. *Acad. Med.*, 77, 232–237.

Losada, M. (1990). Collaborative Technology and Group Process Feedback: Their Impact on Interactive Sequences in Meetings. Paper presented at the Association for Computing Machinery Conference on Computer Supported Cooperative Work, October 7–10, Los Angeles, CA.

Lowyck, J. and Elen, J. (2004). Linking ICT, knowledge domains, and learning support for the design of learning environments. In *Instructional Design: Addressing the Challenges of Learning Through Technology and Curriculum*, edited by N. Seel, and S. Dijkstra, pp. 239–256. Mahwah, NJ: Lawrence Erlbaum Associates.*

Magliano, J. P., Trabasso, T., and Graesser, A. C. (1999). Strategic processing during comprehension. *J. Educ. Psychol.*, 91, 615–629.

Mathieu, J. E., Heffner, T. S., Goodwin, G. F., Salas, E., and Cannon-Bowers, J. A. (2000). The influence of shared mental models on team process and performance. *J. Appl. Psychol.*, 85, 273–283.

Mehrens, W.A., Popham, J. W., and Ryan, J. M. (1998). How to prepare students for performance assessments. *Educ. Measure. Issues Pract.*, 17(1), 18–22.

Meloy, J. M. (1994). *Writing the Qualitative Dissertation: Understanding by Doing.* Hillsdale, NJ: Lawrence Erlbaum Associates.

Merrill, M. D. (2002). First principles of instruction. *Educ. Technol. Res. Dev.*, 50(3), 43–55.*

Michaelsen, L. K., Knight, A. B., and Fink, L. D. (2004). *Team-Based Learning: A Transformative Use of Small Groups in College Teaching.* Sterling, VA: Stylus Publishing.

Miles, M. B. and Huberman, A. M. (1994). *Qualitative Data Analysis: An Expanded Sourcebook*, 2nd ed. Thousand Oaks, CA: SAGE.

Miles, M. B. and Weitzman, E. A. (1994). Appendix: choosing computer programs for qualitative data analysis. In *Qualitative Data Analysis: An Expanded Sourcebook*, 2nd ed., edited by M. B. Miles and A. M. Huberman, pp. 311–317. Thousand Oaks, CA: SAGE.

Moallem, M. (1994). An Experienced Teacher's Model of Thinking and Teaching: An Ethnographic Study on Teacher Cognition. Paper presented at the Association for Educational Communications and Technology Annual Meeting, February 16–20, Nashville, TN.

Morgan, D. L. (1996). *Focus Groups as Qualitative Research Methods*, 2nd ed. Thousand Oaks, CA: SAGE.

Morris, L. L., Fitz-Gibbon, C. T., and Lindheim, E. (1987). *How to Measure Performance and Use Tests.* Newbury Park, CA: SAGE.

Myllyaho, M., Salo, O., Kääriäinen, J., Hyysalo, J., and Koskela, J. (2004). A Review of Small and Large Post-Mortem Analysis Methods. Paper presented at the 17th International Conference on Software and Systems Engineering and their Applications, November 30–December 2, Paris, France.

Newell, A. and Rosenbloom, P. (1981). Mechanisms of skill acquisition and the law of practice. In *Cognitive Skills and Their Acquisition*, edited by J. R. Anderson, pp. 1–56. Hillsdale, NJ: Lawrence Erlbaum Associates.

Nitko, A. (2001). *Educational Assessment of Students*, 3rd ed. Upper Saddle River, NJ: Prentice Hall.

Noldus, L. P. J. J., Trienes, R. J. H., Hendriksen, A. H. M., Jansen, H., and Jansen, R. G. (2000). The Observer Video-Pro: new software for the collection, management, and presentation of time-structured data from videotapes and digital media files. *Behav. Res. Methods Instrum. Comput.*, 32, 197–206.

O'Connor, D. L. and Johnson, T. E. (2004). Measuring team cognition: concept mapping elicitation as a means of constructing team shared mental models in an applied setting. In *Concept Maps: Theory, Methodology, Technology, Proceedings of the First International Conference on Concept Mapping* Vol. 1, edited by A. J. Cañas, J. D. Novak, and F. M. Gonzalez, pp. 487–493. Pamplona, Spain: Public University of Navarra.*

Olansen, J. B. and Rosow, E. (2002). *Virtual Bio-Instrumentation.* Upper Saddle River, NJ: Prentice Hall.

Olkinuora, E., Mikkila-Erdmann, M., and Nurmi, S. (2004). Evaluating the pedagogical value of multimedia learning material: an experimental study in primary school. In *Instructional Design: Addressing the Challenges of Learning Through Technology and Curriculum*, edited by N. Seel and S. Dijkstra, pp. 331–352. Mahwah, NJ: Lawrence Erlbaum Associates.

O'Neal, M. R. and Chissom, B. S. (1993). A Comparison of Three Methods for Assessing Attitudes. Paper presented at the Annual Meeting of the Mid-South Educational Research Association, November 10–12, New Orleans, LA.

O'Neil, H. F., Wang, S., Chung, G., and Herl, H. E. (2000). Assessment of teamwork skills using computer-based teamwork simulations. In *Aircrew Training and Assessment*, edited by H. F. O'Neil and D. H. Andrews, pp. 244–276. Mahwah, NJ: Lawrence Erlbaum Associates.*

Paas, F. (1992). Training strategies for attaining transfer of problem-solving skill in statistics: a cognitive load approach. *J. Educ. Psychol.*, 84, 429–434.

Paas, F. and van Merriënboer, J. J. G. (1993). The efficiency of instructional conditions: an approach to combine mental-effort and performance measures. *Hum. Factors, 35*, 737–743.*

Paas, F. and van Merriënboer, J. J. G. (1994a). Instructional control of cognitive load in the training of complex cognitive tasks. *Educ. Psychol. Rev.*, 6, 51–71.

Paas, F. and van Merriënboer, J. J. G. (1994b). Variability of worked examples and transfer of geometrical problem-solving skills: a cognitive load approach. *J. Educ. Psychol.*, 86, 122–133.

Paas, F., Tuovinen, J. E., Tabbers, H., and Van Gerven, P. W. M. (2003). Cognitive load measurement as a means to advance cognitive load theory. *Educ. Psychol.*, 38, 63–71.

Paterson, B., Bottorff, J., and Hewatt, R. (2003). Blending observational methods: possibilities, strategies, and challenges. *Int. J. Qual. Methods*, 2(1), article 3.

Patton, M. Q. (2001). *Qualitative Research and Evaluation Methods*, 3rd ed. Thousand Oaks, CA: SAGE.

Paulsen, M. F. (2003). An overview of CMC and the online classroom in distance education. In *Computer-Mediated Communication and the Online Classroom*, edited by Z. L. Berge and M. P. Collins, pp. 31–57. Cresskill, NJ: Hampton Press.

Pavitt, C. (1998). *Small Group Discussion: A Theoretical Approach*, 3rd ed. Newark: University of Delaware (http://www.udel.edu/communication/COMM356/pavitt/).

Pelto, P. J. and Pelto, G. H. (1978). *Anthropological Research: The Structure of Inquiry*, 2nd ed. Cambridge, U.K.: Cambridge University Press.

Perez-Prado, A. and Thirunarayanan, M. (2002). A qualitative comparison of online and classroom-based sections of a course: exploring student perspectives. *Educ. Media Int.*, 39(2), 195–202.

Pirnay-Dummer, P. (2006). Expertise und modellbildung: Mitocar [Expertise and Model Building: Mitocar]. Ph.D. dissertation. Freiburg, Germany: Freiburg University.

Popham, J. W. (1991). Appropriateness of instructor's test-preparation practices. *Educ. Meas. Issues Pract.*, 10(4), 12–16.

Prichard, J. S. (2006). Team-skills training enhances collaborative learning. *Learn. Instruct.*, 16, 256–265.

Qureshi, S. (1995). Supporting Electronic Group Processes: A Social Perspective. Paper presented at the Association for Computing Machinery (ACM) Special Interest Group on Computer Personnel Research Annual Conference, April 6–8, Nashville, TN.

Rayner, K. (1998). Eye movements in reading and information processing: 20 years of research. *Psychol. Bull.*, 124, 372–422.

Reigeluth, C. M. (1989). Educational technology at the cross-roads: new mindsets and new directions. *Educ. Technol. Res. Dev.*, 37 (1), 67–80.*

Reilly, B. (1994). Composing with images: a study of high school video producers. In *Proceedings of ED-MEDIA 94: Educational Multimedia and Hypermedia*. Charlottesville, VA: Association for the Advancement of Computing in Education.

Reiser, R. A. and Mory, E. H. (1991). An examination of the systematic planning techniques of two experienced teachers. *Educ. Technol. Res. Dev.*, 39(3), 71–82.

Rentsch, J. R. and Hall, R. J., Eds. (1994). *Members of Great Teams Think Alike: A Model of Team Effectiveness and Schema Similarity among Team Members*, Vol. 1, pp. 22–34. Stamford, CT: JAI Press.

Rentsch, J. R., Small, E. E., and Hanges, P. J. (in press). Cognitions in organizations and teams: What is the meaning of cognitive similarity? In *The People Make the Place*, edited by B. S. B. Schneider. Mahwah, NJ: Lawrence Erlbaum Associates.

Robinson, R. S. (1994). Investigating Channel One: a case study report. In *Watching Channel One*, edited by De Vaney, pp. 21–41. Albany, NY: SUNY Press.

Robinson, R. S. (1995). Qualitative research: a case for case studies. In *Instructional Technology: Past, Present and Future*, 2nd ed., edited by G. J. Anglin, pp. 330–339. Englewood, CO: Libraries Unlimited.

Ross, S. M. and Morrison, G. R. (2004). Experimental research methods. In *Handbook of Research on Educational Communications and Technology*, 2nd ed., edited by D. Jonassen, pp. 1021–1043. Mahwah, NJ: Lawrence Erlbaum Associates.

Rourke, L., Anderson, T., Garrison, D. R., and Archer, W. (2001). Methodological issues in the content analysis of computer conference transcripts. *Int. J. Artif. Intell. Educ.*, 12, 8–22.

Rowe, A. L. and Cooke, N. J. (1995). Measuring mental models: choosing the right tools for the job. *Hum. Resource Dev. Q.*, 6, 243–255.

Russo, J. E., Johnson, E. J., and Stephens, D. L. (1989). The validity of verbal protocols. *Mem. Cogn.*, 17, 759–769.

Salas, E. and Cannon-Bowers, J. A. (2000). The anatomy of team training. In *Training and Retraining: A Handbook for Business, Industry, Government, and the Military*, edited by S. T. J. D. Fletcher, pp. 312–335. New York: Macmillan.

Salas, E. and Cannon-Bowers, J. A. (2001). Special issue preface. *J. Org. Behav.*, 22, 87–88.

Salas, E. and Fiore, S. M. (2004). Why team cognition? An overview. In *Team Cognition: Understanding the Factors That Drive Process and Performance*, edited by E. Salas and S. M. Fiore. Washington, D.C.: American Psychological Association.

Salomon, G. and Perkins, D. N. (1998). Individual and social aspects of learning. In *Review of Research in Education*, Vol. 23, edited by P. Pearson and A. Iran-Nejad, pp. 1–24. Washington, D.C.: American Educational Research Association.*

Salvucci, D. D. (1999). Mapping eye movements to cognitive processes [doctoral dissertation, Carnegie Mellon University]. *Dissert. Abstr. Int.*, 60, 5619.

Sapsford, R. and Jupp, V. (1996). *Data Collection and Analysis*. London: SAGE.

Savenye, W. C. (1989). *Field Test Year Evaluation of the TLTG Interactive Videodisc Science Curriculum: Effects on Student and Teacher Attitude and Classroom Implementation*. Austin, TX: Texas Learning Technology Group of the Texas Association of School Boards.

Savenye, W. C. (2004a). Evaluating Web-based learning systems and software. In *Curriculum, Plans, and Processes in Instructional Design: International Perspectives*, edited by N. Seel and Z. Dijkstra, pp. 309–330. Mahwah, NJ: Lawrence Erlbaum Associates.

Savenye, W. C. (2004b). Alternatives for assessing learning in Web-based distance learning courses. *Distance Learn.*, 1(1), 29–35.*

Savenye, W. C. (2006). Improving online courses: what is interaction and why use it? *Distance Learn.*, 2(6), 22–28.

Savenye, W. C. (2007). Interaction: the power and promise of active learning. In *Finding Your Online Voice: Stories Told by Experienced Online Educators*, edited by M. Spector. Mahwah, NJ: Lawrence Erlbaum Associates.

Savenye, W. C. and Robinson, R. S. (2004). Qualitative research issues and methods: an introduction for instructional technologists. In *Handbook of Research on Educational Communications and Technology*, 2nd ed., edited by D. Jonassen, pp. 1045–1071. Mahwah, NJ: Lawrence Erlbaum Associates.

Savenye, W. C. and Robinson, R. S. (2005). Using qualitative research methods in higher education. *J. Comput. Higher Educ.*, 16(2), 65–95.

Savenye, W. C. and Strand, E. (1989). Teaching science using interactive videodisc: results of the pilot year evaluation of the Texas Learning Technology Group Project. In *Eleventh Annual Proceedings of Selected Research Paper Presentations at the 1989 Annual Convention of the Association for Educational Communications and Technology in Dallas, Texas*, edited by M. R. Simonson and D. Frey. Ames, IA: Iowa State University.

Savenye, W. C., Leader, L. F., Schnackenberg, H. L., Jones, E. E. K., Dwyer, H., and Jiang, B. (1996). Learner navigation patterns and incentive on achievement and attitudes in hypermedia-based CAI. *Proc. Assoc. Educ. Commun. Technol.*, 18, 655–665.

Sax, G. (1980). *Principles of Educational and Psychological Measurement and Evaluation*, 2nd ed. Belmont, CA: Wadsworth.

Schneider, W. and Shiffrin, R. M. (1977). Controlled and automatic human information processing. I. Detection, search, and attention. *Psychol. Rev.*, 84, 1–66.

Schweiger, D. M. (1986). Group approaches for improving strategic decision making: a comparative analysis of dialectical inquiry, devil's advocacy, and consensus. *Acad. Manage. J.*, 29(1), 51–71.

Seel, N. M. (1999). Educational diagnosis of mental models: assessment problems and technology-based solutions. *J. Struct. Learn. Intell. Syst.*, 14, 153–185.

Seel, N. M. (2004). Model-centered learning environments: theory, instructional design, and effects. In *Instructional Design: Addressing the Challenges of Learning Through Technology and Curriculum*, edited by N. Seel and S. Dijkstra, pp. 49–73. Mahwah, NJ: Lawrence Erlbaum Associates.

Seel, N. M., Al-Diban, S., and Blumschein, P. (2000). Mental models and instructional planning. In *Integrated and Holistic Perspectives on Learning, Instruction, and Technology: Understanding Complexity*, edited by J. M. Spector and T. M. Anderson, pp. 129–158. Dordrecht: Kluwer.*

Segers, M., Dochy, F., and Cascallar, E., Eds. (2003). *Optimising New Modes of assessment: In Search of Qualities and Standards*. Dordrecht: Kluwer.

Shepard, L. (2000). The role of assessment in a learning culture. *Educ. Res.*, 29(7), 4–14.

Shiffrin, R. M. and Schneider, W. (1977). Controlled and automatic human information processing. II. Perceptual learning, automatic attending, and a general theory. *Psychol. Rev.*, 84, 127–190.*

Shin, E. J., Schallert, D., and Savenye, W. C. (1994). Effects of learner control, advisement, and prior knowledge on young students' learning in a hypertext environment. *Educ. Technol. Res. Dev.*, 42(1), 33–46.

Smith, P. L. and Wedman, J. F. (1988). Read-think-aloud protocols: a new data source for formative evaluation. *Perform. Improv. Q.*, 1(2), 13–22.

Spector, J. M. and Koszalka, T. A. (2004). *The DEEP Methodology for Assessing Learning in Complex Domains*. Arlington, VA: National Science Foundation.*

Spradley, J. P. (1979). *The Ethnographic Interview*. New York: Holt, Rinehart and Winston.*

Spradley, J. P. (1980). *Participant Observation*. New York: Holt, Rinehart and Winston.*

Stahl, G. (2006). *Group Cognition: Computer Support for Building Collaborative Knowledge*. Cambridge, MA: MIT Press.*

Staller, L. (2005). Understanding analog to digital converter specifications. [electronic version]. *Embedded Syst. Design*, February, 24, http://www.embedded.com/.

Stelmach, L. B., Campsall, J. M., and Herdman, C. M. (1997). Attentional and ocular movements. *J. Exp. Psychol. Hum. Percept. Perform.*, 23, 823–844.

Stevenson, W. G. and Soejima, K. (2005). Recording techniques for electrophysiology. *J. Cardiovasc. Electrophysiol.*, 16, 1017–1022.

Strauss, A. L. and Corbin, J. M. (1994) Grounded theory methodology: an overview. In *Handbook of Qualitative Research*, edited by N. K. Denzin and Y. Lincoln, pp. 273–285. Thousand Oaks, CA: SAGE.*

Sweller, J. (1988). Cognitive load during problem solving: effects on learning. *Cogn. Sci.*, 12, 257–285.*

Sweller, J., van Merriënboer, J. J. G., and Paas, F. (1998). Cognitive architecture and instructional design. *Educ. Psychol. Rev.*, 10, 251–295.

Sy, T. (2005). The contagious leader: Impact of the leader's mood on the mood of group members, group affective tone, and group processes. *J. Appl. Psychol.*, 90(2), 295–305.

Taylor, K. L. and Dionne, J. P. (2000). Accessing problem-solving strategy knowledge: the complementary use of concurrent verbal protocols and retrospective debriefing. *J. Educ. Psychol.*, 92, 413–425.

Thompson, S. (2001). The authentic standards movement and its evil twin. *Phi Delta Kappan*, 82(5), 358–362.

Thorndike, R. M. (1997). *Measurement and Evaluation in Psychology and Education*, 6th ed. Upper Saddle River, NJ: Prentice Hall.*

Tiffin, J. and Rajasingham, L. (1995). *In Search of the Virtual Class: Education in an Information Society*. London: Routledge.

Titchener, E. B. (1900). The equipment of a psychological laboratory. *Am. J. Psychol.*, 11, 251–265.*

Tuovinen, J. E. and Paas, F. (2004). Exploring multidimensional approaches to the efficiency of instructional conditions. *Instruct. Sci.*, 32, 133–152.

Underwood, G., Chapman, P., Brocklehurst, N., Underwood, J., and Crundall, D. (2003). Visual attention while driving: sequences of eye fixations made by experienced and novice drivers. *Ergonomics*, 46, 629–646.

Underwood, G., Jebbett, L., and Roberts, K. (2004). Inspecting pictures for information to verify a sentence: eye movements in general encoding and in focused search. *Q. J. Exp. Psychol.*, 57, 165–182.

Urch Druskat, V. and Kayes, D. C. (2000). Learning versus performance in short-term project teams. *Small Group Res.*, 31, 328–353.

Van der Vleuten, C. P. M. and Schuwirth, L. W. T. (2005). Assessing professional competence: from methods to programmes. *Med. Educ.*, 39, 309–317.

Van Gerven, P. W. M., Paas, F., van Merriënboer, J. J. G., and Schmidt, H. (2004). Memory load and the cognitive pupillary response in aging. *Psychophysiology*, 41, 167–174.

van Gog, T. (2006). Uncovering the Problem-Solving Process to Design Effective Worked Examples. Ph.D. dissertation. Heerlen: Open University of the Netherlands.

van Gog, T., Paas, F., and van Merriënboer, J. J. G. (2005a). Uncovering expertise-related differences in troubleshooting performance: combining eye movement and concurrent verbal protocol data. *Appl. Cogn. Psychol.*, 19, 205–221.*

van Gog, T., Paas, F., van Merriënboer, J. J. G., and Witte, P. (2005b). Uncovering the problem-solving process: cued retrospective reporting versus concurrent and retrospective reporting. *J. Exp. Psychol. Appl.*, 11, 237–244.

Van Maanen, J. (1988). *Tales of the Field: On Writing Ethnography*. Chicago, IL: The University of Chicago Press.

van Merriënboer, J. J. G. (1997). *Training Complex Cognitive Skills: A Four-Component Instructional Design Model for Technical Training*. Englewood Cliffs, NJ: Educational Technology Publications.*

van Merriënboer, J. J. G., Jelsma, O., and Paas, F. (1992). Training for reflective expertise: a four-component instructional design model for complex cognitive skills. *Educ. Technol. Res. Dev.*, 40(2), 1042–1629.

Van Someren, M. W., Barnard, Y. F., and Sandberg, J. A. C. (1994). *The Think Aloud Method: A Practical Guide to Modeling Cognitive Processes*. London: Academic Press.

VanLehn, K. (1996). Cognitive skill acquisition. *Annu. Rev. Psychol.*, 47, 513–539.*

Wainer, H. (1989). The future of item analysis. *J. Educ. Meas.*, 26(2), 191–208.

Webb, E. J., Campbell, D. T., Schwartz, R. D., and Sechrest, L. (1966). *Unobtrusive Measures: Nonreactive Research in the Social Sciences*. Chicago, IL: Rand McNally.

Webb, N. M. (1982). Student interaction and learning in small groups. *Rev. Educ. Res.*, 52(3), 421–445.

Weitzman, E. A. and Miles, M. B. (1995). *A Software Sourcebook: Computer Programs for Qualitative Data Analysis*. Thousand Oaks, CA: SAGE.

Willis, S. C., Bundy, C., Burdett, K., Whitehouse, C. R., and O'Neill, P. A. (2002). Small-group work and assessment in a problem-based learning curriculum: a qualitative and quantitative evaluation of student perceptions of the process of working in small groups and its assessment. *Med. Teacher*, 24, 495–501.

Wolcott, H. F. (1990). *Writing Up Qualitative Research*. Newbury Park, CA: SAGE.*

Woods, D. R., Felder, R. M., Rugarcia, A., and Stice, J. E. (2000). The future of engineering education. Part 3. Development of critical skills. *Chem. Eng. Educ.*, 34, 108–117.

Tamara van Gog, Fred Paas et al.

Woolf, H. (2004). Assessment criteria: reflections on current practices. *Assess. Eval. Higher Educ.*, 29, 479–493.*

Worchel, S., Wood, W., and Simpson, J. A., Eds. (1992). *Group Process and Productivity.* Newbury Park, CA: SAGE.

Yeo, G. B. and Neal, A. (2004). A multilevel analysis of effort, practice and performance: effects of ability, conscientiousness, and goal orientation. *J. Appl. Psychol.*, 89, 231–247.

* Indicates a core reference.

# 56

# Foundations for the Future*

*ChanMin Kim and JungMi Lee*
Florida State University, Tallahassee, Florida

*M. David Merrill*
Florida State University, Tallahassee, Florida

*J. Michael Spector*
Florida State University, Tallahassee, Florida

*Jeroen J. G. van Merriënboer*
Open University of the Netherlands, Heerlen, the Netherlands

## CONTENTS

## ABSTRACT

In this chapter the editors and editorial assistants of this *Handbook* address five questions as a way of speculating about the future of scientific inquiry per-taining to educational communications and technology: (1) What have been the most significant developments in educational communications and technology in the last five years? (2) What are likely to be the most significant developments in the next

---

* The authors of this chapter are listed in arbitrary alphabetical order because they contributed equally.

five years? (3) What significant research findings have occurred in the last five years? (4) What are likely to be the most significant research issues in the next five years? (5) What are the most critical foundational aspects and factors for future research and development in educational communications and technology? In addition to addressing these questions, we also comment on the proper study of instructional design and how best to prepare educational technology practitioners and researchers.

## KEYWORDS

*Core reference:* A reference that is of central interest to researchers in a particular area and generally considered to be a primary source of data or information; core references are indicated by an asterisk in the reference section of each chapter in this *Handbook*.

*Keyword:* A word or phrase that is critically important to a topic area or which has a particular definition important for understanding issues and further discussion.

## INTRODUCTION

When we accepted the task of editing this third edition of *Handbook*, we decided that our basic perspective would be that the *Handbook* was *owned* by our professional community. This meant that its contents should be largely driven by the interests of the community, so we conducted a survey hosted by the Association for Educational Communications and Technology (AECT), the sponsor of the *Handbook*, to determine how previous editions were used and what the community would like to see in this edition, and we responded accordingly.

A second aspect of community ownership was that our own views and biases should not dominate. We broadened this notion to include the concept that no one's views should dominate, and we operationalized this notion in the form of a rule that no one could be lead author on more than one chapter. We actively recruited a broader group of contributors than in past editions, and we encouraged experienced authors to coauthor with more junior authors to ensure diversity of content and views. We sincerely hope that we have achieved these objectives.

Now it is our turn, though, to collectively comment on what we regard as important foundation issues for the future of research and development pertaining to

educational communications and technologies.* We decided to do this by addressing five questions: (1) What have been the most significant developments in educational communications and technology in the last five years? (2) What are likely to be the most significant developments in the next five years? (3) What significant research findings have occurred in the last five years? (4) What are likely to be the most significant research issues in the next five years? (5) What are the most critical foundational aspects and factors for future research and development in educational communications and technology? Our various responses to these questions are woven into subsequent sections of this chapter. We conclude with thoughts about the study of instructional design and technology and how best to prepare practitioners and researchers.

## SIGNIFICANT DEVELOPMENTS IN THE LAST FIVE YEARS

With regard to instructional strategies and learning technologies, the major developments in the last five years took place in the field of Web-based learning and more broadly in e-learning. Although many interpret the "e" in e-learning to refer to the Internet, we interpret the "e" to refer more traditionally to *electronic*, which includes the Internet and many other digital technologies. The focus quickly shifted from the Web as a medium for information distribution to a medium to sustain learning networks, in which social interaction between learners is at least as important, if not more important, than the content to be learned.

Content has become readily available and rich in representational formats. One consequence is that the emphasis in educational research and development is shifting from a content-centric perspective to a user-centric perspective—it is what one does with the content that has become the focus of interest for many developers and researchers, and of course what one does is often done in concert, collaboration, or competition with others. Socially situated activities with rich content have become the focus of much educational technology research and development.

---

* In this chapter we make frequent use of the terms *educational technology*, *instructional design*, and *instructional technology*. In some cases, we make no effort to distinguish these terms as we individually have slightly different meanings for these terms. Roughly speaking, *educational technology* is broader in scope than *instructional technology*, with the latter focused on the use of technology to support specific, intended, and planned learning outcomes. Instructional design, broadly speaking, is the discipline devoted to the study of these technologies and their use in support of learning and instruction.

A movement to merge computer-based technologies with the psychology of learning has been ongoing for many years. An increased emphasis on using new instructional technologies to support learning (blogs, podcasts, wikis, and so on) creates a rich area for educational technology research as there are always new tools and interventions to test; however, it also creates a burden for practitioners to learn how to make effective use of new technologies. The burden is perhaps most strongly felt by teachers, who are continually challenged to keep up with their students and with technology trends.

Technological advances have certainly made it possible to provide educational resources and access to learners separated from their co-learners, tutors, and teachers by time, distance, culture, and language. Although many schools and universities now make regular use of online learning management systems, the challenge is to create meaningful learning environments and experiences.

Technology advances have also occurred with regard to the affective aspects in learning—namely, in using technology to optimize affective responses such as with pedagogical agents (Craig et al., 2004; Kim and Baylor, 2006). Affective aspects such as attitudes, motivation, and emotions obviously influence the process of learning, so it has been a natural extension of educational technology research to develop affective supports for learning. Recently, advanced technologies such as virtual humanlike animations have been developed for more active interaction with learners. Examples of these technologies include affective computing at MIT (http://affect.media.mit.edu/index.php), persuasive technologies at Stanford University (http://captology.stanford.edu/), virtual humans at the University of Southern California (http://www.ict.usc.edu/content/view/32/85), and anthropomorphized interfaces at Utah State University (http://www.create.usu.edu/).

With regard to instructional models and design and development practices, there has been a significant reduction in the gap and tension between constructivist and engineering models of instructional design. For a long time, constructivist and systems approaches were perceived as incompatible and often as antagonist perspectives about the planning and implementation of support for learning. More recently, whole-task models (van Merriënboer, 1997; van Merriënboer and Kirschner, 2007; see also Chapter 35 in this *Handbook*) as well as models for model-facilitated learning (Milrad et al., 2002; Seel, 2003; Seel et al., 2000; Spector, 2006; Spector and Koszalka, 2004) and problem-based learning (Jonassen, 2000; see also Chapter 38 in this *Handbook*) more and more combine a systematic and systemic approach to the design of instruction with constructivist learning principles. This *rapprochement* (perhaps the wrong word but conveys the coming to terms with those previously regarded as belonging to an enemy camp) of constructivism and systems thinking is in part a response to efforts to support learning in and about complex, dynamic, and ill-structured tasks. Innovative learning environments have been developed that take into consideration the rich variety and diversity of all components of a system, including interrelationships among the components and relationships with other systems and users (see Dörner, 1996). These considerations include cognitive, physical, and affective elements within each person involved, as well as social and cultural relationships.

With regard to research methods, the balance between research on instructional strategies and technologies, on the one hand, and research on instructional models and design and development practices, on the other hand, drastically changed. Design experiments and developmental research gained in importance, which may be seen as a shift from model building to model testing and a sign that the field is maturing into a real design science (see Chapters 47 and 54 in this *Handbook* for elaborations of this line of thought).

## LIKELY DEVELOPMENTS IN THE NEXT FIVE YEARS

Will the future resemble the past? Affirmation of the general principle that the future will resemble the past is essential for inductive reasoning and considered a cornerstone of progress in science; however, there is no *evidence* to support this principle of induction, as David Hume pointed out in *An Enquiry Concerning Human Understanding* (Hume, 1777/1910). Nonetheless, we naturally form expectations about the future, and these expectations appear quite useful in coming to understand our worlds. Still, we ought to be modest in making claims about the future; the truth is that we do not *know* what the future will be like, nor do you.

With regard to instructional strategies and technologies, mobile devices such as portable digital assistants (PDAs), smart mobile phones, and e-paper are likely to become increasingly important to learning and instruction. These technologies are likely to offer new ways to extend learning to informal settings outside schools as well as to changing and dynamic work situations. Powerful mobile technologies enable rich learning scenarios in which information provision, collaboration, and work on real-life learning tasks can be combined with each other.

Web-based technologies are likely to continue to expand in terms of access, use, and functionality. More efficient and powerful Web-based technologies will be developed. Blogs will become more commonplace and easier to use. Virtual environments in which participants can dynamically exchange thoughts and reactions will become commonplace in both instructional and work environments. Such developments are likely to mean the end of emphasis on the "e" in e-learning. In short, we will come to expect nearly all learning to be e-learning—that is, facilitated by or supported with some form of electronic technology. With the withering away of e-learning and our fascination with electronic technologies, we are likely to see increased emphasis on learning and performance outcomes, supported of course by a rich variety of *e-solutions*.

Another important technology development will involve open educational resources, such as Wikipedia (http://en.wikipedia.org/wiki/Main_Page). An increasing number of educational institutions will make their learning content freely available to the public via the Internet. With the accessibility of more and more *open* content, learner support, guidance, and assessment in resource-based learning (RBL) will become increasingly important (see Chapter 40 in this *Handbook*).

In the next five years, instructional models will be better adapted to support the design and development of highly flexible learning scenarios and just-in-time/task performance and instructional supports. Indeed, this will be one outcome of recent interest in and emphasis on design research. Instructional models will become more flexible with regard to time, place, and content and will also allow for richer varieties and mixes of learning support, including more support for guided and self-directed learning. The combination of place- and time-independent accessibility, as well as new learning technologies that allow for individual adaptation and personalization, will allow for cost-effective forms of *mass customization*. In the past, adaptive and personalized instruction have been conceptualized and implemented on an individual basis, in response to a particular learner's experience, proficiency, and (mis)understanding. Constructing intelligent tutoring systems based on robust student models proved to be much more difficult than imagined and has only succeeded with regard to a narrow range of learning tasks and situations. As intelligent tutoring technology has matured, content databases have become much more vast and more widely accessible, as have databases containing information about individual experience and training. This combination of events provides the foundation for systems capable of personalization on a grand scale. Commercial examples already exist (e.g., Dell Computer's build-to-order system), so educational applications will be emerging soon.

## SIGNIFICANT RESEARCH FINDINGS IN THE LAST FIVE YEARS

Questions of conscience occur to researchers just as they occur to others. One such question is this: What will come from what one is now doing and likely to do tomorrow? Indeed, what has resulted from what we, as a community of researchers, have done that can be considered significant contributions to learning and instruction? It is hoped that this *Handbook* is filled with good examples. We shall mention a few.

One important research result is that the limitations of constructivist learning principles, such as discovery methods and inquiry learning, are becoming more clear (Kirschner et al., 2006). Whereas the debate on this issue will probably never be fully resolved, the identification of conditions under which particular instructional strategies do or do not work is a major concern in the field of educational communications and technology. The fact that the issue is being refocused in terms of evidence of learning rather than in terms of advocacy for a particular position is encouraging. The classical model for instructional design research (Reigeluth, 1983) is alive and well, which bodes well for the future of educational technology research, in our view.

Merrill's (2002) work on the *first principles of instruction* made it possible to identify similarities between models and approaches that at first sight seemed to have little in common. In particular, his analyses of current instructional models show that learning tasks based on real-life problems and situations are a particularly powerful driving force for learning. This finding is echoed in research on problem-based learning (Jonassen, 2000), and in whole-task training (van Merriënboer and Kirschner, 2007; see also Chapter 35 in this *Handbook*).

Another important finding relates to the *expertise reversal effect* (Kalyuga et al., 2003). Many researchers have long argued that prior knowledge is the most important factor influencing learning, with the tacit assumption that instructional methods that work for novice learners are unnecessary but harmless for more advanced learners. In contradiction to this, the expertise reversal effect shows that methods that work well for novice learners may have counterproductive effects for advanced learners and *vice versa*. This finding is supported by research pertaining to the progressive development of mental models in individual learners (Seel et al., 2000). Seel and colleagues noticed that a conceptual model was often useful for learners new to a domain and lacking relevant knowledge and experience (devised in accordance with a cognitive apprenticeship instructional model), but that the same model often conflicted with those constructed internally by more experienced and knowledgeable learners and detracted from learning in those cases. What works for one may not work for all.

## LIKELY RESEARCH ISSUES IN THE NEXT FIVE YEARS

Having reviewed some of the more significant developments and findings in recent years and provided some sense of likely technology developments in the next five years, we are in a position to speculate about likely research issues that will soon be emerging.

An important research issue for the next five years concerns *technology integration* in rich learning scenarios. In the field of educational communications and technology, there has always been a focus on particular media and particular technologies; however, in future learning scenarios, wired and wireless as well as formal and informal networks will connect people, resources, and tools thanks to the availability of interconnected sets of (mobile) devices. There is now much talk about technology integration but very little real work is going on. First, we need a robust definition of technology integration that is relevant for learning and instruction. This is likely to be a real issue given the increasing variety of technologies and means for supporting learning. As a step toward such a definition of technology integration, we would like to offer the notion that technology is successfully integrated into learning and instruction when the interest and focus are not on the technology but rather on that which the technology makes possible—the affordance (e.g., the dialog itself in a video-based dialog via the Internet or formulation and testing of a hypothesis in a Web-based interactive simulation). In an odd sort of way, successful integration is blind to the technologies involved. We believe that technology integration—what it is, what makes it more or less effective, how and why it contributes to learning—is a particularly rich area for research in the coming years.

Research will more and more focus on strategies and models for complex learning, because general problem-solving and reasoning skills and self-directed learning skills are needed to cope with fast changes in technologies and jobs. Indeed, society increasingly demands workers who are able to cope with complexity and make rapid and flexible adjustments to changing work situations. Such models increasingly aim at learning in rich (simulated) task environments, gaming environments, social networks, and so forth.

Related to increasing interest in complex learning will be increasing emphasis on assessing learning and performance in ill-structured problem and task domains. Without reliable means to determine the relative progress of learning and performance with regard to problems that have multiple solutions and solution approaches, it will not be possible to devise systematic and systemic means of supporting learning effectively (Spector, 2006; Spector and Koszalka, 2004).

Associated with rapid technological and societal changes, life-long learning in informal and professional settings will become increasingly important. This poses new challenges to the field of educational communications and technology, which in the past mainly focused on learning in more or less formal and much less dynamic settings. A consequence of this emphasis on complex and informal learning will be new demands for skilled instructional and performance technologists as well as focused research in these areas. We will address some of these demands subsequently.

## CRITICAL FOUNDATIONS FOR RESEARCH AND DEVELOPMENT

Perhaps the most critical foundation for research and development in educational communications and technology are sound scientific and engineering practices. Science basically involves the development and testing of theories that explain or predict a range of phenomena. Engineering involves the systematic application of these theories in the design and development of solutions to practical problems. Without firm grounding in both science and engineering, instructional design (broadly conceived) is not likely to thrive or contribute significantly to improving learning and performance.

We know that technology will change. Technology will change what we do and what we can do. This is true for learning and instruction just as it is true for shopping and entertainment. Learning tools are changing. Learning tasks are changing. Learning perspectives are changing. The task is to have a strong foundation when these "winds of changes shift" (to borrow from Bob Dylan's "May You Stay Forever Young"). Part of a stable foundation is firm grounding in science and engineering and a realistic and humble sense of what works when and why. The willingness to be wrong and explore alternatives is an important piece of the foundation.

Critical for future research is to find an optimal balance, and to create good interfaces, between different types of research. Educational communications and technology is an eclectic field, in which proper theory and model development is only possibly through a measured interplay among, for example, experimental studies, proofs of concept, design experiments, and developmental research. Fruitful interfaces between research communities require common vocabularies and design languages. As humble instructional technology researchers, we should be sufficiently flexible to choose useful parts from different paradigms for specific instructional and research purposes. We might even occasionally consider trying to disprove or discredit our hypotheses rather than exclusively seeking confirmatory evidence.

For a long time, atomistic approaches dominated the field of educational communications and technology. The new focus on integrated learning objectives, higher order skills (problem solving, reasoning, creativity) and transfer of learning requires a reconsideration (Spector, 2001; Spector and Anderson, 2000). Holistic approaches to learning and instruction are expected to offer better opportunities to support complex learning.

Finally, enormous progress is being made in brain research, and methods for neurocognitive imaging (e.g., functional MRI) yield more and more knowledge of the role that different parts of the brain play in learning. Without doubt, this will influence the field of learning and instruction in the coming decade. There is much that we do not know about the physical mechanisms involved in learning. A particular goal of educational technology research in the next five years ought to be develop close ties with brain researchers and participate actively in that community of scholars.

## THE STUDY OF INSTRUCTIONAL DESIGN

We have made frequent use of the terms *educational technology*, *instructional design*, and *instructional technology* in this chapter. In some cases, we used these terms interchangeably, although we believe they have slightly different meanings. Roughly speaking, *educational technology* is broad in scope and includes technologies that support any kind of learning in any environment. The term *instructional technology* is more narrowly focused on the use of technology to support specific, intended, and planned learning outcomes. Instructional design, broadly conceived, is the discipline devoted to the study of these technologies and their creation and use in support of learning and instruction. What, then, constitutes the proper study of instructional design/systems/technology? One could focus on the objects involved, such as learning activities, materials, supports, technologies, and so on. These certainly need to be categorized and characterized. A more challenging enterprise is studying these various kinds of objects in use. What do particular

learners do with specific objects and how does that contribute to improved learning or performance?

One could focus on processes involved in developing these various objects. Some processes might be more efficient than others. Some processes might jeopardize quality while others might not be replicable. Closely related is the question of how design processes are best supported. What are the requirements for useful design models and tools?

Both the objects involved in instructional design and the processes used to develop those objects are influenced by many factors, such as tasks to be taught, target group characteristics, and learning contexts. In modern society, these factors are subject to enormous changes, such as a change from well-structured procedural tasks to ill-structured problem-solving tasks, from rather homogeneous target groups (in terms of age, prior knowledge, cultural background, etc.) to highly heterogeneous target groups, and from formal settings to informal and professional settings that are becoming increasingly important for lifelong learning. These changes have great impact on the study of objects and processes in instructional design.

Finally, the study of instructional design includes the study of designers. The performance of instructional designers may vary greatly depending on their experience. Even more important, only a very small part of all instruction is developed by designers with some formal preparation. By far the biggest part of instruction is developed by designers-by-assignment and teachers. Moreover, instruction may be developed by one individual but will more typically be developed by a team including content experts, programmers, graphical artists, and so forth. Changes in objects and processes of instructional design will no doubt have an important impact on the work of designers and design teams, the division of roles in design teams, and required instructional design competencies of team members.

Yet another conceptualization of the enterprise of instructional design is to consider three distinct activities: (1) developing tools and artifacts to support instruction, (2) demonstrating the utility and efficacy of these tools in designing and developing instruction, and (3) predicting and evaluating the impact of the use of these tools on learning and instruction. This way of thinking about instructional design proceeds roughly along a continuum from the practice of instructional development (using instructional technology) to instructional technology research (the study of what works when and why) and eventually to theories about various aspects of instructional design (determining how can we make tools and technologies that systematically improve learning and instruction). One might argue that such a continuum might correspond to undergraduate education, to master's-level training, and to doctoral-level training. How might we think about training at these three levels?

## PREPARING PRACTITIONERS AND RESEARCHERS

How can we adequately prepare practitioners and researchers for productive careers in the first half of the 21st century? Graduate programs of study in instructional design/systems/technology vary considerably and are undergoing continual change. Various professional associations are developing suggested curricula standards for educational technology programs—for example, the IEEE Technical Committee on Learning Technology (LTTC; http://lttf.ieee.org/).

Evidence shows that most instructional design practitioners have very little formal preparation. They have become instructional designers by being assigned that position or job—possibly as a reward for superior performance on the job or possibly because no one else was available or wanted the task. Actually, this fits the general picture that nowadays employees change jobs more often. In addition, knowledge of instructional design/systems/technology is becoming obsolete at an increasingly faster rate—just as the knowledge in many other professional fields. This clearly indicates a need for increasingly more flexible educational technology programs, in terms of both time and place, but also in terms of content (e.g., via accreditation of prior learning, or APL).

The further development of electronic job aids, performance support systems, and computer-based design tools may also contribute to lifelong learning in the field of instructional design/systems/technology. This signifies an interesting and growing relationship between the fields of educational communications and technology and human performance technology (HPT; see www.ispi.org). On the one hand, life-long learning in nonformal settings is best supported by a combination or integration of approaches rooted in both disciplines; on the other hand, HPT may contribute to the development of more flexible approaches to teaching educational technology.

It is common for people to believe that they know how to teach something at which they are reasonably competent. This belief in rampant in universities—because so-and-so is an expert logician, many believe that person will be a good logic instructor. The transition from people believing they are good at teaching things they know and understand to believing that they know how to plan effective instructional supports and learning activities is all too easy. The real-world situation is that instructor training is grossly neglected outside teacher preparation programs, and in those programs all too little emphasis is placed on instructor competencies (Klein et al., 2004).

*Designers-by-assignment** (in contrast with those who made a career choice to pursue instructional design and who have significant professional preparation) have managed to develop some impressive learning environments, especially when working in a well-defined area with prior examples of effective instruction. Changes in society, however, increasingly demand new training environments for new tasks—prior training models and methods are not easily applied in such situations, and designers-by-assignment struggle to develop effective instruction. What is needed is widespread recognition that professional preparation is required for instructional designers—that instructional design is an established *trade* with established *competencies* (Richey et al., 2001; see also Chapter 42 in this *Handbook*). In addition, what is also required are professional preparation programs that train practitioners in those competencies. Many graduate programs in instructional design do address competencies at the master's level, but the emphasis in many graduate programs is on research as opposed to practice. The best programs emphasize both practice and research in recognition of the dual need for research to inform practice and for practice to inform research.

What are the requirements for effective preparation in instructional design? As just suggested, it is important to realize that practitioners have different requirements than do researchers, for whom this *Handbook* is written. Serving both in the same graduate program is a challenge. A more natural progression in terms of instructional design education and training might be to address basic competencies in an undergraduate program. This is especially true if one believes that instructional design is a profession with associated knowledge and skills (e.g., theories, principles, models, standards, competencies), with professional societies organized around that body of knowledge and skills, with examples of best practice and what works, and with research aimed at improving practice and fundamental understanding. This would seem to be the case with instructional design, so we find the paucity of undergraduate programs in instructional design or educational technology to be an anomaly. A relatively

---

* The term *designer-by-assignment* was introduced by M. David Merrill to describe the common practice of assigning a subject-matter specialist or someone with particular technology skills the task of designing and developing instructional materials and associated technology support.

new undergraduate program in educational science at the University of Freiburg is aimed at this gap (http://www.ezw.uni-freiburg.de/), and we need more such programs at the undergraduate level. That we do not have more programs should cause some concern within the instructional design community. The IEEE Technical Committee on Learning Technology (http://lttf.ieee.org/) agrees and has initiated an effort to specify curriculum standards for undergraduate preparation of educational technologists. It is hoped that this effort will lead universities to develop associated programs of study. When the initial effort completes its work (probably in 2008), the committee will then address graduate and postgraduate programs of study for professional educational technologists.

A common conception of an instructional technologist is someone who knows how to use particular technologies. As technologies become easier to use and more widely accessible, the number of instructional technologists, according to this common conception, will increase. Developments in instructional technology often follow developments in computer science with about a generation delay. As computer science matured as a discipline, it shifted its focus from training programmers to studying computing and the use of programs and other tools.

Instructional technology is reaching a similar crossroads. Designers-by-assignment constitute a significant practitioner group. Even with successful programs like the one at the University of Freiburg, and even with new undergraduate programs in educational technology that follow new and innovative curriculum standards, we will still have many designers-by-assignment. One response from academia would be for graduate training in instructional design to shift its focus from training instructional designers to the study of instruction and instructional technologies, including training advanced students in the creation of instructional design tools.

If one obtains a master's degree in instructional technology and goes to work in a training department, one is likely to spend little time developing instruction—that will be left to the designers-by-assignment. One is more likely to quickly become a training manager responsible for hiring and overseeing designers-by-assignment. Do graduate programs in instructional design/systems/technology properly prepare professionals for such positions? At best, one might argue that a few programs include some emphasis on being an effective training manager. Even fewer focus on training graduates to create tools to be used by instructional designers—especially by designers-by-assignment.

At the master's level, the emphasis should shift from training students to be users of instructional technology to preparing them to manage, supervise, and inspire those who use instructional technology (designers-by-assignment). The emphasis for master's students includes a detailed study of empirically verified theory and a challenge to develop technology-based, learning-oriented instructional design and development tools that can be used by designers-by-assignment and nonspecialists

What constitutes a proper dissertation study? Too many projects at American institutions consist of a single empirical study or survey; this is less true in European institutions which typically involve doctoral students in a series of studies and publications. A doctoral student in instructional design should be able to identify, modify, and develop an instructional design theory (this corresponds to an advanced instructional design competency according to the International Board of Standards for Training, Performance, and Instruction; see Richey et al., 2001). A doctoral student should conduct extensive product and research literature reviews related to the theory of interest. In addition, a doctoral student should conduct additional original empirical research related to the theory development. Doctoral students might also develop tools that implement the theory in an appropriate context or setting. The students could then demonstrate the use of these tools for the design of instruction and evaluate or supervise the evaluation of instructional products developed by the use of these tools in a field setting.

What is the proper study of instructional design? If we conceive of instructional design as that discipline that studies instructional technology, then we might conclude that the focus of instructional design ought to be on tools and artifacts, with particular emphasis placed on the creation, use, and impact of tools and artifacts, much as one would expect to find in an advanced engineering program. The goal of the engineer or designer is to design useful artifacts and tools, and then to predict their performance and their impact on those who use them (Vincenti, 1990).

## CLOSING WORDS

In closing, we hope this volume helps to establish meaningful and useful foundations for ongoing and future research and development with regard to educational communications and technologies. We hope; we do not know. We are grateful for the contributions of so many talented researchers. Working on this research handbook these last two-plus years has been a growing experience for all of us. Of course, we had our ideas about the various topics discussed herein, and we began with excellent input and guidance from

David Jonassen. The excellent response to the AECT-hosted survey about *Handbook* usage gave us a sense that we had undertaken a significant enterprise that was of keen interest to our community of researchers, practitioners, teachers, and students.

# REFERENCES

Craig, S. D., Graesser, A. C., Sullins, J., and Gholson, B. (2004). Affect and learning: an exploratory look into the role of affect in learning with AutoTutor. *J. Educ. Media*, 29(3), 241–250.

Dörner, D. (1996). *The Logic of Failure: Why Things Go Wrong and What We Can Do to Make Them Right* (R. Kimber and R. Kimber, trans.). New York: Holt, Rinehart and Winston.*

Hume, D. (1777/1910). *An Enquiry Concerning Human Understanding*, http://eserver.org/18th/hume-enquiry.html.

Jonassen, D. H. (2000). Toward a design theory of problem solving. *Educ. Technol. Res. Dev.*, 48(4), 63–85.*

Kalyuga, S., Ayres, P., Chandler, P., and Sweller, J. (2003). The expertise reversal effect. *Educ. Psychol.*, 38 (1), 23–31.

Kim, Y. and Baylor, A. (2006). A social-cognitive framework for pedagogical agents as learning companions. *Educ. Technol. Res. Dev.*, 54(6), 569–596.

Kirschner, P. A., Sweller, J., and Clark, R. E. (2006). Why minimal guidance during instruction does not work: an analysis of the failure of constructivist, discovery, problem-based, experiential, and inquiry-based teaching. *Educ. Psychol.*, 46(2), 75–86.*

Klein, J. D., Spector, J. M., Grabowski, B., and de la Teja, I. (2004). *Instructor Competencies: Standards for Face-to-Face, Online and Blended Settings*. Greenwich, CT: Information Age Publishing.

Merrill, M. D. (2002). First principles of instruction. *Educ. Technol. Res. Dev.*, 50(3), 43–59.*

Milrad, M., Spector, J. M., and Davidsen, P. I. (2002). Model facilitated learning. In *Learning and Teaching with Technology: Principles and Practices*, edited by S. Naidu, pp. 13–27. London: Kogan Page.

Reigeluth, C. M. (1983). Instructional design: what is it and why is it? In *Instructional-Design Theories and Models: An Overview of Their Current Status*, edited by C. M. Reigeluth, pp. 3–36. Hillsdale, NJ: Lawrence Erlbaum Associates.*

Richey, R. C., Fields, D. C., and Foxon, M. with Roberts, R. C., Spannaus, T., and Spector, J. M. (2001). *Instructional Design Competencies: The Standards*, 3rd ed. Syracuse, NY: ERIC Clearinghouse on Information and Technology.

Seel, N. M. (2003). Model centered learning and instruction. *Technol. Instruct. Cogn. Learn.*, 1(1), 59–85.*

Seel, N. M., Al-Diban, S., and Blumschein, P. (2000). Mental models and instructional planning. In *Integrated and Holistic Perspectives on Learning, Instruction and Technology: Understanding Complexity*, edited by M. Spector and T. M. Anderson, pp. 129–158. Dordrecht: Kluwer Academic Publishers.

Spector, J. M. (2001). Philosophical implications for the design of instruction. *Instruct. Sci.*, 29(4), 381–402.

Spector, J. M. (2006). A methodology for assessing learning in complex and ill-structured task domains. *Innov. Educ. Teaching Int.*, 43(2), 109–120.

Spector, J. M. and Anderson, T. M., Eds. (2000). *Integrated and Holistic Perspectives on Learning, Instruction and Technology: Understanding Complexity*. Dordrecht: Kluwer.*

Spector, J. M. and Koszalka, T. A. (2004), *The DEEP (Dynamic and Enhanced Evaluation of Problem Solving) Methodology for Assessing Learning in Complex Domains*, NSF EREC 03-542 Final Report, http://idde.syr.edu/NSF-DEEP/.

van Merriënboer, J. J. G. (1997). *Training Complex Cognitive Skills: A Four-Component Instructional Design Model for Technical Training*. Englewood Cliffs, NJ: Educational Technology.*

van Merriënboer, J. J. G. and Kirschner, P. A. (2007). *Ten Steps to Complex Learning*. Mahwah, NJ: Lawrence Erlbaum Associates.*

Vincenti, W. G. (1990). *What Engineers Know and How They Know It: Analytical Studies from Aeronautical History*. Baltimore, MD: The Johns Hopkins University Press.

---

* Indicates a core reference.

# Glossary of Terms*

*Abstract mathematical knowledge:* Mathematics as a body of knowledge that may be experienced as experientially real.

*Activation principle:* Learning is promoted when learners activate relevant cognitive structures.

*Active learning:* Proponents of experiential learning often refer to active learning, and by this phrase they refer to the participatory nature of experiential learning; learners take an active role in their own learning, and this often also implies that learners have to take some responsibility for their own learning and advancement of understanding.

*Adaptive hypermedia systems (AHS):* Combining micro-adaptive systems and hypermedia systems to provide adaptive/adaptable, hybrid features by presenting learners with choices, along with guidance.

*Adaptive instructional systems:* Any forms of educational intervention aimed at accommodating individual learner differences.

*Adaptivity:* The capability exhibited by an organic or an artificial organism to alter its behavior according to the environment. In the context of an instructional system, this capability allows the system to alter its behavior according to learner needs and other characteristics. This is typically represented within a learner model.

*Analytical science:* Within this perspective researchers aim to develop, test, and justify theories; *see also* design science and situated science.

*Animated pedagogical agents:* Talking heads with speech, facial expressions, and gestures that implement pedagogical strategies.

*Application principle:* Learning is promoted when learners engage in the application of their newly acquired knowledge or skill.

*Apprenticeship:* A process through which a more experienced person assists a less experienced one by way of demonstration, support, and examples.

Also, a traditional learning paradigm in which a student learns by working with a master; this method of education was practiced widely in the Middle Ages. Also, a skilled practical trade through participation in practice.

*Aptitude-treatment interactions (ATI):* Adapting specific instructional procedures and strategies to specific learner characteristics (or aptitudes).

*Articulation:* In cognitive apprenticeship, verbalizing the results of reflective acts.

*Artifacts:* Designed objects or systems, including those created in the process of design and those resulting from the act of design.

*Assessment:* The systematic observation of achievement using any of a number of formats, including paper, technology, or live judgment.

*Assessment criteria:* Describe the aspects of performance that will be assessed.

*Assessment of learning:* Measuring learning achievement, performance, outcomes, and processes by many means.

*Assessment standards:* Describe the quality of performance on each of those aspects that can be expected of participants at different stages (e.g., age, grade) based on a participant's past performance (self-referenced), peer group performance (norm-referenced), or an objective standard (criterion-referenced).

*Asynchronous learning:* Communication between learners and instructors that does not take place simultaneously or in real time; an example of asynchronous learning is when a learner engages in a self-paced, self-service learning module without communicating with another person.

*Attention:* Arousal and intention in the brain which influence an individual's learning processes; without active, dynamic, and selective attending of environmental stimuli, it follows that meaning generation cannot occur.

---

* This glossary of terms represents a consolidated list of keywords with definitions taken from the individual chapters of this *Handbook*. The editors have made only very occasional and very minor changes to definitions provided by authors. Multiple definitions by different authors are indicated by the use of "Also" within a definition.

817

*Authenticity:* Learner-perceived relations between the associated practices and one's projected or envisioned use value of those practices.

*Authoring tool:* A software application used by non-programmers to assemble digital media files into displays, presentations, and interactive exercises.

*Automated instructional design (AID):* Leveraging technology to automate the instructional design as part of the process of learning content development.

*Automated knowledge:* About how to do something; with repetition it operates outside of conscious awareness and executes much faster than conscious processes.

*Baddeley's memory model:* An information-processing model that emphasizes the different short-term memory stores for visual (the sketchpad) and auditory (the phonological loop) information.

*Behaviorism:* An objectivist and monist perspective with regard to individual actions and decisions.

*Blended learning environment:* A learning environment that combines face-to-face instruction with technology-mediated instruction.

*Blog:* From the term "Web log"; originally a Web-based diary but now often used to refer to the software designed to support it that presents Web pages in a reverse chronological order.

*Change agentry:* The activity of facilitating change.

*Clinical education:* Supervised acquisition of clinical skills.

*Coaching:* In cognitive apprenticeship, assisting and supporting learners' cognitive activities.

*Cognitive abilities:* Abilities to perform any of the functions involved in cognition whereby cognition can be defined as the mental process of knowing, including aspects such as awareness, perception, reasoning, and judgment.

*Cognitive apprenticeship:* An apprenticeship process that utilizes cognitive and metacognitve skills and processes to guide learning.

*Cognitive constructivism:* A form of realism that stress the reorganization of mental structures of an individual making sense of the world.

*Cognitive load theory:* A cognitive model of information processing that emphasizes a conceptual mental workload in understanding human thought. Also, an instructional design theory based on our knowledge of human cognitive architecture.

*Cognitive models:* Descriptions of human thought processes via metaphorical constructs that may or may not represent actual biological structures; the value of any model is judged by its utility in representing or predicting actual thought, not by the degree of accuracy in depicting brain structure.

*Cognitive task analysis:* Interview and observation protocols for extracting implicit and explicit knowledge from experts for use in instruction and expert systems.

*Cognitive training model:* A five-task instructional design model.

*Cognitivism:* An objectivist and rationalist perspective with regard to individual cognitive structures.

*Collaboration:* Activity involving multiple people developing shared meaning while working together on a common problem; often involves harmonious cooperation but is not contingent upon it.

*Collaborative learning:* Students working together to maximize their own and each other's learning (i.e., to achieve shared learning goals; synonymous with cooperative learning for many).

*Collective data collection:* Obtaining data from individual group members; data are later aggregated or manipulated into a representation of the group as a whole.

*Community of practice:* A group of people bound by participation in an activity common to them all; may be formal or informal.

*Competency:* A knowledge, skill, or attitude that enables one to effectively perform the activities of a given occupation or function to the standards expected in employment.

*Competency development:* A feature of the holistic approach, indicating that educational programs should be aimed at the development of competencies rather than teaching different topics in different courses.

*Competitive learning:* Students working individually to achieve a grade or recognition attainable by or restricted to only a few.

*Complex:* Pertains to a group of multiple independent entities with interrelated functions seeking a common goal through adaptive processes.

*Complex performance:* Refers to real-world activities that require the integration of disparate measurement instrumentation as well as the need for time-critical experimental control.

*Complex tasks:* Tasks where performance requires the integrated use of both controlled and automated knowledge to perform tasks that often extend over many hours or days.

*Complicated:* Consisting of many interconnecting parts or elements; intricate; involving many different and confusing aspects.

*Component investigation:* The identification or confirmation through research of steps (procedural models) and factors (conceptual models) critical to the instructional design process.

*Computer-mediated communication (CMC):* Communication between two or more individuals with text-based tools such as e-mail, instant messaging, or computer-based conferencing systems.

*Computer-supported cooperative learning:* The instructional use of technology combined with the use of cooperative learning.

*Conceptual model:* A theoretically based explanation of a natural phenomenon.

*Conditions-based instruction:* Described by Gagné as internal and external conditions of learning; states possessed by the learner, such as prior knowledge, are internal conditions, and instructional supports designed to promote learning are external conditions.

*Construction-integration model:* A cognitive model for understanding the processing of text; this model suggests a continual multilevel process of building and confirming a cohesive mental model from a text document and a reader's prior knowledge.

*Constructive controversy:* Occurs when group members have different information, perceptions, opinions, reasoning processes, theories, and conclusions, and they must reach agreement to make progress or proceed.

*Constructivism:* A point of view related to cognitive development; cognitive development depends on a child's actions on his or her own surroundings to change and actively learn from those surroundings (Piaget) and the strong relationship between a child's surroundings and his cognitive development (Vygotsky). Also, a set of assumptions about human learning emphasizing the central role of the mind's active construction of new knowledge.

*Contextualism:* A philosophical worldview in which any event is interpreted as an ongoing act inseparable from its current and historical context and in which a radically functional approach to truth and meaning is adopted; the root metaphor of contextualism is the act in context, and the truth criterion of contextualism is successful working or effective action.

*Cooperative learning:* Students working together to maximize their own and each other's learning (i.e., to achieve shared learning goals; synonymous with *collaborative learning* in this chapter).

*Core reference:* A reference that is of central interest to researchers in a particular area and generally considered to be a primary source of data or information; core references are indicated by an asterisk in the reference section of each chapter in this *Handbook*.

*Curriculum design:* A process of conceiving a plan to define a set of courses constituting an area of specialization that supports the specified learning goal.

*Cybernetics:* System theory concerned with the issues of regulation, order, and stability that face us in the treatment of complex systems and processes.

*Cycle of instruction:* The activation-demonstration-application-integration cycle of first principles.

*Declarative knowledge:* Knowledge about what or why; hierarchically structured and formatted as propositional, episodic, or visuospatial information that is accessible in long-term memory and consciously observable in working memory.

*Demonstration principle:* Learning is promoted when learners observe a demonstration of the skills to be learned.

*Descriptive accounts:* Analysis of naturally occurring instances of human activity.

*Descriptive contextualism:* A variant of contextualism that has as its primary goal an understanding of the complexity and richness of a whole event through an appreciation of its participants and features. It seeks the construction of knowledge that is specific, personal, ephemeral, and spatiotemporally restricted, like a historical narrative.

*Design and development research:* Research that seeks to create knowledge grounded in data systematically derived from practice and based upon a systematic analysis of specific cases.

*Design and development team:* The group of people and skill sets involved in the research-based development of artifacts and systems in education.

*Design-in-the-large (DIL):* Refers to the goal of changing existing situations into preferred ones; *see* design-in-the-small (DIS).

*Design-in-the-small (DIS):* Refers to the design of a specific innovation; *see* design-in-the-large (DIL).

*Design language:* A set of abstractions used to give structure, properties, and texture to solutions of design problems; designs are expressed in terms of design languages.

*Design layer:* One aspect of a decomposed design problem that can be approached using one or more design languages; a subdomain of the larger problem to which one or more design languages pertains.

*Design principles:* Research-based guidelines for instructional design; design principles can be articulated at different grain sizes: Specific principles characterize rationales for designing specific features in a learning environment; pragmatic principles connect rationales behind several features; meta-principles synthesize a cluster of pragmatic principles.

*Design science:* Within this perspective researchers aim to build and evaluate artifacts for well-defined contexts of use; *see* analytical science and situated science.

*Design theory:* The concepts and principles that help to develop strategies and methods for designing.

*Development model:* A recommended set of activities or tasks that define a process for successful instructional design.

*Direct process measure:* Continuous elicitation of data from the beginning to end of a group process. Direct process measures involve videotaping, audiotaping, direct researcher observation, or a combination of these methods.

*Discovery learning environment:* Environment that provides students with a set of events or data that they can explore independently or in a prestructured way to discover the regularities in these data; a rich learning environment that facilitates children's own constructive endeavors to learning experiences.

*Distance education:* An educational program characterized by the separation, in time or place, between instructor and student and in which communications media are used to allow interchange.

*Distributed perspective:* An analytic approach to understanding human activity that distributes agency across people and material artifacts.

*Domain-specific theories:* Theories on instruction that are tailored to a specific subject matter domain.

*Dual-coding theory:* A cognitive model of information processing that emphasizes the unique contributions of verbal and visual subsystems in understanding human cognition.

*Dualism:* When two apparently related items are treated as separate and distinct (e.g., mind/body or individual/environment).

*Dynamic pretest:* A test delivered online that can literally adapt courseware to learner deficiencies identified through online testing and scale courseware to match specific learner needs.

*Educational communications:* Forms, means, and methods of expressing and sharing ideas, information, and knowledge to support learning and instruction.

*Educational technology research:* Research focus on describing, predicting, understanding, and designing effective applications of technology to serve the goals of education, training, and performance support.

*Educational technology:* The disciplined application of scientific principles and theoretical knowledge to support and enhance human learning and performance.

*Effect size:* A statistical measure of the difference between the mean of the control group and the mean of the experimental group in a quantitative research study.

*e-Learning principles:* Prescriptive principles for designing e-learning; *see* multimedia learning principles.

*Electronic performance support systems (EPSS):* An enabler of work tasks delivered by electronic technology provided to individuals or teams at the time of need on the job; typical support includes procedural guidance or references to factual information needed to complete tasks.

*Embodiments:* Tactile or visual models that are meant to represent mathematical relationships and concepts in a ready apprehensible form.

*Emergent modeling:* A dynamic approach to modeling in mathematics education, in which the models that the students use develop from models of informal mathematical activity into models for more formal mathematical reasoning.

*Empiricism:* An epistemology that states that knowledge comes from experience and through the senses.

*Epistemology:* How we come to know about what exists.

*Ergonomics of learning environments:* The applied science that helps illuminate the relationships between a learner and a learnplace.

*Evaluation:* The process of gathering information about the merit or worth of a program for the purpose of making decisions about its effectiveness or for program improvement.

*Experiment:* A design that involves the comparison of one treatment to another, using two or more different groups.

*Expertise development:* Acquisition of knowledge and skill in a domain.

*Exploration:* In cognitive apprenticeship, forming and testing a personal hypothesis in pursuit of learning.

*External validity:* The degree to which the results of an experiment can be generalized to other settings.

*Extraneous load:* In cognitive load theory, the workload component associated with information that is not directly relevant to a particular content area.

*Feedback:* Information on goal attainment designed to help workers, teams, or functional units monitor and evaluate their progress in achievement of desired accomplishments. Feedback may be quantitative or qualitative; it may or may not include explanations to guide performance; it may be directed to individual, team, unit, or organizational levels; and it may be provided through personal communications or through impersonal channels such as charts and graphs posted in work areas or by computer.

*Feedback (cybernetic definition):* Output of a system that is "fed back" to the controller of the system as an input signal to regulate the system with regard to a reference value.

*Feedback (instructional context):* Post-response information that is provided to a learner to inform the learner on his or her actual state of learning or performance.

*First principles of instruction:* Five principles fundamental to effective, efficient, and engaging learning.

*Flexible learning:* Learning that is relatively free of logistical and educational constraints.

*Formalism:* The formal structure and abstract principles that underlie the conceptual framework of the content area; for example, the concept of erosion is a formalism in science, division is a formalism in mathematics, and metaphor is a type of formalism in language arts.

*Four-component instructional design model (4C/ID):* An instructional design model that distinguishes recurrent from non-recurrent tasks and emphasizes whole-task practice on complex cognitive skills.

*Functional contextualism:* A philosophy of science and variant of contextualism that has as its primary goal the prediction and influence of events with precision, scope, and depth using empirically based concepts and rules. It seeks the construction of knowledge that is general, abstract, and spatiotemporally unrestricted, like a scientific principle.

*Gaming:* Taking part in open-ended activities that give opportunity to elicit conceptual learning.

*Generational differences:* The theory that people born within an approximately 20-year time period share a common set of characteristics based on the historical experiences, economic and social conditions, technological advances, and other societal changes they have in common; the term first came into popularity in the 1960s when it was used to distinguish the rebellious Baby Boomer generation from their parents.

*Germane load:* In cognitive load theory, the workload component associated with strategies that require processing, but in doing so make the relevant content more accessible.

*Goal setting theory:* Guidelines for optimizing worker or team performance through setting of specific and difficult goals. Goal setting theory considers the effects of self-efficacy, goal commitment, feedback, and incentives on goal effectiveness.

*Group:* Two or more individuals working together to achieve a common goal.

*Group-based learning (asynchronously):* A mode of learning that enables individuals to learn in groups with online technologies in their own time, at their own pace, and from their own place.

*Group-based learning (synchronously):* A mode of learning which enables individuals to learn in groups with online technologies at the same time and at the same pace as that of the group but from their own place.

*Group learning process:* Actions and interactions performed by group members during the group learning task.

*Groupware authoring:* Concurrent process of creating learning content in a team environment with multiple authors often serving in different roles such as writers, graphic artists, instructional designers, etc.

*Hard technologies:* Represent devices may be used in adaptive systems to capture learner information (e.g., eye-tracking devices) or present content to a learner (e.g., tactile tablet); can be used to detect and classify learners' performance data or affective states such as confusion, frustration, excitement, disappointment, boredom, confidence, contentment, and so on.

*Hierarchical hypertext:* A hypertext structure in which content is ordered relative to the concepts presented. The concepts presented on a screen link to superordinate (more general) concepts, or subordinate (more specific) concepts.

*Holistic data collection:* Obtaining data from the group as a whole. As this type of data collection results in a representation of the group rather than individual group member, it is not necessary to aggregate or manipulate data.

*Human cognitive architecture:* The manner in which structures and functions required for human cognitive processes are organized.

*Hybrid learning environment:* Alternative term for blended learning environment.

*Hypertext:* Text-based informational screens that are presented using a computer. Informational screens are connected to each other using links.

*Hypertext/hypermedia:* Pages of text and other media with hot spots that users can click on and access other pages.

*Idealism:* A view of reality as mental, implying that the world is not separate from the mind.

*IMS learning design:* A formal instructional design language that is used to specify the design of a teaching and learning process in a machine interpretable way.

*Incentives:* Tangible and social rewards intended to optimize performance of individuals or teams; may include money, feedback, and social recognition.

*Indirect process measure:* Discrete measure at a specific point in time during the group process; often involves multiple points of data collection.

Indirect process measures may measure processes, outcomes, products, or other factors related to group process.

*Information processing:* The modeling of sensory input and cognitive transformations as a series of processing stages.

*Informative tutoring feedback:* Multiple-try feedback strategies providing elaborated feedback components that guide the learner towards successful task completion without offering immediately the correct response.

*In-program learner behaviors:* Measures of learner activities and outcomes while engaged in an instructional task.

*Inquiry learning:* Students actively learn by asking questions and interpreting answers or by formulating and testing hypotheses. Also, an "approach to learning that involves a process of exploring the natural or material world, and that leads to asking questions, making discoveries, and rigorously testing those discoveries in the search for new understanding" (National Science Foundation).

*Instructional design:* A purposeful activity that results in a combination of strategies, activities and/or resources to facilitate learning. Also, creating blueprints for effective, efficient, and engaging instruction. Also, the systematic process of analyzing, designing, developing, implementing, and evaluating instruction; also known as instructional systems design.

*Instructional design model:* A coherent set of mostly prescriptive theoretical statements on the appropriateness of particular instructional approaches or interventions.

*Instructional designer:* A person with the knowledge and skills to design effective instruction.

*Instructional strategies:* The prescribed sequences and methods of instruction to achieve a learning objective.

*Instrumentation:* Hardware devices used to assist with the process of data acquisition and measurement.

*Integrated curriculum:* A curriculum based on a whole-task approach aimed at the integration of supportive contents with whole tasks, knowledge, skills, and attitudes and at integrating first-order skills with higher-order skills.

*Integration principle:* Learning is promoted when learners integrate their new knowledge into their everyday life.

*Intelligent tutoring systems:* Intelligent computer systems that model the learner's knowledge and skills at a fine-grained level and that adaptively respond.

*Interactive learning task:* Tasks providing multiple response steps or tries and instructional components such as feedback, guiding questions, prompts, simulation facilities, and so on.

*Interactive multimedia:* The use of more than one form of media (such as text, visuals, video, animation, and audio) in a way in which a user has a great deal of control over the choice or progress of the program.

*Interactive simulation:* Learners manipulate components and parameters of a complex system and observe what happens when system output is generated.

*Internal validity:* The degree to which the results of a study can be attributed to the treatment rather than extraneous or confounding variables.

*Intrinsic load:* In cognitive load theory, the workload component associated with a particular content area and its level of complexity.

*Keyword:* A word or phrase that is critically important to a topic area or which has a particular definition important for understanding issues and further discussion.

*Knowledge-based system:* A computer program that can reason, based on a database of knowledge acquired from a human expert (also known as an expert system).

*Knowledge communities:* Technology focused in bringing communities of people together to both generate and share knowledge about a shared interest.

*Knowledge generation:* Generation of understanding through developing relationships between and among ideas.

*Knowledge integration:* The process of adding, distinguishing, organizing, and evaluating accounts of phenomena, situations, and abstractions.

*Knowledge management:* A collection of technologies and organizational processes aimed at capturing, disseminating and archiving performance related knowledge within an organization.

*Knowledge, skills, and attitudes (KSAs):* Used in the traditional approach for specifying team competencies; recent research now expands the skills beyond those specifically attributed to the team task to include psychomotor and cognitive competencies.

*Learner model:* A representation of the learner that is maintained by an adaptive system. Learner models can be used to provide personalized instruction to a particular individual and may include cognitive and noncognitive aspects of the learner. Learner models have been used in many areas, such as adaptive educational and training systems, help systems, recommender systems, and others.

*Learning content management system (LCMS):* A multi-user software application in which learning developers can create, store, reuse, manage, and deliver digital learning content from a central object repository (database).

*Learning environment:* A system that incorporates a set of features including a navigation system. Learning environments can deliver curriculum in any topic area.

*Learning hierarchy:* Description of successively achievable intellectual skills, each stated as a performance class in which achievement of a superordinate skill is in part dependent on the internal condition of having learned necessary subordinate skills.

*Learning management system (LMS):* A computer-based system to support or replace classroom-based learning; examples include Blackboard, Moodle, Sakai, and WebCT.

*Learning object:* A digital resource that can be reused to mediate learning.

*Learning places (learnplaces):* The immediate physical setting for someone's learning activity, including the tools and artifacts, digital and material, that come to hand.

*Learning style:* There is no single agreed-upon definition of learning style; a general definition is that it is a description of the attitudes and behaviors that determine an individual's preferred way of learning. Also, a learning style involves a theoretical model that proposes that individuals have preferred ways in which they learn; learning styles typically involve visual representation, vocal explanations, and practical examples; experiential learning proposes several ways in which an educator can accommodate these learning styles, although all such styles have a bias toward practical expression and place less emphasis on theoretical expressions of learning.

*Lethal adaptation:* An alteration to an innovation that undermines the expected benefits of the innovation.

*Library media center:* A physical repository of instructional materials and technology resources found in most American public schools, usually managed by a library media specialist.

*Linear hypertext:* A hypertext structure in which links allow the reader to move forward and backward through the content, as if turning the pages of a book.

*Log files:* A sequence of behavioral data stored in a permanent file, offering time- or location-stamped records of human choices made through computer interfaces with learning environments.

*Long-term memory:* A component of the information-processing model of cognition that represents information stored, presumably for the life of an individual. Also, the store holding all knowledge acquired during the processes of learning.

*Loose coupling:* An organizational arrangement characterized by significant freedom between levels in the hierarchy.

*Macro-adaptive systems:* Allowing different alternatives for choosing instructional goals, curriculum content, and delivery systems by grouping students.

*Mathemagenic methods:* Instructional methods that explicitly aim at the transfer of learning; these methods promote learners to invest effort and time in the development of general or abstract cognitive schemas.

*Meaning making:* The process of connecting new information with prior knowledge, affected by one's intention, motivation, and strategies employed.

*Memory:* The mental faculty of retaining and recalling past experiences.

*Mental model:* A mental representation that people use to organize their experience about themselves, others, the environment, and the things with which they interact; its functional role is to provide predictive and explanatory power for understanding these phenomena.

*Micro-adaptive systems:* Diagnosing the learner's specific learning needs during instruction and providing instructional prescriptions for the needs.

*Minimalist principles:* Instructional design principles for sparse instruction.

*Mixed-methods research:* Studies that combine qualitative and quantitative data collection methods. Also, studies that rely on quantitative and qualitative as well as other methods for formulating research questions, collecting and analyzing data, and interpreting findings.

*Model:* An artifact representative of a real object or of an internal interpretation of something real, often represented on a computer screen. Also, structured representation of a system in terms of variables or concepts and their (quantitative or qualitative) relations that can be used for predicting system behavior by means of simulations.

*Model research:* Research that addresses the validity or effectiveness of an existing or newly constructed development model, process, or technique.

*Model validation:* Experiments, quasi-experiments, interviews, and expert reviews that are used for verification and evaluation of a particular design and development technique.

*Modeling:* In cognitive apprenticeship, demonstrating thought processes. Also, the process of creating simulations as a means for learning.

*Motivation processes:* Interest and attribution are two essential and linked components of motivation processes; they are activated by arousal and intention through the descending reticular activation system.

*Multimedia learning principles:* Likely effects of text, animation, audio, and graphics on learning.

*Mutual adaptation:* The coevolution of both an innovation and the environment in which it is implemented.

*Natural information processing system:* The procedures by which natural systems such as human cognition and evolution by natural selection process information.

*Naturalistic evaluation:* An evaluation approach that relies on qualitative methodology but gives evaluators freedom to choose the precise method used to collect, analyze, and interpret their data.

*Novice developer:* A person who has little or no training in instructional design yet has the responsibility of creating learning content using authoring tools.

*Objectivism:* An ontological and epistemological view that contends that reality exists outside of the individual and consists of specific entities.

*Online/offline measures:* Online measures are recorded during task performance, offline measures are recorded after task performance.

*Ontology:* A shared and agreed-upon explicit formal representation of a domain. Also, what exists in the world.

*Open educational resource:* A learning object that can be freely used, reused, adapted, and shared.

*Open-ended learning environment:* Instructional projects based, to varying degrees, on constructivist principles in which learners self-discover concepts and principles while engaged in authentic learning tasks.

*Open source software (OSS):* Software that has OSI open source licenses attached; these licenses state that the source code of a program should always be available to everyone and that everyone can change the source code.

*Open standard (OS):* Commonly agreed-upon and published specifications of the conventions used in a community to ensure the quality and interoperability of products and services.

*Outcome-referenced models:* Approaches to instructional design in which (1) consideration of the nature of the learning tasks and the conditions required to support them are central, and (2) learning outcomes are categorized to represent not only qualitative differences in the acquired capability (as a category of task or goal) but also external conditions that support learning and different learner states; the latter are referred to as internal conditions, which also facilitate learning.

*Participation models of authenticity:* Models that establish a sense of authenticity by engaging learners in the authentic practices as they work on real-world tasks as part of authentic communities and in contexts that value the outcomes of those tasks.

*Participatory design:* A user-centered design approach in which users are actively involved in the design process of a system or product that addresses their specific needs.

*Part-task models:* Instructional models that apply an atomistic approach in which complex contents and tasks are reduced into increasingly simpler elements until a level where the distinct elements can be taught to the learners.

*Pebble-in-the-pond instructional design:* A content-first approach to designing instruction.

*Performance:* Ability of student or trainee to demonstrate accomplishment in either a very specific domain such as a formal examination, across domains and subject matters, or realistic contexts.

*Performance improvement:* An approach to optimizing organizational outcomes that uses a systemic comprehensive methodology to define and resolve gaps at the organizational, process, and individual worker levels.

*Perturbances:* Events that cause a small disruption in organizational function; useful for encouraging reflection on an organization's purposes.

*Phonological loop:* In Baddeley's memory model, a short-term memory component devoted to retaining auditory information.

*Positive interdependence:* When individuals perceive that they can reach their goals if and only if the other individuals with whom they are cooperatively linked also reach their goals.

*Pragmatism:* The view that knowledge is derived from interaction among groups of individuals and the artifacts in their environment, which together create a reality.

*Precedent:* Artifacts and the memory of designing them or examining them.

*Prescriptive accounts:* Designed tools, strategies, and interventions.

*Problem-based learning:* Acquiring knowledge as part of a learner group by analyzing a problem, studying privately, using various learning resources, and collectively synthesizing knowledge. Also, an instructional method that initiates students' learning by creating a need to solve an authentic problem; during the problem-solving process, students construct content knowledge and develop problem-solving skills as well as self-directed learning skills while working toward the solution to the problem.

*Problem-centered instruction: See* task-centered instruction principle and strategy.

*Problem solving:* A process of understanding the discrepancy between current and goal states of a problem, generating and testing hypotheses for the causes of the problem, devising solutions to the problem, and executing the solution to satisfy the goal state of the problem.

*Process-tracing techniques:* Records performance process data such as verbal reports, eye movements, and actions that can be used to make inferences about the cognitive processes or knowledge underlying task performance.

*Programmed technologies:* Process-based methods and approaches to support learning and instruction, often represented in the form of algorithms and implemented in computer software.

*Punctuated equilibrium:* A view of organizational change characterized by long periods of stasis and short periods of change.

*Qualitative research:* Research that emphasizes verbal descriptions or narrative accounts of observed or recorded events; sometimes called naturalistic. Also, research on human systems; hallmarks include researcher as instrument, natural settings, and little manipulation. Also, often conceived of as more traditional, or positivistic, typified by experimental or correlational studies; data and findings are usually represented through numbers and results of statistical tests.

*Quasi-experiment:* An experimental design in which participants are not randomly assigned to treatments.

*Rapid prototyping:* A user-centered design approach in which users participate in a rapid, iterative series of tryout and revision cycles during the design of a system or a product until an acceptable version is created.

*Rationalism:* An epistemological view where reason is the principle source of knowledge.

*Realism:* A form of objectivism that assumes that there is some sort of reality that is separate from the mind and that knowing involves a correspondence between the word and the mind.

*Reasoning:* Formulating and substantiating conclusions based on given information.

*Reculturing:* Changes that involve examining the assumptions and purposes of an organization.

*Redundancy:* The presentation of information multiple times either in the same or in different forms; the value of redundancy in communication is context dependent and debated.

*Reflection:* In cognitive apprenticeship, self-analysis and self-assessment. Also, a key element in the model of experiential learning where the learner has some inner mental consideration of the consequences of the actions they have taken in practical learning; there are some implied mental models that are necessary for reflection to be an effective element within learning in the experiential approach.

*Relational hypertext:* A hypertext structure with links allowing the reader to access information on other screens that have some logical, conceptual, or hierarchical connection to the content on the current screen.

*Resource:* Media, people, places, or ideas that have the potential to support learning.

*Resource-based learning:* The use and application of available assets to support varied learning needs across contexts.

*Restructuring:* Changes that involve organizational structure, new work patterns, or new functions.

*Scaffolding:* Process through which individuals are supported in identifying, interpreting, or otherwise using resources. Also, support that is provided to help learners reach skill levels beyond their current abilities; essential to scaffolding is the fading of the support inversely to the learners' acquisition of the skill that is being supported.

*Scaled instructional strategies:* Hypothesis that the application of first principles has an accumulating performance effect for complex skills.

*Schemata:* Schemata are data structures for representing both generic and specific knowledge.

*Science learning:* Understanding concepts related to biology, physics, chemistry, and astronomy.

*Self-paced learning (offline):* A mode of learning that enables individuals to study with portable technologies in their own time, at their own pace, and from their own place.

*Self-paced learning (online):* A mode of learning that enables individuals to study online and in their own time at their own pace and from their own place.

*Self-regulated learning:* When learners set their own goals for learning and then attempt to plan, monitor, regulate, and control their cognition, motivation, behavior, and context.

*Self-regulation:* Active participation in terms of behavior, motivation and metacognition in one's own learning process.

*Sensory memory:* A component of the information-processing model of cognition that describes the initial input of information (such as vision or hearing).

*Serious games:* Games that help students learn new content, strategies, and skills that are relevant to academic and practical subject matter.

*Shared mental models:* Crucial in the work of a team, as members of the team need to share an accurate model of the problem to be addressed and the associated task to assess the problem, determine their own roles and responsibilities, and coordinate their efforts over time.

*Short-term memory:* A component of the information-processing model of cognition that describes a person's attention.

*Simulation:* A working representation of reality; used in training to represent devices and process and may be low or high in terms of physical or functional fidelity. Also, an executable (runnable) model; computer software that allows a learner to manipulate variables and processes and observe results. Also, a computer-based model of a natural process or phenomenon that reacts to changes in values of input variables by displaying the resulting values of output variables.

*Simulation models of authenticity:* Models that build on the assumption that classroom activity should be made to resemble as much as possible the activities in which real-world practitioners engage.

*Situated learning:* A perspective on learning that emphasizes its social and physical context.

*Situated science:* A perspective in which the scientific inquiry and attitude are carried into (instead of applied to) the field of the project and of practice, modifying each other over time as the project unfolds; *see* analytical science and design science.

*Situatedness:* The context or constellation of influential events and elements that govern and shape human life.

*Situational embodiment:* When to-be-learned content is experienced in relation to a particular context of use that provides legitimacy to the content and student actions, a meaningful goal, and a set of actions for the learner, and on which learner actions have some consequence.

*Situativity theory:* A form of realism that stresses an individual's direct perception of events and phenomena.

*Socio-cultural/historicism:* A relativist perspective that emphasizes relations and processes between the individual and society.

*Soft-skills simulation:* Simulations designed for the specific purpose of teaching interpersonal skills such as leadership, coaching, facilitating, and so on.

*Soft technologies:* Algorithms, programs, or environments that broaden the types of interaction between students and computers; for example, an adaptive algorithm may be employed in a program that selects an assessment task that provides the most information about a particular learner at a particular point in time.

*Software features:* Specific applications of technology intended to advance learning; features include designed artifacts such as modeling tools, simulations, micro-worlds, visualizations, collaboration tools, reflection prompts, games, and embedded assessments.

*Storyboard:* A document that details and specifies on-screen text, narrative scripts, and interaction in a paper-based format before it is converted into an online course.

*Structure–guidance–coaching–reflection cycle:* Instructional assistance within the activation–demonstration–application–reflection cycle of instruction.

*Student modeling:* Student models store information about students including domain competence and individual domain-independent characteristics; student modeling is the process of building and updating the student model.

*Subject-matter expert (SME):* A person with extensive experience who is able to rapidly and successfully perform a class of tasks.

*Synthetic learning environments:* A learning environment characterized in terms of a particular technology, subject matter, learner characteristics, and pedagogical principles; a synthetic experience, as opposed to a real-world interaction with an actual device or process, is created for the learner through a simulation, game, or other technology.

*System:* An interdependent entity that is responsive, systematic, and bound by the open or closed nature of the context in which it is located.

*Systemic change:* The process of changing a system from one paradigm to another by applying systems thinking and systems theory.

*Systems design:* The process for determining what characteristics a new system should have.

*Systems theory:* An interdisciplinary field with applications in both the hard and soft sciences; it focuses on understanding relationships among components comprising the whole.

*Task-centered instruction principle:* The central principle that learning is promoted when learners are engaged in a task-centered approach.

*Task-centered instructional strategy:* Teaching component skills in the context of a progression of real-world whole tasks.

*Task complexity:* Can be defined subjectively (individual characteristics, such as expertise or perception), objectively (task characteristics, such as multiple solution paths or goals), or as an interaction (individual and task characteristics).

*Team evolution and maturation (TEAM) model:* Offers stages that have been observed in team performance that take into account time, experience, and training.

*Technology:* The application of scientific or other organized knowledge to practical tasks.

*Technology-enhanced learning environments:* Technology-based learning and instructional systems through which students acquire skills or knowledge, usually with the help of teachers or facilitators, learning support tools, and technological resources.

*Technology-oriented research:* Research that aims to develop new technological knowledge, methods, and artifacts to change the world as it exists with the final aim to improve the way we live.

*Theoretical foundation:* A related set of rules and principles that can be brought to bear as a basis for making predictions and providing explanations for a variety of phenomena.

*Theoretical statement:* Formal expression about the relationship between at least two variables or instantiations of variables.

*Theory:* An integrated and internally coherent set of theoretical statements that provides a sufficient basis for empirical research in which these statements can be tested.

*Theory development:* Systematic effort to generate (coherent sets of) theoretical statements.

*Theory-oriented research:* Directed at the development of theories about the world as it exists, with the final aim to predict or understand events.

*Tool research:* The research-based design and development of products and tools to enhance learning.

*Tools:* Devices that aid individuals to engage and manipulate resources and ideas.

*Topic-centered instructional strategy:* Teaching component skills in sequence prior to their application to a whole task.

*Transactional leader:* Exerts influence by setting goals, clarifying desired outcomes, providing feedback, and exchanging rewards and recognition for accomplishments; one of two leadership styles that hold the potential for more effective team performance, moving away from a traditional top-down directive approach; *see* transformational leader.

*Transformational leaders:* Exerts influence by broadening and elevating followers' goals and providing them with the confidence to go beyond minimally acceptable expectations specified in the exchange; one of two leadership styles that hold the potential for more effective team performance, moving away from a traditional top-down directive approach; *see* transactional leader.

*Uncertainty:* Nonlinear patterns that are usually the result of unpredictable interactions.

*Unit of analysis:* Boundaries of phenomena of interest.

*Usability:* The ease with which humans can use a system or a product to accomplish their goals efficiently, effectively, and with satisfaction.

*User-centered design:* A design philosophy and approach that places users at the center of the design process from the stages of planning and designing the system requirements to implementing and testing the product.

*User control:* The need for the reader to determine the sequence and pacing of information accessed in a hypertext.

*Validation (validity):* The process and outcome of collecting and interpreting results of assessments or measurement so that inferences from findings are warranted by evidence.

*Visual sketchpad:* In Baddeley's memory model, a short-term memory component devoted to visual and spatial information.

*Visuals:* A form of media in which information is presented visually; text may or may not be considered a visual form.

*Web log file:* A data file residing on a Web server that contains a record of all visitors to the site hosted by the server, where they came from, what links they clicked on, and other information.

*Whole-task models:* Instructional models that apply a holistic approach in which complex contents and tasks are analyzed in coherence and taught from their simplest, yet meaningful version towards increasingly more complex versions.

*Working memory:* The structure that processes information coming from either the environment or long-term memory and that transfers learned information for storage in long-term memory.

*Zone of learnability:* In the construction–integration model of text processing, a hypothesized optimal overlap between a text document and a reader's prior knowledge.

*Zone of proximal development (ZPD):* A term coined by Vygotsky to describe the space between a learner's current skill level and the next skill level which the learner cannot reach without assistance.

# Author Index

## A

Forrester, J. W., 461, *466*
Foshay, R., 189, *195*
Foshay, W. R., 174, 178, 180, *183*, 673, 682, *684*, 749, *760*,
Foster, E., 522, *524*
Fowles, M. E., 360, *363*, *604*, 637, *644*
Fowles-Winkler, A., *293*
Fowlkes, J. E., 323, *325*
Fox, E. J., 57, 58, 59, 62, 63, 64, *64*, *65*, 570, 574, *575*
Fox, H. C., *313*
Foxon, M., *28*, *575*, *815*
Francis, D. J., 543, *562*
Francis, J. B., 570, *575*
Franklin, S., 44, *52*, *221*
Franz, T., *325*
Fraser, W., 37, *37*
Frederiksen, J. R., 146, 158, *161*, 217, *224*, 282, *292*, 459, 460, 462, 463, 465, *467*, *468*, *484*
Fredrick, L. D., 62, *65*
Fredricks, J., *160*
Free Software Foundation, *357*, *364*
Freebody, P., 545, *562*
Freedman, D., 230, *230*
Freeh, V., *364*
Freeman, M., *602*
Freidus, H., 622, *631*
French, J. R. P., 621, 628, *631*
Frensch, P. A., 786, *802*
Fretz, E., *160*, *467*, *658*
Freudenthal, H., 547, *563*
Frick, T. W., 177, *183*, 274, *274*, 394, *398*, 662, 665, *668*, *669*, *670*, *758*
Fried, R. G., *604*
Friedland, R., 252, *256*
Friedman, A., 46, *52*
Friedman, S. L., *27*
Friedman, T. L., 736, *758*
Friend, R., 119, *123*
Friesen, 347, 350, 351, *352*
Frizell, S., 255, *256*
Fröschl, C., 281, 282, *292*
Fry, E. B., 191, *196*
Fry, R., 34, 35, *37*
FSF-DEF, *357*, *364*
Fu, W.-T., 788, *801*
Fuks, H., 242, 245, *248*
Fullan, M., 622, 623, 624, 625, 626, *631*
Fullick, P., *313*
Funk, J. B., 416, *420*

Furst, E. J., *26*
Fussell, S. R., 780, *801*

# G

Gabbard, R., 205, *208*, 215, *221*
Gabbay, J., 245, *248*
Gabbitas, B., *536*
Gabriel, R. P., *644*
Gadde, L. E., 628, *630*
Gaffney, T., *604*
Gage, N. L., *616*
Gagné, E., 387, *396*
Gagné, R. M., 25, 27, 31, *32*, 77, *81*, 96, 174, 180, *183*, 191, 194, *195*, 213, 222, 306, *314*, 384, 386, 387, 388, 389, 394, *395*, *396*, *397*, 399, 446, *455*, 472, *481*, 530, *534*, 583, 592, 636, *644*, 649, *657*, 678, *684*, 707, 710, *712*
Gaimari, R., *224*
Gainer, L., *801*
Gal, S., *110*
Galanter, E. H., 190, *195*
Galbraith, J. K., 5, *19*
Galbraith, P., *437*
Galinsky, M., 321, *325*
Gall, J. P., *96*, 201, 202, *208*, 757
Gall, M. D., *757*, 768, 769, 773, 775, *800*
Gallagher, S. A., 486, 487, 489, 490, 491, 497, *502*, *505*
Gallese, V., *381*
Gallimore, R., 427, 428, 432, *437*, *439*
Gallini, J. K., 43, *52*
Gallivan, M. J., *357*, *364*
Gallwey, W. T., 442, *455*
Galvao, J. R., 318, *326*
Gamblian, V., 585, *592*
Gamma, E., 147, *159*, 790, *801*
Gamson, Z., 609, *616*
Ganesan, R., 573, *575*
Ganeshan, R., *294*
Garcia, C. E., 95, *96*
Garcia, F. J., 358, *363*
García, P., 312, *314*
Garcia, R., *364*
García-Barrios, V. M., 285, *292*
Gardner, A., *535*
Gardner, D. L., 309, *314*
Gardner, H. E., 71, 73, *81*, *96*, 98, 106, *109*

Garfield, J., 73, *81*
Garfinkel, H., 780, *801*
Garfinkel, R. S., *565*
Garg, A., 321, *326*
Garhart, C., 410, *420*
Garibaldi, A., *421*
Garland, N. J., 487, *502*
Garofalo, J., *314*
Garrett. S., *81*, *108*
Garrison, D. R., 219, 222, 270, 271, 274, 275, *422*, *804*
Garrison, J., 65, 69, 79, *81*
Garrison, S., *108*, *534*
Garstens, H. L., *396*
Garton, L., *423*
Garzotto, F., 471, 475, 476, *481*, *643*
Gasevic, D., *353*, *364*
Gaßner, K., *343*
Gaver, M., *239*
Gaver, W. W., 262, *266*
Gavurin, E. I., 191, *195*
Gearhart, M., 420
Gee, J. P., 105, *109*, 169, *170*, 212, 218, 222, 302, *303*, 318, 320, 321, *326*, 710, *712*
Geer, C. H., 229, *230*
Geis, G. L., 509, *524*
Gemeny, B. A., *325*
General Medical Council, 556, 557, 560, *563*
Gentner, D., 27, 322, *326*, 458, *466*
Georgoudi, M., 59, *66*
Gerace, W. J., *563*
Gergen, K. J., 59, *65*
Gerhard, M., 324, *326*
Gerjets, P., 201, *208*, 785, *802*
Gernsbacher, M. A., *222*
Gertner, A., *292*
Gery, G., 510, 519, 520, *524*, 655, *657*, 665, *669*
Getsie, R. L., 389, *396*
Ghaziri H. M., 242, *247*
Ghelani, T., *535*
Gholson, B., *52*, *221*, 222, *292*, *815*
Giarratano, J. C., 242, *248*
Gibbons, A. S., 330, *342*, 346, 347, *353*, 356, *364*, 635, *643*, 636, 637, 638, 639, 642, *644*, *645*, 690, 708, *712*
Gibbons, N. J., 338, 339, *342*
Gibson, G. V., *184*
Gibson, I. W., 498, *500*
Gibson, J. J., *81*, 98, *109*, 254, *256*, 262, *266*

# O

# Subject Index